An Etymological Dictionary of MODERN ENGLISH

By

Ernest Weekley

With a new biographical memoir of the author by
MONTAGUE WEEKLEY

IN TWO VOLUMES:
Volume II. L - Z

Dover Publications, Inc., New York

Published in Canada by General Publishing Company, Ltd., 30 Lesmill Road, Don Mills, Toronto, Ontario.
Published in the United Kingdom by Constable and Company, Ltd.

This Dover edition, first published in 1967, is an unabridged and unaltered republication of the work originally published in London by John Murray in 1921. The work was originally published in one volume and is now published in two volumes. A new biographical memoir of the author was written by Montague Weekley especially for this Dover edition.

Standard Book Number: 486-21874-0
Library of Congress Catalog Card Number: 67-26968

Manufactured in the United States of America
Dover Publications, Inc.
180 Varick Street
New York, N. Y. 10014

ETYMOLOGICAL DICTIONARY

L. Fifty. From Roman symbol resembling, but not ident. with, L.

la¹. Interj. See *law²*.

la² [*mus.*]. See *gamut*.

laager. SAfrDu. *lager*, camp, Du. *leger*; cf. *leaguer*.

labarum [*hist.*]. Imperial standard of Constantine the Great (†337 A.D.), with Christian symbols added to orig. Roman. G. λάβαρον, of unknown origin.

labdanum. MedL. form of *ladanum*, resinous gum, L., G. λάδανον, from λῆδον, mastic, Pers. *lādan*.

labefaction. From L. *labefacere*, to cause to totter, *labare*.

label. OF. (cf. F. *lambeau*, shred), narrow strip, fillet (her.), ? dim. from OHG. *lappa*, shred, rag; cf. *lappet*. Current sense is developed from that of strip of parchment to bear seal attached to document.

labial. MedL. *labialis*, from *labium*, lip. Hence *labialization* (phon.), influence of labial consonant on adjacent vowel, e.g. the *-u-* of F. *buvant*, for OF. *bev-*, L. *bib-*, is "rounded" by influence of lip-consonants *b* and *v*.

labile. Easily displaced. L. *labilis*, from *labi*, to slip. Cf. *lapse*.

laboratory. MedL. *laboratorium*, from *laborare*, to work; cf. F. *laboratoire*, It. Sp. *laboratorio*. *Elaboratory* is also found (17 cent.).

labour. F., L. *labor-em*, toil, distress, ? cogn. with *labare*, to sink, totter. For med. sense cf. *travail*. Pol. sense from c. 1880. *Labour lost* is in *Piers Plowm*. With *labour of love* (1 *Thess.* i. 3) cf. It. *con amore*. F. *labour*, *labourer*, like their Rom. cognates, are chiefly used of agricultural toil, esp. ploughing. This is also the oldest E. sense of the verb, still conspicuous in *AV.*, and may be the source of naut. to *labour*, pitch and roll heavily. To *labour a point*, *laboured style*, are aphet. for obs. *elabour*, F. *élaborer*.

elabourer: to elaborate; labour painfully, travell thoroughly; to worke exactly, doe a thing fully, and finely (Cotg.).

labret. Savage ornament for lip. Dim. from L. *labrum*.

laburnum. L. (Pliny), cogn. with *labrusca*, wild vine.

labyrinth. L., G. λαβύρινθος, spec. the Cretan labyrinth of Daedalus. See *clew*. Prob. not of G. origin.

lac¹. Resin. Hind. *lākh*, Prakrit *lakkha*, Sanskrit *lākshā*. Cf. *shellac*, *lake²*, *lacquer*.

lac², **lakh** [*Anglo-Ind.*]. One hundred thousand, now esp. of rupees. Hind. *lākh*, Sanskrit *laksha*. Cf. *crore*.

Ditta Mull, and Choga Lall, and Amir Nath, and— oh, lakhs of my friends (Kipling, *Tods' Amendment*).

lace. OF. *laz* (*lacs*), L. *laqueus*, noose, cf. It. *laccio*, Sp. *lazo* (see *lasso*). With to *lace*, beat, cf. *lash¹, ²*. *Lace*, a dash of spirits in coffee, etc., was orig. applied to sugar, app. in sense of accessory; cf. *trimmings* of a leg of mutton.

Lo, alle thise folk so caught were in hir las
(Chauc. A. 1951).

lacerate. From L. *lacerare*, to tear, from *lacer*, torn, G. λακερός, from λακίς, a rent.

lacertian, lacertine. Of the lizard, L. *lacerta*, whence *lacertus*, upper arm (cf. *muscle*).

laches [*leg.*]. Negligence. F. *lâchesse*, from *lâche*, lax, L. *laxus*. Cf. *riches*.

lachryma Christi. It. wine. L., for It. *lacrima di Cristo*, tear of Christ. Cf. Ger. *liebfraumilch*, Virgin's milk, a Rhine-wine. *Lacrymatory shell*, causing partial blindness, is a product of Kultur. L. *lacrima*, *lacruma*, is a Sabine form for OL. *dacruma*, cogn. with G. δάκρυ and E. *tear*.

laciniate [*bot. & zool.*]. Jagged. From L. *lacinia*, lappet, etc.

lack¹. Need. First (12 cent.) as verb. Cf. obs. Du. *laken*, to be wanting, with LG. cognates, also ON. *lakr*, inferior. *Lack-lustre* is after *As You Like It*, ii. 7.

lack². Interj. Only in archaic *good lack!* Perh. connected with *alack* (q.v.); but cf. *lawks*.

lackadaisical. From despondent *lack-a-day*, for *alack-a-day*. See *alack*.

lacker. See *lacquer*.

lackey, lacquey. In 16 cent. esp. running footman, camp-follower. F. *laquais*, perh. orig. adj., as in *valet laquais* (15 cent.); cf. Sp. Port. *lacayo*. OF. *alacays* (whence obs. Sc. *allakey*), Catalonian *alacayo*, suggest Arab. origin with def. art. prefixed. Sard. *allecaju*, a striped fish, E. *lackey moth*, also striped, may point to costume as orig. sense (cf. *tiger*).

laconic. Of Spartan brevity. G. Λακωνικός, of *Laconia* or *Lacedaemonia*.

lacquer. Earlier (16 cent.) *lacker*, OF. *lacre*, Port. *lacre*, sealing-wax, var. of *laca*, lac¹.

lacrosse. F. *jeu de la crosse*, the crook (see *crosier*). The Canadian game is mentioned in 1763.

lacrym-. See *lachrym-*.

lacteal. From L. *lac, lact-*, milk.

lacuna. L., pit, hole, from *lacus*, lake. Cf. Ger. *lücke*, lacuna, cogn. with *loch*, hole. See *lagoon*.

lacustrine [*scient.*]. Irreg. formation from L. *lacus*, lake, after L. *paluster*, from *palus*, marsh.

lad. ME. *ladde*, servant, varlet. ? Corrupt. of ON. *lithi*, follower, from *lith*, people, host. I am led to make this unphonetic conjecture by the fact that the surname *Summerlad* is undoubtedly for ON. *sumar-lithi*, viking, summer adventurer, a common ON. personal name, found also (Sumerled, Sumerleda, Sumerluda, etc.) in E. before the Conquest. The corresponding *Winterlad* once existed, but is now app. obs. *Ladda* also occurs, like *boy* (q.v.), as surname earlier than as common noun. Another conjecture is that it may be for Norw. *askeladd*, male Cinderella in Norw. fairy-tales, or *tusseladd*, nincompoop, in which the second element means hose.

ladanum. See *labdanum*.

ladder. AS. *hlǣd(d)er*; cf. Du. *ladder, leer* (dial. *leder*), Ger. *leiter*; cogn. with to *lean* and ult. with G. κλῖμαξ, ladder. Fig. of means of rising, e.g. to *draw up* (*kick down*) *the ladder, educational ladder*, which has been defined as "the broad highway into a cul de sac."

lade¹. Mill-race, watercourse. AS. *lād*, way, course, cogn. with *lead²*, leat, lode.

lade². To load. AS. *hladan*. Com. Teut.; cf. Du. Ger. *laden*, ON. *hlatha*, Goth. *hlathan* (in compds.). Now usu. replaced, exc. p.p. *laden*, by *load* (q.v.). See also *last²*.

la-di-da, lardy-dardy. ? Imit. of affected, *haw-haw*, type of speech. Dates from the sixties, but its great vogue was due to a music-hall song of 1880—*He wears a penny flower in his coat, La-di-da!*

Last May we went to Newmarket, we had a festive day,
With a decentish cold luncheon in a tidy one-horse shay;
With our lardy-dardy garments we were really "on the spot"
And Charley Vain came out so grand in a tall white chimney-pot (A. C. Hilton, *Light Green*, 1873).

Ladin [*ling.*]. Rom. lang. of the Engadine. It. *Ladino*, L. *Latinus*. Cf. *Romansh*.

ladle. AS. *hlǣdel*, from *lade²*, in obs. sense of baling. Cf. *shovel*.

lady. ME. *levedy*, AS. *hlǣfdige*, from *hlāf*, loaf, and an obs. verb, to knead, cogn. with *dough* (q.v.). Orig. meaning was something like housewife. Cf. *lord, dairy*. Applied already in AS. to the Holy Virgin; hence *Lady Day, Lady chapel, lady-bird* (cf. Ger. *Marienkäfer*, lit. Mary's chafer), and many plant-names (*lady's garter, bed-straw*, etc.). In the oldest of these compds. (e.g. *lady smock*) the absence of '*s* is a survival of the AS. genitive of fem. nouns; cf. *Thursday*, from *Thor* (m.), but *Friday*, from *Freia* (f.). The *lady* of a lobster is supposed to resemble in form a seated female figure. The loafer who says *Carry your bag, lady?* preserves the Chaucerian method of address, which has now given way to the borrowed *madam*. *Old lady of Threadneedle Street*, for Bank of England, is due to Cobbett, who likened the directors to Mrs Partington.

lag. As noun and verb from 16 cent. Of obscure origin, but app. connected with *delay* (q.v.). In childish sense of *last* it may be an arbitrary perversion of that word (*fog, seg,...lag*, first, second,...last, in game counting), and this accounts for some meanings. In sense of convict under sentence of transportation it comes from an obs. *lag*, to carry off, steal (Tusser). It has also been associated with *lack*.

Superfluous lags the veteran on the stage
(Johnson, *Vanity of Human Wishes*).

lagan [*hist.*]. Goods or wreckage lying on bed of sea. OF., MedL. *laganum*, prob. cogn. with *lie¹*. Cf. *flotsam, jetsam*.

lager-beer. Ger. *lager-bier*, brewed for keeping, from *lager*, store, ident. in origin with
laager, leaguer (q.v.).

lagoon. F. *lagune*, It. *laguna*, L. *lacuna*, from
lacus, lake. Esp. in ref. to Venice.

laic. Late L. *laicus*. See *lay*³.

laidly [*archaic*]. Northern var. of *loathly*.

lair. AS. *leger*, couch, burial-place, etc.,
cogn. with *lie*¹. Cf. *laager, leaguer*. Now
usu. of wild beast, but still applied to a pen
or shed for cattle on their way to market.

laird. Sc. form of *lord*; cf. *leddy* for *lady*.
Regularly written *lard* in *Privy Council
Acts*, c. 1550.

laissez-aller, laissez-faire. F., let go, let do.
The latter, in pol. sense now somewhat
discredited, was originated by F. free-
trade economists of 18 cent.

laity. AF. *laité*, from *lay*³ (q.v.) after other
words in *-té, -ty*; cf. *duty*.

lake¹. Of water. F. *lac*, L. *lacus*, G. λάκκος,
pit, pond. Prob. confused also with dial.
lake, stream, AS. *lacu*, cogn. with *leak*.
The *Lake school* (Coleridge, Southey,
Wordsworth) is mentioned by *Edinburgh
Review* in 1817. *Lakeland* was app. coined
by Southey.

lake². Pigment. Var. of *lac*¹ (q.v.).

lakh. See *lac*².

lam. Cf. AS. *lemian*, to lame, cripple; but,
the verb not being recorded in ME., *lam*
is perh. of imit. origin (cf. *bang, slam*).

lama. Buddhist priest. Tibetan *blama*,
with silent *b-*. Quot. 2 (from Yule) shows
an odd confusion with *llama* (q.v.). See
also *Dalai-lama*.

A certain high priest, whom they call *Dalae-Lama*,
or *Lama-lamalow* (*NED.* 17 cent.).

The landlord prostrated himself as reverently, if
not as lowly, as a Peruvian before his Grand Llama
(*Novel reviewed in Academy*, May 17, 1879).

lamantin [*zool.*]. F., manatee (q.v.).

Lamarckian. Of *Lamarck*, F. biologist (†1829).

lamasery. F. *lamaserie*, Buddhist monastery, irreg. from *lama*.

lamb. AS. *lamb*. Com. Teut.; cf. Du. *lam*,
Ger. *lamm*, ON. Goth. *lamb*. *Lamb of God*,
after *John*, i. 29, is found in AS. With
fig. ironic application in *Kirk's Lambs*
(Monmouth's Rebellion), from Paschal
Lamb on their banner, cf. *Nottingham
Lambs*, i.e. roughs.

lambent. From pres. part. of L. *lambere*, to
lick, used also of flames playing over
surface. ? Later sense associated with G.
λάμπειν, to shine.

lambrequin [*archaic*]. Scarf worn over helmet. In US. scalloped drapery. F., in
both senses, obs. Du. *lamperkin*, dim. of
same origin as *label*.

A pair of Gobelins lambrequins yesterday, at
Christie's, fetched £3780 (*Daily Chron.* Nov. 6, 1919).

lame. AS. *lama*. Com. Teut., exc. Goth.,
which has *halts* only (see *halt*¹); cf. Du.
lam, Ger. *lahm*, ON. *lame*. Orig. of gen.
weakness of limbs, paralysis. Cf. Ger.
gelähmt, paralysed.

lamella [*biol.*]. Thin plate. L., dim. of
lamina.

lament. F. *lamenter*, L. *lamentari*, from
lamentum, cry of mourning, from imit. *la!*
Cf. *latrare*, to bark.

lamia. L., witch sucking children's blood,
G. Λάμια, vampire, etc. In Wyc. (*Is.*
xxxiv. 15, *Lam.* iv. 3).

lamina. L., plate, layer, whence F. *lame*,
blade, etc.

Lammas [*archaic*]. Harvest festival (Aug. 1)
with consecration of loaves. AS. *hlāfmæsse*,
loaf mass. With *latter Lammas*, never, cf.
Greek calends.

lammergeyer. Ger. *lämmergeier*, lambs-vul-
ture. Second element prob. belongs to
Ger. *gier*, greed (see *yearn*).

lamp. F. *lampe*, L., G. λαμπάς, from λάμπειν, to shine. To *smell of the lamp* was
said by Pytheas (Plutarch) of preparation
of speeches by Demosthenes. *New lamps
for old* is from story of Aladdin.

lampas¹ [*vet.*]. Mouth-disease of horses. F.
(in OF. also meaning throat, as in *humecter
le lampas*, to wet one's whistle). App. connected with *lamper*, to guzzle, nasalized
form of *laper*, to lap (q.v.).

lampas². Chinese flowered silk. Cf. F. *lampas*, in same sense. Origin obscure. It
may be from *lampas*¹, the pattern being
compared to the swellings of the disease
(cf. *fraise, frill, tripe*).

lampion. F., It. *lampione*, from *lampa*, lamp.

lampoon. F. *lampon*, from *lampons*, let us
guzzle, used as refrain of scurrilous songs.
Cf. *vamose*. For F. verb *lamper* see *lampas*¹.

lamprey. F. *lamproie*; cf. MedL. *lampreda*,
whence AS. *lamprēde*, limpet, OHG. *lam-
preta* (*lamprete*), lamprey. Earlier is MedL.
lampetra, explained as lick-rock, L. *lambere* and *petra*, from lamprey's habit of
clinging to stones by a sucker. The use
of the same word for the limpet (v.s.)
makes this plausible. Earliest E. ref. is to
death of Henry I.

lance. F., L. *lancea*, ? of Celt. origin; cf. It. *lancia*, Sp. *lanza*, Du. *lans*, Ger. *lanze*, etc., partly replacing Teut. *spear*. *Lance-corporal* is a half adaptation of obs. *lance-pesade*, OF. *lancepessade* (*anspessade*), It. *lancia spezzata*, broken lance, exact application of which is unknown. To *break a lance* is from the tourney. The *Lancers* (dance) was introduced by Laborde (1836). *Lancet* is F. dim. *lancette*.

lanceolate [*scient.*]. Late L. *lanceolatus*, from *lanceola*, small lance.

lancet. See *lance*.

lancinating. Acute (of pain). After F. *lancinant*, from L. *lancinare*, to rend, pierce.

land. AS. *land*. Com. Teut.; cf. Du. Ger. ON. Goth. *land*; cogn. with Welsh *llann*, enclosure, church, Breton *lann*, heath, whence F. *lande*, moor. With *how the land lies* (naut.) cf. *coast is clear*. *Landfall*, sighting of land, is from *fall* in sense of hap. The Ir. *Land league* was founded by Parnell (1879). *Landlord*, AS. *landhláford*, land-owner, has reached sense of innkeeper via that of master of the house, host. For naut. *landsman* (earlier *landman*) as opposed to *seaman* cf. *huntsman*, *steersman*, etc. Verb to *land* is for earlier *lend*, AS. *lendan*, from *land*. Some fig. senses, e.g. to *land a fortune*, are app. from angling. To *land* (a person) *one in the eye* is for earlier *lend*, used playfully for *give*. The *landing* of a flight of stairs is characteristic of our love of naut. metaphor. So also a sea-plane "lands" on the water.

> If thou dost any more, I shall lend thee a knock
> (Fielding).

landamman [*hist.*]. Swiss magistrate. Ger. *landamtmann*. See *ambassador*.

landau. First built (18 cent.) at *Landau* (Bavaria). Ger. term is *landauer* (*wagen*). Cf. *berline*.

> Im geöffneten wagen, er war in Landau verfertigt
> (Goethe, *Hermann und Dorothea*, i. 56).

landdrost. SAfrDu., magistrate. Du. *drost*, steward, bailiff, etc., earlier *drossate*, cogn. with Ger. *truchsess*, "the royal server, taster, or foretaster" (Ludw.), usu. rendered in MedL. by *dapifer*. The two elements are cogn. with *dree* and *sit*.

landgrave. Ger. *landgraf*, land count.

landloper. Du. *landlooper*, wastrel, adventurer. Cf. *elope*, *interlope*. Also confused with *landlubber*, for which *lubber* (q.v.) alone is found earlier.

landrail. Bird. See *rail*³.

landscape. Earlier (16 cent.) also *landskip*. Du. *landschap*; cf. AS. *landscipe*, land, Ger. *landschaft*, landscape. See *-ship*. For introduction of Du. art words cf. *easel*, *lay-figure*. Orig. of background of portrait (v.i.).

> The sins of other women shew in landscip, far off and full of shadow; hers in statue, neere hand, and bigger in the life (Overbury, *Characters*).

> All that which in a picture is not of the body or argument thereof is landskip, parergon, or by-work
> (Blount).

> A limit has been reached in this impudent desecration of some of our finest city-scapes
> (*Obs.* Jan. 18, 1920).

landsturm. Ger., land storm, reserve next to *landwehr*. Orig. Swiss (17 cent.) for the *levée en masse*.

landtag. Legislative body of Ger. state. Cf. *reichstag*, *diet*².

landwehr. Ger., land defence (see *weir*), theoretically force for home defence.

lane. AS. *lane*, cogn. with Du. *laan*, ON. *lön*, Norw. *laan*. All orig. in sense of narrow street, as in City.

> It is a long lane that has no turning
> (Foote, *Trip to Calais*, 1778).

langrage, langridge [*mil.*]. Kind of case-shot. On *cartridge*, for earlier *langrel* (Capt. John Smith, 1627), chain-shot. Perh. ident. with Sc. *langrel*, long, lanky.

> *langrel*: is a shot which goes in with a shackle to be shorten'd when put into the piece, and to fly out at length when discharged (*Sea Dict.* 1708).

lang syne. Sc., long since (q.v.). In E. after Burns' song (1788).

language. F. *langage*, from *langue*, OF. *lengue*, L. *lingua*, tongue.

langue d'oc [*ling.*]. Lang. of South of France, so called from *oc*, yes, L *hoc*, this, the North using *oïl* (*oui*), L. *hoc* and OF. derivatives of *ille*.

languish. F. *languir*, *languiss-*, VL. **languire*, for *languëre*, with incept. *languescere*; cogn. with *laxus* and ult. with E. *slack*. Cf. *languid*, *languescent*, *languor*.

laniard. See *lanyard*.

laniary. Of teeth, canine. L. *laniarius*, from *lanius*, butcher, *laniare*, to tear.

laniferous. From L. *lanifer*, wool-bearing, from *lana*, wool.

lank. AS. *hlanc*, slender, flaccid. Ground-sense of flexible appears in cogn. Ger. *lenken*, to turn, bend. See *flank*.

lanner [*archaic*]. Hawk. F. *lanier*, perh. ident. with OF. *lanier*, slothful, as this hawk is called *tardiarius* in MedL. OF.

lanier meant orig. wool-weaver and became a term of reproach in Merovingian times. But the hawk's name may be L. *laniarius*, tearing (see *laniary*), from the bird tearing its prey. At any rate it has been connected with the shrike, or butcher-bird (v.i.). The male is *lanneret*, orig. a dim.

gazza sparviera: a kind of lanaret hauke called a skreeke, or nine murther (Flor.).

lanolin [*chem.*]. Fatty matter from wool. Coined (1885) by Liebreich from L. *lana*, wool, *oleum*, oil.

lansquenet. Mercenary soldier, card-game. F., Ger. *landsknecht*, soldier of the country, "land's knight," orig. contrasted with Swiss mercenaries. For formation cf. *yeoman*. Often *lanzknecht*, *lance-knight*, as though from *lance*, and thus wrongly explained by Scott (*Quentin Durward*, ch. xvii.).

To Hans van Elleran, for the conduict of himself and vij lancequenctes sent northwardes
(*Privy Council Acts*, 1548).

lantern. F. *lanterne*, L. *lanterna*, *laterna*, from G. λαμπτήρ, from λάμπειν, to shine, altered on synon. *lucerna*. *Lanthorn* (16 cent.) is folk-etym., from material formerly used as transparent casing. In arch. used of a structure to admit light. *Lantern-jaws*, having hollowed appearance of old-fashioned lantern, is suggested in *Piers Plowm*.

Hongur...buffetede the Brutiner [Breton] about bothe his chekes;
He lokede lyk a lanterne al his lyf after
(A. vii. 163).

lanthanum [*chem.*]. Discovered and named (1839–41) by Mosander. From G. λανθάνειν, to lurk, because hidden in certain rare minerals.

lanthorn. See *lantern*.

lanuginous [*biol.*]. From L. *lanugo*, *lanugin-*, down, from *lana*, wool.

lanyard, laniard [*naut.*]. Readoption (17 cent.) of F. *lanière*, thong, whence already ME. *lainer* (Chauc. A. 2504). OF. *lasniere*, of uncertain origin, but perh. metath. of OF. *nasliere*, of Teut. origin; cf. Ger. *nestel*, strap, OHG. *nestila*, whence Walloon *nâle*, thong. For *-yard* cf. *halyard*, *whinyard* (also *panyard* for *pannier*, in Pepys).

lanyer of lether: lasniere (Palsg.).

Laodicean [*theol.*]. Lukewarm, after *Rev.* iii. 15–16. From Λαοδίκεια (Latakia), in Asia Minor.

lap¹. Fold, pendent part of garment, as in dims. *lappet*, *lapel*. AS. *lappa*; cf. Du. *lap*, Ger. *lappen*, ON. *leppr*, clout, rag. See also *label*. In ME. used both of the garment folded at breast and used as receptacle, e.g. *lap (bosom) of the Church*, and of the skirt part used for nursing child, e.g. *brought up in the lap of luxury*, *lap-dog*, *lapstone*, held on shoemaker's lap. ? Hence (? or from ME. *wlappen*, to wrap) verb to *lap*, enfold, envelope, wrap, whence again noun *lap*, circuit, as in racing. Cf. *overlap*, exceeding the circuit. For *in the lap of the gods* see *knee*.

lap². To drink with tongue. AS. *lapian*, with cognates in obs. Du. & OHG.; cf. Ger. *löffel* (OHG. *leffel*), spoon. F. *laper* is from Teut. Cogn. with L. *lambere*, to lick, G. λάπτειν. Hence dial. *lap*, liquor, as in *catlap*, poor stuff.

lapel. See *lap¹*.

lapidary. F. *lapidaire*, L. *lapidarius*, from *lapis*, *lapid-*, stone. In Wyc. With *lapidation*, pedantic for stoning to death, cf. *decollation*, *defenestration*.

lapilli. Fragments of stone ejected by volcano. It., pl. of *lapillo*, little stone (v.s.).

lapis lazuli. MedL., stone of azure. See *azure*.

Lapp. Inhabitant and lang. (akin to Finnish) of *Lapland*, fabled home of wizards dealing in winds and storms; cf. sailors' opinion of the Finns. Sw. *Lapp*, perh. orig. term of contempt; cf. MHG. *lappe*, simpleton. Native name is *Sabme*.

The opinion is that they were first termed Lappes of their briefe and short speech (Hakl. iii. 404).

lappet. Dim. of *lap¹* (q.v.).

lapse. L. *lapsus*, from *labi*, *laps-*, to slip, glide, whence also *collapse*, *elapse*, *relapse*. Cf. *lapsus linguae* (*calami*). Also *-lapsarian* in several Reformation compds. connoting different varieties of Calvinists.

Laputan. Chimerical, esp. of extracting sun-beams from cucumbers. From Swift's *Isle of Laputa* (in *Gulliver's Travels*), a satire on the Royal Society.

lapwing. ME. *lappewinke* (Gower), AS. *hlēapewince*, leaper winker, where *wink* has the sense of tottering, wavering (cf. OHG. *winkan*, in same sense). From wavering flight. Mod. form is due to folk-etym. (*lap¹* and *wing*).

lar. Usu. in pl. *lares* (q.v.).

larboard. Altered, on *starboard* (q.v.), from ME. *ladeborde*, *latheborde*, app. from *laden*, to load. Cf. *port*, which now usu. replaces it.

AS. had *bæcbord* (cf. F. *bâbord*), lit. back-board, because behind the steersman. For words altered on their opposites cf. *female, grief, render.* E. *larboard,* F. *bâbord* are now abolished as sounding too like their opposites.

larceny. From F. *larcin,* OF. *larecin,* L. *latrocinium,* from *latro,* thief. Final *-y* may be due to *felony, perjury, robbery,* etc. *Petty larceny* was orig. theft of property of less value than twelve pence.

larch. Ger. *lärche,* introduced into E. by Turner (1548), early Teut. loan from L. *larix, laric-,* whence also Du. *lariks,* It. *larice,* Sp. *lárice.*

lard. F., bacon, L. *laridum,* cogn. with G. adj. λαρινός, fat. Hence verb to *lard,* orig. insert, or stick on, strips of bacon in cooking, make rich (*larding the lean earth,* 1 *Hen. IV,* ii. 2), fig. to decorate; cf. *interlard. Larder* is OF. *lardier* or *lardoir,* storehouse for bacon.

lardy-dardy. See *la-di-da.*

lares. Usu. with *penates* (q.v.). Pl. of L. *lar,* tutelary deity of home.

large. F., wide, fem. of obs. *larc,* L. *largus,* abundant, copious. For current changed meaning cf. *wide.* Earliest E. sense is bountiful (cf. *largesse*). With *at large,* free, cf. F. *élargir,* to set at liberty; hence to *talk* (quote, etc.) *at large,* i.e. without restriction, *gentleman at large,* etc.

largo [*mus.*]. It., in broad, majestic style (v.s.).

lariat. Tethering rope. Sp. *la reata,* with agglutination of art. See *reata.*

larix. Larch (q.v.).

lark¹. Bird. Earlier *laverock,* now poet., AS. *lāwerce.* Com. Teut.; cf. Du. *leeuwerik,* Ger. *lerche* (OHG. *lērahha*), ON. *lævirk;* also Port. dial. *laverca,* from Teut. The bird has remarkably long hind-claws, hence plant-name *larkspur. Larkheel,* used of plants and also of negro heel, occurs as ME. surname.

lark². Spree. Altered (c. 1800) from northern dial. *lake,* sport, and further elaborated to *skylark,* which appears much later. *Lake* is ME. *laik,* ON. *leikr,* play, cogn. with AS. *lāc,* contest, etc., OHG. *leich,* melody, dancing-song, Goth. *laiks,* dance.

How this losell laykis with his lorde (*NED.* 1440).
layke, play: ludus (*Manip. Voc.*).

Laiking about to wakes and fairs
(*Heart of Midlothian,* ch. xxxiii.).

larrikin. Austral. hooligan or hoodlum. First at Melbourne (c. 1870), but given as a Cornish word by Jago (1882). ? From *Larry,* common Ir. form of *Lawrence;* cf. *Hooligan.* The mythical derivation from the Ir. policeman's statement that *the prisoner was a larikin' (larking) in the street* first appears in the *Melbourne Argus,* Nov. 17, 1888.

Larrence: (St Lawrence), "He is as lazy as Larrence" (Jago, *Corn. Gloss.*).

larrikins: mischievious (sic) young fellows, larkers (*ib.*).

larrup [*dial.*]. To thrash. ? Suggested by *lather, leather,* and *wallop.*

larum. Poet. for *alarum* (q.v.).

larva. L., spectre, also mask. Hence "disguised" insect, current restricted sense being due to Linnaeus.

larynx. G. λάρυγξ.

lascar. Shortened from Urdu *lashkarī,* military, Pers., from *lashkar,* army (v.i.). Cf. *lascarine,* native policeman, via Port.

The rebells are very stronge and will fight it out, and about 10 dayes hence the Laskar may sett forward (Peter Mundy, 1632).

No lashkar has yet assembled
(*Westm. Gaz.* May 22, 1919).

lascivious. Late L. *lasciviosus,* from *lascivia,* from *lascivus,* sportful, wanton.

lash¹. Of whip. First as noun (14 cent.), blow, flexible part of whip, whence verb to *lash,* beat. But earlier sense of verb, to move violently (cf. to *lash out, lasher* on Thames), is as old as noun. Contains notions of *slash* (q.v.), also of F. *lâcher,* in sense of letting fly, and is perh. partly imit. (cf. *dash, swish,* etc.). Analogy of dial. *lace,* to flog, suggests connection in some senses with OF. *laz,* thong (see *lace*).

lash² [*naut.*]. To bind, secure. OF. *lachier,* var. of *lacier,* to lace. *Lace* (q.v.) was earlier also in naut. use, while *lash* is found in ME. in gen. sense of *lace.*

lashings [*Anglo-Ir.*]. Abundance, esp. of drink. ? For *lavishings.* Cf. name *Candish* for *Cavendish.*

Some horsekeeper lasheth out provender so
(Tusser).

lashkar. See *lascar.*

laspring. Young salmon. Interpreted in Act of Parliament (1861) as *last spring,* but prob. for earlier *lax pink* (16 cent.). See *lax¹, pink⁴.*

lass. ? Cf. ON. *löskr,* idle, weak, OSw. *lösk kona,* unmarried woman. For obscure origin cf. *boy, girl, lad.*

lassitude. F., L. *lassitudo*, from *lassus*, weary.

lasso. Sp. *lazo*, as *lace* (q.v.).

lassy me. Archaic interj., *alas for me*. Cf. *woe is me*.

last¹. Shoemaker's. AS. *lāst*, footstep, *lǣste* last. Com. Teut.; cf. Du. *leest*, Ger. *leiste*, last, ON. *leistr*, foot, Goth. *laists*, footstep; cogn. with L. *lira*, furrow. The proverb is from L. *ne sutor supra crepidam*.

last². Fixed weight of various wares. AS. *hlǣst*, load, from root of *lade²*. WGer.; cf. Du. Ger. *last*, burden, also spec. weight. Cf. *ballast*.

last³. Superl. of *late*. AS. *latost*, from *late*, with *-t-* lost as in *best*; cf. Du. *laatst*, Ger. *letzt* (OHG. *lazzost*). *Latest* is a new formation. *Of the last* (meaning *first*) *importance* is from archaic sense of final, definitive; cf. *last word* and similar use of F. *dernier*. In to *breathe* (*look*) *one's last* the noun is omitted as being already expressed by the verb.

last⁴. Verb. AS. *lǣstan*, to follow, accomplish, also intrans., to continue; cf. Ger. *leisten*, to perform, execute, Goth. *laistjan*, to follow. Perh. cogn. with *last¹*, if that orig. meant track. The sense-development of this group of words, with which the best authorities also connect *learn* and *lore*, is obscure. The fig. sense appears to have prevailed early over the lit.

latakia. Tobacco from *Latakia* (Laodicea) in Syria.

latch. In ME. snare, noose, OF. *lache*, cogn. with *lace* (q.v.). But in door-sense rather from dial. to *latch*, seize, catch, AS. *læccan*; cf. *catch* of a door, and Sc. *sneck*, ? cogn. with *snatch*. *Læccan*, which has no Teut. cognates, may however be ult. connected with L. *laqueus*, snare, and hence with *lace*.

I latche, I catche a thyng that is throwen to me in my handes or [ere] *it fall to the grounde*: je happe (Palsg.).

latchet. OF. *lachet*, dial. form of *lacet*, dim. of OF. *laz*, thong, whence *lace* (q.v.). Usu. allusive to *Mark*, i. 7.

late. AS. *læt*, tardy, sluggish. Com. Teut.; cf. Du. *laat*, Ger. dial. *lass*, ON. *latr*, Goth. *lats*; all orig. in same sense and cogn. with L. *lassus*, weary. See *let²*. Cf. sense-development of F. *tard*. In sense of recent, e.g. *the late archbishop*, *late* was at first adv., e.g. with *her late husband* (Caxton) cf. *her sometime husband* and similar use of adv. *quondam*.

lateen [*naut.*]. Sail. F. [*voile*] *latine*, Latin sail, "a mizen or smack saile" (Cotg.), It. *latina*, "the mizen saile of a ship" (Flor.), a Mediterranean rig. Quot. below is two centuries earlier than *NED*.

There [off Cape St Vincent] met with divers barckes, both latten and square
        (*Voyage of the Barbara*, 1540).

latent. From pres. part. of L. *latēre*, to lie hid, lurk. Cf. opposite *patent*.

lateral. L. *lateralis*, from *latus*, *later-*, side.

Lateran council. One of the five Councils of the Western Church held at cathedral church of *St John Lateran*, at Rome, built on site of the palace of the *Plautii Laterani*, a Roman family.

laterite [*geol.*]. Red brick-like stone (India). From L. *later*, brick.

lath. AS. *lætt*; cf. Du. *lat*, Ger. *latte*, whence F. *latte* (see *lattice*). The *-th* may be due to cogn. Welsh *llath*. Agreement of AS. & OHG. *-tt-* is abnormal and unexplained.

lathe¹ [*hist.*]. Administrative district of Kent. Late AS. *lǣth*, ON. *lāth*, landed possession. Cf. Dan. *fæl-led*, village common.

lathe². Implement. From 17 cent. only, and, in first occurrence (Cotg.), varying with *lare*. ? Cf. Dan. *lad*, in *dreielad*, turning-lathe, and other compds. It may be a differentiated form of *lath*, as the primitive lathe was worked by a spring-lath. Some authorities identify with ME. *lathe*, barn, cogn. with *lade²*, but it is hard to see the connection.

lather. AS. *lēathor*, washing-soda, foam; cf. ON. *lauthr*, in same sense; cogn. with L. *lavare*, *laut-*, *lot-*, G. λουτρόν, bath, Ir. *loathar*, washing vessel, all from root **lou*, to wash, with instrument. suffix. In sense of thrashing prob. associated with *leather*.

Latin. L. *Latinus* or F. *latin*, replacing AS. *lǣden*. From *Latium*, It. region which included Rome. *Vulgar Latin*, the foundation of the Rom. langs., was the every-day speech of the Roman, as different from Cicero as colloq. English is from Burke. Its forms and vocabulary, often of archaic or dial. origin, are of necessity largely conjectural and marked with an asterisk. *Late Latin*, that of the post-classical authors (c. 175–600 A.D.), is particularly rich in derivatives unknown to the short classical period (c. 75 B.C.–175 A.D.). *Medieval Latin*, the means of communication of medieval scholars and the official language in most Europ. countries, contains many words which are merely latinizations of non-Latin words; its most degraded form is *dog Latin*. *Modern Latin* includes scient. terms to which a Latin appearance is given, e.g. *rafflesia-arnoldi*. *Low Latin*, vaguely used in the past for *Vulgar, Late, Medieval, Latin*, is best avoided on account of its uncertain connotation. In medieval hist. *Latin* is often contrasted with *Greek* (Church, empire, cross); cf. Rum. *látin*, heretic.

latino: the latine toong, latine: also cleere, bright, open, easie, broad, wide (Flor.).

Le latin, ce n'est pas pour nous une langue étrangère, c'est une langue maternelle; nous sommes des Latins. C'est le lait de la louve romaine qui fait le plus beau de notre sang (Anatole France).

latitat [*leg.*]. L., he lies hidden. Writ summoning concealed culprit to appear before King's Bench.

latitude. L. *latitudo*, breadth, from *latus*, wide. First in geog. sense (Chauc.). In gen. sense of breadth, freedom, from c. 1600. Hence *latitudinarian*, spec. (c. 1660) episcopal clergyman indifferent to doctrinal details, etc.

Latonian. Of *Latona* (G. *Leto*), mother of Apollo and Diana.

latrine. F., L. *latrina*, for *lavatrina*, lavatory.

latten [*archaic*]. Mixed metal resembling brass. F. *laiton*; cf. It. *ottone* (with loss of *l*-), Sp. *latón*. In most Europ. langs., but of unknown origin. Besides *laton, alaton*, Oudin has *alatron morisco*, which suggests a possible Arab. corrupt. of *electrum*, commonly used in MedL. of a mixed metal.

latter. AS. *lætra*, compar. of *late*. *Later, latest* are new formations (see *last*[3]). Used for *last* in *latter end, days*; hence *Latter-Day Saints*, name assumed by Mormons.

lattice. F. *lattis*, from *latte*, lath (q.v.).

laud. OF. *laude*, L. *laus, laud-*, praise. Earliest (14 cent.) in *lauds*, first of the canonical hours, ending with *Ps.* cxlviii–cl., sung as one psalm and called *laudes*, from init. *laudate* in many verses.

laudanum. Var. of *labdanum, ladanum* (q.v.), used by Paracelsus of a quack elixir, perh. with a suggestion of *laud* (v.s.), and later applied to opiate of which his remedy was prob. composed.

Laudian [*hist.*]. Of *William Laud*, archbp. of Canterbury (†1645).

laugh. AS. *hliehhan*. Com. Teut.; cf. Du. Ger. *lachen*, ON. *hlæja*, Goth. *hlahjan*. Of imit. origin; cf. L. *cachinnare*. With to

laugh in one's sleeve cf. F. *rire sous cape*. In *laughing-stock*, the second element may be the stump or "butt" used as target (but see *stock*). *Laughter* (cf. Ger. *gelächter*) has the same rare suffix as *slaughter*.

launce. Sand-eel. Also called *lant*, the words being of about same age (c. 1620), so that *launce* may be a pl. (cf. *bodice, quince*, etc.). Or *launce* may be from *lance*, in allusion to shape, in which case *lant* may be a false sing.

launch[1]. Verb. ONF. *lanchier* (*lancer*), to hurl, from *lance* (q.v.), orig. meaning in E. (Chauc.). But naut. sense appears c. 1400 and is responsible for fig. senses, e.g. to *launch forth, out*. With to *launch an enterprise* cf. to *float a company*.

The dog died game...enquired if his hearse was ready, and then, as old Rowe used to say, was launched into eternity

(Gilly Williams, *Letter to George Selwyn*, 1765).

launch[2]. Boat. Sp. *lancha*, pinnace. Cf. Port. *lanchara*, Malay *lancharan*, from *lanchār*, quick.

laundress. Fem. of *launder*, earlier *lavender* (whence name *Lavender*), F. *lavandier*, Late L. *lavandarius*, from *lavare*, to wash. For lengthened *launderer* cf. *poulterer, caterer*. Verb to *launder* is a back-formation.

And laveth hem in the lavandrye

(*Piers Plowm.* C. xvii. 330).

laureate. L. *laureatus*, crowned with laurel (q.v.). First E. *poet laureate* was Ben Jonson, though title was only conferred officially (1638) on his successor, Davenant. In much earlier sense in wider sense.

Fraunceys Petrak, the lauriat poete (Chauc. E. 31).

laurel. By dissim. for *laurer, lorer*, OF. *lorer* (*laurier*), from L. *laurus*. Cf. *poplar*. For fig. senses cf. *palm*.

With laurer crowned as a conquerour

(Chauc. A. 1027).

laurustinus. ModL., from *laurus* (v.s.) and *tinus*, the latter a L. name for the same shrub.

lava. It., "a streame or gutter sodainly caused by raine" (Flor.), from *lavare*, to wash. Applied by Neapolitans to lava-streams of Vesuvius and hence adopted by most Europ. langs.

lavabo [*eccl.*]. L., I will wash, from *Ps.* xxvi. 6, repeated by celebrant in ritual washing of hands.

lavatory. L. *lavatorium*, from *lavare*, to wash. Current sense (Blount) is latest.

Thow shalt make a brasun lavatory [Coverd. laver] with his foot to wasshe with (Wyc. *Ex.* xxx. 18).

lave. F. *laver*, L. *lavare*. AS. also had *lafian*, from L.

laveer [*archaic naut.*]. Du. *laveeren*, earlier *loeveren*, F. *louvoyer*. See *luff*[1].

lavender. AF. *lavendre*, MedL. *lavendula*. In most Europ. langs., e.g. It. Sp. *lavanda* (both archaic), Du. Ger. *lavendel*. Earliest recorded is MedL. *livendula*, perh. connected with *livid* (q.v.). Later forms app. associated with *lavare*, to wash, the plant being used as perfume in bath and to scent clean linen (*laid up in lavender*).

laver[1]. Plant. L. (Pliny).

laver[2] [*Bibl.*]. F. *lavoir*, as *lavatory* (q.v.).

laverock. See *lark*.

lavish. Orig. noun, profusion, excessive abundance. OF. *lavasse*, deluge of rain, *lavis*, torrent of words, from *laver*, to wash. Adj. appears first in *lavish of tongue*.

Ther was no lavas in their speche (Caxton).

law[1]. Late AS. *lagu*, of ON. origin (cf. ON. *lög*, law, pl. of *lag*, thing "laid" down). This replaced AS. *ǣ* (cf. Ger. *ehe*, marriage orig. law), and *gesetnes* (cf. Ger. *gesetz*, law, the thing "set"). The same sense-development appears in E. *doom* (q.v.), G. θέμις, law, and L. *statutum*. Applications of the word have been influenced by (? remotely cogn.) F. *loi*, L. *lex, leg-*. *Law and order* is one of the many phrases (*act and deed, acknowledge and confess*, etc.) which spring up naturally among a bilingual population. The use of *-in-law* to indicate relationship by marriage alludes to canon law. The old Teutons had a complete set of words to express the kinship connections of a clan, but these tended to disappear with the transition from tribal life. With *Lydford (Halifax) law* cf. *Lynch law, Jeddart justice*. In sporting sense of start *law* is from hunting phrase to *give fair law*, the hunted animal being in the position of prisoner on trial. With *lawyer* cf. *bowyer, sawyer, lovyer* (Chauc.). *Law-abiding* is a mod. alteration of *law-biding*, awaiting the due course of law. See *bide*.

Their aunt I am in law, in love their mother
(*Rich. III*, iv. 1).
First hang and draw,
Then hear the cause by Lidford law.

law[2], **la.** Interj. Partly of natural origin; cf. *la*, similarly used in AS. and in F. Also for *lor'*, disguised form of *Lord*, and perh. associated in some uses with *lo* (q.v.).

law[3] [*Sc. & north.*]. Hill. AS. *hlāw*, whence southern *low*, mound.

lawks. In *lawks-a-mussy*. Alteration of *Lord have mercy*, perh. associated with *alack*.

lawn[1]. Fabric, esp. used for bishops' sleeves. Prob. from *Laon* (Aisne), pronounced *lan*, once famous for linen manufactures. Cf. *arras, cambric, shalloon*, etc., and obs. *cloth of Remes* (Reims).

lawn[2]. Turf. For earlier *laund*, open treeless space, still in dial. use, F. *lande*, moor, of Celt. origin and cogn. with *land* (q.v.). *Lawn-tennis* was invented (1874) by Major Wingfield.

laund, or *lawn*: saltus, planities inculta (Litt.).

The game we played was an invention of our own and called field-tennis
(Hickey's *Memoirs*, i. 72).

lax[1]. Salmon. Norw. Sw. *lax*, from ON.; cf. AS. *leax*, Du. *lax*, Ger. *lachs*. One of the few Com. Teut. fish-names; it has also Slav. cognates.

lax[2]. Adj. L. *laxus*, slack, cogn. with *languēre*. Cf. *laxative*, and *laxist* (theol.), opposed to *rigorist*.

lay[1]. Verb. Causal of *lie*[1] (q.v.). AS. *lecgan*. Com. Teut.; cf. Du. *leggen*, Ger. *legen*, ON. *legja*, Goth. *lagjan*. Oldest sense to prostrate, "lay low," as in to *lay a ghost*; later, to set; cf. to *lay (set) great store by*, to *lay (set) one's course*. In to *lay by the heels* there is omission of earlier *fast*. With to *lay eggs* cf. F. *pondre des œufs*, L. *ponere*, to place, lay. Betting sense is from ME. to *lay a wager*, i.e. put down a pledge. To *lay out* (an opponent) is a US. witticism on the *laying out* of a corpse. The connection of noun *lay* (slang), line, course of occupation, e.g. the *kinchin lay*, is not quite clear.

lay[2]. Song, poem. F. *lai*, of uncertain origin. ? Cf. Ger. *leich*, song, melody, cogn. with Goth. *laiks*, dance, AS. *lāc*, sport (see *lark*[2]). The earliest *lais* were Arthurian ballads which reached France from Britain in 12 cent., so that AS. *lāc*, which would regularly give F. *lai*, seems the likeliest etymon.

lay[3]. Adj. F. *lai*, Church L. *laicus*, G. λαϊκός, of the people, λαός. In ME. commonly used, like *lewd* (q.v.), in contrast with *learned*, a use revived in 19 cent. sense of non-expert.

layer. Passive sense, what is laid, for etym. active sense, as in *bricklayer*, dates from c. 1600 and first appears in cookery, spelt *lear, leer*, etc. This is prob. a separate word,

F. *liure*, binding, used of a thickened sauce.

Take codlins...and lay a lear thereof in the bottom of the pye (*NED.* 1615).

There is some chinkes or crevises betwixt one lare and another (Purch. xix. 187).

layette. Baby's outfit. F., dim. of *laie*, Du. *lade*, drawer, box.

lay-figure. For earlier *layman*, Du. *leeman*, "a statue, with pliant limbs for the use of a painter" (Sewel, 1766), of which first element is *lid*, joint (earlier *led*), cogn. with AS. *lith*, limb, and Ger. *glied*, limb (OHG. *gelid*), as in synon. *gliedermann*, *gliederpuppe*.

Rather make use of models of wax than a layman of wood (*NED.* 1688).

laystall [*dial.*]. Refuse heap. From *lay*[1] and *stall*. But perh. altered from earlier (obs.) *laystow*, from *stow*, place.

lazar [*archaic*]. Diseased person, esp. leper. From *Lazarus* (*Luke*, xvi. 20), whence also F. *ladre*, "leprous, lazerous; mezeled, scurvy" (Cotg.). Cf. *lazaret(to)*, It. *lazzaretto*, hospital, esp. for lepers, place of quarantine; *lazzarone*, Neapolitan loafer. *Lazarus* is the G. form of Heb. *Eleazar*, helped by God. But some regard It. *lazzaretto* as altered from *nazaretto*, from the hospital and quarantine station on the island of *Santa Maria di Nazaret*, near Venice.

Lazarist. Member of order founded (1624) by S. Vincent de Paul and established in *Collège Saint-Lazare*, Paris.

lazy. Earliest (1549) *laysy*. ? Back-formation from *layserly*, leisurely, taken as *lazyly*. The -*z*- sound is against connection with F. *lassé*, tired, or Ger. *lässig*, "lazy, weary, or tired" (Ludw.).

layserly: tout à loysir (Palsg.).

lazzarone. See *lazar*.

lea. Meadow-land. Two separate words are here combined—(1) AS. *lēah*, tract of ground, cogn. with OHG. *lōh*, as in *Hohenlohe*, Flem. *loo*, as in *Waterloo*, and ult. with L. *lucus*, grove, (2) AS. **lǣge*, fallow, only in *lǣhrycg*, unploughed ridge at end of field, prob. cogn. with *lie*[1]. There is also dial. *lease*, pasture, AS. *lǣs*, *lǣsw*- (cf. dial. *leasow*), which has been confused with pl. of above words. The -*leigh*, -*ley* of place-names is from the first source.

I'd meet thee on the lea-rig,
My ain kind dearie, O! (Burns).

The years have gathered grayly
Since I danced upon this leaze (T. Hardy).

I hold no leasowes in my lease (Hood).

lead[1]. Metal. AS. *lēad*. WGer.; cf. Du. *lood*, Ger. *lot*, plummet; cogn. with OIr. *luaide*.

lead[2]. Verb. AS. *lǣdan*, causal of *līthan*, to travel; cf. Goth. *galeithan*. Com. Teut.; cf. Du. *leiden*, Ger. *leiten*, ON. *leitha*; cogn. with *load*, *lode*. To *give a lead* is orig. from the hunting-field, to show the way over a fence. To *lead up to* is from cards. *Led captain* (archaic), parasite bully whose sword was at his patron's service, is prob. after *led horse*. *Leading-strings* were orig. used to teach babies to walk. *Men of light and leading* is from Burke, after Milton's *light or leading*, illumination, guidance. *Leading article* is partly due to earlier *leaded article*, from *lead*[1], strip of metal used for spacing between lines. The *leaded article* of the *Times* is mentioned in the *Oracle* (1804). A *leading question* attempts to lead the witness to the desired answer.

leaf. AS. *lēaf*. Com. Teut.; cf. Du. *loof*, Ger. *laub*, ON. *lauf*, Goth. *laufs*. For extended senses cf. F. *feuille*.

league[1]. Measure. OF. *legue*, Prov. *legua*, Late L. *leuca*, *leuga*, of Gaulish origin. Cf. It. *lega*, Sp. *legua*, F. *lieue*. A vague distance, never in offic. use, and esp. poet., perh. orig. an hour's march. *Seven-leaguedboots* renders F. *bottes de sept lieues* in Perrault's *Petit Poucet*.

league[2]. Alliance. F. *ligue*, It. *liga*, var. of *lega*, from *legare*, to bind, L. *ligare*. Cf. Ger. *bund*, league. Mod. disparaging sense (*in league with*) perh. by association with F. Catholic League (1576).

The League of Nations is an experiment
          (D. Lloyd George, in H. of C., July 3, 1919).

leaguer [*hist.*]. Camp, esp. of besiegers. Du. *leger*, camp. Cf. *beleaguer*, *laager*, *lair*.

leak. AS. *hlec*, leaky, is a Com. Teut. word; cf. Du. *lek*, Ger. dial. *lech*, ON. *lekr*. But this is not recorded in ME., the existing word being borrowed from LG. or Du., whence also Ger. *leck* (naut.). First as adj.

Their ship was leake both under and above water
                                        (Purch.).

leal. Northern form of *loyal* (q.v.). *Land of the leal* appears to have been coined by Lady Nairne (1798).

lean[1]. Adj. AS. *hlǣne*, with no certain cognates. First recorded of the kine (*Gen.* xli. 3).

lean². Verb. AS. *hlinian, hleonian*; cf. Du. *leunen*, Ger. *lehnen*, from a Teut. root cogn. with that of *incline, climax*.

leap. AS. *hléapan*. Com. Teut.; cf. Du. *loopen*, Ger. *laufen*, to run, ON. *hlaupa*, Goth. *hlaupan*. *Leap-frog* (*Hen. V*, v. 2) is now (March, 1918) in mil. use for movement of troops passing through and replacing those exhausted by fighting. *Leap-year* (ME.) may be so called from the fact that any fixed festival after February in that year leaps a day instead of occurring on the day following that of its last year's occurrence; cf. Du. *schrikkeljaar*, from *schrikkelen*, to jump. *By leaps and bounds*, app. a misunderstanding of F. *par sauts et par bonds*, by fits and starts, owes its currency to Gladstone.

It is statut and ordaint that during the rein of her maist blissit Megeste, for ilk yeare knowne as lepe yeare, ilk mayden ladye of bothe highe and lowe estait shall hae liberte to bespeke ye man she likes, albeit he refuses to taik hir to be his lawful wyfe, he shall be mulcted in ye sum ane pundis or less, as his estait may be; except and awis gif he can make it appeare that he is betrothit ane ither woman he then shall be free
(*Sc. statute*, 1288, quoted by *Enc. Brit.*).

A little before you made a leap into the dark
(T. Browne, *Letters from the Dead*, 1701).

learic. See *limerick*.

learn. AS. *leornian*, cogn. with *lǽran*, to teach; cf. Ger. *lernen, lehren*. Sense of teach (cf. F. *apprendre*, to learn, teach), now considered a vulgarism, was literary E. up to early 19 cent., and survives in adj. *learned* (= L. *doctus*), which supplanted (from 16 cent.) correct *lered* (cf. Ger. *gelehrt*). With AS. *lǽran*, to teach, cf. also Goth. *laisjan*, causal of a verb preserved only in Goth. *lais*, [I] know, a preterite-pres. verb, ult. cogn. with Ger. *geleise*, track, L. *lira*, furrow.

Who lerneth [*var.* techith] a scornere, doth wrong he to hymself (Wyc. *Prov.* ix. 7).

Be he lewed man, or ellis lered (Chauc. C. 283).

lease. OF. *les, lais*, from *laisser*, to leave, let, VL. **laxiare*, for *laxare*, from *laxus*, loose. *Lessor, lessee* preserve AF. form.

leash. F. *laisse*, app. from *laisser* (v.s.); cf. It. *lascia*, leash. For sense cf. *jess* from *jeter*. Often used in sporting lang. for three because hounds were leashed in threes (cf. *brace*).

leasing [*Bibl.*]. Lying. AS. *léasung*, from *léasian*, to lie, from *léas*, false, etc., cogn. with *loose*.

least. AS. *lǽsest, lǽst*, from same root as *less*, but unconnected with *little*. *Leastways* was orig. two words; *leastwise* is a later formation; cf. *edge-ways* (*-wise*).

leat. Water-course. AS. *gelǽt*, in *wæter-gelǽt*, aqueduct, cogn. with *let*¹.

leather. AS. *lether*, in compds. only. Com. Teut.; cf. Du. *leder, leer*, Ger. *leder*, ON. *lethr*. OIr. *leathar*, Welsh *lledr* are perh. from Teut. *Nothing like leather* has an "anecdotic" explanation of a cobbler who suggested leather as the best material for fortifications.

leave¹. Verb. AS. *lǽfan*, to leave, bequeath, causal of (*be*)*lífan*, to remain, a Com. Teut. word; cf. Du. *blijven*, Ger. *bleiben*, Goth. *bilaiban*. With the causal cf. ON. *leifa*, to leave, Goth. *bilaibjan*. With intrans. sense, to depart, cf. F. *partir*, orig. to divide. AS. *láf*, remnant, gave *lave*, still in Sc. & Ir. use. Unrelated to *leave*².

leave². Noun. AS. *léaf*, cogn. with *lief*, dear, *believe, love*, orig. idea being approval resulting from pleasure. Cf. Ger. *erlauben*, to allow, *urlaub*, permission, furlough (q.v.). In *to take one's leave*, i.e. solicit permission to depart, now associated with *leave*¹, with which it is not connected. *Leave of absence* is 18 cent.

leaven. F. *levain*, L. *levamen*, lit. relief, but here used in its etym. sense of means of raising, from *levare*; cf. synon. Du. *hef*, Ger. *hefe*, cogn. with *heave*. Fig. in ref. to various passages in *NT*. The *Vulg.* word is *fermentum*, for G. ζύμη.

lecher [*archaic*]. First as noun, debauchee, adulterer. OF. *lecheor*, from OHG. *leccōn* (*lecken*), to lick, whence F. *lécher*, It. *leccare*, to lick. Hence *lecherous, lechery*, restricted to one form of self-indulgence, wider sense being preserved in *lickerish* (q.v.).

lectern. Half-restored spelling of ME. *letterone, letrun*, etc., OF. *leitron*, Late L. *lectrum*, from *legere, lect-*, to read. The OF. forms are numerous, some representing MedL. *lectrinum*, suffix of which appears in ModF. *lutrin*.

leteron or *leterun, deske*: lectrinum (*Prompt. Parv.*).

lector. Ecclesiastic in minor orders. L., reader (v.s.). Also applied, from Ger., to univ. reader or lecturer, esp. one teaching his native lang. The first teachers of this type in England were the F. & Ger. tutors appointed at Univ. College, Nottingham (1906).

lecture. F., L. *lectura*, reading (v.s.), still its meaning in F. Current sense comes from that of reading aloud (and expounding).

ledge. ME. *legge*, cogn. with *lay*[1], *lie*[1]. Earliest sense is a transverse strip of wood, as still in EAnglia; cf. MHG. *legge*, edge, layer.

ledge of a dore: barre (Palsg.).

ledger. Earlier also *lidger*. Orig. (church) book lying permanently in one place. From ME. *liggen*, to lie, or *leggen*, to lay (v.s.). Used also techn. of a horizontal timber, flat slab, nether mill-stone, etc., and hist. in *ledger* (permanently resident) *ambassador*. Hence also *ledger lines* (mus.), though the reason is not clear. Cf. obs. *coucher*, which has most of the same senses, and of which *ledger* was prob. a transl.

lee[1]. Shelter. AS. *hlēo*, cogn. with ON. *hlȳ*, shelter, warmth, *hlē*, lee (naut.); cf. Ger. *lau*, lukewarm. The true E. form is *lew*, still in dial. and in *leeward*. The *lee* being the side away from the wind, opposed to the "weather" side, a ship is apt to make *leeway*, i.e. to drift laterally from its course, to rectify which *leeboards* are used. Hence fig. to *make up leeway*.

lee[2]. Sediment. Usu. in pl. ME. *lie*, F., Late L. *lia*, of Celt. origin.

leech[1] [*archaic*]. Physician. AS. *lǣce*. Com. Teut.; cf. OFris. *letza*, OHG. *lāhhi*, ON. *lǣknir*, Goth. *lēkeis*, with corresponding verbs. Also Gael. *leig*, Ir. *liaig*. The blood-sucking worm is usu. regarded as the same word, the healer, but ME. *liche*, obs. Du. *lieke* suggest possibility of a separate origin and assim. to *leech*, physician, by early folk-etym.

Sothli ye schulen seie to me this liknesse, Leeche [Tynd. Visicion], heele thi silf (Wyc. *Luke*, iv. 23).

leech[2] [*naut.*]. Edge of sail. Cf. ON. *līk*, whence Sw. *lik*, Dan. *lig*, bolt-rope, Du. *lijk*, Ger. *liek* (from Du. or LG.). ? Ult. cogn. with L. *ligare*, to bind.

leek. AS. *lēac*. Com. Teut.; cf. Du. *look*, Ger. *lauch*, ON. *laukr*. Cf. *garlic*. Formerly in much wider sense, as in *Leighton*, AS. *lēac-tūn*, vegetable garden. To *eat the leek*, knuckle under, is from Fluellen's handling of Pistol (*Hen. V*, v. 1).

leer. App. from obs. *leer*, cheek, AS. *hlēor*, with Du. & ON. cognates. Cf. fig. use of *cheek*. Orig. sense is to look askance, not in normal direction.

leery [*slang*]. Wide-awake. ? From dial.

lear, learning, cleverness, northern var. of *lore* (q.v.), with sense influenced by obs. adj. *leer*, sidelong (v.s.).

leet[1] [*hist.*]. As in *court-leet*, of manorial court of record. First in AF. *lete*, AL. *leta*. ? From *lathe*[1].

leet[2]. Chiefly Sc., in *short leet*, selection of best qualified candidates. Earlier *lite*, F. *élite* (q.v.).

left. Kentish form of AS. *lyft*, weak, as in *lyftādl*, paralysis; cogn. with LG. *lucht*. Cf. F. *gauche*, left, awkward, and, for converse sense-development, Ger. *linkisch*, awkward, etc., from *link*, left. For pol. sense see *centre*. In a *left-handed* (*morganatic*) *marriage* the bridegroom orig. gave his left hand to the bride.

Each gentleman pointed with his right thumb over his left shoulder (*Pickwick*, ch. xlii.).

In Kiel, where the revolution started, matters appear to be going "left" with a vengeance
(*Daily Chron*. Dec. 2, 1918).

leg. ON. *leggr*, ? cogn. with L. *lacertus*, upper arm. Replaced in most senses native *shank*. In many colloq. phrases of obvious meaning. To *pull* (orig. Sc. to *draw*) *one's leg* suggests tripping up. For *leg-bail*, flight, see *bail*[1].

legacy. OF. *legacie*, MedL. *legatia*, from L. *legare*, to bequeath, from *lex*, *leg-*, law. In ME. used also of office of legate (Wyc. *2 Cor*. v. 20).

legal. F. *légal*, L. *legalis*, from *lex*, *leg-*, law. Cf. *loyal*.

legate. F. *légat*, L. *legatus*, from *legare*, to depute. Orig. (12 cent.) of papal legate only.

legatee. Irreg. formation after *lessee*, *payee*, etc. See *legacy*.

legato [*mus.*]. It., from L. *ligare*, to bind.

legend. F. *légende*, MedL. *legenda*, to be read, from *legere*, to read, also to collect, G. λέγειν. Orig. of lives of saints, esp. *Aurea legenda*, compiled (13 cent.) by Jacobus de Voragine, bishop of Genoa. Also inscription on medal or coin.

legerdemain. From 15 cent. F. *léger de main*, light of hand, app. a mistransl. of earlier *sleight of hand*, the noun *sleight* (q.v.) being rendered by F. adj. *léger*, VL. **leviarius*, from *levis*, light.

legerdemain or sleight of hand: praestigiae (Litt.).

leghorn. Hat, fowl. Obs. It. *Legorno*, port in Tuscany, now *Livorno*, after L. *Liburnus*. Cf. *Tuscan hat*.

legible. Late L. *legibilis*, from *legere*, to read.

legion. F. *légion*, L. *legio-n-*, from *legere*, to choose, G. λέγειν. Orig. a mil. unit, 3000 to 6000 men with cavalry attached. For poet. use cf. *myriad*. The *Légion d'Honneur* was founded (1802) by Napoleon.

A legioun [*Vulg.* legio] is name to me; for we ben manye (Wyc. *Mark*, v. 9).

legislator. L. *legis lator*, proposer of law, *lator* being used as agent. noun to *ferre*, to bear, etc. *Legislate* is back-formation. Cf. *legist*, F. *légiste*, MedL. *legista*, as *jurist*.

legitimate. MedL. *legitimatus*, used for *legitimus*, from *lex*, *leg-*, law. Replaced earlier *legitime* (cf. *legitimist*, F. *légitimiste*, supporter of elder Bourbon branch). First in sense of lawfully begotten, the only meaning given by Johns. (cf. *illegitimate*).

legume [*bot.*]. F. *légume*, vegetable, L. *legumen*, ? from *legere*, to gather.

Leibnitzian. Of *Leibniz*, Ger. philosopher (†1716).

leisure. ME. *leysir*, OF. *leisir* (*loisir*), L. *licēre*, to be lawful, allowed. For formation from infin. and change of suffix in E. cf. *pleasure*.

leitmotif [*mus.*]. Ger., lead motive. Coined by a Wagner enthusiast c. 1870.

leman [*archaic*]. Early ME. *leofmon*, lief man. Although the compd. is not recorded as common noun in AS., it occurs as personal name (9 cent.). Orig. of either sex and used in devotional literature both of Christ and the Virgin. For degeneration cf. *paramour*.

lemma [*math.*]. Assumed proposition. G. λῆμμα, from λαμβάνειν, to take. Also used for heading, argument.

lemming. Arctic rodent. Dan., ON. **lemjandi* (only in pl. *lemendr*), whence also Lapp *luomek*.

lemon[1]. Earlier (c. 1400) *limon*, F., *lime*[3] (q.v.); formerly also, lemon (see *citron*). Cf. It. *limone*, Sp. *limón*, MedL. *limo*.

lemon[2]. Flat-fish, as in *lemon-sole*. F. *limande*, "a burt or bret-fish" (Cotg.); cf. OF. *limande*, flat board, cask-stave. ? From L. *lima*, file; cf. It. *limaria*, "a fish called a tunie" (Flor.).

lemur. Nocturnal mammal (Madagascar). L. **lemur*, ghost (only in pl.), ? cogn. with *lamia*, goblin.

lend. For earlier *lene*, AS. *lǣnan* (see *loan*); cf. Du. *leenen*, Ger. *lehnen*, to enfeoff, ON. *lāna*. The *-d* is due to past *lende* and

association with numerous other verbs in *-end*.

Freond, lǣn [Wyc. leene, Tynd. lende] me thrȳ hlāfas (AS. *Gosp. Luke*, xi. 5).

length. AS. *lengthu*, from *long*. *Lengthy* is US. and was esp. indulged in by Jefferson.

That, to borrow a trans-atlantic term, may truly be called a lengthy work (Southey).

lenient. Formerly in sense of *lenitive*. From pres. part. of L. *lenire*, to soothe, from *lenis*, mild.

Leninism [*hist.*]. Pol. system of *Lenin*, alias Uljanoff (born 1870), dictator of Russia during the Bolshevist régime (1917...).

leno. Cotton gauze. F. *linon* or It. *lino*. See *linen*.

lens. L., lentil, from shape; cf. F. *lentille*, in same sense.

Lent. For earlier *lenten*, AS. *lencten*, spring, Lent; cf. OHG. *lengizin*, ModGer. *lenz*, spring, Du. *lente*. First element is prob. *long* and second an OTeut. word for day, with allusion to lengthening of days in spring. Church sense is peculiar to E. The adj. *lenten* is really the older form of the noun felt as adj. in such compds. as *Lenten fast*, *Lenten entertainment* (*Haml.* ii. 2).

lenticular. Shape of lens or lentil (q.v.).

lentil. F. *lentille*, L. *lenticula*, dim. of *lens*, *lent-*, lentil. First record (13 cent.) in ref. to *Gen.* xxv. 29.

lentisk. Tree. L. *lentiscus*, from *lentus*, pliable, "clammie" (Coop.).

lentitude. Sluggishness. L. *lentitudo*, from *lentus*, slow, etc. (v.s.).

leonid [*astron.*]. L. *leonides*, meteors appearing to radiate from constellation *Leo*, the lion.

leonine. L. *leoninus*, from *leo-n-*, lion. *Leonine city* is that part of Rome which includes the Vatican, walled in by *Leo IV* (9 cent.). *Leonine verse*, with middle as well as final rime, is prob. from some medieval poet, perh. *Leo*, Canon of St Victor, Paris (12 cent.).

leopard. F. *léopard*, Late L., Late G. λεόπαρδος, because supposed to be hybrid of lion and pard (q.v.). Mod. spelling is restored from ME. *libbard*, *leppard*, etc.

Si mutare potest Aethiops pellem suam, aut pardus varietates suas (*Vulg. Jer.* xiii. 23).

leper. Orig. leprosy. F. *lèpre*, L., G. λέπρα, fem. of λεπρός, scaly, from λεπίς, scale. Sense of leprous man arose from attrib. use as in *leper folk*. *Leprosy* is from adj. *leprous*, F. *lépreux*, Late L. *leprosus*.

lepidoptera [*biol.*]. Scale-winged. From G. λεπίς, λεπιδ-, scale (v.s.), πτερόν, wing.

leporine. L. *leporinus*, from *lepus, lepor-*, hare.

leprachaun [*Ir.*]. Elusive fairy appearing as shoemaker. Variously spelt, in 17 cent. usu. *lubrican*. OIr. *luchorpán*, from *lu*, little, *corpan*, dim. of *corp*, body.

leprosy. See *leper*.

leptorrhine [*biol.*]. With long narrow nose. From G. λεπτός, thin. See *rhinoceros*.

Lesbian. Of *Lesbos*, in G. archipelago. Esp. in ref. to Sappho and unnatural vice.

lese-majesty [*leg.*]. Treason. F. *lèse-majesté*, L. *laesa majestas*, violated majesty (see *lesion*). Cf. Ger. *majestätsbeleidigung*.

lesion [*leg. & med.*]. F. *lésion*, L. *laesio-n-*, from *laedere, laes-*, to hurt. Cf. *collide*.

less. AS. *lǣssa*, adj., *lǣs*, adv., used as compar. of *little*, but prob. not connected with it. With double compar. *lesser* cf. *better*. Applied to persons only in *no less a man than* and *St James the less*. *Nothing less* has some of the ambiguity of F. *rien moins*, e.g. *I expected nothing less than five pounds*.

-less. AS. *-lēas*, devoid of, free from, cogn. with *lose, loose*; cf. Ger. *-los*.

lessee. See *lease*.

lesson. F. *leçon*, L. *lectio-n-*, reading, from *legere, lect-*, to read. Orig. sense still in eccl. *first* (*second*) *lesson*.

lessor. See *lease*.

lest. ME. *les the*, short for AS. *thȳ lǣs the*, where *thȳ* is instrument. case of def. art. and *the* is its weakened form used as relative particle. Cf. L. *quominus*, lest, lit. by which the less, of which the AS. phrase was perh. a transl.

let¹. To leave, allow. AS. *lǣtan*. Com. Teut.; cf. Du. *latan*, Ger. *lassen*, ON. *lāta*, Goth. *lētan*; perh. cogn. with *late* (q.v.); cf. sense-development of F. *laisser*, from L. *laxus*, slack. Sense of handing over land in exchange for rent is found in AS.

let² [*archaic*]. To hinder. AS. *lettan*, from *late*; cf. *hinder*. Com. Teut.; cf. Du. *letten*, Ger. *letzen* (*verletzen*, to harm), ON. *letja*, Goth. *latjan*, to delay (intrans.). Now chiefly as noun, e.g. *let or hindrance, let at tennis*.

We are sore let and hindered in running the race that is set before us (*Collect, 4th Advent*).

letch. Craving. ? Connected with F. *allécher*, to allure, ult. from L. *allicere*.

lethal. L. *let(h)alis*, from *letum*, death. Now esp. in *lethal chamber* (19 cent.).

He suspects it of wanting to "lethal chamber" his aunt's "dear old doggie" (Wells, *Mod. Utopia*).

lethargy. F. *léthargie*, L., G. ληθαργία, from λήθαργος, forgetful, from λανθάνειν, to escape notice.

lethe. G. Λήθη, river of Hades producing oblivion, λήθη, in those who drank its waters (v.s.).

Lett, Lettic, Lettish. People and lang. in part of Russ. Baltic provinces. Ger. *Lette*, from native name *Latvi*. The lang. is Aryan, akin to Lithuanian and extinct OPrussian.

letter. F. *lettre*, L. *littera*, letter of alphabet, in pl. epistle, earlier *litera, leitera*. Extended senses as in F. *lettre*, partly after St Paul's use of τὸ γράμμα (2 *Cor.* iii. 6). *Before the letter* (of engravings) means proof taken before title-lettering is inserted. *Letterpress* is matter printed from type, as opposed to illustrations, etc. from plates. Sense of literature appears already in L., e.g. *lettered ease* is Cicero's *otium literatum*.

lettuce. ME. *letus(e)*, pl. of AF. *letue*, F. *laitue*, L. *lactuca*, from *lac, lact-*, milk. Cf. *bodice, quince*, etc.

Therf looves with wylde letuse [*Vulg.* cum lactucis agrestibus] (Wyc. *Ex.* xii. 8).

leucopathy. Albinism. From G. λευκός, white.

Levant. Orig. East in gen., now eastern part of Mediterranean. F. *levant*, east, lit. rising, from L. *levare*.

levant. Verb. ? From Sp. *levantar*, to lift, raise (v.s.), as in *levantar el campo*, to strike camp, "decamp," perh. with suggestion of the *Levant* as usual goal of absconding swindler.

levee. F. *levé*, for *lever*, orig. king's morning reception on rising from bed. *Levee*, embankment, pier (southern US.), is F. *levée*, p.p. fem.

level. OF. *livel* (later, by dissim., *nivel*, now *niveau*), VL. **libellum*, for *libella*, dim. of *libra*, balance. First (14 cent.) in E. of instrument, as in mod. *spirit-level*. For fig. senses (*level-headed*) cf. *balance*. *Level best* is US.

Gentlemen are requested not to shoot at the young man at the piano; he is doing his level best
(*Notice in saloon of Californian mining-camp*).

lever. ME. *levour*, OF. *leveor* (replaced by *levier*), from *lever*, to raise, L. *levare*.

leveret. AF. *leveret*, for F. *levrant*, dim. of *lièvre*, hare, L. *lepus, lepor-*.

leviathan. Late L. (*Vulg. Job*, xl. 20), Heb. *livyāthān*, of uncertain origin and meaning. Perh. connected with Heb. *lāwāh*, to twist, bend.

Super Leviathan, serpentem tortuosum
(*Vulg. Is.* xxvii. 1).

levigate. From L. *levigare*, from *lēvis*, smooth.

levin [*poet.*]. Flash of lightning. ME. *leven*, obs. in 18 cent., but revived by Scott, with whom it is a favourite word. Skeat compares obs. Dan. *löffn*, Sw. dial. *lyvna*, in same sense.

levirate. Custom of brother of dead man marrying latter's widow (Jewish). From L. *levir*, husband's brother.

levitate. From L. *levis*, light, after *gravitate*.

Levite, Leviticus. From *Levi*, son of Jacob, whose descendants formed class of assistant priests.

levity. OF. *levité*, L. *levitas*, from *levis*, light.

levy. F. *levée*, p.p. fem. of *lever*, to raise, L. *levare* (v.s.). Orig. of taxes, then of troops, whence to *levy war* (15 cent.), a sense not found in F.

lewd. AS. *lǣwede*, lay, layman, app. in some way derived from L. *laicus*, lay² (ME. *lewed or lered* corresponds to ON. *leikr ok lærdr*). See quot. s.v. *learn*. Orig. meaning of profane, unlettered, hence coarse, vile, passes into current sense, already found in Chauc. (A. 3145).

I have not leeuyd looues [*Vulg.* laicos panes] at hoond, but oonli hooli breed (Wyc. 1 *Sam.* xxi. 4).

lewis. Machine-gun, from American inventor's name. Cf. *gatling, maxim, nordenfeldt*.

The R.F.C. adopted the Lewis...and the German airmen countered with a modified Hotchkiss
(*An Airman's Outings*).

lexicon. G. λεξικόν (sc. βιβλίον), word (book), from λέγειν, to speak. A Renaissance word; cf. F. *lexique* (Ronsard). Hence *lexicographer*, "a harmless drudge, that busies himself in tracing the original, and detailing the signification of words" (Johns.).

Leyden jar, battery. Invented (1745–6) at *Leyden*, Holland.

li. Chin. unit of length, 100 *li* being about a day's march.

liable. App. from F. *lier*, to bind, L. *ligare*, but not recorded in AF. or Law L. Cf. fig. sense of *bound* (*to*).

liaison. F., L. *ligatio-n-*, from *ligare*, to bind.

Now esp. in *liaison officer*, link and interpreter between allied forces.

This position as "liaison minister" between the House and the War Cabinet
(*Daily Chron.* June 18, 1918).

liane, liana. F. *liane*, app. some native name assimilated to *lier*, to bind (v.s.). *Liana* is perh. due to supposed Sp. origin.

Bois rampants...que les habitants nomment "lienes" (*Histoire des Antilles*, 1658).

lias [*geol.*]. Blue limestone. F. *liais*, OF. *liois* (12 cent.). ? From *lie*, lee²; cf. *lie de vin*, used in F. for a purplish blue.

libation. L. *libatio-n-*, from *libare*, to taste, pour forth, G. λείβειν.

libel. OF. (replaced by *libelle*), L. *libellus*, dim. of *liber*, book. Current sense, from Law L. *libellus famosus*, is the latest. See *library*.

And the preest shal wryte in a libel [*Vulg.* in libello] thes cursid thingis (Wyc. *Numb.* v. 23).

liberal. F. *libéral*, L. *liberalis*, from *liber*, free. For later senses cf. *frank, generous*. As party-name from early 19 cent., being applied by opponents, at first in Sp. or F. form, with suggestion of foreign lawlessness, and coupled by George IV with *jacobin*.

To love her [Lady Elizabeth Hastings] was a liberal education (Steele).

Ce gueux est libéral! ce monstre est jacobin!
(Victor Hugo).

libertin. F., orig. (from 16 cent.) free-thinker, L. *libertinus*, freed man. The change of meaning appears to be due to misunderstanding of L. *libertinus* in *Acts*, vi. 9. Secondary sense of debauchee is almost as early in E.

liberty. F. *liberté*, L. *libertas*, from *liber*, free. In all Rom. langs. Up to 1850 used of county region exempt from authority of sheriff and in other kindred senses. *Liberty of the press* is 18 cent.

libidinous. F. *libidineux*, L. *libidinosus*, from *libido, libidin-*, lust; cf. *libet, lubet*, it pleases; ult. cogn. with *love*.

library. F. *librairie* (in OF. library; now, bookseller's shop), from *libraire*, copyist (now, bookseller), L. *librarius*, of books, from *liber*, book, orig. bark of tree. Cf. hist. of *book, bible, paper*.

libration [*astron.*]. Oscillation. L. *libratio-n-*, from *librare*, from *libra*, balance.

libretto. It., little book. See *libel*.

Libyan. Of *Libya*, NAfr. Sometimes used of group of Hamitic langs. which includes Berber.

licence. F., L. *licentia*, from *licēre*, to be lawful. Later sense of excessive liberty appears in current meaning of *licentious* (v.i.). *Lycence poeticall* (v.i.) is in Palsg. *Licentiate* is etym. one who has received licence (to teach, heal, etc.).

Poets and painters are licentious youths (Denham).

lich, lych. Chiefly in *lich-gate*, at which corpse is set down to await priest's arrival. AS. *līc*, body, living or dead (cf. *corpse*). Com. Teut.; cf. Du. *lijk*, Ger. *leiche*, ON. *līk*, Goth. *leik*; cogn. with *like*, ground-sense being shape. See also *-ly*.

lichen. L., G. λειχήν, ? cogn. with λείχειν, to lick.

lichi. See *litchi*.

licit. L. *licitus*, p.p. of *licēre*, to be lawful.

lick. AS. *liccian*. Aryan; cf. Du. *likken*, Ger. *lecken*, Goth. *laigōn* (in compds.), L. *lingere*, G. λείχειν, Sanskrit *rih*, *lih*, OIr. *ligim*. F. *lécher*, It. *leccare*, are from Teut. To *lick into shape* (cf. L. *lambendo effingere*) alludes to old belief as to cubs (see *cub*), recorded by Aristotle, and said to be traceable in Egypt. hieroglyphics. Sense of thrashing is from cant. *Full lick* is US.

lickerish. For earlier *lickerous*, from ONF. form of *lecherous* (q.v.). Like many adjs. it is both active and passive, pleasant to the taste, fond of good fare (cf. *dainty*).

friand: a sweet-lips, pick-morsell, curious feeder, lickorous companion, dainty-mouthed fellow (Cotg.).

lictor. L., officer bearing the *fasces*, bundles of rods with axe. ? From *ligare*, to bind.

lid. AS. *hlid*; cf. Du. *lid*, Ger. *(augen)lid*, (eye)lid, ON. *hlith*, gate, gap.

Lidford law. See *Lydford*.

lie¹. To recline, be situated, etc. AS. *licgan*. WAryan; cf. Du. *liggen*, Ger. *liegen*, ON. *liggja*, Goth. *ligan*, G. λέχος, bed, Ir. *lige*, couch, Russ. *lejat'*. See *lay¹*.

lie². To speak untruly. AS. *lēogan*, orig. strong. Com. Teut.; cf. Du. *liegen*, Ger. *lügen* (MHG. *liegen*), ON. *liūga*, Goth. *liugan*.

liebig. From *Baron von Liebig*, Ger. chemist (†1873).

lied. Ger., song; cf. AS. *lēoth*.

lief. Adv. Now chiefly in *would as lief*, due to *I'd as lief*, orig. *I had as lief* (cf. Ger. *lieb haben*), being understood as *I would as lief*. AS. *lēof*, dear. Com. Teut.; cf. Du.

lief, Ger. *lieb*, ON. *liūfr*, Goth. *liufs*; cogn. with *love*, and with L. *lubet* (*libet*), it pleases. With archaic *lief or loath* cf. Ger. *lieb oder leid*.

liege. First (13 cent.) in *liege lord*. F. *lige*, "liege, leall, or loyall; subject, vassall; naturall, one's own" (Cotg.); cf. It. *ligio*, "a liegeman, subject, or vassall" (Flor.). From Ger. *ledig*, free. Hence MedL. *ligius*, popularly connected with L. *ligare*, to bind (see *allegiance*). The Ger. word is cogn. with AS. *ālithian*, to set free, ON. *lithugr*, free, and ult. with L. *liber*, for **lithr-*, and G. ἐλεύθερος.

Ligius homo, quod Teutonice dicitur *ledigh-man* (Duc. 1253).

lien [*leg.*]. F., bond, L. *ligamen*, from *ligare*, to bind.

lierne [*arch.*]. Short rib connecting intersection of principal ribs. F., app. from *lier* (v.s.).

liernes: slits, enterlaces, or entertoises of timber (Cotg.).

lieu. F., L. *locus*, place. *In lieu of*, for F. *au lieu de*, is found in 13 cent.

lieutenant. F., place-holder (v.s.); cf. *locum tenens*. From usual pronunc., archaic in US., comes naut. *luff*, as in *first luff*. This is perh. due to association with *leave²*. All senses of the word go back to that of substitute, representative of some higher authority. See *general*.

Hubert archebisshop of Caunterbury was leeftenaunt [*var.* lutenant, levetenaunt] of the pope and of the kyng of Engelond (Trev. viii. 143).

In the absence of meistre Richard Yorke, John Fry to be luffetenand (*York Merch. Advent.* 1474–5).

life. AS. *līf*, life. Com. Teut.; cf. Du. *lijf*, body, Ger. *leib*, body (OHG. *līb*, life), ON. *līf*, life, body; cogn. with *leave¹*, ground-sense being continuance. *For the life of me* goes back to *under pain of life*, where *life* is practically equivalent to *death*. *Life-guard* is prob. adapted from obs. Du. *lijf-garde* (cf. Ger. *leibgarde*), body-guard (v.s.). The orig. Teut. identity of *life* with body (v.s.) appears to have an echo in *life and limb* (cf. F. *corps et membres*), *life and soul*, the latter being used up to 18 cent. in phrase to *keep life* (now *body*) *and soul together*.

lift. ON. *lypta*, whence Sw. *lyfta*, Dan. *löfte*; cogn. with archaic *lift*, sky, AS. *lyft*; cf. Ger. *luft*, air, *lüften*, to lift. See *loft*. With slang sense, to steal, still in *shop-lifter*, cf.

F. *enlever*, to remove, carry off, lit. to raise thence.

ligament, ligature. L. *ligamentum, ligatura*, from *ligare*, to bind, or through F.

ligeance [*hist.*]. See *allegiance, liege*.

light¹. Brightness, bright. AS. *lēoht*, noun being perh. neut. of adj. WGer.; cf. Du. Ger. *licht*; cogn. with ON. *ljōme*, gleam, Goth. *liuhath*, light, L. *lux, luc-*, G. λευκός, white, ἀμφιλύκη, twilight. Sense of window, as in *ancient lights*, is ME. Hence verb to *light*, of which *lighten* is a later extension. *Lightning* is pres. part. of latter. *Light-house* replaced (17 cent.) earlier *pharos* (q.v.).

light². Not heavy. AS. *lēoht*. Com. Teut.; cf. Du. *ligt*, Ger. *leicht*, ON. *lēttr*, Goth. *leihts*; cogn. with L. *levis* (for **leghus*). To *make light of* (Tynd. *Matt.* xxii. 5) is for earlier to *set light*, regard as unimportant. *Light-o'love*, orig. adj., is 16 cent. Verb to *light*, AS. *līhtan*, now gen. replaced by *lighten*, has developed intrans. sense of descend, alight (q.v.), via that of lightening the vehicle, etc. With to *light upon* cf. F. *tomber sur*, in same sense. With *lighter*, boat for lightening vessel, cf. F. *allège*, from *alléger*, to lighten.

lights. Lungs of slaughtered animals. Spec. use of *light²*, the lungs being distinguished from other organs by their lightness. See *lung*.

lign-aloes [*Numb.* xxiv. 6]. Late L. *lignum aloes*, wood of *aloe* (q.v.). Not bot. the same as *aloe*.

ligneous. From L. *ligneus*, from *lignum*, wood. Cf. *lignite* coal, *lignum vitae*, guaiacum.

ligula [*bot.*]. L., narrow strip, tongue, cogn. with *lingua*.

like. Adj. AS. *gelīc*, orig. having the form of, from *līc*, body (see *lich*); cf. Du. *gelijk*, Ger. *gleich*, ON. *glīkr*, Goth. *galeiks*, and, for sense-development, L. *conformis*. *Likely* is thus etym. a redupl. (see *-ly*). Something of orig. sense survives in *his like, the likes of*, and Bibl. *liking* (*Dan.* i. 10). *Likewise* is for earlier *in like wise*, in a similar manner. Verb to *like*, orig. to please, AS. *līcian*, is of same origin, ground-idea being to be like or suitable, as in archaic *it likes me, well-liking*. Mod. sense, to approve, love, is due to misunderstanding of *if you like*, i.e. if it please you, is all the same to you (cf. Ger. *wenn es dir gleich ist*), where *you* is dat. governed by impers. verb *like* used in

subjunct. The same development appears in Norw. *like*, while Du. keeps the orig. construction, e.g. *dat lijkt mij niet*. Hence *likes and dislikes* (19 cent.).

> The victorious cause likide to the goddes [L. diis placuit], and the cause overcomen likide to Catoun (Chauc. *Boethius*).

> I do hear that Sir W. Pen's going to sea do dislike the Parliament mightily (Pepys, Mar. 29, 1668).

likely. ON. *līkligr*, cogn. with AS. *gelīclic* (v.s.). In *a likely young fellow*, etc., now chiefly US., influenced by association with later senses of verb to *like*.

likin. Chin. provincial transit duty. Chin. *li*, equivalent to *cash²*, and *kin*, money.

lilac. OF. (now only in pl. *lilas*), Sp., Arab. *līlǎk*, Pers. *līlak*, var. of *nīlak*, bluish, from *nīl*, blue, indigo (cf. *anil*). Earlier *laylock* is via Turk. *leilaq*.

lillibullero [*hist.*]. Part of meaningless refrain of popular song (c. 1688) against James II's Ir. soldiers. A favourite tune with Uncle Toby.

Lilliputian. From *Lilliput*, land of pygmies in Swift's *Gulliver's Travels* (1726). Cf. *Brobdingnagian*.

lilt. ME. *lülten*, to sound, strike up loudly. Mod. sense from Sc. ? Cf. Du., LG. *lul*, pipe.

> Many floute and liltyng horne (Chauc. *House of Fame*, iii. 133).

lily. AS. *lilie*, L. *lilium*, G. λείριον. In most Europ. langs. *Lily of the valley*, earlier also *convally*, is *Vulg. lilium convallium*, from *convallis*, dale, lit. transl. from Heb. of *Song of Sol.* ii. 1. *Lily-livered* is after *Macb.* v. 3.

limb¹. Of body. AS. *lim*, cogn. with ON. *limr*, and ult. with Ger. *glied* (see *lay-figure*); cf. relation of *time, tide*. *Life and limb* is found in AS. (see *life*). *Limb*, mischievous boy, etc., is for earlier *limb of Satan* as opposed to *member* (in AS. *lim*) of Christ; cf. *imp, limb of the law*. In US. *limb* is often euph. for *leg* (v.i.).

> Punching and kicking the said plaintiff [a lady] in, on and about the plaintiff's head, body, arms and limbs (*New York Sun*, Nov. 10, 1917).

limb² [*scient.*]. L. *limbus*, edge; cf. F. *limbe*. See *limbo*.

limbeck [*archaic*]. Aphet. for *alembic* (q.v.).

limber¹. Of a gun. Earlier (c. 1500) also *lymnar, lymour*, shafts and fore-frame of vehicle, F. *limonière*, in same sense, from *limon*, shaft, thill, MedL. *limo-n-*, of unknown origin. ? Cogn. with L. *limus*, slanting. Hence to *unlimber*, *limber up*.

To certifye what carttes, wagons, limoners or other carriages the Pale [of Calais] was able to furnisshe
(*Privy Council Acts*, 1545).

limber² [*naut.*]. Hole through timbers on each side of keelson to admit water to pump-well. F. *lumière*, lit. light, in same sense. For vowel cf. *limn*.

Just sufficient [water] to sweeten the limbers
(Bullen, *Cruise of Cachalot*).

limber³. Adj. From 16 cent. Sense agrees with Ger. *lind*, *gelind*, cogn. with E. *lithe*¹ (q.v.) and L. *lentus*, "pliant, that boweth easily, limber" (Coop.), with which it is possibly cogn.

limbo. L., abl. of *limbus*, edge, border, in theol. *in limbo patrum* (*infantum*), in the border region of Hades reserved for pre-Christian saints and unbaptized children. Hence fig. confinement, prison, receptacle for what is worn out and worthy of oblivion.

lime¹. Mineral, etc. AS. *līm*, used both for glue, (bird) lime, and calcium oxide. Com. Teut.; cf. Du. *lijm*, Ger. *leim*, ON. *līm*; cogn. with L. *limus*, mud, *linere*, to smear. See also *loam*, *caulk*. With *limelight* (19 cent.) cf. *Drummond light*.

lime². Tree. Earlier (16 cent.) *line*, for obs. *lind*, which survives in adj. form *linden* (q.v.). AS. *lind*. Com. Teut.; cf. Du. Ger. *linde*, ON. *lind*. Common in place-names, e.g. *Lyndhurst*, *Lynwood*. Alteration of *line* to *lime* app. due to compds. in which second element had init. labial, e.g. *lime-bark* (*-bast*, *-wood*).

lime³. Fruit. F., Sp. *lima*, Arab. *līmah*, of Malay or Javanese origin. See *lemon*.

lime-hound [*archaic*]. Also *lyam-*, *lyme-*. From OF. *liem*, var. of *lien* (q.v.). For formation and sense cf. *bandog*.

limehouse [*hist.*]. Used disparagingly by pol. opponents of Mr Lloyd George in ref. to a speech made at *Limehouse* in his less wise days.

These are the youths that thunder at a play-house and fight for bitten apples; that no audience, but the tribulation of Tower-hill, or the limbs of Lime-house, their dear brothers, are able to endure.
(*Hen. VIII*, v. 4).

We do not want war-limehousing during a great crisis (*Nat. News*, Nov. 18, 1917).

limerick. Form of verse. Said to be from refrain *Will you come up to Limerick?*

sung at convivial gathering at which such verses were extemporized. But it seems likely that the choice of the word may have been partly due to the somewhat earlier *learic* (v.i.), coined by Father Matthew Russell, S.J.

A "learic" is not a lyric as pronounced by one of that nation who joke with deefficulty, but it is a name we have invented for a single-stanza poem modelled on the form of the "Book of Nonsense," for which Mr Edward Lear has got perhaps more fame than he deserved (*Ir. Monthly*, Feb. 1898).

liminal [*psych.*]. Minimum stimulus producing excitation. From L. *limen*, *limin-*, threshold, used to render Ger. *schwelle*, threshold, adopted (1824) by Herbart in this sense.

limit. F. *limite*, L. *limes*, *limit-*, boundary, cogn. with *limen* (v.s.) and with *limus*, transverse. Hence *limitation*, which, in such phrases as *he has his limitations*, may go back to spec. ME. sense of district allotted to a *limitour*, or itinerant begging friar. *Limited*, descriptive of commerc. company, is for *limited liability*, legalized 1855. Colloq. use of *the limit* is mod. (not in *NED*.).

limitrophe. Bordering. F., Late L. hybrid *limitrophus*, applied to lands allotted for support of frontier troops, from L. *limes*, *limit-* (v.s.), G. τρέφειν, to support.

limn. For earlier *lumine*, OF. *luminer*, to illuminate (manuscripts), or aphet. for *allumine*, OF. *alluminer*, *enluminer*, from L. *lumen*, *lumin-*, light. The King's *limner* is still a court official in Scotland.

This bisshop hymself schonede not to write and lumine [*var.* lymne, Higd. illuminare] and bynde bookes (Trev. vii. 295).

limnology. Study of lakes and pond-life. From G. λίμνη, lake, marsh.

limousine. Motor-car. F., earlier closed carriage, orig. hood as worn by inhabitants of province of *Limousin*.

limp¹. Verb. From 16 cent. Cf. obs. *limp-halt*, lame, AS. *lemphealt*. ? Cogn. with *lame*.

limp². Adj. From c. 1700. App. shortened from *limber³*.

limpet. AS. *lempedu*, Late L. *lampetra*, whence also *lamprey* (q.v.).

limpid. L. *limpidus*, cogn. with *lymph* (q.v.).

linchpin. From AS. *lynis*, axle-tree; cf. Du. *luns*, Ger. *lünse*. Prob. an ancient word (cf. *nave*), but of obscure hist.

Lincoln green. A green cloth made at *Lincoln*. Cf. earlier *Lincoln say²* (c. 1300).

lincrusta. Trade-name, from L. *linum*, flax, *crusta*, crust. Cf. *linoleum*.

linden. Lime-tree. See *lime*² and cf. *aspen*. Currency of adj. form has been helped by Ger. *lindenbaum*, familiar in folk-songs.

Lindley Murray. US. author of *English Grammar* (1795), long regarded as standard. Cf. *Cocker*.

line¹ [*techn.*]. Long fibre of flax. AS. *līn*, flax, L. *linum*, G. λίνον; prob., like *hemp*, of Eastern origin. Cf. *linen*, *linseed*. *Line* is still used in dial. for *linen*.

line². Length without breadth. Earliest in sense of cord, etc. AS. *līne*, L. *linea*, orig. linen thread, from *linum*, flax (v.s.); cf. Du. *lijn*, Ger. *leine*, ON. *līna*, early Teut. loans from L. Hence to *give line*, from angling. In *by line and rule* (cf. F. *au cordeau*, and similar use of Heb. *qav*, cord, *Is.* xxviii. 10), and *lines* in sense of course of life (*Ps.* xvi. 6, *Vulg. funes*), there is orig. allusion to the marking out of land for settlement. *Hard lines* is app. naut., and may be a jocular variation on *hard tack*, ship's biscuit, taking *tack* in its orig. sense of rope, line. Sense of mark, stroke, direction, is via F. *ligne*, L. *linea*, mil. and nav. uses, as in *ship* (*regiment*) *of the line*, being adopted directly from F. *On these* (*such*) *lines* is from ship-building. To *take one's own line* is from the hunting-field. *Lines of communication* were orig. transverse trenches connecting the *lines of circumvallation*, in great siege-works.

line³. Verb (of clothes). From *line¹*, with orig. ref. to linen as material used for the purpose.

> Did a sable cloud
> Turn forth her silver lining on the night
> (*Comus*, 221).

line⁴. Verb (of bitch). F. *ligner*, for *aligner*, to bring together (see *line²*).

lineage. ME. *linage*, F. *lignage*. See *line²*. Cf. *lineal*, F. *linéal*, Late L. *linealis*.

lineament. F. *linéament*, L. *lineamentum*, contour, outline. Not orig. limited to facial lines. Cf. *delineate*.

linen. Orig. adj., made of flax. AS. *līnen*, from *līn*, flax (see *line¹*); cf. Du. *linnen*, Ger. *leinen*. F. *linge* is also of adj. formation.

He left the linen cloth in their hands and fled from them naked (*Mark*, xiv. 52).

ling¹. Fish. ME. *lenge*; cf. Du. *leng*, Ger. *langfisch*, ON. *langa*; cogn. with *long*.

ling². Heather. ON. *lyng*.

-ling. Dim. suffix. Combined from suffixes *-el* (*-le*) and *-ing*. As applied to persons usu. contemptuous (*starveling*, *shaveling*, *underling*, etc.).

-ling(s). AS. adv. suffix (also *-lang*, *-lung*), cogn. with *long*, by which it is now usu. replaced, e.g. *headlong*, *sidelong*. See *grovel*.

linger. ME. *lengeren*, frequent. of obs. *lengen*, to tarry, AS. *lengan*, to prolong, from *long*. Cf. Ger. *verlängern*, to prolong.

lingerie. F., from *linge*, linen, L. *lineum*, neut. adj. from *linum*, flax. This euph. for under-linen will in course of time become indelicate and make way for something else (cf. *shift*).

Fie, miss. Amongst your "linen," you must say. You must never say "smock"
         (Congreve, *Love for Love*).

lingo. Prov. *lengo*, *lingo*, or Gascon *lengo*, L. *lingua*. A naut. word (17 cent.) from Marseille or Bordeaux.

lingua franca. It., Frankish tongue. A kind of "pidgin" It., with elements from other Mediterranean and Oriental langs., spoken in the Levant. Hence fig. mixed jargon understood by those who would otherwise not be intelligible to each other. The name is prob. due to the Arabs, *Frank* (q.v.) being regular Eastern word for European (cf. *Feringhi*).

linguist. From L. *lingua*, tongue, language, Sabine form of OL. *dingua* (cf. *lacrima*, *dacruma*), cogn. with *tongue*.

linhay [*dial.*]. Open shed with lean-to roof. ? From AS. *hlinian*, to lean, with second element as in archaic *church-hay*.

liniment. F., L. *linimentum*, from *linere*, to smear.

link¹. Connection. ON. **hlenkr*, whence ModIcel. *hlekkr*, Sw. *länk*, Dan. *lænke*; cogn. with AS. *hlencan* (pl.), armour, Ger. *gelenk*, joint, *lenken*, to turn. Hence also archaic and dial. *link*, bunch of sausages. The *missing link* (between man and monkey) dates from c. 1880.

link². Torch, as in *linkman*, *linkboy*. ? From *link¹*, a simple form of torch being a length of tarred rope, ? or from MedL. *linchinus*, for *lichinus*, explained as wick in 15 cent., from G. λύχνος, light, lamp.

links. Grass-covered sand-hills on coast. AS. *hlinc*, acclivity, perh. cogn. with *lean²*. Cf. dial. *linch*, boundary-ridge.

Cowering in a sand-bunker upon the links
         (*Redgauntlet*, ch. xi.).

linn. Waterfall, pool at foot. Mixture of AS.

hlynn, torrent, and Gael. *linne*, pool. The latter is in all Celt. langs. ? and cogn. with G. λίμνη, lake.

Linnaean. System of biol. classification of *Linnaeus*, latinized name of *C. F. Linné*, Sw. naturalist († 1778).

linnet. F. *linotte*, from *lin*, flax, on seeds of which it feeds. Cf. Ger. *hänfling*, linnet, from *hanf*, hemp. Dial. *lintwhite*, linnet, is AS. *līnetwige*, ? flax-twitcher.

The lintwhite and the throstle-cock
Have voices sweet and clear (Tennyson).

linoleum. Patented and named (1863) by a Mr Walton from L. *linum*, flax, *oleum*, oil. Cf. *kamptulicon*, *lincrusta*.

linotype. US. (1888). For *line of type*.

linseed. AS. *līnsǣd*, flax seed. See *line*[1], *seed*. Cf. Du. *lijnzaad*.

linsey, linsey-woolsey. From 15 cent. Skeat derives *linsey* from *Lindsey*, near Kersey (Suff.). See *kersey*. Another theory is that it represents *line*[1] and *say*[2] (q.v.), or that the ending is the adj. -*sy* as in *flimsy*, *tipsy*. *Woolsey*, from *wool*, is a later addition.

linstock [*archaic*]. For firing early cannon. Earlier (16 cent.) *lint-stock*, Du. *lont-stok*, from *lont*, match, whence E. dial. *lunt*.

lunt: the matchcord with which guns are fired
(Johns.).

Hairy-faced Dick, linstock in hand,
Is waiting that grim-looking skipper's command
(Ingoldsby).

lint. ME. *linnet*, from *line*[1]. Flax (plant and material) is still *lint* in Sc. Cf. Burns' *lint-white hair* for *flaxen hair*.

lintel. OF. (*linteau*), VL. *limitale* or *limitellus*, from *limes*, *limit-*, limit.

lion. F., L. *leo-n-*, G. λέων, λέοντ-, prob. of Egypt. origin. In all Rom. & Teut. langs. (e.g. It. *leone*, Sp. *león*, Du. *leeuw*, Ger. *löwe*), whence, or from L., it passed into the Balto-Slavic langs., e.g. Russ. *lev*. AS. had *lēo*, *lēon*, directly from L. The *lions*, in sense of noteworthy objects, were orig. those in the Tower of London, and to *have seen the lions* once meant to be wide-awake, up to snuff, not a new arrival from the country. *Lion-hunter*, seeker after celebrities, seems to be due to Dickens' *Mrs Leo Hunter* (*Pickwick*). Scott uses *lionize* (1809).

I took them and all my ladys to the Tower and showed them the lions and all that was to be shown
(Pepys, May 3, 1662).

The only man unspoilt by lionizing was Daniel
(Sir H. Tree).

lip. AS. *lippa*; cf. Du. *lip*, Ger. *lippe* (a LG. word replacing archaic HG. *lefze*); cogn.

with L. *labrum*, *labium*, lip, *lambere*, to lick, Pers. *lab*, lip. In earlier use fig. for tongue, speech (see *babel*), as in *lip-service*, etc. *To the lips*, usu. with *steeped*, is after *Oth.* iv. 2. *Lip*, impudence, and *stiff upper lip* are both US.

lipography. Omission of letter or syllable in copying. From G. λείπειν, to leave.

lipper. Ripple. Orig. Sc. ? Cogn. with *lap*[2].

liquid. F. *liquide*, L. *liquidus*, from *liquēre*, to be clear. For use in phonology, adapted from G. ὑγρός, wet, cf. F. *mouillé*, wet, in *l mouillée*. *Liquidation*, in commerc. sense, means making clear.

My accounts, which I have let go too long, and confounded my publique with my private so that I cannot come to any liquidation of them
(Pepys, Mar. 31, 1666).

liquor. Restored from ME. *licur*, OF. *licour* (*liqueur*), L. *liquor-em* (v.s.). For degeneration in meaning, e.g. *in liquor*, *the worse* (*better*) *for liquor*, cf. *drink*. So also *liquor traffic*.

liquorice. AF. *lycorys*, OF. *licorece* (replaced by *réglisse*), Late L. *liquiritia*, ult. from G. γλυκύς, sweet, and ῥίζα, root. The Europ. forms, resulting from metath. of *l-r*, are extraordinary, e.g. F. *réglisse*, It. *regolizia*, Ger. *lakritze*, Du. *kalissie-drop*; cf. also Arab. *el-irkasūs*. The Late L. form and ModE. spelling are due to association with *liquor*, and the E. termination is perh. due to *orris* (q.v.).

liquorish. Corrupt. of *lickerish* (q.v.) erron. associated with *liquor*.

lira [*It.*]. Coin worth a franc. L. *libra*, pound; cf. F. *livre* used also for franc.

Lisle thread. From *Lille* (Nord), formerly *l'isle*, the island.

lisp. AS. *āwlyspian*; cf. Du. *lispen*, Ger. *lispeln*, earlier *wlispen*. Imit., cf. *whisper*.

I lisp'd in numbers, for the numbers came
(Pope, *Prol. to Sat.* 128).

lissom. For *lithesome*. Regarded as dial. word in early 19 cent.

list[1]. Noun. AS. *līste*, hem, border; cf. Du. *lijst*, Ger. *leiste*. Orig. sense in *list slippers*, made of edge-strips (cf. archaic F. *tapis de lisières*). Sense of enumeration is from F. *liste*, strip of paper, etc., from Teut. (cf. *enlist*). The *lists* for a tourney are the boundaries of the field, but the application of the word has been influenced by F. *lice* (cf. It. *lizza*, Sp. *liza*), so that we find *lists* treated as sing. (cf. *links*, *shambles*, *works*, etc.). F. *lice* is prob. L. *licia*, pl. of *licium*, thread (whence MHG. *litze*, in same sense), and thus unrelated to *list*.

lice: a lists, or tilt-yard (Cotg.).

liste: a list, roll, check-roll, or catalogue of names, &c. also a list, or selvedge (*ib.*).

list². Verb. AS. *lystan*, to please, from *lust* (q.v.); cf. Du. *lusten*, Ger. *lüsten*, *gelüsten*, ON. *lysta*. Orig. impers., as used archaically by Scott, later sense being due to misunderstanding of *if you list* (cf. *like, please*). Hence *list*, inclination, leaning, now usu. naut., and *listless*, for earlier *lustless*.

lust: when a ship heels a little to either side, they say, she has a lust that way (*Sea Dict.* 1708).

> When, in Salamanca's cave,
> Him listed his magic wand to wave,
> The bells would ring in Notre Dame (*Lay*, ii. 13).

list³, listen. *List* is AS. *hlystan*, from *hlyst*, hearing, from an Aryan root which appears in Ger. *lauschen*, to listen (esp. for prey), Welsh *clust*, ear, ult. cogn. with *loud*. *Listen* is Northumbrian *lysnan*, cogn. with AS. *hlosnian*, from same root.

list⁴ [*naut.*]. See *list²*.

listerize. To treat according to methods of *Lord Lister*, E. physician (†1912).

listless. See *list²*.

lists. See *list¹*.

litany. F. *litanie*, MedL., G. λιτανεία, from λιτανεύειν, to pray, from λιτή, supplication. Usual form up to 17 cent. is *letanie*, and *lētanīa* is found in AS.

litchi, lichi. Chin. fruit. Chin. *li chi*.

> A Canton china bowl of dried lichis
> (Kipling, *Bread upon the Waters*).

-lite. F., G. λίθος, stone.

literal. L. *literalis*, from *litera*, letter (q.v.). Cf. *literary, literature*, etc., the latter of which has replaced ME. *lettrure*, from OF., used for AS. *bōccræft*. *Literally* is often used by the excited in a sense opposite to its real meaning (v.i.).

> The eyes of the whole Irish race are literally fixed upon the contest (J. Dillon, M.P., May, 1918).

litharge [*chem.*]. F., from OF. *litargire*, L., G. λιθάργυρος, from λίθος, stone, ἄργυρος, silver. In Chauc. (A. 629).

lithe¹. Adj. AS. *līthe*, soft, mild; cogn. with Ger. *lind, gelind*, gentle, and with L. *lentus*, soft, slow, etc., *lenis*, gentle. Current sense is latest. See *lissom*.

lithe². Only in archaic *lithe and listen*. ON. *hlȳtha*, to listen, cogn. with *list³*.

> Now lithe and listen, ladies gay (Scott).

lithia. Altered from earlier *lithium*, G. λί-

θειον, neut. of λίθειος, stony, name proposed (1818) by Berzelius to emphasize its min. origin, previously discovered alkalis being vegetable.

lithograph. From G. λίθος, stone. Cf. *lithology*, science of stones; *lithotomy* (med.), cutting for stone, from τέμνειν, to cut.

Lithuanian [*ling.*]. Aryan lang. of Baltic group, cogn. with Lettish and extinct OPrussian.

litigation. Late L. *litigatio-n-*, from *litigare*, to go to law, from *lis, lit-*, lawsuit, and *agere*. Earlier is *litigious*, F. *litigieux*, L. *litigiosus*.

> Not litigious, or ful of stryf (Wyc. 1 *Tim.* iii. 3).

litmus [*chem.*]. ON. *litmose*, lichen used in dyeing, from ON. *litr*, colour, *mosi*, moss. It is much older than *NED.* records, occurring several times in the *Custom Rolls* of Lynn (1303–7), to which harbour it was brought from Norway.

litotes [*gram.*]. Affirmative expressed by negation of contrary, e.g. L. *haud parum*, very much, *nonnulli*, some. G. λιτότης, from λιτός, plain, meagre.

> A citizen of no mean city (*Acts*, xxi. 39).

litre. F., suggested by *litron*, obs. measure, from Late L. *litra*, G. λίτρα, pound. F. from 1799 (cf. *gramme, metre*).

litter. F. *litière*, from *lit*, bed, L. *lectus*; cf. G. λέκτρον. Earliest E. sense is bed; then, portable couch, bedding, strewn rushes, straw, etc., for animals, whence disorderly accumulation of odds and ends; cf. F. *faire litière de*, to trample under foot. With sense of number (of animals) brought forth at one birth cf. similar use of *bed*.

little. AS. *lȳtel*. WGer.; cf. Du. *luttel*, Ger. dial. *lützel*. According to *NED.* not related to synon. ON. *lītill*, Goth. *leitils*. (*A*) *little* (*sugar, patience*, etc.) is for earlier *little of*. *Little go* (first Camb. examination) meant in 18 cent. a private lottery.

littoral. L. *li(t)toralis*, from *litus, litor-*, shore, whence the *lido* of Venice. As noun after It. *littorale*, F. *littoral*.

liturgy. Orig. Communion service of Eastern Church. F. *liturgie*, Church L., G. λειτουργία, public worship, first element ult. from λεώς, λαός, people, second from ἔργον, work.

live¹. Verb. AS. *lifian* (WSax. *libban*), from *līf*. Com. Teut.; cf. Du. *leven*, Ger. *leben*, ON. *lifa*, Goth. *liban*; cogn. with *leave¹*, orig. sense being to remain. *Living* in

Church sense is for *ecclesiastical living*, where *living* means endowment, means of support.

live². Adj. Evolved (16 cent.) from *alive* (q.v.).

livelihood. Altered, under influence of obs. *livelihood*, liveliness, from earlier *lifelode*, AS. *līflād*, life-course; see *lade¹*, *lode*. Cf. OHG. *lībleita*, subsistence.

[Pythagoras] berynge of burthens for to gete his lifelode therwith (Trev. iii. 199).

livelong. In the *livelong day* (*night*). Orig. *lief long*, *lief* (q.v.) being a mere intens. Cf. Ger. *die liebe lange nacht*.

den lieben gantzen tag: the whole liblong day
(Ludw.).

lively. AS. *līflic*, lit. life like, orig. sense surviving in *lively description*. For sense-development cf. *vivid*. *A certain liveliness*, from an Admiralty announcement in the autumn of 1914, seems likely to become a stock phrase.

They [young airmen] are much safer in France than in England, and they are sent across directly they begin to show a certain liveliness
(*Daily Sketch*, July 9, 1918).

liver. AS. *lifer*. Com. Teut.; cf. Du. *lever*, Ger. *leber*, ON. *lifr*. Formerly competed with the heart as seat of passion; hence *white-livered*.

When love's unerring dart
Transfixt his liver and inflamed his heart
(Dryden).

Liverpudlian. Of *Liverpool*, with jocular substitution of *puddle* for *pool*.

livery. F. *livrée*, p.p. fem. of *livrer*, to hand over, deliver, Late L. *liberare*, from *liber*, free. Orig. household allowance, provision of any kind, now limited to costume of servants and provender for horses, as in *livery stable*. The City *Livery Companies* had formerly distinctive costumes for special occasions, an inheritance from the medieval gilds.

That no maner of hand-crafte were any lyvery, but of his owne crafte that he usith
(*Coventry Leet Book*, 1421).

lyvery of cloth or oder gyftys: liberata (*Prompt. Parv.*).

livid. F. *livide*, L. *lividus*, from *livēre*, to be bluish.

livre. F., L. *libra*, pound. Still occ. used in F. for *franc* when stating income in thousands.

lixivium. Lye. L., neut. of *lixivius*, from *lix*, ashes, lye. Cf. F. *lessive*, washing solution, from neut. pl.

lizard. F. *lézard*, L. *lacertus*. Cf. *alligator*.

llama. Sp. from Peruv., app. gen. name for sheep.

Llamas or sheepe of Peru (Hakl.).

llano [*geog.*]. SAmer. prairie. Sp., L. *planus*, smooth.

Lloyd's. Marine insurance. Orig. coffee-house in Lombard St., established by *Edward Lloyd* (fl. 1688–1726). The name is Welsh for gray.

lo. ME. also *low*, *loo*. Prob. for *lōke*, look, but with sound affected (*lo* instead of *loo*) by interj. *lo*, AS. *lā*. For loss of *-k* cf. *ta'en* for *taken*.

loach. Fish (*Lorna Doone*, ch. vii.). F. *loche*. Origin unknown.

load. AS. *lād*, way, journey, conveyance, cogn. with *lead²*, which is still used in the Midlands of carting. Verb, from noun, is much later. Sense has been influenced by *lade²*, which it has almost supplanted. With to *load* a gun cf. F. *charger*, Ger. *laden*, in same sense, all going back to the period when cannon were the only fire-arms. See also *lode*.

loode or caryage: vectura (*Prompt. Parv.*).

loadstone. See *lode*.

loaf¹. Noun. AS. *hlāf*, bread, loaf. Com. Teut.; cf. Ger. *laib*, ON. *hleifr*, Goth. *hlaifs*; cogn. with L. *libum*, cake. See *lord*, *lady*.

If it were not for the loaves and fishes [*John*, vi. 26] the train of Christ would be less (Bp Hall, 1614).

loaf². Verb. NED. rejects connection with LG. *lofen*, Ger. *laufen*, to run, as in *landläufer*, landloper. It would seem however that *loafer* might have been evolved from the latter word; cf. colloq. Norw. *loffe*, to loaf, from US.

The newly invented Yankee word of "loafer"
(Dana, *Two Years before the Mast*, 1840).

loam. AS. *lām*, cogn. with *lime¹*; cf. Du. *leem*, Ger. *lehm* (from Du.), Ger. dial. *leimen*.

loan. ON. *lān*, superseding AS. *lǣn* (whence *lend*); cf. Du. *leen*, Ger. *lehen*, fief. Hence verb to *loan*, now chiefly US.

loath. AS. *lāth*, repulsive, etc., replaced in orig. sense by compds. *loathly*, *loathsome*. Com. Teut.; cf. Du. *leed*, Ger. *leid*, sorrow (but still adj. in *lieb oder leid*), ON. *leithr*. F. *laid*, ugly, is from Teut. Current sense, already in Chauc., as also that of verb to *loathe*, is for earlier impers. use. Cf. construction of *like*.

Hym were looth byjaped for to be (Chauc. H. 145).
I lothe his villanye, or it lotheth me of his villanye: il me faiche de sa vilanie (Palsg.).

lob. For gen. sense of something heavy, pendant, or floppy contained in this imit. word cf. Du. *lob, lubbe,* hanging lip, Dan. *lobbes,* clown, Norw. *lubb, lubba,* tubby person, and see *lubber. Lob-lie-by-the-fire* is Milton's *lubber-fiend* (*Allegro,* 110). The cricket *lob* is from dial. verb to *lob,* to pitch gently. With *lobscouse,* sailor's stew, *loblolly,* sailors' gruel, cf. *lob,* a thick mixture in brewing. *Loblolly* (16 cent.), from dial. *lolly,* gruel, etc., was also applied to the doctor's drenches, hence naut. *loblolly boy,* orig. surgeon's mate in the navy. The existence of the surname *Lobb* suggests that the word is much older than *NED.* records, and that archaic and dial. *Lob's pound,* the lock-up, is of the same type as *Davy Jones' locker.*

lobby. MedL. *lobium* or *lobia,* monastic for *lodge* (q.v.). See also *louver.* Current sense first in Shaks. (*Haml.* ii. 2). The *lobby* of the House of Commons is mentioned in 1640. Hence verb to *lobby* (US.), orig. to frequent *lobby* of Congress in order to solicit votes and influence.

Our recluses never come out of their lobbeis [? = cloisters] (*NED.* 1553).

lobe. F., Late L., G. λοβός, lobe of ear, pod, etc.

lobelia. From *Matthias de Lobel* (†1616), botanist and physician to James I.

loblolly, lobscouse. See *lob.*

lobster. AS. *loppestre,* for *lopust,* corrupt. of L. *locusta,* whence also F. *langouste,* "a kind of lobster that hath undivided cleyes" (Cotg.); cf. OCorn. *legast,* lobster. See *locust.* As nickname for soldier orig. applied (1643) to a regiment of Parliamentary cuirassiers, and later associated with the red coat. Joc. use for *lob-bowler* is 20 cent.

local. F., L. *localis,* from *locus,* place. *Local option* (*veto*), right of majority to decide what minority shall drink, owes its currency to Gladstone (1868), but was first used in a Parliamentary bill in 1879 (Sir W. Lawson).

loch. Gael. & Ir., cogn. with *lake*[1]; cf. Anglo-Ir. *lough.*

lock[1]. Of hair. AS. *loc.* Com. Teut.; cf. Du. *lok,* Ger. *locke,* ON. *lokkr.*

lock[2]. Fastening. AS. *loc;* cf. Ger. *loch,* hole, orig. shut-up place, ON. *lok,* lid. In river sense from c. 1300. The *lock* of a gun, first in *firelock,* must orig. have resembled that of a door (cf. Ger. *schloss* in both senses).

Hence *locker, locket;* the latter is F. *loquet,* latch, of Teut. origin.

The gunner is...to have his shot in a locker near every piece (*NED.* 1642).

Heaving the rest into David Jones's locker, i.e. the sea
(Roberts, *Voyages,* 1726, p. 41; see also p. 89).

lockram [*archaic*]. Fabric. OF. *locrenan,* from *Locronan* (Finistère), i.e. cell of St Ronan, where formerly made.

locomotive. Suggested by L. phrase *in loco movēri.* Orig. philos. term, current sense, for *locomotive engine,* dating from c. 1830.

locum tenens. L., place holding. In MedL. of any deputy. Cf. *lieutenant.*

locus. L., place. *Locus standi* is app. mod.

locust. F. *locuste,* L. *locusta,* lobster (q.v.), locust. The *locust bean,* carob, translates G. ἀκρίς, locust, applied to the pod from some fancied resemblance.

locution. F., L. *locutio-n-,* from *loqui, locut-,* to speak.

lode. Graphic var. of *load* (q.v.), preserving etym. sense of course, direction, e.g. in mining, and locally of watercourse, etc. Hence *lodestar* (Chauc.), guiding star (cf. ON. *leitharstjarna,* Ger. *leitstern*), and *lodestone* (16 cent.), magnet. The former is one of Scott's revivals. With the latter cf. synon. Du. *zeilsteen,* from *zeilen,* to sail.

lodge. F. *loge,* OHG. **laubja* (*lauba*), porch, lobby, etc., whence ModGer. *laube,* summer-house, etc.; cf. It. *loggia,* from Ger. See *lobby.* Prob. cogn. with *loft* and *louver,* but not with Ger. *laub,* leaf, though associated with it in ModGer. sense of arbour. Use in Freemasonry and other societies comes from *lodge* being used (14 cent.) of the shop in which the freemasons (q.v.) worked. Current sense of *lodger* is in Shaks. (*Hen. V,* ii. 1). Verb was orig. trans.; cf. to *lodge a sum of money* (*complaint,* etc.).

Like to the summer's corn by tempest lodg'd
(2 *Hen. VI,* iii. 2).

loess [*geog.*]. Dust deposit. Ger. dial., from *los,* loose.

loft. ON. *lopt,* cogn. with AS. *lyft,* air, upper region, Ger. *luft,* air. Hence *aloft, lofty, lofting-iron,* preserving etym. sense. In ME. and later a gen. term for upper room, attic. See *lift.*

He...carried him up into a loft [*Vulg.* caenaculum], where he abode (1 *Kings,* xvii. 19).

log[1]. Late ME. *logge,* of about same age and meaning as *clog.* ? Norw. *laag,* ON. *lāg,* felled tree, cogn. with *lie*[1]. Presumably introduced with timber from Norway. A ship's *log* is the same word, the apparatus being a quadrant of wood weighted so as to float upright. But some derive the naut. *log* from Arab. *lauḥ*, plank, tablet. Hence *log-book*, orig. for recording rate of progress, and verb to *log*, enter in book. *Log-rolling* (US.) was orig. used of cooperative effort in building log-huts (*You roll my log and I'll roll yours*). *Logwood* is imported in logs.

Stuffe called logwood alias blockewood
(*NED.* 1581).

log[2] [*Bibl.*]. Measure for liquids (*Lev.* xiv. 24). Heb. *lōg*, about three-quarters of pint.

logan-berry. First cultivated by *Judge Logan* (US.).

logan-stone. For *logging-stone*, from Corn. dial. *log*, to rock.

logarithm. Coined (1614) by Napier of Merchiston, from G. λόγος, word, ratio, ἀριθμός, number.

logger-head. First (Shaks.) in sense of blockhead, jolter-head, etc. App. from *log*[1]. In naut. lang. orig. a bar-shot with cannon-ball each end. Hence to *be at logger-heads*; cf. *daggers drawn*.

You logger-headed and unpolished grooms
(*Shrew*, iv. 1).

loggia. See *lodge*.

logic. F. *logique*, MedL. *logica* (sc. *ars*), G. λογική (sc. τέχνη), art of reasoning, from λόγος, word, speech, reason.

logie [*theat.*]. Sham jewellery of zinc. From inventor's name.

logistics [*mil.*]. Art of quartering troops. F. *logistique*, from *loger*, to lodge.

logogram, logograph. Sign representing word, G. λόγος. Cf. *logogriph*, word-puzzle, F. *logogriphe*, from G. γρῖφος, fishing-net, riddle; *logomachy*, word-strife, G. λογομαχία, from μάχη, contest; *logotype* (typ.), as *logogram*.

-logue. F., G. -λογος, from λέγειν, to speak.

-logy. F. *-logie*, G. -λογία, from λόγος, word, discourse (v.s.). Cf. *'ology*.

loin. OF. *loigne* (*longe*), VL. **lumbea*, from *lumbus*, loin.

loiter. Cf. Du. *leuteren*, earlier *loteren*, "morari" (Kil.), also, to totter, dawdle; cogn. with Ger. *lotter*, in *lotterbube*, wastrel, *liederlich*, *lüderlich*, debauched, and obs. E. *lither*.

loll. App. imit. of dangling movement. Cf. obs. Du. *lullebanck*, couch, lounge. *Lollop*

is a natural elaboration. There was also an obs. *lill*, expressing a lighter sense.

His [the wood-pecker's] long tongue doth lill,
Out of the cloven pipe of his hornie bill
(Sylv. i. 5).

Lollard [*hist.*]. Obs. Du. *lollaerd*, from *lollen*, to mutter, mumble; cf. *lull*. Orig. applied (c. 1300) to a Catholic fraternity who devoted themselves to care of sick and funeral rites of poor; later to other orders, with suggestion of hypocrisy. Cf. hist. of *beggar*. *Loller* (v.i.) is slightly earlier in E. The name was punningly explained, by opponents, from L. *lolium*, tare, cockle (v.i.).

"This Loller here wol prechen us somwhat."
"Nay, by my fader soule! that shal he nat!"
Seyde the Shipman; "here shal he nat preche;
He shal no gospel glosen here, ne teche.
We leven alle in the grete God," quod he,
"He wolde sowen som difficulte,
Or sprengen cokkel in our clene corn"
(Chauc. B. 1177).

lollipop. From child-lang. Cf. dial. *lolly*, tongue.

lollipops: sweet lozenges purchased by children
(Grose).

lollop. See *loll*.

Lombard. F., It. *Lombardo*, Late L. *Langobardus*, long-beard, from Ger. tribe which conquered and named Lombardy. Some authorities explain it as long-axe, with second element as in *halberd* (q.v.). Earliest *Lombards* in E. were Italian money-lenders and bankers, whence *Lombard St*. See *China*.

I lerned amonge Lumbardes and Jewes a lessoun,
To wey pens [i.e. pence] with a peys
(*Piers Plowm.* B. v. 242).

London pride. Orig. (c. 1600) equivalent to *sweet william*. ? From flourishing in London gardens.

lone. Aphet. for *alone* (q.v.). Hence *lonely*, *lonesome*. Now poet. exc. in to *play a lone hand*, orig. at the obs. card-game quadrille.

long[1]. Adj. AS. *lang*. Com. Teut.; cf. Du., Ger. *lang*, ON. *langr*, Goth. *laggs*; cogn. with L. *longus*, whence F. *long*, which has also contributed to our word. *In the long run* was earlier (17 cent.) *at the long run*, app. adapted from F. *à la longue*. The *longbow* was distinguished from the cross-bow. With fig. sense of to *draw the longbow* cf. mod. to *throw the hatchet*. *Longcloth* is calico manufactured in long pieces. *Long drawn out* is after Milton.

> He loves your wife; there's the short and the long
> (*Merry Wives*, ii. 1).
> Many a winding bout
> Of linked sweetness long drawn out (*Allegro*, 140).

long². Verb. AS. *langian*, to grow long. Mod. sense is from impers. use; cf. F. *il me tarde*, I long, lit. it is slow to me, and Norw. Dan. *længes* (reflex.), also orig. impers.

> Him wile sone long thar after (*NED.* c. 1200).
> *il me tarde que*: I think long till (Cotg.).

-long. In *endlong*, ON. *endlangr*. But in *headlong*, *sidelong*, substituted for *-ling²* (q.v.).

longanimity. Late L. *longanimitas*, on *magnanimitas*, after G. μακροθυμία.

longevity. L. *longaevitas*, from *aevitas* (*aetas*), age.

longinquity. L. *longinquitas*, from *longinquus*, from *longus*. Cf. *propinquity*.

longitude. L. *longitudo*, from *longus*. Cf. *latitude*. In Chauc.

long-shore. Aphet. for *along-shore*. Cf. *cross-country*, for *across-*.

loo [*archaic*]. For earlier *lanterloo*, F. *lanturelu*, meaningless refrain of popular song temp. Richelieu. Cf. *lillibullero*.

looby. ? Cf. *lob*, *lubber*. But F. *Lubin*, a proper name, ult. from *lupus*, wolf, was in OF. an abusive nickname for a monk or friar, and earliest sense of *looby* (*Piers Plowm.*) is idler, loafer.

loofah. Arab. *lūfah*, plant with fibrous pods, from which flesh-brushes are prepared.

look. AS. *lōcian*; cf. Ger. dial. *lugen*, to look out. To *look sharp* meant orig. to *look sharp(ly)* (to something being done). *Never to look back* (earlier *behind one*), in sense of unchecked success, is perh. from racer leading easily. With to *look down on* (*up to*) cf. *despise*, *respect*.

> Here I experienced the truth of an old English proverb, that standers-by see more than the gamesters (Defoe, *Mem. Cav.* ch. ii.).

loom¹. For weaving. AS. *gelōma*, implement, utensil, of any kind; cf. obs. Du. *allaam* (Vercoullie), with prefix as in AS. *andlōman* (pl.), utensils, apparatus.

loom². Verb. Orig. (c. 1600) naut., and app. in mod. sense of indistinct atmospheric effect; ? cf. ON. *ljóma*, to gleam, cogn. with AS. *lēoma*, ray of light.

> *looming*: an indistinct appearance of any distant object, as the sea-coast, ships, mountains, &c., as "she looms large afore the wind" (Falc.).

loon¹. Lout, etc. In early Sc. (15 cent.) rogue, e.g. *false loon*. Later senses prob. associated with *loon²*. Origin unknown.

loon². Sea-bird. Earlier also *loom*. ON. *lōmr*; ? cf. Du. *loom*, lame, clumsy. Prob. assimilated to *loon¹* in its later sense.

loony [*slang*]. For *lunatic*, associated with *loon¹*.

loop. From c. 1400. Cf. Gael. Ir. *lub*, bend; ult. cogn. with *slip* (q.v.); cf. Ger. *schlupfloch*, "a starting-hole, a loop-hole" (Ludw.), from *schlüpfen*, to slip. We still have this sense of *loop-hole* in to *leave one no loophole*. *Looping the loop*, orig. of switch-back performances, is not in *NED*.

> *lits*: a loop. *De lits van een' mantel*: the loop of a cloak. *Litsgat*: a loop-hole (Sewel).

loose. Adj. ON. *lauss*, cogn. with AS. *lēas* (whence obs. *lease*, loose) and with *lose* (q.v.); cf. Du. Ger. *los*, e.g. *ein loser kerl*, a "loose fish." *At a loose end*, without employment, suggests freedom from tether. Verb is from adj.; cf. Ger. *lösen*, from *los*. Noun *loose* is obs. exc. in to *give a loose to one's feelings* (tongue).

loosestrife. Plant. Early herbalists' transl. of Late L. *lysimachion*, G. λυσιμάχιον, from pers. name Λυσίμαχος, from λύειν, to loose, μάχη, strife.

loot. Hind. *lūt*, ? from Sanskrit *lunt*, to rob.

> Hyder Ali's stragglers, or looties as they were called, committed such repeated depredations
> (Hickey's *Memoirs*, i. 175)

loover. See *louver*.

lop¹. To cut. Skeat quotes *æt loppede thorne* from an AS. charter, which points to an AS. verb *loppian*. Perh. connected with *lop²*, as *lopping* is applied esp. to removal of pendent branches in contrast to *topping* or *cropping*.

lop². To hang loosely, as in *lop-eared*, *lop-sided*. Cf. *lap¹*, *lob*. *Lopsided*, orig. naut., was earlier *lapsided*. Cf. obs. *lop-heavy*.

lope, loup. ON. *hlaupa*, to leap, run; cf. Ger. *laufen* and see *leap*, *elope*, *interlope*. Current application to wolf-like trot suggests association with Sp. *lobo*, wolf, L. *lupus*.

lophiodon. Fossil animal. From G. λόφος, crest, after *mastodon*.

loquacious. From L. *loquax*, *loquac-*, from *loqui*, to speak.

loquat. Fruit. Chin. (Canton dial.) *luh kwat*, rush orange.

lorcha [*naut.*]. Port., Chinese-rigged vessel with hull on Europ. model. Origin unknown.

lord. AS. *hlāfweard, hlāford,* loaf-ward; cf. *lady* (q.v.) and AS. *hlāf-æta,* servant, lit. loaf-eater. Orig. master of the house, husband, application to the Deity being due to its translating L. *dominus,* G. κύριος; cf. *Lord's Supper,* L. *caena dominica.* Sense of noble appears in ME., and *drunk as a lord,* to *live like a lord* are recorded in 17 cent. Verb to *lord* is in *Piers Plowm.*

lore¹. Knowledge, etc. AS. *lār,* cogn. with *learn* (q.v.); cf. Du. *leer,* Ger. *lehre.* Orig. what is taught, doctrine.

lore² [*biol.*]. Strap-like appendage to face. L. *lorum,* strap.

lorette. F., Parisian courtezan, from residence near church of *Notre Dame de Lorette* (*Loretto*).

lorgnette, lorgnon. F., from *lorgner,* to look askance, from OF. *lorgne,* squinting, of unknown origin.

loricate [*biol.*]. Armoured. From L. *lorica,* coat of mail, from *lorum,* strap (cf. *cuirass*).

lorikeet. Small lory (q.v.). After *parrakeet.*

lorimer, loriner [*hist.*]. Maker of metal parts of harness. Still in title of City Company, and as surname; cf. *Latimer,* for *latiner.* OF. *loremier, lorenier* (*lormier*), from L. *lorum,* strap, thong.

loriot. Bird. F., for OF. *l'oriot,* with agglutination of art. See *oriole.*

loris. "Ceylon sloth." Through F. from Du. *loeres,* from *loer,* clown.

lorn. Archaic p.p. of obs. *leese,* to lose (q.v.); cf. *forlorn.*

I'm a lone lorn creetur (*David Copperfield,* ch. iii.).

lorry. Also *lurry.* A 19 cent. railway word of unknown origin. It is perh. a metath. of *rolley, rulley,* recorded somewhat earlier in sense of "tram" in coal-mining. Words of this type are orig. in local use (cf. *bogie, trolley*). ? Or cf. Norw. *lorje,* lighter, earlier *lodje,* of Russ. origin. Obs. *loribus* or *lorry-bus* was coined May 31, 1919.

lory. Bird. Malay *lūrī,* also (correctly) *nūrī.*

lose. AS. *losian,* to be lost. Orig. intrans., mod. sense coming from impers. use (cf. *like, loathe*) and from association with cogn. *leese,* AS. *lēosan* (in compds.), which it has supplanted. *Leese* occurs in *AV.* (1 *Kings,* xviii. 5) where mod. editions have *lose;* cf. Du. *verliezen,* Ger. *verlieren,* Goth. *fraliusan.* With *leese, lorn,* cf. Ger. *verlieren* (OHG. *firliosan*), *verloren,* and E. *was, were.*

losel [*archaic*]. Good-for-nothing. Also *lorel.*

From p.p. *losen, loren,* of obs. *leese,* to lose (q.v.). Cf. older sense of *brothel* (q.v.).

loss. Rather a back-formation from *lost* than from AS. *los,* which is found only in dat., as in *to lose weorthan,* to come to destruction; cf. ON. *los,* breaking-up of army. *At a loss* was orig. of a hound losing the scent (cf. *at fault*).

lot. AS. *hlot,* rendering L. *sors, portio.* Com. Teut.; cf. Du. *lot,* and, with different ablaut, Ger. *loos,* ON. *hlutr,* Goth. *hlauts.* Adopted from Teut. into Rom. langs., e.g. F. *lot,* whence some senses of E. *lot;* It. *lotto,* chance, lottery, whence the name of a game; It. *lotteria,* whence E. *lottery.* Orig. the object (counter, die, straw, etc.) used in drawing (casting) lots, AS. *weorpan hlot* (see *warp*); cf. *the lot fell upon,* to *cast in one's lot with,* orig. of sharing plunder (*Prov.* i. 14), to *have neither part nor lot in* (*Acts,* viii. 21). Hence applied to tract of land orig. assigned by lot; cf. *allotment* and US. *building-lot,* etc. Sense of quantity in gen. from 16 cent. A *bad lot,* applied to a person, is from the auction-room (cf. a *hard bargain*).

lota [*Anglo-Ind.*]. Copper jug. Hind., Sanskrit *lohita,* copper.

Lothario, gay. Lady-killer. Character in Rowe's *Fair Penitent* (1703). The name had previously been used for a similar character in Davenant's *Cruel Brother* (1630).

lotion. L. *lotio-n-,* from *lavare, lot-,* to wash.

lottery. See *lot.*

lotto. See *lot.*

lotus. L., G. λωτός, in legend of lotus-eaters (*Odyssey,* ix. 90 ff.), later identified with Egypt. water-lily and other plants. *Lotus-eaters* was app. coined by Tennyson (1832) from *lotophagi.*

loud. AS. *hlūd.* WGer.; cf. Du. *luid,* Ger. *laut;* cogn. with Goth. *hliuma,* hearing, ON. *hljōmr,* sound, G. κλυτός, renowned, from κλύειν, to hear, L. *inclytus,* from *cluēre,* to be famous; cf. OIr. *cloth,* Sanskrit *ṣruta.* For application to colours, manners, etc., cf. F. *criard.*

lough. E. form (14 cent.) of Ir. *loch* or Welsh *llwch.* See *loch.*

louis. Coin. F. *louis d'or;* also furniture (*Louis quinze,* etc.). From various kings of France. The name is ident. with *Clovis, Chlodowig,* OHG. *Hlūtwīc* (*Ludwig*), whence It. *Ludovico,* lit. famous in war, as G. *Clytomachus.* See *loud.*

lounge. From c. 1500, first in Sc. Perh.

suggested by obs. *lungis*, OF. *longis*, "a dreaming luske, drowsie gangrill" (Cotg.), from *Longius* or *Longinus*, apocryphal name of soldier who pierced Christ's side with a spear. This name is perh. from a misunderstanding of G. λόγχη, lance (*John*, xix. 34), and its sense was popularly associated with L. *longus*.

a lounge, or tall gangrell: longurio (Litt.).

a lungis: longurio (*ib.*).

loup. See *lope*.

lour. See *lower*.

louse. AS. *lūs*. Com. Teut.; cf. Du. *luis*, Ger. *laus*, ON. *lūs*. The analogy of G. φθείρ, louse, from φθείρειν, to destroy, has suggested relation between *louse* and *lose*.

lout. From 16 cent., early examples (*learned and lout, lord and lout*), suggesting alteration of *lewd* (q.v.), influenced in current sense by archaic *lout*, to bend low, AS. *lūtan*.

louver. Also *loover, luffer, louvre*. Of various structures with venetian-blind arrangement for passage of smoke, air, light. OF. *lover, lovier*, from OHG. *lauba* (*laube*), whence also *lodge* (q.v.). The *lodium* by which it is sometimes rendered in medieval glossaries (*NED.*) is prob. an error for *lobium* (see *lobby*). Ger. *laube*, whence (prob. through OF.) obs. Du. *loove*, is used of all kinds of wooden structures attached to a house. Cf. Du. dial. *luif*, "a penthouse" (Sewel). Some regard these words as ult. cogn. with ON. *lopt* (see *loft*).

loove: projectura, compluvium, suggrunda, podium, menianum, pergula: vulgò lobia (Kil.).

lovage. Plant. ME. *loveache*, folk-etym. alteration (*love* and obs. *ache*, parsley, F., L. *apia*) of OF. *levesche, luvesche* (*livèche*), Late L. *levisticum*, unexplained corrupt. of L. *ligusticum*, from *Liguria*, supposed to be home of plant. In most Europ. langs. and with extraordinary perversions, e.g. Ger. *liebstöckel*, "love stick-el."

love. AS. *lufu*; cf. obs. Du. *lieven*, to love, Ger. *liebe*; cogn. with L. *lubet*, it pleases, Sanskrit *lubh*, to desire, and also with *leave*[1], belief, *lief*. The equivalent of *love or money* is found in AS. (v.i.). *There's no love lost between* is recorded since early 17 cent. in two opposite senses, of which the less kindly of course survives. *Love*, no score (tennis, etc.), is due to to *play for love*, i.e. for nothing, which again is evolved from *love or money* (v.s.). *Love-knot* is in

Chauc. (A. 197). With *love-lock* cf. F. *accroche-cœur*, in same sense. *Loving-kindness* was first used by Coverd. (*Ps.* xxv. 6). Current sense of *lovely*, "applied indiscriminately to all pleasing material objects, from a piece of plum-cake to a Gothic cathedral" (Marsh), appears in early ME. For etym. sense see *Philip.* iv. 8 (*Vulg. amabilis*).

Ne for feo [fee], ne for nanes mannes lufon
                        (*NED.* 971).
No love between these two was lost,
  Each was to other kind
                (*Babes in Wood*, 17 cent.).

Lovelace. Lady-killer. From Richardson's *Clarissa Harlowe* (1748).

low[1]. Adj. Late AS. *lāh*, ON. *lāgr*; cf. Du. *laag*, Ger. dial. *lāg*, flat; ult. cogn. with *lie*[1]. With fig. senses cf. those of *high*. To *lie low*, in slang sense, is from *Uncle Remus* (1880). *Low-Churchman*, formerly (c. 1700) equivalent to latitudinarian, was revived in 19 cent. as contrast to *High-Churchman*. *Low Sunday* was perh. named as a reaction from the joys of Easter. In *low water*, "hard up," is obviously naut., and may have meant orig. stranded, high and dry, as left by ebbing tide. The formation of the verb to *lower* (cf. to *better*), for obs. to *low*, is abnormal. ? Can it be partly due to naut. attribution of female sex to boats—"Low her away."

He lowyde him silf, takynge the foorme of a servant (Wyc. *Philip.* ii. 7).

low[2]. Verb. AS. *hlōwan*; cf. Du. *loeien*, MHG. *lüejen*, ON. *hlōa*, to roar; cogn. with L. *clamare*.

low[3] [*geog.*]. Hill, tumulus. Common in topography; cf. *law*[3].

low[4]. Blaze. Chiefly Sc. & north. ON. *logi*; cf. Ger. *lohe* and *lichterloh*. Ult. cogn. with *light*.

The taps o' the mountains shimmer
I' the low o' the sunset sky
               (*Loreley*, trad. A. Macmillan).

lower. To scowl, etc. Earlier *lour*, app. cogn. with Du. *loeren*, to frown, look askance, Ger. *lauern*, to lie in wait (one sense of ME. *louren*), and with *lurk*. Form and sense have been affected by association with *low*[1].

For had he laughed, had he loured,
He moste have ben al devoured
            (Chauc. *House of Fame*, i. 409).
The sky is red and lowering [*Vulg.* rutilat triste caelum] (*Matt.* xvi. 3).

loxodromic [*naut.*]. Of oblique sailing. From G. λοξός, oblique, δρόμος, course.

loyal. F., L. *legalis*, from *lex, leg-*, law. Current sense, from feudalism, is not found in F. Cf. *leal*.

lozenge. F. *losange* (13 cent.), app. connected with OF. *lauze*, roofing slate, Prov. *lauza*, slab, tombstone, L. *lapides lausiae* (1 cent.); cf. It. *losanga*, Sp. *losanje*. The origin of *lausiae* is unknown, but MedL. *lausa* is also used for *alausa*, flat fish, and the analogy of *rhombus* suggests possible connection between shape of slab and that of a flat fish. Orig. term of her. and later of arch., the cough lozenge being named from shape.

losange of spyce: losange (Palsg.).

L. s. d. Initials of L. *librae, solidi, denarii*, whence F. *livres, sous, deniers*.

lubber. Earliest (*Piers Plowm.*) applied to lazy monks; cf. obs. *abbey-lubber*. Perh. OF. *lobeor*, deceiver, parasite, from *lober*, Ger. *loben*, to praise, but associated also with *lob, looby*; cf. Du. *lobbes*, "a clownish fellow" (Sewel). As a sailor's word, now usu. *land-lubber*, from 16 cent. Hence *lubberland*, land of Cockayne (cf. Ger. *schlaraffenland*).

cocagna: as we say lubberland (Flor.).

lubra [*Austral.*]. Woman. Orig. Tasmanian. Cf. *gin*[3].

lubricate. From L. *lubricare*, from *lubricus*, slippery. Much earlier is *lubricity*, used by Caxton for F. *lubricité*, in sense now current.

luce. Pike (fish). OF. *lus, luis*, L. *lucius*. ModF. has *brochet*, from *broche*, spike (cf. E. *pike*).

lucerne. Clover. F. *luzerne*, ModProv. *luzerno*, which also means glow-worm. Origin obscure. ? From glowing appearance of the flower.

lucid. F. *lucide*, L. *lucidus*, from *lux, luc-*, light. *Lucid interval* is after L. pl. *lucida intervalla*, common in medieval works on lunacy.

Lucifer. Morning star. L. transl. of G. φωσφόρος. Also applied, by mystical interpretation of *Is.* xiv. 12, to Satan. Hence *as proud as Lucifer*. Both above senses are in AS. *Lucifer match* is a 19 cent. trade-name (cf. *vesuvian*).

luck. LG. or Du. *luk*, for *geluk*; cf. Ger. *glück*, MHG. *gelücke*. Prob. introduced (15 cent.) as gambling term; cf. *gleek* and to *try one's luck*. To *cut one's lucky*, make off, is 19 cent. London slang.

lucre. F., L. *lucrum*, gain. *Filthy lucre* (*Tit.* i. 11) is Tynd.'s rendering of G. αἰσχρὸν κέρδος.

Lucretia. Pattern of chastity. From victim of Sextus Tarquinius (Livy, i. 57–8).

lucubration. L. *lucubratio-n-*, from *lucubrare*, etym. to work by lamp-light, from *lux, luc-*, light.

Lucullian. Of banquets such as those of L. *Licinius Lucullus*, Roman epicure and great general (†56 B.C.).

lucus a non lucendo. Allusion to methods of early etymologists, who sometimes derived words from their opposites, e.g. *lucus*, a grove, from *lux*, because of its darkness.

lud. Minced pronunc. of *lord*. Usu. of barrister addressing judge.

Luddite [*hist.*]. Machine-breaker in Midlands and north (1811–16). From *Captain* (*King*) *Ludd*, imaginary leader (? named as below). Cf. *Captain Swing, Captain Moonlight*.

A quarter of a century before, one Ned Ludd, a half-witted boy in a Leicestershire village, made himself notorious by destroying stocking-frames. The Yorkshire rioters chose to take a name from this poor creature
(Low & Pulling, *Dict. of Eng. Hist.*).

ludicrous. From L. *ludicrus*, from *ludere*, to play.

lues [*med.*]. Flow, discharge. L., from *luere*, to loose.

luff[1] [*naut.*]. To bring head of ship nearer wind. From noun *luff*, ME. *lof, loof*, F. *lof* (in Wace, 12 cent.), some contrivance for altering course of ship; cf. Du. *loef*, Norw. Dan. *luv*, Sw. *lov*, etc.; cf. OHG. *laffa*, blade of oar; prob. cogn. with E. dial. *loof*, hand; cf. L. *palma*, flat hand, blade of oar.

luff[2] [*naut.*]. Lieutenant (q.v.).

luffer. See *louver*.

lug[1], **lugworm.** Used as bait. In Antrim called *lurg, lurgan*. Origin unknown.

lug[2]. Verb. Cf. Sw. *lugga*, to pull hair, from *lugg*, forelock, which is perh. the same as Sc. *lug*, ear, earlier (15 cent.) lappet, or "ear," of cap; ? cogn. with AS. *lūcan*, to pull up (weeds), Goth. *uslūkan*, to lug out (one's sword). Hence *luggage* (Shaks.).

luge [*Alp.*]. Kind of sleigh. Earlier *lege* (18 cent.), *lige* (1518). Origin unknown.

luggage. See *lug*[2].

lugger. Back-formation (late 18 cent.) from *lugsail* (17 cent.), ? for **luck-sail*, transl. of F. *voile de fortune*; cf. obs. E. *bonaventure*, used of the same, or a similar, sail.

lugsail: voile de fortune (Lesc.).

lugubrious. From L. *lugubris*, from *lugēre*, to mourn.

Luke. *St Luke's summer*, spell of warm weather about *St Luke's Day*, Oct. 18.

lukewarm. From obs. *luke*, tepid, ME. *lewk*. Cf. Du. *leuk*, in same sense. ME. had also *lew*, whence dial. *lew-warm*, from AS. *hlēow*, shelter, lee, cogn. with Ger. *lau*, lukewarm, ON. *hlȳr*, warm, mild. The relation of the two words is obscure.

Thou art lew [*var.* lewk, *Vulg.* tepidus] and nether coold nether hoot (Wyc. *Rev.* iii. 16).

lull. Imit.; cf. Sw. *lulla*, Dan. *lulle*, in same sense, also L. *lallare*. See *Lollard*. With *lullaby* cf. *hushaby* and see *bye-bye*.

lumbago. L., from *lumbus*, loin. Cf. *lumbar*, L. *lumbaris*.

lumber. Earliest (ME. *lomere*) as verb, of clumsy, blundering movement, perh. cogn. with *lame*, of which *lome* is a common ME. var. Later associated with *Lumber*, Lombard, *lumber-house*, pawnbroker's shop, regarded as store-house of disused articles; cf. *Lumber Street* (Pepys, Sep. 16, 1668) for *Lombard Street*, and see *Lombard*. NAmer. sense of rough timber is recorded for 17 cent. Thus *lumber* means orig. trumpery, with idea of unwieldiness due to association with unrelated verb. For intrusive -*b*- of verb cf. *slumber*.

lumbrical. Of, or resembling in shape, an earthworm, L. *lumbricus*.

luminous. F. *lumineux*, L. *luminosus*, from *lumen, lumin-*, light, cogn. with *lux*.

lump¹. Aggregation of no particular shape. Nearest in sense are obs. Dan. *lump*, lump, Norw. & Sw. dial. *lump*, block, etc. ? Cf. Du. *lump*, rag, Ger. *lumpen*, rag. Origin unknown.

lump². Fish. Also *lump-fish*. Prob. from *lump¹*, from uncouth shape; but found in Du. & LG. earlier than in E.

lump³. Verb. Now only (colloq.) in contrast with *like*. Orig. (16 cent.), to look sour, and in early quots. usu. coupled with *lower* (q.v.), from which it may have been coined after *dump, grump*, etc.

lunar. L. *lunaris*, from *luna*, moon. *Lunar caustic*, fused nitrate of silver, is from *luna*, silver (alch.).

Sol gold is and luna silver we threpe
(Chauc. G. 826).

lunatic. F. *lunatique*, Late L. *lunaticus*, from *luna*, from belief that lunatics were moonstruck. Abbreviated *loony* shows association with *loon¹*.

lunch, luncheon. Both words are of same date (late 16 cent.), and it is prob. that *luncheon* was extended from *lunch* by analogy with *punch-eon, trunch-eon*. Earliest sense of both is lump, chunk (see quot. s.v. *truncheon*), and it is supposed that *lunch* may be for *lump* by analogy with *hump, hunch*. But "it is curious that the word (*lunch*) first appears as a rendering of the (at that time) like-sounding Sp. *lonja*" (*NED.*), which is ult. ident. with *loin*. The date of appearance favours Sp. origin.

lonja de tocino: a lunch of bacon (Percyvall).

lopin: a lump, a gobbet, a luncheon
(Hollyband, 1580).

lundyfoot. Snuff. From *Lundy Foot*, Dublin tobacconist (18 cent.).

lune [*archaic*]. Leash for hawk. ME. also *loyne*, OF. *loigne* (*longe*), Late L. *longea*, length of cord.

lunette [*fort.*]. F., dim. of *lune*, moon; cf. *half-moon* in similar sense.

lung. AS. *lungen*; cf. Du. *long*, Ger. *lunge*, ON. *lunga*; ult. cogn. with *light²*. Cf. *lights*, and Port. *leve*, lung.

It was a saying of Lord Chatham that the parks were the lungs of London
(Windham, in H. of C. 1808).

lunge¹. Long tether for training horses to gallop in circle. F. *longe*, halter, as *lune* (q.v.).

lunge². In fencing. Aphet. for earlier *allonge, elonge*, from F. *allonger*, to lengthen, stretch out, from *long*.

allonge: a pass or thrust with a rapier (Johns.).

lunkah. Strong cheroot. Hind. *langka*, name of islands in Godavery Delta where tobacco is grown.

Lupercal [*hist.*]. Roman festival. L. *Lupercalia*, from *Luperci*, priests of some form of nature worship, ? lit. wolf expellers, from *arcēre*, to keep distant.

lupine, lupin. Plant. L. *lupinus*, from *lupus*, wolf, ? or from G. λοπός, pod, altered by folk-etym.

lupus. Skin disease. L., wolf. Cf. *cancer, mulligrubs*.

lurch¹, leave in the. From obs. game *lurch*, supposed to have resembled back-gammon. F. *lourche*; cf. It. *lurcio*. Perh. from Ger. dial. *lurz*, as in *lurz werden*, to be discomfited in a game, MHG. *lorz, lurz*, left, the left hand being emblematic of bad luck (cf. *sinister*). *Lurching* is recorded c. 1350.

But to *leave in the lash*, copiously recorded some years earlier than to *leave in the lurch*, suggests some connection with F. *lâcher*, to let go, as in ModF. *lâcher un ami*, to leave a friend in the lurch. See also *lurch*[2]. Prob. two words have amalgamated. Ger. *im stiche lassen*, to leave in the lurch, is from *stich* in sense of score in card-playing.

I'll play still, come out what will, I'll never give over i' the lurch (*Misogonus*, ii. 4, c. 1550).

lurch[2]. Roll to one side. Orig. naut. and recorded as *lee-larch* (Falc.), which is for earlier *lee-latch* (v.i.), app. from F. *lâcher*, to let go, VL. *laxiare, from *laxus*. Cf. also naut. *lask*, to go large, representing the OF. form (*laschier*) of the same verb. As used of gait, partly due to archaic *lurch*, to prowl, whence *lurcher* (q.v.).

lee-latch: when he who conds would bid the man at helm to look that the ship does not go to leeward of her course, he bids him have a care of the lee-latch (*Sea Dict.* 1708).

lurcher. From archaic *lurch*, to prowl about, which, in later (but now obs.) sense of forestalling, is associated with *lurch*[1]. Supposed to be a var. of *lurk* (q.v.).

lurcher: one that lies upon the lurch, or upon the catch; also a kind of dog used in hunting (Kersey).

lurdan [*archaic*]. Lout, sluggard. OF. *lourdin*, from *lourd*, heavy; cf. ModF. *lourdaud*.

lourdaut: a sot, dunce, dullard, grotnoll, jobernoll, blockhead; a lowt, lob, luske, boore, clowne, churle, clusterfist; a proud, ignorant, and unmannerlie swaine (Cotg.).

lure. F. *leurre*, "a (faulkoners) lure" (Cotg.), MHG. *luoder* (*luder*), bait. Orig. of enticement to hawk to return.

O for a falconer's voice, To lure this tassel-gentle back again (*Rom. & Jul.* ii. 2).

lurid. L. *luridus*, yellowish, wan, cogn. with G. χλωρός. As is common in colour-words the sense has changed considerably, e.g. in *lurid light* (language).

lurid: pale, wan, black, and blew (Blount).

lurk. ? Frequent. of *lour*, with suffix as in *talk, walk*.

luscious. ME. *lucius*, var. of *licius*, aphet. for *delicious*. Sense affected by association with *lush*[1].

lush[1]. Adj. As applied to grass, etc., a reminiscence of Shaks. (v.i.). App. for ME. and dial. *lash*, flaccid, F. *lâche*, L. *laxus*. For change of vowel cf. *lurch*[2].

lasch, or to fresh, onsavery: vapidus, insipidus
(*Prompt. Parv.*).
lush, or slak: laxus (*ib.*).
How lush and lusty the grass looks (*Temp.* ii. 1).

lush[2] [*slang*]. Drink. First in slang dicts. of late 18 cent. ? Shelta *lush*, to eat and drink.

The commander of the forces...expects that no man will remain, on any pretence whatever, in the rear, with the lush (*Charles O'Malley*, ch. cv.).

Lushington [*slang*]. Thirsty person. "The *City of Lushington* was a convivial society which met at the Harp, Russell St, up to 1895, and claimed to be 150 years old" (abridged from *NED.*). If this claim is correct, *lush*[2] may be abbreviated from *Lushington*; but it is more probable that the selection of the name *Lushington* was determined by *lush*[2].

And, after all, when a chaplain is named Lushington...! (E. V. Lucas).

Lusitanian. Of *Lusitania*, L. name of Portugal.

lust. AS. *lust*, pleasure, delight, enjoyment. Com. Teut.; cf. Du. Ger. *lust*, ON. *loste*, Goth. *lustus*; cogn. with *list*[2], *listless*. Current sense, peculiar to E., is due to *lusts of the flesh*, in early use to render L. *concupiscentia carnis* (1 *John*, ii. 16). Hence *lusty*, which has run through a series of senses, beginning with joyful (cf. Ger. *lustig*) and ending with burly.

Thou haddist lust in this lyfe, and Lazar peyne
(Wyc.).

lustration. Purification. L. *lustratio-n-*, from *lustrum*, purificatory sacrifice every five years after census, from *luere*, to wash, cogn. with *lavare*. *Lustrum*, period of five years, is secondary sense.

lustre[1]. Brightness. F., from L. *lustrare*, to shine, cogn. with *lux*, light. Sense of chandelier is current F. meaning. Cf. *lutestring, illustrious*.

lustre[2]. Space of five years. F., L. *lustrum*. See *lustration*.

lustring. See *lutestring*.

lusty. See *lust*.

lute[1]. Instrument. OF. *lut* (*luth*), It. *liuto*, Arab. *al'ūd*, lit. the (aloe) wood. Turk. for lute is *ūd*. Cf. Sp. *laud*, Port. *alaude*; also Du. *luit*, Ger. *laute*.

It is the little rift within the lute
(Tennyson, *Merlin and Vivien*, 240).

lute[2]. Clay for caulking, etc. F. *lut*, L. *lutum*, from *luere*, to wash down.

luteous. Deep orange colour. From L. *luteus*, from *lutum*, a yellow dye-plant.

lutestring. Folk-etym. for *lustring*, F. *lustrine*, It. *lustrino*, as *lustre*[1] (q.v.).

lustring, or lutestring: a sort of silk (Kersey).

Lutetian. Of Paris, L. *Lutetia Parisiorum*.

Lutheran. From *Martin Luther* (†1546). Orig. equivalent to Protestant, now limited to spec. doctrines. The name is ident. with F. *Lothair*, OHG. *Hlut-hēr*, famous army.

luxation. Dislocation. F., L. *luxatio-n-*, from *luxare*, from *luxus*, from G. λοξός, askew; cf. F. *louche*, squinting.

luxury. AF. *luxurie*, L. *luxuria*, from *luxus*, abundance. Earliest E. sense is that of lasciviousness, as in Rom. langs., which express neutral E. sense by derivatives of L. *luxus*; cf. ModF. *luxe*, luxury, *luxure*, lust, etc.

lussuria: leacherie, lust, uncleannes of life, luxurie (Flor.).

LXX. Abbrev. for *Septuagint* (q.v.).

-ly. AS. -*līc*, to form nouns and adjs., -*līce*, to form advs. Ident. with *like* (q.v.) and cogn. with *lich* in *lichgate*; cf. Du. -*lijk*, Ger. -*lich*, Sw. Norw. Dan. -*lig* (from ON. *līkr*), Goth. -*leiks*. It is curious that Teut. uses "body" for the adv. formation, while Rom. uses "mind," e.g. F. *constamment* = L. *constanti mente*.

lyam-hound [*archaic*]. See *lime-hound*.

lycanthropy. Insanity in which patient believes himself a wolf. G. λυκανθρωπία, from λύκος, wolf, ἄνθρωπος, man. Cf. *werwolf*.

lyceum. L., G. Λύκειον, garden where Aristotle taught at Athens, adjacent to temple of Apollo, one of whose epithets was Λύκειος. For later senses cf. *academy*, *athenaeum*. Hence F. *lycée*, public school.

lych. See *lich*.

lychnis. Plant. L., G. λυχνίς, some red flower, from λύχνος, lamp.

lycopodium. Plant, lit. wolf-foot. See *lycanthropy*, *tripod*.

lyddite. Invented by Turpin and first tested (c. 1888) at *Lydd*, Kent.

Lydford law. See *law*[1]. From *Lydford* (Dartmoor), where was held a Stannaries Court of summary jurisdiction. Mentioned in *Piers Plowm*.

Lydford law: is to hang men first, and indite them afterwards (Blount).

Lydian. Of *Lydia*, kingdom of Croesus in Asia Minor. Applied in G. to a mode of music regarded as effeminate.

lye. AS. *lēag*. Com. Teut.; cf. Du. *loog*, Ger. *lauge*, ON. *laug*; cogn. with *lather*.

lyke-wake [*archaic*]. Watch over dead body. See *lich*, *wake*.

lymph. L. *lympha*, water, colourless fluid,

altered from *lumpa*, owing to a legendary connection with *nymph*. Hence *lymphatic*, orig. frenzied, mad, but now applied to the sluggish temperament supposed to result from excess of lymph in tissues.

lynch law. Earlier (1817) *Lynch's law*. Connection with *Charles Lynch*, a Virginian justice of the peace, indemnified (1782) for having summarily imprisoned certain persons, is conjectural only. Another, and more likely, suggestion, is that the phrase comes from *Lynch's Creek* (S. Carolina), which is known to have been a meeting-place of the "Regulators" as early as 1768. This would make the phrase parallel to *Lydford law, Jeddart justice* (cf. to *shanghai*).

lynx. L., G. λύγξ; cogn. with AS. *lox*, Du. *los*, Ger. *luchs*, and prob. with G. λεύσσειν, to see. Earliest records (v.i.) allude to keenness of sight. Hence *lyncaean*, sharp-sighted.

A best that men lynx calles
That may se thurgh stane walles (*NED*. 1340).

lyon. In *Lyon King of Arms*, chief herald of Scotland, in allusion to lion on shield.

lyre. F., L. *lyra*, also the name of a constellation, G. λύρα. Hence *lyric-al*, orig. poetry to be sung to the lyre.

M. For 1000. Init. of L. *mille*, thousand. But orig. for symbol CIↃ (see *D*), an alteration of the G. φ.

ma. 19 cent. abbrev. of *mamma* (q.v.).

ma'am. For *madam* (q.v.). Cf. US. (school)-*marm* and Anglo-Ind. *mem-sahib*.

Mac. Facet. for Scotsman. Gael. Ir. *mac*, son, cogn. with Welsh *ap* (earlier *map*). See also *maid*.

macabre. F., earlier *macabré*, in *danse Macabré* (14 cent.), dance of death. App. corrupt. of *Maccabaeus*; cf. MedL. *chorea Machabaeorum* (15 cent.), dance of death.

L'idée de toutes les Danses macabres est la même: c'est l'égalité des hommes devant la mort, le nivellement du cimetière appliqué aux écrasantes inégalités de la vie (Paul de Saint-Victor).

macaco. Monkey. Port., from native name (Congo). Hence F. *macaque*.

macadam. Road-paving introduced by *J. L. McAdam* (†1836).

macaroni. It. *maccheroni* (*maccaroni* in Flor.), pl. of *maccherone*. Of doubtful origin, perh. from obs. It. *maccare*, to pound. Hence *macaroni*, 18th cent. "blood," belonging to *Macaroni Club* (v.i.) and professing contempt for native cooking. *Macaronic poetry*, usu. jargonized Latin, was invented (1517) by Merlinus Cocceius (Teofilo Folengo), who likened his work to the culinary macaroni.

The Maccaroni Club, which is composed of all the travelled young men who wear long curls and spying-glasses (H. Walpole).

macaroon. F. *macaron*, It. *maccherone* (v.s.).

macartney. Pheasant. From *Earl Macartney* (†1806).

macassar. Oil from *Mangkasara*, district in Celebes, one of the Philippines. Cf. *antimacassar*.

macaw. Port. *macao*, for Tupi (Brazil) *macavuana*. The form is prob. due rather to some fancied connection with *Macao*.

macaw-palm. Of Carib origin; cf. *macoya*, *mocaya*, its name in Guiana.

maccaboy, maccabaw, mackabaw. Snuff. From *Macouba*, in Martinique.

mace¹. Weapon. F. *masse*, VL. **mattea*, whence L. *matteola*, mallet; cf. It. *mazza*, "a clubbe" (Flor.), Sp. *maza*. In House of Commons as symbol of authority.

mace². Spice, husk of nutmeg. False sing. from ME. *macis*, F., L. *macis*, recorded only in Plautus, and prob. invented by him.

macédoine. Mixed dish. F., lit. Macedonia, ? from empire of Alexander being regarded as a miscellaneous collection.

macerate. From L. *macerare*, to steep; ? cf. G. μάσσειν, to steep. Sense of fasting app. due to association with L. *macer*, thin.

machete, matchet. Heavy WInd. cutlass. Sp., dim. of *macho*, hammer, L. *marculus*.

Machiavellian. Of *Niccolò Machiavelli* (†1527), of Florence, author of *Il Principe*.

machicolation [*arch.*]. From F. *mâchicoulis*, aperture for dropping melted lead, etc., on assailants of castle. Second element app. as in *portcullis* (q.v.), first doubtful.

machine. F., L. *machina*, G. μηχανή, from μῆχος, contrivance; ult. cogn. with *may*. In all Rom. & Teut. langs. Earliest (15 cent.) as verb, to contrive, plot, as F. *machiner*. For extended senses cf. *engine*. The *party machine* is from US. politics. *Machine-gun*, "an invention of the Devil" (Sir Ian Hamilton), is recorded for 1890.

-machy. G. -μαχία, from μάχεσθαι, to fight.

mackerel. OF. *maquerel* (*maquereau*). Prob. ident. with F. *maquereau*, pander, from a popular belief as to the habits of the fish. ? The latter ult. from OFris. *mek*, marriage.

mackinaw [*US.*]. Blanket, etc. Name of island between Lakes Huron and Michigan.

mackintosh. Waterproof cloth patented (1823) by *Charles Mackintosh*. The name means son of the thane.

macle [*min.*]. Dark spot, twin crystal. F., L. *macula*, spot.

macramé. Turk. *maqrama*, towel, napkin.

macrocosm. F. *macrocosme* (c. 1200), MedL., G. μακρός, great, long, κόσμος, world, coined on the earlier *microcosm* (q.v.).

mactation. L. *mactatio-n-*, from *mactare*, to slay.

maculate. From L. *maculare*, from *macula*, spot.

mad. AS. *mād*, only in compd. *mādmōd*, folly, so that the mod. word is rather aphet. for AS. *gemǣd*, shortened from *gemǣded*, p.p. of an unrecorded verb. Cf. hist. of *fat*, and perh. of *bad*. Cogn. with OHG. *gameit*, foolish, Goth. *gamaiths*, crippled, and ult. with L. *mutare*, to change. The usual AS. adj. was *wōd*, whence obs. *wood* (v.i.), which is one origin of the name *Wood*. With *madman* cf. *foeman*, *freshman*, *nobleman*. With *madcap*, first in Shaks. (*Love's Lab. Lost*, ii. 1), cf. obs. *fuddlecap*, *huffcap*. *Far from the madding crowd* (Gray's *Elegy*) is usu. misunderstood as *maddening*, whereas it means raving. The line is imitated from Drummond of Hawthornden (v.i.).

Festus with greet vois seyde, Poul, thou maddist, or wexist wood (Wyc. *Acts*, xxvi. 24).

Far from the madding worldling's hoarse discords
(Sonnet, *Dear Wood*).

madame. F., orig. *ma dame*, my lady, L. *mea domina*. The earliest E. example (13 cent.) is in addressing a queen, the word, in its gradual descent to *'m*, never having quite lost its suggestion of respect.

madder. AS. *mædere*; cogn. with ON. *mathra*; cf. Du. *mede*, *mee* (in compd. *meekrap*).

madeira. Wine from *Madeira Islands*, named from timber, Port. *madeira*, L. *materia*, because formerly thickly wooded. *Madeira cake* perh. from being orig. flavoured with the wine.

mademoiselle. F., orig. *ma demoiselle*. See *damsel*.

madia. Plant of sunflower tribe. From Chilian *madi*.

madonna. It., orig. *ma* (*mia*) *donna*. As *madame* (q.v.).

madrassah. Mohammedan college. Arab. *madrasah*, from *darasa*, to study.

madrepore. Coral. F. *madrépore,* It. *madre-pora,* from *madre,* mother, and a second element which may be from L. *porus,* pore, or G. πῶρος, calcareous stone.

madrigal. F., It. *madrigale,* perh. from L. *matricale,* from *mater, matr-,* mother. ? A song in the mother-tongue.

Maecenas. Liberal patron. From name of friend of Augustus and patron of Horace and Virgil.

> Mais sans un Mécénas à quoi sert un Auguste?
> (Boileau).

maelstrom. Du. *maalstroom,* earlier *mael-stroom,* whirlpool, from *malen,* to grind (cogn. with Ger. *mahlen* and ult. with L. *molere*), and *stroom,* stream. Applied by 16 cent. Du. geographers to the famous whirlpool on the west coast of Norway, and adopted, as a literary word, by the Scand. langs.

maenad. Bacchante. L., G. μαινάς, μαιναδ-, from μαίνεσθαι, to rave. Cf. *mania.*

maestoso [*mus.*]. It., majestic.

maestro [*mus.*]. It., L. *magister,* master.

maffick. Back-formation from *mafficking,* applied to wild rejoicing at relief (May 17, 1900) of *Mafeking,* SAfr., besieged by Boers and defended by Baden-Powell. Revived in connection with the scenes that disgraced London in Nov. 1918.

> We trust Cape Town...will "maffick" to-day, if we may coin a word (*Pall Mall Gaz.* May 22, 1900).

mafia. Sicilian lawlessness, gen. understood as name of secret society. Origin unknown.

Mag. Short for *Margaret,* as in *magpie,* whence *mag,* to chatter. With *Mag's* (*Meg's*) *diversions* cf. earlier *Mag's tales,* the name being used as a generic term for a rough and boisterous woman (but see also *Meg*).

magazine. F. *magasin,* It. *magazzino* (cf. Sp. *magacen*), Arab. *makhāzin,* pl. of *makhzan,* store-house, from *khazana,* to store up. Sp. *almacén,* Port. *armazem* keep the Arab. def. art. Orig. warehouse; then, arsenal, etc. For adoption of Arab. word, due to the naut. power of the Moors in Middle Ages, cf. *arsenal.* Sense of publication appears first in 17 cent. applied to "store-houses" of techn. information on mil. or nav. subjects. The *Gentleman's Magazine* (1731) was the first periodical magazine.

> A monthly collection to treasure up, as in a magazine, the most valuable pieces on the subjects abovemention'd (*Gent. Mag.* 1. *Introd.*).

Magdalen-e. *Mary Magdalen,* G. Μαγδαληνή, of *Magdala,* near Sea of Galilee (*Luke,* viii. 2), regarded as ident. with the sinner (*Luke,* vii. 37). See *maudlin.* The *NED.* records the word in the sense of hospital, refuge, from c. 1600 only, but the name of *Nicholas atte Maudeleyne* (*Patent Rolls,* c. 1300) points to its existence much earlier.

mage. F., see *magi.*

magenta. Aniline dye discovered just after battle of *Magenta* (NIt.), where Austrians were defeated by French (1859).

maggot. Metath., perh. due to association with name *Mag* (see *magpie*), of ME. *madok,* dim. of AS. *matha,* worm, maggot, cogn. with Du. Ger. *made.* See *mawkish.* *Maggot* (whim) *in the head* belongs to the old belief in internal parasites as cause of mental or bodily disturbance; cf. *mulli-grubs,* and similar use of Ger. *grille,* grasshopper (see quot. s.v. *bee*).

magi. Pl. of L. *magus,* G. μάγος, OPers. *magus,* member of priestly caste, magician. The three *magi* are mentioned in *Piers Plowm.* and *Simon Magus* by Chauc. It is curious to note that Pers. *magh* is now used of a taverner, the sense of Zoroastrian priest having become contemptuous under the Arabs.

magic. F. *magique* (adj.), Late L., G. μαγική (sc. τέχνη), from μάγος. See *magi.* *Natural magic,* as opposed to *black magic,* was used in ME. almost in sense of natural science. *Magic lantern* appears first in F. *lanterne magique* (*laterna magica*) in 17 cent.

magilp. See *megilp.*

magisterial. MedL. *magisterialis,* from *magister,* master, double compar. from *magnus.*

magistrate. L. *magistratus,* orig. office of magistrate, from *magister.*

magma [*geol.*]. Crude pasty matter. G., from μάσσειν, to knead.

magnanimous. From L. *magnanimus,* from *magnus,* great, *animus,* soul.

magnate. Late L. *magnas, magnat-,* from *magnus,* great. Adopted also as spec. title in Pol. & Hung.

magnesia. MedL., G. Μαγνησία, district in Thessaly. Applied to the lodestone (cf. *magnet*) and to a mineral, perh. manganese, supposed by alchemists to be an ingredient of the philosopher's stone. Hence *magnesium,* by analogy with other chem. words in -*ium.*

magnet. OF. *magnete*, or L. *magnes, magnet-,* G. μάγνης, Magnesian stone (v.s.). In most Europ. langs., but replaced in F. by *aimant,* adamant. *Magnetism,* in hypnotic sense, is due to Mesmer.

Magnificat. L., magnifies, init. word of Virgin's hymn (*Luke*, i. 46–55). Cf. *Benedictus, Sanctus,* etc.

magnificence. F., L. *magnificentia,* from *magnus,* great, *facere,* to do.

magnifico. Honorary title of Venet. magnate (v.s.).

magniloquent. From L. *magniloquus,* from *loqui,* to speak.

magnitude. L. *magnitudo,* from *magnus,* great, cogn. with G. μέγας, and ult. with *much.*

magnolia. From *Pierre Magnol* (†1715), professor of botany at Montpellier. Cf. *fuchsia, dahlia,* etc.

magnum. Two-quart bottle. L. *magnum,* neut. adj. Cf. *magnum bonum,* plum, potato, steel pen; also earlier in the bottle sense.

A magnum bonum of very palatable claret
(Hickey's *Memoirs,* i. 132).

magpie. From *pie*[1] (q.v.) with name *Mag* prefixed. Formerly also *Meg-, Maggot-,* etc. Cf. F. *margot,* magpie, E. *robin redbreast, dicky bird, jackdaw,* etc. The *magpie* at rifle practice is signalled with a black and white disk.

pie: a pye, pyannat, meggatapie (Cotg.).

magus. See *magi.*

Magyar. People and lang. of Hungary. From native name, prob. meaning mountain-dwellers, the race coming from the Ural. The lang. belongs to the Uralo-Finnic group.

maharajah. Hind., Sanskrit *mahārāgā,* great king, cogn. with L. *magnus rex.*

mahatma. Sanskrit *mahātman,* from *mahā,* great (v.s.), *ātman,* soul. First *NED.* records in connection with Madame Blavatsky.

mahdi. Arab. *mahdīy,* passive part. of *hadā,* to lead aright. Applied to Soudan insurgent leader c. 1880, but in earlier use in sense of Mohammedan Messiah.

The test of the validity of the claims of a Mahdi is always held by his followers to reside in his success (*Morn. Post,* Feb. 13, 1918).

mahlstick. See *maulstick.*

mahogany. Earlier (1671) *mohogeney,* described as from Jamaica. Of obscure WInd. origin. In several Europ. langs.,

but F. has *acajou,* from Port. (Brazil), and Sp. *caoba,* from Carib.

Mahometan. From *Mahomet,* early popular form of Arab. *Muhammad;* cf. F. *mahométan.* Now usu. replaced by *Mohammedan.* Earlier still (13 cent.) the prophet was called *Mahoun(d)* from OF. shortened form *Mahon.* Cf. also obs. *maumet,* idol, doll.

mahout. Elephant-driver. Hind. *mahāwat,* Sanskrit *mahā-mātra,* lit. great in measure, hence, high officer. Cf. *mahatma.*

Mahratti [*ling.*]. Lang. of the Mahrattas, a form of Hindi.

mahseer. Fish. Hind. *mahāsir,* ? Sanskrit *mahā ṣiras,* big head.

We are now compelled, if we would catch fish, to seek tarpon in Florida, mahseer in India
(Andrew Lang).

maid, maiden. *Maid* is shortened from *maiden,* AS. *mægden,* girl, virgin, cogn. with OHG. *magatīn* (replaced by dim. *mädchen*). With AS. *mægth,* which did not survive, cf. Ger. *magd,* Goth. *magaths.* All these words are fem. derivatives of an OTeut. word for boy, which appears in AS. *magu,* child, son, ON. *mögr,* Goth. *magus,* ?ult. cogn. with Gael. *mac.* Both *maid* and *maiden* were early applied to the Holy Virgin, and the spec. sense of virgin survives in *old maid, maiden aunt,* as fig. in *maiden over* (*speech*). In ME. both are used also of an unmarried man. For *maidenhead* cf. *Godhead.* With *maiden,* the old Sc. guillotine, cf. *Scavenger's daughter.* With *maidenhair* (fern) cf. synon. Dan. *jomfruhaar,* Icel. *Freyjuhār* (see *Friday*), L. *capillus Veneris* (Pseudo-Apuleius).

I woot wel that the Apostel was a mayde
(Chauc. D. 79).

maieutic. Socratic method of extracting truth. G. μαιευτικός, lit. obstetric, used fig. by Socrates, from μαῖα, midwife.

mail[1]. Armour. F. *maille,* L. *macula,* spot, mesh, applied to chain-armour. *Mailed fist* translates Ger. *gepanzerte faust.*

Fahre darein mit gepanzerter faust
(Kaiser Wilhelm II, Dec. 16, 1897).

mail[2]. Bag, now esp. for letters. ME. *male,* OF. (*malle,* trunk), OHG. *mahala,* leather bag, whence also It. Sp. *mala.* The postal *mail* dates from 17 cent. Hence also *mailcoach, -train, -steamer,* carrying the mail. For sense-development of this word cf. *budget.*

male: a male, or great budget (Cotg.).

mail³. Payment, rent, etc. Now only Sc., exc. in *blackmail* (see *black*). ON. *māl*, speech, agreement. Com. Teut.; cf. AS. *mæthel*, meeting, OHG. *mahal*, assembly, treaty, Goth. *mathl*, meeting-place.

maim. ME. also *mahaym*, *maynhe*, etc., OF. *meshaignier*, *mahaignier*, from adj. *mehaing*, mutilated; cf. It. *magagnare*. Second element as in *barren* (q.v.), first doubtful; if *mes-* is orig., it represents L. *minus*, used as "pejorative" prefix. For final *-m* of E. word cf. *grogram*, *vellum*, etc.

main¹. Strength. Now only in *might and main*, *amain*. AS. *mægen*, strength, cogn. with *may*, *might*, and with OHG. *magan*, ON. *magn*.

main². Adj. Partly evolved from compds. of *main¹*, partly from cogn. ON. adj. *meginn*, *megn*, strong. Orig. sense appears in *main force*, which would appear however to owe something to association with F. *main forte*, strong hand (v.i.). Esp. common in mil. and naut. lang., e.g. *main body*, *mainguard*, *mainmast*, *mainstay*. So also *mainland*, ON. *megenland*, sometimes reduced to *main*, as in *Spanish Main*, SAmer. coast from Panama to Orinoco; cf. mod. use of *main* (pipe for gas, etc.). *In the main* perh. owes something to F. *en moyenne* (OF. *meienne*), on the average, and even *mainmast*, also (c. 1600) *meanemast*, suggests association with the same word; cf. Ger. *mittelmast*, and see *mean²*. The *main chance* is orig. from *main³*, but is now apprehended in the sense of *main²*. *Splicing the mainbrace*, partaking of grog, perh. refers to the strengthening influence of good liquor. Fig. use of *mainstay* is one of our numerous naut. metaphors.

à main forte: by maine force, or great power; with might and maine (Cotg.).

main³. Term at hazard, cock-fighting match. Its regular association with *by* suggests that it is a spec. use of *main²* (cf. *main*-road, *by*-road). In the cock-fighting sense it appears to approach in sense *battle-royal*.

Always have an eye to the main, whatsoever thou art chanced at the by (*Euphues*).

There will be by-battles....And in the afternoon will begin the main match (*NED.* 1716).

maintain. F. *maintenir*, from L. *manu tenēre*, to hold with the hand; cf. It. *mantenere*, Sp. *mantener*. Oldest E. sense is to back up, defend. The orig. significance of the

hist. *cap of maintenance* is unknown. It was also called *cap of estate* (*dignity*).

maize. Sp. *maiz*, earlier *mahiz*, from Cuban dial., prob. ident. with Guiana *marisi*, Carib *marichi*; cf. F. *maïs*, earlier *mahiz*.

majesty. F. *majesté*, L. *majestas*, cogn. with *major*, greater. Earliest sense in E. the greatness of God. *Your Majesty* is a L. construction common to the Rom. langs. and adopted from them by the Teut. Up to time of James I it was in competition with *Grace* and *Highness* as royal title.

majolica. It., from *Majolica*, early name of *Majorca*, Balearic Islands. Named from being the larger island; cf. *Minorca*. ModSp. name is *Mallorca*.

major. L., compar. of *magnus*, its relation to which is obscure. Much less used than *minor*. As mil. title via F. *major*, for *sergent-major*, orig. used of higher rank than at present; cf. *major-general* (see *general*). *Major-domo* is adapted from Sp. *mayordomo*, MedL. *major domus*, mayor of the palace, under the Merovingians. See *mayor*. To *go over to the majority*, to die, is L. *abire ad plures*.

Death joins us to the great majority (Young).

majuscule. F., L. *majuscula* (sc. *littera*), dim. of *major*, *majus*, greater.

make. AS. *macian*. WGer.; cf. Du. *maken*, Ger. *machen*. Orig. sense perh. to render suitable; cf. Ger. *gemach* (adj.), suitable, (noun), room, AS. *gemaca*, fellow, equal (see *match¹*). *Made* is contr. of *makede* (cf. Ger. *machte*). Senses correspond to those senses of L. *facere*, F. *faire*, which are not provided by *do*, and many phrases in which *make* is used are directly translated from F., e.g. to *make believe* (*faire croire*), to *make one's way* (*faire son chemin*), to *make as though* (*faire comme si*). In to *make bold* (*free*) the reflex. is omitted. *On the make* is US. For archaic *makebate*, breeder of strife, cf. *makeshift*, *makeweight*, *makepeace* (now only as surname).

Malacca cane. From *Malacca*, in Malay peninsula. Cf. *Penang lawyer*.

malachite. F., ult. from G. μαλάχη, mallow; from colour.

Melochites is a grene stone...and hath that name of the colour of malewes (Trev.).

malacology. Study of molluscs. From G. μαλακός, soft.

maladroit. F., from *mal*, ill, *adroit* (q.v.).

malady. F. *maladie*, from *malade*, Late L.

male habitus, for *male habens*, rendering G. κακῶς ἔχων. Cf. F. *avoir mal* (*aux dents*, etc.).

Centurionis autem cujusdam servus male habens, erat moriturus (*Vulg. Luke*, vii. 2).

Malaga. In South of Spain. Hence wine, raisins.

Malagasy. People and lang. of *Madagascar*; cf. F. *Malgache*. Perh. cogn. with *Malay*.

malander, mallender [*vet.*]. Eruption behind knee of horse. F. *malandre*, L. *malandria*. Cf. *sallender*.

malapert [*archaic*]. OF., from *mal apert*, opposite of *apert*, able, expert (see *pert*). The sense is rather that of OF. *malappris*, ill taught. For formation cf. *maladroit*, *malcontent*.

malapropism. Verbal confusion. From *Mrs Malaprop* (from F. *mal à propos*, ill to the purpose) in Sheridan's *Rivals* (1775), who indulges in such phrases as *derangement of epitaphs* for *arrangement of epithets*.

malaria. It. *mal' aria*, for *mala aria*, bad air. Both quots. below are from letters written at Rome.

A horrid thing called the "mal'aria," that comes to Rome every summer and kills one (H. Walpole).

I want to go to Naples for fear of the heats and bad air arriving (*ib.*).

Malay [*ling.*]. The lingua franca of the Eastern archipelago. Orig. a Polynesian lang., but now saturated with Arab. (the script of which it has adopted), with strong Pers. & Hind. elements also.

Malayalam [*ling.*]. Dravidian lang. of Malabar.

malcontent. OF. *malcontent* (replaced by *mécontent*); cf. *maladroit*, *malapert*.

male. F. *mâle*, OF. *masle*, L. *masculus*, dim. of *mas*, male.

malediction. Learned form of *malison* (q.v.).

malefactor. L., from *male facere*, to do ill. Replaced ME. *malfetour*, *maufetour*, from OF. Cf. *malefic-ent*, from L. *maleficus*.

malevolent. From L. *male*, ill, *volens*, *volent-*, pres. part. of *velle*, to wish. Cf. *benevolent*.

malfeasance [*leg.*]. F. *malfaisance*, from *malfaire*, to do ill (see *malefactor*).

malic [*chem.*]. F. *malique*, from L. *malum*, apple.

malice. F., L. *malitia*, from *malus*, bad. To *bear malice* is after F. *porter malice* (Palsg.).

Nothing extenuate, Nor aught set down in malice
(*Oth.* v. 2).

malign-ant. From L. *malignus*; cf. *benign*. Current sense of to *malign* is for ME. to *malign against*. Application of *Malignant* to royalists (1641–60) is from earlier theol. sense as in *church malignant*, i.e. of Anti-Christ.

Odivi ecclesiam malignantium [*AV.* of evil doers]
(*Vulg. Ps.* xxv. 5).

malinger. Back-formation from *malingerer*, app. corrupt. of OF. *malingreux*, formerly used of beggar with artificial sores, from *malingre*, sickly, "sore, scabbie, ouglie, loathsome" (Cotg.), of unknown origin.

malingeror: a military term for one who, under pretence of sickness, evades his duty (Grose).

malison [*archaic*]. OF. *malëison*, L. *maledictio-n-*, from *maledicere*, to curse. Cf. *benison*.

malkin, mawkin. Dim. of *Maud*, ME. *Malde*, *Matilda*; also of *Mal* (*Moll*), *Mary*. Archaic and dial. for slut (*Cor.* ii. 1); hence, also mop, scarecrow (*Adam Bede*, ch. vi.). Cf. *grimalkin* and see *scullion*.

Malkyn, or mawte, propyr name: Matildis
(*Prompt. Parv.*).

malkyn, or ovyn swepyr: dorsorium, tersorium (*ib.*).

mall. F. *mail*, mallet, L. *malleus* (see *maul*). From implement used in playing *mall* or *pall-mall* (q.v.). Hence applied to shaded walk where game was orig. played; cf. F. *mail*, in same sense, e.g. Anatole France's *L'Orme du Mail*, the elm-tree on the mall. The *Mall* in St James's Park was made after the older *Pall Mall* had been built over.

The mall [at Tours] without comparison is the noblest in Europe....Here we play'd a party or two
(Evelyn).

Here a well-polish'd mall gives us the joy
To see our Prince his matchless force employ
(Waller, *On St James's Park as lately improved by His Majesty*, 1668).

Mallaby-Deeleys [*neol.*]. Clothes. From *Mr Mallaby-Deeley*, M.P., who inaugurated (Mar. 1920) a great scheme to supply clothes at reasonable prices. See *Punch*, Mar. 10, 1920.

mallard. F. *malart*, ? orig. proper name, OHG. *Madal-hart*, strong in the council (see *mail*[3]). The form *mawdelard* occurs in ME. The application of proper names to birds (*guillemot*, *parrot*, etc.) goes back to pre-historic folk-lore. Cf. also *renard*. But Walloon *marlart* points rather to connection with *male*, OF. *masle* becoming *marle* in Walloon.

malleable. F. *malléable*, from L. **malleare*, from *malleus*, hammer.

mallender. See *malander*.

mallet. F. *maillet*, dim. of *mail*. See *mall*, *maul*.

mallow. AS. *mealwe*, L. *malva*, whence also It. Sp. *malva*, Ger. *malve*. See *malachite*, *mauve*.

malm. Soft rock, etc. AS. *mealm*, in *mealm-stān*; cf. ON. *mālmr*, ore, Goth. *malma*, sand, Ger. *malmen*, to crush; cogn. with *meal*[1].

malmaison. Rose, carnation. From name of Empress Josephine's palace, near Versailles. For formation of name, bad house, cf. E. *Caldecote, Coldharbour*.

malmsey [*hist.*]. From *Monemvasia*, G. Μονεμβασία, now *Malvasia*, in the Morea, which orig. produced it; cf. MedL. *malmasia*, forms of which are found in other Europ. langs., and see *malvoisie*.

Attainted was hee by parliament and judged to the death, and thereupon hastely drouned in a butt of malmesey (Sir T. More).

malnutrition, malodorous. 19 cent. coinages. *Malpractice* was orig. (17 cent.) used of bad doctoring.

malt. AS. *mealt*. Com. Teut.; cf. Du. *mout*, Ger. *malz*, ON. *malt*; cogn. with *melt*. With *maltster* cf. *brewster*, both orig. female occupations.

Maltese. Of *Malta*, whence cat, dog, cross. The latter was that of the Knights of St John, Hospitallers, who held Malta during the Middle Ages. The lang. is corrupt. Arab. mixed with It.

Malthusian. Of *T. R. Malthus*, whose *Essay on Population* (1798) advised limited procreation of children.

maltreat. F. *maltraiter*. See *treat*.

malvaceous [*bot.*]. From Late L. *malvaceus*. See *mallow*.

malversation. F., from *malverser*, from L. *versari*. See *versed*.

malverser en son office: to behave him selfe ill in his office (Cotg.).

malvoisie [*archaic*]. F., OF. *malvesie*, It. *malvasia*, as *malmsey* (q.v.).

With hym broghte he a jubbe of malvesye
(Chauc. B. 1260).

mamelon [*fort.*]. F., mound, lit. nipple of breast, *mamelle*, L. *mamilla*, dim. of *mamma*. Hence also *mamillated*.

Mameluke. Arab. *mamlūk*, slave, p.p. of *malaka*, to possess. The *Mamelukes* were orig. a force of Caucasian slaves. They

seized the sovereignty of Egypt in 1254, and held it, with interruptions, till their massacre by Mohammed Ali in 1811. In most Europ. langs. Cf. hist. of *janizary*.

mamillated. See *mamelon*.

mamma. Natural infantile redupl. Cf. L. *mamma*, G. μάμμη, and similar forms in most langs. Spelling, for *mama* (cf. *papa*), is suggested by L. First *NED.* record is 16 cent., but the word is of course venerable (cf. *bow-wow*).

mammal. Late L. *mammalis*, from *mamma*, breast, ident. with above (cf. *pap*). First in *mammalia* (Linnaeus).

mammee. Fruit. Sp. *mamey*, from Haytian.

mammock [*archaic & dial.*]. Fragment, to mangle (*Cor.* i. 3). ? From *maim*.

mammon. Late L., G. μαμωνᾶς, Aram. *māmōn*, riches, gain. Regarded by medieval writers as name of demon (*God and Mammon*). In Bibl. transl. first used by Tynd., where Wyc. has *riches*.

mammoth. Archaic Russ. *mammot* (*mamant*), of unknown origin.

man. AS. *mann*. Com. Teut.; cf. Du. *man*, Ger. *mann*, ON. *mathr* (for *mannr*), Goth. *manna*; cogn. with Sanskrit *manu*. Used for both L. *homo* and *vir*, though AS. had also *wer* in second sense (see *werwolf*), and in AS. used of both sexes. It is possible that the regular omission of the art. when the word is used in gen. sense, e.g. *man is mortal* (cf. *the child, the lion*, etc.), may be partly due to its employment as indef. pron.; cf. Ger. *man*, F. *on* (L. *homo*). Sense of husband (cf. Ger. *mann*) now only in *man and wife*, of servant, subordinate, in *master and man, officers and men*. *Mankind* replaced earlier *mankin* (see *kin, kind*). *Man-of-war* is 15 cent.; cf. *Indiaman*. *Manhandle*, to move without help of machinery, is from *handle*, but in sense of rough usage it may be altered from Dev. *manangle*, AF. *mahangler*, to mangle (q.v.). The distinction between *manslaughter* (earlier *manslaught*) and murder appears in late ME. For *chessman*, back-formation from *chessmen*, see *chess*. It is possible that in other collocations, e.g. *all the king's horses and all the king's men*, we also have a disguised survival of *meiny*.

He [Henry V] roode forthe tylle he cam to Hampton, and there he mosteryd hys mayne
(Gregory's *Chron.* 1415).

I'll catch you and man-handle you, and you'll die (Kipling, *Light that failed*).

manacle. OF. *manicle*, L. *manicula*, dim. of *manica*, sleeve, etc., from L. *manus*, hand.

manage. Orig. to handle and train horses. It. *maneggiare*, from *mano*, hand. Cf. obs. noun *manage*, horsemanship, F. *manège*, "the manage, or managing of a horse" (Cotg.), It. *maneggio*, the Italians being in 16 cent., as now, the trick-riders of Europe and the instructors of young E. nobles on the grand tour. Later senses of the word have been affected by OF. *menage*, direction, from *mener*, to lead (e.g. to *manage a business*), and still more by F. *ménage* (q.v.), housekeeping, *ménager*, to economize. Dryden repeatedly uses *manage* in the exact sense of *ménager*. To *manage* (contrive) *to* is 18 cent. (*Trist. Shandy*, v. 17).

It is the peculiar praise of us Italians...to manege with reason, especially rough horses (*NED.* c. 1560).
Speak terms of manage to thy bounding steed
(1 *Hen. IV*, ii. 3).

manatee. Cetacean, dugong. Sp. *manati*, Carib. *manattoui*. Cf. OF. *manat* (replaced by *lamantin*).

manat: a monstrous Indian fish that resembles an oxe (Cotg.).

Manchester school [*hist.*]. Applied derisively by Disraeli (1848) to the Cobden-Bright group, which considered that the whole duty of man was to buy in the cheapest market and sell in the dearest.

Niggard throats of Manchester may bawl
(Tennyson).

manchet [*archaic*]. Small loaf. Orig. bread of the finest quality. Var. *mainchet* suggests possible connection with obs. *maine*, in same sense, aphet. for (*pain*) *demaine*, lord's bread, L. *panis dominicus*. Or it may be from an unrecorded AF. **demanchet*; cf. F. *dimanche*, L. *dominica*.

manchette. F., dim. of *manche*, sleeve, L. *manica*, from *manus*, hand.

manchineel. WInd. tree. Earlier *mancinell* (Capt. John Smith), F. *mancenille*, Sp. *manzanilla*, from *manzana*, OSp. *mazana*, L. *Matiana* (sc. *poma, mala*), kind of apple, named from the *Matia* gens.

Manchu. Mongol race which (1646) overthrew the native (Ming) dynasty of China.

manciple. College purveyor (Oxf. & Camb.). OF. *manciple, mancipe* (cf. *participle*), L. *mancipium*, orig. purchase, acquisition, from *manus*, hand, *capere*, to take; hence chattel, slave (cf. *emancipate*).

A gentil maunciple was ther of a temple
(Chauc. A. 567).

Mancunian. Of *Manchester*, MedL. *Mancunium*.

-mancy. OF. *-mancie*, Late L., G. μαντεία, divination.

mandamus [*leg.*]. L., we command. Init. word of (orig. royal) writ to enforce performance of some public duty.

mandarin. Port. *mandarim*, Malay *mantrī*, Hind. *mantrī*, Sanskrit *mantrin*, counsellor, from *mantra*, counsel, from root *man*, to think. For non-Chin. origin cf. *joss, junk*. Chin. title is *Kwan*. *Mandarin*, orange, F. *mandarine*, is prob. allusive to bright yellow robes of mandarins. For current sense of pompous official cf. *alguazil, satrap*.

The mandarins of the Foreign Office
(*Daily Chron.* Nov. 21, 1917).

mandate. L. *mandatum*, p.p. neut. of *mandare*, to command, from *manus*, hand, *dare*, to give. Cf. *maundy*. Pol. sense is after F. *mandat*.

mandible. OF. (*mandibule*), L. *mandibula*, from *mandere*, to chew.

mandolin. F. *mandoline*, It. *mandolino*, dim. of *mandola*, for *mandora*. ? Cogn. with obs. *bandore*. See *banjo*.

mandragore. AS. *mandragora*, Late L., G. μανδραγόρας. *Mandrake*, ME. *mandragge*, is a shortened form, prob. altered on *man* and *drake*, dragon, the plant being supposed to resemble the human form and to have magic powers. *Mandragora*, cause of forgetting, is after *Oth.* iii. 3.

Ruben goon out in tyme of wheet hervest into the feeld, fond mandraggis [Coverd. mandragoras]
(Wyc. *Gen.* xxx. 14).

mandrel. In various mech. senses. Corrupt. of F. *mandrin*, of doubtful origin, ? ult. cogn. with L. *mamphur*, for **mandar*, part of a turner's lathe.

mandrill. Baboon. App. from *man* and *drill*, baboon. The latter is prob. a WAfr. word.

dril: a large over-grown ape, or baboon (Blount).

manducate [*theol.*]. To eat. From L. *manducare*. See *mange*.

mane. AS. *manu*. Com. Teut.; cf. Du. *manen* (pl.), Ger. *mähne*, ON. *mön*. Orig. neck; cf. Sanskrit *manyā*, nape of neck, L. *monile*, necklace, Welsh *mwnwgl*, neck, *mwng*, mane.

manège. Riding-school, horsemanship. F., see *manage*.

Manes. L., deified souls of dead ancestors. From OL. *manis*, good, whence *immanis*, cruel.

manetti. Rose. From *Xavier Manetti*, It. botanist (†1784).

manganese. F. *manganèse*, It. *manganese*, corrupt. of *magnesia* (q.v.). From its resemblance to lodestone.

mange. Earlier also *mangie*, ME. *manjewe*, OF. *manjue*, itch, from OF. tonic stem (L. *mandūc-*) of *manger*, to eat, L. *manducare*, from *mandere*, to chew. Cf. F. *démanger*, to itch.

mangel-(mangold-)wurzel. Ger. *mangold-wurzel*, beet-root, corrupted in Ger. to *mangel-wurzel* by association with *mangel*, want, as though famine food, and hence earlier translated into E. as *root of scarcity* and into F. as *racine de disette*. First element is prob. the proper name *Mangold* (the AS. form of which has given *Mangles*); for second see *wort*[1], *wurzel*.

manger. F. *mangeoire*, from *manger*, to eat. See *mange*. The *dog in the manger* is in F. *le chien du jardinier*, who does not eat cabbages and prevents others from doing so.

Like unto cruell dogges liying in a maunger, neither eatyng the haye theim selves ne sufferyng the horse to feed thereof (*NED.* 1564).

mangle[1]. To mutilate. AF. *mangler*, *mahangler*, frequent. of OF. *mahaignier*, to maim (q.v.).

mangle[2]. For linen. Du. *mangel*, for *mangel-stok*, "a smoothing role" (Hexham), from verb *mangelen*, from obs. *mange*, mangle, mangonel, ult. from G. μάγγανον, pulley, warlike engine. Cf. It. *mangano*, "a kinde of presse to presse buckrom, fustian, or died linnen cloth, to make it have a luster or glasse" (Flor.).

mango. Fruit. Port. *manga*, through Malay from Tamil *mānkāy*.

mangold-wurzel. See *mangel-wurzel*.

mangonel [*hist.*]. OF. (*mangonneau*), dim. from Late L. *mangonum*, as *mangle*[2] (q.v.). Obs. from c. 1600 but revived by the romantics.

mangosteen. Fruit. Malay *mangustan*.

mangrove. Altered on *grove* from earlier *mangrowe* (v.i.), app. related to 16 cent. Sp. *mangle*, Port. *mangue*, prob. of SAmer. origin. Malay *manggi-manggi*, mangrove, not now in use, may have been borrowed from Port.

Amongst all the rest there growes a kinde of tree called mangrowes, they grow very strangely, and would make a man wonder to see the manner of their growing (*NED.* 1613).

manhandle. See *man*.

mania. L., G. μανία, from μαίνεσθαι, to be mad. Sense of "craze" is after F. *manie*.

Manichee. Member of sect regarding Satan as co-eternal with God. Late L., Late G. Μανιχαῖος, from name of founder of sect (Persia, 3 cent.).

manicure. F., from *manus*, hand, *cura*, care; cf. earlier *pedicure*.

manifest. F. *manifeste*, L. *manifestus*, ? struck by the hand, palpable, from *manus*, hand, and root of *-fendere*. Pol. sense of verb after F. *manifester*; cf. *manifesto* (17 cent.), from It.

manifold. From *many* and *fold*[1]. The compd. is in AS. and all Teut. langs.

manikin. Flem. *manneken*, dim. of *man*. First (16 cent.) in sense of lay-figure. Cf. F. *mannequin*, from Flem., now applied in E. to living dress model.

mannequin: a puppet, or anticke (Cotg.).

Manilla, Manila. Capital of Philippines, whence tobacco, cheroots, hemp.

manille. Card game. F., now a game, orig. second-best trump at quadrille and ombre, Sp. *malilla*, dim. of *mala* (fem.), bad.

manioc. Earlier (16 cent.) *manihot* (from F.), *mandioc*, *mandioque* (Purch. xvi. 215), Tupi (Brazil) *mandioca*, root of the cassava plant.

maniple. OF. (*manipule*), L. *manipulus*, handful, from *manus*, hand, *plēre*, to fill, also sub-division of legion. As eccl. vestment symbolically explained as napkin for wiping away tears shed for sins of the people.

manipulation. F., of mod. formation from *manipulus* (v.s.) and orig. applied to "handling" of apparatus. *Manipulate* is back-formation.

manitou. Good (also evil) spirit. NAmer. Ind. (Algonkin).

manna. Late L., Late G., Aram. *mannā*, Heb. *mān*, whence G. μάν, L. *man*, commoner than longer form in LXX. and *Vulg.* Perh. Ancient Egypt. *mannu*, exudation of *tamarix gallica*, whence Arab. *mann*. The explanation in *Ex.* xvi. 15 is an early case of folk-etym., resting on a possible interpretation of the Aram. name. The word is found early in most Europ. langs., e.g. in AS. & Goth.

mannequin. See *manikin*.

manner[1]. Mode. F. *manière*, VL. **manaria*, from *manuarius*, belonging to the hand;

cf. It. *maniera*, Sp. *manera*. Orig. sense, method of handling, hence custom, sort, as in *manners* (used in sing. by Chauc.), *what manner of man, no manner of means*. *To the manner born*, subject by birth to the custom, is now usu. misinterpreted to suggest congenital fitness. With *mannerism* cf. earlier *mannerist* (in art) and F. *maniériste* (neol.).

> Though I am native here,
> And to the manner born, it is a custom
> More honour'd in the breach, than the observance
>   (*Haml.* i. 4).

manner² [*archaic*]. Incorr. for *mainour* in *taken in* (*with*) *the mainour*, caught in the act (*Numb.* v. 13), esp. in possession of stolen property. AF. form of F. *manœuvre* (q.v.); cf. *manure*.

manoeuvre. F., from verb *manœuvrer*, Late L. *manoperare*, for L. *manu operari*, to work by hand; cf. It. *manovra*, Sp. *maniobra*. In E. an 18 cent. mil. and naut. loan-word.

manometer. For measuring force of vapour. F. *manomètre*, from G. μανός, thin, rare.

manor. F. *manoir*, OF. infin., to dwell, L. *manēre*. Cf. *pleasure*.

mansard roof. From *François Mansard*, F. architect (†1666). Cf. F. *mansarde*, garret, *toit en mansarde*.

manse. MedL. *mansa*, from *manēre, mans-*, to remain, dwell. Cf. OF. *mes*, whence ME. *meese* (surviving as surname), Prov. *mas*, as in *Dumas*.

mansion. OF., learned form of L. *mansio-n-*, dwelling-place (v.s.), of which popular form was *maison*. Current sense from c. 1500. *Mansion-house*, now spec. residence of Lord Mayor, was in 16 cent. used chiefly of offic. eccl. residence.

mansuetude. OF., L. *mansuetudo*, gentleness, orig. accustoming to handling, from *manus*, hand, *suescere, suet-*, to be wont.

mansworn [*archaic*]. From obs. *manswear*, to perjure, from AS. *mān*, wickedness, cogn. with Ger. *meineid*, false oath.

mantel. Var. of *mantle* (q.v.), in *mantel-piece* (*-shelf*), F. *manteau de cheminée*. Cf. dim. *mantelet*, moveable shelter. For differentiation of spelling cf. *metal, mettle*.

> They make haste to the wall thereof and the mantelet [*Vulg.* umbraculum] is prepared
>   (*Nahum*, ii. 5, *RV.*).

mantic. Of prophecy or divination. G. μαντικός, from μάντις, prophet.

mantilla. Sp., dim. of *manta*, mantle (q.v.).

mantis. Insect. G. μάντις, prophet, from position of fore-legs suggesting prayer. The G. word is also used of some insect.

mantissa [*math.*]. L., makeweight; perh. Etruscan.

mantle. OF. *mantel* (*manteau*), L. *mantellum*, which passed also into Teut. langs., e.g. AS. *mentel*. Prob. ident. with L. *mantelum*, towel, napkin. Late L. *mantum*, whence It. Sp. *manto, manta*, F. *mante*, is a back-formation. In fig. use esp. of blood (blush) suffusing cheek.

> *manteau*: a cloke; also the mantletree of a chimney
>   (Cotg.).

manton. Gun, pistol. See *Joe Manton*. Also used in F.

mantua. Chiefly in *mantua-maker*. Corrupt. of F. *manteau*, perh. by association with *Mantua* silk. Cf. *paduasoy*.

Mantuan, the. Virgil, born (70 B.C.) at *Mantua*, NIt.

manual. F. *manuel* and L. *manualis*, from *manus*, hand. First in *manual labour* (Hoccleve). *Sign manual*, autograph signature, is via F. With *manual*, book, cf. *handbook*.

manucode. Bird of paradise. F., from ModL. *manucodiata*, Malay *mānuq dēwāta*, bird of the gods, second element from Sanskrit.

manuduction. MedL. *manuductio-n-*, from *manu ducere*, to lead by the hand.

manufacture. F., from L. *manu facere*, to make by hand.

manumit. L. *manumittere*, to send from one's hand. Cf. *manciple, emancipate*.

manure. First (c. 1400) as verb. F. *manœuvrer*, to work by hand. Cf. *inure*. Orig. of tillage in gen. Thus Sylv. (i. 6) speaks of *Nile's manured shoare* where Du Bartas has *marge labouré*.

> The face of the earth [in Guiana] hath not been torned, nor the vertue and salt of the soyle spent by manurance (Raleigh).

manuscript. MedL. *manuscriptum*, written by hand. Cf. *script*.

Manx. Earlier *manks*, metath. of 16 cent. *manisk*, ON. **manskr*, from *Man*. Cf. *hunks, minx*. The lang. belongs to the Goidelic branch of Celt.

many. AS. *manig*. Com. Teut.; cf. Du. *menig*, Ger. *manch* (OHG. *manag*), ON. *mengi*, multitude, Goth. *manags*; cogn. with Ir. *minic*, Gael. *minig*, frequent, Welsh *mynych*, often. Orig. distrib. with sing. as still in *many a*. The *many-headed beast* is from Horace, *belua multorum* *capitum* (*Ep.* i. 1). *Many-sided* in fig. sense is due to Ger. *vielseitig*. As noun, in *a good (great) many, friends a many*, etc., it represents rather archaic and dial. *meny, meinie*, retinue, crowd, orig. household, for which see *ménage, menial*.

Maori. Native name, supposed to mean "of the usual kind."

map. First in compd. *mappemonde*, F., MedL. *mappa mundi*, map of the world. L. *mappa*, napkin, cloth, on which maps were painted, whence also Ger. *mappe*, portfolio, is described by Quintilian as Punic.

> As fer as cercled is the mappemounde
> (Chauc. *To Rosamond*, 2).

maple. AS. *mapel, mapul*, in *mapulder, mapeltrēow*, maple-tree. Cf. *Mapledurham* (Berks), AS. *mapulder-ham*.

mar. AS. *mierran*. Com. Teut.; cf. archaic Du. *marren, merren*, to hinder, OHG. *marren*, to hinder, ON. *merja*, to crush, Goth. *marzjan*, to cause to stumble. From Teut. is OF. *marrir*, whence some senses of E. *mar*; cf. It. *smarrire*, to bewilder. Orig. sense to hinder, impede (v.i.), as in *marplot*. In early use often contrasted with *make*, e.g. to *make a spoon or mar a horn* (cf. to *mend or end*). The *Marprelate* tracts were issued under the pseudonym of *Martin Marprelate* (1588–9).

> You mar our labour. Keep your cabins. You do assist the storm (*Temp.* i. 1).

marabou, marabout. F. *marabou(t)*, Port. *marabute*, Arab. *murābit*, hermit, Mohammedan monk of NAfr.; cf. Sp. *morabito*. The nickname was prob. given to the stork from his dignified and solitary habits. Cf. *adjutant bird*. See *maravedi*.

> We hired another marybuck, because they are people which may travell freely (Purch.).

marah. Heb. *mārāh*, fem. of *mar*, bitter (*Ex.* xv. 23, *Ruth*, i. 20).

maranatha. Church G. μαραναθά, Aram. *māran athā*, Our Lord has come, or *maranā 'thā*, O our Lord, come Thou. Often misunderstood as forming with *anathema* an imprecatory formula.

> Be he cursid, Maranatha, that is, in the comynge of the Lord (Wyc. 1 *Cor.* xvi. 22).

maraschino. It., from *marasca*, a small black cherry, aphet. for *amarasca*, from *amaro*, bitter, L. *amarus*.

marasmus. Wasting away. G. μαρασμός, from μαραίνειν, to wither. Cf. *amaranth*.

Marathi. See *Mahratti*.

Marathon race. Foot-race of 29 miles, the distance covered by Pheidippides in bringing the news of Marathon to Athens.

maraud. F. *marauder*, from *maraud*, "a rogue, begger, vagabond; a varlet, rascall, scoundrell, base knave" (Cotg.). Prob. the proper name *Maraud*, OHG. *Mari-wald*, fame powerful, the selection of the name being perh. due to association with OF. *marrir*, to injure, mar. Cf. *ribald*. The F. word was borrowed by Ger. in Thirty Years' War and punningly associated with *Count Merode*, an Imperialist general noted for his barbarity; hence Sp. *merodear*, to maraud.

maravedi [*hist.*]. Coin. Sp., from Arab. *Murābitīn*, lit. hermits, name of Arab. dynasty, the *Almoravides*, at Cordova (1087–1147). See *marabout*. The origin of the word is Arab. *ribāt*, guard-house on frontier, often occupied by fanatics.

marble. ME. also *marbre*, F., L. *marmor*, G. μάρμαρος; ? cf. μαρμαίρειν, to sparkle. Adopted also by Teut. langs., e.g. AS. *marma*, Ger. *marmel*. The F. form shows unusual dissim. of *m-m*, while E. shows dissim. of *r-r* (cf. *pilgrim*), as do also Sp. *mármol*, and Du. *marmel*, in sense of marble used in play.

marc. Liqueur. F., orig. residue of crushed grapes, from *marcher*, to tread, march.

marcasite [*min.*]. Pyrites. MedL. *marcasita*, whence also forms in Rom. langs. Origin unknown.

marcella. Fabric. From *Marseille*, place of manufacture.

March. ONF. (*mars*), L. *Martius* (*mensis*), month of *Mars*. Replaced AS. *hrēthmōnath*, of uncertain meaning. With *March hare* (see *hatter*) cf. obs. *March mad*.

> Then they begyn to swere and to stare,
> And be as braynles as a Marsh hare
> (*Colyn Blowbols Testament*).

march¹ [*hist.*]. Boundary, frontier, esp. in *Lord of the Marches*. F. *marche*, OHG. *marca*, cogn. with *mark*¹ (q.v.); cf. It. Sp. *marca*. Hence verb to *march*, to be conterminous.

march². Verb. F. *marcher*, to walk, orig. to tread, tramp, "foot-slogging," perh. from L. *marcus*, hammer. Adopted in mil. sense by most Europ. langs.

marchioness. MedL. *marchionissa*, fem. of *marchio*, marquess (q.v.).

marchpane. From 15 cent. Cf. F. *massepain* (earlier also *marcepain*), It. *marzapane*, Sp.

mazapan, Ger. *marzipan*, Du. *marsepein*, etc. A much discussed word of obscure origin, the second element having been assimilated to L. *panis*, bread. Kluge accepts Kluyver's theory that it is ident. with the name of a 12 cent. Venet. coin, the normal MedL. form of which, *matapanus*, is applied to a Venet. coin with image of Christ seated on a throne, Arab. *mauthabān*, a king that sits still. The coin acquired the spec. sense of tenth part, and the name was transferred to the small boxes containing a tenth of a "moggio" of sweetened almond paste imported from the Levant.

marconigram. From *Marconi*, It. inventor, after *telegram*, *cablegram*. *NED.* records it for 1902.

mare. AS. *mere*, *miere*. Com. Teut.; cf. Du. *merrie*, Ger. *mähre*, jade, ON. *merr*. These are fem. forms corresponding to AS. *mearh*, OHG. *marah* (see *marshal*), ON. *marr*, cogn. with Gael. Ir. *marc*, Welsh *march*, all meaning horse, stallion, whence allusion to king Mark's ears in *Tristan and Isold*. *Mare's-nest*, in Fletcher (1619), is later than obs. *horse-nest* (Stanyhurst, 1583).

The grey mare is the better horse (Heywood, 1562).

maremma. It., marsh-land by sea, L. *maritima*.

margarine, marge. F., adopted (1888) as leg. name for butter-substitute made from oleo-margarine. Ult. from G. μαργαρίτης, pearl, adopted by Chevreul in *acide margarique*, from pearly appearance of its crystals.

margay. SAmer. tiger-cat. F. (Buffon), earlier *margaia*, an attempt at Tupi (Brazil) *mbaracaïa*.

marge[1] [*poet.*]. F., as *margin*. Poet. also is *margent*, ME. var. of *margin* (cf. *pageant*, *tyrant*, etc.).

marge[2]. See *margarine*.

margin. L. *margo*, *margin-*, whence also F. *marge*; cogn. with *mark*[1], *march*[1]. Earliest (*Piers Plowm.*) in ref. to books. Current fig. senses are 19 cent.

margrave. Du. *markgraaf*, Ger. *markgraf*, count of the march. Cf. *marquis*. *Margravine* has the fem. *-in*, lost in E. exc. in *vixen*. Ger. *graf* looks akin to AS. *gerēfa*, grieve, reeve, but some high authorities recognize no connection.

marguerite. F., daisy, G. μαργαρίτης, pearl,

daisy, prob. of Eastern origin; cf. Sanskrit *mangarī*, cluster of flowers, pearl.

Maria, black. Police van. Quot. below, which turns up every few years, is app. of the same type as those given s.v. *Jack Robinson*. For sense of large shell cf. *Jack Johnson*.

> Few probably recollect that Black Maria came to us from America. She was Maria Lee—a negress of gigantic stature and enormous strength—who, in the intervals of looking after her sailors' boarding-house at Boston, used to help the police in the frequent scrimmages there
>   (*Pall Mall Gaz.* Sep. 3, 1918).

marigold. From (Virgin) *Mary* and *gold*; cf. obs. *marybud* (*Cymb.* ii. 3).

marinade. F., Sp. *marinada*, from *marinar*, to pickle in brine, from *marino*, of the sea.

marine. F. *marin*, L. *marinus*, from *mare*, sea. Fem. form has prevailed owing to such common combinations as *eau marine*, *armée marine*, whence F. *marine*, navy; cf. E. *mercantile marine*. A *marine-store* orig. dealt in old ships' materials. *Marine* (noun) is for earlier *marine soldier*, often (wrongly) regarded by sailors as half a land-lubber, whence *tell that to the marines* (cf. L. *credat Judaeus*), and *marine*, empty bottle.

mariner. F. *marinier*, MedL. *marinarius* (v.s.). In very early use and much commoner than *sailor*.

Marinism. Affected style of *Marini*, It. poet (†1625). Cf. *Euphuism*.

Mariolatry [*theol.*]. Badly formed (c. 1600) on *idolatry*. Cf. *babyolatry*, etc.

marionette. F. *marionnette*, "little Marian or Mal; also, a puppet" (Cotg.) dim. of *Marion*, dim. of *Marie*, L., G. Μαρία, ident. with Heb. *Miriam*. Cf. *doll*.

marish. Dial. and poet. for *marsh* (q.v.).

Marist. Member of R.C. missionary *Society of Mary* (19 cent.).

marital. F., L. *maritalis*, from *maritus*. See *marry*.

maritime. F., L. *maritimus*, near the sea, from *mare*, sea, with ending as in *finitimus*, near the frontier.

marjoram. Earlier (14 cent.) *majorane*. In most Europ. langs., and, as in the case of other pop. herbs, with very diversified forms due to folk-etym. Cf. F. *marjolaine* (OF. *majorane*), It. *majorana*, *maggiorana*, Sp. *mejorana* (earlier *majorana*, *mayorana*), Du. *marjolein*, Ger. *majoran*, Sw. *mejram*, etc. The *maj-* forms are the older. ? Ult. from L. *amaracus*, marjoram, from *amarus*, bitter.

mark[1]. AS. *mearc*, boundary. Com. Teut.; cf. Du. *merk*, Ger. *mark*, ON. *mörk* (in *Dan-mörk*), Goth. *marka*. Also widely adopted in various senses in Rom. langs.; some .E. senses belong to F. *marque*. See also *march[1]*. Cogn. with L. *margo*, Pers. *marz*, boundary. Replaced in Ger. by *grenze* (whence Du. *grens*), of Slav. origin. From orig. sense are evolved those of sign of boundary, sign in general, trace left by sign, etc. *Beside* (*wide of, to miss, overshoot*) *the mark* are from archery. With *mark of the beast* (*Rev.* xvi. 2) cf. *a marked man* (*Gen.* iv. 15). But a *man of mark* is F. *homme de marque*, man of distinction; cf. to *make one's mark*. Below (*up to*) *the mark* refers partly to *mark* in sense of brand, trade-mark; cf. *up to dick*. *Bless* (*save*) *the mark*, common in Shaks., was a deprecatory phrase of the *absit omen* type, but its origin is obscure. It is now mostly used, after 1 *Hen. IV*, i. 3, as a scornful comment on something quoted. *Mark-worthy* is mod. after Ger. *merkwürdig*. With to *mark*, observe, cf. *remark*, of which it is sometimes an aphet. form.

mark[2]. Coin, of varying value. Recorded early in all Rom. & Teut. langs. Perh. from *mark[1]*. Orig. half-pound of silver.

market. Late AS., ONF., for OF. *marchiet* (*marché*), L. *mercatus*, from *mercari*, to trade; cf. It. *mercato*, Sp. *mercado*, also Du. Ger. *markt*, ON. *markathr*. An early trade-word from Rome (cf. *money*).

markhor. Wild goat (Tibet). Pers. *mārkhōr*, lit. serpent-eater.

marksman. For earlier *markman* (*Rom. & Jul.* i. 1). Cf. *huntsman, helmsman, spokesman*.

marl. OF. and dial. *marle* (*marne*), Late L. *margila* (whence Ger. *mergel*), from *marga*, called a Gaulish word by Pliny.

marline. Du. *marlijn*, from *marren*, to bind (see *moor[2]*), *lijn*, line. But it may be rather for *marling*, from naut. *marl*, to tie, etc., app. frequent. from Du. verb (v.s.), and found earlier (*Prompt. Parv.*) than *marline*. Cf. *marling-spike* (Capt. John Smith).

Marlovian. In style of *Christopher Marlowe* (†1593). Cf. *Harrovian, Borrovian*.

marmalade. F. *marmelade*, Port. *marmelada*, from *marmelo*, quince, by dissim. from L. *melimelum*, G. μελίμηλον, lit. honey apple. An old word in E. (c. 1500), though quot. below has a modern look.

Amongst these came the [Portuguese] captaine

with a piece of bread and marmallet in his hand (Purch. xvi. 194).

marmite [*war slang*]. F., cooking-pot, joc. shell. Cf. E. *coal-box* in similar sense.

marmoreal. From L. *marmoreus*. See *marble*.

marmoset. F. *marmouset*, of obscure origin. Its earliest F. sense (13 cent.) is grotesque carved figure, but it may have orig. meant monkey. App. related to OF. *marmot*, monkey, grotesque statuette, now brat (cf. *marmaille*, swarm of children). Maundeville uses *marmosets* to render F. *marmots*. *Marmot* is of doubtful origin, perh. dim. from OF. *merme*, L. *minimus*, ? or ident. with the next word (q.v.).

cercopithecus: ung marmot (Est.), a marmoset, or a munkie (Coop.).

marmot: a marmoset, or little monkie (Cotg.).

marmotta: a marmoset, a babie for a childe to play withall, a pugge (Flor.).

marmot. F. *marmotte*, Romansh *murmont*, ? from L. *mus, mur-*, mouse, *mons, mont-*, mountain. App. influenced in form by F. *marmot* (v.s.). Cf. OHG. *muremunto* (of which dial. forms are still in use), now replaced by *murmeltier*, as though "murmuring animal." But the Romansh word may itself be due to folk-etym. Identical sense of F. *marmotter* and OF. *marmouser*, to mumble, rather suggests ult. identity of. *marmot* and *marmoset*. The earliest name for the animal is *mus Alpinus* (Pliny).

Maronite. Sect of Syrian Christians. From *Maron*, name of founder (4 cent.). Cf. *Druse*.

maroon[1]. Colour, firework. F. *marron*, chestnut, It. *marrone*, of unknown origin, ? Celt. The colour is no longer ident. with F. *marron*. The fire-work sense seems to be suggested by the popping of the roasted chestnut.

maroon[2]. Fugitive slave (WInd.). F. *marron*, aphet. for Sp. *cimarrón*, wild, untamed. Hence to *maroon*, send astray, spec. put ashore on desert island. Alexander Selkirk, the most famous of marooned sailors, served with Dampier, our earliest authority for the verb.

maroquin. F., from *Maroc*, Morocco.

marque, letters of [*hist.*]. Licence to privateer. Orig. *letters of marque and reprisal*. F. *marque*, Prov. *marca*, from *marcar*, MedL. *marcare*, to seize as pledge. App. from *mark[1]*, but sense-development not clear. Perh. of the character of "Border law."

Litterae marquandi seu gagiandi
(*Procl. of Ed. I*, 1293).
La lei de marke & de represailles (*NED.* 1354).

marquee. False sing. (cf. *burgee, Chinee*) from F. *marquise*, lit. marchioness, also a large tent, app. as suited for a noble lady.

marquetry. F. *marqueterie*, "inlaying, or in-layed worke of sundry colours" (Cotg.), from *marqueter*, to variegate, from *marque*, mark[1].

marquis, marquess. ONF. *markis* (*marquis*), OF. *marchis*, formed, with L. suffix *-ensis*, from Rom. *marca* (see *mark*[1]); cf. It. *marchese*, Sp. *marqués*, MedL. *marchio*, and see *margrave*.

marquis: a marquesse; was in old time the gover-nour of a frontire, or frontire towne (Cotg.).

marquois. Instrument for drawing parallel lines. App. for F. *marquoir*, ruler, marker.

marrow. AS. *mearg*. Com. Teut.; cf. Du. *merg*, Ger. *mark*, ON. *mergr*. With *vege-table marrow* cf. F. *courge à la moelle, con-combre de moelle* (little used).

In 1816 a paper was read before the Horticultural Society on a description and account of a new variety of gourd called "vegetable marrow"
(*Daily Chron.* Aug. 8, 1917).

marry[1]. Verb. F. *marier*, L. *maritare*, from *maritus*, married, ? from *mas, mar-,* male. Has supplanted *wed* but not *wedding*.

Such marriages are made in heaven, though cele-brated on earth (Adm. Monson, 1624).

marry[2] [*archaic*]. Interj. For *Mary* (the Virgin). Later, by association with *St Mary the Egyptian*, extended to *marry-gip*, for which *marry-come-up* was substituted, from the feeling that the *gip* was ident. with the admonition *gip* (*gee up*) to a horse.

marsala. Wine from *Marsala* (Sicily).

Marseillaise. Written and composed (1792) by Rouget de l'Isle, and first sung by "patriots" from *Marseille*.

marsh. AS. *mersc, merisc,* orig. adj. from *mere*[1], cogn. with L. *mare*, sea; cf. Ger. *marsch*, MedL. *mariscus*, whence F. *marais*. Cf. *morass*.

marshal. F. *maréchal*, OHG. *marahscalh*, horse servant. The two elements are cogn. with AS. *mearh* (see *mare*) and *scealc*. Cf. *seneschal* and ModGer. *schalk*, knave. ModGer. *marschall*, borrowed back from F., has given us *field-marshal* (Ger. *feld-marschall*). The word appears in all Rom. langs: with a very wide range of offic.

meanings, which accounts for frequency of E. name *Marshall*. For varied senses and rise in dignity cf. *constable*, and with both cf. synon. ON. *stallari*. The first *air-marshal* (1919) was Sir H. M. Trenchard. Orig. sense survives in *farrier-marshal* (cf. F. *maréchal-ferrant*, farrier). *Marshalsea* (hist.) is for *marshalsy*, orig. court held by steward and knight-marshal of royal house-hold. With verb to *marshal* cf. to *usher*. This has recently acquired new sense from US. railway lang.

As a comparison with these forty trains marshalled per hour...by which 2400 containers would be marshalled and ready for loading per hour, the average marshalling at Nine Elms per hour was 62 wagons (*Westm. Gaz.* Sep. 9, 1919).

marsupial [*zool.*]. From L. *marsupium*, G. μαρσύπιον, dim. of μάρσυπος, bag, purse.

mart. Du. *markt*, market (q.v.), commonly pronounced *mart* and formerly so written. First *NED.* ref. is to the *marts* of Brabant (1437) and Caxton has the *marte* of Ant-werp. Also repeatedly in the *Cely Papers* (15 cent.) in ref. to the wool-*marts* of Flanders, the Celys' own warehouse being in *Mart Lane* (now *Mark Lane*), London.

martagon. Turk's head lily. F., It. *martagone*, Turk. *martagān*, turban of special shape. Cf. *tulip*.

martello tower. Earlier *mortella*, from a tower captured by us (1794) on *Cape Mortella* (myrtle) in Corsica, and regarded as of great defensive power. For the vowel metath. cf. the greengrocer's pronunc. of *broccoli* (*brockilo*).

marten. Orig. the fur. ME. *martren*, OF. *martrine* (sc. *peau*), from *martre*, marten, of Teut. origin; cf. E. (*fou*)*mart* (q.v.), Ger. *marder*. Thought to be ult. Lith. *marti*, daughter-in-law. See names for the weasel in my *Romance of Words* (ch. vii.).

martial. F., L. *martialis*, from *Mars, Mart-* (*Mavors*), god of war. In sense of military only in *court martial, martial law*. For application to character cf. *jovial, mer-curial*.

martin. From name *Martin*, F., L. *Martinus*, from *Mars* (v.s.); cf. *robin, dicky*, etc.; also F. *martin-pêcheur*, kingfisher, *martinet*, house-martin. There may have been spec. ref. to departure of bird about Martinmas (v.i.).

Martin, Saint. Bishop of Tours (4 cent.), whose festival is Nov. 11, *Martinmas*. *St Martin's summer*, Indian summer, is mod.

after F. *été de la Saint-Martin. Saint Martin's bird*, the hen-harrier, is after F. *oiseau de Saint-Martin*, "the ring-taile, or hen-harme" (Cotg.).

martinet. Recorded for 1755 (Swift). If the obscure passage below (1676) refers to the mod. word, connection with F. general *Martinet* (†c. 1715), who improved drill and discipline of F. army temp. Louis XIV, is very doubtful. Moreover the word is not known in F. in this sense, though used of various objects, e.g. cat-o'-nine-tails, peak-halyards, whence E. *martinet*, leech-line of sail. All these are from name *Martin*. Cf. also F. *Martin-bâton*, the (disciplinary) stick.

Oldfox. Prithee don't look like one of our holiday captains now-a-days, with a bodkin by your side, you martinet rogue. *Manly* (aside). O, then, there's hopes. (Aloud) What, d'ye find fault with martinet? Let me tell you, sir, 'tis the best exercise in the world; the most ready, most easy, most graceful exercise that ever was used, and the most—. *Oldfox.* Nay, nay, sir, no more; sir, your servant: if you praise martinet once, I have done with you, sir.—Martinet! Martinet!
(Wycherley, *Plain Dealer*, iii. 1).

martingale. F., in all three senses, viz. strap to keep horse's head down, rope for guying-down jibboom, system of doubling stakes till successful. Dubiously connected, via *chausses à la martingale* (Rabelais), fastened in some peculiar way, with *Martigues* (Bouches-du-Rhône), on the supposition that the inhabitants of that place wore breeches of a special kind. Very doubtful. Some connect it with Sp. *al-martaga*, halter, of Arab. origin.

The impossible martingale of doubles or quits
(G. B. Shaw, in *Daily Chron.* March 7, 1917).

martini-henry. Rifle adopted by British army (1870), the breech being the invention of *Martini* and the barrel of *Henry*.

martlet. OF. *martelet*, var. of *martinet* (see *martin*); cf. dial. *Martlemas*. In her. it represents F. *merlette*, dim. of *merle* (q.v.), blackbird. But the her. bird is footless and must therefore have orig. represented the martin, the swallow-tribe having inconspicuous feet; cf. G. ἄπους, martin, lit. footless.

apodes: Gall. martelets (A. Junius).

martinet: a martlet, or martin (Cotg.).

merlette: a martlet, in blason (*ib.*).

martyr. AS. *martyr*, Church L., adopted in Christian sense from Late (orig. Aeolic)

G. μάρτυρ, for μάρτυς, μάρτυρ-, witness. In most Europ. langs.

marvel. F. *merveille*, L. *mirabilia*, neut. pl. treated as fem. sing. (cf. *force*), from *mirus*, wonderful.

Marxian. Of *Karl Marx*, Ger. socialist (†1883).

Mary. In dial. flower-names *mary* is for the Virgin Mary (cf. *lady*). *Little Mary*, stomach, is from Barrie's play (1903).

marzipan. See *marchpane*.

-mas. In *Christmas, Candlemas*, etc., for *mass*[1].

mascle [*her.*]. Perforated lozenge. OF. (*macle*), L. *macula*, spot, mesh (see *mail*[1]), with intrusive -*s*- perh. due to OHG. *masca*, mesh (q.v.).

mascot. F. *mascotte*, popularized by Audran's operetta *La Mascotte* (1880), Mod. Prov., dim. of *masco*, sorcerer, orig. mask (q.v.). Cf. *hoodoo*.

masculine. F. *masculin*, L. *masculinus*, from *masculus*, male (q.v.).

mash. AS. *māsc-*, in *māxwyrt*, mash-wort, infused malt. First as brewing term. Prob. cogn. with *mix*; cf. Sw. *mäsk*, grains for pigs, Dan. *mask*, mash (from LG.), Ger. *maisch*, crushed grapes.

masher. Orig. US. Also to *be mashed on*, etc. Popular, c. 1882. Origin unknown. Can it be a far-fetched elaboration of to *be spoony on*, mash being regarded as spoon-diet? Cf. to *confiscate the macaroon* for to *take the cake*.

mashie. ? Cf. F. *coup massé* (billiards), orig. stroke made with the large headed cue called a *masse*, mace[1].

mask, masque, masquerade. App. two quite separate origins have contributed to this group. F. *masque*, first in 16 cent. as gloss to L. *larva* (Est.), has been associated with It. *maschera*, Sp. *máscara*, of Arab. origin (v.i.), but must surely be connected with MedL. *mascus, masca*, occurring in 7 cent. as gloss to *larva*. This MedL. word, of doubtful (prob. Ger.) origin, should have given F. **mâque*, so that the -*s*- is app. due to the It. & Sp. words. These represent Arab. *maskharah*, laughing-stock, buffoon, the sense passing on from the actor to his vizard, the opposite of the process perh. exemplified by *person* (q.v.). The E. 16 cent. spelling is indifferently *mask, masque*, and the sense of performance, masquerade, is rather earlier than that of vizard. With *masquerade* cf. F. *mascarade*,

It. *mascherata*, Sp. *mascarado*. It replaced earlier *maskery*.

maskinonge. Large pike of NAmer. lakes. An Odjibwa word, compd. of *kinonge*, pike. Corrupted in Canad. F. into *masque long*, *masque allongé*, whence some of the numerous vars.

mason. F. *maçon*, Late L. *machio-n-* (*macio*, *mattio*), whence also Ger. *steinmetz*, stone-mason. ? Cogn. with *mattock*. Used for *freemason* as early as 1425.

Masorah, Massorah [*theol.*]. Critical notes on text of *OT.* compiled by Jewish scholars in 10 cent. ModHeb. *māsōrāh*.

masque, masquerade. See *mask*.

mass¹. Eucharist. AS. *mæsse*, L. *missa*, from *mittere*, to send, used in sense of dismiss. Spec. sense perh. comes from the dismissory formula *ite, missa est*, at conclusion of service. In most Europ. langs., e.g. F. *messe*, Ger. *messe*, the latter also in sense of festival, fair (see *kermis*). Cf. *Christmas, Michaelmas*, etc.

mass². Agglomeration. F. *masse*, L. *massa*, G. μᾶζα, barley cake, cogn. with μάσσειν, to knead. Hence *massive*. The *masses* were first contrasted with the *classes* by Gladstone (1886). *Mass-meeting* is US.

massacre. F., from OF. *macecre, maçacre*, shambles, slaughter-house (cf. orig. sense of *butchery*). It is difficult to connect this with L. *macellum*, shambles, *macellarius*, butcher, whence Ger. *metzler*, butcher, *metzeln*, to massacre. App. the word first became familiar in E. after the Massacre of St Bartholomew, but *masecrer*, butcher, is found in AF. and occurs as a surname in 1224. Spelman quotes *de emptoribus et machecariis* from a law of Edward the Confessor.

Car tout li bouchier du machacre
Hurtent ensemble leur maillès (OF. *fabliau*).

massage. F., from *masser*, Franco-Ind. adaptation (18 cent.) of Port. *amassar*, to knead, from *massa*, dough. See *mass²*.

massé. F., stroke at billiards with the *masse*, mace¹.

massif. F., solid (see *mass²*). Also used in F. & E. of a cluster of hills or forest.

Two enemy air-ships were observed coming from the direction of the Vesuvius massif
(*Daily Chron.* March 16, 1918).

Massorah. See *Masorah*.

mast¹. Of ship. AS. *mæst*. Com. Teut.; cf. Du. Ger. *mast*, ON. *mastr*; also borrowed by some Rom. langs., e.g. F. *mât*, Port. *masto*. Ult. cogn. with L. *malus*. The single mast of the early ship was the boundary between officers and crew; hence *foremast man*, member of crew, for *before the mast man*. With this cf. *after-guard*, the officers, and orig. sense of *midshipman*.

mast². Of trees. AS. *mæst*. WGer.; cf. Du. *mesten*, Ger. *mästen*, to fatten; cogn. with Goth. *mats*, food.

master. Contains both AS. *mægester*, L. *magister*, and OF. *maistre* (*maître*), L. *magister*; cogn. with *magnus*, great. In most Europ. langs. Earliest E. sense (9 cent.) is schoolmaster, but meanings are very wide, almost superseding those of *lord* (cf. *lord and master*), and with the gen. idea of authority or distinction. Dante (*Inf.* iv. 131) calls Aristotle *il maestro di color che sanno*, the master of those who know. *Masterpiece* is translated from Ger. *meisterstück*, specimen of work entitling member of trade-gild to rank of master. In the navy the officer responsible for navigating the ship was formerly the *master* (now *navigating-lieutenant*), the captain and lieutenants being in charge of the military force on board.

captain: is the commander in chief aboard any ship of war; for those in merchants are improperly call'd so, as having no commissions, and being only masters (*Sea Dict.* 1708).

mastic. F., Late L. *mastichum*, for *masticha*, G. μαστίχη, prob. from root of μασᾶσθαι, to chew, mastic being used as chewing-gum in the East (v.i.). In most Europ. langs.

masticate. From Late L. *masticare*, perh. orig. to chew mastic (v.s.).

mastiff. OF. *mastin* (*mâtin*), orig. an adj., domestic, hence applied to servants, and later to the house-dog. The changed ending is due to OF. *mestif*, mongrel (v.i.), VL. **mixtivus*. OF. *mastin* (cf. It. *mastino*, Sp. *mastín*) is usu. explained as VL. **mansuetinus*, for *mansuetus*, from *mansuescere*, to become accustomed to the hand; cf. OF. *mainpast*, domestic, VL. *manupastus*, fed by hand. The sense-hist. points rather to *mediastinus*, a domestic drudge, though this involves phonetic difficulties.

mastin: a mastive, or ban-dog; a great (countrey) curre (Cotg.).

un chien mestif: a mongrell; understood, by the French, especially of a dog thats bred betweene a mastive or great curre, and a greyhound (*ib.*).

mastodon. F. *mastodonte* (Cuvier, 1806), from G. μαστός, breast, ὀδούς, ὀδοντ-, tooth, from nipple-shaped excrescences on molar teeth.

mastoid [*anat.*]. Breast-shaped (v.s.).

masturbation. L. *masturbatio-n-*, from *masturbari*.

mat¹. Noun. AS. *matte, meatta*, L. *matta*, whence also It. *matta*, Du. *mat*, Ger. *matte*. A Late L. by-form *natta* has given F. *natte*. *Matta* is prob., like *mappa*, which also developed a Late L. *nappa* (see *napkin*), a Punic word. Orig. in E. of roughly plaited sedge, rushes, etc., cf. *matted hair*.

mat². Adj. Dull, dead, of surface. F., orig. mated at chess. See *check*.

matador. Sp., killer, L. *mactator-em*, from *mactare*, to make sacrifice to, kill, whence Sp. *matar*, to slay.

match¹. One of a pair. AS. *gemæcca*, esp. used of male and female animal, husband and wife. Cf. obs. *make*, companion, peer, AS. *gemaca*, cogn. with OHG. *gimahho*, companion, orig. an adj., equal, suitable, whence ModGer. *gemach*, easy, comfortable. Hence verb to *match*, to bring together, associate, from which the abstract senses of the noun, e.g. *cricket* (*matrimonial*) *match*, are evolved. *Match-board* is so called because the tongue of one board matches the groove of the other.

Pray to God to give a wife or husband to your sonne and daughter, and make piety and vertue the chiefe match-makers (Whately, c. 1640).

match². For ignition. F. *mèche*, wick, the earliest E. sense, VL. **mysca* for *myxa*, G. μύξα, mucus, snuff of candle, used in MedL. also for wick of lamp. Hence *matchlock*, early fire-arm which preceded the wheel-lock.

matchet. See *machete*.

mate¹. Chess. See *check*. Fig. sense of discomfort, F. *mater*, is recorded in early 13 cent.

mate². Associate. From LG. or. Du. Cf. ModDu. *maat*, for earlier *gemaat*, cogn. with OHG. *gimazzo*, mess-mate (q.v.), sharer of "meat"; cf. AS. *gemetta*, partaker of food, and formation of *companion*. The *mate* of a ship was orig. the *master's mate*; cf. *boatswain's mate, gunner's mate*, etc. See *meat*.

maté. Shrub (*ilex paraguayensis*) of which leaves are used for infusion like tea. Sp. *mate*, Quichua (Peruv.) *mati*, explained (1608) as the calabash in which the drink is prepared.

Vegetarian stores...are already doing a fair trade in maté (*Daily Chron.* Oct. 16, 1917).

matelassé. Quilted. F., from *matelas*, mattress (q.v.).

matelote. Dish of fish. F., from *matelot*, sailor. This latter is for OF. *matenot*, obs. Du. *mattenoet*, from *maat*, meat, *genoot*, companion; cf. MHG. *mazgenōze*, table-fellow. See *huguenot, mate²*.

material. Late L. *materialis*, from *materia*, matter, as opposed to form; ? from *mater*, mother. *Materialism, materialist*, belong to 18 cent. F. philos. lang. Mod. use of to *materialize*, to "come off," is from US. journalism.

materia medica. MedL. transl. of G. ὕλη ἰατρική.

matériel. F., contrasted as noun with *personnel*.

maternal. F. *maternel*, from L. *maternus*, from *mater*, mother (q.v.).

mathematics. Cf. F. *mathématiques*, the only F. pl. of this form. Replaced earlier *mathematic* (Wyc.), OF., L., G. μαθηματική (sc. τέχνη), from μανθάνειν, to learn.

matico. Peruv. herb used as styptic. Sp., dim. of *Mateo*, Matthew. Said to have been named from Sp. soldier who discovered its property.

matie. Herring when in best condition. Adapted from Du. *maatjes* (*haring*), for earlier *maeghdekens-*, dim. of *maagd*, maid.

matins, mattins. F. *matines*, from L. *matutinus*, the fem. pl. perh. representing *matutinae vigiliae*. From *Matuta*, goddess of dawn, prob. cogn. with *maturus*. Orig. one of the Church offices recited at midnight, in mod. Church of England use applied to a composite of matins, lauds and prime. With *matinée*, afternoon performance, cf. *morning call*, also belonging to the afternoon.

matrass. Long-necked vessel (chem.). F. *matras*, prob. from archaic *matras*, large-headed cross-bow bolt, of unknown origin. The flask may have been named from resemblance in shape, as it is also called a *bolt-head* in E.

matriarch. Coined on *patriarch*, the latter being wrongly taken as a derivative of L. *pater*.

matricide. L. *matricidium*, from *caedere*, to slay.

matriculate. From MedL. *matricula*, register of members of society, dim. of L. *matrix* (q.v.). It is supposed that the orig. sense was scroll of parchment made from the uterine membrane. See *scroll*.

matrimony. OF. *matrimonie*, L. *matrimonium*, from *mater*, *matr-*, mother.

matrix. L., orig. pregnant animal, in Late L. womb, from *mater*, mother. For mech. applications cf. similar use of Du. *moer*, mother (see also *screw*).

matron. F. *matrone*, L. *matrona*, from *mater*, mother. Sense of directress, of hospital, etc., is recorded from 16 cent. *British matron*, in *Mrs Grundy* sense, originated in signature of letter to the press (c. 1882) protesting against the nude in art.

matter. F. *matière*, L. *materia*. Orig. opposed to *form* (cf. *material*). With *it doesn't matter*, for earlier *it makes no matter*, cf. *immaterial*. For med. sense of *corrupt matter* cf. F. *matière*, Norw. Dan. *materie*, similarly used. *Matter of fact*, orig. leg., opposed to *matter of law*, is used as adj. by Steele. With *hanging matter* cf. quot. below.

It is made a gally matter to carry a knife [at Genoa] whose poynt is not broken off (Evelyn).

mattins. See *matins*.

mattock. AS. *mattuc*, app. a dim. Origin unknown. ? Cf. *mason*.

mattoid [*med.*]. It. *mattoide*, from *matto*, mad, MedL. *mattus*, as *mate*[1]. Used by Lombroso of a criminal type.

mattress. OF. *materas* (*matelas*), It. *materasso*, Arab. *matrah*, place where things are thrown down, from *taraha*, to throw. Cf. L. *stratum*, couch, from *sternere*, *strat-*, to strew. Obs. Sp. *almadraque* preserves Arab. def. art.

mature. L. *maturus*, ripe, early (v.i.).

matutinal. Late L. *matutinalis*, from *matutinus*, cogn. with *maturus*. See *matins*.

maudlin. F. *Madeleine*, L. *Magdalena* (see *Magdalen*). Sense of lachrymose, as in *maudlin sentiment*, *maudlin drunk*, from pictures representing tearful repentance of *Mary Magdalene*. The restored spelling, in name of colleges at Oxf. and Camb., has not affected the pronunc.

His [the Shipman's] barge y-cleped was the Maude-layne (Chauc. A. 410).

Maugrabin. African Moor (*Quentin Durward*, ch. xvi.). Really pl. of *Maugrabee* (*Bride of Abydos*, i. 8), Arab. *maghrabīy*, western, from *gharb*, west. Cf. sing. use of *Bedouin*.

maugre [*archaic*]. OF. *maugré* (*malgré*), in spite of, from *mal*, ill, *gré*, pleasing, L. *gratus*. Cf. F. *maugréer*, to grumble.

maul. Hammer. F. *mail*, L. *malleus*, whence also It. *maglio*, Sp. *mallo*; cf. *mallet*. Hence to *maul*, to illtreat, etc., orig. to hammer, batter. See *mall*. It is doubtful whether *mauley*, fist, spelt *morley* by Borrow, belongs here. Some authorities consider it a transposition of Gael. *lamh*, hand, used in tinkers' slang or Shelta.

mawley: a hand. *Tip us your mawley*: shake hands with me (Grose).

maulstick. From Du. *maalstok*, paint stick. Du. *malen*, to paint (cf. Ger. *malen*), orig. to make marks, is cogn. with *mole*[1].

maund [*archaic & local*]. Basket. OF. *mande* (*manne*), from Teut.; cf. AS. *mand*, Du. *mand*, Ger. dial. *mande*.

maunder. Orig. (c. 1600), to mutter, grumble. It may be frequent. of earlier *maund*, to beg, which is app. aphet. for F. *quémander*, from OF. *caimand*, beggar. The sense-development is obscure, but not more so than that of *cant*[2].

Maundy. OF. *mandé*, L. *mandatum*, command. Orig. applied to the washing of the feet of the poor by princes, high ecclesiastics, etc., on the day before Good Friday, the antiphon at the service being taken from the discourse (v.i.) which followed Our Lord's washing of the Apostles' feet. Recorded c. 1300. Hence *Maundy Thursday* (16 cent.), *Maundy ale*, *money*, etc. Cf. OHG. *mandāt*, in same sense.

Mandatum novum do vobis; ut diligatis invicem, sicut dilexi vos, ut et vos diligatis invicem
(*John*, xiii. 34).

mauresque [*arch.*]. F., Moorish.

Maurist. Benedictine of order of *St Maur*, founded 1618.

mauser. Rifle. Adopted by Germans (1871). From inventor's name.

mausoleum. L., G. μαυσωλεῖον, from Μαυσωλός, king of Caria, whose tomb, erected (4 cent. B.C.) at Halicarnassus, by his wife Artemisia, was one of the Seven Wonders of the World.

mauve. F., L. *malva*, mallow. For transference to colour cf. *pink*, *violet*.

maverick. Unbranded calf (US.), said to be from *Samuel Maverick*, Texan rancher (c. 1840), who habitually neglected branding. Hence masterless man.

mavis [*dial.*]. Thrush. F. *mauvis*, with many Rom. cognates, esp. in dial. Hence MedL. *malvitius*; ? cf. Breton *milfid*, *milvid*, lark; ? or related to *malva*, mallow. Commonly coupled by poets with *merle*, blackbird.

mavourneen. Ir. *mo-mhuirnín*, my little dear.

maw. AS. *maga*, stomach. Com. Teut.; cf. Du. *maag*, Ger. *magen*, ON. *magi*, Goth. **mago* (whence Finnish *mako*). *Maw-worm*, hypocrite (lit. intestinal worm), is from name of character in Bickerstaffe's *Hypocrite* (1769); cf. *Tartufe*.

mawkish. Orig. squeamish, nauseating. From dial. *mawk*, maggot (q.v.), ON. *mathkr*.

maxillary. From L. *maxilla*, jaw, cogn. with *mala*, cheek-bone, *mandere*, to chew.

maxim[1]. Axiom. F. *maxime*, L. *maxima* (sc. *sententia*).

maxim[2]. Machine-gun. Named (c. 1885) from inventor, (*Sir*) *Hiram Maxim* (†1916). Cf. *gatling*.

maximalist. Russian extremist, Bolshevik. The more accurate rendering of *Bolshevik* (q.v.) would be *majorist*.

> The Maximalists...decided to demand from the Assembly the dictatorship of the proletariat by handing over all power to the Councils of workmen's and soldiers' delegates, and to leave the hall tomorrow if the majority were not disposed to share their point of view
> (*Pall Mall Gaz.* Aug. 27, 1917).

maximum. L., neut. of *maximus*, superl. of *magnus*, great.

may. AS. *ic mæg*, pl. *magon*, a preterite-present verb. Com. Teut.; cf. Du. *mag*, *mogen*, Ger. *mag*, *mögen*, ON. *mā*, *megom*, Goth. *mag*, *magum*. Orig. to be strong, have power; cf. *might*, *main*[1]. With *maybe* cf. F. *peut-être*, and archaic *mayhap*.

May. F. *mai*, L. *Maius* (sc. *mensis*), from *Maia*, goddess of growth and increase, cogn. with *major*. Replaced AS. *thrimilce*, month in which cows can be milked three times a day. Hence *Mayday*, *Mayqueen*, *Maypole*, connected with popular festival on May 1; also *may*, hawthorn, blooming in May, and verb to *may*, now usu. in to go *a-maying*.

> De moi li porte plus saluz
> Qu'il n'a sor mai botons menuz
> (*Roman de Tristan*, 12 cent.).

mayonnaise. F., ? for **mahonnaise* (sc. *sauce*), in honour of capture of *Mahon*, capital of Minorca, by the Duc de Richelieu (1756). This is quite likely; cf. *mazagran*, coffee with liqueur, from F. victory at *Mazagran*, Algeria.

mayor. ME. *mer*, *meyre*, *mair*, etc., F. *maire*, L. *major*, greater. Altered to *maior*, by etym. reaction, later to *mayor* by the regular substitution of *-y-* for *-i-* between vowels. From L. *major* comes also Ger. *Meyer*, the commonest Ger. surname, if its hundreds of compds. are included.

mazard, mazzard [*archaic*]. Head. From archaic *mazer* (q.v.), drinking-bowl, also used for helmet.

mazarinade [*hist.*]. Song against *Cardinal Mazarin*, ruler of France during minority of Louis XIV.

mazarine. Dark blue. Prob. from *Cardinal Mazarin* or the *Duchesse de Mazarin*. Cf. obs. *mazarine hood*, connected by Kersey with the duchess.

mazda. Electric lamp. OPers., name of good principle in system of Zoroaster.

maze. As noun and verb in 13 cent., with sense of bewilderment, stupefaction. App. ident. with *amaze* (q.v.). Sense of labyrinth is in Chauc.

mazer [*archaic*]. Drinking-bowl, orig. of maple. OF. *masere*, of Teut. origin; cf. ON. *mösurr*, maple, *mösurbolle*, maplebowl, Ger. *maser*, vein pattern in wood. From OF. var. *masdre* comes F. *madré*, veined (like maple). Cogn. with *measles* (q.v.).

mazurka. Pol., woman of province of *Mazuria*, the lake-region famous in the Great War. Cf. *polka*, *schottische*.

> The Mazurs of East Prussia have been attracted into their present home from Masovia proper since the xivth century
> (Lutoshuvski, *Gdansk and East Prussia*, 1919).

mazzard. See *mazard*.

me. AS. *mē* (acc. & dat.). Aryan; cf. Du. *mij*, Ger. *mich* (acc.), *mir* (dat.), ON. *mik*, *mēr*, Goth. *mik*, *miz*, L. *me*, G. ἐμέ, με, Gael. Welsh *mi*, Ir. *mí*, Sanskrit *me* (dat.). Reflex. in poet. use only (v.i.).

> For bonnie Annie Laurie, I'd lay me down and dee.

mead[1]. Drink. AS. *meodu*, *medu*. Aryan; cf. Du. *mede*, *mee*, Ger. *met*, ON. *miöthr*, Goth. **midus* (recorded as MedG. μέδος), G. μέθυ, wine, OIr. *mid*, Welsh *medd*, Russ. *med'*; cf. Sanskrit *mādhu*, sweet, honey. Wide extension shows it to be the oldest of the Aryan intoxicants.

mead[2], **meadow.** AS. *mæd*, of which oblique cases, *mædw-*, give *meadow* (cf. *shade*, *shadow*); cogn. with Du. *matte*, *mat*, Ger. *matte*, mountain meadow, as in *Andermatt*, *Zermatt*. *Meadow-sweet*, earlier *mead-sweet*, is shown by its Scand. equivalents to belong to *mead*[1]; cf. *honeysuckle* and obs. *meadwort*, of which first element is certainly *mead*[1].

meagre. F. *maigre*, L. *macer, macr-,* thin; cogn. with G. μακρός, long, AS. *mæger,* Du. Ger. *mager,* ON. *magr.*

meal[1]. Flour, etc. AS. *melo.* Com. Teut.; cf. Du. *meel,* Ger. *mehl,* ON. *mjöl.* From Aryan root which appears in Ger. *mahlen,* to grind, Goth. *malan,* L. *molere* (see *mill*), G. μύλη, mill. *In meal or in malt,* in one form or another, is app. of recent introduction, ? from dial.

meal[2]. Repast. AS. *mæl,* mark, point of time, measure, hence fixed repast. Com. Teut.; cf. Du. *maal,* meal, time, Ger. *mal,* time, *mahl,* meal, ON. *mál,* time, measure, meal, Goth. *mēl,* time. Thus *meal-time* is a pleon., and orig. sense of word appears in *piece-meal,* a piece at a time, a hybrid which is now the only current representative of a common E. formation (*dropmeal, heapmeal, inchmeal,* etc.). Ger. *mal* survives chiefly in compds., e.g. *denkmal,* memorial, lit. think-mark, and *einmal, zweimal,* etc., once, twice, etc.

All the infections that the sun sucks up
From bogs, fens, flats, on Prosper fall, and make him
By inch-meal a disease (*Temp.* ii. 2).

mealie. Maize. SAfrDu. *milje,* Port. *milho (grande, da India),* Indian corn, lit. (great, Indian) millet (q.v.). Found much earlier as *millie* (Guinea) in Purch.

mealy-mouthed. No connection with *meal*[1]. First element is the Aryan word for honey which appears also in *mildew* (q.v.), cogn. with L. *mel,* G. μέλι, and recorded as Teut. in Goth. *milith,* honey, AS. *milisc,* sweet; cf. also Ir. *mil,* Welsh *mêl. Mealy-mouthed* is for earlier *meal-mouth,* flatterer (*NED.* 1546). The epithet is much older, and is found as a surname three centuries earlier, *Henry Millemuth* being mentioned in *Northumberland Assize Roll* (1279). This is a good example of the light thrown by the study of surnames on the antiquity of words for which dict. records are comparatively recent. Cf. *puss.*

perblandus: very pleasant and curteous in wordes; meale-mouthed, passing faire spoken
(Morel, *Lat. Dict.* 1583).

mean[1]. Verb. AS. *mænan,* to mean, allude to. WGer.; cf. Du. *meenen,* Ger. *meinen;* cogn. with *mind* and Ger. *minne,* love.

mean[2]. Common. AS. *gemǣne.* Com. Teut.; cf. Du. *gemeen,* Ger. *gemein,* Goth. *gamains;* ult. cogn. with L. *communis,* and degenerating senses in E. & Ger. run parallel with those of *common.* Has been confused with *mean*[3] (q.v.), e.g., though the *mean people* in ME. is usu. taken as equivalent to the *common people,* it would appear in quot. below to have rather the sense of "middle class."

Pur fere pes entre les mene [*var.* mesne] genz e le pople de la vile de une part, e les riches humes de la vile de autre part
(Mayor of Lincoln to Archbp of York, c. 1272).

mean[3]. Intermediate, as in *happy mean* (cf. F. *juste milieu*). OF. *meien (moyen),* Late L. *medianus,* from *medius;* cogn. with *mid.* Hence noun *means,* formerly *mean* (see quot. s.v. *mich*), used as F. *moyen, moyenne,* in *by no (all) means, by means of, mean proportional,* etc. *Meantime, meanwhile* are recorded as early as the simple word. *Mean*[3] and *mean*[2] are confused in *mean stature,* now understood as insignificant, but orig. for medium stature.

The territory of an indifferent and meane prince is sauf conduct in lawe (Queen Eliz. 1562).

meander. Orig. noun. L. *Maeander,* G. Μαίανδρος, winding river of Phrygia; cf. F. *méandre,* It. Sp. *meandro.*

measles. ME. *maseles;* cf. Du. *mazelen,* Ger. *masern* (from LG.); cogn. with OHG. *mâsa,* spot, and with *mazer.* AS. *mæsle-* occurs once in a compd. The pronunc. (for normal **masles*) may be due to confusion with ME. *mesel,* leper, OF., L. *misellus,* from *miser,* wretched, which may also have affected fig. senses of *measled, measly.*

measure. F. *mesure,* L. *mensura,* from *metiri, mens-,* to measure; ult. cogn. with Ger. *mass,* measure. Fig. senses are mostly as in F. With *to take one's measure* cf. *to know the length of one's foot.* To *measure one's length* is after Shaks. (*Lear,* i. 4). To *measure oneself with* is developed from earlier to *measure swords with* (*As You Like It,* v. 4). To *tread a measure* is to keep time with the measure of the music. To *take measures* is a metaphor from building, carpentry, etc.

meat. AS. *mete,* food in general. Com. Teut.; cf. OSax. *meti, mat,* OHG. *maz* (surviving in *messer,* knife), ON. *matr,* Goth. *mats.* For limitation of meaning cf. F. *viande.* Orig. sense survives in *sweetmeat,*

meat and drink, to sit at meat, grace before meat, etc., and in meat-offering (Lev. ii. 14), altered to meal-offering in RV.

Mecca. Arab. Makkah, birthplace of Mahomet, hence place of pilgrimage.

Carter St Chapel, the Mecca of the London Welsh
(Daily Chron. June 19, 1917).

mechanic. L., G. μηχανικός, from μηχανή, machine. Early associated with handicrafts and the "lower orders." Pepys calls his wife's painting-master a "mechanique."

A crew of patches, rude mechanicals,
That work for bread upon Athenian stalls
(Mids. N. Dream, iii. 2).

mechlin. Lace from Mechlin, in F. Malines (Belgium).

meconic [chem.]. From G. μήκων, poppy.

medal. F. médaille, It. medaglia, VL. *metallea, from metallum, medal. Adopted by most Teut. langs. With the reverse of the medal, F. revers de la médaille, cf. the seamy side.

meddle. AF. medler, OF. mesler (mêler), VL. *misculare, from miscere, to mix; cf. It. mescolare, Sp. mezclar. AF. regularly substitutes -dl- for -sl-, e.g. we find ME. idle, madle, for isle, male (cf. medlar). Its retention in this case is perh. due to association with middle. See mell, medley. Usual current sense is for earlier reflex.; cf. F. se mêler de quelque chose.

I medyll me with a thyng: je me mesle (Palsg.).

mediaeval, medieval. Coined (19 cent.) from L. medius, middle, aevum, age.

mediator. F. médiateur, Late L. mediator-em, from Late L. mediare, to mediate, from medius, middle. Orig. (c. 1300) applied to Christ. Cf. mediation (Chauc.) and mediate, of much later appearance; also medial, median. Mediatize, in Ger. hist., to annex a principality, while leaving titular rights to the prince, was orig. to change an immediate into a mediate vassal, i.e. a sub-vassal, of the Holy Roman Empire. Ger. mediatisieren was borrowed (1803) in this sense from F. médiatiser.

medic. Grass. L. Medica (sc. herba), Medic.

medicine. F. médecine, L. medicina, from medicus, physician, from mederi, to heal. Medico, doctor, now jocular, is an It. word from the grand tour. Its pl. Medici became the name of a famous It. family. Medicine, savage magic, whence medicine-man, is early travellers' transl. of native words expressing magic remedy.

medieval. See mediaeval.

mediocre. F. médiocre, L. mediocris, from medius, middle, and L. dial. ocris, hill, peak, cogn. with acer, sharp. Thus, halfway up (not hill-top!).

meditate. From L. meditari, or perh. backformation from much earlier meditation (c. 1200). Cf. G. μέδεσθαι, to think about.

mediterranean. Replaced earlier mediterrane, L. mediterraneus, from medius, middle terra, land. Spec. application to one sea is earlier than gen. sense.

medium. L., neut. of medius, middle, cogn. with G. μέσος. For senses cf. mean³, which is derived from it. The spiritualistic medium is referred to by Miss Mitford (1854). With happy medium cf. golden mean, Horace's aurea mediocritas.

medjidie. Turk. order instituted (1851) by Sultan Abdul-Medjid.

medlar. Orig. tree bearing fruit called medle, AF. form of OF. mesle (cf. meddle), from pl. of L. mespilum, G. μέσπιλον; cf. Du. Ger. Sw. Dan. mispel, from L. The Rom. langs. have usu. adopted forms from Late L. *nespila, pl. of *nespilum, due to dissim. (cf. napkin), e.g. F. nèfle, It. nespola, Sp. néspera. F. fruit-names are usu. fem. from L. neut. pl., e.g. pomme, poire, and the tree-names end in -ier, as in OF. meslier, medlar.

medley. AF. medlee, OF. meslée (mêlée), from mesler, to mix (see meddle). Orig. in sense now represented by mêlée, and still so used with archaic tinge. Later esp. of dress and used as equivalent to motley.

The gallant medley on the banks of the Alma
(McCarthy, Hist. Own Times, ch. xi.).

médoc. Claret from Médoc, district in S.W. of France.

medullary. Of marrow, pith, L. medulla, cogn. with medius, middle.

Medusa. L., G. Μέδουσα, one of the three Gorgons (q.v.), whose glance turned to stone.

meed [poet.]. AS. méd, reward. WGer.; cf. obs. Du. miede, Ger. miete, reward, wages; cogn. with Goth. mizdō, G. μισθός, Sanskrit mīdhā, prize, contest.

meek. ON. miūkr, soft, pliant; cogn. with Goth. mūka-mōdei, meekness, archaic Du. muik, soft. First as Church word rendering Vulg. mansuetus.

meerkat. SAfr. mammal. Du., monkey; cf. Ger. meerkatze, lit. sea-cat. But Hind. markat, ape, Sanskrit markaṭa, suggests that OHG. *mericazza* may be an early folk-etym. corrupt. of an Eastern word.

meerschaum. Ger., sea foam (see *mere*[1], *scum*), transl. of Pers. *kef-i-daryā*.

meet[1] [*archaic*]. Adj. AS. *gemǣte*; cf. Ger. *gemäss*, according, orig. commensurate, *mässig*, meet, from *mass*, measure (q.v.). See *mete*.

meet[2]. Verb. AS. *mētan*; cf. OSax. *mōtian*, ON. *mæta*, Goth. *gamōtjan*. See *moot*. Orig. sense, to light upon, fall in with, is now usu. represented by to *meet with*. *Meeting* (*-house*), now usu. limited to dissenters, esp. quakers, has more gen. sense in US.

> An' all I know is they wuz cried
>   In meetin', come nex Sunday
>   (Lowell, *The Courtin'*).

Meg. In *Meg's diversions*, identified by some with *Long Meg of Westminster*, a noted 16 cent. character whose "Life and Pranks" (1582) ran through many editions. *Meg's Diversion* is the title of a play (1866).

megalithic. From G. μέγας, great, λίθος, stone.

megalomania. From G. μέγας, μεγάλ- (v.s.). Cf. F. *folie des grandeurs*, Ger. *grössenwahn*.

> A common intellectual complaint...which I may name (as I see Mr Gladstone has consecrated the word) "megalomania" (Lord Salisbury, 1897).

megalosaurus. From G. σαῦρος, lizard (v.s.).

megaphone. Invented by Edison. From G. φωνή, voice (v.s.).

Megarian. Of school of philosophy founded by Euclides of *Megara* (c. 400 B.C.).

megatherium. Coined by Cuvier from G. μέγας, great, θηρίον, beast.

megilp, magilp [*art*]. Vehicle for oil-colours. Variously spelt, var. *McGilp* suggesting possible derivation from a surname.

megrim. F. *migraine*, "the megrim or head-ach" (Cotg.), Late L. *hemicrania*, from G. ἡμι-, half, κρανίον, skull, because affecting one side of the head (cf. *sinciput*). Now usu. in pl. for the blues, etc. Cf. hist. of *mulligrubs*.

meiosis. G. μείωσις, lessening, putting it mildly (cf. *litotes*), as in to *come off second best, not half*, etc.

meistersinger. Ger., master-singer, applied to artisan poets of the 15 cent. trade-gilds.

melancholy. F. *mélancolie*, L., G. μελαγχολία, from μέλας, μελαν-, black, χολή, bile. In all Rom. langs. and borrowed by Teut. The reference is to the black "humour"

supposed to produce temperament; cf. *phlegmatic, sanguine, choleric*. As adj. replaces *melancholic* from c. 1500.

Melanesian. Coined on *Polynesian* to connote the black (v.s.) islanders of Fiji, New Caledonia, etc. Cf. *melanism*, darkness due to excess of black pigment; *melanochroi*, coined by Huxley from ὠχρός, pale, as name for racial type with dark hair and pale complexion; *melastoma*, tropical shrub, fruit of which blackens the mouth, G. στόμα.

Melchite. Sect of Eastern Christians in communion with R. C. Church. From Syr. *mal'kayē*, royalists, because of orig. adherence to Empire.

mêlée. F., see *medley, mell*.

melianthus. Flower. Coined (1700) by Tournefort from G. μέλι, honey, ἄνθος, flower.

melic[1]. Grass. ModL. *melica* (Linnaeus). Origin unknown. ? Mistake for *medica*, Medic grass.

> From the meads where melick groweth
>   (J. Ingelow, *High Tide on Lincolnshire Coast*).

melic[2]. Of poetry for singing. G. μελικός, from μέλος, song.

melilot. Plant. F. *mélilot*, L., G. μελίλωτος, honey lotus.

melinite. Explosive. F. *mélinite*, from G. μήλινος, quince-yellow, from μῆλον, apple, quince.

meliorate. From Late L. *meliorare*, from *melior*, better. Cf. *meliorism*, halfway between optimism and pessimism; also obs. *melioration*, now replaced by *betterment*.

mell [*archaic & dial.*]. Var. of *meddle* (q.v.), representing OF. *meller*. Cf. *mellay, melly*, archaism revived by Scott in orig. sense of *medley* (q.v.).

mellifluous. From L. *mellifluus*, from *mel, mell-*, honey, *fluere*, to flow. Cf. obs. *melliloquent* and see *mealy-mouthed*.

mellow. ME. *melwe*, ripe, app. from oblique cases (*melw-*) of *meal*[1]. Sense may have been affected by obs. *merow*, AS. *mearu*, cogn. with Ger. *mürbe*, mellow.

> The man that drinks strong beer
>   And goes to bed right mellow,
> Lives as he ought to live
>   And dies a hearty fellow (*Old Song*).

melocoton [? *obs.*]. Peach grafted on quince. Sp., quince, It. *melocotogno*, MedL. *melum cotoneum*. See *melon, quince*.

melodeon, melodion. Coined on *accordion* from *melody* (q.v.).

melodrama. From F. *mélodrame* (18 cent.), from G. μέλος, song. Orig. romantic play with songs interspersed.

melody. F. *mélodie*, Late L., G. μελῳδία, from μέλος, song, ἀείδειν, to sing. Cf. *comedy, ode*. In all Rom. & Teut. langs., with meaning affected by supposed connection with L. *mel*, honey (v.i.).

A torrent of mel-melodies [du Bart. torrent de miel] (Sylv. *Trophies*).

melon. F., Late L. *melo-n-*, from Late L. *melum*, apple (L. *malum*), G. μῆλον. Foreign fruits were usu. regarded as "apples" (see *pomegranate*).

melophone. Kind of accordion. From G. μέλος, song.

melt. AS. *meltan*, strong intrans., *mieltan*, weak trans.; cogn. with L. *mollis*, soft, G. μέλδειν, to melt, and *smelt* (q.v.). Strong p.p. *molten* survives as literary adj.

Albeit unused to the melting mood (*Oth.* v. 3).

melton. Cloth. Formerly used for *Melton jackets* as worn at *Melton Mowbray* (Leic.), famous hunting-centre.

member. F. *membre*, L. *membrum*, limb, including the tongue (*James*, iii. 5–8). Cf. to *dismember*, tear limb from limb. Fig. sense orig. in *member of Christ* (the Church, Satan, etc.); cf. *limb*. *Member of Parliament* is recorded 1454.

membrane. L. *membrana*, from *membrum* (v.s.), app. in sense of coating of limb. Earliest E. sense (c. 1500) is parchment.

memento. L., imper. of *meminisse*, to remember, redupl. formation cogn. with *mens*, mind. Orig. as init. word of two prayers in the Canon of the Mass. Hence *memento mori*, often for object reminding of death, such as skull, skeleton at feast.

A great man must keep his heir at his feast like a living memento mori (*Pendennis*).

memoir. Orig. note, memorandum. F. *mémoire* (masc.), spec. use of *mémoire* (fem.). See *memory*.

memorandum. L., neut. gerund. of *memorare*, to call to mind; cf. *agenda, propaganda*. Orig. put, like *query*, at head of note, etc., in sense of N.B. Cf. *item*.

memory. OF. *memorie* (*mémoire*), L. *memoria*, from *memor*, mindful. *Memorial*, petition, was orig. a statement of facts recalled to the mind of the person petitioned.

Memphian. Vaguely for Egyptian. From *Memphis*, city of Egypt.

mem-sahib [*Anglo-Ind.*]. Native alteration of *ma'am, madam*. Sometimes used colloq. by Anglo-Indians for the "missus." See *sahib*.

menace. F., L. *minacia* (only in pl.), from *minari*, to threaten. In all Rom. langs.

ménage. F., OF. *mesnage*, VL. **mansionaticum*. See *mansion* and cf. obs. *meinie*, household, retinue, OF. *maisniée*, VL. **mansionata*, houseful.

menagerie. F. *ménagerie*, orig. applied to domestic administration (v.s.), care of cattle, etc.

mend. Aphet. for *amend* (q.v.). Orig. to improve a person morally. Obs. or archaic senses are represented by *never too late to mend* (v.i.), *least said soonest mended* (atoned for). With *mend or end* cf. *kill or cure, make or mar*.

It is saide in englissh proverbes, better to amende late than never (*Petition to Lord Mayor*, 1433).

mendacious. From L. *mendax, mendac-*, cogn. with *mentiri*, to lie, and perh. with *memini*, I remember.

Mendelian. Of *Mendel's* (†1884) doctrine of heredity. The name is the Ger. form of *Emmanuel*.

mendicant. From pres. part. of L. *mendicare*, from *mendicus*, beggar, ? from *menda*, fault, lack.

menhir. F., Bret. *men*, stone, *hir*, long. Cf. *dolmen, kistvaen*.

menial. AF., from *meinie*, household (see *ménage*); cf. *domestic* from *domus*. Contemptuous sense from 18 cent.

A mannes owne meynal wittes [*domestici sensus*] beeth his owne enemyes (Trev. ii. 215).

A pamper'd menial forced me from the door
(Moss, *Beggar's Petition*, 1768).

meningitis [*med.*]. From G. μῆνιγξ, membrane (of brain).

meniscus. Concavo-convex lens. G. μηνίσκος, dim. of μήνη, moon.

menology. Calendar of Greek Church. From G. μήν, month.

menshevik. Russ. minority socialist, wrongly rendered by *minimalist* (cf. *bolshevik*). From Russ. *men'she*, smaller. Ult. cogn. with *minor*.

menstruum. L., neut. of *menstruus*, from *mensis*, month. Sense of solvent (chem.) is from alchemistic metaphor.

mensuration. Late L. *mensuratio-n-*, from *mensurare*, to measure (q.v.).

mental¹. Of the mind. F., Late L. *mentalis*, from *mens, ment-*, mind.

mental[2] [*anat.*]. Of the chin. F., from L. *mentum*, chin.

menthol. Coined in Ger. (1861) by Oppenheim from L. *mentha*, mint[1] (q.v.).

mention. F., L. *mentio-n-*, cogn. with *mens*, mind. Orig. (c. 1300) as noun in phrase to *make mention of*, F. *faire mention de*, to recall to mind, L. *mentionem facere*. With *not to mention* cf. synon. Ger. *geschweige*, from *geschweigen*, to pass over in silence.

mentor. F., G. Μέντωρ, adviser, monitor, name assumed in *Odyssey* by Athene disguised as sage counsellor of Telemachus, son of Ulysses. The currency of the word is due to Fénelon's *Aventures de Télémaque* (17 cent.).

menu. F., small, detailed, L. *minutus*.

menura. Lyre-bird. Coined (1800) by Davies, from G. μήνη, crescent moon, οὖρα, tail, from shape.

Mephistophelean. From *Mephistopheles*, the ironic demon of Goethe's *Faust*. Earliest form (*Faustbuch* of 1587) is *Mephostophiles*, whence Marlowe's *Mephostophilis* (c. 1590). Origin of name unknown.

How now, Mephostophilus? (*Merry Wives*, i. 1).

mephitic. From L. *mephitis*, noxious vapour.

mercantile. F., It. *mercantile*, from *mercante*, merchant (q.v.).

Mercator's projection. System of mapdrawing due to *Kremer*, Flem. geographer (†1594), who latinized his name, dealer, huckster, as *Mercator*.

mercenary. L. *mercenarius*, for **mercednarius*, from *merces*, *merced-*, reward (cf. *soldier*). First as noun with allusion to *John*, x. 12.

He was a shepherde, and noght a mercenarie
(Chauc. A. 514).

mercer. F. *mercier*, VL. **merciarius*, from *merx*, *merc-*, merchandize. Usu. of dealer in textiles and now almost confined to silk. In F. usu. in sense of "meane haberdasher of small wares" (Cotg.).

mercerize. Method of treating textiles before dyeing, patented (1850) by *John Mercer*, an Accrington dyer, and put into practice c. 1895.

merchandise. In ME. usu. *marchandise*, F., from *marchand*, merchant (q.v.).

merchant. F. *marchand*, from pres. part. of L. *mercari*, to trade, from *merx*, *merc-*, merchandize; cf. It. *mercante*. Usu. *marchant* in ME., as still in surname. Limitation to wholesale trader appears early in

E., but F. sense survives in some compds., e.g. *corn-merchant*. With *merchantman*, ship (Capt. John Smith), cf. *Indiaman*, *man-of-war*. For *merchant prince* see *Is.* xxiii. 8.

This yeare [1504] the Taylors sued to the Kinge to be called Marchant taylors
(Wriothesley, *Chron.*).

Mercian [*ling.*]. Lang. of *Mercia*, AS. kingdom of the Midlands, chief ancestor of literary E. From AS. *Mierce*, men of the "marches."

mercury. OF. *mercurie* (*mercure*), L. *Mercurius*, orig. god of merchandise, *merx*, *merc-*, later identified with G. Hermes. The name was given in L. to a planet and, like other planet-names, to a metal. *Mercurial*, orig. born under the planet *Mercury* (cf. *jovial*, *saturnine*), owes part of its mod. sense to association with quicksilver. In 17 cent. it was a gen. term for newspaper (see *journal*).

mercy. F. *merci*, L. *merces*, *merced-*, reward (cf. It. *mercede*, Sp. *merced*), which in Church L. was applied to the heavenly reward of those who show kindness to the helpless. Current F. sense is thanks (cf. *grammercy*), that of compassion having been gradually replaced by *miséricorde*, which was even used for *dagger of mercy*. *That's a mercy*, something to be thankful for, preserves F. meaning. With *for mercy's sake* cf. for *goodness* (*pity's*) *sake*. *Mercyseat* (*Ex.* xxv. 17) was first used (1530) by Tynd. after Luther's *gnadenstuhl*, Vulg. *propitiatorium*.

mere[1]. Lake. AS. *mere*. WAryan; cf. Du. Ger. *meer*, ON. *marr*, Goth. *mari-(saiws)*, all meaning sea; also L. *mare* (whence F. *mer*, It. *mare*, Sp. *mar*), OIr. *muir*, Welsh *môr*, Russ. *mor'e*; cogn. with *moor*[1]. Cf. *marsh*.

mere[2]. Adj. L. *merus*, pure, unmixed, esp. of wine. Cf. *pure idiocy*, and Ger. *lauter*, mere, from *laut*, clear, transparent. In some obs. leg. expressions it comes via OF. *mier*.

The meere Irish, commonlie called the wild Irish
(Stanyhurst, c. 1580).

mere[3] [*archaic & dial.*]. Boundary. AS. *gemǣre*; cogn. with L. *murus*, wall. Hence *meresman*, *merestone*, the later one source of name *Marston*.

meretricious. Orig. alluring by outward show. From L. *meretricius*, from *meretrix*, *meretric-*, harlot, from *mereri*, to earn, serve for hire.

merganser. Water-fowl, goosander. Coined (16 cent.) from L. *mergus*, diver, *anser*, duck.

merge. Law F. *merger*, to drown, L. *mergere*, to dip. With *merger* (leg.), extinction or absorption of right, cf. *misnomer, rejoinder*, and other leg. terms from AF. infinitives.

mericarp [*bot.*]. F. *méricarpe*, from G. μέρος, part, καρπός, fruit.

meridian. F. *méridien*, L. *meridianus*, from *meridies*, by dissim. for *medi-dies*, mid-day. As noun ellipt. for *meridian line* (*circle, time*). *Meridional*, southern Frenchman, is a recent adoption of F. *méridional*; cf. F. *midi*, south, esp. of France.

meringue. In Kersey (1706). F., of unknown origin.

merino. Earliest (18 cent.) in *merino sheep*, a spec. breed of Estremadura. Sp. *merino*, overseer of pastures, L. *majorinus*, from *major*. Cf. *mayor*.

merit. F. *mérite*, L. *meritum*, p.p. neut. of *mereri*, to earn, deserve; cf. G. μέρος, part, share. *On its merits* is from leg. *merits* (intrinsic rights and wrongs) *of the cause* (*action*).

> The bench dismissed the case on its merits
> (*Nottingham Ev. Post*, Nov. 19, 1917).

merle [*poet.*]. Blackbird. F., L. *merulus*. Usu. coupled with *mavis*, the collocation having been introduced into E. from the Sc. poets by Drayton.

merlin [*archaic*]. Falcon. ME. *merlion* (Chauc.), F. *émerillon*, OF. *esmerillon*; cf. It. *smeriglione*, Sp. *esmerejón*. These are all dims. from a simplex which appears as OF. *esmeril*, ON. *smyrill*, Ger. *schmerl*. Prob. of Teut. origin.

merlon [*fort.*]. Space between two embrasures. F., It. *merlone*, augment. of *merlo, merla*, battlement, for earlier *mergola*, app. from L. *mergae*, pitchforks.

mermaid. From *mere¹*, in obs. sense of sea, and *maid*. Cf. Ger. *meerjungfrau*. *Merman* is a later formation. Cf. AS. *merewíf*. In early use renders *siren*.

> Chauntecleer so free
> Soong murier than the mermayde in the see
> (Chauc. B. 4459).

mero-. From G. μέρος, part.

Merovingian [*hist.*]. F. *mérovingien*, from MedL. *Merovingi*, descendants of *Meroveus*, OHG. *Mar-wig*, famous fight, reputed ancestor of Clovis. Both elements are common in Teut. names, e.g. Walde*mar*, Lud-

wig. Hence *Merovingian Latin*, as used in charters, etc. of the period (c. 500–800).

merry. AS. *myrge*, whence ME. *murie*, of which *merry* is a Kentish form. Prob. cogn. with OHG. *murg-fāri*, short-lasting, Goth. *ga-maurgjan*, to shorten, and ult. with G. βραχύς, short; cf. ON. *skemta*, to amuse, from *skammr*, short. Orig. pleasant, happy, as in *Merrie England* (14 cent.). *Merry Monarch* shows current sense. With *merry-go-round* cf. dial. *merrytotter*, see-saw (*Prompt. Parv.*), and *merrygo-down* (c. 1500), strong ale. *Merry men* was once the regular epithet of the followers of a knight or outlaw chief. ? Can this be partly due to MedL. *laeticus*, used for *liege*, being interpreted as L. *laetus*.

> The Frense Kyngs host hathe kyllyd the Erle of Armenak and all hys myry mene
> (*Paston Let.* iii. 83).

> *lunette*: the merrie-thought; the forked craw-bone of a bird, which we use in sport, to put on our noses (Cotg.).

> Restless he rolls about from whore to whore,
> A Merry Monarch, scandalous and poor
> (Rochester).

mervousness [*hist.*]. Coined (c. 1882) by the Duke of Argyll to describe the state of mind of Lord Roberts, who had warned the Government of Russian designs on Merv (Turkestan). The Russians took the town in 1883–4. Cf. *jingo*.

mesa [*geog.*]. Steep-sided table-land, esp. in New Mexico. Sp., table, L. *mensa*.

mésalliance. F., with prefix from L. *minus*, as in *mischief*.

meseems [*archaic*]. *Me* is dat.; cf. *methinks*.

mesembryanthemum. Flower. From G. μεσημβρία, noon, ἄνθεμον, flower.

mesentery. MedL., G. μεσεντέριον, from μέσος, middle, ἔντερον, intestine.

mesh. From 16 cent., also *meash, mash*. A North Sea word from obs. Du. *mæsche* (*maas*); cogn. with AS. *masc (recorded as *max*), whence dial. *mash* in same sense; cf. Ger. *masche*, ON. *möskvi*.

mesmerism. From *Mesmer*, Austrian physician (†1815). Cf. *galvanism*.

mesne [*feud.*]. Intermediate (tenure, etc.), not directly from sovereign. Law F. spelling, with unorig. *-s-*, of AF. *meen* (see *mean³*). Has influenced *demesne*.

Mesopotamia. G. μεσοποταμία (sc. χώρα), from μέσος, middle, ποταμός, river, the two rivers being the Tigris and Euphrates. The formation is similar to that of

Twynham, Hants, AS. (*bi*) *twin æum*, (at) two waters, or the Indian *Doab*, ult. cogn. with L. *duo* and *aqua*. Now colloq. *Mespot*.

mesquite. Mexican tree, also grass found near it. Mexican Sp.

mess. Orig. dish of food, what is put on the table. OF. *mes* (*mets*), p.p. of *mettre*, to put, L. *mittere*. With to *make a mess of* cf. to *make a hash of*, to *be in a stew*, etc. (see also *kettle of fish*). Thus we get the odd transition to the current sense of what is disorderly, often disgusting. In mil. and naut. use a *mess* consisted orig., as still in the Inns of Court, of four persons (in *Love's Lab. Lost*, the four Russians are called a *mess* of Russians). Hence pleon. *messmate* (see *mate*¹), and to *lose the number of one's mess*, be killed.

més: a messe, or service of meat; a course of dishes at table (Cotg.).

message. F., VL. **missaticum*, from *mittere*, *miss*-, to send. In OF. & ME. also in sense of *messenger*. The latter word, F. *messager*, has the regular intrusive -*n*- (cf. *passenger*, *harbinger*).

The hooly lawes of oure Alkaron,
Yeven by Goddes message Makomete
(Chauc. B. 332).

Messiah. Aram. *m'shīhā*, Heb. *māshīah*, from *māshah*, to anoint. Substituted in the Geneva Bible (1560) for the *Messias* of earlier transls., which represents the G. & L. adaptations, and remains in the *AV.*, exc. in *Dan.* ix. 25–6.

messieurs. Pl. of *monsieur* (q.v.), used (*Messrs*) as pl. of Mr.

messmate. See *mess*.

messuage. Orig. site, now dwelling-house with appurtenances. AF. *mesuage*, perh. orig. a graphic error for *mesnage* (see *ménage*).

mestizo. Half-caste. Sp., VL. **mixticius*, from *mixtus*; cf. F. *métis*, Prov. *mestis*. See also *mastiff*.

A mestizo is one that hath a Spaniard to his father and an Indian to his mother (Hakl. xi. 321).

meta-. G. μετά, prep. of somewhat vague meaning (see *metamorphosis*).

metabolism [*biol.*]. From G. μεταβολή, change, from βάλλειν, to cast.

metal. F. *métal*, L. *metallum*, G. μέταλλον, mine, cogn. with μεταλλᾶν, to seek after, explore. In all Rom. & Teut. langs. *Heavy metal*, *weight of metal*, allude to aggregate power of a ship's guns. Also

applied in E. to non-metallic matter, substance, esp. of earthy nature, whence mod. *road-metal*. In 16–17 cent. used of the "stuff" of which a man is made, in which sense the differentiated spelling *mettle* is usual since c. 1700, while Shaks. writes *metal*, *mettle* indifferently. Esp. in to *show the mettle one is made of*, *be on one's mettle*.

I did not think Master Silence had been a man of this metal (2 *Hen. IV*, v. 3).

They [the horses] are well made and well metalled
(Purch. xvi. 91).

metamorphosis. L., G., from μεταμορφοῦν, to transform, from μορφή, shape, the prefix being gen. equivalent to L. *trans*-. Cf. *metaphor*, from μεταφέρειν, to transfer; *metathesis*, from μετατιθέναι, to transpose. In some cases the prefix implies next to, e.g. *metatarsus* (anat.), next to the *tarsus*; cf. *metaphysics*.

metaphor. See above. *Mixed metaphor* is euph. for *bull*³.

In 1914 our old regular army crossed swords with a great numerical superiority of the cream of the German host at concert pitch and undamaged by war (*Fortnightly*, July, 1919).

metaphysics. For earlier *metaphysic* (cf. F. *métaphysique*). Applied, from 1 cent. A.D., to thirteen books of Aristotle which, in the received arrangement of his works, follow the books dealing with physics and natural science. These were called τὰ μετὰ τὰ φυσικά, the (works) after the physics, which came to be wrongly interpreted as the works beyond, or transcending, physics.

metatarsus, metathesis. See *metamorphosis*.

métayer. F., MedL. *medietarius*, from *medietas*, half (see *moiety*), the farmer paying a part, theoretically a half, of the produce as rent.

mete [*archaic*]. To measure. AS. *metan*. Com. Teut.; cf. Du. *meten*, Ger. *messen*, ON. *meta*, Goth. *mitan*; cogn. with L. *modius*, peck (cf. Goth. *mitaths*). Only current in to *mete out*, some senses of which are affected by archaic *mete*, boundary, OF. L. *meta*, still used in leg. *metes and bounds*.

Ye shall do no unrighteousness in judgment, in meteyard, in weight, or in measure (*Lev.* xix. 35).

metempsychosis. Transmigration of the soul. G. from μετά, ἐν, in, ψυχή, soul. A Pythagorean belief.

meteor. F. *météore*, G. μετέωρον, neut. adj.,

lofty, from μετά and ἀείρειν, to lift up.
Orig. of any atmospheric phenomenon, as
still in *meteorological*.

-meter. Usu., e.g. in *thermometer, calorimeter,*
etc., from F. *-mètre*, ModL. *-metrum*, G.
μέτρον, measure; but in *gas-meter* (whence
water-meter, electric-light-meter), from verb
mete (q.v.).

metheglin [*archaic*]. Welsh mead. Welsh
meddyglyn, medicine, from *meddyg*, healing,
L. *medicus*, and *llyn*, liquor.

methinks. It seems to me. From obs. *think*,
to seem, AS. *thyncan*; cf. Ger. *denken*, to
think, *dünken*, to seem. See *think*.

Him thought he by the brook of Cherith stood
(*Par. R.* ii. 266).

method. F. *méthode*, L., G. μέθοδος, pursuit
of knowledge, investigation, from μετά
and ὁδός, way. Spec. sense of systematic
arrangement was developed by early
logicians. *Methodist* (Wesleyan) was applied to the members of a rel. society, the
"Holy Club," founded at Oxf. (1729) by
John and Charles Wesley and their friends,
but the word was in earlier use (*new methodists*) to indicate adherence to any new rel.
method, or system of belief.

methyl [*chem.*]. F. *méthyle*, Ger. *methyl*, back-
formation from F. *méthylène*, coined (1835)
by Dumas and Peligot from G. μέθυ, wine,
ὕλη, wood.

meticulous. F. *méticuleux*, L. *meticulosus*,
"timorous, fearefull" (Coop.), from *metus*,
fear. Current sense is 19 cent.

métier. F., trade, calling. OF. *mestier*, usu.
derived from L. *ministerium*, service, but
the very early *maistier* points to *magisterium*, mastery. Prob. both have combined. See *mystery²*.

metonymy [*rhet.*]. Use of adjunct for principal, e.g. *a disgrace to his cloth*. F. *mé-
tonymie*, Late L., G. μετωνυμία, change of
name, ὄνυμα (see *eponymous*).

metre. AS. *mēter*, L. *metrum*, G. μέτρον, measure. Readopted in 14 cent. from F.
mètre, and, for the third time, from the
same word, selected (1799) as offic. unit
of measure. Hence *metric system*, based on
this unit. In metric system the multiples
kilo-, hecto-, deca-, are G., the fractionals,
milli-, centi-, deci-, are L. *Metronome*, F.
métronome, is from G. νόμος, law, rule.

metronymic. Name derived from ancestress,
e.g. *Marriott* from *Mary*, *Meggitt* from
Margaret. Coined, on *patronymic*, from G.
μήτηρ, mother.

metropolis. L., G., from μήτηρ, mother,
πόλις, city. Earlier (15 cent.) is *metropolitan*, bishop having control over bishops
of a province, his see being in the metropolis. Hence joc. *Cottonopolis*, Manchester,
Porkopolis, Chicago.

mettle. See *metal*. *Mettle of the pasture* is
after *Hen. V*, iii. 1.

An Irishman, rich with the mettle of his native
pasture (*Daily Chron.* Sep. 15, 1917).

mew¹. Bird. AS. *mǣw*; cf. Du. *meeuw*, Ger.
mȫwe (from LG.), ON. *mār*; also F. dim.
mouette, from Teut.

mew². Of cat. Imit., cf. Ger. *miauen*, F.
miauler, Pers. *maw*, Arab. *mua*, etc.; also
Chin. *miau*, cat. *Maw, miaw, mewl, mewt*
are also found.

miauler: to mewle, or mew, like a cat (Cotg.).

mew³. Verb. Orig. to moult. F. *muer*, L.
mutare, to change. Hence *mew*, cage or
coop, orig. for moulting birds, esp. falcons,
and verb to *mew* (*up*), now fig. only. The
up is due to association with to *mure* (wall)
up, like a peccant nun. The royal *mews*,
hawk-houses, at Charing Cross (*le Muwes
apud Charrynge, NED.* 1394) were pulled
down (1534) and royal stables erected on
their site; hence mod. sense of *mews*. For
extension from particular to general cf.
spa, bridewell.

Ful many a fat partrich hadde he in muwe
(Chauc. A. 349).

More pity, that the eagles should be mew'd,
While kites and buzzards play at liberty
(*Rich. III*, i. 1).

mews. See *mew³*.

mezzanine [*arch.*]. Entresol (q.v.). F., It.
mezzanino, dim. of *mezzano*, middle, L.
medianus. See *mean³*.

mezzotint. It. *mezzotinto*, half tint, L. *medius*.
See *tint*. Cf. *mezzo-soprano*.

mi [*mus.*]. See *gamut*.

miasma. G., from μιαίνειν, to pollute.

mica. L., grain, crumb, whence F. *mie*,
crumb. Sense-development influenced by
association with L. *micare*, to glisten.

Micawber. Type of man who hopes for
"something to turn up" (*Copperfield*).

It is not safe to trust the tradition of Micawber
against the tradition of blood and iron
(R. Blatchford, Dec. 17, 1909).

mich [*slang*]. See *mooch*.

Heere myching Jonas (sunke in suddaine storme)
Of his deliverance findes a fishe the meane
(Sylv. *Jonas*).

Michael. Archangel. Heb. *Mīkhāēl*, who is
like God? A favourite Europ. name, e.g.

F. *Michel*, Sp. *Miguel*. The popular form
was *Mihel*, etc., preserved in *Saint-Mihiel*
(Meuse) and in our common surname *Miles*.
Der deutsche Michel, orig. (16 cent.) a
clumsy, good-natured man, was adopted
during the War of Liberation (1813) for
a national type; cf. *Jacques Bonhomme,
John Bull, Paddy*, etc. *Michaelmas* is in
AS.

I sent to yow the last lettyr the daye aftyr Seynt
Myhell (*Paston Let*. ii. 246).

Michael has been a slave to his imperial master for
the self-same reason (*Daily Chron.* May 17, 1918).

mickle, muckle [*archaic & dial.*]. AS. *micel,
mycel*. Com. Teut.; cf. OSax. *mikil*, OHG.
mihhil, ON. *mikell*, Goth. *mikils*; cogn.
with G. μεγαλ- (μέγας, great) and prob.
with L. *magnus*. See *much*. Cf. name
Micklejohn, Meiklejohn.

microbe. F., badly coined (1878) by Sé-
dillot from G. μικρός, small, βίος, life.
Cf. *microcephalous*, small-headed, usu.
with *idiot*; *microcosm*, the little cosmos,
man, the vogue of which is due to its use
(c. 1200) by Bernard Silvester of Tours in
De Universitate Mundi; *microscope*, from
G. σκοπεῖν, to look.

micturition [*med.*]. From L. *micturire*, desiderative of *mingere*, to urinate.

mid. Orig. adj. AS. *midd*. Aryan; cf.
OSax. *middi*, OHG. *mitti*, ON. *mithr*, Goth.
midjis, L. *medius*, G. μέσος, Sanskrit
madhya, Zend *maidya*, OCelt. *medio-*, in
place-names, e.g. *Mediolanum*, now *Milan*.
Hence prep. *mid*, for *amid* (q.v.). So *mid-
ship*, for *amidship*, whence *midshipman*,
earlier *midshipsman* (Capt. John Smith),
from station in ship. *Midshipmite* and
middy are in Marryat (*Peter Simple*). The
commoner compds., e.g. *midday, midnight,
midsummer, midwinter*, are found in AS.
Midsummer madness, associated with earlier
midsummer moon, is in Shaks. (*Twelfth
Night*, iii. 4). *Midriff*, diaphragm, is from
AS. *hrif*, belly, cogn. with L. *corpus*. *Midst*
is for obs. *mids*, genitive of *mid*, with excrescent *-t* as in *against*, etc.

Midas. Very rich man. Fabulous king of
Phrygia (cf. *Croesus*). Granted by Dionysos the power of turning all he touched
into gold, and gifted by Apollo with ass's
ears.

midden [*dial.*]. Dunghill. Of Scand. origin;
cf. Dan. *mödding*, from *mög*, muck (q.v.),
dynge, heap, dung (q.v.).

middle. AS. *midel*, from *mid* (q.v.). A WGer.

formation; cf. Du. *middel*, Ger. *mittel*.
Oldest records are all in superl. *middlest*,
later replaced by *middlemost* (see *-most*).
Middleman, orig. two words, is first recorded in current sense in Burke. *Middle-
Age(s)* is 18 cent.; cf. F. *moyen âge*, Ger.
mittelalter, all translating ModL. *medium
aevum*.

middling. Not from *middle*, but from *mid*
(q.v.) and *-ling* (q.v.). Orig. Sc. adj., now
used also as noun to express medium
quality, e.g. of meal.

The best moutoun for ixs, the midiling moutoun
for viiis, and the worst moutoun for viis
(*Reg. of Sc. Privy Council*, 1554).

midge. AS. *mycg, mycge*, gnat; cf. Du. *mug*,
Ger. *mücke*, Sw. *mygg*, Dan. *myg*. *Midget*
is 19 cent.

midriff, midshipman, midst, midsummer. See
mid.

midwife. From obs. prep. *mid*, with, cogn.
with Du. *mede*, Ger. *mit*, and *wife* in orig.
sense of woman. The sense is thus "woman
assisting"; cf. synon. Ger. *beifrau*, and see
obstetric. For formation cf. *cummer* (q.v.)
and numerous Du. & Ger. compds. of
mede-, mit-.

mien. Earlier (16–17 cents.) *mene, meane*,
aphet. for *demean* (q.v.), later associated
with F. *mine*, "the countenance, looke,
cheere, visage" (Cotg.), which is perh. of
Celt. origin; cf. Welsh *min*, lip, OIr. *mén*,
mouth.

miff [*colloq.*]. Tiff, huff. Cf. Ger. *muff, müffig*,
from which the E. word was perh. bor-
rowed (c. 1600).

might[1]. Noun. AS. *miht*, from root of *may*;
cf. Du. Ger. *macht*, Goth. *mahts*, also ON.
mättegr, mighty. The collocation with
main[1] is found in AS. and the contrast
with *right* in ME. The adv. use of *mighty*,
now colloq., is also old (13 cent.).

Sa mighti meke, sa mild o mode (*Cursor Mundi*).

might[2]. Verb. AS. *mihte*, past of *may*.

mignon. Dainty. F., see *minion*. Hence
mignonnette, not much used in F., a pet-
name for *réséda*.

migraine. F., see *megrim*.

migrate. From L. *migrare*, or back-formation
from earlier *migration* (Cotg.).

mikado. Jap., from *mi*, august, *kado*, door;
cf. the *Sublime Porte*.

milady. Cf. *milord*.

milch. AS. *milce*, in *thri-milce*, month of
May, when cows can be milked three times

a day. The usu. AS. adj. is *melc, meolc*; cf. Ger. *melk*, milch, *melken*, to milk; cogn. with *milk* (q.v.).

mild. AS. *milde*. Com. Teut.; cf. Du. Ger. *mild*, ON. *mildr*, Goth. *-milds* (in compds.). Orig. gracious, as epithet of superior, esp. of the Deity and the Virgin, the latter surviving in name *Mildmay*, from obs. *may*, maid.

> It was not so much for myself as for that vulgar child—
> And I said, "A pint of double X, and please to draw it mild" (*Ingoldsby*).

mildew. AS. *meledēaw*, honey dew, with first element as in *mealy-mouthed* (q.v.); cf. Ger. *meltau*, OHG. *militou*, mod. form being assimilated to *mehl*, meal¹; also Du. *meeldauw*, Sw. *mjöldagg*, Dan. *meldugg*. Cf. synon. Port. *mela*, from L. *mel*, and cogn. forms in many It. dials. Lit. sense only is recorded in AS. and survives into 17 cent., transition to mod. sense being due to the stickiness of the substance.

> Downe fell the mildew of his sugred words
>   (Fairfax, *Tasso*, II. lxi. 31).

mile. AS. *mīl*, L. *milia*, pl. of *mille*, a thousand (paces), neut. pl. being taken as fem. sing.; cf. F. *mille*, also Du. *mijl*, Ger. *meile*; no doubt an early loan connected with the Roman roads. Old pl. *mile* survives colloq. (cf. the *Five Mile Act*).

Milesian¹. From *Miledh, Milesius*, Spanish king whose sons were fabled to have colonized Ireland c. 1300 B.C.

Milesian². In *Milesian fables*, licentious tales associated with *Miletus* (Asia Minor).

milfoil. OF. (*millefeuille*), L. *millefolium*, from *mille*, thousand, *folium*, leaf.

miliary [*biol. med.* etc.]. L. *miliarius*, having granular appearance of millet (q.v.).

militant. F., from pres. part. of L. *militare*, to serve as a soldier. Orig. and chiefly in *Church militant*.

military. F. *militaire*, from L. *militaris*, from *miles, milit-*, soldier. *NED.* quotes *Prussian militarism* for 1868. *Militia*, L., had in 16 cent. sense of mil. forces, administration, etc. (cf. F. *milice*), but current restricted meaning appears in 17 cent.

> The least military, but the most martial, of peoples [the British] (John Burns, Nov. 1918).

milk. AS. *meolc*. Com. Teut.; cf. Du. *melk*, Ger. *milch*, ON. *mjölk*, Goth. *miluks*; cogn. with L. *mulgēre*, G. ἀμέλγειν, OIr. *bligim*, to milk. Mod. form is Mercian, the milkman's cry preserving the old southern var.

The *milk of human kindness* is after *Macb.* i. 5. *Milksop* is recorded as surname (13 cent.) earlier than in gen. use; in the *Towneley Mysteries* it is applied to the Infant Christ. For *Milky Way* see *galaxy*; the Europ. langs. have many other fantastic names for it, all containing the idea of way.

mill. AS. *myln*, Late L. *molinum*, from *mola*, mill, cogn. with *molere*, to grind, and with *meal*¹. In all Rom. & Teut. langs. (cf *kitchen, cook*), e.g. F. *moulin*, Ger. *mühle*. Older form survives in names *Milne, Milner*, and in place-names. Not applied to a hand-mill (*quern*) till 16 cent. Later extended to various buildings and apparatus. A *snuff-mill* (*-mull*), Sc., orig. contained a pulverizing apparatus. To *go through the mill* is mod. *Mill*, fight, occurs first as verb, to beat (c. 1700); cf. F. *moulu*, bruised, beaten, lit. ground. *Millboard* is for earlier *milled board*, flattened by a roller. The *nether millstone*, emblem of hardness, is from *Job*, xli. 24.

> God's mill grinds slow, but sure (George Herbert).

millefleurs. Scent. F. *eau de mille fleurs*.

millennium. Coined on analogy of *biennium, triennium*, from L. *mille*, thousand, *annus*, year, to express Christ's reign on earth according to one interpretation of *Rev.* xx. 1–5.

millepede. L. *millepeda*, woodlouse, from *mille*, thousand, *pes, ped-*, foot.

miller's thumb. Fish. In *Prompt. Parv.* From shape, with vague allusion to thumb with which miller tested quality of flour (Chauc. A. 563).

> Come on, churl, an thou darest: thou shalt feel the strength of a miller's thumb (*Ivanhoe*, ch. x.).

millet. F., dim. of *mil*, L. *milium*; cogn. with G. μελίνη.

milliard. F., coined (16 cent.) from *mille*, thousand.

milliary. L. *miliarius*, pertaining to Roman mile (q.v.).

milligramme, millimetre. Prefix denotes $\frac{1}{1000}$. See *metre*.

milliner. For *Milaner*, orig. dealer in *Milan* articles, such as "Milan bonnets," ribbons, gloves, cutlery, etc. *Millayne* (*milleyne*) *nedylles* are mentioned repeatedly in *Nav. Accts.* 1495–97. Regarded as fem. from c. 1700. In Shaks. (*Winter's Tale*, iv. 4).

> He was encountered by the Mylleners and the Venicyans (*NED.* 1529).

million. F., It. *milione*, augment. from L. *mille*, thousand. For pl. *million*, after *hundred, thousand*, cf. *dozen*. *Millionaire* is early 19 cent., F. *millionnaire* (Acad. 1762).

milord. Used on continent of rich E. traveller, *my lord*.

milreis. Port. coin, thousand *reis*, pl. of *real²* (q.v.).

milt. Spleen of animals, soft roe of fish. AS. *milte*. Com. Teut.; cf. Du. *milt*, Ger. *milz*, ON. *milti*; prob. cogn. with *melt*. In sense of roe the earlier word was *milk*, which has been confused with *milt*; cf. Ger. *milch*, Dan. *melk*, in same sense.

lactes: mylke of fyshe (*Voc.*).

lactes: the soft roe, or milt of fish (Litt.).

mime. L. *mimus*, G. μῖμος, buffoon; cf. *pantomime*. Hence *mimic*. Biol. sense of *mimicry, mimetic*, etc., is 19 cent.

miminy-piminy. Formed, after *namby-pamby*, on dial. *mim*, imit. of lips pursed up in "prunes, prisms" style. Also *niminy-piminy*. See *jiminy*.

mimosa. F., ModL. (c. 1600), in allusion to sensitive plant's mimicry of animal life.

mimulus. Plant. ModL. (Linnaeus), from *mimus*. See *mimosa* and cf. pop. name *monkey-musk*.

mina¹. Weight and coin. L., G. μνᾶ, of Babylonian origin.

mina². Bird. Hind. *mainā*.

minaret. Sp. *minarete*, from Turk. form of Arab. *manārat*, from *manār*, light-house, from root of *nār*, fire; cf. F. *minaret*, It. *minaretto*.

minatory. OF. *minatoire*, Late L. *minatorius*, from *minari*, to threaten.

mince. OF. *mincier*, VL. **minutiare*, from *minutus*, small; cf. It. *minuzzare* and ModF. *amenuiser*. Orig. kitchen term as in *mince(d)-meat, -pie*. To *mince matters* was earlier to *mince the matter* (Sir T. More), but its popularity is due to *Oth*. ii. 3. Shaks. also uses *mince, mincing* several times in their current fig. senses. Cf. *diminish, minish*.

a mynsynge pace: le pas menu (Palsg.).

2 doozen of machetos to minch the whale (Hakl. iii. 202).

mind. AS. *gemynd*; cf. OHG. *gimunt*, Goth. *gamunds*, memory. From an Aryan root which appears in L. *mens*, Sanskrit *manas*, mind, ON. *minni*, memory, Ger. *minne*, love (see *minnesinger*). The order of senses

is (1) memory, as in *mindful, to call to mind, time out of mind*, and dial. I *mind the time when...*, (2) opinion, intention, as in *to have a (good, great, half) mind to*, to *speak one's mind*, (3) seat of consciousness. The verb is evolved in ME. from the noun, some current senses, e.g. *mind what I say, mind the step*, springing from the idea of mental attention. The latest development is that of being personally concerned (only in neg. or inter. phrases, e.g. *never mind, do you mind?*)

Cromwell died, people not much minding it
(Josselin's *Diary*, Sep. 3, 1658).

mine¹. Possess. pron. AS. *mīn*, gen. of *I*, *me*. Com. Teut.; cf. Du. *mijn*, Ger. *mein*, ON. *mīnn*, Goth. *meins*. Early superseded by *my* before consonant, exc. predicatively.

mine². Noun. F., borrowed also by all Rom. & Teut. langs. The F. word appears first in verb *miner* (12 cent.), which is prob. of Celt. origin; cf. Gael. Ir. *mein*, ore, Welsh *mwyn*. The Celts worked metals before the Teutons (cf. *iron*), and Greece and Italy are poor in minerals. Hence *mineral*, MedL. *mineralis*.

Thys minerall water is cleare...and springeth out of sande (*NED.* 1562).

Minerva press. Printing-shop in Leadenhall St., which issued many sentimental novels c. 1800. L. *Minerva*, goddess of wisdom, cogn. with *mind*.

minever. See *miniver*.

mingle. ME. *mengelen*, frequent. of obs. *mengen*, AS. *mengan*, from *mang*, mixture. Com. Teut.; cf. Du. Ger. *mengen*, ON. *menga*; cogn. with *among*. *Mingle-mangle*, hotch-potch, is used by Latimer.

mingy [*slang*]. Thinned form of *mangy*.

miniature. It. *miniatura*, MedL., from *miniare*, to rubricate, paint in *minium*, red lead, prob. an Iberian word (cf. river *Minius*, now Port. *Minho*, ? from colour). Orig. applied to the ornamental capitals of MS., and later, perh. by association with *minor, minimus*, to small pictures and portraits in gen.

miniatura: a limning, a painting with vermilion (Flor.).

minié-rifle [*hist.*]. Used to fire *minié-bullet*, from F. inventor's name. Superseded by *enfield*.

minify. Incorr. formed from *minor* after *magnify*.

minikin [*chiefly dial.*]. Dainty, affected. Obs. Du. *minneken*, dim. of *minne*, love. Cf. *minnesinger, minion*.

minim [*mus.*]. L. *minimus*, because orig., in ancient notation, the shortest note. Cf. *minimize*, coined by Bentham; *minimalist*, incorr. rendering of Russ. *menshevik* (q.v.); *minimum* (cf. *maximum*).

mynym of songe: minima (*Prompt. Parv.*).

minion. F. *mignon*, darling, from Ger. *minne*, love; cf. *minikin* and It. *mignone*. Esp. of favourite of the powerful, but used in 16–17 cents. without disparaging sense.

mignone: a minion, a favourit, a dilling, a minikin, a darling (Flor.).

The Minion of Power—in other words, a ribald turncock attached to the waterworks
(Mr Micawber).

minish [*archaic*]. See *diminish, mince*.

minister. L., servant; related to *minor* as *magister* is to *major*. Eccl. sense, after F. *ministre*, is found in pre-Reformation times of an ecclesiastic charged with some spec. function. Sense of high officer of Crown from 17 cent.

miniver, minever. OF. *menu ver*, "the furre minever; also, the beast that beares it" (Cotg.); lit. little grey (see *menu* and *vair*); supposed to have been orig. the skin of the small grey squirrel, F. *petit gris*. ME. *veyre* is used of a stoat or weasel and *miniver* survives in same sense in EAngl. dial. Cf. synon. Ger. *grauwerk*, lit. gray fur.

mink. Cf. Sw. *menk*, mink, LG. *mink*, otter. Now usu. of Amer. species. Early examples all in -*s*.

My russet gown pervild with menks
(*Paston Let.* iii. 470).

minnesinger. Ger., also -*sänger*, from *minne*, love; cogn. with *mind*. Applied to MHG. poets who imitated (c. 1170–1300) the troubadours of Provence. Cf. *meistersinger*.

minnie [*mil.*]. From 1915. Abbrev. of Ger. *minenwerfer*, mine-thrower. See *mine*[2], *warp*.

minnow. ME. *menow*, false sing. from ME. *menuse*, F. *menuise*, "small fish of divers sorts" (Cotg.), VL. **minutia*, neut. pl. There is also an AS. *myne*, but it is uncertain what fish it was and it does not appear to have survived.

pesciolini: all maner of minutes (sic), frye, or small fishes (Flor.).

Hear you this Triton of the minnows? (*Cor.* iii. 1).

minor. L., from a root which appears in L.

minuere, G. μινύθειν, to make less; cf. ME. *min*, less, Ger. *minder*. Hence *minorite*, friar minor, Franciscan. In gen. contrast with *major*. *Minor poet* (19 cent.) seems to imitate *minor prophet*.

minorca. Fowl from island of *Minorca*.

Minotaur [*myth.*]. G. Μινώταυρος, monster fed, in Cretan labyrinth, on human flesh; offspring of Pasiphaë, wife of King Minos, and a bull.

minster. AS. *mynster*, Church L. *monasterium*; cf. OF. *mostier*, whence archaic F. *moutier* (replaced by learned *monastère*), Ger. *münster*, Serb. *Monastir*, etc.

minstrel. OF. *menestrel* (replaced by *ménétrier*, fiddler), Late L. *ministerialis*, from *minister*, servant. Orig. any buffoon or entertainer. For restriction of sense cf. *wait* (Christmas). For rise in dignity, due to Scott & Co., cf. *bard*. See quot. s.v. *wait*.

Cuidam tumblere eodem die facienti ministralciam suam (*Earl of Derby's Exped.* 1390–93).

mint[1]. Plant. AS. *minte*, L. *menta*, G. μίνθα; cf. F. *menthe*, Du. *munt*, Ger. *minze, münze*.

mint[2]. For coin. AS. *mynet*, L. *moneta*; cf. Du. *munt*, Ger. *münze*. For hist. see *money*.

minuet. F. *menuet*, from *menu*, small, L. *minutus*, because danced with short steps. From 17 cent. Form influenced by It. *minuetto*, from F.

minus. L., neut. of *minor* (q.v.). First (15 cent.) in quasi-prep. sense unknown to L. *Plus* and *minus*, with symbols +, −, are first found in Ger. book on commerc. arithmetic (1489). Cf. *minuscule*, small letter, F., L. *minuscula* (sc. *littera*).

minute. Noun. F., Late L. *minuta* (sc. *pars prima*), from *minutus*, small; cogn. with *minor*. Adj. is taken later from L. *minutus*. For sense of detail, as in *official minute*, *minutes of meeting*, cf. *menu*.

My mother took minutes, which I have since seen in the first leaf of her prayer-book, of several strange dreams she had (Defoe, *Mem. Cav.* ch. i.).

minx. Earlier also *minks*. LG. *minsk*, wench; cf. Ger. *mensch* (neut.) in same sense, orig. adj., OHG. *manisc*, from *man*, man. For metath. of -*sk*- cf. *hunks, Manx*.

miocene [*geol.*]. Coined (19 cent.) from G. μείων, less, καινός, new. Cf. *pleiocene*.

miquelet [*hist.*]. Sp. irregular, guerilla soldier, etc. Also *miguelet*. Dim. of Sp. *Miguel*, Catalan *Miquel*, Michael.

miracle. F., L. *miraculum*, from *mirus*, wonderful. Cf. AS. *wundortācen, wundorweorc*.

mirage. F., from *se mirer*, to be reflected, mirrored. See *mirror*.

mire. ON. *mȳrr*, cogn. with *moss*. Allusive uses, *stick in the mire*, etc., are very common in ME.

mirific. F. *mirifique*, L. *mirificus*, from *mirus*, wonderful, *facere*, to make.

mirk. See *murk*.

mirror. OF. *mirĕor* (replaced by *miroir*), L. *mirator-em*, from *mirari*, to contemplate, wonder at.

> Playing, whose end...is to hold, as 'twere, the mirror up to nature (*Haml.* iii. 2).

mirth. AS. *myrgth*, from *merry*, of which it follows the sense-development.

mirza. Complimentary title. Pers. *mirzā*, for *mīrzād*, from *mīr* (from Arab. *amīr*, ameer, emir), *zād* (= natus).

mis-. In majority of compds. is AS. *mis-*. Com. Teut. prefix; cf. Du. *mis-*, Ger. *miss-*, ON. *mis-*, Goth. *missa-*; cogn. with *miss*[1]. This prefix has been confused with the unrelated OF. *mes-* (*més-*, *mé-*), L. *minus*, whence Sp. Port. *menos-* (see *muscovado*), OIt. *menes-* (*mis-*).

misanthrope. F., G. μισάνθρωπος, from μισεῖν, to hate, ἄνθρωπος, man. Cf. *misogynist*.

miscarry. OF. *mescarier*, to go astray. See *mis-* and *carry*. The simplex is not used as intrans. verb exc. in *to carry on* (orig. naut.), where it has become equivalent to *go on*; cf. fig. *such goings* (*carryings*) *on*.

miscegenation. Orig. US. Badly coined from L. *miscēre*, to mix, *genus*, race.

miscellaneous. From L. *miscellaneus*, from *miscellus*, from *miscēre*, to mix.

mischief. OF. *meschief* (*méchef*), from *meschever*, to come to grief, opposite of *achieve* (q.v.). See *mis-*. Orig. evil plight, discomfiture. As euph. for the Devil (*what the mischief!*) from 16 cent.

> In siknesse nor in meschief to visite
> The ferreste in his parisshe, muche and lite
> (Chauc. A. 493).
>
> Souvent celuy qui demeure
> Est cause de son meschef:
> Celuy qui s'enfuyt de bonne heure
> Peut combattre derechef
> (*Satire Ménippée*, 16 cent.).

miscreant. OF. *mescreant*, pres. part. of *mescreire* (*mécroire*), L. *minus* and *credere*, to believe. Orig. epithet of Saracens; cf. It. *miscredente*, heathen. Current sense first in Spenser.

misdemeanour. From *demeanour* with E.

prefix *mis-*. Orig. sense of misbehaviour now restricted to leg. use.

misdoubt [*archaic*]. From OF. *se mesdouter*, to suspect, where the *mes-* appears to have rather intens. than neg. force.

mise [*hist.*]. Agreement, esp. in *Mise of Lewes* (1264). F., p.p. fem. of *mettre*, to put, lay down, L. *mittere*, to send.

miser. L., wretched; cf. It. Sp. *misero*, wretched, avaricious, which prob. suggested adoption of L. word (16 cent.). Also *miserable*, F. *misérable*, L. *miserabilis*; *misery*, OF. *miserie* (replaced by *misère*), L. *miseria*.

> Sir John Hawkins had in him malice with dissimulation, rudenesse in behaviour, and passing sparing, indeed miserable (Purch. xvi. 133).

miserere. Imper. of *misereri*, to have pity. Init. word of *Ps.* li. used as penitential.

misericord [*antiq.*]. Hinged seat in choirstall to lean against. F. *miséricorde*, L. *misericordia*, pity, from *misereri* (v.s.) and *cor*, *cord-*, heart. Also (archaic), dagger of mercy, relaxation room in monastery.

misery. See *miser*.

misfeasance [*leg.*]. OF. *mesfaisance*, from *mesfaire* (*méfaire*), to misdo, L. *minus* and *facere*.

misgive. Orig. (c. 1500) in *my heart misgives me*, i.e. forebodes to me unhappily, from *give* in ME. sense of to suggest.

> My hert gyveth me that yᵉ mater wyll nat reste longe in the case that it is nowe in
> (Berners' *Froissart*).

mishap. As silly euph. for defeat, dates from SAfr. war. See *hap*.

mish-mash. Redupl. on *mash*. Cf. Ger. *misch-masch*.

mishnah. Precepts forming basis of Talmud. Post-Bibl. Heb. from *shānāh*, to repeat.

misnomer. AF. infin., OF. *mesnomer*, L. *minus* and *nominare*. See *mis-*. For infin. as noun in AF. law terms cf. *rejoinder*, *attainder*.

misogynist. From G. μισογύνης, from μισεῖν, to hate, γυνή, woman. An enthusiastic temperance orator, unversed in the classics, once declared himself an "uncompromising beerogynist."

misprision[1] [*leg.*]. OF. *mesprision*, mistake, L. *minus* and *prehensio-n-*. Now chiefly in *misprision of felony*, orig. crime partly due to error, but now concealment.

misprision[2] [*archaic*]. Contempt. On above from OF. *mespriser* (*mépriser*), to despise, L. *minus* and *pretiare*. See *prize*[1].

misrule, lord of. Presiding over Christmas revels. Revived by Scott (*Abbot*, ch. xiv.).

miss[1]. To fail to hit. AS. *missan*. Com. Teut.; cf. Du. Ger. *missen*, ON. *missa*; cogn. with AS. prefix *mis-*. Orig. intrans., as still in adj. *missing*. Current sense, as in *we miss you very much*, is evolved from that of lacking. *A miss is as good as a mile*, for earlier *an inch in a miss is as good as an ell*, is said to be for *Amis is as good as Amile* (from romance of *Amis and Amile*).

miss[2]. Short for *mistress*, perh. orig. due to graphic abbrev. *Mis*, *Mis* (*mistris*), common in 16–17 cents., and app. at first with tinge of contempt.

missal. Church L. *missale*, neut. of *missalis*, of the *mass*[1].

missel-thrush. From obs. *missel*, mistletoe (q.v.), on berries of which it feeds; cf. Ger. *misteldrossel*.

missile. L. *missilis* (adj.), from *mittere, miss-*, to send.

mission. L. *missio-n-* (v.s.). Sense of vocation, usu. contemptuous, is 19 cent.

Everybody had a mission (with a capital M) to attend to everybody-else's business (Lowell).

missionaries: persons sent; commonly spoken of priests sent to unbeleeving countries to convert the people to Christian faith (Blount).

missis, missus. Slurred pronunc. (19 cent.) of *mistress*, *Mrs*.

missive. For *letter missive*, MedL. *littera missiva*, from *mittere, miss-*, to send.

mist. AS. *mist*; cf. Du. *mist*, ON. *mistr*; cogn. with G. ὀμίχλη, Sanskrit *megha*, cloud, mist. *Misty* in fig. sense may have been influenced by *mystic* (v.i.).

Mysty or prevey to mannys wytte
(*Prompt. Parv.*, Harl.).

mister. Thinned form of *master*; cf. *mistress* (ME. *mastris*), *mystery*[2].

mistery. See *mystery*[2].

mistletoe. AS. *misteltān*, from *tān*, twig, final *-n* being dropped because taken as pl. inflexion; cf. ON. *mistilteinn*. Hardly recorded in ME. With *mistel*, whence obs. *missel* (see *missel-thrush*), cf. Ger. *mistel*, perh. from *mist*, dung, the popular belief (already in Theophrastus, 3 cent. B.C.) being that the plant was sprung from bird-droppings. Birdlime is made from the berries, hence L. proverb *turdus sibi malum cacat*. F. *gui*, mistletoe, is L. *viscus*, "bird-lyme, mistleden" (Coop.). Kissing under the mistletoe is app. not of much

antiquity, earliest *NED*. ref. being 19 cent. (Washington Irving).

mistral. Cold N.W. Mediterr. wind. F., Prov. *mistral*, earlier *maistral*, L. *magistralis*.

The wind that blew is called maestral (Smollett).

mistress. OF. *maistresse* (*maîtresse*), fem. of *maistre*, master. For thinned pronunc. cf. *mister*. Formerly used as courtesy title of married and unmarried women indifferently. For euph. use cf. *courtezan*. See also *Mr*.

misunderstanding. For current sense cf. F. *malentendu*.

This misunderstanding between us and our good subjects
(Charles I, quoted by *NED*. from Rushworth).

mite[1]. In cheese, etc. AS. *mīte*; cf. Du. *mijt*, OHG. *mīza*, gnat, F. *mite*, from LG. Prob. from a Teut. root meaning to cut small; cf. ON. *meita*, to cut, Ger. *meissel*, chisel. Application to small child, etc., partly due to *mite*[2].

mite[2]. Small coin, atom. OF., "the smallest of coynes" (Cotg.). Prob. ident. with *mite*[1] (cf. *doit*). Hence *not a mite*. The *widow's mite* is alluded to in *Piers Plowm*. (B. xiii. 196). Du. *zier* has also the double sense of cheese-mite, atom.

Mithraic. From *Mithras, Mithra*, G. Μίθρας, OPers., Sanskrit *Mitrā*, one of the gods of the Vedic pantheon.

mithridatize. To make immune to poison. From *Mithridates VI*, king of Pontus (1 cent. B.C.), who trad. made himself poison-proof.

mitigate. From L. *mitigare*, from *mitis*, mild. With *mitigating circumstances* cf. Ger. *mildernde umstände*.

mitrailleuse. F., from *mitraille*, grape-shot, earlier *mitaille*, "great (or the grossest) file-dust" (Cotg.), from *mite*[2]. The word became known during the war of 1870–1 and is still F. for machine-gun.

mitral valve [*anat.*]. Named from shape (*mitre*).

mitre. F., L., G. μίτρα, girdle, head-band, turban. Orig. an Eastern head-dress, mod. application (in most Europ. langs.) being due to its use in LXX. to describe the ceremonial turban of Jewish high-priest.

mitten. F. *mitaine*, glove without separate fingers, *miton*, glove without fingers, *mitt*, from OF. *mite*, in same sense. Of obscure origin. According to some authorities from *mi*, pet call-name for cat. One has heard children call woolly gloves "pussies." To *give* (*get*) *the mitten* is US. ? in contrast with the *glove*, regarded as a mark of lady's favour.

mittimus. Form of writ. From init. word. L., we send. Cf. obs. *bannimus*, formula of expulsion at Oxf.

mix. Back-formation from *mixt*, F. *mixte*, L. *mixtus*, from *miscēre*, to mix. To *be mixed up with* is a metaphor from the apothecary's shop.

mixen [*dial.*]. Dunghill. AS. *mixen*, from *meox*, dung, ult. cogn. with Ger. *mist*.

> Thet coc is kene on his owune mixenne
> > (*Ancren Riwle*).

mizen. Orig. a sail, now a mast. F. *misaine*, now foremast, It. *mezzana*, name of a sail; cf. Sp. *mesana*, Du. *bezaan*, earlier *mezane* (Kil.), Ger. *besan* (from Du.). It is possible that the It. word, taken as meaning middle (see *mezzo, mezzanine*), is really adopted from Arab. *mīzān*, balance. "The mizen is, even now, a sail that 'balances,' and the reef in a mizen is still called the 'balance'-reef" (W. B. Whall, author of *Shakespeare's Sea Terms Explained*).

> The ship was laid to under a balance mizen, tumbling about dreadfully (Hickey's *Memoirs*, ii. 213).

mizmaze. Mystification. Redupl. on *maze* (q.v.).

mizpah [*Bibl.*]. Heb., watch-tower (*Gen.* xxxi. 48).

mizzle[1]. To drizzle. Cf. Du. dial. *miezelen*, LG. *miseln*; prob. cogn. with *mist*. Pepys speaks of a "cold, misling morning" (Sep. 15, 1665).

mizzle[2] [*slang*]. To slink off. Shelta *misli*, to go.

mnemonic. G. μνημονικός, from μνήμων, mindful, μνᾶσθαι, to remember.

moa. Native Maori name of *dinornis*.

Moabite stone. Erected (c. 850 B.C.) by Mesha, king of *Moab*, with earliest known inscription of Phoenician alphabet.

moan. AS. **mān*, cogn. with *mǣnan*, to moan, whence obs. *mean*, replaced after 16 cent. by *moan*, from noun. Orig. chiefly in *to make moan*.

> If you should die for me, sir knight,
> There's few for you would meane (*Sc. Ballad*).

moat. ME. *mote*, mound, embankment, OF. & AF., hill-fortress surrounded by water. Ident. with F. *motte*, clod, ? of Teut. origin and cogn. with *mud*. For change of sense cf. double meaning of *dike*. Older sense of

F. word appears in common surnames *Lamothe, Delamotte*.

> E si aveit une mote environée de marreis e de ewe;
> e là fist Payn un tour bel e fort
> > (*Hist. de Foulques fitz Warin*).

mothe: a little earthen fortresse, or strong house, built on a hill (Cotg.).

mob[1]. Crowd. Abbreviated (late 17 cent.) from *mobile* (sc. *vulgus*), the fickle crowd. Addison (*Spect.* 135) speaks of "*mob. rep. pos. incog.* and the like." See *mobile* and *vulgar*.

der tolle pöbel: the rascally sort of people; the mobile, mobb, or rabble (Ludw.).

mob[2]. Cap. Archaic Du. *mop*, of unknown origin.

mop: a thrum cap worn by sea men (Hexham).

mop-muts: a night-coif (*ib.*).

mobile. F., L. *mobilis*, from *movēre*, to move. *Mobilize* is 19 cent., F. *mobiliser*.

moccasin. NAmer. Ind., with forms varying in different tribes. Earliest *mockasin* (Capt. John Smith).

Mocha. Arab. port on Red Sea, whence coffee. It is prob. that *mocha*, chalcedony, is of same origin.

mock. F. *moquer*, now only reflex.; cf. synon. Prov. *mochar*, It. *moccare*. Orig. sense perh. to blow the nose, as derisive gesture, from L. *mucus*, whence also F. *moucher*, to blow the nose, of which *moquer* would be a dial. form. Sense of imitating, orig. derisively, as in *mocking-bird, mock heroics* (*modesty*, etc.), is developed in E. *Mock turtle* is first recorded in Mrs Glasse (1763).

moccare: to snuffe or blow the nose, to snuffe a candle. Also to mocke, flout, or skoffe (Flor.).

moucher: to snyte, blow, wipe, or make cleane the nose; also, to snuffe a candle; also, to frumpe, mocke, scoffe, deride (Cotg.).

moco. Kind of cavy. Tupi (Brazil) *mocó*.

mocomoco. Kind of arum. Carib *moucoumoucou*.

mode. F. (m.), manner, mood (gram.), (f.) fashion, L. *modus*, measure, limit, etc.; cogn. with *mete*. See *mood*[2]. *Modish* is in Pepys.

model. F. *modèle*, It. *modello*, dim. from L. *modus* (v.s.); cf. L. *modulus* and see *mould*[2].

moderate. L. *moderatus*, from *moderari*, from *modus*, measure (v.s.). For depreciative sense cf. *mediocre*. Oldest is *moderator*, formerly univ. official acting as umpire in academic disputations. Hence Oxf. *Moderations, Mods*, "first public examination" for degree of B.A.

modern. F. *moderne*, Late L. *modernus*, from *modo*, just now; cf. *hodiernus* from *hodie*, to-day.

modest. F. *modeste*, L. *modestus*, from *modus*, measure. Cf. *moderate*.

modicum. Neut. of L. *modicus*, moderate.

modify. F. *modifier*, L. *modificare*, to limit, moderate (v.s.). In E. orig. to alter in the direction of moderation.

modillion [*arch.*]. Bracket. It. *modiglione*, app. from L. *mutulus*, "in tymber worke a bragget, shouldering, or such lyke" (Coop.), confused with *modulus*.

Mods [*Oxf.*]. See *moderate*.

modulate. From L. *modulari*, to give measure to, from *modulus*, dim. of *modus*.

modus. L., measure, method, esp. in *modus operandi*, *modus vivendi*, the latter app. of quite mod. introduction into E.

Moeso-Gothic [*ling.*]. Formerly used for simply *Gothic*, usu. in allusion to the lang. From *Moesia*, corresponding to Bulgaria and Serbia, where the Goths settled.

moët. Champagne, from firm of *Moët and Chandon*, Reims.

mofette. Exhalation of mephitic gas. F., It. (Naples) *mofetta*, ? cogn. with *mephitic*.

mofussil [*Anglo-Ind.*]. Country, as distinguished from presidency. Arab. *mufaççal*, p.p. of *faççala*, to divide.

mogo [*Austral.*]. Stone hatchet. Native (NSW.).

mogra. Arab. jasmine. Hind. *mōgrā*.

Mogul. Pers. & Arab. *mughul*, for *Mongol* (q.v.). Hence *Great Mogul* (16 cent.), Europ. title of Emperor of Delhi till 1857. Cf. archaic *Great* (*Grand*) *Turk*.

mohair. Mod. spelling is due to association with *hair*. The forms, in most Europ. langs., are numerous and varied, all ult. from Arab. *mukhayyar*, cloth of goats' hair, lit. choice, p.p. of *chayyara*, to choose. Later applied to other fabrics. See *moire*.

Mohammedan. From *Mohammed*, a common Arab. name, lit. (much) praised. Now more usual than the pop. form *Mahometan*.

Mohock [*hist.*]. Aristocratic street ruffian (c. 1700). Transferred use of name of NAmer. Ind. tribe, now written *Mohawk*. Cf. ModF. *apache*, in similar sense, also from a Red Ind. tribe name.

A race called the Mohocks that play the devil about this town every night (Swift).

mohur. Coin. Pers. *muhr*, orig. seal, seal-ring; cogn. with Sanskrit *mudrā*, seal.

moidore. Coin. Port. *moeda d'ouro*, money of gold. See *money*.

Fair rose-nobles and broad moidores
The waiter pulls out of their pockets by scores
(*Ingoldsby*).

moiety. F. *moitié*, L. *medietas*, *-tat-*, half, from *medius*, middle.

moil. Usu. in *toil and moil*. In ME. to wet, bedaub, F. *mouiller*, VL. *molliare, from *mollis*, soft. So *NED.* and Skeat; but I am inclined to think that in current sense *moil* is rather from a common early var. of *mule*. In W. Cornwall to *mule* is to work hard (Smythe-Palmer). Cf. Ger. *ochsen*, to swot, from *ochs*, ox.

A moil or mule: mulus, mula. *A moil or labouring beast*: jumentum. *To moil or drudge*: laborare, q.d. instar muli (Litt.).

moire. F., earlier *mouaire*, from E. *mohair*, with which it was orig. synon.

moist. OF. *moiste* (*moite*), L. *musteus*, like must[1] (q.v.) or new wine, fresh, green, new, senses all found in ME.

Matrymonye I may nyme a moiste fruit
(*Piers Plowm.* B. xvi. 68).

Notemuge to putte in ale,
Wheither it be moyste or stale (Chauc. B. 1953).

Hir hosen weren of fyn scarlet reed,
Ful streite y-teyd, and shoes ful moyste and newe
(*ib.* A. 456).

moke. Perh. from some proper name (? *Moggy*) applied to the ass. Cf. prov. phrase *Mocke hath lost her shoe* (Skelton). *Mocke*, *Mok*, *Mog*, *Mug* all occur as pers. names in 13 cent. and survive in surnames *Mokes*, *Moxon*.

moko. Maori tattooing. Native word.

molar[1]. Tooth. AF. *moeller*, F. *molaire*, L. *molaris*, from *mola*, mill-stone, "grinder."

Otiosae erunt molentes in minuto numero
(*Vulg. Eccl.* xii. 3).

molar[2]. Of mass, L. *moles*. See *mole*[3].

molasses. Earlier (16 cent.) *melasses*, pl. from Port. *melaço*, Late L. *mellaceum*, from *mel*, *mell-*, honey; cf. obs. It. *melazzo*, Sp. *melaza*, F. *mélasse*. ? Form influenced by F. *mollasse*, over soft, "quaggie, swagging" (Cotg.).

mole[1]. Spot. AS. *māl*, spot, blemish, esp. on linen, etc., whence *iron-mole*, now corruptly *ironmould*; cf. OHG. *meil*, Goth. *mail*; also ModGer. *mal*, in current E. sense, which Kluge regards as ident. with *mal*, "point" of time (see *meal*[2]).

Thi best cote, Haukyn, hath many moles and spottes (*Piers Plowm.* B. xiii. 315).

mole². Animal. Earlier also *molde*, short for *mouldwarp* (still in dial.), lit. earth-thrower (see *mould¹, warp*); cf. Ger. *maulwurf*, "a mole, a molewarp, a want" (Ludw.), and similar compds. in other Teut. langs. *Moleskin*, cotton fustian, is fanciful (cf. *doeskin*, kind of cloth).

Makyng mountaines of molehils (Foxe).

mole³. Breakwater. F. *môle*, "a peere; a bank, or causey on the sea-side neer unto a rode or haven" (Cotg.), L. *moles*, heap, mass.

Letters to Boloyne for the making of a jettye or mole (*Privy Council Acts*, 1545).

molecule. F. *molécule*, dim. from L. *moles*, mass. A 17 cent. word coined in connection with Descartes' physical speculations.

molest. F. *molester*, L. *molestare*, prob. from *moles* (v.s.). Cf. *cark, burdensome*.

Molinist [*theol.*]. Adherent of (1) *Luis Molina* (†1600), (2) *Miguel de Molinos* (†1696).

mollify. F. *mollifier*, L. *mollificare*, to make soft, *mollis*; cogn. with *melt*.

mollusc. Adopted by Linnaeus (1758) from L. *molluscus*, from *mollis*, soft.

molly-coddle. Orig. noun, one who coddles himself. From *Molly*, Mary, used contemptuously for a milksop. For change of -*r*- to -*l*- cf. *Sally* (*Sarah*), *Hal* (*Harry*).

Molly: a Miss Molly; an effeminate fellow (Grose).

molly-hawk. Bird, fulmar. Folk-etym. for *mollymawk*, earlier *mallemuck*, Du. *mallemok*, lit. foolish gull.

Molly Maguire [*hist.*]. Name assumed by members of Ir. secret society (1843). Cf. *Luddite, Rebeccaite*.

Moloch. L. (*Vulg.*), G. (LXX.), Heb. *mōlek*, from *melek*, king. Canaanite idol to which infant sacrifices were made. For fig. senses cf. *Juggernaut*.

molten. See *melt*.

moly. Plant. Orig. of fabulous herb by which Ulysses was protected against Circe. L., G. μῶλυ.

That moly
That Hermes once to wise Ulysses gave
(*Comus*, 636).

moment. F., L. *momentum*, for *movimentum, movement, moving power. Sense of time-division orig. in *moment of time* (*Luke*, iv. 5). Sense of "weight" now only in *of great* (*little, any*) *moment*. See also *psychology*.

Momus. L., G., personification of μῶμος, ridicule.

monachal. Church L. *monachalis*, from *monachus*, monk (q.v.).

monad. Unity. L. *monas, monad-*, G. μονάς, from μόνος, alone.

monarchy. F. *monarchie*, L., G. μοναρχία, from μόνος, alone, ἄρχειν, to rule.

monastery. Church L., Late G. μοναστήριον, from μονάζειν, to live alone, μόνος. ME. had also *monaster*, F. *monastère*. See *minster*.

Monday. AS. *mōnandæg*, moon day, rendering Late L. *lunae dies*, whence F. *lundi*, It. *lunedi*, etc. Cf. Du. *maandag*, Ger. *montag*, ON. *mānadagr*. With *Saint-Monday*, holiday observed by workers exhausted by the week-end, cf. F. *fêter Saint-Lundi*, and *Mondayish*, of the weary cleric.

monetary. L. *monetarius* (v.i.).

money. OF. *moneie* (*monnaie*, coin, change, mint), L. *moneta*, ? orig. admonishing goddess (L. *monēre*), to whose temple the Roman mint was attached; cf. It. *moneta*, Sp. *moneda*. See *mint², moidore*. *Moneta* may, however, be an old goddess-name unconnected with *monēre*.

The ointment of saffron, confected at Soli in Cilicia, imported for a good while and carried the praise alone: but soone after that of Rhodes was every mans money (Holland's *Pliny*, 1601).

monger. Now usu. in compds. From AS. *mangian*, to trade; cf. OHG. ON. *mangari*, from L. *mango*, dealer (contemptuous). Common since 16 cent. in nonce-formations implying "one who carries on a contemptible or discreditable 'trade' or 'traffic' in what is denoted by the first element of the compound" (*NED.*).

Professor Weekley is well known to our readers as the most entertaining of living word-mongers
(*Daily News*, Nov. 8, 1916).

Mongol. Native name, said to be from *mong*, brave. Cf. earlier *Mogul*.

mongoose. Mahratti *mangūs*, whence also Port. *mangus*, Sp. *mangosta*, F. *mangouste*.

mongrel. With pejorative suffix (cf. *wastrel*), from obs. *mong*, to mix, cogn. with *among* (q.v.). Orig. of dogs.

monial [*arch.*]. Mullion. OF. *moinel, meinel* (*meneau*), app. from *moien, meien*, mean³, because dividing the window into halves; cf. F. *moyen* (*de fenestre*), "the crosse-barre of a window" (Cotg.); also F. *moineau*, middle tower of bastion, OF. *moienel*. See *mullion*.

moniker [*slang*]. Sign. ? A Shelta word.

He bore the monniker of his experience in blood and wounds (D. Newton, *North Afire*).

moniliform. F. *moniliforme*, from L. *monile*, necklace.

monish [*archaic*]. OF. *monester*; cf. *admonish*, of which it is also an aphet. form.

monism. Theory of one sole cause, etc. From G. μόνος, alone.

monitor. L., from *monēre*, *monit-*, to admonish. In school sense from 16 cent. Also name of lizard supposed to give warning of vicinity of crocodiles. Proper name of turret-ship for heavy guns designed and built (1862) by Capt. Ericsson in 100 days and engaged in first ironclad sea-fight in history, viz. that between the Monitor and the Merrimac in Amer. Civil War (March 9, 1862). For later application to class of ships cf. *dreadnought*.

> The iron-clad intruder will thus prove a severe monitor to those leaders....On these and similar grounds I propose to name the new battery Monitor (Capt. Ericsson).

monk. AS. *munuc*, Church L. *monachus*, Late G. μοναχός, solitary, from μόνος, alone. Orig. hermit, but early extended to coenobite; cf. F. *moine*, It. *monaco*, Sp. *monje*; also Du. *monnik*, Ger. *mönch*, ON. *mūnkr*. *Monkshood* is translated from Ger. *mönchskappe*, from shape.

monkey. LG. *Moneke*, son of Martin the Ape in *Reinke de Vos*, the 15 cent. LG. version of the *Roman de Renart*. Earlier is OF. *Monequin*, *Monekin*, occurring in a F. version of part of the epic, and evidently from Flem. dim. of some pers. name. It. *monicchio*, "a pugge, a munkie, an ape" (Flor.), is from Teut., and related forms are recorded in Sp. & Port. *Moneke* is a Ger. surname with many vars. (*Muncke*, *Münnecke*, *Möhnke*, *Mönnich*, etc.), derived from a Teut. name-element which belongs to Goth. *muns*, mind, ON. *munr*, mind, joy, E. *mind*. Its choice for the ape was perh. due to association with LG. *monnik*, monk (cf. F. *moineau*, sparrow, lit. little monk, from brown-capped head, and see *talapoin*). For formation cf. *Reinke* from name-element *Regin* (see *reynard*) and other similar names in the same poem. For other names from this source cf. *bruin*, *chanticleer*. For mech. applications cf. *crane*, *donkey-engine*, etc. In sense of £500 perh. suggested by earlier *pony*, £25. *Sucking the monkey*, stealing spirits from cask, was orig. a compressed naut. phrase for drinking spirits from coco-shell as monkey does milk. To *get one's monkey up* perh. alludes

to animal side brought uppermost by anger; cf. similar use of G. ὗς, swine, by Aristophanes (*Lysistrata*, 683). For *monkey-puzzle* see *araucaria*.

monniker. See *moniker*.

monochord. F. *monocorde*, MedL., G. μονόχορδος, of one cord, from μόνος, alone; see *cord*, *chord*. Cf. *monochrome*, from χρῶμα, colour; *monocle*, F., from L. *oculus*, eye; *monody*, μονῳδία, solo, lament, from ἀείδειν, to sing (see *ode*); *monogamy* (cf. *bigamy*); *monogram*, *monograph*, the former orig. of signature of Byzantine Emperors, from γράφειν, to write; *monolatry* (cf. *idolatry*); *monolith*, from λίθος, stone; *monologue* (cf. *dialogue*); *monomial* (cf. *binomial*); *monophthong* (cf. *diphthong*); *monopoly*, from πωλεῖν, to sell; *mono-rail* (*NED.* 1897); *monotheism* (cf. *atheism*, *polytheism*); *monotonous*, from τόνος, tone; *monoxylon*, dug-out canoe, from ξύλον, wood.

Monroe doctrine [*hist.*]. In message to Congress of *President Monroe* (Dec. 2, 1823) to the effect that "the American continents should no longer be subjects for any new European colonial settlement, etc."

monsieur. F., acc. of *messire*, L. *meus senior* (see *sir*). Fuller form in title *monseigneur* and It. *monsignore*. Hist. *Monsieur* was title of second son of King of France. *Mounseer* is 17 cent., *mossoo* more recent. Abbrev. *Mons.*, affected by some E. writers, is regarded in F. as intentional impertinence.

monsoon. Obs. Du. *monssoen*, Port. *monção*, Arab. *mausim*, monsoon, lit. season, from *wasama*, to mark; cf. F. *mousson*, It. *monsone*, Sp. *monzón*.

monster. F. *monstre*, L. *monstrum*, portent, marvel, etc., from *monēre*, to warn. Sense of huge size is latest (cf. *enormous*).

monstrance. OF., MedL. *monstrantia*, from *monstrare*, to show. Obs. from 16 cent., but revived by Puseyites. Cf. ModF. *ostensoir*, in same sense.

montagnard [*hist.*]. See *mountain*.

montbretia. Flower. Named after *Coquebert de Montbret*, French botanist (†1801). Cf. *dahlia*, *lobelia*, etc.

monté. Card-game. Sp. *monte*, mountain, from heap of cards left after deal.

montem. Till 1844 Eton festival in which boys went in procession *ad montem*, i.e. to Salthill, near Slough, and collected money to defray expenses of senior colleger at Camb.

montero. From Sp. *montera*, hunter's cap, from *montero*, hunter, lit. mountaineer.

Montessorian. Educational method. From It. originator's name (20 cent.).

montgolfier. Formerly used for balloon, from brothers *Montgolfier*, who invented it (1783).

month. AS. *mōnath*, from *moon* (q.v.). Com. Teut.; cf. Du. *maand*, Ger. *monat*, ON. *mānuthr*, Goth. *mēnōths*; cogn. with L. *mensis*, G. μήν, Sanskrit *mās*. *A month's mind*, sometimes used (e.g. *Two Gent. of Ver.* i. 2) of an inclination, expectation, is prop. the commemoration of the dead by a mass one month after the death, sometimes after a longer interval (v.i.). The custom is still usual in Ireland.

I will that ther be xxli bestowed to brynge me on erthe [i.e. bury me], at the monethe mynd, and the twelve monethe mynd
(*Will of John Denham, Prebendary of Lincoln*, 1533).

monticule. F., Late L. *monticulus*, dim. of *mons*, *mont-*, mountain.

monument. F., L. *monumentum*, from *monēre*, to remind. First in E. (c. 1300) in sense of funeral monument, whence *patience on a monument* (*Twelfth Night*, ii. 4).

moo. Imit. of voice of cow; cf. L. *mugire*. See *baa*.

mooch, mouch. To loaf, earlier to play truant. OF. *muchier* (*musser*), to skulk, hide, from a root which appears in both Celt. & Teut., e.g. OIr. *múchaim*, I hide, Ger. *meuchel-mord*, assassination. Cf. earlier *mich* (q.v.), also L. *muger*, cheat (Festus).

mood[1]. State of mind. AS. *mōd*. Com. Teut.; cf. Du. *moed*, Ger. *mut*, ON. *mōthr*, Goth. *mōths*. The cognates have usu. sense of wrath, courage, also an early E. sense, surviving in name *Moody*. In some phrases, e.g. *lighter* (*merry*) *mood*, it combines with mus. sense of *mood*[2].

mood[2] [*mus., log., gram.*]. Alteration of *mode* (q.v.), due to association with *mood*[1].

moolvee, moulvee. Mohammedan doctor of law. Urdu *mulvī*, Arab. *maulawiyy*, adj., judicial, from *mullah*.

moon. AS. *mōna*. Com. Teut.; cf. Du. *maan*, Ger. *mond*, ON. *māne*, Goth. *mēna*; cogn. with G. μήνη. See *month*. Hence verb to *moon*, to behave as though moonstruck; *mooncalf*, orig. abortive birth attributed to influence of moon; *moonlighting*, perpe-

tration by night of outrages by ruffians taking the name of *Captain Moonlight* (Ireland, c. 1880); *moonlit*, coined by Tennyson; *moonshine*, unreality, orig. *moonshine in the water* (*Paston Let.*). With *moonstruck* cf. *lunatic*.

Mon in the mone stond ant strit, on is bot forke is burthen he bereth (*NED.* c. 1300).

moonshee [*Anglo-Ind.*]. Native secretary or language-teacher. Urdu *munshī*, Arab. *munshi'*, pres. part. of *ansha'a*, to compose.

moor[1]. Noun. AS. *mōr*; cf. archaic Du. *moer*, Ger. *moor*, fen; cogn. with ON. *mōrr*, and with *mere*[1].

moor[2]. Verb. Prob. AS. *marian*, implied in *mærelsrap*, mooring rope; cf. Du. *meren*, earlier *marren*, whence F. *amarrer*, to moor.

Moor. F. *More*, *Maure*, L. *Maurus*, G. Μαῦρος, ident. with μαυρος, black. Cf. *negro*. In most Europ. langs. In 16–17 cents. applied by explorers to all Mohammedans exc. "Turks, Tartars, Persians, Moguls" (Purch.).

moose. NAmer. Ind. (Virginia or New England) *mos*, also *mus*, *muns*, etc. Spelt *moos* by Capt. John Smith (1616).

moot. AS. *mōt*, *gemōt*, meeting, coalescing with cogn. ON. *mōt*; cf. Du. *gemoet*, MHG. *mōz*. See *meet*[2], *witenagemot*. In compds. usu. *-mote*, e.g. *folk-mote*, *hundred-mote* (hist.), exc. in *moot-hall* (Wyc. *Matt.* xxvii. 27). Hence to *moot a question*, as though before judicial assembly, *moot point*, one fit to be there discussed. These phrases are perh. rather due to the practice described below.

The pleadynge used in courte and Chauncery called "motes"; where fyrst a case is appoynted to be moted by certayne yonge men, contayning some doubtefull controversie
(Elyot, *Governour*, i. 148).

moot: a term used in the Inns of Court [still at Gray's Inn], and signifies the handling or arguing a case for exercise (Blount).

mop[1]. Noun. Orig. naut. Earlier (15 cent.) *mappe*, Walloon *mappe*, napkin, L. *mappa*, which in F. gave *nappe*. See *map*, *napkin*. Also in ME. for rag-doll, whence *moppet*.

He [Private Dancox] was one of a party of about ten men detailed as moppers-up
(*Official award of V.C.*, Nov. 27, 1917).

mop[2]. Verb. Chiefly in to *mop and mow* (*Temp.* iv., *Lear*, iv. 1), where *mow* is F. *moue*, a grimace. As it usu. refers to apes, it may be connected with obs. *mop*, fool, Ger. *mops*, fool, pug-dog, of LG. origin, which Kluge regards as cogn. with MHG. *mupf*, *muff*, grimace, whence perh. F. *moue* (v.s.).

mope. Orig. to stray aimlessly, as still in dial. Cf. Sw. dial. *mopa*, to sulk, archaic Dan. *maabe*, to mope; ? cogn. with *mop²*.

mopoke. Owl (New Zeal.), nightjar (Tasm.), other birds (Austral.). Imit. of cry. Also *more-pork*, *mope-hawk*, etc.

moppet. See *mop¹*.

moquette. Fabric. F., for earlier *mocade*, ident. with obs. E. *mockado*. This is usu. associated with *mock*, but is prob. ident. with obs. *moquet*, *mugget*, intestines of calf. Another name for it was *tripe* (q.v.). Cf. also *frill*.

mora. SAmer. tree. Tupi (Brazil) *moiratinga*, tree white.

moraine. Débris deposited by glacier. F., ModProv. *mourenne*, of unknown origin.

moral. F., L. *moralis*, coined by Cicero from *mos*, *mor-*, manner, custom, to represent G. ἠθικός, ethic. Adopted by Rom. & Teut. langs. with very wide range of meanings. Early sense of what is naturally right, as opposed to law and trad. ceremony, appears in *moral victory* (*impossibility*, *certainty*). *Moral courage* (19 cent.) contrasts with *physical courage*. F. distinguishes between *le moral*, temperament, spirit (cf. *le physique*), and *la morale*, morality; and some E. writers are beginning to realize this. From the former comes mil. sense of *demoralize*. With *moral* of a fable (whence *moralize*), cf. *morality*, F. *moralité*, early play with ethical tendency. The *very moral of* is a vulgarism for *model* (cf. *imperence* for *impudence*).

> He [Charles XII of Sweden] left a name at which
>   the world grew pale
> To point a moral and adorn a tale
>   (Johns. *Vanity of Human Wishes*).

morass. Du. *moeras*, corrupted, by association with *moer*, moor, from earlier *marasch*, *maras*, OF. *maresc* (*marais*), marsh (q.v.); cf. Ger. *morast*, earlier *morass*, from Du.

moratorium [*leg.*]. Neut. of L. *moratorius*, from *morari*, to delay. Always in italics before 1914.

Moravian. Protestant sect of emigrants from *Moravia*, MedL. for *Mähren* (in Austria), founded (early 18 cent.) in Saxony by Count Zinzendorf.

morbid. L. *morbidus*, from *morbus*, disease, from root of *mori*, to die. For current fig. sense (from 18 cent.) cf. F. *maladif*.

morbleu. F., altered from *mort-Dieu*, 'sdeath.

morceau. F., see *morsel*.

mordacious. Coined, after *audacious*, *rapacious*, etc., from L. *mordax*, *mordac-*, from *mordēre*, to bite. Cf. *mordant*, pres. part. of F. *mordre*, also *mordent* (mus.), Ger., It. *mordente*.

more. AS. *māra*. Com. Teut.; cf. Du. *meerder* (double compar. for earlier *mere*), Ger. *mehr*, ON. *meire*, Goth. *maiza*. AS. *mā* is itself a compar. ME. usu. (e.g. in Chauc.) has, for number, *mo*, AS. *mā*, compar. adv., *more* being used rather of size, extent, as still in *the more's the pity*, *the more fool you*. The *Coventry Leet Book* has several references to the *more park* and the *little park*.

> Cathay, that is a gret del more than Rome
>   (Maundeville).

> And mo the merrier is a proverbe eke (Gascoigne).

moreen. Fabric. ? Trade-word formed on *moire*.

morello, morella. Cherry. Also obs. *morel*, OF. *morelle* (Cotg.). App. altered from early Flem. *marelle*, aphet. for It. *amarello*, dim. from *amaro*, bitter, L. *amarus*. Cf. *maraschino*.

more-pork. See *mopoke*.

moresque. F., It. *moresco*, Moorish.

morganatic. ModL. *morganaticus*, from MedL. *matrimonium ad morganaticam*, alluding to the *morganaticum*, latinization of Ger. *morgengabe*, morning gift, sum handed over to wife after consummation of left-handed marriage, and dispensing husband from any further pecuniary responsibilities for possible children. See *morn*.

morgen. Measure of land. Ger. Du., also SAfrDu. & US. Orig. what could be ploughed in a morning (v.s.). Cf. similar use of *dies*, *diurnalis* in MedL.

morgue [*US.*]. Mortuary. F., earlier room in prison in which new arrivals were viewed by the staff (cf. *Pickwick*, ch. xl.). Perh. ident. with *morgue*, haughty air, of unknown origin.

moribund. L. *moribundus*, from *mori*, to die.

morion [*hist.*]. Brimmed helmet which (16 cent.) superseded the salade or salet. F., Sp. *morrión* or It. *morione*. Origin unknown. Understood by early etymologists as Moorish, Morian, helmet, which may be right.

morisco. Sp., Moorish. Cf. *moresque*.

Morison's pill. Invented by *James Morison* (†1840). Used ironically by Carlyle of gen. remedy for abuses, etc.

morley. Borrow's spelling of *mauley*. See *maul*.

Mormon. Sect founded (1830) at Manchester, New York, by Joseph Smith, who claimed to have discovered the *Book of Mormon*, which he explained as from E. *more* and Egypt. *mon*, good!

morn. ME. *morwe(n)*, AS. *morgen*. Com. Teut.; cf. Du. Ger. *morgen*, ON. *morgunn*, Goth. *maurgins*; ident. with *morrow*, with which it is often synon. in dial. *Morning* is a ME. formation, after *evening*.

morocco. Leather orig. tanned in *Morocco*.

morose. L. *morosus*, from *mos, mor-*, custom (see *moral*). For limitation of sense (in L.) cf. E. *humorous, moody*.

morphia. Earlier *morphium*, coined from *Morpheus*, Ovid's name for god of sleep and dreams, from G. μορφή, form.

morphology [*biol. & ling.*]. Study of form and structure, G. μορφή.

morris-dance. From 15 cent. Cf. Flem. *mooriske dans*, F. *danse moresque*. In E. associated with Robin Hood characters, but perh. orig. danced by people with blackened faces (cf. "nigger"). Cf. *morris-pike* (*Com. of Errors*, iv. 3).

Morris tube. Invented by *Richard Morris* (†1891).

morrow. ME. *morwe*, from *morwen*, morn (q.v.). The words are still interchangeable in dial. Cf. Ger. *morgen*, morning, to-morrow.

The Kyng, the Quene, and the Prynce remeven to morwen to Hertford (*Paston Let.* i. 335).

morse. Walrus. F., orig. *morce marin* (16 cent.), Lapp *morsa* or Finnish *mursu*. *Sea-morse*, very common in Purch., was gradually pushed out again by the earlier *sea-horse*. Cf. obs. perversion *mohorse* (passim in Purch.).

This yere were take iiij grete fisshes bytwene Eerethe and London, that one was callyd mors marine (Caxton).

Morse code. From name of US. electrician (†1872).

morsel. OF. (*morceau*), dim. of *mors*, bite, L. *morsus*, from *mordēre, mors-*, to bite. Cf. E. *bit* from *bite*. Orig. sense in a *dainty morsel*.

He sendeth his cristal as morselis [*Vulg.* buccellas, lit. little mouths] (Wyc. *Ps.* cxlvii. 17).

mort[1] [*archaic*]. Death (of the deer), as in to *blow a mort*. App. altered, after F. *mort*, death, from earlier *mote*, F. *mot*, word, note of horn.

mot: a motto, a word; also, the note winded by a huntsman on his horne (Cotg.).

mort[2] [*dial.*]. Large quantity. ? Cf. northern dial. *murth, merth*, in same sense, ON. *mergth*, from *margr*, many. Perh. affected by *mortal* in *a mortal deal*, etc., and by F. *mort*, as in *boire à mort*, to drink excessively.

"We have had a mort of talk, sir," said Mr Peggotty (*Copperfield*, ch. xxxii.).

mortal. F. *mortel*, L. *mortalis*, from *mors, mort-*, death. With use as intens., e.g. *a mortal hurry, two mortal hours* (also in F.), cf. *awful, ghastly*, etc. Now differentiated in some senses from native *deadly*.

·Elye was a deedli man lijk us (Wyc. *James*, v. 17).

mortar. Vessel for pounding. AS. *mortere* or F. *mortier*, L. *mortarium*, whence also Ger. *mörser*, Sw. Dan. *morter*. Hence *mortar*, piece of artillery, orig. (16 cent.) *mortar-piece*, from shape (cf. obs. *pot-gun* in same sense). *Mortar*, for building, is the same word, "pounded material," and comes to us from F. *mortier*; cf. Du. *mortel*, Ger. *mörtel*, of later adoption than *mörser* (v.s.). It is curious that we have *mortar-board*, college cap, from this sense, while F. *mortier*, cap worn by some F. judicial dignitaries, is from the first sense.

mortgage. OF. (replaced by *hypothèque*), lit. dead pledge, because the pledge becomes dead to one or other of the contracting parties according as the money is, or is not, forthcoming (Coke). See *gage*[1].

mortify. F. *mortifier*, L. *mortificare*, to make dead. Sense of causing humiliation (cf. fig. to *wound*) also from F.

The Lord mortifieth; and quykeneth
                (Wyc. 1 *Kings*, ii. 6).

mortise, mortice. Cavity in wood to receive *tenon*. F. *mortaise*, Sp. *mortaja*, ? Arab. *murtazz*, fixed in.

mortmain [*hist.*]. Inalienable tenure of land by eccl. (and other) bodies. OF. *mortemain*, dead hand, MedL. *mortua manus*. Prob. extended use of *mortua manus* (feud.), incapable of disposing of property. *Amortize* is used in *Paston Let.* of allotting money in perpetuity to a pious foundation.

mortuary. L. *mortuarius*, from *mors, mort-*, death. As noun euph. for earlier *dead-house*.

mosaic. F. *mosaïque*, It. *mosaico, musaico*, MedL. *mosaicus, musaicus*, of the muses; cf. Late G. μουσεῖον, mosaic, whence Late L. *musivum opus* in same sense. For sense-development cf. *antic, grotesque, miniature*.

moschatel. Plant. F. *moscatelle*, It. *moscatello*, dim. of *moscato*, musk (q.v.).

moselle. Wine from region of river *Moselle*.

Moslem. Arab. *muslim*, pres. part. of *aslama*, to submit, obey. Cf. *Islam, Mussulman, salaam*.

mosque. Earlier (16 cent.) *mosquee*, F. *mosquée*, It. *moschea*, Arab. *masjid*, pronounced *masgid* in NAfr., whence the word reached Europe; often *meskite* in Purch. From verb *sajada*, to prostrate oneself, adore. The word is pre-Mohammedan and is found in an inscription of 1 cent. (Doughty).

mosquito. Sp. Port., dim. of *mosca*, fly, L. *musca*. See *musket*.

moss. AS. *mōs*, bog, sense of plant characteristic of bogs appearing in early ME.; cf. Du. *mos*, Ger. *moos*, ON. *mose*, all in both senses; ult. cogn. with *mire* and with L. *muscus*, moss. Hence Sc. *moss-hag*, hole from which peat has been dug; *moss-trooper*, free-booter infesting mosses, or marshy moors, of the Border. The latter is one of Scott's revivals (*Lay*, i. 19).

most. AS. *mǣst*, superl. of *mā* (see *more*). Com. Teut.; cf. Du. *meest*, Ger. *meist*, ON. *mestr*, Goth. *maists*. Mod. vowel (cf. Sc. *maist*) is due to influence of *more, mo*. Orig. sense of greatest (see *more*) survives in *the most part*.

-most. Altered, by association with *most*, from AS. *-mest*, from double superl. Aryan suffix *-mo-* and *-isto-*, the first of which appears in AS. *forma, hindema*, and L. *primus*, while the second has given *-est*. Forms like *aftermost, innermost, uttermost*, AS. *æftemest, inmest, ūtmest*, add a compar. to the two superl. suffixes. The formation has spread much in E., but is restricted to words of position exc. in the case of *bettermost*.

mote¹. Noun. AS. *mot*, speck of dust; cf. archaic Du. *mot*, sawdust, grit, LG. *mut*, dust. Perh. cogn. with *smut*. Usu. allusive (exc. in dial.) to *Matt*. vii. 3, where *Vulg*. has *festuca*.

> He kan wel in myn eye seen a stalke,
> But in his owene he kan nat seen a balke
> (Chauc. A. 3919).

mote². Verb. Archaic survival of AS. *mōt*, may, must² (q.v.), in *so mote it be*, Amen.

mote³ [*hist.*]. See *moot*.

motet [*mus.*]. F., dim. of *mot*, word, L. *muttum*, grunt, murmur; cf. It. *mottetto*.

moth. AS. *moththe, mohthe*; cf. Du. *mot*, Ger. *motte*. ? Cogn. with *maggot* ? or with *midge*. Up to 16 cent. applied rather to the larva, as enemy of clothes (*Matt*. vi. 20), than to the perfect insect.

mother. AS. *mōdor*. Aryan; cf. Du. *moeder*, Ger. *mutter*, ON. *mōther*, L. *mater*, G. μήτηρ, Sanskrit *mātar-*, OIr. *māthir*. Orig. from baby-sound *ma-* (cf. *father*). Goth. has *aithei* (see *father*). Sense of scum, etc., esp. in *mother of vinegar*, is from some early but obscure metaphor; cf. Ger. *mutter*, Du. *mo(d)er*, It. Sp. *madre*, scum, F. *mère de vinaigre*. *NED*. supposes it to be connected with the lang. of alchemy, but the similar use of G. γραῦς, old woman (v.i.), points to still earlier folk-lore. So also for *mother of pearl* (c. 1500) we find It. Sp. *madreperla*, Ger. *perlenmutter*, etc. *Mother earth* is after L. *terra mater*, a goddess. In *mother-tongue* (*-land, -wit*, etc.) it is equivalent to native.

> ταῖς μὲν ἄλλαις γὰρ χύτραις
> ἡ γραῦς ἔπεστ' ἀνωτάτω, ταύτης δὲ νῦν
> τῆς γραὸς ἐπιπολῆς ἔπεισιν αἱ χύτραι
> (Aristoph. *Plutus*, 1205).

> By the feyth that I owe to Seynt Edward and to the Corone of Inglond, I shal destrye them every moder sone
> (Hen. VI, at St Albans, *Paston Let.* i. 329).

mother Carey's chicken. Sailors' name for stormy petrel. Has been explained as corrupt. of It. *madre cara*, dear mother, i.e. the Holy Virgin, but this is a conjecture unsupported by evidence.

motif [*neol.*]. F., in various artistic and literary senses. See *motive*.

> The skirt was bordered...with large jetted lace motifs (*Times*, May 4, 1906).

motion. F., L. *motio-n-*, from *movēre, mot-*, to move. E. senses, corresponding to those of verb to *move*, express not only L. *motio*, but also *motus*, the latter represented in F. by *mouvement*.

motive. F. *motif*, MedL. *motivus* (v.s.).

motley. I suggest that orig. sense was not variegated, but half and half, then striped, and finally speckled, whence back-formation *mottle*. Cf. *pied*, orig. black and white (see *pie¹*), but used by Browning for "half of yellow and half of red" (*Pied Piper*), and practically equivalent to *motley*. The sense has also been affected by *medley*, from which the early philologists derived it. The fool's dress, with which *motley* was later associated, was half and half, F. *mi-parti* (12 cent.), and this is also the earliest sense of Ger. *halbiert*, which was likewise used of a knight's parti-coloured shield. I propose AF. **moitelé*, formed from *moitié* (AF. *motie*), half, by analogy with *écartelé*, quartered. Chaucer's use of *motley* and *medley* (v.i.) suggests that the former might orig. be worn with dignity, while the latter was a homely "pepper and salt."

A marchant was ther with a forked berd,
In mottelye, and hye on horse he sat
(Chauc. A. 270).

He [the sergeant of the lawe] rood but hoomly in a medlee cote (*ib.* 328).

polimitus: ray [striped] or motlee or medlee (*Voc.*).

Scharlachrot unde brun
War sin mantel gehalbiert (*Wigamur*, 4685).

A worthy fool: motley's the only wear
(*As You Like It*, ii. 7).

motor. L., from *movēre*, *mot-*, to move. Hence *motor-car* (*NED.* 1895), shortened to *motor* (*ib.* 1900); first allowed without red flag Nov. 14, 1896.

mottle. Back-formation from *motley* (q.v.).

motto. It., "a word, a mot, a phrase, a saying, a posie or briefe in any shield, ring" (Flor.), as F. *mot* (see *motet*). In Shaks. (*Per.* ii. 2).

We pulled the Christmas crackers, each of which contained a motto,
And she listened while I read them till her mother told her not to (*Bab Ballads*).

mouch. See *mooch*.

moucharaby. Latticed balcony in NAfr. F., Arab. *mashrabah*, lit. drinking place (see *sherbet*), from porous water-vessels kept in it to cool by evaporation.

moufflon. Wild mountain sheep (Corsica, etc.). F., Late L. *mufro-n-* (5 cent.). Pliny's name is *musmo*.

moujik. Russ. *muzhik*, peasant, dim. of *muzh*, man, husband, ult. cogn. with *male*. For occ. rather contemptuous sense of the Russ. word cf. F. *bonhomme* as in *Jacques Bonhomme*, peasant, churl. Usu. *mousik*, *mowsike* in Hakl.

Kuas [kvass] whereby the musick lives (*NED.* 1568).

mould¹. Humus. AS. *molde*. Com. Teut.; cf. obs. Du. *moude*, Ger. dial. *molt*, ON. *mold*, Goth. *mulda*; cogn. with *meal¹*, *mill*, L. *molere*, to grind, etc.

mould². Form. With excrescent -*d* from F. *moule*, L. *modulus*, dim. of *modus*, measure; cf. *model*.

The glass of fashion and the mould of form
(*Haml.* iii. 1).

mould³. Spot. Only in *iron-mould*. See *iron*, *mole¹*.

mould⁴. On cheese, etc. Back-formation from *mouldy* (q.v.).

moulder. A late word (16 cent.), usu. associated with *mould¹*, but prob. representing Ger. *moder*, decay. Kluge supposes that this word may be from Du. *moder*, mother (q.v.), in fig. sense. For intrusive -*l*- cf. *moult*.

vermodern: to moulder, to moulder away, to fall to dust (Ludw.).

mouldy. Extension of ME. *mould*, p.p. of obs. verb *moul*, to become mildewed, etc., earliest form *muwle*, ON. *mygla*; cf. Sw. *mögla*, Norw. *mugla*; cogn. with *muggy*.

Lat us nat mowlen thus in ydelnesse
(*Chauc.* B. 32).

moult. With intrusive -*l*- from ME. *mout*, AS. *mūtian*, in *bemūtian*, L. *mutare*, to change, whence also F. *muer*, Du. *muiten*, Ger. *mausen* (OHG. *mūzōn*). See *mews*.

mowtyn, as fowlys: plumeo, deplumeo
(*Prompt. Parv.*).

moulvee. See *moolvee*.

mound¹ [*archaic*]. Orb or ball of gold surmounted by cross held in hand by figure of Christ or of royal personage. F. *monde*, L. *mundus*, world.

mound². Hillock. App. due to confusion between obs. Du. *mond*, protection, and E. *mount*, with which it is completely confused in mil. lang. of 16 cent. The word, orig. mil., a rampart, is of late appearance (16 cent.) and is used in dial. in sense of boundary, hedge, etc. Du. *mond* is cogn. with Ger. *mund*, AS. *mund*, guardianship, protection, poet. hand, and perh. ult. with L. *manus*.

mount¹. AS. *munt* and F. *mont*, L. *mons*, *mont-*. In archaic mil. sense used for *mound²* (see quot.). Cf. *mountain*, F. *montagne*, VL. **montanea* (sc. *terra*), whence also It. *montagna*, Sp. *montaña*. In pol. sense used of the *montagnard* party, led by Danton and Robespierre, which occupied the highest seats in the assembly. *Mountain dew*, whisky, is in Scott (*Old Mortality*, *Introd.*).

I...will lay siege against thee with a mount [*Vulg.* agger] (*Is.* xxix. 3).

mount². Verb. F. *monter*, from *mont* (v.s.). In some senses for *amount* (q.v.). Sense of setting in order, set going, is found in F., hence to *mount a picture*, to *mount guard*, orig. to post sentinels. With *mount*, horse, cf. F. *monture*.

Qui veut voyager loin ménage sa monture
(Rac. *Plaideurs*, i. 1).

mountain. See *mount¹*.

mountebank. It. *montambanco*, mount (imper.) on bench, or obs. F. *monte-banc*, mount bench. Orig. a quack, juggler, etc., appearing on a platform at a fair. Cf. F. *saltimbanque*, acrobat, It. *saltimbanco*, jump on bench. The surname *Saltonstall* is similarly formed from OF. *salte-en-estal* (*saute en étal*). See my *Surnames* (ch. xii.).

montar' in banco: to plaie the mountibanke (Flor.).
salta in banco: a mountibanke (*ib.*).

mourn. AS. *murnan*. Com. Teut.; cf. OSax. *mornon*, OHG. *mornēn*, ON. *morna*, to pine, Goth. *maurnan*, to be anxious; cogn. with G. μέριμνα, care.

mouse. AS. *mūs*. Aryan; cf. Du. *muis*, Ger. *maus*, ON. *mūs*, L. *mus*, G. μῦς, Sanskrit, Pers. *mūsh*. See *muscle*.

mousseline. F., see *muslin*.

moustache. F., It. *mostaccio* or Sp. *mostacho* (cf. earlier E. *mustachio*), from G. μύσταξ, μυστακ-, ? cogn. with μάσταξ, jaw.

mouth. AS. *mūth*. Com. Teut.; cf. Du. *mond*, Ger. *mund*, ON. *munnr, muthr*, Goth. *munths*; prob. an old pres. part. (cf. *tooth*). For normal loss of Teut. *-n-* before spirant in E. cf. *tooth, other, five. Down in the mouth* refers to the drooping of the corners of the mouth as sign of dejection.

move. F. *mouvoir*, L. *movēre. The spirit moves me* was orig. Quaker (v.i.). Parl. use (cf. *motion*) is due to earlier sense of urging. Current use of *movies* (US.) is curiously like that of Tudor *motions* for a puppet-play.

The sayd pilotte moved this inquisite [witness] to take one of the sayd barckes. Upon which mocion this said inquysite moved the same to the hole companye of the shypp. And they all agreed therunto (*Voyage of the Barbara*, 1540).

The power of the Lord God arose in me, and I was moved in it to... (George Fox, 1656).

mow¹. Corn-stack. AS. *mūga, mūwa*; cf. ON. *mūgi*, swath of corn, crowd of people.

mow². Verb. AS. *māwan*. WGer.; cf. Du. *maaien*, Ger. *mähen*; cogn. with *mead²*, *meadow*, G. ἀμᾶν, to reap, L. *metere*. See *aftermath*.

mow³. Grimace. See *mop²*. Orig. in to *make the mow*, F. *faire la moue*.

M.P. First *NED*. record is from Byron.

He tells me that he thanks God he never knew what it was to be tempted to be a knave in his life, till he did come into the House of Commons
(Pepys, Oct. 31, 1667).

mpret. Title of ruler of Albania. Alb. prince, L. *imperator*. Cf. *emperor*.

The title which Prince William will bear in Albania is "Mpret," a corruption of "Imperator"
(*Times*, Feb. 23, 1914).

Mr. First *NED*. record is from Cromwell's letters (1538). Orig. abbrev. of *master*, weakened to *mister* by unstressed position. Cf. *Mrs*, orig. for married or unmarried woman, latter use surviving latest in case of actresses (as *Madame* in ModF.), and, within the writer's recollection, of headnurse in ' county" family.

This yeare [1542] was boyled in Smithfeild one Margret Davie which had poysoned her Mrs
(Wriothesley, *Chron.*).
One Mrs Belson, an auncient mayde, refused to take the othe of allegeance (*Egerton Papers*, 1612).
Mrs Veal was a maiden gentlewoman (Defoe).

much. ME. *muche*, for *muchel* (see *mickle*); cf. ME. *lut, lutel*, little. Orig., like *more, most*, of size, as still in place-names, e.g. *Much Hadham*, and surname *Mutch* (see quot. s.v. *mischief*). So also *much of a muchness*, i.e. size. In 16–17 cents. equivalent to *many*, e.g. *much people* (thanks).

Thenne is he a moche fool that pourveyeth not to doo well whilis he is here lyvynge
(Caxton, *Mirror of World*).

mucilage. F., viscous fluid, Late L. *mucilago*, musty liquid, from *mucus*. Has replaced *gum* (for sticking) in US.

muck¹. Uncleanness. Cf. ON. *myki*, dung Not related to *mixen*.

muck². Incorr. for *amuck* (q.v.).

mucous. Esp. in *mucous membrane*. L. *mucosus*, from *mucus*, cogn. with *emungere*, to blow the nose, G. μύσσεσθαι (in compds. only).

mud. Cf. LG. *mod*, mud, Ger. dial. *mott*, bog, peat (see *moat*); also Du. *modder*, whence *Modder River* (SAfr.). With *clear as mud* cf. Ger. *klar wie dicke tinte* (thick ink). *Mudlark* is a joc. formation on *skylark*.

muddle. Orig. to wallow in mud, to make muddy, esp. in archaic to *muddle the water* (see *trouble*); cf. obs. Du. *moddelen*, frequent. of *modden*, to dabble in mud. Later senses perh. affected by *meddle*.

The Northern States will manage somehow to muddle through (Bright, 1864).

mudir. Governor. Turk. use of Arab. *mudīr*, pres. part. of *adāra*, to administer, causative of *dāra*, to go round.

muezzin. Crier who proclaims hour of prayer from minaret, "clarke, sexten, priest, bell-ringer" (Purch.). Arab. *mu'adhdhin*, pres. part. of *adhdhana*, frequent. of *adhana*, to proclaim, from *udhn*, ear.

> The motor-cars, the carts, the clogs and boots, and the steam muezzins calling the faithful to work
> (Arnold Bennett, *Mr Cowlishaw*).

muff. Du. *mof*, Ger. *muff*, Walloon *mouffe*, shortened from F. *moufle* (see *muffle*). Sense of duffer prob. started with "muffing" a catch, as though through wearing mittens. The first record is from the match at Muggleton (v.i.). Connection with obs. *muff*, contemptuous term for foreigner, Du. *mof*, Westphalian, is unlikely, as this died out c. 1650. But it may have survived in dial. and have influenced the other word.

> And being 2000 mofes, had small courage, and seeing the enemy coming on with a new assault, ran away
> (*Letter from Antwerp*, 1585, in *Cal. State Papers*).
> Such denunciations as—"Now butter-fingers"—"Muff"—and so forth (*Pickwick*, ch. vii.).

muffetee. Worsted cuff. From *muff*. Orig. (c. 1700) a neck-wrap.

muffin. Orig. dial. Cf. OF. *pain mofflet*, *moufflet*, soft bread.

muffle. First as verb. Aphet. from F. *emmoufler*, to swathe, from *moufle*, "a winter mittaine" (Cotg.), MedL. *muffula*, whence also Du. *moffel*. Perh. of Teut. origin; cf. Du. *mouw*, MHG. *mouwe*, sleeve. F. *manchon*, muff, is extended from *manche*, sleeve.

mufti. Arab. *muftī*, Mohammedan expounder of law, pres. part. of *aftā*, to give a leg. decision. From 16 cent. Current sense of civil dress (early 19 cent.) may be due to a suggestion of the stage mufti in the flowered dressing-gown and tasselled smoking-cap worn off duty by the officer of the period.

mug. Cf. LG. *mokke*, *mucke*, Norw. *mugga*, Norm. dial. *moque*, Guernsey *mogue*. Origin unknown, but perh. orig. a pers. name (cf. *jug*). Hence perh. *mug*, face, early mugs often representing grotesque faces. With *mug*, muff, duffer, cf. *crock*, and also F. *cruche*, in same sense. To *mug up* (for an examination) may be an obscure metaphor from theat. to *mug up*, make up one's mug (face) with paint.

mugger. Broad-nosed Ind. crocodile. Hind. *magar*. Curiously confused in quot. below with *nuzzer*, ceremonial present.

> Sir Salar Jung was presented to the Queen and offered his mugger as a token of allegiance, which her Majesty touched and restored
> (Quoted from *Standard* by *Punch*, July 15, 1876).

muggins [*slang*]. Juggins (q.v.). Both are existing surnames, and their selection as common nouns is due to phonetic fitness (cf. *Lushington*).

Muggletonian [*hist.*]. Of sect founded (c. 1651) by *Lodowicke Muggleton* and John Reeve, who claimed to be the "two witnesses" of *Rev.* xi. 3–6.

muggy. From dial. *mug*, drizzle, mist, ON. *mugga*; ? cogn. with L. *mucus*. Verb to *mug*, drizzle, occurs in *Gawayne and the Grene Knight* (14 cent.).

mugwort. AS. *mucgwyrt*, midge wort.

mugwump [*US.*]. Boss, also one who stands aloof from politics. NAmer. Ind. *mugquomp*, great chief, used in Eliot's *Massachusetts Bible* (1663) to render E. *duke*.

> It was inevitable that one or other of our mugwumps would emerge from his shell for the purpose of "queering" the national pitch
> (*Globe*, Nov. 30, 1917).

mulatto. Sp. Port. *mulato*, from *mulo*, mule (q.v.), in sense of hybrid, mongrel.

mulberry. From F. *mûre*, mulberry, and E. *berry*, the *l* being due to dissim.; cf. Ger. *maulbeere*, OHG. *mūlberi*, by dissim. for earlier *mūrberi*. Or perh. AS. *mōrberie*; cf. *mōrbēam*, mulberry tree. In any case first element is ult. from L. *morus*, mulberry (tree). See *sycamore*, which Wyc. renders *mulberry* (2 *Chron.* i. 15).

mulch [*gard.*]. Orig. (16 cent.) noun, wet straw, etc. Perh. from ME. adj. *molsh*, cogn. with Ger. dial. *molsch*, beginning to decay.

mulct. L. *mulctare*, from *mulcta*, *multa*, penalty, fine.

mule. OF. *mul* (replaced by *mulet*, whence *muletier*), L. *mulus*, cogn. with G. μύκλος, ass. In most Europ. langs. Orig. offspring of male ass and mare (see *hinny*[1]). Hence a gen. term for hybrid, e.g. Crompton's (spinning) *mule* (1779) was a compromise between the machines of Arkwright and Hargreaves.

mulga. Austral. tree. Native name.

muliebrity, mulierosity [*pedantic*]. From L. *mulier*, woman. Both in Blount. See *Cloister and Hearth*, ch. xxxiii.

mull¹ [*Sc.*]. Headland. ? Gael. *maol*, bald head, or ON. *mūli*, snout. The former word, in sense of tonsure, appears in many Celt. names in *Mal-*, *Mul-*, e.g. *Malcolm*, tonsured servant of St Columb.

mull² [*Sc.*]. Snuffbox. See *mill*.

mull³ [*obs.*]. Thin muslin (*Northanger Abbey*, ch. x.). For earlier *mulmull*, Hind. *malmal*.

mull⁴. Muddle. Prob. coined (19 cent.) from *muddle* on analogy of *mell*, *meddle*.

mull⁵. Verb. First as p.p., in *mulled sack* (1607). Perh. from F. *mollir*, to soften, from *mol* (*mou*), soft, L. *mollis*. Cf. obs. *mull*, to dull, deaden (v.i.).

Peace is a very apoplexy, lethargy; mull'd, deaf, sleepy, insensible (*Cor.* iv. 5).

mullah. Mohammedan learned in sacred law. Pers. Turk. Urdu *mullā*, Arab. *maulā*.

mullein. Plant. OF. *moleine* (*molène*), app. from *mol* (*mou*), soft, L. *mollis*. It has woolly leaves and was formerly called also *mullet*.

lapsus barbatus: i. moleine, i. softe (*Voc. of* 13 cent.).

mullet¹. Fish. F. *mulet*, dim. from L. *mullus*, red mullet.

mullet² [*her.*]. Five-pointed star. F. *molette*, rowel, in OF. also with E. sense. App. dim. from L. *mola*, mill-stone, whence F. *meule*, metal disk.

mulligatawny. Tamil *milagu-tannīr*, pepper-water.

mulligrubs. Orig. stomach-ache. Dial. *mull*, *mould¹*, earth, and *grub*, a worm, from pop. belief that internal pains were caused by parasitic worms. Cf. L. *vermina*, *verminatio*, in same sense. For sense-development cf. *megrims*, *spleen*, *vapours*. Prob. much older than dict. records, as there is a character called *Mulligrub*, "a sharking vintner," in Marston's *Dutch Courtezan* (1605); cf. similar use of *Mawworm* in Bickerstaffe's *Hypocrite*.

He [the cock] shrapeth so longe in the duste and mulle til he fynde a gemme
(Caxton, *Mirror of World*).

vermina: mal de ventre, trenchees (Est.).

Whose dog lies sick o' the mulligrubs? (*NED.* 1619).

mouldigrubs, the frets: bauchgrimmen; les tranchées de ventre (Ludw.).

mulligrubs, e.g. to be in his mulligrubs: böse, sauer, murrisch seyn (*ib.*).

mullion. Evidently connected with earlier *monial* (q.v.). OF. has *moilon* as arch. term, though not in precise sense. The form *munnion*, of somewhat later appearance, is app. a corrupt., like *banister* (q.v.). Both *mullion* and *monial* go back ult. to L. *medius*.

mullock [*Austral.*]. Rock without gold, or refuse of gold-workings. Dial. E., from dial. *mull*, *mould¹*, dust, etc. (cf. *mulligrubs*).

That ilke fruyt [medlar] is ever lenger the wers
Til it be roten in mullok, or in stree (Chauc. A. 3872).

multifarious. From Late L. *multifarius*, from L. adv. *multifariam*. ? Orig. of many tongues, from *fari*, to speak (cf. *nefarious*).

multiple. F., Late L. *multiplus* (cf. *double*, *triple*), for *multiplex*, from *multus*, much, many, *plicare*, to fold, whence *multiplicare*, source of F. *multiplier*, E. *multiply*. *Multiplicand* is from the gerund., to be multiplied.

multitude. F., L. *multitudo*, from *multus*. Sense of "numerousness" survives in *multitude of counsellors* (*Prov.* xi. 14, *Vulg.* *multa consilia*). *Multitudinous*, of the sea, is after Shaks. (*Macb.* ii. 2), and the ἀνήριθμον γέλασμα of Aeschylus.

multure [*archaic*]. Miller's toll of flour. OF. *molture* (*mouture*, grist), MedL. *molitura*, from *molere*, to grind.

mum¹. In *mum's the word*, to *sit mum*. ME. *momme* (*Piers Plowm.*), inarticulate sound, hence fig. silence. Imit., cf. *mumble* and Ger. *mumm*.

mum² [*archaic*]. Beer from Germany. Ger. *mumme*. ? From name of a 15 cent. Brunswick brewer.

mumble. ME. *momelen*, frequent. on *mum¹*; cf. Du. *mommelen*, Ger. *mummeln*.

Of this matere I mihte momele ful longe
(*Piers Plowm.* A. v. 21).

Mumbo-Jumbo. WAfr. bogy-man who deals with refractory wives. Described as Mandingo by Moore and Mungo Park. According to a writer in *Notes & Queries* (July 15, 1916), it is for *mama jombo*, the latter being the name of the tree to which the culprit is tied.

mumchance [*archaic*]. Silent, tongue-tied. Orig. (c. 1500) card-game, Ger. *mummenschanz*, of which second element is F. *chance* and first is app. connected with *mummer* (q.v.). Mod. sense due to association with *mum¹*.

mummer. OF. *momeur*, from *momer*, to "mum," i.e. to act in dumb show (see *mum¹*); cf. Ger. *mumme*, mask, *sich ver-*

mummen, to disguise oneself, put on a mask, because the mummers wore vizards. ? Ult. cogn. with *Momus*.

mummy. F. *momie*, MedL. *mumia*, Arab. *mūmiyā*, embalmed body, from *mūm*, wax. Current sense from c. 1600, but that of medicinal preparation from substance of mummy from c. 1400. It is from this transferred sense, passing into that of glutinous mass, that we have to *beat to a mummy*, now usu. misunderstood.

It must be very thick and dry, and the rice not boiled to a mummy (Mrs Glasse).

mump [*archaic*]. To beg, sponge Du. *mompen*, to cheat, perh. orig. to mumble (cf. *cant²*, *maunder*).

mumps. From obs. *mump*, grimace; cf. *mum¹*. Senses of neck-swelling and melancholy are equally old. Cf. Ger. *mumps*.

recchione: a disease or swelling in the necke called the mumps (Flor.).

mumpsimus. Erron. belief obstinately adhered to. Allusion to story (c. 1500) of illiterate priest who, on being corrected for reading, in the Mass, "quod in ore *mumpsimus*," replied, "I will not change my old *mumpsimus* for your new *sumpsimus*."

Some be too stiffe in their old *mumpsimus*, others be too busy and curious in their newe *sumpsimus* (Henry VIII, *Speech from the Throne*, 1545).

munch. Imit., perh. partly suggested by F. *manger* and *crunch* (q.v.).

I manche, I eate gredylye: je briffe (Palsg.).

Munchausen. Hero of narrative of impossible lies written (1785) in E. by Raspe. The Ger. form would be *Münchhausen*.

mundane. L. *mundanus*, from *mundus*, world, prob. ident. with *mundus*, clean, orderly (cf. *cosmos*).

mungo. Superior shoddy. Perh. from dial. *mong*, *mung*, mixture, with humorous assim. to name *Mungo*, often applied to a dog in Yorks. The Yorks. legend that the word came from the inventor's "it mun go," is, of course, apocryphal.

mungoose. See *mongoose*.

municipal. F., L. *municipalis*, from *municipium*, city with Roman privileges, from *munus*, gift, office, *capere*, to take. Cf. *common*.

munificent. After *magnificent*, from L. *munificus*, from *munus* (v.s.), *facere*, to make.

muniment. AF., L. *munimentum*, defence,

from *munire*, to fortify, applied in MedL. to a title-deed able to be used in defence of rights. In ME. often confused with *monument* (cf. *praemunire*).

monymente, or charterys, or oder lyke: monumen (*Prompt. Parv.*).

munition. F., L. *munitio-n-*, from *munire* (v.s.). See *ammunition*. Hence *munitioneer*, *munitionette*.

All that fight against her and her munition (*Is.* xxix. 7).

Smoking big cigars and shouting for special Scotch as if he was a blinking munitioneer (Heard in the train, 1917).

munnion. Incorr. for *mullion* (q.v.).

munshi. See *moonshee*.

muntjak. Small deer (Java). Native *minchek* (Sunda).

mural. F., L. *muralis*, from *murus*, wall. Esp. in *mural crown*, of embattled pattern, granted to soldier who first scaled hostile wall. Cf. hist. *murage*, toll for upkeep of town walls.

murder. AS. *morthor*. Com. Teut.; cf. Du. *moord*, Ger. *mord*, ON. *morth*, Goth. *maurthr*. The lengthened form is only recorded in AS. & Goth., but MedL. *mordrum*, F. *meurtre* point to its existence in other Teut. langs. Cogn. with L. *mors*, *mort-*, G. βροτός (*μροτός), mortal, Sanskrit *mṛti*, death, Welsh *marw*, Ir. *marbh*, dead.

Mordre wol out, that se we day by day (Chauc. B. 4242).

mure [*poet.*]. F. *murer*, to wall up, Late L. *murare*, from *murus*, wall. Has influenced to *mew up*. Prob. as a rule aphet. for *immure*.

I mure up in stonewall: jemmure (Palsg.).

murex. L., shell-fish producing (esp. Tyrian) purple; cf. G. μύαξ, sea-mussel, and see *mussel*.

Who fished the murex up?
What porridge had John Keats? (Browning, *Popularity*).

muriatic [*chem.*]. L. *muriaticus*, from *muria*, brine, pickle.

muricated [*biol.*]. Spiny. From *murex* (q.v.).

murk, mirk. ON. *myrkr*, darkness; cf. AS. *mirce*.

murmur. F. *murmurer*, L. *murmurare*. Imit. redupl.; cf. Ger. *murmeln*, G. μορμύρειν.

murphy. Potato. Jocular use of familiar Ir. name. The name, sea-warrior, is cogn. with Sc. *Murdoch*, Welsh *Meredith*.

murrain. OF. *moraine*, pestilence (*morine, carcase*), from *mourir*, to die. Not orig. limited to cattle.

En cele an [1316] fut graunt famine, qe poeple saunz noumbre morerent de feim, et fut auxint graunt morine d'autre gentz (*Fr. Chron. of Lond.*).

Dyvers myshappes of werres and moreyn
(Trev. i. 341).

murrey [*archaic*]. Mulberry-coloured. OF. *moré*, from L. *morum*, mulberry.

murrhine. Kind of glass. L. *murr(h)inus*, from *murra*, substance of which precious vases were made.

muscat. Wine, grape. F., Prov., It. *moscato*, having flavour of musk (q.v.). Hence dim. *muscatel*, also archaic *muscadine*, in same sense. Cf. *muscadin* (hist.), lit. musk-comfit, applied to Parisian fop, esp. those of the moderate upper-class party (1794–6).

moscato: sweetened or perfumed with muske. Also the wine muskadine (Flor.).

muscle. F., L. *musculus*, dim. of *mus*, mouse. In all Rom. & Teut. langs. Cf. F. *souris*, "a mouse, also, the sinewie brawn of the armes" (Cotg.), Ger. *maus*, "a muscle, the pulp, the fleshy part, the brawn of the arm or other parts" (Ludw.), Du. *muis*, a mouse, the muscle of the hand, also G. μῦς, mouse, muscle. See also *mussel*. *Muscular Christianity* (1858) is associated esp. with Charles Kingsley.

muscology. From L. *muscus*, moss.

muscovado. Unrefined sugar. Sp. *mascabado*, contracted p.p. of *menoscabar*, to lessen, depreciate, ident. in origin with OF. *meschever* (see *mischief*).

Muscovy. Archaic for Russia. F. *Moscovie*, Russ. *Moscow*. *Muscovy duck*, from tropical America, is an alteration of *musk-duck*.

muse¹. Noun. F., L. *musa*, G. μοῦσα, ult. cogn. with *mind*. The names of the nine are first recorded in Hesiod.

muse². Verb. Archaic F. *muser*, to loiter, lose one's time (see *amuse*); cf. Prov. *musar*, It. *musare*, in same sense. Perh. connected with *muzzle* (v.i.), but higher senses prob. associated with *muse¹*.

musare: to muse, to thinke, to surmise, also to muzle, to muffle, to mocke, to jest, to gape idlie about, to hould ones musle or snout in the aire (Flor.).

musette. F., bagpipe, dim. of OF. *muse*, in same sense, from OF. *muser*, to play music (q.v.).

museum. L., G. μουσεῖον, seat of the Muses.

mush¹. Porridge, etc. Orig. US. Ger. *mus,*

cogn. with AS. *mōs*, food. Perh. associated with *mash*. Very common in Ger. compds. such as *apfelmus*, *erbsenmus*, "pease porridge" (Ludw.).

mush² [*slang*]. Umbrella. Short for *mushroom*.

musha [*Anglo-Ir.*]. Ir. *máiseadh*, lit. if it is so.

mushroom. F. *mousseron*, from *mousse*, moss, prop. applied to variety which grows in moss. For final -*m* cf. *grogram, vellum, venom*.

muscheron, toodys halte: boletus fungus
(*Prompt. Parv.*).

music. F. *musique*, L. *musica*, G. μουσική (sc. τέχνη), art of the muses. In all Rom. & Teut. langs. To *face the music*, ? like a performer in front of the orchestra, is first quoted by *NED.* from Cecil Rhodes.

Music has charms to sooth a savage breast
(Congreve, *Mourning Bride*, i. 1).

Pictures, taste, Shakespeare, and the musical glasses (*Vic. of Wakef.* ch. ix.).

musk. Scent obtained from gland of musk-deer. F. *musc*, Late L. *muscus*, Late G. μόσχος, Pers. *mushk*, Sanskrit *mushka*, testicle. Applied also to various plants with similar odour, and to various musky smelling animals.

musket. In ME. sparrow-hawk, OF. *mousquet*, It. *moschetto*, dim. of *mosca*, fly, L. *musca*; cf. *mosquito*. The hawk was named from its small size. Early fire-arms were given the names of hawks (*falconet, saker*), or of serpents and monsters (*culverin, dragoon*). F. *mousquet* now means only musket, the hawk sense being replaced by *émouchet*.

mousquet: a musket (hawke, or peece) (Cotg.).

Muslim. See *Moslem*.

muslin. F. *mousseline*, It. *mussolina*, from *Mosul*, on the Tigris, near ruins of Nineveh.

musquash. Musk-rat. NAmer. Ind. (Algonkin). Mod. form has been altered on *musk* from earlier *mussascus* (Capt. John Smith).

mussel. AS. *muscle*, Late L. *muscula*, for *musculus*, little mouse, muscle; cf. Du. *mossel*, Ger. *muschel*, from L.; also L. *murex* (q.v.), from G. μῦς, mouse.

Mussulman, Musulman. Pers. *musulmān*, adj., from *muslim*, Moslem (q.v.), from Arab. For ending cf. *Turcoman*. *Mussulmen, Mussulwoman* (Dryden), are due to mistaken association with E. *man*.

must¹. New wine, etc. AS. *must*, L. *mustum* (sc. *vinum*), fresh wine. See *moist*.

must². Verb. AS. *mōste*, past of *mōt* (see *mote²*). Com. Teut. preterito-present verb (cf. *can*, *may*, etc.) not found in ON.; cf. Du. *moet*, Ger. *muss*, Goth. *ga-mōt*. Orig. idea was space, leisure, as in Ger. *musse*, idleness. Now used as present (cf. *ought*), orig. past sense surviving in literary use.

It was necessary to make a choice. The government must either submit to Rome, or must obtain the aid of the Protestants (Macaulay).

must³. Frenzy of elephant, etc. Urdu *mast*, intoxicated, from Pers.

must⁴. Mildew, etc. Back-formation from *musty* (q.v.).

mustachio [*archaic*]. See *moustache*.

mustang. Orig. strayed horse of Sp. conquistadors. Sp. *mesteño*, *mostrenco* both occur in the sense of strayed animal, the former from *mesta*, association of graziers, ? L. *mixta*, the latter perh. from *mostrar*, to show, L. *monstrare*, the finder being expected to advertise a stray horse.

mestengo y mostrenco: a straier; ovis errans
(Percyvall).

mestengo ou mostrenco: appartenent aux foires des bergers; c'est aussi une beste esgarée qui n'a point de maistre, une espave (Oudin).

mustard. OF. *moustarde* (*moutarde*), from *moust* (*moût*), *must¹* (q.v.), the condiment being orig. prepared by mixing the seeds with must. The plant is thus named from the preparation. In all Rom. langs. *Mustard-pot* is in Wyc. The *mustard* seed, κόκκος σινάπεως, of *Matt.* xiii. 31 is prob. the black mustard, which grows to a great height in Palestine.

mustee, mestee. Half-caste, or esp. offspring of white and quadroon. False sing. from *mestese*, mestizo (q.v.). Cf. *Chinee*, *Portugee*, etc.

muster. First as verb. OF. *mostrer*, *moustrer* (replaced by *montrer*), L. *monstrare*, to show; cf. It. *mostrare*, Sp. *mostrar*; also Du. *monster*, Ger. *muster*, pattern, from F. or It. To *pass muster* was orig. of mil. or nav. inspection. With to *muster up* (e.g. courage) cf. to *enlist* (e.g. the public sympathy).

Muster your wits, stand in your own defence
(*Love's Lab. Lost*, v. 2).

musty. For earlier *moisty*, in same sense. See *moist*. Perh. immediately from Gascon *mousti*. The sense has been affected by

F. *moisi*, p.p. of *moisir*, L. *mucēre*, "to be filthie, vinewed, or hoare" (Coop.).

mustye as a vessel is or wyne or any other vitayle: moisi (Palsg.).

Musulman. See *Mussulman*.

mutable. L. *mutabilis*, from *mutare*, to change.

mutch [*dial.*]. Cap. Du. *muts* (see *amice*).

mutchkin [*Sc.*]. About three-quarters of pint. Obs. Du. *mudseken* (*mutsje*), dim. of *muts*, cap (v.s.).

mutsje: a little cap, a quartern (Sewel).

mute. Restored, on L. *mutus*, from ME. *mewet*, F. *muet*, dim. of OF. *mu*, L. *mutus*, ult. cogn. with *mum¹*. As noun used (17 cent.) of actor playing dumb part. The funeral *mute* is 18 cent.

A mute is a dumbe speaker in the play.—
Dumbe speaker! that's a bull
(Brome, *Antipodes*, v. 4, 1638).

mutilate. From L. *mutilare*, from *mutilus*, maimed; cf. G. μύτιλος, hornless.

mutiny. From obs. verb *mutine*, F. *mutiner*, from *mutin*, rebellious, from OF. *mute*, rebellion (*meute*, pack of hounds), for *muete*, Late L. *movita*, from *movēre*, to move. Cf. F. *émeute*, insurrection.

mutograph, mutoscope. Neologisms from L. *mutare*, to change.

mutter. Frequent. formation on imit. sound which appears also in F. *mot* (see *motet*).

mutton. F. *mouton* (OF. *molton*), sheep, of Celt. origin; cf. Gael. *mult*, Ir. *molt*, Welsh *mollt*, ram; perh. ult. cogn. with *mutilate*, in sense of castrate. For limitation of sense cf. *beef*, *pork*, *veal* (see quot. s.v. *beef*).

mouton: a mutton, a weather; also, mutton (Cotg.).

mutual. F. *mutuel*, from L. *mutuus*, cogn. with *mutare*, to change. Orig. of feelings, but now currently for common, as in *Our Mutual Friend*. *Mutual admiration society* was coined by O. W. Holmes.

mutule [*arch.*]. F., L. *mutulus*, modillion.

muzhik. See *moujik*.

muzzle. OF. *musel* (*museau*), snout, dim. of OF. *muse*; cf. It. *muso*, OSp. *mus*. Derived by Diez from L. *morsus*, bite (cf. OF. *jus*, downwards, L. *deorsum*). This etym. is supported by Prov. *mursel*, Bret. *morzeel* (from F.), and ME. var. *mursel*, but is not now generally accepted. Earliest E. sense (Chauc.) is that of contrivance to stop biting. In connection with the etym. proposed by Diez it may be noted that Wyc. has *mussel* as var. of *morsel*.

muzzy [*slang*]. Prob. jocular formation on *muse*[2], *bemused*.

my. Shortened form of *mine* (q.v.), orig. used only before consonants, e.g. *my father*, but *mine enemy*. Ellipt. use as interj., for *my God* (*stars, aunt, hat*), is esp. US.; cf. Norw. Dan. *o du min* (sc. *Gud*).

myall[1]. Austral. aboriginal. Native *mail*, pl. of *namail*, a black, used by the half-civilized natives of their wilder brethren, just as *nigger* is by superior negroes.

myall[2]. Austral. acacia. Native *maiāl*.

myc-, mycet-. From G. μύκης, mushroom.

mylodon [*biol.*]. Extinct animal, with cylindrical teeth. From G. μύλος, mill-stone. Cf. *mastodon*.

mynheer. Dutchman, lit. my sir (master, lord). See *herr, hoar*. Cf. *mossoo, milord*.

myology [*anat.*]. Study of muscles. From G. μῦς, μυ-, mouse, muscle.

myopia. From G. μύωψ, from μύειν, to shut, ὤψ, eye.

myosotis. G. μυοσωτίς, from μῦς, μυ-, mouse, οὖς, ὠτ-, ear.

myriad. G. μυριάς, μυριάδ-, from μυρίος, countless, whence μύριοι, ten thousand. With *myriorama* cf. *panorama*.

myrmidon. Usu. in pl. G. Μυρμιδόνες, Thessalian tribe led against Troy by Achilles. Fabled to have been ants (G. μύρμηξ, ant) changed into men.

myrobalan. Fruit used in tanning. F., L., G. μυροβάλανος, from μύρον, unguent, βάλανος, acorn, date. Cf. It. Sp. *mirabolano*.

myrrh. AS. *myrra*, L., G. μύρρα, of Semit. origin; cf. Arab. *murr*, Heb. *mōr*, cogn. with *mar*, bitter (cf. *marah*). In most Europ. langs.

myrtle. Short for *myrtle-tree* (cf. *bay*[1]), OF. *myrtille*, myrtle berry, dim. from L., G. μύρτος, myrtle, Pers. *mŭrd*, whence also F. *myrte*, It. Sp. *mirto*.

For the nettle shal growe the tre that is clepid myrt (Wyc. *Is.* lv. 13).

myself. For *meself*, altered on *herself*, in which *her* was felt as genitive. Cf. *hisself* for *himself*.

mystagogue. L., G. μυσταγωγός, initiator into Eleusinian mysteries. See *mystery, pedagogue*.

mystery[1]. Secret, etc. L., G. μυστήριον, secret rel. ceremony, cogn. with μύειν, to close (lips or eyes). Adopted by LXX. in sense of secret counsel (of God or king) and later rendered *sacramentum* in *Vulg.*, whence theol. sense-development. Adopted also, after F. *mystère*, as name for medieval rel. play. Owing to the fact that these plays were commonly acted by gilds of craftsmen this sense has been associated with *mystery*[2].

mystery[2] [*archaic*]. Handicraft, as in *art and mystery*. Corresponding to F. *métier*, OF. *mestier*, "a trade, occupation, misterie, handicraft" (Cotg.), in which two words are confused, viz. *ministerium*, service, and *magisterium*, mastership. It is from the latter, OF. *maistier* (13 cent.), that the E. word is chiefly derived. It may in fact be regarded almost as a thinned form of *mastery* (cf. *mister, mistress*), a word naturally occurring in connection with the crafts (v.i.). Mod. form is partly due to association with *mystery*[1], with which it has been associated in the sense of secret of a craft, while Tudor puns on the two words are common.

Et prenoit le dit mestre Fouques pour ses gages et pour la mestrie du mestier xviij den. par jour (*Livre des Mestiers de Paris*).

That great and admirable mystery, the law (Clarendon, 1647).

mystic. F. *mystique*, L., G. μυστικός, from μύστης, priest of mysteries. As noun, with ref. to mystical theol., from 17 cent. *Mystify*, F. *mystifier*, has in E. been associated with *mist*.

mythology. F. *mythologie*, Late L., G. μυθολογία, from μῦθος, fable. In Lydgate. *Myth* is mod.

Mythology...is in truth a disease of language (Max Müller).

n-. In a few words, e.g. *nickname, newt*, the *n-* belongs to preceding *an*. Loss of *n-* is more common, e.g. *apron, auger, adder, umpire, humble-pie*, etc.

nab. Also *nap*. A cant word of late (17 cent.) appearance. Cf. Sw. *nappa*, Dan. *nappe*, to snatch, colloq. Norw. *knabbe*, perh. cogn. with *knap*[2]. Prob. *nobble* is of kindred origin.

nabob. Arab. *nawwāb*, honorific pl. of *nā'ib*, deputy. Orig. deputy governor, applied also in 18 cent. E. to returned Anglo-Indian with large fortune. For -*b*- cf. F. *nabab*, Port. *nababo*, one of which may be immediate source of our word.

nacarat. Bright orange red. F., Sp. *nacarado*, from *nacar*, nacre (q.v.).

nacelle [*aeron.*]. Of aeroplane. F., car of balloon, lit. skiff, L. *navicella*, dim. of *navis*, ship.

The floor of the nacelle was burnt out
(*Royal Flying Corps in War*, 1918).

nacre. Mother of pearl. F., It. *nacchera*, ? from Arab. *nakara*, to hollow out. Orig. applied to the shell.

nadir. F. Sp. It., Arab. *nadīr*, opposite, esp. in *nadīr ez-zemt*, opposite the zenith (q.v.).

nag¹. Noun. Cf. Du. *negge*; cf. Ger. *nickel*, a dim. of *Nikolaus*, Nicholas, applied to an undersized man or horse.

nagge, or lytyl beeste: bestula, equilus
(*Prompt. Parv.*).

nag². Verb. Only dial. till 19 cent. Sw. Norw. *nagga*, to peck, nibble; cogn. with Ger. *nagen*, OHG. *gnagan*, to gnaw (q.v.). Cf. Ger. *necken*, to tease, nag, which is also a dial. word of recent adoption.

nagaika. Russ., whip of *Nogai Tatars* (S. Russ.), perh. named from a famous khan *Nogaĭ* (13 cent.).

The Cossacks drove off the agitators with their nagaikas (*Daily Chron.* June 22, 1917).

nagor. Senegal antelope. Coined by Buffon (1764).

naiad. F. *naïade*, L., G. ναιάς, ναιάδ-, cogn. with ναειν, to flow.

naik. Now sepoy corporal, orig. governor. Urdu *nā'ik*, Hind. *nāyak*, leader, chief, etc., Sanskrit *nāyaka*, leader.

nail. AS. *nægl*, in both senses. Com. Teut.; cf. 'Du. Ger. *nagel*, ON. *nagl*, Goth. *nagls* (in verb *nagljan*); ult. cogn. with L. *unguis*, G. ὄνυξ, Sanskrit *nakha*, OIr. *ingen*. Orig. anat., but secondary sense of pointed spike is developed early in Teut. langs. Cf. relation of L. *ungula* and *unguis*. Also as measure and weight (cf. *clove³*). Used in many fig. phrases of obvious origin. *On the nail* refers to the nail of the hand, and must orig. have alluded to drinking fair and square. Cf. F. *payer rubis sur l'ongle*, a variation on *boire rubis sur l'ongle*, to drink out so that the inverted tankard leaves only one red drop of wine on the thumb-nail (see *supernaculum*). The antiquity of the phrase and its early association with the other *nail* are shown by quot. below. To *nail (a lie) to the counter* alludes to the old-fashioned treatment of spurious coin in banks.

Pro quibus prisis et cariagiis plena fiat solucio super unguem (Robert Bruce, 1326).

nainsook. Fabric. Urdu *nainsukh*, from *nain*, eye, *sukh*, pleasure.

naïve. F., fem. of *naïf*, simple, L *nativus*.

naked. AS. *nacod*. Com. Teut.; cf. Du. *naakt*, Ger. *nackt*, ON. *nökkvithr*, Goth. *naquaths*, all p.p. formations from a lost verb the root of which appears in L. *nudus*, Sanskrit *nagna*, Russ. *nagói*, OIr. *nocht*. Many of the fig. senses occur in AS., e.g. *naked sword*, *naked word*, the latter being the origin of later *naked truth*. In *naked eye* (cf. It. *occhio nudo*), which dates from the telescope, the adj. has the archaic sense of unarmed (v.i.).

Naked as I am I will assault thee (*Oth.* v. 2).

naker [*hist.*]. Kettle-drum. OF. *nacaire*, Arab. *naqārah*. Medieval crusading word revived by Scott.

namby-pamby. Nickname of *Ambrose Philips* (†1749), whose poetic addresses to infant members of the nobility excited the derision of Pope, Carey, and their friends.

Namby-Pamby is your guide,
Albion's joy, Hibernia's pride.
Namby-Pamby Pilly-pis,
Rhimy-pim'd on missy-mis (Henry Carey, 1726).

name. AS. *nama*. Aryan; cf. Du. *naam*, Ger. *name*, ON. *nafn*, *namn*, Goth. *namō*, L. *nomen*, G. ὄνομα, Sanskrit *nāman*, OIr. *ainm*. With *namely*, orig. especially, cf. Ger. *namentlich*, L. *nominatim*. *Namesake* is for earlier *name's sake*, a person named for the sake of someone.

nankeen. From *Nankin* (China), lit. southern capital.

nanny-goat. From *Nanny*, pet-form of *Anne*; cf. *billy-goat*.

nantz [*archaic*]. Brandy from *Nantes* (Loire-Inf.).

nap¹. To take a short sleep. AS. *hnappian*, cogn. with OHG. *hnafizzan*, in same sense; perh. cogn. with Norw. Dan. *nap*, snap, with idea of quick closing of eyes; cf. colloq. Norw. *nippe*, to take a nap, i.e. to nip the eyes to. Orig. in more dignified sense.

Tha se brydguma ylde, tha hnappudon hig ealle & slepun (AS. *Gosp. Matt.* xxv. 5).

nap². On cloth. Du. *nop*, whence *noppen*, to shear. Orig. the knotty matter removed by the process; ? cogn. with *knob* and dial. *knab*, *nap*, hillock. No doubt introduced by Flem. cloth-workers. Earlier is obs. *nopsack*, mattress stuffed with flock.

nope of a cloth: villus (*Prompt. Parv.*).

nap³. Card-game. Short for *Napoleon*.

nape. Ident. with obs. *nap*, bowl, AS. *hnæpp*.
Early var. *naupe* points rather to F. *hanap*
(see *hamper*), from cogn. OHG. *hnapf*.
Prop. the hollow at the base of the skull,
as can be seen from the words used for it
in other langs., e.g. OF. *chaon*, VL.
cavo-n-, and Ger. *nackengrube*, lit. neck
pit. In NIt. nape is represented by derivatives of *cuppa*, in EF. by derivatives of
fossa.

nape of the necke: fossette de la teste (Palsg.).
colodra: a deep pan to milk sheep or goats in
(Stevens).
colodrillo: the pole of the head, the nape of the
neck (*ib.*).

napery. OF. *naperie*, from *nape* (*nappe*),
cloth. See *napkin*. Cf. MedL. *naparia*,
branch of royal household concerned with
the linen, whence name *Napier*.

naphtha. L., G. νάφθα; cf. Arab. Pers. *naft*,
which may, however, be from G.

Napier's bones. For simplifying calculation.
Invented by *Napier* of Merchiston (†1617).

napkin. Dim. from F. *nappe*, cloth, L. *mappa*,
m- having become *n-* by dissim.

napoo. Regarded by Mr Atkins as a current
F. phrase closing a discussion in indefinite
fashion. F. *il n'y en a plus*. Cf. the Ger.
war-word *naplü*, cognac.

Not the napoo victory ensuing from neutral
pressure and semi-starvation, but the full decisive
military victory (*Pall Mall Gaz.* Feb. 15, 1917).

nappy [*archaic*]. Foaming, of ale. Prob. from
nap², in allusion to the "head." Cf. F.
vin bourru, from *bourru*, "flockie, hairie,
rugged, high-napped" (Cotg.).

narcissus. L., G. νάρκισσος, ? from νάρκη,
numbness, alluding to narcotic effects.

narcotic. F. *narcotique*, MedL., G. ναρκωτικός
(v.s.).

nard. OF. *narde* (*nard*), L., G. νάρδος, of
Oriental origin; cf. Heb. *nēr'd'*, Arab. Pers.
nārdīn.

Spikenard, or trewe narde (Wyc. *John*, xii. 3).

narghileh. Hookah. Pers. *nārgilēh*, from
nārgīl, coco-nut, of which the reservoir was
orig. made.

nark [*slang*]. As in *copper's nark*, police spy.
Romany *nāk*, nose.

narration. F., L. *narratio-n-*, from *narrare*,
to relate, from *narus*, for *gnarus*, knowing,
acquainted, ult. cogn. with *know*.

narrow. AS. *nearu*, *nearw-*. Cf. OSax. *naru*.
Statement in *NED*. that it is not found in
other Teut. langs. overlooks MHG. *nerwen*,

to constrict, OHG. *narwa* (*narbe*), scar,
orig. fastening together. Franck regards
Du. *naar*, dismal, as cogn. The *narrow
seas*, opposed to *high* (*broad*) *seas*, are mentioned in 15 cent. The *narrow way* (*Matt.*
vii. 14) renders, already in AS., *Vulg. arcta
via*. For fig. senses cf. *broad*.

narthex [*arch.*]. Ante-nave. G. νάρθηξ, kind
of reed. L. *ferula* was used in same sense.

narwhal. Sw. Dan. *narhval*, ON. *nāhvalr*,
app. corpse whale, from *nār*, corpse, ? in
allusion to colour.

nary [*US. & dial.*]. For *ne'er a*.

nasal. F., MedL. *nasalis*, from *nasus*, nose.

nascent. From pres. part. of L. *nasci*, to be
born.

nasturtium. L., nose-twist, from pungency.
Cf. F. *nasitort*.

Nomen accepit a narium tormento (Pliny).

nasty. ME. also *nasky*, perh. the older form.
Cf. Sw. dial. *naskug*, *nasket*. Origin unknown. For weakening of sense from orig.
filthy, disgusting (still in US.), cf. *dirty*.

maulavé: ill-washed; slubbered, nasky, nasty, foule
(Cotg.).

natal. L. *natalis*, from *nasci*, *nat-*, to be born.

natation. L. *natatio-n-*, from *natare*, to swim,
frequent. of *nare*.

nathless [*archaic*]. AS. *nā thȳ lǣs*, not the
less, where *thȳ*, instrument. of *the*, means
thereby. Cf. *nevertheless*, which has supplanted the earlier phrase.

nation. F., L. *natio-n-*, from *nasci*, *nat-*, to
be born. The old *National Schools* were
founded (1811) by the *National Society*.
Nationalist, now almost monopolized by
Ireland, is recorded in proper sense for
1715. *Nationalize*, now much in vogue
with those who consider that labour is best
avoided by appropriating the results of
others' labour, dates in that spec. sense
from c. 1870.

native. L. *nativus*, from *nasci*, *nat-*, to be
born; cf. *natal*, *nativity*, the latter recorded
in late AS., from OF. The zool. limitation
to the oyster is curious.

His train of camels, laden with snow, could serve
only to astonish the natives of Arabia
(Gibbon, *Decline and Fall*, ch. lii.).

natron [*chem.*]. F., Sp., Arab. *natrŭn*, G.
νίτρον, nitre, Heb. *nether*.

natterjack [*dial.*]. Kind of toad. Perh. for
atterjack, from *atter*, poison, as in dial.
attercop, spider, AS. *ātorcoppe*. Cf. *newt*.
The ending is the name *Jack* (q.v.).

natty. Orig. slang. ? From *neat*².

nature. F., L. *natura*, from *nasci*, *nat-*, to be born. Has superseded native *kind* in many senses. Orig. sense of the inherent appears in *in the nature of things*. Collect. sense of natural phenomena and objects from 17 cent. *Natural*, imbecile, is for ME. *natural fool* (*idiot*). *Naturalism* in art and literature, i.e. exaggerated realism, is adopted from F. *naturalisme*, popularized in F. by Zola's school. *Naturalize*, in current sense, is 16 cent.

naught, nought. AS. *nāwiht*, no whit. See *aught, not*. Hence *naughty*, worthless, now limited to the nursery.

> The other basket had very naughty [*Vulg.* malus] figs (*Jer.* xxiv. 3).

naumachia. Sham sea-fight. L., G. ναυμαχία, from ναῦς, ship, μάχη, fight.

nausea. L., G. ναυσία, sea-sickness, from ναῦς (v.s.).

nautch. Urdu, Hind. *nāch*, Prakrit *nachcha*, Sanskrit *nṛtya*, dancing, acting.

nautical. From F. *nautique*, L., G. ναυτικός, from ναύτης, sailor, from ναῦς, ship.

nautilus. L., G. ναυτίλος, sailor, from ναύτης (v.s.).

naval. F., L. *navalis*, from *navis*, ship.

nave¹. Of wheel. AS. *nafu*. Aryan; cf. Du. *naaf*, Ger. *nabe*, ON. *nöf*, Sanskrit *nābhi*, nave, navel. See *auger, navel*. The wide extension of this word, as of *wheel*, points to early invention of waggons.

nave². Of church. F. *nef*, L. *navis*, ship, cogn. with G. ναῦς. Cf. Ger. *schiff*, in same sense. ? From shape ? or from church being regarded poet. as ship (see *anchorite*), ? or from early Christian confusion between G. ναός, temple, and ναῦς, ship.

navel. AS. *nafela*. Aryan; cf. Du. *navel*, Ger. *nabel*, ON. *nafle*, Sanskrit *nābhīla*; cogn. with L. *umbilicus*, G. ὀμφαλός. See *nave*¹, the navel being the nave, or centre, of the body, or rather, the nave being the navel of the wheel.

> He unseam'd him from the nave to the chaps
> And fix'd his head upon our battlements
>   (*Macb.* i. 2).

navew. Wild turnip. F. *naveau*, dim. from L. *napus*. Cf. F. *navet*, turnip, once in common E. use.

navicular [*biol. & eccl.*]. Boat-shaped. Late L. *navicularis*, from *navicula*, dim. of *navis*, ship.

navigate. From L. *navigare*, from *navis*, ship, *agere*, to drive. Hence *navigator*, now

navvy, applied in 18 cent. to labourer employed in canal construction for inland navigation.

> It was seldom indeed that the bargee or the navigator had much to boast of after a young blood had taken off his coat to him
>   (Doyle, *Rodney Stone*, ch. i.).

navvy. See *navigate*.

navy. OF. *navie*. fleet, from *navis*, ship. The *king's* (*royal*) *navy* dates from 16 cent., the word being also used of any fleet or collection of ships, not necessarily of fighting character.

> It is upon the Navy that, under the good Providence of God, the wealth, prosperity and the peace of these Islands and of the Empire do mainly depend (*Articles of War*).

nawab. Urdu form of *nabob* (q.v.).

nay. ON. *nei*, for *ne ei*, not ever (see *ay*). Orig. differentiated in use from *no* (q.v.). Cf. *yea*.

Nazarite. One who has taken certain vows of abstinence (*Numb.* vi.). From L. *Nazaraeus*, from Heb. *nāzīr*, from *nāzar*, to separate, consecrate, oneself. Often confused, as by Shylock (v.i.), with *Nazarene*, inhabitant of *Nazareth*, follower of Jesus of Nazareth.

> Yes, to smell pork! to eat of the habitation which your prophet, the Nazarite, conjured the devil into
>   (*Merch. of Ven.* i. 3).

N.B. L. *nota bene*, note well.

Neanderthaloid [*ethn.*]. From prehistoric skull found (1857) at *Neanderthal* (Rhenish Prussia).

neap. Of tide. AS. *nēp*, in *nēpflōd*. The simplex is recorded only once, app. in sense of helpless, incapable, in phrase *forthganges nēp*, without power of advancing. Origin obscure; ? cf. Norw. dial. *næpen*, hardly touching, *nöpen*, hardly enough.

Neapolitan. Of *Naples*, L., G. Νεάπολις, new city.

near. Orig. adv. AS. *nēar*, compar. of *nēah*, nigh (q.v.); or cogn. ON. *nǣr*, compar. of *nā*. Already often posit. in ME., but compar. sense is still common in 16–17 cents., esp. in *never the near*, none the nearer. As adj. has almost supplanted correct *nigh*. For sense of stingy and other fig. uses cf. *close*. As applied to animals (*near hind leg*, etc.) it means left, because they are led or mounted from that side. Various adv. senses are now usu. replaced by *nearly* (16 cent.).

Nearctic [*geog.*]. Of arctic regions of NAmer. Lit. new Arctic, from G. νέος, new.

neat[1]. Noun. Now chiefly in *neat cattle* and *neat's-foot-oil*. AS. *nēat*, cattle. Com. Teut.; cf. obs. Du. *noot*, OHG. *nōz*, ON. *naut*, whence Sc. *nowt*. From root of AS. *nēotan*, to enjoy, possess, cogn. with Ger. *geniessen*. Cf. hist. of *fee*, pecuniary, cattle.

I could 'a had as upright a fellow as e'er trod on neat's leather (*Misogonus*, iv. 1, c. 1550).

neat[2]. Adj. F. *net*, "neat, clean, pure" (Cotg.), L. *nitidus*, from *nitēre*, to shine. Cf. *net*[2]. Sense of undiluted (spirit), from c. 1800, is evolved from 16 cent. sense of unadulterated (wine).

neath. Aphet. for obs. *aneath*, beneath (q.v.).

neb [*north. & Sc.*]. Beak, bill. AS. *nebb*; cogn. with ON. *nef*, Du. *neb*, and ult. with *snap* and Ger. *schnabel*, beak. Cf. *nib*, and see quot. s.v. *rid*.

nebula. L., mist; cogn. with G. νεφέλη, Ger. *nebel*, ON. *nifl*. The *nebular hypothesis* (astron.) was first propounded by Kant.

necessary. F. *nécessaire*, L. *necessarius*, from *necesse* (neut. adj.), needful, from *ne* and *cedere*, *cess-*, to give way. With *necessity knows no law* cf. Ger. *not kennt kein gebot* (Bethmann-Hollweg, Aug. 1914).

Thanne is it wysdom, as it thynketh me,
To maken vertu of necessitee (Chauc. A. 3041).

neck. AS. *hnecca*, nape of the neck. Com. Teut.; cf. Du. *nek*, Ger. *nacken*, *genick*, ON. *hnakki*, all meaning nape. *Neck or nothing* implies risking nothing less than one's neck. For *necklace* see *lace*. *Neck-verse* (hist.), usu. first verse of *Ps.* li., by reading which in black-letter criminal could claim "benefit of clergy," is recorded for 15 cent. Mod. to *get it in the neck* appears to allude to "where the chicken got the axe." A further playful variation is "where Maggie wore the beads."

We be clerks all and can our neck-verse
(*Hickscorner*, c. 1500).

Away went Gilpin, neck or nought (Cowper).

With your admirable command of foreign idioms you very possibly know our cant London phrase, "Where Maggie wore the beads." Well, Fritz dear, that is where you are going to get it
(*Globe*, May 24, 1918).

necrology. Obituary. From G. νεκρός, dead person, cogn. with L. *necare*, to kill. Cf. *necromancy*, orig. divination by raising the dead, corrupted into MedL. *nigromantia*, F. & E. *nigromancie*, and translated as *black art*; *necropolis*, cemetery; *necrosis*, mortification, esp. of bones, G. νέκρωσις.

nigromance: nigromancie, conjuring, the blacke art (Cotg.).

nectar. L., G. νέκταρ, drink of the Gods. Hence *nectarine*, orig. adj., as in *nectarine peach*. Cf. *nectary*, honey-secreting organ of plant.

neddy. Donkey. From pet-form of *Edward*. Cf. *cuddy*. In slang also a life-preserver.

need. AS. *nīed*. Com. Teut.; cf. Du. *nood*, Ger. *not*, ON. *nauth*, Goth. *nauths*. Ground-sense is constraint, necessity. In adv. *needs* the *-s* is by analogy with other adv. genitives. *Needs must* is ellipt. for some such phrase as *needs must who needs shall*. The curious use of *he need* for *he needs* (*needeth*) is due to analogy with the preterite-present verbs (*may*, *dare*, etc.) followed by infin. without *to*. With *the needful* cf. G. χρῆμα (in pl.), money, cogn. with κεχρῆσθαι, to need.

Nedes must he rin that the devyll dryvith
(Skelton).

We've been most of us taught, in the course of our lives,
That "Needs must when the Elderly Gentleman drives" (*Ingoldsby*).

needle. AS. *nǣdl*. Com. Teut.; cf. Du. *naald* (as E. dial. *neeld*), Ger. *nadel*, ON. *nāl*, Goth. *nēthla*; cogn. with Du. *naaien*, Ger. *nähen*, to sew. Is to *get the needle*, quite mod. slang, due to some association with *nettle*, used in similar sense in 18 cent.?

ne'er-do-well. Orig. Sc., hence often written *ne'er-do-weel*.

nefarious. From L. *nefarius*, from *nefas*, wrong, from *fas*, right, lit. (divinely) spoken, from *fari*, to speak.

negative. F. *négatif*, Late L. *negativus*, from *negare*, to say no, deny, from *neg* (= *ne*, as in *negotium*); cf. Ger. *verneinen*, from *nein*. Scient. senses (math., photogr., etc.) as contrast to *positive*.

neglect. From L. *neglegere*, *neglect-*, not to pick up, *legere*. Older is *negligence*, through F. *Négligé* is restored from 18 cent. *negligee*, loose gown.

negotiate. From L. *negotiari*, from *negotium*, business, lit. not leisure, *otium*.

negrillo. Dwarf negro. Sp., dim. of *negro* (q.v.). Cf. *negrito*, also Sp. dim., applied to dwarfish negroid race of Polynesia.

negro. Sp., L. *niger*, *nigr-*, black.

Negus. Ruler of Abyssinia. Native for king. Identified by Purch. with *Prester John*.

negus. First compounded by Col. *Francis Negus* (†1732).

neigh. AS. *hnǣgan*, of imit. origin. Similar forms are found in other Teut. langs.

neighbour. AS. *nēah-gebŭr*, lit. nigh boor; cf. obs. Du. *nageboer*, Ger. *nachbar*, ON. *nābūe*. Orig. sense of *neighbourhood* was neighbourly conduct, friendliness. See *bond²* and cf. EAngl. *bor*, as used by Mr Peggotty, from Du.

neither. Altered, on *either* (q.v.), from *nauther*, *nouther*, contr. of AS. *nāhwæther*, not whether (q.v.).

nek [*geog.*]. Between hills (SAfr.). Du., neck. Cf. F. *col*, in same sense.

nelly. Largest kind of petrel. From name *Nelly* (*Helen* or *Eleanor*). Cf. *robin*, *magpie*, etc.

nelumbium. Water-bean. Coined by Jussieu (1789) from Singhalese *nelumbu*.

nem. con. L., *nemine contradicente*, no one contradicting.

Nemean. Of Νεμέα, near Argos, abode of lion killed by Hercules.

nemesis. G. νέμεσις, from νέμειν, to apportion one's due. Personified as goddess of retribution.

nemoral. Of a grove, L. *nemus, nemor-*.

nenuphar. Water-lily. MedL., Arab. Pers. *nīnūfar, nīlūfar*, Sanskrit *nīlōtpala*, from *nīl*, blue, *utpala*, lotus. Cf. F. *nénufar*, It. Sp. *nenufar*.

neolithic [*geol.*]. Of later stone age. From G. νέος, new, λίθος, stone. Cf. *neologism*, F. *néologisme*, from G. λόγος, word; *neophyte*, F. *néophyte*, Church L., G. νεόφυτος (1 *Tim.* iii. 6), new-planted, from φυτεύειν, to plant; *neoteric*, recent, up-to-date, G. νεωτερικός, from νεώτερος, compar. of νέος; *neotropical*, of tropical America (cf. *nearctic*).

nepenthe. For earlier *nepenthes*, L., G. νηπενθές (sc. φάρμακον, *Odyss.* iv. 221), neut. of νηπενθής, from νη-, neg., πένθος, grief.

nephew. F. *neveu*, L. *nepos, nepot-*, grandson, nephew, also prodigal. Used in ME. and up to 17 cent. in L. senses and also of descendant in gen. Replaced cogn. AS. *nefa*, which survives as surname *Neve*, *Neave*; cf. Du. *neef*, Ger. *neffe*, ON. *nefi*, Sanskrit *napāt*, classical Pers. *nabīrah*, colloq. Pers. *navādah*. Perh. ult. helpless, thus *nepos* for *ne potis*.

nephritis [*med.*]. G. νεφρῖτις, from νεφρός, kidney.

ne plus ultra. Trad. inscription on Pillars of Hercules.

nepotism. F. *népotisme*, It. *nepotismo*, from *nepote*, nephew (q.v.). Orig. in allusion to favours conferred by the Pope on his

nephews, often euph. for illegitimate sons. E. use of the word dates from the transl. of *Il Nepotismo di Roma* (1667).

Got my wife to read me in the Nepotisme, whicb is very pleasant (Pepys, Apr. 27, 1669).

Neptunian [*geol.*]. Of action of water. From L. *Neptunus*, god of the sea. Planet was discovered (1846) by Galle.

nereid. L. *nereis, nereid-*, G. Νηρηΐς, daughter of sea-god Νηρεύς, ? cogn. with L. *nare*, to swim.

neroli. Oil from flower of bitter orange. F. *néroli*, from name (*Neroli*) of It. princess to whom its discovery is attributed. Cf. *frangipane*.

nerve. L. *nervus*, sinew. Mod. sense appears in Late G. use of cogn. νεῦρον (see *neurotic*). The meaning which our hardier ancestors attached to the word survives in to *strain every nerve*. *Nervous* is occ. used in orig. sense. A *nervous* (*nervy*) individual is illogically one who has no *nerve*.

nerveux: sinewie, full of sinewes; also, strong, stiffe, pithie, forcible (Cotg.).

nescient. From pres. part. of L. *nescire*, from *ne*, not, *scire*, to know.

nesh [*dial.*]. Soft, timid, delicate, etc. AS. *hnesce*; cf. archaic Du. *nesch*, soft, damp, Goth. *hnasqus*, tender. Very common in ME. and still used occ. by writers of the north and Midlands, e.g. in *Festus* by P. J. Bailey, to whom it would have been an every-day word.

A nesshe answere brekith wrathe
(Wyc. *Prov.* xv. 1).

ness. Promontory. AS. *næss* or ON. *nes*, cogn. with AS. *nasu*, nose. Cf. *Gris Nez*, of which second element is more prob. ON. *nes* than F. *nez*. See *nose*.

-ness. AS. *-nes(s)*, *-nis(s)*; cf. Du. Ger. *-nis*, Goth. *-nassus*, in which *-n-* is orig. part of stem, real Teut. suffix being *-assus* from weak verbs in *-atjan*. Much used in mod. jocular formations, e.g. *Why this thusness?*

nest. AS. *nest*; cf. Du. Ger. *nest*; cogn. with L. *nidus*, Sanskrit *nīḍa*, Ir. *nead*, Welsh *nyth*. Supposed to be ult. cogn. with *nether* and *sit*. Hence *nestle*, to snuggle into a nest.

Nestor. G. Νέστωρ, aged and wise Homeric hero.

Nestorian [*theol.*]. Adherent of *Nestorius*, patriarch of Constantinople (5 cent.).

net¹. Noun. AS. *nett*. Com. Teut.; cf. Du. *net*, Ger. *netz*, ON. *net*, Goth. *nati*; ? cogn. with L. *nassa*, wicker net.

net². Adj. F., clean, clear, neat (q.v.). *NED.* connects with this the verb to *net* (e.g. *a good round sum*), but this has prob. been affected by *net¹* (cf. *to bag*, *to hook*, and other sporting metaphors).

nether. AS. *nither* (adv.), whence *neothera* (adj.). Com. Teut.; cf. Du. *neder*, Ger. *nieder*, ON. *nithr*, from OTeut. *ni-*, downwards, with compar. suffix; cf. Sanskrit *nitarām*. Now almost replaced, exc. poet., by *lower*, but surviving in place-names and in jocular *nether man* (*garments*, etc.). Cf. also *Netherlands*.

A copious Englisg and Netherduytch Dictionarie, by Henry Hexham, 1660.

nettle. AS. *netele*; cf. Du. *netel*, Ger. *nessel*. Dim. of earlier form which appears in OHG. *nazza*. To *nettle*, vex, was orig. to beat or sting with nettles.

I am whipt and scourg'd with rods,
Nettled, and stung with pismires (1 *Hen. IV*, i. 3).

neume, neuma [*mus.*]. Group of notes in plainsong sung on single syllable. MedL. *neuma*, G. πνεῦμα, breath.

neuralgia. From G. νεῦρον, nerve, ἄλγος, pain. Cf. *neurasthenia*, G. ἀσθένεια, weakness; *neuropath*, *neurotic*, etc., a dismal list of neologisms. See *nerve*.

Neurope [*philately*]. For *New Europe*.

There is keen competition to obtain "Neurope" stamps—as the issues of the new states are called (*Daily Chron.* Nov. 13, 1919).

neuter. F. *neutre* or L. *neuter*, for *ne*, not, *uter*, either; cf. formation of *neither*. Hence *neutral*, "exempted or excluded from the sphere of warlike operations" (*NED.*), a comforting definition for Belgians.

névé [*Alp.*]. Granular snow not yet absorbed by glacier. Alpine F. dial., VL. **nivatum*, from *nix*, *niv-*, snow.

never. AS. *næfre*, for *ne æfre*, not ever. In early use emphatic for *not*, as still in *never a word*, *never mind*. *Never so*, as in *Ps.* lviii. 5, is practically equivalent to its app. opposite *ever so*, which has replaced it from 17 cent. For *nevertheless*, orig. written in three words, see earlier *nathless*. *Well, I never* understands *heard of such a thing*. The *Never Never Land*, North Queensland, is dubiously explained (1857) as corrupt. of native name for unoccupied land.

new. AS. *nīwe*. Aryan; cf. Du. *nieuw*, Ger. *neu*, ON. *nȳr*, Goth. *niujis*, L. *novus*, G. νέος, Sanskrit *nava*, Pers. *nŭ*, Gael. Ir. *nuadh*, Welsh *newydd* (cf. name *Newth*);

cogn. with *now*. Pl. noun *news* was coined in 14 cent. after F. *nouvelles* and used by Wyc. to render L. *nova*. *Newspaper* (with *newsletter* in same sense) is recorded for 17 cent., but the thing is much older, for the *Paston Letters* contain an example. *Newsmonger* is in Shaks. (1 *Hen. IV*, iii. 2). *Newfangled* is for earlier *newfangle*, from stem *fang-*, of AS. *fōn*, to take (cf. Ger. *fangen*), orig. sense being ready to grasp at new things. For suffix cf. *nimble*. *New-Englander* is US. citizen from one of the six first States, named (1616) by Capt. John Smith; cf. *New York* (orig. *New Amsterdam*), from *Duke of York* (James II), *New Zealand*, named by Du. navigators from *Zeeland*, lit. sea-land.

So newefangel been they of hire mete
And loven novelrie of propre kynde
(Chauc. F. 618).

newel [*arch.*]. Central pillar of spiral stair. OF. *noiel*, *nouel*, dim. from L. *nux*, *nuc-*, nut. Cf. *noyau*.

newfangled. See *new*.

newfoundland. Dog from *Newfoundland*; cf. synon. F. *terre-neuve*.

Wylde catts and popyngays of the newfound island (*Privy Purse of Hen. VII*, 1505).

If they will take their course toward the Occident, they shall goe in the backe side of the new found land, which of late was discovered by your Graces subjects (Robert Thorne, to Hen. VIII, 1527).

Newgate. Prison, demolished in early 20 cent., near one of the old gates of London. Hence *Newgate Calendar*, first issued in 1773, *Newgate fringe*, *frill*, fringe of beard worn under chin.

Two and two, Newgate fashion (1 *Hen. IV*, iii. 3).

newmarket. Coat of sporting type, as worn at *Newmarket*. Cf. *melton*.

newt. For *an ewt*, which became *a newt*; cf. *nickname*. *Ewt* is for *evet*, *eft*, AS. *efete*.

nevte or *evte, wyrme*: lacertus (*Prompt. Parv.*).

next. AS. *nīehst*, superl. of *nēah*, nigh; cf. Du. *naast*, Ger. *nächst*, ON. *næstr*. Many senses, e.g. *the next way*, *next relative*, now usu. replaced by *nearest*.

It is next kin to an impossibility
(Roberts, *Voyages*, 1726).

nib¹. Of pen. Later form of *neb* (q.v.). Orig. (c. 1600) of sharpened point of quill. Hence also cocoa *nibs*.

nib² [*slang*]. Gentleman. App. thinned form of *nob*, whence also obs. *nab*. Cf. *bilk*. So also for jocular *his nibs*, his lordship, we find earlier *his nabs*.

nibble. Frequent. of *nip* (q.v.); cf. Du. *knibbelen*.

niblick. Recorded 1862. Origin unknown. As golf is prob. of Du. origin, I suggest Du. *kneppelig*, from *kneppel, knuppel*, "a club, trunchion" (Sewel). Cf. Ger. *knebel*, "a knubble or truncheon, a short club" (Ludw.).

nice. OF., foolish, weak, simple, etc., L. *nescius*, ignorant; cf. It. *nescio*, "a foole, an idiot, a natural, a dolt" (Flor.), Sp. *necio*. Earliest sense, foolish, suggests influence of F. *niais*, for which see *eyas*, while some later senses show confusion with *nesh*. The sense-development has been extraordinary, even for an adj. (cf. *quaint*), and the interpretation of 16-17 cent. examples is often dubious. Current sense (from 18 cent.) has perh. been evolved from that of fastidious, as in *not to be too nice about...*, to which is allied the idea of delicate, as in *a nice point (distinction)* and *to a nicety*. In *nice and* it is an adv., now felt as mere intens., e.g. *we must start nice and early*, which orig. meant punctually and early.

Nicene. Of *Nicaea* in Bithynia, where eccl. council (325) dealt with *Arian* (q.v.) controversy and produced the *Nicene Creed*.

niche. F., It. *nicchia*, ? from *nicchio*, mussel shell, L. *mitulus*. For change of init. cf. F. *nèfle*, medlar, It. *nespola*, L. *mespilum*. ? Or rather from VL. **nidiculare*, to nestle; cf. F. *nicher*, VL. **nidicare*.

nicchio: the shell of any shellfish, a nooke or corner. Also such little cubboards in churches as they put images in (Flor.).

nick. App. cogn. with *nock* (q.v.), of which it may in some senses be a thinned form.

God have mercy for that good dice, yet that came i' th' nick (*Misogonus*, ii. 4, c. 1550).

Nick, Old. From 17 cent. For *Nicholas*. The choice of the name may have been suggested by Ger. *Nickel*, goblin, etc. (v.i.).

nickel. Sw. abbrev. of Ger. *kupfernickel*, copper nickel, in which the second element is Ger. *Nickel*, goblin, pet-form of *Niklaus*, a name given to the deceptive ore (1751) by the Sw. mineralogist Cronstedt. Cf. *cobalt*.

nicknack. For *knick-knack*.

nickname. For *eke-name* (see *eke*), an *eke-*

name having become *a neke-name*. Cf. ON. *aukanafn* and see *newt*.

As moche than he ys to blame
That geveth a man a vyle ekename
              (*Handlyng Synne*, l. 1531).

neekname, or eke name: agnomen (*Prompt. Parv.*).

nicolo. Kind of onyx. It., for **onicolo*, dim. from L. *onyx*.

nicotine. F., from *Jacques Nicot*, F. ambassador at Lisbon, who sent (c. 1560) some tobacco plants to Catherine de Médicis. His name is a dim. of *Nicolas*.

nictitate. From MedL. *nictitare*, frequent. of *nictare*, to wink.

niddering [*pseudo-archaic*]. Taken by Scott (*Ivanhoe*, ch. xliii.) from an error in early printed edition of William of Malmesbury. Correct form is *nithing*, ON. *nithingr*, from *nith*, envy, cogn. with Ger. *neid*. This was obs. from c. 1300, but has been revived by hist. writers.

nide. Brood or nest of pheasants. F. *nid* or L. *nidus*.

nidification. From L. *nidificare*, to build a nest, *nidus*.

nid-nod. Redupl. on *nod*.

niece. F. *nièce*, VL. *neptia*, for *neptis*; cogn. with AS. *nift*, Du. *nicht*, Ger. *nichte*, etc. See *nephew*, with which it may also be compared for vagueness of meaning.

niello. Black alloy in metal-work. It., L. *nigellus*, dim. of *niger*, black.

niessen. See *nissen*.

Nietzscheism. Doctrine (superman, blond beast, etc.) of *Friedrich Nietzsche* (†1900).

Mr Weekley has also adopted the foolish idea that Nietzsche gave Germany war-madness; if he had taken the trouble to read Nietzsche and to acquaint himself with the limited spread of Nietzscheism in Germany, he would not have fallen into this popular error (*To-day*, Nov. 11, 1916).

nigella. Plant. L., from *niger*, black. Cf. F. *nielle*, "the herb nigella" (Cotg.).

niggard. First in Chauc., for earlier *nig*, *nigon*, which are app. of Scand. origin; cf. Norw. dial. *gnikka, gnigga*, to be stingy, Ger. *knicker*, "one that would shave an egg or flea a louse for covetousness" (Ludw.). Ground-idea is app. that of rubbing, squeezing.

nigger. Earlier *neger*, F. *nègre*, Sp. *negro*, L. *niger, nigr-*, black.

niggle. Norw. dial. *nigla, nugla*, cogn. with *niggard*.

nigh. Orig. adv. AS. *nēah*. Com. Teut.; cf. Du. *na*, Ger. *nah, nach*, ON. *nā-* in compds.

(see *neighbour*), Goth. *nēhwa*. Hence compar. *near*, superl. *next*.

night. AS. *niht*. Aryan; cf. Du. Ger. *nacht*, ON. *nōtt*, Goth. *nahts*, L. *nox, noct-*, G. νύξ, νυκτ-, Sanskrit *nakta*, OIr. *nocht*. The fact that the Aryans have a common name for night, but not for day (q.v.), is due to the fact that they reckoned by nights (v.i.). Of this we have a trace in *fortnight, sennight*, as in Ger. *Weihnachten*, Christmas. In *nightingale*, the *-n-* is intrusive. The earlier form is *nightegale*, AS. *nihtegale*, from genitive of *niht* and *gale*, singer, from *galan*, to sing, cogn. with *yell*; cf. Ger. *nachtigall*. The *nightjar* is named from the whirring, "jarring," sound made by the male when the female is brooding. The second element of *nightmare* is an obs. name for demon, AS. *mare*, cogn. with obs. Du. *mare*, Ger. dial. *mahr*, ON. *mara*, Pol. *mora*. This is also the second element of F. *cauchemar*, nightmare, from OF. *caucher*, to trample (cf. *incubus, hagridden*). In Du. *nachtmerrie* we have the same popular association as in E. With *nightshade*, AS. *nihtscada*, cf. Du. *nachtschaduwe*, Ger. *nachtschatten*, the second element perh. referring to narcotic properties.

Spatia omnis temporis non numero dierum sed noctium finiunt (Caesar, *De Bello Gallico*, vi. 18).

Nec dierum numerum, ut nos, sed noctium computant. Sic constituunt, sic condicunt: nox ducere diem videtur (Tacitus, *Germania*, xi. 2).

nigrescent. From pres. part. of L. *nigrescere*, to become black, *niger*.

nihilism. From L. *nihil*, nothing, from *ne* and *hilum*, ? the black speck in a bean. In most Europ. langs., but pol. sense chiefly developed in Russ. Turgenev uses *nihilist* in *Fathers and Sons*.

nilgai. See *nylghau*.

nil. L., contr. of *nihil*, nothing. See *nihilism*.

nill. Verb. AS. **nyllan*, neg. of *will*. Now only in *willy-nilly*, will he, nill he; cf. L. *nolens-volens*.

Nil we, wil we, we sal mete (*Cursor Mundi*).

nilometer. Altered on *-meter* from G. Νειλο-μέτριον, Nile measure.

nimble. Formed with agent. suffix *-el* from AS. *niman*, to take, a Com. Teut. verb (cf. obs. Du. *nemen*, Ger. *nehmen*, ON. *nema*, Goth. *niman*) which was replaced in E. by *take* (q.v.), but survived till 17 cent., esp. in slang. See *numb*. Orig. sense was quick

at grasping; hence, alert, active, etc., the sense of cogn. Norw. Dan. *nem*. For intrusive *-b-* cf. *thimble*.

capax, qui multum capit: andgetul, numul, gripul
(*Voc.*).

nimbus. L., cloud, usu. poet. and used of "a clowde that gods discended in" (Coop.), ? due to mixture of *imber*, rain, and *nebula*, cloud.

nimiety. Late L. *nimietas*, from *nimis*, too much.

There's a nimiety—a too-muchness—in all Germans
(Coleridge).

niminy-piminy. Imit. of mincing utterance; perh. partly suggested by *namby-pamby* (q.v.). See *jiminy*.

Nimrod. Now only of a "mighty hunter before the Lord," but earlier (16 cent.) of a "mighty one in the earth" (*Gen.* x. 8–9).

nincompoop. Earlier (17 cent.) *nickumpoop*. First element may be from *Nicodemus*, used in F. for a fool (cf. *noddy*), or from *Nicholas*. With second cf. Du. *poep*, fool, slang E. *poop*, duffer, to *poop*, cheat. Hence *nincompoop* appears to be formed like *tomfool*. *Poopnoddy* is found in same sense.

nine. AS. *nigon*. Aryan; cf. Du. *negen*, Ger. *neun*, ON. *nīu*, Goth. *niun*, L. *novem*, G. ἐννέα, Sanskrit *navan*, Pers. *nuh*, OIr. *noí-n*. *Up to the nines* is for earlier *to the nine(s)*, used by Burns in sense of perfectly, *to a T*. The origin of the phrase is obscure, but the *Book of St Albans*, in the sections on blasonry, lays great stress on the *nines* in which all perfect things (orders of angels, virtues, articles of chivalry, differences of coat armour, etc.) occur. Cf. earlier *to the ninth* (degree), with idea of perfection. The *nine points of the law* which constitute possession were earlier (17 cent.) *eleven*. As *neat* (*grand, right*) *as ninepence* is 19 cent. *Ninepins* is 16 cent.

Wonder last but nine night nevere in toune
(Chauc. *Troilus*, iv. 588).

No man passeth by, whatsoever he be,
But those crows beknave him to the ninth degree
(Heywood, *Epigrams*, 1562).

ninny. Pet-form of name *Innocent*, with allusion to fig. sense of adj. from which it comes. Cf. Walloon *inochain, ninoche*, in same sense, and, for degeneration of sense, *silly, natural*, F. *benêt, crétin*.

Innocent: Innocent, Ninny (a proper name for a man) (Cotg.).

Niobe. Emblem of grief. G. Νιόβη, daughter of Tantalus, changed into stone while weeping for her children.

nip. Earlier also *gnip*, *knip*; cf. Ger. *kneifen*, *kneipen* (from LG.), also Sw. *knipa*, Dan. *knibe*, to pinch. A *nip* (of gin) is short for *nipperkin*, a small measure, app. of Du. origin; cf. Du. Ger. *nippen*, to sip, also Ger. *kneipe*, tavern, *kneipen*, to booze. *Nipperkin* occurs in the transl. of Schouten in Purch. Perh. orig. idea is as in Ger. *schnaps* (q.v.), for which *knips* is used in dial. *Nipper*, small boy, was orig. a thief or pickpocket, one who "pinched" other people's property. All these words belong to a Teut. root containing the idea of pinching.

And divers dying give good gifts,
But their executors nip them
(*Coblers Prophesie*, 1594).

nypper: a cut-purse: so called by one Wotton, who in the year 1585 kept an academy for the education and perfection of pickpockets and cut-purses.... He that could take out a counter, without noise of any of the bells, was adjudged a judicial nypper (Grose).

nipple. Earlier *neble* (Palsg.). App. dim. of *neb*.

nirvana. Buddhist name for extinction of individual and absorption into the divine. Sanskrit *nirvāna*, blowing out, extinction, from *vā*, to blow.

nisi [*leg.*]. L., unless, lit. if not (other cause, etc. is shown). Cf. *nisi prius* (*justitiarii ad assisas capiendas venerint*).

nissen [*neol.*]. Army hut. ? From inventor's name.

In a nissen hut or a pill-box
(*Punch*, Apr. 17, 1918).

nit. Egg of louse. AS. *hnitu*. Com. Teut.; cf. Du. *neet*, Ger. *niss*, ON. *gnit*; cogn. with G. κονίς, κονιδ-, Czech *knida*, Russ. *gnida*, Welsh *nedd*.

nithing [*obs.*]. See *niddering*.

nitid. L. *nitidus*, from *nitēre*, to shine.

nitre. F., L. *nitrum*, G. νίτρον; prob. of Oriental origin; cf. Heb. *nether*, rendered νίτρον by LXX. and *nitrum* in *Vulg.* (*Jer.* ii. 22). Hence *nitrogen*, generating nitre (cf. *oxygen*, *hydrogen*).

nix [*slang*]. Colloq. Du. & Ger., for *nichts*, nothing.

Nizam. Urdu *nizām*, Arab. *nidam*, order, arrangement. As title of ruler of Hyderabad it is short for *nizām-al-mulk*, governor of the empire. Also adopted in Turk. as name for "regular" troops.

no. The adj., as in *nobody*, *no room*, is for earlier *none* (q.v.), the *-n* being orig.

dropped before consonant and kept before vowel (e.g. *none other gods*, *of none effect*). Here belongs *whether or no*, earlier *or non*, a noun being understood. The adv. represents ME. *nō*, for *ne ō*, southern form of *nā*, for *ne ā*, not ever (see *ay*, *nay*). In ME. it is a stronger negation than *nay*, as *yes* is a stronger affirmation than *yea*. The neg. *ne* is Aryan.

n°. Abbrev. of It. *numero* (see *number*).

Noachian. Of Noah. *Noah's ark*, in toy sense, is first quoted by *NED.* from *Cricket on the Hearth*.

nob. Head, etc. Later spelling of *knob*. In sense of swell, "tuft," it is the same word, the suggestion that it is short for *nobleman* being contradicted by Sc. *nab*, in same sense, earlier than our *nob*. So also Sc. has *knabbie*, for *nobby*, smart, etc.

nobble [*slang*]. To "get at" (e.g. a race-horse, the electorate, etc.). App. a mod. frequent. of *nab*.

Nobel prize. Established by will of *Alfred Nobel*. See *dynamite*.

noble. F., L. *nobilis*, from root (*g*)*nosc*-, to know; cf. *notable*. The coin called a *noble* was first minted temp. Ed. III. Among arts esp. applied to fencing and boxing.

Richard Tarlton, master of the noble syence of deffence (*NED.* c. 1588).

nock. Orig. (14 cent.) horn end of a longbow, also *notch* of an arrow. Perh. ident. with Du. *nok*, Ger. *nock*, tip, point. But the Rom. langs. use derivatives of L. *nux*, nut, both for the *nock* of the longbow and the *notch* of the cross-bow; and in the latter sense we find also Du. *noot*, Ger. *nusz*, and even E. *nut*. Unsolved.

nocturnal. Late L. *nocturnalis*, from *nocturnus*, from *nox*, *noct*-, night.

nod. Prob. an E. word, but not found before Chauc. Of obscure origin. With sense of dozing, from nodding of the head which accompanies sleepiness, cf. F. *niquet*, midday nap, from *niquer*, to nod, Ger. *nicken*. The *land of Nod* is a punning allusion to *Gen.* iv. 16.

Indignor, quandoque bonus dormitat Homerus
(Hor. *De Art. Poet.* 359).

noddle. First in late ME., and not orig. jocular (cf. *pate*). ? Evolved from earlier *noll*, AS. *hnoll*, crown of the head, by analogy with such pairs of words as *pool*, *puddle*.

nodyl, or *nodle* of the *heed*, or *nolle*: occiput
(*Prompt. Parv.*).

noddy [*archaic*]. Simpleton. ? Pet-form of *Nicodemus*. I have not found this name in E. in required sense, but *nicodème* is F. for a fool, prob. a reminiscence of a part played in some medieval mystery. Cf. *nincompoop*, and see *booby*.

Do you like the name of Nicodemus? Think it over. Nick or Noddy (*Mutual Friend*, ch. v.).

node. L. *nodus*, knot. Also dim. *nodule*.

noetic. Of the mind. G. νοητικός, from νόησις, from νοεῖν, to perceive. Cf. *nous*.

nog[1]. Peg, stump, snag, etc. Cf. ME. *knag*, in same sense.

nog[2]. Strong ale. An EAngl. word of unknown origin. ? Back-formation from *noggin*.

noggin. Small drinking vessel or measure. Analogy of *peg* suggests connection with *nog*[1]. Cf. *piggin*.

Towe pegenes...towe noogenes (*Manch. Inventory*, 1605, in *Chetham Misc.* 1915, p. 10).

noil. Short refuse wool-combings. A very familiar word in Bradford. ? An OF. dim. of *nœud*, knot, L. *nodus*.

noise. F., now only in *chercher noise*, to pick a quarrel. Of doubtful origin. L. *nausea* fits the form but hardly the sense.

noisette. Rose. First raised in America by a *Mr Noisette*.

noisome. From obs. *noy* for *annoy* (q.v.). Now usu. of smells, but orig. in wider sense of harmful.

The sword, and the famine, and the noisome [*Vulg.* malus] beast (*Ezek.* xiv. 21).

nolens volens. L., cf. *willy-nilly*.

noli me tangere. L., touch me not (*Vulg. John*, xx. 17).

nolle prosequi [*leg.*]. L., to be unwilling to pursue. Of a suit abandoned by plaintiff or prosecutor.

nomad. L., G. νομάς, νομάδ-, from νέμειν, to pasture.

no-man's-land. In early use esp. a piece of waste ground outside north wall of London, used for executions. Now esp. land between opposing trenches.

Quaedam domina nomine Juliana...fuit combusta apud Nonemanneslond extra Londonias
(*NED.* 1320).

nom de plume. Used in E. for F. *nom de guerre*, pseudonym, lit. war-name.

nomenclator. L., a steward or official who announced visitors to his master, and esp. an election helper who prompted the candidate for office as to the names and peculiarities of those whom he was trying to humbug. From *nomen*, name, *calare*, to proclaim.

nominal. L. *nominalis*, from *nomen*, *nomin-*, name. Hence *nominalism*, system of philosophy opposed to realism. Cf. *nominative*, the naming case. *Nominee* is badly formed from *nominate* by analogy with *payee*, *lessee*, etc.

nomology. Science of law or rule, G. νόμος.

-nomy. G. -νομία, from νόμος, law.

non. L., not, in some L. phrases, e.g. *non possumus*, we cannot, *non sequitur*, it does not follow, *non est* (*inventus*), he is not (found), *non compos* (*mentis*), not master (of one's mind). Also very common as prefix, in which case it often represents F. *non*, from L. With L. *non*, for *ne-unum, cf. Ger. *nein*, no, for *ne-ein, not one.

nonage. OF. *non age*, state of being under age.

nonagenarian. From L. *nonagenarius*, from *nonageni*, ninety each.

nonagon. Irreg. formation, after *pentagon*, etc., from L. *nonus*, ninth. Cf. *nonary*, L. *nonarius*.

nonce. In ME. *for the nanes*, *nones*, where *the nanes* is for earlier *then anes*, the once (q.v.), *then* being for AS. dat. *thām*. Cf. *newt*, *nickname*, and see *once*.

A cook they hadde with hem for the nones,
To boille the chiknes with the marybones
(Chauc. A. 379).

nonchalant. F., pres. part. of *nonchaloir*, not to care, from L. *non* and *calēre*, to be hot.

non-com. For *non-commissioned officer*. Cf. F. *sous-off(icier)*.

nonconformist. Orig. (early 17 cent.) clergyman of Church of England refusing to conform with certain ceremonies. After Act of Uniformity (1662) applied to those who were ejected from their livings. The *nonconformist conscience* first blossomed (c. 1890) in connection with Parnell's amours.

nondescript. Coined (17 cent.) in scient. sense of not hitherto described.

none. AS. *nān*, for *ne ān*, not one. As adj. reduced to *no*, exc. in a few archaic phrases before vowel (*none other*, *of none effect*). In *none the better* (*worse*, *less*, etc.), which is found from c. 1800, it appears to be a vague imit. of F. *n'en* in such sentences as *il n'en est pas moins vrai que...*, it is none the less true that....

nonentity. Coined (17 cent.) on *entity* (q.v.).

nones [*eccl.*]. F., L. *nonae*, ninth day before Ides, from *nonus*, ninth. Also Church service at ninth hour, about 3 p.m. See *noon*.

nonesuch. For *none such*. Now usu. *nonsuch*.

> Therefore did Plato from his None-Such banish Base poetasters (Sylv. *Urania*).

nonjuror [*hist.*]. Clergyman deprived of benefice for refusing to take oath of allegiance to William and Mary (1689). See *jury*.

nonpareil. F., for *non pareil*, VL. **pariculus*, dim. of *par*, equal.

nonplus. L. *non plus*, not more. From scholastic disputation.

> *il y perdit son latin*: he was there gravelled, plunged, or at a Non plus (Cotg.).

non plus ultra. For *ne plus ultra*.

nonsense. Cf. F. *non-sens*, not sense.

nonsuch. See *nonesuch*.

nonsuit. Orig. cessation of suit by withdrawal of plaintiff (cf. *nolle prosequi*), now by action of judge.

noodle. From 18 cent. ? Variation on *noddy*.

nook. Orig. corner. Chiefly north. & Sc. Cf. Norw. dial. *nok*, hook, bent figure, ? cogn. with *neck*.

noon. AS. *nōn*, L. *nona* (sc. *hora*), orig. about 3 p.m., but early shifted back to midday. Also in other Teut. langs., and, in sense of Church service, in Rom. langs. (see *nones*).

noose. App. from pl. of OF. *no, nou* (*nœud*), knot, L. *nodus*.

nopal. Sp., Mex. *nopalli*, cactus.

nor. Contr. of ME. *nother* (see *neither*). Cf. *o'er, e'er*, etc.

nordenfelt. Obs. machine-gun. From name (*Nordenfeld*) of Sw. inventor. Cf. *gatling, maxim*.

Nordic [*ethn.*]. ModL. *Nordicus*, of the north.

Norfolk. AS. *Northfolc*. Fuller records the fact that the inhabitants are called "dumplings" from their favourite dish. *Norfolk Howard*, bug, dates from an advertisement in the *Times* (June 26, 1862) announcing assumption of this name by one *Joshua Bug*. *Norfolk jacket* is late 19 cent.

normal. L. *normalis*, from *norma*, carpenter's square. *Normal school* (*college*) is after F. *école normale*, a Republican foundation (1794).

Norman. Orig. in pl., OF. *Normanz*, pl. of *Normand*, Teut. *north man*. Application to a style of architecture, called *roman* in F., is not much earlier than 1800. *Norman*, F. ·dial. of Normandy, should be distinguished from *Anglo-Norman*, its further development in this country.

norn. One of three Fates in Scand. myth. ON. *norn*, app. cogn. with Sw. dial. *norna, nyrna*, to warn secretly (cf. hist. of *fate*). First E. occurrence in Bishop Percy (18 cent.).

Norroy. Third King of Arms, whose jurisdiction is north of the Trent. AF. *nor-roy, -rey*, north king.

Norse. Du. *noorsch*, for *noordsch*, from *noord*, north. *Old Norse* is chiefly represented by Old Icelandic, which preserves the most archaic form of the Scand. langs. Owing to isolation, ModIcelandic has not greatly changed from it. *Norseman* appears to be due to Scott.

north. AS. *north*. Com. Teut.; cf. Du. *noord*, Ger. *nord*, ON. *northr*. Also borrowed, with other points of compass, by Rom. langs., e.g. F. *nord*, It. Sp. *norte*.

> The voiage to the North West...by Martyn Furbusher (*Privy Council Acts*, 1577).

Northumbrian [*ling.*]. AS. dial. spoken *north* of the *Humber*.

Norwegian. Earlier *Norvegian* (from MedL. *Norvegia*), altered on *Norway*, lit. north way, a name from the viking period; cf. ON. *suthrvegar*, Germany, *austrvegr*, the Baltic countries.

nose. AS. *nosu*, cogn. with Du. *neus*. The more usual Teut. form is represented by AS. *nasu*; cf. Du. *nase*, Ger. *nase*, ON. *nōs*, L. *nasus*, Sanskrit *nās* (dual), nostrils. To *pay through the nose* seems to be a playful variation on to *bleed*, in money sense, in which the metaphor was orig. surgical. *Nosegay* is from obs. *gay*, bright object, pretty ornament, a substantival use of adj. *gay*.

> And (as it chaunst) the selfe same time she was a sorting gayes
> To make a poisie (Golding's *Ovid*, 1565).
> He may be led by the nose as quietly as the tamest beare in the Garden
> (Glapthorne, *Hollander*, i. 1, 1640).
> The king is pleased enough with her; which, I fear, will put Madam Castlemaine's nose out of joynt (Pepys, May 31, 1662).
> *he cut off his nose to be revenged of his face*: said of one who, to be revenged on his neighbour, has materially injured himself (Grose).

nosology. Science of disease, G. νόσος.

nostalgia. Home-sickness. From G. νόστος, return home, ἄλγος, pain. Cf. *neuralgia*.

nostoc [*bot.*]. Genus of algae. Name invented by Paracelsus.

Nostradamus. Soothsayer. Latinized name of *Michel de Nostredame*, F. physician and prophet (†1566).

> Nostra damus, cum falsa damus, nam fallere nostrum est;
> Et cum falsa damus, nil nisi nostra damus
> (Jodelle).

nostril. AS. *nosthӯrl*, nose-hole. Cf. *thrill* and dial. *thirl*, to pierce.

> His nosethirles blake were and wyde
> (Chauc. A. 557).

nostrum. L., neut. of *noster*, our (unfailing remedy). From the patter of the quack doctor.

not. Unstressed form of *naught*, *nought*. See *aught*.

notable. F., L. *notabilis*, from *notare*, to note. For sense of prominent man (F. hist.) cf. *noble*.

notary. F. *notaire*, L. *notarius*, clerk, secretary, from *notare*, to note. Cf. *notation*, L. *notatio-n-*.

notch. App. for **otch*, F. *hoche*, earlier *oche*, *osche*, Prov. *osca*, whence ME. *ochen*, to cut, dent. The *n-* may be the indef. art., as in *newt*, *nickname*, or may be due to association with *nock*. Formerly used of a run at cricket, "scored" on a stick, e.g. at Muggleton (see *muff*).

> oche: a nick, nock, or notch; the cut of a tally
> (Cotg.).

note. F., L. *nota*, mark, ? cogn. with *nomen*, name. Earliest sense is mus., as in to *change one's note*. Very common in 16–17 cents. for characteristic, distinctive quality, and now much overworked (with *atmosphere*, *technique*, etc.) in intellectual jargon. Sense of small document arises from that of memorandum jotted down briefly.

nothing. Orig. written as two words. With *nothingarian* cf. *anythingarian*.

notice. F., L. *notitia*, from *notus*, from (g)*noscere*, to know. Cf. *notify*, F. *notifier*, L. *notificare*.

notion. L. *notio-n-* (v.s.). Esp. common in neg. construction with *of*. US. sense of miscellaneous articles springs from that of clever invention.

> Machines for flying in the air and other wonderful notions (Evelyn).

notorious. From MedL. *notorius*, from *notus*, known (v.s.), cf. F. *notoire*, It. Sp. *notorio*.

notwithstanding. From *not* and *withstand*, to oppose, the word now app. governed by the prep. being really the subject of the verb, e.g. *notwithstanding this* is "this not

opposing." Cf. archaic F. *nonobstant*, L. *non obstante* (abl. absolute).

> Not that withstanding she ansuered in this maner e
> (*NED*. c. 1500).

nougat. F., Prov., VL. **nucatum*, from *nux*, *nuc-*, nut; cf. Sp. Port. *nogada*.

nought. AS. *nōwiht*, var. of *nāwiht*. Now usu. represented by *naught*, *not*. See *aught*.

noumenon. G. νοούμενον, neut. of pres. part. pass. of νοεῖν, to apprehend. Introduced by Kant in contrast to *phenomenon*.

noun. AF. form of OF. *non* (*nom*), L. *nomen*, name (q.v.).

nourish. F. *nourrir*, *nourriss-*, L. *nutrire*, to feed. See *nurse*. For fig. senses cf. *cherish*, *foster*.

nous. G. νοῦς, mind. Curiously common in dial.

novel. OF. (*nouveau*), L. *novellus*, dim. of *novus*, new. In sense of fiction orig. applied to short tales, F. *nouvelles*, such as those of Boccaccio, and in 17–18 cents. still contrasted with the *romance*, or long novel.

> A novel is a kind of abbreviation of a romance
> (Lord Chesterfield).

November. L. *november* or *novembris* (sc. *mensis*), from *novem*, nine. Replaced native *blōt-mōnath*, sacrificial (blood) month.

novenary. L. *novenarius*, from *novem*, nine.

novercal. L. *novercalis*, of a step-mother, *noverca*, ? from *novus*, new.

novice. F., L. *novitius*, from *novus*, new. Orig. of probationer in rel. order.

now. AS. *nū*. Aryan; cf. Du. OHG. ON. Goth. Sanskrit *nu*, G. νῦν, L. *nunc*. Use of *now* (*then*) to introduce command goes back to AS. For *nowadays* see *a-*.

> Heugh Beamond is dead; wherffor I wolde ye had hys roome nowe or never (*Paston Let*. iii. 137).

Nowel [*archaic*]. F. *Noël*, Christmas, L. *natalis* (sc. *dies*); cf. It. *natale*, Sp. Port. *natal*, whence *Natal* (SAfr.), discovered on Christmas Day.

nowhere. See *no*, *where*, and cf. obs. *no whither* (2 *Kings*, v. 25).

noxious. From L. *noxius*, from *noxa*, harm, from *nocēre*, to hurt.

noyade [*hist*.]. Wholesale drowning of royalists by Carrier at Nantes (1794). F., from *noyer*, to drown, L. *necare*, to kill. For restriction of sense cf. E. *starve*.

noyau. Liqueur. F., kernel, OF. *noial*, *noiel*, dim. of *noix*, L. *nux*, *nuc-*, nut; cf. Prov. *nugalh*, corresponding to Late L. *nucalis*.

nozzle. Dim. of *nose*.

nuance. F., from *nuer*, to shade, from *nue*, cloud, VL. *nuba for *nubes*.

nub, nubble, nubbly. Vars. of *knob*, etc. Cf. Ger. *knubbe*, knot on a tree.

nubile. F., L. *nubilis*, marriageable, from *nubere*, to marry.

nuchal [*anat.*]. Of the nape. From MedL. *nucha*, Arab. *nukhā*, spinal marrow, whence It. Sp. *nuca*, F. *nuque*, nape.

nucleus. L., kernel, from *nux*, *nuc-*, nut.

nude. L. *nudus*. Orig. (16 cent.) as law term, later adopted as art euph. for naked.

nudge. Cf. Norw. dial. *nugga*, to push. Perh. cogn. with *knock*.

nugatory. L. *nugatorius*, from *nugari*, to trifle.

nuggar. Large boat on Upper Nile. Native name.

nugget. From Austral. gold-fields (c. 1850). App. from E. dial. *nug*, lump, block, ? var. of *nog*[1]. Not connected with *niggot*, a misprint for *ingot* in North's *Plutarch*.

nuisance. OF., from *nuire*, *nuis-*, to harm, VL. *nocere for *nocēre*, cogn. with *necare*, to kill. Current sense perh. affected by obs. *noyance*, aphet. for *annoyance*.

Keepe us from his [Satan's] nusance (Hoccleve).

My book inveighing against the nuisance of the smoke of London (Evelyn, 1661).

null. F. *nul*, L. *nullus*, for *ne ullus*, not any. Orig. leg., as in *null and void*. Cf. *annul*, *nullify*, *nullifidian*, of no faith.

nullah [*Anglo-Ind.*]. Hind. *nālā*, watercourse, ravine.

numb. AS. *numen*, p.p. of *niman*, to take (see *nimble*); cf. Norw. *nummen*, numb, Ger. *benommen*, stunned. See also the earlier *benumb*, from which *numb* is usu. a back-formation. Hence *num(b)skull*.

nommyn, or takyn with the palsy: paraliticus
(*Prompt. Parv.*).

number. F. *nombre*, L. *numerus*, cogn. with G. νόμος, law, νέμειν, to distribute. In all Rom. & Teut. langs., e.g. Du. *nommer*, Ger. *nummer*. In sense of order F. uses *numéro*, from It., whence our abbreviation *No. Number one*, oneself, is recorded c. 1700. Mus. sense (*mournful numbers*) is from 16 cent. The *Book of Numbers* contains a census of the Israelites.

numbles [*archaic*]. See *humble-pie*.

numdah [*Anglo-Ind.*]. See *numnah*.

numeral. Late L. *numeralis*, from *numerus*, number. Cf. *numerate*, *numerical*. *numerous*.

numismatic. F. *numismatique*, from L. *numisma*, *nomisma*, G. νόμισμα, current coin, from νομίζειν, to have in use, from νόμος, law, usage, from νέμειν, to distribute.

nummary. L. *nummarius*, from *nummus*, coin, cogn. with *numerus*, number.

nummulite [*zool.*]. Disk-shaped fossil. From L. *nummulus*, small coin (v.s.).

numnah. Horsecloth, pad under saddle. Var. of *numdah* (Anglo-Ind.), Urdu *namdā*, from Pers. *namad*, carpet, rug.

numskull. See *numb*.

nun. AS. *nunne*, Church L. *nonna*, fem. of *nonnus*, monk. These are orig. pet-terms for elderly people and belong to the baby lang. of remote antiquity; cf. It. *nonno*, *nonna*, grandfather, grandmother, Sanskrit *nanā*, "mammy." Also borrowed afresh in ME. from F. *nonne*, whence Du. Ger. *nonne*. Cf. hist. of *abbot*, *Pope*.

nunatak [*geog.*]. Peak over inland ice of Greenland. From Sw., into which it was introduced from Eskimo by Nordenskjöld.

Nunc dimittis. L., now dismissest thou. Song of Simeon (*Vulg. Luke*, ii. 29).

nuncheon [*dial.*]. ME. *noneshench*, noon draught, AS. *scenc*; cf. Ger. *schenken*, to pour out, obs. E. *skinker*, drawer, tavernwaiter (from Du.). Shortened *nunch* is also current in dial. See *lunch-eon*, which has been affected by it in form and sense. Cf. also synon. dial. *nammet*, i.e. noon-meat.

ressie: an afternoones nunchion or drinking (Cotg.).

Munch on, crunch on, take your nuncheon,
Breakfast, supper, dinner, luncheon
(Browning, *Pied Piper*).

nuncio. It. (*nunzio*), L. *nuntius*, *nuncius*, messenger, whence also F. *nonce*, "a nuntio, messenger, tiding-bringer; and particularly an embassador from the Pope" (Cotg.).

nuncupative. Of will made orally instead of by writing. From L. *nuncupare*, to mention by name, from *nomen*, name, *capere*, to take. For vowel cf. *occupy*.

nunky. Playful for *uncle*. Cf. obs. *nuncle* (*Lear*, i. 4), *naunt*, due to wrong separation of *mine uncle*, *mine aunt* into *my nuncle*, *my naunt*.

Send me word how my nawnte is dysposyd, now the dettes be payd, to perform her nonkilles wyll
(*Stonor Let.* 1467).

nuptial. F., L. *nuptialis*, from *nuptiae*, wedding, from *nubere*, *nupt-*, to wed; cogn. with G. νύμφη, bride.

nurse. ME. *nurice, norice,* F. *nourrice,* foster-mother, L. *nutrix, nutric-,* from *nutrire,* to nourish. Orig. what is now called a wet-nurse. Older form survives in name *Norris.* The verb, ME. *nursh, norsh,* contr. of *nourish,* has been assimilated to the noun. For fig. senses cf. *cherish, nourish.*

And he cam to Nazareth, where he was noursed [Wyc. norischid] (Tynd. *Luke,* iv. 16).

nutrix: a nourice; a nourcerie or place where men plant and graffe trees or hearbes, to the ende afterwarde to remove them and set them in a garden or orcharde (Coop.).

nurture. F. *nourriture,* nourishment, also in OF. training, education, which is earliest E. sense.

nut. AS. *hnutu.* Com. Teut.; cf. Du. *noot,* Ger. *nuss,* ON. *hnot*; cogn. with OIr. *cnú,* Gael. *cnù, cnò,* but not with L. *nux.* To *be* (*dead*) *nuts on* (Grose) seems to be evolved from earlier to *be nuts* (i.e. an enticement) *to,* recorded in a letter from Sir Edward Stafford to Burghley (1587), with which we may cf. US. *as good as pie.* Current slang use of *nut* seems to have arisen from earlier contemptuous sense, *an old nut,* where *nut* prob. means head; cf. *a silly chump.* In AustralE. a *nut* meant (1882) "a long, lank, lantern-jawed, whiskerless youth" (*NED.*). *Nuthatch,* ME. *notehach,* means nut-hacker, the bird having a special gift for breaking nuts. *Nutmeg* is ME. *notemugge,* of which second element is OF. *mugue,* usu. *muguette* (now *noix muscade*), musk nut; cf. Ger. *muscatnuss.* The phon. relation of *mugue* to *musc* is obscure. It has a mod. F. derivative *muguet,* lily of the valley. *In a nutshell* is allusive to the copy of the Iliad which, according to Pliny, was minute enough to be thus contained.

He [Cicero] wroot alle the gestes of Troye sotelliche, as it myghte be closed in a note schale
(Trev. iv. 141).

couplot de bois: a woodden sole, or nut for a scrue (Cotg.).

nutation. Slight oscillation of earth's axis. L. *nutatio-n-,* from *nutare,* to nod, frequent. of *nuere,* cogn. with G. νεύειν.

nutriment. L. *nutrimentum,* from *nutrire,* to nourish. Cf. *nutrition, nutritious.*

nux vomica. MedL., irreg. from *vomere,* to vomit.

nuzzle. Frequent. formation from *nose,* but, in sense of nestling, cuddling up to, associated with *nursle,* frequent. of *nurse.*

nyctalopia. Late L., from G. νυκτάλωψ, used by Galen for blind by night, G. νύξ, νυκτ-, night, ἀλαός, blind, ὤψ, eye. Misunderstood as seeing best by night.

nylghau, nilgai. Pers. *nīl,* blue (cf. *anil*), *gāw,* ox, cow (q.v.).

nymph. F. *nymphe,* L., G. νύμφη, bride, nymph. From first sense comes med. *nymphomania.* Cf. *nympholepsy,* enthusiasm, after *epilepsy.*

o, oh. Not found in AS. Partly a natural interj., partly adopted from L.

o' [*prep.*]. Represents both of (*o'clock, will o' the wisp*) and on (*o' nights*).

O'. Ir. *ó, ua,* descendant, grandson; cf. Gael. *ogha,* whence Sc. *oe, oy,* grandchild.

oaf. Earlier also *auph, ouph,* vars. of *elf* (q.v.). Orig. of a changeling.

The flannelled fools at the wicket,
The muddied oafs at the goal (Kipling).

oak. AS. *āc.* Com. Teut.; cf. Du. *eik,* Ger. *eiche,* ON. *eik.* With *Oakapple Day* (May 29), day of Restoration of Charles II, cf. *Royal Oak,* allusive to tree in which he hid (Sep. 6, 1651) after Worcester. The *Oaks,* race founded in 1779, is named from an estate near Epsom.

to sport oak: to shut the outward door of a student's room at college (Grose).

oakum. AS. *ācumbe, ǣcumbe,* off combing; cf. OHG. *āchambi.* Orig. coarse refuse of flax. First element is *ā-, ǣ-,* privative prefix. See *comb, unkempt.* For formation cf. *offal.*

oar. AS. & ON. *ār.* A viking word. With *oarsman,* for earlier *oarman,* cf. *huntsman, steersman,* etc. To *rest upon one's oars* is mod. for to *lie upon one's oars.*

fretillon: a little busie-bodie, medler, Jacke-stickler; one that hath an oare in everie mans boat (Cotg.).

oasis. L., G. ὄασις, of Egypt. origin; cf. Copt. *ouahe,* dwelling-place, from *ouih,* to dwell.

oast [*local*]. AS. *āst,* cogn. with Du. *eest,* and ult. with L. *aestas,* summer, Ir. *aedh,* heat. Orig. kiln in gen., now for malt or hops.

oat. "A grain, which in England is generally given to horses, but in Scotland supports the people" (Johns.). AS. *āte,* with no known cognates. The fact that it is usu. pl., while all other cereals are sing., suggests that orig. sense was the single grain and not the plant. The Com. Teut. name for the cereal is represented by Sc.

haver (see *haversack*). With *wild oats*,
typical, from 16 cent., of crop that one
will regret sowing, cf. fig. use of F. *folle
avoine*.

oath. AS. *āth*. Com. Teut.; cf. Du. *eed*, Ger.
eid, ON. *eithr*, Goth. *aiths*; cogn. with OIr.
oeth. For later sense cf. *swear*.

ob-. L. prep. *ob*, with gen. sense of towards,
against. Also *oc-*, *of-*, *op-*.

obbligato [*mus.*]. It., obliged, i.e. indispensable accompaniment.

obdurate. L. *obduratus*, p.p. of *obdurare*, to
make hard, *durus*.

obeah, obi. A WAfr. word, with senses of *juju*.

obedient. OF., from pres. part. of L. *oboedire*,
to obey (q.v.).

obeisance. F. *obéissance*, obedience, from
obéir, to obey. With usual E. sense, found
in Chauc., cf. *reverence*, but this meaning
is not found in F. and is due to confusion
with archaic *abaisance* (q.v.).

obelisk. F. *obélisque*, L., G. ὀβελίσκος, dim.
of ὀβελός, spit, pointed pillar, also used
of a critical mark (— or ÷) placed against
a passage of doubtful authenticity, as E.
obelisk is of a reference mark (†).

obese. L. *obesus*, p.p. of *obedere*, to eat all
over. For transition of sense cf. *drunk(en)*.

obey. F. *obéir*, L. *oboedire*, from *audire*, to
hearken (cf. Ger. *gehorchen*, to obey, from
horchen, to hearken).

obfuscate. From L. *obfuscare*, *offuscare*, to
darken, from *fuscus*, dark. Cf. F. *offusquer*.

obi. See *obeah*.

obit. OF., L. *obitus*, departure, decease, lit. a
going to meet, from *obire*. Obs. exc. in
(abbrev.) *post-obit(um)*.

obiter. L., by the way, *ob iter*. Hence *obiter
dictum*, orig. in law, expression of opinion
not regarded as binding or decisive.

obituary. MedL. *obituarius*. See *obit*.

object. First as noun. MedL. *objectum*,
thrown in the way, from *obicere*, *object-*,
from *jacere*, to throw. Cf. synon. Ger.
gegenstand. Used, as early as Shaks., with
of pity (*derision*, etc.) understood. *Objective*, contrasted with *subjective*, in philosophy, etc., is MedL. *objectivus*, but its
currency is from Ger. Mil. sense, short for
objective point, is from F.

It lacks what the Anglo-German jargon calls
objectivity (J. S. Phillimore).

objurgate. From L. *objurgare*, from *jurgare*,
to scold, quarrel, from *jus*, *jur-*, law, *agere*,
to do, etc.

oblate[1]. Person devoted to religious work.

L. *oblatus*, used as p.p. of *offerre*, to offer.
Cf. *oblation*.

oblate[2]. Flattened at poles, as earth. MedL.
oblatus, formed on its opposite *prolate*.

oblation. L. *oblatio-n-*, from *offerre*, *oblat-*, to
offer.

oblige. F. *obliger*, L. *obligare*, from *ligare*, to
bind. Pronounced *obleege* by old-fashioned
people within living memory.

oblique. F., L. *obliquus*, slanting, indirect.
Cf. L. *licinus*, bent.

obliterate. From L. *oblit(t)erare*, to blot out,
efface, from *lit(t)era*, letter, script.

oblivion. OF., L. *oblivio-n-*, from *oblivisci*,
to forget; ? cogn. with *levis*, light, smooth.

oblong. L. *oblongus*, from *longus*, long.

obloquy. Late L. *obloquium*, speaking against,
from *loqui*, to speak.

obmutescence. From L. *obmutescere*, from
mutescere, to become dumb, *mutus*.

obnoxious. L. *obnoxiosus*, from *obnoxius*, exposed to harm, *noxa*. Still occ. in orig.
passive sense.

obnubilate. To dim, etc. From L. *obnubilare*,
from *nubes*, cloud.

oboe. It., F. *hautbois*, hautboy (q.v.).

obol, obolus. Coin. F. *obole*, L., G. ὀβολός.

obscene. F. *obscène*, L. *obscaenus*, ? from
caenum, mud.

obscure. F. *obscur*, L. *obscurus*, from root
scu-, Sanskrit *sku*, to cover; cf. L. *scutum*,
shield, G. σκευή, dress. *Obscurant* was introduced (c. 1800) from Ger., the name
being applied to the opponents of *auf-
klärung*, enlightenment.

obsecrate. From L. *obsecrare*, to entreat in
the name of something holy, *sacer*.

obsequies. F. *obsèques*, MedL. *obsequiae*, due
to confusion between L. *exequiae*, exequies
(q.v.), and *obsequium*, service (v.i.).

obsequious. F. *obséquieux*, L. *obsequiosus*,
from *sequi*, to follow. For degeneration of
sense cf. *officious*.

observe. F. *observer*, L. *observare*, from *servare*, to guard, keep. Orig. to attend to a
law, custom, religious practice, etc. For
sense of mention cf. *remark*.

The new observatorie in Greenewich Park
(Evelyn, 1676).

obsess. From L. *obsidēre*, *obsess-*, to sit down
(*sedēre*) before, besiege. Cf. *beset*. In current use a 19 cent. revival.

obsidian. Volcanic glass. L. *obsidianus*, misprint in early editions of Pliny for *obsianus*,
named from resemblance to stone found
in Ethiopia by one *Obsius*.

obsolete. L. *obsoletus*, p.p. of *obsolescere*, to grow out of use, from *solēre*, to be accustomed.

obstacle. F., L. *obstaculum*, from *obstare*, to stand in the way. *Obstacle race* was coined (1869) by the Hon. Secretary of the London Athletic Club.

obstetric [*med.*]. From L. *obstetricius*, from *obstetrix*, *obstetric-*, midwife, from *obsistere*, *obstit-*, to stand by. Cf. *midwife*.

obstinate. L. *obstinatus*, p.p. of *obstinare*, to persist, from *obstare*; cf. *obstacle*.

obstreperous. From L. *obstreperus*, from *obstreperare*, to make a noise, *strepitus*, against.

> I heard him very obstropulous in his sleep
>   (*Roderick Random*, ch. viii).

obstruct. From L. *obstruere*, *obstruct-*, to build up against. Parliamentary *obstruction* was invented (c. 1880) by the Irish party.

obtain. F. *obtenir*, VL. **obtenire*, for *obtinēre*, from *tenēre*, to hold. For intrans. sense (*custom obtains*) cf. similar use of to *hold*.

obtest. From L. *obtestari*, to call to witness, *testis*.

obtrude. L. *obtrudere*, from *trudere*, to thrust.

obturate. From L. *obturare*, to stop up.

obtuse. F. *obtus*, L. *obtusus*, p.p. of *obtundere*, to beat against, blunt, from *tundere*, to beat, strike. For fig. senses cf. *acute*.

obumbrate. From L. *obumbrare*, to overshadow, from *umbra*, shade.

obverse. L. *obversus*, p.p. of *obvertere*, to turn towards.

obviate. From Late L. *obviare*, to meet, from *via*, way. For current sense cf. to *meet a difficulty*. Cf. *obvious*, from L. *obvius*, what meets one in the way.

ocarina. Mus. instrument of terra cotta. From It. *oca*, goose, L. *auca* (**avica* from *avis*, bird), in allusion to shape.

occasion. F., L. *occasio-n-*, falling towards, juncture, from *occidere*, *occas-*, to fall, from *ob* and *cadere*, to fall.

occident. F., from pres. part. of L. *occidere*, to fall, set (v.s.). Cf. *orient*.

occiput. L., back of the head, from *ob* and *caput*.

occlude. From L. *occludere*, from *ob* and *claudere*, to close.

occult. L. *occultus*, p.p. of *occulere*, to conceal, from *ob* and an unrecorded verb cogn. with *celare*, to conceal.

occupy. From F. *occuper*, L. *occupare*, to take possession of, from *ob* and *capere*, to seize, with vowel change as in *nuncupate*. For

-y cf. *bandy*[1], *levy*, *parry*. Etym. sense survives in mil. lang. Acquired gross sense in 16 cent., and hence, though occurring in *AV.*, almost fell out of use between c. 1600 and Cowper.

> Like heretics we occupy other men's wives
>   (*Hickscorner*, c. 1500).

> A captain! God's light! these villains will make the word as odious as the word "occupy," which was an excellent good word before it was ill sorted
>   (2 *Hen. IV*, ii. 4).

occur. L. *occurrere*, to run against, from *ob* and *currere*, to run. *Occurrence*, incident, was orig. pl. of *occurrent* (cf. *accidence*).

ocean. F. *océan*, L., G. ὠκεανός, stream supposed to encompass the world. Earlier the *ocean sea*, or *sea of ocean*, as opposed to the Mediterranean and other inland seas.

ocellus [*biol.*]. Usu. in pl. L., dim. of *oculus*, eye.

ocelot. Tiger-cat. F., abridged by Buffon from Mex. *tlalocelotl*, from *tlalli*, field, *ocelotl*, jaguar.

och. Interj., Ir. Gael.; cf. *ochone*, *ohone*, Gael. *ochóin*, Ir. *ochón*, alas.

ochlocracy. Rule by the mob, G. ὄχλος.

ochre. Earlier *oker*, F. *ocre*, L., G. ὤχρα, from ὠχρός, pale yellow.

-ocracy. See *-cracy*; *-o-* is from first element of compds.

octad. Eight. L., G. ὀκτάς, ὀκτάδ-. Cf. *octagon*, from γωνία, angle; *octahedron*, from ἕδρα, seat.

octant. Late L. *octans*, *octant-*; cf. *quadrant*, *sextant*. With *octarchy* cf. *heptarchy*. With *octateuch*, first eight books of *OT.*, cf. *pentateuch*, *hexateuch*. Oldest sense of *octave*, F., L. *octavus*, eighth, from *octo*, eight, is the eighth day, or period of eight days, after a Church festival. *Octavo* is for *in octavo*, the sheet being folded so as to make eight leaves; cf. *folio*, *quarto*. *Octette* (mus.) is after *duet*, *quartette*.

October. L. *october* or F. *octobre*, eighth (month). Replaced AS. *winterfylleth*, ? from *fyllan*, to fell. With *octobrist*, Russ. moderate conservative connected with abortive revolution of October 1905, cf. *septembrist*.

> It is most important to avoid any clash between the octobrist and cadet sections
>   (*Daily Chron.* March 17, 1917).

octogenarian. From L. *octogenarius*, from *octogeni*, eighty each.

octopus. G. ὀκτώπους, from ὀκτώ, eight, πούς, foot.

octoroon. Person having one eighth negro blood. Irreg. formed from L. *octo*, eight, after *quadroon*.

octroi. Town duties. F., from *octroyer*, to grant, VL. **auctoricare*, to authorize.

ocular. L. *ocularis*, from *oculus*, eye; cf. *oculist*, F. *oculiste*. Esp. in *ocular demonstration* (cf. *eyewitness*).

od. Hypothetical force supposed to pervade nature and explain mesmerism, etc. Arbitrary coinage of Reichenbach (†1869). Also *odyl*.

odalisque. F., Turk. *ōdaliq*, female slave in seraglio, from *ōdah*, chamber, hall.

odd. ON. *odda-*, as in *odda-mathr*, odd man, umpire (q.v.), *odda-tala*, odd number, from *oddi*, point, angle, triangle; cogn. with AS. *ord*, point, tip, OHG. *ort*, point, angle, whence Ger. *ort*, place. Sense-development starts from the unpaired one of three, extends to the general opposite of *even*, and finally to what appears solitary or unique. For noun use of *odds*, difference, etc., orig. used as sing., cf. *news*. The betting and sporting senses are in Shaks. (*Haml.* v. 2, *Rich. II*, i. 1). *Odds and ends*, for earlier *odd ends*, may have been influenced by *ort* (q.v.). *Oddity* and *oddment* are 18 cent. formations. The *Oddfellows* originated at Manchester (c. 1813), the name having previously been used of various convivial societies.

ode. F., Late L. *oda*, G. ᾠδή, for ἀοιδή, from ἀείδειν, to sing. Cf. *odeum*, theatre for music, L., G. ᾠδεῖον, whence F. *odéon*.

odic. From *od* (q.v.).

odious. F. *odieux*, L. *odiosus*, from *odium*, from *odi*, I hate.

odontic. Of the teeth. G. ὀδοντικός, from ὀδούς, ὀδόντ-, tooth.

odour. F. *odeur*, L. *odor-em*; cf. G. ὄζειν, to smell. In Wyc. (*Rev.* v. 8). *Odour of sanctity*, F. *odeur de sainteté*, alludes to belief in fragrance exhaled by the bodies of the holy after death.

odyl. See *od*.

odynometer. Measurer of pain, G. ὀδύνη.

odyssey. Long adventurous journey. G. Ὀδύσσεια, Homeric poem relating adventures of Ὀδυσσεύς, Ulysses.

oecist [*hist.*]. Founder of ancient G. colony. G. οἰκιστής, from οἶκος, house.

oecumenical. Universal, esp. of councils of early Church. From G. οἰκουμενικός, belonging to ἡ οἰκουμένη, the inhabited (earth), from οἶκος, house, dwelling.

oedema [*med.*]. G. οἴδημα, from οἰδεῖν, to swell.

Oedipus. G. Οἰδίπους, lit. swollen foot, Theban hero who solved riddle of Sphinx. For name cf. E. *Puddifoot*.

oenomel. Drink of wine and honey. Also fig. G. οἰνόμελι, from οἶνος, wine, μέλι, honey.

oenothera. Plant. L., G. οἰνοθήρας, lit. wine catcher (v.s.).

oesophagus. G. οἰσοφάγος, gullet, of which second element is app. cogn. with φαγεῖν, to eat.

of, off. AS. *of*. Aryan; cf. Du. *af*, off, Ger. *ab*, off, away, ON. Goth. *af*, L. *ab*, G. ἀπό, Sanskrit *apa*, away from. *Off* is the stressed form and is often used for *of* in dial. The *off*, right, in speaking of horses and vehicles (see *near*), is extended to cricket, *on* being adopted as its opposite from phrase *off and on*. The latter is prob. naut., of a ship sailing on alternate tacks away from and towards the shore. *Off colour* appears to have been first applied to gems. Orig. sense of *offhand* is forthwith, extempore; hence, without ceremony. Vulg. *what are you doing of?* is for *what are you in the doing of?*

> I was writing of my epitaph (*Timon*, v. 1).

offal. For *off fall*; cf. Du. *afval*, Ger. *abfall*, "the garbage in butchers-shops" (Ludw.). Now (March, 1918) oddly familiar.

> We are not surprised that the fastidious are beginning to object to the use of the term "offal" to describe their meat rations
> (*Daily Chron.* Feb. 27, 1918).

offend. OF. *offendre* (replaced by *offenser*), L. *offendere*, to strike against, stumble, from *ob* and *-fendere*. The *offensive* (mil.) is F. *l'offensive* (sc. *partie*). *Peace offensive* was used (1917) of Ger. intrigue for stalemate; cf. *potato offensive* (1918).

> The time has come for a great evangelical offensive
> (A. C. Dixon, Mar. 30, 1919).

offer. AS. *offrian*, L. *offerre*, from *ob* and *ferre*, to bear, an early loan from Church L.; cf. Du. *offeren*, Ger. *opfern*, to sacrifice. Gen. senses rather from F. *offrir*, VL. **offerire*, for *offerre* (cf. *proffer*). *Offertory*, orig. anthem, Late L. *offertorium*, is from Late L. *offertus*, for *oblatus*. Sense of collection in church is quite mod.

> Wel koude he rede a lessoun or a storie,
> But alderbest he song an offertorie (Chauc. A. 709).

office. F., L. *officium*, service, duty, prob. from *opus*, work, *facere*, to do. Orig. sense in *kind office*. For eccl. sense cf. *service*. Sense of place for transaction of business is in Chauc. (D. 1577). Current sense of *officer*, in ME. any public servant, is from 16 cent. *Officious*, F. *officieux*, L. *officiosus*, friendly, serviceable (cf. *obsequious*), preserves its orig. good sense in diplomacy, being used for informally friendly as opposed to *official*.

officinal. Of herbs, drugs. From L. *officina*, workshop, laboratory, for *opificina*, from *opifex, opific-*, workman, from *opus*, work, *facere*, to do.

officious. See *office*.

offing [*naut.*]. From *off*.

offspring. AS. *ofspring*, from *of* and *spring*; cf. *offshoot*.

offuscate. See *obfuscate*.

oft, often. AS. *oft*. Com. Teut.; cf. obs. Du. *ofte*, Ger. *oft*, ON. *oft, opt*, Goth. *ufta*. Lengthened in ME. to *ofte* before consonant, *often* before vowel. *Oft* survives poet. and in compds. (*oft-times, oft-told*), also in *many a time and oft*.

ogdoad. Set of eight. Late L., G. ὀγδοάς, ὀγδοάδ-, from ὀκτώ, eight.

ogee. Curve (~). From F. *ogive* (q.v.), "an ogive, or ogee in architecture" (Cotg.).

ogham, ogam. Ancient Ir. alphabet. Ir. *ogham*, from myth. inventor *Ogma*.

ogive [*arch.*]. F., earlier also *augive*. ? From Sp. *auge*, highest point, Arab. *auj*, apogee, G. ἀπόγαιον, ? or ult. from L. *alveus*, channel, trough (whence F. *auge*, trough), ? from grooving.

ogle. Late 17 cent. cant word. LG. *oegeln*, frequent. of *oegen*, to look at, from *oege*, eye (q.v.). Cf. Ger. *liebäugeln*, "to ogle, to smicker, to look amorously, to cast sheeps-eyes, to cast amorous looks" (Ludw.).

ogre. F., first used, and prob. invented, by Perrault in his *Contes de Fées* (1697). It occurs in OF. in sense of pagan (? orig. Hungarian), but this is not likely to have been known to Perrault.

oh. See *o*.

ohm. Unit of electrical resistance. From Ger. physicist *G. S. Ohm* (†1854). Cf. *ampère*.

-oid. G. -οειδής, from εἶδος, form.

oidium. Fungus attacking vine. ModL. dim. from G. ᾠόν, egg.

oil. OF. *oile* (*huile*), L. *oleum*, orig. oil of olive (q.v.). Also as early Church word (consecrated oil) in the Teut. langs., e.g. AS. *ele* (see *anele*), Du. *olie*, Ger. *öl*. Often

allusive to night study as in *midnight oil* (17 cent.), also to aggravation or appeasement in *oil on flame* (*troubled waters*). To *strike oil* (US.) is to bore successfully for petroleum. *Oilskin* is 19 cent.

ointment. ME. *oynement*, OF. *oignement*, from *oindre, oign-*, to anoint, L. *ungere*. Altered on obs. *oint*, to anoint, from p.p. of above verb.

o.k. For *orl korrect*. US. since 1790.

okapi. Central Afr. animal resembling zebra and giraffe, discovered (1900) by Sir H. H. Johnston. Native name.

-ol [*chem.*]. Extended use of ending of *alcohol*.

old. AS. *eald* (Merc. *ald*). Com. Teut.; cf. Du. *oud*, Ger. *alt*, ON. *ellri* (compar.), Goth. derivative *altheis*. Orig. a p.p., cogn. with L. *alere*, to nourish, whence *altus*, high, orig. nourished, grown. Prob. sense of measurement, as in *ten years old*, preceded the absolute use. Intens. and endearing senses occur early (v.i.), and Satan is called *se ealda* in AS. As noun only in *of old*, whence adj. *olden* in *olden time*.

Gode olde fyghtyng was there (*NED*. c. 1440).

oleaginous. F. *oléagineux*, from L. *oleaginus*, from *olea*, olive tree.

oleander. MedL., whence F. *oléandre*, It. *oleandro*, OSp. *eloendro*. Late L. *lorandrum*, explained by Isidore as a corrupt., influenced by *laurus*, laurel, of *rhododendron*; cf. F. *laurier rose*, oleander. Further affected by assim. to L. *olea*, olive tree.

oleaster. L., from *olea*, olive tree.

olefiant. Only in *olefiant gas*, choke damp. Coined (1795) by Du. chemists to mean oil-producing.

olent. From pres. part. of L. *olēre*, to smell.

oleograph. Printed imit. of oil-painting. From L. *oleum*, oil.

oleomargarine. Earlier name of *margarine* (v.s.).

olfactory. From L. *olfacere*, to cause to smell, *olēre*; from *odor*, smell, with Sabine *-l-* for *-d-* (cf. *lingua, lacrima*).

olibanum. Aromatic gum. MedL., whence F. *oliban*, It. Sp. *olibano*. Corrupt., ? by association with L. *oleum*, oil, of Late L. *libanus*, frankincense, G. λίβανος.

oligarchy. F. *oligarchie*, Late L., G. ὀλιγαρχία, from ὀλίγος, few, ἄρχειν, to rule.

olio [*cook.*]. Altered from Sp. *olla* or Port. *olha*, hotch-potch, L. *olla*, pot, jar. Cf. *olla podrida*.

olive. F., L. *oliva*, olive, olive-tree; cogn.
with G. ἐλαία. *Olive-branch*, child, is allusive
to *Ps.* cxxviii. 4 (*PB.*). Quot. below is
somewhat earlier than *NED.* in complexion
sense.

> He is of complexion neither white nor blacke, but
> of a middle betwixt them; I know not how to
> expresse it with a more expressive and significant
> epitheton than olive (Coryat, 1615).

oliver [*techn.*]. Tilt-hammer. ? From surname *Oliver*.

Oliver. See *Roland*.

olland [*dial.*]. Ploughland lying fallow. For
old land.

> Fields which ought to be ploughed and are still
> olland or stubble (*Daily News*, Apr. 27, 1917).

olla podrida. Sp., lit. rotten pot; hence,
hotch-potch, lit. or fig. From L. *olla*, pot,
putridus, rotten. Cf. *pot-pourri*.

-ology. G. λογία, from λόγος, word, with
connecting *-o-* of first element. Cf. *-doxy*,
-ism.

> Don't pin your faith too much to ologies and isms
> (*John Bull*, Apr. 28, 1917).

Olympian, Olympic. Of *Olympus*, mountain
in Thessaly, abode of gods; or of *Olympia*,
in Elis, scene of games. Hence also
olympiad, space of four years between
celebrations of *Olympic games*, starting
from 776 B.C.

omadhaun [*Ir.*]. Ir. *amadán*, fool.

ombre [*archaic*]. Card game. F. *ombre*,
hombre, Sp. *hombre*, L. *homo, homin-*, man.

omega. Last letter of G. alphabet (*Rev.* i. 8).
G. ὦ μέγα, big o. In Tynd.

> I am alpha and oo, the bigynnyng and endyng
> (Wyc. *Rev.* i. 8).

omelet-te. F., earlier *amelette*, still in dial.,
metath. of *alemette*, altered from *alemelle*,
alamelle, due to wrong separation of *la
lamelle* (cf. F. *la boutique* for *l'aboutique*,
L. *apotheca*), L. *lamellā*, dim. of *lamina*,
thin plate. Cf. F. *flan*, thin disk of metal,
also omelet, flawn (q.v.). *Amulet, aume-
lette*, etc., were earlier common in E.

> Alumelle [*var.* alumette] frite au sucre
> (*Ménagier de Paris*, 14 cent.).

omen. From 16 cent. L., OL. *osmen*, of
unknown origin.

omer. Tenth part of ephah (*Ex.* xvi. 33). Heb.

omit. L. *omittere*, from *ob* and *mittere*, to
send. Cf. F. *omettre*.

omnibus. From F. *voiture omnibus* (c. 1828),
carriage for all, dat. pl. of L. *omnis*. Cf.
F. *train omnibus*, stopping train. Hence

used as term for all-comprising, general,
etc., as in *omnibus box* (theat.). A "plural"
omnibi is recorded in an advt. in the *Field*,
Sep. 11, 1897.

omnifarious. From L. *omnifarius*, as *multifarious* (q.v.).

omnipotent. F., L. *omnipotens, omnipotent-*,
from *omnis*, all, *potens*, powerful. Cf. *almighty*.

omniscience. MedL. *omniscientia*, all knowledge. See *science*.

omnium gatherum. For earlier (15 cent.)
omnigatherum, mock-L., from *gather*.

omnivorous. See *-vorous*.

omophagous. Eating raw flesh. From G.
ὠμός, raw (see *-phagous*).

omoplate. Shoulder-blade. F., G. ὠμοπλάτη,
from ὦμος, shoulder, πλάτη, blade.

omphalos. Centre, hub, etc. G. ὀμφαλός,
navel.

on. AS. *an, on*. Aryan; cf. Du. *aan*, Ger. *an*,
ON. *ā*, Goth. *ana*, G. ἀνά, Zend *ana*. See
off and *a-*.

onager. L., G. ὄναγρος, from ὄνος, ass, ἄγριος,
wild. Hence fem. *onagra*, pseudo-L.

onanism. From name *Onan* (*Gen.* xxxviii. 9).

once. ME. *ones, anes*, genitive of *one* (q.v.).
For spelling cf. *nonce, pence*. With dial.
onst cf. *against, amongst*, etc.

one. AS. *ān*, of which unstressed form gave
E. *an, a*. WAryan; cf. Du. *een*, Ger. *ein*,
ON. *einn*, Goth. *ains*, L. *unus*, G. dial. οἰνός,
OIr. *óen*. Pronunc. with init. *w-* (cf. dial.
wuts for *oats*) was orig. W. & S.W. dial.
(Tynd. was a Glouc. man), becoming gen.
current c. 1700, but not affecting compds.
alone, only (cf. also colloq. *good un,
young un*). The use of *one* as indef.
pron. has been influenced by unrelated F.
on, L. *homo*. *One-sided* was adapted by
De Quincey from Ger. *einseitig* (cf. *many-
sided*). *Oner*, the epithet applied to Sally
Brass by the marchioness, is regarded by
NED. as from *one*, with idea of unique;
? but cf. dial. *wunner* for *wonder*.

> Then won of the twelve, called Judas Iscarioth,
> went unto the chefe prestes (Tynd. *Matt.* xxvi. 14).

oneiromancy. Divination by dream, G. ὄ-
νειρος.

onerous. F. *onéreux*, L. *onerosus*, from *onus,
oner-*, burden.

onion. F. *oignon*, L. *unio-n-*, unity, also a
large pearl, an onion, from the successive
layers being regarded as forming unity, in
contrast with the garlic, or clove-leek (see
clove[1]).

only. First as adj. AS. *ānlic*, one like.

onomasticon. Vocabulary of names. G. ὀνομαστικόν (sc. βιβλίον), from ὄνομα, name.

onomatopoeia. G. ὀνοματοποιΐα, from ποιεῖν, to make (v.s.). Used by E. poet. theorists of 16 cent.

onslaught. Du. *aanslag* or Ger. *anschlag*, enterprise, from *slagen, schlagen*, to strike, slay. Form and sense have been influenced by obs. *slaught*, slaughter, slaying, cogn. with Ger. *schlacht*, battle. A 17 cent. word from the Low Countries. Cf. obs. mil. *slaught-beam*, barrier, Ger. *schlagbaum*.

anschlag: entreprise, wird sonderlich im kriege gebrauchet, wenn etwas gegen eine festung, oder sonsten gegen den feind unternommen wird
(Fäsch, *Kriegs-Lexicon*, 1735).

onto. For *on to*, indicating motion. Cf. *into*.

ontology. Study of being. From ὄν, ὄντ-, pres. part. neut. of εἶναι, to be.

onus. L., burden.

onward. From *on* and *-ward* (q.v.).

onymous. Having a name. Coined (18 cent.) on its opposite *anonymous*.

onyx. L., G. ὄνυξ, finger-nail, onyx-stone.

oof [*slang*]. Short for Yiddish *oof-tish*, for Ger. *auf (dem) tisch(e)*, on the table. Cf. to *plank down*. Hence *oof-bird*, with allusion to "golden eggs."

oolite [*geol.*]. Concretionary limestone. F. *oolithe*, from G. ᾠόν, egg, λίθος, stone.

oology. Study of birds' eggs (v.s.).

oom. Du., uncle, as in *Oom Paul*, President Kruger. Cf. Ger. *oheim*, E. dial. *eme*, AS. *ēam*, and see *uncle*.

oomiak. Eskimo, woman's boat. Cf. *kayak*.

The canoe is called "kaiak," or man's boat, to distinguish it from "umiak," the woman's boat
(Falc.).

oorali. One of the many forms of *curare* (q.v.).

Oordoo [*ling.*]. See *Urdu*.

ooze. The noun represents (1) AS. *wōs*, juice, sap, now only of tan-vat, whence verb to *ooze*, (2) AS. *wase*, mud, cogn. with ON. *veisa*, stagnant pool, whence Norw. dial. *veisa*, mud-bank. For loss of *w-* cf. dial. *'ooman*. The second word has been confused with AS. *gewǣsc*, alluvium (the *Wash*). *Richard atte Wase*, of Norfolk, is mentioned in *Patent Rolls* (13 cent.).

Right as weodes wexen in wose and in donge
(*Piers Plowm.* C. xiii. 229).

O.P. [*theat.*]. Side of stage *opposite prompter*.

opah. Fish. Prob. native name of Guinea coast.

opal. L., G. ὀπάλλιος; cf. Sanskrit *upala*, gem.

opaque. ME. *opake*, L. *opacus*; now spelt after F. *opaque*.

ope, open. *Ope* is shortened (cf. *awake*) from AS. *open* (adj.). Com. Teut.; cf. Du. *open*, Ger. *offen*, ON. *opinn*; prob. cogn. with *up*. With *open-handed* cf. *close-fisted*. Naut. to *open* (Purch.), come in view of, is evolved from adj. in naut. sense of unobstructedly visible.

Our economic rise has been in a very real sense due to the British policy of the open door
(Zimmermann, *Mitteleuropa*).

opera. It., L., cogn. with *opus, oper-*, work. A 17 cent. borrowing. First in Evelyn.

They sometimes entertaine the people [of Siena] with "operas" as they call them (Evelyn).

Strange to see this house, that used to be so thronged, now empty since the opera begun
(Pepys, July 4, 1661).

operation. F. *opération*, L. *operatio-n-*, from *operari*, from *opus, oper-*, work. In Chauc. Surgical sense from 16 cent. Later is *operate* (c. 1600). *Operative*, workman, is 19 cent. (cf. F. *ouvrier*, L. *operarius*).

operculum [*biol.*]. L., lid, from *operire*, to cover.

operose. L. *operosus*, laborious, from *opus, oper-*, work.

ophicleide. F. *ophicléĭde*, coined (early 19 cent.) from G. ὄφις, serpent, κλείς, κλειδ-, key, the instrument being a development of the earlier "serpent."

ophidian. Of snakes. From G. ὀφίδιον, dim. of ὄφις (v.s.). Cf. *ophiophagus*, snake-eater, scient. name of hamadryad (snake); *ophite*, serpentine rock, also name of early Christian sect reverencing serpent as embodiment of wisdom.

ophthalmia. Late L., G. ὀφθαλμία, from ὀφθαλμός, eye. From 14 cent.

opiate. MedL. *opiatus*, from *opium*.

opinion. F., L. *opinio-n-*, from *opinari*, to be of opinion; cf. *inopinus*, unexpected. With current sense of *opinionated*, orig. holding a spec. opinion, cf. F. *opiniâtre*, obstinate.

opisthograph. Manuscript written on back as well as front. From G. ὄπισθεν, behind.

opium. L., G. ὄπιον, poppy-juice, dim. of ὀπός, vegetable juice.

opodeldoc. Medical plaster. Coined by Paracelsus (16 cent.), perh. from above. Cf. *nostoc*.

opoponax. Gum-resin. L., G. ὀποπάναξ, from ὀπός, vegetable juice, πανακής, all healing. Cf. *panacea*.

opossum. NAmer. Ind. name, variously spelt from c. 1600. With *possum* cf. *coon.*

oppidan. L. *oppidanus,* from *oppidum,* town. Now chiefly of Eton boys lodged in town as opposed to "collegers."

oppilate [*med.*]. To obstruct. From L. *oppilare,* from *ob* and *pilare,* to ram.

opponent. From pres. part. of L. *opponere,* to place against, from *ob* and *ponere.*

opportune. F. *opportun,* L. *opportunus,* from *ob* and *-portunus* as in *importune* (q.v.). *Opportunist* is F. *opportuniste,* coined (1876) by Rochefort in ref. to Gambetta and his followers.

oppose. F. *opposer,* compd. of *poser;* see *pose. Opposite* is immediately from L. *oppositus,* p.p. of *opponere. Opposition* in pol. sense is 18 cent. (Burke).

oppress. F. *oppresser,* MedL. *oppressare,* from L. *opprimere, oppress-,* from *ob* and *premere,* to press.

opprobrium. L., from *ob* and *probrum,* infamy.

oppugn. From L. *oppugnare,* from *ob* and *pugnare,* to fight.

opsimathy. Learning late in life. G. ὀψιμαθία, from ὀψέ, late, μανθάνειν, to learn.

opt. F. *opter,* L. *optare,* to choose; cf. *adopt, co-opt.* Hence *optative* (gram.), mood of wishing, *option.*

optic. F. *optique,* MedL., G. ὀπτικός, from ὀπτός, visible, from stem ὀπ-, as in ὤψ, eye, ὄψομαι, I shall see.

optime. L., best (adv.), esp. in *Senior* (*Junior*) *Optime,* 2nd (3rd) class in math. tripos, Camb.

optimism. F. *optimisme,* coined (1737) by the Jesuit editors of the *Mémoires de Trévoux,* from use by Leibnitz of L. *optimum* (cf. *maximum, minimum*) in connection with his theory that this is the "best of all possible worlds." The vogue of the word is due to Voltaire's satire *Candide ou l'optimisme* (1759). Cf. *pessimism.*

option. See *opt* and *local.*

opulent. F., L. *opulentus,* from *ops, op-,* resources, wealth; cf. Sanskrit *apnas,* wealth.

or¹. Conj. Contr. of ME. *other,* replacing AS. *oththe,* cogn. with OHG. *edo, odo* (*oder*), Goth. *aiththau.* The contr. took place in the second term of an alternative; cf. *nor,* and see *either.*

Other in the worlde other in religion, other clerk other lewed (*Ayenbite of Inwite,* 1340).

or² [*archaic*]. Sooner. Northern form of *ere* (q.v.), with which it forms an app. pleon.

in *or ere,* altered from *or ever* by confusion between *ere* and *e'er.*

or³ [*her.*]. Gold, yellow. F., L. *aurum.*

orache. Plant. ME. also *orage, arache,* etc., F. *arroche,* L. *atriplex, atriplic-,* G. ἀτρα-φάξυς; cf. It. *atrepice.*

oracle. F., L. *oraculum,* divine pronouncement, from *orare,* to speak, pray, from *os, or-,* mouth. Hence to *work the oracle,* allusive to tricks by which response was produced.

oral. From L. *os, or-,* mouth.

orange. F., Sp. *naranja* (Port. *laranja*), Arab. *nāranj,* Pers. *nārang;* cf. It. *arancia,* earlier *narancia,* Hind. *nārangī,* Sanskrit *nāranga;* also MedL. *arangia, arantia,* altered to *aurantia* by association with *aurum,* gold, which perh. also explains F. *orange* for **arange.* Loss of *n-* is due to confusion with indef. art.; cf. *adder, apron,* etc. Pers. has also *turunj,* whence Catalan *taronge.*

Orange. French town (Vaucluse), formerly capital of small principality, which passed (1530) to House of Nassau, whence came William III of England. Hence *Orangemen,* Ir. secret society founded (1795) by the *Orange Lodge* of Freemasons at Belfast, with *orange* colours as punning allusion.

orang-outang. Malay *ōrang ūtan,* man of the woods. In most Europ. langs.

Javani...nomen ei induunt ourang outang, quod hominem silvae significat (*NED.* 1631).

orator. ME. *oratour* (Chauc., Wyc.), OF. (*orateur*), L. *orator-em,* from *orare,* to speak, from *os, or-,* mouth.

oratorio. It. Orig. (16 cent.) semi-dramatic mus. service in the *oratory,* chapel for prayer, of St Philip Neri at Rome, to which belonged also the earliest *oratory,* brotherhood of priests. Church L. *oratorium,* from *orare,* to speak, pray (v.s.).

orb. F. *orbe,* L. *orbis,* circle, disk, etc. Hence *orbit, orbicular.* Poet. sense of eye springs from that of eyeball, perh. influenced by that of star, planet.

orc, ork. F. *orque,* L. *orca,* cetacean. Vaguely used, by association with L. *Orcus,* hell, of myth. monsters in gen.

Orcadian. From L. *Orcades,* the Orkneys.

orchard. AS. *ortgeard,* ? pleon. formation from VL. *ortus,* for *hortus,* garden, and cogn. AS. *geard,* yard, garth; cf. Goth. *aurtigards.* ?Or first element from Teut. by-form of *wort¹* (q.v.); cf. AS. *wyrtgeard.*

orchestra. L., G. ὀρχήστρα, space where chorus danced, from ὀρχεῖσθαι, to dance.

orchid. Coined (1845) by Lindley from ModL. *orchideae* (Linnaeus), incorr. formed from L., G. ὄρχις, testicle, from shape of tuber.

orchil. See *archil*.

ordain. From tonic stem (*ordein-*) of OF. *ordener* (replaced by *ordonner*), L. *ordinare*, from *ordo*, *ordin-*, order. Earliest (13 cent.) in eccl. sense. Cf. *ordination*.

ordeal. Revived by 16 cent. antiquaries from AS. *ordāl*, *ordēl*, judicial test, with artificial spelling and pronunc. (v.i.). Second element is ident. with *deal*¹, *dole*¹, first is only E. survival of prefix *or-*, out, cogn. with Du. *oor-*, Ger. *ur-*, Goth. *us-*; cf. Du. *oordeel*, Ger. *urteil*, judgment, decision, not in the restricted sense which is alone found in AS.

> Whe'r so you list by ordal or by oth
>   (Chauc. *Troil.* iii. 1046).

order. F. *ordre*, L. *ordo*, *ordin-*, from *ordiri*, to begin (to weave). For ending cf. *coffer*. Earliest E. sense (13 cent.) is eccl., as in *holy orders*, to *take orders*, *order of the Temple*, springing from the old belief in the nine *orders* of angels. This is extended to the *order of the Garter*, *Bath*, etc. Etym. sense of sequence, arrangement, appears in *in order to* (*that*), with which cf. archaic to *take order*.

ordinal. Late L. *ordinalis*, from *ordo*, *ordin-* (v.s.). In spec. sense of book of rules represents MedL. *ordinale*.

ordinance. OF. *ordenance* (replaced by *ordonnance*), from *ordener*, to ordain.

ordinary. OF. *ordinarie* (*ordinaire*), L. *ordinarius*, from *ordo*, *ordin-* (v.s.). Eccl. sense of churchman exercising independent authority descended to that of chaplain of Newgate. Naut. sense, now chiefly in *laid up in ordinary*, was orig. regular reserve staff in charge of vessel in harbour. *Farmers' ordinary* is evolved from F. sense of regular allowance. For depreciatory meaning, as in *ordinary* (not *able*) *seaman*, cf. F. *vin ordinaire*.

ordinaire: an ordinarie; a bishop (or his chauncelor, &c.) within his diocesse; also, an ordinarie table, dyet, fare (Cotg.).

ordination. See *ordain*.

ordnance. Contr. of *ordinance* in spec. sense of mil. supplies in gen., now usu. restricted to artillery. The *Board of Ordnance*, first established temp. Hen. VIII, is responsible for maps.

ordure. F., from OF. *ord*, disgusting, etc., L. *horridus*.

ore. Sense from AS. *ōra*, ore, cogn. with Du. *oer*; form from AS. *ār*, brass, bronze, cogn. with obs. Du. *eer*, MHG. *ēr*, ON. *eir*, Goth. *aiz*; cf. L. *aes*, *aer-*, brass.

oread. L., G. ὀρειάς, ὀρειάδ-, mountain nymph, from ὄρος, mountain.

orectic. Appetitive. G. ὀρεκτικός, from ὀρέγειν, to stretch out.

orfray. See *orphrey*.

organ. F. *organe*, L. *organa*, neut. pl., from G. ὄργανον, instrument, cogn. with ἔργον, work. Earliest E. sense is mus., the word being found, in L. form, in AS. Wider sense in *organic*, *organize*, etc.

> El miliu de li suspendimes nos organes
>   (*Oxf. Psalter*, 12 cent.).

organdie. Muslin. F. *organdi*, ? connected with *organzine*.

organzine. Silk thread. F. *organsin*, It. *organzino*, ? from *Urgandisch*, Chin. silk market.

orgasm. F. *orgasme*, "an extreme fit, or expression of anger" (Cotg.), from G. ὀργᾶν, to swell, be excited.

orgeat. F., sirup, from *orge*, barley, L. *hordeum*. A Prov. word.

orgies. F., L., G. ὄργια, secret rites, esp. of Dionysos.

orgulous [*archaic*]. F. *orgueilleux*, from *orgueil*, pride, of Teut. origin; cf. It. *orgoglio*. Revived by Southey and Scott.

oriel. OF. *oriol*, MedL. *aureolum*, by dissim. for Late L. *aulaeolum*, from *aulaeum*, curtain, but used rather as dim. of *aula*, hall. The *oriel* was orig. a side chapel or little sanctum (v.i.).

aulaeolum: sacellum, ab *aula*, ecclesia (Duc.)

A l'uis [entrance] de la chambre out un oriol fermé, Droit devers le chardin [garden]
                        (*Vie de S. Thomas*, 12 cent.).

orient. F., from pres. part. of L. *oriri*, to rise; cf. *occident*. *Orient pearl* is for earlier *pearl of orient*, F. *perle d'orient*, i.e. from the East. *Orientation*, now much overworked, is adapted from F. *s'orienter*, to take one's bearings, prop. to face the east, whence also Ger. *orientierung*.

> It [the Russ. revolution] has changed the face of the earth and the orientation of human society
>   (*Daily News*, Apr. 7, 1917).

orifice. F., Late L. *orificium*, from *os*, *or-*, mouth, *facere*, to make.

oriflamme [*hist.*]. F., OF. *orie flame*, L. *aurea flamma*, golden flame, name of sacred banner of St Denis.

> Gefreiz d'Anjou i portet l'orieflambe (*Rol.* 3093).

origan-um. Wild marjoram. F. *origan*, L. *origanum*, G. ὀρίγανον, ? from ὄρος, mountain, γάνος, brightness.

Origenist [*theol.*]. Follower of *Origen* of Alexandria, Christian Father (3 cent.).

origin. F. *origine*, L. *origo, origin-*, from *oriri*, to rise. *Original* occurs first (c. 1300) in *original sin*.

oriole. Bird. OF. *oriol* (replaced by *loriot*, for *l'oriot*), L. *aureolus*, golden.

Orion. G. Ὠρίων, giant of G. myth. slain by Artemis.

orison. AF. *oreison*, F. *oraison*, as *oration* (see *orator*). Revived (c. 1800) by romantics.

ork. See *orc*.

Orleanist [*hist.*]. F. *orléaniste*, partisan of *Duke of Orleans*, younger brother of Louis XIV, and his descendants.

orlop [*naut.*]. Orig. deck covering whole of hold. Earlier (15 cent.) *overlop*, Du. *overloop*, from *overloopen*, to run over (see *leap*). See also quot. s.v. *bilge*.

ormer. Mollusc, sea-ear. Channel Isl. F., L. *auris maris*. Also called *oreille de mer*.

ormolu. F. *or moulu*, lit. ground gold, from p.p. of *moudre*, OF. *moldre*, L. *molere*.

ornament. Restored from ME. *ournement*, F. *ornement*, L. *ornamentum*, from *ornare*, to adorn, ? contr. of *ordinare*. Has absorbed also ME. *aornement*, OF., from *aorner*, L. *ad-ornare*. Application to persons (*ornament of the bar*, etc.) is 16 cent.

> The synne of aornement, or of apparaille
> (Chauc. I. 432).

ornithology. From G. ὄρνις, ὄρνιθ-, bird. Cf. *ornithorhynchus*, duck-billed platypus (Austral.), from G. ῥύγχος, bill.

orography, orology. From G. ὄρος, mountain.

oronoco, oronooko. Tobacco, from Virginia, and prob. not connected with river Orinoco.

orotund. Playful coinage from L. *ore rotundo* (v.i.), one syllable being lost by dissim. (cf. *heroi-comic*).

> Graiis ingenium, Graiis dedit ore rotundo
> Musa loqui (Hor. *Ars Poet.* 323).

orphan. Late L. *orphanus* (*Vulg.*), G. ὀρφανός, from *ὀρφός, bereft, cogn. with L. *orbus*.

Orphic. G. Ὀρφικός, from Ὀρφεύς, myth. musician of Thrace, later regarded as philosophical adept.

orphrey, orfray [*archaic*]. Rich embroidery. False sing. from ME. & OF. *orfreis* (*orfroi*), from L. *aurum* and an obscure second element. The older form app. survives in

orris, trade-name for various kinds of embroidery, etc.

orpiment. Yellow arsenic. F., L. *auripigmentum*, pigment of gold.

orpin. Plant. F., app. shortened from *orpiment*, with which it is synon. in OF.

orpington. Breed of fowls from village in Kent. Cf. *dorking*.

orra [*Sc.*]. Odd, as in *orra man*. Var. of ME. *odde*; cf. dial. *imperence* and see *moral*. *Orra woman* as offic. designation for single woman is found in 16 cent. Sc.

orrery. Invented (c. 1700) by George Graham and named after Charles Boyle, *Earl of Orrery* (Cork).

orris. Esp. in *orris-root*. Ident. with *iris*, form having perh. been affected by association with *liquorice, licoris*, both plants having sweet root. The It. is *irios*, app. from G. ἴριος ῥίζα, where ἴριος is a var. genitive of ἴρις.

> The nature of the orrice is almost singular: for
> there are but few odoriferous roots
> (Bacon, *Sylva*).

ort [*archaic*]. Fragment of food. Usu. in pl. Cf. archaic Du. *orete, ooraete*, LG. *ort*, Sw. dial. *oräte*, in which first element is cogn. with *or-* of *ordeal* and second with *eat*.

> oor-æte, oor-ete: reliquiae, fastidium pabuli sive
> cibi, esca superflua (Kil.).

orthodox. F. *orthodoxe*, L., G. ὀρθόδοξος, from ὀρθός, straight, right, δόξα, opinion, from δοκεῖν, to seem. Spec. epithet of Eastern (Greek) Church. Cf. *orthoepy*, G. ἔπος, ἔπε-, word; *orthography*, G. γράφειν, to write; *orthopaedy*, G. παιδίον, child, παιδεία, rearing; *orthopterous*, G. πτερόν, wing.

ortolan. F., Prov., It. *ortolano*, lit. gardener, L. *hortulanus*, from *hortus*, garden.

> ortolano: a gardner, an orchard keeper. Also a
> kinde of daintie birde in Italie (Flor.).

orvietan [*hist.*]. Antidote, "Venice treacle." F. *orviétan*, It. *orvietano*, from *Orvieto* (It.), where inventor lived.

oryx. Scient. name of gemsbok. G. ὄρυξ, pick-axe, earlier applied to NAfr. antelope with pointed horns, vaguely used by LXX. and *Vulg.* (*Deut.* xiv. 5) and hence by Wyc. and Coverd.

Oscan [*ling.*]. Ancient It. dial. akin to L.

oscillate. From L. *oscillare*, to swing.

oscitant. Drowsy. From pres. part. of L. *oscitare*, to yawn, from *os*, mouth, *citare*, to put in motion, frequent. of *ciëre*, to stir.

osculate. From L. *osculari*, from *osculum*, kiss, lit. little mouth (v.s.).

osier. F., of unknown origin. Cf. Late L. (8 cent.) *ausaria*, *osaria*, bed of willows.

Osmanli. Of *Osman*, Turk. pronunc. of Arab. *Othmān*. See *Ottoman*.

osmium [*chem.*]. From G. ὀσμή, odour.

osmosis. Intermixture, diffusion. From G. ὠσμός, thrust, push.

osmund. Fern. F. *osmonde* (12 cent.), of unknown origin.

osnaburgh [*archaic*]. Fabric from *Osnabrück* (Westphalia). Cf. *holland*, *arras*, etc.

> Four hundred elles of osenbriges very fine
> (Hakl. xi. 28).

osprey. Ult. L. *ossifraga*, lit. bone-breaker (cf. *saxifrage*), whence also F. *orfraie*, for **osfraie*. Neither the late appearance (15 cent.) in E. & F. nor the forms are at present explained.

> The eagle, and the ossifrage, and the ospray
> (*Lev.* xi. 13).

osram [*neol.*]. Electric lamp with filament of *osmium* and *wolfram*.

osseous. From L. *osseus*, from *os*, *oss-*, bone.

Ossianic. Of *Ossian*, anglicized by Mac-Pherson from Gael. *Oisin*, name of bard whose works he claimed to have collected and translated (1760–3).

ossifrage. See *osprey*.

ossuary. After *mortuary* from L. *os*, *oss-*, bone; cf. F. *ossuaire*.

ostensible. F., MedL. *ostensibilis*, from *ostendere*, *ostens-*, to show, compd. of *tendere*, to stretch. With *ostensory*, monstrance, cf. F. *ostensoir*, MedL. *ostensorium*.

osteology. From G. ὀστέον, bone.

ostiary [*eccl.*]. Doorkeeper. L. *ostiarius*, from *ostium*, door; cf. *usher*.

ostler. Ident. with *hostler*, OF. *hostelier*, from *hostel* (q.v.). Orig. inn-keeper, but early associated with '*osses*.

> 'Osses soon will all be in the circuses,
> And if you want an ostler, try the work'uses
> (E. V. Lucas).

ostracize. G. ὀστρακίζειν, from ὄστρακον, earthen vessel, potsherd, because name of person whose banishment was voted was written on piece of pottery. Perh. orig. shell (see *oyster*).

ostreiculture. See *oyster*.

ostrich. OF. *austruce*, *austruche* (*autruche*), VL. *avis struthio*, from Late G. στρουθίων, ostrich; cf. Sp. *avestruz*. The simplex appears in It. *struzzo*, Ger. *strauss*, AS.

strȳta, whence name *Strutt*. In class. G. usu. ὁ μέγας στρουθός, lit. the big sparrow. Often used allusively to supposed habit of the bird of hiding its head in the sand when cornered.

> How long the German, Austrian and Turkish peoples will be content to bury their heads in this official sand (*Westm. Gaz.* Oct. 3, 1918).

Ostrogoths. Late L. *Ostrogothi*, East Goths, who ruled in Italy 493–555. See *Easter*, *Goth*.

other. AS. *ōther*. An Aryan compar. formation; cf. Du. Ger. *ander*, ON. *annar*, Goth. *anthar*, Sanskrit *antara*, and prob. L. *alter*, *alius*, G. ἄλλος. Loss of Teut. *-n-* before spirant is reg. in E. (cf. *tooth*, *five*). Formerly used, like OF. *autre*, for second. Dial. *tother* is due to wrong separation of ME. *thet* (that) *other*; so also we find commonly *the tone* and *a nother*. For *otherguess* see *guess²*.

> If he had not been in drink, he would have tickled you othergates than he did (*Twelfth Night*, v. 1).

otiose. L. *otiosus*, from *otium*, ease; cf. F. *oiseux*.

otology. Study of the ear, G. οὖς, ὠτ-.

ottava rima [*metr.*]. It. eight-lined stanza, lit. eighth rime.

otter. AS. *oter*, *ottor*. Aryan; cf. Du. Ger. *otter*, ON. *otr*, G. ὕδωρ, water, ὕδρα, hydra, water-snake, OPers. *udra*, otter; ult. cogn. with *water*. Also used, in the Great War, of paravane fitted to merchant-ship.

otto. Obs. bicycle. From inventor's name (1877).

Ottoman. From Arab. *Othmān*, founder (c. 1300) of Turk. dynasty, which took over (1517) the Caliphate from the last Abasside Caliph of Cairo. Cf. *Osmanli*. Hence *ottoman* (c. 1800), suggesting an oriental couch.

> The moonie standards of proud Ottoman
> (Sylv. i. 2).

otto of roses. See *attar*.

oubliette [*hist.*]. Secret dungeon. F. (14 cent.) from *oublier*, to forget, VL. **oblitare*, from *oblivisci*, *oblit-*, to forget. App. introduced by Scott.

ouch [*obs.*]. Brooch, clasp, etc. For *nouch* (cf. *auger*, *apron*), OF. *nouche*, OHG. *nuscha*. Of Celt. origin; cf. OIr. *nasc*, ring.

> And they were set as thikke of nouchis
> Full of the fynest stones faire
> (Chauc. *House of Fame*, iii. 260).

> Thou shalt make them to be set in ouches of gold
> (*Ex.* xxviii. 11).

ought[1] [*dial.*]. For *nought*, as in *oughts and crosses*. *An ought* is for *a nought* (v.s.), helped by the suggestion of O.

ought[2]. Verb. Past tense of *owe* (q.v.). As auxil. verb it represents the past subjunctive. Use of p.p. survives in vulg. *you hadn't ought to* (= F. *vous n'auriez pas dû*). Cf. similar use of F. *devoir*, lit. to owe.

Cicero...ought all he had unto learning
(Florio's *Montaigne*, ii. 12).

ounce[1]. Weight. F. *once*, L. *uncia*, twelfth of pound or foot; cf. *inch*[1].

ounce[2]. Animal. F. *once*, for OF. *lonce* (taken as *l'once*), VL. **luncea*, for *lyncea*, from *lynx*; cf. It. *lonza*, "a beast called an ounce, a panther or cat of mountaine" (Flor.), Sp. *onza*.

our. AS. *ūre*, for *ūsere* (cf. *us*), genitive of *wē*. Com. Teut.; cf. OSax. *ūser*, Ger. *unser*, Goth. *unsara*. For reg. formation of possess. pronouns from genitive of pers. pronouns cf. F. *leur*, L. *illorum*. *Ours* is a double possess. of ME. formation. For dial. *ourn* (due to *mine*, etc.) cf. *hisn*, *hern*.

His conversacioun is in hevene, as ouren shulden be (Wyc.).

ourali. See *curari*.

ousel. See *ouzel*.

oust. AF. *ouster*, OF. *oster* (*ôter*), ? VL. **haustare*, from *haurire*, *haust-*, to drain. Cf. *exhaurire*, "to pille, robbe, or take from one all that he hath" (Coop.). L. *obstare*, to hinder, has also been suggested, but sense-relation is difficult.

out. AS. *ūt*. Com. Teut.; cf. Du. *uit*, Ger. *aus*, ON. Goth. *ūt*. *Outer* is a ME. formation differentiated in sense from orig. *utter*. Verb to *out*, expel, now slangy, is in AS. With *out and out*, *out and away*, cf. *far and away*. With ellipsis of verb *out* acquired interj. force which survives in *out upon*. *Outing* is used by Barbour for an expedition.

Normant escrïent "deus aïe"!
La gent englesche "ut ut" escrie
(Wace, describing Battle of Hastings).
owt, owt: interjeccio (*Prompt. Parv.*).

outcaste. From *caste* (q.v.). Formation influenced by *outcast*.

outfit. Used in US. for anything, from a pocket-knife to a railway.

out-Herod. To exaggerate a part, *Herod* being stock braggart and bully of early rel. drama.

I could have such a fellow whipped for o'er doing Termagant; it out-herods Herod (*Haml.* iii. 2).

outland. AS. *ūtland*, out land, foreign country. Hence *outlandish*, orig. foreign, with sense-development as in *strange*, *uncouth*. *Outlander* (c. 1600) is adapted from Du. *uitlander*.

Most excellent outlandish linnen cloth (Purch.).

outlaw. ON. *ūtlagi*, from *ūtlagr*, outlawed, banished.

output. Till c. 1880 techn. term in iron and coal trades.

outrage. F., from *outre*, beyond, L. *ultra*; cf. It. *oltraggio*, E. *going too far*. Occ. misused as though compd. of *rage*.

outrance. F., only in *à outrance*, from *outrer*, to go beyond (v.s.). Altered in E. to *utterance* (*Macb.* iii. 1), still in use as archaism.

outré. F., exaggerated (v.s.).

outrecuidance [*archaic*]. Arrogance. Archaic F., from *outrecuider*, L. *ultra cogitare* (cf. *overweening*). Revived by Scott (*Ivanhoe*, ch. ix.).

outrigger [*naut.*]. Altered, on *rig*[1], from earlier *outligger* (15 cent.), which is prob. Du. *uitlegger*, lit. outlyer, though this is not recorded so early.

On each side of them [canoes] lye out two pieces of timber (Drake).

These are generally called by the Dutch, and by the English from them, out-lagers (Dampier).

outsider. In disparaging sense (not in *NED.*) from early application to horse "outside the favourites."

outskirt. Now only in pl. From 16 cent. See *skirt*.

outspan [*SAfr.*]. Du. *uitspannen*, to out span, unharness team.

outstrip. From 16 cent. See *strip*[2].

outward. See *-ward*.

ouzel, ousel. AS. *ōsle*, blackbird, cogn. with Ger. *amsel*, with very numerous dial. forms, OHG. *amsala*, of which first element may be cogn. with (*yellow-*)*hammer* (q.v.).

oval. F., from L. *ovum*, egg, cogn. with G. ᾠόν. Cf. *ovate*, L. *ovatus*; *ovary*, F. *ovaire*.

ovation. L. *ovatio-n-*, triumph on smaller scale, from *ovare*, to exult, rejoice, prob. imit. of shout.

oven. AS. *ofn*. Com. Teut.; cf. Du. *oven*, Ger. *ofen*, ON. *ofn*, Goth. *auhns*; cogn. with G. ἰπνός, oven, furnace, Sanskrit *ukha*, cooking-pot, which was no doubt orig. meaning.

over. AS. *ofer*. Com. Teut.; cf. Du. *over*, Ger. *ober*, *über*, ON. *yfer*, Goth. *ufar*; cogn. with G. ὑπέρ, L. *super*, Sanskrit *upari*. These are all orig. compar. formations from element which appears in E. *up*.

overbear. Orig. naut., of an overwhelming wind.

> But yᵉ easte wynde shal overbeare the in to the myddest off the sea (Coverd. *Ezek.* xxvii. 26).

overboard. Two words in AS. See *board*.

overcast. Orig. to cover, as with a garment; now only of sky.

> *ovyr caste*, or *ovyr hyllyd*: pretectus, contectus
> (*Prompt. Parv.*).

overcoat, overshoe. Orig. US., after Ger. *überrock, überschuh*.

overcome. Orig., in AS., to catch up, overtake.

overhaul. Orig. naut., to slacken a rope so as to take off strain, later to pull rigging apart for examination. In sense of overtake it replaces earlier *overhale*.

overlap. See *lap*¹.

overlook. For double sense cf. *oversee*. In dial. used of "evil eye."

> Vile worm, thou wast o'erlooked even in thy birth (*Merry Wives*, v. 5).

overman. Used for Ger. *übermensch* in early transl. of Nietzsche. Replaced by *superman*.

> Nietzsche's overman can only be admired so long as he is an overman (*Times*, Sep. 2, 1914).

overplus. Partial transl. of F. *surplus* (q.v.).

overreach. Orig. to reach beyond. Current fig. sense from 16 cent.

override. Orig. to trample under foot, like bandit cavalry. Cf. *overrun*.

oversea(s). Substituted, during the Great War, for *colonial* (troops), objected to by some. In gen. adj. sense Burke uses *ultramarine*.

> The Overseas Settlement Office, as the Emigration Department is now called
> (*Daily Chron.* Mar. 9, 1920).

oversee. AS. *ofersēon*, to superintend, also to fail to notice; cf. double sense of *oversight*. For first sense cf. *survey, supervise*.

overset. Reg. word for *capsize* (q.v.) up to c. 1760. Cf. *overturn*.

overshoe. Cf. *overcoat*.

overshoot. Orig. from archery, to *overshoot the mark*.

overslaugh [*mil.*]. Passing over one's ordinary turn of duty. Du. *overslag*, from *slaan*, to strike; cf. Ger. *überschlagen*, to omit, skip. In gen. sense in US.

overt. OF., p.p. of *ovrir* (*ouvrir*), app. L. *aperire*, early influenced by opposite

covrir (*couvrir*), to cover (q.v.). For other examples of association of opposites cf. *grief, render*.

overtake. Orig. of running down and catching fugitive; cf. etym. sense of *surprise*.

overture. OF. (*ouverture*), opening, from *ouvrir*. See *overt*.

overween. Now usu. in adj. *overweening*, from AS. *ofer-wenian*, to become insolent. See *ween*, and cf. *outrecuidance*.

overwhelm. See *whelm*.

oviparous. From L. *oviparus*, from *ovum*, egg, *parere*, to bring forth.

owe. AS. *āgan*, to have, own. Com. Teut.; cf. OSax. *ēgan*, OHG. *eigan*, ON. *eiga*, Goth. *aigan*. A preterite-present (cf. *can, may, dare*) which survives only in E. & Scand. (Sw. *äga*, Dan. *eie*, to have, own). Current sense has been evolved like that of *have* in *I have to pay* (*go, confess*, etc.), but orig. sense, which is very common in Shaks., survives in dial. See *own, ought*.

> This is no mortal business, nor no sound
> That the earth owes (*Temp.* i. 2).

Owenism. System of *Robert Owen*, communistic theorist (†1858).

owl. AS. *ūle*. Com. Teut.; cf. Du. *uil*, Ger. *eule*, ON. *ugla*. Orig. imit. of cry; cf. L. *ulula*, owl, *ululare*, to howl. *Drunk as an owl* refers to blinking solemnity of bird. *Owlet* is altered on *owl* from earlier *howlet* (q.v.).

own. AS. *ǣgen, āgen*. Orig. p.p. of *owe* (q.v.); cf. OSax. *ēgan*, Ger. *eigen*, ON. *eiginn*, Goth. *aigan*. From *mine own*, etc., was formed ME. *my nown*, with which cf. Sc. *nainsell*, for *ownself*. With to *hold one's own* (14 cent.) cf. mod. *on one's own* (responsibility, etc.). Verb to *own* is AS. *āgnian*, from adj. Sense of confessing, "owning up," is evolved from that of acknowledging possession and resultant responsibility.

ox. AS. *oxa*. Com. Teut.; cf. Du. *os*, Ger. *ochse*, ON. *uxe*, Goth. *auhsa*; cogn. with Welsh *ých*, Sanskrit *ukshan*. Pl. *oxen* is only survival in current E. of AS. weak pl. in *-an*.

oxalic. F. *oxalique* (Morveau and Lavoisier, 1787), from G. ὀξαλίς, from ὀξύς, sour, acid.

Oxford Movement. High Church movement of Pusey, Newman, Hurrell Froude, etc. at *Oxford* (c. 1853). Cf. *Tractarian*.

oxgang [*hist.*]. AS. *oxangang*, bovate (q.v.). The eighth part of a carucate (q.v.).

oxide. F., coined (1787) by Morveau and Lavoisier from G. ὀξύς, sour, with ending of *acide*.

oxlip. For *oxslip*, AS. *oxanslyppe*. See *cowslip*.

Oxon. Signature of bishop of Oxford (v.i.).

Oxonian. From MedL. *Oxonia*, from *Oxenford*, Oxford. Cf. *Cantab*.

Then he asked me and I were cantibrygion. I sayd no, I was an oxonian (*NED.* 1540).

oxter [*Sc. & north.*]. Armpit. From AS. *ōxta, ōhsta*; cf. Du. *oksel*, Ger. *achsel*, OIr. *oxal*, L. *axilla*.

oxygen. F. *oxygène* (Lavoisier), from G. ὀξύς, sour, -γεν-, producing.

oxymoron [*rhet.*]. Association of incongruous terms, as in *pet aversion, splendide mendax*. Neut. of G. ὀξύμωρος, pointedly foolish, from ὀξύς, sharp, μωρός, foolish.

His honour rooted in dishonour stood,
And faith unfaithful kept him falsely true
                                 (Tennyson).

oxytone [*gram.*]. Accented on last syllable. G. ὀξύτονος, with acute (v.s.) accent. See *tone*.

oyer and terminer [*leg.*]. Commission of judges, to hear and decide. AF. *oyer*, OF. *oïr* (*ouïr*), L. *audire*. Hence also the crier's *oyez* or *o yes!*

oyster. OF. *oistre, uistre* (*huître*), L., G. ὄστρεον, cogn. with ὀστέον, bone, shell.

ozokerit. Fossil resin, "native paraffin." Ger., coined (1833) by Glocker, from G. ὄζειν, to smell, κηρός, bees-wax.

ozone. F., from G. ὄζειν, to smell.

Ps and Qs, to mind one's. App. from confusion between *p* and *q* of children learning to write.

pa. Cf. *papa*.

paauw. Bustard (SAfr.). Du., peacock (q.v.).

pabulum. L., cogn. with *pasci*, to feed.

paca. SAmer. rodent. Sp., from Tupi (Brazil).

pace. ME. *pas*, F., L. *passus*, from *pandere, pass-*, to stretch. To *put through one's paces* is to show the qualities of a horse. With suggestion of speed in to *go the pace*, orig. in hunting, cf. *apace*.

pace. Abl. of L. *pax, pac-*, peace, as in *pace tua*, with all deference to you. Hence *pace Mr Churchill*, etc.

pacha. See *pasha*.

pachisi. Board-game in India. From Hind. *pach(ch)īs*, twenty-five.

pachyderm. G. παχύδερμος, from παχύς, thick,

δέρμα, skin. Adopted as biol. term (1797) by Cuvier.

pacific. F. *pacifique*, L. *pacificus*, peace-making, from *pax, pac-*, peace, *facere*, to make. The ocean was named (c. 1500) by Magellan.

pacifist. A clumsily formed word, perh. first in F. *pacifiste*. The correct form would be *pacificist*.

As quarrelsome as a pacifist (*Windsor Mag.*).

pack. Early (13 cent.) loan from Du., due to the wool-trade with Flanders; cf. Du. LG. *pak*, whence also Ger. *pack*; ? cogn. with *bag*. Also borrowed by Rom. langs. (v.i.), in which, as in Teut. langs., it is commonly associated with hurried departure, e.g. F. *faire son paquet = trousser bagage*. Used of cards from 16 cent., of hounds from 17 cent. In to *pack a jury* there has been contact with obs. *pack*, to make secret arrangements, prob. a vulgar pronunc. of *pact* (cf. *feckless*).

package. Orig. the act of packing.

packet. AF. dim. of *pack*. Hence F. *paquet*, It. *pacchetto*, Sp. *paquete*. *Packet-boat* was orig. (17 cent.) for carrying mails (cf. F. *paquebot*, from E.). It was earlier called *post-bark, post-boat*.

pact. OF. (*pacte*), L. *pactum*, from *paciscere, pact-*, to covenant, cogn. with *pangere, pact-*, to fasten.

Pactolian. Of *Pactolus*, G. Πακτωλός, river of Lydia with golden sands.

Apostles of super-indemnities preaching blue ruin for the enemy combined with Pactolian payments
                        (*Obs.* June 1, 1919).

pad[1]. Cushion, etc. In 16 cent. sense of elastic cushion of foot (of camel, etc.) is app. cogn. with obs. Du. *pad, patte*, "palma pedis, planta pedis" (Kil.), LG. *pad*, and perh. with Ger. *pfote* (see *paw*). F. *patte*, Prov. *pauta* are of Teut. origin. This sense is late in E. and can hardly have given the gen. meaning. With *padding* in literary sense cf. *bombast*.

pad[2]. In *footpad* (q.v.). Cant word from 16 cent. Du. *pad*, road, path (q.v.). Obs. *pad*, highwayman, later *padder*, is for *gentleman of the pad*. With *pad*, horse, cf. *roadster*. See also *hoof*.

pad: the high way, and a robber thereon; *a pad*: an easy pacing horse (*Dict. Cant. Crew*).

pad[3]. Basket. Var. of dial. *ped* (see *pedlar*).

paddle[1]. Noun. Orig. (c. 1400) spade-like implement, e.g. *Deut.* xxiii. 13, where it renders *Vulg. paxillus.* First used in current sense by Capt. John Smith. ? Corrupted from F. *pale, pelle,* shovel, L. *pala,* used of blade of oar or of paddle-wheel. A tract on Florida (1563) describes the native oars as "made after the fashyon of a peele" (see *peel*[4]). To *paddle one's own canoe* is attributed to Abraham Lincoln.

paddle[2]. Verb. App. from *pad*[1] in sense of foot, paw. Cf. LG. *paddeln,* to tramp, and synon. F. *patouiller, patauger,* from *patte,* paw (q.v.).

patouiller: to slabber, to padle, or dable in with the feet (Cotg.).

paddock. Alteration (from 16 cent.) of earlier *parrock,* AS. *pearroc.* See *park.* For change of consonant cf. *pediment.*

puddock, or *purrock*: a small inclosure (Worlidge).

paddy. Malay *pādī,* rice in the straw, prob. cogn. with *batta* (q.v.).

Paddy. Irishman. Short for *Padraig, Patrick,* patron saint of Ireland. Also *Paddy-whack,* explained (1811) as a stout, brawny Irishman. This is also used of (presumably Irish) frenzy of rage and often reduced to *paddy.*

paddymelon. Small kangaroo. Corrupt. of Austral. native name.

padishah. Pers. *pādshāh* (in Turk. *pādishāh*), of which first element is Sanskrit *pati,* lord, ruler. Title of Shah of Persia, also given to Sultan of Turkey and other Eastern potentates. See *shah.*

padlock. From 15 cent. First element is of unknown origin. The only *pad* which is old enough is dial. *pad,* frog, toad, AS. *padde,* and the application of animal names to mech. devices is very common, but it is hard to see connection. ? From orig. shape.

padre. It. Sp. Port., L. *pater.* Title of regular clergy. Its use in E. for army or navy chaplain comes from Port. via Anglo-Ind. Cf. *tank.* In Purch. *padre* occurs passim for Jesuit missionary.

padrone. Master of Mediterranean trading-ship, employer of child-musicians, etc. It., MedL. *patro-n-,* for L. *patronus.* Cf. F. *patron,* the guv'nor.

paduasoy [*archaic*]. Alteration of earlier (17 cent.) *poudesoy,* F. *pou-de-soie, pout-de-soie,* with first element of unknown origin. The alteration is due to confusion with obs. *Padua say,* from obs. *say*[2], serge, manufactured at *Padua.* For a similar corrupt. cf. *mantua.*

paean. L., G. παιάν, hymn, chant, from Ἰὼ Παιάν, init. words of invocation to Apollo under name Παιάν, Homeric name of physician of gods.

paederast. Sodomite. G. παιδεραστής, from παῖς, παιδ-, boy, ἐραστής, lover.

paeon [*metr.*]. Foot with one long and three short syllables. Attic G. παιών, paean (q.v.).

pagan. L. *paganus,* rustic, from *pagus,* canton, district. The trad. view that the rel. sense was due to the lingering of paganism in the rural districts is shown by mod. research to be incorrect, as *paganus,* non-Christian, occurs at a date when paganism was still the recognized religion of the Empire. The Roman soldier used *paganus,* "yokel," as contemptuous name for a civilian, or for an incompetent soldier (v.i.), and, when the early Church adopted *miles* (*Christi*), in the fig. sense of soldier (of Christ), *paganus* was also taken over from colloq. L., as its natural opposite, to connote one who was not a good soldier of Christ. Thus the sense has developed from that of the Kiplingesque "lousy civilian," or the more mod. "d—d conchy." See *NED.* vii. 2. *Addenda,* and Gibbon, ch. xxi., Note q.

Mox infensius praetorianis "vos" inquit "nisi vincitis, pagani, quis alius imperator, quae castra alia excipient?" (Tac. *Hist.* iii. 24).

Apud hunc [sc. Christum] tam miles est paganus fidelis quam paganus est miles infidelis (Tertullian).

page[1]. Lad, etc. F.; cf. It. *paggio,* Sp. *page,* MedL. *pagius.* Origin obscure. Prob. L. *pathicus,* G. παθικός, boy kept for unnatural vice, lit. sufferer. Cf. *Ganymede,* which, besides being used allusively for page, has given obs. *catamite,* synon. with *pathicus.* The word has varied in dignity according to its senses, but was app. at first contemptuous.

page[2]. Of a book. F., L. *pagina,* from root *pag-* of *pangere,* to fasten.

pageant. ME. *pagyn* (Wyc.), AL. *pagina.* It is uncertain whether the earlier sense was scene, tableau, or the wooden structure (often on wheels like the pageants of Lord Mayor's Show) on which popular drama was enacted. If the latter, the sense corresponds exactly with that of L. *pegma,* G. πῆγμα, movable scaffold for theatrical use, which is cogn. with L. *pagina,* page (roots *pag-,* πηγ-, to make fast). The form represents L. *pagina,* which, however, is not found in the required sense exc. in AL. (v.s.).

pegma: a stage or frame whereon pageantes be set and caried (Coop.).

pagination. F., from *paginer*, to number pages, from L. *pagina*, page².

pagne. Loin-cloth, etc. F., Sp. *paño*, L. *pannus*, cloth.

pagoda. Earlier (16 cent.) *pagod*, Port. *pagode*, prob. corrupted from Pers. *but-kadah*, idol house. It was also applied to an idol and to a coin, app. from design stamped on it, whence Anglo-Ind. allusions to *shaking the pagoda-tree*, i.e. getting rich quick in India.

They are Indian and heathenish money, with the picture of a divell upon them, and therefore are called pagodes (*NED.* 1598).

pagurian. Hermit crab. From L., G. πάγουρος, lit. hard tail.

pah¹. Interj. Natural exclamation of disgust (*Haml.* v. 1).

pah², pa. Native fort in New Zealand Maori, from *pà*, to block up.

Pahlavi, Pehlevi [*ling.*]. Archaic Persian. Pers. *Pahlavi*, Parthian, name given by followers of Zoroaster to lang. of their sacred books.

pail. AS. *pægel*, small measure, would give mod. form; but OF. *paele* (*poêle*), frying-pan, etc., L. *patella*, dim. of *patina*, dish, would explain final -*e* always found in ME. Neither etymon will account for sense.

paillasse, palliasse. F. *paillasse*, from *paille*, straw, L. *palea*. Cf. *pallet¹*.

paillette. Spangle. F., dim. of *paille*, straw (v.s.).

pain. F. *peine*, L. *poena*, penalty. Orig. sense in *pains and penalties, under pain of*. With to *take pains, for one's pains*, etc., cf. similar use of *trouble*. See *pine²*.

The honourable knight, Sir Walter Raleigh, returning from his paineful and happie discovery of Guiana (Hakl.).

paint. F. *peint*, p.p. of *peindre*, L. *pingere*; cf. *faint, taint*, etc. To *paint the town red* is US.

painter [*naut.*]. ME. *peyntour* (14 cent.), rope or chain by which anchor is held to ship's side, now called *shank-painter*. Current sense from c. 1700. OF. *pentour, pentoir, pantoire*, etc., used in naut. lang. of various suspensory tackle, ult. from *pendre*, to hang, L. *pendere*. *Cutting the painter*, allusive to separation of colonies from Empire, is late 19 cent., but the phrase is much older (c. 1700) in sense of sending off unceremoniously.

pair. F. *paire*, L. *paria*, neut. pl. of *par*, equal, peer. In ME. used also for a set, as still in *pair of steps* (*stairs*), whence the *two-pair front* (*back*) of lodging-houses. Verb to *pair*, mate, is first in Shaks. (*Wint. Tale*, iv. 4).

pal. E. Gipsy; cf. Turk. Gipsy *pral, plal*, brother; ult. cogn. with Sanskrit *bhrātṛ*, brother.

palace. F. *palais*, L. *palatium*; cf. It. *palazzo*, Sp. *palacio*. Orig. applied to imperial residences on *Mons Palatinus* at Rome, prob. from stake (*palus*) enclosure. With mod. *picture-palace* cf. *gin-palace*, recorded 1835 ("Boz").

paladin. F., It. *paladino*, L. *palatinus*, of a palace. Orig. applied to Charlemagne's twelve peers. The substitution of the It. word for OF. *palaisin* was due to the popularity of the It. poets of the Renaissance.

palaeography, paleography. From G. παλαιός, ancient. Cf. *palaeolithic*, from λίθος, stone; *palaeontology*, from G. ὄντα, neut. pl. of ὤν, being; *palaeozoic*, from ζωή, life.

palaestra. L., G. παλαίστρα, from παλαίειν, to wrestle.

palafitte. Lake-dwelling. F., It. *palafitta*, from *palo*, stake, *pale¹*, *fitto*, fixed.

palanquin. Port. (c. 1500), supposed to be nasalized from Hind. *pālkī* (whence E. *palkee*), Sanskrit *paryaṅka, palyaṅka*, bed. The Port. form is app. due to association with Sp. *palanca*, pole for carrying weights, cowlstaff, VL. *palanga*, G. *φαλάγγη (pl. only), whence also F. *palan*, lifting tackle, etc. Some authorities regard the latter source as the true origin of the word and its resemblance to Hind. *pālkī* as accidental. Sir T. Roe has *palankee*, a compromise between the two words.

palate. Restored spelling of OF. & ME. *palat, palet*, L. *palatum*, cogn. with *palear*, dewlap.

palatial. From L. *palatium*, palace (q.v.).

palatine [*hist.*]. F. *palatin*, L. *palatinus*, from *palatium*, palace. Orig. of the imperial palace of the Caesars. In E. hist. (*earl, county*) it indicates quasi-royal authority. In Ger. hist. of the *Palatinate* of the Rhine (see *palsgrave*). In sense of fur tippet, F. *palatine*, from the *Princess Palatine*, wife of Duke of Orleans (17 cent.).

palaver. Port. *palavra*, word, speech, L. *parabola*, parable (q.v.), whence also Sp. *palabra*, F. *parole*. Used by Port. travellers of parleys with natives in WAfr., and brought thence by E. sailors. Cf. *fetish*.

pale[1]. Noun. F. *pal*, L. *pālus*, stake, ult. cogn. with *pangere*, to fix. Hence *palings*. In sense of limit, boundary, esp. in *within* (*outside*) *the pale*, and often with ref. to the *English Pale* in Ireland. Also (her.) vertical band.

Tithe was paid for the first time within the pale after the synod of Cashel
(Magee, *Speech on Disestablishment of Irish Church*, 1869).

pale[2]. Adj. F. *pâle*, from L. *pallidus*, from *pallēre*, to be pale.

paleography. See *palaeography*.

Palestine soup. See *artichoke*.

paletot. F., OF. *paltoc, palletoc*, whence ME. *paltok*; cf. Sp. *paletoque*. Origin obscure. First element is app. OF. *palle*, cloak, L. *palla*.

palette. F., dim. of *pale*, shovel, oar-blade, L. *pala*.

palfrey. OF. *palefrei* (*palefroi*), Late L. *palafredus*, by dissim. from Late L. *parafredus, paraveredus*, from G. παρά, beside, L. *veredus*, light horse, of Celt. origin and cogn. with Welsh *gorwydd*, horse. Cf. It. *palafreno*, Sp. *palafren*, both corrupted by association with L. *frenum*, bridle; also Du. *paard*, Ger. *pferd* (OHG. *pharifrid*). For dissim. of *r-r* to *l-r* in Rom. forms cf. *pilgrim*.

Pali [*ling.*]. Early literary form of Sanskrit. Short for Sanskrit *pāli-bhāshā*, lang. of canonical texts, lit. line language.

palikar [*hist.*]. Greek or Albanian mil. chief, esp. in War of Independence. ModG. παλικάρι, lad, from G. πάλλαξ, youth. First in Byron.

palimpsest. Parchment twice written on. G. παλίμψηστος, from πάλιν, again, ψῆν, to rub smooth.

palindrome. Word or phrase spelt alike backward or forward, e.g. *Roma tibi subito motibus ibit amor*. G. παλίνδρομος, from πάλιν, again, δραμεῖν, to run. Cf. *palingenesis*, re-birth; *palinode*, recantation.

paling. See *pale*[1].

palisade. F. *palissade*, formed by analogy with other mil. words in *-ade* (q.v.) from *palisser*, to fence, from *palis*, pale, from *pal*, stake. See *pale*[1].

palkee. See *palanquin*.

pall[1]. Noun. AS. *pæll*, cloak, pall, L. *pallium*. Earlier gen. sense survives in poet. and

hist. use only. Used in connection with funerals from 15 cent., but not necessarily of mourning colour.

pall[2]. Verb. Aphet. form of *appal* (q.v.) in etym. sense of losing colour, and hence flavour. Cf. *peal* for *appeal*. Now only fig.

this drinke wyll pall, if it stande uncovered all nyght: ce boire s'appallyra, etc. (Palsg.).

Palladian [*arch.*]. Of *Andrea Palladio*, Roman architect (†1580).

palladium[1]. L., G. παλλάδιον, image of Pallas Athene, supposed to protect citadel of Troy. Hence, national safeguard.

They hadde a relik, heet Palladion,
That was hir trust aboven everychon
(Chauc. *Troil.* i. 153).

palladium[2] [*chem.*]. Metal. Named (1803) by discoverer, Wollaston, in honour of recently discovered asteroid *Pallas*. Cf. *cerium*.

pallet[1]. Straw mattress. AF. *paillette*, dim. of F. *paille*, straw, L. *palea*. Cf. *paillasse*.

pallet[2]. In various techn. senses; ident. with *palette*.

palliasse. See *paillasse*.

palliate. From Late L. *palliare*, to disguise, from *pallium*, cloak.

Surmyse set foorth and palliated with the vesture... of a professed veritee (Hall's *Chron.*).

pallid. L. *pallidus*. See *pale*[2].

pallium. L., cloak, etc. See *pall*[1].

pall-mall [*hist.*]. OF. *palemail*, It. *pallamaglio*, lit. ball mallet (from a Lombard form of Teut. *ball*), name of game popular in 16–17 cents., in England esp. after Restoration; also applied to path or walk where it was played. Evelyn seldom speaks of a French town without some description of its *mall* (q.v.) or *pallmall*. Hoby (1551) calls the game *palla-malla*.

So I into St James's Park, where I saw the Duke of York playing at pele-mele, the first time that ever I saw the sport (Pepys, Apr. 2, 1661).

I walked in the Parke, discoursing with the keeper of the Pell Mell, who was sweeping of it
(*ib.* May 16, 1663).

pallor. L.; see *pale*[2].

palm[1]. Tree. AS. *palm*, L. *palma*, a transferred use of *palma*, palm of the hand (v.i.), from the spreading fronds. An early Christian introduction. In most Europ. langs., and usu. applied also to the willow branches used as substitute for the Eastern tree. In early use as emblem of victory, e.g. to *bear* (*carry off*) *the palm*. With *Palm*

Sunday, found in AS., cf. F. *Pâques fleuries*, lit. flowery Easter. *Palm-oil* is recorded punningly in sense of bribe in 17 cent. (see *palm²*).

In the most high and palmy state of Rome
(*Haml.* i. 1).

palm². Of hand. Restored from ME. *paume*, F., L. *palma* (v.s.), cogn. with G. παλάμη and AS. *folm* (see *fumble*). F. differentiates in spelling *palme*, of tree, *paume*, of hand, the former being a learned word. In E. often used in connection with bribery (v.i.), esp. in to *grease one's palm*. To *palm* (*off*) is from juggling, cheating at cards, etc. *Palmistry* is in Lydgate (*pawmestry*).

Let me tell you Cassius, you yourself
Are much condemned to have an itching palm
(*Jul. Caes.* iv. 3).

palma Christi. Castor-oil plant. From shape of leaves. See *palm¹*.

God prepared a gourd [*marg.* palmcrist]
(*Jonah*, iv. 6).

palmate [*biol.*]. Web-footed, etc. L. *palmatus*, from *palma*, palm².

palmer [*hist.*]. OF. *palmier*, *paumier*, MedL. *palmarius*, from *palma*, palm¹; cf. It. *palmiere*, Sp. *palmero*. Orig. pilgrim returning with palm-branch gathered in Holy Land. The *palmer-worm* (*Joel*, i. 4) is nicknamed from wandering habits.

palmetto. Altered, as though It., from Sp. *palmito*, dwarf fan-palm (see *palm¹*).

palmiped [*biol.*]. L. *palmipes*, *-ped-*, palm-footed. Cf. *palmate*.

palmyra. Kind of palm-tree. Port. *palmeira* or Sp. *palmera*, from L. *palma*, with mod. spelling erron. associated with *Palmyra* (Syria).

palpable. F., Late L. *palpabilis*, from *palpare*, to feel, handle gently. For sense-development cf. *tangible*.

A hit, a very palpable hit (*Haml.* v. 2).

palpebral [*anat.*]. Late L. *palpebralis*, from *palpebra*, eyelid, cogn. with *palpitare*.

palpitate. L. *palpitare*, frequent. of *palpare*. See *palpable*.

palsgrave [*hist.*]. Count palatine. Archaic Du. *paltsgrave* (*paltsgraaf*), MHG. *pfalzgrave* (*pfalzgraf*), lit. palace count. Ger. *pfalz*, hist. palace, now usu. Palatinate, is OHG. *phalanza*, VL. **palantium*, for *palatium*, palace. Cf. *landgrave*, *margrave*.

palstave [*antiq.*]. Kind of celt. ON. *pálstafr*, lit. spade stave, but this may be folk-etym. for AS. *palstr*, spike.

palsy. Contr. of OF. & ME. *paralisie*, VL. **paralysia*, for *paralysis* (q.v.); cf. It. *paralisia*, Sp. *perlesia*.

A man was criplidi n parlesie [*vars.* parlesi, palesy palsy] (*Cursor Mundi*).

palter. From 16 cent. App. frequent. of an unrecorded verb to **palt*. Both this word and *paltry* belong to a word *palt*, rag, app. of LG. origin, and occurring in Fris., Dan., Sw., etc., traces of which are also found in the Rom. langs. (see quot. 2, s.v. *paltry*). Cf. dial. E. *palt*, rubbish. For a semantic parallel cf. the F. series below.

chippe: an old clout, rag, or patch (Cotg.).
chipoter: to dodge, miche, paulter; trifle, &c. (*ib.*).
chipoterie: doging, miching, paultering; trifling, fidling, foolish medling (*ib.*).

paltry. Orig. noun, rubbish, etc. For adj. use and sense-development cf. *trumpery*. See *palter*.

[They] cloute up with stable straw, and such paltry, the reuynes, breaches, and decayes (*NED.* 1566).
paltone: a paltry knave, a dodging varlet, a wrangling companion (Torr.).

paludal [*med.*]. Of a marsh, L. *palus*, *palud-*. Cf. *palustral*, from L. *palustris*.

paly [*her.*]. F. *palé*, from *pal*, pale¹.

pam [*archaic*]. Short for F. *pamphile*, card-game, knave of clubs; cf. Sc. *pamphie*, *pawmie*, in same sense. Synon. Norw. Dan. *fil* preserves the second syllable. L. *Pamphilus* is G. Πάμφιλος, beloved of all. Cf. *pamphlet*. Pam was also used as nickname of *Lord Palmerston* (†1865).

pampa. Sp., Peruv. *bamba*, *pampa*, steppe, flat. Usu. in pl., e.g. *pampas-grass*.

pamper. Orig. to cram with food. Frequent. of obs. *pamp*, *pomp*; cf. Ger. dial. *pampen*, Bav. *pampfen*, to gorge. WFlem. *pamperen* has same meaning. ? Ult. cogn. with *pap*.

I was not to be what Mrs Joe called "Pompeyed" (*Great Exp.* ch. vii.).

pampero. SAmer. wind. Sp., from *pampa* (q.v.).

pamphlet. AL. *panfletus* (14 cent.), from OF. *Pamphilet*, name of MedL. amatory poem *Pamphilus, seu de Amore* (12 cent.), taken as type of small book. With this title cf. OF. & ME. *Catonet*, distichs of pseudo-Cato, *Esopet*, Aesop's Fables. Spec. sense of small polemical brochure is later and has been adopted in F. The above etym. is confirmed by the surname *Pamphlett*, which also represents the medieval dim. of *Pamphilus*, e.g. *John Panfelot* (*Pat. R.* 13 cent.). See also *pam*.

pan. AS. *panne*. WGer.; cf. Du. *pan*, Ger. *pfanne*. Borrowed from Teut. by most Europ. langs. Some authorities consider it a very early loan from VL. *panna* for L. *patina*. In early fire-arms applied to the part that held the priming, whence *flash in the pan*, ignition not accompanied by discharge. Also used, esp. in SAfr., of depression in ground. Verb to *pan out* (US.) is from the washing out of gold-bearing gravel in a pan. *Pancake* occurs as symbol of flatness from c. 1600. See also *pantile*.

pan-. G. πᾶν, neut. of πᾶς, all; also *pant-*, *panto-*. Pan- is common in mod. pol. formations, esp. *Pan-German*, *Pan-Slavonic*. The association of this word with the name of the Arcadian god Πάν has led to his being later regarded as personification of nature.

panacea. L., G. πανάκεια, from πανακής, all-healing, from ἰᾶσθαι, to heal.

panache [*archaic*]. Plume. F., It. *pennacchio*, from *penna*, feather.

panada. Pulped food. Sp. *panada* or It. *panata*, from L. *panis*, bread.

panama. Misnomer for hat made in SAmer., not at *Panama*.

pancratium. Athletic contest. L., G. παγκράτιον, from *παν-*, all, κράτος, strength.

pancreas. Sweetbread. G., lit. all flesh, κρέας.

panda. Racoon-like animal from Nepal. Native name.

pandanus. Tree. Latinized from *pandang* (18 cent.), Malay *pandan*.

The weird pandanus trees, standing on their high wooden stilts (Beatrice Grimshaw).

Pandean. In *Pandean pipes*. Irreg. from *Pan*. See *pan-*.

pandect. F. *pandecte*, L., G. πανδέκτης, all receiver, from δέχεσθαι, to receive. Orig. the compendium of Roman law compiled under Justinian (6 cent.).

pandemic. Universal, esp. of disease. Cf. *endemic*, *epidemic*, and see *pan-*.

pandemonium. Coined by Milton (*Par. L.* i. 756). See *pan-*, *demon*.

pander. G. Πάνδαρος, prince who trad. acted as amatory agent between his niece Chryseis (Cressida) and the Trojan Troilus. Chaucer took the story from Boccaccio. Now usu. as verb, to *pander to*.

pandit. See *pundit*.

pandora [*archaic*]. It., L. *pandura*, G. πανδοῦρα, mus. instrument ascribed to the god *Pan*, but prob. a perversion of some Eastern word. See *banjo*, *mandolin*.

Pandora. First mortal woman, made by Vulcan and endowed with gifts by all the gods and goddesses. The gift of Zeus was a box, containing, according to the earlier version, all human ills, according to the later, all blessings, of which only hope was saved at the opening of the box by Epimetheus. G. Πανδώρα, all-gifted.

pandour [*hist.*]. Brutal Croatian soldier. Serbo-Croat. *pandūr*, earlier *bandūr*, found in most SSlav. langs., and ult. from MedL. *banderius*, one under a banner (q.v.). Orig. a local force raised (1741) by Baron Trenck and afterwards incorporated in the Austrian army. For the word's travels cf. *hussar*.

pandy [*chiefly Sc.*]. Stroke on hand with cane, etc. Short for L. *pande palmam* (*manum*), hold out your hand. Cf. *query*.

Pandy [*hist.*]. Rebel sepoy (Indian Mutiny, 1857). *Pande*, a Brahmin name very common among high-caste sepoys, one of the name being the first to kill an officer at Barrackpur (March 29, 1857). Cf. *Fritz*, *Dago*, etc.

In front of the line of the 34th swaggers to and fro a sepoy named Mungul Pandy
(Fitchett, *Great Mutiny*).

pane. F. *pan*, L. *pannus*, cloth, rag. Used in ME., like F. *pan*, of any flat section or surface, whence current sense. Cf. *panel*.

pan: a pane, piece, or pannell of a wall, of wainscot, of a glasse-window, &c.; also, the skirt of a gown; the pane of a hose, of a cloak, &c. (Cotg.).

panegyric. F. *panégyrique*, L., G. πανηγυρικός, from πανήγυρις, general assembly, from *παν-*, all, ἀγορά, assembly.

panel. OF. (*panneau*), dim. of *pan* (see *pane*). Orig. sense survives in *panel* (lining) of a saddle. In ME. esp. used of strip of parchment containing names of jurymen (*Piers Plowm.* B. iii. 315), whence verb to *empanel*. Hence mod. application to list of doctors accepting government conditions. With commonest current sense cf. that of *pane*.

pang. Altered (15 cent.) from *prang*, for earlier *prong* (q.v.), with *-r-* lost as in *Biddy* (*Bridget*), *Fanny* (*Frances*). Used esp. of *pangs of death* (*childbirth*). For ground-sense of constriction cf. *anguish*, *angina*.

As thow the prongys of deth dede streyn here hert root (*NED.* 1447).

pangenesis. Coined (1868) by Darwin to express his hypothesis of hereditary cells.

pangolin. Scaly ant-eater. Malay *penggōling*, roller, with ref. to habit of rolling itself into a ball.

panic¹. Kind of grass. F. *panique* or L. *panicum*.

panic². Terror, etc. Orig. adj., as in *panic terror*. F. *panique*, L., G. πανικός, of *Pan* (see *pan-*). From belief that mysterious sounds causing groundless fear were due to *Pan*.

panicle [*bot.*]. Cluster. L. *panicula*, dim. of *panus*, swelling, ear of millet.

panification. F., from *panifier*, to make into bread, L. *panis*.

panjandrum. Burlesque title coined (1775) by Foote in the nonsense story, "She went into the garden to cut a cabbage-leaf, etc.," extemporized to test Macklin's memory.

> The great panjandrum himself, with the little round button at top (Foote).

> It becomes immaterial to us whether the Germans... democratize their institutions or lay themselves at the feet of a Teutonic Panjandrum
> (*Westm. Gaz.* Sep. 29, 1917).

panlogism. Ger. *panlogismus*, coined (1853) by Erdmann to express Hegel's philosophy.

pannage [*hist.*]. Right of pasturing swine. AF. *panage*, OF. *pasnage*, Late L. *pastionaticum*, from *pastio-n-*, from *pascere*, *past-*, to feed.

pannier. F. *panier*, L. *panarium*, bread-basket, from *panis*, bread. Also applied in F. & E. to basket-like contrivances for enlarging the hips. With *pannier*, waiter in Inner Temple, cf. "boots," "buttons," etc.

pannikin. Coined (19 cent.) from *pan* after *mannikin*, or, as it is app. a Suff. word, it may have been borrowed from Du. Cf. *cannikin*.

panoply. G. πανοπλία, complete suit of armour of the ὁπλίτης, heavily-armed soldier, from ὅπλα, arms.

> Διὰ τοῦτο ἀναλάβετε τὴν πανοπλίαν τοῦ Θεοῦ
> (*Eph.* vi. 13).

panopticon. Coined (1791) by Bentham as name for ideal circular prison in which captives could be always watched. See *pan-*, *optic*.

panorama. Coined (c. 1789) by patentee, R. Barker, from G. ὅραμα, view, from ὁρᾶν, to see.

pan-pipe. See *pan-*, *Pandean*.

pansophy. Universal knowledge. From G. πάνσοφος, all wise.

pansy. F. *pensée*, "a thought,...also, the flower paunsie" (Cotg.), from *penser*, L. *pensare*, frequent. of *pendere*, to weigh. Cf. *forget-me-not*.

pant. App. shortened from OF. *pantaisier*,

later also *pantiser*, ? VL. **phantasiare*, to have the nightmare. Cf. synon. F. *panteler*, also of obscure formation.

pant-. See *pan-*.

Pantagruelian. From *Pantagruel*, hero of Rabelais' burlesque romance (16 cent.).

pantalettes. Dim. formation from *pantaloons*. Chiefly US.

pantaloon. F. *pantalon*, It. *pantalone*, name of comic old Venetian in the stock It. comedy, from *Pantaleone*, popular saint in Venice and favourite Venet. name. Cf. *harlequin*, *columbine*, *scaramouch*. Hence *pantaloons*, from costume of character (cf. *knickerbockers*). In US. of trousers in gen. and often shortened to *pants*, the latter adopted in shop-E. as euph. for men's drawers.

> The lean and slipper'd pantaloon
> (*As You Like It*, ii. 7).

> The thing named "pants" in certain documents,
> A word not made for gentlemen, but "gents"
> (O. W. Holmes).

pantechnicon. Coined (1830) from G. παν and τεχνικός, relating to the arts, as name of bazaar in Motcomb St., Belgrave Sq., which was later converted into a storehouse for furniture. Now usu. short for *pantechnicon van*.

pantheist. Coined (1705) by Toland from G. παν-, all, θεός, god. Hence F. *panthéiste*, *panthéisme* (c. 1712), the latter being re-adopted by E.

pantheon. G. πάνθειον, temple dedicated to all the gods (v.s.). Esp. that at Rome, orig. built (c. 25 B.C.) by Agrippa and later made into a Christian church. Later sense of memorial to national heroes began at the Church of St Geneviève, Paris.

panther. F. *panthère*, L. *panthera*, G. πάνθηρ, pop. explained as all-animal, but prob. of Oriental origin.

pantile. Prop. tile curved in such a way that the roof presents alternately ridges and channels, or "pans." Cf. Ger. *pfannen-ziegel*. Also incorr. for Flem. paving-tiles, e.g. the orig. *Pantiles* at Tunbridge Wells. In 18 cent. applied to country dissenting chapels, roofed like cottages. Hence to *pantile*, build chapels.

> Some of these [dissenters] had pantiled [i.e. built chapels] at Preston
> (Macfarlane, *Reminiscences*, p. 258).

pantisocracy. Community of universal equality. App. coined by Southey. See *pan-*, *isos(celes)*, *-cracy*.

pantler [archaic]. Altered on butler from ME. panterer, for panter, OF. panetier. See pantry.

panto-. See pan-.

pantofle [archaic]. F. pantoufle, whence also Du. Ger. pantoffel; cf. It. pantofola, Sp. pantuflo. In 17 cent. often pantable. Origin unknown.

pantograph. Copying-machine. F. pantographe (early 18 cent.), all writing. Also incorr. pentagraph as though from G. πεντα-, five.

pantomime. F., actor in dumb show, L., G. παντόμιμος, all mimic. The E. Christmas pantomime, from 18 cent., is evolved from the conventional It. comedy with its stock actors, harlequin, pantaloon, etc.

pantomime: an actor of many parts in one play, one that can represent the gesture and counterfeit the speech of any man (Blount).

pantoum. Malay verse-form, imitated by mod. F. & E. poets. Malay pantun.

pantry. OF. paneterie, MedL. panetaria, from panis, bread, cogn. with pasci, to feed. For extension of sense cf. larder.

pants. See pantaloon.

pap. In both senses, breast-nipple, child's food, from baby lang. Numerous parallels are found in other langs. Though not recorded early it belongs of course to the most remote ages of speech. Cf. papa, mamma.

papa. F.; cf. It. pappa and borrowed forms in other langs., e.g. US. poppa. Orig. a baby word, regarded as courtly in 17 cent., later relegated again to the nursery. Cf. Turk. baba, father, and see pap, pope.

pappa: pap for children. Also the first word children use, as with us dad or daddie or bab (Flor.).

papacy. MedL. papatia. Cf. papal, F., Church L. papalis; papist, F. papiste, MedL. papista. See pope.

papaverous. Of the poppy, L. papaver.

papaw. WInd. fruit. Sp. Port. papayo, whence also F. papaye; of Carib origin. Now found also in Malay archipelago, whither the plant was taken in 16 cent.

paper. F. papier, L., G. πάπυρος, Nile-rush from which paper is made. Of Egypt. origin. In most Europ. langs. Cf. book, code, library, Bible. For newspaper from 17 cent. The trade of the paper-hanger is a reminder of the fact that wall-papers were preceded by "hangings."

I have heard the fame of paper-hangings, and had some thought of sending for a suit
(Lady M. Montagu, 1749).

papier-mâché. Lit. F. for "chewed paper," from mâcher, L. masticare. An E. tradeword, unknown in F., and prob. intended to mean "mashed" paper. Cf. équestrienne, sacque.

papilionaceous. Of the butterfly, L. papilio-n-.

papilla [anat.]. Nipple, etc. L., dim. of papula, blister, etc., of imit. origin (cf. bubble).

papist. See papacy. Always in hostile sense.

papoose. Red Ind. baby. Native (Algonkin) word. From 17 cent.

papoosh. Var. of babouche (q.v.).

pappus [bot.]. Downy appendage. G. πάππος.

papyrus. See paper.

par[1]. L., equal. Esp. in on a par with, below par, the latter a Stock Exchange figure of speech.

par[2]. Journalistic for paragraph. Cf. ad for advertisement.

par-. F., L. per-, through. Now usu. altered back to per-, e.g. perfect replaces ME. parfit.

para. Coin. Turk. pārah, piece, portion.

Pará. Brazil. port on Amazon, whence rubber, etc.

para-[1]. G. παρα-, from παρά, by the side of, cogn. with E. far.

para-[2]. F., It. para, imper. of parare, to ward off, parry, L. parare, to make ready.

parabasis. G. παράβασις, digression, from παραβαίνειν, to step aside.

parable. OF. parabole, L., G. παραβολή, comparison, putting beside, application, from παραβάλλειν, to throw beside. Cf. palaver, parole. Has ousted AS. bīspell, at first used as transl.

parabola [math.]. See parable. "The use of παραβολή, application, in this sense is due to Apollonius of Perga, c. 210 B.C., and, with him, referred to the fact that a rectangle on the abscissa, having an area equal to the square on the ordinate, can be 'applied' to the latus rectum, without either excess (as in the hyperbola), or deficiency (as in the ellipse)" (NED.).

Paracelsian. Of Paracelsus, name assumed by P. A. T. von Hohenheim, Swiss physicist, etc. (1493–1541), as a kind of transl. (L. celsus, high) of his own name.

parachute. F. See para-[2], chute. Coined by Blanchard, F. aeronaut. Recorded in E. 1785.

Paraclete. F. paraclet, Church L., G. παράκλητος, intercessor, lit. one called to help, from παρακαλεῖν, to call in. Cf. advocate. See comforter.

parade. F., It. *parata*, "a warding or defending; a dighting or garish setting forth" (Flor. 1611), from L. *parare*, to prepare, etc. Cf. Sp. *parada*, "a staying or stopping, also a standing or staying place" (Minsh.), which has supplied some of the senses. First in Blount (v.i.).

parade: an appearance or shew, a bravado or vaunting offer; it is also a term of war, and commonly used for that appearance of souldiers in a garrison about two or three of the clock in the afternoon, etc. (Blount).

paradigm. F. *paradigme*, L., G. παράδειγμα, pattern, from παραδεικνύναι, to show side by side.

paradise. F. *paradis*, L., G. παράδεισος, OPers. *pairidaēza*, from *pairi*, around, *diz*, to form, whence ModPers. *firdaus*, garden. The G. word, first in Xenophon, is used of a Pers. enclosed park, and was adopted by LXX. in *OT*. for Garden of Eden, and in *NT*. for abode of the blessed, which is the oldest E. sense (AS.). Cf. Late Heb. *pardēs* (*Neh.* ii. 8). The two elements are cogn. with G. περί, around, and E. *dough*.

I wold not be in a folis paradyce
                 (*Past. Let.* ii. 109).

The Moores are of the opinion that these birds come from the heavenly Paradise (Purch.).

parados [*fort.*]. Rear parapet. F., from *para-*[2] and *dos*, back.

paradox. F. *paradoxe*, L., G. παράδοξος, contrary to opinion, δόξα.

paradoxure. Palm cat. From its incredible (v.s.) tail, οὐρά.

paraffin. Discovered and named (1830) by Reichenbach from L. *parum*, too little, *affinis*, related, because of its little affinity with other bodies.

paragoge [*gram.*]. Addition to word of letter or syllable. G. παραγωγή, leading past, from ἄγειν, to lead.

paragon. OF. (*parangon*), It. *para(n)gone*, "a paragon, a match, an equall, a proofe, a triall, an experience, an equality, a comparison. Also a conferring togither, a touch stone to trie gold or good from bad. Also a like as good as one brings" (Flor.). Of obscure origin. Oldest sense (14 cent. It.) appears to be touchstone. Perh. ult. from G. παρακονᾶν, to sharpen one thing against another, from ἀκόνη, whetstone.

paragraph. F. *paragraphe*, Late L., G. παράγραφος, written beside. Orig. the mark or stroke indicating a new section.

parakeet, paroquet. F. *perroquet* (OF. *paroquet*), It. *parrocchetto*, is explained as a dim. of *parroco*, parson, VL. *parochus* (see *parish*); cf. F. *moineau*, sparrow, from *moine*, monk. Sp. *periquito* is a dim. of earlier *perico*, ident. with *Perico*, familiar for *Pedro*, Peter; cf. *parrot*. Prob. both are of one origin, but, as it is not known which is the older, it is impossible to say in which of the two langs. folk-etym. has been at work. See also *peruke*.

parakite [*aeron.*]. Coined (1875) by Simmons from *parachute*, *kite*.

paralipomena. Supplementary matter, in ME. also title of *Chronicles*, so called by LXX. as containing matter omitted in *Kings*. G., from παραλείπειν, to leave aside.

parallax [*astron.*]. Apparent displacement of object caused by change in view-point. F. *parallaxe*, from G. παραλλάσσειν, to alter, from ἄλλος, other.

parallel. F. *parallèle*, L., G. παράλληλος, beside one another, *ἄλληλος* (pl. only). Hence *parallelepiped*, from ἐπί, upon, πέδον, ground; *parallelogram*, from γραμμή, line.

paralogism. Bad logic, fallacy. F. *paralogisme*, Late L., G. παραλογισμός, from παραλογίζεσθαι, to reason beside.

paralysis. L., G. παράλυσις, from παραλύειν, to loose from beside. See *palsy*.

paramatta. Fabric. ? From *Parramatta* (New South Wales); but perh. only fancy tradename.

paramo [*geog.*]. SAmer. plateau. Sp. *páramo*, of native origin.

paramount. F. *par amont*, upwards, lit. by uphill, L. *per ad montem*. Orig. an adv. in OF. & AF., now adj., esp. in *lord* (*lady*) *paramount*. Cf. obs. *paravail*, F. *aval*, downhill, L. *ad vallem*.

Le seignur paramount destreigne le tenant paravale
                 (*NED.* 1531).

paramour. F. *par amour*, by love, L. *per amorem*. In ME. esp. in to *love par amour*, i.e. sexually, as a lover, as compared with other types of affection. As noun, and with suggestion of clandestine love, already in Chauc., but also applied to the Holy Virgin (by men) and to the Saviour (by women).

parang. Sheath-knife. Malay *pārang*.

paranoia. Insanity, esp. megalomania. G. παράνοια, beside mind, νόος, νοῦς.

paranymph. G. παράνυμφος, (m.) best man, (f.) bridesmaid, from νύμφη, bride.

parapet. F., It. *parapetto*, guard breast, *petto*, L. *pectus*. See *para-*[2]. Cf. *parados*.

paraph. Flourish after signature. F. *paraphe*, It. *parafo*, contracted from L. *paragraphus*.

paraphernalia. MedL., neut. pl. of *paraphernalis*, from G. παράφερνα, from φερνή, dowry. Orig. articles belonging to wife in addition to her dowry, hence personal belongings. Current sense from 18 cent.

paraphrase. F., L., G. παράφρασις, lit. beside phrase.

parasang. Pers. measure of length. G. παρασάγγης (Herodotus, Xenophon), from OPers. Cf. ModPers. *farsang*.

parasite. F., L., G. παράσιτος, from σῖτος, food. Scient. sense from 18 cent.

parasol. F., It. *parasole*, ward off sun, *sole*. Cf. F. *parapluie*, umbrella, *paratonnerre*, lightning conductor. See *para-²*.

paravane [*naut.*]. Device against mines invented (? and named) by Lieut. Dennis Burney, R.N.

The first paravane was fitted on H.M.S. Melampus in Nov. 1915 (*Manch. Guard.* Jan. 10, 1919).

parboil. OF. *parboillir*, to boil thoroughly, Late L. *perbullire*. In ModE. usu. to boil incompletely, the prefix being understood as *part*.

The iiij quarters and hed [of Sir T. Wyatt] was putt into a baskett to Nuwgat to be parboyled
(Machyn's *Diary*, 1650–63).

parbuckle [*naut.*]. To hoist or lower, as brewers' draymen do casks. Earlier also *parbuncle* (Capt. John Smith). ? Connected with *buckle*.

parcel. F. *parcelle*, small part, VL. **particella*, from *pars*, *part-*, part. Orig. sense survives in *part and parcel*, *parcel of ground* (*John*, iv. 5), *parcel-gilt*. Current sense, now esp. associated with brown paper, from 17 cent. *Parcel post* was at first (1883) *parcels post*, a typical example of offic. lang.

parcener [*leg.*]. Archaic for *partner* (q.v.).

parch. ME. *perch*, contr. of *perish* (q.v.), which is in ME. often *persh*, *persch*. Though now referring esp. to effects of heat, it is used in dial. of effects of cold (cf. *perished with cold*). For contr. cf. ME. *norsh*, nourish, *chirche*, cherish. OF. *perir* is common in required sense. See also *pierce*.

A la seconde herbe de ceste plante s'y engendrent de petites chenilles noires, appellees barbotes, qui la perissent, la faisant dessecher (Godef.).

The parching air
Burns frore, and cold performs th' effect of fire
(*Par. L.* ii. 594).

parchment. ME. *parchemin*, F., ult. from *Pergamum*, city of Mysia in Asia Minor (now *Bergamo*), where it was first adopted (2 cent. B.C.) as substitute for papyrus. In most Europ. langs., e.g. It. *pergamena*, Sp. *pergamino*, Du. *perkament*, Ger. *pergament*, the F. form being difficult of explanation.

pard¹ [*poet.*]. Leopard. OF., L., G. πάρδος, of Eastern origin; cf. Pers. *pārs*, panther.

Full of strange oaths, and bearded like the pard
(*As You Like It*, ii. 7).

pard² [*US.*]. Supposed to be short for *pardner*, partner. But perh. suggested by Du. *paard*, horse; cf. US. *old hoss*, as term of endearment.

pardon. First (13 cent.) as noun, earliest in sense of papal indulgence. F., from *pardonner*, Carolingian L. *perdonare*, transl. of OHG. *forgeben* (*vergeben*), to "for-give."

pare. F. *parer*, to make ready, L. *parare*, cogn. with *parere*, to bring forth. Early limited to cutting away in thin layers, e.g. *cheese-paring*, *paring one's nails*, etc.

paregoric. Late L., G. παρηγορικός, encouraging, comforting, from παρηγορεῖν, to exhort (in the ἀγορά, public assembly).

parenchyma [*biol.*]. Fundamental tissue, esp. in bot. G. παρέγχυμα, something poured in beside, from ἐγχεῖν, to pour in.

parent. F., from pres. part. of L. *parere*, to beget, bring forth. Replaced *elder* from c. 1500.

parenthesis. MedL., G. παρένθεσις, from παρεντιθέναι, to put in beside.

parget [*archaic*]. To plaster, daub, etc. OF. *parjeter*, from *jeter*, to throw (see *jet²*). Cf. synon. Ger. *bewerfen*, from *werfen*, to throw, and similar use of *cast* in *rough-cast*. Also *parge*, back-formation.

eine mauer oder wand bewerffen: to rough-cast, parget or plaister a wall (Ludw.).

parhelion. Mock sun, etc. G. παρήλιον, from παρα-, beside, ἥλιος, sun.

pariah. Tamil *paṛaiyar*, pl. of *paṛaiyan*, name of largest of lower castes of Southern India. The exaggerated sense of utter outcaste attached to the word by Europeans is esp. due, says Yule, to Bernardin de Saint-Pierre's "preposterous though once popular tale *La Chaumière indienne* (1791)." Hence *pariah dog*.

Parian. Marble from *Paros*, one of the Cyclades.

parietal [*anat.*]. F. *pariétal*, Late L. *parietalis*, from *paries*, *pariet-*, wall.

parish. F. *paroisse*, Late L. *parochia*, for Church L. *paroecia*, G. παροικία, from οἶκος, house; equivalent to *diocese* (q.v.). In E. a township having its own church, the administrative division of the country being thus based on the eccl. (cf. *vestry*). *Parishioner* is lengthened from earlier *parishen*, F. *paroissien*. *Parochial*, a learned word, is equally old. In sense of provincial, narrow-minded, *NED.*'s first quot. is from Emerson.

His parisshens devoutly wolde he teche
(Chauc. A. 482).

parisyllabic. From L. *par*, *pari-*, equal. See *syllable*.

parity. F. *parité*, Late L. *paritas*, from *par*[1].

park. F. *parc*, of Teut. origin and ult. ident. with E. dial. *parrock*, AS. *pearroc* (see *paddock*); cf. Du. *park*, pen, Ger. *pferch*, sheepfold. Borrowed by all Rom. langs. Oldest E. sense is tract held by royal grant for keeping game, distinguished from a chase or forest by being enclosed. In mil. sense, *artillery park*, from 17 cent. F.

To desolve the parkes of Maribone and Hyde, and having bestowed the dere and pale of the same to their Majesties use... (*Privy Council Acts*, 1554).

A policeman "parked" eight or ten perambulators and mounted guard...while the mothers made their purchases (*Times*, Feb. 1, 1918).

parkin [*north.*]. Kind of ginger-bread. ? From surname *Parkin*.

parlance. OF., from *parler*, to speak (v.i.). Now always with adj. (*common, legal*, etc.).

parle [*poet.*]. Parley. From obs. verb *parle*, F. *parler*, VL. *parabolare*. Cf. *parable*, *parole*, *palaver*.

parlementaire [*mil.*]. F., see *parley*, *parliament*.

parley. OF. *parlée*, p.p. fem. of *parler*, to speak (v.s.). Or it may be directly from the verb, with ending as in *bandy*[1], *levy*, etc.

parleyvoo. F. *parlez-vous?* do you speak? For sense of Frenchman cf. F. *goddam*, Englishman.

parliament. F. *parlement*, from *parler*, to speak. Sense has gradually changed from that of speech, discussion, with the evolution of the institution. According to a 16 cent. F. etymologist "parce qu'on y parle et ment." The form is due to MedL. A *parliamentary train* carried passengers at rate of one penny a mile (7 *and* 8 *Vict.*). The adj. is applied to "language" from 19 cent. only. *Parliament*, kind of ginger-bread, is for earlier *parliament-cake* (? Sc.), reason for name being unknown.

And now [1642] came up the names of parties, Royalists and Parliamentarians, Cavaliers and Roundheads (Whitelocke's *Memoirs*).

parlour. OF. (replaced by *parloir*), from *parler*, to speak; cf. MedL. *parlatorium*, It. *parlatorio*. Orig. room for reception of visitors to monastery, as still in F. See *parle*. Something of orig. sense survives in *Mayor's parlour, banker's parlour*.

parlous. Contr. of *perilous*. Still common in dial., and in *parlous state*, echo of *As You Like It*, iii. 2.

parmesan. F., It. *parmegiano*, of *Parma*. The cheese was known in E. from early 16 cent.

Parnassian. Of *Parnassus*, mountain of central Greece, sacred to Apollo and Muses. Cf. *Olympian*.

I sleepe never on the Mount of Pernaso,
Ne lerned Marcus Tullius Scithero (Chauc. F. 721).

Parnellite [*hist.*]. Follower of *C. S. Parnell*, Ir. politician (†1891).

parochial. See *parish*.

parody. F. *parodie*, L., G. παρῳδία, from παρα-, beside, ῳδή, ode (q.v.). First in Ben Jonson.

parole. F., in sense of *parole d'honneur*, word of honour, from 17 cent. mil. lang., Late L. *paraula*, *parabola*, G. παραβολή. Cf. *palaver*, *parable*.

paronomasia. Word-play. L., G. παρονομασία, from παρα-, beside, ὀνομασία, naming, from ὄνομα, name.

paronymous. Cognate. G. παρώνυμος (v.s.).

paroquet. See *parakeet*.

-parous. From L. *-parus*, from *parere*, to produce, bring forth.

paroxysm. F. *paroxysme*, MedL., G. παροξυσμός, from παροξύνειν, from ὀξύνειν, to sharpen, goad, from ὀξύς, sharp.

parquet. F., orig. small compartment, dim. of *parc*, park (q.v.).

parr. Young salmon. Origin unknown, app. Sc.

parricide. F., L. *parricida*, for earlier *paricida*, the first element of which is an Aryan word for kin cogn. with *pater*, *patr-*, father, but not ident. with it.

parrot. From *Perrot*, *Parrot*, a common ME. dim. of F. *Pierre*, Peter. Cf. F. *pierrot*, sparrow. See also *parakeet*. Replaced (c. 1500) earlier *popinjay*.

My name is Parrot, a byrd of paradyse (Skelton).

parry. From F. *parer*, It. *parare*, "to ward or defend a blow" (Flor.), spec. sense of *parare*, to prepare. Form is explained as from imper. *parez*, defend yourself (cf. *revelly*). But E. often adds *-y* to F. verbs, e.g. *bandy*[1], *levy*, *occupy*.

parse. L. *pars*, in school question *Quae pars orationis?* What part of speech?

Parsee. Descendant of Zoroastrians who fled to India after Mohammedan conquest of Persia (7–8 cents.). OPers. *pārsī*, Persian.

parsimony. F. *parcimonie*, L. *parcimonia*, *parsi-*, from *parcere*, *pars-*, to spare. Not orig. with suggestion of stinginess.

parsimonie: thriftinesse, good husbandrie
(Cockeram's *Dict.* 1623).

parsley. AS. *petersilie*, Late L. *petrosilium*, for *petroselinum*, G. πετροσέλινον, rock parsley (see *celery*). In most Europ. langs.; cf. F. *persil*, whence ME. *persil*, *parsil*, which has contributed to mod. form.

I have porettes and percyl [*vars*. persille, persely]
(*Piers Plowm.* A. vii. 273).

parsnip. ME. *pasnep*, altered on *turnep*, turnip, from OF. *pastenaque*, L. *pastinaca*, from *pastinare*, to dig up, from *pastinum*, "spud" (q.v.). Cf. Du. Ger. *pastinak*, It. *pastinaca*, F. *panais*.

Fair words butter no parsnips
(J. Clarke, *Paroemiologia*, 1639).

parson. ME. also *persone*. Ident. with *person* (q.v.). Sense of holder of parochial benefice appears from 11 cent., but its origin is obscure. According to one theory the *parson* was the non-resident holder of the benefice, often a corporate body, whose work was done by the vicar (q.v.).

Clerici quos personas vocant (*NED.* 1096).

part[1]. Noun. F., L. *pars*, *part-*. Has replaced in most senses native *deal*[1]. Sense of share, now most usual F. meaning, appears in *part or lot* (q.v.), *art* (q.v.) or *part*. L. has theat. sense of rôle, an actor's "share" in the performance; cf. sense of gift, talent, in *man of parts*. In to *take one's part* it represents rather the sense of F. *parti* (see *party*). *Part of speech* renders L. *pars orationis* (see *parse*). With *in good part* cf. L. *in bonam partem*.

part[2]. Verb. F. *partir*, which in OF. meant to divide, separate, from L. *partiri*, from *pars*, *part-*, part. Some obs. or archaic senses (e.g. *knell of parting day*) are now usu. represented by *depart* (q.v.). With fig. sense of *parting of the ways* cf. *crucial*.

partake. Back-formation from *partaker*, earlier *part-taker*, a hybrid compd. Cf. L. *particeps*, Ger. *teilnehmer*.

a parte-taker: particeps (*Cath. Angl.*).

parterre. F., for *par terre*, on the ground, L. *per terram*.

parthenogenesis. Lit. birth from a virgin, G. παρθένος. Cf. *Parthenon*, temple of virgin goddess, Pallas Athene.

Parthian. Chiefly in *Parthian shaft* (*shot*), from skill of horsemen of Parthia (WAsia) in shooting backwards while retreating.

Or like the Parthian I shall flying fight
(*Cymb.* i. 6).

partial. F. *partial*, prejudiced, *partiel*, incomplete, both representing Late L. *partialis*, from *pars*, *part-*, part.

participate. From L. *participare*, from *pars*, *part-*, and *capere*, to take. Cf. *partake*.

participle. ME. also *participe*, F., L. *participium*, sharing (v.s.), as partaking of nature both of verb and adj. For intrusive *-l-* cf. *syllable*. In Wyc.

particle. F. *particule*, L. *particula*, dim. of *pars*, *part-*, part.

parti-coloured. Earlier simply *party*, divided, p.p. of *partir*, to divide, part[2], as still in her. Cf. F. *mi-parti*, lit. half divided.

She gadereth floures, party white and rede
(Chauc. A. 1053)

particular. Restored from ME. *particuler*, OF. (*particulier*), L. *particularis*, concerning a *particle*. Orig. sense survives in *particulars*, small details. *London particular*, orig. a spec. kind of madeira, was used by Dickens of a fog (*Bleak House*, ch. iii.). *Particularism* (pol.) is adapted from Ger. *partikularismus*, a 19 cent. coinage.

Partington. *Mrs Partington* trad. attempted to keep out an Atlantic high tide with a mop. The story comes from Devon (early 19 cent.).

partisan[1]. Adherent. F., It. *partigiano*, from *parte*, part[1]. Cf. *courtesan*. Sense of irregular combatant, commander of a "party," appears in 17 cent.

The fighting [in Finland] is of a partisan character
(*Times*, Feb. 22, 1918).

partisan[2] [*hist.*]. Weapon. OF. *partisane*, It. *partegiana*. Prob. connected with OHG. *parta*, *barta*, halberd (q.v.). In ModF. corrupted to *pertuisane*, as though from *pertuis*, hole. Obs. from c. 1700, but revived by Scott.

On battlement and bartizan (q.v.)
Gleam'd axe and spear and partizan (*Lay*, iv. 20).

partition. F., L. *partitio-n-*, from *partiri*, to divide, from *pars*, *part-*, part. Cf. *partitive* (gram.), F. *partitif*, L. **partitivus*.

Partlet. OF. *Pertelote*, female personal name, wife of Chanticleer in *Roman de Renard*. This has affected archaic *partlet*, woman's ruff, earlier *patlet*, OF. *patelete*, dim. of *patte*, paw, in OF. also a band of stuff.

partner. Appears in 13 cent. as var. of *parcener* (still in leg. use), OF. *parçonier*, MedL. *partionarius*, for **partitionarius*, from *partitio-n-*, division. Usu. explained as alteration of *parcener* due to influence of *part* or to common scribal confusion between *-c-* and *-t-*. But the words are of equal age, and AF. *partener* (*Liber Albus*, pp. 570–1) may represent an OF. *part tenour*, part holder; cf. *partaker* and such native compds. as *share-holder*. Cf. OProv. *partender*, of similar formation.

parsonnier: a partener, or coparcener (Cotg.).

partridge. ME. *pertrich*, *partrich*, F. *perdrix*, L. *perdix*, *perdic-*, G. πέρδιξ, whence also OIt. *perdice*, Sp. *perdiz*. For intrusive *-r-* of F. word cf. *treasure*. For change of vowel sound in E. cf. *clerk*.

parturient. From pres. part. of L. *parturire*, desiderative of *parere*, to bring forth. Cf. *esurient*.

party. Represents both F. *partie*, p.p. fem. of *partir*, to divide, and *parti*, p.p. masc. Usual F. senses are *partie*, part, *parti*, party, faction, but they have become much mixed in E. Sense of friendly gathering is partly due to F. *partie*, game, excursion, etc. Slang sense of individual, e.g. *nice old party*, arises from earlier leg. sense as in *guilty party*, i.e. side, to *be a party to*, etc.; cf. *part*. *Party* (her.) is F. *parti*, divided. See also *parti-coloured*. With *party-wall* cf. *partition wall*.

The party [a shipwrecked sailor] had made him for want of apparell two sutes of goats skinnes
                                        (Hakl. x. 197).

parvenu. F., p.p. of *parvenir*, to arrive, L. *pervenire*. Cf. ModF. slang *arriviste*.

parvis [*archaic*]. Enclosed area in front of cathedral, etc. F., OF. *parevis*, for *pareïs*, L. *paradisus*, medieval name for court in front of St Peter's at Rome. The *parvis* of St Paul's was a great resort of lawyers.

A sergeant of the lawe, war and wys,
That often hadde been at the Parvys
                                        (Chauc. A. 309).

pas. F., step, L. *passus*, from *pandere*, *pass-*, to stretch.

paschal. F. *pascal*, Late L. *paschalis*, from L. *pascha*, G. πάσχα, Heb. *pesakh*, from *pāsakh*, to pass over. In most Europ. langs., with application to various Church festivals and holidays, showing a leaning on *pascere*, to feed.

pash [*dial.*]. Prob. imit.; cf. *bash*, *smash*.

pasha, pacha. Turk. *pāshā*, also *bāshā*, from *bāsh*, head. Cf. obs. *bashaw*, via It. *bassa*; see also *Bashi-Bazouk*, *bimbashi*. Hence *pashalik*, jurisdiction of pasha, formed with *-lik*, suffix of condition.

pasquil [*archaic*]. As *pasquinade* (v.i.).

pasquinade. F., It. *pasquinata*, from *Pasquino* or *Pasquillo*, nickname of a mutilated statue disinterred at Rome (1501), to which it was usual to attach lampoons and satirical compositions. The statue is said to have been named from a schoolmaster, or, according to some, a caustic-tongued tailor, shoe-maker, or barber, who lived near. The name is derived from L. *pascha*, Easter (cf. F. *Pascal*, *Pasquin*, etc.).

Pasquino: a statue in Rome on whom all libels, railings, detractions, and satiricall invectives are fathered (Flor.).

I pass'd by the stumps of old Pasquin at the corner of a streete call'd Strada Pontificia; here they still paste up their drolling lampoons and scurrilous papers (Evelyn).

pass¹. Noun. In sense of mountain passage from F. *pas*, whence also *pace* (q.v.). Hence to *sell the pass*, open a passage to the enemy. But in most senses from F. *passe*, back-formation from *passer*, to pass² (q.v.). Hence to *come* (*bring*) *to pass*, to *such a pass*, a *pass* in fencing, conjuring, football, etc.

pass². Verb. F. *passer*, VL. **passare*, from *passus*, step, pace; cf. It. *passare*, Sp. *passar*. Trans. sense, equivalent to *surpass*, survives in *passeth all understanding* and in adv. *passing*, very, e.g. *passing rich on forty pounds a year*. In some senses it is possible that VL. **passare* is rather from *pati*, *pass-*, to suffer. A *pass-book* is app. so-called because passing between bank and depositor.

passage. F., orig. act of passing, as in *bird of passage*, *rough passage*. With *passage of arms* cf. F. *passe d'armes*, orig. of a tournament.

passé. F., p.p. of *passer*, to pass. Cf. mod. *back number*.

passementerie. F., from *passement*, braid, etc., from *passer*, to pass, from the passing or interlacing of the thread.

passenger. ME. *passager*, F., from *passage*, with intrusive *-n-* as in *messenger, scavenger*, etc. Orig. passer-by, wayfarer, as still in *foot-passenger, passenger-pigeon*.

passepartout. F., master-key, lit. pass everywhere. Also used in F. of an engraved plate with vacant centre, whence E. sense of frame.

passerine. From L. *passer*, sparrow.

passim. L., everywhere, from *pandere, pass-*, to stretch.

passion. F., L. *passio-n-*, from *pati, pass-*, to suffer. Earliest (12 cent.) in ref. to the Passion of the Saviour. With *passion-flower* cf. Sp. *flor de la pasión*, F. *fleur de la passion*. Later senses (from 14 cent.) due to Late L. use of *passio* to render G. πάθος, feeling, emotion.

The passiouns of this tyme ben not evene worthi to the glorie to comynge (Wyc. *Rom.* viii. 18).

passive. L. *passivus*, from *pati, pass-*, to suffer. *Passive resistance* in current sense dates from Education Act of 1902.

In this humour of passive resistance...Isaac sat in a corner of his dungeon (*Ivanhoe*, ch. xxiii.).

passover. First in Tynd. *Ex.* xii. 11, where Wyc. has *Pasch*. See *paschal*.

Est enim Phase (id est transitus) Domini
(*Vulg. Ex.* xii. 11).

passport. F. *passeport*, from *passe*, imper. of *passer*, and *port*, port[1]. Cf. It. *passaporto*.

Patrike Colqhon, Scottisshman, for rasing the date and terme of his pasporte, was this daye committed to the Marshalsey (*Privy Council Acts*, 1554).

past. For *passed*, p.p. of *pass*. Hence *past-master*, prop. one who has passed through the various grades of an art or craft. In freemasonry, etc., one who has filled the office of master. App. adapted from F. (v.i.). Use of *past* as prep. is explained by *NED.* from construction of verb to *pass* with *be*, to indicate completed action, e.g. *he is* (i.e. *has*) *now past the worst*; but it may be an absolute use of the p.p.; cf. F. *passé dix heures, dix heures passées*.

Patelin, advocat, maistre passé en tromperie
(Pasquier, 1561).

paste. OF. (*pâte*), Late L. *pasta*, G. πάστη, barley porridge, from παστός, sprinkled, from πάσσειν, to strew. In sense of counterfeit jewellery from 17 cent. *Pasteboard* was orig. made of sheets pasted together as substitute for the "boards" of a book. Verb to *paste* (slang), to thrash, etc., is the same word (cf. *plaster*), but prob. partly suggested by *baste*[3].

pastel. F., It. *pastello*, dim. from *pasta*, paste.

pastern. ME. *pastron*, OF. *pasturon* (*paturon*), tethering rope (for grazing horse), from *pasture* (*pâture*), pasture (q.v.). In OF. *pasture* was used also of the tether. In both F. & E. the name was later extended to the part of the leg to which the tether was attached. See also *fetlock, pester*.

trainello: a kinde of long horse-fetters or pasterns
(Flor.).

pasteurize. To sterilize by method of *Louis Pasteur* (†1895).

pastiche. F., It. *pasticcio*, medley, jumble, also applied to a composition containing unoriginal features, from *pasta*, paste.

pastille. F., L. *pastillus*, little loaf or roll; cf. *paste*.

pastime. For *pass-time*. Coined on F. *passe-temps*. Cf. Ger. *zeitvertreib, kurzweil*.

pastor. ME. & OF. *pastour*, L. *pastor-em*, shepherd, from *pascere, past-*, to feed. In ME. in lit. sense, as still in *pastoral*.

pastry. Formed in E. from *paste*. Cf. OF. *pasteierie*, from *pasteier*, pastry-cook.

pasture. OF. (*pâture*), food, Late L. *pastura*, from *pascere, past-*, to feed.

pasty. OF. *pasté* (*pâté*), pie, from *paste* (*pâte*), paste. Cf. *patty*.

pat. Imit. of light flat blow; cf. *dab*[1]. Hence *pat* of butter, shaped by patting; cf. *pat-a-cake*. Sense of opportunely, in nick of time, etc., is from to *hit pat*.

I heard my physition so pat to hit my disease
(Lyly's *Euphues*).

Pat. Irishman. See *Paddy*.

Patagonian. Gigantic, in allusion to early travellers' tales of the stature of the *Patagonians*, earlier *Patagons*, from Sp. *patagón*, large clumsy foot. Cf. F. *patte*, paw. See *paddle*[2].

The captaine [Magellan] named these people Patagoni (Purch.).

patavinity. Provincialism in style. L. *patavinitas*, from *Patavium*, Padua. Cf. *solecism*.

patch. Essential senses, piece of cloth, plot of ground, coincide exactly with those of F. *pièce*. It must therefore represent OF. dial. **peche* for *pieche*, a common form. See *piece*. The form *peche* occurs in ME. (*Ancren Riwle*), and *Patch*, the fool (v.i.), is called *Peche* in *Excerpta Historica* (1492). For vowel cf. dial. *cratch*, manger, F. *crèche*, *match*[2], F. *mèche*. The early L. glossaries treat *patch, pece* as interchangeable terms. In OF. quot. below all three words mean rag, shred. *Not a patch on* is 19 cent. Obs. *patch*, fool, booby, is It. *pazzo*, fool, associated with *patch*, with suggestion of parti-coloured garments. It is earliest recorded as name of Wolsey's jester, and survives in *crosspatch*.

Escroele, drapel, ne pieche (Godef.).

rapiecer: to peece, patch, botch, clowt, mend (Cotg.).

The power of this Republic...is spread over a region...of an extent in comparison with which the possessions of the House of Hapsburg are but as a patch on the earth's surface
(Dan. Webster to Austrian Chargé d'Affaires, Dec. 21, 1850).

patchouli. Perfume from EInd. plant, so called in Madras, and said to come from Tamil *pach*, green, *ilai*, leaf.

pate. Orig. in dignified sense. Origin unknown.

His wickednes shall fall upon his owne pate
(Coverd. *Ps.* vii. 16).

pâté. F., see *pasty*, *patty*. *Pâté de foie gras*, patty of fat liver (of geese).

patella [*anat.*]. Knee-cap. L., dim. of *patina*, pan (v.i.).

paten. OF. *patène*, L. *patina*, G. πατάνη, flat dish.

patent. First in *letters patent*, F. *lettres patentes*, L. *litterae patentes*, from pres. part. of *patēre*, to lie open. Orig. royal open letter conferring any right, privilege, etc. Current sense of invention protected by "letters patent" grew out of that of exclusive right, monopoly (16 cent.).

pater. L., father (q.v.). Also short for *paternoster* (q.v.).

paterfamilias. From *familias*, OL. genitive of *familia*, family.

paternal. From L. *paternus*, from *pater*, father; cf. F. *paternel*, It. *paternale*.

paternoster. L. *pater noster*, our father, init. words of Lord's Prayer. Found in AS. Cf. F. *patenôtre*.

path. AS. *pæth*. WGer.; cf. Du. *pad*, Ger. *pfad*; ? ult. cogn. with L. *batuere*, to beat. *Pathfinder* was coined (1840) by Fenimore Cooper.

pathetic. F. *pathétique*, Late L., G. παθητικός, from root παθ- of πάσχειν, to suffer, πάθος, feeling, pathos. Orig. sense of *pathos*, adopted in literary sense in 17 cent., appears in *pathology*, lit. study of suffering.

-pathy. G. -παθεια (v.s.), as in *sympathy*, feeling with. Mod. coinages, e.g. *hydropathy*, *electropathy*, are imitated from *allopathy*, *homoeopathy*.

patibulary. From L. *patibulum*, gibbet.

patient. F., from pres. part. of L. *pati*, to suffer. Cf. *longsuffering*. Sense of one under med. treatment (Chauc.), is evolved from that of sufferer. *My patience*, as interj., appears to be Sc.

She sat, like Patience on a monument,
Smiling at grief (*Twelfth Night*, ii. 4).

patina, patine. Vessel. See *paten*. *Patina*, incrustation on old bronze, is adapted from F. *patine*. Its connection with the vessel sense is doubtful.

patio. Sp., open court of house. ? From L. *patēre*, to lie open.

Patlander. Cf. *Paddy*, *Pat*.

patois. Dial. which has ceased to be literary. F. (13 cent.), of obscure origin. ? From imit. root *pat-*, suggesting chatter; cf. OF. *gabois*, jesting, from imit. root *gab-*.

patriarch. F. *patriarche*, L., G. πατριάρχης, from πατριά, family, -αρχης, ruler. See *father*, *arch²*. Orig. used by the LXX. of the Jewish patriarchs, esp. the twelve sons of Jacob. Early adopted as honorific title of certain bishops of primitive Church, orig. those of Antioch, Alexandria and Rome.

patrician. F. *patricien*, from L. *patricius*, one sprung from the *patres conscripti*, or Senators, as opposed to *plebeius*.

patrimony. F. *patrimoine*, L. *patrimonium*, from *pater*, *patr-*, father. In sense a curious contrast with *matrimony*.

patriot. F. *patriote*, Late L., G. πατριώτης, from πατρίς, fatherland. Earlier (17 cent.) always with adj. (*good*, *true*, *faithful*, etc.). Hence *patriotism*, "the last refuge of a scoundrel" (Johns.).

As much out of harmony with his surroundings as a South American patriot at a Peace Conference
(Kyne, *Long Chance*).

patristic [*theol.*]. Of the Fathers of the Church. Adapted from Ger. *patristisch*, from G. πατήρ, πατρ-, father.

patrol. F. *patrouiller*, app. altered from earlier *patouiller* (see *paddle²*). It is supposed to have been orig. soldier slang, "going the rounds" being described as tramping through the mire. This is easily comprehensible by those who have observed the evolution of slang at the front. Very widely adopted, e.g. It. *pattugliare*, Sp. *patrullar*, Du. *patrouilleeren*, Ger. *patrouillieren*.

patron. F., L. *patronus*, "he that in trouble and perill defendeth" (Coop.), from *pater*, father. In MedL. *patron* of a church, which is the earliest E. sense (c. 1300), that of *patron saint* being rather later (14 cent.). Cf. *padrone*, *patroon*, *pattern*. To *patronize* had orig. no objectionable sense (cf. *condescend*).

He patronizes the orphan and widow, assists the friendless, and guides the widow (Addison).

He found a letter from Lord Clive, who patronised him, desiring him immediately to follow him to Portsmouth (Hickey's *Memoirs*, ii. 125).

patronymic. F. *patronymique*, L., G. πατρω-νυμικός, from πατήρ, father, ὄνυμα, name (see *eponymous*).

patroon [*US.*]. Land-holder under old Du. governments of New York and New Jersey. Du. form of *patron* (q.v.).

patten. F. *patin*, earlier clog, now skate, for which *patten* is still the usual word in Cambridgeshire. Cf. MedL. *patinus*, It. *pattino*, clog. Prob. cogn. with F. *patte*, paw, foot. Cf. sense-hist. of *skate*².

patter¹. To mumble rapidly, etc. From *pater*, short for *paternoster*, from hurried repetition of familiar prayers; but synon. Dan. *pjadre*, Sw. dial. *patra*, point rather to connection with *patter²*. Music hall sense is 19 cent.

He saw him wende into the water
Nakyd and thar in stande and pater
In his prayers (*NED.* c. 1450).

patter². Of rain, etc. Frequent. of *pat*.

pattern. ME. *patron*, F., L. *patronus*, in sense of archetype, model. Cf. *matrix*. F. *patron* has still this sense.

patrone, fforme to werk by: exemplar (*Prompt. Parv.*).

patty. F. *pâté* (q.v.). *Pasty*, *patty*, *pâté* represent three successive borrowings of the same word from F.

patulous. From L. *patulus*, from *patēre*, to spread. Chiefly after Virgil (v.i.).

Tityre, tu patulae recubans sub tegmine fagi
Silvestrem tenui musam meditaris avena (*Ecl.* i. 1).

paucity. F. *paucité*, L. *paucitas*, from *paucus*, few (q.v.).

Pauline. L. *Paulinus*, of *St Paul*, lit. the little, L. *paulus*, cogn. with G. παῦρος. Also member of *St Paul's School*, London.

paulo-post-future [*gram.*]. ModL. *paulo post futurum*, rendering G. ὁ μετ' ὀλίγον μέλλων (χρόνος), the future after a little.

paulownia. Tree. Named (1835) from *Anna Pavlovna*, daughter of Tsar Paul I.

Paul Pry. Title-rôle of comedy by John Poole (1825).

paunch. ONF. *panche* (*panse*), VL. *pantica, for *pantex*, *pantic-*. Cf. It. *pancia*, Sp. *panza*, whence name of Don Quixote's materialistic squire.

pauper. L., poor, from *paucum*, little, *parere*, to produce. Use in E. came from leg. phrase *in forma pauperis*, in the character of a poor man (allowed to sue gratuitously).

pause. F., L. *pausa*, G. παῦσις, from παύειν, to make cease.

For in that sleep of death what dreams may come,
When we have shuffled off this mortal coil,
Must give us pause (*Haml.* iii. 1).

pavan [*archaic*]. Stately dance. F. *pavane*, It. or Sp. *pavana*, prob. from L. *pavo*, peacock. Cf. Ger. *pfauentanz*.

pave. F. *paver*, back-formation from OF. *pavement*, L. *pavimentum*, from *pavire*, to beat down, ram. Sense of hard slabs, etc. is absent from F. *pavé*, road-way, as also from orig. sense of to *pave the way for*, i.e. to make a beaten track. *Paviour*, for earlier *paver*, *pavyer*, is app. modelled on *saviour*.

He [Johnson] said one day, talking to an acquaintance on this subject, Sir, hell is paved with good intentions (Boswell, ch. xxxi.).

Soviet Russia is paved with Bolshevist good intentions (*Times Lit. Sup.* June 19, 1919).

pavid. L. *pavidus*, frightened, from *pavēre*, to quake.

pavilion. F. *pavillon*, L. *papilio-n-*, butterfly, used in MedL. also for tent, though the reason is not clear; cf. It. *padiglione*, Sp. *pabellón*. F. sense of naut. flag may have come from its repeating the colours of the medieval knight's pavilion, erected on the poop.

pavise [*hist.*]. Large shield. F. *pavois*, It. *pavese*, prob. from *Pavia*. Cf. *bayonet*, *pistol*, etc. App. revived by Southey.

pavonazzo. Marble. It., from L. *pavo-n-*, peacock, from markings.

pavonine. L. *pavoninus*, from *pavo-n-* (v.s.).

paw. ME. *powe*, OF. *poe*, ? of Teut. origin and cogn. with Du. *poot*, Ger. *pfote*; cf. Prov. *pauta*, F. *patte*, paw, ? also from Teut. Used as contrast with *hoof*, so that to *paw the ground* (*Job*, xxxix. 21), though expressive, is incorr.

pawky [*Sc.*]. Sly, etc. From *pawk*, *palk*, trick (16 cent.), of unknown origin.

pawl [*naut.*]. Device to prevent capstan from recoiling. Falc. derives it from F. *épaule*, shoulder, and is prob. right. Forms found in several Europ. langs. are prob. from E.

pawn[1]. Pledge. OF. *pan*; cf. Du. *pand*, Ger. *pfand*. Primitive sense and relation of Rom. & Teut. forms is unknown. Some identify it with L. *pannus*, cloth, shred (see *pane*).

pawn[2]. At chess. OF. *paon* (*pion*), L. *pedo-n-*, in MedL. foot-soldier, from *pes*, *ped-*, foot; cf. It. *pedone*, footman, *pedona*, pawn, Sp. *peón*, footman, pawn. Ger. has *bauer*, peasant, in same sense. In quot. below there is prob. association between the two *pawns*.

My life I never held but as a pawn
To wage against thine enemies (*Lear*, i. 1).

pawnee, brandy [*Anglo-Ind.*]. Brandy and water. See *brandy*.

pax [*eccl.*]. Tablet engraved with sacred subject. L., peace; cf. F. *paix*, in same sense.

paxwax. Tendon uniting spine and occiput. App. altered from earlier *faxwax*, from AS. *feax*, hair (as in name *Fairfax*), and *weaxan*, to grow, wax. Cf. synon. Ger. *haarwachs*.

pay[1]. To hand over money. F. *payer*, L. *pacare*, to appease, a sense found in OF. & ME.; cf. It. *pagare*, Sp. *pagar*. Colloq. sense of thrashing goes with to *pay back* (*out*), *pay one in his own coin*, etc. *Paying-guest*, euph. for lodger, dates from c. 1900.

If there be any dogge that is so il taught as he would runne at a sheepe, with your wande you muste all to pay him (Turbervile, 1576).

pay[2] [*naut.*]. OF. *peier*, L. *picare*, from *pix*, *pic-*, pitch, whence F. *poix*. See *devil*. Naut. to *pay out* (rope) belongs to *pay*[1].

paynim [*poet.*]. OF. *paienime*, Late L. *paganismus*, heathendom. See *pagan*. Incorr. use for *pagan* (Wyc. *Matt.* v. 47) prob. arose from attrib. use in *paynim land*, *paynim knight*, etc., and may have been helped by *cherubim*. Its currency, like that of *fairy* (q.v.), is largely due to Spenser.

paynize. To impregnate wood with preservatives. From *Payne*, inventor of process. Cf. *kyanize*, *mercerize*.

pea. False sing. from *pease* (q.v.). Cf. *cherry*, *burgee*, etc.

peace. ME. & OF. *pais* (*paix*), L. *pax*, *pac-*, cogn. with *pangere*, *pact-*, to fix; cf. It. *pace*, Sp. *paz*. Early replaced AS. *frith*, esp. as administrative word, e.g. *breach of the peace* (AS. *frithbræc*), *justice of the peace*, etc. *Peace with honour* became a catchword after Beaconsfield's speech (July 16, 1878), but is much older (v.i.). With *peace*

at any price, dating from Crimean war, cf. *pacifist*.

Ut perpetua fiat in nobis pax cum honore vestro meoque dedecore
(Thibaut de Champagne to Louis le Gros, 12 cent.).

With peace and honour I am willing to spare anything so as to keep all ends together
(Pepys, May 25, 1663).

The peace-mongers were ready to have sacrificed the honour of England (Southey, 1808).

peach[1]. Fruit. F. *pêche*, OF. *pesche*, VL. *pessica*, for *Persica* (sc. *arbor*); cf. It. *persica*, *pesca*.

peach[2] [*slang*]. To inform against. Aphet. for *appeach*, cogn. with *impeach* (q.v.).

Rotty and all his felawshepe that the woman hathe apeched (*Paston Let.* iii. 390).

peacock. ME. *pecok*, *pacok*, *pocok*, extended from *pa*, *po*, etc., AS. *pāwa*, L. *pavo*; cf. F. *paon* (L. *pavo-n-*), Du. *paauw*, Ger. *pfau*. Said to be ult. from Tamil. The simplex survives in surnames *Poe*, *Pay*. With *proud as a peacock* (Chauc.) cf. *peacock in pride* (her.), with displayed tail.

Gold, and sylver, and yver, and apis, and poos [*vars.* pokokis, pekokis] (Wyc. 2 *Chron.* ix. 21).

pea-jacket. Pleon. for earlier *pea*, *pee*, Du. *pij*, rough coat, whence also ME. *courtepy*, cassock, etc. (Chauc. A. 290). Perh. ident. with *pie*[1] (q.v.), ? from orig. colour; ? or ult. cogn. with AS. *pād*, cloak, Goth. *paida*. For pleon. cf. *salt-cellar*. The compd. is of US. formation (c. 1700), prob. suggested by Du. *pij-jakker*.

pije: py-gown, or rough-gown, as souldiers and sea-men wear (Hexham).

peak[1]. Point, etc. Var. (from 16 cent.) of *pike* (q.v.), in sense of sharp or projecting part of anything, e.g. of hat, ship, etc. E. naut. *apeak*, for F. *à pic*, perpendicular, shows identity of the two words. In sense of mountain-top first as adaptation of cogn. Sp. Port. *pico*, esp. the *peak of Teneriffe*, which is commonly *pic*, *pico*, *pike* in 17 cent. E.; but *pike* (q.v.), preserved in Lake country, is from ON. The Derbyshire *Peak*, AS. *Pēaclond*, perh. from a demon named *Pēac* (cf. *Puck*), is quite unconnected with the above.

In this Iland of Teneriffe there is a hill called the Pike, because it is piked (Hawkins' *Voyage*, 1564).

peak[2]. To dwindle. Chiefly in to *peak and pine*, echo of *Macb.* i. 3. Hence also dial. *peaky*, *peakish*, sickly. ? From *peak*[1], with idea of becoming "pointed" and thin.

peal. Aphet. for *appeal* (q.v.), F. *appel*, whence also *appeau*, bird-call. Cf. *peer*³, *pall*².

appeaux: chimes; or, the chiming of bels (Cotg.).

pear. AS. *pere*, L. *pira*, pl. of *pirum*; cf. F. *poire* (OF. *peire*), It. Sp. *pera*; also Du. *peer*, OHG. *bira* (*birne*). For neut. pl. taken as fem. sing. cf. F. *pomme*, L. *poma*.

pearl¹. Gem. F. *perle*; cf. It. Sp. *perla*; also Du. *paarl*, Ger. *perle*, from Rom. VL. **pirula*, dim. of *pira* (v.s.), has been suggested; cf. OHG. *perala*, Port. *perola*. But Sicilian *perna*, Neapolitan *perne*, point rather to L. *perna*, kind of shell-fish, lit. ham; cf. It. *pernocchia*, pearl shell.

Nether caste ye youre pearles [Wyc. margaritis] before swyne (Tynd. *Matt.* vii. 6).

pearl². Loop in embroidery, etc. Corrupted spelling of *purl*¹ (q.v.).

pearmain. Kind of apple, but in ME. synon. with *warden pear*. OF. *parmain*, *permain*. As *warden*² (q.v.) is prob. for *wardant*, keeping, ME. & OF. *parmain* must be from OF. *parmaindre*, to endure, VL. **permanere*, for *permanēre*, whence also ME. verb to *permain*. For formation of adj. from verb-stem cf. *demure*, *stale*.

Law of nature...permaynis for ever (*NED.* 1456).

a parmayn: volemum, Anglicè a warden
(*Cath. Angl.*).

peasant. F. *paysan*, from *pays*, country, Late L. *pagensis*, from *pagus*, canton, district. For -*t* cf. *tyrant*, *pheasant*.

pease. AS. *pise*, L. *pisa*, pl. of *pisum*, G. πίσον. We still say *pease-pudding*, but *pease-soup* has become *pea-soup*. See *pea*. Cf. F. *pois*, OF. *peis*, partly the origin of the E. words.

peat. ME. *pete*, Anglo-L. *peta*, in Sc. documents c. 1200. As the earliest sense is not the substance, but the cut piece of turf, it is prob. of Celt. origin and cogn. with *piece* and F. *petit*.

peavey [*US.*]. Lumberman's hook. Name of inventor.

pebble. For earlier *pebble-stone*, rounded stone found on beach, AS. *papolstān*, *popel-*, whence ME. *pibble-*, *puble-*, the uncertainty of the vowel, and the analogy of *boulder* (q.v.), suggesting that the name is imit. of rattling sound. Cf. also *shingle*².

peccable. Liable to sin. F., MedL. *peccabilis*, back-formation from L. *impeccabilis*, impeccable, from *peccare*, to sin.

peccadillo. Sp. *pecadillo*, dim. of *pecado*, sin, L. *peccatum* (v.s.).

peccant. From pres. part. of L. *peccare*, to sin. In med. use (*peccant humours*), via OF.

peccary. SAmer. animal. Carib *paquira*, variously spelt by early travellers. Current form from F. *pécari* (Cuvier).

peccavi, to cry. L., I have sinned, as repentant ejaculation. The attribution to Sir C. Napier of *peccavi*, "I have Scinde," is apocryphal.

peck¹. Measure. AF. *pek*, chiefly in connection with oats for horses. Perh. cogn. with *peck*², *pick*²; cf. F. *picotin*, "a (French) pecke; or, the fourth part of a *boisseau*" (Cotg.), which is app. cogn. with *picoter*, to peck, pick. The phrase *peck of troubles* (c. 1535) also suggests an orig. sense of dose, allowance, rather than a fixed measure.

peck². Verb. Collateral form of *pick*² (q.v.), with which it often varies in ME. texts. Hence colloq. *peckish*, hungry. Ult. cogn. with *beak*, *peak*¹, *pike*. To *keep up one's pecker* (19 cent.) is app. from the figure of the alert sparrow.

Pecksniffian. From *Pecksniff*, unctuous hypocrite in *Martin Chuzzlewit* (1844). Cf. *podsnappery*, *Stiggins*, etc.

J. R. Macdonald delivered a revolutionary speech, which...lent a Pecksniffian sententiousness to the discussion
(B. Tillett, in *Sunday Times*, June 10, 1917).

pectin-. From L. *pecten*, *pectin-*, comb.

pectoral. F., or L. *pectoralis*, from *pectus*, *pector-*, breast.

peculate. Orig. to rob the state. From L. *peculari*, to embezzle, from *peculium*, private property, from *pecu*, cattle, money. Cf. *chattel*, *fee*, *pecuniary*.

peculation: a robbing of the Prince or Commonwealth (Phillips).

peculiar. OF. *peculier*, L. *peculiaris*, from *peculium* (v.s.). Orig. sense survives in *peculiar to*, belonging exclusively to. The *peculiar people* were in 15 cent. the Jews, the mod. sect (*Plumstead Peculiars*) dating from 1838.

pecuniary. F. *pécuniaire*, L. *pecuniarius*, from *pecunia*, money, from *pecu*, cattle. Cf. *peculate*.

pedagogue. F. *pédagogue*, L., G. παιδαγωγός, lit. boy-leader, from παῖς, παιδ-, boy, ἄγειν, to lead; orig. slave leading Athenian boy to school. Not orig. contemptuous in E.

Cf. *pedagogy*, current serious sense of which is from F. *pédagogie*.

ὥστε ὁ νόμος παιδαγωγὸς ἡμῶν γέγονεν εἰς Χριστόν
(*Gal.* iii. 24).

pedal. F. *pédale*, It. *pedale*, L. *pedalis*, from *pes, ped-*, foot. Orig. (c. 1600) of organ.

pedant. F. *pédant*, It. *pedante*, "a pedante or a schoole-master, as *pedagogo*" (Flor.), app. a popular formation on *pedagogo*.

In Italy, of all professions that of Pedanteria is held in basest repute; the schoolemaster almost in every comedy being brought upon the stage to parallel the Zani, or Pantaloun (Peacham, 1634).

pedate [*biol.*]. L. *pedatus*, from *pes, ped-*, foot. Cf. *palmate*.

peddle. Back-formation from *pedlar* (q.v.). Cf. *beg, cadge*[1].

pedestal. F. *piédestal*, It. *piedistallo*, lit. foot stall[1] (q.v.). Cf. Ger. *fussgestell*, "the basis, foot, footstall or pedestal of a pillar, statue, etc." (Ludw.).

pedestrian. From L. *pedester*, from *pes, ped-*, foot.

pedicel [*bot.*]. Dim. of *pedicle*, L. *pediculus*, foot-stalk (v.s.).

pediculous. L. *pediculosus*, from *pediculus*, louse.

pedicure. F. *pédicure* (18 cent.). Cf. *manicure* and see *cure*[1].

pedigree. AF. & ME. *pe de gru*, F. *pied de grue*, foot of crane, L. *grus, gru-*, from sign ⅄ used in indicating descent. By early etymologists associated with *degree* (of relationship). Cf. surname *Pettigrew*, i.e. crane's foot, or Ger. name *Kranenfuss*.

pedegru or *pedygru, lyne of keendrede and awyncetry*: stema (*Prompt. Parv.*).

pediment [*arch.*]. Triangular space over Greek portico. Earlier *periment*, explained (16 cent.) as "corrupt English," and no doubt for *pyramid*, in which sense it is still in dial. use. For change of consonant cf. *paddock*.

pedlar. For earlier *pedder* (Wyc.), from EAngl. *ped*, basket; cf. dial. *tinkler* for *tinker*. For formation of *pedder* cf. *cadger* (q.v.). Verb to *peddle* is a back-formation, and, in sense of busying oneself with trifles, is associated with *piddle*.

pedometer. F. *pédomètre*, hybrid coinage from L. *pes, ped-*, foot, and *mètre* (see *metre*). Recorded for early 18 cent.

peduncle [*bot.*]. L. *pedunculus*. See *pedicel*.

peek [*archaic*]. To peep. ME. *piken*. In earlier E. *keek, peek, peep* are interchangeable. Their relation to each other is ob-scure. Perh. F. *piquer*, in sense of pricking (through). See *peep*[2].

peel[1]. To strip. F. *peler*, L. *pilare*, to strip of hair, but associated in sense with OF. *pel* (*peau*), skin, L. *pellis*; cf. It. *pelare*, to strip of hair. *Peel* is used earlier indifferently with archaic *pill*, to strip, rob (cf. *caterpillar*), F. *piller*, VL. **piliare*, for *pilare* (v.s.), from *pilus*, hair. In *Is.* xviii. 2 the sense of the orig. is doubtful. Wyc. has *torn* or *to-rent*, Coverd. *pylled*.

As piled as an ape was his skulle (Chauc. A. 3935).

peel[2] [*hist.*]. Small fortified house on Border. In ME. palisade, earlier, stake. OF. *pel* (*pieu*), stake, L. *pālus*; cf. *pale*[1]. Hence *Peel*, alias *Castletown*, in I. of Man.

God save the lady of this pel
(Chauc. *House of Fame*, iii. 220).

peel[3]. In *salmon peel*. Synon with *grilse*. From 16 cent. Origin unknown.

peel[4]. Baker's shovel. F. *pelle*, L. *pala*.

peeler [*slang*]. Policeman, orig. Ir. From *Robert Peel*, secretary for Ireland (1812–18). Cf. *bobby*.

Peelite [*hist.*]. Tory seceding (1846) to *Sir Robert Peel* in support of repeal of corn laws.

peep[1]. Of cry of young birds. Imit.; cf. F. *pépier*, Ger. *piepsen*.

peep[2]. To look out, etc. Tends to replace (from 15 cent.) earlier *keek, peek* (q.v.), with the former of which cf. Du. *kijken*, Ger. *gucken*. Of obscure origin, perh. from interj. *pip, peep*. Primitive sense was prob. that of bobbing up, breaking through; cf. F. *point* in *point du jour*, peep of day (see *pip*[2]). For *peep-bo* see *bo-peep*.

peepul, pipal. Sacred fig-tree, *bo-tree*. Hind. *pīpal*, Sanskrit *pippala*, cogn. with *poplar*.

peer[1]. Noun. OF. *per* (*pair*), L. *par*, equal. Orig. sense still in *peerless*; see also *compare*. Sense of noble is derived from Charlemagne's "twelve peers," regarded as all equal, like the knights of the Round Table.

Nullus liber homo capiatur...nisi per legale judicium parium suorum (*Magna Charta*).

peer[2]. To look narrowly. From 16 cent. Altered from earlier *pire*, cogn. with LG. *piren*, under influence of *peer*[3], which it often approaches closely in sense.

Peering [*quarto* piring] in maps for ports and piers and roads (*Merch. of Ven.* i. 1).

peer[3]. To come into view. Earlier *pear*, aphet. for *appear* (q.v.), or immediately from simple *paroir*. Almost obs. in 17–18 cents., but revived by Romantics. See *peer*[2].

When primrose gan to peare on medows bancke so green (*NED*. 1568).

When daffodils begin to peer (*Wint. Tale*, iv. 3).

peevish. Now in sense of ill-tempered and with suggestion of querulous whining, but orig. synon. with froward, perverse. Earliest form *peyvesshe* (*Piers Plowm.*) suggests F. *pervers* or fem. *perverse*; cf. ME. *traves(s)* for *traverse*. Colloq. *peeved* is a back-formation (? US.).

Symony, lechory, perjory, and doubble variable pevyshnesse (*Paston Let.*).

Sik ane pevyche and cative saule as thyne
(Gavin Douglas).

insanus: madde, peevishe, froward, untractable
(Coop.).

peewit. See *pewit*.

peg. First in *Prompt. Parv.* (v.i.). Cf. dial. Du. *peg*, LG. *pigge*, in same sense. ? Ult. cogn. with F. *pique*, pike; cf. *piquet*, tent-peg, picket. *Peg*, drink (Anglo-Ind.), is from the pegs which orig. showed in tankards how far each person was to drink. To *take a person down a peg or two* is from pegs used in tightening up stringed instruments; cf. to *lower one's tone* and see *pin*. To *peg away* is from industrious hammering in of pegs. To *peg out*, die (US.), is prob. from retiring from some game (cf. to *hand in one's checks*, i.e. card-counters, etc., in same sense).

pegge, or pyn of tymbre: cavilla (*Prompt. Parv.*).

Pegasus. G. Πήγασος, winged horse which sprang from blood of Medusa slain by Perseus. From G. πηγή, spring, in allusion to springs of Ocean near which this took place (so Hesiod). As steed of muses first in Boiardo's *Orlando Innamorato* (15 cent.), though the connection is classical (see *hippocrene*).

pegmatite [*min.*]. From G. πῆγμα, fixed framework, in allusion to closeness of texture.

Pehlevi. See *Pahlavi*.

peignoir. F., from *peigner*, to comb, from *peigne*, comb, L. *pecten*.

peine forte et dure [*hist.*]. Pressing to death as punishment for refusing to plead. Not abolished till 18 cent. F., L. *poena fortis et dura*.

Peishwa. See *Peshwa*.

pejorative [*ling.*]. F. *péjoratif* (neol.), from

L. *pejor*, worse; applied chiefly to depreciatory suffixes, e.g. -*ard*, -*aster*.

pekin. Fabric. F. *pékin*, Jesuit spelling of Chin. *Pē-kīng*, lit. northern capital (cf. *nankeen*). Cf. *pekingese*, breed of dog orig. property of Chin. imperial family.

pekoe. Tea. Chin., lit. white down, because gathered while leaves are still in that condition.

Pelagian [*theol.*]. Follower of *Pelagius*, latinized name of British monk *Morgan* (4–5 cents.) who denied doctrine of original sin. *Morgan* is prob. from Welsh *mōr*, sea.

That arch-heretick was called Pelagius, *a pelago*, his name being Morgan (Howell, 1620).

pelagian, pelagic [*scient.*]. Of the open sea, G. πέλαγος. Esp. in *pelagic sealing*.

pelargonium. Coined (1787) by L'Héritier from G. πελαργός, stork, after *geranium*.

Pelasgian, Pelasgic [*hist.*]. Of the *Pelasgi*, G. Πελασγοί, ancient race supposed to have preceded Hellenes in Greece.

pelerine. Cloak. F. *pèlerine*, fem. of *pèlerin*, pilgrim (q.v.).

pelf. OF. *pelfre*, plunder (11 cent.). ? Ult. from L. *pilare*, to pillage. Cf. *pilfer*.

pelican. Late L. *pelicanus*, G. πελεκάν, cogn. with πελεκᾶς, woodpecker, from πέλεκυς, axe, with allusion to power of bill. Used by LXX. to render Heb. *qāāth*. Hence in AS. and in most Europ. langs. *Pelican in her piety* (her.) alludes to belief as to bird feeding its young with its own blood, app. from an Egypt. tradition relating to another bird.

Pelion upon Ossa. See *Titan*.

pelisse. F., L. *pellicia* (sc. *vestis*), from *pellis*, skin. Cf. *surplice*.

pellagra [*med.*]. Skin-disease. It., ? from *pelle*, skin, on model of *podagra* (q.v.), ? or for orig. *pelle agra*, hard skin.

pellet. F. *pelote*, dim. from L. *pila*, ball; cf. It. *pillotta*, Sp. *pelota*. In missile sense orig. applied to large projectile, such as the stone thrown by a medieval war-engine. For diminution in size cf. *bullet*.

Peletes of iron and of lede for the gretter gonnes
(*Coventry Leet Book*, 1451).

pellicle. L. *pellicula*, dim. of *pellis*, skin.

pellitory. Two distinct plant-names, (1) "pellitory of the wall," alteration of *parietary*, F. *pariétaire*, L. *parietaria*, from *paries*, *pariet-*, wall, (2) "pellitory of Spain," alteration of *pyrethrum* (q.v.), whence ME.

peleter. In both cases the -*l*- is due to dissim. of *r-r* (cf. *pilgrim*).

parietaire: pellitory of the wall (Cotg.).

piretre: herb bartram, bastard pellitory, right pellitory of Spaine (*ib.*).

pell-mell. F. *pêle-mêle*, redupl. on *mêler*, to mix, OF. *mesler*. Cf. *melly*, *mêlée*.

pellucid. L. *pellucidus*, for **perlucidus*. See *lucid*.

Pelmanism. System of mind-training originated (late 19 cent.) by W. J. Ennever, "the name Pelman being selected as a short euphonious name well adapted for business purposes" (*Truth*, June 5, 1918).

Turned a blear-eyed pauper to a swell man
In six sharp weeks of concentrated Pelman
                          (G. Frankau).

peloric [*biol.*]. Anomalous, from G. πέλωρος, monstrous.

pelota. Basque game. Sp. *pelota*, ball. See *pellet*.

pelt¹. Skin. For earlier and obs. *pell*, OF. *pel* (*peau*), L. *pellis*. Back-formation from *peltry*, F. *pelleterie*, from *pelletier*, furrier, from OF. *pel* (v.s.), with intrusive -*et*- common in such F. formations (e.g. *coquetier*, egg-cup, from *coque*, egg-shell). ME. *peltrie* became obs., the word being re-borrowed (c. 1700) from F. trappers of NAmer. Or *pelt* may represent OF. & ME. dim. *pelete*.

pelt². Verb. From c. 1500. Orig. to strike with repeated blows, now with a shower of missiles. ? ME. *pelt*, *pilt*, *pult*, to thrust, L. *pultare*, frequent. of *pellere*, to drive. If this is correct, something of orig. sense may appear in *full pelt*, with which cf. *full lick*. But *pelt* may be, at any rate in its current sense, from *pellet* (v.i.).

In this party I first saw the barbarous custom of pelleting each other, with little balls of bread made like pills, across the table
                   (Hickey's *Memoirs*, ii. 137).

peltate [*biol.*]. L. *peltatus*, from *pelta*, shield, G. πέλτη.

pelvis [*anat.*]. L., basin.

pembroke. Table. ? From *Pembroke*, Wales.

pemmican. NAmer. Ind. (Cree) *pimecan*, from *pime*, fat. Also fig. of condensed matter.

pen¹. Enclosure. AS. *penn*; also verb *pennian*, in compd. only, whence p.p. *pent*. ? Cf. LG. *pennen*, to bolt a door, from *penn*, pin, peg.

pen². For writing. ME. & OF. *penne*, L. *penna*, feather. Cf. sense of F. *plume*, Ger.

feder. A *penknife* was orig. used for sharpening quills.

pen³ [*topogr.*]. Welsh, Corn., hill; cogn. with Ir. *ceann*, head.

penal. F. *pénal*, L. *penalis*, from *poena*, punishment, G. ποινή, fine. *Penal servitude* dates from 1853. With *under penalty* cf. F. *sous peine*. Sporting sense of *penalty*, *penalize* appears first in horse-racing.

penance. OF. (replaced by learned *pénitence*), L. *paenitentia*. See *repent*.

Penates. Household gods. L., from *penus*, sanctuary of temple; cogn. with *penitus*, within.

pence. ME. *pens*, contr. of *pennies*.

penchant. Pres. part. of F. *pencher*, VL. **pendicare*, from *pendēre*, to hang. Cf. *leaning*, *bent*, and Ger. *hang*, inclination.

pencil. Orig. paint-brush (Chauc.). OF. *pincel* (*pinceau*), painter's brush, from L. *penicillus*, dim. of *penis*, tail. Current sense, from c. 1600, is due to association with unrelated *pen²*. Orig. sense survives in *pencilled eyebrows*, and also in optics, the rays of a luminous *pencil* being likened to the hairs of a brush.

The prospect was so tempting that I could not forbeare designing it with my crayon (Evelyn).

Here we din'd, and I with my black lead pen tooke the prospect (*ib.*).

pendant. F., pres. part. of *pendre*, to hang, from L. *pendēre*. In naut. sense, esp. *broad pendant* of commodore, from 15 cent., but perh. orig. corrupt. of *pennon* (q.v.) by association with naut. *pendant*, hanging tackle. Cf. *pennant*.

pendent. Latinized spelling of *pendant* (q.v.).

pending. From obs. *pend*, to hang, F. *pendre*, from L. *pendēre*. Perh. also aphet. for *impending*. Prep. use is after F. *pendant*, a survival of the abl. absolute, e.g. *pendant le procès* corresponds to L. *pendente lite*.

Pendragon [*hist.*]. Welsh *pen*, head, and *dragon*, as symbol on standard. Title of Uther in the *Morte Artur*.

pendulum. Neut. of L. *pendulus*, hanging, from *pendēre*, to hang. Cf. F. *pendule*, It. *pendolo*, Ger. *pendel*, all 17 cent.

That great mathematician and virtuoso Monsr. Zulichem, inventor of yᵉ pendule clock
                 (Evelyn, 1661).

Is this the wisdom of a great minister? or is it the vibration of a pendulum? (*Let. of Junius*, 1769).

Penelope. Wife of Ulysses, who, beset by suitors in absence of her husband, promised to make a choice when her web was completed, and deferred this by un-ravelling every night what she had woven during the day. G. Πηνελόπεια (Hom.).

penetrate. From L. *penetrare*, from *penes*, *penitus*, within, *penus*, sanctuary. Cf. *penetralia*, inmost recesses, *Penates*. See *enter*.

penfold. See *pinfold*.

penguin. Applied (16 cent.) both to the great auk and the penguin, and prob. earlier to other sea-birds. Early writers (16–17 cents.) explain it as Welsh *pen gwyn*, white head, a name supposed to have been given by Welsh seamen, or possibly by Breton fishermen off Newfoundland (Cape Breton). This is prob. correct. A bolder flight of fancy connects it with the mythical discovery of America by Madoc ap Owen in the 12 cent. (see Hakl. viii. 108). The fact that the penguin has a black head is no serious objection, as bird-names are of very uncertain application (cf. *albatross*, *grouse*, *pelican*, *bustard*). F. *pingouin*, earlier (1600) *penguyn*, if not from E., may be Breton *pen gouin*, white head. Cf. *pen³*, *Pendragon*. In sense of *Wraf* (q.v.), *penguin* alludes to the flapper that does not fly.

Pengwyns, which in Welsh, as I have been en-formed, signifieth a white head. From which deri-vation...some doe inferre that America was first peopled with Welsh-men
(Richard Hawkins, c. 1600).

penicillate [*biol.*]. Tufted. See *pencil*.

peninsula. L., from *paene*, almost, *insula*, island; cf. F. *presqu'île*, Ger. *halbinsel*. Spec. ref. to Spain and Portugal dates from *Peninsular War* (1808–14).

penis [*anat.*]. L., lit. tail.

penitent. F. *pénitent*, from pres. part. of L. *paenitēre*, to repent. Displaced earlier *penant*, from OF. (cf. *penance*). *Penitentiary*, prison, earlier eccl. house of discipline for penitents, dates from c. 1800.

pennant [*naut.*]. Compromise between *pendant* (q.v.) and *pennon* (q.v.).

penniform [*biol.*]. From L. *penna*, feather.

pennill. Extemporized verse sung at Eisteddfod. Welsh, ? from *pen*, head.

pennon. Knight's swallow-tail flag. F. *penon*, from L. *penna*, feather, plume; cf. It. *pennone*, Sp. *pendón*. See *pendant*, *pennant*. But OF. var. *panon*, and analogy of *drapeau*, flag, from *drap*, cloth, suggest influence of L. *pannus*, cloth.

penny. AS. *pennig*, earlier *pening*; cf. Du. *penning*, Ger. *pfennig*. For suffix cf. *farthing*, *shilling*. Origin obscure, perh. from *pan*, early coins being sometimes shaped like shallow pans. The value and metal have varied at different periods. Often used in ME. for money in gen., as still in *a pretty penny*, to *get one's penny-worth*, to *turn an honest penny*; cf. F. *un joli denier*. A *pennyweight* was of the weight of a silver penny. For hybrid *dwt* cf. *cwt*.

A peny yn seson spent wille safe a pounde
(*Paston Let.* i. 414).

Freend (quoth the good man) a peny for your thought (Heywood, 1546).

pennyroyal. App. arbitrary corrupt. of *puliol royal*, OF. *pouliol*, from L. *pulegium*, flea-bane, from *pulex*, flea. The adj. prob. from its being regarded as a sovereign remedy. Perh. confused with *pennywort*, said to be named from round leaves, with which Palsg. wrongly identifies it.

penology. Science of punishments. See *penal*.

pensile. L. *pensilis*, from *pendēre*, *pens-*, to hang.

pension. "An allowance made to anyone without an equivalent. In England it is generally understood to mean pay given to a state hireling for treason to his country" (Johns.). F., L. *pensio-n-*, from *pendere*, *pens-*, to pay, orig. to weigh. Earlier used, as in F., of any periodic payment, e.g. for board and lodging, whence *pensioner*, Camb. undergraduate who, not being a scholar or sizar on the foundation, pays for all he has (cf. Oxf. *commoner*). *Grand Pensionary* (hist.) is adapted from Du. *pensionaris*, chief magistrate.

Sir William Byles recently asked Mr Lloyd George what is the amount of the pension being paid by the State to Lord Roberts; and what power, if any, resides in the State to withdraw such pension
(*Times*, Nov. 1, 1912).

pensive. F. *pensif*, from *penser*, to think, L. *pensare*, frequent. of *pendere*, to weigh.

penstock. Floodgate. From *pen¹* and *stock*.

pent. Orig. p.p. of to *pen* or of its obs. var. *pend*. See *pen¹*.

penta-. G. πεντα-, from πέντε, five (q.v.). Hence *pentagon*, *pentameter*, *pentarchy*, etc.

pentacle, pentagram. Five-pointed star used in sorcery (v.s.).

pentad. Number five. G. πεντάς, πεντάδ-. Cf. *triad*, etc.

pentagram. See *pentacle*.

pentateuch. L., G. πεντάτευχος, of five books, from G. τεῦχος, implement, in Late G. book.

Pentecost. Church L., G. πεντηκοστή (sc. ἡμέρα), fiftieth (day). G. name for Jewish Feast of Weeks, celebrated seven weeks after second day of Passover. Found in AS., but now usu. replaced by *Whit Sunday*. Cf. F. *Pentecôte*, Ger. *Pfingsten*.

penthouse. Folk-etym. for earlier *pentice*, *pentis*, aphet. for F. *appentis*, from *appendre*, to hang to; cf. a *lean-to*. Association with F. *pente*, slope, has introduced idea of sloping, whence *pent-roof*. The form *penthouse* is much earlier than dict. records. It occurs (in AF.) in *John of Gaunt's Reg.* (1372–76).

Item, quod appenticia sint ita sublimia quod homines potuerint faciliter sub illis ire et equitare (*Liber Albus*, 259).

appentis: the penthouse of a house (Cotg.).

pentagraph. See *pantograph*.

penultimate. From L. *paene*, almost, *ultimus*, last.

penumbra. Coined (1604) by Kepler from L. *paene*, almost, *umbra*, shade.

penurious. Orig. indigent, from *penury*, L. *penuria*, want, cogn. with *paene*, hardly.

peon. In India, police-man, servant, etc., Port. *peão* or F. *pion*. In Sp. Amer., labourer, Sp. *peón*. Both from MedL. *pedo-n-*, footsoldier, from *pes*, *ped-*, foot (see *pawn²*). Hence *peonage*, servitude for debt, in Mexico.

peony. AS. *peonie*, L. *paeonia*, G. παιωνία, from Παιών, physician of the gods, in allusion to med. properties. ME. had also *pioine*, from OF. (now *pivoine*).

people. F. *peuple*, nation, race, L. *populus*; cf. It. *popolo*, Sp. *pueblo*, Ger. *pöbel*, mob. Has largely replaced native *folk* and is used in many senses for which F. uses *gens*, *personnes*, *on*, *monde*, etc. For vowel cf. *beef*, *retrieve*, etc. Mod. spelling, for ME. *peple*, is an artificial reversion to the *-o-* of *populus*.

peperino [geol.]. Porous rock. It., from *pepe*, pepper, in allusion to small grain.

peperomia. Plant. ModL., from G. πέπερι, pepper.

peplum. Overskirt. L., from G. πέπλος, robe.

pepper. AS. *pipor*, L. *piper*, G. πέπερι, of Eastern origin; cf. Sanskrit *pippalī*. Found very early in most Europ. langs. For *peppercorn* (i.e. nominal) *rent* see below. With *peppermint*, from *mint¹*, cf. Ger. *pfeffermünze*.

Reddendo inde annuatim mihi et heredibus meis...

unam clovam gariofili ad Pascham pro omni servicio (Grant in *Stonor Papers*, c. 1290).

Shalt yearly pay
A peppercorne, a nutt, a bunch of may,
Or some such trifle (*NED.* 1616).

pepsin. ModGer. coinage from G. πέψις, digestion, from πέπτειν, to ripen, cook. Cf. *peptic*, *dyspepsia*.

peptone. Ger. *pepton* (v.s.). Hence *peptonize*, to pre-digest by means of pepsin. For fig. use cf. *pemmican*.

per. L., through, by, in MedL. also with distributive sense. As prefix also intens. in L., as in *perturb* (cf. E. *thorough-*), and this sense appears in chem. terms in *per-*, e.g. *peroxide*, *perchloride*. Many E. words in *per-* are latinized from earlier forms in *par-*, borrowed from F., e.g. *perfect*, ME. & OF. *parfit*, L. *perfectus*. Mod. *as per usual* seems to have been suggested by F. *comme par ordinaire*.

peradventure. Restored spelling of ME. & OF. *par aventure*, often contracted in ME.; cf. *perchance* and obs. *percase*. "It is sometimes used as a noun, but not gracefully nor properly" (Johns.).

Paraunter she may be youre purgatorie
(Chauc. E. 1670).

It is indispensable that the Governments associated against Germany should know beyond a peradventure with whom they are dealing
(Pres. Wilson, Oct. 15, 1918).

perai. SAmer. fresh-water fish. Tupi (Brazil) *piraya*, lit. scissors.

perambulate. From L. *perambulare*, from *ambulare*, to walk, travel. Earlier is *perambulation*, official journey to fix boundaries (see *purlieu*). Current sense of *perambulator*, orig. a traveller, etc., dates from c. 1850–60. *Perambucot* is a mod. portmanteau-word.

percale. Muslin. F.; cf. It. *percallo*, Sp. *percal*. Of Eastern origin; cf. Pers. *parqālah*, a rag.

perceive. F. *percevoir*, with OF. tonic stem *perceiv-*, VL. *percipēre*, for *percipere*, from *capere*, to take. Cf. *deceive*, etc.

per cent. Short for L. *per centum*, still in leg. use.

percept. As philos. term coined (19 cent.) on *concept*. L. *perceptum*, from *percipere*, *percept-*, to perceive. Cf. *perceptible*, *perception*, which are much older.

perch¹. Fish. F., L. *perca*, G. πέρκη, cogn. with περκνός, dark-spotted.

perch². Pole, etc., in various senses, now usu.

associated with land-measurement (rod, pole) and birds. F. *perche*, L. *pertica*, staff, measuring-rod.

perchance. ME. *par chance*, etc. Cf. *peradventure*.

percheron. F., horse from *le Perche*.

Sometimes called the Norman horse, the Percheron comes from the Perche region, south of Normandy (*Daily Mail*, Jan. 23, 1918).

percipient. From pres. part. of L. *percipere*, to perceive.

percolate. From L. *percolare*, from *colare*, to flow, from *colum*, strainer. Cf. *colander*.

percussion. F., L. *percussio-n-*, from *percutere*, *percuss-*, to strike, from *quatere*, to shake, strike.

perdition. F., L. *perditio-n-*, from *perdere*, *perdit-*, to lose, from *dare*, to give. Chiefly in theol. sense, whence its disappearance in orig. sense of destruction.

perdu. In to *lie perdu*. Now usu. treated as F. word, but quite naturalized in 17 cent. in mil. use, esp. in *perdus*, for *enfants perdus*, forlorn hope.

perdurable. See *per-* and *durable*. In Chauc., regarded as obs. by Johns., but revived in 19 cent.

peregrine. L. *peregrinus*, foreigner, from *pereger*, abroad on journey, from *per* and *ager*, field. Hence *peregrine falcon*, caught in passage, instead of being taken from nest like *eyas*; cf. F. *faucon pèlerin*, It. *falcone pellegrino*, and see *pilgrim*.

peremptory. F. *péremptoire*, L. *peremptorius*, destructive, from *perimere*, *perempt-*, to take away utterly, from *emere*, to buy, obtain. Used in Roman law in sense of precluding all further debate.

perennial. From L. *perennis*, lasting through the year(s), from *per* and *annus*, year (cf. *biennial*). Used by Evelyn for evergreen.

perfect. Restored spelling of ME. & OF. *parfit* (*parfait*), L. *perfectus*, from *perficere*, *perfect-*, to do thoroughly. Often intens., e.g. *perfect scandal* (*stranger*, etc.). With *perfectibility*, F. *perfectibilité*, from the jargon of the 18 cent. *philosophes*, cf. E. *perfectionist*, theol. coinage of 17 cent. Wyc. uses *to perfection* (*Job*, xi. 7). *Counsel of perfection* is allusive to *Matt.* xix. 21.

He was a verray parfit, gentil knyght
(Chauc. A. 72).

perfidy. F. *perfidie*, L. *perfidia*, from *perfidus*, treacherous, from *fidus*, faithful, from *fides*, faith. For pejorative sense of *per-* cf. *perjure*.

perfoliate [*bot.*]. With stalk apparently passing through leaf. From L. *per* and *folium*, leaf.

perforate. From L. *perforare*, from *forare*, cogn. with *bore*[1]. Chief current sense came in with improved postage-stamps.

perforce. ME. & F. *par force*. Cf. *peradventure*.

perform. AF. *parfourmer*, altered, by association with other words in *-form*, from AF. *parfourner*, OF. *parfournir*, from *fournir*, to furnish (q.v.). ME. had also *parfurnish* in same sense. In *Wollaton MSS*. I find *parfournir* (1259), *perfourmir* (1342). The transition from *performance* (of solemn ceremonies) to *performing fleas* is easily traced.

For noght oonly thy laude precious
Parfourned is by men of dignitee (Chauc. B. 1645).

perfume. Orig. to fumigate. F. *parfumer*, L. *perfumare*, from *fumus*, smoke, fume; cf. It. *perfumare*, Sp. *perfumar*.

perfunctory. Late L. *perfunctorius* (leg.), from *perfungi*, to get done with, from *fungi*, *funct-*, to perform.

perfuse. From L. *perfundere*, *perfus-*. See *fuse*[1].

pergameneous. Coined (19 cent.) from L. *pergamenum*, parchment (q.v.).

pergola. It., arbour, L. *pergula*, projecting roof, from *pergere*, to go forward, from *per* and *agere*.

perhaps. Coined (15 cent.) from *hap*, chance, after *peradventure*, *perchance*, which it has largely superseded. It occurs only three times in *AV*. Prob. the *-s* imitates the ending of *perchance*, *percase*.

peri. F. *péri*, Pers. *parī*, *perī*, orig. malevolent spirit controlled by Ahriman; cf. hist. of *fairy*, *elf*. App. introduced by Beckford (*Vathek*) and popularized by Byron and Moore.

peri-. G. περί, around. Many compds. correspond in sense with those of L. *circum*.

periagua. See *piragua*.

perianth [*bot.*]. F. *périanthe*, coined on *pericarp* from G. ἄνθος, flower.

periapt. Amulet. F. *périapte*, G. περίαπτον, from ἄπτειν, to fasten.

pericardium [*anat.*]. G. περικάρδιον, (membrane) round the heart, καρδία.

pericarp [*bot.*]. F. *péricarpe*, G. περικάρπιον, pod, from καρπός, fruit.

Periclean. Of Athens in time of *Pericles* (†429 B.C.). Cf. *Augustan*.

pericope. Paragraph. G. περικοπή, from κόπτειν, to cut.

pericranium [*anat.*]. G. περικράνιον, round the skull. Often wrongly used for *cranium*.

peridot. F. *péridot*, OF. *peritot* (13 cent.); cf. MedL. *peradota*. ? Arab. *farīdat*, gem. In ME. chrysolite, reintroduced from F. c. 1700 as jeweller's name for olivine chrysolite.

perigee [*astron.*]. F. *périgée*, MedL. *perigeum*, Late G. περίγειον, neut. of περίγειος, round (near) the earth, γῆ. Cf. *apogee*.

perihelion [*astron.*]. From G. ἥλιος, sun, as *perigee*. Cf. *aphelion*.

peril. F. *péril*, L. *periculum*, from root of *experiri*, to try, experiment, *peritus*, experienced. Ult. cogn. with *fare*. Replaced AS. *fǣr* (cf. Ger. *gefahr*). *At* (*one's*) *peril* is ME.

perimeter. G. περίμετρος, from μέτρον, measure.

period. F. *période*, L., G. περίοδος, circuit, from ὁδός, way. Orig. time of duration. *Periodical*, in literary sense, dates from the magazines (*Spectator*, etc.) of early 18 cent.

peripatetic. F. *péripatétique*, L., G. περιπατητικός, given to walking about, from πατεῖν, to tread. Earliest in ref. to Aristotle, who taught while walking in the Lyceum at Athens.

periphery. OF. *peripherie*, L., G. περιφέρεια, lit. carrying round, from φέρειν, to bear. Cf. *circumference*.

periphrasis. L., G. περίφρασις, from φράζειν, to speak. Cf. *circumlocution, talking round* (a subject).

periplus [*hist.*]. L., G. περίπλους, sailing round, from πλόος, πλοῦς, voyage. Cf. *circumnavigation*.

perique. Tobacco (from Louisiana). Said to be named from *Pierre Chenet*, who introduced tobacco-growing among the Acadian exiles.

periscope. Coined on *telescope*, etc., from G. σκοπεῖν, to look.

perish. F. *périr, périss-*, L. *perire*, lit. to go through. For sense cf. Ger. *vergehen*. In ME. also trans., as still in *perishing cold*. Cf. *parch*. Currency of *perish the thought!* is due to Cibber (v.i.), whose impudent "adaptation" is also responsible for *Richard's himself again*.

Catesby. Be more yourself, my Lord: consider, sir;
Were it but known a dream had frighted you,
How wou'd your animated foes presume on't.

Richard. Perish that thought: No, never be it said,
That Fate itself could awe the soul of Richard.
Hence, babbling dreams, you threaten here in vain:
Conscience avant; Richard's himself again
    (*Rich. III*, v. 3. As it is acted at the Theatre
       Royal. By C. Cibber).

peristeronic [*neol.*]. Of the pigeon, G. περιστερά.

peristyle. F. *péristyle*, L., G. περίστυλον, neut. of περίστυλος, having pillars all round, from στῦλος, pillar.

peritoneum [*anat.*]. L., G. περιτόναιον, what stretches round, from τείνειν, to stretch.

periwig. Earlier (16 cent.) *perwike*, for *peruke* (q.v.).

periwinkle[1]. Plant. AS. *perwince*, L. *pervinca*, perh. orig. a climbing plant and cogn. with *vincire*, to bind; cf. F. *pervenche*, "periwinkle, or pervincle" (Cotg.). Form has app. been influenced by *periwinkle*[2].

And fresshe pervynke riche of hewe
    (*Rom. of Rose*, 1432).

periwinkle[2]. Mollusc, winkle. AS. *pinewincle*, explained as sea-snail, with first element app. from L. *pina*, G. πῖνα, mussel. But there is a gap between this and the mod. word (16 cent.). Form has app. been influenced by *periwinkle*[1], as we find 16 cent. *perwinke* in both senses. These two words are a good example of the perversity of folk-etym., for it seems impossible to find any logical point of contact. See *winkle*.

perjure. F. *perjurer*, L. *perjurare*, from *jurare*, to swear, from *jus, jur-*, law, etc. Cf. *forswear*. *Perjury* is older in E. For pejorative force of *per-* cf. *perfidy*.

perk [*colloq.*]. To be jaunty, hold up the head, whence adj. *perk-y*. Forms are those of obs. or dial. *perk*, perch (noun and verb), ONF. *perque*, and the only ME. record (v.i.) has to do with the popinjay; so that orig. sense may have been suggested by the attitude of the parrot on its perch. On the other hand some early examples suggest rather a metath. of *prick*.

The popejayes perken and pruynen for proude
    (*NED.* c. 1380).

permanent. F., from pres. part. of L. *permanēre*, from *manēre*, to dwell, remain. *Permanent way* (rail.) is contrasted with *construction line*.

permeate. From L. *permeare*, from *meare*, to pass.

Permian [*geol.*]. Strata named (1841) by Murchison from *Perm*, E. Russ., where they are well exemplified. Cf. *Devonian, Silurian.*

permit. L. *permittere*, from *mittere, miss-*, to send; cf. F. *permettre*, It. *permettere*. Etym. sense of allowing to pass appears in noun *permit*, orig. imper. of verb; from init. word of offic. authorization (cf. F. *laissez-passer*, a permit).

permute. L. *permutare*, to change thoroughly.

pern. Honey-buzzard. Incorr. from G. πτέρνις, kind of hawk.

pernicious. F. *pernicieux*, L. *perniciosus*, from *pernicies*, destruction, from *nex, nec-*, slaughter, death. Application to disease, esp. anaemia, is recent.

pernickety [*Sc.*]. Fussy, particular. Introduced into E. by Sc. writers from c. 1880. Origin unknown. It is synon. with Sc. *perjink*, and both words, recorded from c. 1800, may be childish or uneducated perversions of *particular*. Cf. synon. Norw. Dan. *pertentlig*, thought to be corrupted from **pedantlig*, pedantic.

peroration. L. *peroratio-n-*, from *perorare*, to speak right through, from *orare*, to speak, pray, from *os, or-*, mouth; cf. F. *péroraison*.

perpend. L. *perpendere*, to weigh thoroughly, from *pendere*, to weigh.

perpendicular. OF. *perpendiculer* (*perpendiculaire*), L. *perpendicularis*, from *perpendiculum*, plummet, from *pendēre*, to hang. First in astron. (Chauc.); as arch. term introduced (1812) by Rickman. *Perpendicular drinking* is treated as a problem in the *Daily Chron.* Mar. 10, 1919.

perpetrate. From L. *perpetrare*, to accomplish, from *patrare*, to bring about. Criminal suggestion in E. is due to word having first been used (16 cent.) in statutes.

perpetual. F. *perpétuel*, L. *perpetualis*, from *perpetuus*, ? from *petere*, to seek, aim at.

perplex. First as adj. (Wyc.). L. *perplexus*, entangled, from *plectere, plex-*, to weave, plait. Cf. *complex.*

perquisite. L. *perquisitum*, thing eagerly sought, from *perquirere, perquisit-*, from *quaerere*, to seek. Orig. (leg.) property acquired otherwise than by inheritance. Current sense from 16 cent. *Perquisition*, domiciliary search, is from ModF.

perron [*arch.*]. Platform with steps before building. F., augment. of *pierre*, stone, L. *petra*; cf. It. *petrone*. See *Peter.*

perruque. See *peruke.*

perry. OF. *peré* (*poiré*), from *peire* (*poire*), pear (q.v.). Still *péré* in NormF.

perse [*archaic*]. A dark colour, purplish blue. Archaic F. *pers*, which in *Rol.* (11 cent.) means livid. MedL. *perseus, persicus*, point to popular association with *Persia*, or perh. with *peach*[1] (q.v.).

> Il perso è un colore misto di purpureo e di nero
> (Dante).

persea. Tree (NAmer. & WInd.). Orig. sacred tree of Egypt and Persia. L., G. περσέα.

persecute. F. *persécuter*, from L. *persequi, persecut-*, from *sequi*, to follow. Earlier (14 cent.) is *persecution*, esp. in ref. to early Church.

persevere. F. *persévérer*, L. *perseverare*, from *severus*, earnest. Until Milt. usu. accented as in quot. below.

> His onely power and providence persever
> T' uphold, maintaine, and rule the world for ever
> (Sylv. i. 7).

Persian. OF. *persien*, from *Perse*, L. *Persia*, in G. Πέρσις, OPers. *Pārs* (see *Parsee*). OPers. or Zend is an Aryan lang. closely allied to Sanskrit. ModPers. is, owing to the Mohammedan conquest (7–9 cents.), saturated with Arab.

persicaria. Plant, peach-wort. MedL. (see *peach*[1]).

persiflage. F., from *persifler*, to banter, 18 cent. coinage from *siffler*, to hiss, whistle, L. *sibilare.*

persimmon. Amer. date-plum. Earlier *putchamin* (Capt. John Smith, 1612), from NAmer. Ind. (Algonkin of Virginia), with suffix *-min* as in other names of grains and fruits.

persist. F. *persister*, L. *persistere*, from *sistere*, to stand.

person. F. *personne*, L. *persona*, character in play (*dramatis persona*), ? from *personare*, to sound through, with allusion to actor's mask, ? or of Etruscan origin (cf. *histrionic*). Orig. sense survives in *impersonate, personify, in the person of, in one's own person* (v.i.), and there is a suggestion of it in *personage*, F. *personnage*, dramatic character. In ME. often used esp. of physical appearance; hence *personable*, comely, having "a fine person." Current senses of *personal* form a parallel series to those of *general*. *Personally conducted* tours were presumably at first accompanied by Mr Cook *in propria persona*. In gram. sense L. *persona* was adopted by Varro in imitation of G. πρόσωπον, character in play, similarly used by Dionysius Thrax.

persona. L. (v.s.); esp. in Late L. *persona grata* and *in propria persona*.

personnel. F., from *personne* (v.s.). Orig. contrasted with *matériel*.

perspective. F., MedL. *perspectiva* (sc. *ars*), from *perspicere, perspect-*, to see through. Used by Chauc. of an optical instrument.

perspicacious. From L. *perspicax, perspicac-*, clear-sighted, from *perspicere* (v.s.). Cf. *perspicuous*, from L. *perspicuus*, transparent. These two words are sometimes confused in mod. use.

perspire. L. *perspirare*, to breathe through, blow gently. Euph. for *sweat* from 18 cent.

That gross kind of exudation which was formerly known by the name of "sweat";...now every mortal, except carters, coal-heavers, and Irish chairmen, merely "perspires" (*Gent. Mag.* 1791).

persuade. F. *persuader*, L. *persuadēre*, from *suadēre*, to advise. With *persuasion*, religious opinion (16 cent.), cf. *conviction*.

pert. Aphet. for ME. & OF. *apert*, L. *apertus*, open, but used in sense of *expertus*. Orig. sense of ready, skilled, etc. survives in dial. *peart*, but the usual meaning, already in Chauc. (v.i.), is now almost that of the opposite *malapert*. Cf. Ger. *frech*, impudent, orig. bold, reckless, and E. *bold hussy*. *Proud* has degenerated in the same way.

With proude wordes apert (*Plowmans Crede*, 541).
She was proud and peert as is a pye
(Chauc. A. 3950).

pertain. ME. *parteyne*, OF. *partenir*, VL. *pertenīre*, for *pertinēre*, from *tenēre*, to hold. Cf. *pertinent*.

pertinacious. From L. *pertinax, pertinac-*, from *tenax*, from *tenēre*, to hold.

pertinent. F., from pres. part. of L. *pertinēre*, to pertain, belong to.

perturb. F. *perturber*, L. *perturbare*, from *turbare*, to disturb, from *turba*, crowd.

peruke. F. *perruque* (15 cent.), It. *perruca, parruca*, of obscure origin. Sp. *peluca* has suggested connection with L. *pilus*, hair, but Port. has *peruca* and the *-r-* may be original. Connection with *parakeet*, in allusion to tufted crest, is not impossible. The popular E. form was *perwike*, whence *periwig*. Pepys, who had his first wig in 1662, spells it at first *peruke* and later *perriwigg*.

peruse. There is an obs. *peruse*, to use up, e.g. *a bowsprete perused and roteyn* (*Nav. Accts.*, 15 cent.), OF. *paruser*, but this can hardly be connected, though it may have influenced the form. Earliest sense, to go

through, survey, hence, inspect, examine critically, points to *pervise*, from L. *pervidēre, pervis-*, to look through, scrutinize (cf. *revise, survey*). It has always been a word rather written than spoken, and such words sometimes acquire spelling pronunc., *u* and *v* not being distinguished in MS. and print till recent times (cf. *Alured*, mistake for *Alvred*, i.e. *Alfred*). With quot. 3 cf. Watts' "When I survey the wondrous cross."

That every weke Maister Meyre let call viij persons unto the tyme that all the x wardes be perused
(*Coventry Leet Book*, 1510).

Littleton's Tenures...lately perused and amended
(Book-title, 1612).

I climbed the Hill, perused the Cross,
Hung with my gain and his great loss
(Vaughan, 1650).

Peruvian bark. Cinchona (q.v.). From *Peruvia*, latinized form of *Peru*.

pervade. L. *pervadere*, to go through.

perverse. F. *pervers*, L. *perversus*, from *pervertere*, to turn away, whence *pervert*; cf. *froward*, which it has replaced. *Pervert*, noun, iron. for *convert*, is a neol.

pervious. From L. *pervius*, from *via*, way.

peseta. Sp. coin, dim. of *pesa*, weight. See *poise*.

peshitta [*theol.*]. Syriac *Vulgate*. Syriac *p'shīttâ*, simple, plain (sc. *mappaqtâ*, version).

Peshwa, Peishwa. Orig. chief minister of Mahratta princes, becoming hereditary sovereign in 1749. Pers. *pēshwā*, chief.

pesky [*US.*]. App. from *pest*; cf. *plaguy*.

peso. Sp. dollar, lit. weight, L. *pensum*, from *pendere, pens-*, to weigh.

pessary [*med.*]. MedL. *pessarium*, from *pessum*, from G. πεσσός, oval stone.

pessimism. Coined (late 18 cent.) ? by Coleridge, after *optimism*, from L. *pessimus*, worst.

pest. F. *peste*, L. *pestis*, plague, pestilence. Cf. *pestilence*, F., L. *pestilentia*.

Pestalozzian. Of *Pestalozzi*, Swiss educationist (†1827).

pester. Now associated with *pest*, but orig. to hamper, entangle, aphet. for OF. *empestrer* (*empêtrer*), "to pester, intricate, intangle, trouble, incumber" (Cotg.), orig. to fasten (at pasture) with a tether, MedL. *pastorium* (see *pastern*), and representing a VL. type *impastoriare*; cf. It. *pastoiare*, "to fetter, to clog, to shackle, to pastern, to give" (Flor.). In early use chiefly naut. and

found passim in various senses in Hakl.
and Purch.

Confin'd and pester'd in this pinfold here
                        (*Comus*, 6).

pestle. OF. *pestel*, L. *pistillum*, from *pinsere*,
pist-, to pound.

pet¹. Darling. Orig. (16 cent.) Sc. and applied
to tame or household animals and birds
as well as to children. Prob. this is the
earlier meaning (cf. *ducky, my lamb*, etc.).
App. related to obs. *peat*, in same senses,
esp. in *proud peat* (*Heart of Midlothian*,
ch. li.). Origin unknown, but see quot.
below.

peton: a little foot; *mon peton*: my prettie springall,
my gentle impe; (any such flattering or dandling
phrase, bestowed by nurses on their sucking boyes)
                             (Cotg.).

pet². Temper. App. from phrase to *take the
pet*, which began to replace (c. 1600) the
earlier to *take pepper in the nose*. It appears
to be from *pet¹*, in sense of animal, like
F. *prendre la chèvre*, lit. to take the goat,
with which cf. US. *that gets my goat*, though
the metaphor is not clear; cf. also It.
pigliare la monna, to get drunk, lit. take
the monkey.

prendre la chevre: to take in dudgeon, or snuffe; to
take the pet, or pepper in the nose (Cotg.).

petal. F. *pétale*, G. πέταλον, thin plate, neut.
of πέταλος, outspread. Cf. *patulous*.

petard. F. *pétard*, from *péter*, to break wind,
from *pet*, L. *peditum*, from *pedere*; cf. It.
petardo, obs. Sp. *petar*.

For 'tis the sport to have the engineer
Hoist with his own petard (*Haml.* iii. 4).

petasus. G. broad-brimmed hat as worn by
Mercury. G. πέτασος, from root πετ-, to
spread; cf. *petal*.

petaurist. Flying marsupial. G. πεταυριστής,
lit. performer on the spring-board, πέταυρον.

Peter. L., G. Πέτρος, lit. stone, rendering
Syriac *kēfā*, stone (*Cephas*). Hence *Peter's
pence*, tribute to Rome, see of St Peter,
also called *Rome-scot*, dating from AS.
times, abolished in 1534. To *rob Peter to
pay Paul* is prob. merely a collocation of
familiar names, *Pierre et Paul* being used
in F. like *Tom, Dick and Harry* in E.,
though later eccl. senses have been read
into the phrase (v.i.). In *blue Peter* the
choice of the name may be arbitrary (cf.
jolly Roger), but I have sometimes won-
dered whether it is in some way connected
with obs. *beaupers, bewpers*, bunting, mis-

understood as "beautiful Peter" (Piers,
Pearce) and perverted to suit the colour.

descouvrir S. Pierre pour couvrir S. Pol: to build,
or inrich one Church with the ruines, or revenues
of another (Cotg.).

A moderate bargain for Paul the taxpayer may be
a very bad bargain for Peter the consumer
                      (*Obs.* June 22, 1919).

Peterloo [*hist.*]. See *blanket*.

peter out. Orig. US., of stream or lode of ore.
? From F. *péter* (see *petard*); ? cf. to *fizzle
out*.

petersham [*archaic*]. Coat, cloth. From
Viscount Petersham (c. 1812). Cf. *spencer,
raglan*.

A Petersham coat with velvet collar, made tight
after the abominable fashion of those days
                      (*Tom Brown*, ch. iv.).

petiole. Footstalk of plant. F. *pétiole*, L.
petiolus, from *pes, ped-*, foot.

petit. F., see *petty*.

petition. F. *pétition*, L. *petitio-n-*, from *petere,
petit-*, to seek, ask for.

Which kynde of disputyng schole men call *Petitio
principii*, the provyng of two certaine thynges,
eche by the other, and is no provyng at all (Tynd.).

petrel. From 17 cent. App. from *St Peter*,
with suffix as in *cockerel*. Cf. Norw. *Peders
fugl*, Ger. *Petersvogel*, prob. suggested by
the E. word. F. *pétrel* is also from E.

The seamen give them the name of petrels, in
allusion to St Peter's walking upon the Lake of
Gennesareth (Dampier).

Petriburg. Signature of bishop of Peterborough.

petrify. F. *pétrifier*, as though from L. **petri-
ficare*, from *petra*, rock. See *Peter*.

petrol. In mod. use from F. *pétrol*, refined
petroleum. The latter is MedL., from
petra, rock, *oleum*, oil. Hence F. *pétroleuse*
(hist.), female incendiary during Paris
Commune (1871).

petrology. Science of rocks. From L. *petra*,
G. πέτρα.

petronel [*hist.*]. Horse-pistol, carbine. The
derivation usu. given, from F. *poitrine*,
chest, is incorr. Archaic F. *poitrinal* is
due to folk-etym., the weapon perh. being
slung, ? or fired, from the chest. The
earliest (16 cent.) forms are F. *petrinal*, It.
petrinale, pietronello, petronello, Sp. *pedreñal*,
all from L. *petra*, stone, the derivatives of
which, It. *pietra*, Sp. *piedra*, mean gun-
flint. Ger. *flinte*, Du. *vlinte*, musket, were
also introduced when the flint-lock superseded the older matchlock. Cf. Sp. Port.

pedernal, flint for striking fire, gun flint. The E. form is prob. from It.

pedreñal: un poitrinal, sorte de petite arquebuse à rouet (Oudin).

'Twas then I fired my petronel,
And Mortham, steed and rider, fell (*Rokeby*, i. 19).

petrosal [*anat.*]. From L. *petrosus*, stony, from *petra*, stone.

petticoat. Orig. (15 cent.) *pety cote*, i.e. *petty coat*, small coat, a garment worn under armour, but already in 15 cent. also used of female attire, though not at first a skirt. As symbol of womankind contrasted by Shaks. with *breeches* (3 *Hen. VI*, v. 5) (see also quot. s.v. *vessel*). *Petticoat government* is first recorded as book-title (1702). *Petticoat tails*, Scotch tea-cakes, has been explained as OF. *petits gastels* (*gâteaux*), but is prob. one of those fantastic coinages which have to be left unexplained.

pettifogger. From 16 cent. First element is *petty* (q.v.), second may be obs. Du. *focker*, monopolist; cf. *focken*, to cheat, in Flem. pedlar lang. These words are connected by some with *Fugger*, name of family of merchant princes at Augsburg (15–16 cent.). Cf. Ger. *kleinigkeitskrämer*, in somewhat similar sense. E. formerly had *pettifactor*, *pettymarchant*, in sense of huckster.

focker: monopola, pantopola, vulgò fuggerus, fuccardus (Kil.).

Lawyers, breath-sellers and pettifoggers [Mont. gens maniant les procès] (Florio's *Montaigne*, i. 22).

pettish. Now associated with *pet*[1, 2], but it is earlier than these words and is prob. aphet. for *impetuous*, with suffix-change as in *squeamish* (q.v.). In its earliest occurrences it is glossed *impetuosus* (Huloet, 1552), *effraenis, iracundus* (Levins, 1570). Current sense is evidently due to *pet*[2], partly perh. to *petulant*.

pettitoes [*dial.*]. Now pig's trotters, but orig. "giblets" of a pig or other animal. Mod. sense, due to association with *toe*, is as early as Florio (v.i.). OF. *petite oe* (*oie*), lit. little goose, applied to goose-giblets, gave E. (*pygges*) *petytoe* (*Rutland MSS*. 1539). But, as F. *petite oie* means accessories of any kind, e.g. of costume, or even the preliminaries of a battle, and these senses are recorded about as early as that of giblets, it seems possible that OF. *petite oe* may be folk-etym. for OIt. *petito*, little, borrowed from F. *petit*.

Puis apres luy firent servir sept cens cinquante platz de petites oues
        (*Chroniques admirables du puissant roi Gargantua*, ? c. 1530).

peduccii: all manner of feete, or petitoes drest to be eaten, as calves, sheepes, neates, or hogs feete, or pigs petitoes (Flor.).

petto, in. It., in the breast, L. *pectus*.

petty. ME. *pety*, for *petit*, the latter also being fully naturalized and current up to 17 cent. F. *petit* is prob. of Celt. origin and cogn. with *piece*. *Petty* was orig. used without disparaging sense, as still in *petty officer*, *petty cash*. Esp. common in leg. lang., e.g. *petty jury* (*larceny, sessions*, etc.).

petulant. F. *pétulant*, L. *petulans, petulant-*, wanton, malapert, etc., as though from L. **petulare*, dim. of *petere*, to seek. Current sense is due to association with *pettish*.

petunia. Coined (1789) by Jussieu from archaic F. *pétun*, tobacco, Port. *petum*, Guarani (Brazil) *petỹ*.

petuntse. Porcelain earth. Chin. *pai-tun-tz'*, white stone, with formative suffix. Cf. *kaolin*.

pew. ME. *puwe*, OF. *puie*, balcony, balustrade, from *podia*, pl. of *podium*, elevated balcony, imperial seat in theatre, G. πόδιον, base, pedestal, dim. of πούς, ποδ-, foot. From *podium* comes archaic F. *puy*, with wide range of meanings in OF. and found in sense of hill in many geog. names, e.g. *Puy-de-Dôme* (Auvergne). Orig. sense of *pew* as raised place of dignity survives, at any rate up to time of writing, in the *squire's pew*.

Nor was there [in the theatre] any pretty woman that I did see, but my wife, who sat in my lady Fox's pew with her (Pepys, Feb. 15, 1669).

pewit, peewit. Imit. of cry; cf. Du. *kievit*, Ger. *kiebitz*, E. dial. *peeweep*.

pewter. ME. *peutre, pewtre*, etc., OF. *peutre* (12 cent.), for earlier **peltre*; cf. It. *peltro*, Sp. *peltre*. There are also later OF. forms in *esp-*, with which cf. synon. E. *spelter*. Origin unknown, although much discussed. Cf. obscure origin of other alloy metals (*brass, latten*).

pfennig. Ger., *penny* (q.v.).

ph-. L. transliteration of G. φ, and found prop. only in words of G. origin. This *ph-* was replaced in VL. by *f-*, so that in OF. we find *filosofe, fisicien*, etc., which passed into ME.; but these have nearly all been restored. Occ. there are doublets, e.g. *fancy, phantasy, frantic, phrenetic*. In some words init. *ph-* is a barbarism, e.g. *philibeg* for *filibeg*, as also in surnames such as *Phayre*, *Phillimore*, etc.

phaeton. Vehicle, from c. 1740. G. φαέθων, lit. shining, used as name of son of Helios who tried unsuccessfully to drive his father's chariot.

-phagous. L., G. -φαγος, from φαγεῖν, to eat. Also *-phagy*, G. -φαγία.

phalange [*anat.*]. Finger-bone. Back-formation from *phalanges*, pl. of *phalanx* (q.v.).

phalanger. Austral. marsupial. From G. φαλάγγιον, spider's web, in allusion to webbed toes.

phalanx. L., G. φάλαγξ, esp. used of the Macedonian formation.

phallic. G. φαλλικός, from φαλλός, penis, worshipped in Dionysiac festivals as symbol of productiveness.

Phanariot. ModG. Φαναριώτης, inhabitant of *Phanar*, district of Constantinople, Turk. *fanar*, G. φανάριον, light-house, dim. of φανός, lamp.

phanerogamous [*bot.*]. Opposite of *crypto-gamous*. From G. φανερός, visible, from φαίνειν, to show.

phantasm. ME. & OF. *fantasme*, L., G. φάντασμα, from φαντάζειν, to display, from φαίνειν, to show; cf. *phantom*. Hence *phantasmagoria*, coined (1802) by exhibitor of optical illusions in London, as a "mouth-filling and startling term" (*NED.*). According to *Dict. Gén.* F. *fantasmagorie* is recorded for 1801, so that the word was prob. borrowed.

phantom. ME. & OF. *fantosme* (*fantôme*), as *phantasm* (q.v.); cf. It. Sp. *fantasma*. Change of vowel in F. word is unexplained.

Pharaoh. L., G. Φαραώ, Heb. *par'ōh*, from Egypt. *pr-'o*, great house, generic name of line of Egypt. kings. Cf. *faro*.

Pharisee. OF. *pharisé* (replaced by *pharisien*), L., G. Φαρισαῖος, Aram. *p'rishaiyā*, pl. of *p'rîsh*, Heb. *pārûsh*, separated. Rendered *sundor-hālig* in AS. *Gospel Version*.

pharmaceutic. L., G. φαρμακευτικός, from φάρμακον, poison, drug. Older is *pharmacy*, ME. *fermacie*, OF. *farmacie*, Late L., G. φαρμακεία. *Pharmacopoeia* is from -ποιος, making (cf. *poet*).

pharos. L., G. Φάρος, island off Alexandria with light-house built by Ptolemy Phila-delphus. One of the seven wonders of the world.

pharynx. G. φάρυγξ; cf. φάραγξ, chasm.

phase. F., or back-formation from *phases*, pl. of ModL. *phasis*, earlier used for *phase*,

G. φάσις, from φαίνειν, to show. Orig. (17 cent.) of the moon.

phasianine. Of the pheasant (q.v.).

pheasant. ME. *fesan*, *fesand*, etc., F. *faisan*, L., G. φασιανός, of Φᾶσις, river of Colchis, whence the bird was first brought. In most Europ. langs. For *-t* cf. *peasant*, *tyrant*.

phenol [*chem.*]. From G. φαινο-, shining, from φαίνειν, to show. Introduced (1841) as F. formative prefix by Laurent.

phenology. Science of recurring phenomena. Ult. a Ger. coinage.

phenomenon. Late L., G. φαινόμενον, neut. of pres. part. pass. of φαίνειν, to show. Sense of extraordinary occurrence, portent, from 18 cent.

phew. Natural interj. of disgust; cf. Ger. *pfui*.

phial. ME. *fiole*, F., Late L. *phiola*, for *phiala*, G. φιάλη, broad, flat vessel. Cf. *vial*.

Silveren fiols [*var.* viols] twelve
(Wyc. Numb. vii. 84).

Phidian. Of *Phidias*, G. Φειδίας, most famous of G. sculptors (†432 B.C.).

phil-. See *philo-*.

-phil, -phile. Adopted in MedL. from G. φίλος, loving, which is used only in proper names, e.g. *Theophilus*, Θεόφιλος, dear to God. Mod. coinages, e.g. *Hunophil*, with linking -o-, are numerous. Opposite is *-phobe*.

The ententophil Balkan states
(*Daily Chron.* Sep. 3, 1917).

Trigo would have nothing to do with the "phils" and the "phobes" of either side
(*Times Lit. Suppl.* Mar. 20, 1919).

philadelphian [*hist.*]. Sect. From G. φιλαδελφία, brotherly love, from ἀδελφός, brother. Hence name of city in US.

philadelphians: a new sect of enthusiasts, pretenders to brotherly love (*Dict. Cant. Crew*).

philander. G. φίλανδρος, lover of men, from G. ἀνήρ, ἀνδρ-, man; cf. *philanthrope*. Later sense as stock name for lover, whence verb to *philander*, perh. due to wrong interpretation, loving man, or from use of name *Philander* in early romances. Cf. *abigail*.

philanthropy. F. *philanthropie*, Late L., G. φιλανθρωπία, from ἄνθρωπος, man.

philately. F. *philatélie*, coined (1864) by stamp-collector Herpin from G. ἀτελής, free of charge, suggested by F. *franco*, *franc de port*; cf. archaic E. to *frank* a letter, F. *affranchir*, Ger. *freimark*, stamp.

-phile. See *-phil*.

philibeg. See *filibeg*.

philippic. L., G. φιλιππικός, orig. name of orations in which Demosthenes, like an Athenian Lord Roberts, urged his country-men to aim for their liberty against *Philip of Macedon*, father of Alexander the Great. The name means lover of horses (see *hippo-potamus*). To *appeal from Philip drunk to Philip sober* is trad. ascribed to a poor widow against whom the king had given judgment when in his normal condition.

philippina, philopoena. Ger. custom of pre-sent-giving connected with double kernel in nut. Ger. *vielliebchen*, dim. from *viel lieb*, very dear, became by folk-etym. *Philippchen*, little Philip, whence F. *Phi-lippine*, etc.

Philistine. F. *philistin*, Late L., G. pl. Φιλιστῖνοι, Heb. *p'lishtīm*, pl. name of tribe, cogn. with *Palestine*. Current sense of uncultured person, chiefly due to Matthew Arnold, is adapted from Ger. *Philister*, used (orig. at Jena, 17 cent.) in student slang for townee, outsider, and trad. due to the text *Philister über dir*, the Philistines are upon thee (*Judges*, xvi.), chosen by univ. preacher of Jena after a fatal "town and gown" in 1689. So explained as early as 1716.

Phillis. Neat-handed maid (*Allegro*, 87). Earlier stock name for rustic sweetheart, often coupled (by mistaken derivation) with *Philander*. L. *Phyllis*, rustic maid in Virg. and Hor., G. Φυλλίς, from φύλλον, leaf.

philo-, phil-. G. φιλο-, φιλ-, from φίλος, dear, φιλεῖν, to love. Often used to form nonce-words, e.g. the *philo-Hun pacifists*. Oppo-site is *miso-, mis-*, e.g. *misogynist, misan-thropy*.

philology. F. *philologie*, L., G. φιλολογία, love of words, literature, etc.

In conclusion he [Bishop Ussher] recommended to me yᵉ study of philology above all human studies (Evelyn).

philomath. Lover of learning. See *mathe-matics*.

Philomel. F. *philomèle*, L., G. φιλομήλα, under-stood as lover of song, μέλος, but perh. lover of apples, μῆλα. Poet. name for nightingale, whence myth of Philomela and Procne. In ME. usu. *philomene*.

philopoena. See *philippina*.

philoprogenitiveness. Coined (1815) by the phrenologist Spurzheim for the bump in-dicating love of offspring, progeny.

philosopher. AF. *filosofre*, OF. *filosofe* (*philo-sophe*), with *-r-* inserted (as in *barrister*), L., G. φιλόσοφος, lover of wisdom (see *sophist*). Used in Middle Ages of adept in occult science, whence *philosophers' stone* (see quot. s.v. *elixir*), MedL. *lapis philo-sophorum*; cf. F. *pierre philosophale*. Some mod. senses of *philosophy, philosophical* (to *take one's troubles philosophically*) seem to refer esp. to the stoic philosophers.

Thou wert my guide, philosopher and friend
(*Essay on Man*, iv. 390).

philtre. F., L., G. φίλτρον, love-potion, from φιλεῖν, to love.

phit [*neol.*]. Imit. of sound of mod. bullet.

phiz. For *physiognomy*. One of the clipped words of late 17 cent.; cf. *mob*¹, *cit*, etc.

phlebotomy. Blood letting. ME. & OF. *fle-botomie*, L., G. φλεβοτομία, from φλέψ, φλεβ-, vein, τέμνειν, to cut. See *fleam*.

phlegm. ME. & OF. *flemme* (*flegme*), etc., Late L., G. φλέγμα, inflammation, clammy humour, from φλέγειν, to burn; cf. It. *flemma*, Sp. *flema*. One of the medieval four "humours," producing apathy. Hence *phlegmatic*. Sense-development is curious as the word is cogn. with *flame*.

phlogistic. Combustible, fiery. From G. φλογιστός, inflammable (v.s.).

phlox. L., G. φλόξ, lit. flame (v.s.); cf. Ger. *flammenblume*.

-phobe, -phobia. G. -φοβος, -φοβια, from φόβος, fear. Earliest is *hydrophobia* (q.v.). In mod. nonce-words *-phobe* is opposite of *-phil*.

He seems to have a "phobia" of sentimentality, like a small boy who would rather die than kiss his sister in public (*Times Lit. Sup.* June 12, 1919).

phocine. Of the seal, L., G. φώκη; cf. F. *phoque*.

Phoenician. ME. *Fenicien*, etc., OF., from L. *Phoenicia* (sc. *terra*), from G. Φοινίκη, from Φοῖνιξ, Φοίνικ-, a Phoenician, ident. with *phoenix*, but reason for name un-certain. The Phoenicians were trad. the inventors of letters. The lang. is Semit. and akin to Hebrew.

phoenix. AS. & ME. *fenix*, L., G. φοῖνιξ, purple-red (v.s.). Name and myth are found in most Europ. langs.

pholas. Boring mollusc. G. φωλάς, lurking in a hole, φωλεός.

-phone. First in *telephone* (q.v.), from G. φωνή, voice. Hence more recent *micro-phone, radiophone*, etc.

phonetic. G. φωνητικός, from φωνή, sound. Orig. used (1797) by Zoega of ancient inscriptions representing sounds instead of pictures. Since middle of 19 cent. esp. in ref. to spelling and to the scient. study of sound-change in lang. Cf. *phonology* in same sense.

The science of phonology is the entrance to the temple of language, but we must not forget that it is but the outer vestibule, not the inner shrine itself (Whitney).

phonograph. Orig. character representing a sound (*phonography*, phonetic spelling, is recorded for 1701); from 1837 associated with Pitman's short-hand, from 1877 with Edison's talking-machine, but now giving way to *gramophone* (q.v.).

phonopore. Apparatus for transmitting telephonic messages on telegraph wires. From G. πόρος, passage.

-phore, -phorous. From G. -φορος, from φέρειν, to bear, chiefly in scient. terms; cf. *-fer, -ferous*. See *semaphore*.

phosphorus. L., G. φωσφόρος, light-bearing, from φῶς, light (v.s.). Orig. the morning star (cf. *lucifer*), later applied to any luminous substance, and, since its discovery in 1669, to a chem. element.

photograph. From G. φῶς, φωτ-, light, γράφειν, to write, etc. Introduced (1839) by Sir John Herschel, perh. as compromise between rival candidates *photogene*, *heliograph*, and at once adopted into F. *Photogravure*, F., is a hybrid, from *gravure*, engraving.

phrase. F., L., G. φράσις, from φράζειν, to point out, tell. Now often used of stereotyped or meaningless expressions such as *freedom of the seas, democratic control, self-determination of peoples*, etc.

I would warn you in all sincerity not to mistake phrases for facts (D. Lloyd George, Mar. 13, 1918).

phratry. G. φρατρία, clan, division of tribe, from φρατήρ, brother.

phrenetic. Learned form of *frantic* (q.v.).

phrenology. Lit. mental science. From G. φρήν, φρεν-, mind; cf. F. *phrénologie*. Coined (c. 1815) by Gall and Spurzheim.

Phrygian. Of *Phrygia*, in Asia Minor, the national cap of which has been identified in mod. times with the cap of liberty.

phthisis. L., G. φθίσις, from φθίνειν, to waste away. From 16 cent.

phycology. Science of sea-weed, L. *fucus*, G. φῦκος.

phylactery. ME. *filaterie* (Wyc.), L., G. φυ-

λακτήριον, guard, amulet, from φυλάσσειν, to guard; cf. OF. *filatiere* (*phylactère*). Orig. case containing four *OT.* texts, viz. *Deut.* vi. 4–9, xi. 13–21, *Ex.* xiii. 1–10, 11–16.

Ye shall bind them for a sign upon your hand, and they shall be for frontlets between your eyes
(*Deut.* xi. 18 *RV.*).

phylarch. G. φύλαρχος, head of a tribe, φυλή.

Phyllis. See *Phillis*.

phylloxera. Vine-pest. Coined (1834), from G. φύλλον, leaf, ξηρός, dry.

phylogeny. History of race. Ger. *phylogenie* (Haeckel, 1866), from φυλή, tribe.

physeter. Sperm-whale. L., G. φυσητήρ, from φυσᾶν, to blow.

physic. ME. *fisike*, OF. *fisique*, L., G. φυσική (ἐπιστήμη), knowledge of nature, φύσις, from φύειν, to produce, cogn. with L. *fui* and ult. with E. *be*. With *physical*, contrasted with *moral*, cf. F. *physique*, bodily constitution, contrasted with *moral* (of troops, etc.). Sense of healing (early ME.) is evolved from that of familiarity with bodily processes, etc.

physiognomy. ME. *fisnamie*, etc., from OF. (*physionomie*), L., G. φυσιογνωμονία, from φύσις, nature, γνώμων, γνώμον-, judge, interpreter. See *gnomon*. Associated, in a statute of Henry VIII against fortune-telling, with *physyke* and *palmestrye*.

I knowe wele by thy fisnamy, thy kynd it were to stele (*NED.* c. 1400).

physiography. Coined (19 cent.) on *physiology*.

physiology. F. *physiologie*, L., G. φυσιολογία, study of nature (v.s.).

physique. See *physic*.

phytology. Botany. From G. φυτόν, plant.

pi¹ [*math.*]. Ratio of circumference to diameter. Name of G. letter π, p, so used by Euler (1748).

pi² [*slang*]. Schoolboy abbrev. of *pious*. Hence *pi-squash*, prayer-meeting, etc.

piacular. Expiatory. L. *piacularis*, from *piaculum*, from *piare*, to appease. See *expiate*.

piaffe [*equit.*]. From F. *piaffer*, to strut, etc., perh. imit. of stamping.

pia mater [*anat.*]. Membrane of brain. MedL., rendering synon. Arab. *umm raqīqah*, tender mother. Cf. *dura mater*.

piano. It., short for *pianoforte* or *fortepiano*. It. *piano*, soft, *forte*, loud, L. *planus*, smooth, *fortis*, strong. Invented (c. 1710) by Cristofori of Padua. *Pianola* (c. 1900) is app. intended for a dim.

piastre. F., It. *piastra*, short for *piastra d' argento*, leaf of silver, orig. applied in It. to Sp. silver *peso*; cf. It. *piastro*, plaster (q.v.), and see *plate*.

piazza. It., place (q.v.), open square, market place; cf. Sp. *plaza*. In E. also erron. applied to the colonnade of Covent Garden, designed by Inigo Jones, instead of to the market-place itself.

The piazza [market square of Leghorn] is very fayre and comodious, and with the church gave the first hint to the building both of the church and piazza in Covent Garden (Evelyn).

piazza: a market-place or chief street; such is that in Covent-Garden....The close walks in Covent-Garden are not so properly the Piazza, as the ground which is inclosed within the rails (Blount)

pibroch. Series of variations on bagpipe. Gael. *piobaireachd*, from *piobair*, piper, from *piob*, E. *pipe* (q.v.). Popularized in E. by Scott.

pica [*typ*.]. L., magpie. Earlier used, with *pie*[1], in sense of set of rules for fixing Church feasts in accordance with displacement of Easter. Prob. "black and white" is the orig. idea. For application to type cf. *brevier* (q.v.), *primer*.

picador. Sp., pricker, from *picar*, to prick. See *pick*[2], *pike*.

picaninny. See *piccaninny*.

picaresque. F., esp. in *roman picaresque*, rogue novel (e.g. *Gil Blas*), Sp. *picaresco*, prob. from *picar*, to prick (cf. to *pick and steal*).

picaroon. Rogue, esp. pirate. Sp. *picarón*, augment. of *picaro*, rogue (v.s.). First in Capt. John Smith.

piccadill [*obs*.]. Common in 17 cent. Orig. cut edge of ruff, etc.; later, fashionable collar with perforated border. OF. *piccadille*, app. from Sp. *picado*, pricked, cut (v.s.). Hence *Piccadilly*, though exact connection is uncertain.

pickadill: the round hem or the several divisions set together about the skirt of a garment, or other thing; also a kinde of stiff collar, made in fashion of a band. Hence perchance that famous ordinary near St James called *Pickadilly*; because it was then the outmost or skirt house of the suburbs that way. Others say it took its name from this, that one Higgins a tailor, who built it, got most of his estate by pickadilles, which in the last age were much worn in England (Blount).

piccalilli. In 18 cent. also *piccalillo*, *pacolilla*. Prob. arbitrary formation on *pickle*.

piccaninny, picaninny. From 17 cent. Negro dim. of Sp. *pequeño* or Port. *pequeno*, small, of unknown origin; cf. Port. *pequenino*,

tiny. It is uncertain whether the word arose in Sp. or Port. colonies, or in the E. or W. Ind., but it has spread remarkably (WAfr., Cape, Austral., etc.).

piccolo. It., small. Orig. in *piccolo flute*, It. *piccolo flauto*. It. *piccolo* belongs to same group as Sp. *pequeño* (v.s.).

pice. EInd. copper coin, quarter anna. Hind. *paisā*, ? from Sanskrit *pad*, *padī*, quarter.

pick[1]. Noun. Ident. with earlier *pike* (q.v.). Used also in early Sc. for *pike*, weapon.

pick[2]. Verb. In ME. also *pike*. AS. *pȳcan*; cf. ON. *pikka*, to peck, prick, Du. *pikken*, to pick, peck, Ger. *picken* (from LG.), to peck, puncture; also F. *piquer*, It. *piccare*, Sp. *picar*. The relation of all these words is obscure, but they are prob. cogn. with *beak* and with L. *picus*, wood-pecker, and the senses are all developed from the pecking action of a bird. See also *peck*[2], *pitch*[2]. With to *pick a quarrel with* (earlier *on*), cf. to *fasten a quarrel on*. *Pick-me-up* is US. With *pickpocket* (16 cent.) cf. *pick-purse* (Chauc.).

The seyde parsone...hathe pekyd a qwarell on to Mastyr Recheforthe (*Paston Let.* i. 87).

pick-a-back. In 16 cent. also *a pick pack*, redupl. on *pack*, as carried on shoulders, early altered by association with *back*. The dial. and baby vars. are numerous. Cf. Norw. Dan. *med pik og pak*, with bag and baggage.

St Christopher carried Christ a pick-pack
(*NED.* 1677).

pickage [*archaic*]. Due for breaking ground when setting up booth at fair. AF. *picage*, from F. *piquer*, to pick, pierce.

pickaxe. Altered by folk-etym. from ME. *pikois*, OF. *picois*, from *piquer* (v.s.). Cf. *curtle-axe*.

Pickoys with which thei myned down the walles
(*Paston Let.*).

pickerel. Dim. of *pike*; cf. *cockerel*.

"Bet is," quod he, "a pyk than a pykerel"
(Chauc. E. 1419).

picket. Orig. pointed stake, e.g. for picketing horses. For sense of outlying detachment cf. *post*[1, 3]. F. *piquet*, dim. of *pic*, pick, pike, peak. *Picketing*, intimidation by strikers, "peaceful persuasion," is recorded for 1867.

pickle. Orig. brine, Du. *pekel*, earlier *peeckel*; cf. Ger. *pökel*, brine, from LG. or Du. Prob. from Du. *pikken*, to prick, pierce; cf. culinary sense of *piquant*. An unsupported tradition derives the word from a Dutchman, *Beukels*, who discovered (1416) means of preserving herrings. With to *be in a pickle* (Du. *in de pekel zitten*) cf. to *be in hot water* (*in the soup*, etc.). A *young pickle* is "hot stuff," but some would connect this rather with *Puck*. *In pickle* has gen. sense of in preparation, reserve, but *rod in pickle* refers to actual saturation with a view to efficiency.

They answered, that they could not possiblie bee in worse pickle than they were at that present
(Hakl. v. 149, c. 1575).

Most impudent and pickel'd youths (*NED.* 1691).

pickwick [*archaic*]. Trade-name for cheap cigar (c. 1850).

Pickwickian sense. See *Pickwick Papers*, ch. i. Dickens took the name from that of the proprietor of a Bath coach (see ch. xxxv.). It is derived from the village of *Pickwick* (Wilts).

picnic. First in Chesterfield's *Letters* (1748). F. *pique-nique* (17 cent.), redupl. on *piquer*, to pick. Early E. instances are often *pique-nique*, and the word is commonly italicized as foreign. Now widely adopted by Europ. langs.

picot. Small loop, purl. F., from *picoter*, to prick, etc. (v.i.).

picotee. Carnation with variegated edge. F. *picoté*, p.p. of *picoter*, to prick, frequent. of *piquer* (see *pick*²). Cf. *pink*³, ⁴.

picric [*chem.*]. From G. πικρός, bitter.

Pict [*hist.*]. Late L. pl. *Picti*, taken as meaning *picti*, painted, but prob. from Celt. name of tribe; cf. the Gaulish *Pictavi*, whence *Poitou*, *Poitiers*.

picture. L. *pictura*, from *pingere*, *pict-*, to paint; cf. It. *pittura*, F. *peinture* (VL. **pinctura*). With *picture hat* (19 cent.), from pictures of Gainsborough, Reynolds, cf. *Gainsborough hat*. *Picturesque* is altered from F. *pittoresque*, It. *pittoresco*. *Picture-house* (*-palace*) is 20 cent.

piddle. To trifle. Also *peddle*, *pittle*. From 16 cent. App. a dial. word with LG. cognates. In childish use perh. a perversion of *piss*.

pidgin, pigeon. Eastern jargon, esp. in China, made up chiefly of E. words; lingua franca of the East, also called *pigeon English*. Extended, in varying forms, to Africa and Australia. Chin. perversion of E. *business*, in which sense it is also used.

All boys belonginga one place you savvy big master

come now; he now fella master; he strong fella too much....No more um Kaiser. God save um King!
(*Offic. Procl. to inhabitants of Bismarck Archipelago*, Oct. 1914).

pie¹. Now usu. *magpie* (q.v.). F., L. *pica*, cogn. with *picus*, wood-pecker. The comestible *pie* (MedL. *pica*) is the same word, though the reason for the name may be connected with some forgotten piece of folk-lore. It has been suggested that it may have to do with the magpie's habit of making miscellaneous collections. Cf. relation of *haggis* to archaic F. *agace*, magpie, and double sense of obs. E. *chewet* (1 *Hen. IV*, v. 1), jackdaw, round pie, from F. *chouette*, now screech-owl, but formerly chough, jackdaw, a bird which is also a collector of oddments. The identity of the two words is also indicated by F. *trouver la pie au nid*, to discover the secret, and synon. 16 cent. *descouvrir le pasté*. *Printer's pie* (17 cent.), unsorted type, is called *pâté* in French, while *pâté* is also used of a job lot of curiosities which one buys in hopes of finding some good item in the collection, like Little Jack Horner, who had a *finger in the pie*. For archaic *pie*, ordinal, whence oath *by Cock* (*God*) *and pie*, see *pica*.

The nombre and hardnes of the rules called the pie (*Pref. to Book of Common Prayer*, 1548–49).

crostata: a kinde of daintie pye, chewet, or such paste meate (Flor.).

il a discouvert le pasté: he hath found out the mysterie (Cotg.).

pie² [*Anglo-Ind.*]. As *pice* (q.v.).

piebald. Ball'd, i.e. streaked (see *bald*), like a mag-*pie* (see *pie*¹). Prop. black and white only, but cf. extended sense of *pied*. Cf. F. *cheval pie*, in same sense.

piece. Orig. sense is a fixed amount or measure (cf. *of a piece with*), not a bit, though the senses are later confused, e.g. a *three-penny piece* (bit). F. *pièce*; cf. It. *pezza*, Sp. *pieza*, MedL. *pecia*, *petia*; usu. supposed to be of Celt. origin and cogn. with F. *petit*. Sense-development took place mostly in F., in which *pièce* can mean almost anything, and the word partly displaced in E. native *deal*¹. See also *patch*, *meal*². Quot. below for *piece-work* is much older than *NED.* record (1795).

No person of the craft of cappers shall put owt any peece-woork but to suche of the same craft
(*Coventry Leet Book*, 1549).

Thus am I bolde to unfolde a peece of my mynde
(*NED.* 1572).

pièce de résistance. F., chief dish, at which one can cut and come again.

pied. From *pie*[1]. Orig. black and white, later, motley (q.v.), variegated. Cf. F. *tigré*, striped, and see *piebald*.

> Proud-pied April dressed in all his trim
> (Shaks. *Sonn.* xcviii.).

piepowder(s), court of [*hist.*]. Court of summary jurisdiction held at fairs. AF. *pie-poudrous*, way-farer, itinerant merchant, lit. *dustyfoot*, which in ME. was used in same sense.

pier. Orig. (12 cent.) support of bridge; later, jetty, landing-stage, etc. Late AS. *per*, AF. *pere*, MedL. *pera*; cf. OF. (Picard & Walloon) *pire*, *piere*, breakwater. The region of OF. *pire* and its regular association with the Scheldt point to Teut. origin. Ger. *bār*, bear, OHG. *pero*, and Du. *beer*, bear, boar, are found in same sense, and the latter is used of the warlike device called in E. hist. a *cat* or *sow*. Hence the word may be an instance of the fig. use of an animal name. Orig. sense, whether in ref. to a bridge or breakwater, was prob. row of piles or stakes. For E. *p-* corresponding to LG. *b-* cf. *pig*. Also, in building, solid masonry between windows and other openings, whence *pier-glass*, occupying such a space.

> *beer*: a bear, a bore. *Een steene beer*: a brick-bank, a mole, peer (Sewel).

> *beer*: bear, boar, peer head (Wilcocke).

pierce. F. *percer*, OF. *percier*, VL. *peritiare*, from *perire*, *perit-*, to go through; cf. origin of F. *commencer*. See also *perish*, with which early forms of *pierce* often coincide. A *piercing shriek* is one that "goes through" you.

> I panche a man or a beest, I perysshe his guttes with a weapon (Palsg.).

> Emptie a caske and yet not perish [du Bart. percer] it (Sylv. i. 2).

Pierian. Of Πιερία, in N. Thessaly, reputed home of Muses.

> A little learning is a dangerous thing;
> Drink deep, or taste not the Pierian spring
> (Pope, *Essay on Crit.* 216).

pierrot. F. *Pierrot*, stock character of F. pantomime, dim. of *Pierre*, Peter. Cf. *Merry Andrew*.

piety. F. *piété*, L. *pietas*, from *pius*. Doublet of *pity*, with which it is often synon. in ME. Hence *pietist*, *pietism*, esp. of followers of Spener, 17 cent. Ger. mystic. *Pietà*, It.,

is a representation of the Virgin holding the dead body of Christ.

piezometer. For measuring pressure. Coined (1820) by Perkins from G. πιέζειν, to press.

piff. Imit.; cf. F. *pif-paf*, Ger. *piff-paff*, of sound of bullet. Hence prob. *piffle*, dial. word adopted by standard E. c. 1890.

pig. ME. *pigge*, orig. young pig, but now largely replacing *swine*; cf. LG. *bigge*, Du. *big*. Origin unknown. With *pig* of metal, orig. (16 cent.) of lead, cf. earlier *sow*, used of a larger mass. *Please the pigs* is explained in 18 cent. as corrupt. of *pyx* (q.v.), but, if not arbitrary euph. for *please God*, is more prob. connected with the *pixies*. *Pigtail* is used earliest of tobacco.

> When ye proffer the pigge, open the poke [bag]
> (*NED.* c. 1530).

pigeon. F., Late L. *pipio-n-*, young cheeping bird, from *pipire*, to pipe, cheep; cf. It. *piccione*, Sp. *pichón*. Has replaced earlier *culver* and native *dove*. Common from 16 cent. in sense of victim of sharper. *Pigeon-hole*, from likeness to apertures of dovecote, is 19 cent.

> The dowve is a symple byrde, and of her nature nourisshith well the pigeons of another douve
> (Caxton, *Mirror of World*).

pigeon English. See *pidgin*.

piggin [*dial.*]. Pail. ? From *peg*. See *noggin*.

pightle [*loc.*]. Small enclosure. Earliest (early 13 cent.) in MedL. *pictel*, *pigtel*, *pichel*, app. dim. formation cogn. with *piece*; cf. MedL. *pictatium*, piece, patch. Hence the common Yorks. name *Pickles*.

pigment. L. *pigmentum*, from root of *pingere*, to paint. Cf. *pimento*.

pigmy. See *pygmy*.

pignorate. From MedL. *pignorare*, for *pig-nerare*, from *pignus*, *pigner-* or *pignor-*, pledge.

pigsney [*archaic*]. Darling. ME. *pigges neye*, lit. pig's eye, the latter word with prosthetic *n-*, as in *newt*, *nuncle*, etc. Cf. obs. *pinkeny*, little-eye, darling (see *pink-eyed*).

pike. AS. *pīc*; cf. F. *pic* and see *pick*[2], *pitch*[2]. Sense of mountain summit in Lake Country represents a Norse form of the same word (cf. *fell*, *force*, *scree*, *tarn*, and other Norse words in same locality). *Pike*, fish, is short for *pike-fish*; cf. synon. F. *brochet*, from *broche*, spit, etc., in allusion to shape of jaw. *Pike*, weapon, is cogn. F. *pique*; hence *by push of pike* (16 cent.), with which cf. *by dint of sword*. *Pike* is also used by

Mr Weller senior for *turnpike* (q.v.). *Pike, pick, pitch* were formerly used indifferently and are still found in various connected senses in dial.

pikelet [*loc.*]. Short for obs. *bara-picklet*, Welsh *bar apyglyd*, lit. pitchy bread.

> *popelins*: soft cakes...like our Welch barrapyclids
> (Cotg.).

pikestaff. In ME. pointed stick, kind of alpenstock; cf. ON. *pīkstafr*. In 16 cent. shaft of *pike*, spear (v.s.). But in *plain as a pikestaff* it is substituted for *pack-staff*, pole for carrying a pack, distinguished by its plainness from the many medieval staffs of office, etc. Cf. *plain as a pack-saddle* (1553).

> The ant hath circumspection, ye have none;
> You packstaff plain, the ant crafty and close
> (Heywood, *Spider and Fly*, 32).

pilaster. F. *pilastre*, It. *pilastro*, MedL. *pilastrum*, from *pila*, pillar. See *pile²*.

pilau, pilaw, pilaff. Oriental dish. Turk., Pers. *pilāw*. *Pilaff* is through Russ.

pilchard. Earlier (16 cent.) *pilcher*. Origin unknown. Late appearance suggests that it may be a nickname, from dial. *pilch*, to steal.

> *pilcher, a fysshe*: sardine (Palsg.).

pile¹. Pointed stake, javelin (her.). AS. *pīl*, dart, L. *pilum*, javelin; cf. Du. *pijl*, Ger. *pfeil*, arrow, from L. Associated in later senses with *pile²*. Hence *built on piles, pile-driver*.

pile². Heap, etc. F. heap, pyramid, pier of bridge (see also *pile¹*), L. *pila*, pillar, pier, etc. In sense of building, *noble pile*, etc., partly due to obs. *pile*, fortress (v.i.), ident. with *peel²*. *Funeral pile* is prob. partly due to *pyre* (q.v.). *Pile* (of wealth) is US. and used by Franklin. To *pile on the agony* is also US.

> The taking of the tour of Aiton in Scotland with other piles there (*Nav. Accts.* 1485–88).

pile³. Of velvet, etc. L. *pilus*, hair, whence F. *poil*, in same sense.

pile⁴. Haemorrhoid. L. *pila*, ball.

pileate [*biol.*]. L. *pileatus*, from *pileus*, cap. Hence *Mount Pilatus* (Switz.). *Pileus* is also used of various capped fungi.

pilfer. OF. *pelfrer*, from *pelfre*, pelf (q.v.).

pilgarlic [*archaic*]. For *pilled* (peeled) *garlic*. Humorous for a bald-headed person, suggesting an onion.

pilgrim. ME. *pelegrim, pilegrim*, Prov. *pelegrin* or It. *pellegrino*; cf. F. *pèlerin*, Ger. *pilgrim* (usu. *pilger*). All from L. *peregrinus*, from *pereger*, one who is abroad

(see *peregrine*), with dissim. of *r-r*. Orig. consonants survive in Sp. *peregrino*. For final -*m* cf. *grogram, venom*, etc. The very early (c. 1200) adoption of an It. or Prov. word is explained by the pilgrimage route to Rome via Provence, or, if pilgrims crossed the Alps, they would encounter Rumansh *pelegorin*. The Puritans who founded (1620) the colony of Plymouth in Massachusetts called themselves *pilgrims*, but *Pilgrim Fathers* first occurs in a poem of 1799.

> First they fell upon their knees,
> And then on the Aborigines (Anon.).

> The Pilgrim Fathers who landed on Plymouth Rock, of whom York Powell said that it would have been better for the world if Plymouth Rock had landed on them (*Times Lit. Sup.* June 19, 1919).

> They [the Pilgrim Mothers] had not only to endure the privations suffered by the Pilgrim Fathers, but also to endure the Pilgrim Fathers as well
> (Rev. R. W. Thompson, 1920).

pill¹ [*archaic*]. To peel. AS. **pilian*, L. *pilare*, to strip of hair, *pilus*, and thus ident. with *peel¹* (q.v.). Still common in dial. ME. sense of plundering, as in archaic to *pill and poll*, influenced by cogn. F. *piller*, to pillage (q.v.).

> And Jacob took him rods of green poplar...and pilled white strakes in them (*Gen.* xxx. 37).

pill². Medicine. OF. *pile*, L. *pila*, ball, or perh. MedL. *pilla*, for dim. *pilula*, whence F. *pilule*, It. *pillola*; cf. Du. *pil*, Ger. *pille*. Mod. slang sense of ball reproduces orig. meaning; hence to *pill*, blackball (*Newcomes*, ch. xxx.), also to reject at examination, etc. *Pill-box*, small concrete fort, occurs repeatedly in offic. account of awards of V.C. Nov. 27, 1917.

pillage. First (14 cent.) as noun. F., from *piller*, to plunder, VL. **piliare*, for *pilare*, to pill¹; cf. It. *pigliare*, to take, snatch.

pillar. OF. *piler* (*pilier*), VL. *pilare*, from *pila*, pillar, pile²; cf. Sp. *pilar*. *From pillar to post* was orig. a figure from the tennis-court, usu. associated with *toss, bandy¹* (q.v.). The expression is also used of shuttlecock in Marston's *What you will* (iv. 2), the context suggesting that *pillar* and *post* were names for the two ends of the court, ? accidentally derived from some famous tennis-court. The orig. order, *post to pillar* (Lydgate), has been inverted to facilitate the rime with *tost*.

> Every minute tost,
> Like to a tennis-ball, from pillar to post
> (*Liberality and Prodigality*, ii. 4, 1602).

pillion [*archaic*]. First in early Sc. (c. 1500). Gael. *pillean*, in same sense, from *peall*, skin, hide, L. *pellis*. Spenser also uses it in *Present State of Ireland*. Cf. Ir. *pillín*.

pilliwinks [*hist.*]. Instrument of torture, of thumbscrew type. Usu. regarded as Sc., but found first as ME. *pyrwykes*, *pyrewinkes*, with very numerous later vars. in *pirli-*, *penny-*, etc. Origin unknown. Coincidence of earliest forms with those of *periwinkle*[1] suggests possible connection with L. *pervincire*, to bind thoroughly.

pillory. F. *pilori*, with MedL. forms showing association with *pillar*. Also Gasc. *espilori*, Prov. *espitlori*, which are app. much later than earliest F. & E. records. Origin unknown. Not legally abolished till 1837.

pillow. AS. *pyle*; cf. Du. *peluw*, Ger. (poet.) *pfühl* (OHG. *pfulwo*, also *pfuliwi*); a very early WGer. loan from L. *pulvinus*, pillow (cf. *pluck*). Archaic *pillow-bere*, pillow-case (Chauc. A. 694), preserves a ME. word cogn. with Ger. *bühre* (from LG.). With to *take counsel of one's pillow* (16 cent.) cf. to *sleep upon* (a matter).

pilose [*biol.*]. L. *pilosus*, from *pilus*, hair.

pilot. F. *pilote*, It. *pilota*, OIt. *pedota*, app. from G. πηδόν, oar, in pl. rudder; cf. OF. *pedot*. Replaced native *lodesman*, *lodeman*, AS. *lādmann* (see *lodestone*). Quot. below (rather earlier than *NED.*) shows the word as a neologism.

> Wages and vityale of 2 lodesmen alias pylotts
>   (*French War*, 1512–13).

pilule. See *pill*[2].

pimento. Sp. *pimiento* or Port. *pimento*, pepper, L. *pigmentum*, pigment, in MedL. spiced drink; cf. F. *piment*.

pimp. Of obscure origin. Malcolm's *London* quotes in this sense, from *Proteus Redivivus* (temp. Charles II), *pimpinio*, which may be a "latinization" of OF. *pimpreneau*, "a knave, rascall, varlet, scoundrell" (Cotg.), app. ident. with *pimperneau*, a small eel. See *pimpernel*.

pimpernel. Orig. (13 cent.) the great burnet. F. *pimprenelle*, with parallel forms in It. Sp. Ger., etc. The oldest appear to be MedL. *pipinella* (12 cent.), glossed as OF. *piprenelle*, and late AS. *pipeneale*. I suggest that *pipinella* is a dim. of L. *pipinna*, membrum virile (Martial, xi. 72). *Mentula* is also a plant-name in MedL.; cf. also *orchid* and the numerous early plant-names in *-pint*, *-pintle*, one of which, *cuckoo-pint*,

is still in use (T. Hardy). L. *pipinna* is a baby word (cf. F. *faire pipi*, to urinate).

pimping. Cf. Du. *pimpel*, weak little man, *pimpelmees*, tit-mouse, which Franck connects with the imit. *piepen*, to peep, twitter.

pimple. Perh. a thinned form of dial. *pumple*, which is, however, recorded much later. Cf. OF. *pompette*, "a pumple, or pimple on the nose, or chin" (Cotg.).

pin. AS. *pinn*, peg; cf. LG. *pinne*, Du. *pin*, late ON. *pinni*, L. *pinna*, in late sense of pinnacle (*Vulg. Luke*, iv. 9). Earlier used for *peg* in to *take down a pin* (mus.), whence also archaic *in merry pin*. As emblem of trifle from 14 cent., e.g. *not a pin, two pins* being a mod. elaboration. *Pinprick* was first used fig. in 1885 to render F. *politique de coups d'épingle*. So also *pin-money* (16 cent.) is for archaic F. *épingles d'une femme* in sense of toilet accessories, etc.; cf. synon. Du. *speldengeld*, from *speld*, pin. Some senses of verb to *pin* (e.g. a man's arms to his sides) perh. affected by *pinion*[1].

pinne: pinna, spiculum, cuspis, veruculum, aculeus (Kil.).

> To pin ones faith on another's sleeve: or take all
> upon trust, for gospel that he saies
>   (*Dict. Cant. Crew*).

> Des coups d'épée, messieurs, des coups d'épée!...
> Mais pas de coups d'épingle!
>   (*Tartarin de Tarascon*).

pinafore. Earlier (18 cent.) *pin-a-fore*, because *pinned afore* the dress. *Pinbefore* also occurs. See *afore*.

pinaster. L., wild pine, from *pinus*.

pince-nez. F., pinch-nose. Late 18 cent.

pincers. ME. *pinsours*, *pinceours*, from F. *pincer*, to pinch.

pinch. Norm. *pincher*, F. *pincer*, nasalized form of a word which appears in It. *pizzicare*, for earlier *picciare*, "to pinch, to snip" (Flor.); cf. Flem. *pinssen*, Ger. dial. *petzen*, *pfetzen*. Ult. hist. unknown.

at pinch: upon a push, or exigence
                            (*Dict. Cant. Crew*).

pinchbeck. Alloy metal invented by *Christopher Pinchbeck*, Fleet St. watchmaker (†1732). Now usu. fig. (cf. *brummagem*).

Pindari. Mounted marauder of Central India. Urdu *pindārī*, Mahratti *pendhārī*. Perh. from the region of *Pandhār*. But the native belief that the name comes from an intoxicating drink called *pinda* has a curious parallel in *assassin*.

pinder [*loc.*]. Keeper of pound. From AS. *gepyndan* (see *pound*[2], *pinfold*).

pine¹. Tree. AS. *pīn*, L. *pinus*. See also *pine-apple*.

pine². Verb. Orig. trans., to torture. AS. *pīnian*, from *pīn*, pain, L. *poena* (cf. *pain*, *penal*); cf. Du. *pijn*, Ger. *pein*, ON. *pīna*. Borrowed by Teut. from L. with Christianity and first applied to the pains of hell.

He was taken in suspeccion, and so turmentyd and pyned yᵗ he confessyd (*NED.* 1494).

pine-apple. In ME. meant fir-cone; cf. F. *pomme de pin*, in same sense. Applied to fruit of pine-cone shape, which was called by 16 cent. travellers *pina, pine*, after Sp. *piña*, fir cone. Cf. *pineal gland*, F. *pinéal*, also from shape.

Their pines are in shape like a pine-apple [i.e. fir-cone], and of this likenesse, I thinke, these had their names (Purch. xvi. 93).

pinfold, penfold [*dial.*]. Late AS. *pundfald*, associated with *pin* and *pen¹*. See *pound²*, *pinder*.

ping. Imit. of sound of rifle-bullet. Cf. *ping-pong* (c. 1900).

pinguid. Coined on *gravid, languid*, etc. from L. *pinguis*, fat.

pinion¹. Wing, orig. end of wing. OF. *pignon*, VL. **pinnio-n-*, from *pinna*, for *penna*, feather. Hence verb to *pinion*, orig. to fasten wings of bird.

pinion² [*mech.*]. Cog-wheel, esp. in *rack and pinion*. F. *pignon*, from OF. *pigne* (*peigne*), comb, L. *pecten*. Cf. Ger. *kammrad*, lit. comb-wheel, "the cog-wheel in a mill" (Ludw.).

pink¹ [*hist.*]. Ship. Du., earlier *pincke*, whence also Ger. *pinke*, F. *pinque*, It. *pinco*. Also obs. Du. *espinek* (Kil.); cf. ON. *espingr*, which some derive from *espi*, aspen wood. Others connect the name of the vessel with the Teut. name for *finch* (q.v.).

pink², penk. Young salmon, parr, orig. minnow. Cf. Ger. dial. *pinke*, in same senses.

pink³. Flower. From *pink⁴*, to perforate, etc., in allusion to the edges of the flower (cf. *picotee*). Hence name of colour. With *the pink* (of perfection, condition, etc.) cf. *the flower* (of chivalry, etc.).

Merc. Nay, I am the very pink of courtesy.
Rom. Pink for flower.
Merc. Right (*Rom. & Jul.* ii. 4).

pink⁴. To perforate. Cf. LG. *pincken*, nasalized form of word which appears in E.

pick² (q.v.), F. *piquer*, etc. In 17 cent. esp. of piercing with sword, in which sense it was no doubt a soldiers' word from the Low Countries (cf. *cashier², furlough*, etc.).

pink-eyed. Now dial., small eyed. Cf. archaic Du. *pinck-ooghen*, "connivere, nictare, palpebras oculorum alternatim movere; et oculis semiclausis intueri; oculos contrahere; et aliquo modo claudere" (Kil.), from *pincken*, "scintillare, micare" (ib.). The name of *Henry Pinkeneye* (*Hund. Rolls*, 1273) suggests that the word is old. Quot. below may refer rather to the form of ophthalmia called *pink-eye*, from *pink³*.

Blimy if they haven't sent some pink-eyed Jews too (Kipling, *His Private Honour*).

pinnace. Archaic F. *pinace, pinasse*, Sp. *pinaça* (13 cent.), supposed to be connected with *pinus*, pine. But earliest F., E. & AL. forms are in *esp-, sp-*. For similar double forms cf. *pink¹*. In the case of *pinnace* the *esp-, sp-* forms may be due to association with *espy, spy*, as the pinnace is usu. described as *navigium speculatorium, catascopium*; cf. archaic Ger. *speheschifflin*, obs. Du. *bespie-scheepken*, in same sense.

Tote la navie qe homme savoit ordeiner, des galeyes, spynagts, grosses barges, et touz les grauntz niefs d'Espaygne
        (*French Chron. of London*, 1340).

pinnacle. F. *pinacle*, Late L. *pinnaculum*, dim. of *pinna*, point, pinnacle, often confused with *penna*, feather; e.g., in *Vulg. Matt.* iv. 5, *pinnaculum* renders G. πτερύγιον, dim. of πτέρυξ, wing.

pinnate [*biol.*]. L. *pinnatus*, winged, feathered (v.s.).

pint. F. *pinte*; cf. It. Sp. Prov. *pinta*; also obs. Du. LG. HG. *pinte*. Origin doubtful. It may be ident. with *pinta*, mark (v.i.), and have been applied to a mark in a larger measure; cf. AS. *pǣgel*, wine-measure, with Scand. & LG. cognates, supposed to be connected with the *peg* used for marking out the measure in a vessel.

pintado. Guinea-fowl. Port., lit. painted, p.p. of *pintar*, VL. **pinctare*. See *paint*.

pintle [*techn.*]. AS. *pintel*, penis, dim. of **pint*; cf. Du. LG. Ger. *pint*, penis. Chiefly naut. and associated with *gudgeon²* (q.v.).

A pyntell & a gogeon for the rother
        (*Nav. Accts.* 1486).

piolet [*Alp.*]. Ice-axe. F., from Savoy dial., dim. of *piolo*, cogn. with F. *pioche*, mattock, and ult. with *pic*, pickaxe.

pioneer. F. *pionnier*, from *pion*, foot-soldier. See *pawn*[2], *peon*. Fig. sense is in Bacon.

Or fera de ses chevaliers
Une grant masse paoniers
           (*Roman de Thèbes*, 12 cent.).

piou-piou [*hist.*]. F. (slang), infantry soldier, "Tommy." Now replaced by *poilu*.

pious. F. *pieux*, VL. **piosus*, for *pius*, devout, whence OF. *piu*, *pie*, as still in *pie-mère*, pia mater. *Pious founder* is recorded for early 17 cent.

pip[1]. Disease of poultry. Obs. Du. *pippe* (*pip*); cf. Ger. *pips* (from LG.), for MHG. *pfips*; also F. *pépie*, "the pip" (Cotg.), It. *pipita*, "the pip that chickins have" (Flor.), Sp. *pepita*, all from VL. *pipita*, for *pituita*, mucus, "fleume, snevill" (Coop.).

pip[2]. On cards or dice. Earlier (c. 1600) *peep*, ident. with *peep*[2] (q.v.), ? via sense of eyes. In Teut. langs. the *pips* are called "eyes," in Rom. langs. "points," and the words for "point" in the Rom. langs. also mean "peep" of day.

pip[3]. Of fruit. Short for *pippin* (q.v.), with which (c. 1600) it was synon., being often referred to as cry of Irish costermonger. Current sense, from c. 1800 only, has been affected by *pip*[2]. Hence also to *pip*, blackball, defeat (cf. *pill*[2]), now also of bullet-wound, star indicating rank, etc., e.g. to *get one's second pip*.

pipal. See *peepul*.

pipe. AS. *pīpe*, VL. **pipa*, from *pipare*, to pipe, cheep, like a young bird, of imit. origin. Thus all the tubular senses app. start from a small reed pipe or whistle, e.g. the *piping time of peace* (*Rich. III*, i. 1), in contrast with the martial trumpet. Cf. F. *pipe*, It. Sp. *pipa*; also Du. *pijp*, Ger. *pfeife*. *Pipe* (of port) is the same word, via sense of cylinder. *Pipeclay* was orig. used for making tobacco-pipes. To *pipe one's eye* (naut.) is an obscure variation on to *pipe away* (*down*, *to quarters*, etc.), with allusion to the boatswain's whistle. *Piping-hot* refers to the hissing of viands in the frying pan. The *pipe-rolls*, great rolls of the exchequer, may have been named from cylindrical appearance.

He sente hire pyment, meeth, and spiced ale,
And wafres, pipyng hoot out of the gleede [hot coals] (Chauc. A. 3378).

After all this dance he has led the nation, he must at last come to pay the piper himself
           (*NED.* 1681).

pip emma. Mil. slang for P.M. See also *ack emma*.

pipi. Maori name of a shell-fish.

pipistrel. Small bat. It. *pipistrello*, "a night bat or reare-mouse" (Flor.), perverted var. of *vipistrello*, for *vespertillo*, VL. **vespertillus*, for *vespertilio*, bat, from *vesper*, evening.

pipit. Bird like lark. Imit. of cry; cf. *pewit*.

pipkin. Formerly in wider sense, including metal vessels. ? Dim. of *pipe*, cask, not orig. limited to wine. Cf. Sp. *pipote*, keg, from *pipa*, pipe, cask.

pippin. Orig. (c. 1300) *pip*[3], kernel; later applied to seedling apple. F. *pépin*, "a pippin, or kernell; the seed of fruit" (Cotg.); cf. Sp. *pepita*, grain. Origin unknown. Du. *pippeling* shows the same transition of sense, app. due to ellipt. use of some such phrase as *golden pippin apple* (cf. commerc. *real bloods*, i.e. blood-oranges).

A panyer full of pipyns and orynges [for Queen Margaret] (*Coventry Leet Book*, 1457).

piquant. Pres. part. of F. *piquer*, to sting, etc. See *pick*[2].

pique. F., from *piquer*, to prick, sting. To *pique oneself on*, F. *se piquer de*, is prob. from bird pecking and preening its plumage (cf. to *plume oneself on*).

piqué. Fabric. From F. *piquer*, to prick, stitch.

piquet. F. (15 cent.), perh. from *pique*, spade at cards.

piragua, periagua. Boat. Sp., Carib *piragua*, dug-out canoe. Cf. F. *pirogue*.

pirate. F., L. *pirata*, G. πειρατής, from πειρᾶν, to attempt, attack. In most Europ. langs.

Some dishonest booksellers, called land-pirates, who make it their practice to steal impressions of other men's copies (*NED.* 1668).

pirogue. See *piragua*.

pirouette. F., orig. spinning top, teetotum, etc. Also in OF. *pirouet*, Burgund. *pirouelle*, Guernsey *piroue*; cf. It. *piruolo*, "a top or gigge to play withal" (Flor.), dim. of *pirla*, in same sense. ModF. form perh. by association with *girouette*, weathercock.

piscary [*leg.*]. MedL. *piscaria*, fishing rights, from *piscis*, fish. Cf. *pisciculture*; *piscina*, orig. fish-pond, in eccl. sense with allusion to pools of Bethesda and Siloam.

pisé. Rammed earth. F., p.p. of *piser*, L. *pisare*, *pinsare*, to ram.

Pisgah view. From *Mount Pisgah*, Heb. *pisgāh*, cleft, from which Moses viewed Promised Land (*Deut.* iii. 27).

pish. Natural interj.; cf. *tush*, *pooh*, etc.

pismire [*archaic*]. Ant. ME. *mire*, ant, ? ult. cogn. with G. μύρμηξ, ant. First element alludes to urinous smell of anthill; cf. archaic Du. *pismiere*, and ModDu. *zeikmier*, from *zeiken*, to urinate.

piss. F. *pisser*, prob. imit.; cf. It. *pisciare*, Rum. *pisà*. Also adopted, orig. as euph., by most Teut. langs.

pistachio. It. *pistacchio*, L., G. πιστάκιον, from πιστάκη, pistachio tree, from OPers. (cf. Mod. Pers. *pistah*).

pistil [*bot.*]. L. *pistillum*, replacing earlier form *pestel*, *pestle* (q.v.). From resemblance to pestle of a mortar.

pistol. Obs. F. *pistole*; app. shortened from earlier *pistolet*, It. *pistoletto*, dim. from *pistolese*, "a great dagger, hanger, or wood-knife" (Flor.), ? from *Pistoia* (Tuscany), still noted for metal-work and gun-making. For transfer of sense from dagger to small fire-arm cf. *dag*[1] (q.v.). For names of arms taken from supposed place of manufacture cf. *bayonet*, *pavis*.

Pistolet a été nommé premièrement pour une petite dague ou poignard qu'on souloit [used] faire à Pistoye et furent à ceste raison nommez premièrement pistoyers, depuis pistoliers et enfin pistolets; quelque temps après, l'invention des petites arquebuses estant venue, on leur transporta le nom de ces petits poignards; depuis encore on a appelé les escus d'Espagne pistolets, pour ce qu'ils sont plus petits que les autres
(Tabourot des Accords, 1613).

pistole. Coin. Ident. with *pistol* (q.v.), sense of coin perh. originating in mil. slang. *Pistolet* was also used of a coin in F. & E., and Ger. *schnapphahn*, pistol, whence archaic E. *snaphaunce*, was the name of a coin at the period of the Thirty Years War.

pistolet: a pistolet; a dag, or little pistoll; also, the golden coyne tearmed a pistolet (Cotg.).

piston. F., It. *pistone*, var. of *pestone*, from *pestare*, to pound, etc., Late L. *pistare*, frequent. of *pinsere*, *pist-*, to beat, pound. Cf. *pestle*. First (c. 1700) in connection with pumps.

pit. AS. *pytt*. WGer. loan from L. *puteus*, well; cf. Du. *put*, Ger. *pfütze*. The theat. *pit* (from 17 cent.) was earlier *cockpit*, from the *pit* used for cock-fighting and other animal fights. Hence also to *pit* one man against another, like fighting cocks or dogs. *Pitfall*, orig. for animals, is from AS. *fealla*, trap; cf. synon. Ger. *falle*.

Can this cockpit hold
The vasty fields of France? (*Hen. V*, Prologue).

I did go to Shoe Lane to see a cocke-fighting at a new pit there (Pepys, Dec. 21, 1663).

pit-a-pat. Earlier *pit-pat*, redupl. on *pat*.

pitch[1]. Noun. AS. *pic*, L. *pix*, *pic-*. In most Rom. & Teut. langs., e.g. F. *poix*, Ger. *pech*, its preparation from tar being no doubt learnt from the Romans. Cf. *pay*[2].

pitch[2]. Verb. Not found in AS., but app. cogn. with *pick*[2], *pike* (q.v.), of which it represents various senses in ME. The past was *pight*. Orig. to thrust in, fix, e.g. to *pitch a tent*, by driving in the pegs, whence to *pitch the wickets* and noun *pitch* as in *cricket pitch*, *dealer's pitch*, etc. (see also *battle*). Sense of throwing developed from that of actually hitting the mark, *pitching into*; cf. *pitch-and-toss*, in which the first element expresses the idea of throwing at a mark, while the second refers to the game of chance which is the sequel. From sense of throwing comes that of height (mus. & arch.), perh. orig. from falconry (see *tower*). *Pitchfork*, for earlier *pickfork* (*Prompt. Parv.*), has become associated with the *pitching*, i.e. raising into a required position, of sheaves, etc.

I hold a grote I pycke as farre with an arowe as you (Palsg.).

pitchblende. From *pitch*[1]. See *blende*.

pitcher. OF. *pichier* (replaced by *pichet*); cf. It. *picchiere*, MedL. *picarium*, *bicarium*. App. ident. with *beaker* (q.v.).

pith. AS. *pitha*; cf. Du. *pit* and other LG. cognates. Orig. of plants only, but used in ME. of spinal marrow and in fig. sense of mettle, vigour. For current sense of *pithy* cf. synon. Ger. *markig*, lit. marrowy.

But Age, allas! that al wole envenyme,
Hath me biraft my beautee and my pith
(Chauc. D. 474).

pithecanthrope [*biol.*]. "Missing link." Coined (1868) by Haeckel from G. πίθηκος, ape, ἄνθρωπος, man.

pittance. F. *pitance*, pity, pittance; cf. OIt. *pietanza*, pity, pittance, Sp. *pitanza*, charity, pittance, MedL. *pietantia*, suggesting derivation from L. *pietas*, piety, earliest sense of *pittance* being a dole established by pious bequest, whence later meaning of scanty allowance, etc. Prob. the It. is the orig. For sense-development cf. *charity*.

pity. F. *pitié*, L. *pietas*, *pietat-*, piety, which in Late L. assumed sense of compassion, no doubt via that of good works. With *piteous*, ME. & OF. *pitous* (*piteux*), cf. *bounteous*, *courteous*, etc.

pivot. F., of obscure origin, but prob. of

similar sense-development to *pintle* (q.v.); cf. It. *pivolo*, peg, dibble, penis. *Pivotal* men were (1918) released from the army for industrial purposes.

The great translators are "pivotal" men in the history of literature (J. S. Phillimore, Dec. 1918).

pixy. Also dial. *pisky.* Sw. dial. *pyske*, small fairy, dwarf, has been suggested, but the fact that *pixy* is essentially a west country word, its orig. home being prob. Cornwall, suggests rather a Celt. origin.

pizzicato [*mus.*]. It., from *pizzicare*, to pinch (q.v.).

pizzle [*archaic*]. Penis of bull used as flogging instrument. LG. *pesel* or Flem. *pezel*, dim. of a word represented by Du. *pees*, sinew; cf. F. *nerf de bœuf*, lit. sinew of ox, in same sense.

nerf de cerf: a stags pizzle (Cotg.).

placable. OF., L. *placabilis*, from *placare*, to appease, causal of *placēre*, to please.

placard. F., from *plaquer*, "to clap, slat, sticke, or past on; to lay flat upon" (Cotg.), Du. *plakken*, in same sense, prob. imit. of sound of daubing brush. Orig. offic. document with large flat seal. Connection with G. πλάξ, πλακ-, flat surface, has also been suggested.

placate. From L. *placare*. See *placable*.

place. F., VL. **plattia*, for *platea*, broad way, G. πλατεῖα (sc. ὁδός), from πλατύς, flat, wide; cf. It. *piazza*, Sp. *plaza*. Orig. sense survives in *market-place*. Many of the senses are found in F., but in E. the word has completely replaced AS. *stōw* and taken over meanings represented in F. by *lieu* and *endroit*. *Another place*, the House of Lords, is used by Burke. To *take place* is for earlier to *have place*, translating F. *avoir lieu*. *Placeman*, *place-hunter* are early 18 cent.

placenta. [*biol.*]. L., flat cake, from G. πλάξ, πλακ-, flat plate.

placer. Gravel, etc. containing gold. Amer. Sp., from *plaza*, place (q.v.).

placet. Affirmative vote at universities. L., it pleases.

placid. F. *placide*, L. *placidus*, cogn. with *placēre*, to please.

plack [*hist.*]. Small coin (Sc.). Flem. *placke*, *plecke*, whence also OF. *placque*, MedL. *placca*, in similar sense. Orig. something flat.

placket [*archaic*]. Apron or petticoat. For *placard*, in obs. sense of breastplate.

placoid [*zool.*]. From G. πλάξ, πλακ-, flat plate.

plafond [*arch.*]. F., ceiling, orig. floor, for *plat fond*, flat bottom.

plagiary. Now usu. *plagiarist*. F. *plagiaire*, L. *plagiarius*, kidnapper, used also by Martial for literary thief, from *plaga*, net.

plagio-. From G. πλάγιος, oblique, from πλάγος, side.

plague. OF., L. *plaga*, stroke, wound (whence F. *plaie*, wound), cogn. with L. *plangere* and G. πληγνύναι, from πλήσσειν, to strike. For extended sense cf. that of *scourge*. For fig. uses, e.g. *plague take it*, cf. *pest*, *pox*, etc.

Betun with many plagis [var. woundis]
(Wyc. *Luke*, xii. 47).

plaice. OF. *plaiz*, VL. **platissus*, for *platessa*, from G. πλατύς, flat; cf. Du. *pladijs*, from L.

plaid. Orig. garment, covering. Gael. *plaide*; cf. Ir. *ploid*, blanket, Gael. *peallaid*, sheepskin; ult. from L. *pellis*, skin. Cf. *pillion*.

plain. F., L. *planus*, smooth, level, the oldest sense in E., whence noun *plain*, used in OF. & ME. not necessarily of low land, but of any treeless stretch, e.g. *Mapperley Plains* are the highest ground near Nottingham. With mod. use as euph. for *ugly* (v.i.) cf. US. sense of *homely*. *Plainsong* is from F. *plain chant*; cf. It. *canto piano*, MedL. *cantus planus*. For *plain-sailing* see *plane*[3].

Whereas I expected she should have been a great beauty, she is a very plain girl
(Pepys, July 28, 1661).

Plain living and high thinking are no more
(Wordsw. *Sonnets to Liberty*, xiii.).

plaint [*poet.*]. F. *plainte*, p.p. fem. of *se plaindre*, to complain, L. *plangere*, *planct-*, to beat (the breast), or OF. *plaint*, immediately from L. *planctus*; cf. It. *pianto*, Sp. *llanto*. Cf. *plaintive*.

plaintiff. Spec. use of OF. *plaintif*, from *se plaindre*, to complain (v.s.). Cf. *complainant*.

plaister. See *plaster*.

plait. Also *plat*. OF. *pleit*, L. *plicitum*, p.p. of *plicare*, to fold, ? or *plectum*, from *plectere*, to weave. Oldest sense survives in var. *pleat*. See also *plight*[2].

plan. F., substantival use of adj. *plan*, flat, smooth, L. *planus*, applied to a groundplot as opposed to an elevation. In lit. and fig. sense from c. 1700. *According to plan* renders Ger. *plangemäss*, much used (1917–18) of yielding ground.

planchette. F., dim. of *planche*, plank. Invented c. 1855.

plane¹. Tree. F. (now usu. *platane*), L., G. πλάτανος, from πλατύς, broad, in allusion to shape of leaves of Oriental plane.

plane². Tool. F., OF. *plaine*, Late L. *plana*, from *planare*, to smooth, from *planus*, level.

plane³ [*math.*]. Arbitrary 17 cent. var. of *plain*; cf. similar sense of F. *plan*. *Plain-sailing* or *plane-sailing* is navigation by a *plane chart*, representing the earth's surface as plane instead of spherical. Fig. misunderstood as simple, uncomplicated, which is etym. correct.

plane⁴ [*aeron.*]. Verb. F. *planer*, to hover, from *plan*, smooth, level. Also used as aphet. for *aeroplane*.

planesheer [*naut.*]. Ledge below gunwale of earlier man-of-war. Folk-etym. (*plane* and *sheer*) for obs. *plancher*, F., boarding, floor. See *plank*.

planet¹ [*astron. & astrol.*]. F. *planète*, Late L., G. πλανήτης, wanderer, from πλανᾶν, to lead astray. With *planet-struck* cf. *moon-struck*.

planet² [*eccl.*]. Early chasuble in form of traveller's cloak. Ident. with above, "wanderer's" mantle. Cf. *pluvial*.

plangent. From pres. part. of L. *plangere*, to beat.

planish [*techn.*]. To flatten (metal). OF. *planir, planiss-* (replaced by *aplanir*), from L. *planus*, smooth.

planisphere. Flat projection of (part of) sphere. F. *planisphère*. See *plane³*, *sphere*.

planisphere: an astrolabe (Cotg.).

plank. Norman-Picard *planque*, F. *planche*, Late L. *planca*, cogn. with G. πλάξ, πλακ-, flat plate, slab; cf. OIt. *pianca*, Sp. *plancha*. Pol. *plank* (of a platform) is US. With to *plank down* (money) cf. Ger. *auf einem brett bezahlen*, and see *oof*.

Protectionists are insisting on a definite protectionist plank (*Daily Chron.* Feb. 12, 1917).

plankton. Collect. name for floating organic life in sea. Ger., coined by Hensen from G. πλαγκτός, drifting, from πλάζεσθαι, to wander.

plant. AS. *plante*, young tree, sapling (as still in *ash-plant*), L. *planta*, sole of foot, plant (? secondary sense from treading in saplings). Later senses from F. *plante*, plant, or *plant*, act of planting, from verb *planter*. Cf. It. *pianta*, Sp. *planta*; also Du.

plant, Ger. *pflanze*, ON. *planta*, Ir. *cland*, Welsh *plant*, all from L. Sense of apparatus, etc. springs from verbal sense of equipping, establishing, e.g. *planting a new industry* (see *plantation*). Sense of swindle, trap, is developed from that of thieves' hidden ("planted") hoard (18 cent.). With to *plant*, abandon, cf. F. *planter là*.

plantain¹. E. plant. OF., L. *plantago, plantagin-*, from *planta*, sole of foot, in allusion to broad prostrate leaves.

plantain². Banana. Sp. *plátano, plántano*, L. *platanus*, plane¹. The E. form is assimilated to the spelling of *plantain¹*. The Sp. word is perh. also an assimilated form of some native WInd. name (? *palatana*, one of the Carib. vars. of *banana*), as the *plantain* has no resemblance to the *plane*.

Plantons, which the Portugals call baynonas
      (Anthony Knivet, in Purch. xvi. 268).

plantation. Hist. sense of colony, settlement, as in the *Plantation of Ulster* or the NAmer. *Plantations*, is due to the wide meaning assumed by the verb to *plant*. The Colonial Office was formerly the *Plantation Office*.

I wyll appoynte a place, and wyll plante [*Vulg.* plantabo] them, that they maye remayne there
      (Coverd. 2 Sam. vii. 10).

plantigrade [*biol.*]. Walking on the sole of the foot, L. *planta*, like the bear, as opposed to *digitigrade*, toe walking, like the cat. F., coined by Geoffroy and Cuvier (1795).

plaque. F., tablet, etc., from *plaquer* (see *placard*). Now used in E. of commemorative plates on historic houses in London.

plash¹ [*archaic*]. Pool. AS. *plæsc*, cogn. with Du. LG. *plas*, and perh. with *plash³*.

plash². Also archaic and poet. *pleach*. To interweave twigs, etc. of hedge. OF. *pleissier*, VL. **plectiare*, from *plectere*, to weave, cogn. with *plicare*, to fold, and G. πλέκειν, to weave. Cf. the common F. place-name *Plessis*, park, etc., as in *Plessis-lès-Tours* (see *Quentin Durward*, ch. i.). *Pleach* became obs. in 17 cent., its mod. use being an echo of Shaks. (*Much Ado*, iii. 1).

plash³. Splash. Cf. archaic Du. *plasschen*, Ger. *plätschern*, and see *plash¹*, with which it may be connected via the intermediate sense of dabbling. See also *splash*.

plasm. For *protoplasm*. L., G. πλάσμα, from πλάσσειν, to mould. Hence *plasmo-*, in scient. neologisms, and trade-name *plasmon* oats (for porridge).

plaster. AS. *plaster*, in med. sense, VL. *plastrum*, for *emplastrum*, G. ἔμπλαστρον, from ἐμπλάσσειν, to daub over, from πλάσσειν, to mould. Building sense is from corresponding OF. *plastre* (*plâtre*), F. having *emplâtre* in med. sense. The var. *plaister*, chiefly Sc. & north., may be due to analogy of *maister* (*master*), OF. *maistre*. *Plaster of Paris* was orig. made from the gypsum of Montmartre.

plastic. F. *plastique*, L., G. πλαστικός, from πλάσσειν, to mould. Hence *plasticine*, trade-name for substitute for modelling clay.

plastron. Front of fencing jacket or dress-shirt. F., adapted from It. *piastrone*, from *piastra*, breast-plate; cf. *plaster*, *piastre*.

plat¹. Piece of ground (2 *Kings*, ix. 26). Var. of *plot*, due to influence of archaic *plat*, flat surface. The latter is F., ult. G. πλατύς, broad. Now usu. as echo of Milton (*Penseroso*, 73), but once common for *plot*, plan.

This is the platt wich I finde best for this enterprise (Mary Q. of Scots to Babington, July 17, 1586).

plat². See *plait*.

platan-e. Oriental plane-tree. OF. *platan* (*platane*), L. *platanus*, plane¹ (q.v.).

platband [*arch. & hort.*]. F. *plate-bande*, lit. flat band, also flower-border.

plate. OF., orig. fem. of adj. *plat*, flat, Late L. *plattus, G. πλατύς, broad; cf. It. *piatta*, Sp. *plata*, which developed esp. sense of metal plate, hence precious metal, silver, as in *Rio de la Plata* (called *River of Plate* by 16 cent. E. sailors), *plate-ship*, etc. Earliest E. sense was also metallic, e.g. *breastplate*, *plate-armour*. Railway sense, as in *plate-layer*, is a survival of the flat wheel-track formerly used in mines and called a *plate*. To *plate* an inferior metal with a nobler dates from c. 1700. *Plate-glass* is a little later. As prize for horse-race, whence *plater*, from 17 cent.

And thei ordeyneden to hym thritti platis of selver (Wyc. *Matt.* xxvi. 15).

plateau. F., OF. *platel*, dim. from *plat*, flat (v.s.).

platen, platten [*typ.*]. Iron plate pressing paper against type. F. *platine*, from *plat*, flat (v.s.).

platform. F. *plate-forme*, lit. flat form. Earliest E. sense (16 cent.) is ground-plan, design, etc., in various applications. Current senses (railway and elevation for speakers) are 19 cent. In pol. sense of program, set of principles, it is US. (1840–50). See also *plot*.

Also that you doe seeke to observe with the instrument which I deliver you herewith the true platformes and distances (Hakl. iii. 123, 1588).

A sudden plotform comes into my mind
(*Grim the Collier*, ii. 1).

plateforme: a platforme, plot, modell, or draught of a building; also, the foundation thereof; also, a platforme or square bulwarke; also, a certaine thicke boord in the prow of a ship (Cotg.).

platina. Earlier (18 cent.) name for *platinum*. Sp., dim. of *plata*, silver (see *plate*). *Platinum*, first introduced into Ger., was adopted in E. by Davy.

platitude. F., coined from *plat*, flat, dull, after *latitude*, etc.

Platonic. L., G. Πλατωνικός, from *Plato* (†348 b.c.). Esp. in *Platonic love*, i.e. spiritual, without sensuality, a Renaissance idea. Cosmo de' Medici (15 cent.) founded an *Accademia Platonica*.

platoon. F. *peloton*, dim. of *pelote*, a ball, pellet, hence an agglomeration. Earlier also *plotoon*. In E. spec. a half-company, and described by the *NED.* (1908) as obs. in Brit. army. For revival cf. *grenade*, *bomb*.

platten. See *platen*.

platter [*archaic*]. AF. *plater*, from F. *plat*, dish, lit. flat. It may have been modelled on *trencher* or altered from OF. dim. *platel*, now *plateau*, tray.

Geve me here Jhon Baptistes heed in a platter [Wyc. dische] (Tynd. *Matt.* xiv. 8).

platypus. Ornithorhynchus (q.v.). G. πλατύπους, flat-footed.

plaudit. For earlier *plaudite*, imper. of *plaudere*, to clap the hands, appeal of Roman actors at end of play. Cf. *explode*.

Nunc, spectatores, Jovis summi causa clare plaudite (Plautus, *Amphitruo*).

plausible. L. *plausibilis*, deserving applause, acceptable, from *plaudere*, *plaus-*, to clap, applaud (v.s.).

play. AS. *plegian*, with gen. sense of brisk activity without spec. reference to either business or amusement. The main current senses are found already in AS. Cogn. with Ger. *pflegen*, to be busily solicitous for, to be accustomed. *Pleghūs* is found in AS., rendering L. *theatrum*, but some old compds. have been replaced by neologisms, e.g. the place-name *Plaistow*, had the sense of mod. *playground*, and the surname *Playfair* was usual for *playfellow* up to c. 1500.

We could, at that distance, see an engine [fire-engine] play—that is, the water go out
(Pepys, Apr. 29, 1667).

plea, plead. Both are *plaid, plait* in AF. & ME. The noun, archaic F. *plaid,* L. *placitum,* what pleases, hence agreement, decision, is in the *Strassburg oaths* (842). The verb, F. *plaider,* from the noun, is represented in MedL. by *placitare.*

pleach. See *plash*[2].

plead. See *plea.*

pleasance [*archaic*]. Delightful garden, etc., in ME. pleasure, delight, courtesy, etc. OF. *plaisance,* from *plaire, plais-,* to please (q.v.). Such place-names as F. *Plaisance,* Sp. *Plasencia,* It. *Piacenza* have the same origin.

pleasant. F. *plaisant,* pres. part. of *plaire,* to please; in ModF. funny, jocular; cf. *pleasantry,* F. *plaisanterie.*

Now Gilpin had a pleasant wit (Cowper).

please. F. *plaire, plais-,* VL. **placere,* for *placēre,* to please, cogn. with G. πλάξ, flatness. Perh. orig. of smoothing ruffled plumage. Correct OF. infin. was *plaisir,* now only noun, whence E. *pleasure,* for ME. *plesir* (cf. *leisure*). Orig. governed dat. as in *please God.* With *if you please,* for earlier *if it please you,* F. *s'il vous plaît,* cf. *if you like* (see *like*). So also imper. *please* for *may it please you.*

pleat. Var. of *plait* (q.v.), preserving orig. sense of that word. For vowel cf. *plead.* Obs. as literary word in 17–18 cents., but given by Walker (*Pronouncing Dict.* 1791) as a vicious pronunc. of *plait.*

plebeian. F. *plébéien,* from L. *plebeius,* belonging to the *plebs,* common people, cogn. with *plerique,* many, *plēre,* to fill. *Plebiscite,* in current sense, F. *plébiscite,* L. *plebiscitum,* for *plebis scitum,* decree of the people (*sciscere, scit-,* to decree, from *scire,* to know), came into gen. use at time of French Revolution.

plectrum. Quill, etc. for striking cords of lyre. L., G. πλῆκτρον, from πλήσσειν, to strike.

pledge. OF. *plege* (noun), *plegier* (verb), whence archaic ModF. *pleige-r.* Found in Merovingian L. as *plevium, plebium, plevire, plebire* (cf. obs. leg. *plevin,* warrant), app. from a WGer. verb, to incur risk, responsibility, represented by AS. *pleon,* Ger. *pflegen.* If this is right, and the approximate equivalence of E. *pledge* and Ger. *pflicht,* duty, makes it likely, *pledge* is ult. cogn. with *play.* There is a curious contradiction between the archaic to *pledge* (in a bumper) and mod. to *take the pledge* (1840–50).

pledget. Plug, tent[2], of lint, etc., for wound. From 16 cent. ? Dim. of ME. *plege* (not in *NED.*), app. roll (v.i.).

For a plege of lynen, vjs. viiid.
(*York Merch. Advent. Accts.* 1504).

Pleiad. Used, after F. *pléiade,* applied in 16 cent. to seven poets of whom Ronsard was chief, of a "galaxy" of writers. L., G. Πλειάς, Πλειάδες, group of stars, trad. connected with πλεῖν, to sail. In Wyc. (*Job,* xxxviii. 31).

pleio-, pleo-, plio-. From G. πλείων, more, compar. of πολύς, much, many. See *plio-.*

pleistocene [*geol.*]. Coined by Lyell (1839) from G. πλεῖστος, most (v.s.), καινός, new.

plenary. Usu. with *power, indulgence, inspiration.* Late L. *plenarius,* from *plenus,* full.

plenipotentiary. MedL. *plenipotentiarius,* from *plenus,* full, *potentia,* power. Cf. Ger. *vollmacht.*

plenish [*Sc.*]. OF. *plenir, pleniss-,* from L. *plenus,* full. Chiefly in *plenishing,* household gear, esp. as bride's outfit.

plenitude. F. *plénitude,* L. *plenitudo,* from *plenus,* full.

plenteous. Altered, on *beauteous, courteous,* etc., from ME. & OF. *plentivous,* from *plentif,* VL. **plenitivus,* from *plenus,* full. Cf. *bounteous.*

plenty. OF. *plenté,* L. *plenitas, -tat-,* from *plenus,* full. Adj. sense (*where money is plenty*), whence colloq. adv. sense (*plenty large enough*), represents rather OF. adj. *plentif* (cf. *jolly* and see *plenteous*). Though now equivalent to *abundance, plenty* means etym. *enough, fullness,* as still in dial.

Off the Lord is the erthe, and the plente of it
(Wyc. *Ps.* xxiii. 1).

pleo-. See *pleio-, plio-.*

pleonasm. L., G. πλεονασμός, from πλέον, compar. neut. of πολύς, much.

I've only fixed that up temp'r'y, pro tem., for the time being (Author's gardener, 1913).

plesiosaurus. Coined (1821) by Conybeare from G. πλησίος, near, approximating, σαῦρος, lizard.

plethora. MedL., G. πληθώρη, from πλήθειν, to become full. Orig. med. for excess of "humours"; cf. *plethoric.*

pleurisy. F. *pleurésie*, from Late L. *pleurisis*, for *pleuritis*, G. πλευρῖτις, from πλευρά, side, rib, whence also *pleuro-*.

pleximeter [*med.*]. From G. πλῆξις, blow, percussion, from πλήσσειν, to strike.

plexus [*anat.*]. Aggregate of fibres, etc. L., from *plectere*, *plex-*, to plait, weave. Esp. in *solar plexus*, favourite mark of pugilists.

pliable, pliant. F., from *plier*, to bend, ply² (q.v.).

plicate [*biol.*]. L. *plicatus*, from *plicare*, to fold.

pliers. From obs. *ply*, to bend. See *ply*¹.

plight¹ [*archaic*]. Pledge. AS. *pliht*, danger, risk, whence verb *plihtan*, to endanger, later to pledge, promise, esp. with *troth*, in ref. to marriage; cf. Du. *plicht*, obligation, Ger. *pflicht*, duty, and see *pledge*.

> And thereto I plight thee my troth
> (*Marriage Service*).

plight². Condition. ME. *plit*, *plyt*, AF. *plit*, var. of *plait*, *pleat*. From sense of fold was developed that of contexture, "complexion" (q.v.), condition, orig. in neutral sense, current sense and spelling (*sorry plight*, etc.) having been influenced by earlier *plight*¹. *En bon plit*, in good condition, is common in AF.

> *plyte, or state*: status (*Prompt. Parv.*).
> A demie bukram cassok, plaine without plites
> (Ascham).

Plimsoll line, mark [*naut.*]. From *S. Plimsoll*, M.P., to whose exertions the Merchant Shipping Act (1876) against over-loading was chiefly due.

plinth. L., G. πλίνθος, brick, squared stone.

pliocene [*geol.*]. Coined, ? by Lyell, from G. πλείων, more, καινός, new. Cf. *pleistocene*.

plod. In lit. and fig. sense from c. 1560. Of imit. origin, ? or cf. ME. & dial. *plod*, *plud*, puddle, Gael. Ir. *plod*, *pool*, puddle.

plop. Imit.; cf. *plump*, *flop*.

plot. AS. *plot* (of land), which, in view of its solitary occurrence and lack of Teut. cognates, is prob. F. *pelote*, clod, VL. *pilotta*, dim. of *pila*, ball (for extension to something larger cf. *moat*). This reappears in ME. (15 cent.) as *plotte*, prob. a new borrowing from F. The sense of scheme, which might naturally develop from that of flat surface (cf. *plan*), was helped by association with *plat*, the two words being used indifferently (cf. *platform*). The degeneration of sense, like that of *scheme*, *design*, was partly due to association with the related F. *complot*, which had already

acquired the sense of conspiracy, and this was definitely fixed (1605) by Gunpowder Plot. It may be noted that *platoon*, from the dim. *peloton*, was also in earlier E. *plotoon*. With the *plot* of a story we may compare F. *intrigue* (*d'une pièce*), and *nœud* (whence *dénouement*), used in the same sense. The order of senses is thus—patch of ground, flat surface, ground plan of building, design in general, nefarious design. See also *complot*, *plat*, *platform*.

> There have been divers good plottes devised, and wise counsells cast allready, about reformation of that realme (Spenser, *State of Ireland*).

> Our generall [= admiral] had plotted to goe for Newfoundland, and there to revictual, and to depart for the streits of Magellan, which plat, etc.…
> (Hakl.).

plough. AS. *plôh*. Com. Teut.; cf. Du. *ploeg*, Ger. *pflug*, ON. *plôgr*. See also *ear*². With *plough*, Charles' Wain, cf. L. *triones*, Great and Little Bear, lit. plough-oxen. On *Plough Monday*, first after Epiphany, spring ploughing begins. *Plough-tail* is substituted for earlier *plough-start* (see *redstart*, *stark-naked*), with which cf. Du. *Ploegstaart*, a famous wood in Flanders, named from its shape, anglicè *Plug Street*. To *plough* in an examination is an arbitrary variation on *pluck*. For *ploughshare* see *share*, *shear*. See also *Luke*, ix. 62.

plover. F. *pluvier*, Late L. **pluvarius*, from *pluvia*, rain. Cf. Sp. *pluvial*, Ger. *regenpfeifer*, lit. rain-piper, E. dial. *rainbird*. Reason for name doubtful.

pluck. AS. *pluccian*, *ploccan*; cf. Du. *plukken*, Ger. *pflücken*, ON. *plokka*, *plukka*. Prob. all borrowed (cf. *pillow*), in connection with the northern trade with Rome in down and feathers, from VL. **piluccare*, from *pilus*, hair, whence It. *piluccare*, "to pick, or pull out haires or feathers one by one" (Flor.), OF. *peluchier* (cf. ModF. *éplucher*), Norman-Picard *pluquer*. Hence *pluck*, viscera of an animal, as being "plucked" out of the carcase (cf. synon. dial. *gather*), adopted in 18 cent., like mod. *guts*, as a pugilistic word for courage. In this sense it is described as "blackguardly" by Scott, and was not used by ladies before the Crimean War (Hotten). It may have been partly suggested by the much earlier to *pluck up heart* (*courage*, *spirits*).

> The proctor then walks up and down the room, so that any person who objects to the degree being granted may signify the same by pulling or plucking the proctor's robes (*Verdant Green*).

plug. Orig. naut. Du., with LG. cognates; cf. Ger. *pflock*, peg, plug. *Plug*-tobacco is named from shape. To *plug*, work hard, stick to it, orig. in rowing, is partly imit. of sound of oars. With US. *plug*, contemptuous name for horse, cf. Dan. *plag*, foal, Swiss-Ger. *pflag*, sorry nag.

plum. AS. *plūme*, L. *pruna*, neut. pl. treated as fem. sing., G. προῦμνον. For change of -*r*- to -*l*- cf. Ger. *pflaume*, ON. *plōma*. This is perh. due to the word having reached the Teutons via the Balkans, still the great plum country (cf. *silk*). The -*r*- is kept in Du. *pruim*, F. *prune*. Applied, from 17 cent., also to raisins, prob. from their being substituted for the dried plums earlier used for *plum-porridge* (-*cake*, -*pudding*). Cf. *sugar-plum*. As slang name for £100,000 from 17 cent.; in sense of "good thing," prize, from early 19 cent., with allusion to Little Jack Horner.

plumage. F. from *plume* (q.v.).

plumassier. Worker in feathers. F., from *plumasse*, augment. of *plume* (q.v.).

plumb. F. *plomb*, L. *plumbum*, lead. Hence adj., perpendicular, and verb, to sound (depth). Also *plumber*, worker in lead, in ME. usu. *plummer*, as still in surname.

plumbago. L., lead-ore and plant. Has been used of various minerals, current sense of "black lead," graphite, dating from 18 cent.

plume. F., L. *pluma*. Borrowed *plumes* alludes to the jackdaw disguised as peacock. With to *plume oneself on* cf. a *feather in one's cap*, but orig. metaphor was that of a bird *pluming*, "preening," itself; cf. *pique*.

> They and their followers preen and plume themselves...on their aristocratic standpoint
>
> (*John Inglesant*).

plummer-block [*mech.*]. ? From name of inventor.

plummet. OF. *plomet*, *plombet*, dim. of *plomb*, lead, L. *plumbum*. In Wyc. (*Acts*, xxvii. 28).

plump¹. Fat. Late ME. *plompe*, coarse, dull, Du. *plomp*, blunt, clumsy; cf. Ger. *plump*, coarse (from LG.). Later sense of comfortably rounded perh. due to association with *plum* and *plumb*.

plump². To fall with a flop, etc. Imit., but perh. influenced by *plumb*; cf. It. *piombare*, to plunge, and see *plunge*. Here belongs verb to *plump*, in voting, which first appears (18 cent.) in noun *plumper*, undivided

vote, which may also have been influenced by *plump¹*.

plump³ [*archaic*]. Solid cluster, as in *plump of spears*, revived by Scott (*Marmion*, i. 3). Origin obscure; cf. similar use of *clump*.

plunder. First as verb. Ger. *plündern*, from *plunder*, orig. household stuff, etc., now rubbish, lumber, a LG. word. First used in E. in ref. to the Thirty Years War and actively introduced by Prince Rupert of the Rhine.

plunge. F. *plonger*, VL. **plumbicare*, from *plumbum*, lead; cf. It. *piombare*, to plunge, from *piombo*, lead. Hence *plunger*, cavalry man, reckless gambler, both 19 cent.

plunk. Imit., but some senses suggest Picard *plonquer*, dial. form of F. *plonger*, to plunge.

pluperfect. Contr. of F. *plus-que-parfait*, L. *plus quam perfectum* (sc. *tempus*), more than perfect. First in Palsg.

plural. ME. & OF. *plurel* (*pluriel*), L. *pluralis*, from *plus*, *plur*-, more. *Plurality*, holding of more than one benefice, is in *Piers Plowm.* In US. politics it is used of excess of votes over next candidate, when there are several, as opposed to absolute majority.

plus. L., more. Introduced in mathematics, with quasi-prep. force, with *minus* (q.v.).

plush. F. *peluche*, "shag, plush" (Cotg.), VL. **pilucca*, from *pilus*, hair; cf. Sp. *pelusa*, nap, velvet, and see *pluck*.

plutocracy. F. *plutocratie*, G. πλουτοκρατία, power of wealth, πλοῦτος. *Plutocrat* is a back-formation, after *aristocrat*, *democrat*.

Plutonian, Plutonic. From G. Πλούτων, *Pluto*, ruler of Hades.

pluvial. L. *pluvialis*, from *pluvia*, rain. Also (hist.) an eccl. vestment, lit. rain-cloak.

ply¹. Noun. F. *pli*, fold, bend, from *plier*, L. *plicare*. Chiefly in *three-ply*, etc., and archaic to *take a ply*, i.e. bent.

ply². Verb. Aphet. for *apply* (q.v.), in sense of busying oneself, wielding, soliciting, etc. In sense of regular transit between points orig. naut. and also used of Thames watermen.

Plymouth brethren. Sect calling themselves "the Brethren," which arose c. 1830 at Plymouth (Devon). The *plymouth rock* (fowl) is named from US. *Plymouth*, reached by Mayflower, 1620.

pneumatic. F. *pneumatique*, L., G. πνευματικός, from πνεῦμα, breath, spirit, from πνεῖν, to blow.

pneumonia. G. πνευμονία, from πνεύμων, πνεύμον-, lung (v.s.).

po. F. pronunc. of *pot*.

poach[1]. To dress eggs. F. *pocher*, lit. to pouch, pocket, the yolk being enclosed by the white. In OF. & ME. we find *en poche* for poached.

poach[2]. To steal game. Earlier *potch*, app. ident. with above. But dial. senses, to poke, trample, etc., belong to F. *pocher*, to thrust, knock, of Teut. origin (see *poke*[2]). In quot. below the exact sense of F. verb is uncertain. See *foozle* for another possible connection.

pocher le labeur d'autruy: to poche into, or incroach upon, another mans imployment, practise, or trade (Cotg.).

pochard. Diving bird. App. from F. *pocher*, to poke, etc. (v.s.). It is also called *poker*.

pock. Usu. in pl. *pox*, for *pocks*. AS. *pocc*, pustule; cogn. with Du. *pok*, Ger. *pocke* (from LG.), and ult. with *pocket*, *poke*[1]. *Smallpox*, as spec. name of disease formerly called *pockes*, *pox*, is from 17 cent.

pocket. AF. *pokete*, dim. of ONF. *poque* (*poche*). See *poke*[1]. First *NED.* record (1781) for *pocket-handkerchief* is from Fanny Burney.

pock-pudding. Opprobrious Sc. name for Englishman. For *poke-pudding*, bag-pudding, see *poke*[1].

pococurante. It. *poco curante*, little caring, L. *paucum* and pres. part. of *curare*.

pod[1]. Of beans, etc. Replaces (17 cent.) earlier *cod* (*peasecod*). Origin unknown. Prob. much earlier than dict. records.

The poods [of pease in Angola] grow on the roots underneath the ground
(Andrew Battell, in Purch.).

pod[2]. US. name for herd of whales, or seals. Origin unknown.

podagra. Gout. L., G. ποδάγρα, from πούς, ποδ-, foot, ἄγρα, trap.

podestà. It., magistrate, L. *potestas*, -*tat*-, power, from *potis*, powerful.

podge. Var. of *pudge* (q.v.).

podium [*arch*.]. L., G. πόδιον, dim. of πούς, ποδ-, foot. See *pew*.

podophyllin [*chem*.]. Resin from plant *podophyllum*, from G. πούς, ποδ-, foot, φύλλον, leaf.

Podsnappery. From *Podsnap*, character in *Our Mutual Friend*, fond of waving objections aside.

Free-trade Podsnapery waves away such a necessity (*Referee*, April 29, 1917).

poem. F. *poème*, L., G. πόημα, var. of ποίημα, from ποιεῖν, to make. Cf. *poet*, F. *poète*,

L., G. ποητής, for ποιητής (cf. early Sc. *maker*, poet); *poesy*, F. *poésie*, from L., G. πόησις; *poetry*, OF. *poetrie*, Late L. *poetria*. *Poetaster* appears to have been borrowed by Ben Jonson from It. *poetastro* or OF. *poetastre*, formed with pejorative suffix -*aster*. See also *posy*.

pogrom. Russ., from verb *gromit'*, to batter, devastate, cogn. with *gromiét'*, to thunder; cf. *gromila*, burglar. Usu. of massacres of Jews.

The total number of places pogrommed was 353, and the Jews killed 20,500
(*Daily Chron.* Oct. 10, 1919).

poignant. Pres. part. of F. *poindre*, to prick, stab, L. *pungere*.

poilu. F., hairy, from *poil*, hair (of beard), L. *pilus*. The word is not new, e.g. Balzac uses it in the sense of bold, determined. There was perh. orig. a play on *brave à trois poils*, lit. three-pile brave, a metaphor from velvet.

poinsettia. Flower. Named (1836) from discoverer, J. R. *Poinsett*, US. minister to Mexico.

point. F. *point* (m.), prick, dot, etc., L. *punctum*, *pointe* (f.), act of piercing, Late L. *puncta*, from *pungere*, *punct*-, to prick, pierce; cf. It. Sp. *punto*, *punta*, in same groups of senses. In sense of distinguishing mark now only in *strong point*. *Point-lace* is made with needle only. *Point-blank* is from *blank*, the white centre of the target, the marksman being considered close enough to point at this without allowing for curve; cf. F. *de but en blanc*, *à bout portant*, *à brûle-pourpoint*, all in same sense, and obs. F. *de pointe en blanc*. *Point of honour*, F. *point d'honneur*, is adapted from Sp. *pundonor*. Archaic *point device*, exactly, is ME. *at point device*, from OF. *devis*, arranged (see *devise*), and *à point*, just right, to a nicety. See also *edge*. Spec. sense of part of argument or chain of reasoning appears in to *strain a point*, *make a point of*.

pointillism [*art*]. From F. *pointiller*, to cover with *pointilles*, small dots.

poise. OF. *pois* (*poids*), earlier *peis*, L. *pensum*, from *pendere*, to weigh. Cf. *avoirdupois*. The -*d*- in ModF. *poids* is due to mistaken association with L. *pondus*. In E. the idea of weight has passed into that of balance.

poison. F., L. *potio-n*-, drink, from *potare*, to drink. Mod. sense arises from that of magic potion, philtre, etc. Cf. Ger. *gift*, poison, lit. gift.

Je suis roïne, mais le non [name]
En ai perdu par la poison [*also called* lovendrinc]
Que nos beümes en la mer (*Tristan*, 12 cent.).

poissarde [*hist*.]. Parisian market-woman, noisily revolutionary. Fem. of *poissard*, pickpocket, from *poix*, pitch, with allusion to fingers, but in later sense associated with *poisson*, fish, as though fish-wife.

poke[1]. Bag. Now chiefly dial., e.g. *hop-poke* (Kent), or in to *buy a pig in a poke*, i.e. without examination, for which Wyc. has to *buy a cat in the sack* (F. *acheter chat en poche*) (see *bag*); also as name for bonnet (now *poke-bonnet*). ON. *poki*, cogn. with AS. *pohha* (whence obs. *pough*, bag). Or E. word may be ONF. *poque* (see *pocket*), which is of Teut. origin. Cf. *pouch*, and see *pock*.

They walwe as doon two pigges in a poke
(Chauc. A. 4278).

poke[2]. To thrust. Of LG. origin; cf. Du. LG. *poken*, also Du. *pook*, stick, Ger. *pochen*, to knock; cogn. with Norw. *paak*, stick. To *poke fun at* is 19 cent. *Poky*, paltry, petty, is from the idea of "poking," in sense of pottering. The *holy poker* is Ir.

poker. Card-game. Orig. US. Cf. Ger. *poch*, *pochspiel*, a "bluffing" card-game, from *pochen*, to brag, lit. to knock, rap, cogn. with *poke*[2].

polacre, polacca [*naut*.]. Three-masted Mediterranean ship. Cf. F. *polacre*, It. Sp. *polacra*, Du. *polaak*, Ger. *polacke*, all app. meaning Polish (cf. obs. *Polack*, Pole, *Haml*. ii. 2). But it is difficult to see how a Mediterranean rig could be named from Poland. Early authorities all describe the *polacre* as "pole-masted," i.e. with each mast made of one piece of timber, so that the word may be of E. formation from *pole*[1] with jocular assim. to *Polack*.

polarize. F. *polariser*, coined (1811) by Malus, as term in optics, later applied to magnetism and electricity. See *pole*[2].

poldavy [*archaic*]. Coarse canvas. From *Poldavide* (Finistère) in Brittany. Cf. *dowlas*, *lockram*.

polder [*geog*.]. Land reclaimed from sea. Du., earlier *polre*. Perh. ident. with Du. *polder*, fowl-run, MedL. *pullarium*.

pole[1]. Stake, etc. AS. *pāl*, L. *pālus*; cf. Du. *paal*, Ger. *pfahl*, ON. *pāll*, also from L. (see *pale*[1]). Of ship's mast in *under bare poles*. For application to measure cf. *rod*, *perch*, also *yard*, *chain*, etc.

pole[2]. Geographical. F. *pôle*, L., G. πόλος, pivot, axis. Cf. It. Span. *polo*, Du. *pool*, Ger. *pol*, also from L. Orig. (Chauc.) two fixed points in celestial sphere around which the stars appear to revolve.

poleaxe. ME. *pollax*, as though from *poll*, head, but formation from *pole*[1] seems more likely; cf. *halberd*. Orig. warlike weapon, halberd, association with the butcher dating from c. 1700.

polecat. From OF. *pole* (*poule*), hen, from its preying on poultry (q.v.); cf. *goshawk*, *hen-harrier*, etc. See also *catchpole*.

And eek ther was a polcat in his hawe,
That, as he seyde, his capouns hadde y-slawe
(Chauc. C. 855).

polemarch [*hist*.]. Commander-in-chief. G. πολέμαρχος (v.i.).

polemic. G. πολεμικός, from πόλεμος, war. Introduced by controversial theologians of 17 cent.

polenta. It., "a meate used in Italie made of barlie or chesnut flowre soked in water, and then fride in oyle or butter" (Flor.), L. *polenta*, peeled barley, from *pollen*, fine meal.

police. F., civil administration, MedL. *politia*, whence also *policy*[1], *polity* (q.v.). Current sense, and *policeman* for constable, from beginning of 19 cent.

policlinic [*med*.]. Clinic (q.v.) held in private house instead of hospital. Ger. *poliklinik*, from πόλις, city. Erron. *polyclinic*.

policy[1]. Statecraft. OF. *policie*, L., G. πολιτεία, from πολίτης, citizen, from πόλις, city. Sc. sense of improvement on estate is due to confusion with *polish*, *polite*.

policy[2]. Of insurance. F. *police*, altered on *policy*[1]. Ult. MedL. *apodissa*, receipt, for L. *apodixis*, G. ἀπόδειξις, from ἀποδεικνύναι, to make known. Cf. Prov. *podiza*, Port. *apólice*, also It. *polizza*, invoice, Sp. *póliza*. For change of *-d-* to *-l-* in words of G. origin cf. *pilot*. In E. from 16 cent.

poligar. Feudal chief in SInd. Mahratti *pālēgar*, from Tamil *pālaiyam*, feudal estate. Hence *poligar-dog*, from poligar country.

polish. F. *polir*, *poliss-*, L. *polire*, to polish, smooth. To *polish off* was orig. pugilistic.

Polish. From *Pole*, inhabitant of *Poland*, used for earlier *Polack*, *Polonian*, *Polander*. The lang. is Slav. For name of country see *polynia*.

polite. L. *politus*, p.p. of *polire*, to polish. Cf. F. *poli*, It. *pulito*. Perh. associated with G. πολίτης, citizen (cf. *urbane*).

politic. F. *politique*, L., G. πολιτικός, from πολίτης, citizen, from πόλις, city. Replaced, exc. in sense of shrewd, and in *body politic*, by *political*. *Politics, politician* are 16 cent. F. *politique* has the sense of trimmer.

That insidious and crafty animal, vulgarly called a politician (Adam Smith).

polity. OF. *politie*, learned form of *policie*. See *policy*[1].

polka. Dance and jacket. Polish, fem. of *Polak*, Pole, whence also F. & Ger. *polka*. Reached London (1842) from Paris via Prague, Vienna. Cf. *polonaise, mazurka*.

poll[1]. Head. Cf. obs. Du. *pol, polle*, LG. *polle*, also Dan. *puld*, crown of head. Now only of voting by head and in archaic *poll-tax*, capitation. Hence to *poll*, crop the head (2 *Sam.* xiv. 26), now usu. of trees, whence *pollard* (oak, willow), earlier and more gen. sense surviving in *deed poll*, a document executed by one party only, as opposed to an indenture (v.i.).

A deed-poll is that which is plaine without any indenting, so called, because it is cut even or polled (Coke).

poll[2]. Parrot. From name *Poll*, for *Moll* (cf. *Peg* for *Meg*), earlier *Mal*, from *Mary* (cf. *Hal*, from *Harry*). NED. quotes *pretty Pall* for 1630. Hence verb to *poll-parrot*, coined by Rogue Riderhood (*Mutual Friend*).

poll[3]. Pass degree (Camb.). Prob. from G. οἱ πολλοί, the many, the multitude.

pollack, pollock. Kind of cod. Prob. from *poll*[1], with fanciful assim. to *Polack*, Pole. Cf. *pollard*, obs. name for chub.

pollan. Ir. freshwater fish. ? From Ir. *poll*, pool, mire.

pollard. See *poll*[1].

pollen. L., fine flour, dust; cogn. with *pulvis*, dust.

pollicitation [*leg.*]. L. *pollicitatio-n-*, from *pollicitari*, to promise.

pollute. From L. *polluere, pollut-*, from *pro* and *luere*, to wash; cf. L. *lues*, filth.

polly [*neol.*]. Slang for *apollinaris*.

pollywog [*dial.*]. Tadpole. ME. *polwigle*, from *poll*[1] and *wiggle*.

polo. Balti (dial. of Indus valley); cf. Tibetan *pulu*. First played in England at Aldershot in 1871. See *chicanery*.

polonaise. Dress and dance. F., fem. of *polonais*, Polish. Cf. *polka*.

polonium [*chem.*]. From MedL. *Polonia*, Poland. Element discovered and named (1898) by M. and Mme Curie, the latter of Polish nationality.

polony. Corrupt. of *Bologna* (sausage), from place of origin in Italy.

poltergeist. Ger., noisy spirit, from *polter*, uproar, cogn. with *boulder* (q.v.). Cf. Du. *buldergeest*. Introduced, with *spook*, by spiritualists. See also *pother*.

poltroon. F. *poltron*, It. *poltrone*, from *poltro*, "sluggard, idle, lazie, slothfull" (Flor.). Connected by some with It. *poltro*, couch. It. Sp. *poltro*, foal, is another possible starting-point.

poly-. From G. πολύς, πολύ, much, many; e.g. *polyandry*, from ἀνήρ, ἀνδρ-, man; *polyanthus*, from ἄνθος, flower; *polygamy*, from γάμος, marriage; *polyglot*, from γλῶττα, tongue; *polygon*, from γωνία, angle; *polyhedron*, from ἕδρα, base, side; *polymath*, G. πολυμαθής, from μανθάνειν, to learn; *polytheism*, from θεός, god.

polyclinic. General hospital. For *policlinic* (q.v.), with changed spelling and meaning.

polygonum [*bot.*]. From G. πολύγονον, knotgrass, from γόνυ, knee.

Polynesia. Latinized from F. *polynésie*, coined (1756) by de Brosses from G. νῆσος, island.

polynia. Open water amid polar ice. Russ. *polynya*, from root of *polye*, field.

polypus. Octopus, cuttlefish. L., G. πολύπους, from πούς, foot. For application (14 cent.) to growth in nose cf. *canker, lupus*.

polysynthetic [*ling.*]. Applied to langs., e.g. NAmer. Ind., which combine a sentence into a compound word.

polytechnic. F. *polytechnique*, from G. πολύτεχνος, skilled in many arts (τέχνη), first applied to the *école polytechnique*, engineering school founded at Paris (1794). In E. to the *Polytechnic Institution*, founded in London (1838).

polyvalent [*neol.*]. Of inoculation against all zymotics. From pres. part. of L. *valēre*, to be strong.

pom [*neol.*]. Short for *Pomeranian* (q.v.).

pomace. Crushed apples for cider. Prob. plur. of OF. *pomat*, cider, MedL. *pomatium*, from L. *pomum*, apple. Cf. *accidence, bodice*, etc.

pomade. F. *pommade*, It. *pomata*, from *pomum*, apple, from which the unguent is supposed to have been orig. made. *Pomatum* is mod. latinization.

pomander [*archaic*]. Perforated metal ball filled with aromatics, pouncet-box. By dissim. for earlier (15 cent.) *pomamber*, OF. *pome ambre*, apple of amber; cf. MedL. *pomum ambrae*. It was also called a *musk-ball* (*Paston Let.* iii. 464).

pomme de senteurs: a pomander, or sweet-ball
(Cotg.)

pomard, pommard. Burgundy wine. Name of F. village (Côte-d'Or). Cf. *beaune*.

pomatum. See *pomade*.

pombé. Fermented drink in Central and E. Afr. Native (Swahili).

pomegranate. OF. *pome grenade* (now simply *grenade*, q.v.); cf. It. *granata*, Sp. *granada*, from L. *granum*, seed. Called in L. *malum granatum*, seeded apple, and in ME. also *garnade*, *apple-garnade*. Wyc. has *powmgarnet*, *pumgarnade*. Exotic fruits are commonly called "apples"; cf. obs. *pomecitron*, citron, Ger. *pomeranze*, Seville orange, lit. apple orange, *apfelsine*, orange, lit. Chinese apple; also E. *love-apple*, *pineapple*, F. *pomme-de-terre*, potato, etc. See also *melon*, *marmalade*.

pomelo. EInd. name for shaddock, US. for grape-fruit. App. from L. *pomum*, apple (v.s.).

pomeranian. Dog from *Pomerania*, Ger. *Pommern*, orig. name of a Slav. tribe. Cf. *Prussian*.

Pomfret cake. From *Pomfret* (Yorks), AF. *pont fret*, broken bridge, L. *pons, pont-, fractus*. Now latinized to *Pontefract*.

pommard. See *pomard*.

pommel, pummel. OF. *pomel* (*pommeau*), dim. from L. *pomum*, apple, applied to a rounded protuberance; cf. F. *pommette*, cheek-bone, *pomme d'une canne*, knob of walking-stick. Hence verb to *pommel, pummel*, orig. to beat about the head with pommel of sword or dagger.

Pomona. Roman goddess of fruit, from *pomum*, apple. Hence *Pomona green*.

pomp. F. *pompe*, L., G. πομπή, solemn procession, lit. sending, from πέμπειν, to send. *Pompous* is depreciatory as early as Chauc. In the Church Catechism *pomp* has sense of *pompa diaboli*, public spectacle, "show" (v.i.).

That I should forsake the devil and all his workes
and pompes, the vanities of the wicked worlde
(*PB.* 1548–9).

That I should forsake the devill and all his workes,
the pomps and vanities of the wicked world
(*PB.* 1603).

pompadour. Fashion, hair-dressing, etc. From the *Marquise de Pompadour* (†1764), mistress of Louis XV of France. Cf. *dolly varden*.

pompier ladder. From F. *pompier*, fireman, lit. pumper.

pom-pom. Machine gun. Imit. of report. A word from the SAfr. War (1899).

pompon. Tufted tassel. F., perh. slang use of OF. *pompon*, pumpkin.

ponceau. Poppy-colour. F., OF. *pouncel*, dim. of *poun* (*paon*), peacock, L. *pavo-n-*. Cf. F. *coquelicot*, wild poppy, from *coq*, cock[1].

poncho. Cloak. SAmer. Sp. from Araucanian (Chile) native name. Cf. *gaucho*.

pond. Orig. artificially banked pool. Ident. with *pound*[2] (q.v.), which is still used for *pond* in dial. Trace of older sense survives in compds. (*duck-, fish-, mill-*, etc.). For sense cf. also Norw. Dan. *dam*, dam, pond.

ponder. F. *pondérer*, to weigh, L. *ponderare*, from *pondus, ponder-*, weight. Cf. *preponderate, ponderous*.

pone [*US.*]. Maize-flour bread. NAmer. Ind. (Algonkin) *pone, appone, oppone*. Capt. John Smith has *ponap*.

pongee. Fabric. Earlier *paunchee*, NChin. *pvn-chī*, for *pvn-kī*, own loom.

pongo. Native name, in Angola or Loango, for large anthropoid ape, perh. gorilla, with which Andrew Battell's description (Purch.) agrees. Also in recent use as nickname for marine.

You could pass as a naval officer more easily than
you could as a pongo
(Coppleston, *Lost Naval Papers*, 1916).

poniard. F. *poignard*, from *poing*, fist, L. *pugnus*; cf. OF. *poignal*, It. *pugnale*, in same sense. But prob. associated also with *poindre, poign-*, to pierce, stab.

pons asinorum. L., bridge of asses. First (math.) in Smollett. Earlier in logic.

pontiff. F. *pontife*, L. *pontifex*, high priest, which app. means lit. bridge-builder, from L. *pons, pont-*, and *facere*. The first element may perh. be Oscan-Umbrian *puntis*, propitiatory offering; but it may be noted that bridge-building has always been regarded as a pious work of divine inspiration. The L. *pons* (cogn. with *path*) had orig. the same sense as *bridge*[1] (q.v.).

pontoon. F. *ponton*, L. *ponto-n-*, punt[1] (q.v.),

floating bridge, prob. Celt., but associated with L. *pons, pont-*, bridge.

pony. Sc. *powney*, ? OF. *poulenet*, dim. of *poulain*, colt, Late L. *pullanus*, from *pullus*, young animal. But the OF. word is rare, and a pony is not a foal, so that the old derivation from *puny* may be correct. For slang sense of £25 cf. *monkey*, £500. The word is, like *donkey*, of late introduction from dial.

> *pony:* a little Scotch horse (Bailey).

pood. Weight of about 36 lbs. Russ., from LG. or Norse *pund*, pound[1] (q.v.).

poodle. Ger. *pudel*, orig. a water-dog, for *pudelhund*, from LG. *pudeln*, to splash. Cf. Ger. *pudel*, puddle, *pudelnass*, dripping wet.

poof. Imit. of blowing out candle, etc. Cf. *puff* and F. *pouf*.

pooh. Imit. of blowing away; cf. *poof, pfew*, etc. Hence to *pooh-pooh* (19 cent.).

Pooh-Bah. Lord High Everything Else in Gilbert and Sullivan's *Mikado*.

> One of our own Pooh-Bahs, in the person of the Lord Chamberlain (*Daily Chron.* Nov. 3, 1919).

pool[1]. Of water. AS. *pōl*. WGer.; cf. Du. *poel*, Ger. *pfuhl*; cogn. with Gael. Ir. *poll*, Welsh *pwll*, Corn. *pol*, common in place-names, but prob. not with L. *palus*, marsh.

pool[2]. In gambling. F. *poule*, hen, perh. orig. in sense of booty of successful player; cf. Sp. *polla*, hen, also stake at hombre, Walloon *poie*, hen, stake. It may be ult. connected with the OF. *jeu de la galline* (L. *gallina*, hen) in which the bird was both target and prize (cf. *cockshy*). In E. associated with *pool*[1], an association perh. helped by F. *fiche*, counter, being confused with *fish*. Verb to *pool* (funds, resources, ideas, etc.) is quite mod.

> Si Denjean est de ce jeu, il prendra toutes les poules; c'est un aigle (Mme de Sévigné, 1680).

> Industrious creatures that make it a rule To secure half the fish, while they manage the pool
>   (*NED.* 1766).

Poonah. Painting, etc. From *Poonah*, in Bombay Presidency.

poop. F. *poupe*, VL. *puppa, for *puppis*, stern; cf. It. *poppa*, Sp. *popa*.

poor. AF. *poure*, OF. *povre* (*pauvre*), L. *pauper*; cf. It. *povero*, Sp. *pobre*. Completely replaced Teut. word (AS. *earm*; cf. Ger. *arm*, etc.). For adj. use of adv. *poorly* cf. *ill, sickly*.

pop[1]. Imit. of short quick sound, as of pistol, drawn cork, etc., e.g. *pop-gun, pop-corn* (US.), to *pop the question*. Also applied to motion, e.g. to *pop in* (*out, off the hooks*), *pop goes the weasel*, name of country dance and tune (c. 1850), and to putting things away quickly, whence sense of pawning, *pop-shop* (18 cent.). *Popping-crease* at cricket (18 cent.) has the idea of popping, or striking, at the ball.

> Sith you have popt me such a doubtfull question, if you and I were alone by ourselves, I would poppe you such an aunswere, that you should well find that I loved you (Greene, *Heaven and Hell*).

pop[2]. Shortened (19 cent.) from *popular concert*.

pop[3]. Debating society at Eton. ? From *lollipop*, the society having met orig. (1811) at a confectioner's.

pope. AS. *pāpa*, Church L., Late G. πάπας, for πάππας, baby word for father, papa (cf. hist. of *abbot*). In early Church title of bishops, but, since Leo the Great (5 cent.), claimed as exclusive title in Western Church for bishop of Rome. With forms in Rom. langs. cf. Ger. *pfaffe*, priest, shaveling, *pabst*, pope, Russ. *pope*, parish priest, from WGer. The *pope's-eye* of a leg of mutton (17 cent.) is in Ger. *pfaffenbisschen*, parson's bit (cf. *parson's nose* of fowl), and in F. *œil de Judas*. Hostile sense of *popery, popish* dates from Reformation.

Pope Joan. Card game. Name of fabulous female pope; but cf. synon. F. *nain jaune*, lit. yellow dwarf, which may have suggested E. name.

popinjay. Orig. parrot, later applied to the over-conspicuous or noisy (1 *Hen. IV*, i. 3), but in ME. sometimes complimentary, e.g. Lydgate applies it to the Holy Virgin. Very widely diffused, e.g. OF. *papegai, papegau*, It. *pappagallo*, Sp. *papagaio*, Ger. *papagei*, Du. *papegaai*, MedG. παπαγᾶς, Arab. *babaghā*, etc., some forms being assimilated to *jay* and its cognates, others to L. *gallus*, cock (cf. hist. of *cockatoo*). Prob. the name originated in some barbarian lang. as imit. of cry, or it may, like so many bird-names (cf. *parrot*), have been a nickname given by early travellers. ME. *papejay*, from OF., has now an intrusive -n-, as in *nightingale, messenger*. An earlier form survives in surname *Pobgee, Popejoy*, etc. Early Sc. *papingo* (Lyndsay) is OF. *papegau* (v.s.), corresponding to MedL. *papagallus*.

poplar. OF. *poplier* (*peuplier*), from L. *pōpulus*, whence directly dial. *popple* (in place-names, e.g. *Popplewell*); cf. Du. Ger. *pappel*.

poplin. F. *popeline*, earlier *papeline*, It. *papalina*, fem. of *papalino*, papal, because made at Avignon, seat of the Pope during the schism (1309–1408) and regarded as a papal town till 1791.

poppet. Earlier form of *puppet* (q.v.).

popple. Of water. Imit. of motion; cf. *bubble* and Du. *popelen*, to throb, quiver. Partly frequent. of *pop*[1].

poppy. AS. *popæg*, later *popig*, from L. *papaver*, whence also F. *pavot*, exact formation of both words being obscure.

popsy-wopsy. Redupl. on archaic *pop*, darling, short for *poppet*. Cotg. has *pupsie*, for *puppy* (s.v. *chien de damoiselle*).

populace. F., It. *popolaccio*, "the grosse, base, vile, common people, rifraffe people" (Flor.), from *popolo*, people, L. *populus*, with pejorative suffix. Cf. *popular*, *population*, *populous*, etc.

porcelain. F. *porcelaine*, It. *porcellana*, orig. cowrie-shaped shell, Venus shell, from *porcella*, dim. of *porca*, lit. sow, used in L. for *vulva*. The shell takes its name from the shape of the orifice (cf. archaic Dan. *kudemusling*). The china is named from surface resembling the shell. L. *porca*, vulva, is regarded by some as distinct from *porca*, sow, and as cogn. with AS. *furh*, furrow.

porch. F. *porche*, L. *porticus*, colonnade, etc., ? cogn. with *porta*, door.

porcine. L. *porcinus*, of the pig, *porcus*.

porcupine. OF. *porc espin*, parallel name to *porc espi* (*porc-épic*), the former meaning spine (thorn) pig, the latter spike pig; cf. It. *porcospino*, Sp. *puerco espin*. The early vars. are numerous and odd, e.g. *porkpen*, *porkenpick*, *porkpoint*, *porpin*, etc., and Shaks. spelt it *porpentine* (*Haml.* i. 5).

The crest a bluw porpyntyn
(Machyn's *Diary*, 1550–63).

The porkpens come out of India and Africke; a kind of urchin or hedgehog they be
(Holland's *Pliny*, viii. 35).

pore[1]. Noun. F., L., G. πόρος, way, passage, pore.

pore[2]. Verb. ME. *pūren*, *pouren*, to gaze fixedly. Origin unknown.

porism [*math.*]. L., G. πόρισμα, deduction, from πορίζειν, to carry, deduce, from πόρος, way.

pork. F. *porc*, pig, pork, L. *porcus*. For limitation of sense in E. cf. *beef*, *mutton*, *veal*. A *porker* was earlier a *porket*.

It [Trinidad] hath store of deare, wild porks, fruits, fish and foule (Raleigh).

pornography. F. *pornographie*, from G. πόρνη, harlot.

porphyrogenitus [*hist.*]. See *purple*.

porphyry. F. *porphyre*, Late L. **porphyrius*, G. πορφύρεος, purple, whence πορφυρίτης, porphyry. In most Europ. langs.

porpoise. OF. *porpeis*, L. *porcus*, pig, *piscis*, fish. Capt. John Smith has *porkpisce*. Cf. sailors' name *sea-hog*, and Ger. *meerschwein*, whence F. *marsouin*, "a porpose, or seahog" (Cotg.). See *grampus*.

porraceous. From L. *porraceus*, of the leek, *porrum*.

porrect. L. *porrigere*, *porrect-*, to extend, from *pro* and *regere*.

porridge. Altered (16 cent.), partly under influence of dial. *porray*, leek-broth, etc., from *poddish*, *pottage* (q.v.). Cf. dial. *imperence*, *orra*, *moral*; and, for converse change, *eddish*, *paddock*. *Porray* is OF. *porée*, Late L. *porrata*, from *porrum*, leek. Association of *porridge* with oatmeal is Sc., in which *parritch* is often treated as pl.

porre or purre, pese potage: piseum
(*Prompt. Parv.*).

There was boyling on the fyer a pipkin of pease pottage....It was throwne downe, broke, and all the porridge aboute the chamber
(Raymond's *Autob.* 17 cent.).

That is a chip in porridge; it is just nothing
(Dryden).

By reason of their mild nature they [leeks] are much used in porridge, which had its name from the Latin porrum, a leek, tho' now from the French we generally call it pottage (*Dict. Rust.* 1717).

porringer. For earlier *potager*, *poddinger* (v.s.), with intrusive -*n*- as in *passenger*, etc.

menestrino: a little porringer, a pottage dish (Flor.).

port[1]. Harbour. AS. *port*, L. *portus*, cogn. with *porta*, gate, and ult. with *ford*. Reinforced in ME. by F. *port*. Hence *port* side of ship, replacing older *larboard* (q.v.), the "loading side" being naturally turned towards the harbour.

port[2] [*hist.*]. Gate. F. *porte*, L. *porta*; cf. Du. *poort*, Ger. *pforte*, from L. Now only in naut. *port-hole* and archaic mil. *sally-port*. See *port*[1].

port[3]. Bearing. F., from *porter*, to carry, L. *portare*, whence also verb to *port*, now only in mil. to *port arms*. Cf. *portable, portation*. For changed sense of *portly*, orig. majestic, cf. *stout*.

My queen and portly empress (Marlowe).

port⁴. Wine. For *port-wine*, from *Oporto*, Port. *o porto*, the harbour. Cf. F. *vin de porto*, Ger. *portwein*.

portage. In current sense, transporting by land from one navigable water to another, from Canad. F. See *port³*.

portal. OF. (*portail*), MedL. *portale*, from *porta*, gate.

portcullis. OF. *porte-coulisse*, sliding door, from ·*couler*, to flow, L. *colare*; cf. theat. *coulisse*. Replaced in F. by *herse*, lit. harrow.

Porte [*hist.*]. For F. *Sublime Porte* (cf. It. *Porta Sublima*), rendering Turk. Arab. *bāb-i-'āliy*, lit. lofty gate, offic. name of central office of Ottoman government. Cf., in diplomatic lang., the *Ballplatz* (Austria), *Quai d'Orsay* (France), *Vatican* (Papacy), etc.

portend. L. *portendere*, to foretell, archaic form of *protendere, protent-*, to stretch forward, whence also noun *portentum*, portent, omen.

Coming events cast their shadows before
(Campbell).

porter¹. Doorkeeper. F. *portier* (see *port²*).

porter². Bearer. F. *porteur* (see *port³*).

porter³. Beer. For *porter's beer*, ale (Swift), from *porter²*. Cf. *cooper¹*. With *porterhouse*, as in *porterhouse steak* (US.), cf. *alehouse, beerhouse*.

portfire [*mil.*]. Fuse, match. Adapted from F. *portefeu*, lit. carry-fire.

portfolio. In 18 cent. *porto folio*, corrupt. of It. *portafogli*, lit. carry-leaves, pl. of *foglio*, L. *folium*. Cf. cogn. F. *portefeuille*, from which comes current pol. sense.

portico. It., as *porch* (q.v.). Also allusively to the Painted Porch at Athens, resort of Zeno (see *stoic*).

portière. F., MedL. *portaria*, from *porta*, door.

portion. F., L. *portio-n-*, cogn. with *pars, part-*. Orig. share, allowance (cf. *apportion*), as still in eating-houses.

Portland cement. From resembling colour of *Portland stone*, from peninsula of *Portland* (Dorset).

portly. See *port³*.

portmanteau. Orig. for horseman's use. F. *portemanteau*, earlier valise, now clothespeg. Older *portmantle* is still in dial. use.

Portmanteau-word (e.g. *acrobatics, Bakerloo, electrocute, Eurasian, gerrymander, perambucot, squarson*), was coined by Lewis Carroll to explain *slithy, mimsy*, etc. (*Through the Looking-Glass*).

One [word] was ingeniously invented by a maidservant, viz. clantastical, which she contrived should express both fantastical and clandestine
(Pegge, 1803).

The Daily Herald, the Hunshevik Labour paper
(*John Bull*, June 7, 1919).

A depraved motor-car comes, belching out its hideous stench as it petrollicks down the road
(W. de Morgan, *Old Madhouse*, ch. i.).

portolan [*hist.*]. Early book of sailing-directions. It. *portolano*, from *porto*, harbour. For formation cf. *ortolan*.

Portolan charts have naturally a great attraction for collectors in the New World
(*Daily Chron.* Aug. 19, 1917).

portrait. F., p.p. of *portraire*, to portray, L. *protrahere*, to draw forward. Orig. in wider sense, painting, sculpture.

port-reeve [*hist.*]. Mayor. AS. *portgeréfa*, where *port* has sense of borough, prob. extended from that of harbour. See *reeve¹*.

Portugee. Back-formation from *Portuguese*, Port. *portuguez*; cf. *Chinee, burgee, marquee, pea*.

We ought to let the Portugeses have right done them (Pepys, Aug. 12, 1664).

Portuguese man-of-war. Marine hydrozoan with sail-like crest; cf. *nautilus, salleeman*.

posada. Inn. Sp., from *posar*, to lodge (v.i.).

pose¹. To place. F. *poser*, Late L. *pausare*, to halt, rest, which replaced in Rom. langs. L. *ponere, posit-*, to place, also in compds. (*compose, dispose, repose*, etc.). See *pause*. L. *ponere* gave F. *pondre*, to lay (eggs), and survives in *compound, expound, propound*, the nouns *composition, exposition, proposition*, being now felt as belonging to both the *-pound* and *-pose* groups. Current sense of *pose* is from the artist's model.

pose². To non-plus. Aphet. for *oppose* or obs. var. *appose*, to question (see *puzzle*). Hence *poser*, orig. examiner, questioner.

And Pilate apposed him saynge, Art thou the kynge of the Jewes? (Tynd. *Luke*, xxiii. 3).

Sitting in the middes of the doctours, both hearynge them and posing them (Tynd. *Luke*, ii. 46).

posit [*logic*]. L. *ponere, posit-*, to place, lay down.

position. F., L. *positio-n-*, from *ponere, posit-*, to place. With *positive*, F. *positif*, L. *positivus*, cf. "laying down" the law. Scient.

senses, opposed to *negative*, are mod. *Positivism* is the philosophy of Auguste Comte, who published his *Philosophie positive* in 1830.

posology. Science of doses. F. *posologie*, from G. πόσος, how much. Used by Bentham for mathematics.

posse. Short for MedL. *posse comitatus*, lit. force of the county (q.v.), L. *posse*, to be able, from *potis*, powerful, *esse*, to be.

possess. OF. *possesser* (replaced by *posséder*), from L. *possidēre, possess-*, compd. of *sedēre*, to sit; cf. Ger. *besitzen*, to possess, from *sitzen*, to sit. Archaic sense of taking possession, controlling, appears in adj. *possessed* (of an evil spirit) and in *Luke*, xxi. 19. Earlier are *possession, possessor*, also from OF.

posset. ME. *poshote, possot, possyt*. Orig. made with curdled milk. Origin doubtful. There is a rare and doubtful OF. *possette*, which may be a dim. from *posson*, "a little measure for milke, verjuice, and vinegar" (Cotg.). This is a dim. of *pot*; cf. archaic E. *posnet*, cooking pot, OF. *possonet*.

possible. F., L. *possibilis*, from *posse* (*potis esse*), to be able. With *possibilist*, orig. school of Sp. republicans, cf. *opportunist*.

possum. Aphet. for *opossum* (q.v.). Esp. in to *play possum* (US.), with allusion to opossum's trick of feigning death.

post[1]. Wooden pillar, etc. AS. *post*, L. *postis*, reinforced in ME. by OF. *post*, which survives in dim. *poteau*, stake, and compd. *suppôt*; cf. Du. *post*, Ger. *pfosten*, all from L. *postis*, ? and this ult. from *ponere, posit-*, to place. Hence to *post* a bill, defaulter, etc., by notice orig. attached to a post (see *bill[3]*).

> I went to see if any play was acted, but I found none upon the post, it being Passion Week
> (Pepys, Mar. 24, 1662).

post[2]. For letters. F. *poste* (f.), station, It. *posta*, Late L. *posta*, for *posita*, from *ponere, posit-*, to place. Orig. used (c. 1500) of series of mounted men stationed at intervals on road for rapid forwarding of royal messages, etc. (cf. synon. L. *equites positi*). Hence *post-haste, post-chaise*, etc. Later applied to the offic. forwarding of all missives. The name was also given to the messenger, as in *by return of post*, F. *par retour du courrier*. With to *ride post* cf. F. *courir la poste*. To *post*, earlier *post over, the ledger* app. belongs here, with idea of transference; hence *posted* (*up*), also

fig. well-informed. As size of paper (*post octavo*) of Du. or Ger. origin and said to have been named from watermark being a posthorn (cf. *foolscap*).

post[3]. Of soldier. F. *poste* (m.), It. *posto*, station, employment, Late L. *postum*, for *positum* (v.s.). For extension from position of soldier to that of civilian cf. *berth*. Here belong *post-captain, post-rank*, and *last post*, bugle-call.

post-. L. *post*, after, as in *post meridiem* (P.M.), *post mortem*. Hence *post-impressionist* (20 cent.), artist going one better than *impressionist*.

poster. See *post[1], bill[3]*.

posterior. L., compar. of *posterus*, coming after, from *post*, after; cf. *posterity*. *A posteriori* (reasoning) is from result instead of cause (*a priori*).

> The man was laughed at as a blunderer who said in a public business, "We do much for posterity; I would fain see them do something for us"
> (Elizabeth Montagu's *Letters*, Jan. 1, 1742).

postern [*archaic*]. OF. *posterne* (*poterne*), for earlier *posterle*, Late L. *posterula*, backway, from *posterus*, from *post* (v.s.).

posthumous. L. *postumus*, last, last-born, superl. of *posterus* (v.s.), altered in Late L. to *posthumus*, by association with *humus*, ground, and applied to what appears after originator's (father's, author's) death.

postil [*archaic*]. Marginal note, esp. in Bible. F. *postille*, also *apostille*; cf. It. *postilla*, Sp. *postela*, MedL. *postilla* (13 cent.). ? Short for *post illa verba* (*sacrae scripturae*), beginning of priest's explanation after reading text.

postilion. F. *postillon*, It. *postiglione*, "a postilion, a postes guide, a forerunner" (Flor.), from *posta*, post[2]. Cf. *postboy*. For form cf. *vermilion*.

postliminy [*leg.*]. Restoration of the *status quo*. L. *postliminium*, right to return home and resume one's privileges, from *limen, limin-*, threshold.

postmaster[1]. Orig. official in charge of the mounted posts (see *post[2]*), hence jobmaster, because of privilege of hiring out horses.

postmaster[2]. Used (from 16 cent.) at Merton College, Oxf. for scholar. ? From the poor scholars of John Wyllyat's foundation (1380) acting as servitors to the Masters (of Arts) and standing behind them at dinner.

post-obit. Promise to pay after death, L. *post obitum*, of some specified person. Cf. *obituary*.

postpone. L. *postponere*, from *ponere*, to place.

postprandial. Coined (? by Coleridge) from L. *prandium*, late breakfast, lunch, from **pram*, early, *edere*, to eat.

postscript. Shortened from L. *postscriptum*, written after.

postulant. From pres. part. of L. *postulare*, to demand, ? cogn. with *poscere*. Esp. one asking admission to holy orders. Cf. *postulate*, to request, thing requested (logic & math.).

posture. F., L. *positura*, from *ponere*, *posit-*, to place. Fig. sense of affectation, etc. is from the professional contortionist.

posy. In both senses, viz. short motto (on ring, knife), bunch of flowers, contr. of *poesy*. The second sense is connected with the language of flowers.

> And for youre poyesye these lettres v. ye take
> Of this name Maria, only for hir sake (Lydgate).

> A hundreth sundrie flowres bounde up in one small poesie (Gascoigne).

> A paltry ring
> That she did give me; whose posy [*old edd.* poesie] was
> For all the world like cutler's poetry
> Upon a knife: "Love me and leave me not"
> (*Merch. of Ven.* v. 1).

pot. Late AS. *pott*; cf. Du. LG. *pot*, ON. *pottr*, F. *pot*, OIt. *potto*, Sp. *pote*, MedL. *pottus*; also in Celt. langs. (from E.). Origin doubtful, but possibly a monkish witticism from L. *potus*, drink. From cooking use come to *keep the pot boiling*, whence *pot-boiler*, work done for a livelihood, *pot-shot*, for food, not for sport, *pot-luck* (cf. F. *la fortune du pot*). From drinking use come *pothouse, potboy, pot-valiant*, etc. A *pot-hunter* was orig. a parasite (see *chassepot*), later an unsportsmanlike sportsman (v.s.), and finally a seeker after athletic cups, etc., vulg. *pots*, or even scholarships and prizes. A *pot of money*, to *put the pot on*, are from racing slang, orig. from vessel which held stakes. *Pot(t)* paper is from watermark (cf. *foolscap*). For *potsherd* see *shard*. The earliest record for to *go to pot* suggests cooking (v.i.), but Udall may have been punning on *pot*, pit of hell, destruction, common in early Sc.

> The riche and welthie of his subjectes went dayly to the potte, and were chopped up (Udall, 1542).

potable.· F., L. *potabilis*, from *potare*, to drink.

potamic. Fluvial. From G. ποταμός, river.

potash. Earlier (17 cent.) *pot ashes*, from obs. Du. *pot-aaschen*, pot ashes, now *potasch*;

cf. F. *potasse*, It. *potassa*, Sp. *potasa*, Ger. *pottasche*, etc. "Latinized" as *potassium* by Davy (1807).

potation. OF., L. *potatio-n-*, from *potare*, to drink.

potato. Altered from Sp. *patata*, var. of *batata* (q.v.), the sweet potato, to which the name was first applied in E., its transference to the familiar tuber, first brought from Peru to Spain (c. 1580), being esp. E. *Potato-ring*, Ir. disk-ring of 18 cent., is mod. and inaccurate.

> One is almost induced to believe that the lower order of Londoners imagine that *taters*, as they constantly call them in their natural state, is a generical term, and that *pot* is a prefix which carries with it some specifick difference (Pegge).

poteen, potheen [*Ir.*]. Illicitly distilled whisky. Ir. *poitín*, little pot.

> The police at Frenchpark (Roscommon) captured recently upwards of 1000 gallons of "potheen" (*Daily Chron.* June 19, 1919).

potent. From pres. part. of L. *posse* (*potis esse*), to be able. Cf. *potency, potential*; also *potentate*, L. *potentatus*, power, in Late L. individual possessing power.

potheen. See *poteen*.

pother. Tumult. Earlier (17 cent.) also *powther, pudder*, mod. form app. influenced by *bother*. ? Cf. Ger. *polter*, in *poltergeist* (q.v.).

> The great gods
> That keep this dreadful pother [*early edds.* pudder, powther] o'er our heads (*Lear*, iii. 2).

pothook. In writing. See *hanger* (s.v. *hang*).

> *pasté*: a blurre, scraule, pothooke, or ill-favoured whim-whau, in writing (Cotg.).

potiche. Oriental jar. F. (neol.), from *pot*.

potion. F., L. *potio-n-*, from *potare*, to drink.

potlatch. Tribal feast of NAmer. Indians. Chinook *potlatsh*, gift.

potleg. Scrap iron used as bullets in Africa. ? For *pot leg*, ? or corrupt. of some native word.

pot-pourri. Orig. hotch-potch. Now mixture of scents, medley of tunes, etc. F., translating Sp. *olla podrida* (q.v.).

> *pot pourri*: a pot porride; a Spanish dish of many severall meates boyled, or stued together (Cotg.).

pott. Paper. See *pot*.

pottage. F. *potage*, from *pot*, pot. See *porridge*. *Mess of pottage* (Gen. xxv. 29–34) dates from Matthew's *Bible* (1537), though Coverd. has the phrase in another passage (*Prov.* xv. 17).

potter. Verb. Frequent. of dial. *pote*, to thrust, poke, AS. *potian*; cf. Du. *peuteren* "to thrust ones finger into a little hole" (Sewel), LG. *pöteren*, etc.; all app. from a Teut. word meaning small stick (cf. *poke*²).

pottle. OF. *potel*, dim of *pot*, pot.

potto. WAfr. lemur. Native name (Guinea).

potwaller [*hist.*]. Householder entitled to vote, as having a fire-place of his own, lit. *pot-boiler*, from AS. *weallan*, to boil. Now usu. *potwalloper*, from dial. *wallop*, to boil furiously, "gallop." Sometimes misunderstood and wrongly used by mod. speakers.

That was not a potwalloper's agitation, and he [J. Burns] urged those present when the strike was over not to celebrate it by a day's drinking
(*Standard*, Aug. 28, 1889).

pouch. F. *poche*, "a pocket, pouch, or poke" (Cotg.). See *poke*¹.

pouf. Padded head-dress, small round ottoman. F., from *pouffer*, to blow out, puff.

poult. Contracted form of *pullet* (q.v.). Hence *poulterer*, lengthened (cf. *caterer*, *upholsterer*) from earlier *poulter*, the latter surviving as surname.

poult-de-soie. ModF. form of *pou-de-soie*, paduasoy (q.v.).

poultice. Earlier (16 cent.) *pultes*, from L. *puls*, *pult-*, pulse, pottage. Perh. orig. the L. nom. pl. *pultes*, altered on words in *-ice*, *-ess*.

poultry. OF. *pouleterie*, from *pouletier*, poulter. Applied in ME. to the office of poulter, also to the fowl-run and its inmates (see *pullet*). Its connection with the trade of the poulterer persists in the *Poultry* (London and elsewhere).

His lordes sheepe, his neet, his dayerye,
His swyn, his hors, his stoor, and his pultrye [*var.* pulletrie],
Was hoolly in this reves governyng
(Chauc. A. 597).

pounce¹. Fine powder for drying up ink or tracing. F. *ponce*, now usu. *pierre-ponce*, L. *pumex*, *pumic-*, pumice (q.v.).

pounce². Verb. Orig. noun, hawk's claw. App. shortened from *pounson*, var. of *puncheon*¹ (q.v.), which is similarly shortened to *punch*¹. In falconry the heel-claw was the *talon* (q.v.), the others being called *pounces* (15 cent.). Cf. archaic *pounce*, to "punch" a pattern or perforation, whence archaic *pouncet-box* (for *pounced box*), a pomander, made of perforated metal. Verb to *pounce*, now usu. with *upon*, was orig. trans., to seize, clutch.

So muche pownsonynge of chisel to maken holes
(Chauc. I. 418).

My best pownsyd peece [of plate] (*Bury Wills*, 1502).

pound¹. Weight. AS. *pund*, L. *pondo*, abl. of OL. **pondos*, by-form of *pondus*, weight, in *libra pondo*, a pound in weight. A trace of its indeclinable origin survives in its unchanged pl., e.g. *five pound note*. Adopted by all Teut. langs., Du. *pond*, Ger. *pfund*, ON. *pund*, Goth. *pund*, Rom. langs. preserving *libra*. Later sense of money arises from the pound (weight) of silver being used as unit in large sums (see *sterling*). For *pound of flesh* see *Merch. of Ven.* iv. 1. *Pound-cake* contains a pound, or equal quantity, of each principal ingredient. Our abbreviations £ and *lb.* are due to the fact that medieval accounts were kept in L.; cf. *s.*, *d.*, *cwt.*, *dwt.*, etc.

And anum he sealde fif pund
(AS. *Gosp. Matt.* xxv. 15).

pound². Enclosure. AS. *pund*, only in compd. *pundfold*, cogn. with verb *pyndan*, to shut up, whence dial. *pind*, to impound, and the offic. *pinder*, so common as surname in north. Hence to *pound the field*, leave the rest far behind (in hunting). See also *pinfold*, *pond*.

pound³. To pulverize, etc. AS. *pūnian*, with excrescent *-d* as in *sound*², *astound*, "gownd." Cf. Du. *puin*, LG. *pün*, stone rubbish, etc.

Upon whom it shal falle, it shal togidre poune hym
(Wyc. *Matt.* xxi. 44).

poundage [*hist.*]. Tax levied on every *pound*¹ of merchandise.

pour. From 14 cent. Origin unknown. The orig. quality of the vowel cannot be determined, for, although the stock rime in 16–18 cents. is *flower*, *shower*, it is also found riming with *yore*, *door*, etc.

Winter invades the spring, and often pours
A chilling flood on summer's drooping flowers
(Cowper).

pourboire. F., in order to drink. Cf. Ger. *trinkgeld*.

pourparler. Usu. in pl. F. infin., to deliberate, from *pour*, L. *pro*, *parler*, VL. *parabolare*. Cf. *parley*, *parable*, *palaver*.

pourpoint [*hist.*]. Quilted doublet. F., p.p. of OF. *pourpoindre*, from *poindre*, to perforate, stitch, L. *pungere*, to prick. Cf. *counterpane*.

poussette [*dancing*]. F., from *pousser*, to push (q.v.).

pou sto. Basis of operations. From saying attributed to Archimedes—δός μοι ποῦ στῶ, καὶ κινῶ τὴν γῆν, give me where I may stand and I move the earth.

pout[1]. Fish (orig. frog), esp. in compd. *eelpout*, AS. *ǣlepūte*, app. from root indicating power of inflation (v.i.).

pout[2]. Verb. Cf. Sw. dial. *puta*, to be inflated. Ult. cogn. with *boudoir*. Cf. *pot*, lip, in many F. dials., Swiss F. (Geneva), *faire la potte*, to make a face.

poverty. OF. *povreté* (*pauvreté*), L. *paupertas, -tat-*, from *pauper*, poor.

powan. Sc. form of *pollan* (q.v.).

Powans, now placed on the market from Loch Lomond (*Daily Chron.* July 7, 1917).

powder[1]. Noun. F. *poudre*, OF. *poldre, polre*, L. *pulvis, pulver-*, cogn. with *pollen* and ult. with *pellere*, to drive. Often for *gunpowder*, e.g. *food for powder* (Ger. *kanonenfutter*), *not worth powder and shot, keep your powder dry, powder-monkey* (17 cent.).

powder[2] [*archaic*]. To rush impetuously, esp. of horseman. Associated with *powder*[1] (kicking up a dust), but rather from archaic *powder*, vehemence, impetuosity, which is prob. related to *pother*. See also *poltergeist*. Quot. below could readily be rendered by Ger. *kam den hügel herabgepoltert*.

Duke Weymar having got the castle came powdring down the hill upon us with all his forces
(Syd. Poyntz, 1624–36).

power. OF. *poer*, VL. *potēre*, for *posse* (*potis esse*), to be able. ModF. *pouvoir* has inserted *-v-* by analogy with *avoir, devoir, mouvoir*, etc. In sense of pol. state (*European powers*, etc.) from early 18 cent. Archaic sense of armed force, revived by Scott, dates from 13 cent. and survives in colloq. *a power of good*, etc. Mech. & math. uses (*horse-power*, etc.) are from 18 cent.

The powers that be are ordained of God
(*Rom.* xiii. 1).

powwow. NAmer. Ind. palaver or conference. Orig. sorcerer, medicine-man. Algonkin *powwaw, powah*. Cf. *caucus*. Quot. below refers to the Essex Quakers.

Heard & true yᵗ Turners daughter was distract in this quaking busines; sad are yᵉ fits at Coxall [Coggeshall] like the pow wowing among the Indies
(Josselin's *Diary*, 1656).

pox. See *pock*.

Three moneths before this time, the small pockes were rife here (Purch.).

po(u)zzolana. Volcanic ash. It. (sc. *terra*), from *Pozzuoli*, near Naples.

praam, pram. Flat-bottomed boat. Du.; cf. LG. *prame*, MHG. *prām* (*prahme*), ON. *prāmr*, all from OSlav. (cf. Pol. *pram*) and ult. cogn. with *fare, ferry*. A Baltic word.

practice. From verb to *practise* (the differentiated spelling is artificial), OF. *practiser*, for *pratiquer, practiquer* (whence archaic E. *practic*), Late L. *practicare*, from *practicus*, G. πρακτικός, concerned with action, from πράττειν, to do. With senses of *practice* and its derivatives cf. those of the opposite *theory*. Practitioner, now usu. of medicine (cf. doctor's *practice*), is lengthened from earlier *practician*, OF. *practicien* (*praticien*). Practice (arith.) is for *practica Italica*, Italian methods.

If you want any information upon points of practical politics (*Vivian Grey*, ii. 8).

prad [*archaic slang*]. Horse. Du. *paard*, horse. See *palfrey*.

It would never do to go to the wars on a ricketty prad (*Ingoldsby*).

prado. Public walk. Sp., meadow, L. *pratum*, spec. public park of Madrid.

prae-. L., before. See also *pre-*.

praemunire, statute of [*hist.*]. From *praemunire facias*, cause to warn, init. words of writ, the verb being used in MedL. sense which had become confused with that of *praemonēre*. For similar confusion cf. *muniment*.

praenomen. L., see *agnomen*.

praepostor, prepostor. Monitor at some public schools. For L. *praepositor*, agent. noun from *praeponere, praeposit-*, to appoint over, depute. But the sense is rather that of *praepositus* (cf. *prefect*).

praetor. Restored spelling of ME. & OF. *pretour*, L. *praetor-em*, for **prae-itor*, foregoer. Hence the *Pretorian guard*, orig. *cohors praetoria*, attached to the praetor, Roman military commander, later privileged body-guard of Emperor, which took to appointing fresh Emperors at its will. The *praetorium* (*Mark*, xv. 16) was the offic. residence of the Roman governor.

The Pretorians of the Red Guard
(*Daily Chron.* June 22, 1918).

pragmatic. F. *pragmatique*, L., G. πραγματικός, versed in business, from πρᾶγμα, πραγματ-, deed, act, from πράττειν, to do. For depreciatory sense cf. *officious, dogmatic*. *Pragmatism*, philosophy of practical consequences, was coined (1898) by W. James.

The next day I began to be very pragmatical [i.e. busily occupied] (Evelyn).

prahu. Malay vessel. Malay *parāhū*; cf. Port. *parao*, Du. *prauw*, F. *prao*, whence our earlier forms *proa, prow*.

prairie. F., meadow, applied by F. travellers to the plains of NAmer. (cf. *veldt*), VL. **prateria*, from *pratum*, meadow; cf. It. *prateria*, Sp. *pradería*.

praise. OF. *preisier* (*priser*, to value), Late L. *pretiare*, from *pretium*, price, value. Orig. Church word, replacing AS. *herian*, but used also in ME. in etym. sense, to appraise. See *prize*[1]. Noun is from verb.

Prakrit [*ling.*]. Inclusive name for (esp. ancient) vernaculars of Northern and Central India allied to Sanskrit. Sanskrit *prākṛta*, unrefined, as opposed to *saṇskṛta*, refined.

pram[1]. See *praam*.

pram[2]. Mod. for *perambulator*.

prance. First in Chauc. ? OF. *paravancier*, intens. of *avancier*, to advance. This suits first record (v.i.), and would automatically give AF. *p(a)rauncer*; cf. *proffer*, *prune*[2, 3], *plush*, also ME. *aunter* for *adventure*, *paraunter* for *peradventure*.

> Though I praunce al beforn
> First in the trais, ful fat and newe shorn,
> Yit am I but an hors (Chauc. *Troilus*, i. 221).

prandial. See *postprandial*.

prank[1]. Trick, orig. of spiteful nature. A 16 cent. word of unknown origin. ? Altered in some way from dial. *prat*, AS. *prætt* (see *pretty*), which is exactly synon. This is found in 15–16 cents., but disappears, exc. in Sc., after appearance of *prank*. Or it may come from *prank*[2] by analogy with the double sense of *trick*.

prank[2]. To decorate, dress up. ? Cf. Du. *pronk*, Ger. *prunk*, show, ornament, MLG. *prank*, display, Ger. *prangen*, to show off, etc. See *prink*.

mit kleidern prangen: to prank up your self (Ludw.).

prate. Du. *praten*, found also in LG., MHG., and the Scand. langs. Perh. of imit. formation.

pratincole. Bird. ModL. *pratincola*, coined (1756) by Kramer from L. *pratum*, meadow, *incola*, inhabitant.

pratique. Freedom from quarantine. F., intercourse, L. *practica*. See *practice*. In 17 cent. spelt *prattick*.

prattle. Frequent. of *prate*.

praty [*Ir.*]. Potato. Ir. *práta* or (Meath and Ulster) *preáta*, for *patata*, with substitution of -*r*- for -*t*- as in many Gael. words.

pravity. L. *pravitas*. See *deprave*.

prawn. ME. *prayne*, *prane*. Origin unknown.

praxis. G. πρᾶξις, from πράττειν, to do.

pray. ME. also *prey*, OF. *preier* (*prier*), Late L. *precare*, for *precari*, from *prex*, *prec*-,

prayer; cogn. with Ger. *fragen*, to ask. *Prayer* is OF. *preiere* (*prière*), VL. **precaria*. With imper. *pray*, for *I pray you*, cf. *please*. See also *prithee*.

pre-. L. *prae-*, *pre-*, before, or F. *pré-*, from L.

preach. F. *prêcher*, L. *praedicare*, from *dicare*, to proclaim. Early Church word widely adopted, e.g. It. *predicare*, Sp. *predicar*; Du. Ger. *predigen*, ON. *prēdika*, etc. With ironic *preachify* (18 cent.) cf. *speechify*.

preamble. F. *préambule*, MedL. *praeambulum*, neut. of *praeambulus*, going before, from *ambulare*.

This is a long preamble of a tale (Chauc. D. 831).

prebend. F. *prébende*, MedL. *praebenda*, neut. pl., pittance, lit. things to be supplied, from *praebēre*, to offer, for *praehibēre*, from *habēre*, to have. In OF. *provende* is usual (see *provender* and cf. *provost*). A *prebendary* was orig. a canon in receipt of a fixed stipend.

precarious. From L. *precarius*, "that by prayer, instance, and intreatie is graunted to one to use and enjoye so long as hee pleaseth the partie and no longer" (Coop.), from *prex*, *prec*-, prayer.

precede. F. *précéder*, L. *praecedere*, to go before. *Precedence*, in to *take precedence*, survives from the elaborate ceremonial of early times, synon. F. *préséance* (v.i.) suggesting that it may also represent *presidence*. *Precedent* (noun) occurs first (15 cent.) in leg. sense of earlier case taken as parallel or guidance; cf. *unprecedented*.

preseance: precedence, or precedencie; a first, or former place, ranke, seat; a sitting, or going, before others (Cotg.).

precentor. Late L. *praecentor*, from *praecinere*, *praecent*-, from *canere*, to sing.

precept. L. *praeceptum*, from *praecipere*, *praecept*-, to take before, order, from *capere*, to take. Cf. *preceptor*, a word of the *academy*, *seminary* type, almost obs. exc. in connection with the examining body called the *College of Preceptors*; also the hist. *preceptory*, branch community of Templars, MedL. *praeceptoria*.

precession. Of the equinoxes. Late L. *praecessio-n-*, from *praecedere*, *praecess-*, to precede; used by Copernicus (c. 1530) for G. μετάπτωσις (Ptolemy).

précieuse. See *precious*.

precinct. MedL. *praecinctum*, enclosure, lit. girt in front, from *cingere*, *cinct*-, to gird. *Procinct*, *purcinct*, from OF. forms from L. *pro-*, were in earlier use.

preciosity. Daintily affected style. See *precious*.

precious. F. *précieux*, L. *pretiosus*, from *pretium*, price, value. Association with literary daintiness, app. due to Saintsbury (1880), is for F. *précieux*, adopted (1640–50) as title by frequenters of refined literary circles in Paris. But Chauc. (v.i.) uses it in somewhat similar sense. Intens. use, e.g. *precious rascal*, is as old as Lydgate. Corresponding adv. use was app. popularized by Dickens.

I wol persevere, I nam nat precius (Chauc. D. 148).

Mr Chuckster remarked that he wished that he might be blessed if he could make out whether he [Kit] was "precious raw" or "precious deep"
(*Old Cur. Shop*, ch. xx.).

precipice. F. *précipice*, L. *praecipitium*, from *praeceps, praecipit-*, from *caput*, head; cf. *headlong, head-first*. Hence *precipitate* (chem.), substance thrown down from solution, as opposed to *sediment*, deposited from suspension.

précis. F., substantive use of adj. *précis*, precise (q.v.).

precise. F. *précis*, L. *praecisus*, from *praecidere, praecis-*, to cut off (in front), shorten, make exact, from *caedere*, to cut. Oldest is adv. *precisely* (15 cent.). Hence *precisian* (16 cent.), puritan, coined on *Christian*.

preclude. L. *praecludere*, to shut off, from *claudere*, to shut.

precocious. Orig. (Sir T. Browne) of plants. From L. *praecox, praecoc-*, early ripe, from *coquere*, to boil, cook. Cf. Ger. *frühreif* and see *apricot*.

preconize. To proclaim, summon, etc. F. *préconiser*, MedL. *praeconizare*, from *praeco-n-*, public crier.

precursor. L., from *praecurrere, -curs-*, to run before.

predatory. L. *praedatorius*, from *praedari*, to plunder, from *praeda*, booty, prey.

predecessor. F. *prédécesseur*, Late L. *praedecessor-em*, from *prae* and *decessor*, one who goes away, deceases; but often used as equivalent of *precessor, antecessor*.

predestination. F. *prédestination*, Late L. *praedestinatio-n-*, fore-ordaining. First used in theol. sense by Augustine and "popularized" by Calvin.

predial. Agrarian. MedL. *praedialis*, from *praedium*, farm, from *praes, praed-*, pledge, security.

predicament. F. *prédicament*, Late L. *prae-dicamentum* (see *predicate*), used to render Aristotle's κατηγορία, category of predications. Mod. sense is narrowed from gen. sense of class, condition.

Irish ladies of strict virtue, and many northern lasses of the same predicament (*Tom Jones*).

predicate. Late L. *praedicatum*, what is asserted, from *praedicare*, to proclaim. Much older is *predication* (Chauc.), proclaiming, preaching. Cf. *preach*.

predict. L. *praedicere, praedict-*, to say before; cf. F. *prédire*.

predikant. Du., Protestant minister, esp. in SAfr. See *preach*.

predilection. F. *prédilection*; cf. MedL. *praediligere*, to prefer, from *diligere, dilect-*, to love. See *diligent*.

pre-emption. Coined (c. 1600) from *pre-* and *emption* (q.v.).

preen. Thinned form of *prune*[3] (q.v.), partly due to archaic *preen*, pin, etc. (AS. *prēon*, cogn. with Du. *priem*, bodkin, Ger. *pfriem*, awl), with allusion to action of bird's beak; cf. similar use of F. *piquer*, to pique (q.v.). Falconry distinguished the three words (v.i.).

Youre hawke proynith and not pikith and she prenith not bot whan she begynnith at hir leggys
(*Book of St Albans*, 1486).

preface. F. *préface*, L. *praefatio*, fore-speaking, from *fari, fat-*, to speak. Cf. *prologue*.

prefect. Restored spelling of ME. *prefet*, F. *préfet*, L. *praefectus*, high official, from *praeficere, praefect-*, to set over, from *facere*, to make, appoint; cf. *prelate*. Often used to render F. *préfet* (*de département, de police*). Public school sense is 19 cent.

prefer. F. *préférer*, from L. *praeferre*, to bear before. Oldest sense to forward, promote, etc., as in *preferment*.

pregnable. Cf. ME. *prenable*, from OF. But in mod. use a back-formation from *impregnable*.

pregnant. L. *praegnans, praegnant-*, from *prae-* and a second element cogn. with L. *gnatus* (*natus*), born. In fig. senses, e.g. *pregnant sentence* (*example*), influenced by obs. *pregnant*, cogent, pithy, OF. *preignant*, pres. part. of *preindre*, to press, L. *premere* (see *print*).

And that was him a preignant argument
(Chauc. *Troil*. iv. 1179).

raisons pregnantes: plaine, apparent, important, or pressing reasons (Cotg.).

prehensile. F. *préhensile* (Buffon), from L. *prehendere*, *-hens-*, to seize, second element cogn. with G. χανδάνειν, to hold, and ult. with *get*.

prehistoric. Coined (c. 1850) by D. Wilson.

prejudice. F. *préjudice*, harm, injury, the oldest sense (13 cent.) in E., as still in *prejudicial*, *without prejudice*. Current sense, represented in F. by *préjugé*, is restored on L. *praejudicium*, fore-judgment.

prelate. F. *prélat*, L. *praelatus*, p.p. of *prae-ferre*, to put before, prefer; cf. It. *prelato*, Sp. *prelado*. Orig. included abbot, prior, etc.

prelection. L. *praelectio-n-*, reading before, public speech, from *legere*, *lect-*, to read. Cf. *prelector*, *praelector*, reader, lecturer (Oxf. & Camb.).

preliminary. F. *préliminaire*, coined from L. *limen*, *limin-*, threshold.

prelude. F. *prélude*, Late L. *praeludium*, from *ludere*, to play.

premature. L. *praematurus*, from *maturus*, ripe. Cf. *precocious*.

premier. F., L. *primarius*, from *primus*, first. In current sense (early 18 cent.) short for earlier *premier minister*, F. *premier ministre*, used by Evelyn of Sunderland.

premise, premiss. F. *prémisse* (OF. *premesse*), MedL. *praemissa* (sc. *propositio*), from *praemittere*, to send in front. Orig. a term in logic (Chauc.), now usu. spelt *premisses*. Later sense, with differentiated spelling *premises*, arises from use of the word in leg. conveyances of property to avoid re-peating conditions already laid down or items already enumerated; cf. *aforesaid*. Verb to *premise* is from noun.

Les articles et les premesses avant nomez (Procl. of Earl of Glouc. 1259).

Wherfore, the premeses [aforesaid grievances] con-sidred, I desire you, and in the Kings name com-mand you... (Plumpton Let. 1502).

premium. L. *praemium*, booty, reward, from *prae* and *emere*, to buy, obtain. In in-surance sense adapted from It. *premio*. Orig. sense in to *put a premium on*.

premorse [biol.]. L. *praemorsus*, bitten off (in front).

prentice. Aphet. for *apprentice* (q.v.); cf. *prentice hand*.

prep [school slang]. For *preparation*, *pre-paratory*. Cf. *rep*[3].

prepare. F. *préparer*, L. *praeparare*, from *parare*, to make ready (see *pare*). Adv. use of *preparatory* (*to*) is in Evelyn.

prepense. Altered from earlier *purpense*, OF. *pourpensé*. Esp. in *malice prepense*, malice aforethought. For loss of ending cf. *signal* (adj.), *defile*[2], *trove*, etc. *Prepensed*, *pur-pensed* are also found.

preponderate. From L. *praeponderare*, from *pondus*, *ponder-*, weight.

preposition. F. *préposition*, L. *praepositio-n-*, from *praeponere*, *-posit-*, to put before, adopted as rendering of G. πρόθεσις.

prepostor. See *praepostor*.

prepossess. Coined (c. 1600) from *possess*, in archaic sense of taking hold of, occupying.

preposterous. From L. *praeposterus*, lit. be-fore behind; cf. *hindside before*, *cart before the horse*, *topsy-turvy*.

When nature's order doth reverse, and change Preposterously into disorder strange (Sylv. i. 2).

pre-Raphaelite. Title of the "brotherhood" formed (c. 1848) by group of E. painters (Holman Hunt, Millais, Rossetti, etc.), who, encouraged by Ruskin, aimed at re-viving the spirit which distinguished art before *Raphael*, It. *Raffaello* (†1520). *Blackwood* (July, 1850) alludes to their "mountebank proceedings" (cf. *gallipot*).

prerogative. F. *prérogative*, L. *praerogativa* (sc. *tribus*, *centuria*), having the right to vote (lit. be asked) first, from *praerogare*. In the *royal prerogative*, referred to in 13 cent., orig. connection of *rogare*, to ask, with *regere*, to rule, is still traceable.

presage. F. *présage*, L. *praesagium*, from *praesagire*, to forebode, from *sagire*, to perceive.

Presbyterian. From c. 1640 as name of Sc. church governed by "elders," lit. rendering of G. πρεσβύτερος, compar. of πρέσβυς, old man (see *priest*). This was used in NT. of a member of the Sanhedrin, and later of an "elder" of the apostolic Church. In *Vulg. senior* is usual in this sense, and is rendered by Wyc. *elder*, *elder man*, *senior*, *priest* (q.v.). Cf. F. *presbytère*, parsonage, and E. *presbytery*, in various senses.

For his religion it was fit To match his learning and his wit: 'Twas Presbyterian true blue (Hudibras, i. i. 191).

prescience. F., L. *praescientia*, fore-know-ledge. See *science*.

prescribe. L. *praescribere*, to write before, ordain. Replaced earlier *prescrive*, from OF. *Prescription*, limitation (positive or negative), is L. *praescriptio-n-*, in same sense.

present. Adj. F. *présent*, L. *praesens, praesent-*, pres. part. of *praeesse*, to be before, be at hand; cf. *a very present help* (*Ps.* xlvi. I). Hence *presence*, F. *présence*, L. *praesentia*, much used formerly of the being present of a royal or important person, whence sense of bearing, etc. (*fine presence*). Adj. is used as noun in *the present* (cf. *the past*), and archaic *these presents*, OF. *ces présentes* (sc. *lettres*). *Present*, gift, F. *présent*, comes from OF. *en present*, in the presence of (v.i.); cf. L. *praesentare*, to place before, exhibit, whence, through F. *présenter*, gen. senses of verb to *present*. *Presently* formerly meant at once (cf. *anon, by and by*).

Quant que il a tot lor met em present
(*Alexandre*, 12 cent.).

presentiment. OF. (*pressentiment*), "a providence, or fore-feeling" (Cotg.), from L. *praesentire*, to feel before.

preserve. F. *préserver*, Late L. *praeservare*, from *servare*, to protect. Some E. senses represent rather those of F. *conserver*.

preside. F. *présider*, L. *praesidēre*, from *sedēre*, to sit. *President* was formerly used of governor of province, dependency, etc., whence the Indian *Presidencies*. In sense of elective head of republic first used in US., the title app. growing out of that of *president* of the congresses of the various States (from 1774).

presidio. Sp., fort, settlement (esp. in Sp. Amer.), L. *praesidium*, from *praesidēre*, to sit before, protect (v.s.).

press¹. To squeeze, etc. F. *presser*, L. *pressare*, frequent. of *premere, press-*, to press. Hence noun *press*, F. *presse*, receptacle for packing things flat (*linen press*), instrument for squeezing (*winepress*), and, from early 16 cent., instrument for printing; also library bookcase (whence *press-mark*). *Liberty of the press* (1680) is already indicated in *Areopagitica* (1644). *In the press* was formerly *under the press*, F. *sous la presse*. A *pressman* was orig. a printer. *At high pressure* is a steam metaphor.

battitore: a printers presseman (Flor.).

press². As in *press-gang* (17 cent.). Back-formation, partly due to association with *press¹*, from earlier *prest*, OF. (*prêt*), loan, from *prester* (*prêter*), L. *praestare*, to warrant, etc. This is from *praes*, security (see *predial*), for *prae vas*, fore pledge, and distinct from *praestare*, to stand in front.

Prest was used in 15 cent. of earnest-money paid to soldier or sailor on enlistment (cf. to *take the shilling*) and in 16 cent. of the enlistment itself, whence verb *imprest, impress*, to enlist, idea of force gradually coming in with altered form. Hence fig. to *press into the service*.

Shyppys prested for the King in the west countrey
(*NED.* 1513).

soldato: prest with paie as soldiers are (Flor.).

Prester John [*hist.*]. Obs. name for ruler of Abyssinia. OF. *prestre Jean* (see *priest*).

prestidigitator. F. *prestidigitateur*, coined (c. 1830), after L. *praestigiator*, juggler (see *prestige*), by a conjuror named J. de Rovère, from It. *presto* (q.v.) and L. *digitus*, finger. Cf. *phantasmagoria*.

prestige. F., magic, from L. *praestigia*, usu. in pl. *praestigiae*. By dissim. for *praestrigiae*, from *praestringere*, to bind before, blindfold. Current sense in F. & E. is 19 cent.

praestigiae: deceytes; delusions; legierdemaine; sleight conveyances that juglers use (Coop.).

presto. It., quick, L. *praestus*, from *praesto*, at hand, ? for *prae situ* (cf. *on the spot*). Introduced in 16 cent. conjurors' patter.

presume. F. *présumer*, L. *praesumere*, to take before, anticipate, in Late L. to take for granted, dare, whence depreciatory senses. The *heir presumptive* is presumed to be heir if the *heir apparent* is not available.

pretend. F. *prétendre*, to lay claim, L. *praetendere*, to hold before, put forward. This, the oldest sense in E., is preserved in *pretentious, pretension, Pretender*. Current sense, from idea of putting forward false claim, is latest, and is not found in F. It seems to have been affected by *pretext*.

preterite [*gram.*]. F. *prétérit*, L. *praeteritus*, from *praeterire*, to go past.

pretermit. L. *praetermittere*, to omit, lit. to let go past.

preternatural. MedL. *praeternaturalis*, coined, ? by Albertus Magnus (13 cent.), from L. *praeter naturam*, beyond nature.

pretext. F. *prétexte*, L. *praetextum*, from *praetexere*, to weave in front. Cf. fig. sense of *cloak, palliate*.

pretorian. See *praetor*.

pretty. AS. *prættig*, from *prætt*, trick, craft; cf. obs. Du. *pretig, pertig*, funny, roguish, etc. Sense-development, as in the case of most adjs. which can be applied to persons (*nice, proud, quaint*), is curious. With various shades of meaning of *pretty fellow* cf. those of *fine fellow*. *Pretty and* was formerly used like *nice and*. With *pretty hopeless* cf. *jolly miserable, precious rotten*, etc., and see *gey*.

preux chevalier. Nom. of OF. *preu, prou*, Late L. *prodis*, from first element of *prodesse*, to be of value. *Prew, prow*, were once common E. words, though now surviving only as surnames. See also *proud, prude*.

prevail. From OF. tonic stem (*prevail-*) of *prévaloir*, L. *praevalēre*, from *valēre*, to be worth, strong.

prevaricate. From L. *praevaricare*, to practise collusion, lit. to walk crookedly, from *varicare*, to straddle, from *varus*, bent, knock-kneed. Cf. fig. sense of to *shuffle*.

prevenient. Esp. in theol. *prevenient* (antecedent) *grace*. From pres. part. of L. *praevenire*, to come before.

prevent. From L. *praevenire, -vent-*, to come before, anticipate, guard against. Etym. sense in to *prevent one's every wish*. Cf. F. *prévenir*, to warn, predispose. Current sense is latest. *Preventive*, applied to branch of Coast Guard dealing with smugglers, is 19 cent.

Prevent us, O Lord, in all our doings
           (*Communion Service*).
They were called custom-house officers then;
There were no such things as "preventive men"
                     (*Ingoldsby*).

previous. From L. *praevius*, from *prae* and *via*, way; cf. *pervious*. The *previous question* (Burnet) is put to shut out the *main question*. *A little previous*, for premature, is US. slang.

previse. From L. *praevidēre, praevis-*, to foresee.

prey. OF. *preie* (*proie*), L. *praeda*, booty, a common sense of *prey* in ME. Cf. *predatory*.

priapism [*med.*]. L., G. πριαπισμός, from Πρίαπος, god of procreation.

price. OF. *pris* (*prix*), L. *pretium*, reward, value (see *praise*); cf. It. *prezzo*, Sp. *precio*. Correct E. form is *prize*¹ (q.v.); for change of consonant cf. *mice, dice*. ME. senses were much wider than mod., some of them having been absorbed by *praise*. *Priceless*, now a favourite schoolboy word, is first in Shaks. Maxim in quot. below, aimed at Walpole and often erron. attributed to him, evidently refers to his supposed or expressed opinion.

It is an old maxim, that every man has his price
    (Sir W. Wyndham, in H. of C., Mar. 13, 1734).

prick. AS. *prica, pricca*, point, dot; cf. Du. LG. *prik*, prickle, dot, etc. Oldest sense appears to be mark made with sharp point, and the word was used in many senses now replaced by *point, dot*; cf. *prick-song*, for *pricked-song*, marked with dots. Verb is AS. *prician*, from noun, and ME. has a form *pritch* (cf. *pick, pitch*). *Prick-eared* was applied to the Puritans, whose short hair made their ears prominent.

It is hard to thee for to kyke agens the pricke
[*Vulg.* contra stimulum calcitrare]
                 (Wyc. *Acts*, ix. 5).
Alle the dayes of poure men been wikke;
Be war therfore, er thou come to that prikke
                (Chauc. B. 118).
At this the town of Mansoul began to prick up its ears (Bunyan).

pricket [*ven.*]. See *brocket*.

prickle. AS. *pricel*, for *pricels*, instrumental noun from *prician* (v.s.), later treated as dim. *Prickly pear* was earlier *prick-pear* (Richard Hawkins), *prickle-pear* (Capt. John Smith).

pride. AS. *prȳto*, app. from *proud*; cf. ON. *prȳthi*, from *prūthr*, gallant, fine. But the formation by umlaut of an abstract noun from a F. loan-word is abnormal and casts some doubt on the origin of *proud* (q.v.). *Pride of place* is from falconry, *place* being used of height attained.

A falcon towering in her pride of place
                   (*Macb.* ii. 4).

prie-Dieu. F., pray-God.

priest. AS. *prēost*, app. shortened from L. *presbyter* (see *Presbyterian*); cf. OF. *prestre* (*prêtre*), It. *prete*, Sp. *preste*, also Du. Ger. *priester*. Assumed also in the converted countries the sense of L. *sacerdos*, and, like *sacerdotal*, has been associated since the Reformation esp. with Rome; hence depreciatory *priestcraft, priest-ridden*.

prig. In earliest (16 cent.) sense of thief a cant word. In usu. mod. sense perh. partly a violent shortening of *precisian* (q.v.), with which it is used interchangeably in 17–18 cents. Cf. the derivations I have suggested for *fag, fug*. But 17 cent. *prig*, spruce, may belong to *prick*, in obs. sense of attiring carefully (with pins, bodkins, etc.); cf. sense-hist. of *smug*.

These dronken tynckers, called also prygges, be beastly people (Harman's *Caveat*, 1567).

prim. Recorded c. 1700 as verb, to assume a formal or demure look, adj., and noun, "a silly, empty starcht fellow" (*Dict. Cant. Crew*). There is also an obs. 16 cent. *prim*, pretty girl, etc. App. OF. *prim*, first, also thin, sharp, etc., var. of *prin* (as in *prin-temps*), L. *primus*.

prime: thinne, slender, exile, small; whence, *cheveux primes*, smooth, or delicate haire (Cotg.).

prima donna. It., first lady. Cf. *leading lady* (theat.).

prima facie. L., at first sight, abl. of *facies*, face. Recorded 1420.

primage [*naut.*]. Percentage addition to freight. ModL. *primagium*. Analogy of *keelage*, *bottomry*, suggests derivation from It. *primo*, formerly used for keel, *legno*, timber, being understood. See *prime³*.

primary. F. *primaire*, L. *primarius*, from *primus*, first. Has replaced *prime¹* in some senses. *Primary school*, after F. *école pri-maire*, is early 19 cent.

primate. F. *primat*, Late L. *primas*, *primat-*, chief, from *primus*, first. Current sense is earliest (c. 1200), but it is also used in ME. for chief, chief priest. Cf. *primates*, adopted by Linnaeus for highest order of mammals.

This preost was primat in that lond of Madyan (Trev. ii. 325).

prime¹. Noun. AS. *prīm*, L. *prima* (sc. *hora*), one of the canonical hours, later used for early part of the day. In other substantive senses, e.g. *prime of life*, it represents the F. form, fem. of OF. *prin*, L. *primus*, as in *prin-temps*. *Primus* is superl. from OL. *pri*, before, cogn. with *prae*.

prime². Adj. F. (v.s.), used in a few phrases only, in which it is usu. a late borrow-ing from L. *primus* rather than an OF. fem. As descriptive of goods it is perh. rather *prime¹* used attributively; cf. similar use of *choice*, *prize*, etc. *Prime minister* (17 cent.) renders F. *premier ministre*. Here belong *prime cost* (*motive*, *number*, etc.).

prime³. To fill up, e.g. with knowledge or drink. Earliest sense (Douglas, 1513) to load (a ship), which points to connection with *primage* (q.v.). The fig. senses may belong partly to *prime⁵*.

prime⁴. To give first coat of paint. Aphet. for synon. F. *imprimer*, lit. to imprint.

prime⁵. Of guns. Goes with dial. *prime*, to prune trees, both app. representing *prine* for *proin* (v.i.); cf. *rile* for *roil* and see *prune²*. The orig. operation perh. con-sisted in clearing the touch-hole.

Rawlins having proined the tuch-hole, James Roe gave fire to one of the peeces (Purch. vi. 168).

Thirty muskets ready laden and pruned...sixty powder-pots matched and pruned...eight pieces of ordnance ready pruned (*ib.* x. 337).

primer. Prayer-book for laity, elementary book for children (Chauc.). MedL. *pri-marius*, though reason for use in first sense is obscure. With name of type cf. *brevier*, *pica*.

primero. Card game. Altered from Sp. *primera*, fem. of *primero*, first, L. *pri-marius*.

primeur. F., fruit, etc. out of season, from *prime*, first. Often used in journalism of first use of exclusive news.

primeval. From L. *primaevus*, from *primus*, first, *aevum*, age.

primitive. F. *primitif*, L. *primitivus*, from *primus*, first. In sense of pre-Renaissance painter late 19 cent. after F. The *Primitive Methodists* seceded from the main body in 1810.

primogeniture. F. *primogéniture*, MedL. *primogenitura*, after Late L. *primogenitus*, born first, from *gignere*, *genit-*, to bear, beget.

primordial. Late L. *primordialis*, from *primordium*, from *primus*, first, *ordiri*, to begin.

primrose. Altered, by association with *rose*, from ME. & OF. *primerole*, from MedL. *primula*, from *primus*, first. Cf. OF. *primerose*, MedL. *prima rosa*. Though not recorded by *NED.* till 15 cent., *primrose* was a surname in 13 cent. As in most flower-names its orig. application is un-certain. For corrupt. cf. *rosemary*. For *primrose path* see *Haml.* i. 3, *Macb.* ii. 3. *Primrose day* commemorates Benjamin Disraeli, Earl of Beaconsfield († Apr. 19, 1881), who was trad. fond of the flower.

primula. MedL. (v.s.). Hence Ger. *primel*.

primum mobile. MedL. astron. term, now sometimes used for *prime mover* (*factor*).

primus. L., first, cogn. with *prae*, before. Cf. *prior*.

prince. F., L. *princeps*, *princip-*, first, chief, from *primus*, first, *capere*, to take; cf. It. *principe*, Sp. *príncipe*. Cf. Ger. *fürst*, prince, lit. first. Application to Satan in *prince of darkness* (*the air*, *the world*, etc.) is by con-trast with *Prince of peace*. The *Black Prince* is first called by that name by 16 cent. chroniclers.

princeps. L. (v.s.). Esp. in *editio princeps*, *facile princeps*.

principal. F., L. *principalis*, from *princeps*, *princip-* (v.s.). For financ. sense, for earlier *principal sum* (debt), cf. *capital*[3]. *Principality*, like *power*, is also used, by a mystical interpretation of the Pauline Epistles, of one of the nine orders of angels or supernatural forces.

Quoniam non est nobis collectatio adversus carnem et sanguinem; sed adversus principes et potestates (*Vulg. Eph.* vi. 12).

principia. L., beginnings, pl. of *principium* (v.i.).

principle. Altered from F. *principe*, L. *principium*, origin, etc., from *princeps, princip-* (see *prince*). Cf. *participle, syllable.*

prink. To adorn. Thinned form of *prank*[2], associated with obs. *prick*, with idea of pins and bodkins.

Prinkipo [*hist.*]. Small island in Sea of Marmora where the Entente Powers offered to meet the Bolshevist leaders. It has become proverbial for an undignified climb-down.

He was unhesitating in repelling the idea that the Prime Minister was proposing a return to Prinkipo (*Daily Chron.* Nov. 11, 1919).

print. ME. also *prente, preinte*, OF. *preinte*, p.p. fem. of *preindre, priembre*, L. *premere*, to press. Prob. often aphet. for *imprint*, F. *empreinte*. Used in ME. of any stamp or impress, later typ. sense perh. representing obs. Du. *printe* (*prent*), from F. *Printing-house* survives only in *Printing-House Square*, site of Times' office.

preynt: effigies, impressio (*Prompt. Parv.*).

prior. Noun. Orig. second in command under abbot. Late AS. *prior*, L., compar. from OL. *pri*, before, cogn. with *prae*. Hence *priory*, orig. offshoot of abbey. As adj. it is mod. loan from L. With *a priori* cf. *a posteriori*.

Priscian. Roman grammarian (6 cent.). Hence archaic to *break Priscian's head*, violate laws of grammar.

Some free from rhyme or reason, rule or check, Break Priscian's head and Pegasus's neck (*Dunciad*, iii. 162).

prise. See *prize*[3].

prism. Late L., G. πρίσμα, piece sawn off, from πρίζειν, to saw.

prison. F., L. *prensio-n-*, from *prendere, prehendere*, to seize; cf. It. *prigione*, Sp. *prisión*. For *prisoner's base* see *base-ball*.

pristine. L. *pristinus*, cogn. with *priscus, prior*.

prithee [*archaic*]. For earlier *preythe*, (I) *pray thee*.

private. L. *privatus*, lit. bereaved, set apart, from *privare*, to deprive, from *privus*,

single, peculiar; cf. *privation*. *Privatus* is in gen. contrast with *publicus, communis*. *Private* (*soldier*) meant orig. volunteer without recognized rank, free lance; cf. *privateer* (17 cent.), coined, after *buccaneer, volunteer*, for earlier *private man of war* (Pepys, Sep. 26, 1668). See quot. s.v. *purchase*. See also *privy*.

Ludlow mentions it as an example of the growing insolence of the Parliamentary army, that the men would no longer be called "common," but "private" soldiers (*NED.*).

privet. From 16 cent. Earlier called also *prim, print, privie, prinne-print* or *privet-print*. Origin unknown, but current form no doubt due to *private*, the plant's only use being to furnish a good screen.

Set privie or prim (Tusser).

privilege. F. *privilège*, L. *privilegium*, private law, from *lex, leg-*, law; cf. *to be a law to oneself.*

This trouble [a strike] has been fomented because in the engineering trade a privileged class of young men has been created (J. Hodge, July 25, 1918).

privy. F. *privé*, L. *privatus*, private. *Privy council* dates from 1300; cf. *privy purse* (*seal*), the latter distinguished from the *great seal*. With *privy*, latrine, cf. synon. OF. *privaise*.

prize[1]. Reward. OF. *pris* (*prix*). See *price*, of which *prize* is a doublet. Hence verb to *prize*. *Prize-fight*, orig. with swords, is 17 cent., and *prize*, contest (for a prize) is in Shaks. (*Merch. of Ven.* iii. 2). With *prize-pig*, etc., cf. *pris* [Higden, *optimus*] *salmon* (Trev. ii. 79).

prize[2]. Capture. F. *prise*, p.p. fem. of *prendre*, to take, L. *prendere, prehendere*.

de bonne prise: good, or lawfull prize (Cotg.).

prize[3]. To force up. From noun *prise*, lever, lit. hold, ident. with *prize*[2]. Cf. F. *donner prise*, to give a hold, leverage.

pro. Short for *professional*.

pro-. L. *pro*, before, or cogn. G. πρό. Becomes *prod-* before vowel. Much used with sense of *phil-, -phil*, in opprobrious neologisms, e.g. *pro-German*. The L. prep. is used in some familiar phrases, e.g. *pro tem(pore)*. See also *con*[3].

proa. See *prahu*.

probable. F., L. *probabilis*, lit. what may be proved, from *probare*, to prove, from *probus*, good. See *probity*.

probang. Surgical instrument for exploring throat. Altered, on *probe*, from earlier *provang*, inventor's name for it (17 cent.). ? Variation on obs. *provet*, probe, F. *éprouvette*, from *éprouver*, to test, etc., ? or representing an E. pronunc. of F. *provin*, vine-shoot for planting, L. *propago, propagin-*, which its shape may have suggested.

probate. L. *probatum*, from *probare*, to prove, test. Cf. *probation-er* and see *probity*.

probe. First as noun. Late L. *proba*, from *probare*, to prove (v.s.). Also called a *tent*, from *tentare*, to try. For fig. senses cf. *sound*[4].

probity. F. *probité*, L. *probitas*, from *probus*, good (v.s.), from *pro* and Aryan root of *be*.

problem. F. *problème*, L., G. πρόβλημα, lit. thing thrown before (cf. *project*), from βάλλειν, to throw. In Wyc. (*Judges*, xiv. 15). *Problem play* (late 19 cent.) is perh. a transl. of F. *pièce à thèse*, ? or vice-versa.

proboscis. L., G. προβοσκίς, elephant's trunk, lit. food instrument, from βόσκειν, to feed.

procacity. L. *procacitas*, pertness, from *procax*, forward, from *procare*, to ask.

proceed. F. *procéder*, L. *procedere*, to go forward. With *legal proceedings* cf. F. *procès*, lawsuit. *Proceeds*, profit, outcome, was orig. used in sing.

The only procede (that I may use the mercantile term) you can expect is thanks (Howell, 1621).

proceleusmatic [*metr*.]. Animating, esp. foot of four short syllables. From G. προκελεύειν, to incite beforehand.

procellarian [*ornith*.]. From L. *procella*, storm.

procephalic [*ethn*.]. From G. προκέφαλος, long-headed. Cf. *dolichocephalic*.

process. F. *procès* (now lawsuit), L. *processus*, from *procedere, process-*, to proceed, go forward. Etym. sense still in *process of time*. Hence *procession, processional*. F. leg. sense (with which cf. *proceedings*) also appears in *process of law, process-server*.

procès-verbal. F., written statement of grounds of action (v.s.).

prochronism. Coined on *anachronism* (q.v.). *Matinée*, afternoon performance, *May Races*, Camb., held in June, are examples.

proclaim. F. *proclamer*, L. *proclamare*. See *claim*. To *proclaim* (an Irish district as no longer fit to be governed by ordinary law) dates from 1881.

proclitic [*gram*.]. Coined (1801) on *enclitic* (q.v.).

proclivity. F. *proclivité*, L. *proclivitas*, from

proclivus, from *clivus*, slope. Cf. *leaning, penchant, bent, inclination*.

proconsul. L., from *pro consule* (see *consul*). Application to governor of great British dependency is app. due to Macaulay, who used it of Warren Hastings.

procrastinate. From L. *procrastinare*, from *crastinus*, of to-morrow, *cras*.

Procrastination is the thief of time;
Year after year it steals, till all are fled
(Young, *Night Thoughts*, i. 393).

procreate. From L. *procreare*, to beget, from *creare*, to create.

Leveful procreacioun of children (Chauc. E. 1448).

Procrustean. Of *Procrustes*, G. Προκρούστης, lit. stretcher, myth. robber of Attica, who, by stretching or chopping, made his captives fit his bed.

proctor. Contr. of *procurator* (q.v.). Cf. *proxy*. Orig. deputy, attorney. In early use at universities.

Presentibus apud Woodstocke tam procuratoribus scolarium universitatis quam burgensibus Oxon.
(*NED*. 1248).

The sone of the proctour [*var*. procuratour] of myn hows (Wyc. Gen. xv. 2).

procumbent. From pres. part. of L. *procumbere*, to fall forward. Cf. *incumbent*.

procurator. F. *procurateur*, L. *procurator-em*, from *procurare*, to procure. Synon. with *attorney*; hence *by procuration*, by proxy. See *proctor*.

procure. F. *procurer*, L. *procurare*, to care for, bring about, act as agent, from *cura*, care. In current sense the dat. of the person is understood, e.g. *he procured* (*for himself*, F. *il se procura*) *money*. Sense of acting as pander, whence *procuress*, first in Shaks.

prod. Used by Coverd. (1535) of goading oxen. App. cogn. with obs. *proke, prog, brod*, all used in similar senses; the last is cogn. with *brad* (cf. dial. *prodawl*), while *proke* has a LG. cogn. *proken*, perh. ult. allied to *prick*.

prodigal. Late L. **prodigalis*, from *prodigus*, from *prodigere*, to squander, lit. drive forth, from *pro* and *agere*. First in ref. to *Prodigal Son* (*Vulg. filius prodigus*).

prodigy. L. *prodigium*, portent, marvel, from *pro* and OL. **agiom*, thing said; cf. *aio*, I say, and see *adage*. *Prodigy pianist* (*violinist*, etc.) dates from c. 1889. With *prodigious*, immense, cf. *monstrous, enormous*.

prodrome. F., G. πρόδρομος, running before, from δραμεῖν, to run. Cf. *palindrome.*

produce. L. *producere,* to bring forth, etc., from *ducere, duct-,* to lead (cf. *product-ion*). The noun was formerly accented as the verb.

You hoard not health for your own private use,
But on the public spend the rich produce (Byron).

proem. Archaic F. *proême,* L., G. προοίμιον, prelude, ? from οἶμος, way, ? or οἴμη, song. In Chauc. (E. 43). Cf. *preamble.*

profane. F., L. *profanus,* lit. before (outside) the temple (see *fane*). Orig. sense of un-initiated, still in playful use, is developed into that of sacrilegious, blasphemous.

profess. L. *profitēri, profess-,* from *fatēri,* to acknowledge, own. Before 1500 in rel. sense only, to make profession of one's faith, and spec. to take the vows. Later to claim knowledge in some spec. branch, whence *professor, profession,* the latter almost monopolised by the stage, as *trade* by the liquor business; also *professional* (cricketer, beauty, politician, agitator).

All who profess and call themselves Christians
(*Prayer for all conditions of men*).

proffer. AF. *proffrir,* OF. *poroffrir,* from *por* (*pour,* L. *pro*) and *offrir,* to offer. Associated in sense with L. *proferre.* For contr. cf. *prune*[2, 3], *plush, pluck.*

Sun destre guant a Dieu en puroffrit (*Rol.* 2389).

proficient. From pres. part. of L. *proficere,* to advance, be useful, from *facere,* to make.

profile. It. *proffilo,* from *proffilare,* to outline, from L. *filum,* thread. Cf. *purfle.*

profilo: a border, a limning or drawing of any picture (Flor.).

profit. F., L. *profectus,* progress, profit, from *proficere,* to help forward, etc. (see *proficient*). As opposite of *loss* has superseded native *gewinn.* For bad sense cf. to *take advantage. Profiteer* was coined (1915), on *privateer,* to describe those who levied blackmail on the nation's necessity by exacting inordinate prices for their commodities or labour (cf. Ger. *kriegsgewinnler*).

Profiteering is an extravagant recompense given for services rendered
(D. Lloyd George, June 30, 1917).

profligate. L. *profligatus,* from *profligare,* to ruin, cast down, etc., from *fligere,* to strike down. Cf. sense-development of *abandoned, dissolute, roué.*

profound. F. *profond,* L. *profundus,* from *fundus,* bottom. Usu. in fig. senses of native *deep.*

profundis, de. Init. words of *Ps.* cxxx. (cxxix.), *De profundis ad te clamavi, Domine!*

profuse. L. *profusus,* p.p. of *profundere,* to pour forth. Cf. *gushing.*

prog[1] [*slang*]. Food. Orig. a cant word (17 cent.). App. from verb to *prog,* poke about, forage, cogn. with obs. *proke,* to prod. Cf. synon. *grub,* from *grub,* to dig. Perh. vaguely associated with *provender, proviant.*

prog[2] [*Oxf. & Camb.*]. For *proctor.* Also *proggins.*

progeny. OF. *progenie,* L. *progenies,* from *pro-* and *gignere, gen-,* to beget.

proggins. See *prog*[2].

prognathous. Coined (19 cent.) from G. γνάθος, jaw.

A prognathous Westphalian, with a retreating brow and the manners of a hog
(Buchan, *Thirty-nine Steps*).

prognostic. Restored spelling of ME. & OF. *pronostique,* L., G. προγνωστικόν, from προγιγνώσκειν, to know before.

program-me. Late L., G. πρόγραμμα, public written notice, from γράφειν, to write. Spelling *programme* is F.

progress. F. *progrès,* L. *progressus,* from *progredior, progress-,* I go forward, from *gradior,* I step. Lit. sense still in *royal progress, progressive whist,* and in math. *Progressive* was adopted c. 1889 as name of advanced party in London County Council.

prohibit. From L. *prohibēre, prohibit-,* from *habēre,* to have, hold. *Prohibition* (by abstainers of alcoholic refreshment for others) is US. (c. 1850) and triumphant 1919.

project. L. *projectum,* from *proicere, project-,* to throw forward, from *jacere,* to throw. Cf. synon. Ger. *entwurf,* from *werfen,* to throw. Etym. sense appears in *projectile.* In chartography *projection* (on to a plane surface) was orig. the result of geometrical projection.

prolate. L. *prolatus,* used as p.p. of *proferre,* to extend. Cf. *oblate, prelate.*

prolegomena. G. προλεγόμενα, neut. pl. of pres. part. pass. of προλέγειν, to say be-forehand. Cf. *preface.*

prolepsis [*gram.*]. G. πρόληψις, from προλαμβάνειν, to take before, e.g. *scuta latentia condunt,* lit. they hide the concealed shields. Cf. *anticipation.*

proletarian. From L. *proletarius*, from *proles*, offspring. Used in L. of class exempted from taxation and mil. service, and assisting the state only by the production of offspring. The pol. currency of the word (*dictatorship of the proletariat*, etc.) is due to F. economists of the 19 cent.

Such men were y-cleped proletarii, that is geteris of children (Trev. i. 251).

prolific. F. *prolifique*, MedL. *prolificus*, from *proles*, offspring, *facere*, to make.

prolix. F. *prolixe*, L. *prolixus*, lit. flowing forth, from *liquēre*, to be liquid. Cf. *fluent.*

prolocutor. Chairman of Lower House of Convocation. L., fore-speaker, from *loqui*, *locut-*, to speak.

prologue. F., L., G. πρόλογος, lit. fore-speech. From c. 1300.

prolong. F. *prolonger*, Late L. *prolongare*, from *longus*, long.

prolusion. L. *prolusio-n-*, from *proludere*, *-lus-*, to play before. Cf. *prelude.*

promenade. F., from *promener*, OF. *pourmener*, to lead along, cause to walk, Late L. *prominare*, to drive (cattle) onward, from *minari*, to threaten. Ending *-ade* is imitated from words of It. or Sp. origin. The *promenade concert* (1839) is of F. introduction.

Promethean. Of *Prometheus*, demi-god who made man from clay and supplied him with fire stolen from Olympus, for which he was chained by Zeus in Caucasus.

prominent. From pres. part. of L. *prominēre*, to jut out; cf. *outstanding* and see *eminent.*

promiscuous. From L. *promiscuus*, from *miscēre*, to mix.

promise. L. *promissum*, p.p. neut. of *promittere*, lit. to send before. ME. had also *promes*, F. *promesse*, L. *promissa*; cf. It. *promessa*, Sp. *promesa*. Verb, from noun, has expelled ME. *promit*. *Land of Promise* (Coverd.), *Promised Land* (Milt.), are for earlier *Land of Behest*. *Promissory* (note) is MedL. *promissorius.*

promontory. MedL. *promontorium*, altered on *mons*, *mont-*, mountain, from L. *promunturium*, cogn. with *prominent.*

promote. From L. *promovēre*, *promot-*, to move forward, to further. Financ. sense is late 19 cent.

One of the fearful things of the late war is that we had no admirals and generals shot—we only promoted them (Lord Fisher, *Times*, Sep. 11, 1919).

prompt. F., L. *promptus*, p.p. of *promere*, to put forth, from *pro* and *emere*, to take, buy.

First (14 cent.) as verb, to incite (cf. It. *prontare*), hence to supply with words, etc. (15 cent.).

Were it
My cue to fight, I should have known it
Without a prompter (*Oth.* i. 2).

promulgate. From L. *promulgare*, alteration of *provulgare* (from *vulgus*, people), perh. due to confusion with synon. L. *promere legem.*

prone. OF., L. *pronus*, face downwards, cogn. with *pro*. Hence used in connection with downward "bent."

Redi [*var.* proon] in to yvel (Wyc. *Gen.* viii. 21).

prong. From c. 1500. Also *prang*, *sprong*. ? Cf. Du. *prang*, compression, pinch, Ger. *pranger*, pillory, Goth. *praggen*, to compress. See *pang.*

pronoun. Imitated by Palsg. from F. *pronom*, L. *pronomen*. See *noun.*

pronounce. F. *prononcer*, L. *pronuntiare*, to proclaim, announce, from *nuntius*, messenger.

pronunciamento [*pol.*]. Sp. *pronunciamiento*, proclamation, esp. of insurgents (v.s.).

The first place in the *Englishwoman* is naturally claimed by Mrs Fawcett's "pronunciamento" on the General Election (*Daily Tel.* Dec. 3, 1918).

proof. ME. *proeve*, *preve*, F. *preuve*, Late L. *proba*, from *probare*, to prove (q.v.), from *probus*, genuine, true; cf. It. *prova*, Sp. *prueba*. In some senses, e.g. *printer's proof*, *artist's proof*, *proof-spirit*, *armour of proof*, it is rather aphet. for F. *épreuve*, trial, test, from *éprouver*, VL. **ex-probare*. So also *proof against*, F. *à l'épreuve de*, whence numerous compds. in *-proof*.

Mr Thomas says, "It behoves us to make our union blackleg-proof" (*Daily Chron.* July 27, 1917).

prop. Du., earlier *proppe*, "pedamen, fulcimentum, fulcrum, sustentaculum" (Kil.); cogn. with Ger. *pfropfen*, peg, plug, cork of bottle. Thought to be Teut., in which case Ger. *pfropfen*, shoot for grafting, must be a separate word (L. *propago*, *propagin-*). To *prop*, stop suddenly (of a horse), is Austral.

propaedeutic. From G. προπαιδεύειν, to teach before. See *pedagogue.*

propaganda. Short for *Congregatio de propaganda fide*, committee of cardinals established (1622) by Gregory XV to supervise foreign missions (see *propagate*). Sometimes erroneously treated as neut. pl. (*memoranda*, *addenda*, etc.). *Raging, tearing* *propaganda* was app. first used at Birmingham (July 22, 1903) by Mr A. Chamberlain in ref. to his brother's (Joseph) Tariff Reform campaign.

propagate. From L. *propagare* (bot.), from *propago*, slip, shoot for transplanting, from root of *pangere*, to fix, plant.

R^d this day the act for propagation of ye Gospel in New England among the heathen
(Josselin's *Diary*, Nov. 25, 1651).

proparoxytone [*gram.*]. Accented on antepenult. G. προπαροξύτονος. See *paroxysm.*

propel. L. *propellere*, *propuls-*, to drive forward. Hence *propulsion.*

propensity. From L. *propensus*, leaning forward, from *pendēre*, to hang. Cf. *proclivity, bent*, etc.

proper. F. *propre*, L. *proprius*, own; cf. It. *proprio*, Sp. *propio*. Etym. sense survives in *property* and *proper motion*. For sense of special to individual, as opposed to *common*, cf. F. *nom propre*. It occurs in ME. as approving epithet (v.i.), while F. sense of fit, clean, has passed into spec. E. sense of correct, decorous. A *lion proper* (her.) is in natural, as opposed to conventional, colours.

John the propereste profit was (*NED.* c. 1375).

property. F. *propriété*, L. *proprietas* (v.s.). In theat. sense (mod. *props*) recorded c. 1425.

prophet. F. *prophète*, L., G. προφήτης, spokesman or interpreter of a divinity, lit. forespeaker, from φάναι, to speak. Used by LXX. to render Heb. *nābī'*, soothsayer; cf. Arab. *al-nabiy*, the Prophet, Mohammed. In most Europ. langs. The distinction in spelling of *prophesy, prophecy*, since c. 1700, is artificial.

My gran'ther's rule was safer'n 'tis to crow:
Don't never prophesy onless you know (Lowell).

prophylactic [*med.*]. G. προφυλακτικός, from φυλάσσειν, to guard.

propinquity. OF. *propinquité*, L. *propinquitas*, from *propinquus*, from *prope*, near.

propitiate. From L. *propitiare*, to make propitious, *propitius*, prob. from *pro* and *petere*, to seek; cf. G. προπετής, inclined.

propolis. G. πρόπολις, bee-glue, lit. suburb, from πρό, before, πόλις, city.

proportion. F., L. *proportio-n-*, from phrase *pro portione*, in respect of share. For backformation cf. *proconsul*. Sense of absolute size (*gigantic proportions*) grows out of that of relative size (*well-proportioned*).

Proportional representation dates from c. 1884.

propose. F. *proposer*, to put forward. See *pose*. To *propose* (*marriage*) is 18 cent.

proposition. F., L. *propositio-n-*, from *proponere*, *proposit-*, to put forward. See *pose*. Colloq. *tough* (*large, paying*) *proposition* is US.

propound. Earlier (16 cent.) *propoune*, ME. *propone*, L. *proponere*, to put forward. Form influenced by cogn. *compound*[1] (q.v.).

propraetor [*hist.*]. L., orig. *pro praetore*. See *praetor* and cf. *proconsul.*

proprietor. Anomalous formation, substituted (17 cent.) for earlier *proprietary*, F. *propriétaire*, L. *proprietarius*, from *proprietas*, property, from *proprius*, own. First used of the "proprietors" of the NAmer. colonies.

propriety. F. *propriété*, property (v.s.). Current sense (late 18 cent.) due to that acquired in E. by *proper.*

propulsion. See *propel.*

propylaeum [*arch.*]. L., G. προπύλαιον, vestibule, neut. of προπύλαιος, before the gate, πύλη. Also *propylon*, G. πρόπυλον.

propylite [*geol.*]. Volcanic rock. Named (1867) by Richthofen as opening the tertiary volcanic period (v.s.).

pro rata. L., for *rate*[1] (q.v.).

prorogue. F. *proroger*, L. *prorogare*, to extend (term of office), lit. to ask (*rogare*) publicly. To *prorogue Parliament* is to postpone its activities without dissolving it.

proscenium. L., G. προσκήνιον. See *scene.*

proscribe. L. *proscribere*, to "post" as an outlaw, lit. to write before.

prose. F., L. *prosa* (sc. *oratio*), from *prosus*, straightforward, for *prorsus*, for *pro versus*, turned forward. *Prosaic* was earlier the opposite of *poetic* in all senses.

Many works, chiefly prosaic, which widely extended his literary reputation (*NED.* 1830).

prosecute. From L. *prosequi*, *prosecut-*, from *sequi*, to follow. Cf. *pursue.*

proselyte. Late L., G. προσήλυτος, from second aorist stem of προσέρχεσθαι, to come to. Orig. Gentile converted to Judaism (Wyc. *Matt.* xxiii. 15).

prosit. L., may it advantage. From drinking ritual of Ger. students (16 cent.).

prosody. L., G. προσῳδία, from πρός, to, ᾠδή, song. Cf. *accent.*

prosopopoeia [*rhet.*]. Introduction of pretended speaker. L., G. προσωποποιία, from πρόσωπον, person, face, ποιεῖν, to make.

prospect. L. *prospectus*, from *prospicere*, to look forward. To *prospect* in mining (US.) is from the noun, in the sense of spot holding out likelihood of mineral deposit.

What they call a "good prospect," that is, every appearance on the surface of a vein of good metal (Capt. Marryat, 1839).

prospectus. L. (v.s.). Orig. (18 cent.) announcement and outline of literary work.

prosper. F. *prospérer*, L. *prosperare*, from *prosper*, fortunate, ult. from *pro*, before.

prostate [*anat.*]. MedL. *prostata*, G. προστάτης, one standing before.

prosthesis [*gram.*]. Prefixing of letter, e.g. F. *esprit* from L. *spiritus*. L., G. πρόσθεσις, from πρός, to, τιθέναι, to put. Has rather the sense of *prothesis*.

prostitute. From p.p. of L. *prostituere*, to offer for sale, from *pro* and *statuere*, to set up.

prostrate. L. *prostratus*, p.p. of *prosternere*, *prostrat-*, from *sternere*, to strew, lay flat.

protagonist. G. πρωταγωνιστής, actor who plays first part, from πρῶτος, first, ἀγωνιστής, competitor, etc. See *agony*.

protasis [*gram.*]. Late L., G. πρότασις, stretching forward, proposition, from τείνειν, to stretch. Cf. *apodosis*.

protean. Like *Proteus*, G. sea-god with power of change of form.

protect. From L. *protegere*, *protect-*, from *tegere*, to cover. In econ. sense *protection* is 19 cent. The first *Protector* (regent) was John Duke of Bedford, uncle of Henry VI.

protégé. F., p.p. of *protéger*, to protect (v.s.).

proteid. Introduced (1871) by Watts for *protein*, Ger. *protein-(stoffe)*, coined by Mulder from G. πρῶτος, first.

protest. F. *protester*, Late L. *protestare*, for *protestari*, to testify publicly, declare, as in to *protest one's innocence*. Now usu. with *against*. *Protestant* was assumed as title by those German princes and free cities that "protested" against the decision of the Diet of Spires (1529) re-affirming the edict of the Diet of Worms against the Reformation.

proteus [*biol.*]. Name of various protozoa and bacteria. See *protean*.

proto-. From G. πρῶτος, first, superl. from πρό, before.

protocol. F. *protocole*, MedL., Late G. πρωτόκολλον, first leaf, fly-leaf glued inside volume and containing account of MS., from κόλλα, glue. Cf. It. *protocollo*, Sp. *protocolo*.

protocollo: a booke wherein scriveners register all

their writings, any thing that is first made, and needeth correction (Flor.).

protoplasm. Ger. *protoplasma*, coined (1849) by Mohl from G. πλάσμα, thing moulded, from πλάσσειν (cf. *plastic*). Ger. *sprachreiniger* (purists) prefer *urschleim*, original mucus.

protozoa [*zool.*]. Unicellular animals. Coined (1818) by Goldfuss from G. ζῶον, animal.

protract. From L. *protrahere*, *protract-*, to draw forward.

protrude. L. *protrudere*, to thrust forward.

protuberant. From pres. part. of L. *protuberare*, from *tuber*, swelling.

proud. Late AS. *prūd*, *prūt*, OF. *prod*, *prud*, Late L. *prodis*, back-formation from *prodesse* (*pro* and *esse*), to be of value; cf. It. *prode*, "valiant, hardie, couragious, full of prowes, stout, noble, worthie, haughtie, wise, grave, notable, of great worth" (Flor.). The F. word survives in the old nom. *preux*, also in *prud'homme*, arbitrator, and *prude*; cf. archaic E. *prow*, doughty, and *prowess*. See *pride*. As with most adjs. which can be used as pers. epithets, its sense-hist. is very vague. In *proud flesh* orig. idea is over-growth (v.i.).

We at time of year
Do wound the bark, the skin of our fruit-trees;
Lest, being over-proud with sap and blood,
With too much riches it confound itself
(*Rich. II*, iii. 4).

There is such a thing as a man being too proud to fight (Pres. Wilson on the Lusitania massacre).

prove. AS. *prōfian* or F. *prouver*, L. *probare*, from *probus*, good, from *pro*, before (see *probity*); cf. It. *provare*, Sp. *probar*; also Du. *proeven*, Ger. *proben*, *prüfen*. In some senses rather apher. for F. *éprouver* (see *proof*). Incorr. p.p. *proven* only in Sc., esp. in *not proven*. Intrans. use, e.g. he *proved useless*, is for earlier reflex.

provenance. F., from *provenir*, to originate, L. *provenire*, to come forth. Also, with latinized spelling, *provenience*.

It is a penal offence to eat seed-potatoes, whatever their provenance (*Daily News*, May 2, 1917).

Provençal. Of *Provence*, L. *provincia*, first part of Gaul acquired by Romans. Often vaguely as gen. name for the dials. of the *langue d'oc* (Provençal, Gascon, Languedocien, Auvergnat, etc.), esp. as used by the troubadours (12–13 cents.).

provender. OF. *provendre*, var. of *provende*, VL. *probenda*, for *praebenda*. See *prebend*, with which it is synon. in ME. For prefix change cf. *provost*. Hence also It. *profenda*, Ger. *pfründe*, benevolent foundation.

provenience. See *provenance*.

proverb. F. *proverbe*, L. *proverbium*, from *verbum*, word. First (c. 1300) with ref. to Proverbs of Solomon. AS. had *bīspell* and *bīword*, the latter a transl. of the L. word.

proviant [*archaic mil.*]. Commissariat. Ger., from It., as *provender* (q.v.). But explained by some as L. *pro viando*, for travelling.

provide. L. *providēre*, lit. to foresee. *Providence*, the Deity, is ellipt. for *divine providence*. *Universal provider* was first (c. 1879) assumed as title by William Whiteley. *Provision*, orig. foresight, acquires its current sense, now usu. suggesting eatables, from phrase to *make (take) provision*; hence also *provisional*. See *prudent, purvey, purview*.

province. F., L. *provincia. The provinces*, contrasted with London, is imitated from F. *la province*, orig. used of the great semi-independent provinces, contrasted with the central kingdom. Hence *provincial-ism*. For sense of sphere of duty, etc., cf. similar use of F. *district*. This belongs to the etym. sense, L. *provincia*, orig. rule, office, etc., being ult. cogn. with Goth. *frauja*, lord (see *frau*).

provision. See *provide*.

proviso. L. abl. absolute in MedL. *proviso quod*, it being provided that. Hence *provisory*. For origin and substantival use cf. cogn. *purview*.

provisor [*hist.*]. Holder of a "provision," papal grant to benefice on its becoming vacant. Hence *Statute of Provisors* (1350–51). ME. & OF. *provisour*, L. *provisor-em*, provider.

provoke. F. *provoquer*, L. *provocare*, to call forth. For L., F., & obs. E. sense of challenging cf. to *call out*. *Agent provocateur*, police or government agent inciting to crime, is 19 cent. F.

Can honour's voice provoke the silent dust?
(Gray's *Elegy*).

provost. AS. *prafost* or OF. *provost*, Late L. *propositus* (whence also Ger. *probst*), for *praepositus*, one placed before, prefect, whence OF. *prevost* (*prévôt*). For wide application cf. *constable, marshal*, etc. *Provost-marshal* (mil.) is adapted from OF. *prevost des mareschaux* (*de France*) and second element has been confused with that of *court-martial* (v.i.).

prevost des mareschaux: a provost martiall (who is often both informer, judge, and executioner) punishes disorderly souldiers, coyners, free-booters, highway robbers, lazie rogues, or vagabonds, and such as weare forbidden weapons (Cotg.).

prow. F. *proue*, Genoese *proa*, app. VL. **proa*, by dissim. for *prora*, G. πρῷρα, cogn. with πρό, before; cf. It. *prua*, Sp. *proa*.

prowess. F. *prouesse*, from *preux* (q.v.). See also *proud, prude*.

prowl. ME. *prollen*, to go round about, search. The analogy of Sp. *rodar*, to go round (L. *rotare*, from *rota*, wheel), whence also F. *rôder*, to prowl, suggests an OF. **porrouler* or **parrouler*, compd. of *rouler*, to roll (q.v.), with contr. as in *proffer, prune*[2, 3]. Its sound-hist. is that of *roll*, mod. pronunc. being influenced (since c. 1750) by spelling.

Though ye prolle ay, ye shul it never fynde
(Chauc. G. 1412).

The nightly wolf, that round th' enclosure proul'd
To leap the fence, now plots not on the fold
(Dryden).

proximity. F. *proximité*, L. *proximitas*, from *proximus*, nearest, superl. from *prope*, near. Cf. *proxime accessit*, he approached nearest; *proximo* (sc. *mense*, month).

proxy. Contr. of *procuracy*. See *procurator, proctor*.

prokesy: procuration (Palsg.).

prude. F., fem. of *preux* (q.v.). See also *proud*. A complimentary epithet in OF. It is probable that *prud'homme* is for *preux d'homme* (cf. *a broth of a boy*), from which *prudefemme* was formed by analogy, *prude* being a back-formation.

prudent. F., L. *prudens, prudent-*, contr. of *providens*, pres. part. of *providēre*, to foresee, etc.

prune[1]. Noun. F., L. *pruna*, neut. pl. taken as fem. sing. Earliest (14 cent.) E. sense is dried plum. For *prunes and prisms* see *Little Dorrit*, ii. 5. See also *plum*.

prune[2]. To trim trees. ME. *proin*, OF. *prooignier*, later *proignier, progner* (still in dial.), for **por-roignier*, from OF. *roignier* (*rogner*), to clip all round, VL. **rotundiare*, from *rotundus*, round. For contr. cf. *proffer, prune*[3]; for change of vowel cf. *lune*. See also *prime*[5].

He plants, he proines, he pares, he trimmeth round
(Sylv. *Eden*).

prune[3]. To trim the feathers. ME. *proin*, OF. *poroindre*, from *oindre*, to anoint, L. *ungere*.

The mod. F. word is *lustrer*, to gloss. For contr. cf. *proffer*, *prune²*. See also *preen*.

Baingnies le [le faucon] en iaue froide et le metes au soleil en arbre u il se puisse espeluquier et pouroindre (*Aviculaire des oiseaux de proie*).

She [the hawk] proynith when she fetchith oyle with hir beke...and anoyntith hir fete & hir federis (*Book of St Albans*, 15 cent.).

prunella, prunello. Strong fabric for clergymen's and barristers' gowns. App. of E. formation, quasi sloe-coloured, from F. *prunelle*, sloe, dim. of *prune¹*. Commonly misunderstood in quot. below to mean something inferior or indifferent, whereas Pope's allusion is to externals of garb or appearance, as in the case of the cobbler and the "cloth."

Worth makes the man, and want of it the fellow:
The rest is all but leather and prunella
(*Essay on Man*, iv. 204).

prurient. From pres. part. of L. *prurire*, to itch.

Prussian. ModL. *Prussianus*, from MedL. *Prussi*, *Borussi*, etc., latinized from native name of a Lithuanian tribe conquered (12 cent.) by the Teutonic Knights. The lang. (extinct) is Slav. *Prussian blue* was accidentally discovered (1704) at Berlin by Diesbach. Cf. *prussic acid*, F. *acide prussique*, obtained from Prussian blue.

People don't shove quite so selfishly, don't scowl at each other so Prussianly
(*Daily Chron.* July 26, 1917).

pry¹. To be inquisitive. ME. *prien*, to peer inquisitively, look closely. ? Cf. AS. *be-prīwan*, to wink, *prēowt-hwīl*, moment, lit. winking while.

pry² [*dial.*]. Back-formation from *prize³*.

prytaneum [*hist.*]. Public hall of G. state. L., G. πρυτανεῖον, from πρύτανις, prince, chief.

psalm. AS. (*p*)*sealm*, L., G. ψαλμός, twanging of strings, from ψάλλειν, to twitch. Adopted by most Europ. langs., with loss of initial *p-*, which has now been restored (e.g. F. *psaume*, Ger. *psalme*) and is sounded, as in other *ps-* words, exc. in E. In ME. *saume*, from OF., is common. With *psalmody*, from G. ᾠδή, song, cf. *prosody*. *Psalmist* has replaced *psalmwright*, found in AS. *Psalter*, L., G. ψαλτήριον, stringed instrument, used in Church L. & G. for psalm-book, has been replaced in orig. sense by the later borrowed *psaltery*. Both are restored spellings (v.i.).

sauter a boke: psaltier (Palsg.).

pseudo-. From G. ψευδής, false, from ψεύδειν,

to deceive; e.g. *pseudonym*, from ὄνυμα, name. Common as prefix in Wyc. and much used for mod. nonce-words.

pshaw. Natural exclamation of impatience, etc. Cf. *pooh*, *pish*.

psilanthropism [*theol.*]. Doctrine that Christ was mere man, ψιλὸς ἄνθρωπος.

psittacine. Of the parrot, L., G. ψιττακός, prob. of Eastern origin.

psyche. L., G. ψυχή, breath, from ψύχειν, to breathe. Personified in G. myth. as beloved of Eros, whence *Psyche task*, impossible of accomplishment, set as punishment by Venus. Hence *psychiatry*, mental disease treatment, from G. ἰατήρ, healer; *psychical research* (1882), and many scient. and philos. terms in *psycho-*. *Psychology* appears first (16 cent.) in Ger. in latinized form *psychologia* (Melanchthon). *Psychological moment* translates F. *moment psychologique*, taken as moment psychically appropriate, a misunderstanding of Ger. *psychologisches moment*, psychological factor (momentum), used (Dec. 1870) by the *Neue Preussische Zeitung* in ref. to the anticipated effect of the bombardment of Paris on the *moral* of the besieged. The mistake has "passed nonsensically into English journalese" (*NED.*).

psychrometer [*meteorol.*]. Kind of thermometer. From G. ψυχρός, cold.

ptarmigan. Pseudo-G. spelling for Lowland Sc. *tarmigan* (16 cent.), Gael. *tarmachan*; cf. Ir. *tarmanach*. Origin unknown. Early var. *termagant* suggests possibility of nickname based on some folk-lore belief.

pteridology. Study of ferns. From G. πτερίς, πτεριδ-, fern, cogn. with πτερόν, feather, wing.

pterodactyl. Coined (19 cent.) from G. πτερόν, wing, δάκτυλος, finger.

ptisane. Restored from *tisane*, common in ME., F., L., G. πτισάνη, (drink made from) peeled barley, from πτίσσειν, to peel.

ptochocracy. Government by beggars. From G. πτωχός, poor.

Ptolemaic. Of *Ptolemy*, Alexandrian astronomer (2 cent.), whose system was displaced by the Copernican. Also of the *Ptolemies*, G. dynasty in Egypt from death of Alexander the Great to Cleopatra.

ptomaine. It. *ptomaina*, badly coined (1878) by Selmi from G. πτῶμα, dead body, lit. what has fallen, from πίπτειν, to fall. Current pronunc. (for *ptomaïne*) is "illiterate" (*NED.*).

puberty. F. *puberté*, L. *pubertas*, from *puber*, youth, cogn. with *puer*, boy.

public. F., L. *publicus*, altered, by association with *pubes*, adult, from earlier *poplicus*, from *populus*, people. *Public school* (cf. L. *schola publica*) has varied much in sense from 12 cent. onward, its present connotation being chiefly 19 cent. *The public* is first recorded in the Translators' preface to the *AV.* (1611). *Pub* is 19 cent. *Publican*, tax-gatherer (*Matt.* xviii. 17), is L. *publicanus*, from *publicum*, public revenue. Its other sense, suggested by the Bibl. word, is 18 cent. *Publicist*, F. *publiciste*, is prop. a writer on public law.

The teetotaler who exults in his teetotalism, thanking God that he is not as other men are, or even as this publican (E. Pugh).

publish. From F. *publier* (for incorr. -*ish* cf. *distinguish, astonish*, etc.), L. *publicare*, to make public (e.g. *the banns of marriage*). *Publisher* in current sense (corresponding to F. *éditeur*) is 18 cent.

Joseph forsothe...wolde not publiche hire
(Wyc. *Matt.* i. 19).

puce. Colour. F., flea, L. *pulex, pulic-*.

Puck. AS. *pūca*, cogn. with ON. *pūki*, mischievous demon. In ME. synon. with devil, and from 16 cent. with Robin Goodfellow. See *pug*[1]. Also used in dial. of the nightjar or goatsucker, a bird regarded with superstitious dread.

pucka, pukka [*Anglo-Ind.*]. Genuine. Hind. *pakka*, cooked, ripe. See *cutcha*.

No need to ask the young un's breed. He's a pukka Chinn (Kipling, *Tomb of his Ancestors*).

pucker. Frequent. formation from *poke*[1], bag. *Pursy* was formerly used (temp. Eliz.) of puckered cloth; cf. also F. *pocher*, to bag, pucker, It. *saccolare*, from *sacco*, bag. With *to be in a pucker*, agitation, cf. *plight*[2].

saccolare: to pucker or gather or cockle as some stuffes do being wet (Flor.).

pud. Baby word for foot. Cf. Du. *poot*, Ger. *pfote*, paw. See also *pad*.

pudding. F. *boudin*, black-pudding, hog-pudding. Orig. sense was intestine, as still in E. dial., which points to ult. connection with L. *botulus* (see *bowel*). Current E. sense, orig. with cloth replacing bladder, is latest (16 cent.) and has been borrowed by F. (*pouding*), Ger. (*pudding*), and other langs. For E. *p*- cf. *purse*. F. *boudin* has also the subsidiary senses of *pudding*, e.g.

pad (naut.), explosive (mil.), tobacco in roll.

The proof of a pudding is the eating
(Glapthorne, *Hollander*, iii. 1, 1640).

puddle. ME. *podel*, dim. of AS. *pudd*, ditch; cf. Ger. dial. *pudel*. Also applied to mixture of clay, sand, and water, used for making embankments, etc. water-tight. Hence also to *puddle* (molten iron). Cf. Du. *poedeln*, Ger. *puddeln*, to dabble, splash. See *poodle*.

pudendum [*anat.*]. L., neut. gerund. of *pudēre*, to be ashamed.

pudge [*dial.*]. Var. (19 cent.) of *podge*. ? Cf. dial. *puddy*, stumpy, the antiquity of which is shown by its presence in surname *Puddifoot*.

pudibund. L. *pudibundus*, from *pudēre*, to be ashamed.

pudsy [*dial.*]. Chubby. Cf. *pudge*. For -*sy* cf. *fubsy, tootsy-wootsy, tricksy, Betsy*, etc.

pueblo. Sp., population, town, etc., L. *populus*, people. Esp. Indian settlement in Sp. America.

puerile. F. *puéril*, L. *puerilis*, from *puer*, boy.

puerperal. From L. *puerperus*, parturient, from *puer* and *parere*, to bring forth.

puff. Imit. of expulsion of breath and resulting inflation. Cf. *buffoon* and other *buff*- words. In literary and advertising sense from 18 cent. *Powder-puff* is recorded c. 1700.

Panis levis, qui dicitur "pouf" mercatoriis
(*Lib. Albus*, 353).

puffin. Sea-bird. ME. *pofin*, also MedL. *poffo*, AF. *pofoun*. Perh. from *puff*, with allusion to corpulence of the young bird; cf. *plump as a puffin*. But, as the earliest associations of the name are with Cornwall and Scilly, it may be a Celt. word.

pug[1]. As in *pug-dog, pug-nose*. App. in some senses for *puck*, devil, later applied to an ape. Also used as term of endearment, which is perh. chief reason for name *pug-dog* (18 cent.), whence *pug-nose*. In dial. applied also to fox, rabbit, squirrel, and other small animals; cf. *pug engine*, small locomotive.

marmouselle: a little puppy, or pug, to play with
(Cotg.).

'Tis quite impossible she should not command what matches she pleases, when such pugs [=dwarfs] as Miss Hamilton can become peeresses
(Lady M. Montagu, 1742).

pug[2]. Loam, etc. mixed for brick-making. From verb to *pug*, knead clay; ? cf. *puddle*.

pug[3] [*Anglo-Ind.*]. Track of wild beast. Hind. *pag*, footprint.

> The marks of enormous pugs that ran...and disappeared in a narrow-mouthed cave
>   (Kipling, *Tomb of his Ancestors*).

pug[4] [*slang*]. Short for *pugilist*.

puggaree, puggree. Hind. *pagrī*, turban. Adopted as mil. name for sun-veil at time of Indian Mutiny.

pugilist. From L. *pugil*, boxer, cogn. with *pugnus*, fist, *pugna*, fight; cf. G. πύξ (adv.), with the fist.

pugnacious. From L. *pugnax*, *pugnac-* (v.s.).

puisne [*leg.*]. OF. *puisné* (*puîné*), L. *post natus*, younger, junior. See *puny*.

puissant [*archaic*]. F., powerful, VL. **poteans*, **poteant-*, pres. part. of VL. *potēre*, used for *posse*. See *power*.

puke. First in Shaks. (v.i.). ? For **spuke*, cogn. with Ger. *spucken*, to spit, and ult. with L. *spuere*, to vomit. Cf. *tummy* and see *s-*.

> Mewling and puking in the nurse's arms
>   (*As You Like It*, ii. 7).

pukka. See *pucka*.

pule. Imit.; cf. F. *piauler*, also F. dial. *pioler*, *piuler*.

> *piauler*: to peepe, or cheepe (as a young bird); also, to pule, or howle (as a young whelpe) (Cotg.).

pull. AS. *pullian*, to snatch, pluck, with possible LG. cognates. Orig. sense, replaced by that of steady effort, survives in to *pull turnips*, etc., to *pull caps* (wigs), to *have a crow to pull with one*, to *pull to pieces*, to *pull* (a racehorse). With *pull of beer* cf. *draught*, and Ger. *zug*, pull, draught, from *ziehen*, to tug. To *have the pull of* prob. goes back to ME. sense of wrestling, though now felt as associated with pulling of wires or strings; cf. US. *pull*, in politics. *Pull devil, pull baker* prob. comes from a scene in popular drama in which the devil carries off the baker for selling short weight.

pullet. F. *poulette*, dim. of *poule*, hen, Late L. *pulla*, fem. of *pullus*, young animal.

pulley. F. *poulie*; cf. It. *puleggia*, Sp. *polea*, MedL. *polegium*, which some connect with G. πόλος, pole[2], axis. But certainly influenced by association with L. *pullus*, G. πῶλος, colt, names of animals (*crane*, *donkey-engine*, *chevron*) being commonly used for mech. devices. In fact F. *poulain*, ME. *poleyn*, colt, are used in same sense. No connection with *pull*.

> *poulain*: a fole, or colt; also, the rope wherewith wine is let down into a seller; a pully rope (Cotg.).

By a pully-rope [Rab. poulain] wine is let down into a cellar (Urquhart's *Rabelais*, i. 5).

pullicate [*archaic*]. Fabric, chequered handkerchief. From *Pulicat* (Madras).

pullman. Car designed (c. 1870) by *G. M. Pullman* of Chicago.

pullulate. From L. *pullulare*, to sprout, spring forth, from *pullulus*, dim. of *pullus*, young animal.

pulmonary. L. *pulmonarius*, from *pulmo-n-*, lung.

pulp. F. *poulpe*, L. *pulpa*, pulp (vegetable or muscular).

pulpit. L. *pulpitum*, stage, platform, esp. for actors, in Late L. for preachers; cf. F. *pupitre*, Ger. *pult*, desk. Formerly used also of auctioneer's desk. For limitation of sense cf. *pew*.

> Come, get to your pulpit, Mr Auctioneer
>   (*School for Scandal*).

pulque. Fermented drink (Mexico). Amer. Sp., ? from Araucanian (Chile) *pulcu*. According to Platt prob. a Haytian word taken to Mexico by the Spaniards.

pulse[1]. Throb. F. *pouls*, L. *pulsus*, from *pellere*, *puls-*, to drive (cf. *pulsate*). Restored spelling for OF. & ME. *pous*.

pulse[2]. Leguminous seeds. OF. *pols*, *pouls*, collect. pl. from L. *puls*, *pult-*, pottage, etc., whence (in sing.) F. dial. *poul*. Cf. *poultice*.

pulverize. F. *pulvériser*, Late L. *pulverizare*, from *pulvis*, *pulver-*, powder.

pulvinated [*arch. & biol.*]. Bulging. From L. *pulvinus*, cushion.

puma. Sp., from Peruv.

pumice. ME. & OF. *pomis*, learned form of *pounce*[1] (q.v.). AS. had *pumic-stān*. Ult. cogn. with L. *spuma*, foam, from lightness.

pummel. See *pommel*.

pump[1]. For water. First (*Prompt. Parv.*) of ship's pump. Cf. F. *pompe*, Du. *pomp*, Ger. *pumpe*, all of rather late appearance; also Sp. Port. *bomba*. All no doubt of echoic origin, imitating the sound of the plunger. Cf. E. dial. and LG. *plump* in same sense, also It. *tromba*, lit. trump. *Pompe*, *plompe* are used indifferently in *Nav. Accts.* 1495–97. *Pump-room* first occurs at Bath (early 18 cent.).

> Sir John Talbot would fain have pumped me about the prizes (Pepys, Apr. 19, 1668).

pump[2]. Shoe. Back-formation from *pumps*, taken as pl., from Du. *pampoesje*, Javanese *pampoes*, of Arab. origin and ult. ident. with *babouche* (q.v.); cf. Dan.

pampusser (pl.), from Du. For E. vowel cf. *bungalow, pundit*, etc. F. army slang *pompes*, boots, can hardly be connected.

pumpernickel. Westphalian rye-bread. Ger., earlier in sense of booby, from dial. *pumpen*, pedere, *Nickel*, lout, from *Niklaus* (see *nickel*). For application to bread cf. obs. E. *brown George*, army bread, and current *tommy*.

pumpkin. Altered from *pumpion, pompion*, OF. *pompon*, "a pumpion or melon" (Cotg.), nasalized from *popon, pepon*, L. *pepo-n-*, G. πέπων, cogn. with πέπτειν, to ripen, cook.

pun. App. a 17 cent. clipped form (cf. *mob, cit*, etc.) of obs. *punnet, pundigrion*, found in same sense. The latter may be an illiterate or humorous perversion of It. *puntiglio*, fine point, used earlier in sense of verbal quibble. Cf. F. *pointe*, verbal conceit, much used in 17 cent. in very similar sense. Cf. also Ger. *stichwort*, "a pun or quibble" (Ludw.), from *stechen*, to prick.

I shall here define it [a pun] to be a conceit arising from the use of two words that agree in the sound, but differ in the sense (Addison).

punch¹. Tool. Shortened from *puncheon¹*. Cf. *pounce²*.

punch². Beverage. Orig. Anglo-Ind., and trad. (since 17 cent.) derived from Hind. *pānch*, five, in allusion to five (?) ingredients. Cf. *Punjaub*, five rivers, and Anglo-Ind. *punch*, council of five. F. *punch*, Du. *punch*, Ger. *punsch*, Sp. Port. *ponche*, are all borrowed from E. The trad. etym. is supported by the parallel of *charebockhra*, described (1629) by Peter Mundy as a "composition of racke (i.e. arrack), water, sugar and juice of lymes." This is app. Hind. *chār-bakhra*, four parts, and the same mixture is called by Mandelslo *pale-puntz*, app. E. *pale punch*.

punch³. To strike. App. combined from *punch*, to pierce, thrust (from *punch¹*), and *punsh*, a common ME. contr. of *punish*. The latter is still a boxing term. *Bounce, bunch*, were also formerly used in same sense and may have contributed to mod. meaning.

Caym [Cain] his synne was i-punsched seven-fold
(Trev. ii. 230).

I *punch*: je boulle, je pousse (Palsg.).

I *bunche, I beate*: je pousse (*ib.*).

punch⁴. Short, fat person, or animal; esp. in *Suffolk punch*, for earlier *punch horse*.

Ident. with *Punch* (v.i.), a word which became very popular in Pepys' time.

His gun, which from the shortness and bigness, they do call Punchinello (Pepys, April 20, 1669).

Staying among poor people there in the alley, did hear them call their fat child Punch, that word being become a word of common use for all that is thick and short (*ib.* Apr. 30, 1669).

Punch. Short for *Punchinello* (17 cent.), earlier *Polichinello*, altered from Neap. *Polecenella*, name of character in puppet-play, It. *Pulcinella*, perh. dim. of *pulcina*, chicken. The Neap. form is used also of the young of the turkey-cock, the beak of which the Punchinello mask may have resembled. Cf. F. *Polichinelle*. *Pleased as Punch* app. refers to his unfailing triumph over enemies. *Punch and Judy* is 19 cent. for earlier *Punch and his wife*. For It. origin cf. *pantaloon, scaramouch*, etc. Repeatedly mentioned as a novelty by Pepys.

Thence away to Polichinello, and there had three times more sport than at the play
(Pepys, Apr. 9, 1667).

puncheon¹ [*archaic*]. Tool for piercing. F. *poinçon*, awl, Late L. **punctio-n-*, from *pungere, punct-*, to pierce; cf. It. *punzone*, Sp. *punzon*. Now usu. replaced by shortened *punch¹*. See *pounce²*.

puncheon². Cask. The earlier E. & F. forms are ident. with those of *puncheon¹*, and It. *punzone* also has both senses. I suggest as origin F. *Poinson*, a common surname (whence E. *Punshon*), from *Pontius* (Pilate). Pers. nicknames for vessels are numerous (see *jeroboam, jorum, tankard, demijohn*, etc.) and usu. unaccountable.

Punchinello. See *Punch*.

punctilio. Altered from It. *puntiglio* or Sp. *puntillo*, dims. of *punto*, point. Cf. *point of honour*. Hence *punctilious*.

punctual. MedL. *punctualis*, from *punctus*, point, from *pungere, punct-*, to prick; cf. F. *ponctuel*, punctilious. Current sense in E. is latest.

punctuation. MedL. *punctuatio-n-*, from *punctuare*, to punctuate. Orig. of the "pointing" of the Psalms.

puncture. L. *punctura*, from *pungere, punct-*, to prick.

pundit. Hind. *paṇḍit*, Sanskrit *paṇḍita*, learned. For jocular use cf. *mandarin*.

pungent. From pres. part. of L. *pungere*, to prick. Cf. *poignant*, and, for sense, *piquant*.

Punic. L. *Punicus*, earlier *Poenicus*, Carthaginian, orig. *Phoenician* (q.v.). Esp. in *Punic faith*, L. *fides Punica*.

punish. F. *punir*, *puniss-*, L. *punire*, for *poenire*. See *penal*. *Punitive*, now usu. with *expedition*, is MedL. *punitivus*.

Punjaub head [*Anglo-Ind.*]. Form of amnesia prevalent in *Punjaub*. Also called *Burmah head*.

> Then the Doctor...told us that *aphasia* was like all the arrears of "Punjab Head" falling in a lump (Kipling, *Plain Tales*).

punk [*chiefly US.*]. Touchwood. App. for *spunk* (q.v.).

punkah [*Anglo-Ind.*]. Hind. *pankhā*, fan, from Sanskrit *paksha*, wing.

punnet. Chip-basket for strawberries. ? F. dial. (Rouchi) *ponete*, "petit panier où les poules viennent pondre" (Hécart).

punt[1]. Boat. AS. has *punt*, L. *ponto*, pontoon (q.v.). But, as the word is not found again till c. 1500 (*punt-boat*), when it occurs in EAngl., it was prob. borrowed afresh from cogn. Du. *pont*, ferry-boat.

punt[2]. To bet. Orig. to lay stakes at cards. F. *ponter*, from *ponte*, Sp. *punto*, point.

punt[3]. At football. First at Rugby (1845). Cf. dial. *bunt*, to kick, strike. Prob. the words are nasalized forms of *butt*[5], *put* (in orig. sense).

puny. Phonetic spelling of *puisne* (q.v.). Shaks. has both spellings in current sense of *puny*.

> The first-born child [Mont. aisné] shall succeed and inherit all; where nothing is reserved for punies [Mont. puisnés] (Florio's *Montaigne*, ii. 12).

pup. Shortened from *puppy* (q.v.). With to *sell one a pup*, swindle, cf. hist. of *cozen*.

pupa [*biol.*]. L., girl, doll, adopted as scient. term by Linnaeus.

pupil[1]. Scholar. F. *pupille* (m. & f.), ward, minor, L. *pupillus*, *pupilla*, dims. of *pupus*, boy, *pupa*, girl, baby words of the *papa* type. Orig. sense, still in F., survives in *pupilage*. Current sense from 16 cent. The *pupil teacher* system was introduced from Holland (1839–40).

> To visit pupilles and widewes in her tribulacioun (Wyc. *James*, i. 27).

pupil[2]. Of eye. F. *pupille* (f.), L. *pupilla*, "the sight of the eye" (Coop.), ident. with fem. form of *pupil*[1], from reflection of face seen in eye. Cf. obs. use of *baby*, also G. κόρη, girl, doll, pupil of eye.

> They may kiss and coll, lye and look babies in one anothers eyes (Burton).

puppet. Later form of *poppet*, OF. *poupette*, "a little babie, puppet, bable" (Cotg.), dim. from VL. **puppa*, for *pupa*, girl, doll; cf. It. *puppa*, Du. *pop*, Ger. *puppe*, doll, also F. *poupée*. From 16 cent. esp. doll worked by strings, whence fig. use.

puppy. F. *poupée*, doll, plaything (v.s.). Orig. (15 cent.) lady's toy-dog, pet; cf. *pug*[1]. Current sense first in Shaks. In earlier use not distinguished from *puppet*.

pur-. Norm. form of OF. *por* (*pour*), L. *pro*. In OF. & ME. often confused with *par-*, *pre-* (see *appurtenance*, *prepense*).

purana. Myth. Sanskrit poems. Sanskrit, from *purā*, formerly.

Purbeck marble. From *Isle of Purbeck*, peninsula in Dorset. Mentioned 1205.

purblind. Already in Wyc. dim-sighted, one-eyed, squinting, but orig. (13 cent.) quite blind. App. for *pure blind*; cf. dial. *pure well*, quite well. For change of sense cf. *parboil*.

purchase. F. *pourchasser*, to obtain by pursuit, procure (orig. E. sense), from *chasser*, to chase[1] (q.v.); cf. It. *procacciare*, to procure. Current sense is first in *Piers Plowm*. *Not worth an hour's purchase* is fig. application of reckoning price of land by ref. to annual value. In sense of leverage orig. naut., the verb being used of "gaining" power by means of capstan, etc. Up to 17 cent. *purchase* is still often used for piratical gain, booty.

> *pourchasser*: eagerly to pursue, follow, prosecute, solicite; instantly to seek, purchase, procure, compasse (Cotg.).

> Their servants do act only as privateers, no purchase no pay (Pepys, May 21, 1667).

purdah [*Ind.*]. Curtain, esp. for screening women. Urdu, Pers. *pardah*.

purdonium. Trade-name for coal-scuttle, introduced by one *Purdon*.

pure. F. *pur*, L. *purus*, clean, pure. For intens. use, e.g. *pure* (unadulterated) *nonsense*, cf. *clean crazy*, etc.

purée [*cook.*]. F., ? from OF. *purer*, to squeeze out, from L. *pus*, *pur-*, ? or ident. with OF. *porée*, from L. *porrum*, leek. Cf. MedL. *purea*, *porea*, pea-soup. See *porridge*.

purfle [*archaic*]. To decorate with ornamental border. OF. *porfiler*, from *fil*, thread, L. *filum*; cf. It. *proffilare*, Sp. *perfilar*. See *profile*.

> *purfyle off cloth*: limbus (*Prompt. Parv.*).

purgatory. AF. *purgatorie*, F. *purgatoire*; cf. MedL. *purgatorium*, from *purgare*, to purge.

From 13 cent. in sense of abode of minor torment preliminary to heaven.

By God, in erthe I was his purgatorie,
For which I hope his soule be in glorie
(Chauc. D. 489).

purge. F. *purger*, L. *purgare*, for *purigare*, from *purus*, pure; cf. *castigare*, from *castus*. Leg. use, e.g. to *purge one's offence* is 17 cent. *Pride's purge* (1648) is first mentioned under that name by 18 cent. historians; cf. *Black Prince* (*Death*).

Purim. Pl. of *pŭr*, lot, prob. borrowed by Heb. from Assyr. or Pers. See *Esther*, ix. 26.

puritan. Cf. F. *puritain*, applied (16 cent.) opprobriously to Protestants. Orig. in E. of advanced reformers in Church of England. Cf. Ger. *ketzer*, heretic, from G. καθαρός, clean, pure. Depreciatory sense survives in *puritanical*.

purl[1]. Twisted gold wire, etc. as ornamental edging. Earlier (16 cent.) *pirl*, from archaic verb to *pirl* (v.i.). Cf. It. *pirlare*, "to twirle round" (Flor.), from *pirolo*, spinning-top, cogn. with *pirouette*. Hence *pearl-stitch*.

I pyrle wyer of golde or sylver; I wynde it upon a whele, as sylke women do (Palsg.).

purl[2]. Drink. Orig. infusion of wormwood in hot beer. In Pepys. Origin unknown.

purl[3]. To murmur (of brook). Imit.; cf. Norw. dial. *purla*, Sw. dial. *porla*.

purl[4] [*colloq.*]. To bowl over. For *pirl*, to spin round, etc. See *purl*[1].

purlieu. Orig. strip of land on edge of wood disafforested by a new "perambulation," or survey. L. *perambulatio* was rendered (13 cent.) in AF. by *puralee*, a going through, from OF. *pouraller*. This was contracted to *purley*, and later corrupted to *purlieu* by a supposed etym. from L. *purus locus*, by which it is rendered in early L. dicts. For a similar perversion cf. *venue*. For later senses cf. *outskirts*. We also find OF. *paraller*, MedL. *peralare*.

Forests, chaces, and purlewes
(*Rolls of Parl.* 1482).

Purlieu, or *Pourallee*, is a certain territorie of ground adjoining unto the forest...disafforrested again by the perambulations made for the severing of the new forrestes from the old
(Manwood, *Lawes of Forest*, 1598).

purloin. OF. *porloignier*, to remove, put far away, from *loin*, far, L. *longe*. Cf. F. *éloigner*, to remove.

purple. ONorthumb. *purpel*, for AS. *purpure*, L. *purpura*, G. πορφύρα, name of the shellfish, also called *murex*, which gave the Tyrian purple. For dissim. of *r-r* to *r-l* cf. *marble*. In most Europ. langs., esp. with ref. to dress of emperors, kings, cardinals, the last-named still showing the orig. bright red colour. *Born in the purple* renders Late G. πορφυρογέννητος, member of Byzantine imperial family. For *purple patch* see below.

Inceptis gravibus plerumque et magna professis,
Purpureus, late qui splendeat, unus et alter
Adsuitur pannus (Hor. *De Art. Poet.* 14).

Not quite my whole task; but I have a grand purple patch [viz. the relief of Londonderry] to sew on, and I must take time
(Macaulay's *Diary*, Oct. 25, 1849).

purport. OF. *porporter*, to embody, from *porter*, to carry.

purpose. OF. *porpos* (*propos*), from *porposer* (*proposer*). See *pose*. With *to the purpose* cf. F. *à propos*, and with dial. *a-purpose*, for *of purpose*, cf. F. *de propos* (*delibéré*). With *novel with a purpose* (late 19 cent.) cf. *problem play* and Ger. *tendenzroman*.

purpresture [*leg.*]. Encroachment. AF. corrupt. of *purpresure*, from OF. *porprendre*, L. *pro* and *prendere* (for *prehendere*, to take).

purr. Imit.; cf. F. *ronronner*.

purse. AS. *purs*, Late L. *bursa*, G. βύρσα, hide, leather; cf. F. *bourse*, It. *borsa*, Sp. *bolsa*. Orig. a small bag drawn together at the mouth by a thong, *purse-string*, whence *purse-net*, and to *purse*, i.e. wrinkle, *one's brow* (*lips*). Idea of orig. shape also survives in *long purse*. *Purser* (naut.) is 15 cent. Hence *purser's name*, false name given to purser by passenger travelling incognito.

purslane. Herb. OF. *porcelaine* (cf. It. *porcellana*), altered, app. by influence of *porcelain*, from L. *porcilaca*, used by Pliny for *portulaca*.

pursue. AF. *pursuer*, from OF. *porsĕu*, p.p. of OF. *porsivre* (*poursuivre*), VL. *prosequere*, for *prosequi*, to follow up, prosecute. Etym. sense appears in *pursuant*, *pursuance*, and *pursuivant*, orig. junior heraldic officer acting as "follower" of herald, now officer of College of Arms. *Pursue* is sometimes *persue* in ME., OF. *persivre*, to persecute, and *persecute*, *prosecute* often occur in same sense.

The King's army...prosecuted them even unto this cittie (Syd. Poyntz, 1624–36).

pursy. For earlier *pursive*, AF. *pursif*, OF. *polsif* (*poussif*), from L. *pulsare*, to throb, frequent. of *pellere*, *puls-*, to drive. See *push*, and cf. *jolly, testy*. Orig. short-winded, later associated with *purse* and suggesting a swollen bag.

pursy in wynde drawynge: cardiacus
(*Prompt. Parv.*).

One said, yong Mr Leake was verry rich and fatt. "True," said B. Reid, "pursy men are fatt for the most part" (Manningham's *Diary*, 1602).

You must warrant this horse clear of the glanders, and pursyness (*Gentleman's Dict*. 1705).

purtenance [*archaic*]. OF. *partenance*, from *partenir*, to belong. Cf. *appurtenance*. See *Ex*. xii. 9.

Caput cum pedibus ejus et intestinis vorabitis
(*Vulg.*).

purulent. F., L. *purulentus*, from *pus, pur-*.

purvey. AF. *purveier*, OF. *porveoir* (*pourvoir*), L. *providēre*, to provide, by which it is now usu. replaced. Both had in ME. orig. sense of to foresee. Cf. *survey*.

purview. F. *pourvu*, p.p. of *pourvoir*, to provide (v.s.), AF. *purveu est, purveu que*, being used to introduce a provision or proviso. Hence body of statute following preamble. In mod. use, e.g. *within the purview of*, influenced by *view*.

pus. L., cogn. with G. πύον, matter.

Puseyite. Supporter of *Pusey* (†1882), canon of Christ Church, Oxf., and leader of Oxf. (Tractarian) movement.

push. F. *pousser*, L. *pulsare*, frequent. of *pellere, puls-*, to drive. Hence *push*, vigorous effort. Sense of gang, lot (Austral.) is evolved from that of throng, press.

Pushtoo [*ling.*]. Native name of Afghan lang., intermediate between Iranian and Sanskrit.

pusillanimous. From Church L. *pusillanimis*, from *pusillus*, very small (cogn. with *puer*, boy), and *animus*, spirit. Used to render G. ὀλιγόψυχος, small-souled.

puss. As call-name for cat found in many Europ. langs., and even in Afghan. Of course much older than the dicts. (*NED*. 1530). *Pussyfoot* is a neol. (1919) from US., where it was formerly used of a dainty gait.

Ilyf le Messer vulneravit Robertum Pusekat juxta pontem de Corebrigge, ita quod statim obiit
(*Northumb. Assize Roll*, 1256).

George came pussy-footing round the corner of the station in old man Cardigan's regal touring-car
(Kyne, *Valley of Giants*, 1918).

At a demonstration, on Saturday, to celebrate America's going dry...the chairman, Sir A. Pearce Gould, said it was not generally known how the name [Pussyfoot] originated. It was an honoured name given to Mr Johnson by the Red Indians because of his skilful and brave fight against the drink traffic in the United States
(*Daily Chron*. Jan. 19, 1920).

pustule. F., L. *pustula*, ? from *pus*, purulent matter, ? or imit. of "puffing" (cf. *blister*).

put. Late AS. *putian*, also *potian, pȳtan*. Of obscure origin, prob. ult. cogn. with *butt*[5] and synon. F. *bouter*, "to thrust, put, force, push, forward" (Cotg.). Orig. sense, to thrust, propel, survives in to *put the weight*, *put a horse* (at a fence), *put a knife* (*bullet*) *into one*, naut. *put back* (*to sea*), and, with differentiated spelling and pronunc., in the golf *putt*. To *put up with* (an affront) was formerly to *put up*, i.e. to "pocket." To *put upon*, bully, earlier befool, was orig. to *put the ass* (*fool*) *upon*. With to *put one down* (*for an ass*, etc.) cf. similar use of to *write*.

Nor would she [the maid-servant] go into a family that did not put out their linen to wash, and hire a charwoman to scour (Defoe).

putative. F. *putatif*, Late L. *putativus*, from *putare*, to think.

putlock, putlog. Transverse support in scaffolding. App. from *put*; second element doubtful.

putrid. F. *putride*, L. *putridus*, from *putrēre*, from *puter*, rotten; cf. *putēre*, to stink.

putt [*golf*]. See *put*.

puttee. Hind. *paṭṭī*, bandage; cf. Sanskrit *paṭṭa*. Late 19 cent.

puttock [*naut.*]. In *puttock-shrouds*, now replaced by *futtock-shrouds*. Cf. Du. *putting*, in somewhat similar sense.

putty. Earlier also *potee*, F. *potée*, "brasse, copper, tinne, pewter, &c., burnt or calcinated" (Cotg.), lit. potful, from *pot*. Sense has undergone various changes.

puzzle. Aphet. for ME. *opposal*, interrogation, etc., also *apposal*; cf. to *pose* and *poser*. The *NED*. points out that the sense-hist. of *puzzle*, so far as recorded, casts some doubt on this otherwise obvious etym.

What answere I sholde make
Unto hys unkouthe opposaylle (Lydgate).

puzzolana. See *pozzolana*.

pyaemia. Blood-poisoning. From G. πύον, pus, αἷμα, blood.

pycnotic. Of condensation. G. πυκνωτικός, from πυκνοῦν, to condense.

pygmy, pigmy. L., G. πυγμαῖος, dwarfish, dwarf, from πυγμή, measure of length from elbow to knuckles, also fist, cogn. with L. *pugnus*. Orig. of dwarf races of Ethiopia and India mentioned by Herodotus and Homer, now esp. of dwarf races from Equatorial Africa whose existence may have been vaguely known to the ancients.

pyjamas, pajamas. Urdu, Pers. *pāĕ jāmah*, leg garment, trouser. In E. incorr. used of sleeping-suit.

pylon. G. πυλών, gateway, from πύλη, gate.

pylorus [*anat.*]. Lower orifice of stomach. Late L., G. πυλωρός, gate-keeper (v.s.), from οὖρος, watcher.

pyracanth. Shrub. L., G. πυράκανθα, app. from πῦρ, fire, ἄκανθα, thorn, but identity of G. shrub with that known by the Linnaean name is dubious.

pyramid. F. *pyramide*, L., G. πυραμίς, πυραμίδ-, trad. associated with πῦρ, fire (beacon), or πυρός, grain (granary), but prob. of Egypt. origin.

pyre. L., G. πυρά, hearth, funeral pile, from πῦρ, fire. See *pile*².

pyrethrum. Plant. L., G. πύρεθρον, from πυρετός, fever, from πῦρ, fire; from med. properties. Cf. its pop. name *feverfew* (q.v.).

pyrexia. Fever. From G. πύρεξις (v.s.).

pyrites. L., G. πυρίτης (sc. λίθος), fire-stone (v.s.).

pyrotechny. F. *pyrotechnie*, from G. πῦρ, fire, τέχνη, art. Orig. in mil. and chem. senses.

pyroxene [*min.*]. Named (1796) by Haüy, who regarded it as a stranger, G. ξένος, to the igneous rocks.

pyroxylin. Explosive from vegetable fibre. Named (1846) by Pelouze from G. ξύλον, wood.

Pyrrhic. Dance and metrical foot. F. *pyrrique*, L., G. πυρρίχη (sc. ὄρχησις, dance), war-dance of Ancient Greeks, trad. from its inventor Πύρριχος. The phalanx (v.i.) belongs rather to next.

You have the Pyrrhic dance as yet:
Where is the Pyrrhic phalanx gone?
(*Isles of Greece*).

Pyrrhic victory. Gained at too great cost to victor, like that of *Pyrrhus*, G. Πύρρος, king of Epirus (3 cent. B.C.), over the Romans at Asculum. Cf. *Cadmean*.

Ctesiphon, where General Townsend won his Pyrrhic victory (*Daily Chron.* June 27, 1917).

Pyrrhonist. Follower of *Pyrrho*, G. Πύρρων, sceptic philosopher of Elis (4 cent. B.C.).

pyrus [*bot.*]. MedL., incorr. for L. *pirus*, pear-tree; esp. in *pyrus japonica*.

Pythagorean. Of *Pythagoras*, G. Πυθαγόρας, philosopher of Samos (6 cent. B.C.). In

early use with spec. ref. to doctrine of transmigration of souls.

Pythian. From G. Πύθιος, of the Delphic Apollo (v.i.).

python. L., G. Πύθων, name of serpent slain near Delphi by Apollo, prob. from earlier name of Delphi. Mod. sense is 19 cent.

pythoness. OF. *phitonise*, Late L. *pythonissa*, used in *Vulg.* of Witch of Endor (1 *Sam.* xxviii. 7), app. connected with the prophetess of the Delphic oracle (v.s.).

And speke as renably and faire and wel,
As to the Phitonissa dide Samuel (Chauc. D. 1509).

pyx [*eccl.*]. Receptacle for consecrated bread. Also *pyxis*. L., G. πυξίς, box, from πύξος, box-tree. See *box*¹. Also later (16 cent.) used of the "assay-box" at the Mint.

Q-ship. Name given to "mystery ships" which lured the unsuspecting U-boat. *Q*-for *query*, in allusion to enigmatic character. Cf. *hush-boat*.

qua. L., in the capacity of, fem. abl. of *qui*, who, used adverbially.

quack. Imit.; cf. Du. *kwakken*, Ger. *quacken*. In sense of "doctor," short for *quacksalver*, Du. *kwakzalver*, one who sells his salves by his patter. Cf. synon. Ger. *marktschreier*, lit. market shrieker, and see *charlatan*. Du. has also *lapzalver*, charlatan, from *lappen*, to patch, cobble.

quad [*Oxf.*]. Short for *quadrangle*.

quadragenarian. From L. *quadragenarius*, from *quadrageni*, distrib. of *quadraginta*, forty.

quadragesimal. Lenten. Late L. *quadragesimalis*, in allusion to forty days.

quadrangle. F., Late L. *quadrangulum*, from *quadr-* (*quattuor*, four).

quadrant. L. *quadrans*, *quadrant-*, fourth part. The instrument (from c. 1400) is a quarter-circle.

quadrate. L. *quadratus*, from *quadrare*, to square, from *quattuor*, four. *Quadratic equations* (17 cent.) are so called because involving the square of *x*. Cf. *quadrature* (squaring) *of the circle*.

quadrennial. From L. *quadriennium*, four years; cf. *biennial*, etc.

quadriga. L., four-horse chariot, from *quattuor*, four, *jugum*, yoke.

quadrilateral. From L. *quadrilaterus*, from *latus*, *later-*, side. In mil. sense of region defended by four fortresses esp. in ref. to the *Italian quadrilateral* (Mantua, Verona, Peschiera, Legnano).

quadrille[1] [*archaic*]. Card-game which superseded ombre (18 cent.) and was superseded by whist. F., ? Sp. *cuartillo*, quarter, altered by association with *quadrille*[2].

quadrille[2]. Dance. F., Sp. *cuadrilla*, orig. troop of riders in four groups; cf. It. *quadriglio*, "a crue, a troupe, a companie" (Flor.).

quadrillion. Coined on *million, billion*.

quadrivium. L., meeting of four ways, from *via*, way; in MedL. the math. part of the liberal arts, viz. arithmetic, geometry, astronomy, music. Cf. *trivial*.

quadroon. Earlier *quarteron, quatron*, F. *quarteron*, Sp. *cuarterón*, from *cuarto*, fourth, L. *quartus*, because having one-fourth of negro blood. Form has been influenced by numerous words in *quadr-* (v.s.).

quadrumane. Late L. *quadrumanus*, coined, after *quadruped*, from L. *manus*, hand.

quadruped. L. *quadrupes, quadruped-*, from *pes*, foot. *Quadru-* is a var. of *quadri-*.

quadruple. F., L. *quadruplus*. Cf. *double, triple*.

quaere. L., imper. of *quaerere*, to seek. Used as comment on matter to be looked up or further considered. Now usu. *query*.

quaestor [*hist.*]. L., from *quaerere, quaesit-*, to seek. Orig. official in charge of treasury.

quaff. Earlier also *quaft*. Orig. to carouse, the date (16 cent.) and hist. of the word suggesting that it came from the Low Countries (cf. *booze*). This is also the statement of early etymologists. The fact that *quass*, LG. *quassen*, to eat or drink immoderately, is found in the same sense, suggests that *quaff* may have originated in a mis-reading of *quaſſ*.

I quaught, I drinke all out: je boys dautant (Palsg.).

The beastly man muste sitte all day and quasse,
The beaste indeede doth drincke but twice a day,
The beastly man muste stuffe his monstrous masse
             (Turbervile, 1576).

In our fathers days, the English returning from the service in the Netherlands, brought with them the foul vice of drunkenness, as besides other testimonies the term of *carous*, from *gar-aus*, all out, learnt of the High Dutch there, in the same service; so *quaff*, &c.
     (Chamberlayne, *Present State of England*, 1692).

quagga. Kind of zebra. Given (1710) as Hottentot *quacha*, but now current in Kaffir in the form *iquara*. "The true quagga is believed to have been exterminated about 1873" (*NED.*).

quagmire. From 16 cent., cogn. with *quake*.

Earlier also *quakemire, quavemire* (see *quaver*).

Quai d'Orsay [*hist.*]. F. Foreign Office. From address. Cf. *Ballplatz, Porte*, etc.

quail[1]. Bird. F. *caille*, of Teut. origin; cf. It. *quaglia*, OSp. *coalla*, MedL. *quacula*, VL. *quaccola* (*Gloss. of Reichenau*, 9 cent.). Source may be OHG. *quahtela*, imit. of cry; cf. Du. *kwakkel*.

quail[2]. Verb. Obs. from c. 1650, but revived by Scott. Fig. use of obs. *quail*, to curdle, coagulate (still in dial.), F. *cailler*, L. *coagulare*. Cogn. It. *cagliare* has the same double sense.

cagliare: to crud or congeale as milke doth. Also to hold ones peace (Flor.).

You could mark by the change of his skin and by the look out of his eyes how his courage was clabbering to whey inside him, making his face a milky, curdled white (Irvin S. Cobb).

quaint. OF. *cointe*, L. *cognitus*, p.p. of *cognoscere*, to get to know. Cf. *acquaint*. Orig. clever, ingenious, pretty, etc. For vague and wide senses cf. *nice, fine*, etc. Some early dicts. have "*quaint*; see *unknown*," the word having thus gradually reached its opposite.

coint: quaint, compt, neat, fine, spruce, brisk, smirk, smug, daintie, trim, tricked up (Cotg.).

quair [*Sc.*]. See *quire*[2].

quake. AS. *cwacian*; cf. OLG. *quekilih*, vibrating; ult. cogn. with *quaver*. Sometimes treated as strong verb in ME. (see *aspen*). The nickname *Quaker* was given (c. 1650) to the Society of Friends, by whom it is not recognized (cf. *Shaker, convulsionnaire*).

Preacht at Gaines Coln, ye quakers nest, but no disturbance (*Diary* of Ralph Josselin, Vicar of Earl's Colne, Essex, July 3, 1655).

qualify. F. *qualifier*, MedL. *qualificare*, to describe, attribute a quality to, from *qualis*, of what kind. Sense of modifying (a statement) by closer definition is 16 cent. Mod. to *qualify for* (*a position*) is for earlier reflex.

I am qualifying myself to give lessons
            (*Bleak House*, ch. xxxviii.).

quality. F. *qualité*, L. *qualitas*, from *qualis* (v.s.). For *people of quality* cf. similar use of *fashion, rank*, etc., with adj. understood.

Les gens de qualité savent tout sans avoir jamais rien appris (*Précieuses ridicules*, ix.).

qualm. Orig. (16 cent.) sudden faintness or fear, later esp. in *qualms of conscience* (Milt.). Du. *kwalm*, earlier, *qualm*, "a steam, reek, vapour, mist" (Sewel), whence

Ger. *qualm*, vapour, exhalation, the cogn.
MHG. word being *twalm*, swoon. Cf. similar
use of *vapours*. AS. *cwealm*, whence ME.
qualm, pestilence, is a separate word.

*es kam mir plötzlich wie ein qualm, oder nebel, übers
herz gezogen*: I got a sudden qualm; I fell into a
swoon (Ludw.).

quandary. "A low word" (Johns.), first in
Euphues (1579). Of obscure origin, but
perh. a mutilation of some L. term used in
scholastic disputes; cf. *nonplus* and F.
mettre à quia, to nonplus, lit. to reduce to
"because," both of such origin. It is explained (1582) by Mulcaster as "of a Latin
form used English-like," and it seems
possible that the second element is L. *dare*,
to give.

quant [*EAngl.*]. Kind of punt-pole. ? L.
contus, "a long pole to shove forth a vessel
into the deepe" (Coop.), G. κοντός.

qwante, sprete, rodde: contus (*Prompt. Parv.*).

quantity. F. *quantité*, L. *quantitas*, from
quantus, how much, how many. *Negligible
quantity*, orig. math., is after F. *quantité
négligeable*.

quantivalence [*chem.*]. From L. *quantus* (v.s.),
after *equivalence*.

quantum. L., neut. of *quantus* (v.s.). *Quantum suff(icit)* is orig. from med. prescriptions.

quaquaversal [*geol.*]. Turning in all directions. From Late L. *quaquaversus*, lit.
wheresoever towards.

quarantine. It. *quarantina*, from *quaranta*,
forty, L. *quadraginta*, because theoretically of forty days.

fare la quarantana: to keepe lent or fast fortie daies,
properly in time of plague or sicknes, to keepe
fortie daies from companie, namely if one come
from infected places, as they use in Italy (Flor.).

quarenden, quarender. West-country apple,
with many spellings. ME. *quaryndon*.
Origin unknown. ? From *Carentan* (Normandy), ? or *Quarendon* (Bucks).

quarrel¹. Dispute. F. *querelle*, L. *querela*,
complaint, accusation, from *queri*, to complain; cf. *querulous*.

Ye Jewes broughte up...many and grevous quarels
[*Vulg.* causas] agaynst Paul (Coverd. *Acts*, xxv. 7).

quarrel² [*hist.*]. Cross-bow bolt. OF. *quarel,
carrel* (*carreau*), dim. from L. *quadrus*,
square; cf. It. *quadrello*, Sp. *cuadrillo*,
MedL. *quadrellus*. Also (archaic) diamond-
shaped pane, as F. *carreau*, and in similar
senses for which dial. often has *quarry*.

quarreau: is (generally) a little square, or square
thing;...also, a quarrell, or boult for a crossebow,
or an arrow with a four-square head (Cotg.).

Scoured deal, red quarries [floor-tiles], and whitewash (*Daniel Deronda*).

quarry¹. Of hunter. Orig. (ME.) offal of stag
given to hounds (still in Turbervile, 1576);
later, heap of dead game (Shaks. *Cor.* i. 1,
Macb. i. 2), object of pursuit. Earlier
quirrè, OF. *cuirée* (*curée*), from *cuir*, hide,
L. *corium*, because the hounds' reward was
spread on the hide (v.i.). This origin, given
c. 1200, may be popular etym. and *cuirée*
may be for *curée*, from L. *curare*, to clean,
eviscerate; cf. Venet. *curare*, to gut. Both
the F. & L. words have also been associated with VL. **corata*, intestines, from
cor, heart; cf. OF. *coraille*, intestines.

Hert, liver, and lightes,
And blod tille his quirre,
Houndes on hyde he dightes (*NED.* c. 1320).

quarry². For stone. Earlier also *quarrer*, OF.
quariere (*carrière*), from L. *quadrare*, to
square (stones). Also dial. *quarrel* (see
quarrel²).

quarry³. See *quarrel²*.

quart¹. Measure. F. *quarte*, quarter (of
gallon), L. *quarta* (sc. *pars*), fem. of
quartus, fourth.

quart². In fencing. Also *quarte, carte* (q.v.).
Cf. *tierce*.

quartan. Ague or fever with paroxysm every
fourth (third) day. ME. *quartain*, F.
quartaine, L. *quartana* (*febris*), from
quartus, fourth.

quarte. See *quart²*.

quarter. F. *quartier*, L. *quartarius*, fourth
part (of a measure), from *quartus*, fourth.
In F. & E. also vaguely for part. The
sense-development took place in F. Topogr.
sense starts from the four *quarters* of the
compass, e.g. *Sits the wind in that quarter?*
misquotation for *corner* (*Much Ado*, ii. 3).
Connection of to *give quarter* with mil.
quarters, as in *winter quarters, close quarters*
(see *close*), is obscure. The *quarter-deck* is
about half the length of the half-deck,
hence *quarter* for adjacent part of ship's
side. *Quartermaster* was orig. (15 cent.)
naval. A *quarterstaff* was perh. orig. from
a tree of a certain size split in four; cf. dial.
quartercleft, quarterclift, a stout staff; there
are references in *Privy Council Acts* (1548–
9) to *clif staves* for the army. A *bad quarter
of an hour* is after F. *mauvais quart d'heure*

(*de Rabelais*), paying time, with allusion to a trad. incident in the life of Rabelais.

quartier: a quarter, coast, part, region; also, a quarter, or ward, in a town; also, the quarter of a yeere, of a yard; a quarter of the moon; of mutton, &c., the fourth part of any thing thats commonly divided by quarters; also, a trencher; also, quarter, or fair war, where souldiers are taken prisoners, and ransomed at a certaine rate (Cotg.).

quartern. OF. *quarteron*, fourth part, from *quart*, quarter, e.g. *a quartern of gin* is a quarter of a pint and a *quartern loaf* is made from a quarter of a peck of flour.

quartette. F., It. *quartetto*, from *quarto*, fourth.

quarto. L. (*in*) *quarto*, the sheet being folded in four. Cf. *folio*, *octavo*, etc.

quartz. Ger. *quarz*, found in MHG., whence also Du. *kwarts*, F. *quartz*, It. *quarzo*. ? Pet-form (cf. *Heinz* for *Heinrich*, *Kunz* for *Konrad*) of MHG. *querch* (*zwerg*), dwarf, gnome (cf. *cobalt*, *nickel*).

quash. F. *casser*, L. *quassare*, frequent. of *quatere*, *quass-*, to break. See *cashier*[2]. The F. *cour de cassation* has the power of "quashing" a sentence.

Quashee. Nickname for negro. From Ashantee or Fantee *Kwasi*, name commonly given to child born on Sunday.

quasi. L., as if, for *quam si*.

quassia. Named (c. 1761) by Linnaeus from *Graman Quassi*, a Surinam negro (see *Quashee*) who discovered the properties of the root (1730). Cf. *sequoia*.

quaternary. L. *quaternarius*, from *quaterni*, four together, from *quater*, four times.

quaternion. Late L. *quaternio-n-*, set of four (v.s.). In Wyc. (*Acts*, xii. 4). In math. sense introduced (1843) by Hamilton.

quatrain. F., from *quatre*, four, L. *quattuor*.

quatrefoil. F. *quatre*, four, *feuille*, leaf, foil[1]. Cf. *trefoil*.

quattrocento. It., as *cinquecento* (q.v.).

quaver. Frequent. of obs. *quave*, ME. *cwavien*, ult. cogn. with *quake*. Cf. *quiver*[2]. Mus. sense from 16 cent.

quay. F. *quai* (12 cent.), Gaulish *caium* (5 cent.). Earlier spelling, now altered on ModF., was *kay*, *key*, AF. *kaie*. See also *key*[2].

quean [*archaic*]. AS. *cwene*, woman. Aryan; cf. OHG. *quena*, Goth. *qino*, G. γυνή, Zend *qenā*, OIr. *ben*, Welsh *bún*; cogn., but not ident., with *queen* (q.v.). For disparaging sense, which appears early, cf. *hussy*, *wench*, and *Who are you calling a woman?*

To knowe
Other [either] a knyght fro a knave other [or] a
queyne fro a queene (*Piers Plowm.* C. ix. 46).

queasy. Earlier (15 cent.) *coisy*. Orig. ticklish, unsettled. Sir John Paston observes more than once that "the world seems queasy," i.e. things are looking queer. Forms point to F. origin, and obs. *squeasy* suggests OF. *escoisier, to disquiet, from *coisier*, to settle, etc., VL. *quietiare (see *coy*); but *squeasy* occurs later (16 cent.) than *queasy* and may be due to influence of *squeamish*.

queen. AS. *cwēn*, wife (of king or celebrity); cf. OSax. *quān*, ON. *kvæn*, Goth. *qēns*, woman; related by ablaut to *quean* (q.v.).

"What news, Mr Neverout?" "Why, Madam,
Queen Elizabeth's dead"
(Swift, *Polite Conversation*).

queer. First in Sc. (c. 1500). ? Ident. with cant *queer*, not straight, "on the cross," Ger. *quer*, across, athwart, ult. cogn. with *thwart*[1]; cf. to *queer the pitch* (*game*), i.e. to thwart, and similar use of F. *travers*, "crosse, crosse-wise, thwart, overthwart" (Cotg.). *Queer Street* is 19 cent.

Queensberry rules. For fair boxing. Drawn up (1867) by eighth *Marquis of Queensberry* (†1900).

quelch. Occ. for *squelch*. Cf. *s-quash*.

quell. AS. *cwellan*, to kill, destroy. Com. Teut.; cf. Du. *kwellen*, Ger. *quälen*, to torture, ON. *kvelja*. ? Cogn. with *kill*. Wyc. has *man quellers* for *murderers* (*Matt.* xxii. 7).

quench. AS. *cwencan*, in *ācwencan*, to extinguish (fire, light), causal of *cwincan*, to be extinguished (cf. *drench*, *drink*), cogn. with Fris. *kwinka*. For application to thirst cf. similar use of F. *éteindre*, Ger. *löschen*, to extinguish. *Modest quencher* is Dick Swiveller's (*Old Cur. Shop*, ch. xxxv.).

quenelle. Forcemeat ball. F. ? corrupt. of synon. Ger. *knödel*, dim. of *knoten*, knot.

querimonious. From L. *querimonia*, from *queri*, to complain.

quern [*archaic*]. AS. *cweorn*. Com. Teut.; cf. Du. *kweern*, OHG. *quirn*, ON. *kvern*, Goth. *qairnus*; ult. cogn. with Sanskrit *grāvan*, stone. The replacement in the Teut. langs. of this word by derivatives of Late L. *molinum* is a tribute to Roman efficiency (cf. *kitchen*).

querulous. From L. *querulus*, from *queri*, to complain.

query. Altered from *quaere* (q.v.). Cf. *pandy*.

quest. OF. *queste* (*quête*), from *quaerere*, *quaesit-*, to seek; cf. It. *chiesta*, Sp. *cuesta*. Sometimes aphet. for *inquest*, e.g. *crowner's* *quest.* In medieval romance esp. of a knight's enterprise.

question. F., L. *quaestio-n-*, from *quaerere* (v.s.). *Questionnaire* (neol.) is F. Depreciatory sense of *questionable* from c. 1800.

queue. F., OF. *coue, cue*, L. *cauda*, tail; cf. *cue*[1]. As verb early in 1918. Quot. below, from a contemporary of the Revolution, refers to the shortage in Paris c. 1792.

Dès deux heures du matin les femmes se rangeaient deux à deux sur une longue ligne que le peuple désigna sous le nom de "queue"
(Mercier, *Paris pendant la Révolution*).

quhair [*Sc.*]. See *quire*[2].

quibble. Dim. of obs. *quib*, clipped form of L. *quibus*, abl. pl. of *qui*, who, which, occurring frequently in leg. documents and hence suggesting hair-splitting tricks, etc.

quick. AS. *cwic*, living. Com. Teut.; cf. Du. *kwik*, Ger. *keck*, impudent, ON. *kvikr*; ult. cogn. with L. *vivus*, alive, G. βίος, life. Orig. sense in *the quick and the dead*, and in numerous compds., e.g. *quicklime* (cf. F. *chaux vive*), *quicksand, quickset hedge* (cf. F. *haie vive*), *quicksilver* (cf. F. *vif argent*, Ger. *quecksilber*); also in Bibl. to *quicken*. Sense of rapid is evolved from that of lively (cf. *look lively*). With to *cut to the quick* cf. F. *trancher dans le vif*.

Deth come on hem; and go thei doun quyk [*var.* lyvende] in to helle (Wyc. *Ps.* liv. 16).

quid[1]. Of tobacco. Var. of *cud* (q.v.).

quid[2]. Sovereign; earlier (17 cent.), guinea. ? Slang use of L. *quid*, something; cf. F. *quibus* used for *de quoi*, the wherewithal.

quidds: money (*Dict. Cant. Crew*).

quiddity. F. *quiddité*, scholastic L. *quidditas*, formed from *quid*, what, after *qualitas, quantitas*.

quidnunc. L. *quid nunc?* what now? what's the news?

quid pro quo. L., something for something. Orig. substitution, in med. prescriptions, of one drug for another. In sense of blunder rather from scholastic phrase *quid pro quod*, i.e. elementary gramm. blunder, which in F. is altered to *quiproquo*.

quiescent. From pres. part. of L. *quiescere*, to become quiet, from root of *quies*, rest.

quiet. L. *quietus*, p.p. of *quiescere* (v.s.). Cf. *coy*. Hence *quietism*, form of rel. mysticism taught (c. 1675) by Molinos, a Sp. priest. The noun may represent AF. *quiete*, L. *quies, quiet-*, common in phrase *en quiete et peas*.

quietus. From MedL. phrase *quietus est*, he

is quit (of a debt, etc.). In fig. sense first in Shaks. (*Haml.* iii. 1).

quiff [*slang*]. Oiled lock plastered on forehead. An East End word (not in *NED.*). ? From It. *cuffia*, coif. *Quife* occurs as early var. of E. *coif*.

The well-oiled quiff, that outcrop of hair that was once the soldier's pride and glory
(*Star*, Apr. 17, 1918).

quill. Orig. hollow stalk (*Prompt. Parv.*); cf. LG. *quiele*, Ger. *kiel*. Origin unknown. Hence archaic to *quill*, orig. to goffer a ruff. Cf. F. *tuyauter*, to quill, from *tuyau*, "a pipe, quill, cane, reed, canell" (Cotg.).

quillet[1] [*antiq.*]. Small plot of land. Earlier also *coylett*, OF. *coillete* (*cueillette*), crop, from *cueillir*, to gather. See *coil*[1], *cull*.

quillet[2]. Quibble. Short for obs. *quillity*, corrupt. of *quiddity* (q.v.).

Why might not that be the skull of a lawyer? Where be his quiddits now, his quillets, his cases, his tenures, and his tricks? (*Haml.* v. 1).

quilt. OF. *coilte, cuilte* (*couette*), L. *culcita*, cushion. With ME. *quilt-point* cf. *counterpane* (q.v.). With slang (US.) sense of *quilt*, thrash, cf. obs. to *bumbast* (see *bombast*) and F. *bourrer*, "to stuffe with flockes, and haire: also, to beat, or thumpe" (Cotg.).

quinary. L. *quinarius*, from *quini*, distrib. of *quinque*, five. This is assim. for **pinque* and suffers dissim. (VL. *cinque*) in Romanic. See *five*.

quince. Orig. pl. of obs. *quine*, ME. *coyn, quoyne*, OF. *cuin, coin* (*coing*), L. *cotoneum* (Pliny), for *cydoneum*, G. κυδώνιον μῆλον, Cydonian apple, from *Cydonia* (in Crete). Cf. *bodice, lettuce*, and, for converse change, *cherry, pea*. Cf. also Prov. *codoing*, It. *cotogna*, Ger. *quitte* (OHG. *chutina*), Du. *kwee*, AS. *coddæppel*.

quincentenary. Incorr. for *quingentenary*.

quincunx. L., orig. five ounces, from *quinque*, five, *uncia*, ounce; also applied to arrangement of trees like the pips on a five of cards. In spec. sense introduced by Evelyn and common in describing the artificial gardens of the period. Cf. F. *quinconce*.

Le vergier [de l'Abbaie de Thélème], plein de tous arbres fruictiers, tous ordonnez en ordre quincunce
(Rab. i. 55).

quingentenary. Coined from L. *quingenti*, five hundred, after *centenary*, etc.

quinine. From *quina*, Sp. spelling of Peruv. *kina*, bark, whence also by redupl. the earlier *quinquina* (17 cent.).

Quinquagesima [*eccl.*]. L., fiftieth (sc. *dies*), because about fifty days before Easter.

quinquennial. From L. *quinquennis.* Cf. *biennial*, etc.

quinquina. See *quinine.*

quinsy. OF. *quinancie* (12 cent.), MedL. *quinancia*, G. κυνάγχη, lit. dog-throttling, from κύων, κυν-, dog, ἄγχειν, to strangle. Commoner in ME. is *squinacy, squinsy,* F. *esquinancie*, with prefixed *es-*.

> *esquinance*: the squincy, or squinancy (Cotg.).

quint. Sequence of five at piquet. F. *quinte*, from L. *quintus*, fifth.

quinta. Country-house (Sp. & Port.). Orig. farm let for fifth part, *quinta parte*, of produce.

quintain [*hist.*]. F. *quintaine*; cf. It. Prov. MedL. *quintana.* ? L. *quintana* (*via*), market-street of camp, orig. quarters of fifth maniple. It is supposed that this may have been used for warlike exercises, but the hist. of the word has not been traced.

quintal. Hundredweight. F., Arab. *qintār*, L. *centenarium*; cf. It. *quintale*, Sp. *quintal*, MedL. *quintale.*

quintennial. Incorr., after *septennial*, for *quinquennial* (q.v.). Cf. *quintagenarian* for *quinquagenarian.*

quintessence. F., OF. *quinte essence*, MedL. *quinta essentia*, substance of the heavenly bodies (outside the four elements), the discovery of which by distillation was one aim of medieval alchemy.

quintette. F., It. *quintetto*, from *quinto*, fifth.

quintillion. Cf. *quadrillion.*

quintuple. F., from L. *quintus*, fifth, after *quadruple.*

quip. Short for obs. *quippy*, L. *quippe*, forsooth. Prob. associated mentally with *nip, whip*, etc., in sense of sharp and cutting, and often confused with *quibble.*

> Quips and cranks, and wanton wiles (*Allegro*, 27).

quipu. Coloured thread used by ancient Peruvians to record events. Peruv., knot.

quire[1]. Earlier form of *choir* (q.v.).

quire[2]. Of paper. ME. *quaer, quair*, etc., OF. *quaier, caier* (*cahier*), VL. *quaternum*, for *quaternio*, "a quier with foure sheetes" (Coop.). Cf. the *Kingis Quair*, i.e. book, written, when imprisoned in England, by James I of Scotland.

Quirinal [*hist.*]. Former papal palace, on *Mons Quirinalis* (Rome), from *Quirinus*, divine name of Romulus.

quirk. From 16 cent. Orig. sense prob.

twist, turn, flourish, as in *quirk* (ornamentation) of stocking (16 cent.). Later, quibble, quip, verbal conceit, etc. ? Ult. cogn. with Ger. *quer*, slanting, etc. (see *queer*).

> Quirks, it may be explained, are young enemy aviators in an embryonic stage
> (*Sunday Times*, May 20, 1917).

quirt. Riding-whip (US.). Sp. *cuerda*, cord.

> And cantering with him rode the frontier band,
> Whooping and swearing as they plied the quirt
> (Masefield, *Rosas*).

quit. Adj. F. *quitte*, L. *quietus*, discharged; cf. Sp. *quito*, MedL. *quitus.* The verb, F. *quitter*, meant orig. to release, clear (cf. *quittance*); hence, to give up, renounce; and finally, to depart from. In some uses, e.g. *quit you like men*, it is aphet. for *acquit.* Something of earlier sense appears in US. *quit*, to leave off, *quitter*, a shirker. *Quit-rent* (leg.) is paid in lieu of service. In to *be quits with* (cf. to *be even with*) the *-s* may be due to MedL. *quitus* (cf. *quietus*); but *doubles or quits* was earlier *double or quit* (Sidney's *Arcadia*). With to *cry quits* cf. obs. leg. *quitclaim*, to acquit, OF. *quiteclamer.* The noun *quitclaim*, formal release, is still in US. use; cf. synon. Du. *kwijtschelden.*

quitch. Grass. AS. *cwice*, cogn. with *quick.* Also called *couch.*

quite. Ident. with *quit* (q.v.), in sense of clear, unburdened. In early use often coupled with *clear* or *clean.*

quits. See *quit.*

quittance. See *quit.*

quiver[1]. For arrows. OF. *cuivre, cuevre*, said to be of Teut. origin and ult. ident. with AS. *cocor*, Ger. *köcher.* ? Or simply a *cover.* For *quiver full* (of children) see *Ps.* cxxvii. 5.

quiver[2]. To shake. Thinned form of *quaver.*

qui vive. F., who (long) live? The abnormal use of the subjunct. is explained by an ellipsis for *Qui voulez-vous qui vive?* Whom do you wish to live? on which side are you? Quot. below seems to confirm this etym., and is much earlier than any record of the F. phrase.

> Interrogati secundum communem modum loquendi: "*Qui* [sic] *vivat, qui vivat?*" respondebant "Rex, Regina et Dux Burgundie," nomen Dalphini tacentes
> (*Chronique du religieux de Saint-Denis*, 1419).

quixotic. From *Don Quixote*, hero of Cervantes' (†1616) novel. The name means *cuisse* (q.v.), hence Smollett called his imitation *Sir Lancelot Greaves.*

quiz. Orig. (late 18 cent.) eccentric person, oddity. With verb to *quiz* cf. to *fool*, to *gull*, etc. App. of arbitrary formation. *Quoz* was used at same period in somewhat similar sense.

quod [*slang*.]. Perh. orig. the quad-rangle of the prison. From c. 1700.

> *quod*: Newgate; also any prison, tho for debt
> *(Dict. Cant. Crew).*

quodlibet [*archaic*]. Dispute for practice; medley. L., what you will.

quoin. Wedge, esp. arch.; also naut. and in gunnery. Var. of *coin* (q.v.).

quoit. Earliest in AF. *jeu de coytes* (1388). In ME. also *coite*, *quayte*. These forms correspond phonetically to F. *couette*, cushion (OF. *coite*, L. *culcita*). It is not known whether the word was orig. applied to the missile or the target. In 16 cent. we find copious records of *cushion*, some unknown game, in to *miss the cushion, wide of (beside) the cushion*, and both E. *quoit* and F. *coussinet* are used in spec. senses for a flat disk of stone. Early quoits were of stone (v.i.) and were perh. orig. slid instead of thrown, hence dial. *quoiting* for "curling," and verb to *quoit* in Shaks. (v.i.). In naut. F. *coites* (*couettes*) are "deux fortes pièces de bois, qui, placées sous un bâtiment en construction, glissent avec lui quand on le lance à la mer" (Littré). I am aware that this is all rather vague, but it may help some other student to identify *quoit* with F. *couette*, an identity of which I personally am convinced.

> *coytyn*: petriludo (*Prompt. Parv.*).

> Quoit him down[-stairs], Bardolph, like a shove-groat shilling (*2 Hen. IV*. ii. 4).

quondam. L., formerly. In 16 cent. used as a noun (cf. *ci-devant*).

quorum. L., of whom, occurring in commissions appointing certain persons *quorum vos...unum* (*duos*, etc.) *esse volumus*.

> Mr Norbury, the butler, always feels the likeness of the breakfast rally to fish in a drop-net....He must look in at the door to see if there is a quorum. A quarum would do. A cujus is a great rarity
> (W. de Morgan, *When Ghost meets Ghost*).

quota. MedL. (sc. *pars*), from *quot*, how many.

quote. MedL. *quotare*, to distinguish by numbers, from *quot*, how many. Cf. F. *coter*. Orig. to mark with chapter-numbers, marginal references, etc., hence to be able to "give chapter and verse." Mod. business sense reverts to etym. meaning.

quoth. Past tense of obs. *quethe*, AS. *cwethan*.

Com. Teut.; cf. OSax. *quethan*, OHG. *quedan*, ON. *kvetha*, Goth. *qithan*. Cf. *bequeath*. Archaic *quotha* is for *quoth he*.

quotidian. F. *quotidien*, L. *quotidianus*, from *quotidie*, every day, from *quotus*, how many, *dies*, day.

quotient. L. *quotiens*, how many times, from *quot*; altered by association with participial forms in *-ent*.

quotum. L., neut. of *quotus*, from *quot*. Cf. *quota*.

R. The *r-months*, when oysters are in season, are mentioned by Lord Chesterfield. *The three Rs*, reading, 'riting, 'rithmetic, is said to have been first given as a toast by Sir W. Curtis (†1829).

rabbet [*carpent*.]. OF. *rabat*, from *rabattre*, to beat back. *Rebate* is found in same sense.

rabbi. L., G., Heb. *rabbī*, my master, from *rabh*, master, Jewish title of respect for doctors of the law. The *-n* in F. *rabbin*, MedL. *rabbinus*, whence *rabbinical*, may be due to association with *assassin*, *cherubin*, etc.

rabbit. Orig. the young rabbit, as distinguished from the cony. Cf. Walloon *robett*, Flem. *robbe*, dim. *robbeke*; also F. *rabouillère*, rabbit burrow. Prob. nickname from *Robert*, whence comes name *Rabbetts*; cf. *renard*, *robin*, *jackdaw*, etc. The rabbit is called *robert* in Dev.

> The hare and the conie are called in their first yeare *leverets* and *rabets* (Turbervile, 1576).

rabble. Orig. (14 cent.) pack, swarm, of animals, with idea of a string or series strongly suggested. Origin unknown. The analogy of *rascal* (q.v.) suggests an OF. derivative of *râble*, rake, L. *rutabulum*, with suffix as in *canaille*, *valetaille*, *pédantaille*, etc.

rabid. L. *rabidus*, from *rabere*, to be mad; cf. *rabies*, (canine) madness, whence *rage*.

raca [*Bibl*.]. Chaldee *rēkā*, of doubtful meaning. See *Matt.* v. 22.

raccoon. See *racoon*.

race¹. Running, current, channel, etc. ON. *rās*. Cogn. AS. *rǣs* gave ME. *rese*, attack, incursion; cf. Ger. *rasen*, to rave, rage, from LG.

race². Tribe, family. F., earlier (16 cent.) *rasse*, It. *razza* (14 cent.), Sp. Port. *raza*, ? from Arab. *rās*, head, origin.

race³ [*archaic*]. Root (of ginger). OF. *rais*, L. *radix*, *radic-*, root. Cf. *radish*.

raceme [*bot*.]. L. *racemus*, grape, erron. taken to mean cluster. Cf. *raisin*.

rachitis [*med.*]. G. ῥαχῖτις, inflammation of the spine, ῥάχις. Adopted (1650) by Glisson as learned name for *rickets*.

rack¹. Mass of driving cloud. In ME. also crash, collision, rush of wind. Cf. ON. *rek*, wreckage, from *reka*, to drive, cogn. with *wreck*, *wrack*.

The night-rack came rolling up ragged and brown
(Kingsley).

rack². Bar, framework in various senses. Du. *rak*, *rek*, cogn. with Ger. *recken*, to stretch. Hence archaic *at rack and manger*, in the midst of plenty. For mech. *rack and pinion* see *pinion²*.

rak, *schotel-rak*: a rack to put trenchers, plates, or platters in (Hexham).

rack³. Torture. First (15 cent.) as verb. Du. *rekken*, to stretch, cogn. with Ger. *recken*, and ult. with *reach* (cf. *rack²*). Hence *racking headache*, to *rack one's brains*, *rack-rent*. In quot. 2 confused with *rack⁴*.

Here [in America] are no hard landlords to racke us with high rents (Capt. John Smith).

He was often wracked by religious doubts
(*Times Lit. Sup.* Feb. 19, 1920).

rack⁴. In *rack and ruin*. Var. spelling of *wrack* (q.v.).

Alas! all then had gone to wrake,
Wold ye have slayne my son Isaac (ME. *Mystery*).

rack⁵ [*equit.*]. Kind of amble. Now only US., but once common in E. Palsg. has *racquassure*, not otherwise known. Quots. below suggest that the word may have lost an init. *t-*, an abnormal phenomenon (but see *rankle*, *ruff³*, and cf. obs. Sc. *rod*, path, for *trod*).

trac: allure d'une bête de somme (*Dict. Gén.*).

destraqué: put out of a racke, or pace (Cotg.).

traquenard: a racking horse, or guelding, a hackney
(*ib.*).

rack⁶. Liquor. Aphet. for *arrack* (q.v.). Esp. in *rack-punch*.

rack⁷. To draw off wine, etc., from the lees. Prov. (Gascon) *arracar*, from *raca*, dry residue of grapes. ? Cf. F. *drêche*, residue of malt, grapes, etc., also OF. *drache*, *drac*.

racket¹, **raquet**. For tennis. F. *raquette*; cf. It. *racchetta*, "a racket to play at tennis with" (Flor.), Sp. *racheta*. OF. *raquete*, palm of the hand, from Arab. *rāhat*. Cf. F. *paume*, tennis, lit. palm (of the hand).

racket². Disturbance, clamour, wild dissipation; hence, trying situation, as in to *stand the racket*. ? cf. *rake-hell*.

rack-rent. See *rack³*.

raconteur. F. from *raconter*, to recount.

racoon. NAmer. Ind., from a Virginian dial. of Algonkin. Early forms are numerous, e.g. *raugroughcum* (Capt. John Smith), *arrahacoune* (*Travel into Virginia*). Cf. *coon*.

racquet. See *racket¹*.

racy. Of anything having a distinctive flavour associated with its origin, race². *Racy of the soil* is mod., orig. used in ref. to Ireland, and perh. suggested by F. *goût de terroir*, used of wines and also fig.

Turgenev is cosmopolitan in character, while his rivals are racy of the soil that bred them
(*Daily Tel.* Nov. 7, 1917).

rad [*pol.*]. Short for *radical* (*NED.* 1831).

rada. Governing body (1918) of Ukraine. ? Borrowed from Ger. *rat*, counsel.

raddle, **reddle**. Vars. of *ruddle* (q.v.), red ochre. Esp. with ref. to rouged cheeks.

radiant. From pres. part. of L. *radiare*, from *radius* (q.v.). For fig. sense cf. *beaming*.

radical. F., Late L. *radicalis*, from *radix*, *radic-*, root. Earliest (14 cent.) in ref. to *radical humours* (*moisture*). Pol. sense first in *radical reform* (18 cent.).

Radical is a word in very bad odour here, being used to denote a set of blackguards (Scott, 1819).

The word radical in the United States is used to denote an extreme socialist
(*Daily News*, Apr. 16, 1920).

radio-. From *radius*, *radium* (q.v.). Also as abbrev. for *radio-telegram*, wireless.

radish. AS. *rædic*, L. *radix*, *radic-*, root; re-adopted in ME. from F. *radis*, It. *radice*, the true OF. form being *rais* (see *race³*). Ult. cogn. with *wort¹*.

radium [*chem.*]. Isolated by Mme Curie and named from its power of emitting rays without loss. *Radiogram* in telegraphic sense dates from 1907.

radius. L., ray, wheel-spoke, ult. cogn. with *radix*, *ramus*. Cf. *ray¹*. The scient. senses are mostly later than 1600.

radix [*math.*]. L., root. See *radish*.

raffia. Fibre for binding. Malagasy. Also *raphia*, *rofia*.

raffish. From archaic *raff*, as in *riff-raff* (q.v.).

raffle¹. Game of chance. Orig. (Chauc.) dicing game; current sense from 17 cent. F. *rafle*, whence *rafler*, to make a clean sweep. Ult. cogn. with *rifle*, and perh. with Ger. *raffen*, to snatch. Cf. Sp. *rifa*, contest, raffle.

raffle: a game at three dice, wherein he that throwes

all three alike, winnes whatsoever is set; also, a rifling (Cotg.).

               This very night
There will be some great rifling for some jewell
Tis twenty pound a man
               (Brome, *Damoiselle*, ii. 1).

rifa: raffle au jeu de dez (Oudin).

rifas: c'est au jeu de dez, quand on met quelque bague pour jouer en compagnie, & que chacun y entre pour sa part, puis on joue à qui l'aura, & cela s'appelle raffler (*ib.*).

raffle². Lumber, esp. naut. Prob. connected with *raffle¹*.

rafflesia. Plant. Named from its discoverer in Sumatra, *Sir T. Stamford Raffles* (†1826).

raft. ON. *raptr*, orig. beam, rafter (whence Sw. Dan. *raft*). Cf. *loft*.

rafter. AS. *ræfter*, cogn. with *raft*.

rag¹. Tatter, etc. AS. *ragg* (in adj. *raggig*), ON. *rögg*, shagginess. First (13 cent.) used of stone (*Kentish rag, ragstone*, etc.), if this is the same word. With *rag-bolt*, having a jagged head, cf. the *ragged* (serrated) *staff* of the Earl of Warwick. *Rag-tag* (*and bobtail*) is for 16–17 cent. *tag and rag*, riff-raff. *Ragtime* is US. See also *rug, rugged*.

Roches full rogh, ragget with stones (*NED.* c. 1400).

rag² [*slang*]. Short for *ballyrag, bullyrag*.

ragamuffin. Used in *Piers Plowm.* (C. xxi. 283) of a demon, such being often described in ME. as *ragged*, i.e. shaggy. ? Second element suggested by OF. *amuafle*, Saracen chief, but perh. arbitrary (cf. *tatterdemalion*).

rage. F., VL. **rabia*, for *rabies*, madness. For later sense cf. US. use of *mad*; for fig. sense, e.g. *all the rage*, cf. *furore*.

raglan. Overcoat. From *Lord Raglan* (†1855), British commander in Crimea. Cf. *wellington, chesterfield, spencer*, etc.

ragout. F. *ragoût*, from *ragoûter*, to revive the taste, *goût*, L. *gustus*.

raid. Northern form of *road* (q.v.); cf. *inroad*. Orig. a mounted incursion on the Border. Much extended in use even before the War, e.g. *police raid*, to *raid the sinking fund*, etc. *Raider* is now (1917–18) used ironically of the cowardly aliens who have fled from London and made the villages of the home counties uninhabitable.

rail¹. Bar. OF. *reille*, L. *regula*, rule, bar, from *regere*, whence also Ger. *riegel*, bolt. ModF. *rail* is from E. *Railroad* (18 cent.) tended to be replaced by *railway* after the invention of the locomotive engine, but the latter word is recorded as early as

1756. *Railings* are theoretically horizontal, *palings* perpendicular.

rail². Woman's garment. Obs. exc. in archaic *night-rail*. AS. *hrægel*, with numerous compds.; cogn. with OHG. *hregil*.

rail³. Bird. Chiefly in compds. *landrail, corncrake, water-rail*. F. *râle*, OF. *raalle*, MedL. *rallus*. Named from its harsh cry (cf. *corncrake*). Cf. Du. *rallen*, "to jabber or jeer" (Sewel), *ralvogel*, landrail. Perh. ult. as *rail⁴*; cf. the bird's Ger. name *wiesenschnarcher*, lit. meadow-snorer.

rail⁴. Verb. To abuse. Now usu. with prep. (*at, against*). Earlier also to jest, tease, like its doublet *rally²*, the sense of which also appears in *raillery*. F. *railler*, "to jeast, boord, sport, be merrie, or pleasant, with; to deride, mock, flowt, scoffe, gibe at" (Cotg.); ? cogn. with Sp. *rallar*, to scrape, grate, fig. to molest, from L. *rallum*, ploughshare. For metaphor cf. *bore¹, drill¹*. For *rail, rally*, from F. *railler*, cf. *soil², sully*, from F. *souiller*.

raiment. Aphet. for *arrayment*. See *array*.

rain. AS. *regn*. Com. Teut.; cf. Du. Ger. *regen*, ON. *regn*, Goth. *rign*. The chief compds. *rainbow, raindrop, rainwater*, are found in AS. and other Teut. langs., also *rainworm*, the common earth-worm.

Wold he have me kepe nothyng agaynst a raynye day? (*NED.* c. 1580).

raise. ON. *reisa* (cf. Goth. *ur-raisjan*), cogn. with AS. *ræran*, whence *rear¹*, which it has partly supplanted. In Wyc., up to *Jeremiah*, the earlier version has *rear*, the later *raise*. For fig. senses, e.g. to *raise cabbages* (*children, the mob*, etc.), cf. similar use of F. *élever, soulever*. With to *raise the siege* cf. F. *lever le siège*.

raisin. F., grape, VL. *racimus*, for *racemus*; cf. Du. *rozijn*, Ger. *rosine*. Since 13 cent. of dried grapes, but used also by Wyc. of the growing fruit.

raj [*Anglo-Ind.*]. Hind. *rāj*, sovereignty (v.i.).

rajah. Hind. *rājā*, Sanskrit *rājan*, king, cogn. with L. *rex, reg-*, OIr. *rī, rīg*, and also with Celt. *Orgeto-rix, Dumno-rix*, etc. See *rich*.

Rajpoot [*ethn.*]. Warlike Hindu race claiming descent from the four original Kshatriyas who sprang from the sacred fire-pit on the summit of Mount Abu. Hind. *rājpūt*, Sanskrit *rājaputra*, king's son (v.s.).

rake¹. Implement. AS. *raca*. Com. Teut.; cf. WFlem. *raak*, Ger. *rechen*, ON. *reka*, spade, shovel, Goth. *rikan*, to heap up. With mil. & nav. to *rake* cf. to *sweep* (with fire).

rake². Debauchee. Short for *rake-hell* (q.v.).

rake³ [*naut.*]. Slant of ship's extremities (see quot. s.v. *bluff¹*) or masts. From Sw. *raka*, to project (cf. Norw. *rage*), from Ger. *ragen*, to jut out, cogn. with AS. *hrǣgan* in *ofer-hrǣgan*, to tower above. In a *rakish-looking schooner* prob. associated with *rake²*.

rake-hell. Early associated (v.i.) with *rake¹* and *hell*, but perh. altered by folk-etym. from ME. *rakel*, rash, whence dial. *rackle*, reckless.

> O rakel hand! to doon so foule amys
> (Chauc. H. 278).

> Such a feloe as a manne should rake helle for
> (Udall, 1542).

> Is there ony news o' that rackle brother of thine?
> (Lanc. dial., *NED.* 1876).

raki. Drink. Turk. *rāqī*, whence ModG. ῥακί, brandy. ? Cogn. with *arrack*.

râle [*med.*]. F., rattle in throat. ? Cogn. with E. *rattle*, ? or with *rail⁴*.

rallentando [*mus.*]. It., pres. part. of *rallentare*, to slow down, cogn. with *relent* (q.v.).

rally¹. To bring together (again). F. *rallier*, from *re* and *allier*, to ally (q.v.). Hence intrans. to revive. Cf. *rely*.

rally². To banter. See *rail⁴*.

ram. AS. *ramm*; cf. obs. Du. LG. OHG. *ram*; cogn. with ON. *rammr*, strong. The Aryan name is *wether*. In AS. also in sense of *battering-ram*, whence the *ram* of a battle-ship; cf. L. *aries*, ram (zool. & mil.). Hence verb to *ram*, *ramrod* (for earlier *rammer*), and various mech. applications, with which cf. Ger. *rammbock*, builders' rammer, lit. ram-buck.

ramadan. Mohammedan fast of thirty days, of changing date, but supposed to have been orig. instituted in a hot month. Arab. *ramadān*, from *ramada*, to be hot.

ramble. From 17 cent. in lit. and fig. sense. Also *ramel*. Superseded ME. *rumble*, *romble*, in *Piers Plowm.* as var. for *roam*, of which it is perh. a frequent. Change of vowel may be due to Du. *rammelen*, Ger. *rammeln*, used of the night-wanderings of the amorous cat and cogn. with *ram*.

rammeler: a rambler, a night-walker, one that goes catterwauling (Ludw.).

ramekin, ramequin. Cheese, bread-crumbs, etc. made into small mould; also, earlier, a kind of Welsh rabbit. ? Cf. obs. Flem. *rammeken*, grilled bread, etc., given by Kil. as used at Bruges. Some connect it with Ger. *rahm*, cream.

ramify. F. *ramifier*, MedL. *ramificare*, from *ramus*, branch.

ramillie [*hist.*]. Wig. From Marlborough's victory at *Ramillies* in Belgium (1706). Cf. *mayonnaise*, *steenkerk*.

ramose. L. *ramosus*, from *ramus*, branch.

ramp¹ [*fort.*]. Inclined plane. F. *rampe*, from *ramper*, to clamber (v.i.).

ramp² [*her.*]. To stand on hind-legs. F. *ramper*, to crawl, clamber. Chiefly in pres. part. *rampant*, fig. sense of which, e.g. *corruption is rampant*, seems due to association with *rank¹* (cf. Sc. *ramp*, rank). Origin and sense-development are both obscure. In sense of nefarious stunt perh. due to fancied connection with L. *rapere*, to snatch. Wyc. uses *rampant* to render L. *rapiens*, *rapax*.

rampage. Orig. Sc., from *ramp²*.

rampant. See *ramp²*.

rampart. F. *rempart*, OF. *rampar*, from *remparer*, to fortify, from *re* and *emparer*, Prov. *amparar*, L. *ante* and *parare*, to make ready. The *-t* is due to influence of synon. *boulevart* (*boulevard*). Cf. It. *riparo*, "a rampire, a fort, a banke, a fence, a mound" (Flor.). The OF. form survives in dial. *ramper*, raised road. For archaic *rampire* (v.s.) cf. *umpire*.

rampion. Plant. Cf. F. *raiponce*, It. *raponzolo*, Ger. *rapunzel*, MedL. *rapuncium*, all ult. from L. *rapum*, rape, turnip.

ramshackle. Back-formation from *ramshackled*, earlier (18 cent.) *ranshackled*, from obs. *ransackle*, frequent. of *ransack* (q.v.). Of late esp. in the *ramshackle empire* (D. Lloyd George, 1914).

ramson [*dial.*]. Garlic. Orig. pl. in *-en* of AS. *hramsa*, cogn. with G. κρόμυον, onion.

ranch. Sp. *rancho*, rank, row, "a quarter among soldiers, their quarters; also a mess on board a ship" (Stevens); hence, row of huts, etc. Of Teut. origin (see *rank²*). Hence *rancheria*, *ranchero*.

Here the Spaniardes have seated their rancheria of some twentie or thirtie houses (Hakl. 1600).

rancid. OF. *rancide*, L. *rancidus*, "mouldie, putrified, stinking" (Coop.).

rancour. Archaic F. *rancœur*, L. *rancor-em*, "a rotten or stinking savour" (Coop.), used in *Vulg.* for bitterness; cogn. with *rancid*.

rand. AS. *rand*, brim, bank; cf. Du. Ger. *rand*, bank, border, etc. Oldest Teut. sense is shield-rim. The E. word is dial. only, but as Du. is now familiar in connection with the gold-bearing reef of Johannesburg

(Transvaal), whence also ironic *rand-lord*, gold magnate.

randan. Rowing with pair of sculls and two oars (19 cent.). ? Fig. use of archaic *randan*, spree, var. of *random*, ? or for *randem* (v.i.).

randem. Three horses harnessed in a line. Jocular formation on *tandem* (q.v.).

In his dog-cart, randem-tandem (Miss Edgeworth).

random. Earlier (14 cent.) *randon, randun.* Orig. in *at randon*, OF. *à (de) randon*, with impetuosity, in headlong rush, very common in OF. epic poetry and often coupled in rime with *à bandon*, recklessly (see *abandon*). Dubiously referred to OHG. *rand* in poet. sense of shield (see *rand*). Chief current sense is from archery (*random shot*).

randy. Orig. Sc., aggressive, boisterous, and esp. applied to women. ? From obs. *rand*, var. of *rant* (q.v.).

ranee. Hindu queen. Hind. *rānī*, Sanskrit *rājnī*, fem. of *rajah*.

The best man upon the side of the enemy [at the battle of Gwalior, 1858] was the woman found dead, the Ranee of Jhansi (Lord Strathnairn).

range. First as verb. F. *ranger*, to set in a row, from *rang*, rank[2], the senses having been extended in E. to measuring, extending, and hence cruising, roving, etc., also trans. to traverse, explore. With sense-development cf. that of F. *arpenter*, lit. to measure ground as a surveyor, fig. to traverse, stride across, etc. The (kitchen-) *range* is as old as the 15 cent., but its earliest sense is not clear. In some senses the verb is aphet. for *arrange*.

rank[1]. Adj. AS. *ranc*, proud, insolent; cf. Du. LG. *rank*, thin, high-grown. For transition to overgrown, coarsely luxuriant, cf. *proud*. Later senses perh. associated with *rancid*. Intens. use, e.g. *rank heresy*, from 16 cent.

rank[2]. Noun. OF. *ranc (rang)*, earlier *renc*, OHG. *hrinc, hring*, ring, circle (of warriors, etc.). Thus the idea of circle has become that of straight line. See *harangue, ranch*. With *man of rank*, adj. being omitted, cf. *man of family, people of quality*, etc. *Rank and fashion* is perh. modelled on earlier *rank and file* (see *file[3]*), with which cf. *in the ranks, ranker*.

rankle. From obs. noun *rankle*, festering sore, OF. *drancle, draoncle*, MedL. *dracunculus*, lit. little dragon. Cf. F. *furoncle*, fester,

L. *furunculus*, lit. little thief (see *felon*). The loss of *d-* before a consonant is abnormal, but cf. F. *rouchi*, used of the dialect of Valenciennes, said to come from *drouchi*, here, in this place. It would be more satisfactory to find an OF. **raoncle*, L. *ranunculus*, a plant regularly used by early vagrants for the production of artificial sores or "rankles."

ransack. ON. *rannsaka*, from *rann*, house (cf. Goth. *razn*), *sækja*, to seek. In ON. esp. to search a house for stolen goods. For formation cf. Sc. *hamsoken, hamesucken*. Later senses perh. influenced by *sack[1]*.

ransom. ME. *raunson*, F. *rançon*, OF. *reançon*, L. *redemptio-n-*, from *redimere, redempt-*, to buy back, from *emere*, to buy. For final *-m* cf. *grogram, venom*, etc. Use of verb in sense of extortion is after F. *rançonner*, "to ransome, to put unto ransome; also, to oppresse, pole, despoyle, exact, or extort most of his substance from" (Cotg.).

rant. Archaic Du. *randen, ranten*, "to dote, or to be enraged" (Hexham); ? cf. MHG. *ranzen*, to spring about. First in Shaks. (v.i.). Sc. sense of lively tune from c. 1700. *Ranter* was applied (c. 1645) to a sect of Antinomians and again (1814) to Primitive Methodists.

Nay, an thou'lt mouth,
I'll rant as well as thou (*Haml.* v. 1).

ranunculus. L., little frog, also plant. Dim. of *rana*, frog.

ranz-des-vaches. Herdsman's song. Swiss F. (Fribourg). ? First element cogn. with *rant*.

rap[1]. Sharp blow, esp. on door or knuckles. Imit.; cf. *clap, flap*, etc. Hence to *rap out* (let fly) *an oath. Spirit-rapping* dates from c. 1850.

rap[2]. Verb. Only in archaic to *rap and rend*. Sw. *rappa* or LG. *rappen*, cogn. with Ger. *raffen*, "to rap and ran, to catch and snatch" (Ludw.). LG. origin seems most likely, as the earliest form is *rape and ren*, the latter word being the Fris. cogn. of *rend*. Here *rape* is due to association with OF. *raper* and L. *rapere* (see *rape[2]*).

Ye shul nat wynne a myte on that chaffare,
But wasten al that ye may rape and renne
(Chauc. G. 1421)

rap[3]. Counterfeit halfpenny (Ireland, 18 cent.) mentioned by Swift (*Drapier's Let.*). Now only in *not (to care) a rap*. Ger. *rappen, rappe*, Upper Ger. **var.** of *rabe*, raven; orig. used (14 cent.) of counterfeit copper coin stamped with eagle. The word may have been brought from Germany by Irish soldiers of fortune.

rapacious. From L. *rapax, rapac-,* from *rapere,* to snatch. Cf. *audacious.*

rape¹ [*hist.*]. One of six divisions of Sussex. ? AS. *ráp,* rope, for measuring.

rape². Taking by force. AF. from OF. *raper,* to snatch, L. *rapere.* Cf. synon. *ravish.*

rape³. Plant. L. *rapum, rapa,* turnip; cf. G. ῥάπυς. In some senses via Du. *raap.*

rapid. F. *rapide,* L. *rapidus,* from *rapere,* to snatch. The *rapids* on Amer. rivers, named (18 cent.) by F. voyageurs, preserve F. sense of steep.

rapier. F. *rapière,* orig. (15 cent.), adj. qualifying *épée,* sword, ? Ir. *rapaire,* half-pike (see *rapparee*). For vague names of weapons cf. *pistol* (q.v.), *glaive* (q.v.). The sword-dancers' *rapper, raper,* is the same word.

rapine. F., L. *rapina,* from *rapere,* to snatch.

rapparee [*hist.*]. Ir. freebooter, orig. (17 cent.) pikeman. Ir. *rapairidhe,* pl. of *rapaire,* half-pike. For use of pl. cf. *cateran, assassin,* etc.

rappee. Snuff. F. (*tabac*) *râpé,* rasped tobacco, i.e. snuff.

rapport. F., from *rapporter,* to refer, relate. Chiefly in phrases imitating F. *en rapport avec.*

rapprochement. F. See *approach.*

rapscallion. Altered (? by association with *rabble*) from earlier *rascallion,* from *rascal.*

rapt. L. *raptus,* p.p. of *rapere,* to snatch. Orig. carried up to heaven, like Elijah. Hence *rapture* (c. 1600). Cf. fig. senses of *ravish.*

raptorial [*zool.*]. From L. *raptor* (v.s.).

rapture. See *rapt.*

rare. F., L. *rarus,* thinly sown, scarce; hence, precious. *Raree-show* represents the pronunciation of *rare-show* by Savoyard proprietors of peepshows; cf. *galanty-show.* The *raree-show* which the *NED.* quotes from T. Brown is also *rare-show, rary-show,* in an earlier edition.

A pretty closet which...is the raree-show of the whole neighbourhood (Evelyn, 1696).

They [the trippers to Ypres and the Somme] speak of this ghastly evidence of human agony as of some raree-show (*Obs.* Dec. 7, 1919).

rarebit. Perversion of (*Welsh*) *rabbit.* Cf. *catsup* for *ketchup.*

rascal. OF. *rascaille* (*racaille*), rabble (q.v.); cf. F. *râcler,* to scrape, Prov. *rasclar,* VL.

rasculare, from *rastrum,* rake. Applied to individual from 15 cent. (cf. ModF. use of *canaille*). In early use (14 cent.) also for inferior animal, esp. deer, a sense common in Shaks., e.g. *As You Like It,* iii. 3. This may have been its first sense in E. Hence archaic *rascallion,* now usu. altered to *rapscallion.*

And he smoot of the puple seventi men, and fifti thousandis of the raskeyl [*Vulg.* plebs]
(Wyc. 1 *Kings,* vi. 19).

rase. See *raze.*

rash¹. Adj. From c. 1500. Du. *rasch,* "quick or swift" (Hexham); cf. Ger. *rasch,* swift, ON. *röskr,* valiant; cogn. with AS. *horsc,* active, quick-witted.

rash². Noun. Archaic F. *rache,* OF. *rasche*; cf. It. *raschia,* "a scratching" (Flor.). Ult. from L. *radere, ras-,* to scrape.

rasher. From 16 cent. ? From obs. *rash,* to cut, slash, corrupt. of F. *raser* (see *raze*). It may even represent F. *rasure,* "a shaving" (Cotg.); cf. *batter, fritter.* Minsheu's explanation, "rashly or hastely roasted," is not very convincing. Sp. *raja,* slice, has also been suggested (cf. *lunch*).

rasores [*ornith.*]. L., lit. scrapers, name given (1811) by Illinger to his fourth order of birds.

rasp. OF. *raspe* (*râpe*), from OHG. *raspón,* to scrape together. Cf. *rappee.*

raspberry. For archaic & dial. *rasp,* back-formation from earlier *raspis,* app. ident. with ME. *raspise,* a kind of wine, MedL. *raspecia,* of unknown origin. If the berry sense is the earliest there may be connection with OWalloon *raspoie,* thicket, of Teut. origin and cogn. with *rasp.*

framboise: a raspis, hindberry, framboiseberry; also, a pleasing smell or savor in wine, or fruits (Cotg.).

Rasputinism [*hist.*]. From *Rasputin,* an obscene impostor supposed to have influenced the late Russian court. Cf. *Boloism, Leninism.*

Bolshevism is only Rasputinism under another name (*Pall Mall Gaz.* Jan. 26, 1918).

rasse. Civet-cat. Javanese *rase.*

rat¹. Animal. AS. *ræt*; cf. Du. *rat,* Ger. *ratte*; also, F. *rat,* obs. It. *ratto,* Sp. *rato,* MedL. *ratus,* all prob. of Teut. origin, the animal having come from the East with the race-migrations; ? cogn. with L. *radere,* to scrape, *rodere,* to gnaw. The usu. ME. word was *raton,* F. dim. of *rat* (cf. *chat, chaton*), with common var. *rotton,* which survives as surname (see *rattening*). Verb to *rat,* desert, is from belief that rats desert a sinking ship (*Temp.* i. 2) or falling house. To *smell a rat* is 16 cent. With the *Hanover rat*, said by Jacobites to have come over with George I, cf. *Hessian fly. Rats!* is US.

rat². For *rot* (in exclamation); cf. *drat*.

rata. New Zealand tree. Maori.

ratafia. F. (17 cent.). App. connected with F. *tafia*, Creole name for rum.

rataplan. F., imit. of drumming; cf. *rub-a-dub*.

ratchet [*mech.*]. F. *rochet*, ratchet of a clock, dim. from OHG. *rocco* (*rocken*), spindle. Cf. It. *rocchetto*, "the wheele of a mill which causeth the grinding stones to turne and goe" (Flor.).

rate¹. Amount, quantity, etc. OF., MedL. *rata* as in L. *pro rata* (sc. *portione*), from *reri, rat-*, to think, judge (cf. *ratio*). The full *rateporcion* is found in AF. Here belongs *at any rate*. Later applied to degrees of speed. *First-rate, second-rate*, etc., were orig. (17 cent.) naut., the navy being divided into six *rates* or classes. Cf. *rating*, now (nav.) almost equivalent to man.

rate². To chide. ME. also *ret, arate*, of which *rate* may be aphet. form. OF. *reter, areter*, to accuse, blame, L. *reputare*, to repute, in Late L. to impute. It occurs in the Anglo-Norm. transl. of the Laws of the Anglo-Saxons, and is very common in AF. for impute; cf. OSp. *rebtar*, to blame. Associated also with *rate¹* (cf. to *tax one with*). Quot. 1 below is the reply of the lamb to the wolf.

"Que retez ceo," fet il, "a mei? N'ere pas nez si cum jeo cuit" (Marie de France).

["Why do you impute this to me?" said he. "I was not born, as I think."]

ratel. Honey-badger. SAfrDu., of uncertain origin.

rath [*Ir.*]. Earthwork, enclosure. Ir. *ráth*, mound, ult. cogn. with L. *pratum*, meadow.

rathaus. Ger., council-house, town-hall. See *rede*.

rathe [*poet.*]. Quick, hence early. Obs. in 18 cent., exc. in *rathe-ripe*, but revived by Scott as echo of Milton's *rathe primrose* (*Lycidas*, 114). See *rather*.

rather. Compar. of ME. *rathe*, quick, early (v.s.), orig. adv., AS. *hrathe*, corresponding to adj. *hræd*, cogn. with OHG. *hrad*, ON. *hrathr*. For sense-development cf. F. *plutôt* (*plus tôt*, sooner). As strong affirmative (= *not half*) first recorded in Dickens. Sense of inclined towards (*rather nice*) is

ellipt. for *rather than not. Rathest* was in use up to 17 cent.

Aftir me is comun a man which was maad bifor me; for he was rather [*Vulg.* prior] than Y
(Wyc. *John*, i. 30).

ratify. F. *ratifier*, Late L. *ratificare*, from *ratus*, agreed, and *facere*, to make. See *rate¹*.

ratio. L., from *reri, rat-*, to judge, etc. (see *rate¹*); ult. cogn. with *rede*.

ratiocination. L. *ratiocinatio-n-*, from *ratiocinari*, to calculate, deliberate, from *ratio*.

ration. F., L. *ratio-n-*, proportion, ratio. Until recently (1918) usu. pronounced to rime with *nation*, but the mil. pronunc., riming with *fashion*, has now become gen.

rational. L. *rationalis*, from *ratio*. For senses cf. *reason* (q.v.). *Rational dress* dates from 1883. *Rationale*, fundamental reason, etc., is the L. neut. adj. *Rationalist*, free-thinker, is after F. *rationaliste* (16 cent.).

ratline, ratling [*naut.*]. Earlier (15 cent.) also *radelyng*. Prob. the *rat-* and *-line* are both folk-etym. (cf. *marline, bowline*). The analogy of Du. *weveling*, ratline, lit. weaving, suggests that *radelyng* is from dial. & naut. *raddle*, to intertwine, interlace, from *raddle*, or *raddling*, long slender rod used in weaving hurdles, etc., dim. of obs. *rathe*, rail of a cart. Cf. F. *enfléchure*, ratline, app. from *fléchir*, to bend, be flexible, and also OF. *flechiere*, raddling of hedge. The ratlines of early ships are pictured as forming a very wide network.

xxiij lb. raddelyne employed raddelyng of the mayne shrowdes (*Nav. Accts.* 1495–97).

enflecheures: the ratlings; the cordy steps whereby mariners climbe up to the top of a mast (Cotg.).

rattan. Malay *rōtan*, from *rāut*, to trim, strip.

rat-tat. Imit. of sharp knock at door.

ratteen [*archaic*]. Fabric. F. *ratine* (17 cent.), ? from *rat*, rat (cf. *moleskin*).

rattening [*hist.*]. Molestation of non-union workers by tampering with tools in such a way as to cause accidents, esp. at Sheffield (1850–60). See Charles Reade's *Put yourself in his place*. From dial. *ratten*, rat (q.v.).

rattle. Imit.; cf. Du. *ratelen*, Ger. *rasseln*, G. κρόταλον, clapper, etc. Prob. in AS., as the word is much older than *NED.* re-cords, e.g. *rattlebag* (*NED.* 1583) was already a surname in 1273 (*John Rattilbagge* in *Hundred Rolls*). *Rattletrap* is of similar formation. With *rattling* as intens. cf. *thundering*, *clinking*, etc.

ratty. Out of temper. Neol. ? from US.

raucous. From L. *raucus*, hoarse.

ravage. F., from *ravir*, to ravish (q.v.).

rave. F. *rêver*, to dream, OF. also *raver*, *resver*; cf. OF. *desver*, to be mad. Both are of unknown origin. ? VL. **re-aestuare*, **de-aestuare*, from *aestus*, tide, vehemence.

ravel. Du. *rafelen*, to tangle, fray out; cogn. with AS. *ārāfian*, to unwind (thread), ? and ult. with *reeve*².

> Sleep that knits up the ravelled sleeve of care
>   (*Macb.* ii. 2).

ravelin [*fort.*]. F.; cf. It. *rivellino*, earlier *revellino*, *ravellino*, "a ravelin, a wicket, or a posterne gate" (Flor.). Perh. ident. with archaic F. *ravelin*, kind of shoe, OF. *revelin*, AS. *rifeling*, whence ME. *riveling*, shoe of undressed hide. The thing and name are still in use in the Shetlands. The F. terms of fort. are often taken from articles of dress which their shape suggested, e.g. *bonnet à prêtre*, *genouillère*, *fausse-braie*, etc.

raven¹. Noun. AS. *hræfn*. Com. Teut.; cf. Du. *raaf*, Ger. *rabe* (OHG. *hraban*), ON. *hrafn*, Goth. *hrabns* (in pers. names); prob. cogn. with L. *corvus*, G. κόραξ.

raven². Verb. OF. *raviner*, to ravage, from *ravine*, L. *rapina*, from *rapere*, to snatch. Hence *ravenous*, now usu. in sense of hungry.

ravin [*poet.*]. Rapine (v.s.).

ravine. F. *ravine*, in archaic sense of violent rush (of water), or *ravin*, from *raviner*, to tear up, as in *des champs ravinés par un orage*. See *raven*².

ravish. F. *ravir*, *raviss-*, VL. **rapire*, for *rapere*, to snatch. Fig. sense, to delight, transport, is in *Piers Plowm.* (cf. *rapture*).

raw. AS. *hrēaw*. Com. Teut.; cf. Du. *rauw*, Ger. *roh*, ON. *hrár*; ult. cogn. with L. *crudus*, raw, *cruor*, blood, G. κρέας, flesh. Orig. uncooked; hence, undressed, unsophisticated, uncovered, e.g. *raw-boned*, to *touch one on the raw*. *Rawhead* (*and bloody-bones*), spectre, is in Johns.

ray¹. Of light. Archaic F. *rai* (usu. replaced by *rayon*), L. *radius*; cf. It. *raggio*, Sp. *rayo*. Not in common use till 17 cent., and of the sun usu. with ref. to heat rather than light (*beam*).

ray². Fish. F. *raie*, "ray, skate, thornback" (Cotg.), L. *raia*; cf. It. *raja*, Sp. *raya*.

rayah. Non-Mohammedan subject of Sultan of Turkey. Arab. *ra'īyah*, herd, subjects, peasants.

rayat. See *ryot*.

raze. F. *raser*, from L. *radere*, *ras-*, to scrape, cogn. with *rodere*, to gnaw. Now usu. of buildings, fortifications, esp. in *to raze to* (make level with) *the ground*. Cf. archaic naut. *razee*, man-of-war cut down by removal of upper decks, F. *rasé*; *razor*, OF. *rasour* (replaced by *rasoir*).

razzia. F., Algerian Arab. *ghāziāh*, military raid, from *ghasw*, to make war.

razzle-dazzle. Recent US. coinage; redupl. on *dazzle*.

re [*mus.*]. See *gamut*.

re, in re. L., in the matter, *res*, (of).

re-. L. *re-*, *red-* before vowels. In E. often via F. *re-*, *ré-*. Both in L. & F. it is often merely intens.

reach. AS. *rǣcan*, to stretch out (the hand). WGer.; cf. Du. *reiken*, Ger. *reichen*. With obs. past *raught* (Shaks.) cf. *teach*, *taught*. In sense of attaining from AS. *gerǣcan*. With *reach* (of a river) cf. *stretch* (of country) and archaic Du. *rak wegs*, stretch of road, from *rekken*, to stretch. *Reach-me-downs* (mod. slang), ready-made clothes, represents the customer requesting to be supplied with garments which he sees hanging in the shop.

> On voyait chez les fripiers des chapes et des rochets à vendre au "décroche-moi-ça"
>   (Hugo, *Quatre-vingt-treize*).

> The shoddy, ready-made, reach-me-down sort of thing that has so frequently to be doled out now as a makeshift for education
>   (*Sunday Times*, March 9, 1919).

> A stout, fatherly man whose clothes had the appearance of rather being made to measure than reached off a hook (Niven, *S.S. Glory*).

reaction. Orig. (17 cent.) scient. (cf. *reagent*). Now used, after F. *réaction*, in mil. sense. *Reactionary* in pol. sense is 19 cent., after F. *réactionnaire*.

read. AS. *rēdan*, to make out, interpret, etc. Com. Teut.; cf. Du. *raden*, Ger. *raten*, to counsel, ON. *rātha*, Goth. *rēdan*. Orig. sense survives in *to read a riddle*, to *read one a lesson*, *reader*, lecturer, also in such modernisms as *how do you read the matter?* See also *rede*, *riddle*. With use of p.p. in *well-read* cf. *well-spoken*, etc.

ready. Lengthened in ME. from (*i*)-*rede*, prepared, AS. *gerǣde*. Com. Teut.; cf. Du. *gereed*, Ger. *bereit* (MHG. also *gereit*), ON. *greithr*, Goth. *garaiths*. Prob. from root of *ride*, *raid*; cf. relation of Ger. *fertig*, ready, to *fahren*, to travel, fare. *Ready money* is recorded from 15 cent.

real[1]. Adj. F. *réel*, Late L. *realis*, from *res*, thing. As trade description perh. influenced by ME. *real*, *rial* (royal), stock epithet for superior merchandise. Adv. use, e.g. *real nice*, is US. With *really?* cf. F. *vraiment! Realism* (philos. & art) as opposite of *idealism* is 19 cent. *Realize*, to convert into cash, is after F. *réaliser*, first used in this sense (1719) in connection with Law's financ. projects.

real[2]. Coin. Sp., lit. royal, L. *regalis*.

realgar [*chem.*]. Sulphide of arsenic. MedL., ult. Arab. *rehj al-qhār*, powder of the cave. In Chauc. (G. 813).

realm. OF. *reame*, *reeme*, L. *regimen*, *regimin-*, later becoming *realme*, *reiaume* (*royaume*), under influence of *real*, royal; cf. It. *reame*, OSp. *realme*. Mod. form, later influencing pronunc., is due to influence of ME. *real*, royal, usual early forms being *reame*, *reme*.

If Gloster live, Leyster will flie the realme.
If Gloster live, thy kingdome's but a dreame
                (*Look about you*, 1600).

realpolitik. Ger., practical politics. Cf. *realschule*, school not following the classical curriculum of the *gymnasium*.

ream[1]. Of paper. OF. *raime*, *remme* (*rame*), Sp. *resma*, Arab. *rizmah*, bundle; cf. It. *risma*, "a reame of paper" (Flor.).

ream[2]. To widen. Dial., exc. in ref. to clearing out bore of gun. ME. *remen*, to open up, AS. *rȳman*, from *room*.

reaming. Chiefly Sc., esp. in *reaming full*, from dial. *ream*, cream, AS. *rēam*. Com. Teut.; cf. Du. *room*, Ger. *rahm*, ON. *rjōmi*.

reap. AS. *repan*, *rīpan*, cogn. with *ripe*.

rear[1]. Verb. AS. *rǣran*, causal of *rise*. ME. also *arear*, AS. *ārǣran*. Now replaced in many senses by *raise* (q.v.), or used with slight differentiation, e.g. to *rear* (*raise*) *children*. Intrans. sense, of horses, is prob. via reflex.

rear[2]. Behind. Aphet. for *arrear*, F. *arrière*, L. *ad retro*. With *rear-* for F. *arrière* in *rearguard* (earlier also *rearward*), cf. *van-* for F. *avant* in *vanguard*; but it may be noted that OF. has also the simple *rière* and *rière-garde* (*Rol.*). A *rear-admiral* is to an *admiral* as a *major-general* is to a *general*.

rearmouse, **reremouse** [*archaic & dial.*]. Bat[2]. AS. *hrēremus*, perh. altered, after *hrēran*, to move (cf. *flittermouse*), from earlier *hreathemūs*.

reason. F. *raison*, L. *ratio-n-*, from *reri*, *rat-*, to judge; cf. It. *ragione*, Sp. *razón*. *It stands to reason* is for earlier *it stands* (conforms) *with reason*. Cf. *rational*.

I have no other but a woman's reason:
I think him so because I think him so
             (*Two Gent. of Ver.* i. 2).

reata, **riata**. Tethering rope. Sp., from *reatar*, to tie, from *re-* and L. *aptare*. Cf. *lariat*.

Réaumur. F. physicist (†1757) who introduced a type of thermometer.

reave, **reive**. AS. *rēafian*, to plunder. Com. Teut.; cf. Du. *rooven*, Ger. *rauben*, ON. *raufa*, Goth. (*bi*)*raubōn*; cogn. with *rob*, F. *dérober*, and ult. with L. *rumpere*, *rup-*; see also *robe*, *rove*. The spelling *reive* is Sc. and due to the revival of the word by Scott. See also *bereave*. The use of the p.p. *reft*, in *reft asunder*, also due to Scott, is due to confusion between this verb and *rive* (q.v.).

rebate. F. *rabattre* (see *abate*). See also *rabbet*.

Rebeccaite [*hist.*]. Welsh rioter destroying turnpike gates (1843). With allusion to *Rebekah* (*Gen.* xxiv. 60).

rebeck [*archaic*]. Early fiddle. F. *rebec*; cf. It. *ribe*(*c*)*ca*, "a rebeck, or a croud, or a kit" (Flor.), Port. *rebeca*, MedL. *rebeca*. Unexplained alteration of OF. *ribibe*, ult. from Arab. *rebāb*.

rebel. F. *rebeller*, L. *rebellare*, from *bellum*, war. Noun *rebel* is from earlier adj., F. *rebelle*, L. *rebellis*, formerly common in predicative use accompanied by *to*, *against*.

reboisement. Reafforestation. F., from *bois*, wood.

rebound. See *bound*[2]. *At the rebound*, common in 16–17 cent. and perh. orig. from tennis, is now only used of emotional reaction.

rebuff. OF. *rebuffe* (replaced by *rebuffade*), It. *ribuffo*, from *buffo*, puff.

rebuke. AF. *rebukier*, OF. *rebuchier*, to repulse, of doubtful origin. Current sense is earliest (14 cent.) in E. and suggests connection with F. *bouche*, mouth; cf. to *cast in one's teeth*, and It. *rimboccare*, "to twit or hit one in the teeth, also to retort backe word for word" (Torr.). *Rebuché*, "hebetatus," occurs in the *Oxf. Glossary*.

rebus. Picture puzzle. F. *rébus* (1512), L. *rebus*, abl. pl. of *res*, thing, "dans l'expression *de rebus quae geruntur*, employée par les clercs de Picardie pour désigner les pièces satiriques à devinettes qu'ils composaient pendant le carnaval" (*Dict. Gén.*). For the *rebus* below see *curry*[1].

Car en rebus de Picardie
Une faux, une estrille, un veau,
Cela fait estrille-Fauveau (Marot).

rebut. F. *rebouter*, from *bouter*, to thrust, butt[5].

recalcitrant. F. *récalcitrant*, from pres. part. of L. *recalcitrare*, to kick out, from *calx, calc-*, heel.

recall. See *call*. *Beyond recall* is an echo of Milton.

Other decrees
Against thee are gone forth without recall
(*Par. Lost*, v. 885).

recant. L. *recantare*, from *cantare*, to sing (cf. *palinode*). A Reformation word.

recapitulate. From Late L. *recapitulare*, from *capitulum*, heading, chapter. Cf. *capitulate*.

recast. In current literary sense a metaphor from metal-founding.

recede. L. *recedere*, to go back. See *cede*.

receipt. Restored on L. *recept-* from ME. *receite*, OF. (*recette*), L. *recepta*, from *recipere, recept-*, to receive, from *capere*, to take. Cf. *conceit, deceit*. Earliest E. sense (Chauc.) is formula, prescription, now often replaced by *recipe* (q.v.).

receive. OF. *receivre*, L. *recipere*, and *receveir* (*recevoir*), VL. **recipĕre*. Cf. *conceive, deceive*. The senses are mostly developed in F. With *receiver* (of stolen goods) (14 cent.) cf. archaic & Sc. *resetter, receter*, OF. *recetour*, L. *receptor-em*.

Commonlie the lytle thieff is hanged, bod his ressetyr and hys mayntynur is savid
(*NED.* c. 1440).

recension. L. *recensio-n-*, from *recensēre*, to review, from *censēre*, to criticize.

recent. F. *récent*, L. *recens, recent-*. First (16 cent.) in Sc.

receptacle. L. *receptaculum*, from *recipere, recept-*, to receive. Cf. *reception, receptive*, the former, in sense of ceremonial gathering (19 cent.), after F. *réception*.

recess. L. *recessus*, "going awaye, or going back; retyring. The secretest or innermost place of anye rome" (Coop.), from *recedere, recess-*, to withdraw. In parl. sense from 17 cent. Cf. *recessional* (hymn), sung as clergy and choir retire from chancel to vestry; but not in eccl. use.

Rechabite. Teetotaler, member of benefit society founded 1835. See *Jer.* xxxv.

réchauffé. F., p.p. of *réchauffer*, to warm up again. See *chauffeur*. Current in ME. (v.i.).

Allso that no cooke sell no maner rechaufid meit
(*Coventry Leet Book*, 1421).

recherché. F., p.p. of *rechercher*, to seek out. Cf. *exquisite* and see *search*.

recidivist [*neol.*]. Relapsing criminal. F. *récidiviste* (neol.), from *récidiver*, "to recidivate, relapse, fall back or again" (Cotg.), MedL. *recidivare*, from L. *recidivus*, from *recidere*, from *cadere*, to fall. Cf. *relapse, backsliding*.

recipe. L., take, imper. of *recipere*, used by physicians as heading of prescriptions. See *receipt*.

recipient. F. *récipient*, from pres. part. of L. *recipere*, to receive.

reciprocal. From L. *reciprocus*, app. from *re-*, back, and *pro-*, forward. *Reciprocity* in econ. sense is 18 cent.

recite. F. *réciter*, L. *recitare*, from *citare*, to cite (q.v.). *Recitative* (mus.) is It. *recitativo*.

reck. AS. *reccan*. Com. Teut.; cf. obs. Du. *roeken* (Du. *roekeloos*, reckless), OHG. *ruohhen* (Ger. *ruchlos*, reckless), ON. *rækja*.

reckon. AS. *gerecenian*. WGer.; cf. Du. *rekenen*, Ger. *rechnen*; also Goth. *rahnjan*; cogn. with *reck*, also with AS. *racu*, account, and ult. with *rake*[1], orig. sense having been a bringing together. US. use (see *calculate*) was formerly literary E.

reclaim. F. *réclamer*, L. *reclamare* (see *claim*). Orig. (13 cent.) to call back (a hawk), hence to reduce to obedience, reform. Cf. F. *réclame*, advertisement, calling to oneself.

reclame: a sohoe, or heylaw; a loud calling, whooting, or whooping to make a hawke stoope unto the lure; also, a claime, a challenge (Cotg.).

recline. L. *reclinare*. Cf. *decline, incline*.

recluse. F. *reclus*, L. *reclusus*, from *recludere, reclus-*, from *claudere*, to shut. Cf. *anchorite*.

recognize. From OF. *reconoistre* (*reconnaître*), *reconoiss-*, L. *recognoscere*, from *cognoscere*, to know; cf. *cognizance* (q.v.). For senses cf. *acknowledge*. Earlier is *recognizance* (v.i.), of which the verb is rather a back-formation.

For he was bounden in a reconyssaunce,
To paye twenty thousand sheeld anon
(*Chauc.* B. 1520).

recoil. F. *reculer*, from *cul*, L. *culus*, posteriors. For change of vowel cf. *foil*[2], *soil*[1].

recollect. From L. *recolligere, recollect-*, lit. to collect again. For senses cf. to *pull oneself together*.

recommend. Earlier *recommand*, F. *recommander*, orig. to entrust; hence, to introduce (favourably). See *command, commend*.

recompense. F. *récompenser*. See *compensate*.

reconcile. F. *réconcilier*, L. *reconciliare*. See *conciliate*.

recondite. L. *reconditus*, p.p. of *recondere*, from *condere*, to put away, hide, compd. of *dare*, to give.

reconnoitre. F. *reconnoître*, archaic spelling of *reconnaître*, to recognize. From early 18 cent. (War of Spanish Succession). Cf. *reconnaissance*, earlier also *reconnoissance*. *Recognize* was used earlier in same sense.

> He [a commander] ought himself to recognize all avenues, whereby his enemies may come at him
> (1657).

reconography [*neol.*]. Reconnaissance sketching. Title of book mentioned in *Times Lit. Sup.* Jan. 23, 1919.

reconstruction. In current sense of re-organization after war first used in US., after Civil War of 1861–65.

record. First (13 cent.) as verb. Archaic F. *recorder*, from L. *recordari*, lit. to get by heart, *cor, cord-*; cf. It. *ricordare*, Sp. *recordar*. Hence noun *record*, sporting sense of which is late 19 cent., the gramophone *record* being still more recent. The offic. *recorder* was orig. one skilled in law appointed by civic magistrates to "record" their proceedings. The *Recorder* of London is still appointed by the Court of Aldermen. The obs. mus. *recorder* is from ME. sense of verb, to practise a tune.

recount. OF. *reconter* (replaced by *raconter*). See *count²*.

recoup. Orig. to deduct. F. *recouper*, from *couper*, to cut. See *coppice*.

recourse. F. *recours*, L. *recursus*, from *recurrere, recurs-*, to run back. For sense cf. *resort*.

recover. F. *recouvrer*, L. *recuperare*, to get back, ult. cogn. with *capere*, to take. Intrans. sense, to revive, etc., is for earlier reflex.

recreant [*poet.*]. OF., pres. part. of *recreire*, later *recroire*, to yield in trial by combat, lit. take back one's pledge, from OF. *creire*, L. *credere*, to believe. Cf. *miscreant*. The p.p. *recru*, in ModF. worn out, exhausted, was used in OF. in same sense.

> Ja bons vassals nen iert vifs recrëuz (*Rol.* 2088).

recreate. From L. *recreare*, to refresh, lit. to create again.

recrement. Waste product. F. *récrément*, L. *recrementum*, from *cernere*, to sift out, separate. Cf. *excrement*.

recriminate. From MedL. *recriminari*, from *crimen, crimin-*, charge, crime. Cf. F. *récriminer*, "to recriminate, retort a crime, accuse an accuser" (Cotg.).

recrudescence. From L. *recrudescere*, to become raw, *crudus*, again. Chiefly in bad sense, of sore, disease, etc.

recruit. Obs. F. *recrute*, dial. var. of *recrue*, p.p. fem. of *recroître*, to grow again, L. *recrescere*. Orig. reinforcement collectively (see *crew*). Adopted as noun and verb by most Europ. langs. in 17 cent. Fig. sense (to *recruit one's health*) also occurs in 17 cent. E. Racine describes verb *recruter* as a barbarous word coined by the *gazettes de Hollande*.

> Presently came orders for our sending away to the fleete a recruite of 200 soldiers
> (Pepys, June 2, 1666).

rectangle. Late L. *rectiangulum*, from *rectus*, straight, right, *angulus*, angle. Cf. *rectilinear*; *rectify*, F. *rectifier*, Late L. *rectificare*; *rectitude*, F., Late L. *rectitudo*.

recto [*typ.*]. L. *recto* (sc. *folio*). Cf. *verso*.

rector. L., from *regere, rect-*, to rule, guide. Earliest (13 cent.) in E. in eccl. sense of incumbent whose tithes are not impropriate. Also at Sc. universities and schools, and at two Oxf. colleges (Lincoln, Exeter), used of the Head. So also F. *recteur*, Ger. *rektor*.

rectum [*anat.*]. L. (sc. *intestinum*), from *rectus*, straight.

recumbent. From pres. part. of L. *recumbere*, to recline. Cf. *incumbent*.

recuperate. From L. *recuperare*, to recover (q.v.), get back. For intrans. use cf. *recover*.

recur. L. *recurrere*, to run back.

recusant. From pres. part. of L. *recusare*, to refuse, from *causa*; cf. *accuse*. Orig. (c. 1550) of Roman Catholic "refusing" to attend service of Church of England. Cf. rare verb to *recuse*, F. *récuser*.

red. AS. *ꝺ̄ead*. Com. Teut.; cf. Du. *rood*, Ger. *rot*, ON. *rauthr*, Goth. *rauths*; cogn. with L. *ruber, rufus*, G. ἐρυθρός, Gael. Ir. *ruadh* (cf. Rob *Roy*), Welsh *rhudd*. Often as intens., e.g. *red ruin* (republican). Spec. application to violent revolutionaries (*red flag*, etc.) dates from adoption (1793) of the Phrygian cap or *bonnet rouge* in France, but in 17 cent. the *red flag* was the naval signal for fight. *Redcoat* dates esp. from the Cromwellian troopers, though recorded for 16 cent. The *Red Cross* (of Geneva) was adopted (1863) by the Geneva Conference as symbol securing immunity for hospitals and wounded. Turkey uses similarly the *Red Crescent*. *Redhanded*, for earlier *redhand* (Sc. law), was coined by Scott. *Red letter* refers to indication of saints' days and feasts in eccl. calendars. With *redpole*, from *poll*[1], cf. *redstart*, from AS. *steort*, tail, rump (cf. *wheatear*). *Redskin* is 17 cent. (cf. F. *peau-rouge*). *Red tape* in fig. sense is 19 cent.

She is nother fyshe nor fleshe, nor good red hearyng
(Heywood's *Proverbs*, 1546).

Send the papers to the Christchurch museum in New Zealand as an example of the red tape-worm of England (*Times*, Oct. 26, 1917).

redaction. F. *rédaction*, L. *redactio-n-*, from *redigere*, *redact-*, to reduce, from *re-* and *agere*.

redan [*fort.*]. Outwork forming salient angle. F., earlier *redent*, "a double notching, or jagging as in the teeth of a saw" (Cotg.), from *dent*, tooth. Cf. synon. F. *ouvrage à scie*.

redd [*dial.*]. See *rid*.

reddle. Var. of *raddle*, *ruddle*.

rede [*poet.*]. Archaic spelling of *read* (q.v.), differentiated to express earlier sense of counsel, etc. Obs. in 17–18 cents., but revived by Scott.

redeem. F. *rédimer*, L. *redimere* (see *ransom*). For vowel cf. *esteem*. *Redeeming feature* (*quality*), *past redemption*, are 19 cent. *Redeemer* has replaced earlier *redemptor*, F. *rédempteur*.

redemptorist. Member of *Congregation of the Most Holy Redeemer* (Naples, 1732).

red-gum. Rash on skin of children. Folk-etym. for ME. *radegound* (*Piers Plowm.*), lit. red pus (see *groundsel*).

redif. Soldier of Turk. reserve. Arab. *redif*, one who follows, second. Cf. *nizam*.

redingote. F., from E. *riding-coat*.

redintegrate. From L. *redintegrare*, to make whole, *integer*, again.

redolent. Now always with *of*. OF., from pres. part. of L. *redolēre*, from *re-* and *olēre*, to smell.

redoubt. Artificial spelling of *redout*, F. *redoute*, It. *ridotto*, from L. *reducere*, *reduct-*; cf. F. *réduit*, nook, refuge.

reduite: a blockhouse, or little fort (Cotg.).

redoubtable. ME. *redoutable*, F., from *re-*

douter, to fear, from *douter*, to doubt, in OF. to fear (see *doughty*). For restored *-b-* cf. *doubt*.

redound. F. *rédonder*, L. *redundare*, "to overflow, reflow or return backe, to redounde" (Coop.), from *re-* and *undare*, from *unda*, wave. Formerly common in lit. sense (cf. *redundant*). For current fig. sense cf. F. *rejaillir*, to gush back.

L'éclat n'en rejaillit qu'à votre déshonneur
(Mol. *Don Juan*, iv. 6).

redowa. Dance. F. or Ger., from Bohem. *reydovák*, from *reydovati*, to whirl round.

redress. Formerly current in various senses of F. *redresser*, to put right again (see *dress*). Now usu. in spec. connection with wrongs, grievances, etym. sense surviving with *balance*.

I called the New World into existence to redress the balance of the Old (Canning, 1826).

redshort [*metall.*]. Swed. *rödskört*, red brittle. Cf. *coldshort*.

reduce. L. *reducere*, to lead back. Lit. sense appears in to *reduce a dislocation*, to *reduce to the ranks*; cf. *reduced circumstances* (19 cent.).

reductio ad absurdum. L., reduction to the absurd. Orig. in geom.

redundant. See *redound*. For sense cf. *superfluous*.

reduplication [*ling.*]. Formation of past tense by doubling of root-syllable, e.g. L. *tango*, *tetigi*, G. λύω, λέλυκα; also in Teut. langs., e.g. *hold*, *held* (AS. *hēold*, for **hehold*). Also a common phenomenon of baby speech (*papa*, *mama*), esp. in imit. words (*bow-wow*, *gee-gee*), and in popular words formed either by rime (*hurly-burly*, *roly-poly*) or by variation of orig. vowel (*see-saw*, *zigzag*). In the last class of formations the fuller vowel is usu. the original. See *duplicate*.

reebok. SAfr. antelope. Du., roebuck. Cf. *springbok*, etc.

reed. AS. *hrēod*. WGer.; cf. Du. Ger. *riet* (usual Ger. word is *rohr*). *Reedy voice* is from mus. sense of *reed*.

Thou trustest in the staff of this broken reed [*Vulg.* baculum arundineum confractum], on Egypt
(*Is.* xxxvi. 6; cf. 2 *Kings*, xviii. 21).

reef[1]. In sail. ME. *riff*, ON. *rif*, in same sense, prob. ident. with *reef*[2]. F. *ris* (Wace) is from pl. (cf. *lis*, lily). *Reefer*, midshipman (attending in tops during reefing of sail), is first in Marryat. Hence *reefer*, coat of naut. cut (late 19 cent.).

reef². Rock. Earlier (16 cent.) *riff*, Du. *rif*, ON. *rif*, reef, rib; cf. Ger. *riff*, from Du. Prob. ident. with *reef¹*. In gold-mining sense orig. (c. 1850) in Austral.

reek. AS. *rēocan*, to smoke. Com. Teut.; cf. Du. *rieken*, to smell, *rooken*, to smoke, Ger. *riechen*, to smell, *rauchen*, to smoke, ON. *rjūka*, to smoke. Now usu. replaced by *smoke*, exc. in picturesque and fig. use. Noun *reek* is still in gen. Sc. use; cf. *Auld Reekie*, Edinburgh.

reel¹. For thread. AS. *hrēol*; cf. ON. *hrǣll*, Fris. *raial*. *Off the reel* is 19 cent. Hence verb to *reel*, in early use, but owing something of later senses to *reel²*.

reel². Dance. Perh. from *reel¹*, with idea of spinning round; but cf. obs. E. *ray*, dance, MHG. *reie* (*reigen*, *reihen*).

reeve¹ [*hist.*]. Steward, etc. AS. *gerēfa*, whence also archaic *grieve*. Cf. *portreeve*, *sheriff*. In AS. a high official, used later in various senses. The resemblance to Ger. *graf* (Du. *graaf*, LG. *grave*, *greve*), count, earlier used of various officials, is thought by the best authorities to be accidental, but the correspondence in sense is remarkable, e.g. archaic E. *dike-reeve* (EAngl.) = LG. *dīk-grēve*, Ger. *deich-graf*.

reeve² [*naut.*]. Verb. From 17 cent. It. *refare*, "to thrid" (Torr.), from *refe*, "any kinde of twisted sowing thred" (Flor.), ? Ger. *reif*, band, rope; ? cf. dial. *reeve*, rope (of onions). Not connected with *reef¹*. With past *rove* cf. naut. *stove* (from *stave*).

Reeving is...drawing a rope thorow a blocke or oylet to runne up and down (Capt. John Smith).

reeve³. Bird. Fem. of *ruff¹* (q.v.).

refectory. MedL. *refectorium*, from L. *reficere*, *refect-*, to remake, repair. For sense cf. *restaurant*.

refer. F. *référer*, from L. *referre*, lit. to carry back. Cf. *relate*. *Referee* was orig. used (early 17 cent.) of parl. official dealing with monopolies; cf. earlier *referendary*. *Referendum* (late 19 cent.) is a Swiss institution (cf. *plébiscite*).

refine. F. *raffiner*, from *affiner*, from *fin*, fine²; cf. It. *raffinare*, Sp. *raffinar*. Orig. of metals.

reflect. L. *reflectere*, to bend back, as still in scient. sense, and in to *reflect* (credit, dishonour, etc.) *upon one*, whence *reflection*, animadversion. *Reflex*, L. *reflexus*, reflected, is 19 cent. in sense of involuntary.

reform. F. *reformer*, to form again, *réformer*,

to improve, L. *reformare*, from *forma*, shape. *Reformation*, in Church sense, was borrowed (16 cent.) from Ger. (Luther). *Reformatory* is 19 cent.

refract. From L. *refringere*, *refract-*, to break back, from *frangere*. *Refractory* is altered from earlier *refractary*, F. *réfractaire*, L. *refractarius*.

refrain¹. Verb. From tonic stem (OF. *refrein-*) of F. *refréner*, L. *refrenare*, to restrain, from *frenum*, bridle, ? cogn. with *frendere*, to gnash the teeth. Current sense is for earlier reflex. (*Gen.* xlv. 1).

refrain². Noun. F., lit. break back, from OF. *refraindre*, VL. **refrangere*, for *refringere*; cf. Prov. *refranh*, Sp. *refran*. OF. & ME. also had *refrait*, *refret*, L. *refract-*.

refrain d'une balade: the refret, burthen, or downe of a ballade (Cotg.).

refresh. OF. *refrescher* (replaced by *rafraîchir*), from *frais*, fresh. Earliest (14 cent.) in sense of physical restoration, etc. With *refresher* (leg.) cf. AF. *refreschement*, instalment of pay (14 cent.).

His memory had received a very disagreeable refresher on the subject of Mrs Bardell's action
                                        (*Pickwick*, xxxi.).

refrigerate. From L. *refrigerare*, from *frigus*, cold. *Refrigerator* is substituted for earlier *refrigeratory* (c. 1600).

reft. See *reave*.

refuge. F., L. *refugium*, from *fugere*, to flee. *Place* (*port*, *house*) *of refuge* are modelled on *city of refuge* (*Vulg.* urbs fugitivorum). *Refugee*, 17 cent. also *refugie*, F. *réfugié*, was first applied to F. Huguenots who migrated after Revocation of Edict of Nantes (1685).

refund. L. *refundere*, lit. to pour back, in Law L. to pay back; cf. F. *verser*, to pay in, lit. to pour. Associated in sense with *fund*.

refuse. Verb. F. *refuser*, L. *refusare*, ? from *refundere*, *refus-*, to cast back, etc. (v.s.). Noun is from F. *refus*, and perh. in earlier adj. sense (*refuse goods*) from p.p. *refusé* with *-é* lost as in *costive*, *signal²*, *trove*, etc. To *have the refusal* (option of acquiring) is 16 cent. *The great refusal* is Dante's *gran rifiuto* (*Inf.* iii. 60), alluding to Celestine V's resignation of the Papacy.

refute. L. *refutare*, to repel. Cf. *futile*.

regal. Archaic F. *régal*, L. *regalis*, from *rex*, *reg-*, king.

regale. F. *régaler*, It. *regalare*, "to present or give guifts unto, to bestow a largesse upon"

(Flor.), prob. from *gala* (q.v.), but naturally associated with *regal* (v.i.).

se regaler: to make as much account, and take as great a care, of himselfe, as if he were a king (Cotg.).

regalia. L., neut. pl. of *regalis*, royal. Earlier used also of royal rights and privileges. In sense of cigar it is Sp., royal privilege.

regard. First (14 cent.) as noun. F., from *regarder*, to look at, consider, from *garder*, to heed, etc. See also *reward*. For sense-development cf. *respect*. It seems possible that *kind regards* (cf. *best respects*), as epistolary formula (18 cent.), may be partly due to Port. *recados* (pl.), "a greeting, commendation, salutation" (Vieyra), used by several early E. travellers and spelt *recarders* by Fryer (17 cent.). This is from *recadar*, to send a message, VL. *recapitare.

regatta. Orig. boat-race on Grand Canal of Venice. It. (Venet.), struggle, match; app. related to archaic E. *regrater* (q.v.). According to the *NED.* the first E. *regatta* was held on the Thames, June 23, 1775 (see *Annual Register*); but quot. 3 relates to 1768.

rigatta: the play that children cal at musse. Also a strife or contention for the maistrie, a coping or bickering together (Flor.).

rigattare: to wrangle, to shift for, to play at musse. Also to sell by retaile as hucksters and brokers use... to proule and shift for by prouling, to contend, to cope or fight for the maistrie (*ib.*).

He [the Earl of Lincoln] planned what was termed a Regatta, to which all the gentlemen of the neighbourhood who kept boats were invited
(Hickey's *Memoirs*, i. 96).

regenerate. From L. *regenerare*, from *genus*, *gener-*, race, breed.

regent. F. *régent*, from pres. part. of L. *regere*, to rule. Hence *regency*, esp. in France (1715–23) and England (1810–20), in each case with suggestion of debauchery.

regicide. Coined (16 cent.) on *homicide*.

régie. Department controlling tobacco. F., p.p. fem. of *régir*, to rule, from L. *regere*.

régime. F., L. *regimen*, "regiment, rule, governaunce" (Coop.), from *regere*, to rule. Esp. (hist.) the *old régime*, in France before Revolution.

regiment. F. *régiment*, Late L. *regimentum*, in various senses of *regimen* (v.s.), e.g. *monstrous regiment of women* (Knox). Mil. sense from 16 cent. With *regimentals* cf. *canonicals*.

region. F. *région*, L. *regio-n-*, from *regere*, to rule. Cf. *kingdom*.

register. F. *registre*, OF. also *regestre*, MedL. *registrum*, *regestrum*, altered from Late L. *regesta*, neut. pl., from *regerere*, *regest-*, to record, from *gerere*, to carry (out), execute, etc. Some senses (organ, stove) app. influenced by association with *regere*, to rule, control. *Registrary*, MedL. *registrarius*, is replaced by *registrar*, exc. at Camb.

Every parson vicare or curate within this diocese shall for every churche kepe one boke or registre wherin ye shall write the day and yere of every weddyng christenyng and buryeng
(T. Cromwell, 1538).

regius. L., royal. Title of five professors instituted by Hen. VIII.

regnant. From pres. part. of L. *regnare*, to reign, from *regnum*, kingdom, from *regere*, to rule. Usu. after noun and esp. in *queen regnant*. Cf. hist. *regnal year*, MedL. *regnalis*.

regorge. Cf. *disgorge*.

regrater [*hist.*]. Retailer, with suggestion of forestalling and monopoly. Still in dial. use for huckster. F. *regrattier*, from *regratter*, explained as from *gratter*, to scratch, scrape. But AF. *regatour* and It. *rigattare*, Sp. *regatear*, suggest that *regratter* may be folk-etym. Cf. also It. *recatare* (v.i.), ult. ident. with F. *racheter*, to buy back (see *cater*). See *regatta*. For another doubtful -*r*- cf. *broker*.

recatare: to buie and sell againe by retaile, to regrate, to retaile. Also to forestall markets (Flor.).

Some hundreds of years ago we had statutes in this country against forestalling and regrating
(*Daily Chron.* July 17, 1919).

regress. L. *regressus*. Cf. *egress*, *progress*, etc.

regret. F. *regretter* (11 cent.), orig. to bewail the dead. Of Teut. origin; cf. AS. *grǣtan*, OSax. *grātan*, MHG. *grazen*, ON. *grāta*, Goth. *grētan*, to weep, rage, etc.; also Sc. *greet²*, to weep.

regular. OF. *reguler* (*régulier*), L. *regularis*, from *regula*, rule, from *regere*. Earliest E. sense (14 cent.), belonging to a religious order or rule, as opposed to *secular*. With *a regular fraud* cf. *a genuine humbug*. Cf. *regulate*, from Late L. *regulare*, whence US. *regulator*, vigilante, agent of lynch-law.

We daily hear of new irregularities committed by the people called regulators (*Boston Chron.* 1768).

regulus [*chem.*]. L., dim. of *rex*, *reg-*, king (cf. *basilisk*). Orig. applied to metallic form of antimony, from its ready combination with gold, the royal metal. Also applied to the basilisk and the crested wren.

regurgitate. From MedL. *regurgitare*, from Late L. *gurgitare*, from *gurges, gurgit-*, abyss, gorge.

rehabilitate. See *habilitate*.

rehearse. OF. *rehercier*, to repeat, lit. to rake or harrow over again (see *hearse*). Very common in ME., theat. sense from 16 cent only (*Dream*, iii. 1).

> Whoso shal telle a tale after a man,
> He moote reherce, as ny as ever he kan,
> Everich a word (Chauc. A. 731).

reichstag [*hist.*]. Ger. parliament. From *reich*, empire, ult. cogn. with *rajah*, and *tag*, assembly, lit. day (see *diet*[2]). Cf. *landtag*, and Austr. *reichsrat*, from *rat*, counsel, "rede."

> He [Bismarck] was a man of infinite humour, who called his hound Reichstag (H. Macfall).

reify. To materialize. Coined (c. 1850) from L. *res*, thing, after *nullify*.

reign. F. *règne*, L. *regnum*, from *regere*, to rule. Cf. It. *regno*, Sp. *reino*.

reim [*SAfr.*]. Thong, strap. Du. *riem*.

reimburse. Coined from archaic *imburse* (Johns.), after F. *rembourser*, from *bourse*, purse (q.v.).

rein[1]. Of horse. F. *rêne*, OF. *resne, reigne*, etc.; cf. It. *redina*, Sp. *rienda*, VL. **retina*, from *retinēre*, to hold back; cf. *retinaculum*, "anye thing that holdeth back" (Coop.).

rein[2]. Loin. See *reins*.

reindeer. ON. *hreindȳri*, whence also Du. *rendier*, Ger. *renntier*, altered on *rennen*, to run. ON. had also the simple *hreinn*, whence AS. *hrān* (King Alfred), F. *renne* (via Ger.).

reinette. Apple. See *rennet*[2].

reinforce. For earlier (16 cent.) *renforce*, F. *renforcer*, from *re-* and OF. *enforcier*, to strengthen, from *force* (q.v.).

reins [*archaic*]. Loins. F., L. *renes*, kidneys. For Bibl. use (*Ps.* vii. 2) as seat of feelings cf. *heart, liver, stomach, bowels*.

reinstate. From archaic *instate* (cf. *install*). See *state*.

reintegration. For *redintegration* (q.v.); cf. F. *réintégration*, MedL. *reintegratio*.

reis[1]. Port. money of account. Port., pl. of *real*[2] (q.v.). Cf. *milreis*.

> It takes one thousand reis to make a dollar
> (Mark Twain).

reis[2]. Arab. skipper, pilot. Arab. *rāis*, from *rās*, head.

reitbuck. SAfr. antelope. Du. *rietbok*, reed buck.

reiter [*hist.*]. Ger., rider, trooper.

reiterate. From Late L. *reiterare*, from *iterare*, "to doe a thing eftsoones or agayne" (Coop.), from *iterum*, again.

reive. See *reave*.

reject. From L. *reicere, reject-*, to throw back, from *jacere*. *Rejectamenta* is ModL.

rejoice. OF. *rejoïr* (*réjouir*), *réjoïss-*, from *re-* and *éjoïr*. See *enjoy, joy*. ME. had also *rejoy* (Chauc.).

rejoin. See *join*. Sense of replying, orig. leg., esp. of defendant's answer to plaintiff, is AF. With *rejoinder*, from infin. *rejoindre*, cf. *remainder*.

rejuvenate. Coined (c. 1800), after *renovate*, from L. *juvenis*, young. Cf. *rejuvenescence*, from MedL. *rejuvenescere*.

relapse. From L. *relabi, relaps-*, to slip back, "backslide," orig. (16 cent.) into heresy.

relate. F. *relater*, from L. *relat-*, p.p. stem of *referre*, to refer, bear back. For senses cf. *refer, report*, and F. *rapporter*. With *relation*, kinsman (c. 1500), cf. concrete use of *acquaintance*. *Relative* (pronoun) is in Wyc.

relax. L. *relaxare*, from *laxus*, lax, loose. Cf. F. *relâcher*.

relay. Orig. (c. 1400) set of fresh hounds. OF. *relai* (*relais*), from *relayer* (13 cent.), from OF. *laier*, to let (see *delay*). ModF. *relais* is due to association with OF. *relaissier*, to release, *laissier* and *laier*, though quite distinct in origin, being used indifferently in OF.

release. OF. *relaissier*, VL. **relaxiare*, for *relaxare* (whence *relâcher*). Cf. *lease*. Current idiotic use of the verb started with the film manufacturers.

> Only this morning a daily paper of some standing remarked that the government had not "released" any colonial mutton last week
> (*Globe*, Feb. 21, 1917).

relegate. From L. *relegare*, from *legare*, to send.

relent. Ult. from L. *lentus*, slow, viscous; cf. F. *ralentir*, to slacken, from OF. *alentir* (12 cent.).

> He stired the coles, til relente gan
> The wex agayn the fir (Chauc. G. 1278).

relevant. From pres. part. of L. *relevare*, to raise up, hence to be of help, importance. Cf. It. *rilevante*, "of importance, of woorth, of consequence" (Flor.).

reliable. Chiefly current since 1850 and often criticized as a bad US. formation. It is, however, quite legitimate (cf. *available*, *laughable*, etc.) and is recorded in E. for 1569. Cf. *reliance*, first in Shaks. See *rely*.

relic. F. *relique*, orig. (12 cent.) in pl., from L. *reliquiae*, from *relinquere*, *reliqu-*, to leave. Earliest in F. & E. in ref. to saints.

relict. L. *relictus*, p.p. of *relinquere* (v.s.). In spec. sense of widow it represents MedL. *relicta* (sc. *mulier*) or OF. *relicte*.

relief. F., from tonic stem (OF. *reliev-*) of *relever*, to raise up, L. *relevare*, from *levis*, light. Thus to *relieve* is the opposite of to *aggravate*. Etym. sense appears in plastic *relief*, It. *relievo*, raised or embossed work, whence idea of variety, contrast, as in *unrelieved monotony*. To *relieve a man of his purse*, to *relieve one's mind*, go back to orig. sense of lightening. Quot. below, referring to change of sentinel, is commonly misused.

For this relief much thanks (*Haml.* i. 1).

religion. F., L. *religio-n-*, from *religens*, careful, opposite of *negligens*, and prob. cogn. with *diligens*. To *get religion* is US. (c. 1850). *Religiosity* is in Wyc.

relinquish. OF. *relinquir*, *relinquiss-*, VL. **relinquire*, for *relinquere*.

reliquary. F. *reliquaire*, MedL. *reliquiarium*, receptacle for relics.

relish. ME. *reles* (early 14 cent.), archaic F. *relais*, from OF. *relaissier*, to leave (behind). See *release*, which is also recorded in same sense. It is supposed that orig. meaning was after-taste, but this sense is not recorded in E. or F.

reluctant. From pres. part. of L. *reluctari*, to struggle against, from *luctari*, to struggle.

rely. In ME. in sense of *rally*[1]. F. *relier*, L. *religare*, to bind together. From 16 cent. to *rely on* (also *to*), perh. with idea of rallying to, falling back on, one's supports. Now always with *on*, *upon*, perh. owing to association with to *depend on*, *upon*.

remain. From tonic stem (*remain-*) of OF. *remanoir*, L. *remanēre*, from *manēre*, to dwell, stay; also OF. *remaindre*, VL. **remanere*, whence *remainder* (orig. leg.); cf. *misnomer*, *rejoinder*, etc., and see *manor*. The publisher's *remainder* is 18 cent. (*Mortal*) *remains* is late (c. 1700) and prob. after F. *restes* (*mortels*).

remand. Late L. *remandare*, to send back word; hence, to refer back, remit.

remanet. L., it remains. Cf. *deficit*.

remark. F. *remarquer*, to mark, notice (see *mark*[1]). Later sense of commenting, etc.

arises from that of calling attention to spec. points. Cf. *observe*.

remedy. AF. *remedie*, L. *remedium*, from root of *medēri*, to heal; cf. F. *remède*. Leg. sense also in ME.

remember. OF. *remembrer*, from Late L. *rememorari*, from *memor*, mindful; cf. *memory*. The *King's remembrancer* was orig. a debt-collector.

remind. Coined (17 cent.) from *mind*, perh. after obs. *rememorate* (v.s.).

reminiscence. F. *réminiscence*, Late L. *reminiscentia*, from *reminisci*, to remember, cogn. with *mens*, mind.

remise [*archaic*]. Coachhouse. F., from *remettre*, to put back.

remiss. L. *remissus*, p.p. of *remittere*, to send back, also to slacken, abate, leave off, etc. Cf. *remission*, earliest (13 cent.) in *remission of sins*.

remit. L. *remittere*, to send back. In E. chiefly in secondary L. senses; earliest as *remission* (v.s.). Hence *remittance* and colonial *remittance man*. With *remittent* (fever) cf. *unremitting*.

remnant. Earlier *remenant* (Chauc.), OF. *remanant*, pres. part. of *remanoir*, to remain (q.v.).

remonstrate. From MedL. *remonstrare*, to demonstrate, point out (a fault); cf. F. *remontrer*.

remora. Sucking-fish, believed by ancients to delay vessel. L., from *mora*, delay.

remorse. OF. *remors* (*remords*), Late L. *remorsus*, from *remordēre*, to bite again. In ME. esp. in *remorse* (*prick*) *of conscience* (Chauc.), rendered in ME. by *ayenbite of inwit*.

remote. L. *remotus*, p.p. of *removēre*, to remove.

remount. In mil. sense (c. 1800) after F. *remonte*.

remove. OF. *remouvoir*, L. *removēre*, from *movēre*, to move. ME. had also *remeve* from tonic stem *remeuv-* (cf. *retrieve*). As name of form, usu. between fourth and fifth, *remove* appears to have originated at Eton.

remunerate. From L. *remunerare*, from *munus*, *muner-*, reward.

renaissance. F., from *renaître*, *renaiss-*, from *naître*, to be born, OF. *naistre*, VL. **nascere*, for *nasci*. In OF. in sense of spiritual re-birth.

renal [*anat.*]. F. *rénal*, Late L. *renalis*. See *reins*.

renard. See *reynard*.

renascence. In ref. to the revival of learning substituted (1869) by Matthew Arnold for *renaissance*.

rencounter [*archaic*]. F. *rencontre*, from *rencontrer*, to meet, from *re-* and OF. *encontrer*, to encounter (q.v.).

rend. AS. *rendan*, to tear, cut; cf. OFris. *renda*. No other known cognates.

render. F. *rendre*, VL. *rendere, for *reddere*, to give back, *re-* and *dare*, altered by influence of its opposite *prendere* (*prehendere*), to take; cf. It. *rendere*, Port. *rendar*. The senses were developed in F.

rendezvous. F. *rendez-vous* (16 cent.), imper. of *se rendre*, to betake oneself, proceed (to a spot). Common in 17 cent. as *randevoo*.

rendition. Surrender, rendering. Obs. F., from *rendre*, to render.

renegade. Sp. *renegado*, orig. Christian turned Mohammedan, p.p. of *renegar*, L. *renegare*, to deny again. Cf. *desperado*. Replaced (16 cent.) earlier *renegate* (Chauc.), from MedL., whence also *runagate* (q.v.).

renew. Formed in ME. from *new* after L. *renovare*.

rennet[1]. For cheese-making. From *renne*, obs. form of *run*[1]; cf. Ger. *renne*, rennet, *gerinnen*, to clot, curdle. Also ME. & dial. *runnet*.

rennet[2]. Apple. F. *reinette*, *rainette*, usu. explained as named, from spotted skin, from *rainette*, frog, dim. of archaic *raine*, L. *rana*; but perh. dim. of *reine*, queen.

renounce. F. *renoncer*, L. *renuntiare*, to protest against. Cf. *announce*, *pronounce*.

renovate. From L. *renovare*, from *novus*, new.

renown. OF. *renon* (*renom*), from *renommer*, to make famous, from *nommer*, to name, L. *nominare*, from *nomen*, *nomin-*, name. Cf. *noun*.

rent[1]. Fissure, etc. From obs. *rent*, to tear (Chauc.), var. of *rend*, due to the p.p.

rent[2]. Of house. F. *rente*, income, yield, VL. *rendita, p.p. of *rendere. See *render* and cf. *tent*. In ME. of revenue in gen. Cf. It. *rendita*, "a rent, a revenue, an income, a profite" (Flor.). *Rental*, register of rents, rent-roll (*Piers Plowm.*), is AF.

Is it leful to geve to Cesar rente?
(Wyc. *Matt.* xxii. 17).

rentier. F., man of independent means, esp. with money in the *rentes*, public funds (v.s.).

renunciation. L. *renuntiatio-n-*, from *renuntiare*, to renounce.

rep[1] [*archaic*]. Bad character. For *reprobate*,

but prob. suggested by *demi-rep* (q.v.). See also *rip*[2].

rep[2]. Fabric. Cf. F. *reps*, Du. *rips*, Norw. *ribs*, *rips*, *reps*, of various "ribbed" fabrics. Prob. cogn. with *rib*. For app. pl. forms cf. *baize*, *chintz*, "*cords*."

rep[3] [*school slang*]. For *repetition*. Cf. *prep*.

repair[1]. To mend. F. *réparer*, L. *reparare*, from *parare*, to prepare. Cf. *pare*, *prepare*.

repair[2]. To resort. OF. *repairier*, Late L. *repatriare*, to return to one's fatherland, *patria*. Cf. It. *ripatriare*, "to settle, place, or dwell in his owne native countrie againe" (Flor.), and E. *repatriate*.

En cest païs avez estet asez,
En France ad Ais bien repairier devez (*Rol.* 134).

repand [*biol.*]. L. *repandus*, bent back.

repartee. F. *repartie*, "an answering blow, or thrust (in fencing &c.) and thence, a returne of, or answer in speech" (Cotg.), p.p. fem. of *repartir*, to start back, hence to return a thrust, to retort. Cf. *riposte*.

repast. OF. (*repas*), from *repaître*, to feed, Late L. *repascere*, from *re-* and *pascere*, *past-*, to feed.

repatriate. See *repair*[2].

repeal. AF. *repeler*, F. *rappeler*, from *re-* and *appeler*. See *peal*, *appeal*. As noun esp. in *Repeal of the Union*, urged (1830) by O'Connell.

repeat. F. *répéter*, from L. *repetere*, lit. to try again, from *petere*, to assail, seek. *Repeating* watches are 17 cent., *repeating* rifles 19 cent.

repel. L. *repellere*, from *pellere*, *puls-*, to drive. Cf. *repulse*, which now usu. replaces *repel* in mil. sense.

repent. F. *se repentir*, from *re-* and OF. *pentir*, VL. *paenitire, for *paenitēre*, cogn. with *paene*, almost. Orig. reflex., as usu. in *AV*. Has nearly supplanted native *rue*[2].

repertory. L. *repertorium*, from *reperire*, *repert-*, to find. Cf. F. *répertoire*.

repetition. F. *répétition*, L. *repetitio-n-*. See *repeat*.

repine. Coined (16 cent.) from *pine*[2], after *repent*, *reproach*, *reprove*, etc.

replenish. OF. *replenir*, *repleniss-*; cf. archaic *plenish* (q.v.).

replete. F. *replet*, L. *repletus*, from *replere*, *replet-*, to fill again; cf. *complete*. Now usu. with *with*, for earlier *of* (Chauc.).

replevin [*leg.*]. Recovery of distrained chattels on security. AF., from OF. *replevir*, from *plevir*, to pledge (q.v.).

replica. It., from *replicare*, to reply (q.v.).

reply. F. *replier*, to fold back, in OF. also to reply (cf. ModF. *répliquer*), L. *replicare*, from *plicare*, to bend, fold. For metaphor cf. *retort*. Spec. leg. sense survives in *plaintiff's counsel then replied*; cf. *replication*, formal reply of plaintiff to plea of defendant.

report. OF. *reporter*, *raporter* (*rapporter*), L. *reportare*, to bring back (e.g. a message). Sense of noise springs from that of carrying back, re-echoing, a sound (v.i.). Current sense of *reporter* is 19 cent.

And that he wolde been oure governour,
And of our tales juge and reportour
                                        (Chauc. A. 813).

The ragged hills and rocky towers reporte,
By ecchoes voyce, the quest of noble hounds
                                        (*NED.* 1589).

repose. F. *reposer*. See *pose*. Intrans. sense is for earlier reflex. (cf. F. *se reposer*). In some senses, e.g. to *repose confidence in one*, rather directly from L. *reponere*, *reposit-*. Cf. *repository*, OF. *repositoire*, L. *repositorium*.

repoussé. F., p.p. of *repousser*, to push back, repulse. Cf. *relief*.

reprehend. L. *reprehendere*, "to pluck back againe; to take holde again; to blame, to rebuke" (Coop.); cf. F. *reprendre*, "to reprehend, blame, check, rebuke, reprove, carpe, controll" (Cotg.). *Reprehensible* is in Wyc. (*Gal.* ii. 11).

represent. F. *représenter*, orig. to bring into presence, hence to make clear, demonstrate, symbolize (cf. *representative*), stand in place of. First *NED.* quot. in parl. sense is from Oliver Cromwell.

repress. From L. *reprimere*, *repress-*, to press back, from *premere*.

reprieve. Orig. (c. 1500) to remand (to prison). Altered, app. by association with ME. *preve*, prove, from earlier *repry*, F. *repris*, p.p. of *reprendre*, to take back. The fact that *reprove* (ME. *repreve*) was a regular rendering of F. *reprendre*, to reprehend, may have helped the confusion.

They were repryed, and sent unto the Toure of London (*NED.* 1494).

reprimand. F. *réprimande*, from *réprimer*, to repress (q.v.).

reprisal. Orig. (15 cent.) in *letters of marque* (q.v.) *and reprisal*. F. *représaille*, It. *ripresaglia*, "booties, prayes, prizes, prisals" (Flor.), from *riprendere*, to take back. Cf.

to *get a bit of one's own back*. E. spelling has been affected by *reprise* (F.), used in various senses, including that of *reprisal*.

reproach. F. *reprocher*, VL. *repropiare*, from *prope*, near; cf. *approach*. Orig. sense, as still in F., e.g. *reprocher à quelqu'un sa faiblesse*, is to bring near, home. Cf. Ger. *vorwerfen*, to reproach, lit. to throw before.

It shall not be reproched to me that ye fyghte me a foot and I on horsbacke (Caxton).

reprobate. L. *reprobatus*, p.p. of *reprobare*, to reprove, reject, which in Late L. had sense of to cast away from God. Orig. in Bibl. lang., e.g. 2 *Cor.* xiii. 5, where Tynd. and Coverd. have *castaway* and Wyc. *reprevable*.

reprove. F. *réprouver*, L. *reprobare* (v.s.). Cf. *approve*.

The stoon whom men bildinge reproveden
                                        (Wyc. *Luke*, xx. 17).

reptile. F., Late L. *reptile* (sc. *animal*), neut. of Late L. *reptilis*, from *repere*, *rept-*, to creep. ? Cogn. with *serpent*. The *reptile press* renders Ger. *reptilienpresse*, coined (1869) on Bismarck's use of *reptilien*.

republic. F. *république*, L. *res publica*, public thing, common weal. In US. politics *Republican* is now opposed to Democrat, as Conservative to Liberal. The *republic of letters* is first in Addison.

repudiate. From L. *repudiare*, from *repudium*, divorce, cogn. with *pudor*, shame.

repugn. F. *répugner*, L. *repugnare*, "to repugne, to resist, to say contrary" (Coop.), from *pugnare*, to fight. Now esp. in *repugnant, repugnance*.

repulse. From L. *repellere*, *repuls-*; cf. F. *repousser*.

repute. F. *réputer*, L. *reputare*, "to consider and weigh diligently" (Coop.), from *putare*, to think.

request. First (14 cent.) as noun. OF. *requeste* (*requête*); cf. *quest*, *require*. With *in request* (16 cent.) cf. *in requisition* (early 19 cent.).

requiem. L., acc. of *requies*, rest, quiet, init. word of Introit in the Mass for the Dead, *Requiem aeternam dona eis, Domine.* Cf. *dirge, magnificat*, etc.

requiescat. L., may he begin to rest (*in pace*, in peace).

require. From tonic stem (*requier-*) of F. *requérir*, VL. *requaerire* for *requirere*, from *quaerere*, to seek; cf. *inquire*. Now often peremptory, orig. sense having been taken over by *request*. With *requirement* cf. *re-quisite*.

One thing have I desired of the Lord, which I will require (*Ps.* xxvii. 4, *PB.*).

requisite. L. *requisitus*, p.p. of *requirere* (v.s.). *Requisition*, in mil. sense, is late 18 cent.

requite. Coined (16 cent.) from obs. *quite*, early var. of *quit* (q.v.).

reredos. AF. *areredos*, *reredos; cf. AL. *retrodorsorium*. Lit. rear back (see *rear*² and *dorsal*). ME. had several other compds. in *rere-*, now obs. or replaced by *rear-*. *Reredos* was also obs. by 1550, exc. in sense of back of open fire-place, but was revived by eccl. antiquaries of 19 cent.

Item, for makyng of the rerdose in the kechyn
(*York Merch. Advent. Accts.* 1433–4).

reremouse. See *rearmouse*.

rereward [*archaic*]. For *rearguard* (1 *Sam.* xxix. 2)

rescind. F. *rescinder*, L. *rescindere*, "to cut or breake in sunder; to abolish or fordoe" (Coop.), from *scindere*, *sciss-*, to cut; cf. *rescission*, annulment.

rescript. L. *rescriptum*, "the letters of a prince making aunswere to other letters; the emperours letters" (Coop.), from *rescribere*, *rescript-*, to write back. In E. first (16 cent.) in Papal sense.

rescue. From stem of AF. *rescure*, OF. *rescourre* (archaic *recourre*), from *re-* and *escourre*, L. *excutere*, to strike out; cf. It. *riscuotere*. The noun was in ME. *rescous*, OF. *rescousse* (archaic *recousse*), representing VL. *re-ex-cussa*. *Rescue home* is late 19 cent.

research. Sense of original, esp. scient., investigation, is 19 cent. Much overworked since c. 1880. See *search*.

reseda. Colour. F. *réséda*, mignonette, L. *reseda*, "a certain herbe dissolving impostumes" (Coop.), imper. of *resedare*, to allay, in formula *reseda morbis*, used as charm when applying the leaves as poultice (Pliny, xxvii. 131).

resemble. F. *ressembler*, from *re-* and *sembler*, to seem, L. *similare*, *simulare*, from *similis*, like, from *simul*, together.

resent. F. *ressentir*, from *re-* and *sentir*, to feel. Orig. to feel strongly in any way, current sense suggesting that "our sense of injuries is much stronger and more lasting than our sense of benefits" (Trench). Cf. *retaliate*.

I resented as I ought the news of my mother-in-law's death (Archbp. Sancroft).

reserve. F. *réserver*, L. *reservare*, from *servare*, to save. Cf. *preserve*. Mil. sense of noun from 17 cent. With *reserved* (in manner), first in Shaks. (*All's Well*, v. 3), cf. Ger. *zurückhaltend*, lit. holding back. *Mental reservation* is recorded from 16 cent., usu. with depreciatory sense of casuistry.

reservoir. F. *réservoir*, from *réserver* (v.s.).

reset [*leg.*]. To receive stolen goods (Sc.); earlier, to harbour. See *receive*.

reside. F. *résider*, L. *residere*, from *sedere*, to sit. *Residency*, earlier used indifferently with *residence*, is now obs., exc. in EInd.

residue. F. *résidu*, L. *residuum*, neut. of *residuus*, remaining, from *residere* (v.s.). Cf. *sediment*.

resign. F. *résigner*, L. *resignare*, to unseal, cancel, from *signum*, sign, seal.

resilient. From pres. part. of L. *resilire*, to jump back, recoil, from *salire*, to jump.

resin, rosin. F. *résine* (OF. also *raisine, roisine*), L. *resina*; cf. G. ῥητίνη. *Rosin* is the older form in E. and Wyc. has both. With quot. below cf. *treacle*.

Whether resyn is not in Galaad
(Wyc. *Jer.* viii. 22).

resipiscence. L. *resipiscentia*, from *resipiscere*, to return to a better frame of mind, from *re-* and incept. of *sapere*, to know.

resist. F. *résister*, L. *resistere*, to stand against, withstand. *Line of least resistance* is late 19 cent. from scient. *line of resistance*.

resolve. L. *resolvere*, from *solvere*, *solut-*, to loosen; cf. *dissolve*. Orig. sense of disintegrating passes, via that of solving a problem, to that of deciding a course of action. Cf. F. *résoudre*, with same senses. Only the secondary sense now appears in *resolute*. *Resolution* in parl. sense is recorded c. 1600. *Resolute*, to pass resolutions, occurs in 16 cent. E., but is now only US. (cf. *sculp*).

resonant. From pres. part. of L. *resonare*, to resound.

resort. F. *ressortir*, to rebound, go back again, from *re-* and *sortir*, to go out; in OF. esp. to have recourse to (a feudal authority), whence E. to *resort to* (counsels, methods, etc.). The noun is earlier in E. (Chauc.), *in the last resort* rendering F. *en dernier ressort*, "finally, fully, without farther appeale, or scope left for any appeale" (Cotg.). See *sortie*.

resource. F. *ressource*, "a resource, new spring, recovery, uprising, or raising against" (Cotg.), from OF. *resourdre*, to rise again, from *re-* and *sourdre*, L. *surgere*, etym. sense appearing in (lost) *without re-source*, F. *sans ressource*. Cf. *source*.

respect. F., L. *respectus*, from *respicere*, *respect-*, to look back at, regard, consider. For gen. senses cf. *regard*. With *respectable* cf. F. *considérable*, Ger. *angesehen*, E. *looked up to*, and, for its degeneration, cf. *honest*. F. *respectable* is still a dignified epithet. See *respite*.

Non est personarum acceptor Deus
(*Vulg. Acts*, x. 34).

Thucydides was a great and respectable man
(Langhorne's *Plutarch*, 1770).

respire. F. *respirer*, L. *respirare*, from *spirare*, to breathe. Cf. *spirit*. The *respirator* was invented by Julius Jeffreys (1835).

respite. OF. *respit* (*répit*), "a respite; a delay, a time or terme of forbearance" (Cotg.), L. *respectus*. Cf. *re-consideration*. *Respect* is common in same sense in 16 cent.

resplendent. From pres. part. of L. *resplendēre*, from *splendēre*, to shine, be splendid.

respond. L. *respondēre*, from *spondēre*, to pledge; cf. origin of *answer*, *answerable*, *responsible*. ME. had *respoun(d)*, OF. *respondre* (*répondre*). *Responsions*, preliminary examination (Oxf.), lit. answers, is recorded only from early 19 cent.

ressaldar [*Anglo-Ind.*]. Native captain in Indian cavalry. Urdu *risāladār*, from *risālah*, squadron, from Arab. *arsala*, to send, with agent. suffix as in *sirdar*, *chokidar*, etc.

rest¹. Repose. AS. *ræst*. Com. Teut.; cf. Du. *rust*, Ger. *rast*, orig. stage of journey; also ON. *röst*, Goth. *rasta*, stretch of road, mile; cogn. with Goth. *razn*, house (see *ransack*). App. a word from the nomadic period; cf. Pers. *manzil*, home, orig. place of dismounting. *Rest-day* is in AS., rendering of *sabbath*. *Rest cure* is late 19 cent. In the verb there has been association with *rest²,³*, e.g. *his eyes rested* (F. *s'arrêtèrent*) *on the object*, *he rested his elbow on the table*, etc. Shaks. *rest you merry* (*happy*, *fair*) is ellipt. for trans. use. Quot. 2 is now often wrongly punctuated.

God rest you merry, sir (*As You Like It*, v. 1).

God rest you merry, gentlemen (*Xmas carol*).

rest². Remainder. F. *reste*, from *rester*, to remain, L. *restare*, lit. to stand back. Has affected sense of *rest¹*. The verb was formerly used in concluding letters for *I remain*, etc.; cf. *rest assured*.

rest³. Of lance. Aphet. for *arrest*; but the simple *rest* is recorded earlier, and It. *resta*, Sp. *ristre*, have same sense; cf. *rest-harrow*, a tough shrub which is a nuisance to farmers (MedL. *resta bovis*, AF. *reste-beof*). See *rest²*.

arrest (*arrêt*): the rest whereon a man of armes setleth his lance (Cotg.).

arreste-bœuf: the herbe rest-harrow, petty-whinne, graund furze, cammocke (*ib.*).

restaurant. F., pres. part. of *restaurer*, to restore. Current sense in Paris from c. 1765, but found earlier (17 cent.) in sense of strengthening diet.

restitution. F., L. *restitutio-n-*, from *restituere*, to re-establish, restore, from *statuere*, to set up. From 13 cent.

restive. OF. *restif* (*rétif*), "restie, stubborn, drawing backward, that will not goe forward" (Cotg.), from *rester*, to rest²; cf. Sc. *reist*, to stand stock-still. The sense has changed curiously. See also *rusty²*.

Like froward jades that for no striking sturre,
But waxe more restife still the more we spurre
(Sylv. i. 2).

restore. OF. *restorer* (*restaurer*), L. *restaurare*, to repair, cogn. with G. σταυρός, stake. For sense of giving back cf. *restitution*. *Restoration* was substituted (1660) for earlier *restauration*.

The happy restoration of his Majesty to his people and kingdoms (*Journal of H. of C.*, May 30, 1660).

restrain. F. *restreindre*, *restreign-*, L. *restringere*, *restrict-*, whence also later *restrict*. See *strain*. *Restraint of princes* is still used for embargo in mercantile insurance.

result. L. *resultare*, to leap back, from *saltare*, frequent. of *salire*, *salt-*, to leap.

resume. F. *résumer*, from L. *resumere*, to take back. For sense of recommencing cf. F. *reprendre*. Cf. *résumé*, F. p.p.

resurge. L. *resurgere*, *resurrect-*, to rise again. Cf. *resurrection*, F. *résurrection* (12 cent.). *Resurrection* is used by Tynd. where Wyc. has *rysyng agein* and the AS. *Gospels* have *æriste*. *Resurrection-man*, *resurrectionist*, body-snatcher, are 18 cent.

resuscitate. From L. *resuscitare*, from *suscitare*, to raise up, arouse, from *sub* and *citare*, to summon, cite (q.v.).

ret [*techn.*]. To steep flax. Archaic Du. *reten*, " to hickle or cleans flax " (Hexham); cogn. with *rot*; cf. Sw. *röta*, Dan. *röde*, Du. *roten*,

Ger. *rösten* (for *rötzen*, MHG. *retzen*); also F. *rouir*, from Teut., *routoir*, retting-pond.

Both France and Holland send their flax to be retted in it [the river Lys]
(*Daily Chron.* Aug. 2, 1917).

retable [*eccl.*]. Appendage to altar. F., altered from OF. **rieretable*, rear-table; cf. Prov. *reiretaule*, MedL. *retrotabulum*; also ME. *rerefront*, app. draping of retable. Introduced (19 cent.) by eccl. antiquaries. Cf. *reredos*.

retail. OF. *retailler*, to cut up (see *tailor*). In E. sense ModF. has *détail*.

destailler: to retaile, or passe away by parcels
(Cotg.).

retain. F. *retenir*, VL. **retenire*, for *retinēre*, to hold back; cf. *contain*, *detain*, etc. With *retainer*, kept fighting-man, cf. *retinue*.

cliens: one that belongeth or retayneth to an noble man; also a client reteyning a lawyer (Coop.).

retaliate. From L. *retaliare*, from *talis*, such, like. Orig. of requiting in kind, good or evil.

His Majesty's desire to retaliate...his subjects' true affections (Speed, 1611).

retard. F. *retarder* or L. *retardare*, from *tardus*, slow.

retch. AS. *hrǣcan*, from *hrāca*, spittle; cf. ON. *hrǣkja*, to spit. Not recorded in ME. The spelling (for *reach*) is accidental.

retiary. Spider. L. *retiarius*, gladiator armed with net, *rete*.

reticent. From pres. part. of L. *reticēre*, from *tacēre*, to be silent.

reticulate [*biol.*]. L. *reticulatus*, from *reticulum*, dim. of *rete*, net.

reticule. F. *réticule*, L. *reticulum* (v.s.). Earlier (c. 1800) is corrupted *ridicule* (see *Oliver Twist*, ch. xlii.).

retina [*anat.*]. MedL., from *rete*, net; cf. F. *rétine*.

retine: the fift thinne membrane of the eye (Cotg.).

retinue. ME. *retenue* (Chauc.), F., p.p. fem. of *retenir*, to retain (q.v.).

retire. F., to pull back, from *tirer*, to draw (see *tire²*). Orig. trans., current sense for earlier *reflex*.

retort. From L. *retorquēre*, *retort-*, to twist back. Cf. *retort*, glass vessel with bent neck, MedL. *retorta*.

This is called the retort courteous
(*As You Like It*, v. 4).

retract. From L. *retrahere*, *retract-*, to draw back. In spec. sense of revoking, recanting, it represents the frequent. *retractare*,

"to unsay that one hath sayd" (Coop.). Hence *retractation*, orig. of St Augustine's *Retractiones*, re-handlings.

retreat. First as noun. F. *retraite*, from *retraire*, to draw back, L. *retrahere*. Orig. (14 cent.) in mil. sense, esp. in to *blow the retreat*. Cf. E. *withdraw*, now euph. in mil. sense.

retrench. F. *retrancher*, to cut off. See *trench*. Cf. to *cut down* (expenditure). *Retrenchment* was added, at the instigation of Joseph Hume, to the *Peace and Reform* program of the Whigs.

retribution. F. *rétribution*, L. *retributio-n-*, from *retribuere*, to pay back (see *tribute*). For degeneration cf. *retaliate*, *resent*.

retrieve. From OF. tonic stem (*retreuv-*) of F. *retrouver*, to find again (see *trove*). For vowel cf. *beef*, *people*, and see *contrive*. Orig. (c. 1400) of dogs used to restart the game; but *retriever*, in mod. sense, is 19 cent.

retro-. L., backward (see *rear²*). Earliest (15 cent.) in *retrograde* (astron.), L. *retrogradus*, from *gradus*, step. Cf. *retrogression*. *Retrospect* is coined on *prospect*. Hence *retrospective*, now usu. substituted for earlier *retroactive*.

retroussé. F., turned up (see *truss*).

return. F. *retourner*, from *tourner*, to turn (q.v.). *Many (happy) returns of the day* is in Addison's *Freeholder* (May 28, 1716). Sense of report occurs orig. (15 cent.) of sheriff's return of writ to court with report on its execution, later extended to his announcement of election of M.P. The tobacco called *returns* was orig. refuse. With *returns*, profits, cf. *revenue*.

retuse [*biol.*]. L. *retusus*, from *retundere*, to beat back. Cf. *obtuse*.

reunion. F. *réunion*, which, like many F. words in *re-*, *ré-*, has partially lost sense of repetition.

Reuter. News agency founded (1850–60) by P. J. von Reuter.

revanche. From OF. *revanchier*, L. *revindicare* (see *revenge*). Mod. sense is that of return match or game, and not "revenge." Hence Ger. rendering of *la Revanche* is as incorr. as that of our own journalists who translate *en revanche*, on the other hand, by "in revenge."

reveal¹. Verb. F. *révéler*, L. *revelare*, to draw back the veil, *velum*. With *revelation*, orig. (14 cent.) in ref. to divine agency, cf *apocalypse*.

reveal² [*arch.*]. Vertical side of doorway. For obs. *revale*, from OF. *revaler*, to bring down. See *vail¹*.

réveillé, revelly. F. *réveillez-(vous)*, imper. of *se réveiller*, to wake up, from *veiller*, to watch, L. *vigilare*. But not used in mil. F., which has *réveil* and *diane*.

revel. First (14 cent.) as verb. OF. *reveler*, to make tumult, have a spree, L. *rebellare*, to rebel. The current sense is the oldest (14 cent.) in E., though that of riot also occurs occasionally (v.i.), and it would appear that the word has been associated with F. *réveillon*, a Christmas Eve supper, and with the gen. idea of night jollifications (cf. *wake*). See also *riot*, which runs parallel with *revel*, though with converse sense-development.

> Men wene and the Dwke of Southfolk come ther schall be a schrewd revele (*Paston Let.* ii. 83).

> *vegghie*: watches, sentinels, wakes, revels a nights (Flor.).

revelly. See *réveillé*.

revendication. F., as *revindication*.

revenge. First (14 cent.) as verb. F. *revancher*, OF. *revanchier, revengier*, L. *revindicare*, from *vindicare*. Cf. *vengeance, vindicate*.

revenue. F. *revenu*, p.p. of *revenir*, to come back, L. *revenire*. Cf. *income, returns*. Sense of public income (*inland revenue, revenue officer*, etc.) is latest (17 cent.).

reverberate. From L. *reverberare*, lit. to beat back.

revere. F. *révérer*, from L. *revereri*, from *vereri*, to fear. Much earlier are *reverence* (13 cent.) and *reverend, reverent*. With *reverence*, bow (*Piers Plowm.*), cf. *curtsy, obeisance*. *Reverend*, as title of clergy, dates from 15 cent., *reverent* being erron. used earlier in same sense.

reverie. F. *rêverie*, from *rêver*, to dream (see *rave*). Current in ME. in sense of wild joy, etc., and app. confused with *revelry*. Readopted in mod. sense in 17 cent.

revers. F., L. *reversus* (v.i.).

reverse. F. *reverser*, from L. *versare*, frequent. of *vertere*, to turn. With mil. sense of defeat, disaster, cf. euph. *setback*.

revert. OF. *revertir*, VL. **revertire*, for *revertere* (v.s.).

revet [*mil. & arch.*]. To face with masonry. F. *revêtir*, OF. *revestir*, from L. *vestire*, to clothe.

> She [H.M.S. Cochran] grounded on a revetment (*Daily Chron.* Feb. 19, 1919).

review. First as noun. F. *revue*, p.p. fem. of *revoir*, to see again, revise, etc. (see *view*). In literary sense from 18 cent.

revile. OF. *reviler*, from *vil*, vile.

revindicate. See *vindicate*.

revise. F. *reviser*, L. *revisere*, frequent. of *revidēre*, to review. The *Revised Version* was executed 1870–84.

revive. F. *revivre*, Late L. *revivere*, from *vivere*, to live. Trans. sense originated through conjugation of intrans. with verb to *be*, e.g. *she was* (mod. *had*) *revived*. *Revival* in rel. sense is quoted by *NED.* from Cotton Mather (1702).

revoke. F. *révoquer*, L. *revocare*, to call back.

revolt. F. *révolter*, It. *rivoltare* (earlier *revoltare*), L. *re-* and *volutare*, frequent. of *volvere*, to roll; cf. *revolution*. For strong sense of *revolting* (from c. 1800) cf. *disgusting, repulsive*.

revolution. F. *révolution*, Late L. *revolutio-n-*, from *revolvere* (v.s.). Orig. (14 cent.) astron. Pol. sense from c. 1600.

revolve. L. *revolvere* (v.s.). *Revolver* was coined (1835) by Colt.

revue [*theat.*]. F., review (of recent and topical events).

revulsion. L. *revulsio-n-*, from *revellere, revuls-*, to tear back.

reward. ONF. form of *regard*, which is common in same sense in AF. Cf. *award* and see *guard*. Orig. of any form of requital, now limited in the opposite direction to *retaliate*. Gen. sense springs from that of looking favourably on; cf. *for a consideration*. Has almost supplanted *meed* (Wyc. *Matt.* v. 12).

reynard, renard. F. *renard*, OF. *regnard, renart*, orig. *Renart le goupil*, Renard the Fox, in the famous beast-epic, *Roman de Renart* (13 cent.), OHG. *Reginhart*, strong in counsel (cf. *Reginald*), used as pers. name of the fox. The popularity of the poem was so great that *renard* has quite supplanted OF. *goupil*. Cf. *chanticleer, bruin, monkey*. The form *Reynard* was used by Caxton after Du. *Reynaert*; cf. dim. *Reineke* in LG. version *Reineke de Vos*.

> "Oh, Mus' Reynolds, Mus' Reynolds!" said Hobden, under his breath. "If I knowed all was inside your head, I'd know something wuth knowin'"
> (*Puck of Pook's Hill*).

rhabdomancy. Use of divining-rod. From G. ῥάβδος, rod.

Rhadamanthine. Inflexible. From *Rhadamanthus*, G. Ῥαδάμανθος, one of the judges of the lower world. Cf. *Draconic*.

Rhaeto-Romanic [*ling*.]. Romance dials. of S.E. Switzerland, esp. Romansh (Grisons), Ladin (Engadine). From L. *Rhaetia*, name of the region.

rhapsody. L., G. ῥαψῳδία, from ῥαψῳδός, esp. reciter of Homeric songs, from ῥάπτειν, to stitch, ᾠδή, song.

rhatany. Astringent shrub. Altered from Sp. Port. *ratania*, Peruv. *rataña*.

rhea. SAmer. ostrich. Adopted (1752) from myth. G. name Ῥέα.

rheim. Var. of *reim* (q.v.).

Rhemish Bible. E. transl published (1582) at *R(h)eims*.

Rhenish. ME. *rinisch*, MHG. *rīnisch* (*rheinisch*), altered on L. *Rhenus*, Rhine.

Half the money would replenish
Their cellar's biggest butt with Rhenish
                     (*Pied Piper*).

rheo-. From G. ῥέος, stream.

rhesus. EInd. monkey. From *Rhesus*, myth. king of Thrace. Cf. *entellus*.

rhetoric. F. *rhétorique*, L., G. ῥητορική (sc. τέχνη), from ῥήτωρ, orator, teacher of eloquence. One of the three arts of the medieval trivium.

rheum [*archaic*]. Restored from ME. *rewme*, OF. *reume* (*rhume*), L., G. ῥεῦμα, flow, from ῥεῖν, ῥευ-, to flow. *Rheumatics, rheumatism*, was formerly supposed to be caused by a "defluxion of rheum."

rhine [*dial*.]. Large open drain (Somerset, etc.). Altered from earlier *rune, roine*, AS. *ryne*, cogn. with *run*[1].

rhinegrave [*hist*.]. Du. *Rijngrave*, Ger. *Rheingraf*, Rhine count. Cf. *margrave, palsgrave*.

rhino [*slang*]. Money. From 17 cent. App. connected by some obscure joke with *rhinoceros*, as *rhinocerical*, wealthy, also occurs. *Ready rhino* is in T. Brown's satirical lines on the Treaty of Ryswick (1697).

rhinoceros. Late L., G. ῥινόκερως, lit. nosehorn, from ῥίς, ῥιν-, nose, κέρας, horn. Cf. *rhinoplastic*, of nose-modelling.

rhizome [*bot*.]. G. ῥίζωμα, from ῥιζοῦσθαι, to take root, from ῥίζα, root.

Rhodes scholarships. Established at Oxf. for colonial, US. (and orig. also Ger.) students by will of Cecil Rhodes (†1902).

rhodium[1]. Rosewood. ModL. (sc. *lignum*), from G. ῥόδον, rose.

rhodium[2] [*chem*.]. Discovered and named (1804) by Wollaston from G. ῥόδον (v.s.).

rhododendron. G., lit. rose tree, δένδρον (v.s.).

rhodomontade. Incorr. for *rodomontade* (q.v.).

rhomb, rhombus. L., G. ῥόμβος, anything that can be twirled, from ῥέμβειν, to revolve.

rhondda [*neol*.]. From *Lord Rhondda*, foodcontroller (1917), who gave his life for his country.

Captain Wright said the Food Control Department had given a new word to the language. If a soldier lost anything, he said it was "rhonddaed"
                (*Daily Chron.* Feb. 15, 1918).

rhotacism [*ling*.]. Conversion of other sounds into *r*. From G. ῥωτακίζειν, from the letter ῥῶ, ῥ.

rhubarb. F. *rhubarbe*, MedL. *rheubarbarum*, altered from *rhabarbarum*, foreign "rha," G. ῥᾶ, said to be from the ancient name of the river Volga. Cf. *rhapontic*, lit. Pontic "rha." From the correct form comes It. *rabarbaro*, "the drug rewbarbe" (Flor.), whence Ger. *rhabarber*. Orig. the drug imported into Europe through Russia; later applied to cultivated plant of same genus.

rhumb, rumb [*archaic naut*.]. Sp. Port. *rumbo*, L. *rhombus*; cf. F. *rumb*, "a roombe, or point of the compasse; a line drawn directly from wind to wind in a compasse, travers-boord, or sea-card" (Cotg.). A word borrowed from the early Sp. & Port. navigators. But Jal regards OF. *rum*, room, space, a common naut. word (see *run*[2]), as the origin, and supposes *rhumb* to be an artificial spelling due to a mistaken etym. This view is supported by chronology and by the double meaning of OF. *arrumer*, to "rummage" (q.v.), stow, and also, "to delineate, or set out, in a seacard, all the rums of windes" (Cotg.).

rhyme, rime. The older spelling is *rime*, F. (12 cent.), L., G. ῥυθμός, measured motion, rhythm, cogn. with ῥεῖν, to flow; cf. It. Sp. *rima*. The persistence of this form was partly due to association with AS. *rīm*, number, and its restoration by mod. writers is due to a mistaken notion of its origin; cf. Ger. *reim*, from F., but also associated with OHG. *rīm*, number, sequence. The half-restored spelling *rhyme* was introduced c. 1600. In MedL. *rithmus* was used of accentual, as opposed to quantitative, verse, and, as accentual verse was usually rhymed, the word acquired the meaning which it has in all the Rom. & Teut. langs.

> For oother tale certes kan I noon,
> But of a rym I lerned longe agoon
>   (Chauc. B. 1898).

absurdus: against all ryme and reason (Coop.).

rhynch-. From G. ῥύγχος, snout.

rhythm. From 16 cent., orig. as etymologizing var. of *rhyme* (q.v.).

> And what were crime
> In prose, would be no injury in rhythm
>   (*NED.* 1677).

ria [*geog.*]. Estuary, such as those on the Sp. coast south of the Bay of Biscay. Sp., fem. form of *rio*, river, L. *rivus*.

riant. F., pres. part. of *rire*, to laugh, VL. *ridere, for *ridēre*.

rialto. Exchange, mart. From the *rialto* of Venice (*Merch. of Ven.* i. 3), from the canal, *rivus altus*, deep stream, which it crosses.

riata. See *reata*.

rib. AS. *ribb*. Com. Teut.; cf. Du. *rib*, Ger. *rippe*, ON. *rif*. In joc. sense of wife with allusion to *Gen.* ii. 21. Bibl. *fifth rib* (2 *Sam.* ii. 23) is an error of the *AV.* translators for *belly*, which is restored in the *RV.*

ribald. OF. *ribauld* (*ribaud*), "a rogue, ruffian, rascall, scoundrell, varlet, filthie fellow; also, a ribauld, fornicator, whoremunger, bawdyhouse hunter" (Cotg.); cf. It. Sp. *ribaldo.* Prob. a spec. application of the common personal name *Ribaud*, OHG. *Ric-bald*, mighty-bold; cf. AS. *Ric-beald.* This occurs as a surname in the *Pipe Rolls* (12 cent.), i.e. a century older than the dict. records of the common noun. The choice of the name would be due to OF. *riber*, to wanton, ? from OHG. *hrīpa*, prostitute. Cf. *maraud*.

riband. Archaic form of *ribbon* (q.v.).

ribband [*naut.*]. Prob. from *rib band*, which suits the sense.

ribbon. From 16 cent. for earlier *riband*, OF. *riban*, var. of *ruban*. The *-d* of *riband* is excrescent, though the second element of the F. word is prob. Ger. *band*, ribbon. *Ribbonman* (hist.) is from the *Ribbon society*, an Ir. secret association of northern Catholics (early 19 cent.). *Ribbons*, reins, is early 19 cent. slang.

ribes. Gooseberries and currants. MedL., Arab. *ribās*, sorrel.

ribston. Pippin from *Ribston Park*, Yorks.

Ricardian. Of *David Ricardo*, economist (†1823). Cf. *Marxian.*

rice. OF. *ris* (*riz*), It. *riso*, VL. *oryzum, for *oryza*, G. ὄρυζα, prob. of Oriental origin. In most Europ. langs., e.g. Rum. *oriz.* *Rice-paper* is not made from rice, but from the pith of a reed found in Formosa.

rich. AS. *rīce*, powerful, noble, rich. Com. Teut.; cf. Du. *rijk*, Ger. *reich*, ON. *rīkr*, Goth. *reiks*; cogn. with L. *rex*, Celt. *-rix*, in names, and ult. with *rajah*. Traces of orig. sense still survive in application to sound, colour, odour, etc. *Riches*, now taken as pl., is F. *richesse* (cf. *laches*), and *rich* is sometimes via F. *riche* (from Teut.).

Richard. F., OHG. *Ric-hart*, mighty-strong (see *ribald*). As one of the commonest names it is applied, in pet-form *Dicky* (q.v.), to various animals and objects. For *Richard Roe* see *John Doe*. For *Richard's himself again* see *perish.*

> Throw us out John Doe and Richard Roe,
> And sweetly we'll tickle their tobies! (*Ingoldsby*).

ricinus. L., castor-oil plant.

rick[1]. Stack. AS. *hrēac*; cf. Du. *rook*, ON. *hraukr.* The form *reek* was literary up to 1700. For shortened vowel cf. dial. *ship* for *sheep*. See also *ruck*[1].

rick[2]. To sprain. Var. of obs. *wrick*, ME. *wricken*, cogn. with *wring*, *wriggle.*

rickets. Softening of the bones. Orig. (17 cent.) a Dorset word, perh. corrupt. of *rachitis* (q.v.). Hence *ricketty.* ·

> This nation was falling into the rickets, the head bigger than the body
>   (Burton, *Parl. Diary*, Jan. 12, 1657).

rickshaw. See *jinricksha.* Written '*rickshaw* by Kipling.

ricochet. F., orig. of flat stone skipping over water, making "a duck and a drake" (Cotg.); earlier (15 cent.) in *chanson* (*fable*) *du ricochet*, with recurring refrain. ? From L. *recalcare*, to retread.

rictus. L., from *ringi*, to open the mouth. In current sense it is rather from F.

rid. ON. *rythja*, to clear (land), cogn. with Ger. *reuten*, *roden*, as in *Baireut*, *Wernigerode*, *Rütli*; cf. E. *-royd*, clearing, common in northern place-names. In some senses it falls together with unrelated Sc. *redd*, to clear, tidy, Du. *redden*, cogn. with AS. *hreddan*, to rescue, Ger. *retten.* In to *be* (*get*) *rid of* we have the p.p. *Good riddance* was earlier *fair*, *gentle*, *riddance* (*Merch. of Ven.* ii. 7).

> Ich sende min engel biforen thine nebbe, the shal ruden thine weie to-fore the (*NED.* c. 1200).

riddle¹. Enigma. AS. *rǣdels*, from *rǣdan*, to read (q.v.); cf. Du. *raadsel*, Ger. *rätsel*. For loss of *-s* cf. *burial*. Wyc. has *redels* (*Judges*, xiv. 16).

riddle². Sieve. Late AS. *hriddel*, for earlier *hrīder*; cogn. with Ger. *reiter*, "a ridle, range, sieve, bolter or searce" (Ludw.), and ult. with L. *cribrum*, whence F. *crible*. Now dial. in lit. sense, but still common in *riddled with wounds* (holes); cf. F. *criblé de blessures* (*de petite vérole*).

riddlemeree. Rigmarole. Fanciful variation on *riddle my riddle*.

ride. AS. *rīdan*. Com. Teut.; cf. Du. *rijden*, Ger. *reiten*, ON. *rītha*. Naut. sense, to *ride* (*at anchor*) is also AS. Archaic *ride and tie* refers to practice of two people using one horse, one riding on ahead and tying up the horse for his companion to find and ride in his turn. To *ride for a fall*, so as to have an excuse for retiring, is from the hunting-field. In to *ride to death*, *hobby* (q.v.) is understood. With *rider*, corollary, etc., for earlier *rider-roll*, cf. *rider*, strengthening timber added to ship. *Little Red Riding-Hood* was used (1729) in transl. of Perrault's *Petit Chaperon Rouge*.

ridge. AS. *hrycg*, spine, back. Com. Teut.; cf. Du. *rug*, Ger. *rücken*, ON. *hryggr*. Northern form is *rig* as in *rigs o' barley* (Burns); cf. northern *rig and fur*, i.e. ridge and furrow, for ribbed stockings.

ridiculous. From L. *ridiculus*, from *ridēre*, to laugh.

riding [geog.]. ON. *thrithjungr*, third part, from *thrithi*, third, init. consonant having been absorbed by final of *north, east, west*, with which it is always compounded into one word in early records.

Omnes comitatus, hundredi, wapentakii, et thre-thingii (*Magna Charta*).

ridotto [archaic]. Entertainment. It., "a company, a knot, a crue or assemblie of good fellowes. Also a gaming or tabling house, or other place where good companie doth meete" (Flor.). As *redoubt* (q.v.).

rifacimento. It., remaking.

rife. Late AS. *rīfe*; cf. archaic Du. *rijf*, LG. *rīfe*, ON. *rīfr*, copious, abundant.

riffraff. From phrase *riff and raff* (14 cent.), every scrap, etc., OF. *rif et raf*, for which Cotg. has also *rifle et rafle*, app. connected with *rifle* and *raffle*, but perh. a redupl. on one of the two syllables only. Sense of scum, refuse of society, is 15 cent.

rifle. F. *rifler*, "to rifle, ransacke, spoile,

make havock or clean work, sweep all away before him" (Cotg.), in OF. also to scratch; cogn. with *raffle* (q.v.). Of Teut. origin; cf. Ger. *riefe*, groove (from LG.), ON. *rifa*, cleft, AS. *gerifian*, to wrinkle. With sense of making grooves in bore of fire-arm (17 cent.) cf. archaic sense of F. *rifler*, to score the back (by flogging).

rift. ON. *ript*, breach (of contract), whence Norw. Dan. *rift*, cleft; cogn. with *rive* and *rifle*. Now chiefly fig.

rig¹. Verb. From 15 cent., with Sc. var. *reek* from c. 1600. Origin doubtful. Prob. not orig. naut. ? Cf. Norw. dial. *rigga*, to bind, wrap up. To *rig the market*, *thimble-rig*, may belong here or to *rig²*.

He is ffast ryggynge hym [equipping himself] ther ffore (*Stonor Let.* 1478).

rig². Fun, trick, etc. From 18 cent. Esp. in to *run a rig*. From obs. verb *rig*, to romp, be wanton, of unknown origin. Perh. ident. with *rig¹* (cf. senses of *trick*).

He little dreamt, when he set out,
Of running such a rig (*John Gilpin*).

rig³. See *ridge*.

rigadoon [archaic]. Dance. F. *rigaudon*, said to be named from *Rigaud*, a dancing-master, who, according to Mistral, lived at Marseille (17 cent.). But the E. word is recorded earlier (1691) than the F. (1696).

right. AS. *riht*, straight, erect, just. Com. Teut.; cf. Du. Ger. *recht*, ON. *rēttr*, Goth. *raihts*; cogn. with L. *rectus* and *regere*. The double sense (straight, just) appears in all the Teut. langs., that of opposite to *left* being of somewhat later development. Cf. F. *droit*, L. *directus*, in the three main senses of the E. word. For noun sense cf. F. *droit* (e.g. *droits de l'homme*). Orig. sense of straight survives in math., also in *right away*, *right in the middle*, etc. (cf. also US. *come right in*). For pol. sense see *centre*. *Righteous* is altered, after adjs. in *-eous*, from ME. *rightwise*, AS. *rihtwīs*; cf. OHG. *rehtwīsig*, knowing the right (see *wist*, *wot*, *wise²*). *Right-hand man* was orig. mil. and about equivalent to *fugleman*. Pepys (Dec. 4, 1665) speaks of his brother-in-law, Balthasar Saint-Michel, being made a right-hand man in the Duke of Albemarle's guards.

rigid. L. *rigidus*, from *rigēre*, to be stiff.

rigmarole. Altered from *ragman-roll*, used in sense of list, catalogue, in 16 cent.; also earlier, a roll used in a medieval game called *ragman*. The earliest trace of *ragman* is its use (*rageman*) as title of a statute of Edward I (1276) appointing justices to hear complaints as to wrongs suffered in the previous twenty-five years, but allusions to the game are almost of same date. Origin doubtful. Perh. *ragman* = devil (see *ragamuffin*).

rigour. OF. (*rigueur*), L. *rigor-em*. Esp., since 15 cent., in *rigour of the law*. Cf. *rigid*.

rigsdag. Dan., cogn. with *reichstag* (q.v.).

rig-veda. Chief sacred book of the Hindus. Sanskrit, praise-knowledge.

riksdag. Sw., cogn. with *reichstag* (q.v.).

rile. Earlier *roil*, to disturb, make muddy (still in dial. & US.). From OF. *rouil*, mud, lit. rust, from *rouiller*, VL. **rubiculare*, from *rubigo*, rust.

rill. From 16 cent.; cf. Du. *ril*, Ger. *rille*, from LG., perh. cogn. with MHG. *rinnelin*, from *rinnen*, to trickle, run. Cf. *runnel*.

rim. AS. *rima*, in *dægrima*, dawn, *sǽrima*, coast; cf. ON. *rime*, strip of land; ult. cogn. with Ger. *rand*, edge, rim.

rime¹. See *rhyme*.

rime². Frost. AS. *hrīm*; cf. Du. *rijm*, ON. *hrīm*; ? ult. cogn. with Ger. *reif*. Chiefly Sc. till 18 cent.

rind. AS. *rind*, bark; cf. Du. *run* (earlier *rinde, rende*), Ger. *rinde*.

rinderpest. Ger., from *rinder*, pl. of *rind*, ox, cogn. with obs. E. *rother*, AS. *hrȳther*, ? and with *runt*.

ring¹. Noun. AS. *hring*, in the chief mod. senses. Com. Teut.; cf. Du. Ger. *ring*, ON. *hringr*. See also *harangue*, *rank²*, *ranch*. It is interesting to note that a word meaning circle has given the longitudinal *rank* and the square (prize-)*ring*. With *ring-leader* (c. 1500) cf. ME. to *lead the ring* (14 cent.). Ger. *rädelführer*, ringleader, from dim. of *rad*, wheel, is 16 cent. Both are app. from dancing. The commercial *ring* is 19 cent. *Ringstraked* (Gen. xxx. 35) is for -*streaked*. With *ringdove*, from neck-mark, cf. It. *colombo torquato*, lit. collared dove.

Should'st thou be the ringleader in dancing this while? (*Misogonus*, ii. 5, c. 1550).

If we had not been there to keep the ring, to see a certain measure of fair play
(D. Lloyd George, Aug. 4, 1917).

ring². Verb. AS. *hringan*; cf. ON. *hringja*. Prob. of imit. origin. Orig. intrans., as in to *ring true* (*false*).

rink. Orig. Sc. Earlier *renk*, course for tilting (Barbour), racing, etc., OF. *renc*, *rank²*. For later vowel cf. *ink*. In ice sense first of curling (Burns), *skating-rink* being 19 cent. For early Sc. sense cf. cogn. It. *arringo*, tilting-ground.

rinse. F. *rincer*, OF. *reïncier, recincier*; cf. MedL. *recincerare, resincerare*, as though from L. *sincerus*, pure, but these are etymologizing forms. Prob. *recincier* is VL. **requinquiare*, from Late L. *quinquare*, to purify, with allusion to the five-year periods between lustrations. Another suggestion is VL. **recencare*, by assim. from **recentare*, from *recens*, fresh.

riot. F. *riotte*, also OF. *rihote, ri(h)ot*; cf. Prov. *riota*, It. *riotta*. Origin unknown. Earliest E. sense (13 cent.) is debauchery, *riotous living* (Vulg. *vivendo luxuriose*). To *run riot* was in ME. used of hounds running on wrong scent. The *Riot Act*, part of which must be read to mob before active measures are taken, was passed in 1714. See *revel*, which has followed the opposite sense-development.

rip¹. Verb. Late ME., of LG. or Scand. origin; cf. Fris. *rippe*, to tear, Flem. *rippen*, to strip off roughly, Dan. *rippe op*, of a wound. Usu. with preps. *up*, *out*, etc. Hence perh. *rip*, broken water, esp. in *tide-rip*. With *let her rip* (US.) cf. *tear²* used of motion. With current sense of *ripping* cf. *stunning, rattling, thundering*, etc.

rip². Rake, wastrel. From 18 cent. and app. first used of inferior animal, jade. Perh. fig. use of one of the mech. senses of *rip* (cf. *screw*). Later associated with *rep¹*.

riparian. From L. *riparius*, from *ripa*, bank of river.

ripe. AS. *rīpe*. WGer.; cf. Du. *rijp*, Ger. *reif*; cogn. with *reap*. For fig. senses cf. *mature*.

riposte. F., It. *risposta*, answer, from *rispondere, rispost-*, to answer, L. *respondēre*. Cf. *repartee*.

ripple¹ [techn.]. To comb flax. Cf. Du. *repelen*, Ger. *riffeln*, "to hatchel flax" (Ludw.), Sw. *repa*.

ripple². Of water. App. from *rip¹* (q.v.). Not recorded till 17 cent., and then of stormy or dangerous agitation of water, in which sense it is very common in Hakl. and Purch.

Ripuarian [hist.]. From MedL. *Ripuarius*, name of a tribe of Rhine Franks. Connection with L. *ripa*, bank, is doubtful.

rise. AS. *rīsan.* Com. Teut.; cf. Du. *rijzen,* Ger. *reisen,* to travel, orig. to rise for a start ("to arise and go"), ON. *rīsa,* Goth. *ur-reisan.* The simple verb is very rare in AS., so that *rise* may often be aphet. for the commoner *arise.* For fig. senses cf. those of F. *se lever* (*relever, soulever, élever*). To *get a rise out of one,* to *rise to it,* are angling metaphors.

risible. F., L. *risibilis,* from *ridēre, ris-,* to laugh.

risk. F. *risque,* It. *risco, risico,* earlier also *rīsigo*; cf. Sp. *riesgo.* Of doubtful origin. A second meaning of the word in the Rom. langs. is cliff, rock. An ingenious suggested etym. is G. ῥιζικόν, from ῥίζα, root, used of a submarine hill, cliff, and in ModG. in sense of fate, chance.

risorgimento [*hist.*]. It., uprising (of Italy against Austria, c. 1850–60), from *risorgere,* L. *resurgere.* Cf. *irredentist.*

The risorgimento and its whole sequel are at stake (*Obs.* Nov. 14, 1917).

risotto [*cook.*]. From It. *riso,* rice.

risqué. F., risky.

rissole. F., OF. *roissole, roussole,* perh. from *roux,* red, russet. It occurs as *russole, rishew* in ME.

rite. L. *ritus,* prob. cogn. with G. ἀριθμός, number. *Ritualist, ritualism,* acquired current sense c. 1850 (cf. *Oxford movement*).

ritornello [*mus.*]. It., dim. of *ritorno,* return. Cf. F. *ritornelle.*

rittmeister [*hist.*]. Ger., cavalry captain, lit. *ride-master.*

ritual. See *rite.*

rival. F., L. *rivalis,* ? orig. of those living on opposite banks of river, *rivus,* ult. cogn. with AS. *rīth,* stream. This picturesque etym. is not now gen. accepted.

rive. ON. *rīfa,* ? cogn. with Ger. *reiben,* to rub. Now chiefly in poet. p.p. *riven.* Cf. *rift.*

rivelled [*archaic*]. Wrinkled. AS. *rifelede* (see *rifle*).

river. F. *rivière,* orig. land lying along river, from *rive,* bank, L. *ripa,* or L. *riparia* (sc. *terra*); cf. It. *riviera,* shore, river, Sp. *ribera.* *River-horse* translates *hippopotamus.*

riverain. Riparian. F., from *rivière* (v.s.); cf. *riverine,* of E. formation.

rivet. F., from *river,* to clinch, from *rive,* bank, from idea of fixing boundaries, turning up ends. This etym., though rather fantastic, is supported by F. *border un lit,*

from *bord,* bank, used in the exact sense in which Cotg. has *river* (v.i.).

river: to rivet or clench; to fasten or turn back the point of a naile, &c., also to thrust the clothes of a bed in at the sides (Cotg.).

rivière. Necklace of gems. F., river (v.i.).

rivulet. Substituted, after It. *rivoletto,* dim. of *rivolo,* dim. of *rivo,* L. *rivus,* stream, for earlier *riveret,* OF. *riverete,* dim. of *rivière.* The two words are not really connected (see *river*). The river Leen (Nottingham) is *Line Riveret* in Leland (1538).

rix-dollar [*hist.*]. Du. *rijksdaalder,* Ger. *reichstaler,* from *reich,* empire. See *reichstag, dollar, thaler.*

roach. OF. *roche.* Of Teut. origin; cf. Du. *rog,* earlier *roche,* LG. *ruche,* whence Ger. *roche*; also perh. AS. *reohhe,* name of a fish; ? connected with *rough.* With *sound as a roach* cf. F. *frais comme un gardon,* It. *fresco come una lasca.*

gardon: a certaine fresh-water fish that resembles the chevin. Some hold it to be the fresh-water mullet; others the roche, or a kinde thereof. *Plus sain qu'un gardon*: more lively, and healthfull then a *gardon* (then which, there is not any fish more healthfull, nor more lively) (Cotg.).

lasca: a fish which some take for the roch (Flor.).

road. AS. *rād,* riding, hostile incursion, senses found up to 17 cent. (cf. *raid, inroad*); cogn. with *ride.* Sense of sheltered stretch of water, where ships *ride at anchor,* as in *roadstead, Yarmouth roads,* is common in ME., but current sense, partially replacing *way, street,* appears first in Shaks. Cf. *roadway,* with orig. sense of riding way, *road-hog,* inconsiderate motorist.

A rode made uppon the Scottes at thende of this last somer within their grounde by oure brother of Gloucestre (Edward IV, 1481).

chevauchée: a riding, travelling, journying, a road, or course (Cotg.).

roam. Trad. from *Rome,* as place of pilgrimage; cf. OF. *romier,* pilgrim to Rome, Sp. *romero,* It. *romeo,* "a roamer, a wandrer, a palmer" (Flor.). The *NED.* altogether rejects this and suggests ME. *ramen,* ? cogn. with OHG. *rāmen,* to aim at, strive after. It is quite clear that *roam* was early associated with *Rome,* the earliest occurrence of *ramen* (Layamon) being connected in the same line with *Rom-leoden,* people of Rome; cf. obs. *romery,* pilgrimage. The word is also older than dict. records, as *roamer,* quoted by *NED.* from *Piers Plowm.,* was a surname in 1273 (*Hundred Rolls*), surviving as *Romer.* For another word that may have influenced *roam* see *saunter.*

roan[1]. Colour of horse. F. *rouan*; cf. It. *roano*, *rovano*, Sp. *roano*, earlier *ruano*. ? Ult. from L. *ravus*, "a dull or sadde colour mixt with black and yealow" (Coop.).

roan[2]. Leather. ? From *Rouen*, regularly spelt *Roan* in ME. Cf. obs. *roan*, Rouen linen.

roan[3]. See *rowan*.

roar. AS. *rārian*; cf. archaic Du. *reeren*, OHG. *rēren*; of imit. origin. A *roar of laughter* is partly an echo of Shaks., whose *roar* (in quots. below) is the unrelated ME. *rore*, tumult (Chauc.), of Du. origin (v.i.), cogn. with Ger. *ruhr* (esp. in *aufruhr*, uproar); cf. Ger. *rühren*, to stir. See *uproar*. Here belong also partially *roaring blade*, *roaring trade*, and perh. even *roaring forties*.

roere: motus, commotio. *Al in roere stellen*: perturbare, inturbare omnia (Kil.).

If by your art, my dearest father, you have
Put the wild waters in this roar, allay them
(*Temp.* i. 2).

Your flashes of merriment that were wont to set the table in a roar (*Haml.* v. 1).

roast. OF. *rostir* (*rôtir*), OHG. *rōsten*, from *rōst*, *rōste*, gridiron. For quot. below see also *roost*[1].

What so ever ye brage ore boste,
My mayster yet shall reule the roste
(*Debate of the Carpenter's Tools*, early 15 cent.).

rob. OF. *rober* (whence *dérober*), Ger. *rauben*, from *raub*, booty (see also *robe*); cf. It. *rubare*, Sp. *robar*. The E. cognate of *rauben* is *reave*.

roband, robbin [*naut.*]. Earlier also *raband* (Gavin Douglas), ? from obs. *ra*, sailyard, ON. *rā*, and *band*[1]; cf. Du. *raband*, which is perh. source of E. word. Sometimes perverted to *rope-band*. This is the accepted etym., but *robyn* is the earliest E. form (*Nav. Accts.* 1495–97), which suggests that the word may be only a naut. application of the name *Robert*; cf. *wylkin*, ram of iron (*ib.*).

robbin [*naut.*]. See *roband*.

robe. F.; cf. It. *roba*, Sp. *ropa*. From same root as *rob*, orig. sense, still in OF., being booty, "spolia." In E. usu. associated with somewhat rich dress and often with allusion to station, profession, etc.

Robert [*slang*]. Policeman. See *bobby*.

robin. Personal name *Robin*, OF. dim. of *Robert*, ident. with *Rupert*, OHG. *Hrode-berht*, glory bright. Like other common font-names has been widely applied. The bird *robin* is short for *Robin redbreast* (cf. *Dicky bird*, *Jack daw*, etc.). With *Robin Goodfellow*, Puck, cf. *Hob goblin*. Also in many plant-names. *Round robin*, in current sense, is naut. (18 cent.), but the adoption of the name seems to have been suggested by some earlier use (v.i.). *Robin Hood* is mentioned in *Piers Plowm*.

Certayne fonde talkers...applye to this mooste holye sacramente names of despitte and reproche, as to call it Jake in the boxe, and round roben, and suche other not onely fonde but blasphemous names (Coverd. 1546).

The Hectoures boate brought a peticion to Sir Henrie Middeton, signed by most of them, in the manner of a circle, because itt should not bee knowne whoe was the principall of the mutiny (Jourdain's *Journ.* 1612).

robust. F. *robuste*, or L. *robustus*, from *robur*, strength. Hence *robustious*, common in 17 cent., but now usu. an echo of *Haml.* iii. 2. This word may have influenced later senses of *boisterous*.

roc. From *Arabian Nights*, but known in several Europ. langs. previously. Arab. *rokh*, whence OF. *ruc*, used by Marco Polo (†1323).

rochet[1]. Eccl. vestment. F., dim. of OF. *roc*, mantle, Ger. *rock*, coat; cf. It. *rocchetto*, "a bishops or cardinals rochet" (Flor.), Sp. *roqueta*; cogn with AS. *rocc*, upper garment.

rochet[2]. Red gurnard. F. *rouget*, from *rouge*, red.

rock[1]. Stone. ONF. *roque* (*roche*); cf. It. *rocca*, Sp. *roca*. ? Ult. from G. ῥώξ, ῥωγ-, cleft, from ῥηγνύναι, to break; cf. ῥωγὰς πέτρα, cloven rock, and relation of *cliff* to *cleave*[1]. *The Rock* is Gibraltar.

rock[2] [*archaic*]. Distaff. Not recorded in AS., but prob. Com. Teut.; cf. Du. *rok*, Ger. *rocken*, ON. *hrokkr*; also It. *rocca*, Sp. *rueca*, from Teut.

rock[3]. Verb. Late AS. *roccian*, cogn. with Ger. *rücken*, to move jerkily, ON. *rykkja*.

rocket[1]. Plant. F. *roquette*, It. *ruchetta*, dim. of *ruca*, L. *eruca*, "the herb rockat" (Coop.).

rocket[2]. Firework. It. *rocchetta*, dim. of *rocca*, distaff, in allusion to shape. Cf. relationship of F. *fusée*, rocket, to *fuseau*, spindle. See *rock*[2].

rococo. F., playful alteration of *rocaille*, rock-work, ornamentation of pebbles and shells, popular in 18 cent. F. arch.

rod. AS. *rodd*, cogn. with *rōd*, rood (q.v.). For use as measure cf. synon. *pole*, *perch*, also *yard*[1]. The senses of *rod* are those of the continental cognates of *rood*.

rodent. From pres. part. of L. *rodere*, to gnaw, cogn. with *radere*, to scrape.

rodomontade. F., It. *rodomontata*, from *Rodomonte*, braggart Saracen in Ariosto's *Orlando Furioso*; cf. *gasconnade*. The name means "roll mountain" and is of a type often given to the "fire-eater" of early comic drama. Cf. *Shakespear*.

roe[1]. Deer. AS. *rā*, *rāha*. Com. Teut.; cf. Du. *ree*, Ger. *reh*, ON. *rā*.

roe[2]. Of fish. Cf. ON. *hrogn*, Ger. *rogen* (OHG. *rogo*), and E. dial. *roan*, *rown*. With prevailing form cf. Flem. *vog*.

roer [*SAfr.*]. Long-barrelled Boer rifle. Du., reed, tube, Ger. *rohr*, as in *feuerrohr*, lit. fire-tube.

Roffen. Signature of bishop of Rochester, AS. *Hrofesceaster*.

rogation. L. *rogatio-n-*, supplication, from *rogare*, to ask. *Rogation days*, three days preceding Ascension.

Roger, jolly. Pirate flag (18 cent.). Reason unknown. Cf. *blue Peter, Davy Jones, round robin*, etc. Earliest name (1723) was *Old Roger*. An earlier slang sense of the name was penis, while from 1915 it was used at the front for gas-cylinder.

Roger de Coverley. *Roger of Coverly*, the name of a tune and dance (17 cent.), was later adopted by Addison for character in *Spectator*. Fryer associates the name with Lancs, Thoresby with *Calverley* (Yorks).

rogue. Cant word for vagabond (16 cent.). Distinct from F. *rogue*, arrogant, but perh. connected with *rogation*, petition. Cf. F. *roi Pétaud*, king of the beggars, which some connect with L. *petere*, to ask. Hence *rogue's march*, played in "drumming out"; also *rogue elephant* (*horse, cabbage*, etc.).

And so they lewter in suche rogacyons
Seven or eyght yeres, walkyng theyr stacious,
And do but gull, and follow beggery
                              (*NED.* c. 1540).

roil. See *rile*.

roister. Verb is from archaic *roister*, noisy bully, etc., for obs. *reister*, German trooper, OF. *reistre* (*reître*), German trooper serving in France (16 cent.), Ger. *reiter*, rider. For intrusive *-s-* cf. *filibuster*, for change of vowel cf. *boil*[2]. *Roisterkin* was used in same sense, also *rutter* and *rutterkin*, synon. with *reister*, though of separate origin. The etym. usu. given, from F. *rustre*, rustic, is based on Cotgrave's *rustre*, "a ruffin, royster, hackester, swaggerer," which cer-

tainly has nothing to do with his *rustault*, "a clowne, boore, churle, hob, hinde, swayne, lobcock." It may be a dial. var. of *reistre*, "a reister, or swart-rutter, a German horseman," or a separate word, from Du. *ruiter*, whence obs. E. *rutter* (v.s.) and *roiter*.

rokelay [*dial.*]. Sc. var of *roquelaure* (q.v.).

roker. Fish. Norw. *rokke* or Sw. *rocka*, ray[2], cogn. with *rough*, formerly used in same sense. Cf. *roach*.

Roker, when controlled, fetched 69s. a kit
                    (*Daily Chron.* March 3, 1919).

Roland for an Oliver. *Roland*, nephew of Charlemagne, and *Oliver*, nephew of Girard of Roussillon, fought for three days without being able to decide which was the better man. They then became brothers-in-law and fell with the other paladins at Roncevaux. References to the two are common in ME.

rôle. F., orig. the "roll" (v.i.) on which an actor's part was written.

roll. First (early 13 cent.) as noun, parchment scroll, etc., whence *Master of the Rolls*, keeper of various records (cf. *custos rotulorum*). F. *rôle*, L. *rotulus*, dim. from *rota*, wheel. Formerly much used in the sense of list, e.g. *roll-call*, to *strike off the roll*(s) of solicitors. Later of many objects suggesting shape of parchment roll, and in senses for which F. uses rather the dim. *rouleau*. Adopted by most Europ. langs. The verb is F. *rouler*, VL. **rotulare*, from *rotula*, little wheel. A *rolling-pin* was orig. the pole round which a banner was rolled.

rollick. Early 19 cent. Origin unknown. ? Mixture of *romp* and *frolic*.

rollock. See *rowlock*.

roly-poly. Redupl. on *roll*. App. used in 18 cent. of a game like roulette.

rom. Male gipsy. Romany *rom*, man.

Romaic. Of mod. Greece. G. Ῥωμαϊκός, Roman, used esp. of the Eastern Empire. Cf. *Romaika*, national dance.

Roman. Restored after L. from ME., F. *Romain*, L. *Romanus*. *Roman type* imitates that of Rome, as opposed to gothic (black-letter) and italic; cf. *roman numerals*, as opposed to arabic. The *Holy Roman Empire* is adapted from Ger. *Römisches Reich*, claiming to represent (800–1806) the empire of Charlemagne.

romance. OF. *romanz*, orig. adv., in phrase *romanz escrire*, L. *Romanice scribere*, to write in the vernacular, as distinguished from literary L., tongue. This became a noun and evolved a sing. *roman*, epic narrative, etc., now novel, or *romant*, whence archaic E. *romaunt*. The older word survives in E. *romance* and in F. derivative *romancier*, romance-writer, novelist. Orig. sense appears in *Romance languages*, also called *Romanic*, i.e. those derived from vernacular Latin (French, Provençal, Italian, Spanish, Portuguese, Rumanian, etc.). The medieval *romances* were heroic narratives, usu. in verse, but the word was readopted later, after F. *roman*, to describe the long-winded novels of the 16–17 cents. *Romantic* has been used since 17 cent. in sense of fanciful, exaggerated (cf. F. *romanesque*), its spec. literary sense, as opposed to classic, dating from use of F. *romantique* and Ger. *romantiker* in early 19 cent. The sense-development of the F. word, used by Rousseau of the Swiss scenery, was due to the spec. sense it had acquired in E.

Frankysche speche ys cald romaunce;
So sey this clerkes & men of Fraunce
                (Robert of Brunne, c. 1330).

romanesque [*arch.*]. In ModF. only in sense of romantic, fanciful (v.s.).

Romanic [*ling.*]. See *romance*.

Romansh, Rumansh [*ling.*]. Grisons form of *romance* (q.v.). See *Rhaeto-Romanic*.

romantic. See *romance*. Current sense was developed first in E. (17 cent.), whence it was borrowed back by F.

Romany. Gipsy *romani*, pl. of *romano*, adj., from *rom* (q.v.). Made current by Borrow.

romaunt. See *romance*.

Romic. Phonetic notation based on Roman alphabet by Sweet (1877).

romp. From c. 1700. Altered from *ramp²*; cf. *rampage*. To *romp in* (*home*), win in a canter, is late 19 cent.

ramp: a Tomrig, or rude girl (*Dict. Cant. Crew*).
rampant: uppish, over-bold, over-pert, over-lusty
                                          (*ib.*).

rondeau [*metr.*]. F., earlier *rondel* (whence ME. *roundel*), from *rond*, round.

rondeau de rime: a rime, or sonnet that ends as it begins (Cotg.).

rondo [*mus.*]. It., F. *rondeau*.

Röntgen rays. Discovered (1895) by *Röntgen*, of Marburg.

rood. AS. *rōd*, the Cross, *holy rood*, orig. sense of rod, wand, etc., appearing only in *seglrōd*, yard of sail; cf. Du. *roede*, Ger. *rute*, senses of which go with those of *rod*

(q.v.). Now differentiated, as superficial measure, from *rod*, linear measure, but *rood* is still used for latter in dial. *Roodscreen* is mod. after ME. *rood-loft*.

roof. AS. *hrōf*; cf. Du. *roef*, cabin, coffin-lid, ON. *hrōf*, boat-shed. For Com. Teut. word see *thatch*. Orig. sense of *roof* was app. internal, rather than external, e.g. *roof of the mouth* is found in AS.

rooinek [*hist.*]. SAfrDu., red neck, nickname for British soldier, replacing earlier *rooibatje*, red coat.

rook¹. Bird. AS. *hrōc*; cf. Du. *roek*, OHG. *ruoh*, ON. *hrōkr*. Perh. of imit. origin (cf. *crow¹*). For *rook*, predatory sharper, cf. fig. senses of *hawk*, *pigeon*.

rook². At chess. Cf. OF. *roc*, It. *rocco*, "a rooke to play at chesse with" (Flor.), Sp. *roque*; also Ger. *roch*, ON. *hrōkr*; all ult. from Pers. *rukh*, *rokh*, in same sense, supposed by some to be altered from Hind. *rath*, chariot, whence *rut*, Indian name of the piece.

rooky [*army slang*]. Corrupt. of *recruit*.

room. AS. *rūm*, space, wide place, etc. Com. Teut.; cf. Du. *ruim*, Ger. *raum*, ON. *rūm*, Goth. *rūm*. Orig. sense survives in *to make room, no room, roomy, in his room*, etc., sense of apartment being late (15 cent.) and esp. E.

Sit not down in the highest room [AS. *Gosp.* setl, Wyc. place, *Vulg.* in primo loco] (*Luke*, xiv. 8).

roost¹. For fowls. AS. *hrōst*; cf. archaic Du. *roest*, "gallinarium, sedile ovium, pertica gallinaria" (Kil.). Orig. sense prob. loft, upper room, as still in dial. Hence *rooster*, US. euph. for *cock*. For *to rule the roost* see *roast*, but I am not sure whether *roost* is not the orig. figure (cf. *cock of the walk*).

roost². Tidal race (Orkney and Shetland). ON. *röst*; ? cogn. with *race¹*.

root¹. Of plant. Late AS. *rōt*, from ON.; cf. LG. *rut*. The native cognate is *wort¹* (q.v.). *Root of the matter* is lit. transl. of Heb. *shōresh dābār* (*Job*, xix. 28). In math. & ling. sense from 16 cent., with symbol √ for *r*.

root². To grub up, "rout out." Altered, by association with *root¹*, from earlier *wroot*, AS. *wrōtan*, from *wrōt*, snout, cogn. with Ger. *rüssel*; cf. Du. *wroeten*, "suffodere rostro humum" (Kil.). Hence *rootle*.

Right as a sowe wroteth in everich ordure, so wroteth hire beautee in the stynkynge ordure of synne (Chauc. I. 157).

das wühlen der schweine mit dem rüssel: the rooting, or routing, of swine (Ludw.).

rope. AS. *ráp.* Com. Teut.; cf. Du. *reep,* Ger. *reif,* usu. hoop, ON. *reip,* Goth. *raip* (in *skauda-raip,* shoe-thong). To *give rope* is prob. from training colts (cf. *end of one's tether*), but now often contains a play on the hangman's rope. To *know the ropes* is naut. With cow-boy to *rope in* cf. to *round up. On the high ropes* may be from rope-dancing.

roquefort. Cheese from F. village of *Roquefort* (Aveyron).

roquelaure [*hist.*]. Mantle. From *Duc de Roquelaure* (†1738). Cf. *spencer,* etc.

roquet. At *croquet,* of which it is an arbitrary alteration. Cf. *ruff*[3].

rorqual. F. (Cuvier), Norw. *röyrkval,* from ON. *reythr,* in same sense, and *hvalr,* whale. First element orig. meant red.

rorty [*slang*]. ? Rimed on *naughty.*

rosace. F., rose-window.

rosaceous. From L. *rosaceus,* from *rosa,* rose.

Rosalie [*hist.*]. French bayonet. Cf. *Josephine,* field-gun, also *Archie, Rupert,* etc.

rosary. Rose-garden, L. *rosarium.* Later used as fanciful title of book of devotion, hence series of prayers, string of beads for counting them; cf. F. *rosaire,* "a rosarie, or Our Ladies psalter" (Cotg.), Sp. *rosario.* Quot. below appears to be considerably earlier than *NED.* records.

I send them a pauper [paper] of the rosery of our Lady of Coleyn [Cologne]
(*Plumpton Corr.* 1485-6).

Roscian. Of *Roscius,* Roman actor (†62 B.C.).

rose. AS. & F., L. *rosa,* from G. ῥόδον, which is prob. of Eastern origin. As emblem of secrecy in *sub rosa, under the rose,* a phrase which prob. originated in Germany. With *bed of roses* cf. *crumpled rose-leaf,* supposed to cause discomfort to sybarite. *Rose of a garden-can* may have been suggested partly by F. *arroser,* to water, *arrosoir,* watering-pot, from L. *ros,* dew. *Rosewood* is named from its fragrance. With *rose-coloured spectacles* cf. F. *voir tout couleur de rose.* For *Wars of the Roses* see 1 *Hen. VI,* ii. 4, but the earliest authority for the story is 16 cent.

rosemary. Altered, after *rose* and *Mary,* from earlier *rosmarine,* OF. *rosmarin* (*romarin*), L. *ros marinus,* lit. sea-dew; cf. It. *rosmarino.* Also in the Teut. langs.

roseola. German measles. ModL., F. *roséole,* prob. coined (from *rose*) on *rougeole,* measles.

Rosetta stone. With inscription giving clue to Egypt. hieroglyphics. Discovered (1798) at *Rosetta,* Egypt. In British Museum.

rosette. F., dim. of *rose.*

Rosicrucian. Member of supposed mystic order, trad. founded (1484) in Germany by *Christian Rosenkreuz,* and known in 17 cent. E. as the *Rosy Cross;* cf. F. *rose-croix,* Sp. *rosacruz.*

rosin. See *resin.*

rosinante. Sorry jade. Name of Don Quixote's charger. Sp. *Rocinante,* from *rocín,* jade, *ante,* before. With *rocín* cf. F. *roussin* and ME. *rouncy,* of unknown origin.

Al fin le vino á llamar Rocinante, nombre, á su parecer, alto, sonoro y significativo de lo que había sido cuando fué *rocín,* antes de lo que ahora era, que era antes y primero de todos los rocines del mundo (*Don Quijote,* cap. i.).

rosolio. Liqueur. It., earlier *rosoli,* L. *ros solis,* because orig. made from the plant sundew, latinized as *rosa solis.*

roster [*mil.*]. Du. *rooster,* list, table, lit. gridiron ("roaster"), with allusion to parallel lines on the paper.

rostrum. L., beak (cogn. with *rodere,* to gnaw), the platform for speakers in the Forum being adorned with beaks of ships taken from the Antiates (338 B.C.).

rot. AS. *rotian.* Com. Teut.; cf. Du. *rotten,* OHG. *rozzen,* ON. *rota.* The p.p. is *rotted, rotten* being ON. *rotinn,* app. an old strong p.p. of cogn. origin. See also *ret. Rot, rotter,* in slang senses, are 19 cent., app. first at Camb.

rota. L., wheel. First used (1659) as title of pol. club founded by J. Harrington to advocate rotation in holding of state offices. Harrington also first (1656) used *rotation* (v.i.) in this sense.

You'l find it set down in the Harrington's moddle Whose brains a Commonwealth doth so coddle, That't has made a Rotation in his noddle
(*Rump Song,* 1659).

rotation. L. *rotatio-n-,* from *rotare,* to revolve, from *rota,* wheel, ult. cogn. with Ger. *rad,* Gael. Ir. *roth,* Welsh *rhod. Rotation of crops* is 18 cent. See *rota.*

rotch, rotgee [*ornith.*]. Little auk. From Fris. *rotgies,* pl. of *rotgoes,* brant-goose.

rote[1] [*hist.*]. Fiddle of medieval minstrel. OF., of Celt. origin; cf. Welsh *crwth,* Ir. *cruit.* Also found early in Ger. & Du. Revived by Scott. See *crowd*[2].

rote[2]. Orig. habit, practice. Now esp. in *by rote.* App. var. of *route,* in sense of travelled way. Cf. *routine,* for which Cotg.

gives *par rotine*, "by rote." But the vowel suggests rather L. *rota*, wheel, used in MedL. for a regular course.

rotgee. See *rotch*.

Rotten Row. Occurs as street-name in many towns, in the north usu. *ratton raw*. Origin obscure. Perh. orig. street of ruinous houses inhabited by *rattens*, i.e. rats.

rotunda. Altered on L. from earlier *rotonda*, esp. the Pantheon, fem. of It. *rotondo*, round, L. *rotundus*, from *rota*, wheel. *Rotund style* (*oratory*) is after Horace's *ore rotundo* (*Ars Poet.* 323).

roturier. F., plebeian, from *roture*, L. *ruptura* (sc. *terrae*), earth-breaking, agriculture.

> *roture*: yeomanrie; the estate, condition, or calling of such as are not of gentle bloud; also, socage, or such an ignoble tenure (Cotg.).

rouble. Earlier (16 cent.) *robell*, *rubble*, etc. Russ. *rublè*. Current spelling is F.

roucou. Tree and dye. F., Tupi (Brazil) *urucú*.

roué. F., p.p. of *rouer*, to break on the wheel, *roue*, L. *rota*. Nickname given (c. 1720) to dissolute friends of the Regent, Duke of Orleans.

rouge¹. Colour. F., red, L. *rubeus*, ult. cogn. with *red*.

rouge². Football scrimmage. An Eton word of unknown origin.

rough. AS. *rūh*. WGer.; cf. Du. *ruig*, Ger. *rauh*. Orig. of surface, later senses developing as those of *smooth*. With *rough-shod*, orig. of horse shod with nails projecting from shoe, cf. to *rough* (a horse). *Rough*, dangerous character, is prob. for *ruffian*, as we do not use adjs. in this way in sing., e.g. we speak of *the rich and the poor*, but not of *a rich, a poor*. *Rough-and-tumble* is from the prize-ring. To *rough it* was orig. (18 cent.) naut.

roulade [*mus.*]. F., from *rouler*, to roll.

rouleau. F., dim. of *rôle*, roll.

roulette. F. dim. of *rouelle*, dim. of *roue*, wheel, L. *rota*.

Roumanian. Now usu. *Rumanian* (q.v.).

Roumansh [*ling.*]. See *Romansh*.

round¹. Circular, etc. F. *rond*, OF. *roond*, L. *rotundus*, from *rota*, wheel; cf. It. *rotondo*, Sp. *redondo*. Sense of symmetry extends to that of completeness in *round dozen, round numbers, a good round sum*, and a further shade appears in sense of plain, unadorned, e.g. a *round unvarnished tale* (*Oth.* i. 3). Noun sense, ammunition, arises from that of serving *round*. *Round* of a ladder is prob. altered from *rung* (q.v.). To *bring*

up with a round turn (naut.) is done by throwing a rope round a belaying-pin. As adv. & prep. *round* is aphet. for *around*, F. *en rond*. With to *get round one* cf. *circumvent*. With to *round up* (cattle), orig. US., cf. to *rope in*. *Roundhead* (hist.) is of the same date as *cavalier* in spec. sense. *Roundhouse*, orig. (16 cent.) in sense of lock-up, is after Du. *rondhuis*, guard-house; its naut. sense appears in Capt. John Smith. The *Round Table* is in Wace's *Brut* (1155); in connection with pol. conference it is late 19 cent. For some fig. senses of *round* cf. *square*.

> What creature's this with his short hairs,
> His little band and huge long ears,
>   That this new faith hath founded?
> The Puritans were never such,
> The Saints themselves had ne'er so much.—
>   Oh, such a knave's a Roundhead
>   (*Rump Song*, 1641)

round² [*archaic*]. To whisper. ME. *roun*, AS. *rūnian*, to whisper, conspire (see *rune*); cf. Ger. *raunen*, "to round, or whisper, something in one's ear" (Ludw.). For excrescent *-d* cf. *sound¹*, *bound³*. Very common up to 17 cent., usu. with *in one's ear*.

roundel. OF. *rondel*, rondeau (q.v.). *Roundelay* is OF. *rondelet*, with ending assimilated to *lay²*, or perh. suggested by *virelay* (q.v.).

roup [*Sc.*]. To sell by auction, lit. to cry, shout. Du. *roepen*; cf. AS. *hrōpan*, Ger. *rufen*, Goth. *hrōpjan*. Cf. obs. *outroop*, auction, Du. *uitroep*, "publick crying out of goods to be sould" (Hexham).

> *enchere*: a bidding, or outbidding; also, any port-sale, outrope, or bargaining, whereby he that bids most for a thing is to carry it (Cotg.).

rouse¹ [*archaic*]. Carousal. Aphet. for *carouse*, phrase to *make* (*take*) *carouse* being understood as to *make* (*take*) *a rouse*. Prob. associated also with Sw. Dan. *rus*, Du. *roes*, Ger. *rausch*, fit of drunkenness. See *row³*. First in Shaks.

> The king doth wake to-night, and takes his rouse
>   (*Haml.* i. 4).

rouse². Verb. Orig. (15 cent.) intrans., of hawk ruffling its feathers, or, trans. (16 cent.), of starting game. Origin unknown, but, as term of ven., prob. OF. Hence *arouse*, suggested by *a-wake*, *a-rise*.

> I rowse, I stretche my selfe, as a man dothe whan he gothe to prove a maystrie [in wrestling] (Palsg.).

roustabout. Wharf labourer (US.), handy man (Austral.). Dial. E. *rouse-about*, restless person (18 cent.), from *rouse²*, becoming *roust* in US. by association with *rout²*, *root²*.

rout¹. Noun. F. *route*, in archaic sense of band, company, esp. of predatory soldiers, L. *rupta* (sc. *pars*, etc.), from *rumpere*, *rupt-*, to break; cf. It. *rotta*, Sp. *rota*, Ger. *rotte* (from It.). For sense cf. *detachment*. In 17 cent. of fashionable assembly, whence *rout-seat* (*-cake*). In sense of complete defeat from c. 1600, after OF. *route*, now replaced by *déroute*.

And to the paleys rood ther many a route
Of lordes, upon steedes and palfreys
(Chauc. A. 2494).

rout². Verb. Esp. in to *rout out*. Var. of *root²*.

route. F., L. *rupta* (sc. *via*), broken way; cf. origin of *causeway*. Now with restored F. pronunc. and spelling, but in mil. use made to rime with *shout*, as *rout¹*, and formerly also spelt *rout*.

routine. F., from *route*. Cf. *rote²*.

rove. Orig. term in archery, to shoot at random. In current sense app. from OF. *roer*, *rouer*, to wander, prowl (replaced by *rôder*), L. *rotare*; perh. influenced by obs. *rave*, to wander, ON. *ráfa*. It has naturally been associated with *rover*. For unoriginal *-v-* cf. *rove*, "burr" of a rivet, ON. *rô*. But it may represent an orig. OF. *-th-* from L. *-t-* (cf. *savory*, *flavour*).

a veue de païs: at randon, roaming, at rovers, at large (Cotg.).

rover. Orig. pirate, Du. *roover*, cogn. with E. *reaver* (see *reave*). Hence obs. verb to *rove*, practise piracy, which has influenced *rove*, to wander, e.g. in *roving commission*.

row¹. Series. AS. *ráw*, rare and doubtful var. of *ráew*, whence obs. *rew*, in same sense; cogn. with Du. *rij*, Ger. *reihe*.

And leet comande anon to hakke and hewe
The okes olde, and leye hem on a rewe
(Chauc. A. 2865).

row². Verb. AS. *rôwan*, cogn. with *rudder* (q.v.). *Rowlock* (*rollock*, *rullock*) is altered on *row* from earlier *oarlock*, AS. *árloc*, lit. oar-fastening, the oar being orig. secured to the gunwale by a thong or withe; cf. synon. AS. *árwiththe*, lit. oar-withe.

row³. Disturbance. "A very low expression" (Todd). App. back-formation from *rouse¹* (q.v.); cf. *cherry*, *pea*, etc. *Row-de-dow* is partly suggested by *rowdy*.

rowan, roan. For *rowan-tree*, orig. Sc. & north., spelt *rountree* by James I. Of Scand.

origin; cf. Norw. *rogn*, Dan. *rön*, Sw. *rönn*. Ult. cogn. with *red*, from berries.

rowdy. Orig. US., lawless backwoodsman (early 19 cent.). Origin unknown.

rowel. OF. *rouelle*, dim. of *roue*, wheel, L. *rota*. But in the spur sense F. uses *molette*, whence *mullet²*.

rowlock, rollock. See *row²*.

roxburghe. Book-binding. From third *Duke of Roxburghe*, bibliophile (†1804). The *Roxburghe club* was inaugurated at the sale of his books (1812).

royal. F., L. *regalis*, from *rex*, *reg-*, king. The *Royal Society* was incorporated (1662) by Charles II, the name, for earlier *Philosophic Society*, being app. suggested by Evelyn. *Royal road*, only fig. in E., is F. *chemin royal*, "the Kings high-way" (Cotg.). *Royalty* on minerals, later on books, is extended from the sense of right granted to individual by the crown. With *royal*, of extra size, etc., cf. *imperial*, and see *battle*.

King Edward made a siege royall
And wanne the towne [of Calais]
(Libel of English Policie, 1432).

A reame of paper roiall, j reame and vij quires of small paper (*Nav. Accts.* 1485–88).

Royston crow. From *Royston* (Camb. & Hertf.). Cf. *Cornish chough*.

rub. Orig. (14 cent.) intrans., and containing idea of friction with rough surface. Hence noun *rub*, inequality on bowling-green, very common in fig. sense in 16–17 cents. (see quot. s.v. *bias*), as in *there's the rub* (*Haml.* iii. 1). Of obscure origin; app. cogn. with Norw. *rubba*, to scrub, EFris. *rubben*.

rub-a-dub. Imit. of drum.

rubber¹. Caoutchouc. For earlier *india-rubber*, named from its use in erasing. Hence US. *rubberneck*, inquisitive person, who cranes his neck as though it were made of rubber.

rubber². At whist, etc., orig. (c. 1600) the deciding game at bowls. Earliest form, *a rubbers* (v.i.), suggests perversion from F. *à rebours*, backwards, altered by association with *rub*. *At reburs*, *robours* occurs in ME., though not with bowls.

Since he hath hit the mistress so often i' the fore-game, we'll e'en play out a rubbers (Dekker, 1602).

rubbish. In 15 cent. also *robous*, *robys*, *rubbes*, etc. Earliest form is AF. *rubbous*; cf. MedL. *rubbosa*. In early use synon. with *rubble*, both being applied to waste building-material. App. pejorative formation from OF. *robe*, goods, plunder (see *rob*, *robe*); cf. It. *roba*, goods, *robaccia*, rubbish.

rubble. ME. *robyll*, *rubel*, etc. Evidently cogn. with *rubbish*.

rubescent. From pres. part. of L. *rubescere*, to become red, *ruber*.

Rubicon. Small stream flowing into Adriatic and marking southern boundary of Cisalpine Gaul. Crossed by Caesar when he left his province to attack Pompey.

rubicund. F. *rubicond*, L. *rubicundus*, from *ruber*, red.

rubidium [*chem.*]. Named by Bunsen from L. *rubidus*, red.

rubric. F. *rubrique*, L. *rubrica* (sc. *terra*), red ochre, from *ruber*, red. ME. had also *rubrish*, OF. *rubriche*. Earliest E. sense is connected with red-printed directions in liturgical books.

ruby. OF. *rubi*, back-formation from *rubis* (used as sing. in ModF.), pl. of OF. *rubin*, VL. *rubinus (*lapis*), from *ruber*, red; cf. It. *rubino*, Sp. *rubin*, Du. *robijn*, Ger. *rubin*, obs. E. *rubine*.

ruche. Frill. F., lit. bee-hive (of plaited straw), OF. *rusche*, ? ident. with OF. *rusche*, *rousche*, rush[1] (cf. *frail*[2]).

ruck[1]. Crew, band. Esp. in the *common ruck*. Orig. stack, heap. Of Scand. origin and cogn. with *rick*[1]; cf. Norw. dial. *ruka*, ON. *hruga*, heap.

Pitt cole the rooke costes at pittes iijs. vjd. A rooke of colles ought to bee ij yeardes high and a yeard and quarter square (*Rutland MSS.* 1610).

ruck[2]. Crease. Norw. *rukka*, ON. *hrukka*, wrinkle. Of late appearance (Grose), but prob. old in dial. Cf. dial. *runkle*, wrinkle, Ger. *runzel*, and L. *ruga*, furrow, wrinkle.

ruckle [*archaic*]. To gurgle, sound the death-rattle. Cf. Norw. dial. *rukla*, in same sense, Ger. *röcheln*, "the rattling in the throat of a sleeping or dying person" (Ludw.); ? ult. cogn. with L. *rugire*, to roar.

rucksack. Swiss Ger. (16 cent.), from *rücken*, back, with Upper Ger. *u* for *ü*. A tourist word (cf. *alpenstock*).

ruction. "A memory of the Insurrection of 1798, which was commonly called 'the Ruction'" (Joyce).

It were after the rising 'rection i' th' north, I remember well (*Misogonus*, iv. 1, c. 1550).

It was in the time of the 'ruction
(Lover, *Legends of Ireland*).

rudd. Fish. Cogn. with obs. *rud*, red, AS. *rudu*, cogn. with *red*. Cf. *ruddock*.

rudder. AS. *rōthor*, steering-oar. Com. Teut.; cf. Du. *roer* (earlier *roder*), Ger. *ruder*, oar; also ON. *rōthr*, act of rowing; ult. cogn. with L. *remus*, G. ἐρετμόν, OIr. *ráme*. See *row*[2].

ruddle. Red ochre for marking sheep. From AS. *rudu*, red. Also *raddle*, *reddle*.

ruddock [*dial.*]. Robin. AS. *rudduc* (see *rudd*).

ruddy. AS. *rudig*, from *rudu*, red. In earliest use esp. of complexion.

It schal be clere, for hevene is rodi
(Wyc. *Matt.* xvi. 2).

rude. F., L. *rudis*, rough, raw; cf. *erudite*. Perh. slightly influenced by obs. *roid*, turbulent, OF. *roide* (*raide*), "rough, fierce, rude, uncivill, violent" (Cotg.), L. *rigidus*.

Rudesheimer. Wine. Ger. *Rüdesheimer* (sc. *wein*), from *Rüdesheim*, on Rhine.

rudiment. L. *rudimentum*, "the first teaching, or instruction" (Coop.), from *rudis*, rough.

rue[1]. Plant. F., L. *ruta*, G. ῥυτή; cf. It. *ruta*, Sp. *ruda*; also AS. *rŭde*, Ger. *raute*, all from L. Often used with punning allusion to *rue*[2].

I'll set a bank of rue, sour herb of grace;
Rue, even for ruth, shortly shall be seen
In the remembrance of a weeping queen
(*Rich. II*, iii. 4).

rue[2]. To repent. AS. *hrēowan*; cf. Du. *rouwen*, Ger. *reuen*; also ON. *hryggth*, sorrow, ruth. Archaic noun *rue*, AS. *hrēow*, survives in *rueful*. The verb was orig. impers.; cf. Ger. *es reut mich*.

If I made you sori in a pistle, now it rewith me not [*Vulg.* non me paenitet] (Wyc. 2 *Cor.* vii. 8).

ruelle. F., morning reception held by lady while still in bed, from *ruelle*, passage between bed and wall, lit. alley, dim. of *rue*, street, L. *ruga*, furrow. Often in ref. to F. literary circles of 17–18 cents., and formerly used in E. in bedroom sense.

Wo in winter-tyme, with wakynge a nightes,
To ryse to the ruel to rocke the cradel
(*Piers Plowm.* C. x. 79).

ruff[1]. Fish. Prob. for *rough*; hence ModL. *aspredo* (16 cent.), scient. name, from *asper*, rough.

aspredo: a fish called a ruffe or a goldfish (Flor.).

ruff[2]. Neckwear of 16 cent. Orig. used in sense of *ruffle* for wrist. See *ruffle*[1].

ruff[3]. At whist. Orig. a card-game. F. *ronfle*, "hand-ruffe at cards" (Cotg.); cf. It. *ronfa*, "a game at cardes called ruffe or trumpe"

(Flor.). These are perh. arbitrary perversions of F. *triomphe*, It. *trionfo* (see *trump²*). The nasal is also lost in Du. *troef*.

ruff¹. Bird. Perh. named from the *ruff* of feathers developed by male bird in breeding season. But the existence of the fem. *reeve²* is against this and points to Teut. origin with vowel-change as in *fox, vixen.*

ruffian. From 16 cent. Cf. F. *rufian*, It. *ruffiano*, Sp. *rufián*, MedL. *ruffianus*, all esp. in sense of pander; ? cogn. with *ruffle³*, ? or with second element of *dandruff*. Sense of word in E. has been affected by association with *rough.*

ruffle¹. For wrist. Appears later than *ruff²*, but app. belongs to *ruffle²*, in sense of creasing, wrinkling.

ruffle². Verb, as in to *ruffle the surface.* Much older (13 cent.) than *ruff²*, *ruffle¹*. Cf. LG. *ruffelen*, to crumple, curl, ON. *hrufla*, to scratch, and second element of *dandruff.*

I ruffle clothe or sylked [? read *sylkes*], *I bring them out of their playne foldynge*: je plionne (Palsg.).

ruffle³. To swagger. Orig. to contend. App. cogn. with Ger. *raufen*, to pluck, tear out, whence *sich raufen*, to fight; cf. Ger. *rupfen*, to pluck (a fowl), *raufbold*, ruffler, ruffian. Became obs. in 17 cent., but was revived by Scott.

ruffelyn or debatyn: discordo (*Prompt. Parv.*).

rufous. From L. *rufus*, red, cogn. with *ruber.*

rug. From 16 cent. Of Scand. origin. Cf. Norw. dial. *rogga*, coarse coverlet, *skinn-rugga*, skin rug, Sw. *rugg*, coarse hair; cogn. with *rag* (q.v.).

rugby. Football. From *Rugby School*, where, in 1823, W. W. Ellis "first took the ball in his arms and ran with it" (*Inscription on Doctor's wall*).

rugged. App. related to *rug*, as *ragged*, with which it was earlier synon., to *rag*. It is much older than *rug*. ME. had also *ruggy*; cf. Sw. *ruggig.*

Tho came this woful Theban Palamoun,
With flotery berd and ruggy [*var.* rugged] asshy heeres (Chauc. A. 2882).

Bourbon l'Archambaut, from whose antient and ragged castle is deriv'd the name of the present royal family of France (Evelyn).

rugger. For *rugby* (q.v.). Cf. *soccer.*

rugose. L. *rugosus*, from *ruga*, furrow, wrinkle.

ruin. F. *ruine*, L. *ruina*, from *ruere*, to rush down.

rule. OF. *reule* (replaced by *règle*), L. *regula*,

from *regere*, to govern, direct. Main senses appear in L., including that of carpenter's *rule*; cf. *by rule and line.* To *rule out* is to cancel by a ruled line.

The ruling passion conquers reason still (Pope).

rum¹. Spirit. Short for earlier *rumbullion*, app. a jocular formation (? or F. *bouillon*, hot drink) from *rum²*; cf. *rum bouse*, wine, lit. good liquor (16 cent.).

rum². Adj. App. spec. use of obs. *rum*, good, a very common cant word (16 cent.) which was prefixed, with varying sense, to a great number of nouns and is supposed to be ident. with *rom* (q.v.). The *Dict. Cant. Crew* gives fifty-two such compds., including *rum cove*, which orig. meant a great rogue.

Rumanian [*ling.*]. Lang. of *Rumania*, a Romance lang., but, owing to geog. position, now largely of alien vocabulary.

Rumansh. See *Romansh.*

rumb. See *rhumb.*

rumble. Imit.; cf. Du. *rommelen*, Ger. *rummeln*. Hence archaic *rumble* of a carriage, prob. from its noisy character, also called (c. 1800) *rumbler* and *rumble-tumble.*

rumbo [*archaic*]. From *rum¹.*

rumbustious. Joc. alteration of *robustious.*

ruminate. From L. *ruminari*, to chew the cud, from *rumen*, *rumin-*, throat, used of first stomach of a ruminant.

rummage. First (1526) as noun. OF. *arrumage* (*arrimage*), from *arrumer* (*arrimer*), to arrange the cargo in the hold; cf. Sp. *arrumar*, in same sense. An older F. form is *arruner*, from OF. *run*, hold of a ship (see *run²*), from AS. *rūm*, room (q.v.), or one of its cognates; for formation cf. *arranger*. Quot. 1 shows that *rummage* must have been preceded in E. by an unrecorded **runage*, the MedL. form occurring several times in the same text and always in connection with wine-casks. The word, first used of casks, prob. came to England with the wine-trade. Later senses arise from the general dragging about and confusion incident on the stowing of cargo (see quot. 5). *Rummage sale* was orig. used of sale at docks of unclaimed goods. With Furetière's definition cf. quot. 3.

Ad ducendum dicta dolia usque navem et pro runagio dictorum doliorum (*Earl of Derby's Exped. to Prussia and Holy Land*, 1390–93).

Arrumeurs sont de petits officiers établis sur les ports, et surtout en Guyenne,...qui ont soin de placer et de ranger les marchandises dans un vaisseau, et surtout celles qui sont en tonneaux, et qui sont en danger de coulage (Furetière).

The romeger whiche they appoynted...to romege caske wares in the said shippe (*NED.* 1544).

And that the masters of the ships do looke wel to the romaging, for they might bring away a great deale more than they doe, if they would take paine in the romaging (Hakl. 1560).

to rummage the hold: changer l'arrimage (Lesc.).

rummer. Du. *roemer*, whence also Ger. *römer*, "a rummer, brimmer, or primmer; a wide-footed drinking-glass" (Ludw.), trad. associated with *Römer*, Roman, but from Du. *roem*, glory, boast, etc.; cf. *bumper*. Quot. below is in transl. from Du. Current spelling is associated with *rum*[1].

They...will drincke up whole romers full of aquavite at a draught (Purch.).

rumour. F. *rumeur*, L. *rumor-em*.

rump. ME. *rumpe*, from Scand.; cf. Dan. *rumpe*, Sw. *rumpa*; cogn. with Du. *romp*, Ger. *rumpf*, trunk (of body).

This fagge end, this rump of a Parliament with corrupt maggots in it (*NED.* 1649).

Boys do now cry, "Kiss my Parliament!"
(Pepys, Feb. 1660).

Now if you ask who nam'd it "Rump," know 'twas so stil'd in an honest sheet of paper (call'd "The Bloody Rump") written before the tryal of our late Soveraign of glorious memory: but the word obtain'd not universal notice till it flew from the mouth of Major General Brown at a publick assembly in the daies of Richard Cromwell
(*Pref.* to *Rump Songs*, 1662).

The situation in Rump Austria is utterly desperate
(*Obs.* Jan. 18, 1920).

rumple. Also earlier *rimple*; cf. Ger. *rümpfen*, Du. *rimpelen*; also AS. *hrimpan*, only in p.p. *gehrumpen*.

rumpus. Swiss Ger. (Basel), ? orig. students' slang use of G. ῥόμβος, spinning-top, also commotion, disturbance.

rum-tum. Light sculling boat, first built and named at Putney (c. 1888). Fanciful formation on *rum*[2], suggested by *funny* (q.v.). Said to have been named by a music-hall gent of sporting proclivities.

run[1]. Verb. AS. *rinnan* (usu. in form *yrnan*), strong intrans., *earnan*, *ærnan* (metath. of **rennan*), weak trans. Com. Teut.; cf. Du. *rinnen* (obs.), *rennen*, Ger. *rinnen*, *rennen*, ON. *rinna*, *renna*, Goth. *rinnan*, *rannjan*. The rarity of *rinnan* and absence of **rennan* in AS. point to the words having been rather borrowed from ON. Fig. senses, e.g. to *run to earth*, to *run down*, to *make the running*, are characteristic of E. love of hunting and racing. *In the long run* was

orig. *at long run*, perh. after F. *à la longue*. To *have a run for one's money* (even if you lose your bet) is racing slang. Cf. *out of the running*. The *runner up* was orig. in coursing. To *feel run down* likens the body to a clock.

Write the vision, and make it plain upon tables, that he may run that readeth it (*Hab.* ii. 2).

run[2] [*naut.*]. "The aftmost or hindmost part of a ship's bottom, where it grows extremely narrow, as the floor approaches the stern-post" (Falc.). OF. *run*, ship's hold, lit. room (q.v.). See also *rummage*. Falc. still has *rum*, *reun*, as synonyms of *cale*, hold, and also *donner rum à une roche*, to give room (a wide berth) to a rock. It is even likely that *the run of* belongs here (see quot. 3).

rum: the hole, or hold of a ship (Cotg.).

Le soubs-tillac ou la marchandise se met; le run, c'est encore plus bas, ou on jette les plus grosses besongnes (Godef. 1622).

Pour son entree, et aussi pour avoir le run de la riviere, il paiera quarante solz parisis (Godef. 1415).

runagate [*archaic*]. Folk-etym. for ME. *renegat*, later replaced by *renegade* (q.v.). *Agate* is a ME. adv., on the way, road (see *gate*[2]), and *run-agate* was no doubt suggested by *run-away*.

runcinate [*bot.*]. Saw-toothed. From L. *runcina*, plane, formerly understood as meaning saw.

rundale. Joint occupation of land in small strips, esp. in Ireland. From *run*[1] and *dale* (*deal*[1]), division, share. Cf. synon. Sc. *runrig*.

rune. Dan., ON. *rún*, mystery, dark secret; cf. AS. *rún* (see *round*[2]). Spec. sense of letter of earliest Teut. alphabet was adopted (17 cent.) from Dan. writers on Norse antiquities. Cf. Ger. *rune*, similarly borrowed by 17 cent. antiquaries. Evelyn speaks of *runic characters*.

rung. AS. *hrung*; cf. Du. *rong*, Ger. *runge*, Goth. *hrugga*. In E. now only of ladder, but in Sc. still used for a cudgel, staff.

runlet[1] [*archaic*]. Cask. OF. *rondelet*, double dim. of *rond*, round.

runlet[2]. From *runnel* (q.v.), after *streamlet*, etc.

runnel. For earlier *rinel*, *rindle*, AS. *rinnelle*, brook, from stem of *run*[1]; cf. Ger. *rinne*, channel, gutter.

runt. Small cattle. Du. *rund*, ox; cf. Ger. *rind* (as in *rinderpest*), obs. E. *rother*. Also applied to uncouth or undersized person, and (17 cent.) to a species of pigeon, app. from its stout build.

a runt or a bullocke: een rundt ofte een jongen os (Hexham).

rupee. Urdu *rūpiyah*, Sanskrit *rūpya*, wrought silver, from *rūpa*, form. From c. 1600. The E. form is perh. from the pl. *rūpe*.

Rupert [*hist.*]. Ger. stationary balloon. Perh. from *Prince Ruprecht of Bavaria*, commanding one of the great blocks of German armies. Cf. *Archie*.

Rupert's drop. Glass toy invented, or introduced, by *Prince Rupert* (17 cent.).

rupture. F., L. *ruptura*, from *rumpere, rupt-*, to break.

rural. F., L. *ruralis*, from *rus, rur-*, country. Not orig. distinguished in sense from *rustic*. *Rural dean* is 15 cent., *ruridecanal* 19 cent.

> Here is a rural fellow
> That will not be denied your highness' presence
> (*Ant. & Cleop.* v. 2).

Ruritanian. Of imaginary kingdoms, like *Ruritania*, in Anthony Hope's *Prisoner of Zenda*.

rusa. EInd. deer. Malay *rūsa*. Cf. *babiroussa*.

ruse. Orig. to drive (fall) back in battle, but in ME. chiefly as hunting term, used of the doubling of the game. F., from *ruser*, OF. *reüser*, ? L. *recusare*. VL. **retusare*, from *tundere, tus-*, to beat, has also been suggested, and is phonetically less objectionable.

rush[1]. Plant. AS. *rysc*, rare var. of *risc*, also *rix*, as still in dial. ME. has *rish* and *rush*, and both -*i*- and -*u*- forms are found in cogn. Du. & Ger. words. The final prevalence of *rush* may be partly due to OF. *rousche*, from Teut. *Rushlight* is for earlier *rush-candle*, the pith of a rush dipped in tallow.

rush[2]. Verb. AF. *russher, russer*, F. *ruser* (see *ruse*). First in Barbour, both as trans., to drive back, and intrans., to dash forward, the former sense corresponding exactly with his use of *ruse* and with earliest examples of OF. *reüser*. For -*sh* cf. *push*. "The development of some of the senses may have been helped by a feeling of phonetic appropriateness" (*NED.*). "A new species of robbery called the 'rush'" is described in the *Gent. Mag.* 1785.

rusk. Sp. or Port. *rosca*, coil, twist, spec. of bread; cf. OF. *tourte*, coarse bread, L. *torta*, twisted.

Russ. Russ. *Rusi*, native name of the people.

Russian (in Shaks.) is MedL. *Russianus*. *Muscovite* was more usual in 16–17 cents. *Russia leather* is mentioned by Sir Thomas Browne. The lang. is Slav.

russell cord. ? From maker.

russet. OF. *rousset*, dim. of *roux*, red, L. *russus*. Earliest E. sense is a fabric; cf. *blanket, scarlet*, etc. Cf. *Dan Russel the fox* (Chauc.).

rust. AS. *rūst*; cf. Du. *roest*, Ger. *rost*, and cogn. ON. *ryth*; ult. cogn. with *red, ruddy*. See also *rusty*.

rustic. L. *rusticus*, from *rus*, country.

> He [Milton] had incurred *Rustication*, a temporary dismission into the country, with perhaps the loss of a term (Johns.).

rustle. Imit.; cf. synon. Du. *ritselen*, Ger. *rauschen*. US. *rustler* shows association with *bustle*[1], *hustle*.

rusty[1]. Of bacon. Altered from *reasty, resty*, F. *resté*, p.p. of *rester*, to remain, be left over (see *rest*[2]).

> And then came haltyng Jone,
> And brought a gambone
> Of bakon that was reasty (Skelton).

rusty[2]. Of temper. Orig. of horses, esp. in to *ride rusty*. Altered from earlier *reasty, resty*, pop. form of *restive* (q.v.). Thus ident. with *rusty*[1].

rut[1]. Sexual excitement of deer. F., OF. *ruit*, VL. **rugitus*, for *rugītus*, from *rugire*, to roar.

rut[2]. In road. F. *route*, "a rutt, way, path, street, course, passage" (Cotg.). For the vowel cf. obs. *ruttier*, sailing instructions, F. *routier*. For fig. sense cf. *routine* and *groove*.

ruth. Now archaic, exc. in *ruthless*. Formed in early ME. from *rue*[2] by analogy with other words in -*th*; cf. ON. *hryggth*. Replaced earlier *rue* (see *rue*[2]).

Ruthene [*ethn.*]. Member of Little Russian race, esp. in Austria. MedL. *Rutheni*, for *Russi*; cf. MedL. *Prutheni*, for *Prussi*.

ruthless. See *ruth*.

rutilant. F., from pres. part. of L. *rutilare*, to gleam, cogn. with *ruber*, red.

rye. AS. *ryge*; cf. Du. *rogge*, Ger. *roggen* (OHG. *rocko*), ON. *rugr*, with Slav. cognates.

rye-grass. For earlier *ray-grass*, from obs. *ray*, darnel, perh. aphet. for obs. *ivray*, F. *ivraie*, L. *ebriaca* (sc. *herba*), from its intoxicating properties. This may have been understood as *ive ray*, *ive* being also an obs. plant-name. But Dan. dial. *radgræs*, from

Ger., suggests rather connection with Ger. *raden*, corn-cockle, OHG. *rāto*.

ivroye: darnell, ray, iveray (Cotg.).

ryot. Ind. peasant. Urdu *raiyat*, ult. Arab. (see *rayah*).

s-. This is by far the largest init. in E. and occupies about one-seventh of the dict. It includes a large number of words of imit. and echoic origin (*slam*, *squeal*, *sizzle*, etc.) and many others which have been altered or influenced by such associations. There are also many long-standing words in *s-* of which the origin has not been actually cleared up, though in many cases it is easy to point to related words in Scand. and other Teut. langs. Initial *s-* also differs from other sounds in its detachable character, and also in the fact that it is often prefixed as an intensive, esp. in *scr-*, *spl-*, *squ-*. The classical example of the first phenomenon is the infantile *tummy*, while *s-mash*, *s-quash*, *s-cratch*, *s-crunch*, etc. illustrate the second. So also *Nottingham* was orig. *Snottingham*; *queasy*, *squeasy*, *quinsy*, *squinsy*, occur indifferently in early texts. Machyn in his *Diary* (1550–63) writes *storch* for *torch* and *trong* for *strong*, and both Palsgrave and Addison use *scuttle-fish*. We find the same tendency in proper names, e.g. in ME. Rolls the same individual will be entered as *Stacey* (from Eustace) or *Tacey*, *Spink* (chaffinch) or *Pink*, *Turgis* (AS. *Thurgisl*, Thor hostage) or *Sturgess*. The same peculiarity is noticed in F. (see *Excalibur*, *scaffold*) and far back in the Aryan langs., e.g. *foam* is cogn. with L. *s-puma*, *s-now* with L. *nix*, *niv-*. As I write (1917) there is a slang tendency to say *snice* for *nice*, etc. It will thus be seen that the *s-* words form a thorny district of etymology. It should be noted also that a large number of words in *sc-*, *sp-*, *st-*, correspond to OF. words which were normally spelt *esc-*, *esp-*, *est-*, e.g. *scarlet*, *spice*, *state*. This phenomenon is due to the VL. tendency to prefix a vowel sound in order to facilitate the pronunc. of L. *sc-*, *sp-*, *st-*. ModF. has now usually lost the *-s-* (*écarlate*, *épice*, *état*).

The freyght and all hoder [other] scostys therof
                                  (*Cely Papers*, 15 cent.).

Sabaoth. L. (*Vulg.*), G. (LXX.), Heb. *çebāōth*, pl. of *çābā*, host, army. By early writers often confused with *sabbath*.

sabbath. L., G., Heb. *shabbāth*, from *shābath*, to rest. Orig. Saturday, which is still the meaning of It. *sabbato*, Sp. *sábado*, while L. *sabbatum* is also the first element of F. *samedi*, Ger. *samstag*. Mod. sense dates from Reformation, the old *Lord's Day* being still preferred by some sects. F. *sabbat* is applied only to the Jewish sabbath, or to a sorcerers' revel, "witches' sabbath," a relic of medieval superstition as to the Jews. *Sabbatarian*, in various senses, is 17 cent. *Sabbatical year*, one off in seven for hard-worked professors, is US.

Sabine [*ling.*]. Ancient Italic dial., traces of which are found in L.

sable. OF. (replaced by cogn. *zibelline*, It. *zibellino*); cf. MedL. *sabellum*, Du. *sabel*, Ger. *zobel*; all from Russ. *sobol'*, name of the animal. Her. sense of black is perh. due to the fur being artificially darkened in order to make a stronger contrast with the ermine which commonly accompanied it.

sabot. F., cogn. with *savate* (q.v.), both with orig. *ç-*. *Sabotage*, malicious damage (done by strikers), is from slang *saboter*, to work badly, from contemptuous slang sense of *sabot*, rubbish, etc.

No longer will the [Russian] army be handicapped by the sabotage of the central authorities
                           (*Daily Chron.* Mar. 16, 1917).

sabre. F., Ger. *säbel*, "a sable, sabre, falchion, hanger, cutlass, scimiter" (Ludw.), introduced (c. 1500) from the East (cf. *hussar*), and applied to the Turk. curved sword; cf. Russ. *sablja*, Pol. *szabla*. Origin unknown. The archaic *shabble* (Scott) is It. *sciabla*, prob. from Hungar. *száblya*. *Sabretache* is F., Ger. *säbeltasche*, from *tasche*, pocket.

sabulous. L. *sabulosus*, from *sabulum*, sand.

sac. F., sack. In sense of dress in Pepys (Mar. 2, 1669).

saccate [*bot.*]. Dilated. MedL. *saccatus*, from *saccus*, sack, bag.

saccharine. Adj. From MedL. *saccharum*, G. σάκχαρον, sugar (q.v.). As noun for *saccharin*, F., discovered and named (1880) by Péligot.

sacerdotal. F., L. *sacerdotalis*, from *sacerdos*, *sacerdot-*, priest, lit. offerer of sacrifices, from *sacer*, sacred, *dare*, to give.

sachem. From early 17 cent. NAmer. Ind. (Narragansett), cogn. with *sagamore*.

sachet. F., dim. of *sac*, sack, bag.

sack¹. Bag. AS. *sacc* or F. *sac*, L. *saccus*, G. σάκκος, Heb. *saq*; cf. Assyr. *saqqu*. In most

Europ. langs., including Celt. & Slav. "This remarkable word has travelled everywhere, together (as I suppose) with the story of Joseph" (Skeat). The penitential *sackcloth* of the Bible was of goats' or camels' hair. *Sack*, plunder, F. *sac*, It. *sacco*, orig. in to *put to sack*, is the same word; cf. sporting use of *bag*. Also *sack*, garment, sometimes *sacque*, a word belonging to the same kind of F. as *équestrienne*.

on luy a donné son sac [et ses quilles] &c.: he hath his passport given him, he is turned out to grazing; (said of a servant whom his master hath put away) (Cotg.).

à sac, à sac: the word whereby a commander authorizeth his souldiers to sack a place or people (*ib.*).

sack² [*archaic*]. Sp. wine. Orig. (16 cent.), *wyne sek*, F. *vin sec*, dry wine; cf. Ger. *sekt*, orig. used of Sp. wine, Du. *sek*, "sack (a sort of wine)" (Sewel), mod. Ger. sense, champagne, being due perh. to a blunder of the actor Devrient when playing Falstaff. The altered form *sack* is from a mistaken idea that the wine was strained through a sack or bag.

sackbut. Kind of trombone. F. *saquebute*, from OF. *saquier*, to drag, *bouter*, to shove, the same word (*saqueboute*) being used in OF. for a hooked lance with which a horseman could be brought down; cf. Sp. *sacabuche*, sackbut, pump-tube, prob. from F. In *Dan.* iii. it is a mistransl., due to superficial resemblance of form, of L. *sambuca*, G. σαμβύκη, a stringed instrument, of Aram. origin. Wyc. has *sambuke*, Coverd. *shawme*. See *hackbut*.

sackless [*archaic & dial.*]. Innocent. AS. *sacléas*, from *sacu*, dispute at law, crime (see *sake*).

sacque. See *sack*¹.

sacrament. F. *sacrement*, L. *sacramentum*, an oath, pledge, etc., from *sacrare*, from *sacer*, holy, ult. cogn. with *saint*; cf. F. *serment*, oath, OF. *sairement*. Adopted in early Church L. as rendering of G. μυστήριον, mystery.

sacrarium. L., sanctuary, from *sacer*, holy.

sacré. F., sacred, euph. for *sacré nom de Dieu*, etc.

sacred. Orig. p.p. of ME. *sacre*, to bless, F. *sacrer*, L. *sacrare* (v.s.). The verb also survives in *sacring-bell*.

sacrifice. F., L. *sacrificium*, from *sacer*, holy, *facere*, to make.

sacrilege. F. *sacrilège*, L. *sacrilegium*, from *sacrilegus*, stealer of sacred things, from *legere*, to gather.

sacristan. MedL. *sacristanus*, for Late L. *sacrista*, keeper of holy things, whence also archaic *sacrist*. See *sexton*, and cf. *sacristy*, of which the pop. form was *sextry*.

sacrosanct. L. *sacrosanctus*, from *sacer*, holy, *sanctus*, holy; cf. F. *sacro-saint*.

sacrum [*anat.*]. L. *os sacrum*, lit. sacred bone.

sad. AS. *sæd*, sated. Com. Teut.; cf. Du. *zat*, Ger. *satt*, ON. *sathr*, Goth. *saths*, all in sense of satiated; cogn. with L. *sat*, *satis*. Current sense of E. word was reached via that of settled, orderly, sober (as in *sad-coloured dress*), esp. in *sad and wise*. In dial. still freely used of physical objects in sense of dense, heavy, etc., e.g. *sad pastry*. Mod. *fed up* is a parallel to the curious hist. of this word. Shaks. plays on old and current senses (*Rom. & Jul.* i. 1).

The grace of God...send sadnesse and substance of lyfelode to oure newe fraternitie (*York Merch. Advent.* 1430).

I wys she ys no thyng so sadde as I wold she wer (*Paston Let.* ii. 264).

saddle. AS. *sadol*. Com. Teut.; cf. Du. *zadel*, zaal, Ger. *sattel*, ON. *söthull*, ult. cogn. with *sit* and L. *sedēre*; cf. L. *sella*, saddle, for *sedla*. Fig. to *saddle* (e.g. with blame) is evolved from older to *lay the saddle on the right horse*. With *saddlebow* cf. F. *arçon*, from *arc*, bow, whence *désarçonner*, to unsaddle, unhorse. *Saddlebag* (incorr. *saddleback*) upholstery imitates the carpet material used for saddle-bags carried on camels in the East.

Sadducee. Late L., Late G. Σαδδουκαῖος, Late Heb. *Çaddūqī*, from pers. name *Çaddūq*, Zadok (2 *Sam.* viii. 17), from whom the priesthood of the captivity claimed descent. Orig. one of the three Jewish sects (cf. *Essene, Pharisee*).

sadism [*med.*]. Sexual perversion with love of cruelty. F. *sadisme*, from Count (commonly called Marquis) *de Sade*, who died (1814) in a lunatic asylum, author of infamous books.

safari. Procession, caravan. Arab., from *safara*, to travel.

Long safaris of surrendered askaris and porters (*Daily Chron.* Nov. 30, 1917).

safe. F. *sauf*, L. *salvus*, cogn. with G. ὅλος, whole; cf. It. Sp. *salvo*, and see *salver*. With *safe and sound* (13 cent.) cf. F. *sain et sauf*. With *safe conduct*, altered from

ME. *sauf condut, saf coundyte* (13 cent.), F. *sauf-conduit*, cf. *safeguard*, F. *sauvegarde*. Noun *safe*, orig. for meat (*Prompt. Parv.*), is for earlier *save*, from verb.

saffron. F. *safran*, ult. Arab. *za'farān*. In most Europ. langs.

sag. From 15 cent., also *sack*. Cf. Du. *zakken*, Sw. *sacka*, to subside, also in spec. naut. sense; cogn. with Norw. dial. *sakka*, ON. *sökkva*, to sink. "It seems possible that the word is orig. WScand., and has passed (? as a naut. term) into Sw. Du. LG., and (perh. through LG.) into E." (*NED.*). Ger. has *sacken* (naut.) from LG. All cogn. with *sink*.

The sagge of the sea to leewards (Hakl. iii. 259).

saga. ON., medieval prose narrative (Iceland and Norway). Introduced by 18 cent. antiquaries (cf. *rune, berserk*, etc.). See *saw²*.

sagacious. From L. *sagax, sagac-*, from *sagire*, to discern acutely, ult. cogn. with *seek*. Orig. of animals.

sagamore. From c. 1600. NAmer. Ind. (Penobscot) *sagamo*, sachem.

sage¹. Plant. F. *sauge*, L. *salvia*, from *salvus*, in allusion to preserving properties; cf. It. Sp. *salvia*, Ger. *salbei*, etc. For vowel cf. *safe, chafe*.

sage². Wise. F., VL. **sapius*, for *sapiens*, from *sapere*, to know; cf. It. *saggio*, Sp. *sabio*. As noun orig. applied to the *Seven Sages*.

saggar, seggar [*techn.*]. Fireproof clay enclosing fine porcelain in oven. Corrupt. of *safeguard*.

sagittary. L. *sagittarius*, archer, from *sagitta*, arrow.

sago. Malay *sāgŭ*; cf. F. *sagou*, Ger. *sago*, etc. From 16 cent.

Sahara. Arab. *çaḥrā*, desert.

Lybia he calleth Sarra, for so the Arabians call a desert (Purch.).

sahib. Urdu, Arab. *çāḥib*, friend, used as respectful address to Europeans and also in some native titles (*Tippoo Sahib, Nana Sahib*). Now common in the services for "white man."

If ever I do meet one performing such a feat, I shall say, "There goes a sahib—and a soldier" (Ian.Hay, *First Hundred Thousand*).

sail. AS. *segl*. Com. Teut.; cf. Du. *zeil* (earlier *seghel*), Ger. *segel*, ON. *segl*. Sense of ship (*forty sail, sail ho!*) may go back to the period of the single sail. With the verb,

AS. *seglian*, cf. F. *cingler*, OF. *singler*, nasalized from ON. *sigla*. *Sailor*, earlier (15 cent.) *sailer*, is much later than *seaman*, *mariner*, which explains its absence from the surname list (*Saylor* means leaper, dancer; see my *Surnames*, p. 118).

sainfoin. F., lit. wholesome hay, L. *sanum* and *foenum*, but often understood as *saint foin* and rendered in E. by *holy hay*.

saint. F., L. *sanctus*, from *sancire*, to consecrate (cf. *sanction*), cogn. with *sacer*. In most Europ. langs. In ME. it regularly coalesces with following name (see *tawdry* and cf. educated pronunc. of name *St John*). Quot. below shows origin of *Tooley St.*

In saynt Towlles [Saint Olave's] in the Oll' Jury
                        (Machyn's *Diary*, 1550–63).

Saint Bernard. From Hospice of the *Great St Bernard*, pass between Italy and Switzerland. Cf. Ger. *bernardiner* (dog).

Saint-Leger. Race established (1776) by *Colonel St Leger*.

Saint Lubbock. Bank holiday (q.v.); cf. *Saint Monday*, F. *fêter saint Lundi*.

Saint Michael. Orange. One of the Azores.

Saint-Simonian. Of *Saint-Simon*, F. socialist (†1825). Cf. *Fourierism*.

sais. See *syce*.

sake. AS. *sacu*, dispute at law, accusation, crime. Com. Teut.; cf. Du. *zaak*, Ger. *sache*, ON. *sök*, Goth. *sakjō*, quarrel; ult. cogn. with *seek*. See *forsake, namesake*. Sense has become much limited and the word is now only used with *for*, earlier meanings being replaced by *case, cause*. Ger. *sache*, thing, affair, still preserves sense of quarrel, cause, etc.; for sense of thing cf. F. *chose*, L. *causa. For consciences sake* is in *Piers Plowm.*

saké. Fermented drink from rice. Jap. *sake*.

saker [*hist.*]. Cannon. Earlier, kind of hawk, F. *sacre*, "a saker; the hawk, and the artillerie, so called" (Cotg.), It. *sacro*, Arab. *çaqr*. Cf. *musket, falconet, culverin*, etc.

saki. SAmer. monkey. F. (Buffon) for Tupi (Brazil) *çahy*.

sal, saul. EInd. tree. Hind. *sāl*, Sanskrit *sāla*.

salaam. Arab. *salām*, peace, as greeting; cf. Heb. *shālōm* (*Judges*, vi. 23–4). Du. *soebatten*, to address cringingly, from Malay *sobat*, friend, may be regarded as a parallel.

salacious. From L. *salax, salac-*, lustful, from *salire*, to leap.

salad. F. *salade*, L. *salata* (sc. *herba*), from *salare*, from *sal*, salt.

> My salad days,
> When I was green in judgment, old in blood
>   (*Ant. & Cleop.* i. 5).

salade [*hist.*]. See *sallet*.

salamander. F. *salamandre*, L., G. σαλα-μάνδρα, lizard supposed to be able to endure fire, prob. of Eastern origin.

sal ammoniac. See *ammonia*.

salary. F. *salaire*, L. *salarium*, soldiers' pay, orig. allowance for salt. Cf. *batta*.

sale. Late AS. *sala*, from ON. See *sell*.

Salem. Nonconformist chapel, from *Jerusalem* (see *Heb.* vii. 1), ? cogn. with *salaam*; cf. *Bethel*.

salep. Meal from dried tubers; cf. F. Sp. *salep*, Turk. *sālep*, Arab. *tha'leb*, for *khasyu'th-tha'lab*, orchis, lit. fox testicles.

saleratus [*US.*]. ModL. *sal aeratus*, aerated salt.

salet [*hist.*]. See *sallet*.

Salian[1]. From L. *Salii*, priests of Mars, ? lit. leapers, from *salire*.

Salian[2]. As *Salic*.

Salic [*hist.*]. F. *salique*, MedL. *Salicus*, Salian Frank, tribe near Zuyder Zee whence sprang the Merovingians. Perh. from the river *Sala* (now Yssel) which runs into the Zuyder Zee. Esp. in *Salic law*, erron. supposed to refer to exclusion of females from succession, invoked (1316) by Philip V of France.

salicional. Organ-stop. Ger. *salizional*, from L. *salix*, willow, because suggesting tone of willow-pipe.

salicyl [*chem.*]. F. *salicyle*, from L. *salix*, *salic-*, willow.

salient. From pres. part. of L. *salire*, to leap, whence F. *saillir*, to jut out, which has given the E. sense. Now very familiar as noun (mil.).

saliferous. From L. *sal*, salt, after F. *salifère*.

saline. VL. **salinus*, from *sal*, salt; cf. *salinae*, salt-pans. So also F. *salin*, It. Sp. *salino*.

saliva. L., spittle.

salleeman, sallyman. Sailor's name for marine hydrozoan, for *Sallee man*, i.e. pirate from *Sallee* (Morocco). Cf. *Portuguese man-of-war*.

sallender. Disease in hock of horse (16 cent.). Cf. F. *solandre*. App. in some way associated with obs. *malander* (q.v.) which occurs much earlier (*Prompt. Parv.*).

> *selenders*: are chops or mangy sores in the bending of a horse's hough, as the malenders are in the knees
>   (*Gent. Dict.* 1705).

sallet, salade [*hist.*]. Gen. name for helmet between the *bascinet* and the *morion*; orig. a plain steel cap. F. *salade*, It. *celata*, "a scull, a helmet, a morion, a sallet, a head-piece" (Flor.), from *celare*, to hide (or Sp. *celada*, from *celar*), perh. because orig. worn under a hood, or, like the bascinet, under the ornamental tilting-helm. Cf. It. *secreta*, "a thinne steele cap, or close skull, worne under a hat" (Flor.), and obs. F. *secrete*, *segrette*, "an yron scull, or cap of fence" (Cotg.). *Jacks and sallets, jakked and salleted*, is the regular 15 cent. description of warlike array (passim in *Paston Let.*), corresponding to F. *jacques et secretes* of the same period.

sallow[1], **sally.** Willow. AS. *sealh*; cf. OHG. *salaha* (surviving in *salweide*, sally-withy), ON. *selja*; cogn. with L. *salix*, G. ἑλίκη, Gael. *seileach*, Ir. *saileach*, Welsh *helyg*. F. *saule*, "a sallow, willow, or withy tree" (Cotg.), is from Teut.

sallow[2]. Adj. AS. *salo*, *salu*; cf. archaic Du. *zaluw*, OHG. *salo*, ON. *sölr*. F. *sale*, dirty, is from Teut. For form of *sallow*[1,2] (-*ow* for ME. -*we*) cf. *fallow*, *farrow*, *swallow*, etc.

sally. F. *saillie*, p.p. fem. of *saillir*, to rush, L. *salire*, to leap. Cf. *sortie*. Fig., outbreak (of wit, etc.), from 17 cent. In early use both noun and verb are usu. followed by *out*. Hence also *sally* (bell-ringing), first movement, later applied to the woolly grips on the rope.

Sally Lunn. Said (by Hone, 1827) to be named from a young woman who first cried them at Bath c. 1780–90.

salmagundi. F. *salmagondi*, earlier *salmigondin*, "a hachee" (Cotg.), app. connected with It. *salame*, salted meat, from *sal*, salt. Cf. also F. *salmi(s)*, explained as shortened from *salmigondis*, but perh. the original of that word. As the latter is app. first recorded in Rabelais, it may be one of his fantastic coinages. For fig. sense cf. *gallimaufrey*.

salmi. See *salmagundi*.

salmiac. Ger. *salmiak*, for *sal ammoniak*.

salmon. ME. also *samon*, *saumon*, F., L. *salmo-n-*; cf. L. *salar*, trout; both prob. from Celt. For Teut. name see *lax*[1].

saloon. F. *salon*, from *salle*, hall, OF. *sale*, Ger. *sal*, cogn. with AS. *sæl*, ON. *salr*; cf. Goth. *saljan*, to dwell. *Salon* was naturalized in 18 cent. E., but is now used only of France, esp. in ref. to art and literature. Later spec. senses of *saloon* are mostly US.

saloop. Var. of *salep.*

Salopian. Of Shropshire, esp. of Shrewsbury School. AF. *Sloppesberie*, for AS. *Scrobbes-byrig*, by confusion of -*r*-, -*l*-, was further corrupted to *Salop*-. For inserted vowel cf. F. *canif*, knife, *semaque*, (fishing) smack, etc.

salpiglossis. Plant. Irreg. from G. σάλπιγξ, trumpet, γλῶσσα, tongue.

salsify. Vegetable. F. *salsifis*, earlier *sasse-fique*, *sassefrique*, etc., It. *sassefrica*, from L. *fricare*, to rub, prob. in allusion to some med. property. Cf. *saxifrage* (q.v.).

sassifrica: as *sassifraga* (Flor.).

salt. AS. *sealt*. WAryan; cf. Du. *zout*, Ger. *salz*, ON. Goth. *salt*, L. *sal*, G. ἅλς, Ir. *salann*, Welsh *halen*, Russ. *sol'*. Earliest E. sense is the current one of sodium chloride, but many other chem. senses date from ME. Earliest allusive sense is *salt of the earth* (*Matt.* v. 13). With *true to one's salt* cf. *salary*. *Worth one's salt* is app. mod. and naut. *With a grain of salt*, sometimes latinized as *cum grano salis*, is 17 cent. *Above* (*below*) *the salt* refers to the large salt-cellar halfway down a medieval table. With *salt*, sailor, cf. *tar*. To *salt* (a mine) is perh. allusive to the *salt-lick* which attracts deer and cattle. With *salted*, of horses immune to disease, cf. fig. use of *seasoned*.

It is...a foolish bird that staieth the laying salt on his taile (*Euphues*).

manger à un grain de sel: to eat a man at a mouthfull (the cracke of a braggadochio;) also to eate his meate hastily, or greedily, without staying for any sawce, or seasoning, other than a corne of salt will yeeld him (Cotg.).

saltarello [*mus.*]. It., from *saltare*, to dance.

saltation. L. *saltatio-n-*, from *saltare*, frequent. of *salire*, to leap.

salt-cellar. Altered (16 cent.), on *cellar*, from *salt-seller*, pleon. for ME. *saler*, *seler*, F. *salière*, "a salt-seller" (Cotg.), from L. *sal*, salt. For pleon. cf. *pea-jacket*.

saltern. Salt-works. AS. *sealtern*, second element, *ærn*, dwelling, cogn. with ON. *rann*, house (see *ransack*).

saltigrade [*biol.*]. Going by jumps, L. *per saltum*; cf. *plantigrade*.

saltire [*her.*]. F. *sautoir*, St Andrew's Cross (×), orig. stirrup-rope, Late L. *saltatorium*, from *saltare*, frequent. of *salire*, to leap. Also in F. a sash worn cross-wise.

saltpetre. Altered, on *salt*, from earlier *sal-petre* (Chauc.), F. *salpêtre*, MedL. *sal petrae*,

salt of stone, because found as incrustation on rocks.

salubrious. From L. *salubris*, from *salus*, health, cogn. with *salvus*, safe.

salutary. F. *salutaire*, L. *salutaris*, from *salus* (v.s.).

salute. L. *salutare*, to hail, wish health, *salus*.

salvage. OF., from *salver* (*sauver*), Late L. *salvare*, from *salvus*, safe. Immediate source is prob. MedL. *salvagium*.

salvation. Restored from ME. *sauvacion*, OF. *sauvacion*, *salvatiun*, etc., L. *salvatio-n-*, from *salvare* (v.s.), used in Church L. to render G. σωτηρία. The *Salvation Army* (1878) is now translated into most Europ. langs., e.g. F. *armée de salut*, Ger. *heils-armee*.

salve¹. Ointment. AS. *sealf*; cf. Du. *zalf*, Ger. *salbe*; ult. cogn. with Sanskrit *sarpis*, clarified butter. Replaced by *ointment*, exc. in compds. With verb, now also usu. fig., cf. Goth. *salbōn*, to heal. In some uses, e.g. to *salve one's conscience*, evidently associated with *salve²* (cf. *salvo²*).

salve². To rescue. Back-formation from *salvage*.

salver. Altered, on *platter*, *trencher*, from F. *salve*, Sp. *salva*, "a taste, a salutation" (Percyvall), from *salvar*, to save, orig. applied to the "pre-gustation" of food and drink, partly as precaution against poison. See *credence* and cf. Ger. *credenzen*, to pour out, from It.

salvia. Plant. L., sage¹.

salvo¹. Of artillery. It. *salva*, "a volie or tire of ordinance" (Flor.), orig. salute; cf. L. *salve!* hail! For incorr. -*o* in words from Sp. & It. cf. *bastinado*, *ambuscado*, etc.

salvo² [*leg.*]. Saving clause. L., abl. of *salvus*, safe, in such phrases as *salvo jure*, without prejudice to the right. Cf. *save²*.

A salvo to conscience (*NED.* 1874).

sal volatile. ModL. (17 cent.), volatile salt.

Sam, Uncle. First came into use, as nickname for US. government and contrast with *John Bull*, during war with Britain (1813). No doubt suggested by initials US. Hence *Sammy*, Amer. soldier, used in first US. offic. message from front (Oct. 17, 1917).

Sam, upon my [*slang*]. App. for earlier *salmon* (in 16 cent. cant), explained by contemporary writers as for *Salomon*, i.e. Solomon. To stand *Sam*(*my*), 19 cent. slang, may be of different origin.

salmon: the beggers sacrament or oath
(*Dict. Cant. Crew*).

Samaritan. Usu. allusive to *Luke*, x. 33. Late L., G., from Σαμαρεία, Samaria.

sambo. Of part negro blood. Sp. *zambo*. As nickname for negro perh. Foulah *sambo*, uncle. But a WAfr. tribe called the *Samboses* is mentioned repeatedly in the narrative of the Hawkins voyage of 1564, and *Sambo* would be a natural back-formation from this (cf. *Chinee*).

Sam Browne. Mil. belt. From *Sir Samuel Browne*, Indian general (19 cent.).

sambur. Indian elk. Hind. *sābar*, *sāmbar*.

same. ON. *samr*. Com. Teut.; cf. AS. *swā same*, likewise, OHG. *sama*, Goth. *sama*; cogn. with L. *similis*, G. ὁμός, Ir. *som*, also with *some*, *-some*.

Samian. Of *Samos*, G. island.

samite [*poet.*]. OF. *samit*, whence also Ger. *samt*, velvet; cf. It. *sciamito*, Sp. *jamete*, MedL. *examitum*, MedG. ἑξάμιτον, app. six-thread, ἕξ and μίτος; cf. *dimity*, *twill*, *drill*⁴. Obs. from c. 1600 till revived by Tennyson.

samlet. Young salmon (Walton); cf. earlier *salmonet*.

Sammy [*neol.*]. US. soldier. See *Sam, uncle*.

Samnite [*ling.*]. Ancient Italic dial.

samovar. Russ., lit. self-boiler (v.i.), with first element ult. cogn. with *same*.

Samoyede [*ling.*]. Turanian lang. of Mongol race in Siberia. Russ., lit. self-eater (v.s.), cannibal, a meaning given by Purch. (1613).

sampan. Chin. boat. Chin. *san-pan*, three-board.

samphire. Altered, perh. after archaic *camphire*, camphor, from 16 cent. *sampere*, *sampier*, etc., F. (*herbe de*) *saint-Pierre*, "sampire" (Cotg.), a name perh. due to association of *Peter* with *rock*.

sample. Aphet. for ME. *essample*, illustration, parable, etc. (see *example*), current sense being later (15 cent.). Cf. *sampler*, OF. *essemplaire*, exemplar.

exemplaire: a patterne, sample, or sampler (Cotg.).

Samurai. Jap., orig. mil. retainer of the daimio.

sanatorium. ModL. (19 cent.) from *sanare*, to cure. Also in Ger.

sanbenito [*hist.*]. Worn, under Inquisition, by impenitent heretic at auto-da-fé. From resemblance to scapular introduced by *St Benedict*.

My description to crown,
All the flames and the devils were turn'd upside-down
On this habit, facetiously term'd San Benito
                              (*Ingoldsby*).

sanctify. Restored from ME. *saintify*, OF. *saintifier* (*sanctifier*), L. *sanctificare*, from *sanctus*, holy, *facere*, to make.

sanctimonious. From *sanctimony*, L. *sanctimonia*, holiness. Not always disparaging, though first occurrence (*Meas. for Meas.* i. 2) has current sense.

sanction. F., L. *sanctio-n-*, law, decree, from *sancire*, *sanct-*, to ratify, make sacred. Current sense of authoritative permission is latest.

sanctity. Restored from ME. *sauntitè*, F. *saintetè*, L. *sanctitas*, *-tat-*.

sanctuary. Restored from ME. *sayntuary*, *sentery*, etc. (see *sentry*), OF. *saintuaire* (*sanctuaire*), L. *sanctuarium*, irreg. from *sanctus*, holy; cf. It. Sp. *santuario*. Orig. in rel. sense, esp. of the Jewish *holy of holies*. Right of sanctuary in criminal cases was abolished 1625, in civil cases 1696–7 and 1722, but the abbey of Holyrood is still theoretically a sanctuary for debtors.

sanctum. L., holy (place). Fig. sense is 19 cent. Prob. for earlier *sanctum sanctorum*, rendering G. τὸ ἅγιον τῶν ἁγίων, Heb. *qōdesh haqqodāshīm*.

sanctus. L., init. word of "angelic hymn" (*Is.* vi. 3) concluding preface of eucharist.

sand. AS. *sand*, *sond*. Com. Teut.; cf. Du. *zand*, Ger. *sand*, ON. *sandr*. US. sense of pluck is a mod. variation on *grit*. *Jolly as a sandboy* is explained (1823) in a *Slang Dict.* with ref. to the cheerful ragamuffins "who drive the sand-laden neddies through our streets." With US. *sandman*, personification of sleepiness, Ger. *sandmann*, cf. Norw. *Ole Lukoie*, the dustman, Olaf Shut-eye, and see *Wee Willie Winkie*. To *sand-bag* is chiefly US. See also *ostrich*.

Nos tamen hoc agimus, tenuique in pulvere sulcos
Ducimus, et litus sterili versamus aratro
                            (Juv. vii. 49).

With sweating browes I long have plowd the sands
                          (Greene, 1590).

While the [German] revolution was being side-tracked in Parliament, it was being sand-bagged in the proletariat (*Daily News*, Mar. 12, 1919).

sandal. F. *sandale*, L. *sandalia*, pl. of *sandalium*, G. σανδάλιον, dim. of σάνδαλον, perh. of Pers. origin.

sandal-wood. For earlier *sandal*; cf. MedL. *sandalum*, OF. *sandle*, *sandre*, whence ME. *sanders*; also It. *sandalo*, Sp. *sándalo*, Ger. *sandel*, from OF., and Arab. *çandal*. Ult. Sanskrit *kandana*.

sandarac. Resin; earlier red arsenic sulphide.

L. *sandaraca*, G. σανδαράκη, prob. a foreign word. In all Rom. langs.

sandblind [*archaic*]. Purblind. First element is AS. *sam-*, half, common in such compds.; cf. dial. *samsodden*, imbecile, lit. half cooked; cogn. with L. *semi*.

sandwich. Recorded 1762. "Said to be named from John Montagu, 4th *Earl of Sandwich* (1718–92) who once spent twenty-four hours at the gaming-table without other refreshment than some slices of cold beef placed between slices of toast" (*NED.*). This explanation has the merit of being contemporary (Grosley's *Londres*, 1770).

Sandy. Nickname for Scotsman. For *Alexander*, whence also *Sanders*, *Saunders*. Cf. *Paddy* and see also *Sawney*. A Borderer named Sandy Armstrong is mentioned in *Privy Council Acts* 1557–8.

You'll please to remember the Fifth of November,
Sebastopol powder and shot,
When General Liprandi met [at Inkermann] John,
Pat and Sandy,
And a jolly good licking he got (*Top.* song, 1854).

sane. L. *sanus*, healthy, ult. cogn. with *sacer* (cf. relation of *whole* to *holy*); cf. F. *sain*. Spec. sense of E. word is due to influence of earlier *insane* (q.v.).

sangar [*mil.*]. Breastwork of stone. A Pushtoo word.

sangaree. Sp. *sangría*, drink composed of red wine and lemon, lit. bleeding.

sang-de-bœuf. In ref. to porcelain. F., lit. bullock's blood. Cf. *pigeon's blood ruby*.

sang-froid. F., cold blood.

Sangrado. Ignorant doctor. Character in Lesage's *Gil Blas* (c. 1700); from Sp. *sangrador*, bleeder.

sangrail [*poet.*]. OF. *saint graal* (see *grail*, *holy*). The form *sangreal* (Scott, Meredith) is due to the spurious etym., royal blood, OF. *sang-reial*.

sanguinary. F. *sanguinaire*, L. *sanguinarius*, from *sanguis*, *sanguin-*, blood.

sanguine. F. *sanguin*, from L. *sanguineus* (v.s.), applied to one of the four "humours" of medieval physiology.

Of his complexioun he was sangwyn
(Chauc. A. 333).

sanhedrim. Supreme council of Jews with 71 members. Late Heb. *sanhedrīn*, G. συνέδριον, council, from σύν, together, ἕδρα, seat. Incorr. -*m* of E. form is due to *cherubim*, etc.

A war cannot be carried on by a Sanhedrim
(D. Lloyd George).

sanicle. Plant. F., MedL. *sanicula*, from *sanus*, whole, from healing properties.

sanitary. F. *sanitaire*, from L. *sanitas*, health, from *sanus*, healthy. This word, after its great 19 cent. vogue, is being cut out by the more fashionable *hygienic*.

sanity. L. *sanitas*, -*tat*-, whence also F. *santé*, health. See *sane*.

sanjak. Division of vilayet. Turk. *sanjāq*, lit. banner.

sans. F., without, OF. *sens*, VL. **sene*, for *sine* (*si ne*, if not), with adv. -*s*. Fully naturalized, as *saun*, *saunce*, etc., from 14 to 16 cent., but now usu. only as echo of *As You Like It*, ii. 7. *Sans peur et sans reproche* was orig. applied to Bayard. *Sans phrase* is from *la mort sans phrase*, attributed to Sieyès voting death of Louis XVI. The writer often passes a house called *Sans-gêne* (for F. *gêne*, constraint, see *gehenna*) which before the War was called *Sans-souci* (solicitude), the name given by Frederick the Great to his palace at Potsdam.

sansculotte [*hist.*]. F. revolutionary (1789), lit. without breeches (*culotte* from *cul*, posterior); usu. explained as wearing trousers instead of the knee-breeches of the upper classes. But in caricatures of the time the "nether garments" are conspicuous by their absence.

Sanskrit [*ling.*]. Sanskrit *saṃskṛta*, put together, perfected, from *sam-*, together, cogn. with *same*, *kṛ*, to perform, cogn. with *create*. Cf. *Prakrit*. Ancient sacred, and (till 18 cent.) secret, lang. of India, and oldest member of Aryan family. Mentioned by Purch. (1617).

Santa Claus. Orig. US., Du. dial. *Sante Klaas*, Du. *Sint Klas*, Saint Nicholas. Cf. Ger. *Niklaus*, patron saint of children (Dec. 5).

santon. Europ. name for *marabout*. Sp. *santón*, hypocrite, from *santo*, saint, whence also F. *santon*.

sap[1]. Of plants. AS. *sæp*. WGer.; cf. Du. *sap*, Ger. *saft*, juice (OHG. *saf*); cogn. with ON. *safi*, and perh. with L. *sapere*, to taste (get to know), *sapa*, must boiled thick, whence, by association with Teut. word, F. *sève*, sap. Some authorities regard the Teut. words as borrowed directly from L. *sapa* with other wine-words. *Sapgreen*, after Du. *sapgroen*, was orig. prepared from juice of buckthorn-berries.

sap[2]. To undermine. Earlier (16 cent.) *zappe*, It. *zappare*, from *zappa*, spade, whence also F. *saper*; cf. Sp. *zapa*, spade, Late L. *sappa* (6 cent.), of unknown origin. With *sap*, to "swot," cf. synon. F. *piocher*, from *pioche*, pick, mattock. The Royal Engineers were, till 1859, *Sappers* and Miners. In fig. sense, to exhaust, "undermine," prob. coloured by *sap*¹.

sap³ [*slang*]. Simpleton. Short for dial. *sapskull*, from *sap*¹, in sense of soft wood.

sanserif [*typ*.]. Without *serif*, *ceriph* (q.v.). Is recorded earlier than the word from which it is app. derived.

sapajou. SAmer. monkey. F., from Cayenne.

sapan-wood. Adapted (16 cent.) from Du. *sapan hout*, Malay, from some SInd. lang.; cf. Tamil *shappangam*.

sapid. L. *sapidus*, savoury. See *sapient*.

sapient. From pres. part. of L. *sapere*, to know, orig. to taste (see *sap*¹).

sapling. From *sap*¹.

sapodilla. Tree. Sp. *zapotillo*, dim. of *zapote*, Mex. *zapotl*.

saponaceous. From L. *sapo-n-*, soap.

sapor. L., savour, from *sapere*, to taste.

sapota. See *sapodilla*.

sapperment. Ger. oath, disguised for *sakrament*.

Sapphic. F. *saphique*, L., G. Σαπφικός, from Σαπφώ, poetess of Lesbos (c. 600 B.C.).

sapphire. F. *saphir*, L., G. σάπφειρος, Heb. *sappīr*, ? Sanskrit *sanipriya*, lit. dear to the planet Saturn.

sapraemia [*med*.]. Septic poisoning. From G. σαπρός, putrid. Cf. *anaemia*.

saraband. Dance. F. *sarabande*, Sp. *zarabanda*, ? from Pers. *sarband*, lit. head-band.

Saracen. AS., Late L. *Saracenus*, Late G. Σαρακηνός; cf. F. *Sarrasin*, It. *Saracino*, Sp. *Saraceno*. Numerous ME. vars., chiefly from OF., with attempt at association with *Sara*, wife of Abraham (cf. *Hagarene* and *Hagar*). Origin uncertain, perh. from Arab. *sharqī*, eastern; cf. *Oriental*, *Anatolian* (from G. ἀνατολή, rising, east), *Easterling*, etc.

Saratoga trunk [*US*.]. From *Saratoga Springs*, summer resort in New York State.

sarawak [*nonce-word*]. From *Sarawak*, Borneo, where Rajah Brooke established a kind of kingdom (1841).

> There is only one place now in the world that two strong men can Sar-a-whack
>   (Kipling, *Man who would be King*).

sarbacane [*hist*.]. Blow-pipe, ear-trumpet. F., altered (on *canne*), from earlier *sarbatenne*, "a long trunke to shoot in" (Cotg.),

Sp. *cerbatano*, Arab. *zabaṭāna*. ? Cf. *sumpitan*.

sarcasm. Earlier (16 cent.) *sarcasmus*, Late L., Late G. σαρκασμός, from σαρκάζειν, to speak bitterly, lit. to tear flesh, σάρξ, σαρκ-.

sarcenet. See *sarsenet*.

sarcoma. Fleshy tumour. G. σάρκωμα, from σάρξ, σαρκ-, flesh.

sarcophagus. L., G. σαρκοφάγος, lit. flesh eating (v.s.), coffin made of a stone reputed to consume the body. Hence Ger. *sarg*, F. dim. *cercueil*, coffin.

sard. Gem. F. *sarde*, L. *sarda*, synon. with *sardius*, sardine¹.

Sard. Sardinian. It. *Sardo*.

Sardanapalian. Of Σαρδανάπαλος, G. name for *Assur-bani-pal*, last king of Nineveh (9 cent. B.C.), famous voluptuary.

sardelle. It. *sardella*, dim. of *sarda*, sardine².

sardine¹. Gem (*Rev*. iv. 3). G. σάρδινος, var. reading of σάρδιος, sardius (q.v.).

sardine². Fish. F., It. *sardina*, L.; cf. G. σαρδίνη, from σάρδη, app. from *Sardinia*, G. Σαρδώ.

> Pro C piscium salsorum...vocatorum "sardyns"
>   (*Earl of Derby's Exped.* 1390–93).

sardius. Gem, sardine¹. L. (*Vulg. Ezek.* xxviii. 13), G. σάρδιος, from Σάρδεις, Sardis, in Lydia. Cf. *chalcedony*, *agate*, *jet*¹.

sardonic. F. *sardonique*, from L. *sardonius*, lit. Sardinian. Said to be due to a poisonous plant, *herba Sardonia*, death from which was preceded by convulsive grinning.

sardonyx. L., G. σαρδόνυξ, compd. of σάρδιος and ὄνυξ.

saree, sari. Bright-coloured wrap. Hind. *sārhī*.

sargasso. Gulf-weed. Port. *sargaço*, ? from *sarga*, kind of grape.

sarissa [*hist*.]. Macedonian pike. G. σάρισσα.

sark [*Sc*.]. Shirt. ON. *serkr*, cogn. with AS. *serc*; cf. *berserk*.

Sarmatian. From L., G. Σαρμάται, orig. Scythian inhabitants of Poland, whence poet. use for Polish.

sarmentose [*bot*.]. L. *sarmentosus*, from *sarmentum*, twig, from *sarpere*, to prune.

sarong. Malay garment. Malay; cf. Sanskrit *sāranga*, variegated.

sarracenia. Plant. Named (1700) by Tournefort from *Dr Sarrazin*, of Quebec, who sent him the plant. Cf. *fuchsia*, etc.

sarsaparilla. Sp. *zarzaparrilla*, from *zarza*, bramble (? Basque *sartzia*), *parra*, vine-trellis. So explained in 16 cent.

sarsen [*loc.*]. Sandstone boulder (Wilts). For *Saracen*.

The inhabitants calling them "Saracens' stones" (*NED.* 1644).

sarsenet, sarcenet [*archaic*]. Fabric. AF. *sarzinett*, from ME. *sarsin*, Saracen (v.s.), perh. after OF. *drap sarrasinois*. Cf. *tartan*.

sartorial. From L. *sartor*, tailor, from *sarcire*, *sart-*, to patch.

Sarum. Signature of bishop of Salisbury. Also in *Sarum missal* (*use*). MedL., from first element of *Sarisburie*, now, by dissim. of *r-r*, *Salisbury*.

sash[1]. Attire, orig. part of turban. Earlier *shash*, Arab. *shāsh*, muslin, turban-sash. For loss of *-h-* by dissim. cf. *sash*[2].

tiara: a turban, a shash (Litt.).

sash[2]. Of window. Earlier (17 cent.) *shash*, back-formation from *shashes*, F. *châssis*, "a frame of wood for a window" (Cotg.), taken as pl. Cf. *cuish*, and, for loss of *-h-*, *sash*[1]. See *chassis*.

sasin. Ind. antelope. Nepalese.

saskatoon. Canadian berry. NAmer. Ind. (Cree) *misāskwatomin*.

sassaby. SAfr. antelope. Sechwana *tsessébe*.

sassafras. Sp. *sasafras*, a NAmer. tree which "hath power to comfort the liver" (Gerarde, 1597). Usu. thought to be corrupted, perh. by influence of some native name, from Sp. *sassifragia*, obs. for *saxifraga*, saxifrage (q.v.). Capt. John Smith (i. 207) even calls the tree *saxefrage*.

Sassenach. Gael. *Sasunnach*, English, from *Sasunn*, Saxon; cf. Welsh *Seisnig* and Welsh names *Sayce*, *Seyes*, etc. Popularized by Scott (cf. *Southron*), but much used in invective by fervent Irishmen.

All loved their McClan, save a Sassenach brute
Who came to the Highlands to fish and to shoot
(*Bab Ballads*).

sassy [*WAfr.*]. Wood, bark, used as ordeal poison. Said to be WAfr. adaptation of E. *saucy*!

Satan. L. (*Vulg.* in *OT.* only), G. Σατᾶν (once in LXX., once in *NT.*), Heb. *ṣāṭān*, adversary (in general), from *ṣāṭan*, to plot against, but also spec. (e.g. in *Job*) the enemy of mankind. Usu. rendered διά-βολος by LXX. Wyc. has *Satanas*, G. Σατανᾶς (*NT.*), replaced, from Tynd. onward, by *Satan*. *His Satanic Majesty* is jocular after *His Catholic Majesty*, etc. With *Satanic School*, applied by Southey to Byron, Shelley, etc., cf. *Satanism*, F.

satanisme, worship of Satan, esp. in ref. to alleged 19 cent. perversion.

satchel. OF. *sachel*, L. *saccellus*, dim. of *saccus*, sack. In Wyc. (*Luke*, x. 4).

sate. Altered (17 cent.) after *satiate* or L. *sat, satis*, from earlier *sade*, lit. to make sad (q.v.). First in Shaks. (*Haml.* i. 5).

assouvir: to fill, content, satiate, satisfie; also, to cloy, glut, sade (Cotg.).

sateen. Mod., after *velveteen*.

satellite. F., L. *satelles*, *satellit-*, attendant, member of bodyguard. Or rather, being gen. used in L. form till c. 1800, back-formation from L. pl. *satellites* (cf. *stalactite*). As astron. term adopted (1611) by Kepler.

Or ask of yonder argent fields above,
Why Jove's satellites are less than Jove?
(*Essay on Man*, i. 42).

satiate. From L. *satiare*, from *satis*, enough. Has influenced *sate* (q.v.). Cf. *satiety*, F. *satiété*, L. *satietas*.

satin. F., archaic It. *setino* (sc. *panno*, cloth), from *seta*, silk, L. *saeta*, lit. bristle, hair, whence F. *soie*, silk, Ger. *seide*, etc. Hence *satinet*, F.

satire. F., L. *satira*, for *satura*, (poetic) medley, fem. of *satur*, full, as in *satura lanx*, full dish, hotch-potch, from *sat*, enough. Often wrongly associated with *satyr* (q.v.) and the G. satyric drama. For sense-development cf. *farce*.

satisfy. OF. *satisfier*, irreg. from *satisfacere* (whence F. *satisfaire*), lit. to make enough. Oldest sense of *satisfaction* (13 cent.) is performance of penance.

satrap. L., G. σατράπης, from OPers. *kshathra-pāvan-*, country protector. In Wyc. (*Dan.* iii. 3), where the orig. author has committed an anachronism by connecting a Pers. title with the Babylonian empire. Sense of domineering official appears in MedL. and all Rom. langs.

Satsuma ware. From name of province in island of Kiusiu, Japan.

saturate. From L. *saturare*, to satiate, its orig. E. sense (16 cent.), from *satur*, full, from *sat*, enough.

Saturday. AS. *Sætern(es)dæg*, half-transl. of L. *Saturni dies*, day of (the planet) Saturn (v.i.); cf. Du. *zaterdag*, LG. *saterdag* (for Ger. *samstag* see *sabbath*); also Gael. Ir. *dia Sathairn*, Welsh *dydd Sadwrn*. *Week-end* has now supplanted *Saturday-to-Monday*.

Saturn. L. *Saturnus*, Italic god of agriculture, perh. the sower (*severe*, *sat-*), later identified with G. Cronos, deposed by his son Zeus. Also planet, whence AS. *Saturnes steorra* and medieval alchem. name for lead (cf. *mercury*). Hence *Saturnalia*, L., neut. pl. of *Saturnalis*, feast of unrestrained merry-making in December; *Saturnian*, early L. metre, or in ref. to the "golden age" of Saturn; *saturnine*, MedL. *Saturninus*, born under the planet Saturn (cf. *jovial*, *mercurial*).

Mars iren, Mercurie quyk-silver we clepe,
Saturnus leed, and Juppiter is tyn (Chauc. G. 827).

satyr. F. *satyre*, L., G. σάτυρος, silvan god. Often confused with *satire* (v.i.). With *satyriasis*, priapism, cf. *nymphomania*.

The savage Satyre himselfe, whose cynicall censure is more severe than need (Greene, 1593).

sauce. F., L. *salsa*, fem. of *salsus*, salted; cf. It. Sp. *salsa*. With fig. *saucy*, *saucebox*, cf. *piquant*, *spicy*, etc. *Saucer* (14 cent.), F. *saucière*, vessel for sauce, acquired current sense in 18 cent., when tea-drinking became gen.

saucy to perte or homlye: malapert (Palsg.).

sauerkraut. From 17 cent. Ger., sour herb. Hence F. *choucroute*, made to conform with *chou*, cabbage, cole.

saumur. Wine. From *Saumur* (Maine-et-Loire).

saunter. From c. 1660, to roam, loiter, an earlier and rare *saunter*, to muse, hesitate, being perh. a different word. Etymologists of 17 cent. agree in deriving it from F. *sainte-terre*, Holy Land (v.i.). Although this etym. is now derided, it may be partly true. I suggest as origin Sp. *santero*, "sometimes an hermit, sometimes one that lives with the hermit, and goes about questing for him and his chappel" (Stevens). This word was also used of a "shrine-crawler" in gen. We may compare It. *romigare*, "to roame, to roave or goe up and downe solitarie and alone as an hermite" (Flor.), from *romito*, "a hermit" (*ib.*), whence *romito del sacco*, "a begging hermite" (*ib.*). This *romito* is from L. *eremita* (see *hermit*).

Our late visionaries and idle santerers to a pretended new Jerusalem (*NED.* 1688).

saurian. From G. σαῦρος, lizard.

sausage. ME. *sausige*, ONF. *saussiche* (F. *saucisse*), Late L. *salsicia*, from *salsus*, salted; cf. It. *salsiccia*, Sp. *salchicha*.

Another view is that the It. word is the original and represents a compd. of *sal*, salt, and It. *ciccia*, dried meat, VL. **isicium*, for *insicium*, from *insecare*, to cut.

sauté [*cook.*]. F., p.p. of *sauter*, to leap, L. *saltare*.

sauterne. Wine. From *Sauterne* (Gironde).

sauve-qui-peut. F., save (himself) who can.

savage. F. *sauvage* (OF. *salvage*), L. *silvaticus*, from *silva*, wood; cf. It. *selvaggio*, Sp. *salvaje*. In E. at first parallel with *wild*, from which it is now differentiated in stronger senses.

Savage trees, as okes, chestnuts, cypresse
(*NED.* 1580);

savannah [*geog.*]. Obs. Sp. *zavana* (*sabana*), said (16 cent.) to be Carib.

savant. F., pres. part. (obs.) of *savoir*, to know, VL. **sapēre*, for *sapere*.

savate. Kick, in F. form of boxing, orig. old shoe; cf. It. *ciabatta*, Sp. *zapata*, MedL. *sabbatum*; ? from Turk. *shabata*, galosh; cf. *sabot*. Hence F. *savetier*, Prov. *sabatier*, shoemaker.

save¹. Verb. F. *sauver*, L. *salvare*, from *salvus*, safe, cogn. with *salus*, health. Earliest in rel. sense, *Saviour* replacing AS. *hǣlend*, healer; cf. It. *salvatore*, Sp. *salvador*, L. *salvator*, used in Church L. to render G. σωτήρ. To *save one's face* (late 19 cent.) was orig. Anglo-Chin., after Chin. *tiu lien*, to lose face, and similar metaphors. Current sense of to *save appearances* is quite altered; it was orig. used, after G. σώζειν τὰ φαινόμενα, of an hypothesis adequately explaining observed facts. *God save the king* is after OF.

"Dex saut," fait il, "le roi Artus"
(*Tristan*, 12 cent.).

When they come to model Heaven
And calculate the stars; how they will wield
The mighty frame; how build, unbuild, contrive
To save appearances (*Par. L.* viii. 80).

The purely saving-face proposal that commissioners should be appointed (*Westm. Gaz.* Feb. 7, 1918).

save². Quasi-prep. For earlier *safe*, *sauf*, used, like F. *sauf*, *sauve*, in constructions like the L. abl. absolute, e.g. *sauf l'honneur* = *salvo honore*. But it also represents the p.p., as in AF. *sauvé et excepté*, with ending lost as in *costive*, *trove*, etc. In ME. it is followed both by nom., e.g. *save I* (Chauc.), and acc., the latter construction being partly due to its being felt as imper. of verb. For *saving* as prep. cf. *excepting*, *providing*. *Saving clause*, from the verb, contains the same idea.

saveloy. Mod. corrupt. (first in *Pickwick*) of obs. *cervelas*, *cervelat*, F. *cervelas*, It. *cervellata*, from *cervello*, brain, L. *cerebellum*. Said to have been made orig. of pigs' brains.

cervellato: a kind of dry sausage (Flor.).

savey, savvy. To know; gumption. Orig. negro or pidgin after Sp. *sabe usted*, you know. Cf. *compree*.

savin-e. Shrub. OF. *savine* (replaced by *sabine*), L. *Sabina* (sc. *herba*), Sabine herb; cf. It. *savina*, Sp. *sabina*, Ger. *sabenbaum*, Du. *zevenboom*; also AS. *safene*.

savoir faire. F., to know (how) to do; cf. *savoir vivre*, to know (how) to live.

savory. ME. *saverey*, Late AS. *sætherie*, from very early OF., L. *satureia*. For -*th*- altered to -*v*- cf. *gyve* and numerous examples in dial. and childish speech, e.g. *wiv*, with. But OF. also had *savoreie*, perh. influenced by *saveur*, savour, the correct OF. form being *sarrie*, whence ModF. dim. *sarriette*.

savour. F. *saveur*, L. *sapor-em*, from *sapere*, to taste, know.

savoy. Cabbage from *Savoy* (16 cent.). Cf. *Brussels sprouts*, etc. Also *Savoy cake* (*biscuit*). Cf. *Madeira cake*.

savvy. See *savey*.

saw¹. Tool. AS. *saga*. Com. Teut.; cf. Du. *zaag*, Ger. *säge*, ON. *sög*; cogn. with L. *secare*, to cut.

I thought everybody know'd as a sawbones was a surgeon (*Pickwick*, ch. xxx.).

saw² [*archaic*]. Saying. AS. *sagu*, cogn. with *say¹*; cf. obs. Du. *zage*, Ger. *sage*, ON. *saga* (q.v.). Now chiefly after *As You Like It*, ii. 7.

sawder [*slang*]. Chiefly in *soft sawder* (*Sam Slick*), app. from obs. form of *solder*. Being first recorded in Lover, the metaphor may be orig. Ir. (cf. *blarney*).

Sawney. Archaic nickname for Scotsman; cf. *Sandy*. Current sense of simpleton must be due to antiphrasis, ? or confused with *zany*. "Sawney the Scot, or the Taming of a Shrew," was an adaptation of Shaks. seen by Pepys (Apr. 9, 1667). Couplet below may have suggested the famous definition of oats in Johns.

Therefore, since Sawny does like Dobbin feed,
Why should we wonder at their equal speed?
(T. Brown).

saxe. Porcelain, etc. F., Saxony.

saxhorn. Invented by *C. J. Sax* (†1865), a Belgian.

saxifrage. F., L. *saxifraga* (sc. *herba*), stone-breaker, from *saxum*, rock, *frangere*, to break, explained by Pliny as named from its med. use against stone in the bladder; for formation cf. *feverfew*. But, as the *NED.* remarks, *saxum* is not *calculus*, and the plant may rather have been named from its action on rocks. Cf. Ger. *steinbrech*, "the herb stone-break, saxifrage, or parsley pert" (Ludw.).

Saxon. F., L. *Saxo-n-* (cf. G. Σάξονες), from WGer. name of tribe, AS. *Seaxan*, OHG. *Sahsūn*, trad. connected with AS. *seax*, axe, knife (cf. *Frank*, *Lombard*). See also *Anglo-Saxon*, for which it was used by early etymologists. In mod. philology *Old Saxon*, the language of the *Heliand* (Saviour), a Biblical poem composed in 9 cent., is equivalent to Old Low German, and is of great value for comparative purposes as containing some words not recorded in AS. or Du. See also *Sassenach*. *Saxon*, Englishman, as opposed to Celt, is mod. (first in Burns), sense of base oppressor (chiefly Ir.) being due to its repeated use in contrast with *Gael* in the *Lady of the Lake*.

The filthy compound of burglary and murder, and sodomy, bigamy and infidelity, child-murder, divorce and sexual promiscuity that covers the standing pool of Saxon life
(Irish Bishop, Dec. 1919).

saxophone, saxtuba. Inventions of son of *C. J. Sax* (see *saxhorn*).

say¹. Verb. AS. *secgan*. Com. Teut.; cf. Du. *zeggen*, Ger. *sagen*, ON. *segja*. With to *have a say* cf. to *be in the know*. For an early example of parenthetic *I say* see *Ps.* cxxx. 6.

say² [*archaic*]. Fabric. F. *saie*, L. *saga*, pl. of *sagum*, mil. cloak, G. σάγος; cf. It. *saja*, Sp. *saya*. In E. prob. confused with OF. *seie* (*soie*), silk, for which see *satin*. Colchester was once famous for "bays and says" (see *baize*).

sayyid, seyd. Title of Mohammedan claiming descent from elder grandson of Prophet. Cf. *Cid*.

sbirro. It., police-officer. Earlier also *birro*, "a serjeant, a catchpoale, a paritor" (Flor.), from his red cloak (see *biretta*).

sc. Abbrev. of *scilicet* (q.v.).

sc-. AS. *sc-* becomes regularly *sh-*, so that mod. words in *sc-* are almost all of foreign (often Scand.) origin.

scab. Orig. disease, itch. ON. **skabbr* (cf.

Sw. *skabb,* earlier *skabber),* cogn. with AS. *sceabb* (whence *shabby).* Or perh. from AS. with pronunc. influenced by cogn. L. *scabies* (see *scabious),* which it rendered in Bibl. lang. Sense of blackleg, non-unionist, is US.

scabbard. ME. also *scauberc, scaberge,* etc., AF. *escaubert,* OF. *escalberc, exalberge,* by dissim. for **escarberc,* from OHG. *scār,* blade, share[1], *bergan,* to hide. Cf. *hauberk,* the final of which is similarly changed in ModF. *haubert* (so also *échafaud,* scaffold). For dissim. of *-r-* in other words derived from *bergan* cf. *belfry, harbinger,* and F. *héberger* (OF. *herberger), auberge.* Cf. also archaic F. *échaugette,* sentry-box, OF. *escalgaite, escargaite,* OHG. *scārwaht,* company watch. The *NED.* is mistaken in thinking that the word is not recorded in OF. (see *Romania,* 1909, p. 391). Also *escarberge* is found in a secondary sense.

Not the courage that throws away the scabbard, much less that which burns its ships (Mahan).

scabious. F. *scabieuse,* MedL. *scabiosa* (sc. *herba),* supposed to be effective against skin disease, *scabies,* from *scabere,* to scratch.

scabrous. F. *scabreux,* Late L. *scabrosus,* from *scaber, scabr-,* rough, cogn. with above. Mod. sense of risqué is after F.

scad. Horse-mackerel. Dial. (Corn.) for *shad.*

scaffold. ONF. *escafaut* (F. *échafaud),* earliest OF. *escadafaut* (cf. Prov. *escadafalc),* with *es-* prefixed to OF. *chafault, cadefaut* (cf. Prov. *cadafalc),* corresponding to It. *catafalco,* catafalque, VL. **catafalcum,* whence also various forms in Rom. langs., and also Du. *schavot,* Ger. *schaffot.* Ult. source obscure, perh. G. κατά and L. *fala, phala,* wooden tower, gallery. Orig. used in F. & E. of any raised platform, esp. for drama, execution associations dating from 16 cent.

Somtyme to shewe his lightnesse and maistrye He pleyeth Herodes, on a scaffold hye
(Chauc. A. 3384).

Tu n'aprendras de moy comment jouer il fault Les miseres des Roys dessus un eschafault
(Joachim du Bellay).

scagliola. Plaster-work. It. *scagliuola,* dim. of *scaglia,* scale[2], chip of marble.

scalade [*hist.*]. See *escalade.*

scald[1]. With hot water. ONF. *escalder* (*échauder),* Late L. *excaldare,* to wash in hot water, from *calidus,* hot, whence F. *chaud.*

scald[2]. Scabby; chiefly in *scald-head.* For *scalled.* See *scall* and cf. *bald.*

scald[3]. Poet. See *skald.*

scale[1]. Of balance. ON. *skāl,* bowl; cf. AS. *scealu,* cup, shell (see *shale),* Du. *schaal,* Ger. *schale* (OHG. *scala);* also OF. *escale* (*écale),* cup, husk (v.i.), of Teut. origin and one source of the E. word. Cogn. with *scale*[2]. *Balance* likewise goes back to a dish, bowl, L. *lanx,* "a dish, a potenger, a ballance" (Coop.). See also *shell.* To *throw the sword into the scale* is from the story of Brennus, the Gaulish chief, when the Romans were weighing the ransom of the Capitol (4 cent. B.C.).

scale[2]. Of fish, etc. OF. *escale* (*écale),* husk, chip, OHG. *scala* (v.s.). ModF. has, in gen. sense of scale[2], *écaille,* OF. *escaille.* In some med. uses confused with *scall.* Hence also *scaleboard,* for bonnet-boxes.

And anon ther felden from his yghen as scalis [*Vulg.* squamae, G. λεπίδες] (Wyc. *Acts,* ix. 18).

scale[3]. Measure, graduation. It. or L. *scala,* ladder, cogn. with *scandere,* to climb. Cf. F. *échelle,* ladder, scale (OF. *eschiele),* Sp. *escala.* With verb to *scale,* OF. *escaller,* It. *scalare* or Sp. *escalar,* cf. *escalade.*

Next the forseide cercle of the A. b. c., under the cros-lyne, is marked the skale, in maner of 2 squyres or elles in manere of laddres (Chauc. *Astrolabe).*

scalene [*math.*]. Late L., G. σκαληνός, uneven, etc.

scall [*dial.*]. Skin-disease (*Lev.* xiii. 30). ? ON. *skalle,* (naturally) bald head, whence Sw. *skalle,* skull; cogn. with *scale*[1, 2], *shell.* See *scald*[2].

scallawag. See *scallywag.*

scallion [*archaic*]. ONF. *escalogne,* OF. *eschaloigne,* VL. **escalonia,* for *Ascalonia* (sc. *caepa,* onion), from *Askalon,* Palestine; cf. It. *scalogno,* Sp. *escalona.* See *shallot.*

scallop, scollop. OF. *escalope,* shell (in ModF. only in cook. sense), cogn. with *scale*[1, 2], but with unexplained suffix. Cf. Du. *schelp,* shell. Esp. cockle-shell worn by pilgrim as sign that he had been to the shrine of St James of Compostella. Ornamental sense from resemblance to undulating edge of shell.

S. Jacobs schelpe: S. James his shell (Hexham).

scallywag. Orig. US., loafer, also applied to undersized cattle, prob. the orig. sense. ? From *scall.*

scalp. Orig. skull, cranium (*Ps.* vii. 17 in *Early Eng. Psalter,* 13 cent.). Later sense has developed from Bibl. *hairy scalp* (Coverd.) in *Ps.* lxviii. 21. Contr. of *scallop*, which, in 14 cent., was used of shell-shaped vessel. Cf. Ger. *hirnschale*, brain pan, from *schale*, shell, scale. To *scalp* is 17 cent. For fig. use cf. to *be on the war-path, happy hunting-grounds*, to *bury the hatchet*, etc.

scalpel. L. *scalpellum*, dim. of *scalprum*, from *scalpere*, to cut.

scammony. Drug. L., G. σκαμμωνία.

scamp¹. Noun. Orig. cant for rogue, highwayman (Grose). From obs. *scamp*, to run wild, go on the highway, OF. *escamper*, *eschamper*, to decamp. See *scamper*. For formation of noun from verb cf. *tramp*.

scamp². Verb. Of recent adoption from dial. ? From ON. *skemma*, to shorten, whence also *skimp*, *scant*.

scamper. Frequent. of obs. *scamp* (see *scamp¹*). The latter is recorded for 16 cent. in *scampant*, used in imit. of *rampant* in a rogue's burlesque coat of arms. Cf. also obs. Du. *schampen*, "to escape or flie, to be gone" (Hexham), from OF.

scan. Earlier also *scand*, L. *scandere*, to climb, also to analyse verse, the oldest sense in E. (14 cent.). Current sense, reached via that of examining, criticizing, is late (18 cent.).

scandal. ME. *scandle* (*esclandre*), ONF. *escandle* (*esclandre*), Church L. *scandalum*, G. σκάνδαλον, cause of stumbling, supposed to have meant orig. the spring of a trap and to be cogn. with L. *scandere*, to climb. Mod. form is due to L. *scandalum* and learned F. *scandale*, readopted in 16 cent., whence also Ger. *skandal*, uproar, Du. *schandaal*. See also *slander*. In *Gal.* v. 11, where *AV.* has *offence*, *RV.* *stumbling-block*, *Rhemish V.* has *scandal*. *Scandalum magnatum* (leg.), slander of magnates, is described by *NED.* as obs. exc. hist., but I remember its use in the trial of an excited taxpayer who audibly cursed in church during the prayer for the Queen and the Royal Family.

scandaroon. Carrier pigeon. From *Scanderoon*, *Iskanderŭn*, seaport in Syria, one of the many places named from *Alexander*. Due to news of vessels being transmitted to Aleppo by pigeon-post.

"What news from Scandaroon and Aleppo?" says the Turkey merchant (T. Brown, c. 1700).

This [Aleppo] is the native country of the carrier-pigeon, formerly used by the Europeans for conveying expeditiously the news of a ship's arrival at Scanderoon. The pigeon thus employed was one that had left young ones at Aleppo
              (Russel, *Travels to Aleppo*).

Scandinavian. From Late L. *Scandinavia*, for *Scadinavia*; from a Teut. compd. represented by AS. *Scedenig*, ON. *Skāney*, southern extremity of Sweden. Second element means island (cf. *ait*, *Jersey*, etc.) and is ult. cogn. with L. *aqua*. In linguistics used to include ON., Norw., Dan., Sw., Faroese.

scanmag [*slang*]. *Scandalum magnatum*. See *scandal*.

scansorial [*ornith.*]. From L. *scansorius*, from *scandere*, *scans-*, to climb.

scant. ON. *skamt*, neut. of *skammr*, short; cogn. with OHG. *scam*. See *scamp²*, *skimp*, and cf. *thwart¹*. As naut. verb very common in ref. to wind "shortening" (Hakl.).

scantling. Perversion of obs. *scantillon*, ONF. *escantillon* (*échantillon*), pattern, sample, dim., with prefixed *es-*, from OF. *chant*, *chantel* (*chanteau*), cantle (q.v.). In some senses coloured by mistaken association with *scant*.

scape¹. Aphet. for *escape*, esp. in *hairbreadth scape* (*Oth.* i. 3). Hence *scapegoat*, coined by Tynd. (*Lev.* xvi.) to render *Vulg. caper emissarius* (cf. F. *bouc émissaire*), which is supposed to be a mistransl. of Heb. *Azazel* (*RV.*), perh. a proper name. *Scapegrace*, one who escapes Divine grace, appears to have been coined after earlier *scapethrift* and *wantgrace*. It is first recorded c. 1800, but is prob. older in dial.

scape². Shaft of column, stalk. L. *scapus*, G. σκᾶπος, cogn. with *shaft*.

scape³. Back-formation from *landscape*, used for forming new compds. (*seascape*, *cloud-scape*) and nonce-words (see *earth*).

scaphoid. Shape of boat, G. σκάφη.

scapular. Orig. short cloak worn by monks (of St Benedict) when at work. MedL. *scapulare*, from *scapula*, shoulder, only in pl. in L. Cf. *scapulary*, F. *scapulaire*.

scar¹. Of wound. Obs. *scar*, cleft, incision, for *scarth*, dial. for cleft, ON. *skarth*, cleft, cogn. with *score*. Influenced by obs. *escar*, *eschar*, OF. *escare* (archaic F. *eschare*), scab resulting from burn, L., G. ἐσχάρα, hearth.

escara vel eschara: ignis, focus; also a crust that is made on a wound by a searing iron; an escar (Litt.).

scar², scaur. Rock. ON. *sker*, skerry, cogn. with *shear*.

scarab. From F. *scarabée*, L. *scarabaeus*, cogn. with G. κάραβος, beetle, crab. Obs. exc. in ref. to Egypt. gems.

scaramouch. F. *Scaramouche*, It. *Scaramuccia*, lit. skirmish (q.v.), one of the stock characters of the It. pantomime (cf. *harlequin, pantaloon*). He was represented as a cowardly braggart dressed in black, in derision of the Spanish don. The name became popular, in its It. form, after visit of It. players to London (1673), and *Scaramouch* also appears in the orig. dialogue of the Punch and Judy show.

Scarborough warning [*archaic*]. Short notice. Cf. *Jeddart justice, Lydford law*.

scarce. ONF. *escars* (archaic F. *échars*), VL. **excarpsus*, from **excarpere*, to pluck out, select. Cf. It. *scarso*, "scarse, hard, covetous, sparing, miserable, scant" (Flor.); also MedL. *scarpsus, scarsus*. To *make oneself scarce* is US.

scare. Noun. ME. *skerre*, ON. *skirra*, from *skiarr*, shy, timid, whence Sc. adj. *scaur* (Burns). From the noun, very common in late 19 cent. journalese, is formed *scaremonger*, freely applied up to July 1914 to the late Lord Roberts.

scarf[1]. Article of dress. ONF. *escarpe* (*écharpe*), var. of OF. *escrepe*, orig. purse hanging from neck, of Teut. origin and cogn. with *scrip*[1]. This is the received etym., but cf. AS. *sceorp*, dress, ornament. For final consonant cf. *scarf*, var. of *scarp*. Ger. *schärpe*, LG. *scherfe*, are from F.

eine scharpe, scharfe oder scherfe: a tippet (Ludw.).

scarf[2]. Joint of two timbers, orig. naut. Cf. synon. F. *écart*, corrupt. of *écarf*, from *écarver*, to scarf, OF. **escarver*; also Du. *scherf*, Sp. *escarba*. Sw. *skarfa*, Norw. Dan. *skarve* (verbs), have a more gen. sense.

scarf-skin. Cf. Du. *scherf*, shred, shard, cogn. with AS. *sceorfan*, to scrape, scarify.

scarify. F. *scarifier*, L. *scarificare*, for *scarifare*, G. σκαριφᾶσθαι, from σκάριφος, pencil, stilus.

scarious [*biol.*]. Of dry appearance. ModL. *scariosus*, of unknown origin.

scarlatina. It. *scarlattina*, fem. of *scarlattino*, dim. of *scarlatto*, scarlet.

scarlet. Orig. rich fabric, not necessarily red. OF. *escarlate* (*écarlate*); cf. It. *scarlatto*, Sp. *escarlata*; also Du. *scharlaken*, Ger. *scharlach* (MHG. *scharlat*), ON. *skarlat*. All ult. from Pers. *saqualāt, siqualāt*, whence also obs. *ciclatoun*. The Pers. word is Arab.

siqlāt, and this is prob. from G. κυκλάς, κυκλάδ-, from κύκλος, circle (cf. *cloak*), whence also the *Cyclades*. *Scarlet and green*, very common in ME. descriptions of gorgeous apparel, is prob. for *scarlet in grain*. For *Scarlet Woman* see *Rev.* xvii. 1–5.

His robe was of syklatoun (Chauc. B. 1924).

scarp [*fort.*]. It. *scarpa*, whence also F. *escarpe*, escarp (q.v.). Often *scarf* in 16 cent.

scart [*Sc.*]. Cormorant, shag. Altered from *scarf*, ON. *scarfr*.

scarus. Fish. L., G. σκάρος, from σκαίρω, I leap.

scat [*hist.*]. Tribute. ON. *skattr*. Com. Teut.; cf. AS. *sceatt*, Du. *schat*, Ger. *schatz*, treasure, Goth. *skatts*, piece of money.

scathe. ON. *skatha* (impers.). Com. Teut.; cf. AS. *scathian*, Du. Ger. *schaden*, Goth. *skathjan*; cogn. with G. ἀσκηθής, unscathed. Replaced by *harm, hurt*, in gen. use, sense of blasting originating from Milton's *scathed oaks* (*Par. L.* i. 613).

scatology. Obscene literature. Neol., from G. σκῶρ, σκατ-, dung.

scatter. From 12 cent. Supposed to be ident. with *shatter*, and perh. ult. with G. σκεδαννύναι. Archaic *scattergood*, spendthrift, quoted by *NED.* for 1577, was already an established surname in 13 cent.

scaur. See *scar*[2].

scavenger. For ME. *scavager* (cf. *messenger*), from *scavage*, London toll levied on foreign merchants, AF. *scawage*, from ONF. *escauwer*, to inspect, of Du. origin and cogn. with E. *shew, show*. Orig. a kind of customs inspector, who was also entrusted with the care of the streets. Current sense appears in AF. much earlier than in records of the E. word, e.g. in the *Serement de Scawageours* (*Liber Albus*). The *Scavenger's daughter*, instrument of torture, is jocular for *Skeffington's gyves, irons*, its inventor having been Lieutenant of the Tower temp. Hen. VIII.

scazon [*metr.*]. Modified iambic trimeter. Pres. part. of G. σκάζειν, to limp.

scenario. It., from *scena*, scene (q.v.). Cf. *scenery*, formerly *scenary* (Johns.).

scene. F. *scène*, L. *scena*, G. σκηνή, booth, stage. All senses are orig. theat., e.g. to *make a scene*, F. *faire une scène à quelqu'un*.

scent. Artificial spelling of ME. *sent*, orig. hunting term, from F. *sentir*, to smell, whence many fig. uses. Sense of (fragrant) perfume is developed late (18 cent.). But the noun is not found in OF. and there has evidently been strong contact with archaic F. *sente*, path, track, L. *semita*, as may be seen by a comparison of passages below.

Ayant recouvré la sente
Par où le lièvre s'absente
       (Gauchet, *Plaisir des Champs*, 1583).
When they have well beaten and founde the tracke or sent of the harte (*NED.* 1576).

sceptic. F., L. *scepticus*, from G. σκέπτεσθαι, to investigate, cogn. with σκοπεῖν, to look. Applied to disciples of Pyrrho (4 cent. B.C.).

sceptre. F., L., G. σκῆπτρον, staff, sceptre, cogn. with σκήπτεσθαι, to lean upon.

schako. See *shako*.

schanse [*hist.*]. Current during SAfr. war. Du., see *sconce²*.

schedule. Altered, on MedL. *schedula*, from ME. *sedule*, F. *cédule*, L. *scedula*, dim. of *sceda*, *scheda*, "a leafe of paper, a scrowe, a shedule" (Coop.). In all Rom. langs.; also Du. *cedel*, *ceel*, Ger. *zettel*, "a note, cedule, schedule" (Ludw.). Current sense springs from that of explanatory label attached to large document (cf. *syllabus*).

scheme. MedL. *schema*, diagram, arrangement, G. σχῆμα, form, figure. Orig. rhet. & scient., current sense of (nefarious) design being early 18 cent.

schenectady [*golf*]. Putter, now barred. From *Schenectady*, New York State.

scherzando [*mus.*]. It., from Ger. *scherz*, sport, jest.

schiedam. Gin. From *Schiedam*, Holland.

schipperke. Small dog. Du. dial., lit. little skipper. Said to be bred esp. by Du. boatmen.

schism. F. *schisme*, L., G. σχίσμα, cleft, rent, from σχίζειν, to split, used in Church L. of separation of any body of Christians from the Church.

I recollected that in most schism shops the sermon is looked upon as the main thing (So⋅they).

schist [*geol.*]. F. *schiste*, L., G. σχιστός (sc. λίθος), split stone (v.s.).

schloss. Ger., castle, orig. lock. See *slot²*.

schnaps. Ger., LG. *snaps*, from *snappen*, to snap, swallow. Cf. *nip*.

schnorrer. Jewish beggar. Yiddish, from Ger. *schnurren*, to beg, orig. with the *schnurrpfeife*, instrument played by vagrant musician; of imit. origin.

scholar, scholiast. See *school*. *Scholarship* in sense of free education is 16 cent.

school¹. Place of learning. ME. *scole*, OF.

escole (*école*), L. *schola*, G. σχολή, leisure, a sense passing into that of otiose discussion, place for holding such. In most Europ. langs., with the range of senses which appears in *final honours school*, *ragged school*; cf. double sense of *scholar*. Replaced AS. *lārhūs*, lore-house.

The schoolmaster is abroad (Brougham, 1828).

school². Of whales. Du. *school*, crowd, etc. See *shoal²*.

Bristlings of water, which, if it were faire weather, would seeme a skull of fish (Hakl.).

schooner. Earlier *scooner*, *skooner*, type of vessel first built (c. 1713) at Gloucester (Massachusetts), and named there prob. from verb to *scon*, send over the water, still in Sc. use. For the idea cf. *sloop*, perh. cogn. with *slip*, F. *goélette*, schooner, orig. kind of sea-gull (skimming the water), and contemporary (Apr. 1918) *scooter*. The "anecdote" usu. given dates from 1790 and is prob. apocryphal (cf. *chouse*).

schorl [*min.*]. Tourmaline. Ger. *schörl*, earlier *schürl*, *schrull*, etc., of obscure origin.

schottische. Ger., Scotch (sc. dance). Perh. introduced in Paris, which would account for pronunc.

schuyt [*naut.*]. Du. *schuit*, flat bottomed river-boat. Also found in E. as *scout*, *scoot*, *shout*; cf. ON. *skūta*.

sciamachy. G. σκιαμαχία, fight with shadows, G. σκιά. Cf. *sciagraphy* (also *skia-*).

Skiagrams of the elbow-joints and knee-joints were produced (*Daily Chron.* June 27, 1919).

sciatica. MedL. (sc. *passio*), fem. of MedL. *sciaticus*, corrupt. of L., G. ἰσχιαδικός, is-chiatic (q.v.).

He hath hadde a cyetica that hath letted hym a gret while to ride (*Paston Let.* i. 50).

science. F., L. *scientia*, from *scire*, to know, ult. cogn. with *scindere*, to cut, divide. Distinction from *art* is in Trevisa (1387). The *dismal science*, economics, is from Carlyle.

scilicet. L., to wit, for *scire licet*, it is permitted to know. Cf. *videlicet*.

scilla. Plant. L., G. σκίλλα.

scimitar. Cf. F. *cimeterre*, It. *scimitarra*, Sp. *cimitarra*, all with many early vars. Described in 15 cent. as Turkish sword, but no Oriental etymon has been found, unless we accept Pers. *shamshīr*. My own conjecture is that it is no more Oriental than *assagai* is Zulu, but simply E. *smiter*, which was used for *scimitar* in 16–17 cents.

(also *smeeter* in Cotg.) and may easily have been a sailors' word much earlier. If borrowed by the Rom. langs. it would normally become *semiter*, *cimeter*; cf. F. *semaque*, (fishing-)smack, *senau*, snow². Cf. Ger. *hauer*, *haudegen*, lit. hewer, "a falchion, simitar, sable or sabre" (Ludw.). Adrian Junius equates OF. *semitaire* with Du. *half-houwer*, evidently misled by the *semi-*.

> In an instant whipt of all their heads with their slicing shamsheers or semiters
> (Herbert's *Trav.* 1634).

scintillate. From L. *scintillare*, from *scintilla*, spark.

scio-. See *sciamachy*.

sciolist. Smatterer. From Late L. *sciolus*, dim. of *scius*, from *scire*, to know.

scion. F., shoot, esp. for grafting, OF. *cion*, *chion*, dim. of some lost word of Teut. origin, ult. cogn. with synon. AS. *cīth*. For fig. sense cf. *imp*, *offspring*, Ger. *sprössling*, and fig. use of *stock*, with which *scion* is often associated.

scire facias [*leg.*]. L., make (him) to know, characteristic words of writ. Cf. *venire facias*.

scirrhous [*med.*]. F. *scirrheux*, from G. σκίρρος, hard tumour, from σκιρός, hard.

scission. F., L. *scissio-n-*, from *scindere*, *sciss-*, to cut, cogn. with G. σχίζειν, Ger. *scheiden*.

scissors. ME. *cisours*, *sysowres*, archaic F. *cisoires*, large shears (for F. *ciseaux*, scissors, see *chisel*), from Late L. *cisorium*, from *-cidere*, *-ciss*, to cut, form taken in compds. by L. *caedere*. Since 16 cent. confused with L. *scissor*, cutter, tailor, from *scindere*, *sciss-*, to cut. See quot. s.v. *tweezers*.

sciurine [*biol.*]. Of the squirrel (q.v.).

sclaff [*golf*]. Sc., to strike with flat surface. Imit., cf. *slap*.

Sclavonic. See *Slav*.

sclerosis [*med.*]. G., from σκληρός, hard.

scoff¹. Derision. First (c. 1300) as noun. Cf. synon. ON. *skop*, *skaup*, OHG. *scoph*, OFris. *schof*. *NED.* suggests also connection with AS. *scop*, poet (cf. *scold*).

scoff² [*slang*]. To eat, "grub." SAfrDu., for Du. *schoft*, cogn. with *schuiven*, to shove, in ref. to spell of work. *Scaff* was used earlier in same sense in Sc. Cf. also naut. Norw. *skaffe*, from Du.

> *schoft*, *eetmael*: eating-time for labourers, or workmen foure times in a day (Hexham).

When a waggon stops at the door, he [the Boer] concludes of course that the passengers want to scoff (to eat) (Lady Barnard's *SAfr. Journ.* 1798).

scold. First (13 cent.) as noun. App. ON. *skáld*, poet, skald. "The sense-development postulated is strange, but the probability of the sense 'lampooner' as an intermediate stage seems to be indicated by the fact that the derivative *skáldskapr*, lit. skaldship, poetry, has in the Icel. lawbooks the specific sense of libel in verse" (*NED.*). Cf. Prov. *tenzone* and early Sc. *flyting*. Synon. Du. *schelden*, Ger. *schelten* are thus unrelated.

scollop. See *scallop*.

scolopendra. Centipede, millipede. L., G. σκολόπενδρα.

sconce¹. Candlestick-bracket, orig. screened lantern. OF. *esconse*, monastic L. *sconsa*, for *absconsa*, from *abscondere*, to hide away.

sconce² [*hist.*]. Small fort (*Hen. V*, iii. 6). Earlier *scans*, *scance* (*Cal. State Papers*, 1585), Du. *schans* or Ger. *schanze*, "a sconce, a strong hold, a fort, a fence" (Ludw.). Orig. sense of Ger. word was bundle of brushwood, rough basket for holding earth or stones (cf. *fascine*, *gabion*). The word is esp. common in connection with the Thirty Years War, and the above etym. is already in Minsh. (1617).

sconce³ [*archaic*]. Head. ? Jocular use of *sconce¹*. Hence, according to Minsh. (earliest authority for the word), to *sconce*, fine (Oxf.), "to set up so much in the butterie booke upon his head."

scone, scon. Orig. Sc. Shortened from obs. Du. *schoonbrot*, fine bread, cogn. with Ger. *schön*, fine. *Schonrogge*, fine rye, was similarly used in LG. of a three-cornered cake of fine rye-flour.

scoop. App. two separate words are here combined. *Scoop* for water (orig. naut.) is of LG. origin, cogn. with Du. *schoep*, baler, bucket, and Ger. *schöpfen*, to draw water; *scoop*, shovel (also orig. naut.), is Du. *schop*, shovel, cogn. with *shove* and with dial. Ger. *schüppe*, "a scoop, a wooden shovel" (Ludw.). To the first group belongs also OF. *escope* (*écope*), scoop for liquids, which may be partly responsible for the E. word. The journalistic *scoop* is US.

scoot. Current form is from US., but *scout* was used in 18 cent. naut. E. in same sense. Sw. *skjuta*, to shoot (intrans.). With

scooter, motor-boat, a coinage of the War, cf. *schooner*. Also *skoot* (q.v.).

Our scooters were busily employed [at Zeebrugge] (*Ev. News*, Apr 24, 1918).

scope. Orig. mark to shoot at, but current sense is earliest (16 cent.) in E. It. *scopo*, "a marke or but to shoote at, a scope, purpose, intent or roome" (Flor.), G. σκοπός, cogn. with σκοπεῖν, to look. For extended senses cf. *range*.

-scope. From G. σκοπεῖν, to look. Extended from *microscope, telescope* to many mod. inventions, e.g. *laryngoscope, periscope*, etc.

scorbutic. Cf. F. *scorbut*, scurvy, Du. *scheurbuik*, ? for earlier **scheur-bot*, lit. rend-bone, with second element assimilated to *buik*, belly; cf. archaic Du. *scheurmond*, scurvy of mouth, *scheurbeen*, scurvy of bones. Prob. a Du. sailors' word adopted by other Europ. langs., e.g. It. *scorbuto*, Ger. *scharbock*. But some authorities regard MedL. *scorbutus* as orig. form and derive it from Russ. *scrobot'*, scratching. As in the case of so many naut. words the origin is obscured by uncertainty of chronology and influence of folk-etym.

scorch. App. altered (by influence of OF. *escorcher*, now *écorcher*, to flay, Late L. *excorticare*, from *cortex, cortic-*, bark) from earlier *skorken, skorkle*, cogn. with ON. *skorpinn*, shrivelled. Chauc. (*Boeth.*) has *scorchith*, var. *scorklith*, for L. *torret*. Like *parch, singe*, used earlier also of effects of cold. Slang senses are late 19 cent.

Hogs grease healeth burns and scaldings, yea though one were scortched and sendged with snow (Holland's *Pliny*, xxviii. 9).

score. ON. *skor*, notch, tally, cogn. with *shear*. Oldest sense (11 cent.) is twenty, perh. from counting sheep, etc. orally and notching a stick at each twenty. Runs at cricket were formerly *notches* (*Pickwick*, ch. vii.) scored on a stick. So also *on the score* (account) *of*. With to *go off at score*, orig. of horses, cf. sporting use of *scratch*. For gen. sense-development cf. *tally* (q.v.).

Score it upon my taille [tally] (Chauc. B. 1605).

Our fore-fathers had no books but the score and the tally (2 *Hen. VI*, iv. 7).

scoria. L., G. σκωρία, refuse, from σκῶρ, dung.

scorn. Earlier (c. 1200) *scarn*, OF. *escarnir, eschernir*, of Teut. origin; cf. OHG. *skernōn*, obs. Du. *schernen*; also It. *schernire*, "to scorne, to flout" (Flor.), from Teut. Later uses perh. coloured by OF. *escorner* (*écorner*),

to disgrace, lit. unhorn, It. *scornare*, "to skorne, to mock, to deride" (Flor.).

Heaven has no rage like love to hatred turned, Nor hell a fury like a woman scorned (Congreve, *Mourning Bride*).

scorpion. F., L. *scorpio-n-*, from *scorpius*, G. σκορπίος. In all Rom. & Teut. langs. In mil. slang used of natives of Gibraltar, *rock-scorpions*.

scorzonera. Plant, "viper's grass." It., from *scorzone*, "a snake, an adder" (Flor.), ? from Late L. *curtio-n-*; because used as antidote against snake-bite.

scot. Contribution, as in to *pay one's scot, scot and lot*, and esp. *scot-free* (cf. AS. *scotfrēo*). ON. *skot*, cogn. with *shot* (q.v.). Some senses via synon. OF. *escot* (*écot*), from Teut.; cf. Ger. *schoss*, "scot, cess, tribute" (Ludw.), and *schossfrei*, scot-free, a compd. found also in Du. & Sw.

Scot. AS. *Scottas* (pl.), Irishmen, Late L. *Scotti, Scoti* (c. 400), of uncertain origin. Irish Gaels settled in N.W. of Great Britain in 6 cent., whence later meaning. *Scotch* is contr. of *Scottish*, and *Scots(man)*, as in *Scots Greys* (*Fusiliers*), of northern *Scottis*; cf. Sc. *Inglis*, English. The Sc. lang., called *Inglis* by Barbour, is a dial. of north. E. strongly saturated with ON. With *Scotch cousin*, distantly connected, cf. F. *oncle à la mode de Bretagne*. With *Scotch collops* cf. *Irish stew*. *Scotched collops* is an etymologizing perversion (*NED.*).

scotch. To cut. From c. 1400, and therefore hardly for obs. *scorch*, to slash, score (v.i.), which is recorded much later (16 cent.). The latter word is supposed to be an extension of *score* due to *scratch*. I suggest that *scotch* is AF. **escoche*, from F. *coche*, "a nock, notch, nick" (Cotg.). This would also explain *scotch*, a support, check (see *s-*). To *scotch the snake* (*Macb.* iii. 2) is Theobald's emendation of *scorch*.

Scotist. Adherent of *John Duns Scotus*. See *dunce*.

scoto-. From G. σκότος, darkness.

Scott, great. ? Euph. alteration of *Great God!*

scoundrel. From 16 cent., orig. in sense of mean fellow; very common in Cotg. App. from AF. *escoundre* (Rymer's *Foedera*), OF. *escondre*, common in sense of evasion, excuse, L. *ex* and *condere*, to hide. For formation cf. *wastrel*. But late appearance makes this origin dubious.

scour[1]. To cleanse. OF. *escurer* (*écurer*), "to scowre, fey, rinse, cleanse" (Cotg.),

? from *ex* and OF. *curer*, L. *curare*, to care
for; cf. MedL. *scurare*, Du. *schuren*, Ger.
scheuern (? from OF.). Some regard the
Teut. forms as the original; cf. synon. ON.
skora, AS. *scorian*, to reject. With fig.
sense of *offscouring* (1 Cor. iv. 13) cf. *scum*.

Richard Gwyn esquier have not eskoored his ditch
(*Stiffkey Papers*, 1614).

scour². To move swiftly. App. combined
from obs. noun *scour*, rush, onset, ON.
skūr, storm, shower, and ME. *discoure*,
discure, discover (see quot. s.v. *scout¹*), used
in ME., and in Shaks., of reconnoitring
(2 *Hen. IV*, iv. 1). For form cf. *curfew*, and
archaic *scomfit* for *discomfit*. See also
scurry. Influenced by *scour¹*. It may also
be partly from OF. *escourre*, to run out,
the normal E. form of which would have
been *scur*. Cf. F. *courir le pays*, to scour
the country.

The discurrouris saw thame cumande
(Barbour's *Bruce*).

Send twa skowrrouris to wesy [examine] weyll the
playne (Blind Harry's *Wallace*).

scourge. AF. *escorge*, from OF. *escorgiee*
(*écourgée*), from *ex* and OF. *corgiee*, scourge,
VL. **coriata*, from *corium*, hide; cf. OIt.
scuriada and E. *excoriate*. It is uncertain
whether the hide was orig. that of the
implement (cf. *cowhide*) or of the sufferer.

scouse [naut.]. For earlier *lobscouse* (see *lob*).
? *Scouse* from *couscous* (q.v.).

scout¹. Watchman, etc. Orig. act of spying,
reconnoitring. OF. *escoute* (*écoute*), from
écouter, to listen, VL. **excultare* for *aus-
cultare*. For sense-development cf. *vedette*,
sentry, *recruit*, etc. Hist. of E. word ranges
from *scout-watch* (14 cent.), sentinel, to the
boy scouts, organized (1908) by General
Baden Powell. For former use at cricket
see *Pickwick*, ch. vii. ? Hence also the
Oxf. *scout*, corresponding to the Camb.
gyp.

escoute: a spie, eave-dropper, prying companion;
also, a scout, scout-watch, or sentinell; the discoverer, or fore-runner, of an armie (Cotg.).

scout². To reject with scorn (from c. 1700),
? ident. with *scout*, to deride, taunt (*Temp.*
iii. 2). *NED.* derives from ON. *skūta*,
taunt, which, considering the late appearance of the word, is unlikely. It. *scuotere*,
to shake, L. *excutere*, satisfies both senses,
if we suppose that Shaks. *scout* had the
sense of F. *berner*, "to flout" (Cotg.), lit.
to toss in a blanket, *berne*, cloak (cf. MedL.

sagatio, tossing in a blanket, from *sagum*,
soldier's cloak). It. *scuotere* is used in sense
of to disregard, make light of (punishment).

scow. Flat-bottomed boat. Du. *schouw*,
earlier *schoude*, cogn. with LG. *schalde*,
punt-pole. *Scowbanker*, though used as
naut. form of abuse, is unconnected; it is
of Austral. origin, var. *skullbanker*, and
means loafer.

scowl. Of Scand. origin; cf. synon. Norw.
skule; ult. cogn. with AS. *sceolh*, ON.
skjālgr, oblique, used as in Ger. *scheel
ansehen*, to look askance, scowl at. See
also *skulk*.

scrabble. Du. *schrabbelen*, frequent. of *schrab-
ben*, to scrape, scratch. In sense associated with *scribble*.

scrag. Lean individual (whence *scraggy*), neck
of mutton. For earlier *crag*, in both senses,
the lean person perh. being likened to the
neck of mutton. See *craw*. Cf. to *scrag*,
throttle, orig. slang for to hang.

scramble. ? Altered, by influence of *scrabble*,
in sense of clawing, from earlier *scamble* in
same sense. *Scramble* and *scamble* are used
early (16 cent.) both of clambering and of
struggling for money.

fare alla grappa piu: to play at musse, to shuffle,
or skamble for (Flor.).

to scamble: certatim rapere (Litt.). *to scramble*:
certatim rapere (*ib.*).

The ragged bramble
With thousand scratches doth their skin be-
scramble (Sylv. *Handicrafts*).

scran [slang]. Broken victuals, "grub,"
? cogn. with *scrannel*. Hence Anglo-Ir.
bad scran to.

scrannel. Lean, meagre (*Lycidas*, 124). In
mod. use only as echo of Milton, ? coiner
of the word; cf. Norw. *skran*, lean, shrivelled,
ON. *skrælna*, to shrivel.

scrap¹. Fragment. ON. *skrap*, leavings at
table, cogn. with *scrape*. Hence *scrap of
paper*, used in E. by Herr von Bethmann-
Hollweg (Aug. 4, 1914).

In a world full of smouldering prejudices a scrap
of paper may start the bonfire
(Zangwill, *Children of Ghetto*, Bk ii, ch. ii, 1892)

We were determined, at any rate, that *this* treaty
should not be a scrap of paper
(D. Lloyd George, in H. of C., July 3, 1919).

scrap². Fight, orig. nefarious scheme (cant).
App. from *scrape*.

They are in great fear Sir Robt. Payton should
bring them into yᵉ scrappe (*NED.* 1679–80).

scrape. AS. *scrapian* or ON. *skrapa*, cogn. with Du. *schrapen*, Ger. *schröpfen*, earlier *schrepfen* (from LG.), and ult. with *sharp*. With to *scrape acquaintance*, "a low phrase" (Johns.), cf. obs. to *scratch acquaintance*. With *scrape* as accompaniment of bow cf. synon. Norw. *skrabud*, lit. scrape out. See also *scrap*[1, 2].

scratch. Combination of earlier *scrat* (still in dial.) and *cratch*; cf. Sw. *krata*, Ger. *kratzen*, Du. *krassen* (earlier *kratsen*), all from a Teut. root which appears in F. *gratter*, to scratch (grate²). For *scrat* see *s-* and cf. *scrag*. Hence to *scratch* (erase) a name, *scratch*, line, as starting point in racing or between two pugilists. The latter was earlier used of the crease at cricket, and to *come up to the scratch* may belong to any of these forms of sport.

Scratch, Old. The devil. Altered (cf. *scratch*) from earlier *Scrat*, ON. *skratte*, goblin, monster, used in ME. in sense of hermaphrodite. Cf. Ger. dial. *schrat*, *schretel*, wood-spirit, satyr.

scrawl[1]. To write badly. App. a new sense given to ME. *scrawl*, var. of *crawl*, by association with *scribble*, *scrabble*, *scroll*. See *s-*.

griffonner: to write fast, and ill; to scrible, to scrall it (Cotg.).

grouiller: to move, stirre, scrall (*ib.*).

scrawl[2] [*Linc.*]. Small crab (Tennyson, *Sailor Boy*). ? Cf. OF. *escrouelle*, "a little shrimp-resembling worme" (Cotg.), which is prob. cogn. with *scrawl*[1] and ult. with *crab*[1].

scream. Imit.; cf. *screech*, *shriek*, and Sw. *skräna*, to scream.

scree [*north. dial.*]. ON. *skritha*, land-slip, cogn. with AS. *scrīthan*, to glide, Ger. *schreiten*, to stride. Back-formation from pl. *scree(th)es* in which consonant is lost as in *clo(th)es*.

screech. Earlier *scritch*. Imit.; cf. *scream*, *shriek*; also ON. *skrækja*. Shaks. wrote *scritch-owl*.

screed. Northern var. of *shred*. Current sense springs from that of list on long strip. Perh. partly due to obs. *screet*, writing, list, Port. *scritto*.

screen. OF. *escren* (*écran*), OHG. *scerm* (*schirm*). Orig., in F. & E., of a fire-screen; cf. It. *schermo*, "a fence, a defence, a warde, a shelter" (Flor.), and see *skirmish*. For *screen*, sieve, cf. double sense of ME. *riddle*, sieve, curtain, the common idea being that of separation.

screever [*slang*]. Pavement artist. From East End *screeve*, to write, ? It. *scrivere*, L. *scribere*. Cf. *scriving-board* for plan of vessel (ship-building).

screw. OF. *escroue* (*écrou*, female screw, nut); cogn. with Du. *schroef* (earlier *schrūve*),. Ger. *schraube* (MHG. *schrūbe*), all supposed by some authorities to come from L. *scrofa*, sow, used fig. of mech. appliance. Cf. Sp. *puerca*, female screw, L. *porca*, sow, and It. dial. derivatives of *scrofa* in same sense. See also *porcelain*, *scroll*. The naut. *screw*, at first manual, is as old as 1788. To *put on the screw* is from torture (thumb-screws, etc.). To *screw up one's courage* is an echo of Shaks. (v.i.). Senses of inferior horse and salary are both 19 cent. slang of obscure origin (? for former cf. *rip*²). *Screwed*, drunk, is perh. a variation on "tight."

Screw your courage to the sticking place
                       (*Macb.* i. 7).

scribble. MedL. *scribillare*, from L. *scribere*, to write; cf. OHG. *scribilōn*, F. *écrivailler*. Orig. as stock formula in ending a letter.

Scribylld in the moste haste at my castel or manoir of Aucland, Jan. 27, 1489, Your own trewe luffer and frende, John Duresme (*Paston Let.* iii. 363).

scribe. F., L. *scriba*, from *scribere*, to write, orig. to scratch (cf. *write*). Earliest in Bibl. use, *Vulg. scriba* rendering G. γραμματεύς, Heb. *sōphēr*, professional interpreter of law, from *sāphar*, to write.

scrim. Upholstery lining. Origin unknown.

scrimmage. Alteration of obs. *scrimish*, for *skirmish* (q.v.); cf. F. *escrime*, fencing. Pegge (*Anecdotes*) gives *skrimidge* as a cockneyism for *skirmish*. In football sense earlier *scrummage* (*Tom Brown*), whence *scrum*.

scrimp. As adj. from c. 1700. Cf. Dan. Sw. *skrumpen*, shrivelled, Ger. *schrumpfen*, to shrivel (MHG. *schrimpfen*); ult. cogn. with AS. *scrimman*, to be paralysed, shrink.

scrimshaw. Naut. slang (19 cent.) for small objects, ornaments, etc., made by sailors in their leisure. Also *scrimshander*. Cf. mil. slang *scrimshanker*, shirker, of later appearance. Origin unknown.

It was the army that gave us "strafe" and "blighty" and "napoo" and "wind-up" and "skrimshanker" (*Sat. Rev.* Aug. 11, 1917).

scrip[1] [*archaic*]. Wallet. OF. *escrepe*, ON. *skreppa* (see *scarf*[1]). In ME. usu. coupled with *burdon* (pilgrim's staff) after OF. *escrepe et bordon*. Immediate source of E.

word is MedL. *scrippum*, "sacculus in quo quae ad victum necessaria erant recondebant peregrini" (Duc.).

scrip². Paper securities. "A Change Alley phrase for the last loan or subscription" (Grose). Short for *subscription* (*receipt*); cf. *tec* for *detective*, *flu* for *influenza*.

script. Restored in ME. from earlier (13 cent.) *scrite*, OF. *escrit* (*écrit*), L. *scriptum*, from *scribere*, to write. So also OF. *escript*, learned spelling of *escrit*. Cf. *scriptorium*, MedL. for writing-room of monastery, etc., also used of the "work-room" of the great *Oxford Dictionary*.

scripture. L. *scriptura*, writing (v.s.). First in Bibl. sense, but also used by Chauc. of writing in gen.

scrive. See *screever*.

scrivello [*WAfr.*]. Elephant's tusk under 20 lb. Port. *escrevelho*, ? var. of *escaravelho*, pin, peg.

scrivener. Lengthened from obs. *scrivein*, OF. *escrivain* (*écrivain*), Late L. *scribanus*, scribe. For leg. sense cf. Sc. use of *writer*.

scrofula. From Late L. pl. *scrofulae* (whence AS. *scrofel*), dim. of *scrofa*, sow, supposed to be subject to the disease.

scroll. Earlier (15 cent.) *scrowle*, lengthened from obs. *scrow*, list, etc., OF. *escroue* (*écroue*, prison register), from L. *scrobis*, trench, also female pudendum, ? whence sense of parchment made from uterine membrane (cf. *matriculate*). Form is due to analogy with *rowle*, *roll*, and this has also affected sense, e.g. *scroll* of a violin.

And heven vanysshed awaye as a scroll when hitt is rolled togedder [*Vulg.* sicuti liber involutus]
(Tynd. *Rev.* vi. 14).

scrooge. See *scrouge*.

scroop. To creak, grate. Imit., after *scrape*.

scrotum [*anat.*]. L., ? ident. with *scortum*, hide, skin.

scrouge, scrounge, scrooge. To push, jostle. Earlier *scruze* (Spens.), perh. suggested by *screw* and *squeeze*. Pegge (*Anecdotes*) gives it as a cockneyism for *crowd* (cf. Mrs Gamp's *scroud*). In mod. mil. slang, to acquire unlawfully.

The present crime-wave has its psychological origin in the army habit of scrounging
(*Westm. Gaz.* Jan. 1920).

scrub¹. Noun. Var. of *shrub*. Orig. dwarf tree, whence fig. sense of undersized person (16 cent.). Collect. sense is Austral.

scrub². Verb. Obs. Du. *schrubben*. Orig. a naut. word borrowed in 16 cent., but also

found (once) in ME., with var. *shrub*, in sense of currying a horse. Analogy of *brush*, *broom*, suggests ult. connection with *scrub¹*.

scruff. Altered from earlier *scuff*, *scuft*, cogn. with ON. *skopt*, Goth. *skuft*, hair, Ger. *schopf*. *Noddle* (in quot. below) was earlier used in sense of nape.

einen beym schopf fassen: to take hold of one by his noddle (Ludw.).

scrummage. See *scrimmage*.

scrump. Something shrivelled; cf. *scrimp*.

scrumptious. Orig. US., fastidious, ripping. ? Ident. with dial. *scrumptious*, stingy (see *scrimp*), with sense-development something like that of *nice*. ? Current sense influenced by *sumptuous*.

scrunch. Intens. of *crunch*. See *s-*.

scruple. L. *scrupulus*, *scripulus* (dim. of *scrupus*, sharp stone), small weight, orig. pebble, "a little sharpe stone falling sometime into a mans shooe" (Coop.); cf. *calculate*, *stone*, *carat*, etc. Sense of compunction, F. *scrupule*, is from fig. sense of cause of uneasiness (Cic.). Both groups of meanings are in all the Rom. langs. and in Ger.

A sicle, that is, a nounce, hath twenti half scripilles
(Wyc. *Ex.* xxx. 13).

This shal not be to thee...into scripil of herte [*Vulg.* in scrupulum cordis] (*ib.* 1 *Sam.* xxv. 31).

scrutiny. OF. *scrutinie*, Late L. *scrutinium*, from *scrutari*, to examine closely. Cf. OHG. *scrutōn*, to examine, and L. *scruta*, rubbish, perh. cogn. with *shred*.

scud. First as verb, chiefly naut., but orig. (16 cent.) of the running of a hare. This fact, and existence of synon. dial. *scut*, to scuttle, point to connection with *scut* (q.v.), for which the *Prompt. Parv.* gives the meaning hare.

Masid as a Marche hare, he ran lyke a scut
(Skelton).

scudo. It. coin, lit. shield, L. *scutum*; cf. OF. *escu* (*écu*), crown-piece.

scuffle. Cf. Sw. *skuffa*, to push, and E. dial. *scuff*, to brush against, drag the feet; cogn. with *shove*. Cf. *shuffle*.

scull. Oar. From 14 cent. Connection with obs. *scull*, bowl, OF. *escuele* (v.i.), has been suggested; but the connection is not obvious, unless the blades of sculls were formerly much hollower than now.

scullery. OF. *escuelerie*, from *escuele*, bowl, dish, L. *scutella*, dim. of *scutra*, cogn. with *scutum*, shield. Earlier (14 cent.) also *squillery*.

scullion. Not orig. connected with *scullery*, but app. a composite from F. *souillon*, scullion, orig. dish-clout, "swab," from *souiller*, to soil² (q.v.), and OF. *escouvillon* (*écouvillon*), oven-brush, mop, etc., dim. from L. *scopa*, broom. Cf. obs. *malkin*, *maukin*, kitchen-maid, mop, orig. dim. of *Mary*, also Du. *schoelje*, varlet, ident. with *scullion*.

sculp. To carve. L. *sculpere*. A 16 cent. word now regarded as jocular back-formation from *sculpture*.

sculpin. Small spiny fish. Corrupt. of Sp. *escorpina*, L. *scorpaena*, cogn. with *scorpion*.

sculpture. L. *sculptura*, from *sculpere*, *sculpt-*, to carve, cogn. with *scalpere*, to cut. Used by Evelyn for engraving.

scum. Orig. foam, froth. Of LG. origin; cf. Du. *schuim*, Ger. *schaum* (OHG. *scūm*), as in *meerschaum*; also, from Teut., OF. *escume* (*écume*), which may be one source of E., It. *schiuma*, Sp. *escuma*. Cf. *skim*.

scumble [*paint*]. To soften effect by a film of more opaque colour. From *scum*.

scuncheon [*arch*.]. Also *scunch*, *squinch*. OF. *escoinson* (*écoinson*), "a scunche; the backe part of the jaumbe of a window" (Cotg.), from *coin*, corner, wedge. For formation cf. *écusson*, escutcheon.

scupper¹ [*naut*.]. First in *scupper-nail* (*skopor nayll*, 1485), also *scupper-leather*, both compds. occurring repeatedly in *Nav. Accts.* 1485–97. Connection with *scoop* (q.v.) seems likely. Or it may be an altered use of OF. *escubier* (*écubier*), hawse-hole.

scupper² [*mil. slang*]. To surprise and massacre. First recorded in connection with the Suakin exped. (1885). Also *cooper*. Origin unknown.

scurf. Late AS. *scurf*, altered under Scand. influence from *sceorf*, *scruf*; cf. Sw. *skorv*, Dan. *skurv*; cogn. with Du. *schurft*, Ger. *schorf*, and ult. with *scarf-skin*.

scurrilous. From archaic *scurril-e*, archaic F. *scurrile*, L. *scurrilis*, from *scurra*, buffoon.

scurry. Back-formation from *hurry-skurry*, redupl. on *hurry* (q.v.). Cf. *harum-scarum*. Perh. partly suggested by *scour²*.

scurvy. First as adj. From *scurf*. For fig. senses cf. *shabby*, lit. scabby. As name of disease (see *scorbutic*) it varies in 16 cent. with *scorbute*, *scurby*, *scorby*, etc., regarded by sailors as a "scurvy" disease. *Scurvy-grass*, supposed remedy for the disease, was earlier *scruby-grass*.

scut. Tail of hare, deer, etc. App. from ME.

scut, short, short garment, hare (*Prompt. Parv.*), ? ult. cogn. with *short* and *skirt*.

scutage [*hist*.]. Tax on knights' fees. MedL. *scutagium*, from *scutum*, shield.

scutch. To beat (flax, etc.). OF. *escoucher*, whence *escouche* (*écouche*), scutching instrument, VL. *excuticare*, from *cutis*, skin.

scutcheon. Aphet. for *escutcheon* (q.v.).

scutella, scutellate, scutellum [*biol*.]. L. *scutella*, little dish, dim. of *scutra*, but used in scient. lang. as though from *scutum*, shield.

scutter. Mod. alteration of *scuttle³*.

scuttle¹. Receptacle, now usu. for coal. AS. *scutel*, L. *scutella*, dish (see *scullery*), whence also Du. *schotel*, Ger. *schüssel*, dish.

scuttle² [*naut*.]. OF. *escoutille* (*écoutille*), hatchway, "cover or lid of a hatchway, sometimes taken for the hatchway itself" (Lesc.), Sp. *escotilla*; orig. the lid of the hatchway, which appears to be also its first sense in E. (v.i.); cf. F. *panneau*, hatchway, lit. panel. ? From Du. *schutten*, to shut (cf. dial. *shuttle*, part of flood-gate). Later sense is square hole, in hatchway or elsewhere, whence to *scuttle* (a ship).

A chayne of yron for the skottelles of the haches
(*Nav. Accts.* 1495–97).

The mildest-manner'd man
That ever scuttled ship or cut a throat
(*Don Juan*, iii. 41).

scuttle³. To make off, etc. Also (17 cent.) *scuddle*, frequent. of *scud* (q.v.).

scye [*tailoring*]. Armhole. Sc. & Ulster dial. word, of unknown origin.

Scylla. Rock on It. side of Straits of Messina, opposite whirlpool of Charybdis.

Incidis in Scyllam cupiens vitare Charybdim
(Gualtier de Chastillon, 13 cent.).

scyphi-, scypho-. From L. *scyphus*, G. σκύφος, cup.

scythe. Altered, on L. *scindere*, to cut (cf. *scissors*), from *sithe* (Johns.), AS. *sīthe*, for **sigthi*, cogn. with ON. *sigthr*, and ult. with Du. *zeis*, Ger. *sense*, and L. *secare*, to cut. As attribute of Death it is borrowed from the Time of the ancients.

Scythian. From L., G. Σκυθία, part of Russia orig. inhabited by nomad race. Sometimes used for the Ural-Altaic group of langs.

se-. OL. *se*, *sed*, without, apart, prob. cogn. with *se*, self, thus *seditio* = going for oneself, on one's own.

sea. AS. *sǣ*. Com. Teut.; cf. Du. Ger. *see*, lake, sea, ON. *sǣr*, Goth. *saiws*, sea, marsh. The last is perh. the orig. Teut. sense. The compd. *high sea* (cf. F. *haute mer*, L. *altum* *mare*) is found in AS. The compds. of *sea* are very numerous and the allusive and fig. uses are indicative of a maritime nation. Current sense of *seaboard* is 19 cent., perh. due to F. *bord de la mer*. *Sea-change*, magic transformation for the better, is an echo of *Temp*. i. 2. *Sea-coal* is usu. understood as sea-borne, but the character of the earliest records (13 cent.) points rather to its having been orig. obtained from beds denuded by sea action. With *sea-horse*, walrus, *sea-hog*, porpoise, *sea-lion*, seal, cf. *hippopotamus*, *porcupine*, *chameleon*, and see *walrus*. *Sea-kale* is said by Evelyn to grow near the coast. *Sea-green* is sometimes used, after Carlyle, with allusion to Robespierre, who dressed in that colour. *Sea-king* is mod., after ON. *sǣkonungr* (cf. *rune*, *berserk*, etc.). *Sea-lawyer*, argumentative sailor, was earlier a name of the shark. *Seaman*, in AS., is much older than *sailor*; with *seamanlike*, in E. sense, cf. *chivalrous*, *sportsmanlike*. *Sea-plane* (not in *NED*.) is a small return made by aeronautics for numerous borrowings from the naut. vocab. *Sea-power* owes its currency to Mahan (1890). The *great sea-serpent* is mentioned in Goldsmith's *Nat. Hist*. (1774). Up to c. 1800 *sea* was often sounded *say*, the older pronunc., e.g. in Cowper's *Alexander Selkirk*, l. 3. For a similar uncertainty cf. *tea*.

> The sea-green incorruptible Mr Snowden
>   (*Pall Mall Gaz*. Jan. 9, 1918).

seal[1]. Animal. AS. *seolh*, *sēol-*; cf. archaic Du. *zele*, OHG. *selah* (replaced by LG. *robbe*), ON. *selr*.

seal[2]. Imprint. OF. *seel* (*sceau*), L. *sigillum*, engraved figure, etc., dim. of *signum*, sign. In all Rom. & Teut. langs. (e.g. Du. *zegel*, Ger. *siegel*), no doubt as inheritance from Roman officialdom; cf. hist. importance in E. *great seal*, *privy seal*. In *hand and seal*, the first word refers to the signature. *His fate is sealed* refers to the seal on the execution warrant. *Sealed book* was orig. used of the MS. copy of *Book of Common Prayer* (1662), and of printed copies, bearing the Great Seal, sent to various eccl. authorities. In to *seal eyes* we have rather archaic *seel*, *sele*, to sew together the eyelids of a young falcon, earlier *sile*, F. *ciller*, from *cil*, lash, L. *cilium*.

> She that so young could put out such a seeming
> To seal her father's eyes up (*Oth*. iii. 3).

seam. AS. *sēam*. Com. Teut.; cf. Du. *zoom*,

Ger. *saum*, ON. *saumr*; cogn. with *sew*, L. *suere*, Sanskrit *syūman*, seam. *Seam-stress*, *sempstress*, is a double fem. (cf. *songstress* and see -*ster*). Current sense of *seamy side* is hardly that of Shaks.

> Some such squire he was
> That turn'd your wit the seamy side without,
> And made you to suspect me with the Moor
>   (*Oth*. iv. 2).

séance. F., from archaic *seoir*, to sit, L. *sedēre*. Orig. of meeting of deliberative or learned society, but since c. 1845 of spiritualistic meeting.

sear[1]. To burn. AS. *sēarian*, from *sēar*, dry, sere (q.v.). Orig. intrans., to wither. Fig. sense is chiefly after 1 *Tim*. iv. 2 (*Vulg*. *cauteriare*).

sear[2]. Part of gun-lock controlling trigger. F. *serre*, talon, in OF. part of lock, from *serrer*, to grasp, Late L. *serare*, from *sera*, bolt. Cf. *serried*, *seraglio*.

search. OF. *cerchier* (*chercher*, by assim.), Late L. *circare*, from *circa*, around (see *joust* for similar formation); cf. It. *cercare*, to seek, Sp. *cercar*, to surround. The sense is now that of F. *fouiller*, orig. sense of *chercher* being already provided for by E. *seek*. Quot. below preserves orig. sense.

> [We] spent all the day in searching the head of the falles, but could not finde it (Hakl. xi. 5).

season. F. *saison*, L. *satio-n-*, sowing, in VL. seed-time, from *serere*, *sat-*, to sow; cf. It. dial. *sason*, Sp. *sazón*. This is the accepted etym.; but it seems possible that the origin is rather VL. **satio-n-*, dissim. of *statio-n-*, station, whence It. *stagione*, season. With *for a season* (*Luke*, iv. 13) cf. *season-ticket*. *Out of season*, i.e. out of due time, is in *Piers Plowm*. To *season* (a dish), OF. *saisonner* (replaced by *assaisonner*), springs from earlier F. sense of maturing, bringing to perfection by observing proper seasons; this orig. sense appears much later in E., as in *seasoned timber* (*troops*). For application to horses cf. *salted*. We usu. understand by *seasoning* a heightening of flavour, but it also had the sense of moderating (v.i.).

> Earthly power doth then show likest God's
> When mercy seasons justice (*Merch. of Ven*. iv. 1).

seat. ON. *sǣti*. Com. Teut.; cf. rare AS. *gesǣt*, Du. *gezeet*, Ger. *gesäss*; cogn. with *sit* (q.v.). Orig. act of sitting, as still in *a good seat on horseback*, or that on which one sits, e.g. *seat of one's trousers*. More extended and dignified meanings are after

F. *siège*, L. *sedes*, as in *sedes belli*, seat of war.

sebaceous [*biol.*]. From L. *sebaceus*, from *sebum*, tallow.

sebesten. Fruit. Arab. *sabastān*, Pers. *sapistān*, ? for *seg-pistān*, dog's teats.

secant [*math.*]. From pres. part. of L. *secare*, to cut.

seccotine. Coined (1894) by inventor from It. *secco*, dry, L. *siccus*.

secede. L. *secedere*, to go apart. Hence *secession*, esp. in ref. to US. hist. (1861–65), whence colloq. US. *secesh-er*.

secern. L. *secernere*, to separate away.

seclude. L. *secludere*, from *claudere*, to shut.

second. F., L. *secundus*, from *sequi*, *secu-*, to follow. As noun for MedL. *secunda minuta*, lit. second minute, i.e. further subdivision. In gen. sense AS. had *ōther*, other (cf. OF. *autre*, second, Ger. *anderthalb*, one and a half, also *second self* for L. *alter ego*, G. ἄλλος αὐτός, ἕτερος αὐτός). The *second* in a duel orig. fought. Here, and in verb to *second* (one's efforts), we have some influence of the subsidiary sense of L. *secundus*, favourable, orig. following. With *secondary education* (c. 1860) cf. *primary*. *Second sight* is translated from Gaelic. Verb to *secónd* (mil.), detail for extra-regimental duty, is from F. *second* in phrase *en second* (v.i.). With *seconde* (fenc.) cf. *tierce*, *quarte*.

I have layd doune a resolucon...to purchase them [viz. books] at the second hand, out of libraries that are to be sold (Josselin's *Diary*, 1645).

second captain, or lieutenant en second: one whose company has been broke, and he is joyn'd to another, to act and serve under the captain or lieutenant of it (*Mil. Dict.* 1708).

secret. F., L. *secretus*, p.p. of *secernere*, to separate. Hence *secretary*, F. *secrétaire*, MedL. *secretarius*, confidential agent, also used in F. & E. of a private desk. Offic. title of cabinet minister has developed from that of private secretary to the crown (temp. Eliz.). The *secretary-bird* is so named from head-feathers suggesting a quill behind a writer's ear. Etym. sense appears in med. *secretion*, separation.

sect. F. *secte*, L. *secta*, from *sequi*, to follow (cf. *Shiah*), with sense influenced by a supposed connection with *secare*, to cut (cf. *schism*). So also *sectator* from frequent. *sectari*, to follow. Vulgar use for *sex* has the authority of Chauc. (E. 1171). *Sectary*, used of schismatics from 16 cent., is now

usu. replaced by *sectarian*, orig. applied (temp. Commonwealth) by Presbyterians to Independents. See also *set²*, *suit-e*.

section. F., L. *sectio-n-*, from *secare*, *sect-*, to cut.

sector. L., cutter (v.s.), used in Late L. to render G. τομεύς, cutter, employed by Archimedes in current sense. Spec. mil. sense, now so familiar (not in *NED.*), is after F. *secteur*.

secular. OF. *seculer* (*séculier*), L. *saecularis*, from *saeculum*, century, used in Church L. for this world as contrasted with eternity. Cf. *temporal*. There is an increasing tendency to give to the word the sense of venerable, of long standing, after F. *séculaire*, learned form of *séculier*. *Secularism*, as a "religion," was propounded (c. 1850) by G. J. Holyoake.

secure. L. *securus*, remote from care, *cura*. Traces of etym. sense survive in to *dwell secure* (*Judges*, xviii. 7). Cf. *sure*. AS. had *sicor*, from L., surviving in dial. (Sc. *sicker*).

They were secure where they ought to have been wary, timorous where they might well have been secure (Macaulay).

securiform [*bot.*]. From L. *securis*, axe, from *secare*, to cut.

sedan. First, "covered chairs called 'sedans,'" in 1634. Peter Mundy (1637) speaks of "sidans att London." Later (18 cent.) called *sedan-chair*. App. introduced from Spain by Prince Charles and Buckingham (1623), but popularized by Sir Sanders Duncombe, who secured a monopoly for them (1634). He may have coined the word from It. *sedere*, to sit. Johnson's derivation from *Sedan* (France), often repeated, is a mere guess. Quot. 1 shows it as a new word, quot. 2 its use as a kind of hearse.

Then the Dutch younker tooke her up into a (what doe you call it?) a sedan, and away they went (Glapthorne, *Hollander*, v. 1, 1640).

June 21. Payd for the whole chardges of my Lord George's corps bringinge downe to Belvoyre, cxxxijli. xviijs. ijd. June 23. Payd the men that carried my Lord George in the sedan, jli. xvjs.
(*Rutland MSS.* 1641).

sedate. L. *sedatus*, p.p. of *sedare*, to settle, set, allay, causal of *sedēre*, to sit; cf. synon. Ger. *gesetzt*, lit. set, F. *rassis*. *Sedative* is much older.

sedentary. F. *sédentaire*, L. *sedentarius*, from pres. part. of *sedēre*, to sit.

sederunt. Sitting, meeting. L., sat (v.s.),

preceding in minute-book names of those present.

sedge. AS. *secg*, ident. with rare *secg*, sword, cogn. with *saw*[1] and L. *secare*, to cut. Cf. L. *gladiolus*, which it renders in early glosses.

sedile [*arch*.]. L., from *sedēre*, to sit. Usu. in pl. *sedilia*.

sediment. F. *sédiment*, L. *sedimentum*, from *sedēre*, to sit, settle.

sedition. F. *sédition*, L. *seditio-n-*, from *se(d)-* (q.v.) and *ire*, *it-*, to go.

seduce. L. *seducere*, to lead away. Gen. sense appears in *seductive*, chief current sense in *seduction*.

sedulous. From L. *sedulus*, from adv. *sedulo*, honestly, OL. *se dolo*, without guile.

Stevenson, in one of his essays, tells us how he played the "sedulous ape" to Hazlitt, Sir Thomas Browne, Montaigne, and other writers of the past. And the compositors of all our higher-toned newspapers keep the foregoing sentence set up in type always, so constantly does it come tripping off the pens of all higher-toned reviewers

(Max Beerbohm, *Christmas Garland*).

sedum. L., house-leek, with var. *sadum*. Prob. not a L. word.

see[1]. Verb. AS. *sēon*. Com. Teut.; cf. Du. *zien*, Ger. *sehen*, ON. *sjā*, Goth. *saihwan*. In sense of to escort (*see out*, *home*, etc.) first in Shaks. Sense of to experience, now chiefly with *better days*, *service*, is in AS. *Let me see* is 16 cent. *Seer* orig. rendered L. *videns* (*Vulg.*), G. βλέπων (LXX.).

Cometh and goo we to the seer

(Wyc. 1 *Kings*, ix. 9).

see[2]. Noun. OF. *sie*, VL. **sedes* (for *sēdes*), from *sedēre*, to sit. Replaced in F. by *siège*, VL. **sedicum*, as in *le saint siège*.

Fro the fyrst gotun of Pharao, that sat in his see, unto the fyrst gotun of the caitiff woman that was in prisoun (Wyc. *Ex.* xii. 29).

seed. AS. *sēd*. Com. Teut.; cf. Du. *zaad*, Ger. *saat*, ON. *sāth*, Goth. *sēths* (in *manasēths*, mankind); cogn. with *sow*[2]. Bibl. sense of offspring is also AS. *Seedcake* was perh. orig. emblematical of sowing (v.i.), the conclusion of which was celebrated by a feast. With colloq. *seedy* cf. *run to seed*.

Wife, some time this week, if the weather hold clear,
An end of wheat-sowing we make for this year.
Remember you, therefore, if I do it not,
The seed-cake and pasties and furmenty pot

(Tusser).

seedy-boy, **sidi-boy** [*Anglo-Ind.*]. Negro. Ironic use of *sidi*, Urdu *sīdī*, Arab. *sayyidī*, my lord (see *Cid*).

seek. AS. *sēcan*, past *sōhte*. Com. Teut.; cf. Du. *zoeken*, Ger. *suchen*, ON. *sēkja*, Goth. *sōkjan*; cogn. with L. *sagire*, to scent out, G. ἡγεῖσθαι, to lead. Mod. form, for *seech* (still in dial.), as in *beseech*, is due to Norse influence. Almost replaced colloq. by to *look for* and *search*, but cf. *hide-and-seek*. Archaic gerundial *to seek* (Chauc.), hard to find, survives as an echo of Porson's epigram—"The Germans in Greek are sadly to seek."

seel [*falc*.]. See *seal*[2].

seem. ON. *sōma*, from *sōmr*, fitting, seemly, cogn. with AS. *sēman*, to reconcile, and with *same*. Orig. sense survives in *beseem*, *seemly*. With archaic *what seemeth him good*, *meseems*, with dat. pronoun, cf. *methinks*. Later senses may have been influenced by obs. *semble*, F. *sembler*, L. *simulare*, from *simul*, together.

seep [*dial. & US.*]. To ooze. Cogn. with *sip*.

Experienced American geologists convinced him that seepages of oil encountered in England came from a true oil-sand (*Daily Chron.* May 30, 1919).

seer[1]. From *see*[1]. Cf. *sightseer*.

seer[2] [*Anglo-Ind.*]. Weight, offic. a kilogram. Hind. *ser*.

seersucker. Fabric. Corrupt. of Pers. *shīr u shakkar*, milk and sugar, striped garment. Cf. *pepper and salt*.

see-saw. Redupl. on *saw*[1]. Jingle sung by children imitating sawyers at work. Cf. synon. Du. *ziegezagen*.

With see saw sack a down, like a sawyer

(*NED.* 1640).

seethe. AS. *sēothan*, to boil (trans.). Com. Teut.; cf. Du. *zieden*, Ger. *sieden*, ON. *siōtha*; cogn. with Goth. *sauths*, sacrifice. Replaced, exc. fig., by *boil*, p.p. *sodden* (*Ex.* xii. 9) having assumed spec. sense.

Thou shalt not seethe a kid in his mother's milk

(*Ex.* xxiii. 19)

segar. Earliest E. spelling of *cigar*.

The incendiary was seized almost in the act of setting fire to the fuse with a lighted segar

(*Obs.* May 14, 1820).

segment. L. *segmentum*, for **secmentum*, from *secare*, to cut.

segregate. From L. *segregare*, to remove from the flock, *grex*, *greg-*.

seguidilla. Dance. Sp., from *seguida*, sequence, from *seguir*, to follow, VL. **sequire*, for *sequi*.

seid. See *sayyid*, *Cid*.

seidlitz powder. Named (1815) as possessing properties like those of medicinal spring at *Seidlitz*, Bohemia.

seigneur. Chiefly in Canada. F., lord, L. *senior-em*, elder. Hence also hist. E. *seignior*. Cf. *alderman*, *priest*.

seine. Net. AS. *segne* or F. *seine*, L. *sagena*, G. σαγήνη. Also in OSax. & OHG.

seisin [*hist.*]. Possession, esp. in ref. to symbolical act (*Puck of Pook's Hill*, ch. i.). F. *saisine*, from *saisir*, to seize. Cf. leg. to *be seized* (put in possession) *of*.

seismic. From G. σεισμός, earthquake, from σείειν, to shake.

seize. F. *saisir*, Frankish L. *sacīre*, to put (into possession), prob. from Teut. **satjan*, to set, as *ponere* is similarly used in same formula; cf. Prov. *sazir*, whence It. *sagire*. In naut. sense, to secure, app. via Du. *seizen*, from F. This sense appears first in noun *seizing* (14 cent.), also in compd. *bowesesynges* (*Nav. Accts.* 1495–97), usu. spelt *bowesesenynges* (*ib.*), with which cf. Du. *seisingen*, "a sort of ship-ropes" (Sewel, 1766), from *seissen*, *seisen*, "to belage, to moor" (*ib.*).

selachian [*zool.*]. Of the shark, G. σέλαχος.

selah [*Bibl.*]. Heb., supposed to be a musical or liturgical direction. See *Psalms* and *Hab.* iii.

seldom. AS. *seldan*, altered after *whilom* (q.v.); cf. Du. *zelden*, Ger. *selten*, ON. *sjaldan*; cogn. with Ger. *seltsam*, strange, rare, Goth. *sildaleiks*, wonderful.

select. From L. *seligere*, *select-*, from *legere*, to pick, choose. *Natural selection* dates from Darwin's *Origin of Species* (1859).

selenite [*min.*]. L., G. σεληνίτης (λίθος), moonstone, because supposed to wax and wane with the moon, σελήνη. Cf. *selenium* (chem.) named (1818) by discoverer Berzelius by analogy with *tellurium*.

Seleucid [*hist.*]. Of dynasty founded (312 B.C.) in Syria by *Seleucus Nicator*, general of Alexander.

self. AS. *self*. Com. Teut.; cf. Du. *zelf*, Ger. *selb*, ON. *sialfr*, Goth. *silba*. Orig. equivalent to L. *ipse*. With later E. sense of same, as still in *self-colour* and pleon. *selfsame*, cf. F. *même*, same, from L. *metipsissimus*, very self. Noun *self* is evolved from second element of *myself*, etc. In AS., and often in ME., *self* was declined with the pronoun to which it was attached; the forms which survive are an accidental collection. Innumerable compds. of *self-* date from

16–17 cents., partly in imit. of G. αὐτο-, the only surviving AS. compd. being *self-will*. *Self-help* was app. coined by Carlyle and popularized by Smiles (1860). The *self-made man* is also a 19 cent. product. *Selfish* is a Presbyterian coinage (17 cent.).

Ic sylf hit eom (AS. *Gosp. Luke*, xxiv. 39).

Seljuk [*hist.*]. Name of reputed founder of certain Turk. dynasties (11–13 cents.) as opposed to *Ottoman*, *Osmanli*.

sell. AS. *sellan*, to give up, sell. Com. Teut.; cf. OSax. *sellian*, to give, OHG. *sellen*, to deliver up, ON. *selja*, to give up, sell, Goth. *saljan*, to offer (sacrifice), all from the Teut. noun which appears in E. *sale*. *Sold*, betrayed (Ben Jonson), and *sell*, trick (Dickens), agree with earliest senses of the word, but are prob. from the later mercantile idea. To *sell one's life dearly* is 13 cent.

sellender. See *sallender*.

s'elp me [*vulg.*]. Contr. of *so help me* (*God*), whence further perversion *swop-me-Bob*.

seltzer. Altered from Ger. *selterser*, from *Selters*, village in Hesse-Nassau with mineral spring. Cf. F. *seltz*, whence *seltzogene*.

selvage. For *self-edge*, after archaic Du. *selfegge*; cf. naut. Du. *zelfkant* (see *cant¹*) and Ger. *salband*, for *selbende*, self end. Hence naut. *selvagee*.

semantic [*ling.*]. G. σημαντικός, significant, from σημαίνειν, to show. In current sense, as pl., adapted from F. *sémantique*, applied by Bréal (1887) to the psychology of lang. as revealed in sense-development. *Semasiology*, from G. σημασία, signification, and *sematology*, from σῆμα, σηματ-, sign, were used earlier in similar sense.

Parti de la chaire de M. Bréal au Collège de France, le mot "sémantique" a fait discrètement son chemin (A. Thomas).

semaphore. F. *sémaphore*, from G. σῆμα, sign, signal.

semblance. Archaic F., from *sembler*, to seem, L. *simulare*, from *simul*, together. But F. usu. has *semblant*, which also appears earlier (13 cent.) in E.

semeiology, semiology. Science of signs, G. σημεῖον.

semester. Univ. half-year. Ger., L. *semestris* (*cursus*), six months (course), from *sex* and *mensis*.

semi-. L., half, cogn. with G. ἡμι-, Sanskrit *sāmi-*, AS. *sām-* (see *sandblind*), OHG. *sāmi-*. Used to form a few compds. in ME.

and an ever-increasing number from 16–17 cents. onward.

seminal. F. *séminal*, L. *seminalis*, from *semen*, *semin-*, seed, from root of *serere*, to sow.

seminar. Ger., "seminary," group of advanced students working with professor.

seminary. L. *seminarium*, seed-plot, also fig. In E. esp. of college for training R.C. priests, and, up to c. 1850, school for "*young ladies*" (*Old Cur. Shop*, ch. viii.). For converse metaphor cf. *nursery* (for plants).

Taking your grafted trees out of the seminary, you shall transplant them into this nursery (Evelyn).

semiology. See *semeiology*.

Semitic [*ling.*]. From Late L. *Sem*, G., Heb. *Shem*, eldest son of Noah. First used, in Ger. *semitisch*, for group of langs. including Hebrew, Aramaic, Arabic, Ethiopic, ancient Assyrian. Cf. *Hamitic*, *Japhetic*.

semolina. Altered from It. *semolino*, from *semola*, bran, L. *simila*, wheat-meal. Cf. *simnel*.

sempiternal. F. *sempiternel*, MedL. *sempiternalis*, from L. *sempiternus*, from *semper*, always, with ending as in *aeternus*.

sempstress. See *seam*.

sen. Copper coin. Jap.

senary. L. *senarius*, from *seni*, distrib. of *sex*, six.

senate. F. *sénat*, L. *senatus*, lit. council of old men, from *senex*, old. Hence governing body, esp. of univ. Sense of upper legislative body first in US., whence adopted, at Revolution, by France.

send. AS. *sendan*. Com. Teut.; cf. Du. *zenden*, Ger. *senden*, ON. *senda*, Goth. *sandjan*, all causals of a lost Teut. verb meaning to go; cf. AS. *sīth*, Goth. *sinths*, journey, Ger. *gesinde*, retinue, orig. leader's train of warriors. Used already in AS. of Divine ordinance, whence *Godsend*, *send him victorious*, etc. To *send mad* (*to sleep*, *into fits*) is 19 cent.

sendal [*hist.*]. Fabric. OF. *cendal*; cf. It. *zendale*, Sp. *cendal*; also Ger. *zindel*; ult. from G. σινδών, fine linen, lit. stuff of *India* (q.v.). Cf. *Scinde*. Obs. from 16 cent., but revived by mod. poets.

And the body taken, Joseph wlappide it in a clene sendel (Wyc. *Matt.* xxvii. 59).

senescent. From pres. part. of L. *senescere*, from *senex*, old.

seneschal. OF. *seneschal* (*sénéchal*), of Teut. origin, with second element as in *marshal*

(q.v.) and first cogn. with L. *senex*, old. Cf. Goth. *sinista*, eldest. Found in Frankish L. as *siniscalcus*, and adopted by all Rom. langs. Ger. *seneschall*, like *marschall*, is borrowed back from F.

senhor. Port., see *senior*.

senile. L. *senilis*, from *senex*, old.

senior. L., compar. of *senex*, old; cogn. with archaic G. ἔνος, Gael. *sean*, Ir. *sen*, Sanskrit *sana*, and with *seneschal*, *sennachie*. Hence titles of respect, F. *sire*, *sieur*, *seigneur*, It. *signor*, Sp. *señor*, Port. *senhor*, with their derivatives. Also used by Tynd., in his orig. transl., for Bibl. *elder*.

senna. Arab. *sanā*. ME. had also *sené*, *senny*, via F. *séné*.

sennachie [*Sc.*]. Gaelic teller of tradition. Gael. *seanachaidh*, from *sean*, old (see *senior*). Cf. Gaulish name *Seneca*.

sennight [*archaic*]. For *seven night*, a compd. already existing in AS. Cf. *fortnight*.

sennit, sinnet, cinet [*naut.*]. Plait of rope, grass, etc. Explained, since Falc., as *seven knit*, but Capt. John Smith defines it as of two, four, six, eight, or nine strings, and Cotg. as of three. If var. *sidnet* (v.i.) is genuine, above etym. is impossible.

sidnet or sinnet: is a line or string made of rope-yarn, of two, six, or nine, platted one over another (*Sea-Dict.* 1708).

señor. Sp., see *senior*.

Senoussi. See *Senussi*.

sense. F. *sens*, L. *sensus*, from *sentire*, *sens-*, to feel; ult. cogn. with *send* and with Ger. *sinn*, sense. Ellipt. use for *good sense* is first in Shaks. In 16 cent. also as verb, but now only as Americanism. *Sensible* still preserves its three orig. meanings of perceptible to the senses, capable of feeling (*sensitive*), actually perceiving, from the last of which is evolved current use for intelligent, discreet, "only in low conversation" (Johns.). From Late L. *sensatus*, gifted with sense, comes *sensation-alism*, of which latest sense belongs to second half of 19 cent. *Sensual-ity* is from Late L. *sensualis*. *Sensuous* was coined by Milton, to avoid the associations of *sensual*, and revived by Coleridge.

sensitive plant. From 17 cent., also *sensible* (v.s.), orig. as rendering *mimosa*.

sentence. F., L. *sententia*, opinion, from *sentire*, to feel (v.s.). Hence esp. opinion as result of deliberation, judicial decision, quoted saying, gram. proposition. *Sententious*, F. *sententieux*, "sententious, grave, wise, pithie, instructive" (Cotg.), had orig. no suggestion of pompousness.

sententious. See *sentence*.

sentient. From pres. part. of L. *sentire*, to feel (v.s.).

sentiment. ME. *sentement*, OF. (*sentiment*), from *sentir*, to feel. Current spelling of F. & E. is due to It. *sentimento*. Sense of sensibility is 18 cent., e.g. Sterne's *Sentimental Journey* (1768), whence is borrowed sense of F. & Ger. *sentimental*.

The word "sentimental" so much in vogue among the polite...I am frequently astonished to hear such a one is a "sentimental" man; we were a "sentimental" party; I have been taking a "sentimental" walk (*NED.* 1749).

sentinel. F. *sentinelle* (f.), It. *sentinella*, whence also Sp. *centinela*, "the watch or guard" (Percyvall). In earlier use (16 cent.) also abstract (to *keep sentinel*) and collect. (v.i.), and used (1600) in Holland's *Livy* for a sentry-box on a city-wall. Cf. hist. of *sentry*, with which it is quite unconnected, though regularly associated with it. Also spelt *centinel*, *centronel*, the latter prob. by association with *century*, detachment of troops, and even *centrell*, by association with *sentry*. OF. *sentinelle* also means sentry-box, and I take orig. It. word to be a dim. of *sentina*, latrine, used as nickname for sentry-box on rampart. This may seem fantastic, but those acquainted with medieval architecture are aware that the external latrine is not, to the amateur eye, distinguishable from a sentry-box. A very good example may be seen in King's Hostel, Trin. Coll., Camb. OF. also has *sentinelle*, sink, jakes. The attempt to connect this word, and the following, with F. *sentier*, path, as though sentinel's beat, disregards their hist. entirely, the current sense being the latest in development.

The vanitie and madness of a sergeant who standing centenel would needs force the governours centenel from his ground, they being 20 and ours but 3
(Raleigh's *Guiana*, 1596).

casino: sentinelle, ou maisonnette de sentinelle sur la courtine, ou sur les rempars et bastions (Duez).

sentry. Quite unconnected with *sentinel*, though naturally associated with it by early etymologists. Also frequently spelt *centry*. It is the popular form of *sanctuary*, as in *sentry-fields*, common in dial. for Church fields (also *centry-gate*, *centry-garth*). The order of senses is sanctuary, place of safety, shelter for watchman,

watchman; cf. F. *guérite*, sentry-box, in OF. sanctuary, refuge (from *guérir*, to save), which would now also prob. mean sentry if *sentinelle* had not been introduced from It. Cf. archaic F. *prendre la guérite*, to take sanctuary, make off. Cf. also L. *custodia*, keeping, watch and ward, watch-tower, the watch, watchman. *Sentry go* was orig. imper., as order to soldier to relieve previous sentry.

He hath no way now to slyppe out of my hands, but to take sentrie in the Hospital of Warwick
(Nashe, 1590).

garite (*guérite*): a place of refuge, and of safe retyrall in a rowt, disaster, or danger; also, a sentrie, or little lodge for a sentinell, built on high
(Cotg.).

Through the thick senteries and stations thick
Of angels watching round (*Par. L.* ii. 412).

Senussi, Senoussi. Mohammedan sect and league (NAfr.), named from founder, born in Algeria (c. 1800).

sepal [*bot.*]. F. *sépale*, ModL. *sepalum*, coined (1790) by Necker, after *petalum*, from G. σκέπη, covering. See *NED.* viii. 2 addenda.

separate. From L. *separare*, from *se-* (q.v.) and *parare*, to make ready. Cf. *sever*.

sepia. L., G. σηπία, cuttle-fish.

sepoy. Port. *sipae*, Urdu, Pers. *sipāhī*, horseman, soldier, from *sipāh*, army. Cf. *spahi*.

Sadhu Sing had been a sipahee, or soldier
(*Surgeon's Daughter*, ch. xiii.).

sept [*antiq.*]. Division of Ir. clan. Artificial spelling of *sect*. So also OF. *sette*, sect, set, and It. *setta*, are sometimes latinized *septa* in medieval documents. Cf. AF. *quipte* for *quitte*.

There are another sect of the Borkes, and divers of the Irisshery, towards Sligoo (*NED.* 1536).

September. L., from *septem*, seven. Replaced AS. *hærfestmōnath*, *hāligmōnath*. Hence *septembrist*, Port. revolutionary (1836), September massacrer (Paris, 1792).

septenary. L. *septenarius*, from *septeni*, distrib. of *septem*, seven (q.v.).

septennial. From L. *septennium*, space of seven years.

septentrional. L. *septentrionalis*, from *septentriones*, orig. *septem triones*, seven plough-oxen, the Great Bear. *Trio* is derived by Roman writers from *terere*, *tri-*, to pulverize, etc., *a terenda terra*.

septic. G. σηπτικός, from σήπειν, to putrefy.

septillion. F., from *sept*, seven, after *million*, etc.

septuagenarian. From L. *septuagenarius*, from *septuageni*, distrib. of *septuaginta*, seventy.

Septuagesima. L. (sc. *dies*). It is uncertain whether this and *Sexagesima* were merely suggested by *Quadragesima*, *Quinquagesima*, or whether as (about) seventieth and sixtieth days before octave of Easter. Both conjectures are in Alcuin (8 cent.).

Septuagint. L. *septuaginta*, seventy, from the (untrue) tradition that the G. version of the *OT.* was the work of 72 Jews of Palestine who completed the task in 70 days. Abbrev. LXX.

They were thre skore and ten that tornede Holy Writte out of Ebrew in to Grewe (Trev. ii. 245).

septum [*scient.*]. Partition. L., from *saepire*, to enclose, from *saepes*, hedge.

sepulchre. F. *sépulcre*, L. *sepulcrum*, from *sepelire*, *sepult-*, to bury. Orig. only of Holy Sepulchre. Cf. *sepulture*, OF., L. *sepultura*.

sequacious. From L. *sequax*, *sequac-*, from *sequi*, to follow.

The degrading sequacity which was the prescribed attitude of Oxford towards German scholarship till the day before yesterday (J. S. Phillimore, 1918).

sequel. F. *séquelle*, L. *sequela*, from *sequi*, to follow.

sequela [*med.*]. After-result. L. (v.s.).

sequence. F. *séquence*, Late L. *sequentia*, from *sequi* (v.s.).

sequester. Late L. *sequestrare*, to separate, put in safe keeping, from *sequestor*, attorney, mediator, third person called in as umpire, from *sequi*, to follow. *Sequestrate* is of later formation.

sequin [*hist.*]. F., It. *zecchino*, from *zecca*, mint, Arab. *sikkah*, coining die. Cf. *chicken-hazard*.

sequoia. Tree, wellingtonia. Named (1847) by Endlicher after *Sequoiar*, a Cherokee Indian. Cf. *quassia*.

serac [*Alp.*]. Ice-tower on glacier. Swiss F. *sérac*, kind of cheese. From shape.

seraglio. It. *serraglio*, "an inclosure, a close, a padocke, a parke, a cloister or secluse" (Flor.), from L. *sera*, lock; erron. used, owing to superficial resemblance of form and sense, to render *serai* (q.v.).

serai. Turk. *serāī*, orig. Pers., lodging, residence, palace. Esp. of Sultan's palace at Constantinople, wrongly called *seraglio* (q.v.). Cf. *caravanserai*.

serang [*Anglo-Ind.*]. Lascar boatswain. Pers. *sarhang*, commander.

serape. Shawl. Mex. Sp.

seraph. First used by Milton as sing. of older *seraphim* (pl.), found in AS., Late L. (*Vulg.*), G. σεραφίμ (LXX.), Heb. *serāphīm* (only in *Is.* vi.), pl. of *sārāph*, regarded by some as ident. with *sārāph*, serpent, used in apposition with *nāhāsh*, serpent (*Numb.* xxi., *Deut.* viii.). For earlier use as sing. cf. *cherubim*, also F. *séraphin*, It. *serafino*, Sp. *serafín*, all sing.

seraskier. Turk. pronunc. of Pers. *ser'asker*, from *sar*, head, *'askar*, army. Cf. *sirdar*, *askari*.

Serbian. Has now replaced earlier *Servian*, an incorr. form perh. due to some vague association between *Slavs* and *serfs*. From native *Srb*, *Serb*. The lang. is Slav.

Serbonian bog. Milton's name (*Par. L.* ii. 592) for *Lake Serbonia* (Egypt), G. Σερβωνίς (λίμνη).

Whatever else we do, we must get out of the Serbonian bog (*Obs.* Nov. 16, 1919).

sere[1]. Adj. AS. *sēar*, dry, withered; cogn. with Du. *zoor*, whence F. *saur*, in *hareng saur*, red herring. Cf. *sear*[1]. Now only poet., esp. in *the sere*, *the yellow leaf* (*Macb.* v. 3).

sere[2]. See *sear*[2].

serenade. F., It. *serenata*, from *sereno*, the open air, lit. serene. App. associated with *sera*, evening, from L. *serus*, late (whence F. *soir*). Cf. *aubade*.

serene. L. *serenus*; cf. F. *serein*, It. Sp. *sereno*. Hence *all serene*, "a street phrase of very modern adoption, the burden of a song" (Hotten, 1859). With *serenity*, as title, F. *sérénité*, L. *serenitas*, of Roman Emperor, Pope, etc., cf. *illustrious* and its Ger. rendering *durchlaucht*.

serf. F., L. *servus*, slave, orig. (cattle) keeper, from *servare*, to preserve. Described by Todd as obs., but revived by hist. writers and in ref. to Russia.

serge. F., L. *serica* (sc. *lana*), from the *Seres*, G. Σῆρες, prob. the Chinese (see *silk*); cf. Rum. *sárică*. In most Europ. langs., from F. In Chauc. (A. 2568).

sergeant, serjeant. F. *sergent*, L. *serviens*, *servient-*, pres. part. of *servire*, to serve. Earlier spelling usu. *sargent*, as still in surname (cf. *Clark*, *Darby*, etc.). In current use *serjeant* is limited to leg. applications. The earlier senses, in F. & E., are servant, soldier, officer. As mil. word it has been borrowed from F. by most Europ. langs. The law sense, E. from 13 cent., is after

Law L. *serviens ad legem*. For wide range of meanings of the title cf. those of *marshal*, *constable*. The *sergeant-major* was orig. a commissioned officer (see *general*).

sergent: a sergeant, officer, catchpole, purysuyvant, apparitor; also (in Old French) a footman, or souldier that serves on foot (Cotg.).

sericulture. Production of raw silk. Altered from F. *sériciculture* (see *serge*, *silk*).

series. L., from *severe*, to join, connect, cogn. with G. εἴρειν, to bind, Lithuanian *serit*, thread. *Seriatim* is MedL., after *gradatim*, etc. *Serial* is 19 cent. and, in chief current sense, was perh. first used of Dickens' novels.

serif. See *ceriph*.

serin. Bird of canary tribe. F., ? VL. **citrinus*, lemon-coloured.

seringa. Shrub. F., Port., L. *syringa* (q.v.).

serio-. Earliest in *serio-comic* (18 cent.).

serious. F. *sérieux*, MedL. *seriosus*, from L. *serius*, orig. heavy, cogn. with Ger. *schwer* (cf. sense-development of *grave³*).

serjeant. See *sergeant*.

sermon. F., L. *sermo-n-*, discourse; ? cogn. with *swear*. First in E. (12 cent.) in Church sense.

sero-. From *serum* (q.v.).

serotinous [*bot.*]. Late-flowering. From L. *serotinus*, from *sero*, adv. of *serus*, late.

serous. See *serum*.

serow. Asiatic antelope. Native name (N.W. Himalayas).

serpent. F., L. *serpens*, *serpent-*, pres. part. of *serpere*, to creep, cogn. with G. ἔρπειν, Sanskrit *sṛp*, ? and with *reptile*. With *serpentine* (rock) cf. *ophite*.

serpiginous [*med.*]. Of ringworm, MedL. *serpigo*, from *serpere*, to creep (v.s.).

serpula. Marine annelid. Mod. use of L. *serpula*, small serpent.

serra. Port. for *sierra* (q.v.).

serrated. From L. *serratus*, from *serra*, saw, ? imit. of rasping sound (Isidore).

serrefile [*mil.*]. F., rear soldier of file, lit. lock file; cf. Port. *serrafila*.

serried. From obs. *serry*, F. *serrer*, to lock, from L. *sera*, bolt, bar. First in Milt., but ME. had *sarray*, and *serr* was in use in 16–17 cents. Mod. currency is due to Scott.

serum [*med.*]. L., whey, watery fluid, cogn. with synon. G. ὀρός.

serval. Afr. bush-cat. F., used by Buffon of Asiatic lynx, Port. (*lobo*) *cerval*, lit. wolf hunting deer; cf. F. *loup-cervier*, L. *lupus cervarius*, from *cervus*, deer.

servant. F., pres. part. of *servir*, to serve. ModF. uses in domestic sense only later fem. *servante*. In Bibl. E., since Wyc., often for L. *servus*, G. δοῦλος.

Servantes be not so delygent as thei were wonto bee (Stonor Let. 1470).

serve. F. *servir*, L. *servire*, from *servus*, slave, serf (q.v.). Senses were mostly developed in L. & F. and those of *service* run parallel. In liturg. sense AS. had *serfise*, L. *servitium*. To *serve one out*, orig. from pugilism, is an ironic application of naut. to *serve out* (*grog*, etc.). With *serve you right* cf. earlier to *be well* (*ill*) *served* (by one's adherents, friends, etc.).

A plenteous victualler, whose provisions serve
Millions of cities that else needes must starve
                          (Sylv. *Colonies*).

Servian. See *Serbian*.

service¹. See *serve*.

service². Tree. Orig. *serves*, pl. of obs. *serve*, AS. *syrfe*, VL. **sorbea*, from *sorbus*, L. name of tree.

sarves, tree: alisier (Palsg.).

serviette. F., from *servir*, to serve. Common in Sc. from 15 cent., but in E. a late 19 cent. refinement now considered vulgar.

servile. F., L. *servilis*, from *servus*, slave.

Servite. From MedL. *Servitae*, members of order called *Servi Beatae Mariae*, founded 1233.

servitor. ME. & OF. *servitour* (*serviteur*), Late L. *servitor-em*, from *servire*, to serve. Formerly, at Oxf., student theoretically performing menial work in exchange for pecuniary help.

servitude. F., Late L. *servitudo*, from *servire* (v.s.).

sesame. ME. *sesam*, L. *sesamum*, G. σήσαμον, EInd. plant, prob. of Oriental origin; cf. Aram. *shumshemā*, Arab. *simsīm*. Mod. trisyllabic form, after G. σησάμη, is due to its use in *Ali Baba* in transl. (1785) of Galland's *Mille et une nuits*. Cf. *shibboleth*.

sesqui-. L., for **semis que*, a half in addition. Esp. after Horace, in *sesquipedalian*, from L. *sesquipedalis*, of a foot and a half.

Telephus et Peleus, cum pauper et exsul, uterque
Projicit ampullas, et sesquipedalia verba,
Si curat cor spectantis tetigisse querela
                          (Ars Poet. 96).

sess. See *cess*.

sessile [*bot.*]. L. *sessilis*, sitting down, stunted, from *sedēre*, *sess-*, to sit.

session. F., L. *sessio-n-*, from *sedēre*, *sess-* (v.s.). Cf. *assize*. *séance*.

sesterce [*hist.*]. L. *sestertius* (sc. *nummus*), for *semis tertius* (see *sesqui-*), i.e. two and a half (*asses*). *Sestertium*, thousand sesterces, is genitive pl. (in *mille sestertium*) taken as neut. sing.

sestet. It. *sestetto*, from *sesto*, sixth, L. *sextus*.

sestina [*metr.*]. It., poem of six-lined stanzas, from *sesto* (v.s.).

set[1]. Verb. AS. *settan*, causal of *sit*. Com. Teut.; cf. Du. *setten*, Ger. *setzen*, ON. *setja*, Goth. *satjan*. The article on this verb is the longest in the *NED*. Many of the senses are now usu. replaced in colloq. E. by *put*. The vulgar confusion with *sit* appears in AS., but in some cases, e.g. *the jelly sets*, intrans. is for earlier reflex. So also in *the sun sets* (not in AS.), with which cf. ON. *setjask* (see *bask*, *busk*[2]). Intrans. to *set out* (on a journey) is evolved from earlier trans. sense of fitting out an expedition; hence a *pretty set-out*, commotion. To *set to* is from earlier reflex.; cf. F. *se mettre à*.

set[2]. Noun. As act of setting, from *set*[1], e.g. in *dead set*, orig. cant for a scheme regarded as certain. But in sense of number, group, from OF. *sette*, ident. with *sect* (q.v.) and thus ult. with *suit-e*. Cf. MedL. *secta*, *setta*, in early wills, e.g. *cum lecto ejusdem settae* (temp. Rich. II), where a mod. upholsterer would say *suite*. But there has been much confusion between the two words, and derivatives of the verbs cogn. with *set*[1] occur in this sense in other Teut. langs. So also with *sett*, an archaic form surviving in various techn. senses, e.g. the paving *sett* is prob. from *set*[1], but the tennis *sett* (16 cent.) from OF. *sette*, sequence.

setaceous [*biol.*]. From L. *seta*, *saeta*, bristle, hair.

seton [*surg.*]. Thread run through skin to keep wound open. F. *séton*, It. *setone*, MedL. *seto-n-*, from *seta* (v.s.).

settee[1] [*naut.*]. It. *saettia*, "a very speedie pinnace, bark, foyst, brigandine, or barge" (Flor.), L. *sagitta*, arrow.

settee[2]. Couch. From early 18 cent. ?Altered from *settle* by analogy with obs. *settee*, part of head-dress (v.i.). The essential feature of the *settee* appears to have been the division in the middle (see Cowper's *Task*, i. 75), so there may be some vague association with *section*; cf. analogous uses of F. *coupé*. The two words occur together in quot. below, though in a totally different sense.

The settée, coupée place aright
        (*Mundus muliebris*, 1690).

setter. Dog. From *set*[1]. Earlier a kind of spaniel.

When he approcheth nęere to the place where the birde is, he layes him downe, and with a marcke of his pawes, betrayeth the place of the byrdes last abode, whereby it is supposed that this kinde of dogge is called Index, setter (*NED.* 1576).

setterwort. Cf. *settergrass*, ME. *satur-*, with cogn. LG. & MHG. forms. Origin unknown. ? From *satyr*.

settle[1]. Noun. AS. *setl*; cf. Ger. *sessel*, Goth. *sitls*; cogn. with *sit*, *saddle*, and with L. *sedēre*, to sit.

settle[2]. Verb. AS. *setlan*, from above, affected in some senses by ME. *saughtle*, to reconcile, frequent. of *saught*, of Scand. origin, and ult. cogn. with L. *sancire*. Cf. Ger. *siedeln*, to settle (in country).

setwall. Plant (red valerian), orig. drug. AF. *zedewale*, OF. *citoual*, *citouar*, Arab. *zedwār*, whence MedL. *zedoarium*, zedoary.

seven. AS. *seofon*. Aryan; cf. Du. *zeven*, Ger. *sieben*, ON. *sjau*, Goth. *sibun*, L. *septem*, G. ἑπτά, Sanskrit *sapta*, Gael. *seacht*, Welsh *saith*, etc. Regarded, ? owing to story of Creation, as perfect or sacred number, and hence used of a great many perfect sets (champions, sages, virtues, wonders of the world, etc.). Cf. similar uses of *nine*. The story of the *Seven Sleepers*, Christians of Ephesus who took refuge, during the Decian persecution, in a cave where they slept for some centuries, is in Ælfric (10 cent.). The Mohammedan *seventh heaven* is borrowed from Judaism. *Seventy-four* (*-gun ship*), standard line-of-battle ship c. 1800, is in Hickey's *Memoirs* (i. 263).

"No power on earth, I thought, could have prevented those two from going into action." "Seventy-fours at least—both of 'em!" laughs Harry (*Virginians*, ch. xxxiv.).

sever. F. *sevrer*, in ModF. only to wean, VL. **seperare*, for *separare*, to separate (v.i.).

several. OF., Late L. *separalis*, from *separ*, separate, from *se-* (q.v.) and *par*, equal. For orig. sense, as in *conjointly and severally*, cf. *divers*.

Captain Monson went forth severally to seeke his owne fortune in the Alcedo (Purch. xvi. 25).

severe. F. *sévère*, L. *severus*, strict, etc., from *se-*, without, and an obscure second element perh. cogn. with ON. *værr*, tranquil, tolerant. To *leave severely alone* is first quoted by *NED.* from C. S. Parnell. Phrase below has also been attributed to Horace Walpole.

Summer, as my friend Coleridge waggishly writes, has set in with its usual severity (Lamb).

Sèvres. Porcelain, from *Sèvres* (Seine-et-Oise).

sew. AS. *sīwian, sēowian.* Com. Teut., but not used exc. in Scand. & Fris.; cf. Fris. *siije,* OHG. *siuwan,* ON. *sȳja,* Goth. *siujan;* cogn. with L. *suere,* G. κασσύειν, Sanskrit *siv,* and ult. with *seam.*

sewer¹. Drain. AF. *sewere,* OF. *esseveur,* from *essever,* to drain, VL. **exaquare,* from *aqua,* water. For form cf. *ewer.* Till 16 cent. chiefly in MedL. (*sewera*) and AF. (*sewere*) leg. documents. Also *shore,* as in *Shoreditch,* partly due to the *common shore* (of the sea) being regarded as place where filth could be deposited. But OF. *essuiere,* sink, from *essuyer,* to dry, L. *exsucare,* from *sucus,* sap, can hardly be left out of account.

sewer². [*hist.*]. Attendant at table. Aphet. for AF. *asseour,* lit. putter, from F. *asseoir,* L. *assidēre,* from *sedēre,* to sit.

seware at mete: depositor, dapifer (*Prompt. Parv.*).

sewin¹. Bull-trout. In Welsh use, but app. not Welsh.

sewin². In pheasant-shooting. Corrupt. of obs. *sewel, shewel,* scare-crow, cogn. with *shy¹.* Cf. synon. Ger. *scheusal.*

sex. F. *sexe,* L. *sexus,* ? cogn. with L. *secare,* to cut, divide. *Fair* (*weak, soft,* etc.) *sex* is common in 17 cent. *Sexual* is Late L. *sexualis.*

sexagenarian. From L. *sexagenarius,* from *sexageni,* distrib. of *sexaginta,* sixty.

sexagesima. See *septuagesima.*

sexennial. From L. *sexennium,* six years. Cf. *biennial,* etc.

sext [*eccl.*]. L. *sexta* (sc. *hora*), sixth. Cf. *nones.*

sextant. L. *sextans, sextant-,* sixth part. Cf. *quadrant.* As instrument named (c. 1600) by Tycho Brahe.

sextet. Altered, on L. *sex,* six, from *sestet* (q.v.).

sextile [*astron.*]. L. *sextilis,* from *sextus,* sixth. In classical L. only as name for August.

sextillion. After *million,* etc.

sexton. Contr. of AF. *segerstain,* OF. *se-crestein, segrestein* (replaced by learned *sacristain*), MedL. *sacristanus,* from *sacer, sacr-,* holy. Cf. *sacristan.*

sextuple. From L. *sex,* six, after *quintuple,* etc.

seyd. See *sayyid.*

sforzando [*mus.*]. It., from *sforzare,* to force, VL. **ex-fortiare;* cf. F. *efforcer* (OF. *es-forcier*).

sgraffito. It., ? as synon. *graffito* (q.v.); ? or both rather from G. γράφειν, to write.

sh-. Exc. for a few foreign words, all words in *sh-* are AS., the digraph representing an original *sc-* which persists in doublets and cognates of Scand. origin.

sh! Imposing silence. Usu. written *hush.* Cf. *st!*

shabby. From dial. *shab,* AS. *sceabb,* scab (q.v.). "A word that has crept into conversation and low writing; but ought not to be admitted into the language" (Johns.). *Shabby-genteel* is recorded for 1754.

shabrack [*mil.*]. Saddle-cloth. Ger. *scha-bracke* or F. *schabraque,* of Eastern Europ. origin; cf. Magyar *csabrág,* Turk. *chābrāq.*

shack¹ [*dial.*]. Person of disreputable appearance. Short for *shackrag* (c. 1600), i.e. shake-rag. Cf. *wag.*

shack² [*US.*]. Shanty. ? From Mex. *jacal,* Aztec *xacalli,* wooden hut.

shackle. AS. *scacul,* bond, cogn. with ON. *skökull,* pole of wagon; cf. LG. *schakel,* hobble, Du. *schakel,* link of chain.

shad. Fish. AS. *sceadd;* cf. Norw. dial. *skada;* also Gael. Ir. *sgadan,* herring.

shaddock. EInd. fruit. Named (17 cent.) after *Capt. Shaddock,* who introduced it into the WIndies from the EIndies.

shade. AS. *sceadu, sceadw-,* whence also *shadow,* the two representing all senses of L. *umbra.* Com. Teut.; cf. Du. *schaduw,* Ger. *schatten,* Norw. *skodde,* mist, Goth. *skadus;* cogn. with G. σκότος, darkness, Gael. *sgáth,* Welsh *ysgod,* etc. With *shade,* gradation of colour, cf. synon. F. *nuance,* from *nue,* cloud. *Shady,* inferior, appears first in univ. slang. The *shadow of death* (*Ps.* xxiii. 4, and elsewhere), renders G. σκιὰ θανάτου (LXX. & NT.), now usu. regarded as mistransl. of a Heb. word for intense darkness. *May your shadow never grow less* is Oriental.

Coming events cast their shadows before
　　　　　　(Campbell, *Lochiel's Warning*).

shadoof. Irrigation machine. Egypt. Arab. *shādūf.*

shadow. See *shade.* With to *shadow* (c. 1600) cf. to *dog.*

shaft. AS. *sceaft*, shaft of spear, pole, etc. Com. Teut.; cf. Du. *schacht*, Ger. *schaft*, ON. *scapt*; cogn. with L. *scapus*, scape². All senses may be brought under orig. idea of cylindrical rod, passing into that of cylindrical cavity (*shaft* of mine), the latter sense being represented in Ger. by *schacht*, the LG. doublet of *schaft*. For a similar transference of meaning cf. *socket*, and, for the converse, *spigot*.

shag. Orig. matted hair. AS. *sceacga*, head of hair, cogn. with ON. *skegg*, beard, and with AS. *sceaga*, small wood, shaw, also ult. with *shock*³. Not recorded by *NED*. between AS. and 16 cent. Hence perh. *shag*, kind of cormorant with shaggy crest.

shagreen. Quasi-phonetic spelling (17 cent.) of *chagrin* (q.v.).

shah. Restored form of earlier (16 cent.) *shaugh, shaw*. Pers. *shāh*, shortened from OPers. *kshāyathiya*, king, cogn. with Sanskrit *kshatra*, dominion, G. κτᾶσθαι, to possess.

The King of Persia (whom here we call the great Sophy) is not here so called, but is called the Shaugh (Hakl. iii. 174, 1574).

Shaitan. Arab. *shaiṭān*, from Heb. *sāṭān*, Satan.

shake. AS. *sceacan*, cogn. with ON. *skaka*, LG. *schacken*; not found in HG. & Goth. To *shake down*, settle, whence a *shakedown*, is a metaphor from measuring corn (*Luke*, vi. 38). *No great shakes* is perh. from dicing. With *Shaker*, of various rel. bodies, cf. *Quaker*, with which it was synon. in 17 cent.

shako. F. *schako*, Magyar *csákó (-süveg)*, peaked cap, from *csák*, peak, Ger. *zacken*, earlier *zacke, zack*. Cf. *zigzag*.

shale. AS. *scealu*, scale¹, shell, as in *stānscalu*, or perh. from cogn. Ger. *schale*, as in *schalstein*, laminated limestone.

shall. AS. *sceal*, orig. a preterite (cf. *may, can*, etc.), with later past tense *sceolde*, whence *should*. Com. Teut.; cf. Du. *zal*, Ger. *soll*, ON. Goth. *skal*; ? cogn. with L. *scelus*, guilt. Orig. sense of owing (as late as 15 cent.) appears in AS. *scyld*, Ger. *schuld*, debt, guilt; cf. Ger. *soll und haben*, debit and credit. A trace of this survives in use of *shall* in 2nd and 3rd persons (thou *shalt not steal*, etc.), and in *sha'n't*. The correct alternation with *will* can, it is said, only be confidently executed by a Londoner.

And by that feith I shal to God and yow
(Chauc. *Troil.* iii. 1649).

shalloon. Fabric. Earlier *chalouns* (Chauc.), from *Chalons-sur-Marne* (Marne), a town named from the *Catalauni*. Cf. Ger. *schalaune*.

shallop. F. *chaloupe*, orig. ship's boat, Du. *sloep*, sloop (q.v.); cf. It. *scialuppa*, Sp. *chalupa*, Ger. *schaluppe*, from F. But some authorities regard Du. *sloep* as from F. *chaloupe*, in which case the origin must be sought elsewhere. Connection has been suggested with OF. *chaloppe*, shell (of nut), var. of *escalope*, of Teut. origin (see *scale²*, *scallop*). *Shallop* and *sloop* are treated as synonyms in early dicts.

shallot. Earlier *eschalot*, OF. *eschalotte* (*échalotte*), variation on *eschalogne*, scallion (q.v.).

shallow. Not found in AS., but evidently cogn. with *shoal¹* (q.v.). The form points to AS. **sceal*, **scalw-* (cf. *fallow*).

sham. Slang of late 17 cent., usu. assumed to be northern form of *shame*. ? Originating in mock assumption of *shame*, modesty (so explained by North, 1734). In view of the obscure origin of most cant words the above explanation is to be regarded as dubious.

Shamming is telling you an insipid, dull lie, with a dull face, which the sly wag, the author, only laughs at himself (Wycherley, 1677).

shamah. Ind. song-bird. Hind. *çāmā*.

Shamanism. Primitive spiritualistic religion, orig. of Ural-Altaic peoples of Siberia. From Russ. *shaman*, priest-doctor, a Mongolian word, perh. ult. from Pali *samana*, Buddhist monk, Sanskrit *sramaṇa*.

The yellow-skinned, slant-eyed, nomadic, shamanistic Kirghiz-Kaizat of Western Siberia and Turkestan (*Times Lit. Suppl.* March 13, 1919).

shamble¹. Noun. Usu. in pl. *shambles*. AS. *sceamel*; cf. archaic Du. *schamel*, Ger. *schemel*, footstool. WGer. borrowing of L. *scamellum*, dim. of *scamnum*, bench. In E. bench for sale of meat, hence meat-market, butchery, as in the *Shambles* at Nottingham. Later used of slaughter-house and often fig. With *a shambles* cf. *a works, a links*, etc.

shamble². Verb. From 17 cent., first as adj., in *shamble legs*, app. from *shamble¹*. *NED*. compares WFris. *skammels*, lit. shambles¹, used of ill-formed legs (cf. also F. *bancal*, crooked-legged, from *banc*, bench). But gloss below suggests possibility that the verb arose from the movement of the weaver at his loom, the connection with *shamble*[1] remaining.

schæmelen: insilia; ligna pedibus textorum subjecta, quibus telae alternis vicibus, sive alternatim contrahuntur & aperiuntur (Kil.).

shame. AS. *sceamu*. Com. Teut.; cf. Du. *schamen* (verb), Ger. *scham*, ON. *skömm*, Goth. **skama* (only in verb *skaman*). The E. word has the double sense expressed in F. by *pudeur, honte*, and in Ger. by *scham, schande* (derivative of *scham*). *Shamefaced* is folk-etym. for *shamefast* (Chauc. A. 840), AS. *scamfæst*, firm in modesty (cf. *steadfast*).

There is a common saying amongst us, Say the truthe and shame the divel (Latimer, 1552).

shammy. Leather. Quasi-phonetic spelling of *chamois* (q.v.). Earlier also *shamoy*.

shampoo. Orig. a form of massage (Anglo-Ind.). Hind. *shāmpo*, imper. of *shāmpnā*, to press. Cf. *dekho*, look (mil. slang), imper. of *dekhna*, to look.

The barbers of this place are much spoken of for their neatenesse in shaveinge and artificiall champinge (Peter Mundy, 1632).

shamrock. Ir. *seamróg*, dim. of *seamar*, clover; cf. Gael. *seamrag*. Trad. used by St Patrick as symbol of Trinity.

Shandean, Shandeian, Shandeism. From Sterne's *Tristram Shandy* (1759–67).

shandrydan. From c. 1800. Also (north-west dial.) *shandry, shandry-cart*. Origin unknown.

shandygaff. App. first (c. 1850) at Oxf. Origin unknown. Cf. Lond. slang *shant*, pot (of beer).

shanghai [*naut.*]. From *Shanghai*, China. Orig. US., but *shanghai*, catapult, is recorded earlier in Austral. Cf. *stellenbosch* and obs. *barbadose*, to transport to the plantations (in *Barbados*).

shank. AS. *sceanca*, leg. WGer.; cf. Flem. *schank*, leg-bone, Ger. dim. *schenkel*, thigh; cogn. with Ger. *schinken*, ham, and prob. with ON. *skakkr*, crooked (cf. the Rom. names for leg, e.g. F. *jambe*, supposed to be cogn. with G. καμπή, curve, and Celt. *cam*, crooked). Gradually superseded in gen. sense by *leg* (q.v.), but survives in surnames *Cruikshank, Sheepshanks*, etc.

And aye, until the day he dy'd,
He rode on good shanks naggy (*Sc. song*, 1724).

shanker [*med.*]. Obs. form of *chancre*.

shanty[1]. Hut. Orig. US. & Canada. ? Corrupt. of F. *chantier*, workshop, used in Canada of woodcutters' forest quarters.

Cf. *shantyman*, lumberman, Canad. F. *homme de chantier* (see *gantry*). Others derive it from Ir. *sean toig*, old house, cogn. with L. *senex* and *tectum* respectively.

shanty[2]. See *chanty*.

shape. AS. *gesceap* (noun), *scieppan* (verb), the latter orig. strong; cf. archaic p.p. *shapen*, whence mod. form of the verb. Orig. to create, hence to mould, form. Com. Teut.; cf. Du. *scheppen*, Ger. *schöpfer*, creator, *schaffen*, to create, procure, ON. *skepja*, Goth. *gaskapjan*; cogn. with *-ship*. With *shapely* cf. L. *formosus*, from *forma*, shape.

shapoo. Tibetan *sha-pho*, wild sheep.

shard[1], **sherd** [*archaic*]. AS. *sceard*, cleft, fragment (cf. *potsherd*), from *shear*.

shard[2]. Beetle-wing. Ghost-word evolved from *shardborn beetle* (*Macb.* iii. 2), which means born in dung, AS. *scearn*; cf. AS. *scearnbudda*, dung-beetle, whence mod. dial. *shornbug* and synon. F. *escarbot*.

share[1]. Of plough. AS. *scear*, cogn. with *shear, share*[2]. See *scabbard*.

share[2]. Portion. AS. *scearu*, cutting, division (v.s.), only recorded in obs. sense of the fork of the legs, and in compds., e.g. *land-scearu*, boundary (whence name *Landseer*); cf. Du. *schaar*, Ger. *schar*, troop, detachment. In ME. orig. naut., portion of booty, whence *share and share (a)like* (16 cent.), *lion's share*, etc.

Common mariners and souldiers are much given to pillaging and spoiling, making greater account of the same then of their shares (Hakl. xi. 51).

shark. Although recorded as fish-name somewhat earlier than in sense of greedy parasite, I think the latter is the orig. sense, and that the word comes, perh. via Du., from Ger. *schurk(e)*, "a shark, sharper, rook, rake, rogue" (Ludw.), whence also *shirk* (q.v.), It. *scrocco*, as in *mangiare a scrocco*, "to feede scotfree at another mans charge" (Flor.), and F. *escroc*, a sharper. The change of vowel is normal (cf. *clerk, Derby*, etc., and see *serve*). This word may easily have been current among seamen before being recorded, and the quots. (v.i.) suggest a naut. nickname rather than a foreign word. Job Hortop (Hakl.) saw "monstrous fish called 'sharkes'" off Sierra Leone in 1568, though the account of his adventures was written later. The early travellers usu. call the fish *tuberon, tiberon*, from Sp. It may also be noted that the F. name *requin*, also (16 cent.) *requien*, is prob. a nickname. It is explained (17 cent.) by Furetière as for *requiem*, which is quite possible.

There is no proper name for it that I knowe, but that sertayne men of Captayne Haukinses doth call it a "sharke" (*NED.*, from a broadside, 1569).

The shark hath not this name for nothing, for he will make a morsel of anything that he can catch, master, and devour (*ib.* 1655).

Jaws...of such strength that a leg or an arm, bone and all, is but an easy morsel; wherefore called shark by the seamen

(Fryer's *E. Ind. and Pers.* 1672–81).

Sharon, rose of. See *Song of Sol.* ii. 1. *Sharon* is a fertile strip on the coast of Palestine. The flower is unidentified.

sharp. AS. *scearp*. Com. Teut.; cf. Du. *scherp*, Ger. *scharf*, ON. *skarpr*; cogn. with AS *scearpian*, to scarify, and ult. with *scrape*. *Sharper* was prob. suggested by earlier *sharker*, which, in its turn, owes something to Du. *schaker*, robber. *Sharpset*, eager for food, was in 16 cent. used of hawks, but may have orig. been a metaphor from the saw.

shatter. Later var. (14 cent.) of *scatter*, with which it was at first synon., as still in dial. (see *Lycidas*, 5).

shave. AS. *sceafan*, to scrape, pare down; orig. strong, as still in p.p. *shaven*. Com. Teut.; cf. Du. *schaven*, Ger. *schaben*, ON. *skafa*, Goth. *skaban*; cogn. with L. *scabere*, to scratch. Cf. noun *shave*, as in *spokeshave*, AS. *sceafa*. With *young shaver*, from fig. to *shave*, steal, swindle, cf. *nipper*. With *a close shave*, from sense of brushing lightly against, cf. F. *friser la corde*, to escape hanging, lit. to brush against the rope.

Shavian. For formation, from (*G. B.*) *Shaw*, cf. *Borrovian*, of *George Borrow*, *Harrovian*, of *Harrow*.

shaw[1] [*dial.*]. Small wood (Johns.). AS. *sceaga*, cogn. with *shag* and with ON. *skōgr*, wood, so common in northern place-names (*Briscoe, Ayscough*, etc.).

shaw[2] [*Sc.*]. Potato-haulm. ? Sc. form of *show*.

shawl. Pers. *shāl*. In most Europ. langs.

shawm. ME. *shalmeye*, OF. *chalemie*, unexplained var. of OF. *chalemel* (*chalumeau*), dim. from L. *calamus*, reed (cf. *calumet*); cf. Du. Ger. *schalmei*, from F. Current form is back-formation from pl. *shalmys* (cf. *cuish*).

How many notes a sackbut has, and whether shawms have strings

(Arthur Hilton, *Vulture and Husbandman*).

shay. See *chay*. Pegge (*Anecdotes*) gives *shay* and *po*(*st*)-*shay* as cockneyisms.

she. AS. *sīo*, *sēo*, fem. of def. art. (orig. demonstr. pron.), substituted for AS. pron. *hēo*, which tended to become indistinguishable from masc. The same substitution is found in other langs. (Du. *zij*, Ger. *sie*, G. *ἡ*, etc.). Application to ship is in Barbour (*scho*), but in 16–17 cents. *he* is more usual; cf. *Indiaman, man-of-war*, etc. Use of *he-, she-*, in names of animals, is peculiar to E.

The bestes all, bath sco and he,
War brogt for wit him to see

(*Cursor Mundi*, 13 cent.).

shea. WAfr. tree. Mandingo word, so spelt by Mungo Park.

sheading. Division of I. of Man. Var. of *shedding*, from *shed*[1].

sheaf. AS. *scēaf*, sheaf of corn. Com. Teut.; cf. Du. *schoof*, Ger. *schaub*, wisp (*schober*, haycock, etc.), ON. *skauf*, fox's brush. In ME. also esp. of two dozen arrows (Chauc. A. 104).

shealing. See *shieling*.

shear. AS. *scieran*. Com. Teut.; cf. Du. Ger. *scheren*, ON. *skera*. Replaced, exc. in spec. senses, by *cut*. Hence *shears*, scissors, also *share*[1,2]. See also *sheer*[2]. *Shorn of one's strength* is from story of Samson. The *shorn lamb* proverb was app. adapted by Sterne (v.i.) from F. *à brebis tondue Dieu mesure le vent*.

"God tempers the wind," said Maria, "to the shorn lamb" (*Sent. Journey*).

sheat-fish, sheath-fish. Large freshwater fish. Cf. Ger. *scheiden* (OHG. *schaide, scheide*), also *scheidfisch*. ? Cogn. with *shad*.

scheide oder scheidfisch: the shad or shad-fish (Ludw.).

sheath. AS. *scǣth*; cf. Du. *scheede, schee*, Ger. *scheide*, ON. *skeithir* (pl.); cogn. with *shed*[1], with idea of separation. Goth. has *fōdr*, whence F. *fourreau* (dim.), It. *fodero*.

sheath-fish. See *sheat-fish*.

sheave. Grooved wheel of pulley. Unexplained var. of *shive* (q.v.), with orig. sense of disk. Both were used in ME. of a slice of bread.

shebeen [*Anglo-Ir.*]. Cabin where whisky is sold without licence. Ir. *sibin, séibín*, lit. little mug; cf. *colleen, poteen*, and, for sense, Ger. *krug*, pothouse, lit. mug.

Shechinah. See *Shekinah*.

shed[1]. Verb. AS. *scēadan*, to divide, hence to sprinkle, scatter. Com. Teut., though app. not recorded in ON.; cf. Du. Ger. *scheiden*, Goth. *skaidon*, to divide; cogn. with G. σχίζειν, to split. Orig. sense appears in *watershed* (cf. Ger. *wasserscheide*).

shed². Noun. Earlier (15–16 cents.) *shad*, var. of *shade*, in sense of shelter. Current sense is due to influence of earlier *schudde* (whence dial. *shud*), ult. cogn. with Ger. *schutz*, protection.

schud, or lytyl howse: teges (*Prompt. Parv.*).

sheen. Orig. adj., as noun first in Shaks. (*Haml.* iii. 2), who prob. apprehended it as belonging to *shine*. AS. *scíene*, beautiful, splendid. Com. Teut.; cf. Du. *schoon* (see *scone*), Ger. *schön*, Goth. *skauns*; prob. cogn. with *show* (cf. *shapely*, *sightly*). Being often used as epithet of the sun it was naturally associated with *shine*.

Sheeny [*slang*]. Jew. East End slang (early 19 cent.). ? From Yiddish pronunc. of Ger. *schön*, beautiful, used in praising wares. (A guess.) ? Cf. *smouch*.

sheep. AS. *scæp*, *scéap*. WGer.; cf. Du. *schaap*, Ger. *schaf*. For the Aryan name of the animal see *ewe*. To *cast sheep's eyes* is in Skelton (cf. *ogle*). Current sense of *sheepish* (in ME. meek, docile, etc.) is 17 cent.

sheer¹. Adj. Cogn. with dial. *shire*, AS. *scír*, bright, pure. Com. Teut.; cf. OSax. *skîr*, Ger. *schier*, ON. *skírr*, Goth. *skeirs*; ult. cogn. with *shine*. For sense-development cf. *mere*, *pure*, and Ger. *lauter*, lit. pure, e.g. *aus lauter bosheit*, from sheer malice. A *sheer precipice* is one that is all precipice without any interruption. *Sheer*, which has ousted *shire*, is prob. AS. **scǽre*, corresponding to ON. *skǽrr*, cogn. with above.

sheer². Verb. Accidental (naut.) spelling of *shear*, to divide, used to indicate a slanting course, esp. in to *sheare off* (Capt. John Smith), also earlier to *sheer up to* (*out, by, away*); cf. to *cut off* (intrans.). Hence also the *sheer*, curve of upper works, of a ship; cf. synon. F. *tonture*, "the sheer of the wales and deck" (Lesc.), from *tondre*, to shear. A *sheer-hulk* is an old dismasted ship used as platform for mounting *shears*, i.e. a naut. crane of the form of a pair of shears, or scissors. In the famous song it is prob. often understood as "mere" hulk.

Here, a sheer hulk, lies poor Tom Bowling
(Dibdin, 1790).

We have strawed our best to the weed's unrest,
To the shark and the sheering gull
(Kipling, *Price of Admiralty*).

sheet¹. Cloth. AS. *scíete*, *scéat*, napkin, winding-sheet, whence *sheeted dead* (*Haml.* i. 1). Used in AS. *Gospels* for the *linen cloth* of *Mark*, xiv. 51. Connection with beds appears in ME. Hence *sheet of paper*, *water*, etc. For cognates see *sheet²*.

sheet² [*naut.*]. AS. *scéata*, synon. with *scéat* (v.s.), and with additional sense of foot of sail, whence app. transferred to the rope. For a similar transfer of sense cf. *shroud*. A later development appears in *stern-sheets* (15 cent.), app. part of boat to which sheets were formerly attached. The naut. sense appears in some of the Teut. cognates, e.g. Du. *schoot*, lap, sailrope, Ger. *schoss*, bosom, lap (LG. *schôte*, sailrope), ON. *skaut*, bosom, skirt, sailrope, Goth. *skauts*, hem of garment. Cf. also L. *sinus*, bosom, hollow of sail. Synon. F. *écoute* (OF. *escoute*), It. *scotta*, Sp. *escota* are from Teut. Late ME. had also *shutte*, *shoot*, etc., from LG. Here belongs *sheet-anchor*, also earlier *shute anker*, *ankers called shutte* (*Nav. Accts.* 1495–97), though the reason for the name is obscure. It may have been suspended near the sheets (cf. *bow-anchor*, *bower²*). For fig. use, already (*shote ancre*) in Sir T. More, cf. *mainstay*.

The biggest anchor of all is the sheat-anchor, frequently by seamen call'd their Last Hope, being us'd in the greatest extremity (*Sea Dict.* 1708).

sheikh. Arab. *shaikh*, lit. old man, from *shākha*, to grow old. Cf. *priest, alderman, seneschal, senate*, etc. Hence *Sheiku 'l Islam*, chief of Islam, supreme rel. authority.

sheiling. See *shieling*.

shekel. Heb. *sheqel*, from *shāqal*, to weigh. Cf. *pound¹*. Earlier *sicle* (Wyc.), through OF.

Shekinah. Visible manifestation of God "between the cherubim." Late Heb. *shekīnāh*, from *shākan*, to dwell.

Sheldonian theatre. At Oxf., "built (1669) by the munificence of *Dr Gilbert Sheldon*, Abp. of Canterbury" (Evelyn).

sheldrake. App. from dial. *sheld*, *shell*, dappled, pied; cf. Du. *verschillen*, to diversify, from ODu. *skela*, division, ult. cogn. with *skill*. But cf. ON. *skjöldóttr*, dappled, of which first element means shield, and see *skewbald*.

shelf. First in Chauc. LG. *schelf*, in same sense, cogn. with AS. *scylf*, as in *stānscylf*, rocky crag. The two are associated in *shelf* (of rock) which is not recorded till 16 cent.

and then only in sense of sandbank, submerged rock, also commonly called *ledge*, *flat* (passim in Purch.). Both are prob. from a Teut. root *skelf-*, to split. See also *shelve*.

Jove in heaven would smile to see Diana set on shelfe (Gascoigne, 1575).

shell. AS. *sciell*; cf. Du. *schel, schil*, ON. *skel*, sea-shell, Goth. *skalja*, tile, and other cognates s.vv. *scale*[1], *shale*. The school form called the *shell* was orig. held at the shell-shaped end of the school-room at Westminster. A *shell-jacket* fits like a shell. In sense of missile *shell* was orig. (17 cent.) applied to a hand-grenade. *Shellback*, sailor, is mod.

The world is suffering from shell shock
               (D. Lloyd George, Feb. 14, 1920).

shellac. For *shell lac*, rendering F. *lac en écailles*, lac in thin plates. See *lac*[1].

Shelta [*ling.*]. Cryptic Gael. Ir. tinkers' lang. Origin of name unknown.

shelter. Late 16 cent. ? Evolved from Ger. *schilterhaus*, var. of *schilderhaus*, sentry-box, orig. small wooden structure for sentinel in bad weather (Grimm), from *schilden*, to protect, shield. Cf. Du. *schilderhuis*. The date favours Du. or Ger. origin. At any rate it must be cogn. with *shield*.

shelty. Shetland pony. Orkney or Caithness pronunc. of ON. *Hjalti*, Shetlander. Cf. *Shetland, Zetland*, ON. *Hjaltland*.

shelve. To slope (c. 1600). ? Can hardly come from *shelf*, the essence of which is to be horizontal. ? Cf. Ger. *scheel*, oblique (MHG. *schel, schelw-*, whence dial. *schelb*), cogn. with AS. *sceol*. On the other hand it may have been orig. applied to a "shoaling" shore, and Purch. renders L. *vada* by "shallow places, quicke sand, or shelves." To *shelve*, postpone, is to put on the shelf (in current sense).

Shemitic. See *Semitic*.

she-oak. Austral. tree. From *she*, earlier applied to plants as to animals. "There is no foundation for the allegation that the word is a corruption of a native Australian or Tasmanian name" (*NED.*).

There are two kinds of holly, that is to say he holly and she holly (Gascoigne, 1575).

Sheol [*theol.*]. Heb. *sheōl*, the underworld, Hades. Substituted for *hell* in many passages of *RV*.

shepherd. AS. *scēaphirde*. See *herd*. For fig.

senses cf. *pastor*. For mil. sense of to *shepherd* cf. to *round up*.

We headed 'em off, and the other Johnnies herded 'em behind (Doyle, *Trag. of Korosko*, ch. ix.).

sheraton. Furniture. From *T. Sheraton*, cabinet maker (†1806). Cf. *chippendale*.

sherbet. Turk. Pers. *sherbet*, Arab. *sharbah*, from *shariba*, to drink. Cf. *sirup, shrub*[2], *sorbet*.

Sherbecke...is only honey and water
               (Capt. John Smith).

sherd. See *shard*[1].

shereef. Arab. *sharīf*, noble, from *sharafa*, to be exalted. Orig. descendant of Mohammed through his daughter Fatima.

sheriff. AS. *scīrgerēfa*, shire reeve[1] (q.v.). For extended senses cf. *marshal, sergeant, steward*, and other offic. titles. Mod. pronunc. (v.i.) is due to spelling. See *shrievalty*.

Our pair of new sheriffs
Hang by them like sleeves (*Rump Song*, c. 1659).

sherry. Back-formation from *sherris*, Sp. (*vino de*) *Xeres*, (wine from) *Xeres* (now *Jerez*), L. (*urbs*) *Caesaris*, commonly written *Sherries* in 17 cent. E. Cf. *cherry* for loss of -s.

shew. See *show*.

shewbread [*Bibl.*]. First in Tynd. (*Ex.* xxv. 30), after Ger. *schaubrot* (Luther), lit. show-bread, rendering L. *panes propositionis* (*Vulg.*), G. ἄρτοι ἐνώπιοι (LXX.), lit. from Heb. AS. has *offring-hlāfas*, Wyc. *loovis of proposicioun*. Tynd. had used *halowed loves* in his *NT*. transl. (*Matt.* xii. 4).

Shiah. Branch of Mohammedans (chiefly Pers.) recognizing Ali as successor of Prophet (see quot. s.v. *Bedouin*). Arab. *shī'ah*, sect, from *shā'a*, to follow. Hence *Shiite*. Cf. *Sunnite*. The distinction is really ethnic, between Persian and Arab, Aryan and Semite.

shibboleth. Test-word (*Judges*, xii. 4–6). Heb. *shibbō-leth*, ear of corn, rustling stream (both from idea of growth). The latter sense is preferred by mod. commentators because of the local circumstances. But cf. *sesame* (q.v.) and It. *cicera*, chick-pease, used as test-word by Italians in the massacre of Frenchmen in Sicily (1282), commonly called the Sicilian Vespers. Similar tests are applied at the police-station when a "drunk" professes strict sobriety.

shicer [*slang*]. Orig. Austral., unproductive gold-claim. Ger. *scheisser*, cacator.

shield. AS. *scield*. Com. Teut.; cf. Du. Ger. *schild*, ON. *skjöldr*, Goth. *skildus*.

shieling, shealing [*dial*.]. Shepherd's hut. Dim. of dial. *shiel*, app. from an AS. cognate of ON. *skále*, whence synon. dial. *scale*. Both are common in place-names, e.g. *Shields, Greenshields, Seascale, Winterscale*, etc.

shift. First as verb. AS. *sciftan*, to divide, apportion, arrange (for sense-development cf. *devise*). Com. Teut.; cf. Du. *schiften*, to divide, Ger. *schichten*, to classify, ON. *skipta*, to divide, change. Current sense, to remove, etc., is latest. With *shift*, evasion, cf. *shuffle*, and with *shift*, chemise, orig. euph. for smock, cf. It. *mutande*, "thinne under-breeches" (Flor.). In to *make shift, shift for oneself*, etc., there seems to be confusion with synon. F. *chevir* (cf. *venir à chef*, to manage), whence ME. *cheve*. To *make shift* corresponds exactly to archaic F. *faire chevisance*.

Send me word howghe ye doo and howghe ye have schevyte for yourself syn ye departid hens
(*Paston Let.* ii. 142).

Shiite. See *Shiah*.

shikaree. Urdu, Pers. *shikári*, from *shikár*, hunting, sport.

shillelagh. Cudgel from wood of *Shillelagh* (Co. Wicklow).

shillibeer. Funeral conveyance, formerly also omnibus. From *G. Shillibeer*, coach-proprietor (†1866). Cf. *tilbury*.

shilling. AS. *scilling*. Com. Teut.; cf. Du. *schelling*, Ger. *schilling*, ON. *skillingr*, Goth. *skilliggs*; also adopted by Rom. langs. Origin uncertain. ? Root *skell-*, to resound (cf. *chink*²), ? root *skel-*, to divide (cf. Dan. *skillemynt*, change, Ger. *scheidemünze*, change, cogn. with *shed*¹). With to *take the shilling*, enlist, cf. *press*².

Tha behēton hig hym thritig scyllinga
(AS. *Gosp. Matt.* xxvi. 15).

When I die, I'll leave him the fee-simple of a rope and a shilling (Farquhar, 1700).

shilly-shally. Redupl. on *shall I?*

I don't stand shill I, shall I, then; if ·I say't, I'll do 't (Congreve, 1700).

shimmer. AS. *scymrian*, cogn. with *scímian*, to shine, whence obs. *shim*; cf. Ger. *schimmern*.

shimmy [*dial*.]. For *chemise*. Cf. *burgee*, *cherry*, etc.

shin. AS. *scinu*, also *scinbán*, shinbone. WGer.; cf. Du. *scheen, scheenbeen*, Ger. *schiene, schienbein*. Orig. sense perh. edge, plate; cf. Du. Ger. sense of splint, greave, railway metal, that of *shin* being represented by the compd. Cf. *bladebone*.

shindy, shine. App. these belong together. Both meant orig. (early 19 cent.) spree, jollification, with later change of sense as in *row*³ (cf. *tea-fight*). From *shine*¹ (cf. F. *éclat*, shining, outburst).

shine¹. To gleam. AS. *scínan*. Com. Teut.; cf. Du. *schijnen*, Ger. *scheinen*, ON. *skína*, Goth. *skeinan*. Ult. cogn. with *shimmer*. With to *take the shine out of*, i.e. reduce splendour, cf. synon. F. *décatir*, a metaphor from the cloth-trade.

shine². See *shindy*.

shingle¹. Wooden tile. ME. *scincle*, L. *scindula*, for *scandula*, "a shingle or tile of wood cleft" (Coop.), whence also Ger. *schindel*.

shingle². Stones on beach. Earlier (16 cent.) *chingle*, app. of echoic origin (*chink*²). Synon. Norw. *singel* is also echoic. Cf. *boulder, pebble*.

shingles [*med*.]. Corrupt. of MedL. *cingulus*, for *cingulum*, girdle, used to render G. ζώνη, in same sense, the eruption surrounding the body like a belt.

Shintoism. From *Shinto*, native religion of Japan. Chin. *shin tao*, way of the gods.

ship. AS. *scip*. Com. Teut.; cf. Du. *schip*, Ger. *schiff*, ON. Goth. *skip*. It. *schifo*, F. *esquif* are from Teut. With *shipshape* cf. *seamanlike*.

-ship. AS. *-scipe*, cogn. with *shape*; cf. Du. *-schip* (see *landscape*), also Du. *-schap*, Ger. *-schaft*, ON. *-skapr*.

shire. AS. *scír*, offic. charge, district; cogn. with OHG. *scíra*, offic. charge. Unconnected with *shear*. *The shires*, orig. used by people of EAngl., Kent, Surrey, etc. in ref. to those counties which end in *-shire*, now usu. means the hunting-country of the Midlands, whence also *shire horse*.

shirk. Var. of *shark* (q.v.). As verb orig. to live as a parasite.

shark, or hanger on: parasitus, aeruscator (Litt.).
shirk: parasitus, gnathonicus (*ib·*
shurk: a sharper (*Dict. Cant. Crew*).

Shirley poppy. First grown (1880) at *Shirley*, near Croydon, by Rev. W. Wilks, secretary of Horticultural Society.

shirt. AS. *scyrte*; cf. Du. *schort*, Ger. *schürze* (MHG. *schurz*), apron, ON. *skyrta*, shirt, whence E. *skirt*. All cogn. with *short* (q.v.); cf. hist. of *kirtle*. To *get one's shirt out*, whence *shirty*, bad-tempered, is 19 cent. *Shirt of Nessus*, maddening poison of cause of which the victim is unconscious, is from the story of Hercules and the centaur.

shit. AS. *scītan, in *besciten* (p.p.). Com. Teut.; cf. Du. *schijten*, Ger. *scheissen*, ON. *skīta*; prob. cogn. with *shed*[1], in orig. sense of separation (cf. L. *excrementum*, from *excernere*, to separate).

shittim [*Bibl.*]. Heb. *shittīm*, pl. of *shittāh*, acacia.

shive. Thin bung, also (dial.) slice of bread. AS. *scīfe; cf. Du. *schijf*, "shive of a pulley" (Hexham), Ger. *scheibe*, "any round and flat thing" (Ludw.); cogn. with G. σκοῖπος, potter's disk. Also *sheave*.

shiver[1]. Splinter; chiefly in *to shivers*. Early ME. *scifre*, cogn. with *shive*, *sheave*, and with Ger. *schiefer*, slate (q.v.). Hence *shiver my timbers*, "a mock oath attributed in comic fiction to sailors" (*NED.*).

shiver[2]. To tremble. ME. *chevere*, *chivere*, also *chivel*, in same sense. ? Cf. F. *chevroter*, to quaver (of the voice), which the *Dict. Gén.* connects with the bleating of the goat, *chèvre*.

shoal[1]. Shallow. Earlier *sho(a)ld*, *shald*. AS. *sceald* (adj.), cogn. with LG. *schol*, shallow. The regular Hakl. & Purch. spelling is *shoald*. Noun sense is later.

shoal[2]. Of fish. From 16 cent. A peculiar use of *shoal*[1], suggested by synon. Du. *school*, school[2], which is cogn. with AS. *scolu*, multitude, from root **skel-*, to divide. Cf. F. *banc de sable*, shoal of sand, *banc de harengs* (*maquereaux*, *morues*), shoal of herring (mackerel, cod).

shock[1]. Of corn. ? Orig. some def. number of sheaves. Cf. LG. *schok*, shock of corn, sixty, Du. *schok*, sixty (earlier also shock of corn), Ger. *schock*, sixty, Sw. *skock*, crowd, sixty, Norw. *skok*, sixty, flock. Reckoning by sixties is said to have spread from Babylon into the Europ. langs. Relation of *sheaf* to *shove* suggests that *shock* belongs to *shake*; for def. sense cf. *score*.

shock[2]. To collide, etc. First (16 cent.) in mil. sense (cf. neol. *shock-troops* for Ger. *sturmtruppen* or *stosstruppen*). F. *choquer*, perh. from OF. *choque*, tree-stump; cf. OF. *choper*, to stumble, from *chope*, tree-stump. With nursery use of *shocking* cf. *naughty*.

With *shilling shocker* (neol.) cf. *penny dreadful*.

shock[3]. Of hair. Back-formation from obs. *shock-dog*, app. ident. with earlier *shough*, said to have been an Iceland dog, ? cogn. with *shag*. Cf. myth. *shuck-dog* (Norf.).

As hounds and greyhounds, mongrels, spaniels, curs, Shoughs, water-rugs, and demi-wolves, are cleped All by the name of dogs (*Macb.* iii. 1).

shod. Old p.p. of *to shoe*, esp. in *dryshod*, *roughshod*, *slipshod*.

shoddy. From 19 cent. Yorks dial. word of unknown origin. ? Cogn. with *shed*[1] in orig. sense of separating.

shoe. AS. *scōh*. Com. Teut.; cf. Du. *schoen* (orig. pl.), Ger. *schuh*, ON. *skōr*, Goth. *skōhs*, ? from root *skeu, to cover. Distinction from *boot* is mod. With *another pair of shoes* cf. F. *autre paire de manches*, "an other manner of matter" (Cotg.). Chaucer's saying (v.i.) is as old as Plutarch. For *shoeblack*, from street cry, cf. *sweep*.

But I woot best where wryngeth me my sho
(Chauc. E. 1553).

Who waitth for dead men shoen shall go long barefoote (Heywood, 1546).

shoful [*Yiddish*]. False coin. Ger. *schofel*, worthless, Heb. *shāphāl*, low. Also applied, for reason not known, to hansom cab.

shog [*dial.*]. Cf. Du. *schok*, shake, jolt, OHG. *scoc*, oscillation. Cf. *jog*.

shogun. Hereditary commander of Jap. army (see *tycoon*). Jap. (*sei-i-tai*) *shōgun*, (barbarian-subduing) chief, Chin. *chiang chiin*, lead army.

shoo. Instinctive. Cf. Ger. *schu*, It. *scioia*.

shoot[1]. To spring forth, impel missile, etc. AS. *scēotan*. Com. Teut.; cf. Du. *schieten*, Ger. *schiessen*, ON. *skjōta*. The correspondence of *to shoot* (rubbish) with Ger. *schütten*, *ausschütten*, suggests that some unrecorded AS. verb has been absorbed (cf. OSax. *skuddian*, to shake).

shoot[2]. In *to shoot the rapids*. See *chute*. But *to shoot*[1] is similarly used in 16 cent. E., esp. in connection with the "overfall" under London Bridge, so that two words have been combined.

The Duke of Somersett was had from the Tower of London by water and shott London bridge at v of the clock (Wriothesley, *Chron.* 1551).

We turned down the river, shooting the over-fals with more celeritie than when we came up
(Purch. xvi. 394, Guiana).

shoot[3] [*slang*]. Lot. See *shot*.

shop. AS. *sceoppa*, treasury (only in *Luke*,

xxi. 1), cogn. with Ger. *schopf*, porch, etc., *schuppen*, shed (from LG.), and with E. dial. *shippen*, cow-shed, AS. *scipen*. But the lateness of the word (13 cent.), and rarity of AS. *sceoppa*, point rather to our having taken it from cogn. OF. *eschope* (*échoppe*), booth, stall (12 cent.), "a little (and most commonly) low shop" (Cotg.), of Teut. origin. For *shop-lifter* (17 cent.) see *lift*.

shore[1]. Edge of land. Cf. Du. *schor*, earlier *schoor*, "alluvies, terra alluvione aggesta" (Kil.). A LG. word of unknown origin. The late appearance (14 cent.) and Du. sense are against connection with *shear*.

shore[2]. Prop. Cf. Du. *schoor*, ON. *skortha*, ? cogn. with AS. *scorian*, to project.

shore[3] [*dial.*]. See *sewer*[1].

short. AS. *sceort*, cogn. with OHG. *scurz*, ? VL. **excurtus*, from *curtus*, short, whence Du. *kort*, Ger. *kurz*. But it seems unnatural for the Teut. langs. to have borrowed an adj. in this way, and the origin of *curt* (q.v.) suggests that *short* may be Teut. and cogn. with *shear*. See *shirt*, *skirt*. To *fall short* is from archery (cf. *beside the mark*). In *shortcake* the adj. is perh. of different origin (see *coldshort*). *Short-lived* (first in Shaks.) is for *short lifed*. *Shortage* is US., *shortcoming* is Sc., *shorthand* is early 17 cent.

shot. Missile, act of shooting, etc. AS. *sceot*, *gesceot*, from *shoot*[1]; cf. OSax. *-scot*, Ger. *geschoss*, ON. *skot*. Archaic *shot*, contribution, in to *pay one's shot* (Pepys, Nov. 30, 1667), is the same word, AS. *sceotan* having also the sense of contributing; cf. *scot* (q.v.) and Ger. *zuschuss*, "one's scot, part, portion, or quota" (Ludw.). Here belongs slang *whole shoot*, earlier (17 cent.) *whole shot*. With *shot silk* cf. *bloodshot* and Ger. *durchschiessen*, to interleave. A *shotten herring* is one that has shot its spawn.

What's the shot, hostess? he says, I'll begone
(*Misogonus*, ii. 1, c. 1550).

should. See *shall*.

shoulder. AS. *sculdor*. WGer.; cf. Du. *schouder*, Ger. *schulter*. With *cold shoulder* (orig. Sc.) cf. *Neh*. ix. 29, where *Vulg*. has *humerum recedentem dare*.

shout. From 14 cent. ? From an unrecorded AS. cognate of ON. *skúta*, taunt.

shove. AS. *scúfan*. Com. Teut.; cf. Du. *schuiven*, Ger. *schieben*, ON. *skúfa*, Goth. *afskiuban*, to shove off. Replaced by *push*, exc. in colloq. and naut. lang., and not used in *AV*.

shovel. AS. *scofl*, from *shove*; cf. Du. *schoffel*, Ger. *schaufel*. ME. also *schole*, *shoul*, etc. *Shovel-board* (game) is altered from *shove-board*.

"I," said the owl, "With my spade and showl."

show, shew. AS. *scēawian*, to look at. WGer.; cf. synon. Du. *schouwen*, Ger. *schauen*, ult. cogn. with L. *cavēre*, to beware. The causal sense, to make to look at, appears in E. c. 1200. Colloq. uses of noun *show* (to *boss*, *run*, *give away the*) are US. Cf. *side-show*, a coinage of the proprietor of the "greatest show on earth." See also *shewbread*.

What may be termed my side-shows, or temporary enterprises (Barnum).

shower. AS. *scúr*. Com. Teut.; cf. Du. *schoer*, Ger. *schauer*, ON. *skúr*, Goth. *skúra* (only in *skúra windis*, wind-storm).

shrapnel. Invented (c. 1803) by *Gen. H. Shrapnel*.

shred. AS. *scrēad* (in pl. only). WGer.; cf. Du. *schroot*, Ger. *schrot*; from a Teut. root, to cut, whence Ger. names *Schröder*, *Schröter*, *Schröer*. See *screed*.

shrew. AS. *scrēawa*, shrew-mouse, reputed to have dangerous powers. Not found between AS. and 16 cent., though Trevisa (i. 335) has *wel schrewyd mys* to render *mures nocentissimi*. Hence applied to a spiteful person, male or female, e.g. *Henry le Shrewe* lived in Sussex in 1293 (*Coram Rege Roll*). Now only a "peevish, malignant, clamorous, spiteful, vexatious, turbulent woman" (Johns.). *Shrewd*, for *shrewed* (cf. *dogged*), orig. meant malignant, malicious, esp. in *shrewd turn* (*Hen. VIII*, v. 3). F. *malin*, shrewd, shows a similar sense-development. It is possible that the AS. sense of *shrew*, which has no Teut. cognates, is a nickname; cf. MHG. *schröuwel*, devil. See also *beshrew*. Another AS. name for the animal was *scirfemūs*, from *sceorfan*, to gnaw.

shriek. Imit., cf. *screech* (q.v.), also earlier *screek*, *shrike*.

shrievalty. From *shrieve*, obs. var. of *sheriff*, with F. ending after *mayoralty*.

shrift. AS. *scrift*, from *shrive* (q.v.). Hence *short shrift*, period allowed culprit to make confession before execution.

shrike. Butcher-bird. From cry; cf. AS. *scrīc*, *scrēc*, thrush, Norw. *skrike*, jay.

shrill. Imit., cf. Sc. *skirl*, LG. *schrell*.

shrimp. Cogn. with *scrimp* and AS. *scrimman*, to shrink. Sense as in quot. below, now felt as transferred from that of the crustacean, is prob. direct from etym. sense.

We borel [homely] men been shrympes
(Chauc. B. 3145).

shrine. AS. *scrīn*, L. *scrinium*, coffer, etc.; cf. Du. *schrijn*, Ger. *schrein*, ON. *skrīn*; also F. *écrin* (OF. *escrin*), It. *scrigno*, Sp. *escrinio*. An early Church word from L., but used in gen. sense of casket, etc. in some of the above langs.

shrink. AS. *scrincan*, with Scand. cognates; ult. cogn. with *scrump*. It had a causal *shrench* (cf. *drink, drench*). Fig. senses perh. with allusion to the snail (see *horn*).

shrive [*archaic*]. AS. *scrīfan*, to decree, "prescribe," penance, L. *scribere*, to write; cf. Du. *schrijven*, to write, describe, Ger. *schreiben*, to write, ON. *skrifa*, to write, *skripta*, to confess, lay penance. Replaced Teut. word for scratching inscriptions, exc. in E. (*write*), in which it assumed spec. sense. See *scribe*.

shrivel. From 16 cent. Cf. Sw. dial. *skryvla*, to wrinkle.

shroud. AS. *scrūd*, garment, cogn. with *shred*; cf. ON. *skrūth*, fittings, shrouds of ship. Sense of winding-sheet is late (16 cent.), also that of veil, screen, etc., whence verb to *shroud*, replacing ME. *shride*, AS. *scrȳdan*. For naut. use cf. sense-development of *sheet²*.

Shrovetide. From 15 cent. From *shrive* (q.v.), with ref. to practice of confession before Lent. Use of past tense is anomalous, but cf. *spokesman*.

shrub¹. Plant. AS. *scrybb*, with LG. & Scand. cognates. Cf. *scrub¹,²* and see *Salopian*.

shrub². In *rum-shrub*. Var. of obs. *shrab*, Arab. *shurb, sharāb*, drink; cf. *sherbet, syrup*.

shrug. Orig. (c. 1400), to shiver, shudder, a sense curiously exemplified in quot. below. ? Cogn. with Ger. *schrecken*, to frighten, orig. to jump with fright (cf. *heuschrecke*, grasshopper).

Those on board felt the old ship [Vindictive] shrug as the explosive tore the bottom-plates and bulkheads from her (*Admir. Offic.* May 15, 1918).

shuck [*dial. & US.*]. Husk. Hence *shucks*, rubbish. ? Metath. of *scutch* (q.v.), in sense of husking corn.

shudder. ME. *schodren*; cf. LG. *schuddern*, whence Ger. *schaudern*. A frequent. from the simplex which appears in Du. *schudden*, Ger. *schütten*, to shake, whence frequents. *schütteln, schüttern*.

shuffle. From 16 cent. Cf. LG. *schuffeln, schüffeln*, with same set of senses; cogn. with *scuffle, shove* (cf. *shuffle-board* for *shovel-board*). To *shuffle off*, with dir. object, is usu. an echo of *Haml.* iii. 1. Sense of prevaricating is from cards (v.i.).

The author...employs all his art, shuffling and cutting, to bring his peer off this business with honour (North's *Examen*).

shun. AS. *scunian*, usu. in compds.; ? cf. Sc. *scunner*, to loathe. Not found in other Teut. langs.

'shun. For *attention* (mil.).

He called out, "Shun!" and I shunted (Kipling).

shunt. A dial. word, to go (push) aside, recorded from c. 1200, and adopted with railways (1840–50). In earliest *NED.* quots. for current sense it is in inverted commas. Perh. from *shun*. For fig. senses cf. US. to *side-track, switch off*.

shunt: a country word for to shove (Kersey).

shut. AS. *scyttan*, cogn. with *shoot¹*. Orig. to put a bar, bolt, in position.

[I] did give him half-a-pint of wine, and so got shut of him (Pepys, Aug. 19, 1663).

shute [*dial.*]. Channel, gutter, inclined trough for "shooting" goods. Combines *shoot¹* and *chute*.

shuttle. AS. *scytel*, missile, cogn. with *shoot¹*, applied in ME. to weaver's instrument shooting backwards and forwards across warp. Hence *shuttlecock*, knocked to and fro as at badminton.

shyttel cocke: volant (Palsg.).

shy¹. Adj. AS. *scēoh* (rare); cogn. with Du. *schuw*, Ger. *scheu*, and AS. *scyhhan*, to take fright. The latter did not survive, mod. to *shy* (of horse) being from adj. In view of the rarity of the AS. word, and of *shy* in early ME., it seems likely that the chief origin is cogn. OF. *eschif*, from Teut., with *-f* lost as in *jolly, testy*, etc. Cf. *eschew*. For *fight shy* cf. quot. s.v. *aloof*.

shy². To throw. From 18 cent. Analogy of *cockshy* (see *cock¹*) suggests that the verb was developed in some way from earlier *shycock*, one hard to catch, perh. orig. one given to *fighting shy*, from *shy¹*.

shie, shy: to shy at a cock, to throw at a cock with a stick (Grose).

si [*mus.*]. See *gamut*.

siamang. Ape. Malay *siy-āmang*, from *āmang*, black.

Siamese. Of *Siam*; esp. in *Siamese twins* (1814–74), who were united at waist.

sib [*archaic*]. Akin. AS. *sibb*, race. Com. Teut.; cf. OSax. *sibbia*, Ger. *sippe*, ON. *sifjar* (pl.), Goth. *sibja*. See *gossip*.

sibilant. From pres. part. of L. *sibilare*, whence F. *siffler*, to whistle, hiss. Of imit. origin (cf. Ger. *zischen*).

Pour qui sont ces serpents qui sifflent sur vos têtes? (Rac.).

sibyl. L., G. Σίβυλλα, prophetess, said to be Doric Σιοβόλλα for Attic Θεοβούλη, divine wish.

sic. L., so, thus.

sicca [*Anglo-Ind.*]. In *sicca* (newly coined) *rupee*. Pers. Arab. *sikkah* (see *sequin*).

siccative. Late L. *siccativus*; from *siccare*, from *siccus*, dry.

Sicilian Vespers [*hist.*]. Massacre with vesper-bell as signal. See *shibboleth*.

sick. AS. *sēoc*. Com. Teut.; cf. Du. *ziek*, Ger. *siech*, ON. *sjūkr*, Goth. *siuks*. Replaced by *ill* (see *unwell*) exc. in higher style and US., but surviving in *sick-bay*, *sicklist*, *sickroom*. The *Sick Man of Europe* (Turkey) is due to Nicholas I of Russia (1854). With later sense in to *feel sick* cf. F. *se trouver mal*. To *sickly o'er* is an echo of *Haml*. iii. 1.

We hope that the pale cast of Lord Robert Cecil's thought will not sickly o'er the American resolution (*Morn. Post*, Nov. 21, 1917).

sickle. AS. *sicol*, L. *secula*, from *secare*, to cut. Early WGer. loan-word; cf. Du. *sikkel*, Ger. *sichel*. Other early loans of the same class are *flail*, *stubble*.

side. AS. *sīde*. Com. Teut.; cf. Du. *zijde*, Ger. *seite*, ON. *sītha*; cogn. with AS. *sīd*, long, wide, whence dial. *side*, in same sense (cf. L. *latus*, side, *lātus*, wide). This appears in *country-side*, suggesting a wide expanse. *Side-slip* once meant illegitimate child (cf. *by-blow*). *Side*, swagger, contains a punning reference to *putting on side* at billiards. It may be connected with dial. *side* (v.i.) in sense of proud. As adv., boastfully, *side* is used by Dunbar (cf. to *talk tall*). With *sidesman*, for earlier *sideman*, standing by the churchwarden, cf. *huntsman*, *spokesman*, etc. *Sidelong* is altered from much earlier *sideling* (14 cent.), whence is evolved verb to *sidle* (cf. *grovel*). For *side-track* (US.) see *shunt*.

In Lincolnshire and most northern parts they use the word *side* for long...and for high...and by metaphor for proud, as a *side woman*, i.e. a haughty proud woman: which in Sussex is *sidy*, as a *sidy fellow*, i.e. an imperious surly fellow
(White Kennett, c. 1700).

sidereal. From L. *sidereus*, from *sidus, sider-*, constellation.

sidi-boy. See *seedy-boy*.

sidle. See *side*.

siege. F. *siège*, seat, siege, VL. *sedicum*, for *sedes*, seat. Used of "sitting down" before a fortress. Orig. sense also appears as late as Shaks. (*Oth*. i. 2). To *lay* (*raise*) *siege* after F. *mettre* (*lever*) *le siège*.

sienna. Pigment. For It. *terra di Siena*, from *Sienna*, in Italy.

sierra [*geog.*]. Sp., L. *serra*, saw. See *serrated*.

siesta. Sp., sixth (hour), L. *sexta* (*hora*).

sieve. AS. *sife*. WGer.; cf. Du. *zeef*, Ger. *sieb*; cogn. with dial. *sye*, to strain, and Ger. *seihen*, to filter.

sift. AS. *siftan*, cogn. with *sieve*; cf. Du. *ziften, zichten*, Ger. *sichten* (from LG.).

sigh. ME. *sighe, sihe*, back-formation from *sihte*, past of obs. *siche*, AS. *sīcan*, to sigh.

sight. AS. *sihth, gesihth*, from *see*[1]; cf. Du. *zicht*, Ger. *sicht*. Sense of large quantity, arising from that of view, was once literary. With *sightly* cf. *shapely*.

To the citie of the living God, the celestiall Jerusalem, and to an innumerable sight of angels
(Tynd. *Heb*. xii. 22).

sigil. Late L. *sigillum*, from L. pl. *sigilla*, dim. of *signum*, sign.

sigma. L., G. σῖγμα, G. letter *s*.

sign. F. *signe*, L. *signum*. In some cases (e.g. *tavern sign*) prob. aphet. for *ensign* (cf. *gin*[1], *vie*). Earliest sense as verb was to mark with the cross, and most of our ancestors "signed" their letters in the same way, instead of "subscribing" their names.

signal[1]. Noun. F., Late L. *signale*, neut. of *signalis*, from *signum*, sign.

signal[2]. Adj. F. *signalé*, "notable, famous" (Cotg.), p.p. of *signaler*, to mark out, signalize, with *-é* lost as in *defile*[2], *costive*, *trove*.

signature. F., MedL. *signatura*, from *signare*, to mark, sign.

signet. F., dim. of *signe*, sign. Hist. smaller seal of sovereign, whence Sc. *writer to the signet*.

Donnee souz le signet de nostre anel en absence de nostre prive seal
(*John of Gaunt's Reg*. 1372–76).

signify. F. *signifier*, L. *significare*, from *signum*, sign, *facere*, to make.

Signior [*hist.*]. In *Grand Signior*, Sultan of Turkey, adapted from It. *gran signore*, great lord.

signor. It., for *signore*, L. *senior-em* (see *senior*).

sika. Deer. Jap., deer.

Sikh. Sect established (16 cent.) in Punjab by Nanak Shah. Hind. *sikh*, disciple.

silage. For *ensilage*. See *silo*.

silence. F., L. *silentium*, from *silēre*, to be silent. Replaced AS. *swīge*, cogn. with Ger. *schweigen*.

silene. Plant. Named by Linnaeus, from G. Σειληνός, foster-father of Bacchus.

silesia. Fabric. From *Silesia*, Germany, latinized from Ger. *Schlesien*.

silhouette. From *Étienne de Silhouette*, F. politician (†1767), though the sense of the joke is variously given.

silica. From L. *silex, silic-*, flint.

siliquose [*bot.*]. From L. *siliqua*, pod.

silk. AS. *sioloc, seoloc*; cf. ON. *silki*, OSlav. *shelkŭ* (whence Russ. *shelk'*), L. *sericum* (see *serge*). It is supposed to have passed into Slav. via some lang. which confused -*r*- and -*l*- (cf. *plum*), and hence via the Baltic trade into AS. & ON. The other Europ. langs. have names derived from L. *saeta*, hair, bristle, e.g. F. *soie*, Ger. *seide*. To *take silk* is to become a K.C., who has the right to wear a silk gown. *Silken, silkworm*, are found in AS.

sill. AS. *syll-e*, beam acting as foundation of wall; cf. archaic Du. *sulle, sille*, Ger. *schwelle*, threshold, ON. *svill, syll*; cogn. with Goth. *gasuljan*, to found[1]. All from L. *solea*, foundation of wall (Kluge), from *solum*, ground, and hence cogn. with F. *seuil*, threshold. Current sense, as in *window-sill*, is ME.

sillabub. Also (16 cent.) *sillibouk*, app. happy belly (see *silly*), from obs. *bouk*, AS. *būc*, cogn. with Du. *buik*, Ger. *bauch*, ON. *bukr*, trunk; cf. dial. *merribouk* in similar sense. The fact that *sillibouk* also occurs c. 1550 (*Misogonus*, iv. 1) in the sense of jolly wench suggests a sense-development like that of *fool* (gooseberry).

laict aigre: whay; also, a sillibub, or merribowke (Cotg.).

sillery. Champagne from *Sillery* (Marne), village near Reims.

silly. ME. *seely*, AS. *gesǽlig*, happy, from *sǽl*, time, happiness; cogn. with Ger. *selig*, happy, blessed, ? and ult. with L. *salvus*, G. ὅλος, whole. Earlier senses survive in *silly sheep, silly Suffolk*. For change of sense cf. *simple, innocent, crétin*, etc., and, for instability of adjs., *quaint, nice, buxom*,

etc. The *silly season* (Aug. & Sept.) was named by *Punch*.

A piece of invention contrived (according to custom) to amuse the ignorant at this barren season of news (*Daily Journal*, Sep. 6, 1725).

silo. Pit for storing grain, etc. Sp., L., G. σιρός, pit for corn. Cf. *ensilage*.

silt. Sediment deposited by sea-water. App. cogn. with *salt*. Cf. Norw. Dan. dial. *sylt*, salt-marsh, beach, also Du. *zult*, Ger. *sülze*, salt pan.

Silurian [*geol.*]. Of rocks first studied in part of Wales orig. inhabited by the *Silures*. Cf. *Devonian*.

silurus. Sheat-fish. L., G. σίλουρος.

silvan. L. *silvanus*, from *silva*, wood.

silver. AS. *siolfor, seolfor*. Com. Teut.; cf. Du. *zilver*, Ger. *silber*, ON. *silfr*, Goth. *silubr*, with cognates in Balto-Slav. langs. Prob. taken over in prehistoric times from some non-Aryan race (cf. *hemp*). With Sc. sense of *siller* cf. F. *argent*. The *silver age*, following the golden age, is also used of the decadent period of L. literature, from the death of Augustus to that of Hadrian.

simar. See *cymar*.

Simeonite [*theol.*]. Adherent of *Charles Simeon*, Low Church clergyman (†1836).

simian. From L. *simia*, ape, ? from G. σιμός, flat-nosed. Cf. F. *singe*.

similar. F. *similaire*, from L. *similis*, from *simul*, together (cf. G. ὁμοῖος from ὁμοῦ); cogn. with *same*.

simile. L., neut. of *similis* (v.s.).

simmer. Earlier (15 cent.) *simper*. Imit., cf. Ger. *summen*, to buzz.

simnel [*archaic*]. OF. *simenel*, dim., with dissim. of *l-l*, from L. *simila*, fine flour, cogn. with G. σεμίδαλις; cf. Ger. *semmel*, "a simnel, a simnel-bread" (Ludw.).

Simon Pure. Name of Quaker in Mrs Cent-livre's *Bold stroke for a wife* (1717), who is impersonated by another character in part of the play. Cf. *Mrs Grundy*.

simony. Traffic in Church appointments. F. *simonie*, Church L. *simonia*, from *Simon Magus* (*Acts*, viii. 18–19).

simoom. Arab. *semūm*, from *samma*, to poison.

simper. From 16 cent., and later than obs. *simper-de-cocket*, flirt, etc. Cf. obs. Du. *simpellije, zimperlije*, Ger. *zimperlich* (from LG.), Scand. dial. *simper, semper*, all in similar senses and prob. imit. of an affected "sipping" motion of the lips. Cf. Ger.

sipp, zipp, Dan. *sippe,* Sw. *sipp,* etc., all used of a simpering person.

faire la petite bouche: to simper (Cotg.).

simple. F., L. *simplus* or *simplex* (cf. *double, duplex*), cogn. with *simul, semel,* and *singuli,* all from an Aryan **sem* (= one) which appears in G. ἁ-πλόος, simple, ἑ-κατόν, one hundred. Disparaging sense (cf. *silly*) is linked with that of devoid of duplicity, which appears earliest in E. The *simple life* (1901) renders Pastor Wagner's *la vie simple.* Archaic *simples,* medicinal herbs, is a spec. use of *simple,* medicament of one ingredient only. Hence obs. to *simple,* gather remedies.

simpleton. "A low word" (Johns.). Jocular formation on *simple,* intended to suggest a surname. Cf. *lushington, singleton, skimmington,* also obs. *simpkin, simkin,* "a fool" (*Dict. Cant. Crew*), from *Simple Simon.*

simulacre. OF., L. *simulacrum,* from *simulare* (v.i.).

simulate. From L. *simulare,* to make like; cf. *similar.*

simultaneous. Coined (17 cent.), after *momentaneous,* from L. *simul,* at the same time, cogn. with *similis,* like. Cf. F. *simultané.*

simurgh. Gigantic bird of Pers. legend. Pers. *sīmurgh,* from Pers. *murgh,* bird, and doubtful first element. Cf. *roc.*

sin. AS. *synn,* from a lost stem **sundj-.* Com. Teut.; cf. Du. *zonde,* Ger. *sünde,* ON. *synth*; ? cogn. with L. *sons, sont-,* guilty, and ult. with *authentic.* See *sooth.* Occ. euph. for the *devil* (*like sin, ugly as sin*).

Had I been, for my sins, born of the male race
(Frances Burney, *Diary,* 1772).

sinapism [*med.*]. Mustard plaster. F. *sinapisme* (see Cotg. *sinapiser*), L., from G. σίναπι, mustard, prob. of Egypt. origin.

since. Contr. of obs. *sithence,* for ME. *sithens,* formed, with adv. -s (cf. *against, needs,* etc.), from *sithen,* AS. *siththan,* from *sīth,* late, and instrument. case of demonstr. (cf. Ger. *seitdem*). Or from obs. *sin* (cf. *auld lang syne*), contr. of *sithen,* with -s as in cogn. Du. *sinds,* which comes to the same thing. Cf. Ger. *seit, sint* (archaic), and Goth. *thanaseiths,* further, in which the elements of *since* are reversed. For causal use cf. F. *puisque.*

sincere. F. *sincère,* L. *sincerus,* pure, from *sine* and a second element which may be cogn. with *caries,* decay.

sinciput [*anat.*]. L., front of head, from *semi,* half, *caput,* head (cf. *occiput*). But some connect the first element with *suinus,* from *sus,* pig, and regard the word as playful, "boar's head."

sine [*math.*]. L. *sinus,* in sense of bosom, fold of garment, used to render Arab. *jaib* in geom. sense (see *jibbah*).

sinecure. Orig. eccl. From L. (*beneficium*) *sine cura,* benefice without cure (of souls).

sine die. L. without (fixed) day. See *adjourn.*

sine qua non. Scholastic L., without which not, with *causā* understood, after Aristotle's ὧν οὐκ ἄνευ.

sinew. AS. *sinu, sinw-*; cf. Du. *zeen, zenuw,* Ger. *sehne* (OHG. *senewa*). ME. had also *sine. Sinews of war* is after L. *nervi belli pecunia* (Cic.).

sing. AS. *singan.* Com. Teut.; cf. Du. *zingen,* Ger. *singen,* ON. *syngva,* Goth. *siggwan.*

singe. Earlier *senge,* AS. *sencgan,* causal of *singan* (v.s.), to cause to sing, make hiss; cf. Du. *zengen,* Ger. *sengen.*

Singhalese. See *Cingalese.*

single. OF., from L. *singuli,* one at a time, cogn. with *simple* (q.v.). Contrasted with *double* in many compds. and techn. expressions, where F. has *simple, singulier.* The *single-stick* is so called because used with one hand, while the quarterstaff required two. To *single out,* for earlier to *single* (Shaks.), was orig. a hunting term, to mark, spot.

singlet. "A waistcoat not lined as opposed to a doublet" (Grose).

singleton. At cards, etc. Jocular formation from *single* after surname *Singleton.* Cf. *simpleton, lushington.*

singular. OF. *singuler* (*singulier*), L. *singularis,* whence also F. *sanglier,* (orig. solitary) wild boar, OF. *sengler.* For sense of remarkable cf. *unique.*

Sinhalese. See *Cingalese.*

sinister. Restored from OF. *senestre* (*sinistre*), L. *sinister, sinistr-,* on the left hand, taken as bad omen, although in some periods of folk-lore the opposite is the case. With her. senses, as in *bend* (incorr. *bar*) *sinister,* indicating illegitimacy, cf. *dexter.*

sink. AS. *sincan.* Com. Teut.; cf. Du. *zinken,* Ger. *sinken,* ON. *sökkja,* Goth. *sigqan.* As trans. verb has supplanted obs. *sench* (cf. *drink, drench,* and Ger. *senken*). Some fig. senses, e.g. to *sink one's title* (the *shop,* etc.), prob. from naut. lang. With adj. use of old p.p. *sunken* cf. *drunken.*

Hence noun *sink*, orig. pit, cesspool, etc.
The first *sinking fund* was established in
1716.

sinnet. See *sennit*.

Sinn Fein[*neol.*]. Ir., we ourselves. Pol. society
(1905). *Shin Fain; or Ourselves Alone* was
the title of an Ir. play published 1882 by
T. S. Cleary. Already (since Easter, 1916)
current abroad (v.i. and cf. *boycott*).

Les forts de Verdun tombent un à un, nous sommes
acculés, la bête enragée nous presse...il ne nous
reste qu'à être fusillés dans le dos: Sinn Fein s'en
charge (R. C. Escouflaire).

sinology. Study of the Chinese, G. Σῖναι.
Cf. Ger. *apfelsine*, orange.

sinople. Green (her.). Archaic F., also
sinopre, whence obs. E. *sinoper*, red, confused with *cinnabar*. Coloured earths from
Sinope, G. colony in Paphlagonia.

sinter [*geol.*]. Ger., see *cinder*.

sinuous. F. *sinueux*, L. *sinuosus*, from *sinus*,
bay, bend, fold, etc. (see *sine*).

sip. Thinned form of *sop*, *sup*, expressing less
vigorous action. Cf. colloq. Dan. *sippe*.

sipahee. Archaic var. of *sepoy* (q.v.).

siphon. F., L. *sipho-n-*, G. σίφων, pipe, tube.

sippet. "A lytell soppe" (Palsg.). Wyc. has
supett (2 *Sam.* xiii. 8). See *sip*.

si quis. L., if anyone (should have found, etc.).
See quot. s.v. *bill*[3].

sir. Reduced form of *sire* (q.v.). In ME. and
up to 17 cent. also used as title of priests.

sircar. See *sirkar*.

sirdar. Urdu, Pers. *sardār*, commander in
chief, from *sar*, head, and agent. suffix as
in *ressaldar*, etc. In ref. to Egypt first
(1898) of Lord Kitchener. Cf. Serb. *serdar*,
burgomaster (esp. in Montenegro), which
has reached Serbia from Persia via Turkey
and Albania.

sire. F., L. *senior*, with abnormal development due to its unstressed position as
title; cf. *sieur*, for normal *seigneur*, L.
senior-em, which has also contributed to
sir. *Sire*, *sir*, now differentiated in senses,
were used indifferently in early ME. Of
animals (correlative to *dam*) from 16 cent.

siren. F. *sirène*, L., G. Σειρήν (*Odyss.* xii.
39 ff.). Steam-boat sense, with allusion to
alluring voice, is late 19 cent. With incorr.
syren cf. *sylvan*, *tyre*.

Sirius. L., G. Σείριος, the dog-star, lit.
scorching.

sirkar [*Anglo-Ind.*]. Government. Urdu,
Pers. *sarkār*, from *sar*, head (cf. *sirdar*), and
agent. suffix.

sirloin. Earlier (16 cent.) also *surloyn*, from
OF. *surloigne*, over loin (q.v.). Current
spelling (cf. incorr. *sirname*) is due to the
etym. myth variously connected with
Henry VIII, James I, Charles II.

sirocco. It., also *scirocco*, from Arab. *sharq*,
east, from *sharaqa*, to rise (of the sun).

sirrah [*archaic*]. Extended from *sir*; cf. US.
sirree. Skeat's suggestion that it is Prov.
sira (= F. *sire*) is made doubtful by late
appearance (16 cent.). Still, it may have
been a sailor's word picked up at Bordeaux
or Marseille (cf. *lingo*).

sirup. See *syrup*.

sirvente. Troubadour lay, usu. satirical.
F., from Prov. *sirventes*, *serventes*, adj.,
from *servir*, to serve.

sisal. Fibre, hemp, etc. From *Sisal*, Yucatan.

siskin. Bird, aberdevine. Ger. dial. *sisschen*,
zeischen (cf. obs. Flem. *sijsken*), dim. of
zeisig, siskin, canary, of Slav. origin (cf.
Russ. *chizhek'*).

sister. ON. *systir*. Aryan; cf. AS. *sweostor*
(whence ME. *swuster*, *suster*), Du. *zuster*,
Ger. *schwester*, Goth. *swistar*, L. *soror*
(**swesor*), Sanskrit *svasr*, Russ. *syestra*, OIr.
siur, etc. Sense of nun is in AS. The
sisters, head-nurses, of St Bartholomew's
Hospital, are mentioned 1730–1.

Sistine. It. *sistino*, from *Sixtus*, name borne
by several popes. The *Sistine Madonna*
was taken from church of *San Sisto* at
Piacenza.

sistrum. Timbrel. L., G. σεῖστρον, from
σείειν, to shake.

Sisyphean. Of *Sisyphus*, G. Σίσυφος, king of
Corinth, condemned in Hades to roll uphill
a stone which always rolls down again from
the top. Cf. *tantalize*.

sit. AS. *sittan*. Com. Teut.; cf. Du. *zitten*,
Ger. *sitzen*, ON. *sitja*, Goth. *sitan*; cogn.
with L. *sedēre*, G. ἕζεσθαι. For vulg. confusion with *set* cf. *lie*, *lay*. Slang *sitter*, easy
task, is allusive to shooting a sitting bird.

Sits the wind in that corner (*Much Ado*, ii. 3).

site. AF., L. *situs*, position, situation.
ModF. *site* is from cogn. It. *sito*.

sith [*archaic*]. See *Ezek.* xxxv. 6. Obs. c.
1700 but revived by 19 cent. poets. See
since.

sit(i)ophobia. Morbid aversion to food, G.
σῖτος.

situate. From Late L. *situare* (*situs*, place).

Siva. Third deity of Hindu triad. Sanskrit,
auspicious.

six. AS. *siex*, *sex*. Aryan; cf. Du. *zes*, Ger. *sechs*, ON. *sex*, Goth. *saihs*, L. *sex*, G. ἕξ, Sanskrit *shash*, Gael. *se*, etc. *At sixes and sevens* occurs first (Chauc.) in to *set on six and seven*, hazard all one's chances, evidently from dicing.

aleam omnem jacere: to put in adventure; to set at sixe and seven (Coop.).

sixte [*fenc.*]. F., sixth. Cf. *tierce*, etc.

sizar [*Camb. & Dubl.*]. From *size* (q.v.), in sense of allowance.

size. Aphet. for *assize* (q.v.). The form *sise* also occurs in OF.; cf. MedL. *sisa*. Ground-sense is anything fixed or settled, idea of magnitude springing from that of fixed standard, allowance, the latter esp. at Camb. Painters' *size* represents F. *assise*, layer (cf. *coat* of paint).

Rottans [rattans] for water-caske, which make excellent hoopes, and are heere of all assises in great abundance (Purch. 1612).

Where life still lives, where God his sises holds
(Sylv. i. 2).

sizzle. Imit., cf. Ger. *zischen*, to hiss.

sjambok. SAfrDu., Malay *samboq*, *chamboq*, Urdu *chābuk* (whence obs. E. *chawbuck*). Prob. taken to SAfr. by Portuguese (cf. *assagai*, *kraal*).

skald. Norse poet. ON. *skāld* (9 cent.), of unknown origin. App. introduced into E. by Bishop Percy. Cf. *rime*, *berserk*, *viking*.

skat. Card game. Ger., It. *scarto*, cogn. with F. *écarté*.

skate[1]. Fish. ON. *skata*; cf. Jutland *ska*.

skate[2]. For ice. Back-formation (cf. *cherry*, *pea*, etc.) from earlier *scates*, Du. *schaats*, ONF. *escache* (*écache*, *échasse*, stilt), whence also obs. E. *scatch*, stilt, Sc. *sketch*, skate. F. *échasse*, orig. wooden leg, is of Teut. origin, LG. *schake*, shank, leg. The earliest *skates* were made of animals' shank-bones; cf. ON. *īsleggr*, skate, lit. ice-leg, and F. *patin*, skate, from *patte*, paw. *Skating* was popularized at the Restoration (cf. *pall-mall*, *yacht*), Charles II's followers having learnt the art in Holland.

The strange and wonderful dexterity of the sliders on the new canal in St James's Park, performed before their Maties by divers gentlemen and others with skeets, after the manner of the Hollanders
(Evelyn, Dec. 1, 1660. See Pepys, same date).

skean. See *skene*.

skedaddle. Became current (1861–65) in US. mil. slang (cf. *vamose*), but app. earlier in north. E. dial. in sense of to spill.

skein. OF. *escagne* (*écagne*), Prov. *escanha*, also *escanh*, ? VL. *scamnium, from *scamnum*, stool (see *shamble*[1]), which is conjectured to have also been applied to a winding instrument. This hypothesis is supported by the fact that Prov. *escavel*, winder, skein, corresponding to F. *écheveau*, the usual F. word for skein, represents phonetically L. *scabellum*, a dim. of *scamnum*, stool. Cf. also Ger. *haspel*, yarn-winder, in OHG. also skein, derived from *haspe*, hasp of a door, an equally inexplicable connection, and synon. Port. *serilho*, VL. *sericula, from *sera*, bolt. In the absence of exact knowledge as to what was the form and mechanism of the primitive yarn-winder, the above etym. remains only a promising conjecture.

skeleton. G. σκελετόν (sc. σῶμα), dried up (body), from σκέλλειν, to dry up. *Skeleton in the cupboard* (*house*), introduced into literary use by Thackeray, is perh. due to *skeleton at the feast*, memento mori, from a practice of the ancient Egyptians recorded by Plutarch.

skellum [*archaic*]. Rogue. Du. *schelm*, Ger., rascal, devil. A fairly common word in narratives of soldiers of fortune of the Dugald Dalgetty type.

skelter. From *helter-skelter*.

Skeltonic. Of *John Skelton*, burlesque poet (†1529).

skene. Gael. Ir. *scian*, *sgian*, knife; cf. Welsh *ysgien*. Esp. in *skene dhu*, black knife, worn in Highlander's stocking.

skep. Beehive. From earlier (now dial.) sense of basket, orig. measure. ON. *skeppa*, cogn. with Du. *schepel*, Ger. *scheffel*, bushel, all perh. ult. from L. *scapha*, vessel.

skerry [*geog.*]. Rock, rocky islet. Orkney dial., ON. *sker*. Cf. *holm*.

sketch. Earlier *schitz* (Pepys, *Navy Mem.* p. 129), Du. *schets*, It. *schizzo*, L. *schedium*, extempore poem, from G. σχέδιος, extempore. F. *esquisse*, Ger. *skizze*, are from It. Cf., for Du. art-words, *easel*, *lay-figure*, *landscape*.

skew. First as verb, to move sideways, dodge. OF. *escuer*, for *eschuer* (see *eschew*).

skewbald. Bay and white in patches. Altered, on *piebald* (prop. black and white), from ME. *skewed*, *skued*, perh. from OF. *escu* (*écu*), shield, L. *scutum*. Cf. L. *scutulatus*, colour of a horse, from *scutula*, platter, also F. *luné*, from *lune*, moon, *roué*, from *roue*, wheel, both used of the markings of a horse, also Ger. *spiegel*, mirror, similarly used, and possible origin of *sheldrake*. Cf. also ON. *skjaldhvalr*, dappled whale, from *skjald*, shield.

skewer. App. altered from *skiver* (still in dial. use), ? from ON. *skifa*, to split (cf. *shiver*¹). Cf. (*n*)*ewt* for *evet*.

ski. Norw., ON. *skīth*, snow-shoe, billet of cleft wood, cogn. with AS. *scīd*, whence obs. *shide*, billet of wood; ult. cogn. with *shed*¹. Introduced 1880–90.

skiagraphy. For *sciagraphy*. See *sciamachy*.

skid¹. Orig. billet of wood used as support. App. connected with *ski* (q.v.). Hence verb to *skid*, as though wheels were braked with a skid, now esp. of rubber tires.

skid². Var. of *scud*.

skiff. F. *esquif*, It. *schifo* or Sp. *esquife*, OHG. *scif*, ship. Orig. small boat of a ship.

skill. ON. *skil*, distinction, difference, hence "discernment." Etym. sense appears in archaic *it skills not*, orig. makes no difference. For sense-development cf. Ger. *gescheidt*, clever, from *scheiden*, to divide.

The serious thing is the discovery—now past doubt—that the British have lost their skill in fighting; and the whole world knows it and is regulating itself accordingly
(Col. John Hay, June 15, 1900).

skillet. Small cauldron. Earlier *skelet* (c. 1400), ? dim. of dial. *skeel*, bucket, etc., ON. *skjōla*, pail.

skilly [*slang*]. Gruel. Short for earlier *skilligalee*, orig. naut., fanciful formation, ? on *skillet*, which I have always heard pronounced *skilly* by old country-women.

skim. OF. *escumer* (*écumer*), from OHG. *scūm* (*schaum*), froth, scum (q.v.). For vowel cf. *brisk*, *whisky*, etc. In reading orig. (18 cent.) to *skim over*, like a swallow, not with idea of taking cream.

escumement: a foaming; also, a scumming, or skimming (Cotg.).

skimble-skamble. Redupl. on *scamble* (q.v.).

skimmington [*dial.*]. Procession in ridicule of unhappy couple, orig. character personating the wife, shown in a frontispiece of 1639 as beating her husband with a *skimmer*. For form cf. *simpleton*, *singleton*, *lushington*.

skimp. "Not in general use until very recently" (*NED.*). App. altered from *scamp*² and associated with *scrimp*.

skin. ON. *skinn*, cogn. with Ger. *schinden*, to flay. Has partly replaced native *hide*. The *skin of one's teeth* is a lit. rendering, in the

Geneva Bible (1560), of the Heb. (*Job*, xix. 20), not followed by *Vulg.* and LXX. With *skinflint* cf. F. *tondre sur un œuf*, "to make commodity of any thing, so bare soever it be" (Cotg.).

skink. Lizard. F. *scinque*, earlier *scinc*, L., G. σκίγκος.

skinker [*archaic*]. Drawer, tapster. From archaic *skink*, to pour out, Du. *schenken*. See *nuncheon*.

skip¹. Verb. ? OF. *esquiper*, to depart by ship (see *equip*). This suits one of the ME. senses, still preserved in US. to *skip*, abscond, but will not account for earliest sense. Hence archaic *skipjack*, whippersnapper, also name of fish.

And whanne the apostlis Barnabas and Poul herden this...thei skipten out among the puple
(Wyc. *Acts*, xiv. 13).

skip². Basket. Var. of *skep* (q.v.).

skip³ [*curling*]. Short for *skipper*, captain.

skip⁴. College servant (Dubl.). For archaic *skip-kennel*, lackey, lit. jump gutter, with which cf. F. *saute-ruisseau*, street urchin.

skipper. Du. *schipper*, from *schip*, ship, whence also OF. *eschipre*. In sport first at curling (*skip*³).

skippet [*antiq.*]. Small case for documents. Also *skibbet*. ? Dim. of *skip*².

skirl [*Sc.*]. Esp. of the bag-pipe. An imit. word of Scand. origin. Cf. *shrill*.

skirmish. Earlier (14 cent.) *scarmoch*, F. *escarmouche*, It. *scaramuccia*, "a skirmish, a fight, a fray" (Flor.). The -*ish* forms and the verb are influenced by OF. *eskermir*, *eskermiss-*, to fence, OHG. *scirman* (*schirmen*), to defend, from *scirm*, *scerm*, defence, screen (cf. *regenschirm*, umbrella). The relation of It. *scaramuccia* to this is obscure. See also *scrimmage*, *scaramouch*. The verb must be much older than dict. records, as the group of surnames derived from it (*Scrimygour*, *Scrimshire*, *Skrimshaw*, *Skurmer*, etc.) is well exemplified in 13 cent.

skirr, scurr. To move swiftly. ? OF. *escourre*, L. *ex-currere*. See also *scurry*.

skirret. Herb. Earlier *skirwhitte*, *skirwit*, etc., supposed by *NED.* to be an etymologizing corrupt. (? as though *sheer white*) of synon. OF. *eschervis* (*chervis*), ? ult. ident. with *caraway* (q.v.). It is more prob. a popular name expressing some belief as to its med. properties, *shire wit*, clear wit, from obs. *shire*, to purify, cogn. with *sheer*¹. Cf. *wormwood*.

skirt. ON. *skyrta*, shirt (q.v.); cf. Ger. *schürze*, apron. Sense of border, edge, esp. in *outskirts*, *skirting-board*, and in verb to *skirt*, appears earliest (14 cent.) in ref. to side-flaps of a saddle. Cf. similar use of *hem*. With vulg. sense as emblem of female sex cf. similar use of Norw. Dan. *skjört*, also *skjörteregiment*, petticoat government. *Skirt-dancing* was introduced (1892) by Miss Loie Fuller.

orae: the edges, the brimmes, the borders, the skirtes, the hemmes (Coop.).

skit, skittish. ? Connected with ON. *skjóta*, to shoot. Cf. dial. *skite*, to dart swiftly, whence frequent. *skitter*, also *skite*, trick, skit. *Skittish*, frivolous, occurs c. 1400, but is a century later in ref. to horses, this sense perh. being suggested by synon. OF. *escouteux* (*écouteux*), supposed to mean a horse that listens to every sound. Mod. sense of *skit* (*upon*), which it is not easy to connect with *skittish*, is early 18 cent.

schifo: coie, quaint, disdainfull, nice, skittish, fonde, frowarde, puling, queasie, akeward (Flor.).

skittle. From 17 cent., also *kittle*. If the *skittle* was orig. the projectile, it may be Sw. Dan. *skyttel*, shuttle, also used in archaic Dan. for ball. With *beer and skittles* cf. L. *panem et circenses* (Juv.).

skive [*techn.*]. ON. *skífa*, to split. See *shive*.

skoal [*archaic*]. Health-drinking (Longfellow, *Skeleton in armour*). ON. *skál*, bowl. See *scale*[1].

skoot. Var. of *scoot* (q.v.).

"Do you skootamote?" will probably be heard frequently in the near future
           (*Daily Chron.* Aug. 21, 1919).

skrimshanker. See *scrimshaw*.

skua. Gull. From Faroese *skúgvur*, ON. *skúfr*.

skulk. Cf. Norw. *skulka*, to lurk, Sw. *skolka*, Dan. *skulke*, to play truant. These app. from LG. *schulen*, to lurk, look askance (see *scowl*), with suffix as in *lurk*, *walk*, etc.

skull. From 13 cent., earliest *schulle*. ? OF. *escuele*, *escule*, bowl, L. *scutella*, dim. of *scutra*, dish (whence *scullery*); cf. synon. Ger. *hirnschale*, *hirnbecken* (basin), also obs. E. *scull*, *skull*, helmet, with which cf. *bascinet*. In most Europ. langs. the words for skull, head, were orig. names of vessels, and *skull* replaced AS. *héafod-bolla*, *-panne*. Our word might also be Sw. *skulle*, cogn. with *scale*[1].

beckeneel: the scull or pan of the head; head-peece, helm, or murion (Hexham).

skunk. NAmer.Ind. *segankw*, *segongw*. Noted for offensive smell.

Skupshtina. Serb. national assembly. From OSlav. *kup*, heap, whence Serbo-Croat. *skupa*, together, *skupiti*, to gather. For prefix cf. *Sobranje*, *soviet*.

sky. Orig. cloud, current sense springing from *the skies*, the clouds, hence upper region of air. ON. *ský*, cogn. with AS. *scuwa*, shade, shadow. Has replaced *heaven* exc. in poet. style. For naut. *sky-lark*, to frolic, see *lark*[2]. *Sky-pilot* was orig. a sailors' word.

Skye terrier. From *Skye*, Hebrides.

slab[1]. Noun. Of doubtful origin. First used (13 cent.) of metal, and hence, if applied orig. to molten mass, perh. connected with *slab*[2]. *Slab-sided* is US.

slab[2]. Adj. Before 19 cent. only in *Macb.* iv. 1. App. related to *slabber*, *slop*, and *slaver*. Cf. dial. *slab*, puddle, *slabby*, viscid, etc.

slabber. See *slobber*.

slack[1]. Adj. AS. *slæc*, *sléac*. Com. Teut.; cf. Du. *slak*, Ger. dial. *schlack*, ON. *slakr*; ult. cogn. with *lax*[2]. Orig. of persons and conduct, so that sense-development is unusual.

slack[2]. Refuse coal. Cf. Du. *slak*, Ger. *schlacke*, dross, orig. splinter broken off, from *schlagen*, to strike.

slade [*dial. & poet.*]. Dingle, etc. (the dial. senses are innumerable). AS. *slæd*, *sléad*, with cognates in Scand. dials.

slag. LG. form of *slack*[2].

slake. AS. *slæcan*, *slacian*, from *slack*[1]. Orig. to slacken; hence, diminish vehemence; cf. *slack-lime*, *slaked-lime*, also *slake-water*, earlier form of naut. *slackwater*.

slam. Imit., cf. Norw. dial. *slamra*. *Grand* (*little*) *slam* at cards is from obs. name for a game called ruff and honours.

slammerkin [*dial.*]. Slovenly. Cf. dial. *slammock*, *slommock*, also *shammock*, in same sense. First as surname (Gay's *Beggars' Opera*, 1727), but this is prob. from the colloq. word. Cf. Ger. *schlampe*, slut.

slander. F. *esclandre*, altered from *escandle*, L. *scandalum*, scandal (q.v.).

slang. Orig. a cant word. ? Cogn. with *sling*; cf. Norw. dial. *slengjeord*, neologism, *slengjenamn*, nickname, and colloq. E. to *sling language* (*words*, etc.), to *sling the bat*, talk the vernacular (Kipling); see quot. s.v. *sling*[1]. Some regard it as an argotic perversion of F. *langue*, language (see *s-*).

slant. Evolved from earlier *aslant* (q.v.). Cf. *squint*. *Slantindicular*, portmanteau-word on *slanting, perpendicular*, is US.

slap. Imit., cf. Ger. *schlapp, klaps*. With *slap-up* cf. *bang-up*. *Slapdash* is used by Dryden.

slash. Not recorded till 16 cent., exc. once in Wyc. (1 *Kings*, v. 18). ? OF. *esclachier*, to break. In some senses intens. of *lash*[1] (see *s-*). For intens. use of *slashing* cf. *ripping*, etc.

slat[1]**.** Narrow strip. ME. *sclat*, OF. *esclat* (*éclat*), fragment, from *éclater*, OF. *esclater*, from *ex-* and an imit. root. In E. orig. roofing slate, later sense app. due to Ir. *slat*, lath.

By the sclattis [AS. watelas, Tynd. tylynge] thei senten him doun with the bed (Wyc. *Luke*, v. 19).

slat[2]**.** To flap (naut.). Prob. imit., cf. frequent. *slatter*.

slatch [*naut.*]. Var. of *slack*[1].

slate. OF. *esclate*, fem. form of *esclat* (see *slat*[1]). Cf. relation of Ger. *schiefer*, slate, to *shiver*[1]. To *slate*, assail vigorously, originated in Ir. It is explained (1865) as equivalent to "bonneting," knocking a man's hat (? *slate*) over his eyes, but is perh. rather from missile use of *slate* (cf. to *stone*). With fig. *clean slate*, orig. in ref. to score chalked up in tavern, cf. to *pass the sponge over*.

slatter. See *slat*[2].

slattern. From dial. *slatter*, to spill, slop things about, as in a *dirty slattering woman* (Ray, 1674).

slaughter. ON. *slātr* (for **slahtr*), butcher-meat, cogn. with *slay*[2]; cf. Ger. *schlachten*, to slaughter. Orig. connected with butchers and cattle; for sense-development cf. *massacre, carnage, butchery*.

Slav, Slavonic, Sclav- [*ling.*]. MedL. *Sclavus*, Late G. Σκλάβος, also (later) MedL. *Slavus*, whence F. *slave*. Group of races and langs. represented by Russ., Pol., Czech, Bulgar., Serbo-Croat., etc.

slave. F. *esclave*, OF. also *esclaf*, as *Slav*, the Slavs of central Europe having been reduced to slavery by conquest. The word, now in most Europ. langs. (It. *schiavo*, Sp. *esclavo*, Du. *slaaf*, Ger. *sklave*, etc.), prob. started in this sense from the Byzantine Empire. Cf. AS. *wealh*, foreigner, Briton, slave. *Slavey*, orig. male or female servant, dates from c. 1800.

slaver. Of Scand. origin; cf. synon. ON. *slafra*; cogn. with *slobber*.

slay[1]**, sley, sleigh** [*techn.*]. Part of loom. AS. *slege*, cogn. with *slay*[2].

slay[2]**.** Verb. AS. *slēan*, to smite, kill. Com. Teut.; cf. Du. *slaan*, Ger. *schlagen*, to strike (*erschlagen*, to slay), ON. *slā*, Goth. *slahan*. Replaced by *kill* exc. in higher style. They are about equally common in *AV*.

sleave. Floss silk. Only as (usu. muddled) echo of *Macb.* ii. 2 (see quot. s.v. *ravel*). From AS. *slǣfan* (in *tōslǣfan*), causal of *slīfan* (see *sliver*).

sleazy. Of loose texture. Assimilated to obs. *sleazy*, Silesia, as in *Sleasie or Silesia linen cloth* (Blount, 1670), but doubtfully ident. with it.

sled. Du. *slede, slee*, cogn. with *slide*; cf. Ger. *schlitten*, ON. *slethi*. See also *sledge*[2], *sleigh*.

sledge[1]**.** Hammer. AS. *slecg*, cogn. with *slay*[2]. With pleon. *sledge-hammer* (15 cent.) cf. *pea-jacket, salt-cellar*, etc.

sledge[2]**.** Sled (q.v.). Du. dial. *sleeds*, of Fris. origin.

sleek. Later var. of *slick* (q.v.).

sleep. AS. *slāpian, slǣpan*. Com. Teut. exc. Scand.; cf. Du. *slapen*, Ger. *schlafen*, Goth. *slēpan*. Orig. strong and weak, the old strong past surviving in dial. *he slep*, the weak forms perh. being due to a lost causal (cf. *fall, fell*). With fig. senses cf. *dormant*. With *sleeper*, horizontal beam, etc. (from c. 1600), cf. *joist*. With *sleepy pears* cf. *sad pastry*. With *sleeping sickness*, now of spec. Afr. disease, cf. ME. *sleeping evil* (Trev.).

sleet. Cf. LG. *slōte* (Ger. *schlosse*), hail, Du. *sloot*, also Dan. *slud*, Norw. dial. *sletta*, sleet.

sleeve. AS. *slīefe*, cogn. with Fris. *slefe, sliv*, sleeve, and with archaic Du. *slove, sloof*, covering.

sleigh. Sledge (orig. US.). Du. *slee*, for *slede*, sled. Cf. *snickersnee*.

sleight. ON. *slǣgth*, from *slǣgr*, sly, crafty; cf. *sloyd*. Now esp. in *sleight of hand* (see *legerdemain*).

slender. Earlier also *sclendre* (Chauc. A. 587). App. of OF. origin, but OF. *esclendre* is only recorded by Palsg. Kil. gives obs. Du. *slinder*, but this is prob. from E.

sleuth. Chiefly in *sleuth-hound*, and in mod. US. for detective. ON. *slōth*, track, trail, whence also *slot*[3].

slew, slue [*naut.*]. To turn. Hence *slewed*, drunk (naut.). Origin unknown.

sley. See *slay*[1].

slice. OF. *esclice*, shiver, splinter (*éclisse*, splint), from *esclicier*, OHG. *slīzan* (*schleissen, schlitzen*), to slit (q.v.).

James the second was slaine by the slice of a great peece of artillerie, which by overcharging chanced to breake (Holinshed).

slick. First as verb, to make smooth, sleek. AS. -*slȳcian*, in *nīgslȳcod*, new sleeked; cf. Norw. dial. *slikja*; cogn. with Ger. *schleichen*, to creep, glide. Adv. (orig. US.) may have been influenced by cogn. Ger. *schlecht, schlicht*, which in compds. has preserved its orig. sense, e.g. *slick away* renders Ger. *schlechtweg* (see *slight*).

slide. AS. *slīdan*; cf. LG. *slijden*, MHG. *slīten* (whence *schlitten*, sledge[2], *schlittschuh*, skate[2]). *Sliding scale*, app. first used in current sense by Carlyle, was earlier (c. 1700) equivalent to math. *sliding-rule*.

slight. ME. also *sleght*, ON. **sleht-* (*slettr*). Com. Teut.; cf. Du. *slecht*, Ger. *schlecht, schlicht*, Goth. *slachts*; ult. cogn. with *slick, sleek*. Orig. smooth, sleek, as still in Ger. *schlicht*, while var. *schlecht* means bad (v.i.), exc. in compds. (*schlechthin, schlechterdings*, straightway) and in *schlecht und recht*, plainly. Later sense of slender, weak, passed into that of trifling, inferior, base, whence to *put a slight on* and verb to *slight*. Common 17 cent. sense of razing a fortress is app. from Ger. For range of senses cf. *nice, silly, quaint, slim*, etc.

[David] chose fyve slighte stones out of the ryver (Coverd. 1 *Sam*. xvii.).

schlechten oder rasiren (eine festung): to slight a fortification (Ludw.).

slim. Du., crafty, awry, cogn. with Ger. *schlimm*, bad. Orig. sense was crooked, oblique. Mod. sense of cute, from SAfrDu., was current in 17 cent. E., as still in dial. & US.

slime. AS. *slīm*. Com. Teut.; cf. Du. *slijm*, Ger. *schleim*, mucus, ON. *slīm*; ult. cogn. with L. *limus*, "mudde, slime, clay in water" (Coop.).

sling[1]. To hurl. ON. *slyngva*, cogn. with Ger. *schlingen*, to twist, wind, also MHG. to throw (for double sense cf. hist. of *throw, warp*). Ger. *schlange*, snake, is cogn. From Teut. comes OF. *eslinguer* (naut.). With noun, suspensory noose of various kinds, cf. synon. Ger. *schlinge*. The sense-hist. of *sling, throw, warp*, suggests that the starting-point of the whole group may have been the elementary noose-like weapon

which was twisted round and round before discharge (cf. L. *telum torquēre*). To *sling*, suspend, is from the noun.

But Eneas be war he abyes
The bolde wordes that [he] dede sclyng
              (*NED*. c. 1400)

sling[2]. In *gin-sling* (obs. US.). ? From Ger. *verschlingen*, to swallow (? cf. *schnaps*). This for earlier *verschlinden*, also Du., cogn. with OSax. *slund*, gulp. *Sling* alone occurs in E. 18 cent. slang with sense of nip, gulp.

slink. AS. *slincan*, to creep, crawl (of reptiles); cf. LG. *slinken*, Ger. *schleichen*; cogn. with *sling*[1] (cf. *slink*, abortive calf, etc., prematurely "slung" or cast).

slip. Only *slipor*, slippery, is found in AS. Cf. Du. *slippen*, Ger. *schlüpfen*, to slip, *schleifen*, to whet, ON. *sleppa*, Goth. *sliupan*; also AS. *slūpan*. With to *give the slip* cf. to *slip a hound*. Sense of narrow strip corresponds with that of Ger. *schleife*, band, *schleppe*, train of dress, *schlippe*, alley (E. dial. *slipe*). No continental lang. has the earliest E. sense of slip for grafting. It is possible that *a slip (of a girl)*, earlier also applied contemptuously to boys, is not a fig. use of *slip*, shoot, scion, but short for *slipstring*, formerly used like *waghalter* (see *wag*) and *crackrope*. Ground-sense of the word is prob. that of making smooth, and the group is ult. cogn. with L. *lubricus*, "slipper" (Coop.). *Slippery* is a 16 cent. extension of obs. & dial. *slipper* (v.s.) after Ger. *schlüpfrig*.

The slyper [*var*. slideri] mouth werchith fallingis
              (Wyc. *Prov*. xxvi. 28).

slipe [*dial*.]. See *slype*.

slipper. From *slip* (v.i.).

slipshod. Cf. obs. *slipshoe* and AS. *slȳpescōh*. In Shaks. (*Lear*, i. 5).

slipslop. Redupl. on *slop*[2].

slit. Cf. obs. *slite*, AS. *slītan*; cogn. with Ger. *schlitzen*, and with *slice*.

slither. For earlier *slidder* (see quot. s.v. *slip*), frequent. of *slide*.

Thou toke mi saul dede fra,
Mi fete fra slitheringe als-swa (ME. *Psalt*. lvi. 13).

sliver. From dial. *slive*, to cleave, divide, AS. *slīfan* (in *tōslīfan*, to split). Cf. *sleave*.

slobber, slubber. Also earlier *slabber*, cogn. with *slab*[2], and ult. with *slip, slop*[2].

sloe. AS. *slāh*. WGer.; cf. Du. *slee*, Ger. *schlehe*.

slog. Orig. pugil., also dial. & US. *slug*. ? From Du. *slag*, blow, Ger. *schlag*, cogn with *slay*², with vowel change as in *bluff*. In dial. also to plod; cf. *foot-slogger* (mil.).

slogan. Gael. *sluagh-ghairm*, host cry. An early form *slughorn* misled Chatterton and Browning (*Childe Roland*).

sloid. See *sloyd*.

sloop. Du. *sloep*; cf. LG. *slupe*, Sw. Dan. Norw. *slup*; perh. cogn. with *slip* (cf. *schooner*, but see also *shallop*). App. borrowed from Du. in EIndies. Scot's *Relation of Java* (1602–5) has *a small slup or pinnace* rather earlier than *NED.* quots.

sloops: are vessels attending our men of war, and generally of about 66 tuns. See *shallops*
                       (*Gent. Dict.* 1705).

slop¹. Loose outer garment. AS. *slop*, in *oferslop*, prob. cogn. with *slip* (cf. origin of *smock*). In 16–17 cents. often in sense of baggy breeches. Cf. F. *salopette*, workman's slop, of Teut. origin.

The business of slopps, wherein the seaman is so much abused by the pursers (Pepys, Mar. 16, 1662).

slop². Liquid, orig. mud, etc. AS. *sloppe*, in *cūsloppe*, cowslip (q.v.); cogn. with *slip*, *slobber*, *slab*².

slop³ [*slang*]. Policeman. For *ecilop*, i.e. *police* spelt backward.

slope. Back-formation from *aslope* (q.v.). Cf. *slant*, *squint*. Slang to *slope* was orig. US.

slosh, slush, sludge. ? Cf. Norw. dial. *sluss*, mire, ? ult. cogn. with *sleet*. Also (naut.) applied to refuse grease, whence *slush-lamp*, *slushy*, ship's cook.

slot¹. For pennies. Orig. (14 cent.), and still in dial., groove or hollow between the breasts. OF. *esclot*, in same sense, perh. ident. with *slot*³.

slot² [*techn.*]. Bar, rod. Du. LG. *slot*, cogn. with Ger. *schloss*, lock, *schliessen*, to shut.

slotte or schetyl of a dore: verolium (*Prompt. Parv.*).

slot³. Track of animal. OF. *esclot*, ON. *slōth*, sleuth.

sloth. ME. formation from *slow*, replacing obs. *sleuth*, AS. *slǣwth*. As name of animal translates Port. *preguiça*, L. *pigritia*, laziness, given to it by early Port. explorers.

slouch. Orig. noun, lout (Barclay, 1515), as still in US.; also *slouk* (*Manip. Vocab.*). Cf. Norw. Dan. *sluköret*, LG. *slukorig*, slouch-eared, Norw. dial. *slauk*, languid person, cogn. with *slug*¹. With *slouch hat* cf. earlier *slouch-eared* (16 cent.).

slough¹. Mire. AS. *slōh*, ult. cogn. with Ger. *schlingen*, to swallow up; cf. L. *vorago*, "a swallow or gulfe" (Coop.), from *vorare*,

to devour, and OHG. *schlūch*, abyss, from *schlucken*, to swallow.

slough². Scarf-skin of snake. Cogn. with Ger. *schlauch*, wine-skin, hose, in MHG. snakeskin. Hence verb to *slough* (med.).

Slovak [*ethn.*]. Native name of Slav race in Hungary. Cf. *Slovene*.

sloven. Earlier (15 cent.) *sloveyn*, *slovayne*. App. from Du. *slof*, careless, Flem. *sloef*, squalid, with AF. suffix (F. *-ain*, L. *-anus*); ? cogn. with Ger. *schlaff*, slack, flaccid.

Slovene [*ethn.*]. Serbo-Croatian or Wend. Ger., OSlav. *slovēne*, Slav.

slow. AS. *slāw*, sluggish, obtuse. Com. Teut.; cf. Du. *sleeuw*, *slee*, OHG. *slēo*, ON. *slǣr*, *sljār*, *sljōr*. *Slow-coach* (fig.) is first in Dickens (*Pickwick*, ch. xxxiv.).

slow-worm. AS. *slāwyrm*, app. slay worm, being ignorantly regarded as dangerous. In earliest records used as gloss to names of lizards (*rĕgulus*, *stellio*) to which deadly powers were attributed. But synon. Norw. *slo* or *ormslo* is explained as ult. cogn. with *slick*, *sleek*, and this is confirmed by Ger. *blindschleiche* (associated with *schleichen*, to creep, glide).

sloyd, sloid. Training in manual dexterity. Sw. *slöjd*, sleight.

slubber. Older form of *slobber* (q.v.). Hence *slubberdegullion* (also *slabber-*), with which cf. *tatterdemalion*. But both words suggest an imit. of a F. formation, as in *chien de voleur*, *fripon de valet*, etc. ? Second element from OF. *goalon*, "a sloven; one that weares his clothes unhandsomely, or puts them on carelessly; so tearmed about Blois" (Cotg.).

trainquenailles: scoundrells, ragamuffins, base rascalls, slabergudgions (Cotg.).

sludge. See *slosh*. The Manchester *sludge-boats* remove the city's "muck."

slue. See *slew*.

slug¹. Sluggard. Cf. Norw. dial. *sluggje*, slow person, Sw. dial. *slogga*, to be slow, and E. verb to *slug*, as in *slug-a-bed*. Hence also *sluggard*, *sluggish*. For later zool. application of *slug* cf. *sloth*.

slug². Roughly shaped bullet. ? Connected with *slug*³. Late appearance (17 cent.) makes Du. or Ger. origin likely.

slug³ [*US.*]. See *slog*.

slughorn. See *slogan*.

sluice. OF. *escluse* (*écluse*), Late L. *exclusa*, from *excludere*, to shut out, whence also Du. *sluis*, Ger. *schleuse*. The Battle of Sluys (1340) is in F. hist. *la bataille de l'Écluse*.

slum. From c. 1800. Orig. cant, room, also with other, app. unrelated, senses. To *go slumming* is recorded by *NED.* for 1884, the pastime owing its inception to Besant and Rice's East End novels.

slumber. ME. *slumeren*, frequent. of *slumen*, from AS. *slūma*, sleep; cf. Du. *sluimeren* (also earlier *sluimen*), Ger. *schlummern* (also earlier *schlummen*). For -*b*- cf. *chamber*, *timber*, etc. Prevalence of frequent. form in all three langs. is due to the idea of dozing, intermittent sleep.

slump. In current sense, lit. small land-slide, US. Cf. dial. *slump*, to sink in with a flop, an imit. word (cf. *plump*²) with Scand. & Ger. cognates, one of which may be the source of the US. word.

Preacht at Wakes [Colne] church, snowy; the way bad, twice I slumpt in and was wett
　　　　　　　　　　(Josselin's *Diary*. 1659).

slur¹. To smear, now usu. fig. From ME. *sloor*, mud (*Prompt. Parv.*). With to *cast a slur* cf. *aspersion*.

slur². To pass lightly over, orig. to slip a die out of the box without its turning, to slide about; cf. LG. *sluren*, Du. *sleuren*, to drag, trail; ? cogn. with *slur*¹. The two verbs cannot be distinguished in some senses.

slush. See *slosh*.

slut. Cf. synon. Ger. dial. *schlutte*, *schlutz*, with app. related words in Scand. langs. Perh. ult. cogn. with *slattern*, but not connected with *sloven*. *Sluttish* is in Chauc.

sly. ME. also *sleh*, *sley*, ON. *slǣgr*; cf. *sleight*. Orig. skilful, expert. For degeneration of sense cf. *crafty*, *cunning*, etc. Perh. ult. cogn. with *slay*², and meaning skilled in striking; cf. synon. Ger. *schlau*, *verschlagen*. *Slyboots* app. contains some suggestion of furtive tread (*pussyfoot*); cf. synon. Ger. *leisetreter*, lit. light treader.

Therfor be ye sligh as serpentis and symple as dowves (Wyc. *Matt.* x. 16).

slype [*arch.*]. Covered way from transept to chapter-house. A 19 cent. spelling of *slipe*, long narrow strip (of ground, etc.), cogn. with *slip*.

smack¹. Flavour. AS. *smæc*. WGer.; cf. Du. *smaak*, Ger. *geschmack*. ? Orig. imit. of smacking of lips. Verb was earlier *smatch*, AS. *gesmæccan*.

smack². Of lips, whip. Imit.; cf. Du. *smak*, Ger. dial. *schmacke*, also colloq. Ger. *schmatzen*, to eat noisily.

baiser: to kisse, to smoutch, to smacke (Cotg.).

smack³. Fishing-boat. Du. LG. *smak*, whence Sw. *smack*, Dan. *smakke*; also F. *semaque*, Sp. *esmaque*, from Teut.

small. AS. *smæl*. Com. Teut.; cf. Du. *smal*, Ger. *schmal*, narrow, slender, ON. *smalr*, Goth. *smals*. As adv. now only in to *sing small* (v.i.). Archaic *small-clothes*, knee-breeches, is in Dickens usu. *smalls*. With fig. sense of *small beer* cf. US. *small potatoes*. For *small-pox* (1518) see *pock*. *Small talk* is first recorded in Chesterfield's *Letters*.

To suckle fools and chronicle small-beer (*Oth.* ii. 1).
She has brown eyes and speaks small like a woman
　　　　　　　　　　(*Merry Wives*, i. 1).

smallage [*archaic*]. Celery. Earlier *small ache*, F. *ache*, VL. *apia, for *apium*, "perseley, smallage" (Coop.).

smalt. Glass coloured deep blue. F., It. *smalto*, of Teut. origin, cogn. with *smelt*².

smaragd [*archaic*]. OF. *smaragde*, as *emerald* (q.v.).

smart. First as verb. AS. *smeortan*, to be painful. WGer.; cf. Du. *smarten*, Ger. *schmerzen*. *Smart-money* was orig. (17 cent.) compensation for disablement (mil. & nav.). Orig. sense of adj. was sharp, stinging, as still in *smart rap over the knuckles*, etc.; later, brisk, forward, clever, trim in attire, the last sense ascending from the kitchen to the drawing-room c. 1880. Ult. cogn. with L. *mordēre*, to bite.

smash. Late (18 cent.) intens. of *mash*; cf. *s-plash*, *s-quash*, *s-crunch*, etc. Sense prob. associated with *slash*, *dash*, *crash*, etc.

smatter. In late ME. to talk ignorantly; earlier, to dirty, defile. For current sense cf. to *dabble*. ? Cogn. with *smut*.

smear. AS. *smeoru*, fat, ointment. Com. Teut.; cf. Du. *smeer*, Ger. *schmer*, ON. *smjör*, butter, Goth. *smairthr*; cogn. with Gael. *smier*, marrow, G. μύρον, ointment. See *anoint*.

smelfungus. Grumbler. Sterne's name, in *Sentimental Journey*, for Smollett, allusive to the latter's captious tone in his *Travels* (1766).

smell. Early ME., but not recorded in AS. and with no known cognates. As noun has largely replaced *stink*.

smelt¹. Fish. AS. *smelt*; cf. Dan. *smelt*, obs. Ger. *schmelz*.

smelt². Verb. Of LG. origin; cf. Ger. *schmelzen*, to melt (q.v.). Cf. *smalt*.

smew. Saw-billed duck. Also called *smee*, *smeeth*. ? Cogn. with *smooth*

smilax. G. σμῖλαξ, bindweed.

smile. Cf. OHG. *smīlan*, Dan. *smile*, Norw. & Sw. *smila*, all prob. of LG. origin. To *come up smiling* (after reverses) is from the prize-ring.

smirch. From 15 cent. Orig. *smorch*, app. OF. *esmorche*, var. of *amorce*, bait, priming, from L. *mordēre*, *mors-*, to bite. This is used by Rabelais (i. 13) in an unquotable passage in the sense of *smirch*. No doubt there has been association with *smear*.

smirk. AS. *smearcian*, ? cogn. with *smierian*, to smear, anoint, with idea of "oily smile."

smite. AS. *smītan*, to smear; cf. Du. *smijten*, to throw, strike, Ger. *schmeissen*, to throw, smite (OHG. *smīzan*, to smear), Goth. *-smeitan*, to smear. For sense-development cf. ironic use of *anoint* and cf. F. *frotter* (see *baste*[3]).

smith. AS. *smith*. Com. Teut.; cf. Du. *smid*, Ger. *schmied*, ON. *smithr*, Goth. *-smitha*, with cogn. verbs. Orig. craftsman in metal; cf. Ger. *geschmeidig*, malleable. With *smithy*, ON. *smithja*, cf. Ger. *schmiede*.

smitham. Small coal; earlier, dust of lead ore, ground malt. Var. of AS. *smedma*, fine powder, spelling being due to association with *smith*; cf. archaic Dan. *smitten*, Sw. dial. *smitter*, fragment, ult. cogn. with *mite*[1].

smithereens [*Anglo-Ir.*]. Ir. *smidirín*, small fragment (v.s.). Cf. *colleen*, *poteen*, etc.

Smith's prizes [*Camb.*]. Founded (1768) by Robert Smith, Master of Trinity.

smock. AS. *smoc*, prob. cogn. with *smūgan*, to creep, as being a garment into which one inserts the head. Cf. *slop*[1]. See also *smug*, *smuggle*. Norw. *smokk*, finger-stall, is prob. the same word.

smog. Portmanteau-word, "what one eminent doctor has called 'smog'—coal-smoke-fog" (*Daily Chron.* Dec. 2, 1919).

smoke. AS. *smoca*; cf. Du. *smook*, Ger. *schmauch*. As verb AS. had *smēocan* (strong intrans.), whence dial. to *smeek*, *smocian* (weak trans.), whence to *smoke*. Has largely supplanted *reek*. To *smoke* (tobacco) appears c. 1600 (cf. F. *fumer*, Ger. *rauchen*) for earlier to *drink* (tobacco).

smolt. Young salmon intermediate between parr and grilse. ? Cf. *smelt*[1].

smooth. AS. *smōth*, found only once, the usual form being *smēthe*, whence dial. *smeeth*, common in place-names, e.g. *Smithfield*, *Smedley*.

smother. Early ME. *smorther*, stifling smoke,

from stem of AS. *smorian*, to smother, suffocate, whence dial. to *smore*; cf. Du. *smoren*, Ger. *schmoren* (from LG.).

> Thus must I from the smoke into the smother
> (*As You Like It*, i. 2).

smouch [*slang*]. Jew. Earlier *smouse*, Du. *smous*, "a German Jew" (Sewel), ident. with Ger.-Jewish *schmus*, patter, profit, Heb. *sh'mū'ōth*, tales, news (? cf. *sheeny*). Sewel (1708) explains *smous* as formed from *Moses*, with which it has at any rate been associated. Cf. SAfr. *smouse*, pedlar.

smoulder. First (14 cent.) as noun, smother, smoky vapour. App. cogn. with *smother* and with Du. *smeulen*, to smoulder. Obs. from c. 1600, but revived by Scott.

> Where be much hete, being a fatte man, he was smoulderid to death (Leland, c. 1540).

> This word [smouldering] seems a participle; but I know not whether the verb smoulder be in use (Johns.).

smouse. See *smouch*.

smudge, smutch. ? Related to *smut* ? or to *smoke*. The latter is favoured by dial. *smudge*, to smoke (herrings), and US. *smudge*, smoky fire to keep off mosquitos. But there may be two separate words *smudge*, and influence of *smirch* also seems likely.

smug. From 16 cent., trim, neat, gradually shading into self-complacent, and, at universities, swot. Cf. Ger. *schmuck*, trim, elegant, cogn. with *schmiegen*, to press closely against (cf. *smock*).

> *sie hatte ihren schmuck angelegt*: she had smugged up her self (Ludw.).

smuggle. From 17 cent. LG. *smukkeln*, *smuggeln*, whence also Ger. *schmuggeln*, Du. *smokkelen*; cogn. with *smug*, with idea of secrecy. ? Cf. slang *smug*, to steal, hush up.

smut. From 17 cent., in all senses. Of LG. origin, cogn. with ME. *smoten*, to besmirch (Trev.); cf. Ger. *schmutz*, "smut, dirt, nastiness" (Ludw.).

> I saw the new play my wife saw yesterday, and do not like it, it being very smutty
> (Pepys, June 20, 1668).

smutch. See *smudge*.

snack. Orig. snap, bite, hence share, as in to *go snacks*. From dial. verb to *snack*, bite, snap; app. cogn. with *snatch* and ult. with *snap*; cf. Du. *snakken*, Norw. dial. *snaka*. See also *sneck*.

snaffle. From 16 cent. Cf. Du. *snavel*, snout, Fris. *snaffel*, mouth, Ger. *schnabel*, beak, all ult. cogn. with *neb*. For transference of sense cf. *muzzle*.

snag. Prob. of Scand. origin; cf. Norw. dial. *snage*, sharp point, stump, ON. *snagi*, point.

snail. AS. *snægel*; cf. LG. *snäl*, Ger. dial. *schnägel*, ON. *snigill*; cogn. with synon. Ger. *schnecke, schnake*, and with *snake*.

snake. AS. *snaca*; cf. LG. *schnake*, ON. *snākr*, and OHG. *snahhan*, to creep; cogn. with *snail*, ? and ult. with *nag*, cobra (q.v.).

snap. LG. Du. *snappen*, cogn. with Ger. *schnappen*, to snap, *schnabel*, beak. In some senses partly an intens. of *knap*². Very common in compds. indicating instantaneous action, e.g. *snapshot, snap vote*, etc., esp. in US.

snaphaunce [*hist.*]. Robber, firelock. Corrupt. of Du. *snaphaen*, or Ger. *schnapphahn*, lit. snap-cock; for formation cf. *catchpole*. The firelock may have been named from the robber (F. *chenapan*, rogue, is from Ger.), or have been an independent formation from the *hahn*, cock (of a gun), snapping on the flint. The Ger. word corresponds to the *petronel* of the Rom. langs.

chien: a dogge; also, the snaphaunce of a pistoll (Cotg.).

snare. ON. *snara* or AS. *sneare*, cord, noose; cogn. with Du. *snaar*, string, and ult. with Ger. *schnur*.

snark. Imaginary animal. Coined (1876) by Lewis Carroll in the *Hunting of the Snark*. Cf. *jabberwock*.

Our Liberal contemporaries are engaged in explaining every day that the Snark is undoubtedly a Boojum (*Obs.* Jan. 25, 1920).

snarl. Extended from obs. *snar*, cogn. with Ger. *schnarren*, to snarl, rattle; prob. imit.

snatch. Cogn. with *snack* (q.v.). Tusser has *snatch* for *snack*, light refreshment. With *by snatches* (16 cent.) cf. synon. L. *raptim*.

sneak. First as verb (Shaks.). App. cogn. with AS. *snīcan*, to creep, crawl, whence ME. *snike*. But the latter does not appear after 13 cent., and to this gap must be added the difference of vowel. Cf. *snake, snail*.

sneck [*Sc.*]. Latch, or catch, of door. Cogn. with *snatch, snack*. Cf. similar use of *catch, snap* (e.g. of bracelet).

sneer. Cf. Fris. *sneer*, scornful remark, *sneere*, to scorn. ? Cogn. with *snarl*. Earlier sense was to snort. Cf. F. *ricaner*, to sneer, OF. to bray, etc. Mod. contempt is less noisy but more intense.

sneeze. Altered from obs. *fnese*, AS. *fnēosan*

(only in noun *fnēosung*), cogn. with Du. *fniezen*, ON. *fnȳsa*, and ult. with Ger. *niesen*. The alteration was perh. due to sense of phonetic fitness, helped by scribal confusion between *fn, ſn*. Var. *neese* is in *AV.* (*Job*, xli. 18).

He speketh in his nose,
And fneseth faste and eek he hath the pose [cold]
(Chauc. H. 61).

snib [*dial.*]. See *snub*.

snick. To cut. ? Suggested by *snickersnee*, ? or by *nick*. Now esp. at cricket.

snicker. Var. of *snigger* (q.v.); cf. Sc. *nicker*, in similar sense; ult. cogn. with *neigh*.

snickersnee [*archaic*]. Large knife, orig. fight with knives. Altered from obs. *snick-a-snee*, earlier *snick-or-snee*. Orig. from Du. *steken*, to thrust, stick (cf. Ger. *stechen*), *snijden, snijen*, to cut (cf. Ger. *schneiden*); cf. *cut-and-thrust*. The *st-* of the first word was later assimilated to the *sn-* of the second. In quot. 1 the speaker is a Dutchman.

It is our countrie custome onely to stick or snee (Glapthorne, *Hollander*, i. 1, 1640).

Among other customs they have in that town [Genoa], one is, that none must carry a pointed knife about him; which makes the Hollander, who is us'd to snik and snee to leave his horn-sheath and knife a ship-board when he comes ashore (Howell).

snider. Rifle. Invented by *Jacob Snider* (†1866).

sniff. Imit., cf. *snuff-le, snivel*.

snifting [*techn.*]. In *snifting-valve*. From dial. *snift*, to sniff; cf. Sw. *snyfta*.

snigger. Imit., also *snicker, nicker*.

sniggle. To fish for eels. From *sniggle*, dim. of dial. *snig*, eel (*Cath. Angl.*); ? cogn. with *snake*.

snip. Cf. Du. LG. *snippen*, Ger. dial. *schnippen*; cogn. with *snap*. As name for a tailor in Ben Jonson.

snipe. App. Scand.; cf. ON. *mȳrisnīpa*, Norw. *strandsnipa*; cogn. with Du. *snip*, Ger. *schnepfe*, "a snipe, snite" (Ludw.); ult. cogn. with *neb*; cf. F. *bécasse*, snipe, from *bec*, beak. The AS. name was *snīte*, whence dial. *snite* (v.s.). To *snipe*, shoot at individual, is 18 cent., latest fig. sense of spiteful attack or unpatriotic faultfinding being 20 cent.

I really beg, for the common cause of the country, that there should be an end of this sniping (D. Lloyd George, May 9, 1918).

snip-snap-snorum. Card-game (18 cent.). LG. *snipp-snapp-snorum* (or *-snurr*), a jingle on *snippen* or *snappen*, to snap up.

snivel. AS. *snyflan*, in *snyflung*, running at nose, from *snofl*, mucus; cogn. with *sniff*, *snuffle*. For fig. senses cf. *drivel*.

snob. Orig. (18 cent.) nickname for shoemaker; later, vulgarian (esp. at Camb.). Chief current sense is due to Thackeray (*Book of Snobs*, 1848). ? Cogn. with *snub*, to cut short (cf. *snip*, tailor).

snood [*poet.*]. AS. *snōd*, head-dress, fillet. Not found in ME. and now only as Sc. or poet. word.

snooker. Elaboration of pool and pyramids. Late 19 cent. Origin unknown. ? Arbitrary (cf. *spoof*).

snook-s. Derisive gesture. Late 19 cent. Origin unknown. Cf. F. *faire un pied de nez*, Ger. *eine lange nase machen*. Perh. name *Snook-s* felt as phonetically appropriate (cf. *Walker*).

snooze. Cant word (18 cent.) of unknown origin.

snoozle [*colloq.*]. ? Combination of *snooze*, *snuggle*, *nuzzle*.

snore. Imit., cf. *snort*, dial. *snork*, and Ger. *schnarchen*, "to snore or snort" (Ludw.).

This millere hath so wisely bibbed ale,
That as an hors he snorteth in his sleepe
(Chauc. A. 4162).

But give to me the snoring breeze
And white waves heaving high
(Allan Cunningham).

snort. Imit. (v.s.). For intens. *snorter* cf. *ripper*, *screamer*, etc.

snot. AS. *gesnot*; cf. Du. LG. *snot*, MHG. *snuz*; cogn. with *snout*. For *snotty*, contemptuous name for midshipman, cf. colloq. F. *morveux*, brat, with suggestion of lacking pocket handkerchief.

snout. Early ME. *snute*. Cf. Du. *snuit*, Ger. *schnauze*, Dan. *snude*, Sw. Norw. *snut*. Existence of AS. *snӯtan*, to wipe the nose, suggests that the word represents an unrecorded AS. *snūt*.

snow[1]. AS. *snāw*. Com. Teut.; cf. Du. *sneeuw*, Ger. *schnee* (OHG. *snēo*, *snēw-*), ON. *snær*, Goth. *snaiws*; cogn. with L. *nix*, *niv-*, Gael. Ir. *sneacht*, Welsh *nyf*, Russ. *snieg'*, etc. To *snow under* is US. (cf. to *freeze out*).

snow[2] [*naut.*]. Kind of brig. Du. *snauw* or LG. *snau*, whence also Ger. *schnaue*, F. *senou*. Orig. LG. sense is snout, beak, the build being somewhat pointed, for speed.

snub. ON. *snubba*, to check, rebuke. Ground-sense is to shorten, as in *snub nose* (cf. Norw. dial. *snubbnos*), and naut. & US.

sense of pulling up short. *Snib*, *snip* were also used in same sense.

He schuld snybbe the maydenes that thei schuld not be redy to telle swech tales
(Capgrave, *St Augustine*, c. 1450).

snuff. Earliest sense, wick of candle (Wyc. *Ex.* xxv. 38). App. the same word as *snuff*, sniff, snort (see *snivel*); cf. F. *moucher*, to snuff a candle, to wipe the nose, and Norw. Dan. *snyde* in same senses; cogn. with Ger. *schnupfen*, cold in the head, *schnuppe*, snuff of candle. Wyc. (*Ex.* xxv. 38) has to *snot out* as var. of to *snuff out*. Sense of powdered tobacco is Du. *snuf*, *snuif*, short for *snuiftabak*, tobacco for sniffing. Formerly often *snush*, with which cf. Sc. *sneeshing*, because helping to sneeze. *Up to snuff* is recorded c. 1800. ? Cf. F. *ne pas se moucher du pied*.

schnupftoback: a sneezing-powder; a snuff or snush (Ludw.).

snuffle. Frequent. of *snuff*; cf. Du. *snuffelen*, Ger. *schnüffeln*. Cf. *snivel*.

snug. Orig. (16 cent.) naut., as in to *make all snug*, to *snug down*. Cf. Sw. *snygg*, archaic Dan. *snyg*, tidy, LG. *snügger*, Du. *snugger*, sprightly. Hence to *snuggle*.

so. AS. *swā*. Com. Teut.; cf. Du. *zoo*, Ger. *so*, ON. *svā*, Goth. *swa*. See *as*. With *so and so* cf. *such and such*.

soak. AS. *socian*, cogn. with *suck*.

To dinner at Trinity-house, where a very good dinner among the old sokers (Pepys, Feb. 15, 1664).

soap. AS. *sāpe*. Com. Teut.; cf. Du. *zeep*, Ger. *seife*, ON. *sāpa*. L. *sapo* (whence F. *savon*, It. *sapone*, Sp. *jabón*) is of Teut. origin and occurs first in Pliny, the Romans app. not knowing the use of soap. Cf. *lather*.

soar. F. *essorer*, VL. **exaurare*, from *aura*, air; cf. It. *sorare*.

sob. Imit., cf. Fris. *sobje*, to suck *Sob-stuff* (neol.) is US.

sobeit. For *so be it*. One of our few surviving subjunctives.

sober. F. *sobre*, L. *sobrius*, opposite of *ebrius*, drunk, with which it is no doubt cogn. Found very early in extended sense of grave, sedate, etc., e.g. *in sober earnest*, *sober as a judge*, the latter prob. not the opposite of *drunk as a lord*.

Sobranje. Bulg. national assembly. From prefix *so-* (as in *soviet*) and *berem*, I gather, cogn. with G. φέρειν, E. *bear*[2]. Thus "conference." Cf. Russ. *sobirat'*, to gather.

sobriquet, soubriquet. F., "a surname; also, a nick-name, or by-word; and, a quip or cut given, a mock or flowt bestowed, a jeast broken on a man." In OF. a chuck under the chin, with which cf. synon. It. *sottobecco*, lit. under (the) beak. For sense-development we may compare Ger. *spitzname*, lit. sharp-pointed name, but the form of the F. word is unexplained. The second element may have orig. meant brisket; cf. OF. *soubarbe, soubride*, both used of a sudden check to a horse.

soc, socage [*hist.*]. See *soke*.

soccer, socker. Association football. Cf. *rugger*.

social. F., L. *socialis*, from *socius*, companion, cogn. with *sequi*, to follow. It is uncertain whether *socialism, socialist* originated (c. 1835) in F. or E. No doubt they contain a reminiscence of Rousseau's *Contrat Social* (1762). *Sociology* is F. *sociologie*, coined by Comte.

society. F. *société*, L. *societas* (v.s.). Cf. *association*.

Socinian [*theol.*]. Of *Faustus Socinus*, latinized name of *Sozzini*, It. theologian of 16 cent., who denied divinity of Christ.

sociology. See *social*.

sock¹. For foot. AS. *socc*, slipper, L. *soccus*, light shoe. In *sock and buskin*, comedy and tragedy, with allusion to light shoe of ancient comic actors (*Allegro*, 131).

sock². To beat, to give *socks*. Cant, of unknown origin.

> sock: a pocket, also to beat. *I'll sock ye*: I'll drub ye tightly (*Dict. Cant. Crew*).

sock³. "Tuck." Orig. Eton slang. Origin unknown.

sockdologer [*US.*]. Knock-out blow, "whopper." Said to be arbitrary formation from *doxology*, regarded as final.

socker. See *soccer*.

socket. AF. *soket*, orig. spear-head of shape of small ploughshare, dim. of F. *soc*, ploughshare, of Celt. origin (cf. Gael. *soc*). The transfer of sense from the blade to the cylinder receiving it is easily paralleled (cf. *shaft*).

> [Pugio] brevem formam habens vomeris, unde vulgariter "vomerulus" vocatur, Gallice "soket"
> (Matthew Paris).

socle [*arch.*]. F., It. *zoccolo*, pedestal, little sock, L. *socculus*, dim. of *soccus*, sock¹.

socman [*hist.*]. See *soke*.

Socratic. Of *Socrates* (†399 B.C.), esp. with ref. to eliciting truth by question and answer.

sod¹. Of grass. Also (17 cent.) *sad*. Cf. Du. *zode*, Ger. *sode* (from LG.), OFris. *sātha, sāda*. The cogn. forms all point to connection with *seethe*, but the reason for this is unknown. Cf. *sud, sodden*.

sod². For *sodomite*.

soda. It., also Sp. & MedL.; cf. F. *soude*, which could represent L. *solida*, but this will not account for the forms in the other langs. With *sodium* (Davy, 1807) cf. *potassium*.

sodality. L. *sodalitas*, from *sodalis*, companion.

sodden. Orig. p.p. of *seethe* (q.v.).

sodium. See *soda*.

sodomy. F. *sodomie*, from *Sodom* (*Gen.* xviii.–xix.).

Sodor. In bishopric of *Sodor and Man*. From ON. *suthreyjar*, southern islands (Hebrides), episcopally united with Man in 11 cent.

sofa. F., Arab. *ṣoffah*; cf. It. Sp. *sofa*.

soffit [*arch.*]. F. *soffite*, It. *soffito*, lit. fixed under, from L. *sub* and *figere*, to fix. Cf. *suffix*.

soft. AS. *sōfte*, more usu. *sēfte*, survival of the *-o-* form being due to influence of adv. WGer.; cf. Du. *zacht*, Ger. *sanft, sacht* (LG.); ? cogn. with Goth. *samjan*, to please. As applied to persons shows the usual degeneration (cf. *silly*) from orig. gentle, compassionate, etc., via effeminate (Shaks.). Burton already has "silly, soft fellows" with mod. sense of both adjs.

soho. AF. hunting cry (14 cent.). Cf. *tally ho, yoicks*.

soi-disant. F., lit. self-saying.

soil¹. Ground. AF. *soil*, VL. *solium*, for *solum*, ground. Or perh. simply OF. *soul*, L. *solum*, with the E. fondness for *-oi-*, as in *recoil, foil², obs. moil*, mule, *soil³*, etc.

soil². To stain. F. *souiller* (whence also *sully*); cf. Prov. *sulhar*. Prob. of Teut. origin; cf. OHG. *bisuljan*, OSax. *salwian*, Goth. *bisauljan*, AS. *sylian*, from *sol*, mud, wallow, Norw. dial. *söyla*, to defile. Hence *soil*, filth, esp. in *night-soil*, and to *take soil* (of hunted animal), to seek refuge in pool, wallow.

soil³ [*archaic*]. To fatten (cattle) on green food. F. *saouler, soûler*, from *saoul, soûl*, satiated, L. *satullus*, dim. of *satur*, from *satis*, enough, cogn. with *sad*.

soirée. F., from *soir*, evening, L. *serum* (sc. *tempus*), late. Cf. *matinée*.

sojourn. OF. *sojorner* (*séjourner*), VL. **sub-diurnare*, from *diurnus* (see *journal*). As in *succour* E. preserves the fuller first syllable.

soke, soc [*hist.*]. Right of, district under, local jurisdiction. MedL. *soca*, AS. *sōcn*, cogn. with *seek*. Orig. sense of pursuit, attack, survives in Sc. *hamesucken* (leg.), assault on a man in his own house.

sol [*mus.*]. See *gamut*.

sola. Urdu *solā*, Hind. *sholā*, plant from the pith of which light hats are made; hence *sola topee*, the latter, Hind. *ṭopī*, hat, perh. from Port. *topo*, top.

solace. Archaic F. *soulas*, L. *solatium*, from *solari*, to comfort, console.

solan. Gannet. Now usu. *solan-goose*. Earlier *soland*. ON. *sūla*, second element perh. ON. *önd, and-*, duck (cf. Ger. *ente*). If so, *solan-goose* contains three bird-names.

solandra. Shrub. From *Solander*, Sw. botanist (†1782).

solar. L. *solaris*, from *sol*, sun; cogn. with G. ἥλιος, Goth. *sauil*, ON. *sōl*. *Solar plexus*, complex of nerves at pit of stomach, is app. from central position. *Solar myth* is 19 cent.

solarium. L., "a dial; also the sollar of an house" (Coop.), from *sol* (v.s.). In current use for terrace for sun baths. *Sollar, soller*, upper room, etc. (Wyc. *Acts*, i. 13), is still in dial. use.

soldan [*hist.*]. OF. form of *sultan* (q.v.); cf. It. *soldano*, Sp. *soldán*. In ME. more usu. *sowden* (still as surname), OF. *soudan*. Spec. of the Sultan of Egypt.

soldanella. Bindweed. It., of obscure origin, ? ult. from L. *solidus*; cf. various names for *comfrey* (q.v.).

solder. Restored from earlier *soder, soudur*, etc., F. *soudure* (cf. *batter, fritter*), from *souder*, L. *solidare*, to make solid. ME. had the verb *sold, soud*, now replaced by *solder*.

soldier. Restored from ME. & OF. *soudeour, soudier*, etc. (with more than seventy E. vars.), from *soude, solde*, pay (cf. It. *soldo*, Sp. *sueldo*), ult. ident. with *sou* (q.v.). ModF. *soldat* is It. *soldato*, lit. paid.

I can not wele gide or rewle sodyours
(*Paston Let.* ii. 308).

Some of them be but yonge sawgeres, and wote full lytyll what yt meneth to be as a sauger, nor for to endure to do as a sawger should be (*ib.* iii. 155).

soldato: prest with paie as soldiers are (Flor.).

Und sein sold
Muss dem soldaten werden; darnach heisst er
(Schiller, *Picc.* ii. 7).

soldo. It. coin. See *sou*.

sole¹. Of boot. F., VL. *sola*, for *solea*, from *solum*, ground. *Sole*, fish, is the same word, from shape.

sole². Adj. Restored from ME. & OF. *soul* (*seul*), L. *solus*.

solecism. L., G. σολοικισμός, from σόλοικος, speaking incorrectly, orig. in the corrupt Attic of the Athenian colonists of Σόλοι in Cilicia. Cf. *barbarism, anglicism, laconic, patavinity*.

solemn. OF. *solemne* (replaced by *solennel*), L. *sollemnis, sollennis*, appointed, festal, from OL. *sollus*, whole, entire, and *annus*, year. Now usu. with suggestion of gloom, austerity, but orig. sense survives in verb to *solemnize* (marriage). See also *sullen*.

solen. Razor-fish (mollusc). G. σωλήν, tube, shell-fish, etc.

sol-fa [*mus.*]. See *gamut*.

solfatara. Volcano vent. Name of sulphurous volcano near Naples, from It. *solfo*, sulphur.

solfeggio [*mus.*]. It., from *sol-fa*.

solferino. Colour. Discovered soon after battle of *Solferino* (1859). Cf. *magenta*.

solicit. F. *solliciter*, L. *sollicitare*, from OL. *sollus*, whole, *cière, cit-*, to set in motion. Leg. sense of *solicitor* appears in 16 cent., the King's *general attorney* and *general solicitor* being mentioned in an act of 1533-4.

To the memory of Hobson Judkin Esq., late of Clifford's Inn, the honest solicitor
(*Epitaph in St Dunstan's, Fleet St.*).

solid. F. *solide*, L. *solidus*, cogn. with OL. *sollus*, whole, G. ὅλος. *Solidarity*, much used of late, is F. *solidarité*, a coinage of the *Encyclopédie* (1765).

solifidian [*theol.*]. One who believes in salvation by faith alone (*Rom.* iii. 28). A Reformation coinage on L. *solus*, alone, *fides*, faith.

soliloquy. Late L. *soliloquium*, coined by St Augustine (? on G. μονολογία) from *solus*, alone, *loqui*, to speak.

soliped [*zool.*]. With uncloven hoof, solid ungulate. MedL. *solipes, soliped-*, for *solidipes*.

solitary. F. *solitaire*, L. *solitarius*, from *solus*, alone. *Solitaire*, gem, game for one person, etc., is a later borrowing from F. *Solitude*, though in Chauc., was not in common use till 17 cent.

solivagant. From L. *solivagus*, wandering alone, from *vagari*, to wander.

sollar, soller [*dial.*]. See *solarium*.

solleret [*hist.*]. Part of armour. OF. dim. of *soler* (*soulier*), shoe, ? VL. **subtelare*, from *subtel*, the instep, lit. under heel (*talus*), ? or connected with *sole*[1].

solo. It., L. *solus*, alone.

Solomon's seal. Plant. Translates MedL. *sigillum Solomonis*, variously explained.

Solon. Sage. G. Σόλων, early lawgiver of Athens, one of the seven sages.

so-long [*colloq.*]. ? Corrupt. of *salaam*. Cf. *compound*[2], *go-down*, etc.

solstice. F., L. *solstitium*, from *sol*, sun, *sistere*, to stand.

soluble, solution. See *solve*.

solus. L., alone.

solve. L. *solvere*, *solut-*, to loosen, from *se-*, apart, *luere*, to pay, release. OF. *soudre* had also spec. sense of pay; cf. *solvent*.

somatic. G. σωματικός, from σῶμα, body.

sombre. F., cf. Sp. *sombra*, shade. App. in some way connected with L. *umbra*, shade, but origin of init. *s-* is unknown.

sombrero. Broad hat. Orig. (16 cent.) parasol. Sp., from *sombra*, shade (v.s.).

some. AS. *sum*. Com. Teut., but now mostly dial. in related langs.; cf. Du. *som-* (in *somtijds*, *somwijlen*), OHG. *sum*, ON. *sumr*, Goth. *sums*; cogn. with Sanskrit *sama*, any, every. US. sense, (of) some (consequence), has lately become colloq. E. *Something* was in ME. and later very common as adv., as still in *something like* (cf. *somewhat*). Dial. *summat* is for *some whit*.

> That night, I tell you, she looked some
>   (Lowell, *The Courtin'*).

-some. AS. *-sum*. Com. Teut.; cf. Du. *-zaam*, Ger. *-saam*, ON. *-samr*, Goth. *-sams*; ? cogn. with *same*, *seem*. But in *foursome* the suffix is the word *some* orig. preceded by genitive of numeral.

somersault. Corrupt. of F. *soubresaut*, Prov. *sobresaut*, L. *super* and *saltus*, leap; cf. It. *suprasalto*, F. *sursaut*. Further corrupted to *summerset*, *somerset*. Cf. *fault* for restored *-l-*.

somnambulism. Coined from L. *somnus*, sleep, *ambulare*, to walk. Replaced earlier *noctambulation* (Bailey). *Somnus* is cogn. with AS. *swefn*, sleep, dream.

somnolent. F., L. *somnolentus*, from *somnus* (v.s.).

son. AS. *sunu*. Com. Teut.; cf. Du. *zoon*, Ger. *sohn*, ON. *sunr*, Goth. *sunus*; cogn. with Sanskrit *sūnu*, and ult. with G. υἱός. Found in the same langs. as *daughter*.

sonant. From pres. part. of L. *sonare*, to sound.

sonata. It., from *sonare*, to sound. Cf. *cantata*.

song. AS. *sang*, *song*, cogn. with *sing* (q.v.). *For a song* is in Shaks. (*All's well*, iii. 2). With *songstress*, a double fem. (*-ster*, *-ess*), cf. *sempstress*.

sonnet. F., It. *sonetto*, dim. of *suono*, sound, L. *sonus*. First in title of Surrey's poems (1557), but orig. used of various short poems.

sonorous. From L. *sonorus*, from *sonor*, sound, cogn. with *sonus*.

> Here let the mountains thunder forth sonorous,
>   Alleluia;
> There let the valleys sing in gentler chorus,
>   Alleluia (J. M. Neale).

sonsy [*Sc. & Ir.*]. Buxom. From *sonse*, plenty, Gael. Ir. *sonas*, good fortune.

soon. AS. *sōna*, at once; cf. OSax. OHG. *sān*. For fig. sense of *sooner* cf. *rather* (cf. also F. *plus tôt*, *plutôt*).

soot. AS. *sōt*; cf. Du. dial. *zoet*, ON. *sōt*; ? cogn. with *sit*, as meaning what settles, sediment.

sooterkin [*archaic*]. Imaginary afterbirth attributed to Du. women. App. archaic Du. *soetken*, darling, dim. of *soet* (*zoet*), sweet, but the E. sense is not known in Du. Howell (1621) calls it *zucchie*.

sooth. AS. *sōth*, orig. adj., true; cf. OSax. *sōth*, ON. *sannr*, Goth. *sunjis*, Sanskrit *satya*, all supposed to be, like L. *sons*, guilty, pres. part. formations from the root *es-*, to be (cf. *authentic*). Obs. from 17 cent., exc. in *forsooth*, *soothsayer* (with which cf. Ger. *wahrsager*), but revived by Scott.

soothe. AS. *sōthian*, to show to be true (v.s.). Current sense is reached via that of cajoling a person by assenting to what he says.

> These be they that sooth young youths in all their sayings, that uphold them in al their doings
>   (Lyly's *Euphues*).

sop. AS. *sopp*, bread, etc. dipped in liquid; cogn. with *sup*, *soup*; hence verb to *sop*, AS. *soppian*; cf. Du. *soppen*. With *sopped*, wet through, cf. synon. F. *trempé comme une soupe*.

sophism. Restored from earlier *sofyme*, *sophume*, etc., OF. (*sophisme*), L., G. σόφισμα, from σοφίζεσθαι, to devise, from σοφός, wise. Depreciatory sense springs from bad reputation of the *sophists*, professional teachers, in ancient Greece. Cf. *sophisticate*, earliest E. sense (c. 1400) of which is to adulterate. *Sophister*, OF. *sophistre*, L. *sophista*, has the same intrusive *-r-* as *barrister*. *Sophomore*, second year student (now only US.), is for obs. *sophumer*, from *sophume* (v.s.). Cf. Camb. *soph*.

Sophy [*hist.*]. Surname of Pers. dynasty (c. 1500–1736) founded by *Ismael Safī*, whose name comes from Arab. *safī-ud-dīn*, purity of religion. With the *Grand Sophy* cf. the *Grand Turk*, the *Great Mogul*.

sopite. From L. *sopire*, *sopit-*, to put to sleep (v.i.).

soporific. From L. *sopor*, sleep, ult. cogn. with *somnus* (see *somnambulism*).

soprano. It., from *sopra*, above. Cf. *sovereign*.

sorb. F. *sorbe* or L. *sorbum*, fruit of service-tree.

sorbet. F., as *sherbet* (q.v.).

Sorbonist. From the *Sorbonne*, Paris, orig. theol. college, founded (13 cent.) by *Robert de Sorbon*.

sorcerer. Extended from ME. *sorcer*, F. *sorcier*, VL. **sortiarius*, from *sors*, *sort-*, lot, fate.

sordid. F. *sordide*, L. *sordidus*, from *sordes* (pl.), filth.

sore. AS. *sār*. Com. Teut.; cf. Du. *zeer*, Ger. *sehr* (v.i.), ON. *sārr*. For adv. use, e.g. *sore afraid*, cf. mod. use of *awfully*, etc. Ger. *sehr* has lost orig. sense (exc. in dial. and verb *versehren*, to harm) and means very, being used with any adj., while archaic E. *sore* usu. accompanies adjs. expressing grief, suffering, etc. The E. limitation is prob. due to the adoption of *very* in gen. sense.

sorghum. ModL., from It. *sorgo*, Indian millet, MedL. *surgum*, *suricum*, app. for *Syricum*.

soricine [*biol.*]. Resembling the shrew-mouse, L. *sorex*, *soric-*.

sorites [*log.*]. Chain of syllogisms. L., G. σωρείτης, from σωρός, heap.

sorner [*Sc.*]. Beggar, one who quarters himself on others. From obs. Ir. *sorthan*, free quarters, as privilege of feudal superior and his men. Cf. *cosher¹*, which was used in very similar sense.

sororicide. Cf. *fratricide*. See *sister*.

sorrel¹. Plant. F. *surelle*, dial. name for plant (*oseille*), dim. from OHG. *sūr*, sour.

sorrel². Colour of horse, formerly also of buck in third year (*Love's Lab. Lost*, iv. 2).

OF. *sorel*, dim. of *sor* (*saur*) (whence ME. *sore*, of hawks and horses); of Teut. origin, cogn. with *sere¹* (q.v.).

sorrow. AS. *sorh*, *sorg*. Com. Teut.; cf. Du. *zorg*, Ger. *sorge*, ON. *sorg*, Goth. *saurga*. Unconnected with *sorry*.

sorry. AS. *sārig*, from *sār*, sore. Unconnected with *sorrow*, though early associated with it. For sense of vile, mean, cf. *wretched*, *pitiful*, etc.

sort. F. *sorte*, VL. **sorta*, for *sors*, lot, share; cf. It. *sorta*. Also adopted by the Teut. langs. *Of a sort*, *of sorts*, are both now slightly contemptuous, but *man of sort* was equivalent to *man of quality* in Tudor E. *Out of sorts* meant in 17 cent. out of stock, but fig. sense is recorded still earlier (cf. *indisposed*). Verb to *sort* is from the noun, partly also from L. *sortire*, "to make lottes; to dispose or order" (Coop.), and F. *assortir*.

Another semi-civil war of sorts is making a promising start in the province of Mohileff

(*Daily Chron.* Feb. 6, 1918).

sortie. F., p.p. fem. of *sortir*, to go out, of obscure origin. VL. **surctire*, from *surgere*, *surrect-*, to rise (cf. Sp. *surtir*, to rise, spring forth), has been suggested, but the formation of a VL. verb in *-ire* from a p.p. is abnormal (but cf. *squat*).

sortilege. F. *sortilège*, MedL. *sortilegium*, from *sortilegus*, fortune-teller, from *sors*, *sort-*, lot, *legere*, to choose.

sorus [*bot.*]. Cluster of spore-cases, etc. G. σωρός, heap.

S.O.S. Wireless signal of distress at sea, represented by · · · — — — · · · , etc., a simple and unmistakable message substituted for earlier *C.Q.D.*, come quickly distress.

In January we shall send out the S.O.S., save or starve (Sir Arthur Yapp, Dec. 10, 1917).

sostenuto [*mus.*]. It., p.p. of *sostenere*, to sustain.

sot. In ME. fool. F., ? L. *idioticus*, ? whence also It. *zotico*, earlier *zottico*, "clownish, rusticall, slovenlie, lubberly, homely, unmannerly, blockish, rude" (Flor.).

Sothic (year). From G. Σῶθις, an Egypt. name of Sirius.

sotnia. Squadron of Cossacks. Russ. *sotnya*, hundred, cogn. with L. *centum*.

sotto voce. It., under (L. *subtus*) voice.

sou. F., back-formation from *sous*, pl. of OF. *soul*, *sol*, L. *solidus*, used as name of coin. Cf. *soldier*, *£. s. d.* Formerly, and still occ., used colloq. in pl.

> Not a sous had he got, not a guinea or note
> (*Ingoldsby*).

> He had not given a sous since the war began
> (*Daily Chron.* May 15, 1918).

soubise. Sauce. From F. *Marshal Soubise* (†1787). Cf. *bechamel*.

soubrette. F., from ModProv. *soubret*, coy, from *soubra*, to put on one side. So *Dict. Gén.* Others connect the word with Sp. *sobrina*, niece, L. *consobrina* (see *cousin*).

soubriquet. See *sobriquet*.

souchong. Tea. Chin. *siao-chung*, small sort.

Soudanese. Of the *Soudan*, lit. blacks (Arab.).

soufflé. F., p.p. of *souffler*, to blow, L. *sufflare*, from *sub* and *flare*.

sough. First as verb, to make a rushing sound. AS. *swōgan* (also found in OSax.), cogn. with *swēgan*, to sound. Obs. in E. from 16 cent., but re-introduced by Burns and Scott. Esp. in to *keep a calm sough*, to hold one's tongue.

sought. See *seek*.

soul. AS. *sāwol, sāwl.* Com. Teut.; cf. Du. *ziel*, Ger. *seele*, ON. *sāla*, Goth. *saiwala*. For fig. senses and collocation with *body*, *life*, cf. similar use of F. *âme*, Ger. *seele*. As applied to individual (*good soul, not a living soul, every soul on board*) perh. due to eccl. character of medieval administration (cf. *parish*).

sound¹. Noise. ME. & AF. *soun*, F. *son*, L. *sonus*. For excrescent -*d* cf. dial. *gownd*, *drownd*, and see *bound³*.

sound². Adj. AS. *gesund*, healthy, whence also ME. *isund*. WGer.; cf. Du. *gezond*, Ger. *gesund*; ? cogn. with Ger. *geschwind*, swift, orig. strong. Later sense of genuine, trustworthy, develops into mere intens. (sleep, sherry, thrashing, etc.). In *sound as a bell* there is association with *sound¹*.

sound³. Narrow channel, esp. in Sc. ON. *sund*, swimming, strait (as between Cattegat and Baltic), cogn. with *swim*; cf. AS. *sund*, swimming, water, whence sense of swimming-bladder of sturgeon, cod, etc. By early writers associated with *sound⁴*, as a channel that can be sounded, whereas it is a channel that can be swum. For sense cf. relation of *ford* to *fare* or of L. *vadum*, ford, to *vadere*, to go.

sound⁴. To measure with plummet. F. *sonder*, from *sonde*, plummet-line, app. Teut. and ident. with *sound³*, though it is difficult to see the connection; cf. AS.

sund-līne, sund-rāp (rope). Hence med. to *sound*, probe, a wound, and, with a leaning on *sound¹*, to *sound* the lungs.

sounder [*archaic*]. Herd of wild swine. OF. *sondre*, of Teut. origin; cf. synon. AS. *sunor*, ON. *sonar-* (in compds.), OHG. *swaner*.

soup. F. *soupe*, of Teut. origin and cogn. with *sop*, *sup*; cf. It. *zuppa*, Sp. *sopa*. Du. *sop*, Ger. *suppe*, are from F.

soupçon. F., OF. *sospeçon*, L. *suspectio-n-*, for *suspicio-n-*.

sour. AS. *sūr*. Com. Teut.; cf. Du. *zuur*, Ger. *sauer* (OHG. *sūr*), ON. *sūrr*. Cf. *sorrel¹*. *Sour-dough*, man from Alaska, alludes to use of leaven in baking bread there in winter. As *sour-dough* has long been obs. in E., its US. currency is prob. due to Du. *zuurdeeg* or Ger. *sauerteig*.

> The citee restide a litil in mengyng to gydre of soure dowe, till it were sourdowid all
> (Wyc. *Hos.* vii. 4).

source. F., spring, from *sourdre*, to rise, spring up, L. *surgere*. ME. had also the verb to *sourd*, spring up, well forth.

sourdine [*mus.*]. F., It. *sordina*, from *sordo*, deaf, muffled, L. *surdus*.

souse¹ [*dial.*]. Pigs' feet and ears pickled, brine, etc. for pickling. OF. *soult, souz*, OHG. *sulza*, whence Ger. *sülze, sulze*, "souce, souced pork" (Ludw.); cf. synon. Du. *zult*, and It. *solcio*, from Ger.; cogn. with *salt*.

souse² [*archaic*]. To swoop down. First (15 cent.) as noun. ? In some way connected with F. *sous, dessous*, or perh. with *sus, dessus*, as in *fondre dessus*, to swoop down upon. The *NED.* explanation (from Skeat) that *souse* is altered from *source*, upward flight, is due to misunderstanding of quots. below, in which *mount, source*, are not equivalent, but alternative, to *souse*; i.e. the hawk attacks its prey from below or above, the latter method being the swoop or souse.

> Iff youre hawke nym the fowle a loft, ye shall say she toke it at the mounte or at the souce
> (*Book of St Albans*, 1486).

> The sparowhawkes do use to kill the fowl at the sowrce or souse (Turberville, 1575).

souse³. Thump, flop, etc. Imit., cf. Ger. *saus*, tumult, esp. in *saus und braus*, ON. *sūs*, roar of waves. Strongly associated with *souse¹,²*, e.g. in quot. below, which it would be hard to assign to any of the three.

> Jonas (to them all appease)
> O'er head and eares was soused in the seas
> (Sylv. *Jonas*).

soutache [*neol.*]. Braid, etc. F., Hung. *szuszak*.

soutane. F., cassock, It. *sottana*, from *sotto*, under, L. *subtus*.

souteneur. F., prostitute's bully, from *sou-tenir*, to maintain. See *sustain*.

south. AS. *sūth*. Com. Teut.; cf. Du. *zuid* (as in *Zuider Zee*), Ger. *süd*, ON. *suthr*; from Teut. *sunth-*, ? cogn. with *sun*. Hence F. *sud* (cf. *nord*, *est*, *ouest*). The *southern-wood* (AS.) orig. came from south of Europe. *Southron*, a Sc. alteration, after *Briton*, *Saxon*, of *southern*, was app. popularized by Jane Porter (*Scottish Chiefs*, 1810), who took it from Blind Harry. With *sou'wester*, protection against a south-west gale, cf. Du. *zuidwester*.

souvenir. F., orig. infin., L. *subvenire*, to come to mind.

sovereign. OF. *soverain* (*souverain*), VL. **superanus*, from *super*, above; cf. It. *sovrano*, whence *sovran*, a spelling first used by Milton (*Comus*, 41), Sp. *soberano*. For unoriginal -g- cf. *delight*, *sprightly*, etc., but it may be partly due to influence of *reign*. For sense of coin, temp. Hen. VII, cf. *real*². *Sovereign remedy* is in *Piers Plowm*. *Sovereign good* is also ME., after L. *summum bonum*.

soviet. Russ., council, from prefix *so-*, together (cf. *Sobranje*), and a Slav. root, to speak, which appears in Russ. *otviet*, answer, *priviet*, greeting, etc. Cf. Serbo-Croat. & Sloven. *svet* in same sense.

sow¹. Noun. AS. *sugu*. Com. Teut.; cf. Du. *zeug*, Ger. *sau*, ON. *sȳr*; cogn. with L. *sus*, G. *ῦs*, Zend *hu*. For sense of mass of metal cf. *pig*.

> Ye can be [*read* not] make a silk purse out of a sowe's luggs, a Scotch proverb (*Dict. Cant. Crew*).

sow². Verb. AS. *sāwan*. WAryan; cf. Du. *zaaien*, Ger. *säen*, ON. *sā*, Goth. *saian*, L. *serere*, *sat-*, OSlav. *sejati*, etc.

sowar [*Anglo-Ind.*]. Urdu, Pers. *sawār*, horseman.

soy. Sauce, bean. Jap., colloq. for *siyau-yu*, Chin. *shi-yu*, from *shi*, salted bean, *yu*, oil. Also *soya*, via Du.

spa. From *Spa*, Belgium, famed for mineral springs.

> Th' English Bath and eke the German Spau
>   (*Faerie Queene*, I. xi. 30).

space. F. *espace*, L. *spatium*; cf. It. *spazio*, Sp. *espacio*.

> The spacious times of great Elizabeth
>   (Tennyson, *Dream of Fair Women*).

spade¹. Tool. AS. *spadu*; cf. Du. *spade*, *spa*, Ger. *spaten*; cogn. with G. *σπάθη*, flat blade, sword, etc., whence It. *spada*, Sp. *espada*, F. *épée* (OF. *espede*). To *call a spade a spade*, first in Udall's transl. of Erasmus, is due to the latter having rendered Plutarch's *σκάφη*, trough, bowl, by L. *ligo*, spade, because of connection with *σκάπτειν*, to dig. The proverb is also in Lucian—*τὰ σῦκα σῦκα, τὴν σκάφην δὲ σκά-φην ὀνομάζων*.

spade². At cards. Mistransl. of Sp. *espada*, sword (v.s.), the sign orig. used. Cf. *club*.

spadille. Ace of spades at ombre and quadrille. F., Sp. *espadilla*, dim. of *espada*, spade².

spadix [*bot.*]. L., G. *σπάδιξ*, palm branch.

spae [*Sc.*]. To foretell; esp. in *spae-wife*. From ON. *spā*, to foretell, orig. to pry, spy (q.v.).

spaghetti. It., pl. of *spaghetto*, "a small thred" (Flor.), dim. of *spago*, "any kinde of pack thred" (*ib.*), of unknown origin.

spagyric [*hist.*]. Of alchemy. ModL. *spa-giricus*, prob. coined by Paracelsus.

spahi [*hist.*]. Turkish trooper. F., Turk. *sipahi*, from Pers. (see *sepoy*). Since Crimean War also of F. Algerian cavalry.

spall. Chip of stone. Cf. ME. *spald*, to split, of LG. origin, cogn. with Ger. *spalten*.

spalpeen. Ir. *spailpín*, orig. casual farm labourer, dim. of unknown origin.

span¹. Stretch, etc. AS. *spann*; cf. Du. Ger. *spanne*, ON. *spǫn*. As the AS. word is rare, ME. *span* is prob. rather OF. *espan*, from Teut. Ground-idea is that of stretching from point to point, as in verb (cf. Du. Ger. *spannen*). This was used earlier, after Du., of harnessing horses, a sense now re-introduced (*inspan*, *outspan*) from SAfr. *Spanner*, tool, orig. used for winding up spring of wheel-lock firearm, is Ger., from *spannen*, to stretch. *Span of life* is after Ps. xxxix. 6 (PB., *Vulg. dies mensurabiles*).

span². See *spick*.

spancel. Hobble, esp. for cow. Du. *spanzel*, from *spannen*, to tie, span.

spandrel [*arch.*]. Dim. of AF. *spaundre* (14 cent.), ? from OF. *espandre* (*épandre*), to expand.

spangle. Dim. of AS. *spang*, clasp, buckle; cf. Du. *spang*, Ger. *spange*, "a clasp, tacke, hook, or buckle" (Ludw.), ON. *spǫng*, brooch, spangle, etc.

spaniel. OF. *espagneul* (*épagneul*), lit. Span-ish, L. *Hispaniolus*. Used also in ME. &

OF. for *Spaniard*, the latter representing OF. *Espagnard*, formed like *campagnard*. This is now replaced in F. by *Espagnol*, Sp. *Español*.

spank. Imit. of resonant slap. With *spanking*, as intens. (*a spanking lass*) cf. *dashing*, *thundering*, *whopping*, etc. In some senses, e.g. *spanking pace*, and in naut. uses (*spanker-boom*), partly due to Sc. *spang*, to move rapidly, suddenly, also used for a smart blow. ? Cf. Port. *espancar*, to strike.

span-new. See *spick and span*.

spar[1]. Rafter, pole, etc. (naut.). Com. Teut.; cf. Du. *spar*, Ger. *sparren*, ON. *sparri*. Not recorded in AS., but cf. *gesparrian*, *besparrian*, to bar (a door), and dial. *spar*, *spear*, in same sense. Also OF. *esparre*, "the barre of iron thats nailed on a door" (Cotg.), whence perh. some of the E. senses. ? Cogn. with *spear*.

sperren: to spar, bar or bolt, a door (Ludw.).

spar[2]. Mineral. From LG.; cf. Ger. *sparkalk*, AS. *spœrstān*, *spœren*, gypsum. See *feldspar*, second element of which is perh. cogn.

spar[3]. To box, etc. Earlier (16 cent.) to strike with the spurs (in cock-fighting), orig. (15 cent.) to thrust rapidly. ? From obs. *spar*, long-handled battle-axe, var. of *sparth*, ON. *spartha*.

The last few months in the [US.] Senate have been devoted to sparring for position
(*Westm. Gaz.* June 12, 1919).

sparable. Small headless nail (shoemaking). For *sparrow-bill*, from shape.

spare. AS. *sparian*, in main current senses. Com. Teut.; cf. Du. Ger. *sparen*, ON. *spara*. From an extended form of the Teut. verb come F. *épargner* (OF. *espargner*), It. *sparagnare*. With adj., AS. *spœr*, cf. OHG. *spar*, frugal. Sense of not in use (*spareroom*) is (from 14 cent.) esp. naut.

spare-rib. Also (17 cent.) *ribspare* (still in dial.); cf. LG. *ribbspeer*, Ger. *rippe(n)speer*, with doubtful second element. In E. associated with *spare*, from absence of fat.

spark. AS. *spearca*, with cogn. forms in LG. & obs. Du., but not in other Teut. langs. Hence *sparkle*. Sense of smallest trace (*without a spark of*) is in AS. *Spark*, gallant, now disparaging, is prob. fig. use of same word (v.i.). It is even used of a lady in *Appius & Virginia* (Prol.). *Mr Sparks*, the wireless operator (naut.), is a neol.

This honourable sparke [the Earl of Cumberland]

was further kindled and enflamed by former disasters (Purch. xvi. 12).

Coronell Mustin was shot dead and many a brave sparke more (Sydenham Poyntz, 1624–36).

sparling [*archaic*]. Fish (smelt), also *spirling*, *spurling*. Cf. OF. *esperlinge* (*éperlan*), of Teut. origin; also Du. *spiering*, Ger. *spierling*.

sparrow. AS. *spearwa*. Com. Teut.; cf. Fris. *sparreg*, Ger. *sperling* (dim. of dial. *spar*), ON. *spörr*, Goth. *sparwa*; cogn. with OPruss. *spurglis*. Hence *sparrowhawk*, earlier *sparhawk*, AS. *spearhafoc*. For *sparrowgrass* see *asparagus*.

sparse. L. *sparsus*, from *spargere*, to scatter; cf. F. *épars* (OF. *espars*), It. *sparso*. Earlier as verb (Coverd.). In ref. to population, congregation, etc., orig. US.

spart. Esparto (q.v.). Cf. *sparterie*, F. *esparterie*, from Sp.

Spartacist [*pol.*]. Ger. Bolshevist (Nov. 1918). From *Spartacus* (†71 B.C.), ringleader in the Roman Servile War.

Spartan. Of endurance, frugality, etc., characteristic of inhabitants of *Sparta*. Cf. *laconic*.

sparus. Sea-bream. L., G. σπάρος.

spasm. F. *spasme*, L., G. σπασμός, from σπᾶν, to tug.

spat[1]. Spawn of shell-fish. ? Cogn. with *spit*[2].

spat[2]. Sharp blow, smacking sound. Imit.

spat[3]. Short gaiter. Short for *spatterdash*, *spatterplash*, etc., defence against spatterings.

pero: a shoo of raw leather worn by countrey folks in snow and cold weather, a start-up, a spatterplash (Litt.).

spatchcock. Fowl dressed in summary fashion. Orig. Ir., now chiefly Anglo-Ind. ? For *dispatch cock* (v.i.), but perh. rather altered from earlier *spitchcock* (q.v.). Hence to *spatchcock*, interpolate, esp. (journ.) "cook" a telegram.

spatch cock: abbreviation of a dispatch cock, an Irish dish upon any sudden occasion (Grose).

Did or did not the Hearst papers spatchcock statements into cable dispatches from London?
(*Daily Chron.* Nov. 7, 1916).

spate. Sudden rise of river. Orig. Sc., of unknown origin.

spathe [*bot.*]. From L., G. σπάθη, flat blade, etc. See *spade*[1].

spatial. From L. *spatium*, space.

spatiate [*archaic*]. To stroll. From L. *spatiari*, from *spatium*, space. Cf. *expatiate* (q.v.).

spatter. Orig. to scatter, fly, in fragments. Cf. LG. Du. *spatten*, to burst, "to spatter, to bedash" (Sewel). Current senses associated with *spit*², *sputter*.

spatula, spatule. L., dim. of *spatha*. See *spade*¹. Hence *spatulate* (biol.), broadended. For Late L. sense of *shoulder-blade* (see *epaulet*) cf. Ger. *schaufel*, shoulderblade (of game), lit. shovel.

spavin. ME. *spavayne*, etc., OF. *espavain*, var. of *esparvain* (*éparvin*, *épervin*), "a spavin in the leg of a horse" (Cotg.). App. connected in some way with OF. *esparvier* (*épervier*), sparrowhawk, OHG. *sparwari* (*sperber*); cf. Sp. *esparaván*, sparrowhawk, spavin. Ger. dial. *spatz*, spavin, is app. ident. with *spatz*, sparrow. App. from forgotten piece of folk-lore (cf. *frog*²).

spawn. First (c. 1400) as verb. App. for **spaund*, AF. *espaundre*, to shed the roe, OF. *espandre* (*épandre*), to shed, spill out, L. *expandere*.

spay [archaic]. To castrate (female animal). AF. *espeier*, OF. *espeer*, to cut with sword, *espee* (*épée*). Cf. L. *spado*, "a gelding, be it man or beast" (Coop.). See *spade*¹.

speak. AS. *sprecan*, later *specan*. WGer.; cf. Du. *spreken*, Ger. *sprechen*; ? cogn. with ON. *spraka*, to crackle. For archaic past *spake* cf. *brake*. For loss of *-r-* cf. *pang*. With use of p.p. as active (*plain-spoken, out-, well-, blunt-*, etc.) cf. Ger. *pflichtvergessen*, duty forgetting. The oldest of these is *fair-spoken* (15 cent.). *Spokesman*, for obs. *speakman*, is also anomalous (cf. *shrovetide*). Trans. sense, to address, survives in *speak one fair* and naut. to *speak a ship*. The *Speaker* of the H. of C. is first mentioned 1376–7.

spear. AS. *spere*; cf. Du. Ger. *speer*, ON. *spjör* (pl.); ? cogn. with *spar*¹, ? or with L. *sparus*, dart.

spec. For *speculation*. Orig. US. (18 cent.).

special. As *especial* (q.v.). *Special pleading*, calling attention to specific circumstances (leg.), has, from late 19 cent., sense of exparte argument, sophistry. *Special constables* date from 1801.

specie. L., abl. of *species* (v.i.), in phrase *in specie*, orig. in kind, in actual form; from c. 1600 esp. of actual minted metal, as compared with paper money or bullion. For E. word from L. abl. cf. *effigy*, *quarto*, *propaganda*.

species. L., appearance, kind, from *specere*, to behold; cf. F. *espèce*, It. *specie*, Sp.

especie, and see *spice*. See also *genus*. Hence *specific*, having to do with one kind, *specify*, *specimen*, etc.

specious. F. *spécieux*, L. *speciosus*, "beautifull, fayre, goodly to see to, well favoured, honest" (Coop.), from *species* (v.s.). For degeneration of sense cf. *sanctimonious* and many other adjs.

And they knew him, that it was he which sate for alms at the Specious Gate of the Temple
(*Acts*, iii. 10, *Rhemish Version*).

speck¹. Spot. AS. *specca*, spot, not found in other Teut. langs., though Du. has *spikkel* (earlier *speckel*), speckle. Prob. ident. with dial. *speck*, patch on shoe (cf. F. *tache*, spot, speck, in OF. also patch). Origin unknown.

speck². Blubber of whale. Du. *spek*, fat, bacon; cf. Ger. *speck*, AS. *spic*, bacon. Hence *specksioneer*, chief harpooner, corrupt. of Du. *speksnijder*, *-snijer*, blubber cutter. For full account see Melville's *Moby Dick*, ch. xxxii.

In the British Greenland Fishery, under the corrupted title of *Specksioneer*, this old Dutch official is still retained (Melville, *loc. cit.*).

spectacle. F., L. *spectaculum*, from *spectare*, to look, frequent. of *specere*. *Pair of spectacles* (15 cent.) appears to have been an advance on the single glass (v.i.).

Poverte a spectacle is, as thynketh me,
Thurgh which he may his verray freendes see
(Chauc. D. 1203).

spectator. L., beholder, on-looker. As title of periodical first in 1711 (Addison).

spectre. F., L. *spectrum*, apparition, appearance, from *specere*, *spect-*, to behold. From *spectrum* come also scient. words in *spectro-*, e.g. *spectroscope*.

specular. Of a mirror, L. *speculum*, from *specere* (v.s.). Cf. Ger. *spiegel*, from L.

speculate. From L. *speculari*, to watch, spy from watchtower, *specula* (v.s.). Financ. sense is 18 cent.

speech. AS. *sprǣc*, later *spǣc* (see *speak*). Sense of oration is 16 cent.

speed. AS. *spēd*, *spēd*, from *spōwan*, to succeed. WGer.; cf. Du. *spood*, OHG. *spuot*, whence Ger. *sputen*, to hasten (trans.). Oldest sense of success survives in to *wish one good speed* and perh. in plant-name *speedwell*. Some senses of verb (AS. *spēdan*) suggest influence of F. *expédier*, "to expedite, achieve, dispatch" (Cotg.); cf. obs. *dispeed*, to dispatch (Purch.).

speer [Sc.]. To inquire. AS. *spyrian*. Com. Teut.; cf. Du. *speuren*, to track, Ger. *spüren*, ON. *spyrja*. See *spoor*.

I spere, I aske: je demande. This terme is fare northyrne, and nat usyd in commyn speche (Palsg.).

spell¹. Magic formula. AS. *spell*, narrative, saying, etc.; hence, set of words. Com. Teut.; cf. OSax. OHG. *spel* (Ger. *beispiel*, example, parable), ON. *spjall*, Goth. *spill*. Cf. *gospel*.

spell². Verb. OF. *espeler* (*épeler*), for earlier *espeldre*, to explain, of Teut. origin, from above.

spell³. Turn of work. First as verb, earlier *spele*, AS. *spelian*, to act for, from *spala*, substitute, deputy.

spellican. See *spillikin*.

spelt. Kind of grain. AS. *spelt*, Late L. *spelta*. WGer., from L.; cf. Du. *spelt*, Ger. *spelt, spelz*; also F. *épeautre*, It. *spelta*, Sp. *espelta*. Never in current E. use.

spelter. Alloy, orig. zinc. Cogn. with *pewter* (q.v.).

spence [archaic]. Larder, etc. Aphet. for *dispense*. Cf. obs. *spencer*, steward, whence surname. See *spend*.

spencer. Short overcoat; later, bodice. From second *Earl Spencer* (†1834). Cf. *sandwich*. Cf. naut. *spencer*, kind of sail, also from a surname.

Spencerian. Of *Herbert Spencer*, sociologist (†1903).

spend. AS. *spendan* (in compds.), L. *expendere*, to weigh out, pay, whence also Ger. *spenden*. The E. word is also, and chiefly, aphet. for OF. *despendre* (replaced by *dépenser*). Fig. senses, e.g. *spent*, exhausted, occur early. *Spendthrift* replaced (16 cent.) earlier *scattergood*, found as (still surviving) surname c. 1300.

Spenserian [metr.]. Stanza as used in *Faerie Queene*, imitating It. *ottava rima*.

spergula. MedL. for *spurry* (q.v.). ? Suggested by MedL. *sparagus*, asparagus.

sperm. F. *sperme*, L., G. σπέρμα, from σπείρειν, to sow. Hence *spermaceti*, MedL., lit. sperm of whale (see *cetacea*), due to erron. belief as to nature of substance, and *spermaceti whale* (17 cent.), now reduced to *sperm-whale*.

spew. AS. *spīwan* (strong), *spēowan* (weak). Com. Teut.; cf. OSax. *spīwan*, Ger. *speien*, ON. *spýja*, Goth. *speiwan*; cogn. with L. *spuere*, which has influenced var. *spue*.

sphaer-. See *sphere*.

sphagnum. Bog-moss, now (1918) used as

surgical dressing. From G. σφάγνος, kind of moss.

sphenoid [scient.]. From G. σφήν, wedge.

sphere. Restored from ME. *spere* (astron. geom.), OF. *espere* (F. *sphère*), L., G. σφαῖρα, ball. *Sphere of influence*, in ref. to conflicting colonial ambitions, is late 19 cent.

And after that the melodye herde he
That cometh of thilke speres thryes three
(Chauc. *Parl. of Fowles*, 60).

sphincter [anat.]. L., G. σφιγκτήρ, band, from σφίγγειν, to bind tight.

sphinx. L., G. Σφίγξ, the strangler, from σφίγγειν (v.s.). Orig. myth. monster with head of woman and body of winged lion, which infested Thebes till its riddle was solved by Oedipus.

sphragistic. Of a seal (for stamping), G. σφραγίς.

sphygmo-. From G. σφυγμός, pulse, from σφύζειν, to throb.

spicate [bot.]. From L. *spica*, spike, ear of corn.

spice. OF. *espice* (*épice*), var. of *espèce*, species (q.v.), early druggists recognizing four species, viz. saffron, clove, cinnamon, nutmeg. For fig. sense of *spicy* cf. *piquant*.

Justice, all though it be but one entier vertue, yet is it described in two kyndes or spices
(Elyot, *Governour*, ii. 187).

spick and span. For *spick and span new*, ME. *span-new* (Chauc.), *spon-new*, ON. *spán-nȳr*, lit. chip-new (cf. Ger. *span*, chip, shaving). *Spick* is ident. with *spike*, nail. Cf. Ger. *nagelneu*, "brand-new, fire-new, spick- and span-new" (Ludw.), *spanneu*, "span-new, spick-new, fire-new or brand-new" (*ib.*), Du. *spikspeldernieuw*, "spick and span new" (Sewel), lit. spike splinter new, also F. *battant neuf*, lit. beating new (from the anvil).

They say *bran-span-new* in Yorkshire
(Pegge, Additions to Grose).

spiculate [bot.]. L. *spiculatus*. See *spicate*.

spider. ME. *spithre*, AS. **spīthre*, **spinthre*, from *spinnan*, to spin. Cf. Du. *spin*, Ger. *spinne*.

spiffing [slang]. Cf. dial. *spiff*, well-dressed man. Origin unknown.

spiflicate. From 18 cent., "to confound, silence, or dumbfound" (Grose). ? Fanciful formation on *suffocate*. Cf. dial. *smothercate*.

spigot. Also ME. *speget* (*Voc.* 771, 27). Usu. associated with *spike*; cf. Prov. *espigou*, bung, Port. *espicho*, "a spigot, a pin or peg put into the faucet to keep in the liquor" (Vieyra). But the earliest E. sense is the vent, not the plug, as is shown by quot. below, and by the gloss *clipsidra, ducillus*, in *Prompt. Parv.* (see *clepsydra*). This suggests Du. *spiegat*, scupper hole. But I have no evidence that this was ever connected with casks. The Du. word is now felt as "spit hole," but the first element **is** really *spie, spij*, plug, peg, cogn. with *spike*; cf. obs. Du. *spuntgat*, bunghole, from *spunt*, plug. The second element was orig. *-gote*, ident. with E. *gut* (q.v.), in sense of channel, passage.

My wombe is as must with out spigot [*Vulg.* spiraculum] (Wyc. *Job*, xxxii. 19).

spike. L. *spica*, also *spicum*, ear of corn, whence also F. *épi* (OF. *espi*), It. *spiga*, Sp. *espiga*. Sense of pointed nail, etc. (orig. naut.) corresponds to Sw. Norw. *spik*, with which cf. Du. *spijker*, Ger. dial. *speicher*. These are perh. also ult. from L., though they may be Teut. and cogn. with *spoke*. In naut. *handspike, marlinspike* second element was earlier *speek*, Du. *spaak*, spoke (q.v.). Guns were *spiked* by driving a big nail into the touch-hole (see *cloy*).

speeks: are like great iron pins, with flat heads
(*Sea-Dict.* 1708).

spikenard. Late L. *spica nardi*, rendering G. νάρδου στάχυς, ear of nard (q.v.). Cf. OF. *spicanarde*, Ger. *spikenarde*, etc.

spile. Splinter, vent-peg. Cf. Du. *spijl*, skewer, etc

spill[1]. Verb. AS. *spillan*, to destroy, wreck, kill, squander; cf. Du. LG. *spillen*, ON. *spilla*; also AS. *spildan*, OSax. *spildian*, obs. Ger. *spilden*. Cf. F. *gaspiller*, to squander, from Teut.

My sone, ful ofte for to muche speche
Hath many a man been spilt, as clerkes teche
(Chauc. H. 325).

spill[2]. Splinter, pipe-light. Cogn. with *spile*, ? and ult. with Ger. *spalten*, to split.

spill[3] [*techn.*]. Thin cylindrical rod. Du. *spil*, spindle; cf. Ger. *spille*, OHG. *spinala*; cogn. with *spin*.

spillikin, spellican. Orig. (1734) *spilakee*; from *spill*[2].

spin. AS. *spinnan*. Com. Teut.; cf. Du. Ger. *spinnen*, ON. *spinna*, Goth. *spinnan*; with other vague cognates, but app. not, like *weave*, Aryan. Fig. senses all start from the spinning-wheel. *Spinning-house*, prison for prostitutes (Camb.), was suggested by synon. Du. *spinhuis*, "the house of correction for naughty women" (Sewel).

Hue spak to the spynnesters [*var.* spinnere] to spynnen hit oute (*Piers Plowm.* C. vii. 222).

spinach. OF. *espinache, espinage*, also *espinar* (*épinard*); cf. It. *spinace*, Sp. *espinaca*, Du. *spinazie*, Ger. *spinat*. Early associated with L. *spina*, from prickly seeds, but perh. of Eastern origin; cf. Arab. *isfināj*, Pers. *isfānāj*, but these words are of doubtful antiquity. Or it may be connected with *Hispanicum olus*, Spanish herb (16 cent.); cf. OF. *herbe d'Espaigne*, "spinage" (Cotg.).

spindle. AS. *spinel*, from *spin* (cf. *shovel*). Intrusive *-d-* appears also in Du. Ger. Sw. *spindel*. Cf. *spill*[3]. With *spindleshank* cf. Ger. *spindelbein*, Du. *spillebeen*, F. *doigts fuselés*, taper fingers (see *fuse*[2]). With *spindle side*, formerly contrasted with *spear side*, cf. *apron-strings*, and rather crude use of *ventre* and *verge* in archaic F.

spindrift. Sc. var. of *spoondrift* (see *spoon*[2]). Now common in E., "probably at first under the influence of W. Black's novels" (*NED.*).

spine. OF. *espine* (*épine*), L. *spina*, thorn, backbone. Latter sense in E. is direct from L., F. having in this sense *échine* (see *chine*[2]).

spinel. Kind of ruby. F. *spinelle*, It. *spinella*, dim. from L. *spina* (v.s.).

spinet. OF. *espinete* (*épinette*), "a paire of virginals" (Cotg.), prob. from inventor, *Giovanni Spinetti*, of Venice (fl. c. 1500). So explained 1608.

spinifex [*bot.*]. ModL., from *spina*, spine, *facere*, to make.

spinnaker [*naut.*]. "Said to have been a fanciful formation on *Spinx*, mispronunciation of *Sphinx*, the name of the first yacht which commonly carried the sail" (*NED.*). ? Suggested by naut. *spanker*.

spinney. OF. *espinei* (whence place-name *Épinay*), VL. *spinetum*, from *spina*, thorn.

Spinozist. Follower of *Spinoza*, Sp. Jew philosopher (†1677).

spinster. From *spin*, with fem. ending *-ster* (q.v.). As formal description, of unmarried woman from 17 cent., or perh. earlier, as it is in Minsh.

spinster: this onely addition is given to all unmarried women, from the Viscounts daughter downward (Blount).

spinthariscope. Coined (1903) by Crookes from G. σπινθαρίς, spark.

spiracle. L. *spiraculum*, from *spirare*, to breathe.

spiraea. Flower. L., G. σπειραία, from σπεῖρα, spire².

spiral. See *spire²*. With *spiral staircase* cf. Ger. *wendeltreppe*, from *winden*, to wind.

spirant [*gram.*]. From pres. part. of L. *spirare*, to breathe.

spire¹. Pointed summit, etc. Earlier also *spear*. AS. *spīr*, stalk, of long grass, in ME. shoot, sprout; cf. Du. Ger. *spier*; ult. cogn. with *spar¹*. Steeple sense from 16 cent., so also Sw. *spira*, Dan. Norw. *spir*.

spire². Coil, convolution. F., L., G. σπεῖρα, coil, winding. Hence *spiral*.

Made so fairly well With delicate spire and whorl
(*Maud*, ii. ii. 1).

spirit. L. *spiritus*, from *spirare*, to breathe, used in *Vulg.* to render G. πνεῦμα (for sense-development cf. *animus*). Partly also via OF. *esperit*, *espirit* (*esprit*). Replaced, in certain senses, native *soul*, *ghost*, but has not been gen. adopted by the other Teut. langs. In ref. to temperament from medieval science, which believed in three "spirits" (see *animal*) or subtle fluids pervading the individual, as it did in four "humours." Alcohol sense (c. 1600) from earlier use by the alchemists, who recognized four, viz. quicksilver, orpiment, sal ammoniac and brimstone (Chauc. G. 822 ff.); cf. similar use of Ger. *geist*. To *spirit* (*away*), abduct, was orig. used (17 cent.) of kidnapping boys for the WInd. plantations, as though they had been supernaturally removed. Littleton has *plagiarius*, "a spirit, who steals other mens children or servants." *Spiritualism*, in table-rapping sense, appears 1855. *Spirituel* (F.) has developed also the spec. sense of *esprit*, wit, intellect.

spirometer. Irreg. formation from L. *spirare*, to breathe.

spirt. See *spurt*.

spit¹. Cooking implement, sandy point. AS. *spitu*. WGer.; cf. Du. *spit*, Ger. *spiess*; cogn. with Ger. *spitz*, pointed (cf. *Spitzbergen*), whence *spitze*, lace. Cf. also OF. *espiet*, spear, from Teut.

spit². To expectorate. North. AS. *spittan*, imit. More usual in AS. were *spǣtan*, whence dial. *spet*, and *spīwan* (see *spew*). Cf. also Ger. *spucken*, dial. *spützen*, *spitzen*, Dan. *spytte*, etc. With vulg. *the very spit of*

cf. F. *il est son père tout craché*. With *spitfire* cf. earlier *shitfire* (Flor. s.v. *cacafuoco*).

spit³. As in *two spit deep* (c. 1500). From dial. to *spit*, dig with a spade (*Piers Plowm.*), AS. *spittan*, cogn. with Du. *spitten*, "to spit, as to spit turf" (Hexham), and perh. with *spit¹*.

spitchcock. Mode of preparing eels. Perh. for *spit-cook* (v.i.), because roasted. The 17 cent. dicts. show that a *spitchcock-eel*, "anguilla decumana" (Litt.), was of the largest size. See also *spatchcock*.

spitchcock: anguille des plus grosses, qu'on rôtit ordinairement (Miège, 1679).

spite. Aphet. for *despite* (q.v.). With *in spite of* cf. Ger. *trotz*, in spite of, orig. noun, "bravado, hectoring, scorn, sham, spite, despite or despight" (Ludw.). Froissart tells us that a friar attached to the household of John of Gaunt was killed by Wat Tyler's men "en despit de son maistre," i.e. to show their hatred and scorn for his master.

spittle. Altered, on *spit²*, from earlier *spattle*, AS. *spātl*, cogn. with *spǣtan*, to spit.

spittoon. App. coined (c. 1840) in US., the land of accurate expectoration. The earlier E. term (17 cent.) was *spitting-box*.

spitz. Pomeranian dog. Ger., also *spitzhund*, from *spitz*, pointed (see *spit¹*).

splanchno-. From G. σπλάγχνα, inward parts.

splash. Intens. of *plash³*. See *s-*. For fig. senses cf. *dash*.

splay. In *splay-foot*. From verb to *splay*, to slope (arch.), aphet. for *display* (q.v.), in sense of spreading out. OF. had also *espleier*, now only in *aigle éployée* (her.), spread-eagle.

In like wise at the est ende of the same brigge another myghty stonewerk with ij displaies
(*Contract for Newark Bridge*, 1485).

spleen. OF. *esplen*, L. *splen*, "the spleene, the milte" (Coop.), G. σπλήν, regarded in ME. as seat of morose feelings (cf. *heart*, *liver*, *kidney*), in which sense it has been borrowed back by F.

splendid. F. *splendide*, L. *splendidus*, from *splendēre*, to be bright. *Splendacious* is a jocular formation after adjs. in -*acious* (cf. rustic *boldacious*).

splenial [*anat.*]. From G. σπλήνιον, bandage.

splice. Orig. naut. Archaic Du. *splissen*, cogn. with *split*; cf. Ger. *spleissen*, "to split, or slit, wood or hoops" (Ludw.), also "to splice ropes; to open the twists at the end of both ropes, and make them fast into one another" (*ib.*). Fig. to marry (*Peregrine Pickle*, ch. vii.).

splint, splinter. *Splint* is the earlier, having in ME. also the sense of overlapping strip or narrow plate in the jointing of armour, while *splinter* was used in some of the senses of *splint*, as still in *splinter-bar*. A LG. word; cf. Du. *splint, splinter*, "assula, schidium, aculeus ligneus" (Kil.). ? Cogn. with *split*; cf. Ger. *splitter*, splinter. In armour sense *splent* is earlier, via OF. *esplente*.

split. From 16 cent. Orig. naut., esp. in sense of suffering shipwreck, splitting on a rock (common in Shaks.). Du. *splitten*. With slang to *split on*, whence *split*, informer, detective, cf. to *break with*. The silly fuss about the *split infinitive* dates from 1899, one purist stating that "words fail to adequately express" his abhorrence of it. See also *splice*.

splodge, splotch. The latter is earlier (Holland's *Pliny*). ? Imit., with suggestion of *splash, blotch*.

splutter. "A low word" (Johns.). Imit., cf. *sputter*.

spode. Porcelain. From *J. Spode* (†1827). Cf. *wedgwood*.

spoil. OF. *espoillier*, L. *spoliare*, from *spolium*. Also aphet. for *despoil*. Earliest sense, booty stripped from vanquished enemy (*spoiling the Egyptians*), hence to damage, and, from 17 cent., to harm by indulgence; cf. similar use of *spill* in quot. s.v. *sprig*. So also F. *gâter*, lit. to lay waste, has later senses of E. *spoil*. With to be *spoiling for a fight* (US.) cf. sporting sense of *stale*.

spoke. AS. *spáca*. WGer.; cf. Du. *speek*, Ger. *speiche*. Hence *spokeshave* (c. 1500). To *put a spoke in one's wheel* is an illogical mistransl. of Du. *een spaak in het wiel steken*, where *spaak* (perh. cogn.) means bar, pole; cf. F. *mettre des barres dans les roues*. See also *handspike* (s.v. *spike*).

spokesman, -spoken. See *speak*.

spoliation. L. *spoliatio-n-*. See *spoil*.

spondee [*metr.*]. F. *spondée*, L., G. σπονδεῖος, from σπονδή, solemn drink-offering, from σπένδειν, to pour out.

spondulicks [*slang*]. Orig. US. Origin unknown. First element may be Du. *spaan*, chip, used in Du. dial. for money, "chips."

spondylus [*zool.*]. Genus of bivalves. L., G. σπόνδυλος, spine.

sponge. AS. *sponge, spunge*, and OF. *esponge*

(*éponge*), L. *spongia*, G. σπογγιά, from synon. σπόγγος. To *chuck up the sponge*, in acknowledgement of defeat, appears to have been refined in the contemp. prize-ring (v.i.). Slang sense of parasite is opposite to 17 cent. use, in which the victim was called the *sponge* (to be squeezed); cf. obs. *sponging-house* (for debtors), from extortion practised there.

In the fourth [round] Clark's seconds threw in the towel (*Daily Chron.* March 13, 1917).

Germany throws up the sponge
(*Sunday Times*, Oct. 13, 1918).

sponson [*naut.*]. Lateral extension of steamer before and abaft paddle-boxes. ? Sailors' corrupt. of *expansion*.

sponsor. L., from *spondēre, spons-*, to promise, vow.

spontaneous. From L. *spontaneus*, from *sponte*, (of one's own) accord, abl. of **spons*, cogn. with Ger. *widerspenstig*, obstinate. *Spontaneous combustion* occurs first (18 cent.) in ref. to such cases as those of Mr Krook (*Bleak House*) and Jacob Faithful's mother.

spontoon [*hist.*]. Kind of half-pike. F. *sponton, esponton*, It. *spuntone*, from *punto*, point.

spoof. Invented by Arthur Roberts (born 1852).

I knew at times she was deceiving me, and I spoofed (Witness in treason trial, March 7, 1917).

spook. Orig. US. (c. 1800). Du., cogn. with Ger. *spuk*, night-wandering spectre, a LG. word of unknown origin.

spool. Bobbin, reel. ONF. *espole*, of Teut. origin; cf. Du. *spoel*, LG. *spole*, Ger. *spule*.

spoom. See *spoon²*.

spoon¹. Noun. AS. *spōn*, thin piece of wood, chip (cf. *spick and span*). Com. Teut.; cf. Du. *spaan*, Ger. *span*, ON. *spōnn, spānn*, all in orig. sense, that of (orig. wooden) spoon being found also in Norw. & ON. With to *make a spoon or spoil a horn* cf. obs. to *make a bolt or a shaft*. To *spoon*, make love, is developed, via earlier *spoony*, silly, from *spoon*, simpleton (18 cent. slang), with which we may compare slang use of *stick²*; ? hence also *wooden spoon* (Camb.), formerly (1824) simply the *Spoon*.

Therfore bihoveth hire a ful long spoon
That shal ete with a feend (Chauc. F. 602).

spoon² [*naut.*]. To scud before the wind (in Hakl., Purch., Capt. John Smith). Perh. from the "spooning" of the water by the dipping prow. Later *spoom*, a landsman's perversion, after *spume*, foam. Hence *spoondrift*, now usu. *spindrift* (q.v.).

spoonerism. Accidental transposition of sounds, orig. type of which is said to be *Kinkering congs their titles take*, attributed to *Rev. W. A. Spooner*, of New Coll., Oxf.

spoony. See *spoon*[1].

spoor. Du., the word reaching us from SAfr. Com. Teut.; cf. AS. ON. *spor*, Ger. *spur*, whence *spurlos*, without leaving a trace, as in the genial suggestion (*spurlos versenken*) of Count Luxburg, Ger. minister to the Argentine, with regard to neutral shipping. See also *speer*. The word belongs to the primitive Teut. hunting vocab.

sporadic. MedL., G. σποραδικός, from σπείρειν, to sow, scatter.

spore. From G. σπορά, seed (v.s.).

sporran. Gael. *sporan*, purse, from Late L. *bursa*. Familiarized by Scott.

sport. Aphet. for *disport* (q.v.), with spec. sense-development which has led to its being borrowed by several other langs. Sense of abnormal plant, etc. (19 cent.) app. goes back to obs. *sport of nature*, rendering L. *lusus naturae*. To *sport*, display, etc., is used by Steele (1712). With *sportsmanlike* cf. *seamanlike*, *workmanlike*.

to sport timber: to keep one's outside door shut (Grose).

The rise of Germany is a freak, a sport, and does not belong to the real terrene scheme of evolution (*Westm. Gaz.* Feb. 22, 1918).

That every child born in the country should have a sporting chance (Prince of Wales, Dec. 18, 1919).

spot. From 12 cent., first in sense of blemish, stigma, etc. (as in *spotless*, *unspotted*). Cf. ON. *spotti*, small piece, Norw. dial. *spott*, spot, speck, piece of ground, also Fris. & obs. Du. *spot*, speck. If ult. cogn. with *spit*[2], it may be also ult. ident. with Ger. *spott*, derision, which some authorities connect with L. *spuere*, *sput-*, to spit; cf. use of F. *conspuer*, L. *conspuere*, "all to bespitte" (Coop.). For later sense-development cf. Ger. *fleck(en)*, which has the same group of meanings, e.g. *fleck-fieber*, "the spotted feaver" (Ludw.), though this was prob. not the cerebro-spinal meningitis now called by that name. To *knock spots out of* is US., perh. from use of playing-cards as pistol targets.

ich will den spott nicht auf mir sitzen lassen: I will not suffer that spot, blur or blemish, in my reputation (Ludw.).

spouse. OF. *spos*, *espos*, *spose*, *espose* (*époux*, *épouse*), L. *sponsus*, *sponsa*, lit. promised, vowed, from *spondēre*. Cf. *espouse*.

spout. First (14 cent.) as verb. Cf. Du. *spuit*, earlier *spuyt*, "sluce to let in or out water" (Hexham); cogn. with *spit*[2]. From 16 cent. also of a "shoot" for corn and hence of a pawnbroker's lift for pledged articles. Application to pretentious oratory, etc., is 18 cent., but *spout* is found in early 16 cent. as illiterate form of *spute*, for *dispute*.

I forbad all spouting in sophistry;
Now they spout in spouting who may spout most high (Heywood, *Spider & Fly*, xxxix. 4).

Mr Hull, pawnbroker, committed suicide by hanging himself within his "spout"
(*NED.*, from *Gent. Mag.* Oct. 1855).

sprag [*dial. & US.*]. Prop. brake. Origin unknown. To "sprag the wheel of progress" was used by Capt. W. A. Redmond in H. of C., Mar. 25, 1919.

sprain. App. OF. *espreindre* (*épreindre*), *épreign-*, to press, VL. **expremere*, for *exprimere*, though, as the E. word is first recorded c. 1600, retention of *s-* is anomalous. For formation and sense cf. *strain*, which has taken over the usual meaning of *épreindre*.

spraints [*sport.*]. OF. *espraintes*, "the dung of an otter, or other such vermine" (Cotg.), var. of *espreintes*, p.p. fem. pl. of *espreindre* (v.s.).

sprat. AS. *sprott*; cf. Du. *sprot*, Ger. *sprotte* (from LG.). Orig. sense was perh. small fry, the sprat being regarded as the young of the herring. This points to connection with AS. *spryttan*, to germinate, sprout.

sprawl. AS. *sprēawlian*; cf. Fris. *spraweli*; ? cogn. with *spread*.

spray[1]. Sprig, etc. Cf. AS. *spræc*, mod. dial. *sprag*, also in Sw. dial. As earliest records (from 13 cent.) have collect. sense, young shoots, small growth, etc., ult. identity with *spray*[2] is possible, with ground-idea of what is scattered or sprinkled.

spray[2]. Of water. From 16 cent. Cf. LG. *sprei* (noun), obs. Du. *sprayen*, MHG. *sprǣjen*, to sprinkle, ult. cogn. with synon. Ger. *sprühen*, *spreuen*, and with *spreu*, chaff.

The sprie of the sea, which the winde blew about us like raine (Purch. 1615).

spread. AS. *sprǣdan*. WGer.; cf. Du. *spreiden*, *spreien*, Ger. *spreiten*. With *spread-eagle* cf. F. *aigle éployée* (her.), lit. splayed eagle. With *spread-eagleism*, bombast (US.), allusive to the "bird of freedom," cf. *jingoism, chauvinism, junkerism.*

spree. From c. 1800. Earlier also *spray.* Orig. Sc. ? Ident. with *spreagh,* foray, cattle-raid, alteration of *spreath,* Gael. *spréidh,* cattle, from L. *praeda,* prey.

sprig. In Langland in spec. sense (v.i.), otherwise not recorded till 16 cent. ? Altered from earlier *spring,* in same sense. For fig. senses (*sprig of nobility*) cf. *scion.*

Ho so spareth the sprigge [*var.* spring] spilleth hus children (*Piers Plowm.* C. vi. 139).

sprightly. From *spright,* perverted form of *sprite* (q.v.).

spring. AS. *springan,* to leap, burst forth, fly up, etc. Com. Teut.; cf. Du. Ger. *springen,* ON. *springa. Spring* has also replaced the causal *sprenge,* AS. *sprengan* (cf. Ger. *sprengen,* to sprinkle, burst, gallop, etc.), as in a *sprung bat* (*mast, leak*), and to *spring a trap* (*mine, new theory,* etc.). The noun, AS. *spring, spryng,* esp. of water, developed sense of beginning, as in *dayspring* (see 1 *Sam.* ix. 26), whence *springtime,* earlier *springing time* (Trev. i. 65), *spring of the year* (Palsg.), now simply *spring* (replacing *lent*); cf. also *spring-tide,* used in 16 cent. both for springtime and as opposite of *neap-tide.* Sense of growth, shoot, appears in dial. *spring,* wood, copse (common in Bucks), and in *offspring.* See also *sprig, springald.*

springald [*archaic*]. From *spring,* with suffix -*ald,* AS. -*weald,* powerful, which in late formations is pejorative (cf. -*ard*). First element has prob. sense of growth, shoot, etc., rather than of jumping (cf. *stripling, scion, imp*). Obs. from 17 cent., but revived by Scott. Though not recorded by *NED.* till c. 1440, it was a common nickname by 13 cent. and survives in surnames *Springall, Springle, Springett,* etc.

springbok. SAfrDu., spring buck.

springe [*archaic*]. Snare. ME. *sprenge,* from AS. *sprengan,* to cause to jump; cf. synon. OHG. *sprinka,* Ger. *sprenkel.* See *spring.* Esp. with *woodcock,* as echo of *Haml.* i. 3.

sprinkle. Earlier *sprenkle,* frequent. of *sprenge* (see *spring*); cf. Ger. *sprenkeln,* to sprinkle, from *sprengen.*

sprint. Earlier (14 cent.) *sprent,* to dart forward rapidly, which, being chiefly used in past, was prob. associated with obs. *sprenge* (see *spring*). Of Scand. origin; cf. ON. *spretta,* for earlier **sprinta.* App. a

northern dial. word introduced into gen. sporting use c. 1870.

And furth scho sprent as spark of gleid or fyre
                              (Gav. Douglas).

sprit. Pole. In ME. chiefly naut. (cf. *bowsprit*). AS. *sprēot,* pole; cf. Du. Ger. *spriet,* the latter, like most Ger. naut. terms, from LG.; cogn. with *sprout.*

sprite. F. *esprit,* L. *spiritus.* Orig. var. of *spirit* in gen. sense. Hence *spright, sprightly.*

Upon his schelde a dove whyte,
Sygnyfycacioun of the holy spryte (*NED.* 14 cent.).

sprocket [*techn.*]. Projection, in various senses, orig. carpentering term. ? Cf. dial. *sprag,* prop, brake.

sprout. AS. *sprūtan* (in p.p. *āsproten,* sprouted out). WGer.; cf. Du. *spruiten,* Ger. *spriessen.*

spruce. From earlier *pruce,* from *Pruce,* Prussia (see *s-*). In many names of commodities brought over by the Hanse merchants (*beer, board, leather, fir*). Current sense app. from use of *spruce leather* in dress.

If I sent over see my servauntz to Bruges,
Or into Pruslonde [*var.* Spruce land] my prentys
                      (*Piers Plowm.* B. xiii. 392).

spruit [*SAfr.*]. Watercourse. Du., as *sprout.*

spry. A dial. word re-introduced from US. Origin unknown.

spud [*slang*]. Potato. ? Slang application of *spud,* weeding instrument, used in ME. (*Prompt. Parv.*) of an inferior dagger (? cf. ON. *spjōt,* spear, spit[1]). See *parsnip.*

spue. See *spew.*

spume [*poet.*]. OF. *espume,* L. *spuma,* foam.

spunk [*slang*]. Spirit, mettle (esp. US.). Orig. spark (Sc.), touchwood. ? Cf. US. *punk,* touchwood, obs. E. *funk,* spark, Ger. *funke,* spark. But Sc. origin points rather to Gael. *spong,* tinder, Ir. *sponc,* ult. ident. with *sponge.*

spur. AS. *sporu.* Com. Teut.; cf. Du. *spoor,* Ger. *sporn,* archaic *spor* (OHG. *sporo*), ON. *spori*; cogn. with *spurn* and L. *spernere,* with ground-idea of kick, and perh. with *spoor.* Cf. F. *éperon* (OF. *esporon*), from OHG. *On the spur of the moment* is elaborated from archaic *on the spur,* in great haste. Widely extended senses (biol. & geog.) are characteristic of a horsy race.

Dittes leur que je leur mande que il laissent à l'enfant gaegnier ses esporons, car je voel, si Diex l'a ordonné, que la journée soit sienne (Froissart).

spurge. Plant. OF. *espurge* (*épurge*), from *espurger*, to purge, L. *expurgare*, from med. properties.

spurious. From L. *spurius*, "base borne, counterfayte" (Coop.).

spurlos versenken [*hist.*]. Ger., to sink without leaving a trace. See *spoor*.

spurn. AS. *spornan, spurnan*, to strike with foot. Com. Teut.; cf. OSax. *spurnan*, OHG. *spornōn*, ON. *sporna*; cogn. with *spur*, also with L. *spernere*, to disdain, which may have influenced the E. word via AF. *esperner*, to reject (*Liber Albus*, p. 47).

spurry. Plant. Du. *spurrie*, cogn. with MedL. *spergula*.

spurt¹. Of blood, etc. Also *spirt*. Cogn. with Ger. *spritzen*, to squirt, etc., MHG. *sprützen*, whence It. *spruzzare*, "to spout, to spirt" (Flor.), and ult. with *sprout*.

spurt². Sudden effort, as in obs. by *fits and spurts*. Also *spirt*. Prob. ident. with *spurt¹*, though it may be connected with *sprint* (q.v.).

sputter. Frequent. of *spout*; or imit.; cf. Du. *sputteren*.

sputum [*med.*]. L., from *spuere*, to spit.

spy. OF. *espie*, from *espier* (*épier*), OHG. *spehōn* (*spähen*); cf. Du. *spieden* (earlier *spien*), ON. *spœja*. This group of words contains the only Teut. trace of Aryan *spec-*, to examine, etc. Like *scout* (q.v.) *spy* was orig. fem. and abstract (v.i.). In ModF. replaced by *espion*, It. *spione*, from Teut.

A eus fu venue une espie (*Tristan*, 4273).

squab. Unfledged bird, esp. young pigeon, short fat person, sofa, sofa-cushion. Cf. obs. *quab*, sea-slug, tadpole, flabby mass. Senses point to imit. origin, with floppy suggestion; cf. Ger. *kaul-quappe*, tadpole.

squabash [*slang*]. Portmanteau-word on *squash, bash*, first used (1818) by Prof. Wilson. Cf. *stramash*.

Utterly to squabash and demolish every gainsayer (*Ingoldsby*).

squabble. Imit. of noisy confusion. Cf. Sw. dial. *sqvabbel*.

squad. F. *escouade*, altered, on Sp. *escuadra*, from *escadre*, It. *squadra*, squadron (v.i.), whence also obs. E. *squader*.

squadron. It. *squadrone*, from *squadra*, square (q.v.). Hence also F. *escadron* (mil.), *escadre* (nav.), and dim. *escadrille*; also Ger. *schwadron* (mil.), *geschwader* (nav.). Now applied, like other nav. terms, to the air-service.

The strength of the German aviation service—rather more than 200 squadrillas
(*Daily Chron.* Dec. 12, 1917).

squails. Obs. parlour game, orig. dial. for skittles. Cf. obs. *skayles*, skittles, for *kailes*, cogn. with Ger. *kegel*, "a keil, keal, or (nine) pirl" (Ludw.). Cf. *squail*, to throw a loaded stick.

squalid. L. *squalidus*, from *squalēre*, to be dry, dirty.

squall. Imit., cf. *squeal*, also Gael. *sgal*, howl, shriek. ? Hence sudden gust, from sound. With to *look out for squalls* (Marryat) cf. synon. F. *veiller le grain*.

squaloid. Like the shark, L. *squalus*.

squamose [*biol.*]. L. *squamosus*, from *squama*, scale.

squander. From late 16 cent., to scatter (*Merch. of Ven.* i. 3), esp. money. Origin obscure. ? Cogn. with Ger. *verschwenden*, "to squander, confound, run out, lavish, dilapidate, dissipate, destroy, spend, mis-spend, spill, waste" (Ludw.), causal of *verschwinden*, to disappear.

square. OF. *esquerre* (*équerre*, carpenter's square, which is earliest sense of E. word), VL. **exquadra*, from *quadrus*, from *quatuor*, four; cf. It. *squadra*, Sp. *escuadra*. Fig. senses (*on the square*, to *act squarely*, to *square the authorities*, etc.) are from math. (cf. fig. uses of *straight*). These often run parallel with those of *round*, e.g. a *square meal*, but a *round sum*, while we can tell a man *squarely* or *roundly* what we think of him. With obs. to *square*, swagger, and current to *square up to*, cf. F. *se carrer*, "to look stately, surly, or big on't" (Cotg.).

square toes: an old man; square toed shoes were anciently worn in common, and long retained by old men (Grose).

squarrose [*bot.*]. L. *squarrosus*, scurfy.

squarson. Portmanteau-word on *squire, parson*. Attributed to Bishop Wilberforce, Sydney Smith, and others. Cf. *squishop*.

squash¹. Verb. OF. *esquasser*, VL. **exquassare*, from *quatere, quass-*, to shatter; but more often intens. of *quash* (q.v.). Hence prob. *squash*, peascod, etc.

Some had their braines dasht out, some their heads all to squasht [*var.* quashed]
(Stubbes, *Anat. of Abuses*).

squash². Gourd. From NAmer. Ind. (Narragansett) *asquutasquash*, from *asq*, uncooked.

squat. OF. *esquatir*, from *quatir*, to press flat (whence *se quatir*, to crouch), VL. **co-*

active, from *coactus*, p.p. of *cogere*, to compress, etc. (*co-agere*). Trans. in ME., and used by Wyc. for L. *conquassare* (2 *Sam.* xxii. 8); current sense is from reflex. *Squatter* was orig. (18 cent.) US., of unauthorized occupier of land. From Austral. sense of crown-tenant come joc. *squatterarchy*, *squattocracy*.

squatter. Verb. Imit. of flapping, splashing movement.

squaw. NAmer. Ind. *squaws*, *squa*, woman, with many other forms in various Algonkin dials.

squawk. Imit., cf. *squall*, *squeak*.

squeak. Imit., cf. Ger. *quieken*, "to skreek like a pig" (Ludw.). Hence *squeak*, slight chance, in allusion to thinness of sound, as now in *narrow squeak*.

squeal. Imit., cf. *squeak*. Both *squeak* and *squeal* are used in slang of turning informer, the latter esp. US. Of late (1917–18) *squeal* has also been much used of terrified protests by an enemy subjected to homoeopathic treatment.

squeamish. Altered from earlier *squamous*, *squeamous*, *esquaymous*, AF. *escoymos*. Earliest sense fastidious, esp. in diet. ? From AS. *sceamu*, shame, whence *scamisc*, causing shame, and ME. *schamous*; cf. Ger. *schamhaft essen*, *die schüssel nicht rein ausessen*, "to leave manners in the dish" (Ludw.). Also dial. *swamous*, modest, shy.

Si il poy mange e beyt poy, lors est gageous ou escoymous (Bozon, 13 cent.).

squeegee. Swab. Orig. naut. ? From *squeege*, colloq. for squeeze; but this will not explain var. *squilgee*.

squeeze. Intens. of earlier *queise* (15 cent.), app. cogn. with AS. *cwīesan* (in compd. *tōcwȳsan*). Cf. dial. *squench*, for *quench*.

squelch. Also occ. *quelch*. Imit.

squib. Explosive, lampoon. From early 16 cent., second sense app. fig. from first. ? Imit. of explosive noise. Raleigh describes the Armada, attacked off Calais by our fireships, as "driven with squibs from their anchors."

squid. Cuttle-fish. ? Sailors' name on *squit*, dial. for *squirt*.

Squides, a rare kind of fish, at his mouth squirting matter forth like ink (*NED.* 1620).

squiffy. Slang (19 cent.), of unknown origin.

squilgee. See *squeegee*.

squill. Sea-onion. L. *squilla*, G. σκίλλα; cf. F. *squille*, It. *squilla*, etc.

squinch, **scunch** [*arch.*]. Back-formation from *scuncheon* (q.v.). This is the word which now appears in *lepers' squint*.

squint. Back-formation from earlier *asquint* (q.v.). See also *squinch*.

squire. OF. *escuyer* (*écuyer*); cf. *esquire*, which appears later in E. Earliest sense is gentleman attendant on knight, whence to *squire*, escort (Chauc. D. 305). Later applied to various court and household officials, which suggested Spenser's *squire of dames*. With Ir. *squireen* cf. *colleen*, *dudeen*, etc.

He was sent to apprehend
One Joseph Clark, of Herridge End,
For stealing deer of Esquire Dounes,
Where he was shot and died o' th' wounds
(*Epitaph, Prestbury Churchyard*, 1750).

squirm. Orig. (16 cent.) of eels. Imit. of wriggling movement, perh. with a suggestion of *worm*; cf. synon. dial. *squiggle*, with a suggestion of *wriggle*.

squirrel. OF. *escureul* (*écureuil*), VL. **scuriolus*, dim. of *sciurus*, G. σκίουρος, app. from σκιά, shade, οὐρά, tail, but this is prob. folk-etym. for some foreign name (cf. *butter*); cf. Sp. *esquirol*. The Teut. name is represented by AS. *ācweorna*, Du. *eekhoorn*, Ger. *eichhorn*, OSw. *ekorni*, of which first element is app. *oak*.

squirt. Earlier (14 cent.) *swirt*, to spatter, etc., as still in dial.; cf. synon. LG. *swirtjen*.

squish. Marmalade (Oxf. & Camb.). From *squish*, to squeeze, squash, of soft mud, etc.

squitch [*dial.*]. Var. of *quitch*, couch-grass.

st! To impose silence; cf. *sh!* Usu. written, less exactly, *hist*.

stab. Noun is in *Prompt. Parv.*, but early examples of verb are Sc. Northern var. of *stob*, stake, etc., cogn. with *stub*.

Stabat Mater (*dolorosa*). L., Stood the Mother (full of sorrow). Init. words of sequence composed (13 cent.) by Jacobus de Benedictis.

stabilize. In current mil. sense (1918) neol. after F. *stabiliser* (cf. *consolidate*).

stable[1]. Noun. OF. *estable* (*étable*, cowshed, sty), L. *stabulum*, standing-place, from *stare*; cf. It. dim. *stabbiolo*, pig-sty, Sp. *establo*.

For whan the grete stiede
Is stole, than he taketh hiede,
And makth the stable dore fast (Gower).

stable[2]. Adj. OF. *estable* (*stable*), L. *stabilis*, from *stare*, to stand.

stablish [*archaic*]. Aphet. for *establish*, in *AV. & PB.*

staccato [*mus.*]. It., p.p. of *staccare*, for *distaccare*, to detach. Cf. opposite *legato*, lit. bound. For fig. use (e.g. of musketry) cf. *crescendo*.

stachys. Plant. L., G. στάχυς, prop. ear of corn.

stack. ON. *stakkr*, haystack; cogn. with synon. Russ. *stog*. Also applied to mass of chimneys, columnar rock; for latter sense cf. Faroese *stakkur*.

stad [*SAfr.*]. Native village. Du. (see *stead*). Cf. *kraal*.

staddle [*dial.*]. Support, platform for rick, etc. AS. *stathol*, cogn. with *stand*.

stadholder, stadtholder [*hist.*]. Chief magistrate of Du. Republic, title conferred on William of Orange (1580). Du. *stadhouder*, lit. place-holder, locum tenens, lieutenant, viceroy. Cf. Ger. *statthalter* (till Nov. 1918 of Alsace-Lorraine) and see *stead*.

stadhous, stadthouse [*hist.*]. Du. *stadhuis*, town-house, townhall. See *stead*.

stadium. L., G. στάδιον, rendered *furlong* in *AV*.

staff. AS. *stæf*. Com. Teut.; cf. Du. *staf*, Ger. *stab*, ON. *stafr*, Goth. *stafs*; ult. cogn. with *stable*. *Stave* is back-formation from pl. For mus. sense cf. *bar*. Mil. sense (from 18 cent. only), now also civil, is due to Du. or Ger., in which idea of command is developed from that of staff of office, baton.

The Germans call a regiment, and all that belongs to it, the colonel's staff (*den regiment oder colonel-stab*), for with that soldiers are to be ruled
(*NED.* 1700).

staffage [*art*]. Accessories. Ger., from *staffieren*, OF. *estoffer* (*étoffer*), to pad.

stag. AS. *stagga*. Orig. sense prob. male, as in US. *stag-party*; cf. dial. senses of young horse, bull, boar, cock, etc.; also ON. *steggr*, male-bird, Icel., tom-cat, whence E. dial. *steg*, gander. In slang also informer, outside broker.

stage. OF. *estage* (*étage*, story of house), VL. *staticum*, from *stare*, to stand. In ME. floor, raised platform, relative height, etc. In theat. sense from 16 cent. (cf. *pageant*), with extended senses corresponding to those of F. *scène*. Idea of horizontal, for orig. perpendicular, extension, as in *stage of a journey*, *stage-coach*, *by easy stages*, appears c. 1600 and is due to use of the word in OF. & ME. in sense of *stadium* (which it may even in this sense represent phonetically). *Old stager*, now felt as belonging to "the profession," is in Foxe

(1570) in sense of old inhabitant, "fossil"; cf. OF. *estagier*, resident, MedL. *stagiarius*, aged monk permanently lodged in infirmary.

stagger. For earlier *stacker* (Chauc.), ON. *stakra*, frequent. of *staka*, to push, stagger; cf. Du. *staggelen*. To *stagger belief* is perh. due to Burke.

Stagirite. Aristotle, born at *Stagīra*, Macedonia.

stagnate. From L. *stagnare*, from *stagnum*, pool. Cf. dial. *stank*, pond, OF. *estanc* (*étang*).

staid. For *stayed*, p.p. of *stay²*. Cf. *sedate*, *demure* (q.v.), F. *rassis*, Ger. *gesetzt*, all in similar sense.

stain. Aphet. for *distain*, OF. *desteindre* (*déteindre*), prop. to unstain, lose colour or tint (q.v.), but used with *sur* in a sense approximating to E. Sense of losing, removing, defacing, colour is also earliest in ME., and this is still the prevailing sense of the noun (cf. *stainless*).

I stayne a thynge, I change the colour of it with shedynge any thynge upon it: je destayns (Palsg.).

stair. AS. *stæger*, flight of stairs, staircase. This is still the sense of Sc. *stair*, while in E. a pl. form has been current from 14 cent.; cogn. with AS. *stīgan*, to ascend (Com. Teut.; cf. Du. *stijgen*, Ger. *steigen*, ON. *stīga*, Goth. *steigan*). Cf. Du. *steiger*, stairs. *Staircase* is 17 cent. Formerly also of stone steps, as still on Thames (*Wapping Old Stairs*).

staith [*dial.*]. Landing-stage, embankment. ON. *stöth*, cogn. with AS. *stæth*, bank, and with *stand*; cf. Ger. *gestade*.

stake. AS. *staca*, post "stuck" in ground; cogn. with *stick*¹·²; cf. Du. *staak*; also OF. *estache*, It. *stacca*, Sp. *estaca*, from Teut. In early use of post to which criminal was bound for execution, esp. by burning. With *to stake*, hazard (Palsg.), cf. cogn. Du. *staken*, to fix, place; cf. F. *mettre en jeu*, whence *enjeu*, stake. See also *sweep*. In *at stake* there is a tinge of the burning or baiting metaphor (v.i.). Earliest sense of verb *to stake* is to mark out a boundary (cf. US. to *stake out*, *pull up stakes*).

Have you not set mine honour at the stake,
And baited it with all th' unmuzzled thoughts
That tyrannous heart can think
(*Twelfth Night*, iii. 1).

stalactite, stalagmite. Back-formations from ModL. *stalactites*, *stalagmites* (Olaus Wormius, 17 cent.), from G. σταλακτός, dropping, σταλαγμός, a dropping, from σταλάσσειν, to drop, drip. Cf. *satellite*.

stale. Orig. of liquor that has stood long enough to clear. OF. *estale*, verbal adj. of *estaler* (*étaler*), to spread out, display, fix, as still in *mer étale*, smooth sea, from OHG. *stal*, fixed place, stall¹ (q.v.). Hence also archaic *stale*, decoy, AF. *estale*, corresponding in sense to Ger. *stellvogel*, decoy fowl, from *stellen*, to place, from OHG. *stal* (v.s.); cf. AS. *stælhrān*, decoy reindeer, Du. *stel*, trap (in SAfr.). So also *stalemate*, incorr. for earlier *stale* (15 cent.), AF. *estale*, from *estaler*, or perh. OF. *estal*, fixed position, as in obs. Sc. *in stale*, in ambush, in battle array. Dial. *stale*, urine, is also OF. *estal*, from stopping to urinate. Thus all senses of *stale* belong ult. to OF. *estaler* and hence to Teut. *stal*, fixed place.

Tary a whyle, your hors wyll staale (Palsg.).

fare tavola: to make a stale at the play of chesse, to be idle, neither win nor lose (Flor.).

stalk¹. Noun. Dim. of ME. & dial. *stale*, stalk, handle, AS. *stalu*, cogn. with synon. Ger. *stiel*; cf. Sw. *stjälk*, Norw. dial. *stelk*, Dan. *stilk*. AS. has also *stela*.

stalk². Verb. AS. *stealcian*, to walk stealthily (in synon. *bestealcian*), in ME. esp. to approach game; cogn. with *steal* (cf. *lurk*, *talk*, *walk*). Hence *stalking-horse*, orig. trained to conceal fowler, later applied to a camouflaging framework. Later sense of taking long ungainly strides is influenced by stalk¹.

he stalketh lyke a crane: il va a grans pas comme fait une grue (Palsg.).

stall¹. Noun. AS. *steall*, standing place, position, esp. for cattle. Com. Teut.; cf. Du. *stal*, Ger. *stall*, cattle-shed, stable, ON. *stallr*; also OF. *estal* (*étal*, butcher's stall), It. *stallo*, place, *stalla*, stable, from Teut.; cogn. with *stand*. For sense of canon's (knight's) seat in church, etc., cf. MedL. *stallus*, F. *stalle*, later theat. development being 19 cent. Dealer's *stall* is prob. via OF. (v.s.). Also used of various receptacles (v.i.). Cf. *install*, *forestall*.

I stall an ox to fede him fatte: je mets en estal (Palsg.).

They be made glovelike, and for eche finger a stall (*NED*. 1568).

stall². Verb. In to *stall off*, keep off (sport.). Orig. to keep off by trickery, from slang *stall*, confederate, orig. decoy (see *stale*).

stallion. Altered from earlier *staloun*, OF.

estalon (*étalon*); cf. It. *stallone*. Because kept in a stall¹.

stalwart. Sc. form of *stalworth*, AS. *stælwierthe*, serviceable, sturdy, from *stæl* (*stathol*), stability, etc. See *worth¹* and cf. *steadfast*. Both forms were revived by Scott.

A rycht stalwart castell (Barbour).

stambouline. Frock-coat of Turk. official. From *Stamboul*, Turk. name of Constantinople.

stamen [*bot.*]. L., thread, fibre. Hence pl. *stamina*, now treated as sing., physical (moral) fibre.

stamina. See *stamen*.

stammel [*hist.*]. Bright red, orig. fabric (cf. *scarlet*). OF. *estamel*, cogn. with *estamine* (*étamine*), from L. *stamen* (v.s.).

stammer. AS. *stamerian*, from *stamor*, *stamm*, indistinct in speech; cf. Du. *stamelen*, Ger. *stammeln*; ult. cogn. with Ger. *stumm*, dumb.

stamp. Early ME., but prob. of AS. origin; cf. AS. *stempan*, to pound. Influenced by F. *estamper* (ModF. also *étamper*), to stamp, impress, from Teut. Cf. Ger. *stampfen*, ON. *stappa*; also It. *stampare*, to tread, print, Sp. *estampar*, from Teut. The same root, without the nasal, appears in *step*. Hence noun *stamp*, with which cf. Ger. *stempel*, impress, F. *estampe*, print, It. *stampa*. Postal sense dates from Rowland Hill (1837), the detachable scrap of paper replacing the offic. impress. *Stamp-collecting* dates from c. 1860.

stampede. Orig. US. Earlier also *stampedo*, Sp. *estampida*, stamping, uproar, used in Mex. Sp. in spec. sense.

stance. Sc., position. OF. *estance*, from *ester*, to stand, L. *stare*. Cf. *stanza*. Golfing sense is mod.

stanch. See *staunch*.

stanchion. Earlier *stanchon*, OF. *estanson* (*étançon*), from *estance*, prop, lit. standing, "stance," from *ester*, to stand, L. *stare*.

stand. AS. *standan* (*stōd*, *gestanden*). Com. Teut.; cf. OSax. *standan*, OHG. *stantan*, ON. *standa*, Goth. *standan*. The Teut. langs. had also a shorter form from the same root, appearing in Du. *staan*, Ger. *stehen*, etc., mod. conjugation of which is mixed up with the longer (cf. the parallelism of *go*, *gang*); cogn. with L. *stare*, G. ἱστάναι, Sanskrit *sthā*. *As* is omitted in to *stand security* (*godfather*). *All standing* (naut.) is opposite of dismantled, the verb being much used in naut. lang., e.g. to *stand by* (*after, off and on*, etc.), and *standby*, orig. attendant ship. For sense of costing see *cost*. *It stands to reason* is for earlier *stands* (is consonant) *with reason*. In to *stand in awe, in need*, the person was orig. dat. and *awe, need*, nom.; cf. to *stand one in* (*good*) *stead*, and, for a similar change of construction, see *like*. Earliest trans. sense was to face, confront (an opponent), which passes into that of endure, sustain, e.g. the price of a drink. To *stand a candle on the floor* (*a child in the corner*) is mod. (Dickens). *Standpoint* is also mod., after Ger. *standpunkt*.

Of him tham stod selcut gret agh (*Cursor Mundi*).
If ye will have it to be made here, it will stand ye in 6 marks or more (*Plumpton Let.* 1476).

standard. OF. *estandart, estendart* (*étendard*), royal banner, from *estendre*, to extend; cf. It. *stendardo*, Sp. *estandarte*; also Du. *standaard*, Ger. *standarte*, from OF. or Sp. But strongly influenced, esp. in secondary senses, by *stand*, e.g. its first occurrence in E., with ref. to the Battle of the Standard (1138), has a contemporary explanation from *stand*. Development of E. sense of official exemplar of weight, measure, quality, etc., whence many extended uses, is app. also due to *stand* (cf. a *standing example*). *Standardize*, orig. an engineer's word, is now overworked.

Standardized air-raid warnings
(*Ev. News*, May 29, 1918).
Quelquefois il y a un peu d'hésitation devant le néologisme: une Académie vient de déférer "standardisation" à un tribunal (*Débats*, Jan. 30, 1919).

standish [*archaic*]. Inkstand, but orig. a case containing writing materials (Pepys, July 16, 1662). Of obscure origin. First element might be *stand* or *stone*, but there is no record of *dish* in such a sense. ? Connected with OF. *estain* (*étain*), pewter (see *stannary*).

standish: un grand écritoire, comme ceux qui sont faits d'étain (Miège).

stang [*dial.*]. Pole. ON. *stöng*; cogn. with AS. *stæng*, Du. *stang*, Ger. *stange*, and ult. with *sting*, as *stake* with *stick*. Hence to *ride the stang*, be carried round for public derision, for which US. has substituted to *ride on a rail*.

stanhope. Vehicle. First built for *Fitzroy Stanhope* (†1864). Cf. *stanhope lens, press*, invented by third *Earl Stanhope* (†1816).

stank [*dial.*]. See *stagnate*.

stannary [*hist.*]. From MedL. *stannaria*, the Stanneries, tin-mining district of Cornwall and Devon, from L. *stagnum, stannum*, tin, whence also F. *étain* (OF. *estain*), pewter. The L. word is prob. of Celt. origin.

stanza. It., lit. standing, stopping place, from L. *stare, stant-*, to stand; cf. OF. *estance* (*étance*), support, Sp. *estancia*, dwelling, Sc. *stance* (q.v.). Cf. sense-development of *verse, strophe*. First in Shaks. (*Love's Lab. Lost*, iv. 2).

staphylo- [*med.*]. From G. σταφυλή, bunch of grapes.

staple. AS. *stapol*, post, as still in place-names (*Stapleton, Stapleford*, etc.); cf. Du. *stapel*, leg of chair, stocks, Ger. *staffel*, step, rung of ladder (whence *staffelei*, easel), ON. *stöpull*, pillar, steeple. Ground-sense is something fixed. ME. sense of mart is via OF. *estaple* (whence F. *étape*, halting-place), from LG. Adj. is from noun used attributively as in *staple commodities*. As the great Flem. *staples*, or marts, were chiefly concerned with the wool-trade (cf. *woolstapler*), the word acquired a spec. connection with one commodity and came to mean its fibre. Ult. cogn. with *step*. Sense-development is not unlike that of *stock*. Spec. sense of bent iron holdfast perh. comes from some meaning otherwise lost in E.; cf. It. *staffa*, stirrup, staple, from OHG.

star. AS. *steorra*. Com. Teut.; cf. Du. *ster*, Ger. *stern* (OHG. *sterro*), ON. *stjarna*, Goth. *stairnō*; cogn. with L. *stella* (**sterla*), G. ἀστήρ, Sanskrit *star*. Fig. senses from astrol., e.g. to *thank one's stars, my stars!* now extended to *my stars and garters*, with jocular allusion to insignia; cf. *star-gazer*. The *Stars and Stripes*, adopted 1777, were at first thirteen, one (star and stripe) for each of the orig. states of the Union; cf. the *Star-spangled Banner*, by F. S. Key (1814). Sense of exceptional person is now chiefly theat.; hence to *star the provinces* (Thackeray). The *Star-chamber*, earlier *sterred chambre*, was in MedL. *camera stellata*, in AF. *chambre esteillee* (both 14 cent.), app. from its ornamentation. With *star* on horse's forehead (blaze[2]) cf. It. *stellato*, horse similarly marked, from L. *stella*, star.

starboard. AS. *stēorbord*, steer board, steer side, the steering paddle of an early Teut. ship being worked on the right, the steersman having his back to the *larboard* (q.v.), whence its obs. name *backboard* (F. *bâbord*); cf. Du. *stuurboord*, Ger. *steuerbord*, ON. *stjornborthi*; also It. *stribordo*, Sp. *estribor*, F. *tribord* (OF. *estribord*), from Teut.

starch. First as verb, to stiffen, strengthen. AS. *stercan* (found only in p.p.), from *stearc*, stiff, stark (q.v.).

stare. AS. *starian*; cf. Du. *staren*, OHG. *starēn*, ON. *stara*; cogn. with Ger. *starr*, rigid, as in *starr anschauen*, "to stare upon" (Ludw.); cf. *stark staring mad*. With *staring colour* cf. F. *couleur voyante*.

stark. AS. *stearc*, stiff, rigid. Com. Teut.; cf. OSax. Ger. *stark*, ON. *sterkr*, all rather with sense of strong; cogn. with Goth. *gastaurknan*, to stiffen. Also as intens., e.g. *stark mad* (see *stare*). But *stark-naked* is for ME. & dial. *start-naked* (13 cent.), from AS. *steort*, tail, rump (cf. *redstart*, bird), cogn. with Du. *staart* (as in *Ploegstaart*, plough-tail, *Wood*, anglicè *Plug Street*), Ger. *sterz*, ON. *stertr*.

starling[1]. Bird. AS. *stærling*, from *stær*, whence ME. & dial. *stare*; cf. Ger. *star*, ON. *stari*; cogn. with L. *sturnus*, "a bird called a sterling or stare" (Coop.), whence F. dim. *étourneau* (OF. *estournel*).

starling[2] [*techn.*]. Pile-work protecting bridge. Corrupt. of *staddling* (see *staddle*).

Stadelinges and ground workys of the same brigge (*NED.* 1482).

starosta [*Russ.*]. Mayor, local director. Pol., from *stary*, old.

start. ME. *sterten* (Kentish), AS. *styrtan*, to move with a bound. WGer.; cf. Du. *storten*, Ger. *stürzen*, to precipitate, rush. From sport. sense (c. 1600) comes gen. idea of beginning, setting out (c. 1800). Hence *from start to finish*. Trans. in to *start a hare* (Chauc.), also common in naut. lang. in sense of fracturing, etc.

Wrong is often a good starter, but always a bad stayer (D. Lloyd George, May 24, 1918).

startle. AS. *steartlian*, frequent. of *start*. Orig. intrans. For trans. sense (first in Shaks.) cf. *stagger*.

And the heerd starteled and ran hedlyng into the see (Tynd. *Mark*, v. 13).

starve. AS. *steorfan*, to die (orig. strong, *stearf, storfen*). WGer.; cf. Du. *sterven*, Ger. *sterben*. Orig. sense survives in dial., e.g. *starved with cold*, current sense (from 16 cent.) being due to ellipsis of *with hunger*. *Starvation*, oldest formation in -*ation* from a native word (exc. perh. *flirtation*), was either coined by, or reproached against,

"Starvation Dundas," who feared (in H. of C., March 6, 1775) that a bill for restraining trade with New England colonies might not be effectual in producing famine in those regions.

-*ation* is a modern finish, which has been in much use since *starvation* was heard in Parliamentary language (Pegge, *Anecdotes*).

stash [*slang*]. ? Coined on *stow, squash*[1]. Cf. *stow it*.

-**stat.** In names of scient. instruments, e.g. *aerostat*. G. -στατης, from root of ἱστάναι, to cause to stand.

state. OF. *estat* (*état*) and L. *status*, from *stare*, to stand; cf. It. *stato*, Sp. *estado*. Sense of magnificence, whence *stately*, springs from that of (high) rank or condition; cf. *state-room*, orig. captain's cabin (Pepys). For gen. senses cf. F. *état*, Du. Ger. *staat* (from OF.). Hist. *States-General* is after F. *États-généraux*, Du. *staaten generaal*, as *statesman* is after F. *homme d'État*. See *estate*, which in early use is not differentiated from *state*. So also a *statesman*, yeoman (Cumb. & Westm.), owns an *estate*. Hence verb to *state*, orig. to put in position, hence fix, set out in detail, etc.

stater. Coin. G. στατήρ, from ἱστάναι, to fix, weigh.

statics. From G. στατικός, causing to stand, also skilled in weighing (v.s.). Orig. science of weight and equilibrium.

station. F., L. *statio-n-*, from *stare, stat-*, to stand; cf. It. *stazione*, Sp. *estación*. Ground-idea is standing-place, stopping-place, many current uses being orig. mil. or nav. (v.i.). Hence *stationer*, MedL. *stationarius*, tradesman with a station or shop (as opposed to itinerant dealer), esp. one licensed to sell books in univ. towns. *Stationers' Hall*, where register of copyrights is kept, is head-quarters of *Company of Stationers* (booksellers, printers, binders, etc.), founded 1556.

Zabulon in the brynke of the see shal dwelle, and in the stacioun of shippes (Wyc. *Gen.* xlix. 13).

statistics. Older (16 cent.) is *statist*, orig. politician, It. *statista*, from *stato*, state. Current sense is due to Ger. *statistik*, which in 18 cent. had sense of gen. study of resources, etc. of a state. Cf. F. *statistique*, from Ger.

Statists and politicians, as though it were their business to deceive the people, as a maxim do hold that truth is to be concealed from them

(Sir T. Browne).

stato-. From G. στατός, standing. Cf. *statics*.

statthalter [*hist.*]. See *stadholder*.

statue. F., L. *statua*, from *stare*, *stat-*, to stand. *Statuesque* was coined (? by Coleridge) on *picturesque*.

stature. F., L. *statura*, from *stare* (v.s.).

status quo (**ante**). L., state in which (before). Cf. *in statu quo*.

statute. F. *statut*, Late L. *statutum*, decree, from *statuere*, to set up, establish, from *stare*, *stat-*, to stand. Cf. origin of *law*.

staunch, stanch. Adj. OF. *estanche* (*étanche*), water-tight, from *estancher* (*étancher*), to stanch, stop a flow, ? VL. *stagnicare* (cf. *stagnate*). Current sense, with which cf. fig. to *hold water*, is of naut. origin.

stauro-. From G. σταυρός, cross.

stave. Back-formation from pl. of *staff* (q.v.). Hence naut. to *stave* (*in*), orig. break the staves of a cask, with naut. past tense *stove*; also to *stave off*, keep off, orig. with a staff, and perh. at first in ref. to beating dogs off the animal being baited.

stavesacre. Plant. Folk-etym. for ME. *staphysagrye*, etc., L., G. σταφὶς ἀγρία, wild raisin. Cf. Du. *staverzaad*, corrupted on *zaad*, seed.

stay¹. Support. AS. *stæg*. Com. Teut.; cf. Du. Ger. ON. *stag*; also F. *étai* (OF. *estai*), Sp. *estay*, from Teut. Orig. naut. (cf. *mainstay*), but later used of any support, e.g. *pair of stays* (c. 1600). Hence verb to *stay*, support, as in to *stay one's stomach*, later to check, suspend, as in to *stay one's hand*, *stay of execution*, where there is association with *stay²*.

stay². To remain. OF. *ester*, to stand (still in leg. use), L. *stare*. This was in NE. dial. *esteir*, with p.p. *estei*, whence noun *esteie*, pause, sojourn, stay, which may be the immediate origin of the E. word. In AF. the stem became *esté-*, *estei-*, and the pres. was *estai-*. For trans. sense (to *stay the course*) cf. *stand*.

Vet s'en li rois sanz plus ester (*Tristan*, 3142).

Li rois n'a pas fait longe estee (*ib.* 3148).

stchi. Russ., cabbage soup, lit. kale.

stead. Chiefly in compds. (*bedstead, farmstead*) or phrases (*instead, in good stead*; cf. *bestead*). AS. *stede*, place, assigned position, hence settlement, village, etc. Com. Teut.; cf. Du. *stad*, town, *stede*, *stee*, place, Ger. *statt*, place (whence *anstatt*, instead), *stadt*, town (merely a var. spelling), ON. *stathr*,

place, Goth. *staths*, place; ult. cogn. with *stand*. With *steadfast*, AS. *stedefæst*, cf. *stalwart*, and synon. Ger. *statthaft*, *standhaft*; with *steady*, of late appearance (Palsg.), cf. Ger. *stetig*, constant, persistent. *Steady progress* is etym. a contradiction in terms.

steak. ON. *steik*, cogn. with *steikja*, to roast on a spit, and with *stick²*. The *Beef-steak Club* was founded by the great Earl of Peterborough as a protest against new-fangled foreign ways (see *macaroni*).

steal. AS. *stelan*. Com. Teut.; cf. Du. *stelen*, Ger. *stehlen*, ON. *stela*, Goth. *stilan*. For ME. use as verb of motion, to *steal away* (*after, out of the room*, etc.), cf. sense-development of *furtive* and Bibl. *thief in the night*. Hence *stealth*, retaining also etym. sense up to 18 cent. Cf. Ger. *verstohlen*, "stealingly, by stealth" (Ludw.). To *steal a march on* is mil., to move troops without enemy's knowledge.

A despot big with power obtained by wealth,
And that obtained by rapine and by stealth
(Cowper).

steam. AS. *stēam*, vapour, fume, cogn. with Du. *stoom*. *Steam-engine*, earlier *fire-engine*, is recorded for 1751, *steamboat* for 1787. Later compds. run into hundreds, and fig. senses are also numerous.

What an instance of the tragic irony of history is contained in the recorded use of the phrase *the steam-roller* to signify the supposed irresistible advance of the Russian hosts (Sir E. Cook).

Les Russes marchent sur Posen. Vous allez voir fonctionner le rouleau compresseur, comme disent les Anglais (Margueritte, *L'Embusqué*, ch. xix.).

stearin [*chem.*]. F. *stéarine* (Chevreul), from G. στέαρ, tallow.

steatite [*min.*]. Soapstone. L. *steatitis*, from G. στέαρ, στεατ- (v.s.).

steed. AS. *stēda*, stallion, cogn. with *stud²* (q.v.). After 16 cent. only poet. or jocular.

steel. AS. *style*, *stēle*. Com. Teut.; cf. Du. *staal*, Ger. *stahl*, ON. *stāl*.

The stern joy that warriors feel
In foemen worthy of their steel
(*Lady of Lake*, v. 10).

steelyard. From *steel* and *yard¹* (*NED*.). Current form was prob. fixed by the hist. *Steelyard*, London, head-quarters of the Hanse merchants, which is supposed to be a mistransl. of LG. *stālhof*, lit. sample yard, first element being mistaken for LG. *stāl*, steel, in which the Hanse merchants dealt (*Staelhoeff alias Stylgerd*, in Rymer, 1474).

The earliest known ref. (1394) to this is, however, MedL. *Curia Calibis* (*chalybis*), court of steel. The *Stilliarde beme*, public balance kept at the Steelyard, is mentioned 1531. With regard to the etym. of *steelyard*, the hist. of *lanyard*, *poniard*, *whinyard*, and the existence of the earlier *stelleer* (v.i.), make one chary of accepting the too obvious origin proposed by the *NED*.

romaine: a Roman beam, a stelleere (Cotg.).

steenbok. SAfr. antelope. Du., stone buck.
steenkerk, steinkerk [*hist.*]. Cravat. From F. victory (1692) at *Steenkerke* (stone church), Belgium. Cf. *magenta*, *ramillie*, etc. According to Voltaire the looseness of the *cravate à la Steinkerque* imitated the disorderly dress of the *maison du Roi*, household troops, going into action hurriedly.
steep¹. Adj. AS. *stēap*, lofty, precipitous; cogn. with *stoop*, and with Ger. *Hohenstaufen*. US. slang sense, orig. of price, was perh. suggested by Du. *stijf*, stiff (but cf. *tall*).
steep². Verb. Of late appearance (c. 1400). Cf. Sw. *stöpa*, Dan. *stœbe*, to soak (barley for malting); ? cogn. with *stoup* (q.v.) and AS. *stēap*, vessel.
steeple. AS. *stēpel*, tall tower, from *steep¹*. A *steeple-chase* had orig. a visible steeple as goal. With *steeplejack* (19 cent.) cf. *lumberjack* (US. & Canada).
steer¹. Noun. AS. *stēor*, bullock. Com. Teut.; cf. Du. Ger. *stier*, bull, Goth. *stiur*; cogn. with ON. *thjŏrr*, and perh. with G. ταῦρος. In US. and Colonies for male cattle in gen.
steer². Verb. AS. *stiēran*, from *stēor*, rudder (in *stēoresman*). Com. Teut.; cf. Du. *stuur*, Ger. *steuer*, ON. *stȳri*, Goth. *stiurjan*, to establish. Perh. orig. (guiding) staff; cf. G. σταυρός, cross. Ships were steered from the *steerage* before the deck-wheel was introduced.
steeve [*naut.*]. To point upward, or not straight forward (of bowsprit). ? From Du. *stevenen*, to point prow (*steven*) of ship. See *stem¹*.
stegano-, stego-. From G. στέγειν, to cover.
steinberger. Hock from *Steinberg*, near Wiesbaden.
steinbock. Ger., as *steenbok* (q.v.).
steinkerk. See *steenkerk*.
stele [*antiq.*]. Upright (inscribed) slab. F. *stèle*, G. στήλη.

stellar. Late L. *stellaris*, from *stella*, star.
stellenbosch [*mil. slang*]. To relegate to place where incompetence is less harmful. From *Stellenbosch*, Cape Colony, said to have been used for this purpose in Kaffir wars. Cf. F. *limoger* (neol.), to relegate to *Limoges*. This is the accepted (journalistic) explanation, but quot. below suggests an earlier ironic allusion. ? Cf. to *go to Bath*.

When the village [Stellenbosch] was first built, there was a variety of manufactures attempted there,—but this was speedily discouraged....It therefore soon became the asylum only for old age, —and under these oaks the evening of life is spent peacefully, coolly, and I trust happily, as people are supposed to live to a more advanced period of life here than in any other part of the colony (Lady Barnard's *SAfr. Journ.* 1797).

stellio. Lizard. L., from *stella*, star, from markings.
stem¹. Noun. AS. *stemn*, *stefn*. Com. Teut.; cf. Du. *stam*, Ger. *stamm*, ON. *stamn*, *stafn*, the last only in naut. sense of end-post of ship. In latter sense Du. & LG. have *steven*, borrowed by Ger. Both senses are very rare in E. between AS. and 16 cent. Naut. *stem* was orig. at both ends of ship (v.i.); cf. F. *étambot*, sternpost, from Teut. Hence also verb to *stem* (*the tide, current*), which has been confused with *stem²*.

The kele with the ij stems (*Nav. Accts.* 1495–97).

stem². Verb. ON. *stemma*, to check; cf. Ger. *stemmen*, "to stem, hem, or stop the course of a thing" (Ludw.); cogn. with *stammer*. See *stem¹*.
stemson [*naut.*]. From *stem¹*, after *keelson*.
stench. AS. *stenc*, cogn. with *stink* (cf. *drench*, *drink*). Not orig. limited to unpleasant smell. Cf. OHG. *stank* (v.i.).

Thaz hūs was gifullit fon themo stanke thera salbūn (Tatian, *John*, xii. 3).

stencil. Exc. for isolated occurrence (1707) of *stanesile*, a 19 cent. word, which makes connection with rare ME. *stansel*, to adorn with spangles, etc. very unlikely. This is OF. *estenceler* (*étinceler*, to sparkle), from VL. *stincilla, for *scintilla* (see *tinsel*). I suggest obs. Du. *stemsel*, "forma, formula, baston sur quoy ils cousent les souliers" (*Trium Ling. Dict.* 1587), "ora sive limbus calcei" (Kil.). The connection between a shoe-last and a stencil is that both serve to multiply a fixed pattern; cf. F. *calquer*, to stamp, trace (a drawing, etc.), from L. *calx, calc-*, heel. ? Ult. cogn. with *stamp*.

stenography. From G. στενός, narrow. From c. 1600.

stentorian. From Στέντωρ, G. warrior with powerful voice (*Iliad*, v. 785).

step. AS. *stæppan*, orig. strong, with past *stōp*. WGer.; cf. Du. *stappen*, Ger. *stapfen*, esp. in ref. to footprints; cogn. with *stamp*. For fig. senses of noun cf. *grade*, also F. *pas*, *démarche*.

step-. AS. *stēop-*, cogn. with *āstȳpan*, to bereave, make orphan; cf. synon. OHG. *stiufen*, *irstiufen*. Orig. of children, and then, by an easy transition, of parents (for converse case cf. *grandchild*). Com. Teut.; cf. Du. Ger. *stief-*, ON. *stjūp-*. Johns. regarded *stepmother* as the only current compd. of the group.

stephanotis. Mod., from G. στέφανος, crown.

steppe. Russ. *step'*, of unknown origin.

-ster. AS. *-estre*, fem. agent. suffix, corresponding to masc. *-ere*; cf. LG. Du. *-ster*. Use as masc. suffix is prob. due to trades orig. carried on by females (*baxter*, *brewster*), the only word preserving orig. sense being *spinster*. With addition of *-ess* is formed double fem. suffix (*sempstress*, *songstress*). From 16 cent. used (? influence of *-aster*) in jocular and contemptuous formations (*punster*, *rhymester*, *trickster*).

stercorary. From L. *stercus*, *stercor-*, dung.

stere. Cubic metre. F. *stère*, from G. στερεός (v.i.).

stereo [*typ*.]. Short for *stereotype* (v.i.).

stereo-. From G. στερεός, solid. Hence *stereoscope*, invented and named (1838) by Wheatstone, perfected (c. 1860) by Brewster; *stereotype*, F. *stéréotype*, invented (c. 1798) by Didot. For fig. use of *stereotyped* cf. *cliché*.

sterile. F. *stérile*, L. *sterilis*, cogn. with G. στεῖρος, Sanskrit *starī*, barren cow, Goth. *stairō*, barren woman. *Sterilize*, in med. sense, is late 19 cent.

sterlet. Small sturgeon. Russ. *sterlyad'*.

sterling. Orig. the E. silver penny of the Norman dynasty. Prob. late AS. **steorling*, from *steorra*, star, with which some of the early Norman pennies are marked (cf. *copeck*, *crown*, *rose-noble*, *angel*, etc.). The excellence of the E. coin led to wide continental currency; hence OF. *esterlin* (c. 1100), MedL. *sterilensis*, *sterlingus* (12 cent.), It. *sterlino*, MHG. *sterling*. Erron. derived, as early as c. 1300, from the *Easterlings* (Hanse merchants), and in early Sc. associated with *Stirling*. A *pound*

sterling was orig. a *pound* (weight) *of sterlings*. Fig. senses are opposite of *counterfeit*, *foreign*.

Deux centz livres d'esterlinges
               (*John of Gaunt's Reg.* 1372–6).

stern[1]. Adj. AS. *stierne*, *styrne*; cogn. with Ger. *starr*, stiff, G. στερεός, solid, rigid, and with *stare*.

stern[2]. Noun. ON. *stjörn*, steering, from *stȳra*, to steer. Sense of steering gear, helm, survived till 17 cent. With *sternson* cf. *stemson*. In *stern chase*, "if he (the enemy) be right ahead of you" (Capt. John Smith), perh. sometimes associated by landsmen with *stern*[1].

And withe that the Spanyard shotte by them on sterne, and stayed and came by them agayne
          (*Voyage of the Barbara*, 1540).

We...altered course to S.E. parallel to them, and settled down to a long stern chase
          (Sir D. Beatty, March 3, 1915).

sterno-. From L. *sternum*, G. στέρνον, chest, breastbone.

sternutation. L. *sternutatio-n-*, from *sternutare*, frequent. of *sternuere*, to sneeze; cogn. with G. πτάρνυσθαι.

stertorous. From L. *stertere*, to snore.

stet [*typ*.]. L., let stand.

stethoscope. F. *stéthoscope*, invented and named (c. 1819) by Laennec, from G. στῆθος, chest.

stevedore. Sp. *estivador*, from *estivar*, to stow a cargo, L. *stipare*, "to stop chinkes or cleftes" (Coop.).

stew[1] [*archaic*]. Brothel. From OF. *estuve* (*étuve*), "a stove, hot-house, hot bath" (Cotg.); cf. It. *stufa*, "a stufe, a bath, a whot house" (Flor.), Sp. *estufa*; cogn. with *stove*[1] (q.v.). The public hot-air baths acquired a reputation like that of our massage establishments some time ago. Cf. also *bagnio*. For later senses see *stew*[2]. With *to be in a stew* cf. *to be in a sweat*, but perh. rather from later cooking sense (*stew*[2]; cf. *to make a hash*).

stew[2]. To boil slowly. Developed (15 cent.) from *stew*, to bathe in hot vapour, etc. (see *stew*[1]). To *stew in one's own juice* is a variation on an earlier figure (v.i.).

In his owene grece I made hym frye
For angre and for verray jalousye (Chauc. D. 487).

stew[3] [*archaic*]. Fishpond, tank (Chauc. A. 350). OF. *estui* (*étui*, case), trough or tub in which fish were kept for kitchen purposes. Of obscure origin, perh. ult. from *stow*.

steward. AS. *stigweard*, major-domo, caterer, lit. sty-ward, *sty*[1] (q.v.) being used in wider sense than now. For wide range of senses cf. *marshal*, *sergeant*, etc. From Sc. form *stewart* came the royal house sprung from *Walter* (*the*) *Stewart*, who married (1315) Marjorie de Bruce, daughter of King Robert.

stibium [*chem.*]. Black antimony. L., from G. στίβι, στίμμι.

stichomythia. Dialogue in alternate lines. G. στιχομυθία, from στίχος, row, line (cf. *acrostic*), μῦθος, speech, "myth."

stick[1]. Verb. AS. *stician*, to pierce, remain fixed, hence (in ME.) to (cause to) adhere. Has absorbed cogn. dial. *steek*, which corresponds to Ger. *stechen*, to pierce, sting, stitch. Cf. Du. *stikken*, to embroider, Ger. *stecken*, to stick (fast), put, *sticken*, to embroider, Goth. *stiggan*, to thrust; cogn. with *sting*, *stitch*; also with *stigma*, *instigate*, *distinguish*, etc. To *stick* (endure) *it* appears to be a mod. variation on to *stand it*. With Austral. to *stick up* (coach, bank) cf. US. to *hold up*. *Stuck-up* is 19 cent.

Like a stuck pig the woman star'd (*NED.* 1702).
He [Dominie Sampson] became totally incapable of proceeding in his intended discourse...and was ever after designated as a "stickit" minister
(*Guy Mannering*, ch. ii.).

stick[2]. Noun. AS. *sticca*, cogn. with *stick*[1]. Naut. for mast, as in to *up stick and run*.

That sort of alternative which is commonly called a cleft stick (Cowper).

stickle. For earlier *stightle*, to arrange, control (cf. Yorks surname *Pickles* from *pightle*), frequent. of obs. *stight*, AS. *stihtan*, cogn. with Du. *stichten*, Ger. *stiften*, to set in order, establish. Oldest sense of *stickle* (Palsg.) is to see fair play between combatants, and Flor. uses *sticklers* to render Montaigne's *personnes tierces* (ii. 27) in duels, with which cf. *umpire*. The early lexicographers associated it with the *stick* or wand used for parting combatants (cf. archaic Ger. *stanger*, *stängler*, stickler, second in duel, from *stange*, staff, stick).

arbitrer: to arbitrate, stickle (Cotg.).

stickleback. From AS. *sticel*, prick, sting, from *stick*[1]. Pop. form *tittlebat*, *tiddlebat*, illustrates moveable character of *s*- (q.v.) and occ. confusion between final dental and palatal (cf. *scabbard*).

stiff. AS. *stīf*. WGer.; cf. Du. *stijf*, Ger. *steif*; cogn. with L. *stipes*, stake, stem. With

stiffnecked cf. Ger. *hartnäckig*, obstinate, whence surname *Harnack*. Both correspond to L. *dura cervice* (*Vulg.*), G. σκληρο-τράχηλος, lit. transl. from Heb. *Stiff upper lip* is US.

stifle[1], **stiffle**. Joint between femur and tibia of hindleg of quadruped, esp. horse. Recorded c. 1320. Origin obscure. ? OF. *estival*, boot, whence Ger. *stiefel*.

stifle: is the part of the hind-leg which advances towards a horse's belly (*Gent. Dict.*).

stifle[2]. Verb. Earlier (14 cent.) *stuffle*, either frequent. of *stuff*, or from cogn. OF. *estouffer* (*étouffer*), "to stifle, smother, choake" (Cotg.).

A monke fil doun of a brigge into a water and was i-stufled [*var.* y-stoffed, L. suffocatus]
(Trev. vi. 449).

Stiggins. Alcoholic hypocrite (*Pickwick*).

stigma. L., G. στίγμα, mark, brand (of infamy), from στίζειν, to puncture. Hence *stigmatize*, to brand. In R.C. Church also of miraculous marks reproducing the wounds of Christ.

stile, style. AS. *stigel*, from *stīgan*, to ascend (cf. *stair*). To *help a dog over a stile* is in Heywood (1562).

Fleete houndes goe away with the game, when the rest neede helping over a stile a mile behind
(Peacham, 1634).

stiletto, style. It., "a little poynard, dagger, poynado, bodkin, needle, or pinne, or stabber" (Flor.). Dim. of *style*[1] (q.v.).

still[1]. Adj. AS. *stille*. WGer.; cf. Du. *stil*, Ger. *still*; from the root expressing fixity to which *stall*[1] belongs. Sense of dead only in *stillborn*, *still life*, the latter after Du. *stilleven*, whence also Ger. *stillleben*; cf. synon. F. *nature morte*. Hence adv. *still*, preserving something of orig. sense in *stock still*, also in poet. use for constantly, usu. a Shaks. echo (e.g. *Temp*. i. 2). With poet. *stilly* (18 cent.) cf. Shaks. *vasty*.

still[2]. Noun. From archaic verb to *still*, aphet. for *distill* (q.v.). Hence *still-room*, now house-keeper's store-room.

stilling [*dial.*]. Support for casks. Du. *stelling*, "a stilling, stand, gauntree" (Sewel), from *stellen*, to place (see *stale*).

stilo-. See *stylo-*.

stilt. Of LG. origin; cf. Du. *stelt*, Ger. *stelze*. Orig. (14 cent.) plough-handle, crutch.

stilton. Cheese from Vale of Belvoir (Leic.) made famous (18 cent.) by a coaching-inn at *Stilton* (Hunts), the owner of which came from the Belvoir country.

stimulus. L., goad. Orig. med. Cf. *stimulate*, to spur on, *stimulant*, excitant, with alcoholic sense from 19 cent.

stimy [*golf*]. See *stymie*.

sting. AS. *stingan*, to pierce; cf. ON. *stinga*; ult. cogn. with *stick*[1]; cf. synon. F. *piquer*, Ger. *stechen*, both orig. to puncture.

stingaree. Fish. US. & Austral., for *sting-ray* (Capt. John Smith), from *ray*[2].

stingo. From 17 cent. From *sting*, as having a "bite."

stingy. App. from *stinge*, dial. form of *sting*. It has in dial. the sense of crabby, irritable, and current sense may be partly due to association with *stint*. For softening of -*g*- cf. *dingy, tinge*. For specialization of sense cf. *miser*. Ger. *frech*, insolent, orig. greedy, shows opposite sense-development; cf. Du. *vrek*, "niggardish, stingy" (Sewel).

stink. AS. *stincan*, to smell, as in *swōte stincan*, to smell sweet (see *stench*). WGer.; cf. Du. Ger. *stinken*. For offensive sense, which appears already in AS., cf. *smell*, which tends in the same direction. In both cases this is orig. due to context, to *stink (smell) of*.

stint. First (c. 1200) as verb, to desist, come to an end, later trans., to discontinue, check, etc. AS. *styntan*, to blunt, dull, cogn. with *stunt*[1] (q.v.); cf. ON. *stytta* (*stynta), to shorten, ? also Ger. *stutzen*, to stop short, also to dock, crop, lop, etc. Sense has been affected by obs. *stent*, limit, allowance, aphet. for *extent*. *Extented*, for *stinted*, occurs in *Coventry Leet Book* (1480, p. 445).

limiter: to limit, bound, stint (Cotg.).

If the summe which the debtor oweth be above the stint, he shall not be released (Coryat, i. 280).

stipend. L. *stipendium*, from *stips, stip-*, wages, *pendere*, to weigh, pay. A *stipendiary magistrate* is distinguished from the "great unpaid."

stipes [*bot.*]. L., stem, stalk.

stipple. Du. *stippelen*, frequent. of *stippen*, to speckle, from *stip*, point; cogn. with Ger. *steppen*, to stitch, embroider.

stipulate. From L. *stipulari*, "to require and demaunde a thing to be given to him, or done for him with ordinary words of the law" (Coop.). Connection with L. *stipula*, straw, is rejected by mod. authorities, perh. too readily, for the derivation of leg. expressions from symbolic acts is common in primitive lang. (cf. F. *rompre la paille*, used of making a formal decision).

stir. AS. *styrian*; cf. ON. *styrr* (noun); cogn. with Du. *storen*, Ger. *stören*, to disturb, ? and ult. with *storm*. Noun-sense of uproar, commotion, is partly due to dial. *stour* (see *storm*).

stirk [*dial.*]. Bullock. AS. *stirc, styrc*, calf; cf. Du. dial. *sterke*, Ger. *stärke*, maiden heifer, Bavar. *sterch*, breeding sheep (swine).

stirp. Stock, lineage. L. *stirps, stirp-*, "the stemme of a tree, a stocke in kindred" (Coop.).

stirrup. AS. *stigrāp*, mount rope (see *stair, stile*); cf. Flem. *steegreep*, Ger. *stegreif*, ON. *stigreip*; also Du. *stijgbeugel*, Ger. *steigbügel*, with second element cogn. with *bow*[1]. Orig. a help for mounting, primitive races riding without stirrups. With *stirrup-cup* (F. *coup de l'étrier*) cf. Ger. *aus dem stegreif*, impromptu.

stitch. AS. *stice*, puncture, stab, cogn. with *stick*[1]; cf. Ger. *stich*, stitch, sting, pricking. Oldest sense in *stitch in the side*, for which *stitchwort* is a remedy.

stithy [*archaic*]. Anvil. ON. *stethi*, cogn. with *stand*, whence E. dial. *stith*, the lengthened *stithy* being influenced by *smithy*, for which it is used by Shaks. (*Haml.* iii. 2). Obs. from 17 cent. and app. revived by Scott.

stiver [*archaic*]. Small coin. Du. *stuiver*; ? cogn. with ON. *stȳfa*, to cut off (cf. *doit*). Now only in *not a stiver*.

stoa. See *stoic*.

stoat. ME. *stote* (15 cent.). Origin unknown.

stoccado [*archaic*]. Altered from It. *stoccata*, "a foyne, a thrust, a stoccado given in fence" (Flor.), whence also F. *estocade*. From *stocco*, "a tuck, a short sword," of Teut. origin; cf. Ger. *stock*, stick.

stock. AS. *stoc*, trunk, log, pillory. Com. Teut.; cf. Du. *stok*, Ger. *stock*, ON. *stokkr*. For genealogical sense cf. L. *stirps*, F. *souche*, Ger. *stamm*. As emblem of lifelessness in *stocks and stones* (Aelfric, *Deut.* xxviii. 36, *Vulg. lignum et lapis*). *Laughing-stock* is by analogy with earlier *whipping-stock*, whipping-post. The *stock-dove*, wood pigeon, is named from nesting in hollow trees. Used of many supporting frameworks, e.g. *on the stocks* (orig. in shipbuilding), and for the massive part of an implement. *Stock, lock and barrel* is app. a mod. variation on *stock and block* (17 cent.). As name of flower short for *stock-gilliflower*, with woody stem; cf. *stock*, stiff cravat, etc. (17 cent.). For sense of property, store (peculiar to E.), cf. *fund*, lit. foundation. Hence *live-stock* and spec. Austral. application to cattle (*stock-yard*, *-whip*, *-rider*). Adj. use, like that of *staple*, is due to attrib. use of noun, e.g. *stock merchandise* (*argument*). With *stockfish*, dried cod, cf. Du. *stokvisch*, Ger. *stockfisch*, the name being variously explained.

stockade. F. *estacade* (archaic var. *estocade*), Sp. *estacada*, from *estaca*, stake, from Teut. Cf. *palisade*.

stockinet. For *stocking net*. Cf. *bobbinet*.

stocking. From archaic *stock*, hose, divided into *upper stock* and *nether stock*, the latter being the *stocking*. Similarly F. has *haut de chausses*, breeches, *bas de chausses*, "a stocking, or netherstocke" (Cotg.), whence mod. *bas*. For use of *stock* in this sense cf. Ger. *strumpf*, stocking, for *hosenstrumpf*, hose stump, hose trunk, and see *trunk-hose*.

stodge. To fill up, cram. From 17 cent. Perh. suggested by *stuff* or *stow*.

stoep [*SAfr.*]. Raised verandah. Du., cogn. with *step*. Hence US. *stoop*.

stoic. L., G. στωικός, from στοά, the Porch, where Zeno lectured at Athens (c. 300 B.C.). In Wyc. (*Acts*, xvii. 18).

stoke. Back-formation from *stoker*, Du., from *stoken*, to poke, feed a fire, from *stok*, stick.

stole[1]. Vestment. L. *stola*, G. στολή, cogn. with στέλλειν, to array; cf. F. *étole* (OF. *estole*). Used in *Vulg.* & AS. (*Mark*, xii. 38) in spec. Church sense.

stole[2] [*hist.*]. In *Groom of the Stole*, high royal officer. For *stool*, in sense of *close-stool*.

For cariage of the Quenes stole from London to Oxonford, and from Oxonford to Langley, xiiijd.
        (*Privy Purse Exp. of Eliz. of York*, 1502).

And when my honourable lord saies it shall be thus, my worshipfull rascall (the grome of his close stoole) saies it shal not be thus
        (*Eastward Hoe*, ii. 1).

Bid Essex, Percy, and your quondam grom
O'th stool to wait us in the Princes room
        (*Pyms Juncto*, 1640).

stolid. OF. *stolide*, L. *stolidus*, ult. cogn. with *still*[1].

stomach. F. *estomac*, L., G. στόμαχος, orig. throat, gullet, from στόμα, mouth. In L. also fig. for pride, indignation, inclination, etc. (cf. *bowels*, *heart*, *kidney*, *liver*), as in archaic *stomachful*, spirited, etc., Bibl. *proud stomach*.

I have doon my devoyr to know my Lady Wulgrave's stomacke (*Paston Let*. iii. 120).

I know I have the body of a weak, feeble woman; but I have the heart and stomach of a king—and of a king of England too
        (Elizabeth at Tilbury, 1588).

stomato-. From G. στόμα, στόματ-, mouth.

stone. AS. *stān*. Com. Teut.; cf. Du. *steen*, Ger. *stein*, ON. *steinn*, Goth. *stains*; cogn. with G. στία, pebble. With *stone-blind*, *-deaf*, etc., in which *stone* gradually becomes mere intens. (*stone-broke*), cf. Ger. *steinalt*, *steinreich*, etc. The *stone weight* was orig. a stone (cf. origin of *calculate*, *yard*[1], etc.). The *stonechat* is named from its note suggesting the knocking together of pebbles. For *stonecrop*, AS. *stāncropp*, see *crop*. With metaphor in quots. 2, 3, cf. G. πάντα λίθον κινεῖν.

I have a counterpais wheith of the wheight stone that the wooll was weyed with, and...se that the stone be kept that the shipman brings
        (*Paston Let*. 1469).

remuer toute pierre: to attempt all meanes, prove all courses, try all wayes (Cotg.).

I will leave no stone unmoved that I conceave may knocke your fathers fightinge designes on the head, and preserve him (*Verney Papers*, 1639).

stook. Of corn. Cf. Flem. *stuik*, Ger. dial. *stauche* (OHG. *stūhha*); ? ult. cogn. with *stand*.

stool. AS. *stōl*, seat, esp. throne. Com. Teut.; cf. Du. *stoel*, Ger. *stuhl*, ON. *stōll*, chair, seat, Goth. *stōls*, throne; cogn. with OSlav. *stolŭ*. Change of sense in E. is due to adoption of *chair* from F.

Betwen tuo stoles lyth the fal (Gower).

stoop[1]. Verb. AS. *stūpian*, to bow, bend; cf. Flem. *stuipen*, ON. *stūpa*; cogn. with *steep*[1]. Sense of swoop (falc.) from 16 cent.

stoop[2] [*US.*]. See *stoep*.

stoop and roop [*Sc.*]. Completely, neck and crop. Cf. early Sc. *stout and rout*, Ger. *stumpf und stiel*.

stop. AS. *stoppian* (in *forstoppian*, to plug up). WGer.; cf. Du. *stoppen*, Ger. *stopfen*. An early loan from VL. *stuppare, to plug up, from *stuppa*, *stupa*, tow, G. στύπη, στύππη, whence also F. *étouper* (OF. *estouper*), It. *stoppare*, Sp. *estopar*. As AS. *stoppian* is unrecorded, and *forstoppian* occurs once only, it seems likely that the E. word is an early naut. loan from Du. or LG. All meanings spring naturally from ground-sense, as in *stopgap*. Intrans. use appears 16 cent., no doubt for reflex. See also *estop*.

storax. Gum-resin. L., G. στύραξ. Cf. *styrax*.

store. First (13 cent.) as verb, to supply, furnish; earlier also *astore, enstore.* OF. *estorer,* from L. *instaurare,* "to newe make or beginne againe, to repaire" (Coop.), cogn. with G. σταυρός, post, stake. Cf. sense-development of *stock,* with which the noun *store* often runs parallel, e.g. *store-cattle,* to *set* (no) *store by,* with which cf. mod. to *take* (no) *stock in.* In AF. we find *estor mort* contrasted with E. *live-stock.*

His lordes sheepe, his neet, his dayerye,
His swyn, his hors, his stoor [live-stock], and his
    pultrye,
Was hoolly in this reves governyng
                              (Chauc. A. 597).

storey. See *story².*

stork. AS. *storc.* Com. Teut.; cf. Du. *stork,* Ger. *storch,* ON. *storkr.* ? Ult. cogn. with Ger. *starr,* stiff.

storm. AS. *storm.* Com. Teut.; cf. Du. *storm,* Ger. *sturm,* ON. *stormr;* cogn. with *stir.* Cf. OF. *estour(m),* onset, from Teut., whence E. dial. *stour,* disturbance, etc. *Storm-troops* (neol.) renders Ger. *sturm-truppen, stosstruppen* (shock-troops). *NED.* quotes mil. sense, furious onset, first from Oliver Cromwell, no doubt a Dugald Dalgetty word from the Thirty Years' War. *Storm and stress* was orig. used by Lewes (*Life of Goethe,* 1855) to render Ger. *sturm und drang,* the title of a play by Klinger (1776), taken as symbolical of a new literary movement to which the earlier works of Goethe and Schiller also belonged.

Storthing. Norw. parliament (now *storting*), from *stor,* great, powerful, ON. *storr,* great, whence Sc. *stour,* vigorous, etc. See *thing.*

story¹. Narrative. AF. *estorie,* OF. *estoire,* L. *historia,* whence learned F. *histoire.* In ME. not differentiated from *history* (our island story). Cf. *storied,* ornamented with scenes or sayings from history and legend. As euph. for lie from 17 cent.

Dedes that wolde deie, storye kepeth hem evermore
                              (Trev. i. 7).

story², storey. Of house. App. ident. with *story¹,* though sense-development is obscure. *NED.* suggests that the word may orig. have referred to tiers of "storied" windows or sculptures corresponding to the different floors. The etym. seems to be proved by several records of AL. (h)*istoria* in same sense from 12 cent. onward, while E. *story* is not recorded till c. 1400.

stoup [*archaic*]. ON. *staup,* bucket. Com. Teut.; cf. AS. *stēap,* Du. *stoop,* Ger. dial.

stauf. Later sense of drinking vessel prob. from Du. Revived by Romantics and as Church word, the latter for obs. *stop,* representing cogn. AS. *stoppa.*

stout. OF. *estout,* proud, fierce, from Teut.; cf. Du. *stout,* Ger. *stolz,* ON. *stoltr,* proud; these are prob. early loan from L. *stultus,* foolish, a sense also of *stolz* in MHG. ME. sense of strong, vigorous, became euph. for fat c. 1800 (cf. F. *fort,* similarly used, esp. in fem.). Orig. sense survives in *stout-hearted, stoutly.*

stout: very strong malt-drink (*Dict. Cant. Crew*).

stove¹. Noun. From 15 cent., hot air bath, sweating-room, etc. Du. *stoof,* earlier *stove,* "stew, hot hous, or bain" (Hexham); cf. Ger. *stube,* "a stove; a room, or apartment, wherein there is a stove, or furnace, to warm it" (Ludw.), ON. *stofa, stufa,* AS. *stofa,* hot air bath, which did not survive. Perh. all from VL. **ex-tufare,* from G. τῦφος, vapour. For the connection between the stove and the room cf. OHG. *kemenāte,* room, cogn. with *chimney,* Ger. dial. *pesel,* room, ult. ident. with F. *poêle,* stove. See also *stew¹.*

Here [at Cairo] are many bath-stoves very artificially built (Purch.).

stove². Verb. Incorr. naut. use of incorr. past of *stave* as pres.

stow. From obs. *stow,* place, AS. *stōw,* common in place-names, ult. cogn. with *stand.* Cf. *bestow.* Naut. sense (from 16 cent.) perh. due rather to cogn. Du. *stouwen,* "to stow up, to cram, press or pack up close" (Hexham); cf. Ger. *stauen,* "to stow goods in a ship" (Ludw.), from LG. *Stowaway* is 19 cent.

strabism. L., G. στραβισμός, from στραβίζειν, to squint.

strad. Short for *stradivarius* (q.v.).

straddle. Frequent. formation from *stride. Stridling* is used in same sense in Purch. Sense of shooting on each side of object from 1916.

The sheds and hangars were well straddled
                    (*Admir. Report,* Jan. 1, 1918).

stradiot [*hist.*]. Also *estradiot.* It. *stradiotto,* "a kind of soldiers that the Venecians use, a boote-haler, a freebooter" (Flor.), G. στρατιώτης, soldier. Comines tells us that they were orig. Greek mercenaries.

stradivarius. Violin by *Antonio Stradivari* (17 cent.).

strafe. "From Ger. phrase *Gott strafe England*, 'God punish England,' a common salutation in Germany in 1914 and the following years" (*NED.*). Cf. *hate*.

One [letter] contained this reference to Mr Lloyd George: "God strafe his — eyes"
(*Nottingham Guardian*, Feb. 5, 1917).

straggle. ? For **strackle*, frequent. of obs. *strake*, to rove, cogn. with *stretch*; cf. Ger. *landstreicher*, "a rambler or vagabond" (Ludw.). For change of consonant cf. *stagger*.

straight. ME. *streght*, p.p. of *stretch*; cf. Ger. *strack*. In early use as adv. Sense of undiluted, uncompromising, etc. (*straight ticket, whisky straight*) is US. Often absent-mindedly confused with *strait* (v.i.).

strack: strait, straight, streight, right or direct
(Ludw.).

Englishmen, Scotsmen, Welshmen must be more straightened and hard-pressed if Ireland is still privileged (*Obs.* Mar. 31, 1918).

strain¹. Verb. OF. *estreindre* (*étreindre*), to grip, L. *stringere*, "to straine, to wring, to trusse" (Coop.). In some senses there has been contact with *sprain* (q.v.). With to *strain a point* (16 cent.) cf. similar use of *stretch*. To *strain at* (*Matt.* xxiii. 24), usu. misunderstood, means to strain liquor if a gnat is found in it. This sense of *strain* is in Chauc. Cf. Du. *muggenzifter*, "a caviller, a capricious biggot" (Sewel), lit. midge-sifter.

Ye blinde gydes, which strayne out a gnat [*Vulg.* excolantes culicem], and swalowe a cammyll
(Tynd.).

strain². Of melody. From *strain¹*, in obs. to *strain* (*uplift*) *one's voice*, orig. to tighten up the cords of a musical instrument. Hence *in the same strain*, etc.

strain³. Race, breed. AS. *strēon, gestrēon*, gain, property, procreation; ult. cogn. with L. *strues*, heap. Current form, for *streen*, is due to *strain¹*.

Bountee [goodness] comth al of God, nat of the streen
Of which they been engendred and y-bore
(Chauc. E. 157).

strait. OF. *estreit* (*étroit*), L. *strictus*, p.p. of *stringere*, to tighten. For gen. senses cf. native *narrow*. *Strait-laced* is earlier (16 cent.) in fig. than in lit. sense. With *strait waistcoat* (18 cent.) cf. F. *camisole de force*, Ger. *zwangsjacke*. With *straitened circumstances* cf. L. *res angusta domi*. As noun

usu. in pl., e.g. *in great straits*. Geog. *strait* (usu. pl.) represents also OF. *destreit* (*détroit*), defile, isthmus, narrow channel (cf. naut. *narrows*).

strake [*naut.*]. Longitudinal timber (see *garboard*). In dial. also section of wheel-rim. ME. *strake*, cogn. with *stretch*. Early confused with unrelated *streak*, e.g. in *ring-straked* (*Gen.* xxx. 35, *Vulg. maculosus*).

stramash. Chiefly Sc. ? Fanciful formation on *stour* (see *storm*) and *smash*. Cf. *squabash*.

Seaforth profited by the confusion to take the delinquent who had caused this "stramash" by the arm (*Ingoldsby*).

stramonium. Thorn-apple. ModL. (16 cent.); cf. It. *stramonio*, Sp. *estramonio*. ? Cf. synon. Russ. *durman*, from Tatar *turman*, a medicine for horses.

strand¹. Of sea. AS. *strand*; cf. LG. Du. *strand*, Ger. *strand* (from LG.), ON. *strönd*, border, coast. Formerly used also of river bank, whence the *Strand*. Fig. use of verb is app. 19 cent. (cf. F. *échouer*, to come to grief, lit. run ashore).

strand². Of rope. ? OF. *estran, estrange*, rope, of Teut. origin; ? cf. Ger. *strähne*, skein, plait, ? or *strang*, rope, string.

strange. OF. *estrange* (*étrange*), L. *extraneus*, from *extra*, outside; cf. It. *strano*, Sp. *estraño*. For sense-development cf. *outlandish, foreign*. *Stranger*, OF. *estranger* (*étranger*), meant orig. foreign-er.

strangle. OF. *estrangler* (*étrangler*), L. *strangulare*, G. στραγγαλᾶν, from στραγγάλη, halter, from στραγγός, twisted. *Stranglehold* is from wrestling.

strangury [*med.*]. L., G. στραγγουρία, from στράγξ, στραγγ-, drop squeezed out, οὖρον, urine.

strap. Dial. var. of *strop* (q.v.), first (16 cent.) as naut. word. With *strapper, strapping* (fellow, lass) cf. *whopper, spanking*, etc. For *strap-hanger* see Whitmanesque ode in *Punch*, Nov. 8, 1905.

a strapping girl: grandis virgo (Litt.).

strapeze [*neol.*]. Portmanteau-name (*strap, trapeze*) for accommodation provided for majority of travellers by London Tubes and public vehicles.

strappado [*hist.*]. Altered from It. *strappata*, form of torture, from *strappare*, to drag, pull, of Teut. origin; cf. Ger. *straff*, tight, from LG. From It. *strapazzo*, "abuse, drudgery, ill-using" (Flor.), comes synon. Ger. *strapatze*.

stratagem. F. *stratagème*, L., G. στρατήγημα, piece of generalship, from στρατηγός, general, from στρατός, army, ἄγειν, to lead. Cf. *strategy*, generalship.

strath [*Sc.*]. Gael. *srath*, wide open valley; cf. Welsh *ystrad*; cogn. with *street*. For *strathspey*, dance, *NED.* quotes (c. 1625) *stravetspy*, which, if a genuine form, suggests that the dance-name has been assimilated to the place-name.

stratocracy. Government by the army, G. στρατός.

stratum. L., p.p. neut. of *sternere*, to lay down, spread out.

straw[1]. Noun. AS. *strēaw, strēow*, cogn. with *strew* (q.v.); cf. L. *stramen*, straw, litter, cogn. with *sternere, stra-*, to strew. Com. Teut.; cf. Du. *stroo*, Ger. *stroh*, ON. *strā*. For *bricks without straw* see *Ex. v. Man of straw*, dummy, hence person without means, is a leg. fiction; cf. synon. Ger. *strohmann*. Orig. sense was prob. scarecrow, as in Luther. The *last straw* is allusive to proverb of camel. *Strawberry*, AS. *strēawberige*, is prob. from the tiny strawlike particles which cover the fruit (AS. *strēaw* is used for the "mote" of *Matt.* vii. 3); also AS. *strēawberiewīse*, from *wīse*, growth, cogn. with *wesan*, to be. The persistence of the name, to the exclusion of synon. AS. *eorthberge* (cf. Ger. *erdbeere*), may be partly due to the old practice of using straw to protect the fruit. *Strawberry leaves*, noble rank, from ornamentation of coronet of duke, marquis, earl.

straw[2]. Verb. Archaic var. of *strew* (q.v.).

stray. Aphet. for *astray, estray*, OF. *estraier*, to wander, etc., derived by *NED.* from L. *extravagare* (cf. Prov. *estragar*). Continental authorities regard OF. *estraier*, ownerless horse, as the earliest word, and derive it from VL. *stratarius, from *strata*, street, road. In OF. there has been association with *estreer*, to surrender a fief, hand over derelict property (esp. of foreigner) to lord of manor, supposed to represent VL. *extradare. Something of this sense appears in the earliest E. record (1228), and is present in *waive, waif*, regularly coupled with *stray*, an association which appears in the mixed form *straif* (Cowell). The complete history of the word remains to be written.

streak. AS. *strica*, stroke of pen, line of motion, cogn. with *strike*; cf. Du. *streek*, Ger. *strich*, "a streak or stroke" (Ludw.).

The *silver streak*, English Channel, appears to be due to Gladstone (1870).

stream. AS. *strēam*. Com. Teut.; cf. Du. *stroom*, Ger. *strom*, ON. *straumr*; ult. cogn. with G. ῥεῖν, to flow, Sanskrit *sru*.

street. AS. *strǣt*, Late L. *strata* (sc. *via*), strewn (paved) way, whence also OF. *estree*, It. *strada*, Sp. *estrada*. Orig. of Roman road, as in *Watling* (*Icknield*) *Street*; cf. Du. *straat*, Ger. *strasse*, ON. *strǣti*, also Arab. *çirāṭ*, testifying to the superiority of the Romans as road-makers. In the Middle Ages a *road* or *way* was merely a direction in which people rode or went, the name *street* being reserved for the made road. Cf. hist. of *route*. The form of the Ger. word (-*sz*- for L. -*t*-) points to very early adoption. The *man in the street* is described by Greville (1831) as a Newmarket expression, but currency and mod. sense are due to Emerson.

strength. AS. *strengthu*, from *strong*; cf. *length*. *On the strength of* meant orig. fortified by (cf. 1 *Kings*, xix. 8).

strenuous. From L. *strenuus*; cogn. with G. στρηνής, strong.

Not the doctrine of ignoble ease, but the doctrine of the strenuous life (Roosevelt, 1899).

Strephon. Lover. From Sidney's *Arcadia*.

strepitous. From L. *strepitus*, noise.

strepto- [*biol.*]. From G. στρεπτός, twisted, from στρέφειν, to turn.

stress. OF. *estrecier*, VL. *strictiare, from *strictus*, p.p. of *stringere*, to clutch, compress, etc. Cf. *distress*, of which *stress* is usu. an aphet. form (cf. *sport, stain*, etc.), as in *stress of weather* (*circumstances*). To *lay stress on* was orig. to put strain, burden, on; hence, rely on, emphasize.

stretch. AS. *streccan*, prob. from *strec*, strong, rigorous. WGer.; cf. Du. *strekken*, Ger. *strecken*; ? ult. cogn. with *stark*. With to *stretch a point* cf. *strain*. With *stretch of country* (*water*) cf. similar use of *reach*. See also *distraught, straight*.

strew. AS. *strewian*, cogn. with *straw* (q.v.). Com. Teut.; cf. Du. *strooien*, Ger. *streuen*, ON. *strā*, Goth. *straujan*; cogn. with L. *sternere, str-*, G. στορέσαι, Sanskrit *str̥*. Orig. weak, *strewn, strown* being of later formation. For orig. sense cf. F. *joncher*, to strew, *jonc*, rush, reed.

stria [*scient.*]. Stripe, line. L., groove or ridge. Hence *striated*.

stricken [*archaic*]. See *strike*.

strict. L. *strictus*, p.p. of *stringere*, to tighten, constrain, etc., cogn. with G. **στράγγειν.* For senses cf. *rigid.* Hence *stricture* (med.).

stricture. Criticism. From L. *stringere*, *strict-*, to scrape, touch lightly (see *strigil*). Orig. sense of incidental comment has changed by association with the unrelated *stringere*, to tighten, etc. (v.s.).

stride. AS. *strīde*, pace, measure, whence verb *strīdan.* App. cogn. with Du. *strijd*, Ger. *streit*, ON. *strith*, all in sense of struggle, contention, trouble. From this sense, unrecorded in AS. for *stride*, but recorded for *strith*, may have developed that of striving forward, advancing. Cf. sense-development of E. *travel* and that of L. *contendere*, to strive, contend, also "to go towarde a place" (Coop.). *Striding* still suggests vigour and determination. LG. *striden* has the same double sense. *In one's stride*, i.e. without change of gait, is orig. from the hunting-field.

strident. From pres. part. of L. *stridere*, to creak. Cf. *stridulent, stridulous.*

strife, strive. OF. *estrif, estriver*, in which the *-f-, -v-*, is perh. for an orig. *-th-.* Of Teut. origin; cf. Ger. *streiten*, to contest, strive, and see *stride.* The verb should be weak (*strived*), but has been assimilated to *drive.*

strigil. Skin-scraper. L. *strigilis*, horse-comb, from *stringere* (see *stricture*). Cf. F. *étrille*, horse-comb.

strigose [*biol.*]. From L. *striga*, "a rew of things layed in length" (Coop.).

strike. AS. *strīcan* (trans.), to wipe, (intrans.), to go, move. WGer.; cf. Du. *strijken*, to smooth, stretch out, Ger. *streichen*, to stroke, stretch out, also to lash; cogn. with ON. *strjūka*, to stroke, rub, wipe; cf. also Goth. *striks*, stroke (of pen); ult. cogn. with *streak.* For sense-development cf. that of *smite* (q.v.) and double sense of cogn. *stroke.* Earlier sense of making smooth, level, appears in *strike* (levelled measure) *of corn*, also in to *strike sail* (*one's colours*), and (18 cent.) in to *strike* (*tools*), with which cf. Ger. *die waffen streichen*, to lay down one's arms. Mod. to *down tools* keeps the same figure. Sense of moving forward survives in *stricken* (far advanced) *in years*, also in to *strike for*, go towards (cf. Ger. *landstreicher*, tramp). *Stricken field* is one of Scott's revivals, from obs. Sc. to *strike a battle* (Barbour).

string. AS. *streng.* Com. Teut.; cf. Du.

streng, Ger. *strang*, ON. *strengr*; cogn. with *strangle* (q.v.) and L. *stringere*, to wring, tighten, etc. *First* (*second*) *string* is allusive to *two strings to one's bow.* Some fig. senses now felt as mus., e.g. *highly strung*, *strung up to*, were perh. also orig. from archery. The verb, orig. weak, has been influenced by *sing*, etc. With to *pull the strings* cf. *wire-pulling.*

> Hee had so plotted the voyage that still hee would have a string left in store for his bow
> (*Purch.* xvi. 83).

stringent. From pres. part. of L. *stringere*, to tighten, etc. Cf. *strict.*

string-halt [*vet.*]. Dry spavin (*Gent. Dict.* 1705). App. from *string* in sense of sinew. Found in early 16 cent., *spring-halt* (*Hen. VIII*, i. 3) being app. due to folk-etym.

strip[1]. To denude. AS. *strīpan*, in *bestrīpan*, to plunder. WGer.; cf. Du. *stroopen*, "to flea (flay), to skin, or to pill" (Hexham), Ger. *streifen.* Hence noun *strip*, section peeled off, with which cf. Ger. *streif*, *streifen*, "a stripe or streak" (Ludw.). But the exact relation of the verb and noun, as well as their connection with *stripe*, is obscure.

strip[2] [*obs.*]. To move swiftly (ME.), later to outstrip. Of obscure origin, but app. cogn. with *strip*[1], *stripe*; cf. Ger. *streifen*, to rove, wander, etc., app. with ground-idea of lines of movement in various directions. Now only in *outstrip.*

> Before he reacht it, he was out of breath,
> And then the other stript him
> (*Beaumont & Fletcher*).

stripe. Of Du. or LG. origin and cogn. with *strip*; cf. Du. *streep*, earlier *strijpe*, LG. *stripe.* In ME. of the mark of a blow, hence for the blow itself. See *strip*[1].

> *strypynge or scorgynge with a baleys* [rod]: vibex
> (*Prompt. Parv.*).

stripling. From noun *strip* in sense of something elongated and slender, though this is recorded much later. Occurs as surname in 13 cent. (*Pat. Rolls*). Cf. *thread-paper*, used of a long, thin person.

strive. See *strife.*

strob- [*biol.*]. From G. στροβεῖν, to whirl round.

stroke. First as verb. AS. *strācian*, cogn. with *strīcan*, *strāc*, to strike. For double sense of smooth, caressing action and of blow (e.g. *on the stroke of twelve*) cf. *strike*, *smite.* In quot. below both senses occur

Sense of mark arises from that of movement (*stroke of the pen*).

> And what man that is wounded with the strook [of the sword]
> Shal never be hool, til that yow list of grace
> To stroke hym with the plat [flat] in thilke place
> Ther he is hurt (Chauc. F. 160).

> The oars were silver,
> Which to the tune of flutes kept stroke
>   (*Ant. & Cleop.* ii. 2).

stroll. Earlier *strowl, stroil.* A cant word introduced from continent c. 1600, hence prob. of Ger. origin. Cf. Ger. *strolch,* vagabond, from Swiss-Ger. *strolchen,* also *strollen.*

stroma-. From G. στρῶμα, anything spread, from στρωννύναι, to spread.

stromb-. From G. στρόμβος, spiral.

strong. AS. *strang.* Com. Teut.; cf. Du. Ger. *streng,* strict, stern, ON. *strangr;* ult. cogn. with *string.* Orig. compared *strenger, strengest* (cf. *old, elder, eldest*). *Going strong* is from racing. For *stronghold* see *hold*[1]. *Strong-minded* (18 cent.) is app. due to misinterpretation of F. *esprit fort,* free-thinker.

strontium [*chem.*]. Named (18 cent.) from *Strontian,* Argyll, where found.

strop. Older form of *strap.* AS. *strop,* with Du. & Ger. cognates. WGer. loan from L. *struppus,* garland, fillet, thong. Cf. OF. *estrope,* perh. immediate source of ME. word.

strophe. G., from στρέφειν, to turn. Orig. of movement of chorus, hence applied to lines sung during movement.

strow. Archaic var. of *strew* (q.v.).

structure. F., L. *structura,* from *struere, struct-,* to build.

struggle. ME. *strogelen,* in Chauc. (E. 2374). Of obscure origin. Palsg. (p. 707) has *scruggell.* Perh. largely suggested by *strong, strife,* and obs. *tuggle,* from *tug. Struggle for life* (Darwin) has been adopted into many Europ. langs., e.g. F. *struggle-for-lifeur* (Daudet, 1889), man determined to get on.

Struldbrug. Mortal condemned to immortality. Coined by Swift (*Gulliver's Travels*).

strum. Imit.; cf. earlier *thrum, drum.*

strumous [*med.*]. From L. *struma,* tumour; cogn. with *strues,* heap, *struere,* to build.

strumpet. ME. *strompet* (*Piers Plowm.,* Chauc.). Origin unknown. Gregory's *Chronicle* (c. 1450) has *streppett* in same sense.

strut[1]. Verb. ME. *strouten,* AS. *strūtian,* to stick out stiffly; cf. Dan. *strutte,* Ger. *strotzen,* to swagger, look big; cogn. with AS. *thrūtung,* anger, arrogance, and ult. with *throat* (q.v.) (cf. F. *se rengorger,* to "bridle," from *gorge,* throat). Thus *strut* referred orig. rather to the air or attitude than to the gait, current sense appearing in Anglo-Ir. of 16 cent.

sie strotzet einher: she struts it. *ein strotzender weiberrock*: a strutting, or flaunting, petti-coat (Ludw.).

strut[2]. Timber support. App. from *strut*[1]; but it corresponds in sense with Du. *stut,* "a prop, support, stay" (Sewel), Ger. *stütze,* "a stay, prop, support" (Ludw.), which are cogn. with ON. *stythja,* to support, AS. *studu,* post, buttress. Cf. also Ger. *stutzen,* "to strut" (Ludw.), whence *stutzer,* a fop, masher, which only add to the puzzle.

struthious [*zool.*]. Of the ostrich (q.v.), L. *struthio.*

strychnine. From G. στρύχνος, night-shade.

stub. AS. *stubb* (also *stybb*); cf. LG. *stubbe,* ON. *stubbi;* cogn. with L. *stipes,* G. στύπος.

stubble. OF. *estouble* (*étouble, éteule*), VL. **stupila,* for *stipula,* "stubble, or straw left in the fielde after corne is reaped" (Coop.); cf. It. *stoppia,* also Ger. (orig. LG.) *stoppel,* from L. With *stubble goose,* fed on the stubble, cf. *green goose,* ? *wayzgoose.*

> For of thy percely yet they fare the wors,
> That they han eten with thy stubbel goos
>   (Chauc. A. 4350).

stubborn. ME. *stoburn, stiborn,* app. from *stub,* but of obscure formation. Cf. Ger. *störrig,* stubborn, from *storren,* tree-stump, stub. The *-n* is prob. excrescent. Orig. sense was often stronger, e.g. ruthless, implacable, etc.

> Plain matters of fact are terrible stubborn things
>   (Budgell, 1732).

stucco. It., OHG. *stucchi,* crust, coating, usu. piece, whence Ger. *stück,* piece; cf. Du. *stuk,* AS. *stycce,* ON. *stykke,* all in sense of piece; cogn. with *stock.*

stud[1]. Nail, etc. AS. *studu,* post, support (for cognates see *strut*[2]). App. this was applied later to any kind of strengthening device such as a rivet, large-headed nail, and finally support for collar. Hence *studded with,* as though sprinkled with nails with conspicuous heads.

stud[2]. Of horses. AS. *stōd;* cf. OHG. *stuot* (whence Ger. *stute,* mare, *gestüte,* stud), ON. *stōth;* cogn. with *steed* and with ME.

stot, nag, cob (Chauc. A. 615). Orig. sense is herd, and the word is cogn. with AS. *stōd*, place (in place-names), and with *stand*. Ger. *Stuttgart* means herd-yard.

studding-sail. Earliest is Sc. *stoytene-sale* (v.i.), ? from Du. *stooten*, to push, urge, etc., or LG. *stöten*, cogn. with Ger. *stossen*. The regular ME. term was *bonnet* (found in most Europ. langs. in same sense). OF. (Wace, 12 cent.) has *estouin, estouinc*, and it seems possible that naut. *stunsel* may represent a dim. of this and that *studding-sail* is a meaningless elaboration. The OF. word survives, corrupted, in *bonnette en étui*, "studding-sail" (Falconer).

For mair speid the galliasse pat furtht hir stoytene salis (*Complaynt of Scotlande*, 1549).

student. From pres. part. of L. *studēre*, to be zealous, from *studium*, eager attention, study, whence OF. *estudie* (*étude*) and E. *study*. With use of latter for room (from c. 1300) cf. F. *étude*, lawyer's chambers, It. *studio*, "a studie, or place to studie in" (Flor.), not recorded in E. till 1819. Orig. sense persists in *studied* (*insult, careless-ness*, etc.). ME. *studiant* represents OF. *estudiant* (*étudiant*).

stuff. OF. *estoffe* (*étoffe*), L. *stuppa, stupa*, tow, G. στύπη. For wide senses cf. those of *matter*. F. *étouper*, to stop with tow, *étouffer*, to choke, stifle, are of kindred origin. Orig. sense persists in to *stuff*, upholster (cf. F. *étoffer*), to *stuff up*, while *stuffy* corresponds to F. *étouffer*. Cf. It. *stoppa*, tow, *stoffa*, stuff, Sp. *estopa*, tow, *estofa*, padded fabric; also Du. *stof*, Ger. *stoff*, from OF. The remarkable sense-development of the noun (*that's the stuff to give 'em*) is very similar to that of Ger. *zeug*, orig. equipment, but now used of anything. *Sterner stuff* is after *Jul. Caes.* iii. 2. *Stuffy*, bad-tempered, is US. (18 cent.). Cf. *stop*.

The gap that has been caused by the defection of Russia has been filled by the much sterner stuff we have received from America
(General Smuts, July 24, 1918).

stuggy [*dial.*]. Var. of *stocky*, stumpy and strong. See *stock*.

Like enough we could meet them, man for man, and show them what a cross-buttock means, because we are so stuggy (*Lorna Doone*, ch. v.).

stultify. From L. *stultus*, foolish.

stum. Unfermented grape-juice. Du. *stom*, lit. dumb; cf. Ger. *stumm*, dumb; orig. checked in speech; cogn. with *stammer*

and *stem²*. Ground-sense of checking, arresting, appears in Ger. *ungestüm*, impetuous, reckless.

stumble. ME. *stomelen*, cogn. with above. *Stumbling-block* was coined by Tynd. to render *Vulg. offendiculum* (G. πρόσκομμα) and used by later translators for *Vulg. scandalum*.

Sed hoc judicate magis, ne ponatis offendiculum fratri, vel scandalum (*Rom.* xiv. 13).

stump¹. Of tree, etc. From 14 cent. Cf. Du. *stomp*, Ger. *stumpf*, ON. *stumpr* (? from LG.). Orig. sense, what is left of amputated limb, felled tree, appears in Ger. *stummel*, whence *verstümmeln*, to mutilate. *Stump speech*, to *stump the country* are US., a tree-stump being the natural perch of the orator in country regions. To *be stumped*, at a loss, was orig. US., perh. in ref. to ploughing newly cleared land. With to *stump up* ? cf. to *plank down*, ? or to *fork out*.

stump². For drawing. F. *estompe*, from *estomper*, app. Du. *stompen*, to blunt (v.s.).

stun. ME. *stunien, stonien*, OF. *estoner* (*étonner*), to astonish (q.v.); cf. Ger. *staunen*, to amaze, from Swiss F. F. *étonner*, VL. **ex-tonare*, to thunder-strike, had stronger sense up to 17 cent. With intens. *stunning* cf. *ripping*, and synon. F. *épatant*, from *épater*, to flop, flatten. See also *torpedo*.

Fouke, santz plus dire, leva le grand potence [crutch], si fery sire Gyrard desouth l'oryle, qu'il chay [fell] tot estonee à terre
— (*Foulques Fitz Warin*)

Stundist. Russian sect (1861). From Ger. *stunde*, hour, lesson, the movement originating among Ger. colonists. Cf. AS. *stund*, point of time, Du. *stond*, hour, time, ON. *stund*, period; prob. cogn. with *stand*.

stunt¹. To check growth. Cf. AS. *stunt*, dull, stupid, but mod. sense rather from cogn. ON. *stuttr*, short. See *stint*.

stunt². Feat, performance, etc. US., orig. college athletic slang (late 19 cent.), ? from Ger. *stunde* or Du. *stond* in sense of lesson (see *Stundist*); but *stump* was used earlier in a similar sense.

It's the army side of the efficiency stunt
(H. G. Wells, *Britling*)

Poets are a flying corps....In prose the "stunting" genius is less indispensable
(J. S. Phillimore, 1918).

stupe¹ [*med.*]. Surgical dressing. L. *stupa, stuppa*, tow. Cf. *stupeous* (entom.).

stupe[2] [*dial.*]. Back-formation from *stupid*.

stupid. L. *stupidus*, from *stupēre*, "to be astonied or amased" (Coop.). Orig. sense appears in *stupor*, *stupefy* (F. *stupéfier*), and *stupendous*, from L. *stupendus*. *Stupendous* occurs on nearly every page of Evelyn's foreign diary.

sturdy[1]. Adj. OF. *estordi* (*étourdi*), reckless, bewildered, heedless, etc. Mod. sense via that of *contumax* (*Prompt. Parv.*). For curious sense-development of adjs. that can be applied to persons cf. *nice*, *quaint*, *stout*, etc. Cf. It. *stordire*, "to astonish, to become or make giddie, dull or dizie in the head" (Flor.), OSp. *estordir*. The sense (F. *étourdi* = stunned) points to an origin like that of *stun* (q.v.). VL. *exturbiditus* has been suggested, also L. *turdus*, thrush, OF. *estordir* being used esp. of effect of alcohol (see quot. s.v. *amethyst*); cf. *soûl comme une grive*, drunk as a thrush.

sturdy[2]. Vertigo in sheep. OF. *estordie* (v.s.).

sturgeon. F. *esturgeon*, MedL. *sturio-n-*, OHG. *sturio* (*stör*), whence also It. *storione*, Sp. *esturión*. WGer.; cf. AS. *styria*, Du. *steur*. App. the "stirrer," disturber.

stutter. Frequent. of obs. *stut*; cf. Du. *stuiten*, to rebound, Ger. *stutzen*, to stop short, hesitate; cogn. with Ger. *stossen*, to collide, strike against, which is Com. Teut.; cf. ON. *stauta*, Goth. *stautan*; ult. cogn. with L. *-tud-*, in *tundere*, *tutud-*, to strike. Cf. also Du. *stutteren*, Ger. *stottern*, frequent. forms.

My dull, stutting, frozen eloquence (Sylv. i. 7).

sty[1]. For pigs. AS. *stig* (see *steward*). In other Teut. langs. in wider sense (pen, etc. for pigs, cattle, fowls, geese, etc.); cf. ON. *stia*, OHG. *stīge*, still in *hühnersteige*, fowl-house; also It. *stia*, "a cage, a pen, a frank or coope for poultrie" (Flor.), from Teut. Thought to belong to a Teut. word for score, twenty, which appears in Ger. *stiege* (dial. also *steig*), with which cf. Crimean Goth. *stega*, twenty (16 cent.). Others connect it with AS. *stīgan*, to ascend, which assumes fowl-house to be orig. sense. In this case the sense of twenty may have come from normal number of steps of ladder to roost (cf. hist. of *score*), Ger. *stiege* having also the spec. sense of ladder, narrow stair.

sty[2]. On eye. AS. *stīgend*, whence obs. *styan*; cf. Norw. *sti*, LG. *stige*, archaic Du. *styghe*, "hordeolum" (Kil.). App. from *stīgan*, to rise, with idea of swelling. From *styan* was formed dial. *styany* (*styan-eye*), which, being interpreted as *sty-on-eye*, gave the current back-formation.

hordeolum: a little swelling in the eye-lids, like a barley-corn; a stian or stithe (Litt.).

Stygian. See *Styx*.

style[1]. In writing, etc. Incorr. for earlier *stile*, OF. (*style*), L. *stilus*, incorr. *stylus*, "an instrument to write in tables" (Coop.), also fig., "a style; a maner or forme of wordes in speakyng; an elegant form or order in speakyng or writyng; the facion and maner of ones pennyng" (*ib.*). Cf. *stiletto*. In some current senses (whence *stylish*) an adj. (e.g. *good*) is understood (cf. *fashion*, *quality*, *rank*). The once common sense of description, title (*under the style of*), now survives chiefly in the verb, esp. the p.p. *styled*. *Stylize*, to conventionalize (art), is from Ger. *stilisieren*.

style[2] [*bot.* & *dialling*]. G. στῦλος, pillar. Cf. *stylite*, ascetic residing on a pillar.

style[3]. See *stile*.

stylet. See *stiletto*.

stylo-. See *style*[1, 2].

stylobate [*arch.*]. F., L., G. στυλοβατής, from στῦλος, pillar, βαίνειν, βατ-, to progress.

stylus. See *style*[1].

stymie [*golf*]. Earlier in sense of person partially blind, from dial. *styme*, in *not to see a styme* (13 cent. E.). Golf sense app. from inflicting a kind of blind shot on adversary.

styptic [*med.*]. F. *styptique*, from G. στύφειν, to contract, astringe.

styrax. Tree. G. στύραξ. Cf. *storax*.

Styx. G. Στύξ, Στυγ-, cogn. with στύγος, hatred.

suasion. L. *suasio-n-*, from *suadēre*, to persuade, ? cogn. with *suavis*. Chiefly in *moral suasion* (17 cent.).

suave. F., L. *suavis*, cogn. with *sweet*. For degeneration of sense cf. *bland*.

sub. Short for many compds. of *sub-*, e.g. *subaltern*, *subscription*, *substitute*, *subsist-money* (advance wages).

Alderman. "Then you have 19*s*. a week left."—Applicant. "Ah, but the wife subs off me, you know" (*Daily Chron.* Apr. 24, 1918).

sub. L., under. In *sub judice*, *sub poena*, *sub rosa* (see *rose*), etc.

sub-. L. (v.s.), cogn. with G. ὑπό (cf. *supposition*, *hypothesis*, *subcutaneous*, *hypodermic*), becoming also, by assim., *suc-*, *suf-*, *sug-*, *sup-*, *sur-*, *su-*. F. *sou(s)-* is for OF. *souz-*, *soz-*, L. *subtus*, which as prefix replaced *sub-* in VL. In some cases (*subdeacon, subdean*) the mod. E. word is restored from F. forms in *sous-*.

subadar [*Anglo-Ind.*]. Native officer of sepoys. Earlier, governor of province. Urdu, from *çūbah*, province (Arab.), and *-dar* from Pers. Cf. *sirdar*, etc.

subaltern. Orig. adj., subordinate. Late L. *subalternus*, succeeding in turn (see *sub-*, *alternate*). Mil. sense from 17 cent.

subaudition [*gram.*]. Implication, supplying mentally. App. adopted by Horne Tooke from synon. L. *subauditio-n-*.

subclavian [*anat.*]. See *clavicle*.

subconscious. App. coined by De Quincey.

subdolous. From L. *subdolus*, from *dolus*, cunning. *Subdolent* (v.i.) is a nonce-word.

With another professional glance, subdolent but correct (Q. *Foe-Farrell*).

subduce, subduct. To withdraw, remove. L. *subducere, subduct-*, from *ducere*, to lead.

subdue. ME. *sodue* (see *sub-*), OF. *souduire*, L. *subducere* (v.s.), app. confused in AF. with L. *subdere*, to subdue, from *dare*, ? or with *subjugare*. *Subdued* in fig. sense is perh. due to Coleridge.

subfusc. L. *subfuscus* (*suffuscus*), from *fuscus*, grey, dusky.

subjacent. From pres. part. of L. *subjacēre*, to lie below. Cf. *adjacent*.

subject. Restored spelling of ME. *soget*, *suget*, F. *sujet*, L. *subjectus*, p.p. of *subicere*, to subject, from *jacere*, to throw. Some senses direct from L. *subjectum*, rendering Aristotle's τὸ ὑποκείμενον, as philos. & gram. term. Cf. *object*, with which it is often synon., though usu. contrasted. With senses of verb cf. *submit*. Current sense of *subjective, objective*, is largely due to Kant. *Subject matter*, earlier (14 cent.) *matter subject*, is MedL. *subjecta materia*; cf. G. ὑποκειμένη ὕλη (Aristotle).

subjugate. From L. *subjugare*, from *jugum*, yoke.

subjunctive. L. *subjunctivus* (*modus*), mood of "subjoined" clauses, rendering G. ὑποτακτικός.

sublime. F., L. *sublimis*, lofty, perh. from *limen* in sense of lintel. Chem. use of verb (L. *sublimare*), orig. of raising into vapour to be later precipitated, is much older (Chauc. G. 774). For *Sublime Porte* see *Porte*.

Le magnifique et le ridicule sont si voisins qu'ils se touchent (Fontenelle, 1683).

Du sublime au ridicule il n'y a qu'un pas
(Napoleon I).

submarine. Coined from *marine*, on *subterranean*. Cf. F. *soumarin*, Ger. *untersee-*. Verb to *submarine* dates from 1914. Quot. 1 is from a project by the virtual founder of the Royal Society, which orig. met informally at Wadham Coll. Oxf., where Wilkins was Warden.

Concerning the possibility of framing an ark for submarine navigations (John Wilkins, 1647).

He saw the sliding submarine
  Wrest the green trident from the hold
Of her whose craven tradesmen lean
  On yellow men and yellow gold
        (G. S. Viereck, New York, 1915).

submerge. L. *submergere*, from *mergere*, to plunge. Intrans. use, described by *NED.* as rare, is now common in connection with submarines. *Submerged tenth* is app. due to General Booth (*In Darkest England*, 1890).

A German named Flack has invented a submersible vessel (*Pall Mall Gaz.* 1866).

submit. L. *submittere*, to send (put) under. Intrans. sense springs from reflex. (*Eph.* v. 22); cf. F. *soumettre*, to subdue, *se soumettre*, to be submissive. Orig. trans. sense in to *submit* (an argument, project, etc.).

subordinate. From Late L. *subordinare*, from *ordinare*, to ordain. *Insubordination*, from F., is first recorded in Burke (*French Revolution*).

suborn. L. *subornare*, orig. to equip, etc., from *ornare*, to adorn. Only secondary sense of priming a (false) witness has passed into E.

subpoena. L. *sub poena*, under penalty, init. words of writ commanding presence.

As for the supena, the writ is not retorned in
        (*Plumpton Let.* c. 1475).

subreption [*leg.*]. Concealment of facts. L. *subreptio-n-*, from *subripere*, from *rapere*, to snatch.

subrogate [*leg.*]. To substitute. See *surrogate*.

sub rosa. App. a Renaissance coinage. See *rose*.

Entrust it under solemn vows
Of *Mum*, and *Silence*, and the Rose
        (*Hudibras*, III. ii. 1493).

subscribe. L. *subscribere*, to write under, put down one's name (for). Hence *subscription*.

I made a gathring for the Indians. I gave 5 l....
and yʳ was underwritt more 32 l.
        (Josselin's *Diary*, 1651).

subsequent. F. *subséquent*, from pres. part. of L. *subsequi*, to follow under.

subservient. From pres. part. of L. *subservire*,

to help, be instrumental. For degeneration of sense cf. *officious*.

subside. L. *subsidere*, from *sidere*, to settle, sit down, cogn. with *sedēre*, to sit.

subsidy. AF. *subsidie*, L. *subsidium*, help, lit. sitting under (v.s.); cf. F. *subside*, It. *sussidio*, Sp. *subsidio*. Hence *subsidiary*, *subsidize*.

subsist. L. *subsistere*, to stand firm, support, lit. stand under, from *sistere*, to stand. Hence *subsistence* (usu. with *means*), in sense of *sustenance*.

substance. F., L. *substantia*, from *substare*, to be present, lit. stand under; used to render G. οὐσία, lit. being. Hence *substantial*, *substantive*, in gram. sense (*Piers Plowm.*), for Late L. (*nomen*) *substantivum*, self-existing, as opposed to adjective.

Ibi dissipavit substantiam [G. οὐσίαν] suam vivendo luxuriose (*Vulg. Luke*, xv. 13).

substitute. From L. *substituere*, *substitut-*, to appoint under, from *statuere*, to appoint, set up.

subsultory. Of earthquakes. From L. *subsilire*, *subsult-*, to take sudden leaps, from *salire*, to leap.

subsume [*log.*]. ModL. *subsumere*, after *assume*, *presume*.

subtend. L. *subtendere*, to stretch under. Cf. *hypotenuse*.

subter-. L., under, from *sub*, as *inter* from *in*.

subterfuge. L. *subterfugium*, from *subterfugere*, to flee under.

subterranean. From L. *subterraneus*, from *sub* and *terra*, ground. Cf. *mediterranean*.

subtle. Restored spelling of ME. *sotil*, *sutel*, OF. *soutil* (*subtil*), L. *subtilis*, for **subtexlis*, from *texere*, to weave (cf. *finespun*, *-drawn*); cf. It. *sottile*, Sp. *sutil*. Earlier also *subtile*, direct from L., whence techn. words in *subtil-*, with gen. sense of attenuation.

subtract. From L. *subtrahere*, *subtract-*, to draw away, from *trahere*. Infantile *substract* was once literary. It is due partly to *abstract*, partly to F. *soustraire*, VL. **substustrahere* (see *sub-*).

If like proportionals be substracted from like proportionals (Barrow).

subulate [*biol.*]. From L. *subula*, awl.

suburb. OF. *suburbe*, L. *suburbium*, from *sub* and *urbs*, city. Cf. *suburbicarian* (eccl.), of parishes round Rome. *Suburban*, in disparaging sense, due to Byron (*Beppo*), is in curious contrast with 17 cent. *suburbian*, riotous, disorderly.

subvention. F., Late L. *subventio-n-*, from *subvenire*, to help, lit. to come under. Cf. *subsidy*.

subvert. L. *subvertere*, to overthrow, lit. turn from under.

subway. Hybrid coinage (19 cent.).

succade [*archaic*]. Candied fruit, etc. Also *succate*, *sucket*. Very common as early trade-word. Cf. OF. *succade*, MedL. *succatum*, from L. *sucus*, sap. This word has perh. contributed to dial. *sucker*, lollipop.

succedaneum. L., neut. of *succedaneus*, succeeding, acting as substitute.

succeed. F. *succéder*, to follow after, L. *succedere*, from *sub* and *cedere*, to move. Later sense of accomplishing aim (also found in archaic F.) is due to ellipsis of adv. Cf. *success*, F. *succès*, now only in sense of *bon succès*. So also Ger. *erfolg*, success, from *folgen*, to follow. *Succession* has kept etym. sense, as in *apostolical succession* (19 cent.), *succession of crops* (18 cent.); also *successive*.

The voyage of Master Benjamin Wood into the East Indies and the miserable disastrous successe thereof (Purch.).

Nothing succeeds like success (Helps).

succentor. Precentor's deputy. Late L., from *succinere*, to accompany, from *sub* and *canere*, to sing.

succès d'estime. F., favourable reception of play, etc. due to high repute of author.

succinct. Lit. girded up. L., p.p. of *succingere*, from *sub* and *cingere*, to gird.

succory. Altered, on Du. *suikerei*, from *sycory*, early var. of *chicory* (q.v.).

succotash. Mess of vegetables. NAmer. Ind. (Narragansett) *msiquatash*.

succour. Verb is OF. *socorre*, *socorir* (*secourir*), L. *succurrere*, lit. to run under, from *sub* and *currere* (cf. *subsidy*, *subvention*). Noun is back-formation from ME. *socors*, *succors*, felt as pl., OF. *socors* (*secours*), MedL. *succursus*. There was perh. also a tendency to make noun and verb uniform, as in vulg. to *summons*, which shows opposite working of analogy.

succubus. Altered, after *incubus* (q.v.), from Late L. *succuba*, strumpet, and applied to fiend in female form having intercourse with men.

That fend that gooth a nygt,
Wommen wel ofte to begile,
Incubus hatte [is called] be rygt;
And gileth men other while,
Succubus is that wight (Trev. i. 419).

succulent. L. *succulentus*, from *sucus*, sap.

succumb. L. *succumbere*, from *sub* and *-cumbere*, to lie. Till 19 cent. regarded as Sc.

Succomb is used by Foote, in his farce of the Knights, but has always been accounted as peculiarly Scottish (Sinclair, 1782).

succursal. F. *succursale* (sc. *église*), from MedL. *succursus*, succour. In F. & E. also of branch business.

such. AS. *swilc*, *swylc*, compd. of *so* (q.v.) and *like*, so that *suchlike* is pleon.; cf. Du. *zulk* (earlier *sulic*), Ger. *solch* (OHG. *solih*), ON. *slīkr*, Goth. *swaleiks*. For loss of -*l*- cf. *which*.

suck. AS. *sūcan*, also *sūgan*; latter form is cogn. with Du. *zuigen*, Ger. *saugen*, ON. *sūga*; also with L. *sugere*, OIr. *súgim*, and ult. with *soak*. *Suckle* is back-formation from *suckling* (cf. Du. *zuigeling*, Ger. *säugling*), which is older than dict. records (*Prompt. Parv.*), since it was a surname in 13 cent. *Sucking dove* is allusive to *Mids. N. Dream* (i. 2).

suction. L. *suctio-n-*, from *sugere*, *suct-*, to suck.

sud. See *suds*.

Sudan. See *Soudanese*.

sudarium. Cloth with which St Veronica wiped the face of Christ on the way to Calvary. L., from *sudor*, sweat. Cf. *sudatory*, *sudorific*.

sudd. Vegetable obstruction in White Nile. Arab., from *sadda*, to obstruct.

sudden. F. *soudain*, VL. **subitanus*, for *subitaneus*, from *subire*, to go stealthily. Spelt *sodain* up to 17 cent. (cf. *sullen*).

subito: sodeinly, upon a sodayne (Coop.).

sudorific. See *sudarium*.

suds. Orig. (16 cent.) dregs, esp. (in EAngl.) ooze left by flood; cf. archaic Du. *sudde*, "palus, lacus" (Kil.), Ger. *sud* (*oder sod*), "a sud, a seething" (Ludw.), *seifensod*, "soap-sud" (*ib.*), from *sieden*, to boil, seethe (q.v.).

sue. AF. *suer*, from tonic stem *su-* of OF. *sivre* (*suivre*), VL. **sequere*, for *sequi*, to follow. Orig. to follow in gen. sense, also used for *ensue*, *pursue*, for which it is sometimes aphet. See *suit*.

Seke he pees and parfijtly sue it (Wyc. 1 *Pet.* iii. 11).

To pursue for your pardon (*Plumpton Let.* 1461).

suède. F., in *gants de Suède*, Swedish gloves.

suet. Dim. of AF. *sue*, *seu*, OF. *sieu* (*suif*), L. *sebum*, tallow, etc., whence It. *sevo*,

"tallow, fat, sewet or grease to make candles" (Flor.), Sp. *sebo*.

suffect [*Roman hist.*]. Additional consul. L. *suffectus*, from *sufficere*, to substitute.

suffer. F. *souffrir*, VL. **sufferire*, for *sufferre*, from *sub* and *ferre*, to bear. *Sufferance*, earlier *suffrance*, F. *souffrance*, is respelt on the verb.

suffete [*hist.*]. Magistrate of Carthage. L. *suffes*, *suffet-*, of Phoenician origin; cf. Heb. *shōphēt*, judge.

suffice. F. *suffire*, *suffis-*, L. *sufficere*, from *sub* and *facere*, to make. Hence *sufficient*, much used by the uneducated for *enough*. *Suffice it to say* is one of our few surviving subjunctives.

Schewe to us the fadir, and it suffisith to us (Wyc. *John*, xiv. 8).

suffix. From L. *suffigere*, *suffix-*, to fix under.

suffocate. From L. *suffocare*, from *sub* and *fauces* (pl.), throat. Cf. *throttle*.

suffragan. OF. (*suffragant*), MedL. *suffraganeus*, bishop liable to be summoned by his metropolitan to give his "suffrage" at synods. Current sense from temp. Hen. VIII.

suffrage. F., L. *suffragium*, vote, ? from *fragor*, uproar, cogn. with *frangere*, to break. Hence *suffragette* (1906), app. coined on *midinette*, Parisian shop-girl who goes out to lunch at noon, a word rather in evidence at the time. Cf. *munitionette* (*Nottingham Ev. Post*, June 4, 1918).

suffuse. From L. *suffundere*, *suffus-*, from *sub* and *fundere*, to pour.

sufi. Mohammedan mystic, "often erron. associated with *sophy*" (*NED*.). Arab. *çūfī*, lit. man of wool, *çūf*.

sugar. Ult. Arab. *sukkar*, cogn. with G. σάκχαρ (cf. *saccharine*), Pers. *shakar* (cf. *jaggery*), Sanskrit *ṣarkarā*, orig. pebble, grit. In all Europ. langs., Sp. *azúcar*, Port. *assucar* retaining Arab. def. art. (cf. *assagai*).

suggest. From L. *suggerere*, *suggest-*, from *sub* and *gerere*, to bear. Earlier is *suggestion* (Chauc.), from F., usu. with implication of evil prompting. Cf. mod. use of *suggestive* as euph. for prurient.

suicide. From 17 cent., "the slaying or murdering of himself; self-murder" (Blount). ModL. *suicidium*, barbarously formed on *homicidium*, etc.; cf. F. *suicide*, It. Sp. *suicidio*. Prob. an E. coinage, which "may as well seem to participate of *sus*, a sow, as of the pronoun *sui*" (Phillips). Replaced earlier *self-murder*, with which cf. Ger. *selbstmord*.

suit. AF. *siute*, OF. *sieute* (*suite*), VL. **se-quita*, following, series, from **sequere*, to follow (see *sue*). Cf. MedL. *secta* and see *set*[2]. Leg. senses, whence fig. that of wooing (*suitor*), go with *sue*. To the dress sense, complete "set" of armour, garments, belongs chief current use of the verb, to harmonize, as in archaic to *suit with*.

> En cele temps [1321] multz des gentz de mesters en Loundres furent vestuz de suite [i.e. adopted livery] (*Fr. Chron. of Lond.*).

> What? I love, I sue, I seek a wife
> (*Love's Lab. Lost*, iii. 1).

suite. Later adoption of F. *suite* (v.s.) in spec. senses in which *suit* was used up to 17–18 cents.; cf. to *follow suit*, *long suit*.

sulcated [*biol.*]. From L. *sulcatus*, from *sulcus*, groove, furrow.

sulky. From 18 cent., orig. in sense of keeping aloof, whence name of vehicle for one person only (US. 1756), with which cf. synon. F. *désobligeant* and the contrasted *sociable* (tricycle). Origin unknown. ? From obs. *sulk*, furrow, L. *sulcus*, with suggestion of "lonely furrow" (cf. *groovy*).

sullen. Earlier *solein* (cf. *sudden*), pop. form of *solemn*, of which it has taken over the secondary sense, morose, gloomy. Influenced also by ME. *solein*, unique, solitary, app. AF. from L. *solus*, alone. For later senses cf. *surly*. With *the sullens* cf. *the dismals* (*dumps*). Shaks. describes the curfew as *solemn*, Milt. as *sullen*.

> *agelastus*: that never laugheth, sadde, soleyne
> (Coop.).

> *vultuosus*: of a grave and solemne countenance (*ib.*).

> *sullen*: acerbus, agelastus (Holyoak).

> *vultuosus*: of a sullen, grim countenance (Litt.).

> Put on sullen black incontinent (*Rich. II*, v. 6).

> Customary suits of solemn black (*Haml.* i. 2).

sully. F. *souiller*, to soil[2] (q.v.). First in Shaks.

sulphur. Restored from ME. & OF. *solfre* (*soufre*), L. *sulfur*, *sulphur* (prop. *sulpur*); cf. It. *solfo*, Sp. *azufre* (with Arab. def. art.). Replaced cogn. AS. *swefl*, with which cf. Ger. *schwefel*, Goth. *swibls*, etc.

Sulpician. Member of congregation of secular priests founded (1642) by priest of parish of *Saint-Sulpice*, Paris.

Sultan. F., Arab. *sulṭān*, king; cf. It. *sultano* (whence fem. *sultana*), Sp. *sultán*, and see earlier *Soldan*. *Sultana raisin* is a 19 cent.

trade-name, but the word was also used of 18 cent. confections.

sultry. From obs. verb to *sulter*, app. dial. form of *swelter* (q.v.). Now often playful for fig. senses of *hot*.

sum. F. *somme*, L. *summa* (sc. *res*, *pars*), from *summus*, for **supmus*, superl. from stem of *super*, *superior*; cf. It. *somma*, Sp. *suma*. Orig. sense of amount in *sum-total* (MedL. *summa totalis*), *sum and substance* (Shaks.), to *sum up*. Hence to *do sums* was orig. to practise addition only. To *sum up*, in sense of giving an epitome, was earlier to *sum*, and perh. owes something to F. *résumer*, prop. to take up again.

sumach. Tree. In ME. used of the leaves as prepared for tanning. F. *sumac*, Arab. *summāq*, whence also It. *sommaco*, Sp. *zumaque*.

summary. MedL. *summarius*, from L. *summarium* (noun only), from *summa*, sum. In leg. sense, implying omission of unnecessary formalities, first in adv. use (Palsg.).

summer[1]. Season. AS. *sumor*. Com. Teut.; cf. Du. *zomer*, Ger. *sommer*, ON. *sumar*; cogn. with Sanskrit *samā*, half-year, year, OIr. *sam*, summer. *Summer*, *winter*, the orig. divisions of the year, are connected with many more allusions than *spring*, *autumn* (see *Lent*, *harvest*). A young lady's age is reckoned fig. by summers, an old man's by winters. *Summer-time*, in latest sense, was first adopted May 21, 1916.

summer[2] [*archaic*]. Beam. F. *sommier*, orig. pack-horse (cf. *gantry*), from *somme*, burden, Late L., G. σάγμα. Cf. *breastsummer*.

summit. F. *sommet*, dim. of OF. *som*, *son*, L. *summum*, neut. of *summus*, highest (see *sum*).

summon. OF. *somondre* (*semondre*), VL. **summonere*, for *summonēre*, from *sub* and *monēre*, to warn, admonish. *Summons* is OF. *somonse* (*semonce*, rebuke), VL. **summonsa*, for *summonita*. Vulg. to *summons* was once literary.

summum bonum. L., highest good, in ethics (Cicero).

sump [*dial. & techn.*]. Swamp, pit, etc. LG. *sump*, cogn. with *swamp*; cf. Ger. *sumpf*.

sumpitan. Malay blow-pipe. Malay, from *sumpit*, narrow. ? Ult. cogn. with *sarbacane*.

sumpsimus. Correct expression replacing incorrect. Allusive to *mumpsimus* (q.v.).

sumpter [*archaic*]. OF. *sommetier*, driver of

packhorse (see *summer²*). Hence name *Sumpter* (cf. *Palfreyman, Runciman*, etc.). Later applied to the animal, earlier *sumpter-horse*.

sumptuary. Only of laws (v.i.).

sumptuous. F. *somptueux*, L. *sumptuosus*, from *sumptus*, expense, from *sumere*, *sumpt-*, to take.

sun. AS. *sunne*. Com. Teut.; cf. Du. *zon*, Ger. *sonne*, ON. *sunna*, Goth. *sunnō*; ult. cogn. with L. *sol*, G. ἥλιος, Sanskrit *svar*, to shine. *Sunrise, sunset* prob. contain an orig. subjunctive, as in *ere the sun rise* (v.i.). *Sunstroke* is for earlier *stroke of the sun*, rendering F. *coup de soleil*. *Sundowner* (Austral.) is a tramp who times himself to reach a homestead at *sundown*, when it is too late to send him further. A *place in the sun* renders Ger. *platz an der sonne*, a phrase current in Ger. before its use by William II (at Hamburg, Aug. 27, 1911). The "empire" allusion was to Spain before the 19 cent.

They ben huntyd tofore the sonne ryse [*var*. bifore the sonne riseth] (Trev.).

The sun never sets in the Spanish dominions
(Capt. John Smith).

Vous avez un empire auquel nul roi ne touche,
Si vaste que jamais le soleil ne s'y couche!
(Hugo, *Hernani*, ii. 2; Spain, anno 1519).

Snobs are...recognized throughout an empire on which I am given to understand the sun never sets
(Thackeray).

C'est là ma place au soleil; voilà le commencement et l'image de l'usurpation de la terre
(Pascal's *Pensées*).

Retire-toi de notre soleil; il n'y a pas de place pour toi (Vigny, *Chatterton*, i. 5).

Sunday. AS. *sunnandæg*, sun day, rendering Late L. *dies solis*, Late G. ἡμέρα ἡλίου; cf. Du. *zondag*, Ger. *sonntag*, ON. *sunnudagr*. The first *Sunday School* was established (1783) by Robert Raikes, of Gloucester. With *Sunday clothes* (1642) cf. F. *s'endimancher*, to dress in one's best.

sunder. Late AS. *syndrian, sundrian*, for *āsyndrian* (also *ge-, on-, tō-*), from adj. *sundor-*, separate, cogn. with Du. *zonder* (prep.), Ger. *sonder* (prep.), ON. *sundr* (adv.), Goth. *sundrō* (adv.). Cf. also Ger. *sondern*, but, *sonderbar*, remarkable, *besonders*, especially.

sunder, in. For earlier *asunder* (q.v.).

sundry. AS. *syndrig*, separate (v.s.). For orig. sense, as in *all and sundry*, cf. *divers, several*.

Rather I wish ten thousand sundrie deaths
Then I to live and see my daughter thine
(*Tancred & Gismund*, 16 cent.).

sunn [*Anglo-Ind.*]. Fibrous plant. Hind. *san*, Sanskrit *ṣāṇa*, hempen.

Sunni. Orthodox Mohammedan (Turks and most Arabs), accepting the *sunna*, trad. teaching of Mohammed, as of equal authority with the Koran. Arab. *sunnī*, lawful, from *sunna*, form, rule. See *Shiah*.

sup. AS. *sūpan*, to take liquid in mouthfuls, cogn. with *sop*. Hence ME. *soup*, as in dial. *soop*, vowel being later shortened by association with *supper* (q.v.). Com. Teut.; cf. Du. *zuipen*, Ger. *saufen*, ON. *sūpa*. From the verb comes the noun *sup*, now dial., exc. in *bite* (orig. *bit*) *or sup*. *Sup*, to take *supper* (q.v.), is back-formation from noun.

super. Short for *supernumerary* (theat.), *superfine* (commerc.).

super-. L. *super*, above, cogn. with G. ὑπέρ and with *over* (cf. *hyperaesthesia, supersensitive; overflowing, superfluous*). Many E. compds. correspond to F. words in *sur-*, e.g. *surnuméraire, surfin* (v.s.).

superannuated. Orig. (17 cent.) impaired by age. Coined, on MedL. *superannatus*, from *super* and *annus*, year. Cf. *annual*.

superb. L. *superbus*, haughty, magnificent, from *super*.

supercargo. Also earlier *supracargo*, adapted from Sp. *sobrecargo*, lit. over cargo. Both forms are in Dampier.

supercilious. Late L. *superciliosus*, from *supercilium*, "the over brow; severitie, gravitie" (Coop.), from *cilium*, eyelid. Cf. F. *sourcilleux*, "surly, or proud of countenance" (Cotg.), and see *arch¹*.

supererogation. Usu. with *works*. Late L. *supererogatio-n-*, from *supererogare*, to pay over, in addition, from *erogare*, from *rogare*, to ask.

superficial. Late L. *superficialis*, from *superficies*, surface, from *facies*, face.

superfluous. From L. *superfluus*, from *superfluere*, to overflow; cf. F. *superflu*, It. Sp. *superfluo*.

superintend. Church L. *superintendere*, from *intendere*, to attend to, from *tendere*, to stretch. Cf. F. *surintendant*, superintendent.

superior. ME. & OF. *superiour* (*supérieur*), L. *superior-em*, compar. from *super*.

The right honourable member for Stroud is the "superior person" of the House of Commons
(Disraeli, 1864).

superlative. ME. *superlatif*, F., L. *superlativus*, from *super* and *latus* used as p.p.

of *tollere*, to take away. First as gram. term.

> Ther nys no thyng in gree superlatyf,
> As seith Senek, above an humble wyf
> (Chauc. E. 1375).

superman. Coined (1903) by G. B. Shaw, after F. *surhomme* (Lichtenberger, 1901), to render Ger. *übermensch*, used by Nietzsche (†1900) to express an ideal very popular with those to whom nature has denied a pair of shoulders and other virile attributes. Nietzsche took it from Goethe, the latter from Herder, with whom it is a favourite, and it is recorded in Ger. as early as 1527. This foolish word has led to any number of nonce-formations of which the lang. is getting very tired.

> Is the food-controller to be a minister or a super-minister? (*Obs.* Nov. 19, 1916).

supernaculum [*archaic*]. Mock L. (16 cent.), rendering Ger. *auf den nagel trinken*, i.e. to show the tankard is empty by the solitary drop it leaves on the thumb-nail; cf. F. *boire rubis sur l'ongle* and see *nail*. For the custom see *Vivian Grey*, vi. 1.

> *boire la goutte sur l'ongle*: to drinke all but a drop to cover the nayle with (Cotg.).

supernal. OF., from L. *supernus*, from *super*. Cf. *infernal*.

supernumerary. Late L. *supernumerarius*, soldier additional to strength of legion, from *numerus*, number.

superpose. See *pose*.

superscribe. L. *superscribere*, to write over. Cf. *subscribe*. Much earlier is *superscription* (Wyc. *Luke*, xx. 24).

supersede. OF. *superseder*, L. *supersedēre*, to sit above, be superior, also to desist, refrain. For latter sense see *surcease* and cf. leg. *supersedeas*, you shall desist. Development of current sense is somewhat obscure. Influence of *cedere*, to yield, appears in MedL. *supercedere*.

superstition. F., L. *superstitio-n-*, lit. standing over; cf. It. *superstizione*, Sp. *superstición*. Earlier is *superstitious* (Chauc.). Many theories have been propounded as to the sense-development, but none are at all convincing. The ground-sense of L. *superstes* is survivor. If orig. sense of *superstitio* was prophetic frenzy, the parallel of *ecstasy* would suggest itself.

supertax [*neol.*]. For earlier *surtax* (cf. *surcharge*), F. *surtaxe*.

supervene. L. *supervenire*, from *venire*, to come. Cf. F. *survenir*.

supervise. From MedL. *supervidēre*, *supervis-*, from *vidēre*, to see. Cf. *oversee*, *survey*.

supine. L. *supinus*, lying on one's back, from root of *super*, over. As gram. term for L. *supinum* (sc. *verbum*), applied in L. also to the gerund.

supper. F. *souper*, orig. infin. (cf. *dinner*), prob. of Teut. origin and cogn. with *sup*, *soup*. The supper of the F. peasant is still regularly soup.

supplant. F. *supplanter*, L. *supplantare*, to trip up, from *sub* and *planta*, sole of the foot. Earliest (13 cent.) is *supplanter*, with ref. to Jacob.

> Juste vocatum est nomen ejus Jacob: supplantavit enim me in altera vice (*Vulg. Gen.* xxvii. 36).

supple. F. *souple*, L. *supplex*, *supplic-*, submissive, from *sub*, under, *plicare*, to fold. Cf. *suppliant*. Hence *supplejack*, name for various twining shrubs and for cane made from them.

supplement. L. *supplementum*, from *supplēre*, *sub* and *plēre*, to fill. Cf. *complement*.

suppliant. F., pres. part. of *supplier*, L. *supplicare*, whence also *supplicate*, for which ME. had also *supply*. See *supple*.

supplicat [*univ.*]. Petition for degree. L., he supplicates (v.s.).

supply. OF. *supplier*, var. of *suppleier* (*suppléer*), irreg. from L. *supplēre*, *sub* and *plēre*, to fill. Cf. It. *supplire*, Sp. *suplir*; also F. *emplir*, to fill, L. *implēre*.

support. F. *supporter*, L. *supportare*, from *sub* and *portare*, to carry. Oldest sense (Wyc.) is to endure, put up with, now regarded rather as a gallicism.

suppose. F. *supposer* (see *pose*). Like all compds. of *-pose* it has taken over the senses of L. *-ponere*. Current senses of *supposition* are chiefly due to adoption of *suppositio* in MedL. to render G. ὑπόθεσις.

supposititious. From L. *supposititius*, from *supponere*, *supposit-*, to substitute, lit. put under.

suppress. From L. *supprimere*, *suppress-*, lit. to press under, from *premere*, to press.

suppurate. From L. *suppurare*, from *sub* and *pus*, *pur-*, pus.

supra-. L. *supra*, above, cogn. with *super* and ult. with *sub*.

supreme. L. *supremus*, superl. formation from *super*, over; cf. F. *suprême*. Early use chiefly in connection with the *supremacy* of Hen. VIII over the E. Church. F. *suprématie* is from E.

sur-. F *sur-*, OF. also *sour-*, L. *super-* (q.v.).

surah [*neol.*]. Fabric. ? For *surat*.

sural [*anat.*]. Of the calf of the leg, L. *sura*.

surat. Cotton fabric. From *Surat*, Bombay.

surcease [*archaic*]. Altered, on *cease*, from F. *sursis*, p.p. of *surseoir*, "to surcease, pawse, intermit, leave off, give over, delay or stay for a time" (Cotg.), L. *supersedēre*, to supersede (q.v.).

surcingle. OF. *surcengle*, from *cengle* (*sangle*), girth, L. *cingula*, from *cingere*, to gird.

surcoat [*hist.*]. OF. *surcot*(*e*). See *sur-*, *coat*.

surd. L. *surdus*, "deafe; also that speaketh not, or sowneth not, that maketh no noyse" (Coop.). Math. sense of "irrational" is due to use of L. *surdus* to render Arab. *aҫamm*, deaf, as in *jathr aҫamm*, surd root, the Arab. being translated from G. ἄλογος (Euclid), speechless, unutterable, irrational.

sure. F. *sûr*, OF. *sëur*, L. *securus*, secure (q.v.). Gradual change of sense in ellipt. *Well, I'm sure! To be sure*, is curious. For senses of *surety* cf. *security*.

surf. Late 17 cent., usu. *surf of the sea*, and recorded, I believe, by no gen. E. dict. before Dyche and Pardon (1792), though *surff of the sea* is in the *Gent. Dict.* (1705). Replaced earlier *suff*(*e*) *of the sea*, which occurs passim in Hakl. and Purch. The -*r*- is prob. due to influence of *surge* (q.v.), *sea-surge* and *surge of the sea* occurring in practically the same sense in Hakl. and Purch. Orig. sense is app. the pull of the water (v.i.); cf. synon. F. *ressac*, lit. backpull, rendered *surf* by Romme (1798). Origin unknown.

We were nowe so neere the shore that the countersuffe of the sea would rebound against the shippes side (Hakl. xi. 406).

The sea threw me against the beach...every suffe washed mee into the sea again
(David Middleton, 1610, in Purch.).

There running, in fine weather, but little surf, or suff as seamen call it (Roberts, *Voyages*, 1726).

surface. F., from *face*, after L. *superficies*, from *facies*, face.

surfeit. OF. *surfet* (*surfait*), p.p. of *surfaire*, to overdo, L. *super* and *facere*.

surge. From F. *surgir*, from L. *surgere*, to rise, whence also F. *sourdre*, to spring up (of water), with OF. stem *sourg-*, *surg-*. Cf. *source* and see *surf*.

surge of the sea: vague (Palsg.).

The captaine commanded them to keepe it [the boat] off, for feare of the great surge that went by the shore (Hakl. xi. 311).

surgeon. AF. *surgien*, *surigien*, etc., for F. *chirurgien*, chirurgeon (q.v.).

surly. From 16 cent., orig. in sense of haughty, imperious. Earlier *serly*, "imperiosus" (*Manip. Vocab.*), *syrlie* (Spenser), formed from *sir* by analogy with *lordly*, *kingly*, etc.; cf. Ger. *herrisch*, arrogant, from *herr*, sir. In Shaks. it always means arrogant, imperious. Later sense-development has been like that of *sullen*. See quot. from Cotg. s.v. *square*.

That surlie and imperious colleague of his sirnamed Imperiosus (Holland's *Pliny*).

The surly surges [du Bart. l'orgueil plus escumeux] of the waters fall (Sylv. *Ark*).

surmaster. Second master of St Paul's School. It looks rather like an erron. adaptation by Colet of F. *sousmaître*.

Twoo techers perpetuall, oon callid the maister, and that other callid the ussher or surmaister
    (Dean Colet, c. 1512).

soubs-maistre: an under master; or an usher in a schoole (Cotg.).

surmise. OF., p.p. fem. of *surmettre*, to accuse, lit. to put on, lay to one's charge, from L. *mittere*. This is orig. E. sense (c. 1400), passing (16 cent.) into that of supposing, conjecturing. *Wild surmise* is from Keats' *Sonnet on Chapman's Homer*.

My mortall enemie hath...falsely surmised mee to bee a fayned person (Perkin Warbeck).

surmullet. Red mullet. F. *surmulet*, from *sur*, reddish (see *sorrel²*).

surname. From *name*, after F. *surnom*, whence also ME. *surnoun*; cf. MedL. *supernomen*, *supranomen*, It. *soprannome*, Sp. *sobrenombre*. For incorr. *sirname* cf. *sirloin*.

surpass. F. *surpasser*, to over-pass. For archaic adv. use of *surpassing* cf. *exceeding* and see *pass²*.

Thy very streets are paved with gold, Surpassing clear and fine (*Jerusalem*).

surplice. OF. *sourpeliz*, *surpelis*, MedL. *superpellicium* (sc. *vestimentum*), from *pellicia*, fur garment, from *pellis*, skin; cf. It. *superpellicio*, Sp. *sobrepelliz*. So called because worn over furs in unheated medieval churches.

surplus. F., from *sur* and *plus*, more.

surprise. First as noun. F., p.p. fem. of *surprendre*, lit. to overtake, from L. *prehendere*, to seize. Cf. *apprise*, *comprise*.

surrebutter, **surrejoinder** [*leg.*]. Plaintiff's reply to defendant's *rebutter*, *rejoinder*. See *rebut*, *rejoin*.

surrender. OF. *surrendre*, to hand over (see *render*). Cf. MedL. *super reddere*, also *sursum reddere*, corresponding to AF. *susrendre*.

surreptitious. From L. *surreptitius*, for *subrepticius*. See *subreption*.

surrogate. L. *surrogatus*, from *surrogare*, for *subrogare*, "to substitute, to make a deputie, to put in another mans roume" (Coop.), from *rogare*, to ask, appoint.

surround. OF. *suronder*, to overflow, Late L. *superundare*, from *unda*, wave. Current sense (from c. 1600) is due to erron. association with *round*.

Prees et pastures et terres semez, ajoignnauntz as ditz rivers, sount grandement destourbez, surondez, gastez, et destruitz (*Liber Albus*, temp. Rich. II).

to surround or overflowe: rondt-om vloeyen, over-vloeyen, ofte omçingelen (Hexham).

surtout [*archaic*]. F., over-all. *Tout* is VL. **tottus*, for *totus*.

surveillance. F., supervision, esp. in *surveillance de la haute police*, from *surveiller*, from *veiller*, to watch, L. *vigilare*.

survey. AF. *surveier*, OF. *surveeir*, from *veeir*, *veoir* (*voir*), to see, L. *videre*. Cf. *supervise*, *oversee*. Older than *survey* is *surveyor*, as offic. title (15 cent.).

survive. F. *survivre*, L. *supervivere*, to overlive. *Survival of the fittest* was used by Spencer for Darwin's *natural selection*.

susceptible. Late L. *susceptibilis*, from *suscipere*, to receive, lit. undertake, from *sub* and *capere*.

suspect. F. *suspecter*, from L. *suspicere*, *suspect-*, lit. to look up at, from *sub* and *specere*. Earlier (14 cent.) is adj. *suspect*, regarded with *suspicion*. As noun dates chiefly from F. use at time of Revolution, as in the *loi des suspects*.

suspend. F. *suspendre*, L. *suspendere*, to hang up, from *sub* and *pendere*. *Suspenders*, braces, is US. *In suspense* was orig. leg., in abeyance. *Suspension bridge* dates from 1821.

sus. per coll. Abbrev., in jailer's book, for L. *suspensio per collum*, hanging by the neck.

suspicion. Respelt, on L. *suspicio-n-* (see *suspect*), for ME. *suspecioun*, OF. *sospeçon* (*soupçon*), L. *suspectio-n-*.

suspire [*poet.*]. L. *suspirare*, from *sub* and *spirare*, to breathe; cf. F. *soupirer* (OF. *sospirer*).

sustain. OF. *sostenir*, VL. **sustenire*, for *sustinere*, from *sub*, under, *tenere*, to hold;

cf. It. *sostenere*, Sp. *sostener*. For sense-development cf. *suffer*. Orig. sense of up-keep appears in *sustenance*, *sustentation*.

susurration. L. *susurratio-n-*, from *susurrare*, from *susurrus*, murmur, whisper, of imit. origin.

sutler [*hist.*]. Du. *zoetelaar* (earlier *soeteler*), cogn. with Ger. *sudeln*, to befoul, in MHG. to cook badly, from *sieden*, to seethe, boil. Cf. relation of L. *lixa*, "a scullion, drudge, or slave to carie woodde and water in an armie, or to a kitchen" (Coop.), with *lixare*, "to seeth or boyle" (*ib.*). Sc. form in quot. below is app. due to confusion with *scullion*.

The skuddileris [*orig.* lixae] and kitchine boys
      (Leslie's *Hist. of Scotl.* 1596).

suttee. Hind., Sanskrit *satī*, virtuous woman, fem. of *sat*, good, wise, etc., lit. existing, orig. pres. part. of *as*, to be.

suture. F., L. *sutura*, from *suere*, *sut-*, to sew.

suzerain. F., coined (c. 1300) from *sus*, up, by analogy with *souverain*, sovereign. *Sus* is L. *susum*, *sursum*, for *subversum*, earlier *-vorsum*, from *sub* and *vertere*, to turn.

svelte. F., It. *svelto*, p.p. of *svellere*, to drag upwards, VL. **exvellere* (cf. F. *élancé*, slender).

swab. From a LG. root suggestive of swaying and flapping, whence ME. *swabble*; cf. LG. *swabben*, to splash, Sw. Norw. *svabb*, mop, Du. *zwabber*, "swabber, the drudge of a ship" (Sewel). For contemptuous or invective use cf. origin of *scullion*.

swaddle. Frequent. of *swathe*. Earliest (12 cent.) in *swaddle-band*, later replaced by *swaddling clothes* (Coverd. *Luke*, ii. 7); cf. AS. *swethel*, bandage, etc.

swag. From 16 cent. of swaying, tottering motion, as in *swag-bellied* (*Oth.* ii. 3). App. cogn. with *sway*; cf. synon. Norw. dial. *svaga*, *svagga*. Earliest sense (1303) is that of bulging bag, which, though not again recorded till 19 cent., seems to account for the burglar's *swag* and the Austral. bushman's bundle.

He said he'd "done me wery brown" and nicely
    "stow'd the swag."
—That's French, I fancy, for a hat—or else a
    carpet-bag (*Ingoldsby*).

swagger. First in Shaks. (*Mids. N. Dream*, iii. 1). Though it has the form of a frequent. of *swag* (v.s.), sense suggests rather connection with Sc. *swack*, to fling, brandish, obs. Du. *swacken*, "vibrare" (Kil.). Cf. *stagger*. Adj. use arose at Camb.

Swahili [*ling.*]. Lang. of Zanzibar and neighbourhood. From Arab. *sawāḥil*, pl. of *sāḥil*, coast.

The Suaheli tongue, which is the *lingua franca* of the east of Africa, as Hausa is of the west (James Platt, *Notes & Queries*, Apr. 2, 1898).

swain. ON. *sveinn*, boy, attendant, cogn. with synon. AS. *swān*, which it has replaced. Cf. *boatswain*, *coxswain*. App. obsolescent in Spenser's time and revived by him in sense of rustic, shepherd, esp. pastoral sweetheart.

Hym boes [behoves] serve hym-self that has na swayn (Chauc. A. 4027).

swallow[1]. Bird. AS. *swealwe*. Com. Teut.; cf. Du. *zwaluw*, Ger. *schwalbe* (OHG. *swalwa*), ON. *svala*. It reaches Greece a season earlier than these islands, hence ἔαρ, spring, in the G. proverb—μία χελιδὼν ἔαρ οὐ ποιεῖ.

swallow[2]. Verb. AS. *swelgan*. Com. Teut.; cf. Du. *zwelgen*, Ger. *schwelgen*, to feast, ON. *svelga*. Orig. strong, with p.p. *swolgen*, which has influenced pronunc.

swami. Hind. *swāmī*, master, lord, Sanskrit *svāmin*. Orig. Hindu idol, but used in E. of theosophical wonder-worker.

swamp. Orig. (Capt. John Smith) in ref. to Virginia. Of LG. origin (see *sump*) and ult. cogn. with AS. *swamm* (Du. *zwam*, Ger. *schwamm*), sponge; cf. G. σομφός, spongy, porous.

swan. AS. *swan*. Com. Teut.; cf. Du. *zwaan*, Ger. *schwan*, ON. *svanr* (poet.); "app. at first applied to the 'musical' swan" (*NED.*) and cogn. with Sanskrit *svānati*, (it) sounds, and L. *sonare*, to sound. Cf. relation of Ger. *hahn*, cock, to L. *canere*, to sing. The singing of the swan before death is alluded to by Chauc., but *swan-song* was adapted (? by Carlyle) from Ger. *schwanengesang*, "the singing of a swan; the contentedness and fine sayings of a dying person" (Ludw.). See Aeschylus *Agam.* 1445. *Swan-hopping* is a corrupt. of *swan-upping*, the taking up of swans to mark their beaks with sign of ownership.

Toujours, en parlant des dernières heures d'un beau génie qui s'éteint, on dira: "C'est le chant du cygne" (Buffon).

swank. A midl. & S.W. dial. word adopted early in 20 cent. ? Cf. Sc. *swank*, active, *swanking*, strapping, *swankie*, smart fellow, of LG. origin and ult. cogn. with Ger. *schwenken*, to brandish, flourish, from *schwingen*, to swing. ? Or simply a perversion of synon. *swagger*.

swap, swop. A "low word" (Johns.). Orig. to strike, make rapid motion; also used of striking (hands in token of) a bargain (v.i.), whence current sense. In the ballad of Chevy Chase it occurs as var. of *swack* (see *swagger*), in ref. to swords. Of imit. origin. Cf. F. *toper*, Ger. *topp*, similarly used of striking a bargain.

Swete, swap we so, sware with trawthe (*NED.* 14 cent.).

swap, or *strak*: ictus (*Prompt. Parv.*).

They will either beg them [beads, etc.], or make a swap with you in private (Purch.).

It was not best to swap horses when crossing a stream (Abraham Lincoln).

sward. AS. *sweard*, skin, bacon-rind. Com. Teut.; cf. Du. *zwoord*, bacon rind, Ger. *schwarte*, "the sward, or rind, of a thing" (Ludw.), ON. *svörthr*, scalp, whale-skin. Current sense is due to ME. *sward of the earth*. AS. had also *swearth*, whence dial. *swarth*, in both senses.

sward of flesh: coriana (*Prompt. Parv.*).

turfe, flag, or *sward of erth*: cespes (*ib.*).

swarm[1]. Of bees. AS. *swearm*. Com. Teut.; cf. Du. *zwerm*, Ger. *schwarm*, ON. *svarmr*. Usu. connected with Sanskrit *svar*, to be noisy; but *NED.* suggests a possible ground-idea of confused or irregular movement and ult. connection with *swerve*; cf. Icel. *svarmla*, *svarfla*, to dash hither and thither, Norw. dial. *svarma*, *svarva*, to be giddy, stagger, Ger. *schwärmen*, to wander, rave, become frenziedly enthusiastic. See also *swarm*[2].

swarm[2]. To climb. Orig. (16 cent.) naut., with var. *swarve* (v.s.). Perh. ult. cogn. with *swarm*[1].

swart. AS. *sweart*. Com. Teut.; cf. Du. *zwart*, Ger. *schwarz*, ON. *svartr*, Goth. *swarts*. This is the true Teut. word for *black*, which has now replaced it in E. It is used by early voyagers for "Blacks." *Swarthy* is 16 cent.

swash. App. imit. of blow; cf. *swap*, *dash*[1]. Chiefly in *swash-buckler*, a compd. of the *Shake-spear* type; cf. such ME. surnames as *Crakesheld*, *Breakspear*, Ger. *Hauenschild*, etc., and see my *Surnames* (ch. xii.).

tranche-montaigne: a swash-mountaine, terrible swash-buckler, horrible swaggerer (Cotg.).

swastika [neol.]. Gammadion, fylfot. Sanskrit svastika, from svasti, well being, from sū, good, as, to be. The emblem is of prehistoric (? even palaeolithic) antiquity.

swat¹. To hit. Chiefly US., from E. dial. Esp. in swat that fly (1911).

swat². See swot.

swath, swathe. AS. swæth, track, trace, used in ME. of space covered by sweep of scythe. Cf. LG. swad, furrow, measure, Du. zwad, swath, Ger. schwaden. The form swathe is partly due to swathe, band (v.i.).

swathe. AS. swathian, from swath, band, occurring only in dat. pl. as gloss to John, xi. 44; cf. swaddle. ? Cogn. with swath.

sway. From c. 1500. LG. swājen, to be moved hither and thither by the wind (whence also Sw. svaja, Dan. svaie); cf. Du. zwaaien, to totter, also trans., as in den rijkstaf zwaaien, to wield the sceptre, which shows origin of sway, rule, empire. Distinct from ME. sweghe, to move, sink.

swear. AS. swerian. Com. Teut.; cf. Du. zweren, Ger. schwören (OHG. swerian), ON. sverja; cogn. with Goth. swaran. See answer. For secondary sense of using bad language, orig. invoking sacred names, cf. oath, and also double sense of F. jurer. With archaic I'll be sworn cf. I'll be bound.

sweat. As noun replaces ME. swote, AS. swāt, by analogy with the cogn. verb, AS. swātan. Com. Teut.; cf. Du. zweeten, Ger. schwitzen, ON. sveita; cogn. with L. sudor, G. ἱδρώς, Sanskrit svid, to sweat. Sweater, profiteering employer, appears to be due to an error of Kingsley's (Alton Locke). In earlier use it was applied to a workman doing overtime. The garment originated c. 1880 ? at Camb. Old sweat, soldier, is for earlier swad (c. 1750), of unknown origin.

In sudore vultus tui vesceris pane
(Vulg. Gen. iii. 19).
The most sweated toiler in the world, the working-man's wife (Daily Chron. Feb. 17, 1919).

swede. For Swedish turnip. Swede is obs. Du. Swede (Zweed); cf. Ger. Schwede. This is prob. a back-formation from AS. Swēothēod or ON. Svíthjóthr, Swedish people, from AS. Swēon (pl.), ON. Svíar, with which cf. L. Suiones and archaic Suiogothic, used by early philologists for OSwedish. With Swedish drill cf. sloyd.

Swedenborgian. Of Emanuel Swedenborg or Svedberg, Swedish mystic (†1772).

sweep. ME. swepen, altered, perh. by influence of past swepe, AS. swēop, from swopen (see swoop), AS. swāpan (trans. & intrans.), whence Sc. soop (esp. in curling). For intrans. senses cf. cogn. ON. svīpa, to move swiftly, Ger. schweifen. With (chimney-)sweep for (chimney-)sweeper cf. shoeblack, both prob. from street cries. Sweepstake, orig. he who sweeps up, wins, all the stakes (cf. to sweep the board), is recorded much earlier than the simple stake (in sense of wager, etc.). It was also a ship-name (in Pepys), dating back to Nav. Accts. of 1495, and, as a surname, is recorded as early as 1379 (Yorks Poll-Tax). Current sense from 18 cent.

sweet. AS. swēte (adj.), from swōt, sweetness. Com. Teut.; cf. Du. zoet, Ger. süss, ON. sǣtr, Goth. sūts (for *swotus); cogn. with L. suavis (for *suadvis), G. ἡδύς, Sanskrit svādu. Sweetbread (16 cent.) is of doubtful origin; the second element may be AS. brǣde, roast meat, and the first may be related to synon. LG. sweder, Ger. dial. schweder, sweeser, Du. zweezerik, earlier zweesrik, "sweet bread of veal" (Sewel, 1766), also zweeserkens. The last (app. = sisterkins) is also applied to the testicles, as was broederkens in archaic Du. The two glands of the pancreas form a pair united by a ligament. With sweetheart cf. earlier dear heart in same sense. Sweetmeat preserves earlier gen. sense of meat. To be sweet on is 17 cent.

Delicacie his swete toth hath fostred (Gower).

The two noblest of things, which are sweetness and light (Swift, Battle of Books).

swell. AS. swellan. Com. Teut.; cf. Du. zwellen, Ger. schwellen, ON. svella, Goth. uf-swalleins (noun). See also sill. Hence swell, "a well dressed man" (Grose), "a man who by excessive dress apes a higher position than he actually occupies" (Hotten), thus, a puffed-up individual. Orig. sense appears in swell-mobsman, with which cf. synon. Ger. hochstapler, lit. high rascal. Swelled head (cf. too big for one's boots) was earlier swell-head (app. US.), but see quot. below, in a much earlier sense.

swelled head: a disorder to which horses are extremely liable, particularly those of the subalterns of the army. This disorder is generally occasioned by remaining too long in one livery-stable or inn, and often arises to that height that it prevents their coming out of the stable door. The most certain cure is the unguentum aureum—not applied to the horse, but to the palm of the master of the inn or stable (Grose).

swelter. Frequent. of obs. *swelt*, AS. *sweltan*, to perish, cogn. with AS. *swelan*, to be burnt, from *swol*, burning; cf. dial. *sweal*, *swale*, to burn, singe. Com. Teut.; cf. Du. *zwoel*, *zoel*, "sultry, sweltry" (Sewel), Ger. *schwül*, "sweltry" (Ludw.), ON. *svæla*, fume, smoke. See *sultry*.

After a swelting day, some sultry shower
Doth in the marshes heapes of tadpols poure
(Sylv. *Colonies*).

swerve. AS. *sweorfan*, to scrub, scour. Com. Teut.; cf. Du. *zwerven*, "to swerve or swarve, wander, stray" (Sewel), OHG. *swerban*, to swerve, ON. *sverfa*, to scour, Goth. *swairban*, to wipe (in compds.). Relation of senses is difficult to trace, but we have something like it in *sweep*. See also *swarm*[1, 2].

swift[1]. Rapid. AS. *swift*, cogn. with *swīfan*, to move, sweep. Hence name of bird.

swift[2] [*naut.*]. To make taut, etc. Cf. ON. *svipta*, to reef, Du. *zwichten*, in *het zeil zwichten*, "to take in the sail" (Sewel, 1766), Ger. *schwichten* (from LG.), Dan. *svigte*; perh. ult. cogn. with *swift*[1].

swig. From 16 cent., drink, liquor. ? Cf. Norw. Dan. *svik*, tap, for cognates of which see *switch*. In the earliest examples in *NED. tap* would make equally good sense (v.i.).

Long accustomed to the olde sowre swyg of Moses lawe (Udall).

swill. AS. *swillan*, to wash (trans.). Hence *swill*, hog-wash. As verb app. associated with Du. *zwelgen*, "to swallow down, to swill" (Sewel), for which see *swallow*[2].

Those that the sea hath swill'd (Sylv. i. 1).

swim[1]. To float in water. AS. *swimman*. Com. Teut.; cf. Du. *zwemmen*, Ger. *schwimmen*, ON. *symja*, Goth. *swam* (pret.). See also *sound*[3]. *In the swim* (*with*) is from angling sense of *swim*, part of river from fishing point of view (cf. *birds of a feather*).

swim[2]. In *swimming in the head*, etc. ? From AS. *swīma*, dizziness; cf. Du. *zwijm*, ON. *svime*, obs. Ger. *schweimel*; ult. cogn. with Ger. *schwinden*, to disappear, *schwindeln*, to be giddy. Orig. idea is that of vacuity; cf. F. *s'évanouir*, to vanish, faint, ult. from L. *vanus*, empty. But *NED.* treats this word as ident. with *swim*[1] (cf. Ger. *verschwommen*, blurred).

schweimel, *schwiemel*, *oder schwindel*: a giddiness, or swimming, of the head (Ludw.).

swindler. Ger. *schwindler*, picked up (1762) from Ger. Jews in London. Re-borrowed by Ger., and other langs., from E. From *schwindeln* (see *swim*[2]). *Swindle* is a back-formation (cf. *beg*, *cadge*, *peddle*).

This name is derived from the German *schwindlin* (sic), to totter, to be ready to fall; these arts being generally practised by persons on the totter, just ready to break (Grose).

swine. AS. *swīn*. Com. Teut.; cf. Du. *zwijn*, Ger. *schwein*, ON. *svīn*, Goth. *swein*. Orig. adj. from *sow*[1]; cf. L. *sus*, *suinus*.

swing. AS. *swingan*. Cf. OSax. *swingan*, Ger. *schwingen*; cogn. with Ger. *schwenken*, to waver, with which cf. Du. *zwenken*, to swing. *Full swing* is prob. from bell-ringing. Naut. to *swing* (hang up) *a hammock* suggests that to *swing a cat* (1665) may be for orig. *cot*[2]. With *Captain Swing* (hist.), leader of rick-burners (1830–32), cf. *Captain Moonlight*, and see *Luddite*.

Moreton preaches in a little conventicle you can hardly swing cat round in (T. Brown, c. 1700).

to swing: to be hanged (Grose).

I'll burn them precious stacks down, blow me!
   Yours most sincerely, Captain Swing
                      (*Ingoldsby*).

swinge [*archaic*]. To thrash. ME. *swenge*, AS. *swengan*, causal of *swing* (cf. *sing*, *singe*). Now chiefly as adj., e.g. *swingeing majority* (cf. *thumping*, *spanking*, etc.).

swingle. For beating flax. From *swing* or *swinge*; cf. Ger. *schwengel*, swingle-tree. Also in *swingle-tree* (of carriage), for second element of which cf. *boot-tree*, *cross-tree*, etc.

swink [*archaic*]. Toil. AS. *swinc*, also verb *swincan*; cogn. with *swing*.

swipe. First as noun. ME. *swipe*, stroke, cogn. with *sweep*.

swipes [*slang*]. Thin beer. Orig. naut. Cf. synon. Norw. *skvip*; cogn. with Norw. dial. *skvipa*, to sprinkle.

swipes: purser's swipes; small beer; so termed on board the king's ships (Grose).

swirl. Orig. Sc. Cf. Norw. dial. *svirla*, from synon. *svirra*; cogn. with Ger. *schwirren*, to whiz, warble. For association between sound and movement cf. *warble*.

swish. Imit. of sound of rod, scythe, etc.

Swiss. F. *Suisse*, for *homme de Suisse*, man of Switzerland. Often with implied sense of door-keeper, mercenary soldier (*Swiss Guard*).

Point d'argent, point de Suisse (F. *proverb*).

switch. Of late appearance (Shaks.). App. from Du. *zwik*, peg, spigot, earlier *swick*, "scourge, swich, or whip" (Hexham), also "small pearcer to give vent to a barrill of beere" (*ib.*). This is LG. *swik*, from Ger. *zwick*, var. of *zweck*, aim, orig. wooden pin in centre of target, cogn. with *zwicken*, to pinch, and with E. *twitch*. The peg sense suits the mech. applications of *switch*. These are chiefly US., though *switch* occurs in connection with coal-mining in 18 cent. E. Cf. similar use of *point* in E. railway lang., and of *aiguille*, needle, in F. For fig. senses cf. *shunt*, *side-track*. A *switch-back* was orig. (US.) a zig-zag mountain railway with abrupt reversal of direction. It seems doubtful whether the sense of pliant wand, scourge (Kil.), can belong to the same word. In any case an E. *sw-*, for Ger. *zw-* (= E. *tw-*) is abnormal, and can only be explained by substitution of this sound in LG. Cf. relation of E. *twig* to Ger. *zweig*, prob. cogn. with above.

swither [*Sc.*]. To hesitate. ? Cf. AS. *swethrian*, to retire, dwindle, etc.

> The Pope, the swithering neutrals,
> The Kaiser and his Gott (Kipling, 1917).

Swithun, Saint. Bishop of Winchester (9 cent.).

> This night with us being called St Swithin's day, at night it rained; the old saying is it raines 40 days after (Josselin's *Diary*, July 15, 1662).

Switzer [*archaic*]. Ger. *Schweizer*, from *Schweiz*, Switzerland, OHG. *Schwīz*, orig. name of one canton (*Schwyz*).

swivel. Orig. naut. (14 cent.), from AS. *swīfan*, to revolve, cogn. with *sweep*.

swiz [*slang*]. Schoolboy perversion of *swindle*.

swizzle [*slang*]. "In North America, a mixture of spruce beer, rum, and sugar was so called. The 17th regiment had a society called the Swizzle Club, at Ticonderoga, A.D. 1760" (Grose). ? Arbitrary from *swig*.

swoon. First (13 cent.) in *swooning*, ME. *swowenynge*, app. from AS. *geswogen* (whence obs. *aswoon*), p.p. of a lost verb. The revival of dial. *swound*, with excrescent *-d*, is app. due to Coleridge.

> It [the ice] cracked and growled, and roared and howled,
> Like noises in a swound (*Ancient Mariner*).

swoop. AS. *swāpan*, to sweep (trans.), to rush, dash. Cf. intrans. senses of *sweep* (q.v.), which has replaced ME. *swope* in gen. senses.

swop. See *swap*.

sword. AS. *sweord*. Com. Teut.; cf. Du. *zwaard*, Ger. *schwert*, ON. *sverth* (but Goth. has *hairus*).

swot [*school slang*]. "This word originated at the Royal Military College, Sandhurst, in the broad Scotch pronunciation of Dr Wallace, one of the professors, of the word *sweat*" (Hotten, from *Notes & Queries*, i. 369).

sybarite. G. Συβαρίτης, inhabitant of Σύβαρις, in SItaly, famed, like Capua, for luxury.

sybil. Incorr. for *sibyl*.

sycamine [*Bibl.*]. In *AV.* (*Luke*, xvii. 6) for G. συκάμινος, perh. from Heb. *shiqmīm*, pl. of *shiqmāh*, sycamore (q.v.). It is not known what tree is really meant by the G. word.

sycamore. Earlier *sicomore* (Wyc.), OF., L., G. συκόμορος, as though from σῦκον, fig, μόρον, mulberry, but prob. folk-etym. for Heb. *shiqmāh* (v.s.).

syce [*Anglo-Ind.*]. Groom. Hind. *sāïs*, from Arab., from *sāsa*, to tend a horse.

sychnocarpous [*bot.*]. From G. συχνός, many together, καρπός, fruit.

sycophant. G. συκοφάντης, informer, lit. fig-shower, said to have meant orig. one who laid information as to (forbidden) export of figs from Attica. From σῦκον, fig, φαίνειν, to show. Perh. rather successful tree-shaker (see *pagoda*).

sycosis [*med.*]. Skin-disease. G., fig-like ulcer (v.s.).

syenite [*geol.*]. L. *Syenites* (sc. *lapis*), from *Syene*, now Assouan (Egypt).

syl-. For *syn-* before *l-*.

syllable. F. *syllabe*, with *-l-* inserted as in *participle*, *principle*, L., G. συλλαβή, from συλλαμβάνειν, to take together.

syllabub. See *sillabub*.

syllabus. A ghost-word due to misprint in 15 cent. ed. of Cicero—"indices...quos vos Graeci (ut opinor) *syllabos* appellatis" (*Ad Atticum*, iv. 4), where correct reading is *sittubas*, acc. pl. of *sittuba*, G. σιττύβη, piece of parchment used as label-tag of MS. First in Blount and evidently regarded as kindred with *syllable*. Cf. *collimate*.

syllepsis [*gram.*]. L., G., as *prolepsis*. Cf. *zeugma*.

> Mr Weller took his hat and his leave (*Pickwick*).

syllogism. L., G. συλλογισμός, a reckoning together, from λογίζεσθαι, to reckon, from λόγος, word, reckoning.

sylph. Coined by Paracelsus (16 cent.), ? with suggestion of *sylvanus* and *nympha*. Cf. *gnome*.

sylvan. Incorr. for *silvan*. Hence *Sylvanus Urban*, pseudonym of editor of *Gentleman's Magazine* (18 cent.).

Sylvanus Urban had not a more indefatigable correspondent (*Ingoldsby*).

sym-. For *syn-*, before labial.

symbol. F. *symbole*, L., G. σύμβολον, token, watchword, from συμβάλλειν, to agree, lit. cast together. Applied (3 cent.) by Cyprian of Carthage to the creed. *Symbolism*, in art and literature, dates from movement in F. literature c. 1890.

symmetry. F. *symétrie*, L., G. συμμετρία, from μέτρον, measure.

sympathy. F. *sympathie*, L., G. συμπάθεια, from πάθος, feeling. Cf. *compassion, fellow feeling*. The current over-working of *sympathetic* in "intellectual" jargon is due to Ger. *sympathisch*.

symphony. F. *symphonie*, L., G. συμφωνία, from φωνή, sound.

symposium. L., G. συμπόσιον, convivial gathering of the educated, lit. a drinking together (G. πόσις, drinking, from root of πίνειν, to drink). Esp. as title of one of Plato's dialogues, whence current sense.

symptom. F. *symptôme*, L., G. σύμπτωμα, from συμπίπτειν, to fall together, happen.

syn-. G. σύν, together, OAttic ξύν, cogn. with L. *cum, com-, con-*.

synaeresis [*gram.*]. G. συναίρεσις, contraction, from αἱρεῖν, to take.

synagogue. F., L., G. συναγωγή, assembly, bringing together, from ἄγειν, to drive; lit. transl. of late Heb. *keneṣeth*.

synchronize. G. συγχρονίζειν, from χρόνος, time.

syncope. G. συγκοπή, from συγκόπτειν, to dash together.

syncretism [*philos.*]. F. *syncrétisme*, "the joyning, or agreement, of two enemies against a third person" (Cotg.), from G. κρητισμός, lying, from κρητίζειν, to lie like a Cretan. See *Tit.* i. 12.

syndic. F. *syndique*, L., G. σύνδικος, one helping in a trial, from δίκη, judgment; also, advocate, judge. Like most offic. titles (*sergeant, marshal, steward*, etc.) its applications are very wide. With F. *syndicat*, mercantile trust, also association of workmen in particular trade, cf. more recent *syndicalisme*, applied to similar

scheme for blackmailing the public. Both now unpleasantly familiar in E.

syne. In *Auld lang syne*. Sc. form of *since* (q.v.) without adv. -*s*.

synecdoche [*rhet.*]. Part for whole or vice-versa. L., G. συνεκδοχή, receiving together, from σύν, ἐκ, and δέχεσθαι, to receive.

synod. F. *synode*, L., G. σύνοδος, going together, from ὁδός, way. Orig. eccl. council, now esp. of Presbyterians (but see quot.).

The Synod of the Presbyterian Church of England was changed at its annual meeting this week to the name of General Assembly
(*Daily Chron.* May 6, 1920).

synonym. F. *synonyme*, L. (neut. pl.), from G. συνώνυμος, of same name, ὄνυμα (Aeolic).

synopsis. G. σύνοψις, seeing together (see *optic*). Cf. *conspectus*. *Synoptic* (theol.) is applied to the first three Gospels.

syntax. F. *syntaxe*, L., G. σύνταξις, from τάσσειν, to arrange.

synthesis. G. σύνθεσις, putting together, from τιθέναι, to put. Cf. *analysis*.

syntonic [*wireless*]. Used (1892) by Lodge, at suggestion of Myers.

syphilis. Coined (1530) by Fracastoro, physician of Verona, in title of poem, *Syphilis, sive Morbus Gallicus*. The hero's name, *Syphilus*, may be intended as "pig-lover."

syphon. See *siphon*.

syren. See *siren*.

Syriac [*ling.*]. Form of *Aramaic* (q.v.). See *Dan.* ii. 4.

syringa. From *syrinx* (q.v.).

syringe. Restored from F. *seringue*, "a siringe, or squirt" (Cotg.), from *syrinx* (q.v.).

syrinx. G. σῦριγξ, σύριγγ-, shepherd's pipe, from συρίζειν, to play on the pipes of Pan. Hence applied to various tubular objects.

syrup, sirup. F. *sirop*, MedL. *sirupus*, Arab. *sharāb*, from *shariba*, to drink; cf. It. *siroppo*, Sp. *jarope*; also *sherbet, shrub²*. Orig. of med. potion, with later sense-development like that of *treacle* (q.v.).

systaltic. G. συσταλτικός. See *systole*.

system. F. *système*, L., G. σύστημα, what stands together, from ἱστάναι, to set up. For formation and senses cf. *constitution*.

systole. G. συστολή, from συστέλλειν, to draw together. Cf. *diastole*.

systyle [*arch.*]. Building with columns close together. From G. στῦλος, pillar, *style²*. Cf. *peristyle*.

syzygy [*astron.*]. Conjunction. G. συζυγία, from σύν and ζυγόν, yoke.

T, to a. ? For earlier *to a tittle*. Cf. Ger. *genau bis aufs tüttelchen*, exact to the dot on the i.

ta. Natural infantile sound of gratitude. Recorded from 18 cent.

taal. Du., language, applied in E. to the SAfrDu. patois. See *tale*.

tab. A dial. word of obscure origin, often interchangeable with *tag*. ? Ult. cogn. with Du. *tepel*, nipple, Ger. *zipfel*, lappet, etc., and with It. *zaffo*, "ear" of a tab (from Teut.). Latest (mil.) sense, esp. in ref. to red tabs of staff (v.i.), is quite mod.

crampon de cuir: a loope, or tab, of leather (Cotg.).

The army had not ceased chuckling over this gem of red tabdom (*Daily Chron.* Jan. 22, 1919).

tabard [*hist.*]. OF. *tabar(t)*; cf. It. *tabarro*, Sp. *tabardo*. Orig. coarse sleeveless upper garment worn by peasants (Chauc. A. 541). Later knight's surcoat (whence *Tabard Inn*). Her. sense from 16 cent. Origin unknown.

tabaret. Striped fabric. Trade-name from *tabby*. Cf. *tabinet*.

tabasco. Trade-mark for a pepper-sauce condiment. *Tabasco*, name of a river and state in Mexico.

tabby. F. *tabis*, earlier *atabis*, striped taffeta, from Arab. '*attābiy* (quarter of Bagdad where it was manufactured), whence also It. Sp. *tabi*. Cf. *calico*, *fustian*, *muslin*, *surat*, etc. Hence *tabby-cat* (17 cent.), earlier described as *tabby-coloured* or "streakt"

tabby: an old maid; either from Tabitha, a formal antiquated name; or else from a tabby cat, old maids being often compared to cats (Grose).

tabernacle. F., L. *tabernaculum*, dim. from *taberna*, hut, booth (see *tavern*). Earliest (13 cent.) in *OT*. sense.

tabes [*med.*]. L., consumption, wasting.

tabinet. Fabric. Earlier also *tabine*. App. from *tabby*.

table. F., L. *tabula*, board (also for games), writing tablet, list, picture, etc.; cf. It. *tavola*, Sp. *tabla*; also Du. Ger. *tafel* (see *tafferel*), AS. *tabule*. To *turn the tables* (*upon*) is from reversing the position at backgammon, earlier called *tables* (Chauc.). *Table-land* is first recorded (Dampier) as name for *Table Mountain*, at the Cape, so may be adapted from Du. *Table-rapping*, *table-turning*, date from 1850–60. Spec. sense of *table-talk* dates from Luther's *Colloquia Mensalia* (1567).

tableau. F., picture, dim. from *table*.

table d'hôte. F., host's table.

tablet. F. *tablette*, dim. of *table*. Earliest (14 cent.) in E. in ref. to the two Mosaic tablets of stone.

tabloid. Trade-word for concentrated drug, coined on *tablet*. For recent fig. uses cf. *pemmican*.

In a report published on the 13th inst....occurred the word "tabloid," the origin of which is most interesting. It was coined by Messrs Burroughs, Wellcome & Co., and was registered as their trademark in 1884 (*Ev. Stand.* Apr. 19, 1920).

taboo, tabu. Tongan *tabu* (adj.). Found in various forms (*tapu*, *tambu*, *kapu*) throughout the South Sea Islands. First in Cook's *Voyage* (1777) and adopted as E. verb before 1800 (Burke).

tabor. OF. *tabour* (*tambour*), of Oriental origin; cf. Pers. *tabīrah*, *tabūrāk*, drum, Arab. *ṭanbūr*, lute. Prob. imit. See *tambour*.

tabouret. Stool. F., lit. little drum (v.s.).

tabula rasa. L., scraped tablet. Cf. *clean slate*, F. *table rase*.

tabular. L. *tabularis*, from *tabula*, table (q.v.). Cf. *tabulate*.

tacamahac. Resin and tree. Obs. Sp. *tacamahaca* (*tacamaca*), Aztec *tecomahiyac*.

tache [*archaic*]. Buckle, link (*Ex.* xxvi. 6). OF. *tache*, aphet. for *attache*. Cf. *tack*[1].

tachometer. From G. τάχος, speed, whence also scient. words in *tachy-* (adj. ταχύς).

tachy-case [*neol.*]. For *attaché-case*, small bag as carried by embassy attaché.

tacit. L. *tacitus*, from *tacēre*, to be silent. Cf. *taciturn*, L. *taciturnus*.

tack[1]. Fastening. ONF. *taque*, doublet of *tache* (see *attach*, *attack*). Hence verb to *tack*, sew together, shift the tacks (naut.) so as to change direction. Cf. fig. to *be on the right tack*. It is curious that Sp. *puntear*, from *punto*, stitch, has the same two senses.

tack[2]. Food. Esp. in naut. *hard-tack*, ship's biscuit, *soft-tack*, bread. App. short for *tackle*, used in same sense (v.i.).

tackle. Of LG. origin. Cf. LG. *takel*, rope, pulley, etc.; earlier, equipment in general; cogn. with *take*, in sense of laying hold. This appears in the verb (wrestling, football, and John Willet). From 13 cent., chiefly naut., whence many, and various, fig. senses. Borrowed by several naut. langs.

"Rare tackle that, sir, of a cold morning," says the coachman (*Tom Brown*, i. 4).

tact. F., L. *tactus*, touch, from *tangere, tact-*. Cf. Ger. *takt*, time (mus.). We still say of a *tactless* man that he has a heavy "touch."

tactics. Renders G. τὰ τακτικά, lit. matters of arrangement, from τάσσειν, τακτ-, to arrange. Cf. *syntax*.

tadpole[1]. Young frog. ME. *taddepol*, lit. toad head (*poll*[1]). The numerous dial. names all allude to the head.

tadpole[2]. Pol. scheming nonentity. *Tadpole* and *Taper* are characters in Disraeli's *Coningsby* (1844).

The wretched old party game of reds and blues, tadpoles and tapirs (sic) (*Ev. News*, July 25, 1917).

tael. Chin. money of account, orig. the *liang*, or ounce, of standard silver. Port., Malay *tahil*, weight.

taenia [*arch. & biol.*]. L., G. ταινία, fillet, ribbon.

tafferel, taffrail [*naut.*]. Orig. panel picture; later (c. 1700) flat part of stern usu. ornamented with picture or carving. Du. *tafereel*, dim. of *tafel*, table, picture. Cf. synon. naut. F. *tableau*. *Taffrail* (19 cent.) is altered on *rail*[1].

taffeta. OF. *taffetas*, ult. from Pers. *tāftah*, p.p. of *tāftan*, to shine, also to twist, spin; cf. It. *taffetà*, Sp. *tafetán*.

taffrail. See *tafferel*.

taffy. Earlier form of *toffee*.

Taffy. Welshman. Cf. *Paddy, Sandy, Sawney*.

Taffy was once a Cottamighty of Wales (*Rump Songs*, 1639–61).

Taffy: a Welshman or David (*Dict. Cant. Crew*).

tafia. Rum distilled from molasses. Described in 1722 as native WInd. name (see *ratafia*), but also found in Malay.

tag[1]. End, point. Orig. (14 cent.) pendent point of "dagged" garment. Perh. altered from obs. *dag* (*Piers Plowm.*) under influence of *tack*[1], in sense of sharpened point; ? or from LG. and ult. cogn. with Ger. *zacke*, point, jag. Some senses are associated with *tab*. Hence *tag, rag and bobtail* (Pepys), earlier (16 cent.) *tag and rag, tagrag*. Shaks. has *tag* for rabble (*Cor.* iii. 1). Another var. is *tag, rag and cut-tail*.

tag[2]. Game of touch. ? Ult. from L. *tangere*. Cf. *tig*.

taguan. Flying squirrel. Philippine name.

tail[1]. Caudal appendage. AS. *tægel*. Com. Teut., but not in gen. use in mod. Teut. langs.; cf. LG. *tagel*, rope's end, etc., OHG. *zagel*, tail, ON. *tagl*, horse-tail, Goth. *tagl*, hair. Orig. sense was prob. hair, hairy tail.

From 13 cent. in sense of train of followers, with which cf. mod. cricket use. Sense of inferior part, residue, appears in *tailings*, with which cf. *middlings*. In connection with *pasha* it refers to the number of horsetail banners which indicate his rank.

Some learned writers have compared a scorpion to an epigram...because as the sting of the scorpions lyeth in the tayl, so the force and virtue of an epigram is in the conclusion (Topsell).

tail[2] [*leg.*]. Limitation in inheritance of freehold. F. *taille*, tax, assessment, from *tailler*, to cut; cf. AF. *fee taylé*, MedL. *feodum taliatum*. See *entail*.

tailor. F. *tailleur*, tailor, cutter (of anything), from *tailler*, to cut (see *tally*). See quot. s.v. *turn*.

taint. Aphet. for *attaint* (q.v.). Cf. to have a "touch" of. Some senses slightly influenced by obs. *taint*, colour, tint (q.v.).

Car si l'avait atainte et la pluie et la bise (*Berthe au grand pied*).

Cold and wet lodging had so tainted their people (*New England's Memorial*).

La première atteinte que nous donnons à la vérité (Bossuet).

And the truth With superstition and tradition taint (Milt.).

Taiping [*hist.*]. Chin. revolutionary (1850–65). Chin. *t'ai p'ing*, lit. great peace, the leader having assumed the title *T'ai-p'ing-wang*, prince of great peace, and aiming at the establishment of a *T'ai-p'ing-choo*, great peace dynasty.

take. ON. *taka*, gradually replacing AS. *niman* in ME.; cogn. with Goth. *tēkan*, to touch (see also *tackle*), and with root *tag* of L. *tangere*, to touch (cf. *tagax*, thievish). The sense-development is remarkable, e.g. the combination to *take up* has 52 varieties of meaning. "It is one of the elemental words of the language" (*NED.*). The development of many of the senses can be understood by a comparison with F. *prendre*. Poet. p.p. *ta'en* is ME. *y-tan*, for *y-taken*.

My modyr wepyth and takyth on mervaylously (*Paston Let.* iii. 37).

takin. Horned ruminant from Tibet. Native name.

talapoin. Monkey, orig. Buddhist monk (Pegu). Port. *talapão*, OPeguan *tala pōi*, my lord. Purch. has *talapoye*.

talar. Long robe. L. *talaris*, from *talus*, ankle.

talbotype [*phot.*]. Patented (1841) by *W. H. F. Talbot*.

talc. F., It. *talco*, Arab. *ṭalq*, from Pers.; cf. Sp. *talco*, Du. Ger. *talk*.

tale. AS. *talu*, speech, number. Com. Teut.; cf. Du. *taal*, speech, Ger. *zahl*, number, ON. *tala*, speech, number. For double sense cf. cogn. *tell*, also Ger. *zählen*, to count, *erzählen*, to relate, recount. So also OF. *conter*, L. *computare*, now artificially differentiated into *conter*, to relate, *compter*, to count. With *old wives' tale* (Marlowe) cf. F. *conte de bonne femme*. For degeneration of sense cf. *story*[1]. To *tell tales*, betray, is 14 cent.

Thereby hangs a tale (*Shrew*, iv. 1).

And I will my nese Annes have a pare bedes of coral gawdid with gold & my boke of the talys of Cantyrbury (*Will of Sir Th. Cumberworth*, 1451).

talegalla. WGuinea brush-turkey. F. *talégalle*, coined (1828) by Lesson from Malagasy *talèva*, coot, and L. *gallus*, cock.

talent. F., L. *talentum*, money of account, G. τάλαντον, balance, weight, sum. In most Europ. langs., having in OF. and other Rom. langs. sense of will, inclination, which is also common in ME. Current fig. sense is from *Matt.* xxv. 14–30. AS. had *talente*, from L. pl.

tales [*leg.*]. Jurymen, orig. those added on emergency. L., pl. of *talis*, such, in *tales de circumstantibus*, such of those standing round. See *Pickwick*, ch. xxxiv.

taliacotian operation [*med.*]. Surgical reconstruction, esp. of nose. From *Tagliacozzi*, surgeon of Bologna (†1599).

talion, law of. Adapted from F. *loi du talion*, L. *talio-n-*, from *talis*, like. An eye for an eye, etc. Cf. *retaliate*.

talipot. Palm. Hind. *tālpāt*, Sanskrit *talapattra*, leaf of the palmyra or fan-palm.

talisman. Sp., or It. *talismano*, Arab. *tilsam*, G. τέλεσμα, lit. payment, in Late G. religious rite, etc., from τελεῖν, to accomplish, from τέλος, end, initiation. Cf. *telegraph*.

talk. Early ME. frequent. formation on *tale* or *tell*; cf. *lurk*, *walk*. *Talkative* (15 cent.) is a curious hybrid. *Talkee talkee* is negro redupl.

tall. AS. *getæl*, swift, prompt; cogn. with OHG. *gizal*, swift; cf. Goth. *untals*, uncompliant. Orig. sense may appear in Chauc. (v.i.). For later developments cf. *buxom*, *deft*, *pretty*, *proper*, and many other adjs. applied to persons. Usual ME. sense survives in archaic *tall fellow of his hands*,

used by Holland to render L. *promptus manu*; cf. *tall ship*, common in Hakl. & Purch. Current sense appears in Palsg.

She made hym at hir lust so humble and talle
                (Chauc. *Compl. of Mars*, 38).

Tall words and lofty notions (*NED*. 1670).

tallage [*hist.*]. Tax. OF. *taillage* from *tailler*, to cut, whence MedL. *tallagium*; cf. F. *taille*, "a task, or tax; a tallage, tribute, imposition" (Cotg.). See *tally*.

tallboy. High chest of drawers (18 cent.), tall drinking glass (17 cent.). App. *tall boy*, as playful name, perh. partly suggested by surname *Tallboys* (F. *taille-bois*).

tallet [*west-country*]. Hay-loft. Welsh *taflod*, *taflawd*, Late L. *tabulata*, boarding. See *table* and cf. OIr. *taibled*, storey.

tallith. Fringed shawl or scarf worn by Jews at prayer. Rabbinical Heb. from *ṭāla·l*, to cover.

tallow. ME. *talgh* (14 cent.), LG. *talg*, tallow being extensively imported from the Baltic. Hence also Du. *talk*, Ger. Sw. Dan. Norw. *talg*.

tally. AF. *tallier*, F. *tailler*, to cut (cf. *rally*[2], *sully*, etc.). The noun, in sense of double notched stick used for "scoring," one half being kept by each party, is prob. older in E. Hence *tallyman*, selling on tick. With F. *tailler* cf. It. *tagliare*, Sp. *tajar*, VL. *taliare*. Usu. derived from L. *talea*, rod, slip for grafting. My own opinion is that VL. *taliare* is from *talis*, like, and that the orig. idea was to cut into equal lengths or portions. Cf. *retaliate*. For orig. sense of noun *tally* cf. synon. Norw. Dan. *karvestok*, Ger. *kerbholz*, lit. carve-stick, -wood, and see *score*.

tally-ho. F. *taïaut* (Mol.), OF. *thialau*, with many vars. Prob. a meaningless exclamation. Cf. *yoicks*.

talma. Cloak. From *Talma*, F. tragedian (†1826). Cf. *roquelaure*.

Talmud. Body of Jewish trad. law. Late Heb. *talmūd*, instruction, from *lāma·d*, to teach.

talon. F., heel, VL. **talo-n-*, from *talus*, ankle; cf. It. *talone*, Sp. *talón*. Sense of claw, orig. heel-claw of falcon, is developed in E. only.

The grete clees [of a hawk] behynde...ye shall call hom talons (*Book of St Albans*).

talus. F., slope, OF. *talu*, VL. **talutum*, from *talus*, ankle, taken in sense of heel (*talon*). Orig. in fort., later in geol.

tamandua. Ant-eater. Port., from Tupi (Brazil). Earlier is *tamandro* (Purch. xvi. 220).

tamarack. Amer. larch. Native Ind. name in Canada.

tamarau. Diminutive Philippine buffalo. Native name.

tamarin. Marmoset. F., from Carib dial. of Cayenne.

tamarind. Cf. F. *tamarin* (OF. *tamarinde*), It. Sp. *tamarindo*, MedL. *tamarindus*, Arab. *tamr-hindī*, date of India, whence *tamarindi* (Marco Polo).

tamarisk. Late L. *tamariscus*, var. of *tamarix*, *tamaric-*, whence F. *tamaris*.

tamasha [*Anglo-Ind.*]. Entertainment, function. Urdu, Pers., Arab., from Arab. *masha*, to walk.

tambouki [*SAfr.*]. Grass of *Tembu-land*, from tribal name.

tambour. F., drum, also in *tambour de Basque*, tambourine. Nasalized form of *tabor*, ? partly due to L. *tympanum*. Also of drum-shaped embroidery frame and as techn. term of arch. *Tambourine* is F. *tambourin*, prop. the Provençal drum, but used in E. for the *tambour de Basque*. Ben Jonson has *timburine*, prob. by association with *timbrel*.

tame. AS. *tam*. Com. Teut.; cf. Du. *tam*, Ger. *zahm*, ON. *tamr*, Goth. *tamjan* (verb); cogn. with L. *domare*, G. δαμᾶν.

Tamil [*ling.*]. Chief Dravidian lang. of S.E. India. Sanskrit *Dramila, Draviḍa*.

Tammany [*US.*]. From pol. associations of *Tammany Hall*, New York, centre of Democratic activity, orig. head-quarters of Society of *St Tammany*, "tutelar saint" of Pennsylvania, the name being taken from that of an Indian chief with whom Penn the Quaker negotiated for grants of land (17 cent.).

tammy[1]. Fabric. Prob. for obs. *tamin*, F. *étamine* (OF. *estamine*), whence ME. *stamin*. Ult. from L. *stamen*, thread.

tammy[2], tam o' shanter. Lowland bonnet as worn by hero of Burns' poem. Hence *black and tam*, Oxford undergraduette (1920).

tamp [*techn.*]. To ram. F. *étamper*, OF. *estamper*, of Teut. origin (*stamp*).

tamper. Var. of *temper* (q.v.), in sense of working in clay, whence fig. sense of meddling. Cf. F. *tremper dans une affaire*, to be mixed up in a business.

A fork and a hooke, to be tampring in claie
(Tusser).

Hee would needs be handling and tempering with the weapons of his said guest (Holland's *Pliny*).

tampion, tampon, tampkin. See *tompion*[2].

tan. AS. **tannian* (cf. *tannere*, tanner); cf. MedL. *tannare*, F. *tanner*. Of Celt. origin, from Bret. *tann*, oak; cf. Corn. *glas-tannen*, ilex. The earliest *tan* was oak-bark (cf. name *Barker*, i.e. *Tanner*). Cf. *tawny*. The latest (1920) sense of *black and tan*, members of auxiliary Royal Irish Constabulary, is prob. due to orig. extempore uniform of the force being army khaki with black leather belt.

tanager. Bird. ModL. *tanagra* (Linnaeus), for Tupi (Brazil) *tangara*.

Tanagra. Terra-cotta statuette from *Tanagra* in Boeotia.

tandem. L., "at length."

tandem: a two-wheeled chaise, buggy, or noddy, drawn by two horses, one before the other: that is, at length (Grose).

tandsticker. Sw. *tändstickor*, pl. of *tändsticka*, match, from *tända*, to light, *sticka*, splinter, thus approx. tinder-stick.

tang[1]. Sharp point, sting, pungent flavour. ON. *tangi*, point. For series of senses cf. F. *pointe* and *piquant*. ? Cogn. with *tongue*.

tang[2]. Imit. of sound (cf. *twang*), but in some senses, e.g. *tongue with a tang* (*Temp.* ii. 2), closely associated with *tang*[1].

tang[3] [*dial.*]. Sea-weed. See *tangle*[2].

tangena, tanghin. Poison and shrub. F. *tanghin*, Malagasy *tangena*.

tangent. From pres. part. of L. *tangere*, to touch.

Having twelve times described this circle, he lately flew off at a tangent (Humphrey Clinker).

tangerine. Orange from *Tangier(s)*, F. *Tanger*.

tangible. L. *tangibilis*, from *tangere*, to touch.

tangle[1]. To embarrass, etc. From 14 cent., with var. *tagle* (whence Sc. *taigle*), of which it is app. a nasalized form. *Tagle* is aphet. for AF. *entagler*, to entangle (*Lib. Alb.*, *Lib. Cust.*), and this, I suggest, is from *tackle*, in the sense of rope, so that the formation, and sense, would run parallel with those of *pester* (q.v.). *Tangle*[2], from which Skeat derives it, is a purely Sc. word of much later appearance.

Qe ne soient appellez ne appellours, et qe ne soient entaglez de plee de la coroune
(*Lib. Cust.*, p. 298, temp. Edw. II)

tangle[2]. Sea-weed. Sc. (16 cent.), prob. via Orkney or Shetland dial. from ON. *thön gull*, from *thang*, bladder-wrack; cf. Norw. *taangel*, Faroese *tongul*.

tango. SAmer. dance (v.i.).

A negro dance from Cuba, introduced into South America by mariners who shipped jerked beef to the Antilles, conquered the entire earth in a few months (Ibañez, *Four Horsemen*).

tangram. Chin. puzzle. The Chin. name is *ch'i ch'iao t'u*, seven ingenious plan, and *tangram* is app. an E. or US. coinage on *anagram*, *cryptogram*, etc.

tanist [*hist.*]. Successor apparent to Celtic chief. Ir. Gael. *tánaiste*, lit. parallel, second.

tank. Orig. Anglo-Ind., pool, cistern, a very common word in Hakl. & Purch., Port. *tanque*, L. *stagnum*, whence F. *étang* (OF. *estanc*), Sp. *estanque*. Some authorities regard *tank* rather as a native word (Guzerati, Mahratti), with which the Port. word accidentally coincided (for a similar problem see *palanquin*). *Tanks* first went into action at Pozières ridge, Sep. 5, 1916.

It was decided [Feb. 1916] that one hundred Tanks —the name was adopted for the sake of secrecy— should be built (*Times Lit. Sup.* Jan. 22, 1920, reviewing Sir A. G. Stern's *Tanks* 1914–18).

tankard. Cf. OF. *tanquart*, archaic Du. *tanckaert*, MedL. *tancardus*. I take it to be a joc. metath. (? due to the fame of the Crusader *Tancred*), of L. *cantharus*, "a tankerd" (Coop.), G. κάνθαρος, suggested by the pers. name *Tankard*, once common and still a surname (also *Tancred*, *Tanqueray*). This is OHG. *Thanc-ward*, lit. thought keeper. With this conjecture cf. *jack*, *jug*, *toby-jug*, *bellarmine*, *goblet*, *puncheon*, etc. From L. *cantharus* come OF. *canthare*, "a great jugge, or tankard" (Cotg.), It. *cantharo*, "a tankard" (Flor.). A similar metath. is seen in Norw. Dan. *kopper*, pox, for earlier *pokker*.

tanner [*slang*]. Sixpence (c. 1800). Orig. unknown.

tannin. F. *tanin*, from *tan*, tan.

tanrec. Insectivorous mammal. F., from Malagasy.

tansy. OF. *tanesie*, aphet. for *atanesie*, Late L., G. ἀθανασία, immortality, from ἀ-, neg., θάνατος, death. Either in ref. to med. virtues or persistence of flowers (cf. *everlasting*, *immortelle*).

tantalize. From punishment of *Tantalus*, king of Phrygia and son of Zeus, who was condemned to remain athirst in water up to his chin and with fruit hanging just above his mouth. *Tantalus*, spirit-stand which looks accessible but is not, is late 19 cent. *Tantalum* (chem.) was named

(1802) by Ekeberg from its incapacity to absorb acid when immersed in it.

The fugitive pippin, swimming in water not of the purest, and bobbing from the expanded lips of the juvenile Tantalus (*Ingoldsby*).

tantamount. Orig. as verb, AF. *tant amounter*, to amount to as much; cf. It. *tanto montare*.

His not denying tant-amounteth to the affirming of the matter (Fuller).

tantara, tantarara. Imit. of flourish of trumpet, or roll of drum. Cf. L. *taratantara* (Enn.).

tantivy. Orig. adv., at full gallop. ? Imit. of huntsman's horn. Hist. application to Tory High Churchmen temp. Charles II and James II is due to a caricature of 1680–1 described below.

From thence to London it rode tan-tivy
          (*The Rump*, Dec. 26, 1659).

About half a dozen of the tantivies were mounted upon the Church of England, booted and spurred, riding it, like an old hack, tantivy to Rome
          (North's *Examen*).

tantony [*archaic*]. For *St Anthony*. Esp. in *tantony pig*, Saint Anthony being patron of swineherds. Stow connects the saying esp. with the hospital of *St Anthony*, London. Cf. *tawdry*.

If any gave to them bread, or other feeding, such would they know, watch for, and daily follow, whining till they had somewhat given them; whereupon was raised a proverb, "Such an one will follow such an one, and whine as it were an Anthonie pig" (*Survey of London*).

tantrum. Also (18 cent.) *tantarum*. Origin unknown. Cotg. has *trantran* in sense of *tantara*.

Taoism. One of the three religions of China (cf. *Buddhism*, *Confucianism*). From Chin. *tao*, path, right way, as in *tao tē king*, book of reason and virtue, containing the teachings of Lao-tsze (6 cent. B.C.).

tap¹. For liquids. AS. *tæppa*. Com. Teut.; cf. Du. *tap* (see *tattoo¹*), Ger. *zapfen*, ON. *tappi*. Orig. sense prob. plug (see *tompion*). For transition of sense cf. *shaft*, *socket*.

tap². To strike lightly. F. *taper*, of imit. origin; cf. *rap¹*, *rub-a-dub*, etc.

tapa, tappa. Polynesian cloth. Native name.

tape. AS. *tæppe*, of unknown origin. ? Cogn. with *tapis*.

taper¹. Candle. AS. *tapur*, ? dissim. of **papur*, L. *papyrus*. The same dissim. occurs in some of the more remote cognates of L. *pōpulus*, poplar. *Papyrus* is rendered *taper* in early glossaries (11 cent.) and had the sense of candle-wick. Cf. Ger. *kerze*, taper, from L. *charta*, paper. Adj. sense of slender is evolved from earlier *taperwise*. Hence also verb to *taper*. Cf. F. *fuselé*, taper (of fingers), from *fuseau*, spindle.

taper². See *tadpole²*.

tapestry. ME. *tapesry, tapysserie*, etc., F *tapisserie*, from *tapis* (q.v.).

tapinocephalic [*anthrop.*]. From G. ταπεινός, low, κεφαλή, head.

tapioca. Sp. or Port., Tupi-Guarani (Brazil) *tipioca*, meal of cassava root, from *tipi*, residue, *og*, to squeeze out. Spelt *tockawhoughe* by Capt. John Smith.

tapir. Tupi (Brazil) *tapira*.

tapis. F., carpet, Late L. *tapetium* (for *tapete*), G. ταπήτιον, dim. of τάπης, tapestry, perh. of Pers. origin and cogn. with *taffeta*; cf. Sp. *tapiz*; also AS. *teped* (Late L. *tapetum*), Du. *tapijt*, Ger. *teppich*. Older F. sense was table-cover, whence *sur le tapis*, before the meeting.

tar. AS. *teru, teoru*; cf. Du. LG. *teer*, also Ger. *teer* (from LG.), ON. *tjara*; prob. cogn. with *tree*. With *tar, tarpaulin*, sailor (17 cent.), cf. earlier *tar-breech* and F. *cul goudronné*. In to *lose the ship for a ha'porth of tar, ship* is for *sheep*, orig. allusion being ? to use of tar as sheep-ointment, ? or in marking sheep (with the latter cf. *tarred with the same brush*).

> And rather thus to lose ten sheepe than be at the charge of a halfe penny worth of tarre
> (Capt. John Smith).

taradiddle. "A fib or falsity" (Grose). Playful elaboration of *diddle* (q.v.).

tarantass. Vehicle. Russ., from Tyoorkish.

tarantula. MedL., from *Taranto*, Apulia, L. *Tarentum*, where the spider is found. Hence *tarantism*, dancing mania, It. *tarantismo*, and *tarantella*, It., dance and melody supposed to be a cure for the spider's bite.

taraxacum. Dandelion. MedL., Arab., from Pers. *talkh chakōk*, bitter herb.

tarboosh. Fez. Arab. *ṭarbūsh*.

tardigrade [*zool.*]. F., L. *tardigradus*, slow-stepping.

tardy. F. *tardif*, from *tard*, late, L. *tardus*. Cf. *jolly, testy*.

tare¹. Plant. Orig. (c. 1330) a small seed. Later (1388) in the sense of a kind of vetch, and used in the second Wyc. version (*Matt.* xiii. 25) for earlier *cockle, darnel*, rendering L., G. ζιζάνια. Origin unknown.

> But ther-of sette the millere nat a tare
> (Chauc. A. 4000).

tare² [*archaic*]. Reduction (for packing, vehicle, etc.) from gross weight. F., "losse,

diminution, decay, impairement, want, or waste in merchandize" (Cotg.), It. or Sp. *tara*, Arab. *ṭarḥah*, from *ṭaraḥa*, to reject. Now only in archaic *tare and tret*.

target. Orig. shield. Dim. of archaic *targe*, F., ON. *targa*, shield, cogn. with OHG. *zarga*, edge, border (cf. OHG. *rand*, shield, lit. edge). AS. also had *targe*, from ON. The hard -*g*- of *target* is due to OF. *targuette* or It. *targhetta*. Sense of shield-like mark for archery is 18 cent.

targum. Collection of Aram. *OT.* versions, paraphrases, etc., handed down orally after Captivity and reduced to writing c. 100 A.D. Chaldee, from *targēm*, to interpret. Cf. *dragoman*.

tariff. It. *tariffa*, "arithmetike or casting of accounts" (Flor.), Arab. *ta'rīf*, explanation, definition, from *'arafa*, to make known; cf. Sp. Port. *tarifa*. *Tariff-Reform* was orig. (c. 1890) US. and a movement *towards* free trade.

tarlatan. Fabric. F. *tarlatane*, earlier *tarnatane*, prob. of EInd. origin.

tarmac. Road-material. Registered name for *tar-macadam*.

tarn. ON. *tjörn*, whence Norw. *tjörn, tjern*. A dial. word introduced into E. by the Lake Poets (cf. *gill², fell³*).

tarnation. US. for *darnation*, i.e. *damnation*. Influenced by *tarnal*, eternal.

tarnish. F. *ternir, terniss-* (c. 1200), from *terne*, dull, dingy, ? from OHG. *tarnan*, to hide, darken, cogn. with AS. *dernan* (see *darn¹*). For vowel cf. *varnish*.

taro. Plant. Polynesian (Capt. Cook).

taroc, tarot. Playing-card. F. *tarot*, It. **tarocco* (pl. *tarocchi*), of unknown origin.

tarpaulin. Used by Capt. John Smith as equivalent to *awning*. Second element is prob. ME. *palyoun*, canopy, a pop. form of *pavilion*, with which cf. Norw. Dan. Sw. *paulun*, canopy, and cogn. forms in LG. To derive *tarpauling* from synon. Lincolnshire *pauling* is like deriving *tobacco* or *potato* from "Lincolnshire" *bacca* and *tater*. ? Unless the Lincolnshire word is an early loan from Scand. (v.s.).

tarpon. Jew-fish. Cf. Du. *tarpoen*. Prob. from some native NAmer. name.

tarragon. Plant (used for flavouring vinegar). Ult. Arab. *ṭarkhōn*, which is prob. G. δράκων, lit. dragon, the plant having been early associated with δρακόντιον, or *arum dracunculus*. Cf. MedL. *tragonia*, Sp., F. *estragon*, It. *taracone*, etc.

tarras. See *trass*.

tarry. In ME. also trans., as still in archaic to *tarry one's leisure*. The phonetic history of the word is that of obs. *tary*, *tarre*, to vex, persecute, egg on, etc., corresponding to AS. *tergan* and OF. *tarier*. But there is no approach in these to the sense, which is exactly that of OF. *targier*, VL. **tardiare*, from *tardus*, late. This does not suit the phonetics.

Tarshish, ship of [*Bibl.*]. Large merchant-ship such as those of *Tarsus* in Cilicia. Cf. *argosy* (q.v.), earlier *Aragousey shippe* (*Privy Council Acts*, 1545–6).

tarsia. It., "a kind of painting, in laying or setting in of small pieces of wood, ivorie, horne, or bone...as in tables, chesse-boordes and such" (Flor.).

tarsus [*anat.*]. G. ταρσός, flat of the foot between toes and heel. Hence *tarso-* in scient. words.

tart¹. Adj. AS. *teart*, severe (of punishment, etc.), only found once in ME. in a passage of doubtful meaning, but common from 16 cent. in lit. and fig. senses. ? Cogn. with *tear²* (as *bitter* with *bite*). The gaps in its hist. want filling up.

tart². Noun. F. *tarte* (13 cent.), MedL. *tarta* (c. 1100). Connection with OF. *torte* (*tourte*), Late L. *torta panis*, kind of loaf (*Vulg.*), ? lit. twisted bread, is doubtful, though both It. & Sp. have *torta*, tart, pasty, in early use (Flor., Minsh.). Connection of Late L. *torta* with *torquēre*, *tort-*, to twist, is also doubtful, the Rom. forms pointing to orig. *ō*, not *ŏ*.

tartan¹. Fabric. ME. & OF. *tartarin*, MedL. *tartarinum*, rich material imported from China via *Tartary*, also called *tarterne* in ME. Occurs several times as *tartar* in *Sc. Treas. Accts.* of 15 cent. For later application to a coarser material cf. *buckram*, *camlet*, etc. ? Partly due to F. *tiretaine*, a mixed fabric, OF. var. *tertaine*, with which cf. 16 cent. Sc. *tertane*. *Tartaryn*, *tartayne*, *tyrtaine* all occur in will of Lady Clare (†1360).

Item, for v elne of tartar to lyne a gowne of cloth of gold to the King (*Sc. Treas. Accts.* 1473).

For iij elnis of heland tertane to be hois [hose] to the Kingis grace (*ib.* 1538).

tartan² [*naut.*]. Mediterranean vessel. F. *tartane*, It. (Sp.) *tartana*, ? from Arab. *tarīdah*, whence also ME. *tarette*. Cf. MedL. *tarida*, *tareia*, "navis onerariae species, eadem quae tartana vocitata, ut quidam volunt" (Duc.).

tartar [*chem.*]. F. *tartre*; cf. It. Sp. *tartaro*, MedL. *tartarum*, MedG. τάρταρον, ? of Oriental origin, cogn. with Arab. *durdī*, tartar, Pers. *durd*, sediment, dregs.

Tartar. MedL. *Tartarus*, app. altered, on *Tartarus*, hell, from the orig. ethnic name, which is *Tātār* in Pers. Most of the Europ. langs. have both *Tart-* and *Tat-* forms. First used (13 cent.) in ref. to the hordes (Mongols, Tartars, Turks, etc.) of Jenghiz Khan. The lang. is Turanian. With *to catch a Tartar* cf. F. *tenir le loup par les oreilles*, "to bee in danger; (for if you hold him he bites you by the fingers, if you let him goe he will goe neere to devoure you)" (Cotg.). See Terence, *Phormio*, 506.

This noble kyng, this Tartre Cambyuskan
(Chauc. F. 28).

Nor will I in haste My dear liberty barter,
Lest, thinking to catch, I am caught by a Tartar
(*Song*, c. 1700).

Tartarus. Hell. L., G. Τάρταρος.

Tartu(f)fe. Hypocrite. F., title-rôle in Molière's comedy (1664); cf. It. *Tartufo*, character in It. comedy, prob. from *tartuffo*, truffle.

tasimeter. From G. τάσις, tension, from τείνειν, to stretch.

task. ONF. *tasque*, for OF. *tasche* (*tâche*), metath. of *taxe*, tax (or VL. **tasca* for *taxa*). This metath. is common in F., e.g. *lâche*, OF. *lasche*, VL. **lascus*, for *laxus* (*lacsus*). *Task* has also the sense of *tax* in ME. and to *take one to task* is very similar in meaning to *to tax one* (*with*).

tass [*archaic*]. Cup, goblet. F. *tasse*; cf. It. *tazza*, Sp. *taza*, MedL. *tassa*; all from Arab. *ṭass*, *ṭassah*, basin, Pers. *tast*, goblet.

tassel¹. Pendent ornament. OF. *tassel*, tassel, orig. little heap, dim. of *tas*, heap (whence ME. *tass*, heap, bunch), of Teut. origin. OF. *tassel* also means clasp, prob. from the practice, often referred to in OF., ME. & Prov., of making the fastenings of a mantle of a tress of hair. The equivalents in the Europ. langs. all mean bunch, tuft, e.g. F. *houppe* (Du. *hoop*, heap, bundle), Ger. *quast*, orig. bundle of leaves, twigs, It. *fiocco* (see *flock²*), Sp. *borla* (see *burlesque*).

tassel² [*archaic*]. As in *tassel-gentle*. See *tercel*.

tasset [*hist.*]. Kind of kilt of overlapping armour plates. OF. *tassete*, dim. of synon.

tasse. Orig. purse, pouch. Connection of sense is not clear, but Sp. *escarcela*, purse, pouch, also means tasset; cf. also It. *scarsella*, a pocket, *scarselloni*, "bases or tasses for a horseman" (Flor.). OF. *tasse*, pocket (cf. It. *tasca*, Ger. *tasche*), is of doubtful origin.

taste. OF. *taster* (*tâter*), to touch, handle, VL. *taxitare*, frequent. of *taxare*, to handle, touch, from root of *tangere*; cf. It. *tastare*, "to feel, handle, touch, grope for, try" (Flor.), whence Ger. *tasten*, to feel. To *taste of*, fig., still corresponds to F. *tâter de*. For fig. sense of noun (*good taste*, etc.) cf. F. *goût*, Ger. *geschmack*, the latter cogn. with E. *smack*¹, which *taste* has superseded.

> Lat thyn hand upon it falle,
> And taste it wel, and stoon thou shalt it fynde
> (Chauc. G. 502).

tat¹. See *tatting*.

tat² [*Anglo-Ind.*]. Pony. Short for *tattoo*, Hind. *ṭaṭṭū*.

> She was mounted on a tatoo, or small horse belonging to the country (*Surgeon's Daughter*, ch. xiii.).

tat³. In *tit for tat*. See *tit*².

ta-ta. Baby lang. for good-bye. First recorded by *NED*. as used by Mr Weller sen., but prob. older! Cf. *bow-wow*, *gee-gee*.

Tatar. See *Tartar*.

Tatcho. Hair tonic named by G. R. Sims. Romany, true, genuine, etc.

tatler. See *tattle*.

tatter. From 14 cent., also *totter*. In earliest use applied contemptuously to the "dags" (see *tag*¹) of slashed garments. Cf. ON. *toturr*, *töturr*, also OF. *tatereles*, the latter prob. of Teut. origin; also AS. *tætteca*, ? rag. *Tatterdemalion* (c. 1600) appears to be formed from *tatter* with fantastic second element as in *ragamuffin*, *slubberdegullion*, *hobbledehoy*; but it may be noted that *Tatar*, Tartar, was a contemporary word for vagabond, gipsy, in several Europ. langs., while Dekker uses *tatterdemalion* rather in the sense of rogue, gipsy, and Capt. John Smith applies *tattertimallion* to the Tartars.

tatting. Early 19 cent. Perh. connected with *tattle*. Cf. synon. F. *frivolité*.

tattle. Orig., in Caxton's *Reynard the Fox* (1481), to stammer, prattle, as rendering of Flem. *tatelen*, now usu. *tateren* (Du.), with which cf. LG. *tateln*, *täteln*, to gabble, quack; of imit. origin. Later senses influenced by *tittle*, a much older word in E. (see *tittle-tattle*). Hence *tattler* (1 *Tim*. v. 13)

or *tatler*, used as name of periodical founded (1709) by Steele and Addison.

tattoo¹ [*mil.*]. Earlier *taptoo*, "lights out," first recorded (1644) in order of Colonel Hutchinson to garrison of Nottingham, the original of which may be seen framed in the City Library. Du. *tap toe*, lit. (shut the) tap to, already at an earlier date in colloq. Du. use for "shut up." See *tap*¹, and cf. Ger. *zapfenstreich*, "the taptow" (Ludw.). Orig. E. sense was signal for closing the taps, i.e. taverns. Immediate source of form *tattoo* may be obs. Sp. *tatu* (Stevens).

> The ladies became grave, and the devil's tattoo was beat under the table by more than one (Lady Barnard's *SAfr. Journ.* 1797).

tattoo². Marking of skin. Polynesian, first recorded (*tattow*) in Capt. Cook (1769).

tatty [*Anglo-Ind.*]. Grass screen. Hind. *ṭaṭṭī*.

tau. G. ταῦ, name of letter T, τ. Esp. in *tau-cross*, St Anthony's cross. *In signo tau*, in the sign of the cross, is on a very ancient tomb in Southwell Priory, Notts.

taunt¹. To provoke, etc. From c. 1500. App. from F. phrase *tant pour tant*, in sense of tit for tat. But no doubt associated with F. *tancer*, to rebuke, scold, VL. **tentiare*, from *tendere*, *tent-*, to strive. There is a tendency in E. to confuse *-aunce*, *-aunt* (see *jaunt*), and *taunt* might be a back-formation like *romaunt*.

> When they rebuked me so sore, I wold not render taunt for taunt (*NED*. c. 1550).

> *tanser*: to chide, rebuke, check, taunt, reprove, take up (Cotg.).

taunt² [*naut.*]. Very tall (of masts). From phrase *all ataunt*, *all ataunto*, under full sail, with all rigging in use, F. *autant*, as much, in OF. to the full, esp. in *boire autant*, whence ME. *drink a tante*.

tauromachy. G. ταυρομαχία, from ταῦρος, bull, μάχη, fighting.

taut. Now chiefly naut. in lit. and fig. sense. Earlier *taught* (Capt. John Smith), ME. *toght*, app. cogn. with AS. *téon* (**teohan*), to pull. This verb is Com. Teut.; cf. OSax. *tiohan*, Ger. *ziehen*, ON. *toginn* (p.p.), Goth. *tiuhan*; cogn. with L. *ducere*. Related are *tie*, *tight*, *tough*, *tow*², *tug*.

> Thanne shal this cherl, with bely stif and toght
> As any tabour, hyder been y-broght
> (Chauc. D. 2267).

tautology. Late L., G. ταυτολογία, from ταὐτό, τὸ αὐτό, the same.

tavern. F. *taverne*, L. *taberna*, "a little house or lodging made of boardes" (Coop.), ? cogn. with *tabula*, plank, ? or with *trabs*, beam. Cf. *tabernacle*.

taw[1]. To prepare (leather). AS. *tāwian*; cf. Du. *touwen*, OHG. *zawjan*, Goth. *taujan*, to do, make. Ground-sense app. to prepare, etc.; for restriction to leather cf. *curry*[1], and Ger. *gerben*, to tan, lit. to make ready, "yare." Cogn. with *tool*.

taw[2]. A marble, *alley*[2]. Skeat suggests *tau* (q.v.), used for T-shaped mark, and compares the golf *tee*[3]; but both of these are rejected by the *NED*. Earliest sense of *taw* (Steele) is app. the marble, not the mark. Also *tor*[2].

tawdry. Aphet. for *St Audrey*, i.e. *Etheldreda*, AS. *Æthelthryth*, patron saint of Ely. Orig. in *St Audrey's lace* (Palsg.). Bede tells us that Etheldreda died of a tumour in the throat, which she regarded as a punishment for her early love of necklaces. The immediate source of the word is from *St Audrey's fair*, held in her honour, at which necklets were sold, a practice very likely going back to the legend mentioned above. Cf. obs. *bartholomew ware*, from *St Bartholomew's Fair*, Smithfield. For sense-development we may compare *gorgeous*, and, for the treatment of the first element, *Tooley St.*, for *St Olave St.* See *saint*.

You promised me a tawdry-lace and a pair of sweet gloves (*Wint. Tale*, iv. 4).

tawny. F. *tanné*, p.p. of *tanner*, to tan (q.v.). In OF. the vowel was nasalized (cf. *pawn*[1]).

taws, tawse [*Sc.*]. Earliest (Gavin Douglas) of whip for spinning a top. Treated by Sc. writers as pl. From *taw*[1].

tax. First (13 cent.) as verb. F. *taxer*, L. *taxare*, to censure, reckon, value, etc., in MedL. to impose a tax. In ME. *tax*, *task* (q.v.) are synon. Its use in *Luke*, ii. for G. ἀπογράφειν (Wyc. *discryve*) is due to Tynd. Archaic *taxed cart* was a vehicle, for agricultural or business purposes, on which a lower duty was charged.

taxi. For *taximeter* (q.v.), *taxi-cab*. Also used, by airmen, as verb.

Softly she nosed to the ground, taxied her distance and stopped (Corbett-Smith, *Marne and after*).

taxidermy. Mod., from G. τάξις, arrangement, δέρμα, skin.

taximeter. F. *taximètre*, from *taxe* in sense of tariff, rate of payment. Introduced in London March 1907.

taxonomy [*scient.*]. Classification. F. *taxonomie*, irreg. from G. τάξις, arrangement.

tazza. It. See *tass*.

Tchech, Tschekh. See *Czech*.

tchin. Russ., rank.

tea. Du. *thee*, Malay *te*, *teh*, Chin. dial. *t'e* (Amoy), for Mandarin *ch'a*, whence Port. *cha*, Russ. *chaï*, Pers. Urdu *chā* (10 cent.), Arab. *shay*, Turk. *chāy*; cf. *chah*, tea, in E. mil. slang. The Port. form, also found earlier in E. and other Europ. langs., came from Macao, the Russ. came overland from China. The Du. form has, owing to Du. traders being the chief importers (16 cent.) from the far East, prevailed in most Europ. langs. (F. *thé*, It. *tè*, Sp. *te*, Ger. *tee*), It. having also *cià*. The earlier E. pronunc. was indifferently *tay*, *tee* (cf. *sea*). *Storm in a tea-cup* is 19 cent. for 17 cent. *storm in a cream-bowl*; cf. L. *fluctus in simpulo* (ladle) *excitare* (Cic.).

That excellent, and by all physicians approved, China drink, called by the Chineans *Tcha*, by other nations *Tay* alias *Tee*
      (*Mercurius Politicus*, Sep. 30, 1658, *advt.*).

I did send for a cup of tee (a China drink) of which I never had drunk before (Pepys, Sep. 25, 1660).

Here, thou, great Anna! whom three realms obey,
Dost sometimes counsel take—and sometimes tea
            (*Rape of Lock*, iii. 8).

He thank'd her on his bended knee;
Then drank a quart of milk and tea (Prior).

teach. AS. *tǣcan*, not found in other Teut. langs., but cogn. with Ger. *zeigen*, to show, and G. δεικνύναι; also with *token*.

Teague [*archaic*]. Irishman. From common Ir. name *Tadhg*, later identified with *Thaddeus*. Cf. *Paddy*, *Taffy*, etc.

teak. Port. *teca*, Malayalam *tēkka* (Tamil *tēkku*).

teal. ME. *tele*, prob. from AS.; cf. synon. Du. *taling*, *teling*.

team. AS. *tēam*, in current sense, also progeny, etc., cogn. with *tēon*, to draw (see *taut*). Com. Teut.; cf. Du. *toom*, Ger. *zaum*, ON. *taumr*, all in sense of rein, bridle. This, app. the ground-sense, is not recorded in AS., nor is the E. sense found in other Teut. langs.

teapoy [*Anglo-Ind.*]. Small tripod table. From Hind. *tin-*, *tir-*, three, and Pers. *pāï*, foot. Cf. *charpoy*, *tripod*. Spelling has been assimilated to *tea*.

tear[1]. Noun. AS. *tēar*. Com. Teut.; cf. OFris. *tār*, (poet.) Ger. *zähre* (orig. pl. from OHG. *zahar*), ON. *tār*, Goth. *tagr*; cogn.

with L. *lacrima* (OL. *dacruma*), G. δάκρυ, Welsh *deigr*.

tear². Verb. AS. *teran*. Com. Teut.; cf. Du. *teren*, Ger. *zehren*, to destroy (also *zerren*, to distort), Late ON. *tära*, to use up (cf. *wear and tear*), Goth. *gatairan*, to destroy; cogn. with G. δέρειν, to flay. Past *tare* (Bibl.) has been altered to *tore* after p.p. (cf. *bare, brake, sware,* etc.). For intrans. sense, to rush violently, cf. Ger. *ausreissen*, "to shew a fair pair of heels" (Ludw.), lit. to tear out.

tease. AS. *täsan*, to tease (wool). WGer.; cf. Du. *teezen*, to pull, scratch, OHG. *zeisan*, to tease (wool). For current fig. sense cf. *heckle*. F. *attiser*, to stir up (for which see *entice*), has perh. also helped the fig. sense; cf. techn. *teaser*, fireman, stoker, F. *tiseur* (techn.). In lit. sense ME. usu. has *toose,* whence name *Tozer* and dog-name *Towzer* (cf. *tousle*).

The teasers of the plot, who would let no sort of people rest (North's *Examen*).

teasel. Large thistle used in "teasing" cloth. AS. *täsel*, with instrument. suffix as in *shovel*.

teat. F. *tette*, of Teut. origin; cf. It. *tetta*, Sp. *teta*. This replaced AS. *titt*, which survives as *tit, tet*, in dial. Cf. Du. dial. *tet*, Ger. *zitz*. All prob., like L. *mamma*, breast, from baby lang.

tec [*slang*]. Detective. Cf. *scrip²*, *flu*.

technical. From G. τεχνικός, from τέχνη, art, craft. For F. *technique*, technics, see *-ics*.

tectonic. Late L., G. τεκτονικός, from τέκτων, carpenter, builder.

Teddy-bear. Orig. US., named (c. 1907) in allusion to the President, *Theodore* (*Teddy*) *Roosevelt* (†1919).

Te Deum. Init. words of ancient L. hymn, *Te Deum laudamus*. Recorded in AS.

tedious. Late L. *taediosus*, from *taedium*, from *taedere*, to weary.

tee¹. The letter T., used of various T-shaped objects, e.g. *tee-square*. Cf. *ess, tau*.

tee². Mark aimed at (curling, bowls, quoits). Perh. orig. a T-shaped mark (v.s.).

tee³. Golf. App. distinct from *tee*¹,², as *NED.* has *teaz*, noun and verb, for 1673. For back-formation cf. *pea, burgee, Chinee*, etc. If the verb is older, it may be obs. *teise*, to bend a bow (OF. *teser*, L. *tensare*), which is used by Gavin Douglas of poising a spear before hurling it.

tee-hee. See *te-hee*.

teem. AS. *tïeman*, from *team* (q.v.) in AS. sense of progeny.

teen [*archaic*]. Affliction, etc. AS. *tēona*, hurt, trouble; cogn. with ON. *tjōn*, loss.

-teen. AS. *-tȳne, -tēne*, from *ten*; cf. Du. *-tien*, Ger. *-zehn*, L. *-decim*. Hence *in one's teens*. Shifting of accent to suffix in the E. compds. (exc. in mechanical counting) is due to wish to differentiate clearly from *-ty* (cf. *July*).

Twelve years they sate above Kings and Queens,
Full twelve, and then had enter'd their teens
               (*The Rump*, Dec. 26, 1659).

teeny. See *tiny*.

teetotal. Playful elaboration of *total*, perh. suggested by *teetotum*. In anti-alcoholic sense said (on his tombstone) to have been first used (1833) by "Dicky Turner," of Preston, a working-man temperance agitator, but the word must have been earlier in colloq. use. Quot. below is the reported opinion of a Kentucky backwoodsman.

These Mingoes...ought to be essentially, and particularly, and tee-totally obfisticated off of the face of the whole yearth (*NED.* 1832).

teetotum. Earlier *T-totum* (Defoe), orig. the lucky side only of the instrument, which was also called a *totum*. The four sides were orig. marked T (*totum*), A (*aufer*), D (*depone*), N (*nihil*). Those of the F. *toton*, formerly *totum*, "a kind of game with a whirle-bone" (Cotg.), were, according to Littré, marked T (*totum*), A (*accipe*), D (*da*), R (*rien*). Cf. Du. *aaltolletje*, "a whirl-bone or totum" (Sewel, 1766), lit. all-top.

teg [*dial.*]. Sheep (earlier also doe) in second year. Origin unknown.

tegument. L. *tegumentum*, from *tegere*, to cover.

te-hee. Imit. of derisive titter.

"Tehee!" quod she, and clapte the wyndow to
               (Chauc. A. 3740).

teil [*Bibl.*]. Obs. name for lime-tree. OF. (replaced by *tilleul*), L. *tilia*, "a teyle" (Coop.). Erron. used in *AV*. (*Is.* vi. 13) for Heb. *ēlāh*, elsewhere rendered oak. For this *Vulg.* has *terebinthus* (so Wyc., Coverd., and *RV*.).

telaesthesia. Coined (1882) by Myers, along with *telepathy*, from G. αἴσθησις, perception. Cf. *aesthetic* and see *tele-*.

tele-. G. τῆλε, far off. *Telegraph* (18 cent.) was orig. used of the semaphore, whence *Telegraph Hill* in many localities. *Telephone* was also used of several sound instruments before being adopted for that invented

(1876) by Bell. *Telepathy* was coined (1882) by Myers (cf. *telaesthesia*). These are all imitated from the much earlier *telescope*, It. *telescopio* (Galileo, 1611), which is in Milton. Cf. Ger. *telefunken*, name of a wireless company, from *funke*, spark.

telega. Vehicle. Russ. *teljēga*. In Hakl.

teleo-. From G. τέλεος, perfect, complete, from τέλος, end. Hence *teleology*, doctrine of final causes, ModL. *teleologia* (Wolf, 1728).

tell. AS. *tellan*, cogn. with *tale* (q.v.). Ground-sense is to mention in order, hence double meaning (to count, recount). Com. Teut.; cf. Du. *tellen*, to count, Ger. *zählen*, to count (*erzählen*, to relate), ON. *telja*, to count, relate; cogn. with Goth. *talzjan*, to teach. The counting sense survives in *all told, gold untold*, the *tellers*, in the H. of C., to *be told off*, *telling one's beads*, etc., and in to *tell one thing from another*. Cf. also a *telling shot*, one that counts.

tellurium [*chem.*]. Discovered and named (1798) by Klaproth, from L. *tellus, tellur-*, earth, in contrast to *uranium* (q.v.).

telpher. Overhead line. For *telephore*. See *tele-, -phore*.

Telugu [*ling.*]. Dravidian lang. of India. Cf. *Tamil*.

temerity. From L. *temeritas*, from *temere*, blindly, rashly.

temper. First as verb. AS. *temprian*, L. *temperare*, to proportion duly, regulate, perh. from *tempus*, time. Hence also F. *tremper*, used esp. of tempering metals, which has affected the sense-development of the E. word. *Temper* is now often for *bad temper*, and to *be in a temper* is equivalent to its logical opposite to *be out of temper*, with which cf. to *keep one's temper*, i.e. one's mental balance. *Temperance* was one of the four cardinal virtues, its use for total abstinence being 19 cent. *Temperament* was in medieval physiology used for *complexion* (q.v.), and was interchangeable in most senses with *temperature*. Current use as euph. or excuse for cowardice, immorality, etc., is adopted from Ger.

So ill-tempered I am grown that I am afeard I shall catch cold (Pepys, June 28, 1664).

tempest. OF. *tempeste* (*tempête*), VL. **tempesta*, for *tempestas*, season, weather, storm, from *tempus*, time. For transition of sense in L. cf. Ger. *gewitter*, storm, from *wetter*, weather.

template. See *templet*.

temple[1]. Building. AS. *templ*, L. *templum*, reinforced in ME. by F. *temple*. ? Orig. the section of earth and sky marked out by the augur for observing the flight of birds (cf. *contemplate*), from an Aryan **temp-*, cogn. with *tend-*, stretch. The *Temple*, London, was orig. the property of the *Knights Templars* (organized c. 1118, suppressed 1312), who were named from occupying at Jerusalem a building near Solomon's Temple. The *Good Templars*, teetotal body, were established (1851) in US.

Le pavement du chemyn par entre la Barre du Novel Temple de Lundres (*NED*. 1314–15).

temple[2]. Of head. OF. (*tempe*), L. *tempora*, pl. of synon. *tempus*, neut. pl., as often, becoming fem. sing. in VL. Sense, *tempora capitis*, ? imitated from G. τὰ καίρια, lit. the seasonable (places to strike an enemy); ? or as *temple[1]*, with orig. sense of stretched, thinnest, part; cf. synon. AS. *thunwange*, Ger. dial. *dünnung*, ON. *thunnvangi*, lit. thin cheek, cogn. with Ger. *dünn*, thin, *dehnen*, to stretch, L. *tenuis*, thin.

templet. In various techn. senses, the form *template* being due to folk-etym. App. from earlier *temple*, used of various mech. devices (? thing stretched), AS. *timple*, L. *templum*, temple[1]; cf. Rum. *timplar*, carpenter.

tempo [*mus.*]. It., L. *tempus*, time.

temporal[1]. Secular. L. *temporalis*, from *tempus, tempor-*, time, ? from same root as *temple[1]*. For sense cf. *secular*. Wyc. uses it in sense of *temporary*.

temporal[2]. L. *temporalis*, of the temple[2].

temporary. L. *temporarius*, from *tempus, tempor-*, time.

temporize. Cf. F. *temporiser*, MedL. *temporizare*, to put off the time, delay. Cf. *time-serving*.

Why, turne a temporist, row with the tide,
Pursew the cut, the fashion of the age
           (Marston, *What you will*, ii. 1).

tempt. OF. *tempter*, L. *temptare*, to handle, test, etc., intens. of *tendere*, to stretch. The OF. learned form has given way to the pop. *tenter*. Earliest E. sense (13 cent.) is to allure.

Aftyr that thes thingis weren doone, God temptide Abraham (Wyc. *Gen.* xxii. 1).

ten. AS. *tīen*. Aryan; cf. Du. *tien*, Ger. *zehn*, ON. *tīu*, Goth. *taihun*, L. *decem*, G. δέκα, Gael. Ir. *deich*, Pers. *dah*, Sanskrit *daṣa-*.

Upper ten is for *upper ten thousand. Tenpenny* nails were orig. (15 cent.) sold at tenpence a hundred.

tenable. F., from *tenir*, to hold, VL. **tenire*, for *tenēre*.

tenacious. From L. *tenax, tenac-*, from *tenēre*, to hold. Cf. *audacious*.

tenant. F., pres. part. of *tenir*, to hold (v.s.).

tench. OF. *tenche (tanche)*, Late L. *tinca* (Ausonius).

tend¹. To incline, etc. F. *tendre*, L. *tendere*, to stretch, strive, cogn. with *tenuis*, thin, G. τείνειν, to stretch. Current *tendencious* is after Ger. *tendenziös* (cf. Ger. *tendenzroman*, novel with a purpose).

tend². To care for. Aphet. for *attend*, also for some early senses of *intend*. See *tender³*.

tender¹. Adj. F. *tendre*, L. *tener, tener-* *Tenderfoot* is US. for a green hand. *Tenderloin* is US. for undercut, and the Tenderloin district of New York, where are the chief theatres, restaurants, etc., is so named as being the "juiciest" cut from the point of view of graft and police blackmail.

tender². To offer. F. *tendre*, tend¹. For ending cf. *render* from *rendre*. This is prob. due to the F. infin. being first adopted as noun, as in *remainder, rejoinder*, etc. (cf. *legal tender*).

tender³. Of ship or locomotive. From *tend²*, to attend. So also of agent, now only in US. compds. (*bar-tender, bridge-tender*, etc.).

tendon. MedL. *tendo-n-*, G. τένων, τένοντ-, sinew, tendon, from τείνειν, to stretch, confused with L. *tendere. Tenon, tenaunt* are also found as earlier forms.

tendril. Connected rather with F. *tendre*, to stretch, reach (*tend¹*), than with *tendre*, tender, the characteristic of the tendril being its reaching and clutching character, rather than its tenderness. The equivalents in the Europ. langs. all contain the clinging or twining idea. ModF. has *tendron* (more usu. *pampre*), but OF. uses *tendon* in same sense (v.i.).

capreolus: les tendons de la vigne (Est.).

capreolus: the tendrell of a vyne (Elyot, 1538).

La vigne par ses tendrons ou capreoles tortues embrasse toutes choses (Ambroise Paré, 16 cent.).

tenebrous. F. *ténébreux*, L. *tenebrosus*, from *tenebrae*, darkness.

tenement. AF., MedL. *tenementum*, from *tenēre*, to hold. US. *tenement house*, let off in flats, was orig. Sc. (cf. *flat*).

tenet. L., he holds, prob. as init. word of MedL. dissertations. *Tenent*, they hold, occurs earlier in same sense. Cf. *exit, habitat*, etc.

Pseudodoxia epidemica, or enquiries into very many received tenents and commonly presumed truths (Sir T. Browne).

tenné [*her.*]. OF. var. of *tanné*, tawny.

tennis. Earliest form *tenetz* (Gower). Also recorded in *Cronica di Firenze* of Donato Velluti (†1370) as *tenes*, and described as introduced into Italy (1325) by F. knights. App. F. *tenez*, imper. of *tenir*, called out by the server before play. Of this there is no record, but there is plenty of evidence for *accipe* or *excipe* as its transl. The F. name has always been *paume*, palm², but foreigners would naturally call the game by the word they heard regularly employed.

tenon. Projection fitting into *mortice*. F., from *tenir*, to hold.

tenor, tenour. OF. *(teneur)*, L. *tenor-em*, course, gist, from *tenēre*, to hold. As mus. term is found in OF., but in ModF. & E. the senses are assimilated to those of It. *tenore*, MedL. *tenor*, holder, used of the voice to which the *canto fermo*, or melody, was allotted.

They kept the noiseless tenour of their way
(Gray's *Elegy*).

tense¹. Noun. OF. *tens (temps)*, L. *tempus*, time.

tense². Adj. L. *tensus*, p.p. of *tendere*, to stretch. Cf. *tension*, F., L. *tensio-n-*. For pol. sense cf. *détente*.

tent¹. Shelter. F. *tente*, L. *tenta* (sc. *tela*), p.p. of *tendere*, to stretch. Cf. L. *tentorium*, awning.

tent². Roll of lint for insertion in wound; earlier, probe. F., from *tenter*, to try, test, L. *temptare* (see *tempt*).

tent³. Wine. Sp. *(vino) tinto*, dark wine, L. *tinctus*, p.p. of *tingere*, to dye.

tentacle. ModL. *tentaculum*, from *tentare*, var. of *temptare* (see *tempt*).

tentative. MedL. *tentativus*, from *tentare* (v.s.).

tenter. ME. *tentour*, F. *tenture*, stretching, tapestry, from *tendre*, to stretch, L. *tendere*. Hence *tenter-hooks*, by which cloth was stretched after being milled. Part of Spitalfields is still called the *Tenter ground*. Also used of the hooks by which tapestry was fastened (v.i.), a still existing sense not recorded by *NED*. To *be on tenter-hooks* is thus like being *on the rack*. For form cf. *batter, fritter*.

Pro le tenterhukes, pro le hangyngs, et pro le candeles [in the chapel]
(*York Merch. Advent. Accts.* 1490).

tenuity. From L. *tenuitas*, from *tenuis*, thin; cogn. with *tendere*, to stretch.

tenure. OF., from *tenir*, to hold, VL. **tenire*, for *tenēre*, cogn. with *tendere*, to stretch.

teocalli. Mex. temple. From Aztec *teotl*, god, *calli*, house.

tepee. Wigwam. NAmer. Ind. (Sioux).

tephrite [*min.*]. From G. τεφρός, ash-coloured, from τέφρα, ashes.

tepid. L. *tepidus*, from *tepēre*, to be warm.

ter-. L. *ter*, three times, cogn. with *three*.

terai (hat). From *Terai*, jungly belt between Himalayas and plain, from Hind. *tar*, damp.

teraphim. Household gods of Hebrews (*Judges*, xvii. 5). In *AV.* often rendered images, idols. Heb. *t'rāphīm*, pl. in form (cf. *cherubim*), and of doubtful origin and meaning.

teratology. Study of marvels and monstrosities. From G. τέρας, τέρατ-, prodigy.

tercel, tiercel [*archaic*]. Male of the falcon. OF. *tercel*, also *terceul*, MedL. *tertiolus*, from *tertius*, third; cf. It. *terzuolo*, Sp. *terzuelo*. For one of various supposed reasons see quot. below. Hence *tassel-gentle* (*Rom. & Jul.* ii. 2), in which second element means noble.

tiercelet: the tassell, or male of any kinde of hawke, so tearmed, because he is, commonly, a third part lesse than the female (Cotg.).

tercet [*metr.*]. F., It. *terzetto*, "a terset of rymes, rymes that ryme three and three" (Flor.), dim. of *terzo*, third, L. *tertius*.

terebella [*zool.*]. Marine worm. ModL., from *terebra*, borer, cogn. with *teredo*, *terete*.

terebinth. F. *térébinthe*, L., G. τερέβινθος, prob. of foreign origin. Cf. *turpentine*.

teredo [*zool.*]. Boring mollusc. L., G. τερηδών, wood-boring worm, cogn. with τείρειν, to rub, bore.

terete [*biol.*]. From L. *teres*, *teret-*, rounded off, smooth, cogn. with *terere*, to rub, G. τείρειν, and ult. with Ger. *drehen*, to turn, E. *throw, thrawn*.

tergiversation. L. *tergiversatio-n-*, from *vertere, vers-*, to turn, *tergum*, the back.

term. F. *terme*, L. *terminus*, limit, boundary, cogn. with G. τέρμα, limit, and ult. with *thrum*[1]. Hence, limiting condition. For sense of expression and math. use cf. G. ὅρος, boundary, employed in math. and logic, and rendered *terminus* by Late L. philos. writers.

termagant. ME. & OF. *Tervagant*, name of supposed god or idol of Saracens, usu. coupled with *Mahoun(d)*. Sense of fury, braggart, is from medieval stage. Spec. application to female appears in 17 cent. Cf. It. *Trivagante* (Ariosto). Origin unknown. See quot. s.v. *out-Herod*.

termination. L. *terminatio-n-*, from *terminare*, to limit, from *terminus*, boundary, term.

terminology. First (18 cent.) in Ger. *terminologie*, from L. *terminus* in its MedL. sense (see *term*). *Terminological inexactitude*, euph. for lie, was coined by Winston Churchill in a speech on "Chinese slavery."

terminus. L., boundary, end. Adopted in railway sense c. 1836. Much older in learned use, e.g. *terminus a quo* (*ad quem*). See *term*.

termite. White ant. L. *termes*, *termit-*, woodworm, cogn. with *terere*, to rub, bore (see *terete*).

tern. Cf. Dan. *terne*, Sw. *tärna*, Norw. dial. & Faroese *terna* (ON. *therna*). In EAngl. the black tern is called *starn*, AS. *stearn*, *stern*, no doubt ult. cogn. with above. *Tern* is of late appearance (17 cent.), which points to the foreign word having been picked up by sailors.

ternary. Late L. *ternarius*, from *terni*, three at a time, from *ter*, three times.

terne [*techn.*]. Chiefly in *terne-plate*, F. *terne*, dull (see *tarnish*).

terp [*antiq.*]. Prehistoric village-site in Holland. Fris., village, cogn. with *thorp* (q.v.).

Terpsichorean. Of Τερψιχόρη, Muse of dancing, from τέρπειν, to delight, χορός, dance, chorus.

terrace. F. *terrasse*, augment. of *terre*, L. *terra*, earth. Orig. raised promenade, etc.; cf. It. *terraccia*, Sp. *terraza*.

terra cotta. It., cooked earth. Cf. synon. F. *terre cuite*. *Terra* is cogn. with *torrēre*, to parch, dry; cf. *extorris*, banished man.

terra firma. L., firm earth, continent. Cf. It. *terra ferma*, used hist. of mainland possessions of Venice.

terrain. Land, esp. from mil. point of view. F., from *terre*, earth.

terra incognita. L., unknown land.

terramare [*min.*]. Ammoniacal earth found on site of neolithic dwellings in Italy. F., It. dial. *terramara*, from dial. *mara* (*marna*), marl.

terrapin. Small turtle. NAmer. Ind. (Algonkin). In 17 cent. *torope*.

terraqueous. Coined from L. *terra*, earth, *aqua*, water.

terra Sienna. Pigment. It. *terra di Siena*.

terrene. L. *terrenus*, from *terra*, earth.

terreplein [*fort.*]. Orig. inner slope of rampart. F., from It. *terrapieno* (cf. Sp. *terrapleno*), from verb *terrapienare* (cf. Sp. *terraplenar*), to fill up with earth. In F. & E. confused with *plain*, level.

terrestrial. From L. *terrestris*, from *terra*, earth. Cf. *celestial*.

terret. Ring on harness. In ME. also *toret*, *turret*, OF. *touret*, dim. of *tour*, turn (see *tour*).

terrible. F., L. *terribilis*, from *terrēre*, to frighten. For intens. use cf. *awful*, *tremendous*, etc.

terrier[1] [*hist.*]. Register of property, rent-roll, etc. Cf. F. *registre terrier*, MedL. *liber terrarius*, from *terra*, land.

terrier[2]. Dog. F. (sc. *chien*), from *terre*, earth; cf. MedL. *terrarius*. Orig. used for getting badger, etc. out of its "earth." Var. *tarrier* may be partly due to obs. *tarre*, *tary*, to set on.

basset: a terrier, or earthing beagle (Cotg.).

terrier[3]. For *territorial* (soldier). Coined 1908.

terrify. F. *terrifier*, L. *terrificare*, from root of *terror* and *facere*, to make.

terrine. See *tureen*.

territory. F. *territoire*, L. *territorium*, usu. associated with *terra*, earth, but perh. rather from *terrēre*, *territ-*, to frighten, "warn off." In US. hist. of regions not yet incorporated as States. Hence *territorial* (mil.), dating from army reorganization of 1881.

For a Continental European war it [the British Territorial army] may be left out of account
(Bernhardi, *Germany and the Next War*, Transl. p. 135).

terror. ME. *terrour*, F. *terreur*, L. *terror-em*, cogn. with *terrēre*, and ult. with *tremere*, to tremble, *trepidus*, timid. *Terrorism*, *terrorist*, *terrorize*, are due to the *Reign of Terror*, F. *la Terreur* (c. March 1793–July 1794).

Lenin and Trotsky publish their proclamation that the Terror has been a lamentable necessity
(*Obs.* Jan. 18, 1920).

terry (velvet). With uncut loop. ? F. *tiré*, drawn; cf. Ger. *gezogener samt*, drawn velvet.

terse. L. *tersus*, p.p. of *tergere*, to wipe. Current sense comes from that of polished, smooth.

tertian. Orig. in *tertian fever* (Chauc.), with paroxysms every third day, L. *febris tertiana*, from *tertius*, third. Cf. *quartan*.

tertiary. L. *tertiarius*, of the third rank (v.s.). Geol. sense dates from 18 cent.

tertium quid. Orig. used by alchemists of an unidentified element present in a combination of two known elements. L., rendering G. τρίτον τι (Plato), third something.

terza rima [*metr.*]. It., third rime, as in Dante (*a, b, a, b, c, b, c, d, c, ...*).

tessara-. G. τέσσαρα, neut. of τέσσαρες, four, with which it is cogn.

tessellated. From It. *tessellato* or L. *tessellatus*, from *tessella*, dim. of *tessera*, square tablet, die, from Ionic G. τέσσερα (v.s.).

tessera. Of various square objects; also, token, watchword. See above.

test. OF. (*têt*), pot, L. *testum*, var. of *testa*, pot, tile. Orig. (Chauc. G. 818) alchemist's cupel used in treating gold and silver. Hence *brought to the test*, to *stand the test*, the verb to *test* being an Americanism, first recorded as used by George Washington.

Until the year 1894 no one had ever heard of a "Test" match
(P. F. Warner, *Westm. Gaz.* Aug. 19, 1905).

testaceous. From L. *testaceus*, covered with hard shells, tiles (v.s.).

testament. L. *testamentum*, will, from *testari*, to be witness, attest, etc., from *testis*, witness. Used in Church L. to render G. διαθήκη, covenant, will, lit. disposition, arrangement. This was prob. due to the use of διαθήκη, covenant, in the account of the Last Supper. Cf. *testate*, L. *testatus*, p.p. of *testari*, which is much less common than *intestate*. Dial. forms of L. *testis* point to earlier *tr-* and orig. sense of third man (cf. *umpire*).

testamur [*univ.*]. Certificate. L., we testify.

testator. ME. & OF. *testatour*, Late L. *testator-em*, from *testari* (v.s.).

teste. L., abl. of *testis*, witness, used in abl. absolute construction.

tester[1] [*archaic*]. Canopy of bed. OF. *testre*, MedL. *testrum*; cf. OF. *testière*, covering for head (*têtière*, head-stall of horse, etc.); also It. *testeria*, Sp. *testera*, MedL. *testeria*, all in gen. sense of head-cover; also ME.

tester, head-armour of horse (Chauc. A. 2499). See *tête-à-tête*.

j lectum rubeum quiltpoint cum j testro de eadem setta (*Will* temp. Rich. II, Surtees Soc. ii. 41).

tester² [*hist.*]. Coin. Orig. the *teston, testoon*, of Hen. VIII, first E. coin with true portrait, imitated from the *testone* of Galeazzo Maria Sforza, Duke of Milan (†1476) and the F. *teston* of Louis XII and Francis I. The E. form may be for *testern, testorn, teston*. See *tête-à-tête*.

testicle. From L. *testiculus*, dim. of *testis*, witness (to virility). Cf. synon. G. παρα-στάται, lit. by-standers.

testify. From Late L. *testificare*, for *testificari*, from *testis*, witness, *facere*, to make.

testimony. OF. *testimoine* (learned form of *témoin*), L. *testimonium*, evidence of witness, *testis*. Cf. *testimonial*, orig. in *letter testimonial*, bearing witness to status of bearer, after Late L. (*litterae*) *testimoniales*, credentials. The *NED.* does not record sense of subscribed gift, etc. till 19 cent., but quot. below has a suggestion of it.

Item, the xv day of January [1543], to a woman of Lycetershire that whent wyth a testymoniall for burnyng of hyr howsse, iiijd (*Wollaton MSS.*).

testudo [*Roman hist.*]. Shelter for troops attacking fortress. L., tortoise, from *testa*, shell (see *testaceous*).

testy. AF. & ME. *testif*, headstrong, corresponding to OF. *testu* (*têtu*, obstinate). See *tête-à-tête*. For form cf. *jolly, tardy*. Palsg. gives *testyf* as OF.

tetanus. L., G. τέτανος, muscular spasm, from τείνειν, to stretch.

tetchy. Archaic (and earlier) form of *touchy* (q.v.).

tête-à-tête. F., head to head. OF. *teste*, L. *testa*, pot, tile, slang name for head.

tether. Orig. northern. ON. *tjōthr*, cogn. with archaic Du. *tuier* (earlier *tudder*), LG. *tüder, tier*, etc., OHG. *zeotar*, whence Bav. *zieter*, team, with which it is cogn. *The end of one's tether* refers to a grazing horse.

il est au bout de sa corde: he can doe no more, he can go no further; he may put up his pipes, goe shake his eares (Cotg.).

My stocke is worth about 25l. in cowes, hogs, corne on the ground; so God enlargeth my tedder daily, yearly (Josselin's *Diary*, 1660).

tetra-, tetr-. G. τετρα-, from τέτταρες, four.

tetrad. Set of four. G. τετράς, τετράδ- (v.s.).

tetrarch. Late L. *tetrarcha*, G. τετράρχης (v.s. and cf. *monarch*).

Eroude tetrarcha, that is, prince of the fourthe part, herde the fame of Jhesu (Wyc. *Matt* xiv. 1).

tetter [*archaic*]. Eczema, ring-worm, etc. AS. *teter*, cogn. with Sanskrit *dadru*, skindisease; cf. Ger. *zittermal*, ring-worm, of which second element means spot, mole¹.

Teutonic. L. *Teutonicus*, from *Teutones*, from OHG. *diot*, people (see *Dutch*). In ling. conveniently used in E. of that group of the Aryan langs. which includes High German, Low German (English, Dutch), Scandinavian and Gothic. F. uses *germanique*, Ger. *germanisch*, there being in those langs. no confusion with *German* (*allemand, deutsch*). In this Dict. many words are described as Common Teutonic which are not actually found in the scanty records of Gothic, but some of which, by indirect evidence, are believed to have existed in that lang.

text. F. *texte*, L. *textus*, tissue, hence style and matter, from *texere*, to weave, ult. cogn. with G. τέχνη, handiwork, art (cf. *context*). Some senses are due to spec. use of MedL. *textus* for actual wording of Bible, e.g. the *text* of a sermon was orig. quoted in L. from the *Vulg.*, and distinguished from the gloss, or exposition, in the vernacular. A *text-book* was orig. a classic written wide to allow of interlinear glosses. For *textual* cf. *actual, annual*, etc.

textile. L. *textilis*, from *texere, text-*, to weave (v.s.).

texture. L. *textura* (v.s.).

th-. Exc. for a few exotic or unexplained words, all words in *th-* are of E., Scand., or G. origin (þ or ð, θ).

Now I will speak but three words, and I durst jeopard a wager that none here [on the Continent] shall pronounce it after me: "Thwarts [? Thwaites] thwackt him with a thwitle" (Sir Thomas More).

-th¹. Forms abstract nouns from verbs (*birth, death*) or adjs. (*filth, mirth*). In *drought* (Sc. *drouth*), *height, sleight, theft*, has been replaced by *-t*.

-th². In ordinal numbers. AS. *-tha, -the*, cogn. with L. *-tus* (*quintus*), G. -τος (πέμπτος). AS. *fīfta, sixta, endlyfta, twelfta*, in which the orig. Aryan *-t-* was protected by the preceding spirant, have been levelled to *-th*.

thakur [*Anglo-Ind.*]. Title of respect, esp. of Rajpoot noble. Hind. *ṭhākur*, Sanskrit *ṭhakkurra*, deity.

thalamus [*biol.*]. L., G. θάλαμος, inner chamber.

thalassic. F. *thalassique*, from G. θάλασσα, sea. Cf. *thalatto-*, from Attic θάλαττα.

thaler. Ger., earlier *taler.* See *dollar.*

Thalian. Of Θάλεια, Muse of comedy, from θάλλειν, to bloom.

thallium [*chem.*]. Named (1861) by Crookes, from G. θαλλός, green shoot (v.s.), because of its green line in spectrum.

thalweg [*geog.*]. Ger., dale-way.

Thames, to set on fire. From 18 cent. A similar phrase has been used of other rivers (v.i.), e.g. of the Liffey.

> Er hat den Rhein und das meer angezündet
>   (Nigrinus, c. 1580).

than. AS. *thanne*, ident. with *then*, the two not being finally differentiated in spelling till c. 1700. Use after compar. is WGer.; cf. Du. *dan*, Ger. *denn*, similarly used. As *then* was orig. an adv. formation from *that, the*, it seems possible that the construction originated in a kind of relative use; cf. L. *quam*, than, a derivative of *qui*.

thanatism [*neol.*]. Belief in extinction at death, G. θάνατος.

> How do we die? An essay in thanatology
>   (*Book-title*, Mar. 20, 1919).

thane [*hist.*]. AS. *thegn*, servant, attendant, also spec. in *cyninges thegn*, king's man, whence use as title. Mod. form should have been *thain*, which survives as surname, current spelling being largely due to Shaks. (*Macb.*). Com. Teut.; cf. OSax. *thegan*, Ger. *degen* (poet.), ON. *thegn*; cogn. with G. τέκνον, child. For sense-development cf. *knight*. In AS. commonly used of Christ's disciples, e.g. John is called *se deora thegn* (*Blickling Hom.*).

> Ic eom man under anwealde geset, and ic hæbbe thegnas under mē (AS. *Gosp. Matt.* viii. 9).

thank. First as noun, mod. prevalence of pl. having been helped by AS. & ME. use of genitive *thanks* as adv. AS. *thanc*, cogn. with *think*, orig. sense being thought; hence, kind thought, gratitude. Com. Teut.; cf. Du. Ger. *dank*, ON. *thökk*, Goth. *thagks*.

that. AS. *thæt*, neut. of demonstr. pron. and adj. *sē, sēo, thæt*. Orig. hardly distinguished in use from *the*, but by c. 1200 used as equivalent to L. *iste, ille*, F. *ce...là*. For relative use cf. that of Ger. demonstr. and art. (*der, die*), *das*. With use as conj. cf. that of Ger. *dass*, ident. with *das*, also G. ὅτι from neut. of rel. ὅστις and L. conj. *quod* (F. *que*, It. *che*, Sp. *que*) from pron. *quod*. Its orig. pl., AS. *thā*, survives in

dial. *tho, thae*, as in "I wonder who paid for they pigs."

> Anon my wife sends for me, I come, and what was it but to scold at me, and she would go abroad to take the ayre presently [i.e. at once], that she would
>   (Pepys, May 9, 1666).

thatch. Verb. AS. *theccan*, from noun *thæc*, whence dial. *thack*. Current form, for *thetch*, is due to the noun, the consonant of which has been altered on the verb. Com. Teut.; cf. Du. *dak*, Ger. *dach*, roof (*decken*, to cover), ON. *thak*, roof, thatch; cogn. with L. *tegere*, to cover, G. τέγος, roof, Gael. Ir. *tigh*, house. See also *deck¹, roof*.

thaumaturge. MedL., G. θαυματουργός, wonder-working, conjuror, from θαῦμα, θαύματ-, wonder, -εργος, working, from ἔργον, work.

thaw. AS. *thāwian*. Com. Teut.; cf. Du. *dooien*, Ger. *tauen* (also *verdauen*, to digest), ON. *theyja*.

the. Weakened form of *that* (q.v.), also representing masc. and fem. *the, thee*, which replaced, under influence of *thæt*, earlier *sē, sēo*. Aryan; cf. Du. *de, dat*, Ger. *der, die, das*, ON. (*sā, sū*), *that*, Goth. (*sa, sō*), *thata*, G. (ὁ, ἡ), τό, Sanskrit (*sa, sā*), *tat*, also L. *is-te*. *That* survived longer before vowels, as in *that one and that other*, later separated as *the tone and the tother*. In *the more pity, the fewer the better*, etc., *the* represents the old instrument. case, AS. *thȳ, thē*. Cf. Du. *des te*, Ger. *desto*, OHG. *des* (genitive) *diu* (instrument.). Cf. *lest*.

theandric. Church G. θεανδρικός, from θεός, god, ἀνήρ, ἀνδρ-, man.

theanthropic. From Church G. θεάνθρωπος, from θεός, god, ἄνθρωπος, man.

thearchy. Church G. θεαρχία (v.s.).

Theatine. Rel. order founded (1524) at Chiete (formerly *Teate*) in Italy.

theatre. F. *théâtre*, L., G. θέατρον, from θεᾶσθαι, to behold. In most Europ. langs.

> And could not then th'Almightie All-creator,
> Th'all-prudent, be without this fraile theater
>   (Sylv. i. 1).

Thebais, Thebaid. District round *Thebes* (Egypt), formerly favourite abode of hermits and ascetics. Cf. F. *Thébaïde*.

> Swinburne became the book-monk of a suburban Thebais (E. Gosse).

theco- [*biol.*]. From G. θήκη, case.

thee. AS. *thē*, dat. of *thou*, also replacing AS. acc. *thec*; cf. obs. Du. *di*, Ger. *dir, dich*, ON. *thēr, thik*, Goth. *thus, thuk*.

theft. AS. *thīefth*, from *thief*. See *-th¹*.

thegn [*hist.*]. See *thane*.

their. ON. *theirra*, genitive pl. of demonstr., replacing AS. pers. pron. *hira*, ME. *her*.

theist. From G. Θεός, God.

Thelema. Rabelais' *Abbaye de Thélème*, of which the only rule was *Fay ce que vouldras*. G. θέλημα, wish.

The new Thelema of a neurasthenic Rabelais of 1920 (*Athenæum*, May 28, 1920).

them. ON. *theim*, dat. of demonstr., replacing AS. pers. pron. *him*, whence ME. *hem, em*, still in colloq. use, e.g. "That's the stuff to give em."

theme. Restored spelling of ME. *teme*, OF. *te(s)me* (*thème*), L., G. θέμα, proposition, from τιθέναι, to put.

Themis. G. Θέμις, personification of Justice, from τιθέναι, to set.

then. AS. *thanne*, from the root of the demonstr. *that, the*; cf. Du. *dan*, Ger. *dann*, ON. *thā*, Goth. *than*. See *than*.

thence. ME. *thannes, thennes*, for earlier *thenne*, with adv. genitive *-s* (as in *hence*); from demonstr. root *that, the*; cf. Ger. *dannen*.

theo-. From G. θεός, god.

theocracy. G. θεοκρατία, sacerdotal government under divine inspiration.

theodolite. First (1571) in L. form *theodelitus*, prob. invented and named by the E. mathematician Leonard Digges. "Can it have been (like many modern names of inventions) an unscholarly formation from θεάομαι, I view, or θεῶ, behold, and δῆλος, visible, clear, manifest, with a meaningless termination?" (*NED*.). It is just possible that Digges, for some fantastic reason now unknown, named the instrument after the famous OF. theol. poem called the *Tiaudelet*, translated from the Late L. *Theodulus* (9 cent.).

theogony. G. θεογονία, generation of the gods. Cf. *cosmogony*.

theology. F. *théologie*, L., G. θεολογία, an account of the gods, mod. sense being due to spec. application of the word in Church G.

theophany. G. θεοφάνεια, manifestation of God, from φαίνειν, to show.

theorbo, theorbe. Lute. F. *téorbe, théorbe*, It. *tiorba*, "a kind of musicall instrument used among countrie people" (Flor.). Origin unknown.

theorem. L., G. θεώρημα, speculation, proposition to be proved (Euclid), from θεωρεῖν, from θεωρός, a spectator. Current sense of *theoretic* is after Aristotle, who contrasts θεωρητικός with πρακτικός. So also *theory*, from MedL. transl. of Aristotle's θεωρία.

theosophy. MedL., Late G. θεοσοφία, knowledge of things divine. Current use for esoteric Buddhism from c. 1880, the *Theosophical Society* having been founded at New York (1875) by Madame Blavatsky & Co.

therapeutic. G. θεραπευτικός, from θεραπεύειν, to attend, etc., from θέραψ, θεραπ-, attendant, minister.

there. AS. *thǣr*, from root of demonstr. *that, the*; cf. Du. *daar*, Ger. *da* (OHG. *dār*), ON. Goth. *thar*. For formation cf. *where*. Demonstr. origin appears in compds., e.g. *therefor(e)* (= F. *pour cela*), *thereon, therewith*, etc.

theriac [*archaic*]. Antidote. See *treacle*.

therio-. From G. θηρίον, dim. of θήρ, wild beast.

-therium. From G. θηρίον (v.s.).

thermal. From G. θέρμη, heat.

Thermidor [*hist.*]. Eleventh month of F. Republ. Calendar (July 19–Aug. 17). From G. θέρμη (v.s.), δῶρον, gift. Esp. the 9th *Thermidor*, fall of Robespierre and end of Terror.

thermo-. From G. θερμός, hot. Hence *thermometer*, F. *thermomètre*. Earliest form was the air-thermometer of Galileo (c. 1597).

thermos (flask). G. θερμός, hot. Invented by Dewar, patented 1904, name registered 1907.

thero-. From G. θήρ, wild beast.

Thersitical. Scurrilous. From Θερσίτης, lit. the audacious, a G. soldier at siege of Troy distinguished by his evil tongue, like Sir Kay among the Round Table knights.

thesaurus. L., G. θησαυρός, treasure. Used as title by early dict. compilers (Cooper, 1565).

these. AS. *thǣs*, var. of *thās*, pl. of *this* (q.v.). See also *those*.

thesis. G. θέσις, proposition, from τιθέναι, to put. Cf. *theme*.

Thespian. Of Θέσπις, trad. founder of G. tragedy (6 cent. B.C.).

theurgy. L., G. θεουργία, sorcery, from θεός, god, -εργος, working.

thew. AS. *thēaw*, custom, characteristic, quality. WGer.; cf. OSax. *thau*, custom, OHG. *thau*, discipline. In ME. used of good quality, and in 16 cent. of physical endowments. Obs. after Shaks., but revived by Scott, to whom current sense, *thews and sinews*, is due. Orig. sense appears in Sc. *thewless*, feckless. See also quot. s.v. *ethics*.

> If so were that she hadde
> Mo goode thewes than hire vices badde
> (Chauc. E. 1541).

they. ON. *their*, nom. pl. masc. of demonstr., replacing AS. pers. pron. *hīe*. Cf. *their*, *them*.

thick. AS. *thicce*. Com. Teut.; cf. Du. *dik*, Ger. *dick*, ON. *thykkr*; cogn. with Gael. Ir. *tiugh*. For two ground-senses of massive, dense in texture or juxtaposition of parts, cf. those of *thin*. To the latter belong *as thick as thieves*, *thickset*. *Through thick and thin* orig. referred to intervening growth, trees, etc. (v.i.). It is found in the other Teut. langs. also. *The plot thickens* is 17 cent.

> And whan the hors was laus, he gynneth gon
> Toward the fen, ther wilde mares renne,—
> Forth with "Wehee!" thurgh thikke and thurgh
> thenne (Chauc. A. 4064).

> He and I are as great as two beggars
> (Edm. Verney, 1639).

thicket. AS. *thiccet*, from *thick*. Cf. synon. Ger. *dickicht*.

thief. AS. *thēof*. Com. Teut.; cf. Du. *dief*, Ger. *dieb*, ON. *thiófr*, Goth. *thiufs*.

thigh. AS. *thēoh*. Com. Teut.; cf. Du. *dij*, OHG. *dioh*, ON. *thjō*.

thill. Shaft of cart. ? Ident. with AS. *thille*, board, deal² (q.v.).

thimble. AS. *thȳmel*, from *thumb*; cf. ON. *thumall*, thumb of glove. "Perh. a leather thumb-stall was the earliest form of thimble; metal thimbles were app. introduced in the 17 cent." (*NED.*). In *thimble-rig* (19 cent.) second element is *rig²*.

thin. AS. *thynne*. Com. Teut.; cf. Du. *dun*, Ger. *dünn*, ON. *thunnr*; cogn. with L. *tenuis*, Sanskrit *tanu*, and with L. *tendere*, G. τείνειν, Ger. *dehnen*, to stretch. For double meaning cf. *thick*. *Thin red line* (*tipped with steel*) was used by W. H. Russell of the 93rd Highlanders repulsing the Russian cavalry, without forming square, at Balaclava.

thine. AS. *thīn*, genitive of *thou*; cf. Du. *dijn*, Ger. *dein*, ON. *thīn*, Goth. *theins*. See *thy*.

thing. AS. *thing*, deliberative assembly; hence affairs, matters (see *hustings*, *storthing*). Com. Teut.; cf. Du. Ger. *ding*, ON. *thing*, all orig. in sense of public assembly; also Goth. *theihs*, appointed time. For sense-development cf. Ger. *sache*, thing, *sake* (q.v.), also F. *chose*, thing, L. *causa*.

With *the thing* cf. *cheese²*. *Thingum*, whence *thingummy*, *thingumbob*, etc., is 17 cent. With orig. sense of *thing* cf. use of *day* (see *diet²*) and the combination of the two words in Ger. *verteidigen*, to defend, OHG. **vertagedingen*, to summon before the *tageding*, assembly.

think. AS. *thencan*, causal of *thyncan*, to seem (see *methinks*). Com. Teut.; cf. Du. Ger. *denken*, ON. *thekkja*, Goth. *thagkjan*, all causals of verb cogn. with AS. *thyncan* (v.s.). The two were distinct in AS., but fell together in ME. See also *thank*.

third. Metath. of *thrid*, AS. *thridda*, from *three*; cf. Du. *derde*, Ger. *dritte*, ON. *thrithe*, Goth. *thridja*.

thirst. AS. *thurst*. Com. Teut.; cf. Du. *dorst*, Ger. *durst*, ON. *thorsti*, Goth. *thaurstei*; cogn. with Ger. *dürr*, dry, L. *torrēre*, to parch, Sanskrit *trsh*, to thirst. The verb is AS. *thyrstan*, the vowel of which has been adopted by the noun.

thirteen. Metath. of *thriteen*, AS. *thrēotȳne*, from *three*. Superstition as to unlucky number (? from Last Supper) is app. mod.

thirty. Metath. of *thritty*, AS. *thrītig*, from *three*.

this. Neut. sing. of AS. demonstr. *thēs*, *thēos*, *this*, from the same root as *that*, *the*, with suffix corresponding to Goth. *sai*, see, behold; cf. Du. *deze*, Ger. *dieser*, ON. *thesse*. Pl. was *thās*, whence *those*, and *thǣs*, whence *these*.

thistle. AS. *thistel*. Com. Teut.; cf. Du. Ger. *distel*, ON. *thistill*. Recorded as emblem of Scotland from 15 cent., whence *Order of the Thistle*, founded (1687) by James II.

thither. AS. *thider*, earlier *thǣder*, from root of demonstr. *that*, with suffix as in *hither*, to which also the vowel has been assimilated.

thole¹. Peg of rowlock. AS. *thol*; cf. ON. *thollr*, Du. *dol*; ? ident. with ON. *thollr*, fir, tree. In ME. recorded only in non-naut. sense. From Teut. comes F. dim. *tolet*.

thole² [*archaic & dial.*]. To endure. AS. *tholian*. Com. Teut.; cf. OSax. *tholōn*, OHG. *dolōn* (whence Ger. *geduld*, patience), ON. *thola*, Goth. *thulan*; cogn. with L. *tollere*, *tuli*, *tolerare*, G. τλῆναι.

Thomas. G. Θωμᾶς, of Aram. origin, a twin, hence explained by G. Δίδυμος, from δίς, twice. Used for doubter (*John*, xx. 25). *Thomas Atkins* has been used (since 1815) as specimen name in filling up army forms.

Thomist. Follower of *St Thomas Aquinas.* Cf. *Scotist.*

thong. AS. *thwang*, strap; cogn. with ON. *thvengr*, and with Ger. *zwingen*, to constrain (see *twinge*).

Thor. ON. *thōrr*, thunder (q.v.). Cf. *Thursday.*

thorax. L., G. θώραξ, breastplate.

thorium [*chem.*]. Discovered and named (1828–9) from *Thor* by Berzelius, and adapted (1885) to incandescent mantles by Welsbach.

thorn. AS. *thorn.* Com. Teut.; cf. Du. *doorn*, Ger. *dorn*, ON. *thorn*, Goth. *thaurnus*; with Slav. cognates. *Thorn in the flesh* (2 *Cor.* xii. 7) renders G. σκόλοψ, stake, pale.

Picolominie all the while sate upon thornes studying how to get away (Sydenham Poyntz, 1624–36).

thorough. Var. of *through* (q.v.) in stressed position. *Thoroughfare* is found as verb in AS. *Thorough-paced* was orig. (17 cent.) used of horses.

Constantius was a thorough-pac'd Christian (Fuller).

thorp [*poet.*]. AS. *throp, thorp*, village. Com. Teut.; cf. Du. *dorp*, Ger. *dorf*, ON. *thorp*, Goth. *thaurp.* Current form (cf. *-throp, -thrupp*, etc. in place-names) is partly due to Norse influence. Obs. from c. 1600, but revived by Wordsworth.

those. AS. *thās*, pl. of *this*, in northern ME. gradually replacing *tho*, AS. *thā*, pl. of *that.* It is thus a doublet of *these*, from which it is now differentiated in sense.

thou. AS. *thū.* Aryan; cf. archaic Du. *du*, Ger. *du*, ON. *thū*, Goth. *thu*, L. *tu*, G. σύ (Doric τύ), Gael. Ir. *tu*, Pers. *tū*, Sanskrit *tva.*

though. AS. *thēah.* Com. Teut.; cf. Du. Ger. *doch*, ON. *thō* (for *thauh*), Goth. *thauh.* Current form (ME. also *thei, thagh*, etc.) is from ON.

thought. AS. *thōht, gethōht*, from *think*; cf. Du. *gedachte*, OHG. *gidāht* (whence Ger. *gedächtnis*, memory). In ME. often of mental distress, whence to *take thought* (*Matt.* vi. 31, *Vulg. sollicitus esse*). With *a thought too particular* cf. *a sight too careless.*

thousand. AS. *thūsend.* Com. Teut.; cf. Du. *duizend*, Ger. *tausend*, ON. *thūsund*, Goth. *thūsundi.* Second element is cogn. with *hundred* (cf. ON. *thūs-hundrath*, thousand), first may be cogn. with Sanskrit *tavas*, strong. Orig. sense prob. large number, myriad, there being no gen. Aryan word for 1000.

thrall. ON. *thrǣll*, cogn. with OHG. *dregil*, servant, prop. runner, and with AS. *thrǣgan*, to run. Dial. *thrall*, stand for barrels, etc., is prob. a fig. use of the same word. Cf. mech. uses of *jack*, i.e. servant.

thranite [*hist.*]. G. θρανίτης, rower in upper tier, from θρᾶνος, bench. The lowest tier rower was called *thalamite*, from θάλαμος, chamber, applied to a section of the boat.

thrash, thresh. AS. *therscan, threscan*, to thresh (corn). Com. Teut.; cf. Du. *dorschen*, Ger. *dreschen*, ON. *threskja*, Goth. *thriskan*; orig. to tramp, stamp (whence OF. *trescher*, to dance, It. *trescare*); then, esp. the treading of the corn, the use of the flail (q.v.) being learnt from the Romans. Later flagellating sense, with artificial differentiation of spelling, from 16 cent. We still *thrash out* a question, although we *thresh out* corn. See *threshold.*

thrasonical. From name of braggart soldier in Terence's *Eunuchus.* G. Θράσων, from θρασύς, bold.

thrawn [*Sc.*]. Twisted, distorted. From *thraw*, dial. form of *throw.* For sense cf. *warped.*

thread. AS. *thrǣd.* Com. Teut.; cf. Du. *draad*, Ger. *draht*, wire, ON. *thrathr*; from a root to twist, "throw"; cf. Ger. *drehen*, to twist. With *threadbare* (*Piers Plowm.*) cf. Ger. *fadenscheinig*, lit. thread showing, and F. *montrer la corde.*

threat. AS. *thrēat*, throng, pressure; cf. AS. *thrēotan*, to weary; cogn. with Du. *verdrieten*, Ger. *verdriessen*, to vex, ON. *thrjōta*, to lack, Goth. *usthriutan*, to oppress, ? and ult. with L. *trudere*, to thrust.

three. AS. *thrī, thrīo, thrēo.* Aryan; cf. Du. *drie*, Ger. *drei*, ON. *thrīr, thrjār, thrjū* (Sw. Dan. *tre*, Norw. *tri*), Goth. *threis, thrija*, L. *tres, tria*, G. τρεῖς, τρία, Welsh, Gael. Ir. *tri*, Russ. *tri*, Zend *thri*, Sanskrit *tri.*

threnody. G. θρηνῳδία, dirge, from θρῆνος, lament. See *ode.*

thresh. See *thrash.*

threshold. AS. *thersc-old, -wald, -wold*; cf. ON. *threskjöldr*, OHG. *driscūfli*; first element *thresh*, in orig. sense (see *thrash*), second doubtful.

thrice. ME. *thries*, formed from *thrie*, three, with adv. genitive *-s*, after *ones*, once.

thrift. Formed in ME. from *thrive* (q.v.). Orig. success, prosperity.

thrill. Metath. of earlier *thirl*, AS. *thyrlian*, to pierce, from *thȳrel*, hole (cf. *nostril*), cogn. with *thurh*, through, and ult. with *drill*[1].

thrips. L., G. θρίψ, wood-worm. Erron. sing. *thrip* is back-formation.

thrive. ON. *thrīfa*, to grasp, etc., with sense of reflex. *thrīfask* (cf. *bask*, *busk²*), to grow, increase. *Takask* (see *take*) has same sense in ON.

thro. See *through*.

throat. AS. *throte*; cf. OHG. *drozza* (whence Ger. *drossel*, only in ven.). From a root meaning to swell, also found with init. *s-* in Du. *strot*, It. *strozza* (from Teut.). To *lie in one's throat* was revived by Scott from Shaks., the phrase being app. vaguely due to the earlier to *thrust a lie down the speaker's throat*.

throb. As pres. part. (*throbbant hert*) in *Piers Plowm.*, and then not till 16 cent., with var. *frob*. Of imit. origin. It is like *thud*, with recurrence of the beat suggested by the *-r-*.

throe. ME. *throwe*, spasm, pang, esp. of death or child-birth. From AS. *thrōwian*, to suffer, die, cogn. with ON. *thrā*, violent longing, AS. *thrēa*, punishment, throe, and ult. with *threat*. Mod. spelling, from 17 cent. only, is due to unconscious differentiation from *throw*.

throne. Restored from ME. *trone*, F. *trône*, L., G. θρόνος, elevated seat.

throng. AS. *gethrang*, from *thringan*, to press; cf. Du. *drang*, Ger. *drang*, pressure, *gedränge*, throng. The verb, still in dial. and archaic use, is Com. Teut.; cf. Du. Ger. *dringen*, ON. *thryngva*, Goth. *threihan*.

throstle. AS. *throstle*; cf. LG. *draussel*, Ger. *drossel*, ON. *thröstr*; ? ult. cogn. with L. *turdus*, thrush.

throttle. Formed in ME. from *throat*; cf. synon. Ger. *erdrosseln*.

through. AS. *thurh*, which, when stressed, became *thorough* (cf. *borough*, *furrow*). WGer.; cf. Du. *door*, Ger. *durch*, "through, thorow, or thorough" (Ludw.); cogn. with Goth. *thairh*. Orig. oblique case of a Teut. name for hole, and hence cogn. with *thrill*. The two forms were earlier used indifferently, e.g. Shaks. has *throughfare*. US. sense of finished is found in ME. (v.i.).

He will throughly purge his floor (*Matt.* iii. 12).

I am through with my brother, Edward Plompton, touching Haverary Park (*Plumpton Let.* 1490).

throw. AS. *thrāwan*, to twist, turn. WGer.; cf. Du. *draaien*, Ger. *drehen*; cogn. with L. & G. root which appears in *teredo*. With changed sense (prob. via that of whirling missile before throwing, L. *torquēre telum*,

to hurl a javelin) has replaced *warp* and largely superseded *cast*. Orig. sense survives in *silk-throwing*. See also *thrawn*.

thrum¹ [*archaic*]. Short end, scrap of yarn, etc. Orig. what is left attached to loom when web is cut. AS. *thrum*, ligament. Com. Teut.; cf. Du. *dreum*, Ger. *trumm* (now esp. in pl. *trümmer*, ruins), ON. *thrömr*, edge; cogn. with L. *terminus*.

Thrumb'd halfe with ivie, halfe with crisped mosse (Sylv. i. 7).

thrum². Verb. Imit., cf. *strum*.

thrush¹. Bird. AS. *thrysce*, *thryssce*, app. cogn. with *throstle* (q.v.), though some authorities regard them as quite separate.

thrush². Disease of mouth. From 17 cent., also in 18 cent. used of disease in the "frog" of horse's hoof. Cf. Sw. *törsk*, Dan. *tröske*, also of obscure origin. Norw. has *frösk*, *frosk*, in same sense, phonetically ident. with *frosk*, frog. This fact, and use of L. *rana*, frog, G. βάτραχος, frog, as names for diseases of the mouth, suggests that **frush* may have been the original. See *frog²*. The change of *f-* to *th-* has parallels in hist. *thirdborough*, AS. *frithborh*, peace surety, and naut. *thrap* for *frap*.

thrust. ON. *thrýsta*, ? ult. cogn. with L. *trudere*. In colloq. use mostly replaced by *push*.

thud. From 16 cent. (verb and noun). Imit., or, with new sense developed under imit. influence, from AS. *thyddan*, to thrust.

Thug. Hind. *thag*, cheat, swindler, used instead of the correct name *p'hansigar*, strangler.

thuja, thuya. Shrub. G. θυία, θύα, an Afr. tree, whence also *thyine* (*Rev.* xviii. 12).

Thule. L., G. Θούλη, Θύλη, a land six days' sail north of Britain (Polybius), whence L. *ultima Thule*, variously identified, and used fig. for furthest point.

Tile is the uttermost ylond of occean
(Trev. i. 325).

thumb. AS. *thūma*. Com. Teut.; cf. Du. *duim*, Ger. *daumen*; also ON. *thumall*, thumb of glove; cogn. with L. *tumēre*, to swell, OPers. *tūma*, fat. For excrescent *-b* cf. *dumb*. *Rule of thumb*, skill learned by practice, is 17 cent. *Under the thumb* seems to be evolved, with changed sense, from 17 cent. *under thumb*, secretly, underhand.

Each finger is a thumb to-day, methinks
(*Ralph Royster-Doyster*, 1534).

Thummim [*Bibl.*]. See *Urim*.

thump. From 16 cent. Imit., cf. *bump, thud.* For intens. use (*thumping majority*) cf. *whopping, spanking,* etc.

thunder. AS. *thunor.* Com. Teut.; cf. Du. *donder,* Ger. *donner,* ON. *thōrr* (for *thonr), whence name of god *Thor*; cogn. with L. *tonare,* Sanskrit *tan,* to resound. Early used both of sound and flash, hence *thunderstruck* (cf. similar use of F. *tonnerre,* Ger. *donner*). See also *bolt*[1]. *Thunderer,* the *Times,* is in Carlyle (1840), and was orig. applied to Edward Sterling, who wrote for the *Times* 1830–40. With intens. *thundering* cf. *thumping,* etc. The *Thundering Legion* (hist.) trad. derived its name from a militarily convenient thunderstorm brought on by the prayers of its Christian members. With *thunder and lightning,* black and yellow (in various colloquialisms), cf. *pepper and salt, seersucker.*

thurible. From L. *thuribulum,* from Late L. *thus, thur-,* incense, L. *tus,* G. θύος, sacrifice, from θύειν, to sacrifice.

Thursday. AS. *Thunresdæg* and ON. *Thōrsdagr,* day of Thor or thunder (q.v.); cf. Du. *donderdag,* Ger. *donnerstag.* Teut. rendering of Late L. *Jovis dies,* whence F. *jeudi,* It. *giovedì.*

thus. AS. *thus,* from demonstr. root of *that, the;* cf. Du. *dus.* OHG. has *sus,* from demonstr. *so.*

thuya. See *thuja.*

thwack. Imit. intensification (16 cent.) of earlier *thack,* AS. *thaccian,* to clap, which is also imit. Cf. relation of *tang*[2] and *twang.*

thwart[1]. To impede, etc. First (c. 1200) as adv. ON. *thvert,* across, athwart, orig. neut. of adj. *thverr,* transverse. Hence ME. adj. *thwart,* froward, perverse, "cross," and verb to *thwart* (cf. to *queer the pitch,* and F. *traverser un projet*). Com. Teut.; cf. Du. *dwars* (adv.), Ger. *quer* (OHG. *twer*). These are all shortened from an earlier form which appears in AS. *thweorh,* perverse, cross, Ger. *zwerch-* (OHG. *twerh*), in *zwerchfell,* diaphragm, "cross skin," Goth. *thwairhs,* angry, "cross"; ult. cogn. with L. *torquēre,* to twist.

We frequently chang'd our barge, by reason of the bridges thwarting our course (Evelyn).

thwart[2]. Of a boat. Altered (18 cent.), under influence of *thwart*[1], from earlier *thought* (Capt. John Smith and mod. dial.), for *thoft* (still in dial.), AS. *thofte,* rowers' bench; cf. ON. *thopta,* Du. *docht, doft,* Ger.

duft, ducht (from LG.), from a Teut. root, to squat. AS. *gethofta,* comrade, lit. benchmate, is an interesting parallel to *companion, comrade, messmate,* etc.

thaughts: are the seats on which they sit who row in the boat (Sea-Dict. 1708).

thy. Weakened form of *thine,* orig. before consonants as in Bibl. *thine eyes, thy son.*

Thyestean (feast). From Θυέστης, brother of Ἀτρεύς, who made him eat of the flesh of his own sons.

thyine. See *thuja.*

thylacine. Marsupial wolf (Tasmania). F., coined (1827) by Temminck from G. θύλακος, pouch.

thyme. F. *thym,* L. *thymum,* G. θύμον, from θύειν, to burn sacrifice.

thymele. Altar of Dionysus in G. theatre. G. θυμέλη, altar, from θύειν (v.s.).

thyroid [*anat.*]. From G. θυρεοειδής, shield-shaped (Galen), from θυρεός, oblong shield.

thyrsus. L., G. θύρσος, stem of plant, Bacchic staff.

tiara. L., G. τιάρα, orig. a Pers. head-dress, so prob. of Oriental origin.

tibia. L., shin-bone, flute.

tic. F., in earliest use applied to spasmodic trouble in horses. Hence *tic douloureux,* facial neuralgia. ? Cf. It., *ticchio,* freak, whim.

ticca [*Anglo-Ind.*]. In *ticca-gharry.* Hind. *ṭhīkā,* hire.

tice [*cricket, lawn-tennis*]. From dial. *tice,* aphet. for *entice* (q.v.), or, as it appears earlier (13 cent.), perh. direct from F. *attiser.*

tick[1]. Insect. WGer.; cf. Du. *teek, tiek,* Ger. *zecke;* also F. *tique* (from Teut.). AS. *ticia* (? for *tīca or *ticca) is recorded once. Perh. orig. goat and cogn. with Ger. *ziege,* goat, *zicklein,* kid; cf. synon. Ger. *holzbock,* lit. wood goat.

tick[2]. In *bed-tick.* Cf. Du. *tijk,* Ger. *zieche.* WGer. loan from L. *teca, theca,* G. θήκη, case, from τιθέναι, to put, whence also F. *taie,* pillow-case.

tick[3]. Light touch, sound. Imit., cf. Du. *tikken,* Norw. dial. *tikka,* to tap, touch lightly. Sense of light touch with pen, whence to *tick off,* is 19 cent. See also *tig.*

tick[4]. Credit. A 17 cent. clipped form of *ticket* (cf. *mob, cit,* etc.). Perh. from seamen's practice of getting goods on their pay-tickets (v.i.).

Their families must starve if we do not give them money, or they procure upon their tickets from some people that will trust them (Pepys, Oct. 31, 1666).

ticket. F. *étiquette*, label, etc., OF. *estiquete*, from *estiquer*, to stick, of Teut. origin. US. pol. use is recorded c. 1700; hence prob. *that's the ticket.* The (obs.) *ticket-porters* of London were so called from the badge which showed them to be licensed by the Corporation. Spec. sense of *ticket-of-leave*, written permission, arose in Austral.

tickle. ? Metath., influenced by *tick*[3], of *kittle* (q.v.). But cf. synon. L. *titillare* and dial. *tittle* (14 cent.).

> How he tickles yon trout under the gilles! you shall see him take him by and by
>   (Marston, *Ant. & Mellida*, ii.).

tick-tack. Redupl. on *tick*[3]. Cf. F. *tic-tac*.

tic-polonga. Snake (Ceylon). Sinhalese *tit-polongā*, spot viper.

tidbit. See *titbit*.

tiddler. For *tittlebat*. See *stickleback*.

tiddlywinks. Game, orig. (1870) form of dominoes. ? Suggested by slang *tiddly-wink*, unlicensed drink-shop (pawnshop).

tide. AS. *tīd*, time, as still in many compds. (*eventide*, *Yuletide*, etc.) and to *work double tides*, though this is orig. allusive to the two tides of each day. Com. Teut.; cf. Du. *tijd*, Ger. *zeit*, ON. *tīth*, all meaning *time*, with which they are ult. cogn. From archaic to *tide* (*betide*), happen, comes *tiding*(s), orig. happenings, but found in AS. in current sense. Cf. Ger. *zeitung*, newspaper. Application to sea has a parallel in LG. *tīde*, Du. *tij* (earlier *tijde*), from which it may have been borrowed, the first clear example of *tide* (of the sea) being in Chauc. In pleon. *time and tide*, which occurs much earlier, *tide* has its orig. sense. To *tide over* is naut. (v.i.). A *tide-waiter*, now sometimes fig. for time-server, was a Customs officer who awaited ships coming in with the tide.

> To tide over to a place, is to goe over with the tide of ebbe or flood (Capt. John Smith).

tidivate. See *titivate*.

tidy. Orig. timely, seasonable. From *tide* (q.v.).

> I will do what I can tidily to signify unto your Majesty our state (Lord Wentworth, 1558).

tie. AS. *tēag* (noun), *tīgan* (verb); cogn. with ON. *taug*, rope, Ger. *ziehen*, to draw, and with *tight*, *tow*[2], *tug*, etc. Sense of equality (sport) is evolved from that of connecting link, { ; cf. mod. *bracketted*, i.e. equal.

tier. Orig. naut., of oars or guns. From F. *tirer*, to draw, shoot. OF. has *tire*, sequence, but the E. word (16 cent.) perh. represents rather F. *tir*, shooting, and was orig. applied to a "tire of ordnance," row of guns. Cf. It. *tiro*, "a tyre of ordinance" (Flor.).

> The sayd Philip carried three tire of ordinance on a side, and eleven peeces in every tire
>   (Raleigh, 1591).

tierce. F., fem. of *tiers*, third, L. *tertius*. The cask called a *tierce* is the third of a pipe. For fencing sense cf. *carte*, *quarte*.

tiercel. See *tercel*.

Tiers-État [*hist.*]. F., third estate, i.e. the Commons, as opposed to the clergy and nobility.

> Qu'est-ce que le Tiers-État? Tout. Qu'a-t-il été jusqu'à présent dans l'ordre politique? Rien. Que demande-t-il à devenir? Quelque chose
>   (Sieyès).

tiff[1]. Temper. Prob. imit. of small outburst. Cf. *huff*, *sniff*.

tiff[2], **tift** [*dial.*]. To drink. Hence Anglo-Ind. *tiffin*, lunch, for *tiffing*. For extension from drinking to eating cf. *nuncheon*, *bever*.

> *tiffing*: eating, or drinking out of meal time (Grose).
> The captain, tifting away at the fluids as became an honest sailor (*Tom Cringle's Log*).

tiffany. Fabric. In AF. occ. used for Epiphany and also common in ME. as a female name. OF. *tiphanie*, L., G. θεοφάνια, lit. manifestation of God; cf. F. dial. (Berri) *tiefen*, January. As name for fabric perh. a joc. allusion to etym. sense of "manifestation," ? or associated with *diaphanous*.

> Tiffanie, sarcenet, and cypres, which instead of apparell to cover and hide, shew women naked through them (Holland's *Pliny*).

tiffin. See *tiff*[2].

tig. Game of "touch." Cf. *tick*[3], *tag*[2], and synon. Ger. *zeck*.

tiger. F. *tigre*, L., G. τίγρις, prob. of Oriental origin, ? with orig. sense of swift, whence also river *Tigris*. In most Europ. langs. Often used by early travellers for the jaguar, panther, etc. As archaic name for groom prob. from striped waistcoat or livery.

tight. For earlier *thight*, ON. *thēttr*, watertight, solid, staunch; cf. synon. Ger. *dicht* (from LG.). Change of form is app. due to association with *taut* (q.v.) and obs. *ticht*, p.p. of *tie*, whence also some later senses, chiefly from naut. lang. Orig. sense of dense, compact, appears in *water-tight*; so also a *tight ship*, and hence a *tight little island*. For slang sense of drunk cf. *screwed*.

> *thyht, hoole, not brokyn, not hoole withyn*: integer solidus (*Prompt. Parv.*).

tike. See *tyke*.

tilbury [*archaic*]. Vehicle. Inventor's name. Cf. *shillebeer*.

tilde. Sp., diacritic mark over *n* as in *señor*. Metath. from L. *titulus* (cf. *tittle*).

tile. AS. *tigele*, L. *tegula*, from *tegere*, ˙to cover; cf. F. *tuile*, It. *tegola*, *tegghia*. Early Teut. loan from L.; cf. Du. *tegel*, Ger. *ziegel*, ON. *tigl*. *Slate* (q.v.) is F., the orig. Teut. roof-cover being represented by *thatch* (q.v.).

till¹. Verb. AS. *tilian*, to strive after, labour. WGer.; cf. Du. *telen*, to breed, cultivate, Ger. *zielen*, to aim, and see *till²*. For specialization of sense cf. F. *labourer*, to till, lit. to work. AS. *tilth* is now usu. replaced by *tillage*.

till². Prep. & conj. Northumb. and ON. *til*, corresponding in use to E. *to*, Ger. *zu*, as still in Sc. Orig. a noun; cf. AS. *till*, fixed position, Ger. *ziel*, end, aim, also AS. *til*, serviceable, to the purpose. See also *till¹*.

till³. Noun. Orig. (15 cent.) drawer or compartment in coffer for valuables, private documents, etc. Origin obscure. ? Cf. F. *tille*, boat-locker, which is perh. of Teut. origin and cogn. with *thill*.

tillandsia. Plant. Named by Linnaeus from *Tillands*, Sw. botanist.

tiller. OF. *telier*, *tellier*, orig. weaver's beam, *telier des tisserands*, MedL. *telarium*, from *tela*, web; hence, stock of crossbow. E. naut. use (= F. *barre du gouvernail*) is 17 cent.

Sor le telier a un quarrel assis (*Loherencs*).

arbrier: the tillar of a crosse-bow (Cotg.).

tilt¹. Of cart. Replaces (16 cent.) ME. *teld*, *telt*, AS. *teld*, tent, cogn. with Ger. *zelt*, ON. *tjald*, ? and ult. with L. *tendere*, to stretch (see *tent¹*). Current form is app. due to ME. *tillette* (v.i.), OF. *telele*, var. of *teilete* (*toilette*), dim. of *teile* (*toile*), cloth, L. *tela*.

Cartes with tillettes for shott with all appareile (*Nav. Accts.* 1497).

tilt². To incline, etc. In ME. to overthrow. App. from AS. *tealt*, unsteady, whence *tealtian*, to be unsteady. Current sense perh. orig. from naut. use.

tilt³. Joust. Identified by *NED.* with *tilt²*, which I believe to be an error. First recorded c. 1500, as noun, in sense of encounter, place of encounter (*tilt-yard*). I conjecture connection with OF. *tillet*, *tillot*, from *tilleul*, lime², staves of lime-wood

having been used in the sport (v.i.), perh. as splintering easily. I have not found evidence that the *tilt* was orig. the lance-shaft, but the correspondence of *full tilt* with OF. *pleine hanste* (passim in *Roland*), *bouhort plenier* (*Tristan*), is significant, as both *hanste* and *bouhort* mean shaft of lance, and OF. *bouhorder*, to tilt, is derived from the latter. To *run a tilt* is for earlier *atilt* (adv.). To *tilt at windmills* alludes to Don Quixote.

tiliatus, tiliosus: virgula tiliacea, cujus usus maxime erat in hastiludiis. Cujus vero ligni interdum fuerint ipsae virgulae discimus ex aliis L. remiss. ann. 1375 in Reg. 107, ch. 50: "Iceulx Jehan et Girart prinrent chascun d'eulx un blanc petit tilleul pelé, pour en behourder l'un a l'autre, et en eulx ainsi esbatant et bouhourdant, briserent plusurs tilleux l'un contre l'autre" (Duc.).

tilth. See *till¹*.

Timariot. In *Bride of Abydos* (i. 7). F., It. *timariotto*, from Pers. *tīmār*, fief.

timbale [*cook.*]. From shape. F., kettledrum, bowl, app. a mixed form from OF. *atabal* (q.v.) and L. *tympanum*; cf. It. *timballo*, Sp. *timbal*. See *timbre*.

timber. AS. *timber*, house, building material, trees suitable for the purpose. Com. Teut.; cf. Du. dial. *timmer*, Ger. *zimmer*, room (OHG. *zimbar*), ON. *timbr*, Goth. **timr* (in *timrjan*, to build); cogn. with G. δέμειν, to build, δόμος, house. Cf. also Ger. *zimmern*, to carpenter, *zimmermann*, carpenter. In law *timber* is oak, ash, elm of twenty years' growth or more, with certain additions due to local use in building, e.g. in Bucks the beech is included.

timbre. F., small bell; hence, tone, L. *tympanum*, G. τύμπανον, timbrel, kettledrum. The F. word also assumed the sense of bellhelmet; hence, crest, and finally, stamp, whence E. *timbromania*, stamp-collecting.

timbrel. Dim. of obs. *timbre*, used by Wyc. to render *tympanum* (v.s.).

time. AS. *tīma*, cogn. with ON. *tīmi* (whence Sw. *timme*, Dan. *time*, hour), and with *tide*, the immediate cognates of which represent its senses in the other Teut. langs. In E. it has the double sense of extent and point (F. *temps*, *fois*, Ger. *zeit*, *mal*), and also stands for hour (F. *heure*, Ger. *uhr*). *Good* (*bad*) *time*, now regarded as US., was once current E. (cf. F. *se donner du bontemps*, and to *have a fine time of it*), but *high old time* is genuine US. (see however *old*). *Father Time* represents G. χρόνος. The *Times* dates from 1788. The earliest railway *time-table* appeared 1838, a year before *Bradshaw*. *Time-honoured* is an echo of Shaks. (*Rich. II*, i. 1).

timid. F. *timide*, L. *timidus*, from *timēre*, to fear.

timocracy. F. *timocratie*, MedL., G. τιμοκρατία, from τιμή, honour. In Aristotle, rule by propertied class, in Plato, rule inspired by love of honour.

Timon. Of Athens, famous misanthrope.

> The latter-day Timon of Cheyne Row [Carlyle]
> (*NED.* 1886).

timoneer. F. *timonier*, helmsman, It. *timoniere*, from *timon*, helm, L. *temo-n-*, waggon-pole, helm.

> And teach him the trade of a timoneer
> (*Gondoliers*).

timorous. OF. *timoureus*, MedL. *timorosus*, from *timor*, fear.

Timothy (grass). Introduced from England into US. by *Timothy Hanson* (early 18 cent.).

tin. AS. *tin*. Com. Teut.; cf. Du. *tin*, Ger. *zinn*, ON. *tin*. For slang sense of money, said to have been first applied to the thin-worn silver coinage of the 18 cent. recalled in 1817, cf. *brass*. Contemptuous *tinpot* was orig. applied to music. *Tin hat*, helmet, was theat. before the Great War.

tinamou. Partridge of the pampas. F., from native name.

tinchel [*Sc.*]. Circle of beaters in hunting. Gael. *timchioll*, circuit.

> We'll quell the savage mountaineer,
>   As their tinchel cows the game
> (*Lady of Lake*, vi. 17).

tincture. L. *tinctura*, from *tingere*, *tinct-*, to dye.

tinder. AS. *tynder*, cogn. with *-tendan*, to kindle, whence dial. *tind*. The verb is Com. Teut.; cf. Ger. *zünden*, ON. *tendra*, Goth. *tandjan*. See *tandstickor*. Orig. method of procuring fire by striking flint with steel has given the phrase to *strike a light*.

> Nether men tendyn a lanterne, and putten it undir a busshel (Wyc. *Matt.* v. 15).

tine. Prong. AS. *tind*, cogn. with ON. *tindr*, Ger. *zinne*, pinnacle. For loss of *-d* cf. *woodbine*.

ting. Imit. of thin clear sound. Cf. *tang²* and redupl. *ting-tang*.

tinge. First as verb. L. *tingere*, to dye.

tingle. Modification of *tinkle*, with which it varies in Wyc. Orig. idea of sound, passing into that of sensation, appears in to *make* one's ears tingle. L. *tinnire* has the same double sense.

> A cry that shiver'd to the tingling stars
> (Tennyson, *Morte d'Arthur*).

tink. Imit., the redupl. *tink-tank* (cf. *ting-tang*) representing alternation of lighter and heavier sound.

> I am maad as bras sownnynge or a symbal tynkynge [*Vulg.* tinniens] (Wyc. 1 *Cor.* xiii. 1).

tinker. This, and Sc. *tinkler*, are found much earlier (12 cent.) than *tink*, *tinkle*, from which they are usu. derived, an etym. given in the *Prompt. Parv.* This is not an insuperable objection, as a word like *tinker*, used as trade-name and surname, would naturally get recorded more easily than an onomatopoeic word.

tinkle. Frequent. of *tink* (q.v.). Cf. *tingle*, with which it is used indifferently in ME.

> Bothe his eeris shulen tynclen [*Vulg.* tinnire]
> (Wyc. 1 *Sam.* iii. 11).

tinsel. F. *étincelle*, spark, OF. *estincelle*, VL. **stincilla*, metath. of *scintilla*. ModF. has in this sense *paillette* or *clinquant*.

> *estinceller*: to powder, or set thick with sparkles
> (Cotg.).

tint. Earlier *tinct*, L. *tinctus*, from *tingere*, *tinct-*, to dye. Later form, as art word, due to It. *tinta*.

tintinnabulation. Coined (? by Poe) from L. *tintinnabulum*, bell, imit. redupl. from *tinnire*, to resound, tinkle.

tiny. From earlier (15 cent.) *tine*, used as noun (small quantity) and adj. and always preceded by *little*. ? Aphet. for synon. F. *tantin*, *tantinet*, ever so little, corresponding in sense to L. *tantillus*, from *tantus*, so much. For sense, and regular use with *little*, cf. Sc. *wee* (q.v.). Transition from sense of small quantity to that of small size is like that of Sc. *the bit laddie*. Terence uses *puer tantillus* in same sense as ME. and Shaks. *little tiny child*. But if the etym. I propose for *wee* is correct, *tiny* may be rather connected with *teen* (q.v.).

> *tantino*: a verie little, never so little, a little little quantity (Flor.).

> *tantillus*: so little and small, very little, little tiny (Litt.).

tip¹. Point, extremity. Cf. synon. Du. *tip*, Sw. *tipp*, Norw. Dan. *tip*; also Du. *tepel*, Ger. *zipfel*. In some senses perh. a thinned form of *top*; cf. *tip-top*, which may be redupl. on either word. First appears in *tiptoe* (Chauc.).

tip². Present. From earlier verb to *tip* (c. 1600), hand over, pass, orig. a cant word, as in *to tip the wink*. Here belong *straight tip*, *tipster*.

tip³. To upset, tilt up. Orig. (14 cent.) *type*, with long vowel (still in dial.). Origin unknown, but cf. synon. *top*, *tope* (naut. & dial.). Here belongs *tip-cat*.

tip⁴. To touch lightly. ? Thinned form of *tap²*. Cf. dial. *tip for tap*. Here belongs *tip and run* (cricket), used during the Great War of Ger. nav. dashes at seaside resorts.

tipit, tippit. Provincial game. For *tip² it*, hand it over, pass it on.

tippet. Orig. dim. of *tip¹*. Cf. Ger. *zipfel* in similar senses.

[He] bond the sorys to his hede with the typet of his hood (*Beryn*).

tipple. From 16 cent., but *tipeler* is found as leg. description in 14 cent. (*NED.*) and as surname is recorded early in 13 cent. This proves early existence of verb, unless it is a back-formation like *cadge*, *peddle*. Origin obscure, but ult. connection with *tap¹* seems likely. Cf. Norw. dial. *tipla*, to drip slowly, drink in small quantities. A *tippler* was orig. an alehouse keeper. For a converse sense-development cf. *tobacconist*.

tipstaff [*hist.*]. For *tipped staff*, truncheon with emblem of office, carried by constable, etc. See *tip¹*.

tipsy. From *tip³*, but later associated with *tipple*. For suffix cf. *tricksy*, *popsy-wopsy*.

tirade. F., It. *tirata*, volley, etc., from *tirare*, to fire. See *tire²*.

tirailleur. F., from *tirailler*, frequent. of *tirer*, to shoot. See *tire²*.

tire¹. To weary. AS. *tīorian*, to exhaust, wear away (trans. & intrans.). Ulterior hist. obscure.

tire² [*obs.*]. To tug, tear, etc. F. *tirer*, to draw; cf. It. *tirare*, Sp. *tirar*. Hence *attire*, *retire*. Of obscure origin, but perh. connected with *tire¹*, as the verb has in the older Rom. langs. also sense of vexing, harassing.

tire³. Dress, outer covering of wheel. Aphet. for *attire*. In first sense confused with ME. *tiar*, tiara. For second sense cf. Ger. *radkranz*, lit. wheel-garland. Often incorr. spelt *tyre*.

perruquiere: a tyre-maker, or attire-maker; a woman that makes perriwigs, or attires (Cotg.).

The application of elastic bearings round the tire of carriage-wheels (*NED.* 1845).

tiro. L., young soldier, raw recruit. In MedL. often *tyro*. Hence *tirocinium* (Cowper, 1784), lit. first campaign, novice experience.

Tironian. System of shorthand attributed to Cicero's freedman *Tiro*.

tirra-lirra. Imit. of cheerful song (*Wint. Tale*, iv. 3, *Lady of Shalott*, iii. 4). Cf. OF. *ture-lure*.

tisane. See *ptisane*.

Tishri. Jewish month, called *Ethanim* before Captivity. Late Heb. *tishrī*, from Aram. *shᵉrā*, to begin.

tissue. Earlier *tissu*, F., p.p. of OF. *tistre* (replaced by *tisser*), to weave, L. *texere*. *Tissue-paper* (18 cent.) was perh. orig. used, as now, to insert between layers of fine tissue (fabric); but synon. F. *papier de soie* suggests rather an allusion to the softness and delicacy of the paper itself.

tit¹. Small nag, little girl, bird. Cf. ON. *tittr*, titmouse, Norw. dial. *tita*, of various small fish and other objects. Occurs much earlier in *titmouse*, *titling*.

tit². In *tit for tat*. ? Imit. of light tap. Cf. earlier *tip for tap*, also dial. *tint for tant*, app. after F. *tant pour tant* (see *taunt*).

Titan. One of family of giants, G. Τιτᾶνες, children of Heaven and Earth (Uranus and Gaea), who attempted to scale heaven and overthrow Zeus by piling Mount Pelion upon Mount Ossa. *Weary Titan* is in M. Arnold's *Heine's Grave*. He afterwards applied the epithet to England (*Friendship's Garland*).

titanium [*chem.*]. Named (1795) by Klaproth on analogy of *uranium* (v.s.).

titbit. From 17 cent. (also *tidbit*). Prob. from *tit¹*.

Tite Barnacle. Adhesive and incompetent bureaucrat. See *Little Dorrit*.

tithe. AS. *teogotha*, *teotha*, tenth. Spec. sense of eccl. due has led to the retention of the word, replaced as ordinal by *tenth*. Cf. F. *dîme*, tithe, L. *decima* (sc. *pars*). Hence *tithing* (hist.), AS. *teothung*, aggregate of ten households under system of frankpledge.

Titian hair. Of the red colour common in pictures by *Titian* (†1576).

titillate. From L. *titillare*, to tickle.

titivate. From c. 1800 (also *tidivate*). ? From *tidy* with jocular latinization, ? or fanciful elaboration of synon. dial. *tiff*, F. *attifer*, "to decke, pranke, tricke, trim, adorne" (Cotg.), Merovingian L. *aptificare*, from *aptus*, fit.

title. OF. (*titre*), L. *titulus*, "the title or inscription of a worke or acte" (Coop.).

> And the title of his cause was writun
> (Wyc. *Mark*, xv. 26).

titling. See *tit*¹. Cf. ON. *titlingr*, sparrow.

titmouse. ME. *titmose*, from *tit*¹ and obs. *mose*, AS. *māse*, a Teut. bird-name; cf. Du. *mees*, Ger. *meise*, ON. *meisingr*; also F. *mésange*, "a titmouse, or tittling" (Cotg.), from Teut. Altered on *mouse*, whence incorr. pl. *titmice*. Cf. Norw. Dan. *musvit*, black tit, altered on *mus*, mouse, from earlier *misvitte*. Often shortened to *tit*, whence *tomtit*.

titter. Imit., cf. Ger. *kichern*.

tittle. L. *titulus*, title, in Late L. for any small stroke forming part of, or added to, a letter; cf. Port. *til*, accent, Prov. *titule*, dot of i, Sp. *tilde* (q.v.). In Bibl. use (Wyc. *Matt.* v. 18) it represents Heb. *qōts*, thorn, prick, G. κεραία, horn, L. *apex*, rendered *prica* in AS. See *jot*.

tittlebat. See *stickleback*.

tittle-tattle. See *tattle*. App. the redupl. is on *tittle*, to prate, much older than *tattle*. The NED. quotes *tittler* from *Piers Plowm.*, but it was a surname a century earlier (*Hund. Rolls*). The verb is prob. imit., cf. *titter*.

tittup. To prance along. First (c. 1700) as noun, canter. Perh. imit. of hoof-beat.

titubate. From L. *titubare*, to stagger.

titular. From L. *titulus*, title.

tizzy [*slang*]. Sixpence. ? Argotic perversion of obs. *tilbury*, sixpence, "so called from it's being formerly the fare for crossing over from Gravesend to Tilbury fort" (Grose). Cf. schoolboy *swiz* for *swindle*.

tmesis [*gram.*]. Separation of parts of compound. G. τμῆσις, from τέμνειν, to cut.

T.N.T. Powerful explosive, *tri-nitro-toluene*, from Ger. *toluin*, from *tolu* (q.v.).

to. AS. *tō*. WGer.; cf. Du. *te*, Ger. *zu*. ON. has *til*, Goth. *du*; cogn. with L. enclitic -*do* (as in *quando*), G. -δε. For *all to brake* (*Judges*, ix. 53) see *all*, *to-*.

to-. Obs. prefix. AS. *tō-*. WGer.; cf. OSax. *te-*, Ger. *zer-*; ult. cogn. with L. *dis-*. See *all*.

toad. From AS. *tādige*, with no known cognates. Cf. *tadpole*. *Toady* is for *toad-eater*, orig. mountebank attendant of quack doctor pretending to eat (poisonous) toads in order to advertise his master's infallible antidotes (see quot. s.v. *understrapper*). F. *crapaud*, toad, is used with similar allusion; cf. also F. *avaleur de couleuvres* (adders), toady. For *toadstool* cf. synon.

Du. *paddestoel*, from *padde*, toad, "paddock."

> The Beauclerks, Lord Westmorland and a Mr Jones his tutor or toadeater, were our party
> (Duchess of Devonshire, July 26, 1776).

toast. First (14 cent.) as verb. OF. *toster*, from L. *torrēre*, *tost-*, to parch, etc.; cf. It. *tostare*, "to toste, to bloate, to parch with heate" (Flor.). In ME. used also of a slice of toasted spiced bread with which beverages were flavoured, and, from c. 1700, of a lady regarded as figuratively adding piquancy to the wine in which her health was drunk.

> Go fetch me a quart of sack, put a toast in't
> (*Merry Wives*, iii. 5).

tobacco. Earlier (16 cent.) *tabaco*. Sp., from Carib of Hayti, according to Oviedo (1535) the name of the tube through which the smoke was inhaled, but according to Las Casas (1552) a kind of cigar. Later research suggests the possibility of its being a Guarani word (Brazil). In most Europ. langs. A *tobacconist* was earlier (Ben Jonson) a smoker.

> To the corrupted basenesse of the first use of this tobacco, doeth very well agree the foolish and groundlesse first entry thereof into this kingdome
> (James I).

> Drunkards and tobacconists are ranked together, and not improperly (Adm. Monson, 1624).

toboggan. Canad. Ind. (Micmac) *tobākun*. Spelt *tabaganne* in 17 cent. F.

toby¹. Jug, Punch's dog, both first in Dickens, unless a jug is meant in quot. below. From *Tobias* (cf. *jeroboam*, *tankard*, etc.). Earlier (17 cent.) also buttocks, as in *to tickle one's toby*. *Toby Philpot*, "fill pot" (*Tom Brown's Schooldays*), for a brown jug, goes back to the name of a character in O'Keefe's *Poor Soldier* (1782).

> I am glad you had the Toby
> (Letter of 1673, in *Notes & Queries*, 12 S. v. 118).

toby² [*archaic*]. In *high toby*, *low toby*, profession of mounted highwayman and footpad respectively. From Shelta *tobar*, road, ? deliberate perversion of Ir. *bothar*, road.

toccata [*mus.*]. It., from *toccare*, to touch.

toco, toko [*slang*]. From WInd. phrase *toco for yam*, punishment instead of food, with ref. to slaves. *Toco* is said to be imper. of Hind. *tokna*, to censure.

toco-. From G. τόκος, offspring.

tocsin. F., OF. *toquassen*, Prov. *tocasenh*, touch (q.v.) sign, with second element from L. *signum*, used in Late L. for bell.

tod. Weight, orig. of wool. Fris. & LG. *todde*, small bundle, load, ? cogn. with Ger. *zotte*, shaggy tuft, etc. *Tod*, bush, esp. in *ivy-tod*, is the same word.

to-day. From *to* and *day*; cf. *to-night*, *to-morrow*, also Ger. *heutzutage*, F. *aujourd'hui*, both pleon., as *heute* is for OHG. **hiu-tagu*, and OF. *hui* is L. *hodie*, *hoc die*.

> Yet hadde I levere wedde no wyf to-yeere
> (Chauc. D. 168).

toddle. Orig. Sc. & north. (*NED.*). Of obscure origin, ? ult. cogn. with *totter*. *NED.* records it from c. 1600.

toddy. Orig. Anglo-Ind. name for fermented sap. Earlier *tarrie* (Purch.), *taddy*. Hind. *tārī*, from *tār*, species of palm, Sanskrit *tāla*.

> A kinde of drinke of the pamita tree called "taddy"
> (Jourdaine's *Journal*, 1609).

todea. Fern. Named from *Tode*, Ger. botanist (†1787).

to-do. Cf. *ado* and origin of *affair*.

tody. WInd. bird. From F. *todier*, from L. *todus*, some small bird, adopted as generic name by Linnaeus.

toe. AS. *tā* (for **tāhe*). Com. Teut.; cf. Du. *teen*, *toon* (orig. pl.), Ger. *zehe*, ON. *tā*.

toff. Earlier *toft*, vulgarism for *tuft* (q.v.).

toffee. Later form of northern *taffy*. ? Connected with *tafia*.

toft [*archaic*]. ON. *topt*, homestead, earlier *tomt*; ? ult. cogn. with L. *domus*. Common in place-names and surnames. Hence also Norm. F. *-tot* in place-names (*Yvetot*, etc.).

tog. Usu. in pl. A cant word, perh. from L. *toga*.

> *toge*: a coat (*Dict. Cant. Crew*).

toga. L., cogn. with *tegere*, to cover.

together. AS. *tōgædere*, cogn. with *gather*; cf. Ger. *zusammen*, together, cogn. with *sammeln* (OHG. *samanan*), to gather. Hence *altogether*.

toggle. Cross-bar. Orig. naut. ? Cf. obs. *tuggle*, from *tug*.

toil¹. To work laboriously, orig. to contend, struggle. OF. *touillier*, L. *tudiculare*, to stir, from *tudicula*, machine for crushing olives, from *tudes*, mallet, cogn. with *tundere*, *tutud-*, to beat. Earlier sense survives in Sc. *tulzie*, in which *-z-* is a late printer's substitute for an obs. symbol (as in *Mackenzie*, *Menzies*, etc.) representing the sound of the consonant *y*.

toil². Only in pl., *in the toils*. F. *toile*, cloth, web, L. *tela*, cogn. with *texere*, to weave;

in F. also, in pl., for "toyles; or, a hay to inclose, or intangle, wilde beasts in" (Cotg.).

> The 7 of August [1554] was a general huntinge at Wyndsore forest, where was made a great toyle of 4 or 5 myles longe (Wriothesley).

toilet. F. *toilette*, dim. of *toile*, cloth (v.s.). For curious sense-development in F. & E., wrapper, table-cover, dressing-table, attire, etc., cf. that of *bureau*.

toise [*mil.*]. F., fathom, measure of six feet, L. *tensa* (sc. *brachia*), stretched (arms), from *tendere*, to stretch. Cf. F. *brasse*, fathom, L. *brachia*.

tokay. Wine. From *Tokay*, Hungary.

toke [*slang*]. Bread. ? Alteration of *tack²*.

token. AS. *tācn*. Com. Teut.; cf. Du. *teeken*, Ger. *zeichen*, ON. *teikn*, Goth. *taikns*; cogn. with *teach* (q.v.). Largely replaced by borrowed *sign* (see *Ps.* cxxxv. 9). With *by the same token*, very common in 15 cent., cf. F. *à telles enseignes que*, the proof of this being that.

> An ivel generacioun and avoutiere sekith a tokne
> (Wyc. *Matt.* xii. 39).

> By the same tokyn that I payd hym vj gʳˢ in Ajust
> (*Cely Papers*).

toko. See *toco*.

tolbooth [*hist.*]. From *toll¹* and *booth*. Orig. customs office (Wyc. *Matt.* ix. 9), later, esp. in Sc., town-hall, jail.

> At the last Sturbridge Fayre when the Proctours brought malefactours to the Tolboothe the Mayour refused to take them in
> (*Privy Council Acts*, 1547).

tol-de-rol. Meaningless refrain; cf. synon. F. *flonflon*.

toledo [*hist.*]. Sword (Ben Jonson). From *Toledo*, Spain. Cf. *bilbo*.

tolerate. From L. *tolerare*, cogn. with *tollere*, to lift, bear.

toll¹. Payment. AS. *toll*, *toln*; cf. Du. *tol*, Ger. *zoll*, ON. *tollr*. Early Teut. loan from VL. *toloneum*, for *teloneum*, "the place where taskes or tributes are payed, or tolles taken" (Coop.), G. τελώνιον, from τέλος, tax. For early and wide adoption of L. offic. word cf. *dicker*. Orig. *-n-* appears in OSax. *tolna*, OHG. *zollantuom*; also in AS. *tolnere*, tax-gatherer. Cf. F. *tonlieu*, feudal due, a metathetic form. See also *tolbooth*.

toll². Verb. App. spec. use of obs. *toll*, to draw, allure (still in dial. & US.), cogn. with obs. *till*, to pull, AS. *-tyllan*. Orig. sense may have been that of "alluring" people to church (cf. *peal*); but its supersession, in later funereal sense, of earlier *knell*, *knoll*, is no doubt due to suitability of sound.

Tolstoyan. Of *Count Leo Tolstoy*, a kind of 19 cent. Russ. Rousseau (†1910).

In these [districts], where the Tolstoyan theory holds good, the peasants are fervent believers in the doctrine of universal virtue and prosperity, provided the virtue is not expected from them
(*Sunday Times*, Jan. 6, 1918).

tolu. Balsam. From *Tolu* (now *Santiago de Tolu*), Colombia.

Tom. For *Thomas* (q.v.). With *Tom, Dick, and Harry* cf. F. *Pierre et Paul*, Ger. *Heinz und Kunz* (Henry and Conrad). Coriolanus uses *Hob and Dick* (ii. 3) in same sense, and Gower, in his lines on Wat Tiler's Rebellion, gives a longer list of the commonest names as typical of the mob, viz. *Wat, Tom, Sim, Bet* (Bartholomew), *Gib* (Gilbert), *Hick* (Richard), *Col* (Nicholas), *Geff, Will, Grig, Daw* (David), *Hob* (Robert), *Larkin* (Lawrence), *Hud* (?), *Jud* (Jordan), *Teb* (Theobald), *Jack*. *Tom* is often used for great bells (cf. *Big Ben*), whence *Tom Quad*, Christ Church, Oxf., also for guns (*long tom*), fools (*tomfool, tomnoddy*). *Tom-cat*, for *Tom the cat*, in a child's book of 1760 (cf. *Reynard*), has replaced earlier *gib-cat* (from *Gilbert*). *Tom and Jerry* are the chief characters in Egan's *Life in London* (1821). *Tomboy* was orig. applied to an unmannerly boy. *Tom Tiddler's ground* is also in dial. *Tom Tickler's* (*Tinker's*) *ground*. With *tomtit* cf. *jackdaw, magpie*, etc., and see *jack* for similar groups of senses. With *Tom Thumb* cf. F. *Petit Poucet*, Ger. *Däumling* (dim. of *daumen*, thumb).

Jack and Tom and Will and Dick shall meet and censure me and my government (James I).

A thoughtless young fool,
Bassanio, a lord of the Tomnoddy school
(*Ingoldsby*).

[Soho] was not the crowded haunt of every hungry Tom, Dick, and Harriet that it is to-day
(*Sunday Times*, Apr. 11, 1919).

tomahawk. NAmer. Ind. (Virginia), spelt *tomahack* by Capt. John Smith, with many vars. in the Ind. dials. Its burial was emblematic of a sworn peace. Cf. *pipe of peace*.

toman [*hist.*]. Pers. gold coin nominally worth 10,000 dinars. Pers. *tūmān*, ten thousand, of Tatar origin.

tomato. Earlier (17 cent.) *tomate*, F. Sp. Port., from Mex. *tomatl*. App. altered on *potato*. Known in Europe from 16 cent.

tomb. F. *tombe* (now only poet.), Late L.

tumba, from G. τύμβος, funeral mound; cf. It. *tomba*, Sp. *tumba*; ? cogn. with L. *tumulus*.

tombac. EInd. alloy of copper and zinc. F., Port. *tambaca*, Malay *tambāga*, copper.

tombola. It., lottery, from *tombolare*, to tumble, fall upside down.

tome. F., L., G. τόμος, part of volume, from τέμνειν, to cut. Cf. *section*.

tomentose [*biol.*]. From L. *tomentum*, wadding, cogn. with *tumēre*, to swell.

Tommy. See *Tom. NED.* quotes *Tommy Atkins* from Sala (1883) and *Tommy* from Kipling (1893). For origin of the nickname see *Thomas*. Sense of food, orig. bread only (mil.), is app. via witticism *Tommy Brown* (see *brown*). *Tommy-rot* is 19 cent. (c. 1880).

The "Tommy shop"—an establishment where you can run for a week "on the slate"
(*Daily Chron.* Aug. 1, 1919).

to-morrow. See *to-day*.

tompion[1]. Watch or clock by *Thomas Tompion*, watchmaker temp. Anne.

tompion[2]. Plug fitting mouth of cannon. Also *tampion, tampkin*. F. *tampon*, nasalized form of *tapon*, bung, of Teut. origin and cogn. with *tap*[1]. For vars. cf. *pumpkin*.

tom-tom. Urdu *tam-tam* or Malay *tong-tong*, of imit. origin. Cf. *pom-pom*.

-tomy. Late L., G. -τομία, from τέμνειν, to cut.

ton[1]. Weight. Var. of *tun* (q.v.), differentiation of sense appearing only in 17 cent. Cf. F. *tonne*, in both senses, also dim. *tonneau*, cask, used also in giving *tonnage* of ship, which was orig. calculated in terms of Bordeaux wine-tuns (see *rummage*). Hist. *tonnage* (*and poundage*) was levied on every tun of wine.

ton[2]. F., tone.

tonality [*art jargon*]. After F. *tonalité*, from *ton*, tone.

tondo [*art*]. Circular painting, carving in circular setting, etc. It., for *rotondo*, round.

tone. F. *ton*, L., G. τόνος, stretching, tension, esp. as mus. term, from τείνειν, to stretch. In some senses immediately from L. *tonus*. See also *tune*. For application to colour cf. use of *light and shade* in music. Physiol. sense is perh. direct from G. Hence med. *tonic*. *Tonic stem* of a F. verb is that in which the accent is on the stem in F. & L., with the result that in OF. we have variation of vowel (*je treuve, nous trouvons; je lieve, nous levons*, etc.), as still sometimes in ModF. (*je meurs, nous mou-rons*; *je tiens, nous tenons*, etc.). *Tony* is US., for earlier *high-toned*.

tonga[1] [*Anglo-Ind.*]. Light cart. Hind. *tāngā*.

tonga[2]. Plant and drug (Fiji). Said to be arbitrary invention of one Ryder who first sent specimens to England.

tongs. AS. *tang, tange*. Com. Teut.; cf. Du. *tang*, Ger. *zange*, ON. *töng*; cogn. with G. δάκνειν, to bite. Pl. use is peculiar to E.

tongue. AS. *tunge*. Com. Teut.; cf. Du. *tong*, Ger. *zunge*, ON. *tunga*, Goth. *tuggō*; cogn. with L. *lingua*, OL. *dingua* (cf. *tear*[1]). In many fig. senses, from shape. *Tongue in cheek* is mod. (*Ingoldsby*).

tonic. See *tone*.

to-night. See *to-day*.

tonite. Explosive. From L. *tonare*, to thunder.

tonitrual. Late L. *tonitrualis*, from *tonitrus*, thunder.

tonka bean. Negro name in Guiana. Erron. *tonquin bean*.

tonneau. Of motor-car. F., cask. See *ton*, *tun*.

tonsil. From L. *tonsillae* (pl.).

tonsorial. From L. *tonsorius*, from *tonsor*, from *tondēre, tons-*, to shear, clip, ult. cogn. with G. τέμνειν, to cut.

tonsure. F., L. *tonsura*, from *tondēre, tons-* (v.s.).

tontine. From *Tonti*, Neapolitan banker, who introduced this method of insurance in France (17 cent.).

Tony [*hist.*]. Port. soldier (*Daily News*, June 29, 1917). For *Antonio*. Cf. *Tommy*, *Sammy*, etc.

too. Stressed form of *to*; cf. Ger. *zu* in both senses. Orig. idea is that of addition, super-fluity.

homines nimium sermone blandi: verie faire spoken men; too too smooth tongued, or meale mouthed (Morel, 1585).

tool. AS. *tōl*, from a Teut. verb, to make, prepare, which appears in *taw*[1], with agent. suffix as in *shovel, ladle*. Connection of slang to *tool*, drive (c. 1800), is not clear.

toot. Du. *tuiten, toeten*; cf. Ger. *tuten*, "to blow, or wind, the horn, as post-boys do" (Ludw.), ? of imit. origin; ? but cf. Ger. *tute, tüte, düte*, horn-shaped bag, of LG. origin.

tooth. AS. *tōth* (for **tanth*). Aryan; cf. Du. *tand*, Ger. *zahn* (OHG. *zand*), ON. *tönn*, Goth. *tunthus*, L. *dens, dent-*, G. ὀδούς, ὀδόντ-, Sanskrit *danta*, Welsh *dant*. Prob.

a pres. part., eater (cf. L. *edere*, to eat). Fig. senses often allude to teeth as natural weapon. With current *toothcomb*, for *small tooth comb*, cf. to *comb out*.

The army behind the front is being tooth-combed of all men fit for the fighting-line
(*Daily Chron.* Jan. 25, 1918).

tootle. Frequent. of *toot*.

tootsy, tootsicum. Baby word for foot (19 cent.), prob. evolved from *toddle*.

In this, my unenlightened state,
    To work in heavy boots I comes,
Will pumps henceforward decorate
    My tiddle toddle tootsicums?
          (Gilbert, *Ben Polter*).

top[1]. Summit, etc. AS. *top*. Com. Teut.; cf. Du. *top*, Ger. *zopf*, queue of hair, ON. *toppr*, tuft of hair. The hair sense is perh. the earliest and appears in F. dim. *toupet*, "a tuft, or topping" (Cotg.). See also *tuft*. Prevailing E. sense appears in many phrases, e.g. *top and bottom, top to toe*, to *top and tail* (onions), etc. *Over the top* (of the parapet) is characteristic of the British soldier's dislike for heroics. *Top* is common in naut. lang., e.g. in *top-gallant*, in which the second element has intens. force; cf. naut. use of *royal* (sail), and Du. *bramzeil*, top-gallant, ? from LG. *bram*, display; cf. also cogn. F. *gaillard* used for the fore and after castles of a ship. *Topknot* may be folk-etym. for AF. dim. *topinet*, crest; a *topynet de j basinet*, crest of a helmet, is mentioned in the Earl of Derby's travel-ling accounts (14 cent.). Fig. use of *top-sawyer* is due, according to Grose, to the fact that in Norfolk saw-pits the *top-sawyer* received twice the wages of the *bottom-sawyer*. (*Up to the*) *top-hole* is a recent variation on earlier *top-notch*.

At this moment the Canadians went over
          (*Press Ass.* Nov. 13, 1916).

top[2]. For spinning. Cf. Du. dial. *top, dop*, the latter the earlier form, app. cogn. with Ger. *topf*, pot, used in dial. for top (v.i.); also F. *toupie*, "a gig, or casting-top" (Cotg.), OF. *topet, toupin*, etc., from Teut. App. the orig. *top* was the hollow humming-top. F. *sabot*, wooden shoe, also means "a top, gig, or nun to whip, or play with" (Cotg.), hence *dormir comme un sabot*, sleep like a top.

der topf-kreusel [*-kreisel*] *oder kreusel-topf, damit ein knabe spielet*: a top wherewith a boy plays. *Den topf, oder dopf, treiben oder peitschen*: to scourge, or whip, your top (Ludw.).

topaz. F. *topaze*, L., G. τόπαζος, of obscure origin; ? cf. Sanskrit *tapas*, heat, fire.

tope¹. Mango grove. Tamil *tōppu*, Telugu *tōpu*.

tope². Dome-shaped Buddhist shrine or tumulus. Hind. *tōp*, Sanskrit *stūpa*.

tope³. Verb, whence *toper*. F. *toper*, to accept the stake in gambling, hence to clinch a bargain and "wet" it. Cf. synon. It. *toppare*, Sp. *topar*, and It. *toppa*, done! also Ger. *topp*, from F. Of imit. origin, from striking hands together in token of bargain. Cf. *swap*.

tope⁴. Small kind of shark. According to Ray (1686) a Corn. name.

Mr Adams, a member of the City of London Piscatorial Society has caught a 33¾ lb. tope at Margate
(*Ev. News*, Aug. 15, 1918).

topee. See *sola*.

top-gallant [*naut.*]. See *top¹*.

Tophet. Heb. *tōpheth*, name of place near *Gehenna* (q.v.), where the Jews sacrificed to strange gods (*Jer.* xix.), later used for deposit of refuse and taken as symbol of torment. Trad. derived from *tōph*, timbrel, used in worship of Moloch.

topiary [*gard.*]. Clipping of shrubs into fantastic shapes. L. *topiarius*, from G. τόπια, pl. of τόπιον, dim. of τόπος, place. Cf. F. *topiaire*, "the making of images in, or arbors of, plants" (Cotg.). Currency is due to Evelyn.

topic. From L., G. τὰ τοπικά (neut. pl. of τοπικός), title of work by Aristotle on (κοινοὶ) τόποι, commonplaces, pl. of τόπος. Current sense of *topical* (song) is late 19 cent.

topography. Late L., G. τοπογραφία, from τόπος, place. Cf. *toponomy*, study of place-names, from ὄνομα, name.

topple. From *top¹*, orig. sense being to fall as being *top-heavy*.

topsy-turvy. Earlier (16 cent.) *-tirvy, -tervy*, e.g. *topsy-tyrvy* (Palsg.). Perh. for orig. **top-so-tirvy*, which would have a parallel in earliest form of *upside-down* (q.v.). Second element app. from obs. *terve*, to turn, usu. in compd. *over-terve*, with which cf. AS. *tearflian*, to roll, app. a derivative of the unrecorded simplex (cf. OHG. *zerben*, to rotate). In early works often misprinted *-turn-* (v.i.), unless this is a similar formation from *turn*. A 17 cent. spelling *topside totherway* is an etymologizing guess.

The furious waves
All topsie turned by th' Aeolian slaves
(Sylv. *Jonas*).

toque. F., cf. It. *tocca*, Sp. *toca*, Port. *touca*, all used of form of head-dress. Common (as *tock, tuck*) in Hakl. and Purch., of Turkish or Moorish cap, turban, which suggests Eastern origin.

tor¹ [*west country*]. AS. *torr*, tower, rock, L. *turris*; cf. OWelsh *twrr*, pile, heap, Gael. *torr*, hill, mound, from L. via AS.

tor². In *alley-tor*. See *taw²*.

Torah. Mosaic law, Pentateuch. Heb. *tōrāh*, direction, instruction.

torch. F. *torche*, OIt. *torchio*, VL. **torculum*, from *torcēre* (*torquēre*), to twist, a torch being made of twisted tow; cf. It. *torcia*, "a torch or a linke" (Flor.), Sp. *antorcha*, Port. *tocha*. Connection with *torquēre* seems to be certified by synon. ME. & OF. *tortis*, MedL. *torticius*. *Handing on the torch* is allusive to the G. torch-race, λαμπαδηδρομία.

Et quasi cursores vitai lampada tradunt
(Lucret. ii. 79).

torchon. F., lit. duster, dish-cloth, from *torcher*, to wipe, from *torche* (v.s.), in sense of handful of twisted straw. Cf. *chiffon*.

toreador. Sp., from verb *torear*, from *toro*, bull, L. *taurus*.

toreutic. G. τορευτικός, from τορεύειν, to work in relief.

torment. OF. (*tourment*), L. *tormentum*, orig. warlike implement worked by twisting, for **torquementum*, from *torquēre*, to twist.

tormentil. Plant. F. *tormentille*, MedL. *tormentilla*, prob. from med. virtues against some sort of pain.

tornado. E. perversion, after Sp. *tornar*, to turn, of Sp. *tronada*, from *tronar*, to thunder L. *tonare*. Where Peter Mundy, who knew the origin of the word (v.i.), has *tronado*, the log of the ship he sailed in has *turnatho*.

The ternados, that is thundrings and lightnings
(Hakl.).

"Tronados" in Portugues signifieth only thunder, but is a name given by them for all the fowle weather...by reason of the greate and frequent thunder among the rest (Peter Mundy, 1628).

torpedo. L., numbness, also "a fish that hath the nature to make the handes of them that touche it to be astonyed, though he doe it with a long pole" (Coop.), from *torpēre*, to be torpid. Applied (18 cent.) to a land-mine and (c. 1800) to a drifting sea-mine.

T. They write here one Cornelius-son hath made the Hollanders an invisible eel to swim the haven at Dunkirk and sink all the shipping there. P. But how is't done? C. I'll show you, sir. It is an automat, runs under water with a snug nose, and has a nimble tail made like an auger, with which tail she wriggles betwixt the costs [ribs] of a ship and sinks it straight (Ben Jonson, *Staple of News*, iii. 1).

torpid. L. *torpidus*, from *torpēre* (v.s.). The *Torpids*, Lent races at Oxf., were earlier the clinker-built boats used in the races, and these boats were orig. the second, i.e. slower, boats of each college.

The little gentleman...did not join with the "Torpids," as the second boats of a college are called (*Verdant Green*).

torque. From L. *torques*, twisted collar, from *torquēre*, to twist.

torrefy. F. *torréfier*, from L. *torrefacere*, from *torrēre* (v.i.) and *facere*.

torrent. F., L. *torrens*, *torrent-*, orig. pres. part. of *torrēre*, to burn, hence to boil, bubble, etc. Cf. *burn*[1,2] and see *estuary*.

Torricellian [*phys.*]. Of *Torricelli*, It. physicist (†1647).

I went to yᵉ Philosophic Club, where was examined yᵉ Torricellian experiment (Evelyn, 1660).

torrid. L. *torridus*, from *torrēre*, to parch, etc., ult. cogn. with *thirst*.

Quinque tenent caelum zonae: quarum una corusco
Semper sole rubens, et torrida semper ab igni
(*Georg.* i. 233).

torsion. F., L. *tortio-n-*, from *torquēre*, *tort-*, to twist.

torsk. Fish. Norw. & Sw., ON. *thorskr*; cf. Ger. *dorsch* (from LG.); cogn. with Ger. *dürr*, dry.

torso. It., stalk, cabbage-stump, trunk of body without head and arms. L., G. θύρσος, thyrsus, wand.

tort [*leg.*]. F., MedL. *tortum*, lit. twisted, from *torquēre*, *tort-*. Cf. relationship of *wrong* to *wring*.

White had suffered damage by reason of defendants' tortious and wrongful acts
(Mr Just. Astbury, Apr. 30, 1920).

torticollis [*med.*]. Crick in neck. ModL., from *collum*, neck (v.s.). Cf. earlier F. *torticolis*.

tortilla [*Mex.*]. Cake. Dim. of Sp. *torta*. See *tart*[2].

tortoise. Earlier (14–15 cents.) *tortu*, *tortuce*, *tortose*, etc.; cf. F. *tortue*, Sp. *tortuga*, representing Late L. *tortuca*, ? twisted (see *tort*), ? from crooked feet of SEurop. variety. The sibilant ending of *tortoise* may be due to *tortu's-shell*. But the naming of the animal from so inconspicuous a feature as the feet seems unnatural, and some of the SEurop. forms in *tar-* (e.g. It. *tartaruga*, Sicilian *tartuca*) suggest *-a-* as orig. vowel, with a later assim. to L. *tortus*.

tortuous. F. *tortueux*, L. *tortuosus*, from *torquēre*, *tort-*, to twist.

torture. F., L. *tortura* (v.s.). For sense-development cf. *torment*.

torula [*biol.*]. ModL. dim. from *torus* (v.i.).

torus [*arch. & biol.*]. L., lit. bed, hence cushion, bulge, etc.

torve [*archaic*]. OF., L. *torvus*, "cruell and sturdy in lookes, grimme, sterne, terrible, fell" (Coop.).

Tory. "One who adheres to the ancient constitution of the state and the apostolical hierarchy of the Church of England" (Johns.). Ir. *tóraidhe*, *tóraighe*, pursuer (in compds. only), from *tóir*, pursuit. Orig. applied (c. 1650) to dispossessed Irishmen who became freebooters, rapparees. Hence, by Parliamentarians, to rebel Irish, papist soldiers of Charles I. Pol. nickname (cf. *Whig*) dates from 1679–80, when the "Exclusioners" used it of the supporters of the Duke of York, afterwards James II. Definitely established as name of one of the two great parties at the Revolution (1689). See also *Conservative*.

tosh [*school slang*]. NED. quotes from 1892. Perh. from same word used at some schools (1879 in author's recollection) for penis. A parallel will occur to those familiar with schoolboy lang.

toss. From c. 1500. ? Cf. Norw. **dial.** *tossa*, to spread, strew. Earliest in ref. to the sea (Tynd. *Matt.* xiv. 24, where Wyc. has *throwen*). In current senses the upward motion is emphasized as compared with *throw*, *cast*, *fling*.

tot[1]. Small child. Earliest (1725) in Sc. ? Cf. ON. *tuttr*, as nickname for dwarf, **whence** Dan. *tommel-tot*, Tom Thumb. ? Hence also sense of very small glass (cf. *tallboy*).

tot[2]. To reckon up. From earlier noun *tot*, short for *total*. Perh. partly due to obs. *tot*, to mark an item as paid in sheriff's accounts, which is L. *tot*, so much.

He [Admiral Seymour] had the names of all the Lordes, and totted them whome he thought he might have to his purpose
(*Privy Council Acts*, 1548–9).

total. F., Scholastic L. *totalis*, from *totus*, all. *Totalizator*, machine for registering bets (*pari mutuel*), is after F. *totalisateur*.

tote [*US.*]. To carry, transport. From 17 cent. (Virginia). Cotg. has *tauter*, "to lay a roller &c. under a heavy thing, the better to remove it," and the existence of an OF. word in Virginia would not be unnatural.

> He took around with him on his rambles...old Uncle Mesrour, his executioner, who toted a snicker-snee (O. Henry).

totem. NAmer. Ind. (Algonkin) *aoutem*, hereditary emblem, recorded in F. 1609, the *t-* being supposed to represent the final sound of a possess. pron. (cf. Shaks. *nuncle* for *mine uncle*). Extended use in anthropology (*totemic, totemism*) is app. due to Lubbock.

tother [*dial.*]. See *the, that, other.*

> Thei crieden the toon to the tother
> (Wyc. *Is.* vi. 3).

totter. From c. 1200, orig. to swing, esp. from gallows. ? Ult. ident. with dial. *tolter* and Du. *touteren*, to swing. ? Cf. AS. *tealtrian* and *tilt*[2].

> I have made a pair of galows at the waterside wher I fere me some woll towter tomorrow
> (Sir T. Howard, 1512).

> She fattens them up 'till they're fitted for slaughter, Then leaves them at Tiburn to tittar and tauter
> (*Rump Song*, c. 1653).

> Troy nods from high and totters to her fall
> (Dryden, *Aen.* ii. 384, for L. ruit alto a culmine Troia, ii. 290).

toucan. SAmer. bird. F. (16 cent.), Sp. *tucan*, Tupi (Brazil) *tucana*, Guarani (Brazil) *tucān*, perh. from cry. But it is a curious fact that the EInd. hornbill is also called *toucan*, which has been taken to be Malay *toucan*, carpenter, from the bird's hammering trees with its bill. For a similar puzzle cf. *cayman.*

touch. F. *toucher*; cf. It. *toccare*, Sp. *tocar*. Prob. from an imit. *toc*, ground-sense being to strike; cf. *tocsin* and F. *toquer*, to touch, knock, a Norm.-Pic. form. Chief senses are developed in F. *Touch and go* is app. from some catching game of the "touch wood" type; ? cf. *tip and run*. With *touchstone* cf. F. *pierre de touche*. With *touched*, crazy, cf. earlier *tainted in one's wits*, and see *taint.*

> He [the Duke of Wharton] has touch'd the Duke de Ripperda for three thousand pistoles
> (*British Journal*, Apr. 30, 1726).

touchy. Altered on *touch*, with suggestion of sensitiveness, from archaic *tetchy*, earlier also *titchy*, aphet. for OF. *entechié, entichié*, from *teche*, quality, characteristic, of obscure origin, ? ident. with ModF. *tache*, stain, and ult. with *token*. *Entechié* had also in OF. pejorative sense, as though *mal*

entechié, ill-conditioned, and this sense passed into E.

> Si estoit [Aucasins] entechiés de bones teches, qu'en lui n'en avoit nule mauvaise
> (*Aucassin et Nicolete*, 13 cent.).

chatouilleux à la poincte: quick on the spurre; hence also, *tichie*, that will not endure to be touched (Cotg.).

tough. AS. *tōh.* WGer.; cf. Du. *taai*, Ger. *zäh*. US. sense of street ruffian was perh. suggested by noun use of *rough.*

toupee [*archaic*]. F. *toupet*, top-knot of periwig. See *top*[1].

tour. F. (OF. *torn*), from *tourner*, to turn (q.v.). In 17 cent. esp. of the *grand tour*, through France, Germany, Switzerland and Italy, as conclusion of gentleman's education. Hence *tourist* (c. 1800). F. *tour* has also sense of feat, trick, etc., as in *tour de force.*

tourmaline [*min.*]. F., ult. Sinhalese *toramalli*, cornelian; cf. Ger. *turmalin*, Du. *toermalijn*, It. Sp. *turmalina.*

tournament. OF. *tourneiement, tournoiement*, from *tourneier* (*tournoyer*), from *tourner*, to turn. Cf. F. *tournoi*, from the same verb, whence E. *tourney.*

tourniquet. F., from *tourner*, to turn.

tournure. F., shape, bearing, etc., from *tourner*, to turn. Cf. *contour.*

tousle, touzle. Frequent. of archaic *touse*, to pull, worry, whence dog-name *Towzer*; cogn. with *tease* (q.v.) and with Ger. *zausen*, "to towze, tew, tug, lug, pull, tumble or rustle, one about the hair" (Ludw.). Cf. *wolle zausen*, "to towse wool" (*ib.*).

tout. Orig. to peep, look out for, in which sense obs. *toot*, AS. *tōtian*, occurs earlier. The latter form survives in *Toothill.*

tow[1]. Unworked fibre. In AS. only in compds. *towcræft*, spinning, *towhūs*, spinning-house. Identity of Ger. *werg*, tow, with *werk*, work, suggests connection of *tow* with *taw*[1], *tool*, etc., as being raw material for work.

tow[2]. Verb. AS. *togian*, to draw. Com. Teut.; cf. Du. *togen*, OHG. *zogōn*, ON. *toga*; cogn. with Ger. *ziehen*, to draw, L. *ducere*, also with *tie, tug, taut*. Here belongs Sc. *tow*, rope, esp. for hanging, with which cf. naut. Ger. *tau*, rope (from LG.). As noun esp. in phrase *in tow*, often fig.

toward(s). AS. *tōweard* (see *-ward*). In AS. also as adj., whence common ME. sense of promising, docile, "towardly" (opposite of *froward*); hence, favourable, as still in *un-*

toward. The *-s* of *towards* is the adv. genitive as in *against*, *thence*, etc.

The exceeding greatness of his power to us-ward who believe (*Eph.* i. 19).

towel. Archaic F. *touaille*, of Teut. origin; cf. Du. *dweil*, ON. *thvegill*, OHG. *dwahila*, from *dwahan*, to wash, cogn. with AS. *thwēan*, to wash, *thwēal*, washing. So also It. *tovaglia*, Sp. *toalla*, from Teut. In OF. & ME. also as part of attire (v.i.).

De touailles sont entorteillies lour [the Bedouins'] testes, qui lour vont par desous le menton
(Joinville).

Hir [Hate's] heed y-writhen was, y-wis,
Full grymly with a greet towayle
(*Rom. of Rose*, 160).

tower. F. *tour*, L. *turris*, G. τύρσις; cf. It. Sp. *torre*, also Ger. *turm*, possibly an early loan from OF. AS. had also *torr*, from L. (see *tor*[1]). Hence verb to *tower*, *towering* (ambition, etc.), orig. of hawk (v.i. and see *pitch*[2], *pride*). *Towering passion* was revived by Scott from Shaks. (*Haml.* v. 2).

Like a falcon towring at full pitch ore the trembling fowle (Glapthorne, *Hollander*, iv. 1, 1640).

town. AS. *tūn*, enclosure, court; later, homestead (cf. F. *ville*, town, L. *villa*, country-house). Com. Teut.; cf. Du. *tuin*, garden, Ger. *zaun*, hedge, ON. *tūn*, enclosure, farmhouse; cogn. with AS. *tȳnan*, to fence. Hence *-ton* in place-names; ult. cogn. with Celt. *-dunum* (e.g. *Lyon-s = Lugdunum*), whence *-don* in place-names. Cf. Welsh *Dinas*. For the fence as characteristic of early Teut. settlements, Kluge quotes " Sēo [Bamborough] wæs ærost mid hegge betȳned and thæræfter mid wealle" (*AS. Chron.* 547). Sense of homestead survives in Sc. It is a good example of the possibilities of sense-development that a word which once meant a yard should now be spec. used of the vastest of all cities. At Oxf. and Camb. contrasted with *gown* (with *townee* cf. *bargee*). The latest compd. of *town* is *town-planning* (1906).

toxic. MedL. *toxicus*, from G. τοξικόν, arrow poison, from τόξον, bow (v.i.).

toxophilite. Devotee of archery. From Ascham's *Toxophilus* (1545), lover of the bow (v.s.), coined on *Theophilus*.

toy. App. Du. *tuig*, earlier *tuygh*, " arma, artium instrumenta, armamenta, impedimenta, ornamenta" (Kil.), cogn. with Ger. *zeug*, stuff, implements, frippery, etc., AS. *sulh-ġetēog*, agricultural implements, late

ON. *tȳgi*, tool, equipment; cf. Du. *speeltuig*, Ger. *spielzeug*, toy, plaything. Common from c. 1530 both as noun and verb with abstract and concrete senses—dalliance, fun, whim, etc., trifle, plaything, knick-knack, implement, etc. But the *NED.* points out that its isolated occurrence in ME. (1303) in sense of amorous dalliance raises difficulties in the way of origin and sense-development. To this may be added the fact that *Toy(e)*, presumably connected, has been a not uncommon surname since 12 cent. (Aldwin Toie, *Pipe Rolls*, Devon). My own conjecture is that two separate words have got mixed up.

nugae: fables, trifles, toyes (Coop.).

I look upon Birmingham as the great toy-shop of Europe (Burke, 1777).

trabeated [*arch.*]. Irreg. (for *trabate) from L. *trabs*, beam.

trace[1]. Track, vestige, etc. F., from *tracer*, VL. *tractiare, from *tractus*, a drawing along, from *trahere*, *tract-*, to draw; cf. It. *tracciare*, "to trace, to track, to follow by the footing" (Flor.), Sp. *trazar*. Senses have been influenced by (prob. unrelated) *track* (q.v.). *Tracery* (arch.) was introduced by Wren, who describes it as a masons' term.

trace[2]. Of horse. ME. *trays*, OF. *trais*, pl. of *trait*, "a teame-trace, or trait" (Cotg.), L. *tractus* (v.s.). For adoption of pl. cf. *bodice*, *truce*, etc.

Ful hye upon a chaar of gold stood he,
With foure white boles in the trays
(Chauc. A. 2138).

tracheo- [*anat.*]. From Late L. *trachia*, G. τραχεῖα (sc. ἀρτηρία), fem. of τραχύς, rough.

trachyte [*geol.*] Gritty volcanic rock. F., from G. τραχύς, rough.

track. F. *trac*, "a track, tract, or trace" (Cotg.), ? of Teut. origin and cogn. with Du. *trekken*, to draw, pull, which supposes ground-sense to have been mark made by what is dragged along, ? or from a hunting-cry *trac (cf. Sp. Port. *traque*, sharp report, Port. *traquejar*, to pursue). For sense-development cf. *trace*, *trail*, with which it is mentally associated. Railway *track*, to *make tracks*, are US., also to *die (fall) in one's tracks*, i.e. on the spot where one is wounded. The *beaten track* is after F. *chemin battu*.

tract[1]. Space. L. *tractus*, "a drawyng in length, a space, a countrey, a region, a coast" (Coop.), from *trahere*, to draw.

tract². Pamphlet. Short for *tractate* (15 cent.), L. *tractatus*, from *tractare*, to handle, treat of, frequent. of *trahere*, tract-, to draw. Orig. treatise, spec. current sense dating from c. 1800. The *Tracts for the Times* (1833–41) were started by Newman. Hence *tractarian* (cf. *Oxford movement*).

tractable. L. *tractabilis*, from *tractare* (v.s.). Cf. F. *traitable*, whence archaic E. *treatable*.

tractarian, tractate. See *tract²*.

traction. MedL. *tractio-n-*, from *trahere*, tract-, to draw. Cf. *tractor*.

trade. A LG. word, track, course, cogn. with *tread*. Introduced (14 cent.) by Hanse Merchants. Current sense has developed via that of regular course, occupation. Cf. obs. *common trade*, thoroughfare (*Rich. II*, iii. 3). So also *trade-wind* (17 cent.) had orig. nothing to do with commerce, but was evolved from obs. to *blow trade* (Hakl.), i.e. on one steady course. *Trade union* is 19 cent., *tradesman* still being used locally for artisan. *The Trade*, spec. that of the publican, has been used since 1914 of the submarine service.

A "tradesman," in Scotland, implies one who works with his hands at any handicraft trade; whereas in England, it means a shopkeeper (Sinclair, 1782).

tradition. F., L. *traditio-n-*, from *tradere*, to hand over, *trans* and *dare*, to give.

Some new-comers into honourable professions learn the tricks before the traditions (Mayor of Scarborough, on the bombardment of that fortress, Dec. 16, 1914).

traduce. L. *traducere*, to lead across; hence, to lead along as a spectacle, "to slaunder, to defame" (Coop.). Also, to translate, whence F. *traduire* (cf. Ger. *übersetzen*). Hence *traducian* (theol.), believer in transmission of sin from parent to child.

traffic. F. *trafic*, It. *traffico*, from *trafficare* (early 14 cent.); cf. Sp. Port. *traficar*. A Mediterranean word of uncertain origin. ? VL. **traficare*, from *trans* and *facere* (cf. *transigere*, to transact), ? or Arab. *taraffaqa*, to seek profit. Now often with sinister suggestion.

tragacanth. Medicinal gum. L., G. τραγάκανθα, from τράγος, goat, ἄκανθα, thorn.

tragedy. F. *tragédie*, L., G. τραγῳδία, from τράγος, goat, ῳδή, song, the connection with the goat being variously explained. With loss of -co- in L. *tragicomoedia*, for *tragico-comoedia* (Plautus), cf. *heroi-comic* (s.v. *hero*).

tragelaph. Myth. animal, antelope. L., G. τραγέλαφος, from τράγος, goat, ἔλαφος, deer.

tragopan [*ornith*.]. L., G. τραγόπαν, some Ethiopian bird, from τράγος, goat, Πάν, Pan. Adopted by Cuvier for horned pheasant.

trail. OF. *trailler*, to tow, ? VL. **tragulare*, from *tragula*, a sledge, drag-net (Pliny), cogn. with *trahere*, to draw. Cf. AS. *træglian*, Du. LG. *treilen*, app. of L. origin; also Sp. *tralla*, Port. *tralha*, rope, tow-line. Senses correspond gen. with those of cogn. F. *traîner* (see *train*), while some meanings run parallel with those of *track* and *trace¹*, which also start from the dragging idea.

train. F. *train*, from *traîner*, to drag (behind one), OF. *traîner*, VL. **traginare*, from *trahere*, to draw; cf. It. *trainare*, "to traine, to traile, to draggle or draw along the ground" (Flor.), Sp. *trajinar*, to convey. Some senses correspond with those of cogn. *trail* (q.v.), and of Ger. *zug*, from *ziehen*, to draw. OF. had also *traïne* (fem.). The railway *train* is for earlier *train* (series) *of carriages* (*waggons*). To *train*, drill, educate, etc. (whence ModF. *entraîner*, Ger. *trainieren*), is app. from gardening, the earliest sense in which it is recorded, but perh. influenced also by F. *mettre en train*, to set in train, set going. *Train-band* (hist.) is for *trained band*.

train-oil. For earlier *train*, Du. *traan*, lit. tear (cf. Ger. *träne*), used also of exudations, in which sense it has been borrowed by many Europ. langs. Adoption of a Du. word is due to activity of Hollanders in early whale-fishery.

Two Holland ships which came to make traine oyle of seales (Purch.).

traan (*gesmolten walvisch-spek*): whale-oyl, trane oyl (Sewel).

thran: trane, blubber, fish-oil (Ludw.).

trait. F., line, stroke, feature, p.p. of OF. *traire*, to draw (in ModF. to milk), VL. **tragere*, for *trahere*. Cf. Ger. *zug*, stroke, feature, from *ziehen*, to draw.

traitor. OF. *traitour*, L. *traditor-em*, from *tradere*, to hand over, *trans* and *dare*; cf. It. *traditore*, Sp. *traidor*. ModF. *traître*, L. nom. *traditor*, is due to frequent vocative use (cf. *fils*). See *treason*.

trajectory. From L. *traicere*, traject-, to cast across, from *trans* and *jacere*. Prop. the path of any body moving under action of given forces, but given spec. sense by artillerists.

tram. Of LG. origin; cf. archaic Ger. *tram*, LG. *traam*, balk, handle of barrow, etc., Fris. *trame*, beam, rung of ladder. From c. 1500 in sense of shaft of barrow, also wooden frame for carrying or dragging. Sense of vehicle, first in mining, is app. evolved from *tram-road*, in which the *trams* were heavy wooden rails on which the coal-trams were run. Cf. Ger. *prügelweg*, road made on swampy ground with transverse logs, "corduroy" road, lit. cudgelway. *Tram-car* is for earlier *tramway car*. The persistence of the *Outram* (†1805) myth is due to its inclusion in Smiles' *Life of George Stephenson* (cf. *beef-eater*).

To the amendinge of the highewaye or tram, from the west ende of Bridgegait, in Barnard Castle, 20s.
(*Will*, 1555).

tram: a rafter or joist (Ludw.).

trammel. First (14 cent.) in sense of large fishing-net, trammel-net; cf. F. *trémail*, It. *tramaglio*, Sp. *trasmallo*, all explained as three-mesh, from L. *macula*, mesh. If this is right, I regard *trammel*, clog, hindrance, as a separate word and belonging to *tram* (q.v.), the most elementary form of clog being a stout staff (v.i.).

tramaiolus: baculus collo canis appensus, ne per ea loca currat, quibus nocere posset...nos *tramail* vocamus non solum rete, sed etiam quodvis pedicae genus (Duc.).

cep: the stock of a tree, or plant; also, a log, or clog, of wood; such a one as is hung about the neck of a ranging curre (Cotg.).

trämel: a leaver, bar, pole, stick, club (Ludw.).

tramontane. It. *tramontana*, "the north, the northern wind" (Flor.), *tramontani*, "those folkes that dwell beyond the mountaines" (*ib.*), from L. *transmontanus*, from *trans*, across, *mons*, *mont-*, mountain. Cf. *ultramontane*.

tramp. App. nasalized form of a Teut. verb, to tread, which appears in Ger. *treppe*, stairs, the modification being perh. imit.; cf. relationship of *stamp*, *step*. So also Ger. *trampen*, Norw., Sw. *trampa*, Dan. *trampe*, Goth. *anatrimpan* (*Luke*, v. 1). With *tramp* (17 cent.), for one "on the tramp," and later naut. sense (c. 1880), cf. *scamp*[1]. *Tramp*, *trample* occur as vars. in Wyc. (*Prov.* vi. 13).

trance. F. *transe*, deadly anxiety, orig. passage from life to death, from *transir*, to perish, lit. to go across (now only to chill), L. *transire*, with which cf. poet. F. *trépasser*, to die. Chauc. has it both in F. & E. sense.

tranquil. F. *tranquille*, L. *tranquillus*, from *trans* and an element cogn. with *quies*.

trans-. L. *trans*, across, often *tra-* in compds.; orig. pres. part. of a lost verb which appears in *intrare*, *penetrare*. In many geog. and hist. compds., e.g. *transalpine*, *transpadane* (L. *Padus*, Po), *transrhenane* (L. *Rhenus*, Rhine), etc. Cf. *cis-*.

The object of a translator of poetry is transvaluation (*Times Lit. Sup.* Nov. 20, 1919).

transact. From L. *transigere*, *transact-*, to achieve, come to agreement, etc., from *agere*, to do, drive. Cf. F. *transaction*, compromise, agreement by mutual concession, the earliest sense in E. See *intransigent*.

transcend. L. *transcendere*, to climb beyond, from *scandere*. Mod. sense of *transcendent-al*, beyond experience, is due to Kant, and owes its E. vogue to Emerson.

transcribe. L. *transcribere*, to copy, from *scribere*, to write. Much older (13 cent.) is *transcrit* (from OF.), now restored to *transcript*.

transect. To cut across, from L. *secare*, *sect-*, to cut.

transept. First (16 cent.) as AL. *transeptum*, common in Leland, who perh. coined it from L. *septum*, *saeptum*, hedge, etc., from *saepire*, to enclose. ? Or a pedantic perversion of *transect* (cf. *sept*).

transfer. F. *transférer* or L. *transferre*, from *ferre*, to bear.

transfigure. L. *transfigurare*, from *figura*, form; cf. *transform*, *metamorphosis*. Orig. and chiefly Bibl.

transfix. OF. *transfixer*, from L. *figere*, *fix-*, to fix.

transform. F. *transformer*, L. *transformare*, from *forma*, shape. Cf. *metamorphosis*.

transfuse. See *fuse*[1].

Transfusion of the blood is a late anatomical invention experimented by the Royal Society (Phillips).

transgress. F. *transgresser*, from L. *transgredi*, *-gress-*, from *gradior*, I step. Cf. *trespass*.

transient. From pres. part. of L. *transire*, from *ire*, to go.

transit. L. *transitus*, from *transire* (v.s.). Older is *transitory* (Chauc.). *Transitive* is L. *transitivus*, passing over (Priscian).

translate. Archaic F. *translater*, from L. *transferre*, *translat-*, to bear across (cf. Ger. *übersetzen*). From 13 cent. also in lit. sense, e.g. *translation of Elijah*, as still spec. of transfer of bishop.

transliterate. Coined (? by Max Müller) from L. *littera*, letter.

transmigration. Late L. *transmigratio-n-* (see *migrate*). Wyc. uses *transmigration* for the Babylonish captivity. With *transmigration of souls* cf. *metempsychosis*.

transmit. L. *transmittere*, from *mittere*, to send.

transmogrify. From 17 cent. (*transmografy*), app. arbitrary perversion of *transmigure*, ? altered, after *transfigure*, from *transmigrate*.

The soul of Aristotle was said to have been transmigured into Thomas Aquinas (*NED.* 1687).

transmute. L. *transmutare*, from *mutare*, to change.

transom. ME. *traunson*, *traunsom*. Earliest E. sense, common in 15 cent. wills and inventories, is bolster. App. a corrupt. of F. *traversin*, cross-piece, bolster (cf. *Stemson*, *Stenson*, *Stimpson*, for *Stevenson*), with ending perh. affected by F. *sommier*, transom, mattress, lit. beast of burden (see *sumpter*); in fact the earliest record (1459) is *transomer*. Earlier still occur, app. in the same sense, AF. *traversin* (*Black Prince's Will*) and AL. *transversia* (*Joan of Kent's Will*).

I bequethe to Richard Jaxson, my son, a ffetherbed, ij trawnsoms, a matras, ij pelowes, iiij payer of schetes (*Will of Agas Herte*, of Bury, 1522).

I bequethe to Jone Jaxson my dowghter a fetherbed, a matras, a bolster, ij pelowes, iiij payer of schetes (*ib.*).

traversin: a crosse-beame, or peece of timber in a ship, &c., also, a bed-boulster (Cotg.).

transparent. F., from pres. part. of MedL. *transparēre*, to show through, from *parēre*, to appear.

transpire. F. *transpirer*, to perspire, from L. *spirare*, to breathe. Hence fig. to ooze out.

transpontine. F. *transpontin*, from L. *trans* and *pons*, *pont-*, bridge. In E. spec. of the "Surrey side" and its theatres once famous for lurid melodrama. Nonce-sense in quot. 2, from L. *pontus*, sea, is not given by *NED*.

The Americans are shocked and amazed...at the disclosure of this fantastic transpontine villainy
(*Westm. Gaz.* March 2, 1917).

She [an American writer] has investigated her subject with typical transpontine enthusiasm
(*Times Lit. Sup.* Apr. 15, 1920).

transport. F. *transporter*, L. *transportare*, from *portare*, to carry. The *transportation* of criminals, orig. to Amer. "plantations," dates from 17 cent. For fig. sense cf. *ecstasy*, to *be carried away*, etc.

transpose. F. *transposer*. See *pose*. Cf. *metathesis*.

transubstantiation. MedL. *transubstantiatio-n-*, transmutation, from *substantia*, substance. Current sense from Reformation.

transvase. F. *transvaser*, to pour from one vessel, *vase*, into another.

transverse. L. *transversus*, from *vertere*, *vers-*, to turn.

trap[1]. Snare. AS. *træppe*; cf. obs. Du. *trappe*; also MedL. *trappa*, F. *trappe*, It. *trappola*, Sp. *trampa*. Of Teut. origin and cogn. with Ger. *treppe*, stair (cf. *tramp*). The simplest form of trap is a pitfall giving to the tread. *Trap-door* is in Chauc. Sense of vehicle is for earlier *rattletrap*, used disparagingly of a rickety vehicle, article of furniture, etc. It is uncertain whether *traps*, portable articles, belongs here (? the trapper's outfit) or is short for *trappings*, paraphernalia (v.i.).

trap[2]. Chiefly in *trappings* of horse. Var. of F. *drap*, cloth, for which see *drab*, *draper*.

Grett horses trapyd with velvet to the ground
(Machyn's *Diary*, 1550–63).

trap[3] [*min.*]. Sw. *trapp*, staircase (see *trap*[1]), the rock being named from its stair-like appearance.

trapeze. F. *trapèze*, L., G. τραπέζιον, dim. of τράπεζα, table. Cf. *trapezoid*, suggesting a trapezium. The *trapeze* is named from its shape ▽.

trappings. See *trap*[2].

Trappist. F. *trappiste*, Cistercian monk of reformed order established (1664) by abbot of *La Trappe* (Orne).

trapse, traipse [*colloq.*]. App. from obs. *trape* (Johns.), to trudge, loaf (see *tramp*), was developed a noun *trapes*, slattern, which in its turn was used as verb (cf. *coax*).

trash. From 16 cent. App. earliest sense was broken twigs, etc., as still in dial. and in WInd. *cane-trash*. Hence used for rubbish of any kind. Cf. Norw. *trase*, rag, Norw. dial. *tras*, trumpery, ON. *tros*, rubbish.

Who steals my purse, steals trash (*Oth.* iii. 3).

trass, tarras [*geol.*]. Volcanic earth used for cement. Du. *tras*, earlier *tarrasse*, OF. *terrace*, It. *terracia*, from *terra*, earth.

traumatic [*med.*]. L., G. τραυματικός, from τραῦμα, wound.

travail. F., work, earlier also toil, suffering, whence *en travail*, in child-birth suffering, with which cf. *in labour*. From verb *travailler*, cogn. with It. *travagliare*, Sp. *tra-*

bajar. This is usu. derived from Late L. *trepalium* (6 cent.), an instrument of torture, conjectured to have been an ingenious arrangement of three stakes (L. *palus*). An alternative, and better, etym. is from VL. **trabaculum*, dim. of *trabs*, beam, whence F. *travail*, "the frame whereinto farriers put unrulie horses, when they shooe or dresse them" (Cotg.). Cf. obs. E. *trave*, *travail*, similarly used. This makes an equally good starting-point for the series of senses. That of (orig. toilsome) journeying, which appears early in AF. and is peculiar to E., is now (since 17 cent.) differentiated by the spelling *travel*.

And she sproong, as a colt doth in the trave
(Chauc. A. 3282).
Having travailed about 2 leagues, about noone wee returned to the point (Hakl. xi. 176).
Some cut hoops, others laboured upon the sailes and ship, every man travelling for his life (*ib.* 413).

travel. See *travail*.

traverse. F. *traverser*, VL. *traversare*, for *transversare*, from *vertere*, *vers-*, to turn. For leg. sense, to oppose, deny, frustrate, cf. sense-development of *thwart*[1].

travertin-e. Limestone. F. *travertin*, It. *travertino*, earlier *tivertino*, "a kind of stone to build withall" (Flor.), L. *Tiburtinus*, of *Tibur*, Tivoli.

travesty. First as adj., p.p. of F. *travestir*, It. *travestire*, to disguise, from L. *trans* and *vestire*, to clothe.

trawl. Prob. var. of *trail* (q.v.). This suits the sense, and the vowel has a parallel in *brawl*[1] (q.v.). *Trail, trailnet* are found for *trawl*, and *trawl* is recorded for *trail* of a gun (v.i.) earlier than first *NED.* record (1768) of *trail* in that sense.

The train of artillery within the Tower, consisting of fifty pieces of brass ordnance, mounted on trauling carriages
(Chamberlayne, *Present State of England*, 1692).

tray[1]. Utensil. ME. *trey*, AS. *trīg*, ult. cogn. with *tree*, as being of wood.

tray[2], **trey**. Three at cards, also (ven.) third branch of stag's horn. OF. *trei*, backformation from *treis* (*trois*), L. *tres*, three. For first sense cf. *deuce*.

treachery. F. *tricherie*, OF. also *trecherie*, from *tricher*, to cheat, for which see *trick*[1]. Spelling and sense partly due to association with *treason*.

treacle. OF. *triacle*, antidote against venom, L. *theriaca*, "triakle" (Coop.), from G. θηριακός, from θηρίον, dim. of θήρ, wild

beast; cf. It. *triaca*, "a remedie against poyson, called treacle" (Flor.), Sp. *triaca*, also Arab. *tiryāk* (7 cent.). Later used of many pharmaceutical compounds, and, in E. only, of unrefined molasses. For sense-development cf. *syrup*. John Clerk, treacler and tuthdragher, i.e. druggist and dentist, was a freeman of York in 1422.

Payd for ij boxes of conserves, tryacle, and souger candy, xd. (*Stonor Let.* 1424).
There is no more triacle [Wyc. gumme, resyn, *Vulg.* resina] at Galaad (Coverd. *Jer.* viii. 22).

tread. AS. *tredan*. Com. Teut.; cf. Du. *treden*, Ger. *treten*, ON. *trotha*, Goth. *trudan*. Hence *treadle*, with agent. suffix as in *ladle*, *shovel*; *treadmill*, invented (1822) by William Cubitt of Ipswich.

treason. OF. *traïson* (*trahison*), L. *traditio-n-*, from *tradere*, to hand over, from *trans* and *dare*, to give. Hist. definition dates from Statute of Treasons (1350–51).

treasure. F. *trésor*, L., G. θησαυρός, ? from τιθέναι, to put, lay up. Replaced AS. *goldhord* (*Matt.* vi. 21). For intrusive -*r*-, due to assim., cf. *partridge*. This does not appear in It. Sp. *tesoro*. *Treasure trove*, OF. *trové* (*trouvé*), with ending lost as in *costive, defile*[2], *signal*[2], etc., corresponds to MedL. *thesaurus inventus* (12 cent.). See *trover*.

treat. F. *traiter*, L. *tractare*, "to handle, to touch, to intreate, to use or exercise, to order or governe" (Coop.), frequent. of *trahere*, to draw, drag. All senses develop naturally from that of handling. That of dealing kindly with, entertaining (15 cent.), appears in mod. *school treat*, etc. *Treatise* is OF. *traitis*. With *treaty*, F. *traité*, cf. *tractate*. It was orig. synon. with *treatise*, current sense springing from that of discussion, negotiation, as still in *to be in treaty for*.

At after soper fille they in tretee
What somme sholde this maistres gerdoun be
(Chauc. F. 1219).

treble. OF., L. *triplus*, for *triplex*, three-fold; cf. *double*. Mus. sense app. from the soprano being the third part added in early contrapuntal music to the melody (see *tenor*).

trebuchet [*hist.*]. Missile war-engine. F. *trébuchet*, trap, balance, in OF. war-engine, from *trébucher*, to stumble, from L. *trans* and OHG. *buc*, trunk of body (cf. Ger. *bauch*, belly). Also used for **cucking-stool**.

trecento [*art*]. It., for *mil trecento*, 14 cent. Cf. *cinquecento*.

tree. AS. *trēow*. Aryan, though not found in Du. & Ger. (*boom, baum*); cf. OSax. *trio*, ON. *trē*, Goth. *triu*, G. δρῦς, oak, Pol. *drwa*, wood, Welsh *derwen*, oak, Sanskrit *dru*, tree, wood. Formerly used of wood (whence obs. adj. *treen*), as still in naut. *tre(e)-nail*, *cross-tree*, etc., and in *boot-tree*, *roof-tree*, *saddle-tree*, *swingle-tree*, etc.; also (already in AS.) for the Cross, Rood. *Up a tree* is US., of the hunted animal. With *tree-calf* (book-binding), from tree-like markings, cf. *tree-agate*.

trefa, trifa [*Jew.*]. Meat which is not *kosher* (q.v.). Heb. *ṭ'rēphāh*, from *ṭāraf*, to tear (*Lev.* xvii. 15).

trefoil. AF. *trifoil*, L. *trifolium*, from *tri-* (q.v.) and *folium*, leaf.

trek [*SAfr.*]. Du. *trekken*, to draw, drag, hence journey by ox-waggon.

trellis. F. *treillis*, "a trellis; a lattice before a doore, hole, or window; a grate set thick with crosse-barres of wood" (Cotg.), OF. *treliz*, VL. *trilicius*, for *trilix*, *trilic-*, "tissue made of three threades of divers colours" (Coop.), rendering G. τρίμιτος (see *dimity, samite*). Later form and sense affected by association with F. *treille*, lattice, railing, trellised vine, L. *trichila*, bower, summer-house.

tremble. F. *trembler*, VL. *tremulare*, from *tremulus*, from *tremere*, to quake, tremble.

tremendous. From L. *tremendus*, to be feared, from *tremere* (v.s.). For application to size cf. *enormous, monstrous*.

tremolo [*mus.*]. It., L. *tremulus*, from *tremere* (v.s.).

tremor. OF. *tremour* (archaic F. *trémeur*), L. *tremor-em* (v.s.). Cf. *tremulous*, from L. *tremulus*.

trenail [*naut.*]. See *tree*.

trench. First (14 cent.) as noun, OF. *trenche* (*tranche*, slice), from *trencher* (*trancher*), to cut, app. VL. *trincare*, for *truncare*, from *truncus*, trunk. The alteration of the vowel may be due to L. *trinus*, three at a time, ? thus, to cut in threes. Current senses of noun correspond rather to those of F. *tranchée*, orig. p.p. fem. To *trench upon* (cf. to *cut into*) may be of mil. origin or refer to altering of boundary trenches. Hence also *trenchant, trencher*, F. *tranchoir* (OF. *trencheoir*), wooden platter on which food was cut (cf. Ger. *teller*, plate, F. *tailloir*, from *tailler*, to cut). With *trencher*, college-cap,

cf. *mortar-board*. *Trencher-man*, one who "plays a good knife and fork," is ironic after *bowman, spearman*, etc.

He's a very valiant trencher-man, he hath an excellent stomach (*Much Ado*, i. 1).

trend. AS. *trendan*, to roll, revolve, cogn. with *trundle*, and with Dan. *omtrent*, about, Sw. dial. *trind*, round. In current use it is a naut. metaphor, occurring passim in Hakl. and Purch. of the gen. run or direction of the coast. Cf. also dial. *trendle, trindle*, used of many round objects and implements.

trental [*eccl.*]. Series of thirty masses. Church L. *trentale*, from VL. *trenta*, thirty, for *triginta*.

Trentine [*hist.*]. Of Council of *Trent* (16 cent.), L. *Tridentum*, city in the *Trentino* (Tyrol). Cf. *Nicene*.

trepan[1] [*surg.*]. F. *trépan*, MedL. *trepanum*, G. τρύπανον, from τρυπᾶν, to bore.

trepan[2]. To kidnap. First (17 cent.) as noun (*trapan*), a decoy, swindler. A cant word app. connected with *trap*[1]. Its contemporary synonym was *cony-catch*.

Abetting sham-plots and trapans upon the government and its friends (North's *Examen*).

trepang. Sea-slug, bêche-de-mer. Mal. *trīpang*.

trephine. Improved *trepan*[1]. For *trafine*, coined (1628), after *trepan*[1], by its inventor, Woodall, "*a tribus finibus*, from the three ends thereof." Borrowed by F., whence current spelling.

trepidation. L. *trepidatio-n-*, from *trepidare*, to hurry, be agitated. Cf. *intrepid*.

trespass. OF. *trespasser* (*trépasser*, to pass away, die), MedL. *transpassare*, to pass across. For sense-development cf. *transgress*. Leg. sense, peculiar to E., reverts to etym. sense, but originated as a spec. use of gen. sense of offence.

tress. F. *tresse*, from *tresser* (OF. *trecier*), to weave, plait; cf. It. *trecciare*. The forms point to a VL. *trectiare* or *trictiare*, of obscure origin. ? Or rather from G. τρίχα, three-fold.

trestle. OF. *trestel* (*tréteau*), VL. *transtellum*, dim. of *transtrum*, cross-beam, from *trans*, across.

tret. Only in archaic *tare and tret*. Orig. allowance of 4 lb. in 104 lb. on goods sold by weight. AF., F. *trait*, pull (of the scale), from OF. *traire*, to pull, L. *trahere*. The allowance compensated for the number of "turns of the scale" which would result from weighing the goods in smaller quantities. *Trait* is still so used in F. (v.i.), and *draft*, *draught*, had a similar sense in ME.

Un poids en équilibre ne trebuche point, si on n'y ajoûte quelque chose pour le trait. Les petits poids ne reviennent pas aux grands à cause du trait
(Furetière, 1727).

On appelle trait ce qui emporte l'équilibre d'une balance et la fait trébucher. Pour certaines marchandises où l'on pèse très juste, le vendeur accorde par facture une réduction de tant pour cent ou par pesée qu'on appelle trait (Glauser and Poole, *French Commercial Correspondence*, 1902).

trews. Ir. *trius*, Gael. *triubhas*, from obs. E. *trouse*, trousers (q.v.).

trey. See *tray²*.

tri-. L., from *tres*, three, or G. τρι-, from τρεῖς, three, τρίς, thrice.

triad. L., G. τριάς, τριάδ-, group of three.

trial. AF., from *try* (q.v.).

trialogue. MedL. *trialogus*, mistakenly coined on *dialogus* (see *dialogue*).

triangle. F., L. *triangulum*, from *angulus*, corner. In mil. lang. (hist.) of three halberds to which soldier was tied when flogged.

triarchy. G. τριαρχία, triumvirate. Cf. *monarchy*, etc.

triassic [*geol.*]. Through Ger., from G. τριάς, triad, because divisible into three groups.

tribe. L. *tribus*, ? from *tri-* and root of verb to *be* as in L. *fu-* and in G. φυλή, tribe. Orig. applied to the three divisions of the early Romans. Cf. F. *tribu*, It. *tribù*, Sp. *tribu*, all learned words.

tribrach [*metr.*]. L., G. τρίβραχυς, three short. Cf. *amphibrach*.

tribulation. Church L. *tribulatio-n-*, from *tribulare*, to oppress, from *tribulum*, threshing-machine, cogn. with *terere*, *tri-*, to rub, pound.

tribune. L. *tribunus*, "a protectour of the commons" (Coop.), from *tribus*, tribe. Hence L. *tribunal-e*, judgment seat, of which latest (war) sense is naturally not in *NED*. This was replaced in MedL. by *tribuna*, whence F. & E. *tribune*, platform, rostrum, etc.

tribute. L. *tributum*, from *tribuere*, to give, assign, etc., app. from *tribus*, tribe, though the nature of the connection is not clear. Hence *tributary*.

trice. To pull, now only naut. Du. *trijsen*, to hoist; cf. Dan. *trisse*, naut. Ger. *trissen*, both from Du. or LG., also F. *drisse*,

halyard, of Teut. origin. Hence *in a trice*, earlier *at* (*with*) *a trice*, at one pull.

Sometime thy bedfelowe is colder than is yse,
To him then he draweth thy cloathes with a trice
(*NED*. 1515).

triceps. Muscle. Cf. *biceps*.

trichi. Short for *Trichinopoli* (cheroot), Madras.

trichinosis. From ModL. *trichina*, intestinal worm, from G. τρίχινος, hairy, from θρίξ, τριχ-, hair.

tricho-. From G. θρίξ, hair (v.s.).

trichotomy. Tripartite division. Coined on *dichotomy*, from G. τρίχα, triply.

trick. First (c. 1400) as noun. ONF. *trique*, from *triquier* (*tricher*), to cheat, of doubtful origin; ? VL. *triccare*, for *tricari*, "to trifle, to dallie, to jest and toy with trifling wordes" (Coop.). Verb in E. is from noun. The word has developed many senses not known in F., and it is doubtful whether they all belong here, e.g. archaic *trick*, to adorn, deck out, suggests OF. *estricqué*, "pranked, decked, neat, fine, spruce, trickt up" (Cotg.), p.p. of OF. *estriquer*, to array, put in order, orig. to level corn with a "strike." To *trick*, sketch, a coat of arms, may be Du. *trekken*, to draw (for change of vowel cf. *trigger*), and naut. *trick at the wheel* (*oar*) is prob. also Du. *trek*, pull, spell, etc. In fact Du. *trek*, *trekken* have so many senses in common with *trick* that the possibility of Du. or LG. origin must be allowed for F. *tricher* (OF. also *trechier*).

Nay soft, I pray ye, I know a trick worth two of that (1 *Hen. IV*, ii. 1).

trickle. Orig. (14 cent.) of tears. ? For *strickle*, frequent. of *strike* (q.v.), which in AS. & ME. has also the sense of flow. The loss of *s-* would be due to the word being regularly preceded by *tear-s*.

And whan this abbot hadde this wonder seyn,
His salte teeris trikled [*vars.* trekelede, striked, stikled] doun as reyn (Chauc. B. 1863).

triclinium [*antiq.*]. Couch round three sides of table. L., G. τρικλίνιον, dim. of τρίκλινος, from κλίνη, couch (cf. *clinic*).

tricolour. F. *tricolore* (sc. *drapeau*), adopted at Revolution, Late L. *tricolor*, from *color*, colour. The arrangement of the colours (blue, white, red) dates from 1794.

tricorne. Three-cornered hat. F., L. *tricornis*, from *cornu*, horn.

tricot. F., from *tricoter*, to knit, ? ult. from Ger. *stricken*, to knit.

tric-trac. Form of backgammon. F., imit. of clicking noise made by pieces. Also called *tick-tack*.

tricycle. F., orig. (1827) of a three-wheeled horse-vehicle. Cf. *bicycle*.

trident. F., L. *tridens, trident-*, from *dens*, tooth.

Tridentine. As *Trentine* (q.v.).

triduum. Three days' prayer. L., from *tri-* and *dies*, day. Cf. It. Sp. *triduo*.

triennial. From L. *triennium*, from *annus*, year. Cf. *biennial*, etc.

trierarchy [*hist.*]. G. τριηραρχία, office of *trierarch*, commander of a *trireme* (q.v.).

trifa. See *trefa*.

trifid [*biol.*]. L. *trifidus*, cleft in three, from root of *findere*, to cleave.

trifle. ME. & OF. *trufle*, mockery, deceit, var. of synon. OF. *trufe*; cf. It. *trufa*, "a cozening, cheating, conicatching" (Flor.), obs. Sp. *trufa*, "a gibe, a jesting, or jeering" (Minsh.). Orig. a lying or nonsensical story, ? later sense having been affected by *trivial*. The usual assumption that it is ident. with *truffle* (q.v.) has parallels in the somewhat similar use in F. of *nèfle*, medlar, *prune*, plum, *baie*, berry, *baguenaude*, bladder-nut, etc., and Cotg. gives "waternut" as one sense of *truffe*. If this is correct, the It. & Sp. may be from OF. For application to a sweetmeat cf. *fool²* (q.v.).

trifolium. L., cf. *trefoil*.

triforium [*arch.*]. MedL., used (12 cent.) by Gervase of Canterbury in ref. to Canterbury Cathedral. Revived in same application by 18 cent. antiquaries, but not used as gen. term till 19 cent. The usual explanation from L. *fores*, folding door, does not suit orig. sense. The word may be due to some mistake of Gervase.

trig¹ [*dial.*]. Nimble, trim, etc. ON. *tryggr*, trusty, firm, which, like so many adjs. applied to persons, assumed varied senses in E.

> The captain...slight and trig and trim
> (B. Grimshaw).

trig². To check, prop. Back-formation from dial. *trigger*, brake, skid, etc. (v.i.).

trigger. Earlier (till c. 1750) *tricker*, Du. *trekker*, in gen. and spec. sense, from *trekken*, to pull.

triglyph. L., G. τρίγλυφος, from γλυφή, carving.

trigonometry. ModL. *trigonometria* (16 cent.), from G. τρίγωνον, triangle, -μετρία, measurement.

trilby hat. From Du Maurier's novel *Trilby* (1894).

trilith. Cromlech. G. τρίλιθον. Cf. *monolith*.

trill. It. *trillare*, of imit. origin.

trillion. F. (15 cent.) after *million*. Cf. *billion, quadrillion*, etc.

trilobite [*palaeont.*]. Extinct animal with three-lobed body. Coined (18 cent.) from G. λοβός, lobe.

trilogy. G. τριλογία, series of three tragedies performed at Athens at feast of Dionysus.

trim. AS. *trymman*, to arrange, make firm, from *trum*, firm, strong; but the verb, whence the noun and adj. are evolved, is not recorded between AS. and c. 1500, when it at once becomes very common and developes great variety of meanings. For very wide extension of lit. and fig. senses cf. *dress*, lit. to make straight. Orig. sense survives in naut. to *trim the ship, in fighting trim*, etc. Hist. *trimmer*, "one who changes sides to balance parties" (Johns.), was accepted by Halifax and his friends (1680–90) as meaning one who helps to keep the ship of state on an even keel.

trimeter [*metr.*]. L., G. τρίμετρος, from μέτρον, measure.

trine. L. *trinus*, from *tres*, three.

trinity. F. *trinité*, L. *trinitas*, triad, three together, from *trinus* (v.s.), with spec. sense in early Church L., after similar use of G. τριάς; cf. It. *trinità*, Sp. *trinidad*, Gael. *trionaid*, Welsh *trindod*, etc. *Trinity House* was founded at Deptford by Hen. VIII to regulate British shipping. With *Trinitarian* (17 cent.) cf. *Unitarian*.

trinket. From 16 cent., usu. in pl., in sense of implements, paraphernalia, "traps," etc., and also of small ornaments. App. ident. with ME. *trenket*, shoemaker's knife, ONF. *trenquet* (*tranchet*), from *trancher*, to cut (see *trench*). This curious transition of sense may be explained by the fact that ornamental knives were at one time a regular adjunct to female costume (see Chauc. A. 233), and also by association with *trick*, to decorate, etc. (cf. obs. *trinkle*, for *trickle*).

> Thy purse and eke thy gay gilt knives
> (*Lady Greensleeves*, 1584).

lormier: a worker in small yron, a maker of small yron trinkets, as nayles, spurres &c. (Cotg.).

trinomial [*math.*]. Coined from *tri-* after *binomial*.

trio. F., It., coined from *tre*, three, on analogy of *duo*.

triolet [*metr.*]. F.. from *trio* (v.s.).

Triones [*astron.*]. L., plough-oxen.

trip. OF. *triper*, *treper*, to dance, skip, of Teut. origin, ult. cogn. with AS. *treppan*, to tread (see *tramp*, *trap*¹). Spec. sense of causing to fall is E. only, and suggests rather a thinned form of *trap*¹ (cf. *bilk*). Sense of journey was orig. naut. (cf. to *trip the anchor*), as still in *trial trip*.

tripe. F., entrails (13 cent.); cf. It. *trippa*, Sp. *tripa*; of obscure origin; ? Arab. *therb*, entrails. At one time also applied to a coarse velvet with a surface like that of dressed tripe (cf. *frill*).

triphthong. Coined from *tri-* after *diphthong*.

triple. F., L. *triplus*. See *treble*. Hence *triplet*, *triplicate*.

tripod. L. *tripus*, *tripod-*, G. τρίπους, from πούς, ποδ-, foot. Cf. *trivet*.

tripos. L. *tripus* (v.s.) altered on G. words in -os. At Camb. orig. a B.A. who, seated on a tripod, conducted a satirical dispute (cf. *wrangler*) with candidates for degrees; corresponding to the Oxf. *terrae filius*. The (math.) *Tripos* list was orig. printed on the back of a set of humorous verses composed by the *Tripos*.

Mr Nicholas, of Queens' College, who I knew in my time to be Tripos (Pepys, Feb. 26, 1660).

The Senior Proctor calleth up the Tripos, and exhorteth him to be witty, but modest withall (*NED.* 1665).

triptych. From *tri-*, after *diptych*.

triquetrous [*biol.*]. From L. *triquetrus*, three-cornered.

trireme [*hist.*]. Galley with three banks of oars. F. *trirème*, L. *triremis*, from *tri-* and *remus*, oar.

trisagion [*eccl.*]. G. (τὸ) τρισάγιον, the Eucharistic hymn, neut. of τρισάγιος, from τρίς, thrice, ἅγιος, holy.

trisect. Coined from *tri-*, after *bisect*.

Trismegistus. Epithet of Hermes (q.v.).

tritagonist. G. τριταγωνιστής, actor playing third part. Cf. *protagonist*.

trite. L. *tritus*, p.p. of *terere*, to rub. For sense-development cf. *terse*.

tritoma. Plant. From G. τρίτομος, thrice-cut. Cf. *atom*.

Triton. L., G. Τρίτων, sea-deity, son of Poseidon.

triturate. From Late L. *triturare*, from *tritura*, from *terere*, *trit-*, to rub, pulverize.

triumph. F. *triomphe*, L. *triumphus*, cogn. with G. θρίαμβος, hymn to Bacchus. Orig. L. sense of processional entry of victorious

general survives in *triumphal arch* (*progress*).

triumvir [*hist.*]. L., usu. in pl. *triumviri*, back-formation from *trium virorum*, genitive of *tres viri*, three men. Esp. Pompey, Caesar, Crassus (60 B.C.), Caesar, Antony, Lepidus (43 B.C.).

triune. From *tri-* and L. *unus*, one.

trivet. AS. *trefet*, L. *tripes*, *triped-*, tripod, from *pes*, foot. Hence *as right as a trivet*, ? because a three-legged article will stand firm on any surface.

trivial. L. *trivialis*, "common, used or taught in high wayes, of no estimation" (Coop.), from *trivium*, cross-roads, "also where common recourse of people is" (Coop.), from *tri-* and *via*, way. Influenced also by MedL. *trivium*, three (grammar, logic, rhetoric) of the seven liberal arts.

-trix. L., fem. of *-tor*.

trochaic [*metr.*]. L., G. τροχαικός, from τρέχειν, to run. Cf. *trochee*, F. *trochée*, L., G. τροχαῖος.

troche [*pharm.*]. Shortened from *trochisk*, F. *trochisque*, L., G. τροχίσκος, small wheel, globule, lozenge, dim. of τροχός, wheel, from τρέχειν, to run.

trocho-. From G. τροχός, wheel (v.s.).

troglodyte. Prehistoric cave-dweller. L., G. τρωγλοδύτης, from τρώγλη, hole, δύειν, to get into.

troika. Vehicle. Russ. *troĭka*, from *troye*, set of three, *tri*, because drawn by three horses.

Trojan. L. *Trojanus*, from *Troja*, Troy.

Gif we wil mene that they beeth stronge we clepeth hem Trojans (Trev. ii. 255).

troll¹. Verb, with gen. suggestion of rotary motion, e.g. with ref. to gait, the bowl, a catch in singing, etc. In ME. (*Piers Plowm.*) to saunter. ? OF. *troller* (*trôler*), "hounds to trowle, raunge, or hunt out of order" (Cotg.), Ger. *trollen*, to run with short steps, ? like a *troll*². In angling sense perh. another word, *trowell*, "rotula" (*Manip. Voc.*), OF. *troul*, *trouil* (*treuil*), reel, winch, ? ult. from G. τροχός, hoop, from τρέχειν, to run; cf. Welsh *troell*, "wheel, reel, pulley, windlass" (Spurrell), *troelli*, "to twist, wind" (*ib.*), ? from E. It may be noted that the senses of *troll* are very similar to those of *trundle* (q.v.), and may all have started, like that word, from the name of a circular object, small wheel.

troll². Goblin. ON. *troll*, supernatural giant (also *trolldōmr*, witchcraft), whence Sw. *troll*, Norw. Dan. *trold*, now dwarfish imp.

Introduced, like other words from Norse myth. (*rune*, *norn*, etc.), by mod. antiquaries, but in pop. use (*trow*) in Orkneys and Shetlands from Scand. times.

trolley. ? From *troll*[1]. Orig. vehicle suited to narrow Yarmouth "rows." For local and obscure origin cf. *bogie*, *lorry*, *tram*.

trollop. I suggest this is simply *troll*[1]-*up*, a nickname like *gad-about*. Cf. *startup*, formerly used of an upstart, and now also, like *Trollop*, a surname. So also Du. *klimop*, ivy, lit. climb-up.

trombone. It., augment. of *tromba*, trump[1] (q.v.).

tromometer. For measuring tremor, G. τρόμος, of earth.

tronage [*hist.*]. Due for offic. weighing by the *tron*, still in Sc. use, OF. *trone*, L. *trutina*, G. τρυτάνη.

tronk [*SAfr.*]. Prison. Cape Du., from Port. *tronco*, trunk, used for stocks.

troop. F. *troupe*, "a troope, crue, rout, rabble, throng, or multitude of people, etc." (Cotg.); cf. It. *truppa*, Sp. *tropa*, Late L. *troppus*, flock, ? of Teut. origin and cogn. with *thorp* (q.v.), ? or connected with L. *turba*. Ult. identity of *thorp* and *turba* is possible. *Trooper*, man and horse, first appears (1640) in Sc. *Trooping the colour*(s) is from *troop* in sense of drum-beat, "assembly."

tropaeolum [*bot.*]. Named (1737) by Linnaeus from G. τρόπαιον, trophy, the leaf suggesting a shield and the flower a helmet.

trope. F., L., G. τρόπος, from τρέπειν, to turn.

tropho-. From G. τροφή, from τρέφειν, to nourish.

Trophonian [*myth.*]. Of Τροφώνιος, builder of temple of Apollo, at Delphi, afterwards associated with cave in Boeotia, entry into which deprived of power of ever smiling again.

trophy. F. *trophée*, L., G. τρόπαιον, neut. of τροπαῖος, putting to flight, from τροπή, turning, defeat, from τρέπειν, to turn. Orig. a memorial set up on the battle-field.

tropic. L., G. τροπικός (sc. κύκλος, circle), pertaining to the "turning" of the sun at the solstice, from τρέπειν, to turn.

trot[1]. Of horse. F. *trotter*, OHG. *trottōn*, cogn. with *tread*; cf. It. *trottare*, Sp. *trotar*, MedL. *trottare*, also from OHG. The E. verb must, as is shown by surname *Trotter*, be much older than dict. records (*Piers Plowm.*).

trot[2]. Old woman, hag. ? From *Dame Trote of Salerno*, *Trotula Salernitana*, famous

11 cent. doctoress and witch, often referred to in medieval literature.

troth [*poet.*]. Phonetic var. of *truth*; cf. *trow*.

troubadour. F., Prov. *trobador*, from *trobar*, to find, corresponding to F. *trouvère*, *trouveur*, medieval poet, It. *trovatore*, Sp. *trovador*. See *trover*.

trouble. F. *troubler*, OF. *torbler*, VL. **turbulare*, frequent. of *turbare*, to disturb, from *turba*, disorder, throng, G. τύρβη.

trough. AS. *trog*. Com. Teut.; cf. Du. Ger. ON. *trog*; ult. cogn. with *tray*[1], *tree*.

trounce. ? From *traunce*, earlier form of *trance* (q.v.), which in OF. & ME. had the sense of "extreme fear, dread, anxiety, or perplexity of mind" (Cotg.). For vowel cf. obs. *trance*, to prance, etc., which has a 16 cent. var. *trounce*, and see *jounce*. This suggestion suits the first recorded sense (see quot. 1), which seems to have passed via that of tormenting (see quot. 2) to the current sense of thrashing.

The Lorde trounced [*Vulg.* perterruit] Sisara and all his charettes...with the edge of yᵉ swerde before Barak (*Judges*, iv. 15, 1551).

Lord Jhese Christ, when he was i-pounst and i-pilate,
Was ner so i-trounst, as we have been of years late (*Respublica*, iii. 3, 1553).

troupe. F., troop (q.v.).

trousers. Lengthened from obs. *trouse* (*trews*), spec. used (16 cent.) of close-fitting breeches of Irish. Ir. Gael. *triubhas*, ident. with OF. *trebus* (13 cent.), Late L. *tubraci*, later *tibraci*, derived by Isidore (7 cent.) from *tibia*, thigh, *braccae*, breeches. It may however be of Teut. origin, "thigh breeches"; cf. OHG. *deohproh* in *Cassel Gloss.* (8 cent.). In current sense from c. 1800 (see *sans-culotte*).

Under no circumstances whatever shall any preacher be allowed to occupy the pulpit who wears trousers (*Trust-deed of Bethel Chapel, Cambridge St., Sheffield*, 1820).

trousseau. F., dim. from *trousse*, bundle, truss (q.v.).

trout. AS. *trūht*, Late L. *tructus*, *tructa*, from G. τρώκτης, gnawer, also name of some fish, from τρώγειν, to gnaw; cf. F. *truite*.

trouveur. F., poet, from *trouver*, to find. *Trouvère* is the OF. nom. Cf. *troubadour* and see *trover*.

trover [*leg.*]. Finding and appropriating personal property. Cf. *treasure trove* (q.v.). OF. *trover* (*trouver*), to find; cf. It. *trovare*, Sp. *trovar*; of obscure, though much discussed, origin.

trow [*archaic*]. AS. *trēowian*, to trust, believe, from *trēow*, faith, belief, cogn. with
true. Com. Teut.; cf. Du. *trouwen*, Ger.
trauen, ON. *trūa*, Goth. *trauan*.

trowel. F. *truelle*, Late L. *truella*, for *trulla*,
dim. of *trua*, ladle, etc.

troy weight. From weight used at fair of
Troyes (Aube). Many medieval towns had
their standard weights and coins.

truant. F. *truand*, "a common beggar, vagabond, rogue, a lazie rascall" (Cotg.), of
Celt. origin; cf. Welsh *truan*, wretched,
Gael. *truadanach*, vagabond, earlier E. sense
(13 cent.) of *truant*. For current spec. sense
cf. to *play the wag*, i.e. the rascal (see
wag).

faire l'eschole buissoniere: to play the truant, or
seeke birds nests when he should be at schoole
(Cotg.).

truce. Orig. pl. of *trewe*, AS. *trēow*, fidelity,
agreement, etc., cogn. with *true*. For form
cf. *bodice* (q.v.). Use of pl., already in AS.,
is perh. due to the word being used to
render L. pl. *induciae*. Sing. was also in
use till 16 cent. Cf. F. *trève*, Sp. *tregua*,
Late L. *treuga*, from cogn. Goth. *triggwa*.

Si la guerre dure sanz peas ou trieus
(*John of Gaunt's Reg.* 1372–76).

Mene tyme were truyse [*orig.* induciae] i-take for
two yere (Trev. ii. 413).

I conceive that ye prepared to have ridden with
me this day of trewe (*Plumpton Let.* 1486–87).

truck[1]. Barter, whence the *Truck Acts*,
against payment in goods, to *have no truck
with*, colloq. *truck*, rubbish, and US. sense
of garden produce. F. *troquer*, "to truck,
chop, swab, scorse, barter, change" (Cotg.);
cf. It. *truccare*, Sp. *trocar*, MedL. *trocare*
(13 cent.). Origin unknown. Analogy of
swap suggests connection with Gasc. *truc*,
blow, *truca*, to strike, but quot. 1, if reliable, points to ult. connection with *trudge*.

truccare: to truck, to barter, to change ware for
ware, to swab. Also to trudge, to skud, or pack
away (Flor.).

I hae no trokings wi' night-birds
(*Kidnapped*, ch. xxix.).

truck[2]. Vehicle (18 cent.), orig. small wooden
wheel, as still in naut. *truck*, disk of wood
at mast-head. Short for earlier *truckle*
(q.v.).

Our naval organisation must be revised from truck
to keelson (*Obs.* June 15, 1919).

truckle. Orig. grooved wheel, sheave of
pulley. AF. *trocle*, L. *trochlea*, G. τροχιλία,
from τρόχος, hoop, wheel, from τρέχειν,

to run. Esp. in *truckle-bed* (also called
trundle-bed), a small bed on castors for use
of inferior or servant, which could be run
under the great bed of the master; hence
to *truckle under*, occupy a subordinate
position. See *truck*[2].

The troucle is called *trochlea* vel *rechamus*
(Coop. s.v. *chelonia*).

So all to bed. My wife and I in the high bed in our
chamber, and Willett [the maid] in the trundle-bed
by us (Pepys, Oct. 9, 1667).

There wife and I lay, and in a truckle-bed Betty
Turner and Willett (*ib.* June 11, 1668).

truculent. L. *truculentus*, from *trux, truc-*,
fierce.

trudge. From 16 cent., also *tredge, tridge*, orig.
in sense of starting off. ? Connected with
Du. *trekken*, to march, trek, earlier *trecken*,
"proficisci" (Kil.), *trucken*, cogn. with ON.
tregga, whence synon. dial. *trig*, esp. in to *trig
it*, *trig the country*. See quot. 1 s.v. *truck*[1].
For variation of vowel cf. *trundle*. Another
possibility is that *trudge* represents F.
trousser (*bagage*) with the same phonetic
change as in *forge*[2], *grudge* (q.v.); cf. archaic
to *pack*, be off, trudge. This view is supported by the fact that *truss*, F. *trousser*,
occurs earlier in same sense. No doubt
mod. sense has been affected by *tread*,
tramp.

As for all other, let them trusse and packe (Skelton).

trudgen stroke [*swim.*]. Introduced (c. 1868)
by *John Trudgen*.

true. AS. *getrīewe*, from *trēow*, faith. Com.
Teut.; cf. Du. *getrouw*, Ger. *treu*, ON. *tryggr*,
Goth. *triggws*, all (as orig. *true*) with sense
of faithful, trustworthy, true-hearted. For
later sense of veracious cf. a *faithful report*.
In this sense *true* has gradually superseded
sooth, corresponding in sense to Ger. *wahr*,
L. *verus*. A *true-lover's knot* was earlier
(14 cent.) simply *true-love*, much used in
ornamentation. *Truism* is first quoted by
NED. from Swift.

truffle. From F. *truffe*, app., by metath.,
from L. *tubera*, pl. of *tuber*, "a puffe
growyng on the ground like a mushrome"
(Coop.). For adoption of neut. pl. as fem.
sing. cf. F. *feuille*, L. *folia*, *lèvre*, L. *labra*,
arme, L. *arma*, etc. See also *trifle*. Cf. It.
tartuffo, "a kinde of meate, fruite or roote
of the nature of potatoes, called traffles"
(Flor.), app. L. *terrae tuber*. From a dim.
of this comes Ger. *kartoffel*, potato, dissim.
for earlier *tartoffel* (still in dial.).

trull. From c. 1500. Ger. *trulle*, ? cogn. with *troll*², of which MHG. form was used as term of contempt, and ult. with *droll*. Cf. synon. Rouchi (Valenciennes) *droule*, archaic F. *drôlesse*, harlot, fem. of *drôle*, rascal.

Trulliberian. From *Parson Trulliber* (*Joseph Andrews*, ii. 14).

> In the Common Room the Fellows spent lives of Trulliberian luxury (Goldwin Smith, *Oxford*).

trump¹. Trumpet, by which it is now re-placed exc. poet., e.g. *last trump*. F. *trompe*; cf. It. *tromba*, Sp. *trompa*, OHG. *trumba*; ? of imit. origin (cf. *drum*), ? or ult. akin to *triumph*. For dim. *trumpet*, F. *trompette*, cf. *cornet*¹.

> A clamorous trumpeter of his owne praises
> (*NED*. 1599).

trump². At cards. Earlier *triumph*, on double sense of which Shaks. plays (v.i.). Cf. F. *triomphe*, "the card-game called ruffe, or trump; also, the ruffe, or trump at it" (Cotg.), It. *trionfo*, "a trump at cards, or the play called ruff or trump" (Flor.). Hence *to be a trump*, a "brick." In ModF. *trump* is *atout*, to all. Here belongs to *trump up*, perh. with a leaning on *trump*¹ (cf. to *drum up recruits*) and on *trumpery*.

> Now turn up your trump, your heart—hearts is trump, as I said before
> (Latimer, *Sermon on the Card*, 1529).
> She, Eros, has
> Pack'd cards with Caesar, and false-play'd my glory
> Unto an enemy's triumph (*Ant. & Cleop.* iv. 12).

trumpery. Orig. deception, guile, hence "something of less value than it seems" (Johns.). F. *tromperie*, from *tromper*, to cheat, perh. from *trompe*, trump¹. Cf. Du. *fluiten*, to play the flute, deceive, F. *piper*, to pipe, deceive, ? all orig. fowling meta-phors. For *trumpery* as adj. cf. *paltry*.

trumpet. See *trump*¹.

truncate. From L. *truncare*, from *truncus*, trunk. For app. replacement of this verb in Romanic by *trincare* see *trench*.

truncheon. F. *tronçon*, dim. of *tronc*, trunk, L. *truncus*. Orig. E. & ModF. sense is frag-ment, esp. of spear-shaft.

> *tronson*: a truncheon, or little trunk; a thick slice, luncheon, or peece cut off (Cotg.).

trundle. Phonetic var. of earlier *trendle*, *trindle*, AS. *trendel*, ring, circle, from *tren-dan*, to turn, trend (q.v.). In 16 cent. of a small massive wheel, esp. in *trundle-bed* (see *truckle*). Cf. OF. *trondeler*, "to trundle as a ball" (Cotg.), of cogn. Teut. origin, which has app. influenced the E. word.

trunk. F. *tronc*, L. *truncus*. Sense of chest is due to primitive method of "digging out" a box from a tree-trunk; cf. F. *tronc*, poor-box in church. With *trunk-hose* (surviving in the *trunks* of boxing costume) cf. Ger. *strumpf*, stocking, orig. stump, trunk, and sense-development of *stocking*; also OF. *triquehouse*, gaiter, from *trique*, thick club. *Trunk-sleeves* occurs earlier (temp. Hen. VIII). In *trunk* of elephant there is con-fusion (? due to archaic *trunk*, tube) with *trump*¹, earlier used in same sense.

> *trompe*: a trump, or trumpet; also, the snowt of an elephant (Cotg.).

trunnion. Knob at side of cannon by which it rested on its carriage. F. *trognon*, stock, stump, ? from OF. *tron*, var. of *tronc*, trunk.

truss. F. *trousse*, bundle, package, etc., from *trousser*, "to trusse, tucke, packe, bind or girt in, plucke or twitch up" (Cotg.), OF. *torser*; cf. Prov. *trosar*, MedL. *trossare*. Of obscure origin, perh. from L. *thyrsus*, staff, used for tightening ligature; cf. F. *bâcler*, to pack, from *baculus*, staff. In surg. sense from 16 cent.

trust. ON. *traust*, whence verb *treysta*, giving ME. *trest*, *trist*, later assimilated to noun; cogn. with *trow*, *true*; cf. Du. *troosten*, Ger. *trösten*, to comfort, Goth. *trausti*, covenant. Ground-sense is that of confidence, secu-rity. Commerc. *trust* is chiefly US.

try. F. *trier*, to sift, sort, separate good from bad, as still in whaling, to *try* (*out*) *blubber*, metallurgy, etc.; hence, to test, prove. Cf. Prov. & Catalan *triar* (? from F.), MedL. *triare*. ? Late L. *tritare*, to triturate, thresh corn, from *terere*, *trit-*. Leg. sense was de-veloped in AF. *Trysail* is from the naut. manoeuvre called *trying*, earliest in to *lie a-try*, with one sail, with which cf. to *lie a-hull*, with no sails. *Trial* is AF.

trypograph. From G. τρυπᾶν, to pierce.

tryst. Earlier *tristre* (c. 1225), *treste* (13 cent.), hunting station to which the game was driven; hence, hunting rendez-vous. Cf. OF. *tristre*, *terstre*, *triste*, MedL. *trista*. Archaic F. *tistre* (*titre*), with one -*r*- lost by dissim., survives as term of ven. The fact that the word is only E. & F. (? Norm.) makes Norse origin likely, and ON. *treysta*, to trust, rely, has been suggested, but, in the absence of evidence as to exact orig. sense, this remains a conjecture only.

tsar. Now usual spelling of *czar* (q.v.), of hist. interest only now (July 1918) that the last bearer of the title has been murdered.

tsetse. Fly. From Bechuana lang. of SAfr.

Tsung-li-yamen. Chin. Foreign Office, lit. general management bureau.

tuatara. New Zeal. lizard. Maori, from *tua*, on the back, *tara*, spine.

tub. First in Chauc. Of Du. or LG. origin; cf. Du. *tobbe*, LG. *tubbe*; ? cogn. with Ger. *tobel*, bowl-shaped valley. With *tub-thumper* cf. earlier *tub-preacher*, *pulpit-thumper*. In *Rump Songs* (1639–61) are repeated allusions to preachers standing in (*not* on) a tub and the frontispiece depicts the same.

A bricklayer, called Henry Daunce, sett a tub to a tree, and therein he preached divers Sondayes (Wriothesley, *Chron.* 1538).

tuba. L., trumpet, cogn. with *tubus* (v.i.).

tube. F., L. *tubus*. The *Twopenny Tube* was the title of an article by H. D. Browne in the *Londoner* (June 30, 1900), describing a trial trip in the Central London Railway before it was opened to the public.

The tube-journey can never lend much to picture and narrative: it is as barren as an exclamatory O! (George Eliot, *Felix Holt*, 1866).

tuber. L., hump, swelling, cogn. with *tumēre*, to swell. Hence *tubercle*, *tuberculosis*, the latter orig. applied to any disease connected with formations of tubercles, current sense dating from Koch's discovery of the tubercle-bacillus (1882).

tuberose. Plant with tuberous root. L. *tuberosa*, fem. of *tuberosus*, tuberous (v.s.), but often misunderstood as *tube-rose*.

tuck¹. To gather in folds; earlier, to tug, snatch, and spec. to dress cloth by stretching it on the tenter-hooks (hence name *Tucker*). App. ident. with AS. *tūcian*, to ill-treat (for shortened vowel cf. *suck*), cogn. with Ger. *zucken*, to tug, snatch, intens. of *ziehen*, to pull, and ult. with *tug*, *tie*, etc. Hence *tucker*, frill, as in *best bib and tucker* (1737). From sense of gathering up and putting away, "tucking in," comes *tuck-shop* and Austral. *tucker*, provender.

tuck² [*archaic*]. In *tuck of drum*. F. *toquer*, north. form of *toucher*, to touch (q.v.); cf. *tocsin*. Hence archaic *tucket*, flourish of trumpets.

tuck³ [*hist.*]. Straight sword. F. *estoc*, "a rapier, or tucke" (Cotg.), whence It. *stocco*, "a tuck, a short sword" (Flor.), from LG. *stocken*, to stick, pierce, cogn. with Ger. *stock*, stick. The E. word is from F. dial. var. *étoc*.

tucker. See *tuck¹*.

tucket. See *tuck²*.

tucutucu. Burrowing rodent (Patagonia). Native, from grunt.

Tuesday. AS. *Tīwesdæg*, day of *Tīw*, corresponding to ON. *Týr* (whence *týsdagr*), cogn. with OHG. *Zio* (whence Ger. dial. *zistag*), and with L. *deus*, G. Ζεύς, Δι-, OIr. *dia*, Sanskrit *dyaus*, *div*, heaven. This ancient Teut. divinity was taken as corresponding to Mars, hence *Tuesday* for L. *Martis dies* (whence F. *mardi*). Du. *dinsdag*, Ger. *dienstag* belong to *Thinxus*, Late L. epithet of the same god, *Mars Thinxus*, from Lombard *thing*, public assembly, etc. (see *thing*).

tufa [*geol.*]. It. *tufo*, *tufa*, from L. *tofus*. Earlier (16 cent.) is synon. *tuff*, via F. *tuf*, "a kind of white sand, or soft and brittle stone" (Cotg.).

tuft. F. *touffe*, with excrescent *-t* (cf. *graft¹*), prob. of Teut. origin, cogn. with *top¹* (see *toupet*), and ult. with Ger. *zopf*, "a tuft or tuffet" (Ludw.). Also, ornamental tassel formerly worn at the univs. by titled students, whence *tuft-hunter* (18 cent.), toady to the aristocracy. See also *toff*.

tug. ME. *toggen*, intens. formation from AS. *tēon*, corresponding to Ger. *ziehen* (*zog*, *gezogen*), to pull. See *tie*, *tow¹*, *tuck¹*. Athletic *tug of war* (1876) is a curious example of the way in which the phrase of a minor writer will sometimes become a permanent addition to the lang. (see *Greek*, and cf. *diddle*, *Grundy*).

tuism. Coined (? by Coleridge) from L. *tu*, thou, after *egoism*.

tuition. AF. *tuycioun*, OF. *tuicion*, L. *tuitio-n-*, from *tueri*, to look after. For sense-development cf. *tutor*.

Humbly desiring pardon of your honour for my tediousness, I leave your lordship to the tuition of the Almighty (Hakl. xi. 378).

tulip. From 16 cent. Cf. F. *tulipe* (earlier *tulipan*), It. *tulipano*, Sp. *tulipán*, Ger. *tulpe*, Du. *tulp*, etc., all from *tul(i)band*, vulg. Turk. pronunc. of Pers. *dulband*, turban, which the shape of the flower suggested. Addison has *tulipomania*, the subject of Dumas' *Tulipe noire*. *Tulip wood* is from the *tulip-tree*, a NAmer. magnolia, with tulip-shaped flowers.

tulipan: the delicate flower called a tulipa, tulipie, or Dalmatian cap (Cotg.).

tulle. From *Tulle* (Corrèze). Cf. *jean*, *cambric*, etc.

tulwar. Hind. *talwār*, sabre.

tumble. Frequent. from AS. *tumbian*, to dance, etc., early sense surviving in *tumbler*, acrobat. Cf. Du. *tuimelen*, Ger. *tummeln*, to bustle, *taumeln*, to reel, Sw. *tumla*, Dan. *tumle*, to tumble, roll. F. *tomber*, of LG. origin, has kept to one spec. sense and influenced the E. word. The wide extension of the word (e.g. Rum. *tumbă*, somersault, Calabrian *tummare*, to go head over heels) points to an orig. imit. *tum(b)* of the *flop, bump* type. The glass called a *tumbler* was orig. round-bottomed so that it could not be put down till empty. Slang to *tumble to* is, I believe, for *under-stumble*, a slang perversion of *understand*, which I remember in use nearly fifty years ago. This is further complicated in riming slang into *do you Oliver* (sc. *Cromwell*)?

You unde[r]stumble me well, sir, you have a good wit (*Misogonus*, i. 4, c. 1550).

tumbrel. OF. *tomberel* (*tombereau*), a tip-cart, esp. for dung, from *tomber*, to fall. Esp. of the carts in which victims were taken to the guillotine during the Reign of Terror. Hist. E. sense of instrument for punishment, app. cucking-stool, is found in early 13 cent., but is unknown in F.

tumid. L. *tumidus*, from *tumēre*, to swell. Cf. *tumour*, F. *tumeur*, L. *tumor-em*; *tumefaction*, from L. *tumefacere*, to make to swell. See *thumb*.

tummy. Infantile for *stomach*. See *s-*.

tump. Mound. A dial. word (WMidl.) in use at the Front. Welsh *twmp*, ? cogn. with L. *tumulus*; ? cf. Sicilian *timpa*, hill, a pre-Roman word.

tump of ground: tumulus (Litt.).

tumult. F. *tumulte*, L. *tumultus*, from *tumēre*, to swell.

tumulus. L., "a hillock, a knap, a tump" (Litt.), from *tumēre* (v.s.).

tun. Var. of *ton* (q.v.). AS. *tunne*; cf. Du. *ton*, Ger. *tonne* (OHG. *tunna*), ON. *tunna*; also, from Teut., F. *tonne*, MedL. *tunna*, Gael. Ir. *tunna*. Prob. a seafaring word of LG. origin, adopted early by other Europ. langs. Orig. large cask, application to weight (*ton*) appearing in late ME.

tund [*Winchester school slang*]. L. *tundere*, to beat.

tundra [*geog.*]. Treeless steppe of NRuss. Lapp, orig. compd., *tun-tur*, marsh plain.

[We] came to a playne called Correapin Tundra (Purch. xii. 258).

tune. Phonetic var. (14 cent.) of *tone* (q.v.), with later differentiation of sense.

To be knocked on the head at the tune of 3*s*. 6*d*. a week (Defoe, *Colonel Jack*).

tungsten [*chem.*]. Sw., heavy stone.

tunic. F. *tunique*, L. *tunica*, used of various garments. Of Semit. origin and ult. ident. with G. χιτών.

tunnel. OF. *tonel* (*tonneau*), dim. of *tonne*, tun (q.v.), with ground-sense of cylindrical shape. Earliest E. sense, tunnel-net for partridges, is F. fem. *tonnelle*. Chief current sense has been developed in E. and borrowed, with other railway-words, by F.

Le railway, le tunnel, le ballast, le tender, Express, trucks et wagons; une bouche française Semble broyer du verre ou mâcher de la braise (J. P. G. Viennet, 1855).

tunny. From F. *thon*, "a tunnie fish" (Cotg.), Prov. *ton* or It. *tonno*, L., G. θύννος.

tup [*dial.*]. Ram (Johns.). ? Transferred use of Norw. Sw. *tupp*, cock, cogn. with *top*[1], in sense of crest. The word must be much older than dict. records (14 cent.), as *Tupper*, *Tupman* are well-established surnames and *John Tupp*, "carnifex," was a freeman of York in 1317.

tupelo. Tree. NAmer. Ind.

Tupi [*ling.*]. One of the two chief native langs. of Brazil. Cf. *Guarani*.

Tupperism. In style of *Martin Tupper*, author of *Proverbial Philosophy* (1838–42).

tu quoque. L., thou also, "you're another."

Turanian [*ling.*]. Group of Asiat. langs. (Ural-Altaic) which are neither Aryan nor Semitic. From Pers. *Turān*, realm beyond the Oxus, contrasted with *Irān*, Persia. The chief Turanian literature is in Finnish and Magyar. Pol. and ethn. applied esp. to the Turks (v.i.).

The pan-Turanian camarilla is incorrigible (*Obs.* Feb. 22, 1920).

turban. Pers. *dulband*. In most Europ. langs., the *-r-* for *-l-* appearing first in Port. Earlier E. forms were *tolipan*, *tulban*, etc. See *tulip*.

turbary [*leg.*]. Right of cutting turf or peat. OF. *tourberie*, from *tourbe*, turf (q.v.), peat. Cf. MedL. *turbaria*.

turbid. L. *turbidus*, from *turba*, crowd, disturbance. See *troop*.

turbine. F., L. *turbo, turbin-*, whirlwind, reel, spindle, etc., from *turbare*, to disturb (v.s.).

turbit. Pigeon. App. from L. *turbo*, top[2] (v.s.).

turbot. F. (12 cent. *tourbout*), prob. of Scand. origin, "thorn butt[1]"; cf. synon. Ger. *dornbutt*, and Norw. *pigvar*, turbot, from *pig*, thorn. Cf. *halibut*.

turbulent. F., L. *turbulentus*, from *turba*, crowd, disturbance.

Turco. F. slang for Algerian infantry soldier. Sp. It., Turk.

Turcoman [*ethn.*]. Branch of Turkish race inhabiting Turkestan. Pers. *turkumān*, one like a Turk, from *māndan*, to resemble. Cf *Mussulman*.

turd. AS. *tord*, with Du. & ON. cognates. Occurs passim in Wyc. where *AV*. has *dung*.

turdiform [*ornith.*]. From L. *turdus*, thrush.

tureen. Earlier *terreen*, F. *terrine*, "an earthen pot, or pan" (Cotg.), from *terre*, earth. Mod. spelling perh. due to some fancied connection with *Turin*. Cf. *cayenne*, *paduasoy*, etc.

turf. AS. *turf*, sod, peat. Com. Teut.; cf. Du. *turf*, OHG. *zurba* (replaced by LG. *torf*), ON. *torf*; cogn. with Sanskrit *darbha*, tuft of grass. OF. *tourbe* is from Teut. (see *turbary*). The other langs. have not the sense of greensward. With *the Turf* (18 cent.) cf. *the boards*.

turgid. L. *turgidus*, from *turgēre*, to swell.

Turk. Cf. F. *Turc*, It. Sp. *Turco*, MedL. *Turcus*, Late G. Τοῦρκος, Arab. *turk*; of obscure origin. "Probably the name *Turk* appears first in E. in connexion with the Third Crusade, 1187–92" (*NED.*). It was also used vaguely for Moslem (*Collect for Good Friday*), and for brutal individual, as still playfully. With *Grand* (*Great*) *Turk* (15 cent.) cf. *Great Mogul*. See also *Turki*.

turkey. Short for *Turkey-cock* (*-hen*), orig. applied (16 cent.) to the guinea-fowl, which was often imported through Turkish territory, and later transferred to the Amer. bird. For vague use of the word cf. *Indian* in *Indian corn* (also called *Turkey wheat*), and F. *dindon*, *dinde*, turkey, for earlier *coq* (*poule*) *d'Inde*. See early list of Europ. names below. Horne Tooke, whose father was a poulterer, used to describe him as an "eminent Turkey (i.e. Levant) merchant."

gallina Africana, Numidica, Indica: *Al.* Indianisch oder Kalekuttisch [of Calicut] oder Welsch Hun. *B.* [*Du.*] Calkoensche oft Turckische Henne. *G.* [*F.*] geline ou poulle d'Inde, ou d'Afrique. *It.* gallina d'India. *H.* [*Sp.*] pavon de las Indias. *An.* cok off Inde (A. Junius).

Turki [*ling.*]. Pers. *turki*, Turkish, applied also to the lang. of the Eastern Turks, Turcomans. *Turkic* is also used in a wider sense, while *Turkish* is applied to the lang. of the Ottoman Turks (v.i.).

The Turkish tongue is loftie in sound, but poore of it selfe in substance. For being originally the Tartarian, who were needie ignorant pastors, they were constrayned to borrow their termes of state and office from the Persians, of religion from the Arabians, as they did of maritime names from the Greekes and Italians (George Sandys, 1610).

Turkoman. See *Turcoman*.

turmeric. Earlier (16 cent.) also *tarmaret*, archaic F. *terre mérite*, MedL. *terra merita*, app. a fanciful name for the powdered root of *curcuma*. It may, however, be folk-etym. for some Eastern word.

turmoil. From early 16 cent. as noun and verb, to agitate, disquiet. ? For unrecorded **turmel*, OF. *trumel*, disturbance, tumult, altered like AF. *troboil*, trouble, or associated with *moil*, to drudge, for which it is used in dial. Godef. conjectures for *trumel* the sense of gambling only, but see quot. below, which means that the man sent crazy by love desires fighting, quarrel and turmoil.

Qu'amors desvee
Desirre mellee
Hutin et trumel (Godef.).

turn. AS. *turnian*, *tyrnan*, L. *tornare*, "to turne or worke with the wheele as turners doe" (Coop.), from *tornus*, lathe, G. τόρνος, carpenter's compasses. Replaced native *thrawan* (see *thrawn*), *wendan* (see *wend*). Senses were reinforced in ME. by F. *tourner*; cf. It. *tornare*, Sp. *tornar*, also Ger. *turnen*, to do gymnastics. The very wide senses, largely developed in F. *tour* (OF. *tourn*), *tourner*, start from a handicraft metaphor, which is still apparent in a *well-turned phrase* (*pair of ankles*). A *turncoat* was orig. one who attempted to hide the badge of his leader or party. *Turnpike*, also used for *turnpike road*, was orig. a revolving barrier armed with pikes or spikes, used as a mil. defence. *Turnsole*, plant and dye, is F. *tournesol*, Prov. *tournasol*, turn sun (cf. *heliotrope*).

An exceedingly well-turned-out damsel in a dark blue tailormade (*Daily Chron.* Mar. 19, 1920).

turnip. Earlier (16 cent.) *turnepe*, compd. of obs. *neep*, AS. *nǣp*, L. *napus*, "navew or turnepe, long rapes" (Coop.). First element may be *turn*, from symmetrical shape.

turpentine. Earlier (14 cent.) *terebinthine*, OF., L. *terebinthina* (sc. *resina*), exudation of the *terebinth* (q.v.). Colloq. *turps*.

turpinite. Explosive. From name, *Turpin*, of F. inventor. Cf. *lyddite*.

turpitude. F., L. *turpitudo*, from *turpis*, base.

turquoise. F., "a turqueise or Turkish-stone" (Cotg.), because brought from *Turkestan*.

turret. OF. *tourete* (replaced by *tourelle*), dim. of *tour*, tower (q.v.). Nav. sense from 1862.

turtle¹. Dove. Now usu. replaced by *turtle-dove*. AS. *turtla* (m.), *turtle* (f.), dissim. (cf. *marble*) of L. *turtur*, of imit. origin, from coo of dove (cf. *bulbul*).

turtle². Sea-tortoise. Sailors' corrupt. of F. *tortue*, tortoise (q.v.), assimilated to *turtle¹*, in the same illogical way as F. *langouste*, kind of lobster, becomes *long oyster* (see also *alligator pear*). The word appears to belong to the Bermudas (v.i.), the form *turckle*, found in the same records, being app. due to the turtle's neck being compared to that of a turkey (Purch. xix. 284). Quots. below are earlier than first *NED*. record (1657). Naut. to *turn turtle*, allusive to the helplessness of the turtle when on its back, was earlier (Marryat) to *turn the turtle*.

One turtle (for so we called them) feasted well a dozen messes (William Strachy, describing the Bermudas, 1609, in Purch. xix. 24).

The tortoise, which they [the Bermuda settlers] call a turtle (Norwood's *Summer Islands*, 1622, in Purch. xix. 190).

Turveydropian. Of *Mr Turveydrop*, model of deportment (*Bleak House*). Cf. *Chadbandian*, *Pickwickian*, *Pecksniffian*, etc.

Tuscan. F., It. *Toscano*, Late L. *Tuscanus*, of the *Tusci*, or Etruscans. Name of simplest of five ancient orders of architecture and of the purest It. lang. For *tuscan hat* cf. *leghorn*.

tush. Natural exclamation of impatience, earlier also *twish*. Cf. *tut*. *Tushery*, romantic literature in pseudo-archaic lang., was coined by R. L. Stevenson.

tusk. ME. *tusp*, metath. of AS. *tūx*, var. of *tūsc*, whence archaic *tush*; cf. Fris. *tosk*, LG. *tusk*; ? ult. cogn. with *tooth*. The early voyagers rarely use *tusk* in ref. to the elephant, but usu. speak of "elephant's teeth," while the Ivory Coast is called by them the *Tooth Coast*.

tussle. Frequent. of dial. *touse* (see *tease*, *ousle*).

tussock. From 16 cent., tuft of hair, with vars. *tusk*, *tush*, suggesting ult. identity with *tusk*; but it is hard to trace the connection.

tuske of heer: monceau de cheveulx (Palsg.).

tushe of heyres: crinetum; *tushe of thornes*: dumetum; *tushe of trees*: arboretum (*Manip. Voc.*).

tussore. Hind. *tasar*, coarse brown silk.

tut. Natural exclamation of contempt. Cf. *tush*.

bat: a worde of reproche, as tush, tut (Coop.).

tutelar. L. *tutelaris*, from *tutela*, guardianship, from *tutus*, safe, from *tueri*, to regard, see to. Cf. *tutelage*.

tutor. F. *tuteur*, guardian, L. *tutor-em*, from *tueri* (v.s.). Orig. sense survives at univs. For later sense-development cf. *tuition* and *governess*.

tutti frutti. It., all fruits.

tutty. Oxide of zinc. F. *tutie*, Sp. *tutía*, Arab. *tūtiyā*, prob. of Pers. origin; cf. Sanskrit *tuttha*, blue vitriol.

tu-whit, tu-whoo. Imit. of owl's cry (*Love's Lab. Lost*, v. 2).

twaddle. From c. 1800 for earlier *twattle*, in *twittle-twattle* (c. 1550), a "vile word" (Johns.), variation on *tittle-tattle* (q.v.).

So home, and with my wife, late twatling at my Lady Pen's (Pepys, July 25, 1666).

twain. AS. *twēgen* (m.), which in ME. became merely an alternative for *two* (q.v.), esp. when following the noun.

twang. Imit., the *-w-* expressing the bow-string element which is absent from the percussive *tang²*. Hence *twangle*.

twank [*dial.*]. Imit. of sound which begins with a *twang* and ends like a *spank*.

twankay. Green tea. Chin. *Taung-kei*, dial. form of *Tun-ki*, name of stream where orig. grown.

tway-blade. Plant. From obs. *tway*, apocopated form of *twain*.

tweak. From c. 1600. App. for earlier *twick*, AS. *twiccian*, cogn. with *twitch* (q.v.).

tweed. Originated (c. 1830) in a misreading of *tweel* (*Guy Mannering*, ch. xxvi.), Sc. form of *twill* (q.v.), helped by natural association with the river *Tweed*, which runs through a region where the fabric is made.

tweedle-dee and tweedle-dum. From *tweedle*, imit. of sound of pipe, the phrase being first used (1725) in ref. to two rival musicians (v.i.).

> Some say compared to Bononcini
> That Mynheer Handel's but a ninny;
> Others aver that he to Handel
> Is scarcely fit to hold a candle.
> Strange all this difference should be
> 'Twixt Tweedle-dum and Tweedle-dee! (Byrom).

tweeny [*colloq.*]. For *between-maid*, assisting both cook and housemaid.

tweezers. "The etymology of *tweezers* can best be made clear by starting from F. *étui*, a case, of doubtful origin. This became in E. *etwee*, or *twee*, e.g. Cotg. explains *estui* (*étui*) as 'a sheath, case, or box, to put things in; and (more particularly) a case of little instruments, as sizzars, bodkin, penknife, etc., now commonly termed an ettwee.' Such a case generally opens book-fashion, each half being fitted with instruments. Accordingly we find it called a surgeon's 'pair of twees,' or simply 'tweese,' and later a 'pair of tweeses.' The implement was named from the case, and became *tweezers* by association with *pincers, scissors*, etc." (Weekley, *Romance of Words*, ch. ix.). For change of sense cf. F. *boussole*, compass, It. *bossola*, orig. little box, and see *bodkin*. For double pl. (*tweeses*) cf. *quinces*.

> I did give him [a young man leaving for the Indies] "Lex Mercatoria," and my wife [gave him] my old pair of tweezers (Pepys, Dec. 15, 1667).

Twelfth-night. Eve of *Twelfth-day*, Epiphany, twelfth day after Christmas. Both are found in AS.

twelve. AS. *twelf*, from *two*, with second element as in *eleven* (q.v.). Com. Teut.; cf. Du. *twaalf*, Ger. *zwölf* (OHG. *zwelif*), ON. *tōlf*, Goth. *twalif*; for relation to *two* cf. also L. *duodecim*, G. δώδεκα. Compd. *twelvemonth* occurs in AS.; cf. ON. *tōlfmānuthr*. The jury were formerly called the *twelve men* (see also *Meas. for Meas.* ii. 1).

twenty. AS. *twēntig*, from *two* (*twain*) and *-ty* (q.v.). Com. Teut.; cf. Du. *twintig*, Ger. *zwanzig*, ON. *tuttugu*, Goth. *twaitigjus*.

twice. ME. *twīes*, AS. *twiges*, adv. formation from *twiga, twiwa*, twice, cogn. with *two*. Cf. *once, thrice*.

twiddle. App. imit. of motion which suggests both *twirl* and *fiddle*, in sense of trifling, aimless movement.

twig¹. Noun. AS. *twig*, cogn. with *two*, with orig. sense of dividing, forking; cf. Du. *twijg*, Ger. *zweig*.

> *hop the twig*: weglaufen (Ebers, 1793)

twig². Verb. 18 cent. slang, of obscure origin. ? Ident. with dial. *twick*, to pinch, nip (see *tweak, twitch*).

twilight. Formed in ME., with prefix *twi-*, cogn. with *two*, which enters into many obs. compds.; cf. LG. *twelecht*, whence is imitated Ger. *zwielicht*, replacing MHG. *zwischenlicht*, between-light, with which cf. AS. *twēonelēoht*, Norw. Dan. *tusmörke* (between murk). *Twilight of the gods* comes, via Ger. *Götterdämmerung* (? Wagner), from ON. *ragnar rökkr*, altered from earlier *ragnar rök*, judgment of the gods.

twill. Short for obs. *twilly*, AS. *twili*, formed from *twi-* (v.s.) after L. *bilix*; cf. Ger. *zwilch* (OHG. *zwilīh*), "linnen woven with a double thread" (Ludw.), and see *drill⁴*, *dimity*. See also *tweed*.

twin. AS. *twinn*, twofold, twin, cogn. with *two*, with suffix as in L. *bini*, two at a time. With ME. *twinling* cf. Ger. *zwilling*, twin, OHG. *zwiniling*, Du. *tweeling*; also G. δίδυμος, two-fold, twin, from δίς, twice, cogn. with δύο, two.

twine. AS. *twīn*, cogn. with *two*; cf. Du. *twijn*, Ger. *zwirn*, ON. *tvinni*. So also F. *dédoubler*, to untwine.

> I *twyne threde*, I double it with the *spyndell*: je retors
>   (Palsg.).

twinge. First as verb, to wring, pinch. AS. *twengan*, usu. regarded as cogn. with Du. *dwingen*, Ger. *zwingen*, ON. *thvinga*, all meaning to oppress, but *NED.* doubts connection.

twinkle. AS. *twinclian*, frequent. of **twincan*, whence archaic *twink*, to wink, sparkle, etc.; cogn. with Ger. *zwinken, zwinkern*. With *twinkling*, moment, cf. AS. *beorhthwīl*, lit. bright-while.

> And the devyll...shewed hym all the kyngdoms of
> the erth even in the twyncklynge of an eye
>   (Tynd. *Luke*, iv. 5).

twirl. Of late appearance (c. 1600), replacing (? under influence of *whirl*) ME. *tirl* (still in dial.), earlier *trill* (Chauc.), cogn. with Norw. Sw. *trilla*, Dan. *trille*.

> *girer*: to veere, or turne with the wind, to twirle, whirle, or wheele about (Cotg.).

twist. In ME. as noun and verb, in AS. only in compd. *mæst-twist*, stay of mast. Cogn. with *two* and *twine*. Du. *twist*, Ger. *zwist*, discord, strife, represent another sense-aspect.

> I *twyste threde*, I *twyne threde*: this terme is northren; declared in I *twyne* (Palsg.).

> Twist like plough-jobbers and swill like tinkers
>   (Motteux' *Rabelais*, v. 5).

twit. Earlier *twite*, aphet. for obs. *atwite*, to reproach, AS. *ætwītan*, to reproach with, from *at* and *wītan*, to blame, cogn. with *wīta*, punishment, as in hist. *bloodwite* (q.v.) and dial. to *bear the wite*. Cf. Ger. *verweisen*, "to reproach, upbraid, to cast, hit, or twit in the teeth with" (Ludw.), Du. *verwijten*, Goth. *fraweitan*, all cogn. with *wit*, knowledge, with sense-development like that of L. *animadvertere*, to censure, punish, lit. turn the mind to.

I twyhte one, I caste hym in the tethe, or in the nose: je luy reprouche (Palsg.).

twitch¹. To jerk, etc. Earliest (12 cent.) in compd. *totwitch*. Cogn. with *tweak*, dial. *twick*, Du. *twikken*, Ger. *zwicken*, *zwacken*, "to pinch, twitch, nip" (Ludw.).

twitch². Grass. Dial. var. of *quitch* (q.v.).

twite. Mountain-linnet. Imit. of cry.

twitter. Imit., cf. Du. *kwetteren*, Ger. *zwit-schern*, *zwitzern*.

twizzle. To twirl. Dial. formation on *twist*, *twirl*.

two. AS. *twā*, fem. and neut., replacing masc. *twain*, AS. *twēgen*. Aryan; cf. OSax. *twēne*, *twō*, *twē*, OHG. *zwēne*, *zwō*, *zwei*, ON. *tveir*, *tvār*, *tvau*, Goth. *twai*, *twōs*, *twa*, L. *duo*, G. δύο, OIr. *dá*, Russ. *dva*, Sanskrit *dva*. In Du. & Ger. the current form is the neut. (*twee*, *zwei*), but in some Ger. dials. one still says *zwene männer*, *zwo frauen*, *zwei kinder*. The prevalence of the neut. is due to the practice, found in AS. & OHG., of using it in ref. to words of different gender. It will be noticed that most E. words in *tw-* are related to *two*. Contemptuous 19 cent. *twopenny-halfpenny* is an elaboration of 16 cent. *twopenny*. A further variation is *penny-farthing* (Kipling).

-ty. In numerals. AS. *-tig*; cf. Du. *-tig*, Ger. *-zig*, ON. *tigr*, Goth. *tigus*, the two latter not suffixed; cogn. with *ten* (q.v.).

Tyburn tree [*hist.*]. Gallows (mentioned in 12 cent.) at *Tyburn*, at junction of Oxford St. and Edgware Rd.

Tychonic [*astron.*]. Of *Tycho Brahe*, Dan. astronomer (†1601). Cf. *Copernican*.

Tycoon. Title by which the Shogun of Japan was described to foreigners. Jap. *taikun*, from Chin. *ta*, great, *kiun*, prince.

tyke. ON. *tīk*, bitch; hence, contemptuous northern name for dog. As applied to Yorkshiremen "perh. orig. opprobrious, but now accepted and owned" (*NED.*). Cf. *Hampshire hog*, *Suffolk dumpling*.

They [the Scots at Pinkie] stood very brave and braggart, crying, "Come here, hounds! Come here, tykes" (W. Patten, 1548).

Yorkshire-Tike: a Yorkshire manner of man (*Dict. Cant. Crew*).

tympanum. L., drum, wheel for raising weights, face of pediment, G. τύμπανον, cogn. with τύπτειν, to strike. Cf. *tympany*, morbid swelling, turgidity, from MedL., G. τυμπανίας, dropsy.

Tynwald [*hist.*]. Annual gathering of authorities in Isle of Man. From ON. *thingvöllr*, assembly ground (see *thing*). Cf. place-names *Dingwall*, *Tinwald*, *Tingwall*.

Many English holiday-makers attended the 1000-years-old Tynwald ceremony in the Isle of Man on Saturday (*Daily Chron.* July 7, 1919).

Tyoorkish [*ling.*]. Turano-Mongol lang. spoken by some tribes of Russia and Siberia.

type. F., L., G. τύπος, impression, from τύπτειν, to strike. First (15 cent.) in fig. sense of symbol, etc. (cf. *typify*). Printing sense from 18 cent. For sense-development cf. *stamp*.

typhlitis [*med.*]. From G. τυφλόν, blind gut, neut. of τυφλός, blind.

typhoid. Of the nature of *typhus*, Late L., G. τῦφος, vapour, stupor, from τύφειν, to smoke.

Typhon. G. Τυφῶν, giant, father of the winds, buried under Mount Etna (v.i.), personification of τυφῶν, whirlwind.

typhoon. Combined from Arab. *tūfān*, hurricane, which is prob. G. τυφῶν (v.s.), and Chin. *tai fung*, dial. form of *ta fēng*, big wind. The Arab. word was adopted (16 cent.) via Urdu, and the Chin. name was assimilated to it, current spelling being due to *Typhon*.

A cruell storme called the tuffon, fearefull even to men on land (Purch. 1608).

typhus. See *typhoid*.

tyrant. F. *tyran*, L., G. τύραννος, absolute ruler, with degeneration of sense in Europ. langs. (cf. *despot*). For spurious *-t*, which does not appear in the derivatives, cf. *peasant*, *pheasant*, etc.

The tyrant of the Chersonese
    Was freedom's best and bravest friend;
That tyrant was Miltiades!
    Oh! that the present hour would lend
Another despot of the kind! (*Isles of Greece*).

tyre. Prevalent incorr. spelling of *tire*³ (q.v.).

Tyrian. Of *Tyre*, esp. in *Tyrian purple*.

tyro. Incorr. spelling of *tiro* (q.v.).

Tyrtaean. Of Τυρταῖος, martial poet of the Spartans (7 cent. B.C.).

Tzigane. Hung. gipsy. F., Magyar *czigány*, cogn. with *Zingari* and Ger. *Zigeuner*, "an egyptian or gipsy" (Ludw.).

U-boat. For Ger. *unterseeboot*, undersea boat.

> The U-boats could not stow prisoners. So they reverted to the practice of the Middle Ages
> (*Times Lit. Sup.* Jan. 8, 1920).

ubiety. "Whereness." Coined, on *ubiquity*, from L. *ubi*, where.

ubiquity. F. *ubiquité*, coined from *ubique*, wherever, everywhere. Cowper uses *ubiquarian* (*Tirocinium*, 266) for *ubiquitous*.

> *ubiquitarians*: a late sect holding that Christs body is every where as well as his divinity (Blount).

udal [*hist.*]. Freehold tenure anterior to feudalism still in force in Orkneys (see Scott's *Pirate*). ON. *ōthal*; cf. AS. *æthelu*, lineage, produce, OSax. *ōthil*, OHG. *uodal*; cogn. with *atheling*.

udder. AS. *ūder*. Aryan; cf. Du. *uier* (earlier *uder*), Ger. *euter*, ON. *jūgr*, L. *uber*, G. οὖθαρ, Sanskrit *ūdhar*. A word from the nomadic or pastoral period. For relation of L. -*b*- to Teut. dental cf. *beard*, *red*.

udometer. Rain-gauge. From L. *udus*, damp.

ugh. Natural exclamation of disgust.

ugly. ON. *uggligr*, from *uggr*, fear; cogn. with *awe*; cf. Goth. *ōgan*, to fear. The pugil. *ugly customer* preserves orig. sense.

Ugrian [*ling.*]. Finnic. From name of a tribe of N. Russia. Cf. *Ural-Altaic*.

uhlan. Ger. *ulan*, lancer, Pol. *ulan*, Tatar light horseman, Turk. *oghlan*, young man, Tatar *oglan*, son, child. Hence F. *hulan*, E. *ewe lamb* (slang of the Great War).

> When they are called to the Chan [of the Crim Tatars], he heares them, the soldans, tuians, ulans, marzies...and principall Tartars being present
> (Purch. xiii. 481, *Transl. of Broniovius*).

> Our men went through the uhlans like brown paper
> (Sir P. Chetwode, 1914).

ukase. Russ. *ukaz*, edict, esp. imperial (now, Leninite), from *kazat'*, to indicate (in Serb. to speak, in Czech to preach), whence *ukazat'*, to command; cf. *pokazat'*, to show.

ulcer. F. *ulcère*, L. *ulcus*, *ulcer*-, "a boyle, a sore, a botch" (Coop.), cogn. with G. ἕλκος, sore, wound.

ulema. Corporation of Moslem doctors of sacred law. Arab. *'ulemā*, pl. of *'ālim*, learned, from *'alama*, to know. Cf. *alma*.

ullage. "What a cask lacks of being full" (Phillips). Prov. *ulhage*, from *ulhar*, to fill up; cf. synon. OF. *ouillage*, *ouiller*; from

L. *oculus*, eye, in sense of bung-hole; cf. F. dial. (S.W.) *uyet*, funnel for cask filling.

ulmic [*chem.*]. From L. *ulmus*, elm.

ulnar [*anat.*]. Of the *ulna*, L., smaller bone of fore-arm, cogn. with *ell*, *elbow*.

ulotrichian [*ethn.*]. Woolly-haired. From G. οὐλόθριξ, from οὖλος, whole, thick, fleecy, θρίξ, τριχ-, hair.

ulster. For *Ulster* overcoat. Orig. long frieze coat as worn in *Ulster*. Cf. *inverness*.

ulterior. L., compar. from *ultra*, beyond.

ultimate. From Late L. *ultimare*, to come to an end, from *ultimus*, superl. of *ulterior*. *Ultimatum*, earlier also *ultimat*, comes, via F., from "diplomatic Latin."

ultimo. Abl. of L. *ultimus* (sc. *mensis*). Cf. *proximo*.

ultimogeniture. Borough English (q.v.). Opposite of *primogeniture* (q.v.).

ultra-. L., beyond. Cf. F. *outre*, *outrage*. Hence mod. *ultra*, extremist, *ultraism*, *ultraist*, these perh. suggested by *altruism*, *altruist*.

ultramarine. Orig. adj. qualifying *blue*. Altered from It. *oltra marino*, foreign. from overseas, applied to lapis lazuli. Now replaced by *over-sea* in gen. sense.

ultramontane. F. *ultramontain* (14 cent.), beyond the mountains, esp. the Alps. Connotation varies according to the position of the speaker or writer, but current sense usu. refers to belief in Papal authority. F. *ultramontanisme* is 18 cent.

ultra vires. L., beyond powers.

ultromotivity. Power of spontaneous movement. From L. *ultro*, spontaneously. Cf. F. *de son propre mouvement*, of one's own accord.

ululate. From L. *ululare*, "to houle as a dog or wolf doth" (Coop.), of imit. origin.

umbel [*bot.*]. Earlier *umbella*, L., "the round tuft or hed of fenell, or other herbes, wherein the seede is" (Coop.), also a sun-shade, dim. of *umbra*, shadow.

umber. "Somewhat a sad yellow colour used by painters" (Blount). F. *terre d'ombre*, It. *terra d'ombra*, shadow earth, a pigment used for shading; cf. Sp. *sombra*, umber, lit. shadow.

umbilical [*anat.*]. Of the navel, L. *umbilicus*, cogn. with G. ὀμφαλός, and ult. with *navel* (q.v.).

umbles [*archaic*]. Entrails of deer. See *humble-pie*.

umbo. L., central boss (of shield, etc.), cogn. with *umbilical* and with *nave*[1].

umbraculum [*bot.*]. L., from *umbra*, shade.

umbrage. F. *ombrage*, "an umbrage, a shade, a shadow; also, jealousie, suspition, an incling of; whence *donner ombrage à*, to discontent; make jealous of, or putte buzzes into the head of" (Cotg.). Perh. orig. a term of horsemanship, as in F. *cheval ombrageux*, a horse apt to take fright at its own shadow. See also *dudgeon*².

umbrella. Archaic It. *ombrella* (now *ombrello*), dim. of *ombra*, shade, L. *umbra*, used in sense of L. *umbella* (see *umbel*). Orig. as defence against sun (cf. F. *ombrelle*), the first rain-umbrella used by a man in London having been trad. carried (c. 1760) by Jonas Hanway, the famous traveller and philanthropist (†1786). But women used them from c. 1700. The use in Italy of *umbrellaes* is mentioned by Coryat (1611).

Here [at Marseilles] we bought umbrellos against the heat (Evelyn).

Blest was the prophet [Jonah] in his heavenly shade,
But ah! how soon did his umbrella fade!
      (*Epitaph*, 1684).

The young gentleman borrowing the umbrella belonging to Will's Coffee-house, in Cornhill, of the mistress, is hereby advertised, that to be dry from head to foot on the like occasion, he shall be welcome to the maid's pattens
    (*Female Tatler*, Dec. 12, 1709).

Umbrian. Of *Umbria*, province of Italy. Name of school of painters and of Italic dial. akin to L.

umiak. See *oomiak*.

umlaut [*ling.*]. Ger., from *um*, around, *laut*, sound. Coined (18 cent.) by Klopstock.

umpire. For ME. *noumper*, OF. *nomper* (*non pair*), not equal (see *peer*¹), third (or extra) man called in when arbitrators disagreed. For loss of *n-* cf. *apron*, *auger*, etc.; for ending cf. archaic *rampire* for *ramper* (*rampart*); for sense cf. Sp. *tercero*, "the third, a broaker, a mediator" (Percyvall). Montaigne uses similarly *personne tierce*, rendered by Florio *stickler* (q.v.); *tierz*, arbitrator, occurs in an AF. proclamation of the Earl of Gloucester (1258). Cf. also *arbiter*. The form used in quot. 2 is remade on *un-* and L. *par*, equal, peer. The abstract noun in quot. 3 is a curious formation.

Arbitratores that tyme named, if thei myghten accordyn, and ellys of anoonpier (*Paston Let.* i. 14).

The seide arbitrours might not accorde, an ye as unpar have yeven your decree rightwysly and indifferently (*Coventry Leet Book*, 1464).

The matter betwyxt my servant and John Forest is put to iiij men, and the owmpreght of you
    (*Plumpton Let.* temp. Hen. VII).

umpty, umpteen. Army slang to disguise number of division, brigade, etc. Cf. *iddy-umpty*, colloq. for the Morse *dot-and-dash* notation.

One who served with umpty squadron through the battle of the Somme (*An Airman's Outings*).

un [*colloq.*]. As in *good un to go*. Preserves correct pronunc. of *one* (q.v.). Also, in old southern dial., from AS. *hine*, acc. of *he* (see *him*).

un-¹. Prefixed to adjs., and nouns and advs. derived from them. AS. *un-*. Aryan; cf. Du. *on-*, Ger. *un-*, ON. *ō-*, *ū-*, Goth. *un-*, L. *in-*, G. *ἀ-*, *ἀν-*, Sanskrit *an-*, *a-*. Often in euph. coinages, e.g. *untruth*, lie, *unworthy*, rascally, *unrest*, brigandage; cf. *dis-* (e.g. *disease*), *in-* (e.g. *infamous*). Thus *unsavoury* is euph. for *disgusting*, also orig. euph. In some cases (*uncouth*, *ungainly*, *unkempt*, *unruly*) the simplex is not in use exc. as a nonce-word.

During the recent war the lot of her [Ireland's] uninvaded, unconscribed, unbombed, and uncouponed people was almost that of the spoilt children of Europe (*Daily Chron.* June, 1919).

un-². Prefixed to verbs. AS. *un-*. Com. Teut.; cf. Du. *ont-*, Ger. *ent-* (OHG. *ant-*), Goth. *and-*; cogn. with L. *ante*, G. *ἀντί* (see *answer*).

unaneled [*archaic*]. See *anele*.

unanimous. From L. *unanimus*, from *unus*, one, *animus*, mind.

unbend. In fig. use from the bent bow. Thus to *unbend*, i.e. become almost straight, is not logically the opposite of *unbending*, rigidly straight.

unberufen. Ger., unsummoned, exclamation propitiating Nemesis.

unbosom. Cf. to *make a clean breast*.

uncanny. Sc., "dangerous, incautious, mischievous, untender, careless" (*Sc. Dict.* 1818). See *canny* and cf. synon. Ger. *unheimlich*, lit. unfamiliar. Cf. also *uncouth*.

uncate [*bot.*]. From L. *uncus*, hook.

unchancy. Sc., from orig. sense of *chance* (q.v.). For synon. *wanchancy* see *wanton*.

uncial. L. *uncialis*, as in Late L. *litterae unciales*, "letters an ynche long" (Coop.), used by Jerome and applied to a character resembling a capital used in early MSS. See *inch*¹, *ounce*¹.

uncinate [*bot.*]. L. *uncinatus*, from *uncus*, hook.

uncle. F. *oncle*, VL. *aunclus*, for *avunculus*, "the unkle on the mothers side" (Coop.), dim. of *avus*, grandfather. Introduced into most Teut. langs. in place of native word (e.g. AS. *ēam*, Ger. *oheim*), which is also ult. cogn. with L. *avus*. The pawnbroker as (helpful) uncle is found in E., F., Ger., Norw. Dan.

unco. Sc. form of *uncouth* (q.v.), esp. in *unco guid*, unnaturally righteous.

unconscionable. See *conscience*. Chiefly as echo of Charles II's famous apology.

> He apologized to those who had stood round him all night for the trouble which he had caused. He had been, he said, a most unconscionable time dying (Macaulay).

unconventional. A 19 cent. epithet for a certain type of affectation.

> It is not difficult to be unconventional when your unconventionality is but the convention of your set (Somerset Maugham).

uncouple. Orig. of hounds, from *couple* (q.v.), in etym. sense.

uncouth. AS. *uncūth*, unknown, from p.p. of *cunnan*, to know. For sense-development cf. *strange, outlandish*. Chauc. has it in the sense of rare, splendid (A. 2497 and *House of Fame*, iii. 189). Cf. dial. *unkid*, in which *-kid* is the p.p. of AS. *cȳthan*, to make known.

> *uncowth*: extraneus, exoticus (*Prompt. Parv.*).

> The most uncouth accident that ever befell unto poore men (Purch. xiv. 98).

unction. L. *unctio-n-*, from *ungere, unct-*, to anoint. For fig. senses of *unctuous* cf. "oily," and for degeneration cf. *bland*. With *extreme unction*, after F. *extrême-onction*, cf. *in extremis*.

undate [*bot.*]. From L. *unda*, wave.

undé [*her.*]. F. *ondé*, waved (v.s.).

undecennial. From L. *undecim*, eleven, after *septennial*, etc. Cf. *undecagon*, with G. second element.

under. AS. *under*, under, among, second sense surviving in *under the circumstances*. Com. Teut.; cf. Ger. *unter*, Du. *onder*, ON. *undir*, Goth. *undar*; cogn. with L. *inter, infra*, which correspond to the two Teut. senses. Often, like *over*, used with adj. force, e.g. *under jaw, under dog, under-linen*, etc.

undergrad. Short for *undergraduate*, univ. student *in statu pupillari*.

> The audience was chiefly composed of under-graduates and undergraduettes (the latter from Girton and Newnham) (*Obs.* Nov. 23, 1919).

underhand. Orig. adv., prob. from gambling

trick; cf. F. *sous main*. The opposite of *above-board*.

> *tenir sous main*: to keep in secret, in private, in a corner, in hugger-mugger (Cotg.).

underhung. "Having the underjaw projecting beyond the upper jaw" (Goldsmith, *Animated Nature*).

underlie. In fig. sense from geol.

underling. See *-ling*. In *Piers Plowm.* (B. vi. 47).

undermost. See *-most*.

underneath. See *beneath, nether*.

underpin. From obs. *pin*, to fill in joints.

understand. AS. *understandan*, lit. to stand among. The sense-development is obscure, but cf. G. ἐπίστασθαι, lit. to stand upon, Ger. *verstehen*, corresponding to AS. *forstandan*, to understand, lit. to stand before; also OHG. *antfristōn*, to interpret, with double prefix. *Understandings*, euph. for legs, is 19 cent.

understrapper. ? Orig. a barber's assistant.

> I [a charlatan] shall have occasion now and then for some understrapper to draw teeth for me, or to be my toad-eater upon the stage (T. Brown, 1701).

understudy [*theat.*]. To study a part so as to be able to replace another actor if necessary. Cf. *study* (*Mids. N. Dream*, i. 2).

undertake. Cf. Ger. *unternehmen*, AS. *underniman*, F. *entreprendre*. An *undertaker* was orig. a contractor, projector, etc. For specialization of sense, from c. 1700, cf. *stationer. Funeral-undertaker* was the orig. description in current sense.

> *undertakers*: were such as were employed by the Kings purveyors, as their deputies, and such as undertake any great work, as draining of fens, &c. (Blount, *Law Dict.* 1691).

underwrite. Transl. of *subscribe* (q.v.); cf. Ger. *unterschreiben*, "to subscribe, underwrite, or sign" (Ludw.). It occurs in *Piers Plowm.* in orig. sense. Now esp. to sign a marine insurance policy.

undies [*neol.*]. For *underclothing*. Cf. *nighty* for *nightgown*.

undine. ModL. *undina*, from *unda*, wave. Popularized by the Ger. romance *Undine* (1811) by La Motte Fouqué.

undo. For spec. sense of bringing destruction upon cf. *defeat*.

undose [*biol.*]. L. *undosus*, from *unda*, wave.

undulate. From L. *undulare*, from *undula*, dim. of *unda*, wave.

unearth. ? Orig. from fox-hunting, ? or treasure-seeking. Cf. F. *déterrer*.

unexceptionable. From spec. sense of *exception* (see *except*).

unfortunate. In noun sense in Grose (18 cent.).

unfrock. From *frock* in spec. sense of priestly garb.

ungainly. Orig. unfit, improper. From ME. *ungein*, from ON. *gegn*, convenient, etc., cogn. with *gegna*, to meet, suit, and with *again*. For sense-development cf. *untoward*.

ungual. From L. *unguis*, nail, talon.

unguent. L. *unguentum*, from *unguere*, to anoint. Cf. F. *onguent*.

ungulate. From L. *ungula*, hoof, talon, dim. of *unguis*, nail.

unhand. In theat. sense, *Unhand me, villain*, etc., an echo of Shaks.

> Unhand me, gentlemen.
> By Heaven, I'll make a ghost of him that lets
> [= hinders] me (*Haml.* i. 4).

unhealthy. Euph. (Great War) for region specially exposed to fire.

unhinged. For fig. sense see *hook*.

> Airy subtleties in religion which have unhinged the brains of better heads (Sir T. Browne).

uni-. From L. *unus*, one. Cf. *mono-*.

Uniate. Member of Oriental Christian Church acknowledging Papal supremacy. Russ., from L. *unus*, one.

unicorn. L. *unicornis*, from *uni-* and *cornu*, horn. Cf. synon. G. μονόκερως. The Bibl. *unicorn* (*Deut.* xxxiii. 17) is a mistransl. of Heb. *re'ēm*, aurochs, and is altered to *wild-ox* in *RV*.

uniform. F. *uniforme*, L. *uniformis*, from *uni-* and *forma*, form. Mil. sense is for *uniform coat* (*dress*). Hence *uniformity*, in 17 cent. esp. of rel. conformity.

unify. F. *unifier*, Late L. *unificare*, from L. *unus*, one; cf. It. *unificare*, Sp. *unificar*.

Unigenitus [*hist.*]. L., only begotten, init. word of bull directed by Clement XI against Jansenism (1713).

union. F., L. *unio-n-*, from *unus*, one. Also of workhouse supported by several parishes. The *Union Flag* (incorr. *Jack*) symbolizes the union of England, Scotland and Ireland by combining the crosses of St George, St Andrew and St Patrick. *Unionist*, as party title, came into use after Gladstone's Home-Rule bill (1886). See also *trade*.

> The unionist principle that the better workers must not discredit the worse by exceeding them in efficiency (Herbert Spencer).

unique. F., L. *unicus*, from *unus*, one. Sense has strengthened in E.

unison. F. *unisson*, L. *unisonus*, from *uni-* and *sonus*, sound; cf. It. *unisono*, Sp. *unisón*.

unit. Shortened from *unity*. Cf. *defile*².

Unitarian. Ending perh. suggested by *Arian*, with which it is almost synon. Not in Johns.

> *unitarians*: a numerous sect holding one God without plurality or distinction of persons
> (*Dict. Cant. Crew*).

unite. From L. *unire*, *unit-*, from *unus*, one. *The United States* is for earlier (1777) *The States* (Adams).

unity. F. *unité*, L. *unitas*, from *unus*, one; cf. It. *unità*, Sp. *unidad*. The *dramatic unities* (of time, place, action) appear in 17 cent. F.

universe. F. *univers*, L. *universum*, neut. of *universus*, lit. turned to one, from *vertere*, *vers-*, to turn. L. *universitas*, whole, the state in gen., the world, was also used of a corporation or organized body, mod. sense of *university* being tinged with the idea of universal learning. The first univ. was prob. that of Salerno.

unkempt. Lit. uncombed, from p.p. of AS. *cemban*, to comb (q.v.). Cf. *uncouth*.

> *hure*: a staring, horrid, unkembed, or ill-kept, pate of haire (Cotg.).

unless. For *on less*, earlier *on lesse that*; cf. F. *à moins que*.

unloose. Here *un-* has purely intens. force, as in one sense of *unravel*.

unmentionables. Cf. *inexpressibles* and Calverley's *crurum non enarrabile tegmen* (*Carm. Saec.*). In Hotten also *unutterables*, *unwhisperables*.

unmuzzle. Fig. sense dates from Shaks. Used 1865 by Gladstone of politician no longer restrained by offic. position.

> Ay, marry, now unmuzzle your wisdom
> (*As You Like It*, i. 2).

unorthodoxy. See *doxy*².

> Calvin made roast meat of Servetus for his unorthodoxy (T. Brown).

unpaid, great. The voluntary magistrates as distinguished from stipendiary magistrates.

unquestionably. In philology usu. in ref. to some hazy recollection of an amateur theory propounded in the "correspondence column."

> Dreyfus has nothing to do with "tripod." It comes unquestionably from the city of Trèves
> (*Obs.* Dec. 31, 1916).

> "Odds" is unquestionably a corruption of "orts"
> (*Daily Chron.* Feb. 27, 1918).

unready. In hist. application to Ethelred II preserves fuller orig. sense. Cf. AS. *ungerǣd*, ill-advised.

unreliable. A word coined by Coleridge, to which ignorant objections are often made. De Quincey suggests, "as more correct English," *unrelyuponable*.

unruly. From obs. *ruly*, from *rule*. Cf. *uncouth*, *unkempt*.

> These notable examples of justice have since held us in much better termes of ruly obedience
> (*Purch.* xvi. 67).

> The tongue can no man tame; it is an unruly evil
> (*James*, iii. 8).

unsex. ? A Shaks. coinage.

> Come, you spirits
> That tend on mortal thoughts, unsex me here
> (*Macb.* i. 5).

unsoaped. First in Dickens. Cf. *unwashed*.

> The unsoaped of Ipswich brought up the rear
> (*Pickwick*, ch. xxiv.).

unspeakable. Orig. unutterable, ineffable (1 *Peter*, i. 8), now usu. disparaging, e.g. the *unspeakable Turk* (Carlyle, *Daily News*, Nov. 28, 1876).

unstrung. Now usu. felt as mus. metaphor, but perh. orig. of bow (see *string*).

until. For *unto*, with substitution of northern *till²* (q.v.).

untim(e)ous [*archaic*]. From Sc. *tim(e)ous*, a leg. term coined on *righteous*. App. revived by Scott.

unto. For *und-to*, with first element cogn. with OSax. *und*, OHG. *unz*, Goth. *und*, and with *un-²*.

untoward. See *toward*, and for sense cf. *froward*, for which it is a kind of euph., like *untruth* for *lie*.

untruth. In sense of lie app. due to Dogberry. But in Chauc. (B. 687) in sense of unfaithfulness.

> Moreover, they have spoken untruths
> (*Much Ado*, v. 1).

unvarnished. An echo of *Oth.* i. 3.

unwashed. Used by Shaks. of artisans (v.i.), now esp. in the *great unwashed*, the rabble.

> Another lean, unwash'd artificer
> (*King John*, iv. 2).

unwieldy. From obs. *wieldy*, of which orig. sense was powerful, capable of wielding.

> Ther was greet showvyng, bothe to and fro,
> To lifte hym up, and muchel care and wo,
> So unweeldy was this sory, palled goost
> (*Chauc.* H. 53).

unwieldy: inhabilis (Litt.).

unwritten law. Orig. law approved by

practice or judicial decision, though not in statute form. Applied to right of private vengeance in US.

up. AS. *upp*, *ūp* (adv.). Com. Teut.; cf. Du. *op*, Ger. *auf*, ON. *upp*, Goth. *iup*; cogn. with *over* and with G. ὑπό. To get *the upper hand* is from wrestling.

uppish: rampant, crowing, full of money
(*Dict. Cant. Crew*).

> An absolutely up-to-the-moment drama
> (*Advt.* Dec. 1918).

upas. Malay, poison. The use of the Javan poison tree, *pōhun ūpas*, for poisoning darts is described by Friar Odoric (14 cent.), but the fable of its deadly influence first appeared in the *London Magazine* (1783), and was popularized by Erasmus Darwin in his *Loves of the Plants* (1789). For a similar myth cf. *juggernaut*.

upbraid. App. from *up* and *braid* (q.v.), with idea of "taking up (sharply)." Cogn. ON. *bregtha*, Dan. *bebreide* have the same fig. sense. A parallel form *unbraide* is common in Tudor E.

upheaval. Fig. sense is from geol., in which it is the opposite of *subsidence*.

upholster. First as noun, for *upholdster*, from *upholder*, in ME. a broker, used in *Piers Plowm.* of the traders of Cornhill. For lengthened *upholsterer* cf. *fruiterer*, *caterer*, etc. For mod. limitation of sense cf. *stationer*, *undertaker*. Current sense perh. affected by Ger. *polstern*, to pad, cushion, etc., cogn. with *bolster*.

upholdere that sellyth smale thyngis: velaber
(*Prompt. Parv.*).
upholstar: frippier (Palsg.).
upholster: tapetiarius, plumarius (Litt.).

uphroe, euphroe [*naut.*]. Kind of block. Du. *juffrouw*, lit. young woman, maiden. See *gasket*.

upon. AS. *uppon*, up on.

upright. AS. *ūpriht*. For fig. sense cf. cogn. Ger. *aufrecht*, *aufrichtig*.

uproar. Du. *oproer*, from *op*, up, and *roeren*, to stir, which is cogn. with AS. *hrēran*, to move, Ger. *rühren*, to stir, ON. *hrōra*. So also Ger. *aufruhr*, "an uproar, sedition, tumult" (Ludw.). Unconnected with *roar* (q.v.), though the two have been associated. See also *rearmouse*.

> Ther was a gret up-rore and showtyng at ys sermon
> (*Machyn's Diary*, 1550–63).

upset. ME. *upsetten* means to set up, fix. Mod. sense seems to be due to obs. *overset*, to capsize.

upshot. ? Orig. in sense of target, thing shot at (archery).

I [aye] there's the but; whose h[e]art-white if we hit,
The game is our's. Well we may rage and rove
At Gloster, Lancaster, Chester, Faukenbridge,
But he is the upshot (*Look about you*, 1600).

upside-down. For ME. *up-so-down*, up as though down. Cf. *topsy-turvy* and F. *sens dessus dessous*, where *sens* is for *sen*, *s'en* (Cotg.), app. for *si en*. See quot. s.v. *amiss*.

And he turnyde upsadoun the bordis of chaungeris
(Wyc. *Matt.* xxi. 12).

s'en dessus, dessoubs: upside-downe, topsie turvy
(Cotg.).

upstart. ME. has *startup* in same sense, still surviving as surname. A *Stephen Stertup* is mentioned in the *Pipe Rolls* (12 cent.). Shaks. uses both forms (*Much Ado*, i. 3, 1 *Hen. VI*, iv. 7).

upward(s). See *up* and *-ward*. Often misused in sense of nearly, approaching.

I am a very foolish, fond old man,
Fourscore and upward (*Lear*, iv. 7).

uraemia [*med.*]. From G. οὖρον, urine, αἷμα, blood.

uraeus [*antiq.*]. Head-dress of Egypt. kings. G. οὐραῖος, from οὐρά, tail.

Ural-Altaic [*ling.*]. Finno-Ugrian. From *Ural* and *Altai* mountains. The chief langs. of the group are Finnish and Magyar (Hung.).

uranium [*chem.*]. Discovered (1789) by Klaproth and named after the planet *Uranus* in compliment to Herschel (v.i.).

urano-. From G. οὐρανός, heaven, also (myth.) the father of Saturn, and given as name to planet discovered by Herschel (1781). Cf. *Urania*, muse of astronomy.

urban-e. L. *urbanus*, "of a citie, dwelling in a citie, civile, curteise" (Coop.), from *urbs*, city. For sense of *urbane*, the older form, cf. *civil* and the contrasted *boorish, churlish*. For differentiated spelling and sense cf. *human-e*.

urceolate [*bot.*]. From L. *urceolus*, dim. of *urceus*, pitcher.

urchin. ME. *irchoun*, orig. hedgehog, then, goblin, small boy, ONF. *herichun* (*hérisson*), VL. *(h)ericio-n-*, for *ericius*, cogn. with G. χήρ, hedgehog. The sea-urchin is also in F. *oursin*, as though from *ours*, bear (cf. *ourson*, bear-cub), and this may have affected the E. word. Wyc. (*Is.* xiv. 23) has *irchoun* (*Vulg. ericius*), where Coverd. has *otter* and *AV. bittern*!

herisson de mer: the sea urchin; a fish whose outside somewhat resembles the land-urchin (Cotg.).

Urdu [*ling.*]. Hindustani, the lingua franca of India, a mixture of the vernaculars descended from Sanskrit with the langs. of various invaders (Arab., Pers., Mongol). For *zabān-i-urdū*, language of the camp, horde (q.v.).

Urdu-zabán, camp language, is the proper name of Hindustani, formed in the armies of the Mogul Emperors (Max Müller).

urea [*chem.*]. From G. οὖρον, urine.

ureter, urethra [*anat.*]. From G. οὐρεῖν, to urinate.

urge. L. *urgēre*, cogn. with G. εἴργειν, to shut, compress, and ult. with *wrick*.

uric [*med.*]. From G. οὖρον, urine.

Urim and Thummim [*Bibl.*]. Ornaments of high-priest's breastplate (*Ex.* xxviii. 30). Heb., lights and perfections.

Pones autem in rationali judicii doctrinam et veritatem, quae erunt in pectore Aaron
(*Vulg. Ex.* xxviii. 30).

urine. F., L. *urina*, cogn. with G. οὖρον.

urman [*geog.*]. Tract of coniferous forest in Siberia. Of Tatar origin.

urn. F. *urne*, L. *urna*, orig. vessel of burnt clay; ? cogn. with *urere*, to burn.

urochs. See *aurochs*.

Ursa Major, Minor [*astron.*]. L., Greater (Smaller) Bear.

ursine. L. *ursinus*, of the bear, *ursus*.

Ursuline. Order of nuns (founded 1537) named from *St Ursula* of Cologne.

urticate [*med.*]. To sting like a nettle, L. *urtica*.

urubu. Black vulture. Native Central Amer. name.

urus. See *aurochs*.

us. AS. *ūs* (dat.); cf. Du. *ons*, Ger. *uns*, ON. *oss*, Goth. *uns*. AS. had also acc. *ūsic* (cf. OHG. *unsich*, Goth. *unsis*).

use. The noun is archaic F. *us* (in *us et coutumes*), L. *usus*, from *uti, us-*, to use. The verb is F. *user* (in ModF. to wear out, use up), VL. **usare*, for *uti*. Leg. sense of benefit, enjoyment (of property, etc.) has been affected by OF. *ues*, profit, advantage, L. *opus*, but L. *usus* has this sense also, e.g. *pecuniam publicam in usus suos convertere*. Leg. *user* is the F. infin. (cf. *misnomer, rejoinder*, etc.). Pronunc. of *used to* (*ust*) is due to the *t-* of *to*.

usher. OF. *uissier* (*huissier*), door-keeper, from *uis* (*huis*), door, L. *ostium*; the F. word now only in leg. *à huis clos*, in camera. Sense of assistant-master, peculiar to E., is as old as the 14 cent., the (*h*)*ostiarius* being duly provided for in the foundation deeds of Winchester.

usquebaugh [*archaic*]. Ir. *uisge beatha*, water of life. Cf. F. *eau-de-vie* and see *whisky*.

The prime is usquebaugh, which cannot be made anywhere in that perfection; and whereas we drink it here in *aqua vitae* measures, it goes down there by beer-glassfuls, being more natural to the [Irish] nation (Howell, 1634).

usual. L. *usualis*, from *usus*, use, custom.

usucaption, usucapion [*leg.*]. L. *usucapio-n-*, from *usucapere*, to take by prescription, use.

usufruct [*leg.*]. L. *ususfructus*, "the use and profite of another mans goodes, with the consent of the owner, the stocke or substance being saved" (Coop.), from *usu*, abl. governed by *frui, fruct-*, to enjoy.

usurp. F. *usurper*, L. *usurpare*, from *usu*, by profit, and *rapere*, to seize.

usury[1]. Interest on money. From F. *usure*, L. *usura*, from *uti, us-*, to use, derive benefit from.

usury[2] [*neol.*]. Adaptation of F. *usure*, wear and tear, loss, from *user*, to wear out (see *use*).

The usury of enemy strength has certainly been greater than last year
                              (*Daily Chron.* Nov. 21, 1917).

ut [*mus.*]. Now usu. replaced by *do*. See *gamut*.

utensil. L. *utensilis*, from *uti*, to use. Hence also F. *outil*, tool, and *outillement*, tools, plant, utensils collectively.

uterus [*anat.*]. L., cogn. with G. ὑστέρα.

utility. F. *utilité*, L. *utilitas*, from *utilis*, useful, from *uti*, to use. E. *utilitarian*, F. *utilitaire* are 19 cent., dating from the *Utilitarian Society*, founded by Mill 1822–3. ? Coined by Bentham.

I told my people that I thought they had more sense than to secede from Christianity to become Utilitarians (Galt, *Annals*, ch. xxxv.).
I did not invent the word, but found it in one of Galt's novels, "The Annals of the Parish"
                                            (J. S. Mill).

uti possidetis. L., as you possess.

utmost. Double superl. from AS. *ūt*, out. See *-most*. For sense cf. *extreme*.

Ne gǣst thū thanone, ǣr thū āgylde thone ytemestan [Wyc. last, Tynd. utmost] fēorthlinge
                              (AS. *Gosp. Matt.* v. 26).

Utopia. Title of Sir T. More's imaginary country (1516), from G. οὐ, not, τόπος, place. Widely adopted in Europ. langs.

Utraquist [*hist.*]. Hussite sect claiming communion in both kinds, *sub utraque specie*.

utricle [*biol.*]. F., L. *utriculus*, dim. of *uter*, leather bag, wine-skin.

utter[1]. Adj. AS. *uttera*, compar. from *ūt*, out. *Uttermost* is for earlier *utmost* (q.v.).

utter[2]. Verb. ME. *uttren*, from adv. *utter*; cf. Ger. *äussern*, to utter, express, from *aus*, out; cf. "out with it." AS. had *ūtian*, to expel. To *utter base coin* is a figure something like that of "releasing" films (see *release*). The verb was formerly used of retailing (see *vent*[2]).

They been gretely hurted and in grete damage in utterance and sellynge of their marchandise
                              (*York Merch. Advent.* 1478).
debiter: to sell, or utter by parcels, to passe away by retaile (Cotg.).

utterance [*archaic*]. F. *outrance*, as in *combat à outrance*, from *outre*, beyond, L. *ultra*. Chiefly as echo of *Macb.* iii. 1.

This battle was fought so farre forth to the utterance, that, after a wonderfull slaughter on both sides, when that theyr swordes and other weapons were spent, they buckled togither with short daggers (Holinshed).

uvula [*anat.*]. ModL., dim. of *uva*, bunch of grapes.

uxorious. From L. *uxorius*, from *uxor*, wife.

v-. There are, apart from dial., no words in *v-* of AS. origin, exc. *vane, vat, vixen*, which are southern vars. of *f-* forms. On the obs. Cockney confusion between *w-* and *v-* see Messrs Weller passim, and cf. quot. below. Machyn's *Diary* (1550–63) has *wacabond, welvet, volsake, vomen*, etc., and in 1573 an inhabitant of Nottingham got into trouble for "becallyng the constabelles knaves and 'wellanttes'" (cf. *warmint* for *vermin*). See also *wear*[2].

Villiam, I vants my vig....Vitch vig, sir? Vy, the vite vig in the vooden vig-box, vitch I vore last Vensday at the westry (Pegge, 1803).

V. Five. The Roman symbol for the number.

vac. For *vacation*. Recorded for 1709. Cf. *mob, cit*, etc., of same period.

vacant. F., from pres. part. of L. *vacare*, to be empty, *vacuus*. Cf. *vacancy, vacate, vacation*, the last used by Chauc. in sense of release from activity.

vaccine. L. *vaccinus*, from *vacca*, cow, used (1798) by Jenner in *variolae vaccinae*, cowpox. Hence *vaccination* (1800), adopted by F. and other langs., which replaced earlier inoculation (q.v.).

The small pox is here [at Adrianople] entirely harmless by the invention of *ingrafting*, which is the term they give it (Lady M. Montagu, 1717).

vaccinium [*bot.*]. L., bilberry.

vacillate. From L. *vacillare*, "to wagge or waver, to be lewse" (Coop.).

vacuum. L., neut. of *vacuus*, empty. *Nature abhors a vacuum* was the early scientists' explanation of phenomena now known to be due to atmospheric pressure.

vade-mecum. L., go with me.

vagabond. F., L. *vagabundus*, from *vagari*, to wander.

vagary. Orig. (16 cent.) wandering, roaming, etc. Current sense via that of mental wandering, divagation. App. from L. *vagari*, to wander, though the nature of the borrowing is abnormal. In 17 cent. often *fegary*, *figary*.

They long'd for a vagarie into the country
(*Eastward Hoe*, iii. 2).

vagina [*anat.*]. L., sheath.

vagrant. ME. *vagaraunt*, AF. *wakerant*, very common in rules and enactments, OF. *walcrant*, *waucrant*, pres. part. of *walcrer*, to wander, app. of Teut. origin and cogn. with *walk*. Change of *w-* to *v-* is due to influence of *vagabond*.

Que nulle soit trové wakeraunt apres Curfeu soné a Seynt Martin (*Lib. Albus*, 640).

vague. F., L. *vagus*, wandering. But in some senses, e.g. *into the vague, vague of waters*, it corresponds rather to F. *vague* in *le vague des cieux, terrain vague*, No-man's-land, which is L. *vacuus*, empty.

vail[1] [*archaic*]. To lower, descend. Aphet. for obs. *avale*, F. *avaler*, from *ad vallem*, to the valley, downhill (cf. *amount*).

She charged us to strike our sailes for the King of Spaine and vail the bonnet according to the prerogative they had in these seas (Purch. xix. 137).

vail[2] [*archaic*]. Gratuity. Aphet. for *avail* (q.v.), in sense of profit, perquisite, esp. as received by servants.

vain. F., L. *vanus*, empty, vain. *Vainglory* (13 cent.) is adapted from MedL. *vana gloria*.

vair [*her.*]. Fur, orig. of grey and white squirrel. F., L. *varius*, "of divers colours or facions" (Coop.). Cf. *miniver*.

vakeel [*Anglo-Ind.*]. Agent, representative. Urdu *vakīl*, from Pers. Arab.

valance. App. a pl. form (cf. *bodice*) of unrecorded **valant*, from F. *avaler*, to descend (see *vail*[1]). Cf. F. *pentes*, "valance" (Cotg.), from *pendre*, to hang.

Two pilloo coddes with the valandes
(*Yorks Will*, 1512).

A field-bed of walnut tree, with the canopy, valens, curtaines, and gilt knops (Hakl. xi. 33).

Now are my valence up
(Marston, *What you will*, iii. 1).

I give and bequeath to Jane Colle a suite of wrought curtaines and vallance
(*Will of Dame Mary Saunders, of Maplestead, Essex*, 1668).

The valans of the [book-]shelves being of greene velvet, fring'd with gold (Evelyn).

vale. F. *val*, L. *vallis*; cf. It. Sp. *valle*. Now only poet., e.g. *vale of tears* (*misery*, etc.), or in place-names.

valediction. From L. *valedicere*, to say farewell, *vale*, imper. of *valēre*, to be strong, prosper.

valenciennes. Lace, from place of origin (Nord).

valentine. Orig. person of opposite sex chosen as sweetheart on day of *St Valentine* (Feb. 14), when birds were supposed to mate.

For this was on Seynt Valentynes day
Whan every bryd cometh ther to chese his make
(Chauc. *Parl. Foules*, 309).

valerian. F. *valériane*; cf. It. Sp. MedL. *valeriana*, app. from pers. name *Valerius*; but some of the Ger. & Scand. forms of the name point rather to connection with the saga-hero *Wieland*.

valet. F., OF. *vaslet*, *varlet*, dim. of *vassal* (q.v.). Now usu. as short for *valet de chambre*, gen. sense of F. *valet*, "a groome, yeoman, or household servant of the meaner sort" (Cotg.), being represented by var. *varlet* (q.v.). This is a degeneration from the OF. sense of noble page, young squire, etc.

valetudinary. L. *valetudinarius*, "subject to sickenesse, often sicke, queasie" (Coop.), from *valetudo*, state of health, from *valēre*, to be well.

Valhalla. From ON. *Valhöll*, *Valhall-*, hall of those slain in battle. Cf. AS. *wæl*, slaughter, bodies of slain warriors, and poet. Ger. *wahlstatt*, battle-field. Kluge suggests connection with OHG. *wuol*, overthrow, AS. *wōl*, pestilence. *Valhalla* was introduced by 18 cent. antiquaries (cf. *norn*, *rune*, etc.). See also *Valkyrie*.

vali. Turk. governor. See *wali*.

valiant. F. *vaillant*, OF. pres. part. of *valoir*, to be worth, L. *valēre*. Orig. sense survives in F. *n'avoir pas un sou vaillant*.

valid. F. *valide*, L. *validus*, strong, from *valēre*, to be strong, well.

valise. F., It. *valigia*, "a male, a cloke-bag, a budget, a portmanteaw" (Flor.); cf. Sp. *balija*, MedL. *valesia* (13 cent.). Origin unknown. Synon. Ger. *felleisen*, as though leather-iron, is folk-etym.

Valkyrie [*poet.*]. One of twelve war-maidens hovering over battle-field and conducting the fallen to Valhalla. ON. *valkyrja*, dead chooser, with first element as in *Valhalla* (q.v.), second from stem of *kjōsa*, to choose. Cf. AS. *wælcyri(g)e*, sorceress. *Valkyrie* was introduced with *Valhalla*, both first in Gray's notes to his *Fatal Sisters* (1768).

valley. F. *vallée*, from *val*, vale; cf. It. *vallata*. Has largely replaced native *dean²*, dale.

vallonia. See *valonia*.

vallota. Plant. From *Vallot*, F. botanist (†1671).

vallum. L., "a bulwarke or rampire" (Coop.), from *vallus*, stake, palisade.

valonia. Acorn used in tanning. It. *vallonia*, ModG. βαλανία, from G. βάλανος, acorn.

valour. F. *valeur*, worth, valour, L. *valor-em*, from *valēre*, to be worth, etc. Sense of value is common in ME.

valse. F. form of *waltz* (q.v.).

value. First (c. 1300) as noun. F., p.p. fem. of *valoir*, to be worth, L. *valēre*. Cf. *issue*. For sense-development cf. *esteem*. Current use in "intellectual" jargon is from lang. of painting.

We apologize to Mr Wells for using the word "values," since he dislikes it
(*Times Lit. Sup.* June 5, 1919).

The hooligan sees none of the values of the stranger
(H. G. Wells, *Obs.* Jan. 18, 1920).

valve. L. *valva*, leaf of folding-door, usu. in pl., ? cogn. with *volvere*, to roll.

vambrace [*hist.*]. Guard for fore-arm. Earlier *vaunt-brace*, F. *avant-bras*. Cf. *van¹*.

vamose, vamoose [*US.*]. Sp. *vamos*, let us go, from L. *vadere*. Cf. *absquatulate*, *skedaddle*.

vamp. ME. *vampey*, OF. *avanpié* (*avant pied*), part of foot-gear covering front of foot. Hence to *vamp*, patch (shoes), fig. to patch up (literary work, a mus. accompaniment, etc.). Cf. *vambrace*, *van¹*.

vampey of a hose: avant pied (Palsg.).

It being a new play, or an old one new vamped, by Shadwell (Pepys, Feb. 25, 1669).

vamp: superior pars calcei (Litt.); *to vamp*: interpolo, refarcio (*ib.*).

vampire. F., Magyar *vampir*, found also in all the Slav. langs. Adopted by most Europ. langs., first in Ger. (1732), in an account of the Hungarian vampires. Such

vars. as Russ. *upir*, Pol. *upior*, seem to point to Turk. *uber*, witch. Also applied to a SAmer. blood-sucking bat.

vamplate [*hist.*]. Hand-guard for tilting lance. From *plate*, with prefix as in *vambrace* (q.v.).

van¹. Short for *vanguard*, F. *avant-garde*, "the forward, or vaunt-guard, of an armie" (Cotg.). See *vambrace*, *vamp*, and cf. *vaunt-courier*.

van². Vehicle. For *caravan* (q.v.). Cf. *bus*, *wig*, *loo*.

van³ [*archaic & poet.*]. For *fan* (q.v.). Either a southern dial. var., or adopted from cogn. F. *van*, "a vanne, or winnowing sive" (Cotg.).

vanadium [*chem.*]. Named (1830) by Sw. chemist Sefström from ON. *Vanadīs*, one of the names of goddess Freyja.

Vandal. L. *Vandalus*; cf. AS. *Wendlas* (pl.), ON. *Vendill*, a Ger. tribe. As opprobrious epithet since Genseric's sack of Rome (455). Cf. *Goth*, *Hun*.

Vandyke. In *Vandyke beard* (*brown, collar*, etc.). From *A. Van Dyck*, Flem. painter (†1641). Cf. *Gainsborough hat*. Hence verb to *vandyke*, mark with deep indentations, like a Vandyke collar.

vane. Southern var. of obs. *fane*, AS. *fana*, flag. Com. Teut.; cf. OSax. *fano*, Ger. *fahne*, ON. *-fāni* (in *gunn-fāni*, gonfalon), Goth. *fana*. Cf. Ger. *wetterfähnlein*, "a fane or weather-cock, at the top steeple" (Ludw.).

vang [*naut.*]. Rope for steadying gaff. of synon. *fang*, with sense of catch, or fr cogn. Du. *vang*.

vanguard. See *van¹*.

vanilla. Sp. *vainilla*, dim. of *vaina*, pod, *vagina*, sheath.

vanish. Aphet. for obs. *evanish*, OF. *esvanir*, *esvaniss-* (*évanouir*), from VL. **exvanescere*, for *evanescere*, from *vanus*, empty.

vanity. F. *vanité*, L. *vanitas*, from *vanus*, empty.

The name of that town is Vanity; and at the town there is a fair kept, called Vanity Fair (Bunyan).

van John. Univ. slang (? obs.) for *vingt-et-un*.

vanquish. OF. *vainquir*, *vainquiss-*, var. of *vaincre*, to conquer, OF. *veincre*, L. *vincere*.

vantage. Aphet. for *advantage* (q.v.), esp. in *coign* (q.v.) *of vantage* and in lawn-tennis.

vant-brace [*archaic*]. See *vambrace*.

vapid. L. *vapidus*, "that giveth an ill smacke, that casteth a vapour of an ill savour" (Coop.). Cf. *vappa*, "wyne that hath lost the vertue" (*ib.*).

vapour. F. *vapeur*, L. *vapor-em* (v.s.). With archaic *vapours*, hysteria, etc., from early physiology, cf. *humour*. With *vapour*, boast, etc., very common in 17 cent., cf. mod. to *gas*.

You can do most things with the Briton if you do not approach him in the temper of a nursery governess with the vapours (L. Harcourt, Aug. 1918).

vapulatory. From L. *vapulare*, to be beaten.

vaquero. Sp., cow-boy, from *vaca*, cow, L. *vacca*.

Varangian [*hist.*]. Norse rover (9–10 cent.) reaching Constantinople via Russia, member of body-guard of Byzantine Emperors (see *Count Robert of Paris*). From MedL. *Varangus*, MedG. Βάραγγος, via Slav., from ON. *Vǣringi*, from *vār*, plighted faith (only in pl. *vārar*), cogn. with Ger. *wahr*, true, L. *verus*, OIr. *fír*.

varech. Sea-weed. F., from Scand., cogn. with *wreck*.

variance. OF., L. *variantia*, from *variare*, to vary (q.v.). This is in E. the oldest word of the group. With to *be at variance* cf. to *be at odds* and spec. sense of *difference*.

variant. In ling. applied to a parallel form, e.g. *burden, burthen, tone, tune*, while, in this Dict., *variation* is used for a (usu. playful) elaboration or imitation of phrase, e.g. to *confiscate the macaroon* (take the cake), *where Maggie wore the beads* (in the neck), etc.

varicose. L. *varicosus*, from *varix, varic-*, "a crooked veine swelling with melancholy bloud in the temples, belly, or legges" (Coop.), cogn. with *varus*, "that hath crooked legges; that hath spottes in the face" (*ib.*), whence L. name *Varus*.

variegate. From L. *variegare*, from *varius*.

variola [*med.*]. Smallpox. From L. *varius*. Cf. F. *variole, petite vérole*, and see *vair*.

variorum. L., of various (commentators), for *editio cum notis variorum*.

varlet. Archaic F., noble page, var. of OF. *vaslet*, valet (q.v.). For degeneration in E. cf. *knave*.

varnish. F. *vernis*; cf. It. *vernice*, Sp. *barniz*, MedL. *vernicium, vernix*, MedG. βερνίκη; also Ger. *firniss*, Du. *vernis*, Dan. *fernis*, etc., from F. Earliest (8 cent.) is Late L. *veronix*, of unknown origin. The *varnishing days* of the Royal Academy were instituted in 1809. With fig. sense cf. to *gloss*.

varsity. Aphet. for *university*.

Wee'l down with all the versities
Where learning is profest (*Rump Song*, c. 1640).

varsovienne. F. (sc. *danse*), from *Varsovie*, Warsaw.

vary. F. *varier*, L. *variare*, from *varius*, various. Cf. *vair*.

vascular. From L. *vasculum*, dim. of *vas*, vessel, vase.

vase. F., L. *vas* (v.s.), with sense restricted in E. In US. still usu. pronounced as by the author's father (†1920 aetat. 85).

Her boudoir, a sweet place,
For love or breakfast; private, pleasing, lone,
And rich with all contrivances which grace
Those gay recesses:—many a precious stone
Sparkled along its roof, and many a vase
(*Don Juan*, vi. 97).

vaseline. Trade-name coined (c. 1874) from Ger. *wasser*, water, G. ἔλαιον, oil, and -*ine*!

vassal. F., adherent, warrior; cf. It. *vassallo*, Sp. *vasallo*, MedL. *vassallus*, dim. of *vassus*. Of Celt. origin; cf. Welsh *gwas*, OIr. *fos*, Breton *goaz*, servant, and Gaulish -*vassus*, in names. See *valet, varlet, vavasour*. In OF. & ME. a complimentary term, e.g. *vasselage*, warlike prowess, is contrasted with *vilenie*.

vast. L. *vastus*, "great beyond measure, huge, sometyme desolate" (Coop.), cogn. with *waste* (cf. *devastate*). From 16 cent. and very popular in 17–18 cents., e.g. *vastly obliged*, etc. The extended *vasty* is an echo of Shaks. (1 *Hen. IV*, iii. 1).

vat. Southern var. of Bibl. *fat* (*Mark*, xii. 1). AS. *fæt*, cask. Com. Teut.; cf. Du. *vat*, Ger. *fass*, ON. *fat*; cogn. with Ger. *fassen*, to hold, contain. For v- cf. *vane, vixen*.

Vatican. L. *Vaticanus* (sc. *collis, mons*), hill on which Papal palace stands. Cf. F. *Vatican*, It. Sp. *Vaticano*. The *Vatican* is theoretically an independent sovereignty.

Whether the Sultan as Caliph, shall remain head of a Vatican area in Constantinople and keep a camouflage-sovereignty (*Obs.* Jan. 11, 1920).

vaticinate. From L. *vaticinari*, to prophesy, from *vates*, prophet, -*cinere* (*canere*), to sing.

vaudeville. F., earlier *vau-de-vire*, light popular song such as those ascribed to Olivier Basselin (15 cent.), inhabitant of the valley of *Vire* (Calvados).

Vaudois. F., MedL. *Valdensis*. See *Waldenses*, *voodoo*.

vault¹. Noun. ME. *voute*, OF. *voute, volte* (*voûte*, arched roof), VL. **volta* (for *voluta*), from *volvere*, to turn. For restored -*l*- cf. *fault*. Cf. It. *volta*, "a vault, a cellar, an arche, a bent or bow" (Flor.).

vault². Verb. F. *volter*, "to vault, or tumble; also, to bound, or curvet; also, to turn, or make turn" (Cotg.), from *volte*, It. *volta*, "the turne that cunning riders teach their horses" (Flor.). In E. applied to mode of mounting horse (v.i.), orig. connection with horsemanship appearing in gymn. *vaulting-horse*. Etym. as for *vault¹*. See *Macb.* i. 7.

desultor: a vaulter that leapeth up and doune from an horse (Coop.).

vaunt. Partly aphet. for obs. *avaunt*, OF. *avanter*, to put forward, from *avant*, L. *ab ante*; partly F. *vanter*, to praise, extol (whence *se vanter*, to boast), OF. also *venter*, L. *venditare*, "to do any thing before men to set forth him selfe and have a prayse; to vaunt, to crake, to brag" (Coop.), lit. to push one's wares, frequent. of *vendere*, to sell. Cf. It. *vantarsi*, "to boast, to bragge, to glorie, to vante, to crake" (Flor.), where *vantare* is aphet. for *avantare*, "to brag, to boast, to glorie, to crake, to vaunt" (Flor.), from *avante*, before. The derivation usu. given, from Late L. *vanitare* (Augustine), disregards the hist. of the word, which has reached its present use via the reflex. sense (in OF. & ME.) of putting oneself forward, praising oneself.

Ki traïst altre, nen est dreiz qu'il s'en vant
(*Rol.* 3974).

Their maister wyll perchance avaunte hym selfe to be a good philosopher (Elyot, *Governour*, i. 167).

institor: a marchaunts factour. *Institor eloquentiae*: a marchant of eloquence, a vaunter or setter forth of eloquence (Coop.).

Charity vaunteth not itself, is not puffed up
(1 *Cor.* xiii. 4).

vaunt-courier [*archaic*]. Only as echo of *Lear*, iii. 2. F. *avant-coureur*, "a fore-runner, avant-curror" (Cotg.).

vavasour [*hist.*]. Feudal tenant ranking below baron. F. *vavasseur*, Merovingian L. *vassus vassorum*, vassal (q.v.) of vassals.

vaward [*archaic*]. Contr. of *vanward*, vanguard (see *van¹*).

veal. OF. *veel* (*veau*), L. *vitellus*, dim. of *vitulus*, calf, orig. yearling, cogn. with G. ἔτος, year, and with *wether*. For adoption of F. name cf. *beef, mutton, pork*. As name for animal still in 18 cent.

vector [*math.*]. L., agent. noun from *vehere*, *vect-*, to carry.

Veda. One of the four sacred books of the Hindus. Sanskrit *veda*, knowledge, sacred book, cogn. with L. *vidēre*, E. *wit*. Hence *Vedic*, early Sanskrit.

vedette, vidette [*mil.*]. F., It. *vedetta*, "a watch towre, a prying or peeping-hole" (Flor.), from *vedere*, to see. For sense-development, with change of gender, cf. *spy, scout, sentry, sentinel*.

veer¹ [*naut.*]. To let out rope. Du. LG. *vieren*, esp. in *den schoot vieren*, "to veer the sheets" (Sewel), cogn. with OHG. *fieren*, to give direction to.

haler un chable: to veere a cable; or let it out, or let it runne out (Cotg.).

veer². To turn. Also orig. naut., of the wind. Altered, after *veer¹*, from earlier *vire*, F. *virer* (12 cent.), "to veere, turne round, wheele or whirle about" (Cotg.); cf. It. *virare*, Sp. *virar*. Origin obscure. The same root appears in *environ* and *ferrule*. As OF. *virer* means also to direct, it may be from LG. *vieren* (see *veer¹*). See *wear²*.

vega [*geog.*]. Sp., fertile plain, ? VL. *vica*, from *vic-em*, turn, from rotation of crops.

vegetable. F. *végétable* (adj.), L. *vegetabilis*, from *vegetare*, "to quicken, to make lively and lusty" (Coop.), from *vegetus*, "quicke, sound, lusty, fresh, lively" (*ib.*), from *vegēre*, to be healthy, cogn. with *vigēre*, to flourish. Mod. sense of to *vegetate* is thus very far from orig. Currency of barbarously formed *vegetarian* dates from formation of Vegetarian Society at Ramsgate (1847).

vehement. F. *véhément*, L. *vehemens, -ment-*, explained by some as from *mens, ment-*, mind, with neg. prefix as in *vesanus*, insane. According to others from *vehere*, with idea of bearing onward.

vehicle. L. *vehiculum*, from *vehere*, to carry. Orig. (c. 1600) a means, medium, esp. in medicine.

Vehmgericht [*hist.*]. Secret tribunal in Westphalia (12–16 cents.). Older form of Ger. *Femgericht*, from MHG. *veime, veme*, judgment, of obscure origin; perh. cogn. with Du. *veem*, gild, league, whence *vennoot*, companion, for *veem-genoot*. See *Anne of Geierstein*, ch. xx.

veil. OF. (*voile*), L. *velum*, of which pl. *vela*, treated as fem. sing., gave *voile* (f.), sail, which is orig. sense of L. *velum*; cf. It. Sp. *velo*. Earliest in ref. to garb of nun, to *take the veil* occurring c. 1300. To *pass beyond the veil* is allusive to the Jewish *veil of the Temple*.

vein. F. *veine*, L. *vena*; cf. It. Sp. *vena*.

Thou troublest me; I am not in the vein
(*Rich. III*, iv. 3).

velar [*phonetics*]. Of the soft palate. L. *velaris*, from *velum*, curtain, veil. Cf. *velarium*, awning.

veldt [*SAfr.*]. Older form of Du. *veld*, field (q.v.). For SAfr. sense cf. *prairie*.

velitation. Skirmish, esp. fig. (archaic). L. *velitatio-n-*, from *velites*, pl. of *veles*, light-armed soldier.

velleity [*archaic*]. MedL. *velleitas*, coined after *voluntas*, from *velle*, to wish; cf. F. *velléité*, weak impulse.

velleity, or *woulding*: velleitas (Litt.).

vellum. F. *vélin*, from OF. *vel*, calf (see *veal*). For final *-m* cf. *venom*, *pilgrim*, perh. due to distant assim.; but E. prefers *-m* (cf. *grogram*).

velocity. F. *vélocité*, L. *velocitas*, from *velox*, *veloc-*, swift, ? cogn. with *volare*, to fly. *Velocipede* (? obs.) is F. *vélocipède*, from *velox* and *pes*, *ped-*, foot. "The Velocipede, or swift walker" is the title of an article in the *Observer* (Mar. 14, 1819). From shortened *vélo* is coined *vélodrome*, after *hippodrome*. Cf. more recent *aerodrome*.

velour-s. F., velvet (q.v.).

velvet. Ult. from L. *villus*, shaggy hair; cf. It. *velluto*, in Flor. *veluto*, "a stuffe of silke called velvet," Sp. *velludo*; also F. *velours*, OF. *velous*, L. *villosus*, shaggy. The *-v-* is app. a misreading of the *-u-* (for an opposite case cf. *Alured* for *Alvred*, Alfred) in AF. *veluet*, app. a dim. from F. *velu*, shaggy, VL. *villutus (whence It. Sp. forms above); cf. F. *velvote*, name of various woolly plants, for obs. *veluote*, *veluette*. As *u* only is used for *u*, *v* in medieval MSS., it is prob. that in all the earlier records *veluet* is trisyllabic (v.i.). *Velveteen* is 18 cent.

And by hire beddes heed she made a mewe,
And covered it with vel-u-ett-es blewe
(Chauc. F. 643).

The duchyes met with hym in a chare y-coveryd with blewe felewette (Gregory, *Chron.* 1460).

Not like our author, who is always on velvet, he is aware of some difficulties (Burke, 1769).

venal. L. *venalis*, from *venum*, that which is for sale. Cf. *vend*.

venatic. L. *venaticus*, from *venari*, to hunt. Cf. *venatorial*.

vend. F. *vendre*, L. *vendere*, for *venum dare*.

vendace. Confused, by erron. latinization of loc. *vangis*, with unrelated OF. *vendoise* (*vandoise*), "a dace or dare-fish" (Cotg.).

The annual custom of netting the Castle loch of Lochmaben for the vendace, fabled to have been introduced by Mary Queen of Scots from France (*Daily Chron.* Aug. 21, 1918).

Vendean [*hist.*]. F. *Vendéen*, esp. in ref. to the rising of *La Vendée* against the Republic (1793). Cf. *Chouan*.

vendetta. It., L. *vindicta*, vengeance. See *vindictive*.

veneer. For earlier (18 cent.) *fineer*, Ger. *furnieren*, "to inlay with various sorts of wood, to veneer" (Ebers' *Ger. Dict.* 1796), F. *fournir*, to furnish (q.v.).

venerable. F. *vénérable*, L. *venerabilis*, from *venerari*, to worship, from *venus*, *vener-*, love (cf. *venereal*). Orig. of distinguished ecclesiastics, e.g. Bede, now spec. of archdeacons. Also in ME. with ref. to dignity of age.

venereal. From L. *venereus*, from *venus*, *vener-* (v.s.).

venery[1] [*archaic*]. Hunting. Archaic F. *vénerie*, from OF. *vener*, to hunt, from L. *venari*. Cf. *venison*.

venery[2] [*med.*]. Sexual indulgence. From L. *venus*, *vener-*, sexual love.

venesection [*med.*]. From L. *vena*, vein, *sectio*, cutting. Cf. *phlebotomy*.

Venetian. Esp. in *venetian blind*, *Venetian School* (15–16 cents.). MedL. *Venetianus*, from *Venetia*, Venice. In ME. also *Venicien*, from OF.

vengeance. F., from *venger*, to avenge, L. *vindicare*, from *vindex*, *vindic-*, redresser of wrongs, etc., etym. sense of which appears in *vindicate* (q.v.). *With a vengeance* (cf. archaic *with a mischief*, *plague*, *pox*, etc.) is evolved from Tudor phrase *a vengeance on* (cf. *a mischief*, *plague*, *pox*, etc. *on*). Both sets of phrases are very common in Heywood (c. 1540). *Vengeful* is from archaic verb to *venge*.

A distinguished neutral calls it peace with a vengeance (*Obs.* May 11, 1919).

venial. OF. *venial* (*véniel*), Late L. *venialis*, from *venia*, pardon.

venire facias [*archaic leg.*]. Writ directing sheriff to summon jury. L., that thou make to come.

venison. F. *venaison*, L. *venatio-n-*, from *venari*, to hunt; cf. It. *venagione*, Sp. *venación*. Used in archaic *vert and venison* of game animals collectively.

Venite. L., come. First word of *Ps.* xcv., *Venite, exultemus Domino*.

venom. ME. *venim*, F. *venin*, from L. *venenum*, poison. For *-m* cf. *vellum*, but OF. *venim* (whence *venimeux*) points rather to VL. *venimen (? after *crimen*).

venous. L. *venosus*, from *vena*, vein.

vent[1]. Slit in back of coat. For earlier *fent*, F. *fente*, fissure, from *fendre*, L. *findere*, to cleave.

fent of a gowne: fente (Palsg.).

vent[2]. Orifice, outlet, emission. Partly from F. *vent*, wind (cf. L. *spiraculum*, vent-hole, from *spirare*, to breathe), partly from F. *évent*, exposure to air, from *éventer*, OF. *esventer*, "to puffe, blow, breathe, or yeeld wind; also to divulge, publish, or spread abroad" (Cotg.). From the latter comes to *vent one's spleen*. No doubt also associated with *vent*[1], the spelling of which it has influenced. Finally, fig. sense, esp. in to *find a vent*, has been associated with obs. *vent*, sale, F. *vente*, which is very common (also as verb) in 16–17 cents., occurring passim in Hakl. and Purch. It is impossible to demarcate rigorously the origins and senses of this word. See also quot. s.v. *utter*[2].

We be uncertaine what vent or sale you shall find in Persia (Jenkinson's *Voyages*, 1557–71).

vent for wares: venditio (Litt.).

ventil [*mus.*]. Organ-valve. Ger., L. *ventile*, shutter, from *ventus*, wind.

ventilate. From L. *ventilare*, to fan, winnow corn, from *ventus*, wind (cf. current use of *fan*). Fig. sense of investigating, bringing to notice, etc., common in 17 cent., is now felt as a hygienic metaphor, but was orig. a metaphor from winnowing, found long before the "fresh air" gospel.

ventilare: to van or winnow; to canvass, or sift a point (Litt.).

ventral. L. *ventralis*, from *venter*, *ventr-*, abdomen. Cf. *ventricle*, L. *ventriculus*, "the stomacke; the cell or holow part of the harte" (Coop.); *ventriloquy* (16 cent.), from L. *ventriloquus*, "one possest with a spirit that speaks out of his belly" (Litt.).

venture. Aphet. for ME. *aventure*, adventure (q.v.). *At a venture* is for earlier *at aventure*. The *Merchant Venturers' School* (Bristol) preserves the fame of the Elizabethan *venturers*.

venue [*leg.*]. Esp. in *change of venue*, locality in which a case is tried, now commonly, and absurdly, of locality in gen., esp. with ref. to sport. Usu. explained as ident. with obs. *venue*, *venew*, *veny*, bout in fencing, from p.p. fem. of F. *venir*, to come. I cannot see the connection, but regard it as altered, perh. by association with *venire facias* (q.v.), from earlier AF. *visné*, MedL. *vicinetum*, orig. area from which jury was

summoned, later applied to the jury itself. For a similar disguised ending cf. *purlieu* for *purley*, dial. *vinew*, mouldiness, for *vinny*. Another parallel is obs. *persue* (ven.), track left by wounded animal, earlier *parcy*, F. *percée*.

Triable by enquest in the same shire and visne where the said action shall be taken (*NED*. 1449).

visnetum al. *vicinetum*: a venue or venew, a neighbour-place (Litt.).

It is the proud tradition of the Essex hunt that a fox has never been shot in their venue
            (*Daily Chron.* Feb. 16, 1917).

Venus. Personification of L. *venus*, sexual love. See *venerable*, *venereal*, and cf. *Cupid*.

veracity. F. *véracité*, MedL. *veracitas*, from *verax*, *verac-*, truthful.

verandah. Hind. *varandā*, Port. *varanda*, balcony, etc., of unknown origin. ? Cogn. with It. *verone*, "a building of pleasure jetting or butting out in prospects or galleries" (Flor.). For Port. words via India cf. *padre*, *tank*.

veratrine [*chem.*]. F. *vératrine*, from L. *veratrum*, hellebore.

verb. F. *verbe*, L. *verbum*, word, verb, ult. cogn. with *word*.

verbena. L., "the herbe vervin" (Cotg.). Cf. F. *verveine*, whence E. *vervain*.

verbiage. F. (17 cent.), from OF. *verbier*, to speak.

verbose. L. *verbosus*, from *verbum*, word. *Intoxicated with the exuberance of his own verbosity* was said by Disraeli of Gladstone.

verbum sap. For L. *verbum sapienti satis est*, a word to the wise is sufficient. Cf. *infra dig*.

verdant. After F. *verdoyant*, pres. part. of *verdoyer*, to grow green, from OF. *verd* (*vert*), L. *viridis*. Or simply suggested by much earlier *verdure*, from F. Cf. *verd antique*, ornamental marble, OF., It. *verde antico*, antique green.

verderer [*hist.*]. Royal forester. Extended (cf. *poulterer*) from AF. *verder*, OF. *verdier*, from *verd*, green (v.s.), with allusion to *vert* and *venison* (q.v.).

verdict. ME. & AF. *verdit*, OF. *veir dit*, *voir dit*, true word. Hence MedL. *ver(e)dictum*, to which mod. form has been assimilated. F. *verdict* is from E.

verdigris. OF. *vert de Grece*, Greek green, later *verd-de-gris* (*vert-de-gris*), "verdigrease, a Spanish green" (Cotg.). Cf. MedL. *viride grecum*. The reason for the name is unknown. Synon. Ger. *grünspan* is for *spangrün*, "verdigrease or vertgreece"

(Ludw.), earlier *spanschgrün*, Spanish green (v.s.), MedL. *viride hispanicum.*

verditer. Pigment. OF. *verd de tere (vert de terre)*, earth green.

verdure. F., from OF. *verd (vert)*, green, L. *viridis.*

verecund. L. *verecundus*, from *vereri*, to revere.

verge[1]. Noun. Orig. wand, rod, esp. of office. F., "a rod, wand, stick, small staffe; also, a sergeants verge or mace" (Cotg.), L. *virga.* Hence *verger*, mace-bearer. From the *verge*, or staff of office of the Royal Steward, came the expression *within the verge*, AF. *dedeinz la verge*, AL. *infra virgam*, i.e. subject to the Steward's authority, orig. applied to a twelve-mile radius round the king's court, and, in 18 cent., to the precincts of Whitehall as place of sanctuary. Hence gen. sense of boundary, edge, rim, and finally brink, in to *be on the verge (of)*. A very curious sense-development.

One Elizabeth Cottrell was condemned at the verge holden on Thursday last for stealing one of his majestys dishes
(*Verney Papers*, Jan. 21, 1637).

verge[2]. Verb. L. *vergere*, to turn (cf. *diverge*, *converge*), but much influenced by *verge*[1], esp. in to *verge on*, i.e. border on.

verger. See *verge*[1].

veridical. From F. *véridique*, L. *veridicus*, from *verum*, truth, *dicere*, to say.

verify. F. *vérifier*, MedL. *verificare*, from *verus*, true, *facere*, to make.

verisimilitude. L. *verisimilitudo*, from *verisimilis*, likely to be true. Cf. F. *vraisemblance*, probability.

Corroborative detail intended to give artistic verisimilitude to a bald and unconvincing narrative
(Pooh-Bah).

verity. F. *vérité*, L. *veritas*, from *verus*, true; cf. It. *verità*, Sp. *verdad.*

verjuice. F. *verjus*, "verjuice; especially that which is made of sowre, and unripe grapes" (Cotg.), earlier *vert jus*, green juice.

vermicelli. It., pl. of *vermicello*, dim. of *verme*, worm, L. *vermis.*

vermicular. MedL. *vermicularis*, from *vermiculus*, dim. of *vermis* (v.s.).

vermiform. F. *vermiforme*, MedL. *vermiformis*, worm-shaped, esp. in *vermiform appendix* (18 cent.). Cf. *vermicide*, *vermifuge.*

vermilion. F. *vermillon*, from *vermeil*, L. *vermiculus*, dim. of *vermis*, worm, applied to the cochineal insect. *Vermeil* is occ. used

poet. in E. for ruddy, bright, and also in its secondary sense of silver-gilt.

vermin. F. *vermine*, collect. from OF. *verm (ver)*, worm, L. *vermis.* Applied in ME. to noxious animals in gen. (as still by gamekeepers) and also to parasitic insects, etc. OF. had also the collectives *serpentine*, *sauvagine.*

vermouth. F., Ger. *wermuth*, wormwood (q.v.).

vernacular. From L. *vernaculus*, "that is borne in ons owne house; that taketh beginning in our owne countrey" (Coop.), from *verna*, bond servant. Cf. the *vulgar tongue.*

vernal. L. *vernalis*, from *vernus*, from *ver*, spring, cogn. with G. ἔαρ.

vernicle [*antiq.*]. OF. *veronicle*, var. of *veronique*, portrait of the Saviour imprinted on the handkerchief of St Veronica. See *veronica.*

vernier. Instrument invented by F. mathematician *Vernier* (†1637).

veronal. Drug. Fancy name from L. *ver*, spring.

veronica. Flower. From *St Veronica* (see *vernicle*). The name of the Saint may have sprung from the legend and represent L. *verum*, true, combined with G. εἰκών, image, likeness. Some regard it as altered from *Berenice.*

verrucose. L. *verrucosus*, from *verruca*, wart.

versatile. F., L. *versatilis*, "that turneth or may be turned" (Coop.), from *versare*, frequent. of *vertere*, to turn.

verse. AS. *fers*, L. *versus*, metric line, lit. turning (to the next line), from *vertere*, to turn. Reinforced by F. *vers.* In most Europ. langs. Sense of stanza, peculiar to E., is developed in ME. In AS. also used of clauses of the Creed, and verses of the Psalms corresponding to the Heb. couplet. The whole Bible was first divided into verses in the Geneva Version (1560). With *versicle*, L. *versiculus*, cf. F. *verset*, "a versicle, or short verse" (Cotg.).

versed[1]. Practised. Adapted from F. *versé* or L. *versatus*, p.p. of *versari*, to busy oneself, frequent. of *vertere*, to turn. Cf. *conversant* and pedantic *versant.*

versed[2] [*math.*]. In *versed sine.* Adapted from L. *versus*, turned.

versicoloured. From L. *versicolor*, turning, changing, colour (v.s.).

version. F., L. *versio-n-*, from *vertere*, *vers-*, to turn.

vers libres [*metr.*]. F., free verses, i.e. lines of varying length.

verso. L. (sc. *folio*), abl. of *versum folium*, turned leaf.

verst. Russ. *versta*, via Ger. *werst* or F. *verste*. About two-thirds of a mile. Usu. *werst* in the early travellers.

versus. L., towards, against, from *vertere*, *vers*-, to turn.

vert. F., green. Chiefly in *vert and venison*, where *vert* means green vegetation such as serves as cover to deer. Cf. *verderer*.

'vert. Coined (? c. 1846 by Dean Stanley) of seceders from the Church of England to Rome.

> Old friends call me a pervert; new acquaintances a convert: the other day I was addressed as a 'vert (*NED.* 1864).

vertebra. L., from *vertere*, to turn.

vertex. L., whirlpool, vortex, hence pole of the sky, summit of anything, from *vertere*, to turn. Hence *vertical*, F., Late L. *verticalis*.

vertigo. L., from *vertere*, to turn.

vervain. See *verbena*.

verve. F., with sense in OF. of whim, caprice. In E. very common in current sense from c. 1870. Origin unknown. L. *verba*, words, has been suggested, with a transitional sense of empty chatter which occurs in the *Roman de la Rose* (13 cent.).

very. ME. *verray*, true, real, OF. *verai* (*vrai*), ? VL. *veracus, for *verax*, *verac*-, from *verus*, true, ? or VL. *veraius, from *aio*, I say (cf. *veridicus*). Orig. sense appears in *verily*, *Very God of very God, the very image*, etc. For adv. use cf. US. *real nice*.

Véry light. From F. inventor.

vesica. L., bladder. In arch. sense short for *vesica piscis*, a pointed oval ornament. Cf. dim. *vesicle*.

vesper. L., evening star, cogn. with G. ἕσπερος, Hesperus. Use in pl. for older *evensong* was app. suggested by F. *vêpres*, OF. *vespres*, "even-song, or evening prayer" (Cotg.). This appears first in 17 cent. accounts of travel, and was prob. at first an affectation brought home by those who had done the "grand tour." For pl. cf. *matins*, *nones*, and see *compline*.

vespine. Of the wasp, L. *vespa*.

vessel. Represents both OF. *vaissel* (*vaisseau*), ship, L. *vascellum*, dim. of *vasculum*, dim. of *vas*, vase, etc., and F. *vaisselle* (collect.), pots and pans, plate, L. *vascella*, neut. pl. taken as fem. sing. Both senses appear

c. 1300. The association between hollow utensils and boats appears in all langs. In Bibl. metaphor, with *weaker* (1 *Pet.* iii. 7), *chosen* (*Acts*, ix. 15), *wrath* (*Rom.* ix. 22), it represents the body as containing the soul, and renders L. *vas* (*Vulg.*), G. σκεῦος. The form *wessel* is common up to 16 cent.

> Gevynge honour to the wommans vessel, or body (Wyc. 1 *Pet.* iii. 7).

> But I must comfort the weaker vessel, as doublet and hose ought to show itself courageous to petticoat (*As You Like It*, ii. 4).

> He called me a wessel, Sammy, a wessel of wrath (Mr Weller).

vest. First as verb. OF. *vestir* (*vêtir*), L. *vestire*, from *vestis*, garment, cogn. with G. ἐσθής, Sanskrit *vastra*. Now usu. replaced by *invest*, but surviving in ref. to rights, authority, *vested interests*, with which one is *invested*; cf. *investiture* and fig. sense of *clad* and of F. *revêtu*. As noun, F., It. *veste*, orig. used of various loose garments, current sense being latest. The tailor still preserves the sense of waistcoat, said by Pepys to be due to Charles II.

Vesta. Roman goddess of the hearth and home, corresponding to G. Ἑστία, personification of ἑστία, hearth, household. For application to wax match cf. *lucifer*. Hence *Vestal*, orig. one of the *virgines Vestales* in charge of the sacred fire in the temple of Vesta.

vestiary. OF. *vestiarie* (*vestiaire*), L. *vestiarium*, wardrobe, neut. of *vestiarius*, from *vestis*, garment.

vestibule. L. *vestibulum*, porch, entry.

vestige. F., L. *vestigium*, footprint. In E. usu. fig. and accompanied by neg. Cf. *investigate*.

> There is no footstep in history of any absolute monarchy established in this island (*News-Reader's Pocket-Book*, 1759).

vestment. OF. *vestement* (*vêtement*), L. *vestimentum*, from *vestire*, to clothe. In E. usu. of ceremonial, esp. eccl. garments, current use belonging to the High Church revival.

> This day [Nov. 1, 1552] all copes and vestments were put downe through all England (Wriothesley, *Chron.*).

vestry. OF. *vestiarie*, vestiary (q.v.). Extended sense is connected with the E. system in which the administrative unit is ident. with the Church parish, the *vestry*, or robing-room, of the church being used for the deliberations of the parishioners.

vesture. OF., from *vestir* (*vêtir*), to clothe (v.s.). Chiefly poet. and fig. ModF. *vêture* is used only of assuming monastic garb.

vesuvian. Eruptive match (c. 1850), long disused by all good smokers. Trade-name, from *Mount Vesuvius*.

vet. For *vet*(*erinary*) *surgeon*.

vetch. ONF. *veche* (F. *vesce*), L. *vicia*, "the pulse called a vetch" (Coop.). Var. *fitch* (*Is.* xxviii. 25) occurs in Wyc. and is still in dial. use.

veteran. F. *vétéran*, L. *veteranus*, from *vetus*, *veter-*, old. Cf. *inveterate*.

veterinary. L. *veterinarius*, from *veterina* (*animalia*), "beasts used in cariage, as horses, mules, asses" (Coop.), orig. beasts of a certain age (v.s.).

veto. L., I forbid, formula used by Roman tribunes in opposing measures of the Senate, etc.

vettura. It., carriage, L. *vectura*, from *vehere*, *vect-*, to carry; cf. F. *voiture*.

vex. F. *vexer*, L. *vexare*, to shake, agitate, as still in *vexed question*, *vexation of spirit* (*Eccl.* ii. 17), from **vexus*, from *vehere*, to carry along. Cf. *agitate*, from *agere*, to drive along.

vexillum [*hist.*]. L., military flag, cogn. with *vehere*, to carry.

via. L., by way (of).

viaduct. Coined (early 19 cent.) from L. *via*, way, after *aqueduct*.

vial. Var. of *phial* (q.v.). Esp. in *vials of wrath* (*Rev.* xvi. 1).

viand. F. *viande*, VL. **vivanda*, for *vivenda*, from *vivere*, to live, one -*v*- being lost by dissim., and neut. pl. taken as fem. sing.; cf. It. *vivanda*, Sp. *vianda*. For limitation in ModF. to sense of meat cf. hist. of *meat* in E. See also *vivandière*.

viaticum. L., travelling money, provision for journey, from *via*, way.

vibrate. From L. *vibrare*, to shake, brandish.

viburnum. L., "the wild vine, or bendwith" (Litt.). Hence F. *viorne*, "the hedge-plant called, the travellers joy; also, the hedge-tree called, the way-faring tree" (Cotg.). The statement, in Smythe-Palmer and *NED.*, that the *traveller's joy* was named by Gerarde, seems doubtful. He prob. only fitted the pop. name to a fancied etym.

[It] is commonly called *viorna*, quasi *vias ornans...* and therefore I have named it the "traveilers joie" (Gerarde's *Herbal*, 1597).

vicar. F. *vicaire*, L. *vicarius*, substitute, from *vic-em*, turn. Orig. priest acting in place of absent rector, or as deputy from rel. community to which the tithes were appropriated; hence still distinguished from *rector* (q.v.). For earlier sense cf. *vicar of God*, the Pope, F. *vicaire*, the curé's deputy, and adj. *vicarious*.

The sole proverb of this county [Berks], viz. "The Vicar of Bray will be Vicar of Bray still" (Fuller).

vice¹. Fault; hist. also personification of a vice on medieval stage, hence buffoon. F., L. *vitium*. Hence *vicious*, *vitiate*.

vice². Implement. F. *vis*, screw, "the vice, or spindle of a presse; also, a winding staire" (Cotg.), L. *vitis*, vine, with ref. to spiral tendrils; cf. It. *vite*, "an arbor of vines, the vine it selfe. Also, a vice or a scrue" (Flor.). The second sense given by Cotg. is also found in ME. and is still used by archaeologists.

vice³. Short for *vice*-(*chairman*, etc.).

vice-. L. *vice*, in place of, still used as disyllable in mil. lang., abl. of *vicem* (not found in nom.), orig. used in L. with following genitive. Many E. compds. were orig. in *vis-*, from OF., this form of the prefix surviving only in *viscount*. Compds. of which the simplex does not exist alone in E. are *vicegerent*, from pres. part. of L. *gerere*, to direct, and *viceroy*, from OF. *roy* (*roi*), king. For gen. sense of prefix cf. *vicar*.

vicennial. From L. *vicennium*, twenty years, from *vicies*, twenty times, and *annus*. Cf. *biennial*, *triennial*.

vicesimal. See *vigesimal*.

vice versa. L., position turned, abl. absolute. See *vice-*.

vichy. Mineral water from *Vichy* (Allier).

vicinity. From L. *vicinitas*, from *vicinus*, neighbour, from *vicus*, village (see *wick²*). Cf. *vicinage*, restored from ME. OF. *vesinage* (*voisinage*).

vicious. F. *vicieux*, L. *vitiosus*, from *vitium*, *vice¹*. *Vicious circle* is mod., the early logicians using *circle* alone. In ref. to horses *vicious* may represent rather AF. *wischus*, restive, unbroken, OF. *guiscos*, *guicheux*, perh. ult. cogn. with *wince*, which, up to 18 cent., meant to kick out with the heels, and is ident. with OF. *guenchir*, "to start, shrinke, or wrench aside" (Cotg.).

vicissitude. F., L. *vicissitudo*, from *vicissim*, in turns (see *vice-*).

victim. Currency dates from adoption, in rel. sense, by the Rhemish translators of the

Bible (1582), to render L. *victima*, "sacrificial beast," ult. cogn. with Ger. *weihen*, to consecrate. Hence *victimize*, described (1830) by Bulwer as slang.

victor. L., from *vincere*, *vict-*, to conquer, cogn. with AS. *wīg*, battle, a common element in Teut. names (*Ludwig*, *Wigram*, etc.). Cf. *victory*, F. *victoire*, L. *victoria*.

victoria. Used of various objects (vehicle, plum, fabric) named after *Queen Victoria* (1837–1901). The *Victoria Cross* was instituted Jan. 29, 1856, its first recipients being heroes of the Crimean War.

victorine. Fur tippet. ? From *Victoria*.

victual(s). Restored from *vittle*, ME. & OF. *vitaille* (*victuaille*), L. *victualia*, neut. pl. taken as fem. sing., from *victus*, food, from *vivere*, *vict-*, to live; cf. It. *vettovaglia*, Sp. *vitualla*. OF. form survives in verb *ravitailler*. *Victualler* is also in early use (*Piers Plowm.*), esp. in connection with army and navy, but *licensed victualler* is not recorded by *NED.* till 19 cent.

> I must confess, your wine and vittle
> I was too hard upon a little (Swift).

vicuna. Sp. *vicuña*, "animal Indicum simile caprae" (Minsh.), from Peruv. name. Hence also F. *vigogne*.

vidame [*hist.*]. Noble acting as secular power of a bishop. F., OF. *visdame*, MedL. *vicedominus*.

vide. L., see. Also *v.*; cf. *v.s.*, *vide supra*, *v.i.*, *vide infra*.

videlicet. L., from *vidēre*, to see, *licet*, it is allowed. Cf. *scilicet*.

vidette. See *vedette*.

vidimus. L., we have seen, used to authenticate document. Hence F. *vidimer*, to certify.

vidual. L. *vidualis*, of a widow, *vidua*.

vie. Aphet. from OF. *envier* (*au jeu*), "to vie" (Cotg.), orig. as gaming term, to challenge; cf. F. *à l'envi*, in emulation, also It. *invitare al giuoco*, "to vie or to revie at any game, to drop vie," archaic Sp. *embidar* (*envidar*), "to vie at cards" (Minsh.). OF. *envier*, to challenge, L. *invitare*, is, of course, distinct from *envier*, to envy (q.v.). For loss of *en-* cf. *gin*[1].

vielle [*archaic*]. OF., as *viol*, *fiddle* (q.v.).

view. F. *vue*, p.p. fem. of *voir*, to see, L. *vidēre*. For similar adoption of noun later becoming verb cf. *issue*, *value*. The F. p.p. in *-u* corresponds to It. *-uto*, Sp. *-udo*, VL. *-utus*. Sense-development in F. & E. is wide, but easy to follow. *Viewy* was app.

coined by Newman with ref. to "spurious philosophism." *Viewless* is first in Shaks. (*Meas. for Meas.* iii. 1).

vigesimal. From L. *vigesimus*, var. of *vicesimus*, twentieth.

vigia [*naut.*]. Danger-mark on chart. Sp. Port., look-out, L. *vigilia*; cf. F. *vigie*, "écueil en pleine mer, poste d'un gardien des signaux" (Lesc.), from Sp.

vigil. F. *vigile*, "the eve of a holy, or solemne day" (Cotg.), L. *vigilia*, watchfulness, from *vigil*, alert, cogn. with *vigēre*, to be vigorous. F. has also the popular form *veille*, eve. *Vigilance committee* was orig. US. and concerned with the administration of lynch law. Cf. *vigilante*, also US., from Sp., and recently (1917) adopted by a small but noisy E. party.

Islington Election result—Mr E. Smallwood (Govt.) 2709, Mr A. Baker (Vigilante) 1532
(*Times*, Oct. 24, 1917).

vignette. F., lit. little vine, orig. used of decorative border design on blank page of book. *Vinet* is similarly used in ME. Phot. sense from c. 1860.

> *vignettes*: vignets; branches, or branch-like borders, or flourishes, in painting, or ingravery (Cotg.).

vigogne. F., as *vicuna* (q.v.).

vigour. F. *vigueur*, L. *vigor-em*, from *vigēre*, to flourish.

viking. Introduced, in ON. form *vīkingr*, by early 19 cent. antiquaries and poets; cf. AS. *wīcing*. Usu. referred to ON. *vīk*, creek, inlet, but "current in Anglo-Frisian from a date so early as to make its Scand. origin doubtful; *wīcingsceatha* is found in AS. glossaries dating from the 8th cent., and *sǣ-wīcingas* occurs in the early poem of *Exodus*, whereas evidence for *vīkingr* in ON. and Icel. is doubtful before the latter part of the 10th cent. It is therefore possible that the word really originated in the Anglo-Frisian area, and was only at a later date accepted by the Scand. peoples; in that case it was prob. formed from AS. *wīc*, camp, the formation of temporary encampments being a prominent feature of viking raids" (*NED.*). See *wick*[2]. Sometimes misunderstood as *vi-king*, hence coinage of *sea-king* and nonce-word *viqueen*.

vilayet. Turk. province ruled by a *vali*, *wali* (q.v.). See *blighty*. Suffix *-yet* means district.

vile. F. *vil*, L. *vilis*, "vile, of no value, little worth, good cheape, of little price" (Coop.). Still used in F. of price. Cf. *vilipend*, F.

vilipender, Late L. *vilipendere*, to esteem at a low price, from *pendere*, to weigh.

Does the right honourable gentleman not see that the effect of a speech made by a gentleman in Lord Roberts' position is to vilify a foreign power?
(Swift Macneill, M.P., Nov. 6, 1912).

vill [*hist.*]. AF., territorial unit corresponding to AS. tithing, F. *ville*. Revived by mod. historians.

villa. L., "a manour or house out of a city or town" (Coop.), ? cogn. with *vicus*, settlement, *wick²*. For sense-development of F. *ville* cf. E. *town, -ton, -ham, borough*, etc. Current E. sense is via It. With *villadom* cf. *suburbia*.

Suburban villas, highway-side retreats,
That dread th'encroachment of our growing streets
(Cowper).

village. F., L. *villaticum*, neut. of *villaticus*, of a villa (v.s.); cf. It. *villaggio*, Sp. *villaje*.

villain, villein. OF. *vilain*, peasant, churl (whence ModF. *vilain*, low, ugly), orig. serf attached to a *ville* or manor (see *villa*). For degeneration of sense, perh. in this case helped by association with *vil*, vile, cf. *churl, boor*. An opprobrious epithet early in OF., hence usual E. sense; but AF. *villein* is used by historians in orig. sense; cf. *villeinage*, serfdom. For the extensive proverbial lore dealing with the "villainy" of the *vilain* see Cotg.

vilain: a villaine, slave, bondman, servile tenant. Hence also, a churl, carle, boore, clown; and, a miser, micher, pinchpenny, pennyfather; and, a knave, rascall, varlet, filthie fellow; any base-humored, ill-born, and worse-bred hinde, cullion, or clusterfist (Cotg.).

villanelle [*metr.*]. F., It. *villanella*, "a ballat, such as countrie milke-maids sing" (Flor.), fem. of *villanello*, rustic (v.s.). F. & It. forms were used in 16 cent. E. of a rural song. Current use is 19 cent.

villeggiatura. It., from *villeggiare*, to live in a country villa.

villein. See *villain*.

villosity [*biol.*]. From L. *villosus*, from *villus*, shaggy hair.

vim. Orig. US. ? Acc. of L. *vis*, strength.

vimineous [*bot.*]. From L. *vimineus*, from *vimen, vimin-*, osier.

vinaceous. From L. *vinaceus*, from *vinum*, wine.

vinaigrette. F. from *vinaigre*, (aromatic) vinegar (q.v.).

vincible. Chiefly in *vincible ignorance* (theol.). See *invincible*.

vinculum. L., from *vincire*, to bind.

vindicate. From L. *vindicare*, "to punish; to defend or deliver from danger or wrong" (Coop.), from *vim*, acc. of *vis*, force, *dicere*, to say. Cf. *vindictive*, earlier (16 cent.) *vindicative*, F. *vindicatif*, "vindicative, revenging, wreakfull, avengefull" (Cotg.). See *vengeance*.

vine. F. *vigne*, L. *vinea*, vineyard, vine, from *vinum*, wine (q.v.). In *vineyard* substituted for older *wine-*, AS. *wīngeard*, with which cf. Ger. *weingarten*. The older word survives in name *Wynyard*.

vinegar. F. *vinaigre*, sour wine (see *eager*); cf. It. *vinagro*, "sowre wine, vineger" (Flor.), Sp. *vinagre*. *Vinegar aspect* is after Shaks. (*Merch. of Ven.* i. 1).

vingt-et-un. F., twenty-one. See *van John*.

vinous. F. *vineux*, L. *vinosus*, from *vinum*, wine.

vintage. Earlier *vendage* (Wyc.), F. *vendange*, "vintage, vine-harvest, grape-harvest" (Cotg.), L. *vindemia*, from *vinum*, wine, *demere*, to remove, from *de* and *emere*, to take. Later form is due to influence of *vintner* (q.v.).

vintner. Altered from earlier *vinter*, OF. *vinetier*, from L. *vinum*, wine. Hence *Vintry*, part of the City (cf. *Poultry, Jewry*).

viol. For earlier *vielle*, after later F. *viole*; cf. Prov. *viula*, It. Sp. *viola*, all from a root *vid-*, which appears in MedL. *vidula, vitula*, and in *fiddle* (q.v.), the WGer. name being presumably of L. origin. If so, the three instruments of the early minstrels represent the three Europ. lang. groups, viz. L. (*fiddle*), Teut. (*harp*), Celt. (*rote*). *Violin* is It. dim. *violino*, "an instrument of musicke called a violine" (Flor.), and *violoncello* is It. dim. of augment. *violone*, "a great violl or viole de gamba" (*ib.*). The *viola da gamba* is held between the legs (see *gambit*). ? Ult. from L. *fides*, (lute-)string.

viola¹. Flower. L., violet (q.v.).

viola². Instrument. It., viol (q.v.).

violate. From L. *violare*, "to violate, to corrupt, to defile, to defloure, to breake, as a man doth a law" (Coop.), from *vis, vi-*, force. Earlier are *violence* (13 cent.), *violent. Violent death* is first in Shaks. (*Tit. Andr.* v. 2; *2 Hen. VI*, i. 4).

violet. F. *violette*, dim. of OF. *viole*, L. *viola*, cogn. with G. *ἴον* (see *iodine*). The colour is from the flower (cf. *pink³*).

violin. See *viol*.

violoncello. See *viol*.

viper. F. *vipère*, L. *vipera*, for *vivipara*, viviparous (q.v.). See also *wivern*.

virago. L., "a woman of stoute and manly courage" (Coop.), from *vir*, man. In Wyc. (v.i.).

Haec vocabitur Virago, quoniam de viro sumpta est (*Vulg. Gen.* ii. 23).

virelay [*metr.*]. F. *virelai*, altered on *lai*, lay², from OF. *vireli*, prob. meaningless jingle as refrain of dancing song.

virescent. From pres. part. of L. *virescere*, to become green, *viridis*.

virgate [*hist.*]. MedL. *virgata*, from *virga*, (measuring) rod, rendering AS. *gierdland*, yard¹ land. Cf. *bovate*, *carucate*.

Virgilian. Of *Virgil*, as in quot. below, referring to the *sortes Virgilianae*, i.e. opening Virgil at random as an oracle. King Charles I, at Oxf., is said to have opened at *Aen.* iv. 615. The spelling *Virg-*, for L. *Verg-*, comes via F. from It.

I cannot but suspect Cowley of having consulted on this great occasion the Virgilian lots (Johns.).

virgin. OF. *virgine*, *virgne*, L. *virgin-em*, acc. of *virgo* (whence F. *vierge*); cf. It. *vergine*, Sp. *virgen*. In early use chiefly of the Holy Virgin, and in ME. also used (as was *maid*) of males. Hence unsullied, untouched, as in *virgin forest* (*gold, soil*). The connection of archaic *virginals*, musical instrument, with this word is unexplained (cf. archaic *regals*, used of a small organ).

virginia. Tobacco (mentioned by Capt. John Smith) from *Virginia*, founded 1607 and named after Elizabeth, the *Virgin Queen*. Cf. *virginia creeper*.

viridescent. From pres. part. of L. *viridescere*, to become green, *viridis*.

virile. F. *viril*, L. *virilis*, from *vir*, man. See *werwolf*.

virtu. It. *virtù*, virtue, in spec. sense of knowledge of, and love for, art. Adopted in 18 cent., when Italy was the vogue.

virtue. F. *vertu*, L. *virtus*, *virtut-*, "vertue, strength, puissance, valiantnesse, manlinesse, manhoode, prowesse, power. Helpe. Merit or defect" (Coop.), from *vir*, man. Orig. sense survives in *virtual*, essential, *medicinal virtues, in virtue of*, and in Bibl. lang. Wyc. has *virtue* passim where Tynd. and *AV*. have *power*. Spec. sense of female chastity first in Shaks. (*Much Ado*, iv. 1), but *virtuous* is earlier in this sense. The *seven cardinal virtues*, as opposed to the *seven deadly sins*, are divided into natural (justice, prudence, temperance, fortitude) and theological (faith, hope, charity). For sense-development cf. Ger. *tugend*, virtue, from *taugen*, to be of service, whence also *tüchtig*, doughty.

virtuoso. It., in spec. sense of skilled, learned. See *virtu*. Perh. made current by Evelyn, who uses it repeatedly, while Pepys applies it to the members of the Royal Society.

Such as are skilled in them [antiquities] are by the Italians tearmed *Virtuosi*, as if others that either neglect or despise them were idiots or rakehels (Peacham, 1634).

virulent. L. *virulentus*, from *virus*, poison, venom.

vis. L., strength.

visa. F., L., p.p. fem. of *videre*, to see. Cf. *visé*.

visage. F., from OF. *vis*, face (still in *vis-à-vis*), L. *visus*, from *videre*, to see; cf. It. *visaggio*, Sp. *visaje*. So also Ger. *gesicht*, face, from *sehen*, to see.

visard. See *visor*.

vis-à-vis. F., face to face. See *visage*.

viscacha. SAmer. rodent. Sp., from Peruv.

viscera. L., pl. of *viscus*, "the chiefe intests of a man or beast, as the hart, splene, longes, liver, &c." (Coop.).

viscount. AF. *viscounte*, OF. *visconte* (*vicomte*), from *vice-* (q.v.) and *count¹* (q.v.); cf. It. *visconte*, Sp. *vizconde*. In ME. spec. a sheriff. The form *vice-count* is also found.

viscous. L. *viscosus*, from *viscum*, "mistleden, birdlyme" (Coop.), cogn. with G. ἰξός, mistletoe, from which bird-lime was made.

visé. F., p.p. of *viser*, to inspect, VL. **visare*, from *videre*, *vis-*, to see.

Vishnuism. Worship of *Vishnu*, second of the triad of Hindu deities, Sanskrit *Vishṇu* lit. worker, from *vish*, to be active.

visible. F., L. *visibilis*, from *videre*, *vis-*, to see. *Visible means of subsistence* are referred to in an act of 1824. Cf. *vision*, F., L. *visio-n-*; also aphet. for obs. *avision*, apparition, from OF., app. influenced by *aviser*, to warn.

Visigoth [*hist.*]. Late L. *Visigothus*, Late G. Οὐισίγοθος, with first element prob. meaning west; cf. *Ostrogoth*.

vision. See *visible*.

visit. F. *visiter*, to inspect, search, etc., L. *visitare*, frequent. of *visere*, from *videre*, *vis-*, to see. Early uses are due to frequent occurrence of *visitare* in *Vulg.*, sense of inspecting, testing, passing into that of punishing, requiting. Current sense arises from that of visiting, and comforting, the sick. Cf. *visitation*, offic. inspection, esp. in eccl. sense, *visitor*, inspector.

Ego sum Dominus Deus tuus fortis, zelotes, visitans iniquitatem patrum in filios (*Vulg. Ex.* xx. 5).

visne [*hist.*]. See *venue*.

visor, **vizor**. AF. *viser*, F. *visière*, from *vis*, face, visage (q.v.).

vista. It., sight, view, from L. *vidēre*, *vis-*, to see. A word that came in with It. landscape gardening (17 cent.).

visual. Late L. *visualis*, from *vidēre*, *vis-*, to see. *Visualize* was app. coined by Coleridge.

vital. L. *vitalis*, from *vita*, life. Occ. logically equivalent to its opposite *mortal*, e.g. *vital mistake* (*wound*). As noun in pl., for vital parts. *Vital spark* (*of heavenly flame*) is the first line of Pope's adaptation of the Emperor Hadrian's address to his soul— "animula vagula, blandula."

vitelline [*chem.*]. From L. *vitellus*, yolk of egg, lit. little calf, *vitulus*.

vitiate. From L. *vitiare*, from *vitium*, vice¹.

viticulture. F., from L. *vitis*, vine.

vitreous. From L. *vitreus*, from *vitrum*, glass.

vitriol. F. (13 cent.), MedL. *vitriolum*, from glassy appearance (v.s.). In Chauc. (G. 808). Fig. sense of *vitriolic* is 19 cent.

Vitruvian [*arch.*]. Of *Vitruvius*, Roman architect (1 cent.).

vitta [*biol.*]. L., fillet, strip.

vituline. L. *vitulinus*, of the calf, *vitulus*. See *veal*.

vituperate. From L. *vituperare*, to censure, from *vitium*, fault, *parare*, to make ready (cf. to *find fault*).

Vitus. A Slav. divinity *Svanto-Vid*, worshipped by the Baltic Slavs (Rügen) with epileptic dances, was transformed by early Christian missionaries into *Sanctus Vitus*, whence a popular baptismal name (Ger. *Veit*, It. *Guido*, F. *Guy*). With *St Vitus' dance* cf. F. *danse de Saint-Guy*, Ger. *Veitstanz*.

viva¹. It., pres. subj. of *vivere*, to live. Cf. *vivat*.

viva². Short for *viva-voce*.

vivacious. From L. *vivax*, *vivac-*, from *vivere*, to live. For formation cf. *audacious*.

vivandière. F., fem. of OF. *vivandier*, purveyor, from Late L. *vivenda*, provisions. See *viand*.

vivarium. L., from *vivere*, to live. Hence also F. *vivier*, Ger. *weiher*, fish-pond.

Aviaries, vivaries, fountaines, especially one of five jettos [F. *jet d'eau*] (Evelyn).

vivat. L., pres. subj. of *vivere*, to live. Cf. *qui-vive*.

viva-voce. L., with living voice. Cf. F. *de vive voix*.

vivid. L. *vividus*, from *vivere*, to live. Cf. *vivify*, F. *vivifier*; *viviparous* (see *-parous*); *vivisection* (see *section*). The last dates from c. 1700.

vixen. AS. **fyxen*, fem. of *fox*, with solitary E. survival of Teut. fem. suffix still common in Ger. (*füchsin*, *Zarin*, etc.), cogn. with *-in-* of L. *regina*. Init. *v-* (cf. *vane*, *vat*) is west country. Fig. sense is in Shaks. (*Mids. N. Dream*, iii. 2).

fixen: a froward, peevish child (*Dict. Cant. Crew*).

viz. For *videlicet* (q.v.). Earlier *vidz*, the *z* being orig. not a letter, but a twirl indicating abbrev.

vizard. Var. of *visor*, with excrescent *-d* as in "scholard."

When the house began to fill, she put on her vizard, which of late is become a great fashion among the ladies (Pepys, June 12, 1663).

vizier. Turk. *vezīr*, Arab. *wazīr* (see *alguazil*), from *wazara*, to bear burdens. Title first conferred (754) by Abassid Caliphs in place of earlier *kātib*, secretary.

vizor. See *visor*.

vley, **vly** [*SAfr.*]. Depression, swamp. Contr. of Du. *vallei*, valley.

vocable. F., L. *vocabulum*, cogn. with *vox*, *voc-*, voice. With *vocabulary*, Late L. *vocabularium*, cf. *dictionary*.

vocal. L. *vocalis*, from *vox*, *voc-*, voice.

vocation. F., L. *vocatio-n-*, from *vocare*, to call. Orig. of spiritual "call." Cf. *vocative*, L. *vocativus* (sc. *casus*), calling case.

vociferate. From L. *vociferari*, from *vox*, *voc-*, voice, *ferre*, to bear.

vodka. Russ., brandy, dim. of *voda*, water (q.v.). It is also called endearingly *vodoshka*. For sense-hist. cf. *whisky*.

Ni en matière de musique, ni en matière de vodka, ni en matière d'éloquence, les Russes n'ont la notion de la mesure (R. Herval, *Huit mois de révolution russe*).

voe [*Shetland*]. Inlet. Norw. *vaag*, ON. *vāgr*, creek; cogn. with *vogue*.

vogue. F., from *voguer*, "to saile forth, or forward" (Cotg.), It. *vogare*, "to rowe in a gallie or any bote" (Flor.), from Ger. *woge*, wave, OHG. *wāc*, cogn. with AS. *wǣg*. Orig. sense in *vogue la galère!* ? For metaphor cf. *boom* (see *boom¹*).

voice. OF. *vois* (*voix*), L. *vox, voc-*. Obs. sense of vote (cf. F. *voix*) still in to *have a voice in*.... As verb, to *voice* (a grievance, aspiration, etc.), used by Bacon, and then unrecorded till 19 cent.

void. OF. *voit, vuit* (*vide*), ? VL. **vocitus*, for **vacitus* (cf. *evacuate*); app. influenced also by *viduus*, empty. See *avoid*, of which archaic verb to *void* is sometimes an aphet. form. *Aching void* was serious in 18 cent. (Cowper).

voivode. Ruler, official (Poland and Balkans). Russ. *voyevoda*, with first element cogn. with Russ. *vojna*, war, Serb. *vojsko*, army, second from Russ. *voditi*, to lead. For formation cf. Ger. *herzog*, duke, lit. army-leader, AS. *heretoga*.

volage. F., from *voler*, to fly. Current in ME. (Chauc.), but now re-introduced as a F. word.

volant. F., pres. part. of *voler*, to fly, L. *volare*.

Volapük. Artificial lang. invented (1879) by Schleyer. Supposed to mean, in Volapük, world-speech. Cf. *Esperanto*.

volar [*anat.*]. From L. *vola*, "the palme of the hand, or sole of the foote" (Coop.).

volatile. F. *volatil*, L. *volatilis*, from *volare*, to fly.

vol-au-vent. F., for *vole au vent*, fly in the wind.

volcano. It., "a hill that continually burneth and casteth out flame and smoke" (Flor.), L. *Vulcanus*, Vulcan, whose forge was supposed to be below Etna, to which the name was at first spec. applied.

vole¹. At cards. F., ? L. *vola*, hollow of the hand, ? or from *voler*, to fly.

vole². Field-mouse. Short for *vole-mouse*, Norw. Dan. *vold, voll*, field, plain, ON. *völlr*, cogn. with E. *weald, wold*.

volet [*arch.*]. F., "a shut, or wooden window to shut over a glasse one" (Cotg.), from *voler*, to fly, L. *volare*.

volitant [*biol.*]. From L. *volitare*, frequent. of *volare*, to fly.

volition. MedL. *volitio-n-*, from *volo*, I wish.

volkslied. Coined (1771) by Herder, from Ger. *volk*, people, *lied*, song. Cf. *folklore*.

Volksraad [*hist.*]. Parliament of former SAfr. republics. Du., council of the people (v.s.). *Raad* is cogn. with Ger. *rat*, counsel, E. *rede, read*, etc.

volley. F. *volée*, from *voler*, to fly, L. *volare*. Orig. a term at tennis (v.i.), and still surviving as such in E., of taking the ball in "flight." With shooting sense cf. to "let fly."

perdre la volée pour le bond: to lose an opportunity, by neglecting it, upon a hope that it will returne (Cotg.).

volplane [*aeron.*]. For F. *vol plané*, from *vol*, flight, and p.p. of *planer*, to glide.

volt. Unit of electromotive power. From *Volta*, It. physicist (†1827), whence also *voltage, voltaic*. Cf. *galvanism, ohm, ampère*, etc.

Voltairian. Of *Voltaire* (†1778), i.e. François-Marie Arouet, whose pen-name is said to be an anagram of *Arouet l. j.* (le jeune).

volte [*fenc. & equit.*]. F. *volte*, "the bounding turn which cunning riders teach their horses" (Cotg.). As *vault²* (q.v.).

volte-face. F., It. *volta faccia*, turn face.

voltigeur [*hist.*]. F., orig. member of light company, light bob, from *voltiger*, It. *volteggiare*, to leap, etc. See *vault²*.

voluble. L. *volubilis*, from *volvere, volu-t-*, to turn, roll. Current sense first in Shaks.

A knave very voluble (*Oth.* ii. 1).

volume. F., L. *volumen*, from *volvere*, to roll, the earliest volumes being in roll form. Hence also mass, wreath (of smoke, etc.), orig. conceived as in form of coil.

voluntary. F. *volontaire*, L. *voluntarius*, from *voluntas*, wish, from *volo*, I wish, cogn. with *will*. A *voluntary* in church is supplied by the organist as something outside his compulsory duties. *Volunteer* (F. *volontaire*) has app. been influenced by other mil. words in *-ier, -eer* (*grenadier, carbineer*, etc.).

Orders to disarm and secure malignants in the county and to raise voluntiers for the security and defence of yᵉ same (Josselin's *Diary*, 1650).

voluptuous. F. *voluptueux*, L. *voluptuosus*, from *voluptas*, pleasure, cogn. with *volo*, I wish.

volute. F., It., L. *voluta*, from *volvere, volut-*, to roll.

vomit. From L. *vomere, vomit-*, cogn. with G. ἐμεῖν, to vomit (cf. *emetic*). Hence *vomitory*, exit of Roman amphitheatre. *Vomito*, yellow fever, is Sp. *vómito*.

voodoo. WInd. witchcraft, with human sacrifice and devil-worship. ? Creole F., from *vaudois* (see *Waldenses*), these "heretics" being represented as devil-worshippers by R.C. teachers of negroes. The *NED.* does not, however, mention this theory, but gives a WAfr. (Dahomey) word *vodu* (see *hoodoo*).

Upon her arrest she confessed that she had killed 17 people, and declared that she was a Voodoo priestess (*Daily Chron.* Apr. 4, 1912).

voortrekker [*hist.*]. Early Du. settler in SAfr., pioneer. From Du. *voor*, fore, *trekken*, to journey, trek.

voracious. From L. *vorax*, *vorac-*, from *vorare*, to swallow up, devour.

-vorous. From L. *-vorus*, from *vorare* (v.s.). Cf. *-phagous*.

vortex. L., var. of *vertex*, from *vertere*, to turn. Hence *vorticism* (neol.), art craze.

A little futurism, a little vorticism, a little cubism have all gone to the making of this artist
(Apr. 30, 1919).

vote. L. *votum*, from *vovēre*, *vot-*, to vow, whence also F. *vœu*, prayer, aspiration, etc. This sense is also found in E. (16 cent.) and survives in *votary*, *votaress*, *votive offering*. *Vote* was only Sc. till c. 1600 (see *voice*). F. *vote* is from E.

vouch. OF. *vochier*, ? L. *vocare*, but more usu. aphet. for *avouch* (q.v.). The form of the F. word suggests a VL. *voticare*, metath. of *vocitare*, frequent. of *vocare*. Hence *vouchsafe*, to declare safe, orig. in two words, with *vouch* inflected. For AF. infin. *voucher* used as noun cf. *misnomer*, *rejoinder*, etc.

voussoir [*arch.*]. F., OF. *volsoir*, from VL. *volsus*, for *volutus*, from *volvere*, to roll.

vow. OF. *vou* (*vœu*), L. *votum*, from *vovēre*, *vot-*, to vow. Often aphet. for earlier *avow* (q.v.), esp. as verb, in sense of protesting, asserting strongly.

vowel. OF. *vouele* (*voyelle*), L. *vocalis* (sc. *littera*), from *vox*, *voc-*, voice; cf. It. *vocale*, Sp. *vocal*.

vox humana [*mus.*]. L., human voice.

vox populi. L., voice of the people.

voyage. F., L. *viaticum*, provision for journey, from *viare*, to travel, from *via*, way; cf. It. *viaggio*, Sp. *viaje*. In ME. of any journey, later limitation of sense being characteristic of a seafaring nation.

vraisemblance. F., true seeming, verisimilitude.

vrow, vrouw. Du. *vrouw*, woman. See *frau*.

vulcanize. Coined (1843) by W. Brockedon from *Vulcan*, with allusion to sulphur employed in process (see *volcano*). Cf. *vulcanite*.

vulgar. L. *vulgaris*, from *vulgus*, the common people. For degeneration of sense cf. *mean*[1],

common. Orig. sense in *vulgar fraction*, *tongue* (cf. *vernacular*).

Our intent is to make this art [poetry] vulgar for all English mens use (Puttenham).

Vulgate. L. version of Bible prepared by Jerome (4 cent.). For *editio vulgata*, from *vulgare*, to publish, make common (v.s.). Cf. F. *vulgariser*, to popularize, make accessible.

vulgus [*school slang*]. L. or G. verse exercise (*Tom Brown's Schooldays*, ii. 3). For earlier *vulgars* (16 cent.), sentences in vulgar tongue for transl. into L.

vulnerable. Late L. *vulnerabilis*, from *vulnerare*, to wound, from *vulnus*, *vulner-*, wound.

vulpine. L. *vulpinus*, of the fox, *vulpes*, cogn. with G. ἀλώπηξ.

vulture. OF. *voltour* (*vautour*), from L. *vultur*, cogn. with *vellere*, to tear.

vulva [*anat.*]. L., integument, cogn. with *volvere*, to turn.

---

w-. Exc. for a few exotics (*wapiti*, *wombat*, etc.) all words in *w-* are of AS. or kindred Teut. origin. In a few cases, where the immediate source is the N.E. dials. of OF. (*wage*, *warrant*), they answer to F. words in *g-* (*gage*, *guarantee*), of Teut. origin. For confusion between *w-* and *v-* see *v-*.

Waac. Acrostic for *Women's Auxiliary Army Corps.* "The Waacs in France" is the title of an article in the *Daily Chron.* Nov. 24, 1917. Cf. *Wraf*, *Wren*.

Waacs, Wrens, and Wrafs had not come into existence when Nurse Cavell faced the German rifles
(*Daily Chron.* May 15, 1919).

wabble. "A low, barbarous word" (Johns.). See *wobble*.

wacke [*geol.*]. Ger., OHG. *waggo*, flint.

wad. Cf. synon. Ger. *watte* (from Du.), Norw. Dan. *vat*, F. *ouate*, It. *ovata*. Ult. source unknown, but prob. Oriental. In US. often for a bundle of currency notes.

waddle. Frequent. of *wade*.

waddy. Austral. war-club. Native name.

wade. AS. *wadan*. Com. Teut.; cf. Du. *waden*, Ger. *waten*, ON. *vatha*; cogn. with L. *vadere*, to go (cf. *vadum*, ford).

A crowne! to which who would not wade through blood? (*Coblers Prophesie*, 1594).

wadi. Arab., water-course, whence Sp. river-names *Guadiana*, *Guadalquivir*.

Anzac mounted troops got over this wadi [near Gaza] in the dark (*Daily News*, Apr. 7, 1917).

wafer. ONF. *waufre* (*gaufre*), LG. or Du. *wafel* (whence US. *waffle*, kind of pancake); cogn. with Ger. *wabe*, honeycomb, which is ult. cogn. with *weave*. Orig. small flat cake with honeycomb pattern, as still F. *gaufre*. See *goffer*.

Waff. Acrostic (1915) of *West African Frontier Force*.

waft. From 16 cent. (also *waught*), in obs. naut. sense of convoying ships, very common in early naut. literature. Fletcher calls Charon the "wafter of the souls." App. this sense passed into that of signalling to convoy, indicating direction, etc., in which there was prob. confusion with *wave*[1]. App. from archaic Du. or LG. *wahten*, to watch, guard, etc. (see *watch, wait*). For pronunc. cf. *laughter*.

> I shall conducte and wafft hys vytellars to hys grett army in the water of Brest
> (*French War*, 1512–13).

> The Scots were very busy a wafting her [an English galley] ashore towards them, with a banner of Saint George that they had (W. Patten, 1548).

> I made a weffe with my torbant [turban]
> (Jourdain, 1611).

wag. Cf. Sw. *vagga*, to rock, ON. *vagge*, cradle; cogn. with AS. *wagian* (whence ME. *wawen*), OHG. *wagōn*, whence Ger. frequent. *wackeln*, "to wag, wabble, totter, rock, reel or move" (Ludw.); ult. cogn. with *weigh*. Now rather jocular, and esp. of tails, but see *Matt.* xxvii. 39. *Wag*, jester, orig. rascal, as still in to *play the wag* (truant), is short for *waghalter*, with which cf. synon. *crackrope, crackstring*, whence obs. *crack*, lad (*Cor.* i. 3). Cf. with these Sc. *hempie*, minx, It. *capestro*, wag, lit. halter. With *wagtail* cf. synon. Du. *kwikstaart*, lit. quick-tail (see *redstart*, s.v. *red*), and *rumpevrikker*.

> The gallows groans for this wag as just rope-ripe
> (*Misogonus*, i. 4, c. 1550).

> *cavestrolo*: a wag, a haltersacke (Flor.).

> Wife, the meaning hereof differeth not two pins Between wagging of men's beards and women's chins (Heywood, 1562).

> "Thus we may see," quoth he, "how the world wags" (*As You Like It*, ii. 7).

> *ein ertz-schalck*: an arch-wag, a waghalter (Ludw.).

wage. Noun. ONF. (*gage*), from Goth. *wadi*, pledge, whence MedL. *vadium*; cogn. with *wed*. For pl. often treated as sing. (*Rom.* vi. 23) cf. *links, shambles*, etc. Hence verb to *wage* (war), orig. to declare war, with which cf. *gage of battle*. With *wager* cf.

synon. F. *gageure*. Its earlier sense appears in hist. *wager of battle*.

> *gage*: a gage, pawne, pledge; also, a wager and a stake at play; also, a guerdon, reward, or salary (Cotg.).

> Not a miserable allowance to starve on, but living wages (Lloyd-Jones, *Beehive*, July 18, 1874).

wager. See *wage*.

waggle. Frequent. of *wag*; cf. Ger. *wackeln*.

waggon. Du. *wagen*, carriage, cogn. with *wain* (q.v.). Still in US., after Du., for vehicle in gen.; cf. also *waggonette*. See also quot. s.v. *crambo*. To *hitch one's waggon to a star* is from Emerson.

> O Proserpina,
> For the flowers now, that frighted thou let'st fall From Dis's waggon (*Wint. Tale*, iv. 4).

> From Dort I took wagon [i.e. a coach] to Roterdam (Evelyn).

waif. ONF. for OF. *gaif*, of Teut. origin, but exact source doubtful (see *waive*). Orig. leg., of abandoned property (*waifs and strays*).

> *gayves, choses gayves*: weifes, things forsaken, miscarried, or lost; which not being justly claimed in a yeare and a day, may be lawfully retained by the finder, or by the lord of the mannor wherein they were found (Cotg.).

wail. ON. *væla*, ? orig. to cry *woe*, ON. *væ, vei*. In ME. esp. in *weep and wail*.

> For I moot wepe and wayle while I lyve, With al the wo that prison may me yeve (Chauc. A. 1295).

wain [*archaic*]. AS. *wægn*. Com. Teut.; cf. Du. Ger. *wagen*, ON. *vagn*; ult. cogn. with *way*, with L. *vehere*, to convey, carry, G. ὄχος, vehicle, Sanskrit *vah*, to transport. An ancient Aryan root (cf. *nave*[1], *wheel*), pointing to early invention of vehicles.

wainscot. Du. *wagenschot*, earlier *wægheschot*, of which second element means board. First element may be a Fris. word cogn. with AS. *wāg*, wall, but is explained by Kil. as from archaic Du. *wæge*, *wave*[2], with ref. to marking of grain (v.i.). The word is very old in E., and was orig. applied to a fine kind of boarding imported from Holland.

> *wæghe-schot*: lignum scriniarium, tabula undulata, asser tigrinus, lignum quod sponte fluctuantis maris undas imitatur (Kil.).

waist. ME. *waste*, from *waxen*, to grow, orig. of a man's, rather than woman's, waist, and regarded as the region of greatest circumference. The *waist* of a ship (v.i.) is still its widest part.

> *waste, of a mannys medyl*: vastitas (*Prompt. Parv.*).

Then up they heave him straight, and from the waste
Him suddainly into the sea they cast
(Sylv. Jonas).

wait. ONF. *waitier* (OF. *gaitier*, whence F. *guetter*, to lurk, lie in wait), OHG. *wahtēn*, to stand on guard; cogn. with *wake*[1] and *watch*. Something of orig. sense appears in archaic to *wait on*, escort, and in noun *wait*, now Christmas minstrel, but orig. watchman. With to *lie in wait*, corresponding to F. *aux aguets*, cf. *await* (q.v.).

Mr Robinson. These minstrels do corrupt the manners of the people and inflame their debauchery by their lewd and obscene songs.
Sir Thomas Wroth. Harpers should be included.
Mr —. Pipers should be comprehended.
Alderman Foot. I hope you intend not to include the waits of the City of London, which are a great preservation of men's houses in the night
(Burton, Parl. Diary, Dec. 5, 1656).

waive. ONF. *waiver* (OF. *gaiver*), to renounce, esp. to hand over to the lord of the manor. Of obscure origin. It might come from ON. *veita*, to give, grant (e.g. a fief), via an OF. **gaither*, with the same consonantal change as in *gyve*, *savory* (q.v.). See also *stray*, *waif*. The journalese to *waive aside* (an objection, etc.) is due to confusion with *wave*[1].

wake[1]. Verb. AS. *wacian* (strong intrans.), *weccan* (weak trans.). Com. Teut.; cf. Du. *waken*, *wekken*, Ger. *wachen*, *wecken*, ON. *vaka*, *vekja*, Goth. *wakan*, *wakjan*; cogn. with *watch* and with L. *vigil*. Wyc. has *wake* where Tynd. has *watch*. *Waken* is AS. *wæcnian*, orig. intrans. AS. *wacu*, *wæcce*, watching (in *nihtwacu*), survives as *wake* in dial. sense of jollification and with spec. Ir. sense. Cf. It. *vegghia* (L. *vigilia*), "a watch, a watching, a wake, a waking, a revelling a nights" (Flor.).

wake[2]. Of ship. Du. *wak*, of Scand. origin; cf. Norw. *vaage*, Sw. *vak*, opening in ice, ON. *vök*. Hence also synon. naut. F. *ouaiche*, *houaiche*, OF. *ouage*, which may be partly responsible for E. *wash* (of a ship).

waken. See *wake*[1].

Waldenses [*hist.*]. Body of early Reformers, followers of *Peter Waldo*, or *Valdo*, of Lyons (c. 1170). Hence F. *Vaudois*.

waldhorn [*mus.*]. Ger., wood-horn, hunting-horn.

wale, weal. AS. *walu*, stripe, ridge caused by lash, orig. rod; cf. ON. *völr*, rod, Goth. *walus*, staff. Cf. naut. *wale*, side-timber of ship, now chiefly in compds. *gunwale*, channel[2]. Also *wale-knot*, commonly *wall-knot*. US. to *whale*, thrash, is a wrong spelling.

waler [*Anglo-Ind.*]. Horse imported from *New South Wales*.

wali. Turk., governor; cf. *blighty*, *vilayet*.

walk. AS. *wealcan*, to roll. In ME. also to full (tread) cloth, whence name *Walker*. Com. Teut.; cf. Du. Ger. *walken*, to full, ON. *vālka*, to stamp, wallow; ? cogn. with L. *valgus*, bandy-legged. A *walk over* occurs, when, in the absence of competitors, the solitary starter can traverse the course at a walk. A *walking gentleman* (*lady*) has a silent part on the stage.

Whom [viz. J. Hales] I may justly style a walking library (Anthony a Wood, *Ath. Ox.* xi. 124).

Walker [*slang*]. Also *Hooky Walker*, implying derisive incredulity. The reason for the choice of the name is unknown. Cf. *juggins*, *lushington*, etc.

Mr Weller senior ventured to suggest, in an undertone, that he [Stiggins] must be the representative of the united parishes of Saint Simon Without and Saint Walker Within (*Pickwick*, ch. xliv.).

wall. AS. *weall*, rampart, L. *vallum*, "a bulwarke or rampire" (Thomas), whence also Du. *wal*, Ger. *wall*, Welsh *gwal* (? from E.), etc. Replaced, in gen. sense, AS. *wāh*, but has kept mil. sense in other langs. For wide diffusion of the L. word cf. *street*. To *go to the wall* is a reminiscence of the time when there were no side-walks and the great man and his retinue took the "crown of the causeway," i.e. the middle of the road. With the introduction of side-walks the position was reversed (v.i.). The *wallflower* grows on walls, joc. use for lady not invited to dance being 19 cent.

Two men last night, justling for the wall about the New Exchange, did kill one another, each thrusting the other through (Pepys, Feb. 1, 1664).

wallaby. Small kangaroo. Austral. native name. Hence *on the wallaby track*, on the tramp.

Wallach. See *Welsh*. Gen. sense of foreigner appears in Boh. *Vlach*, Italian.

wallah [*Anglo-Ind.*]. Agent, doer (see *competition wallah*). Chiefly in joc. formations.

"*You* went into action," exclaimed Ethelbert,— "you, a confirmed base-wallah"
(Punch, Oct. 30, 1918).

wallaroo. Kind of kangaroo. Native Austral. name.

wallet. App. ident. with *wattle* (q.v.), as *walet, watel* occur as var. MS. readings in *Piers Plowm.* (C. xi. 269). Shaks. (*Temp.* iii. 3) uses "wallets of flesh" of the Alpine goitre, app. likened to the "wattles" of a turkey.

wall-eyed. ME. *wald-eyed*, ON. *vald-eygthr*, ? for *vagl-*, beam, disease of eye. Some connect the first element with *weld*[1] or *woad*.

gauzo: bleere-eied, pinck-eied, squint-eied, goggle-eied, whal-eied (Flor.).

wall-knot [*naut.*]. See *wale*.

Walloon. F. *Wallon*, people and Rom. lang. of part of Belgium and N.E. France. See *Welsh*.

wallop [*slang*]. To thrash, in ME. to gallop, also to boil furiously. App. connected with AS. *weallan* (see *well*[1]), but of obscure formation (see alternative suggestion s.v. *gallop*). See also *potwalloper*. With intens. use of *walloping* cf. *thumping, spanking*, etc.

wallow. AS. *wealwian*, to roll; cogn. with Goth. *walwjan*, L. *volvere*, to roll.

He walowid to a grete stoon at the dore of the biriel (Wyc. *Matt.* xxvii. 60).

walnut. First element is AS. *wealh*, foreign (see *Welsh*); cf. Du. *walnoot*, Ger. *walnuss* (also *welsche nuss*), ON. *valhnot*; cf. also Pers. *jauzrūmi*, walnut, lit. Roman nut.

Walpurgis night. Ger. *Walpurgisnacht*, witches' revel, esp. on Brocken, on May-day eve. From *Walburga*, E. abbess who migrated to Heidenheim in Germany in 8 cent., by the accident of May 1 being the day of the removal of her bones from Heidenheim to Eichstädt.

walrus. Dan. *hvalros*, inversion of ON. *hross-hvalr*, horse-whale (cf. AS. *horschwæl*). Du. *walrus*, Ger. *walross* are also of Scand. origin, and the E. word may be via Du. The more usual early E. name was *morse* (q.v.).

waltz. From Ger. *walzer* (18 cent.), from *walzen*, to roll, cogn. with *welter*[1]. Some, however, connect both dance and word with the F. *volte* (see *volte, vault*[2]), a popular medieval dance.

Those maniacal turnings and gesticulations which have lately become fashionable in this country, under the appellation of *German vaults* (or rather, *walzen*) (*Domestic Encycl.* 1802).

wampum. NAmer. Ind., from *wompi* (Narragansett), *wapi* (Delaware), white (cf. *wapiti*). The current form is short for *wampumpeag*, white money (i.e. strung shells).

wan. AS. *wann*, black, dark, later sense of pale being connected with earlier via idea of absence of colour; ? cogn. with AS. *wan*, deficient (see *wane, wanton*). An epithet of the sea in Chauc. (A. 2456).

wand. ON. *vöndr*, ? cogn. with *wind*[2] (from pliancy); cf. Goth. *wandus*.

wander. AS. *wandrian*, frequent. formation from root of *wend*; cf. Du. *wandelen*, Ger. *wandeln*, to walk, *wandern*, to wander.

wanderoo. Monkey. Sinhalese *wanderu*, cogn. with Hind. *bandar* (cf. *bandar-log*), from Sanskrit *vana*, tree, forest.

wane. AS. *wanian*, from *wan*, wanting (see *wanton*). Usu. of moon and in contrast with *wax*.

wang-hee. Cane. Chin., ? yellow root.

wangle. First in printers' slang (1888). ? Ident. with dial. (Chesh.) *wangle*, to shake, totter, with var. *wankle* (cf. ME. *wankel*, unstable, Ger. *wanken*, to totter); ? hence, to perform in make-shift fashion, do a thing somehow, also to be a dodger fond of raising trouble.

"You're a bloomin' wangler, Short." "What's that, corporal?" asked the injured Shorty. "A wangler is a bloke who wangles," said Bill illuminatingly; "a nicker, a shirker, a grouser—any bloomin' thing that talks a lot an' don't do much work"
(E. Wallace, *Private Selby*, 1912).

It may be laid down as an axiom that in every shop there is a senior wangler (*Daily Mail*, Mar. 8, 1918).

want. ON. *vant*, neut. of *vanr*, lacking (see *wanton*), whence also *vanta*, to be lacking, and E. to *want*. For sense-development cf. F. *il me faut*, I want, lit. there lacks to me.

wanton. ME., from *wan-*, not, and *towen*, taught, trained, AS. *togen*, p.p. of *tēon*, to draw, educate (see *tow*[2], *tie*); cf. Ger. *ungezogen*, ill-mannered, naughty, corresponding to ME. *untowen*. This is the only E. survival of a Com. Teut. neg. prefix; cf. Du. *wan-* (still in *wanhoop*, despair), OHG. *wan-* (still in *wahnwitz, wahnsinn*, madness), ON. *vanr* (see *want*), Goth. *wans*. ? Ult. cogn. with *vain*. See also *wane, wan*. Orig. of children, associated by Shaks. with (childish) cruelty, and, in moral sense, explained by 17 cent. etymologists as "want one" (of the opposite sex).

A frere ther was, a wantowne and a merye
(Chauc. A. 208).

wap. See *whop*.

wapentake [*hist.*]. AS. *wǣpengetæc, wǣpentæc*, ON. *vápnatak*, from *vápna*, genitive pl. of *vápn*, weapon, *tak*, touching, from *taka*, to take, grasp, etc. Orig. an armed muster with inspection of weapons; cf. Sc. *wapen-shaw* in this sense (*Old Mortality*, ch. i.). Or the touching of arms may have been a sign of homage (v.i.). The *wapentake* of counties subjected to Norse occupation corresponded to the AS. *hundred*.

When any on a certain day and place took upon him the government of the Hundred, the free suiters met him with launces, and he...holding his launce upright, all the rest, in sign of obedience, with their launces touched his launce or weapon (Leigh).

wapiti. Amer. elk. NAmer. Ind. (Cree) *wapitik*, white deer, Rocky Mountain goat. Cf. *wampum*. For transference of name to an animal which is not white cf. *penguin*.

war. ONF. *werre* (F. *guerre*), OHG. *werra*, strife, confusion (cf. Ger. *verwirren*, to perplex), whence also It. Sp. *guerra*. The Teutons had many poetic words for fight (e.g. AS. *gūth, heatho, hild, wīg*, all common in pers. names), but no gen. current term (Ger. *krieg*, orig. obstinacy, etc., only acquired current sense in late MHG.). The borrowing of a foreign word by Romanic was due to the homophony of L. *bellum*, war, and *bellus*, beautiful. For *warfare*, orig. warlike expedition (1 *Cor.* ix. 7), see *fare*. With *warrior* cf. OF. *guerroiour*, from *guerroyer*, to make war, whence obs. E. to *warray*. *War-cry* (cf. F. *cri de guerre*), *warpath, war-paint, war-whoop* were orig. used of Red Indians. *War-lord* (neol.) renders Ger. *kriegsherr*. In the ancient ship-name *Warspite* the second element is dial. *spite, speight*, woodpecker, cogn. with Du. Ger. *specht*. The bird appears in the arms of the ship. A large number of *war-words* date from 1914 onward.

At Sarray, in the land of Tartarye,
Ther dwelte a kyng that werreyed Russye
(Chauc. F. 10).

War [*hist.*]. Acrostic (1915) of *West African Rifles*. Cf. *Waff*.

warble. ME. *werblen*, ONF. *werbler*, Ger. *wirbeln*, to roll, rotate, etc., also to warble; ult. cogn. with *whirl*.

ward. Verb is AS. *weardian*, from *weard* (m.), keeper, *weard* (f.), keeping. From the former comes *ward*, keeper, replaced by *warden* (q.v.), *warder*, exc. in archaic compds. *bearward, gateward*, etc., in *steward* (q.v.), and in names *Hayward* (hedge), *Durward* (door), *Woodward*, etc. The latter gives abstr. *ward*, esp. in *watch and ward* (see *watch*), also *ward* of town (prison, hospital, lock), and *ward*, minor under

guardianship. With *ward-room* of warship cf. *guard-room* of fortress. The whole group is partly due to cogn. ONF. *warder* (F. *garder*), Ger. *warten*, to wait, whence also It. *guardare*, Sp. *guardar*; cf. AS. *weardian* (v.s.), ON. *vartha*, to protect, Goth. *-wards*, keeper. Ult. cogn. with *ware*².

-ward(s). AS. *-weard*. Com. Teut.; cf. Du. *-waart*, Ger. *-wärts*, ON. *-verthr*, Goth. *-wairths*; cogn. with AS. *weorthan*, to become (see *worth*²), and with L. *versus*, towards, *vertere*, to turn. See also *froward, toward*. Much used in nonce-formations, e.g. *Putney-ward* (Carlyle), *Canon Liddon-ward*, of one making for St Paul's to hear the famous preacher.

warden¹. Keeper. AF. *wardein*, corresponding to F. *gardien*, from *garder*; cf. MedL. *gardianus*. Has largely replaced earlier *ward*, e.g. *churchwarden* for *churchward*, the obs. form surviving as surname.

warden², **wardon.** Pear. ME. *wardone*, app. from ONF. *warder* (see *ward*), as being a "keeping" pear. Cf. the etym. I have proposed for *pearmain*, which in ME. was equivalent to *warden*. Hence *warden-pie* (*Wint. Tale*, iv. 3 and *Ingoldsby*).

poire de garde: a warden, or winter peare, a peare which may be kept verie long (Cotg.).

wardrobe. ONF. *warde-robe* (F. *garde-robe*), keep dress.

ware¹. Noun. Usu. in pl., exc. in compds (*hardware, earthenware*, etc.) and in *warehouse*, and esp. of pottery. Replaced in gen. sense by *goods, merchandise*. AS. *waru* (pl.). Com. Teut.; cf. Du. *waar*, Ger. *ware* (from LG.), ON. *vara*. Prob. cogn. with *ware*² with ground-sense of protected property.

ware² [*archaic*]. Adj. (*Acts*, xiv. 6). Now usu replaced by *wary* (see also *aware, beware*). AS. *wær*. Com. Teut., cf. Du. *gewaar*, Ger. *gewahr*, ON. *varr*, Goth. *wars*; cogn. with L. *verēri*, to respect. As verb now only in imper., e.g. *ware wire!* One source of the verb may be cogn. ONF. *warer* (F. *garer*), from Teut. (see *garage*). F. imper. *gare!* corresponds exactly to E. *ware!*

warison [*obs.*]. ONF. from *warir* (OF. *garir*), to protect, save, whence F. *guérir*, to heal, *guérison*, cure (see *garrison*). Erron. used by Scott (*Lay*, iv. 24), as though meaning *war sound!* Cogn. with *ware*², *weir*.

warlock [*archaic*]. Wizard, orig. trucebreaker. AS. *wǣrloga*, from *wǣr*, truth, compact, *lēogan*, to lie². Usual ME. form was *warlow*, surviving as surname.

warm. AS. *wearm.* Com. Teut.; cf. Du. Ger. *warm,* ON. *varmr,* Goth. *warmjan* (verb); cogn. with L. *formus,* G. θερμός, Sanskrit *gharma,* heat, glow. For fig. senses cf. those of *cold.* A *warm man* is "comfortably off." *Warming-pan* is ME.

warn. AS. *warnian,* cogn. with *ware²*; cf. Ger. *warnen,* ON. *varna.* Ground-idea is that of taking heed, providing against. See *garnish.*

warp. AS. *weorpan,* to throw. Com. Teut.; cf. Du. *werpen,* Ger. *werfen,* ON. *verpa,* Goth. *wairpan.* The *warp* of a fabric is that across which the *woof* is thrown. The idea of distortion or bending, orig. naut. and of Scand. origin, is found in the other Teut. langs.; cf. also F. *déjeté,* warped, from *jeter,* to throw. The connection of *warp,* land reclaimed from the sea, is obscure, but this sense is old (v.i.).

warpe, threde for webbynge: stamen (*Prompt. Parv.*).
warpynge of vessellys that wax wronge or auelonge: oblongacio (*ib.*).

warpynge of the see or of oder water: alluvium (*ib.*).
The country here is all "warpe," or reclaimed land (*Daily Chron.* Mar. 26, 1919).

warrant. ONF. *warant* (F. *garant,* surety), OHG. *werento,* from *weren,* to guarantee, whence Ger. *gewähren,* "to warrant, avouch, or assure" (Ludw.). From *garant* was formed *garantir,* whence E. *guarantee,* senses of which are parallel with those of *warrant.* Cf. *warranty,* ONF. *warantie,* from *warantir.* With *I'll warrant* cf. *I'll be bound.* A *warrant officer* has a *warrant* from his superior, not a commission from the sovereign. See also *ware².*

garantir: to warrant, or passe by warrantie, to save harmlesse; to protect, support, defend, keep safe from danger (Cotg.).

warren. ONF. *warenne* (F. *garenne*), from OHG. *weren* (*wehren, gewähren*), to keep safe, preserve (v.s.), cogn. with Goth. *warjan,* to protect, and with *weir.* Cf. *warrant.*

warrior. See *war.*

wart. AS. *wearte.* Com. Teut.; cf. Du. *wrat,* Ger. *warze,* ON. *varta*; ult. cogn. with L. *verruca,* "a wert, a knap of flesh rising in the body" (Coop.).

wary. From earlier *ware²* (q.v.). Cf. *swarthy, vasty,* etc.

A sergeant of the lawe, war and wys (Chauc. A. 309).

was. See *be.*

wash. AS. *wascan,* orig. strong (as in Bibl. *unwashen*). Com. Teut.; cf. Du. *wasschen,* Ger. *waschen,* ON. *vaska*; ult. cogn. with

wet, water. To *wash one's hands of* is after Matt. xxvii. 24. The *wash* of a steamer is perh. rather naut. F. *ouaiche* (see *wake²*).

washer. In mech. sense of disk of metal or leather for tightening joint this can hardly be from *wash.* Form below suggests possible connection with F. *vis,* screw, *vice².*

It [the nave] has likewise in each end of the hole, through which the end of the axletree goes, a ring of iron called the wisher, which saves the hole of the nave from wearing too big (*Gent. Dict.* 1705).

Washingtonia. Californian palm. Named from *George Washington.*

wasp. AS. *wæsp, wæps* (whence dial. *waps*). Com. Teut.; cf. Du. *wesp,* Ger. *wespe,* Norw. Dan. *veps*; cogn. with OSlav. *vôsa,* L. *vespa,* ? and ult. with *weave,* from structure of nest (cf. *wafer*). F. *guêpe* (OF. *guespe*) shows mixture of L. *vespa* with Teut. *w-* (cf. *waste*).

wassail [*archaic*]. AF. *weisseil* (Wace), representing AS. drinking salutation *wes hāl,* be hale (healthy), where *wes* is imper. of *wesan,* to be (whence *was, were*). Cf. AS. *hāl wes thū* (*Luke,* i. 28). See *hale¹, whole.*

waste. ONF. *waster* (F. *gâter,* to spoil), L. *vastare,* to waste, destroy, from *vastus,* vast, desolate. The init. is influenced by OHG. *wastan* (from L.); cogn. with AS. *wēste,* waste, uninhabited, Du. *woest,* Ger. *wust, wüst,* whence *wüste,* wilderness. Sense of prodigality is in Chauc. (c. 593). *Waster,* as term of contempt, may owe something to naut. *waister,* inefficient seaman stationed in waist of ship. *Wastrel* is its dim. (cf. *cockerel, dotterel*). With F. *gâter* cf. It. *guastare,* Sp. *gastar.*

watch. AS. *wæcce* (noun), *wacian* (verb), cogn. with *wake¹*; orig. of night only, hence *watch and ward,* night and day guard; cf. Ger. *wache, wacht* (as in *die wacht am Rhein*), Goth. *wahtwō,* watch, *wahtære,* watchman. The *watch* orig. patrolled the streets, or guarded the camp, at night; hence *watchword.* A *watch* differs from a clock in needing to be "watched" instead of listened to; cf. F. *montre,* orig. clock-dial, from *montrer,* to show, L. *monstrare.*

Watchman, what of the night? (*Is.* xxi. 11).

water. AS. *wæter.* Com. Teut.; cf. Du. *water,* Ger. *wasser,* ON. *vatn,* Goth. *watō*; cogn. with *wet,* with G. ὕδωρ and OSlav. *voda* (see *vodka*). Another Aryan name is represented by L. *aqua,* AS. *ēa* (as in *Twynam,* at two waters), Goth. *ahwa* (cf. Ger. *Eisenach, Fulda,* etc.). Numerous fig.

senses, e.g. *smooth* (*troubled*) *waters*, *high* (*low*) *water*(-*mark*), to *keep one's head above water*, etc., are natural to an island race. For application to gems, with ref. to clearness, cf. similar use of F. *eau*. *Waterlogged* is orig. naut., and app. alludes to the log-like inertia of a ship partly full of water, but Lesc. (1777) has *water-lodged*. The sense-development of *watering-place* is curious.

Watrynge place, where beestys byn wateryd
                       (*Prompt. Parv.*).

watt. Unit of electricity. From *James Watt* (†1819), inventor of steam-engine. Cf. *ampère*, *volt*, etc.

watteau [*dress*]. From name of F. painter of Dresden china style (†1721).

wattle. AS. *watol*, hurdle, roofing wicker (*Luke*, v. 19). The *wattle* plant of Australia, *acacia saligna*, is so called because the early colonists used its flexible branches in building "wattle and daub" huts. ME. *watel*, wallet (q.v.), can hardly be the same word. The analogy of naut. F. *vadel*, *valet*, wad of a gun-mop, suggests connection with *wad*, with sense of bunch. This would account for *wattle* of a turkey (hog). *Wallet* for *watel* may be due to influence of synon. *budget*, *pocket*. Cf. also Ger. *läpplein*, wattle (v.i.), dim. of *lappen*, rag, dish-clout (see also *dewlap*).

goitrons: waddles, or wattles; the two little, and long excrescences, which hang, teat-like, at either side of the throat of some hogs; also, the wenny bags that breed under the throats of the most inhabitants of the Alpes (Cotg.).

das läpplein eines hahnes unter dem schnabel: the waddles of a cock (Ludw.).

wave¹. Verb. AS. *wafian*, to brandish; cf. ON. *vafra*, *vafla*, to waver, MHG. *wabelen*, to wobble; app. cogn. with *weave*, ground-sense of which is movement to and fro. In ref. to *wave-offering* (*Ex.* xxix. 24) Luther has *weben*, to weave.

wave². Billow. Of late appearance (16 cent.), replacing ME. *wawe*, which is cogn. with Ger. *woge* (see *vogue*), AS. *wæg*, and F. *vague* (from Teut.). *Wave* is app. LG. *wacht*, earlier *wach* (Simon Dach), with sound-change as in *waft* (q.v.), and this is cogn. with the words above. App. the substitution is due to Tynd., whose *NT.*, first printed in Germany, has *waves* throughout for Wyc.'s *wawis*.

After hir deeth ful often may she wayte,
Er that the wilde wawes wol hire dryve
Unto the place ther she shal arryve
                       (Chauc. B. 467).

waver. Frequent. of *wave¹*.

wavy. Snow-goose. NAmer. Ind. *wawa*.

wax¹. Noun. AS. *weax*, beeswax. Com. Teut.; cf. Du. *was*, Ger. *wachs*, ON. *vax*; ? ult. cogn. with *wafer*.

wax². Verb. AS. *weaxan*, orig. strong (as in Bibl. *waxen*). Com. Teut.; cf. Du. *wassen*, Ger. *wachsen*, ON. *vaxa*, Goth. *wahsjan*; cogn. with L. *augēre*, *vigēre*, G. αὐξάνειν, Sanskrit *vaksh*, to increase. Now usu. replaced by *grow*, but the senses of the two words are distinct in *AV*. (*grow* = to germinate, flourish, *wax* = to become).

wax³ [*slang*]. Fit of anger. ? Evolved from archaic to *wax wroth*.

way. AS. *weg*. Com. Teut.; cf. Du. Ger. *weg*, ON. *vegr*, Goth. *wigs*; cogn. with *wain* and with L. *via*, way, *vehere*, to transport, Sanskrit *vah*, to carry. An ancient word from the Aryan migration. Compds. with -*fare* are AS. Sense of manner, method, as in *ways and means*, appears in late ME. To *give way*, *have one's way* belong orig. to precedence in a thoroughfare. *Out of the way* is off the beaten track. With *by the way* cf. F. *en passant*. Spec. use of movement of boat appears in to *give way* (in rowing), to *get under way*, often misspelt *weigh* by association with *a-weigh* (of anchor). To *way-lay* is adapted from Ger. *wegelagern*, for earlier *weglagen*, from MHG. *lage*, OHG. *lāga*, lying in ambush. *Wayleave*, right of way, has recently (Mar. 1919) become familiar in connection with inquiry on coal-mining. *Wayward*, now understood as bent on having one's way, is aphet. for *away-ward*, synon. with *froward*. *Waybread*, plant, is AS. *wegbrǣde*, way-breadth, so named from its large flat leaves; cf. Ger. *wegebreit*.

We call it only pretty Fanny's way (Parnell).

Royalties and way-leaves should all be held by the state (*Daily Mail*, Mar. 21, 1919).

-way(s). From *way*, with adv. -*s* (see *against*, *amidst*, *whilst*). Often interchangeable with -*wise*, e.g. *endways*, *endwise*.

wayzgoose. Printers' bean-feast. App. kind of goose forming the chief dish. We find geese described, according to place of feeding, as *grass-*, *green-*, *stubble-*, and there is a small wild goose called the *road-* or *rood-goose*. Hence a *wayzgoose* may have been fed on what Miss Mitford calls "the little greens formed by the meeting of these cross-ways." *Waygoose*, *ways-goose* occur in dial. as synon. with stubble-goose.

> The master printer gives them a way-goose, that is he makes them a good feast
> (Moxon, *Mechanick Exercises*, 1683).

we. AS. *wē*. Com. Teut.; cf. Du. *wij*, Ger. *wir*, ON. *vēr*, Goth. *weis*; cogn. with Sanskrit *vayam*.

weak. ON. *veikr*. Com. Teut.; cf. AS. *wāc*, Du. *week*, Ger. *weich*; cogn. with G. εἴκειν, to yield. Form, for ME. *weik*, has been affected by *weaken*, from AS. *wǣcan*, from *wāc* (v.s.).

weal¹. Prosperity. AS. *wela*, cogn. with *well²*.

weal². Mark of blow. See *wale*.

weald. AS. *weald*, forest, woodland, whence ME. *wald*, *wæld*, now *wold*. Com. Teut.; cf. Du. *woud*, Ger. *wald*, ON. *völlr* (see *vole²*). The spelling is archaic and app. due to Verstegan. In 16–17 cents. often confused with *wild*.

> A franklin in the wild of Kent (1 *Hen. IV*, ii. 1).

wealth. ME. *welthe*, from *weal¹*. Orig. sense was welfare, happiness, as still in *common-wealth* and in *PB*. (e.g. *Prayer for the King's Majesty*). Cf. sense-development of F. *bien*, well, goodness, property.

> For the wealth of our voyage, the health of our men, and safetie of our ships (Hakl. xi. 212).

wean. AS. *wenian*, to accustom, e.g. to a new diet. Com. Teut.; cf. Du. *gewennen*, Ger. *gewöhnen* (MHG. *gewenen*), ON. *venja*. From a Teut. adj. which appears in E. *wont* (q.v.). In current E. sense Ger. uses *entwöhnen*, to unaccustom, with which cf. synon. AS. *āwenian*.

weapon. AS. *wǣpen*. Com. Teut.; cf. Du. *wapen*, Ger. *waffe*, weapon, *wappen*, coat-of-arms (from LG.), ON. *vāpn*, Goth. *wēpna* (pl.); ? cogn. with G. ὅπλον.

wear¹. Of clothes. AS. *werian*, orig. weak (v.i.); cf. OHG. *werian*, ON. *verja*, Goth. *wasjan*; cogn. with *vest*. Secondary sense of using up springs from that of effect of age on clothes; cf. Ger. *abtragen*, to wear out, from *tragen*, to wear, lit. carry.

> A whit cote and a blew hood wered he
> (Chauc. A. 564).
> The House have cut us off £150000 of our wear and tear (Pepys, Oct. 12, 1666).

wear² [*naut.*]. Seamen's pronunc. of *veer²*; with past *wore*, due to association with *wear¹*.

> *to veer* signifie aussi "virer vent arrière." On corrompt souvent ce mot en disant *to weer* (Lesc.).
> He [Nelson] disobeyed the signal without a moment's hesitation and ordered his ship to be wore
> (Southey).

weary. AS. *wērig*, cogn. with *wōrian*, to wander; cf. OSax. *wōrig*, weary, OHG. *wuorag*, drunk. Unconnected with *wear¹*.

weasand [*archaic*]. AS. *wǣsend*, *wāsend*, the latter now represented by dial. *wosen*. App. pres. part. of some lost verb.

weasel. AS. *wesle*. Com. Teut.; cf. Du. *wezel*, Ger. *wiesel*, ON. *hreysi-vīsla*, hole-weasel. ? Cf. OSlav. *vesely*, lively.

weather. AS. *weder*. Com. Teut.; cf. Du. *weder*, Ger. *wetter*, ON. *vethr*; cogn. with *wind¹*, Ger. *wehen*, to blow, Sanskrit *vāta*, wind. Orig. sense of movement of air (*wind and weather*) survives in naut. lang., e.g. *weather side* (opposite of *lee*), to *weather a storm* (*cape*), *weather gage*, to *keep one's weather eye open*, etc. Cf. also Ger. *gewitter*, storm, *wittern*, to wind (game), *verwittert*, weathered (of rocks, walls, etc.). With *weathercock*, from shape, cf. synon. Du. *weerhaan*, Ger. *wetterhahn*. This compd. also preserves the connection between *weather* and *wind*. *Weather-beaten* (cf. Norw. Dan. *veirslagen*) has absorbed also *weather-bitten* (cf. *frost-bitten*, *hard-bitten*), corresponding to Norw. Dan. *veirbidt*, Sw. *väderbiten*.

weave. AS. *wefan*. Com. Teut.; cf. Du. *weven*, Ger. *weben*, ON. *vefa*; cogn. with G. ὕφος, web, and with Sanskrit *ūrṇa-vābhi*, spider, lit. wool-weaver. One of the key industries of primitive races, hence numerous and simple fig. applications.

weazen. See *wizened*.

web. AS. *webb*, cogn. with *weave*; cf. Du. *web*, Ger. *gewebe*, ON. *vefr*.

wed. AS. *weddian*, from *wed*, pledge, which is Com. Teut.; cf. Du. *wedde*, Ger. *wette*, ON. *veth*, Goth. *wadi*; all in sense of pledge, wager, marriage sense developing in E. only from earlier sense of betrothal (v.i.); cogn. with L. *vas*, *vad-*, G. ἆθλον (whence *athletic*). See also *gage¹*. Wyc. always has *wed*, which Tynd. replaces by *marry*. *Wedlock* is AS. *wedlāc*, second element meaning sport, offering, etc. (see *lark²*), occurring also in some pers. names, e.g. *Gūthlāc* (*Goodlake*). Its precise sense here is obscure.

> A mayden, weddid to a man, to whom the name was Joseph (Wyc. *Luke*, i. 27).

wedge. AS. *wecg*. Com. Teut.; cf. Du. *wegge*, simnel-cake, *wig*, wedge, Ger. *weck*, wedge-shaped cake (OHG. *wecki*, wedge), ON. *veggr*, wedge. For Du. & Ger. senses cf. E. dial. *wig* (v.i.).

> *eschaudé*: a kind of wigg, or symnell, fashioned somewhat like a hart; a three-cornered symnell (Cotg.).

wedgwood. From *Josiah Wedgwood* (†1795), a Burslem potter.

Wednesday. AS. *Wōdnesdæg*, day of *Woden*, translating Late L. *Mercurii dies* (F. *mercredi*), day of *Mercury*, with whom *Odin* was identified. Cf. *Wednesbury* (Staffs.), borough of Woden. Corresponding to E. are Du. *woensdag*, ON. *ōthinsdagr*, but Ger. adopted *mittwoch*, mid-week, after Late L. *media hebdomas*, with which cf. It. dial. *mezzedima*. *Woden, Odin*, Ger. *Wotan* (as in the *Wotan line* of 1917), is cogn. with Ger. *wut*, frenzy, archaic E. *wood*, mad.

wee. Orig. Sc. & north., and, in early use, always accompanied by *little* (cf. *tiny*), as in Shaks. (*Merry Wives*, i. 4). *Weeny* is used in SIr. as *wee* in NIr. The analogy of Ger. *winzig*, wee, tiny, from *wenig*, little, a derivative of *weh*, woe, suggests that *wee* is ident. with the northern var (still in dial. use) of *woe*, and that *weeny* is from (? cogn.) ME. *wæne*, misery, sense of small developing from that of pitiable, etc., as in the case of Ger. *wenig*. The two words *wo* and *weane* are sometimes coupled in ME. *Wee Willie Winkie* (Sc.) corresponds to Dan. *Ole Luköie*, Olaf shut-eye, US. *sandman*, sending children to sleep.

"Shut your eyes tight," replied Mr Button, "or Billy Winker will be dridgin' sand in them"
(Stacpoole, *Blue Lagoon*).

weed[1]. Plant. AS. *wēod*; cf. OSax. *wiod*, Du. *wieden*, to weed. Both Spenser and Ben Jonson call tobacco the *sovereign weed*.

weed[2]. Garment. Now only poet., exc. in *widow's weeds*. AS. *wēd*. Com. Teut.; cf. Du. *gewaad*, OHG. *wāt, giwāti*, ON. *vāth*; cogn. with Sanskrit *vā*, to weave. See quots. s.v. *apron, weird*.

After folowed a woman in a mourninge weede, blacke and ragged (Elyot, *Governour*, ii. 423).

wee-free [*pol.*]. Orig. applied to a Sc. church party, and, after election of 1918, to the rump of the old Liberal party.

week. AS. *wicu, wucu*. Com. Teut.; cf. Du. *week*, Ger. *woche* (OHG. also *wehha*), ON. *vika*, Goth. *wikō*. Orig. sense perh. change, alternation (cf. AS. *wice*, office, service), hence cogn. with Ger. *wechsel*, change, and ult. with L. *vicem*. *Week-end* is a northern expression which became gen. c. 1885.

Calidus will tell you that he has been in this hurry for so many years and that it must have killed him long ago, but that it has been a rule with him to get out of the town every Saturday, and make the Sunday a day of quiet, and good refreshment in the country (Law, *Serious Call*, 1728)

ween. Poet. and in *overweening*. AS. *wēnan*, to hope, think, from *wēn*, expectation. Com. Teut.; cf. Du. *wanen*, Ger. *wähnen*, ON. *vǣna*, Goth. *wēnjan*.

weep. AS. *wēpan*, orig. strong (past *wep*; cf. dial. *slep*), from *wōp*, outcry, sense-development showing our progress from a primitive and demonstrative to a restrained race. Cf. F. *pleurer*, to weep, L. *plorare*, to cry out (see *explore*). Com. Teut.; cf. OSax. *wōpian*, OHG. *wuofan*, ON. *œpa*, Goth. *wōpjan*, the verb in each case being derived from a noun (? of imit. origin) indicating outcry. With *weeping willow* cf. F. *saule pleureur*, Ger. *trauerweide*, from *trauer*, mourning.

Thǣr byth wōp and tōtha gristbītung
(AS. *Gosp. Matt.* viii. 12).

weever. Fish. Dial. form of obs. *wiver*, wivern (q.v.), the name being due to the formidable spines.

weevil. AS. *wifel*, beetle. Com. Teut.; cf. archaic Du. *wevel*, "curculio" (Kil.), Ger. *wiebel*, ON. *yfill* (in *tordyfill*, dung-beetle); cogn. with *weave*, from the enclosure of the larva.

weft. AS. *wefta, weft*, cogn. with *weave, woof*; cf. AS. *wefl*, warp.

weigh. AS. *wegan*, to carry, move, weigh. Com. Teut.; cf. Du. *wegen*, to weigh, Ger. *wiegen*, to rock, *wägen*, to weigh, *bewegen*, to move, ON. *vega*, to move, lift, weigh, Goth. *gawigan*, to stir; cogn. with *wain* and with L. *vehere*, to transport. Sense of motion passed into that of lifting (cf. to *weigh anchor*) and then of weighing. To *weigh in* (with an argument, etc.) is fig. from the successful jockey after winning a race. *Under weigh* (naut.) is app. for *way* (q.v.). With *weight*, AS. *gewihte*, cf. Du. Ger. *gewicht*, ON. *vætt*. *Weight of metal* is orig. naut. and refers to weight fired by ship's guns at one discharge. To *pull one's weight* is from rowing; cf. sporting sense of *passenger*. For *weighty*, early mod. E., cf. *wealthy, lengthy*.

weir, wear. AS. *wer*, cogn. with *werian*, to defend. Cf. Ger. *wehr*, defence (as in *landwehr*), dam, *gewehr*, weapon, gun, *wehren*, to defend. The verb is Com. Teut.; cf. OSax. *werian*, to obstruct, ON. *verja*, to defend, Goth. *warjan*, to obstruct, defend. The prevailing spelling, for *wear*, is Sc.

weird. Orig. noun, fate, destiny (see *dree*), adj. use coming from its application to the Norns or Fates, the *weird sisters* (*Macb.*

i. 3), misunderstood later as meaning uncanny, gruesome-looking. AS. *wyrd*, fate,
from *weorthan*, to become, orig. sense of
turning, direction, appearing in cogn.
suffix *-ward(s)*. The verb is Com. Teut.
(see *worth²*). Cf. ON. *urthr*, fate, *Urthr*, one
of the Norns, cogn. with *vertha*, to become.

The wirdes that we clepen destinee
(Chauc. *Leg. Good Women*, 2580).

Makbeth and Banquho met be ye gait thre women
clothit in elrage and uncouth weid. They wer jugit
be the pepill to be weird sisters
(Bellenden's *Boethius*).

welcome. From *well²* and *come* (p.p.); cf. F.
bienvenu, It. *benvenuto*, ON. *velkominn*, all
prob. orig. as greeting. But this has replaced AS. *wilcume*; cf. *wilcuma*, welcome
guest, lit. one coming according to will,
wish (cf. Ger. *willkommen*).

weld¹. Dyers' weed. ME. *welde, wolde*, Sc.
wald; cf. LG. *wolde*, Du. *wouw*, Ger. *wau*,
earlier *waude*, also F. *gaude* (from Teut.).

weld². Verb. For earlier *well*, in sense of
coagulating of melted metal (see *well¹*).
For excrescent *-d* cf. *woold*. Prob., with
other iron-work words (e.g. *coldshort*), from
Sw., which uses *välla*, to well, bubble up,
in same sense.

wellyn metyl: fundo (*Prompt. Parv.*).

wellyn mylke or other lycour: coagulo (*ib.*).

welfare. From *well²* and *fare*. Cf. *farewell*
and Ger. *wohlfahrt*. *Child welfare* is a neol.

welk [*archaic*]. To wither. ME. *welhen, wel-
wen*, ? from *walh*, sickly. Cf. synon. Ger.
welken, from *welk*, faded, ? orig. damp.

verwelcken: to forwelk, flag, wither, dry up, droop,
decay, fade, or fade away, as a flower does (Ludw.).

welkin [*poet.*]. AS. *wolcnu*, pl. of *wolcen*,
cloud. WGer.; cf. Du. *wolk*, Ger. *wolke*,
cloud. For sense-development in E. cf.
sky. Esp. in to *make the welkin ring*.

well¹. For water. AS. *wiella*, well, spring, etc.
Orig. rather of moving water, and cogn.
with *weallan*, to boil, well up, etc. Com.
Teut.; cf. Du. *wel*, spring, Ger. *welle*, wave,
wallen, to boil up (cf. *wallop*), ON. *vell*,
bubbling (whence Sw. *välla*, to weld); ult.
cogn. with L. *volvere*, to roll. Older sense
survives in *well-head, wellspring*.

Dan Chaucer, well of English undefyled
(*Faerie Queene*, IV. ii. 32).

well². Adv. AS. *wel*. Com. Teut.; cf. Du.
wel, Ger. *wo(h)l*, ON. *vel*, Goth. *waila*;
prob. cogn. with *will* and with L. *volo, velle*,
orig. sense being according to wish (cf.

double origin of *welcome*). With interj. use
cf. F. *eh bien!* See *weal¹, wealth*. With
well-known fact cf. *unquestionably*.

welladay, wellaway [*poet.*]. Second is older,
welladay (*Merry Wives*, iii. 3) perh. being
suggested by *woe worth the day* (see *worth²*).
ME. *wei la wei*, northern var. of *wo lo wo*,
AS. *wā lā wā*, i.e. woe lo woe.

For I may synge allas and weylawey
(Chauc. B. 1308).

wellington. Boot. Named from *Duke of
Wellington*. Cf. *wellingtonia*, New Zealand
tree. Cf. also *blucher*.

Welsbach burner. From name of Austrian
inventor. See *thorium*.

Welsh. AS. *wǣlisc*, foreign, from *wealh*,
foreigner, slave, esp. Celt. Cf. Ger. *welsch*,
foreign, esp. Italian, *Welschland*, Italy.
From the Celt. tribe *Volcae*, inhabiting
southern Gaul. Cogn. are *Wallachia, walnut, Cornwall, Walloon*, etc. For sense-
development cf. Arab. *ajam*, foreigner,
Persian. With *Welsh rabbit* (incorr. *rarebit*) cf. *Bombay duck*. *Welsher*, betting
sharper, perh. belongs to the reputation
given to Taffy in the old rime. "The word
is modern, but the practice is ancient"
(Hotten).

welt¹. Seam. ME. *welt* (*of a sho*), "incutium"
(*Prompt. Parv.*), of obscure origin. For
dial. sense of thrash cf. *wale, weal²*, with
which *welt* is perh. cogn.

welt². Ger., world, esp. in *weltmacht*, colonial
power, usu. misunderstood in E. as mean-
ing world domination, *weltpolitik, welt-
schmerz*. The last was coined (1810) by
Jean Paul Richter and popularized by
Heine.

welter¹. To wallow. Frequent. of ME. *welten,
walten*, from AS. *wealt*, unsteady; cogn. with
Ger. *walzen*, "to wallow, or roll" (Ludw.),
ON. *veltask* (reflex.), and ult. with *wallow*
and *walk*. Cf. F. *se vautrer*, to wallow, of
Teut. origin.

welter². In *welter weight*, unusually heavy.
? From *welter¹*, as likely to produce a
wallowing motion.

Theoretically, a welter-weight is that which should
make a horse roll from distress at the finish of a
race, a sight frequently seen
(*Notes & Queries*, Aug. 22, 1903).

wen. AS. *wen*; cf. Du. *wen*, LG. *ween*, Ger.
dial. *wenne*.

wench. ME. *wenche*, app. shortened from
earlier *wenchel*, boy or girl, AS. *wencel*,
child, ? cogn. with AS. *wancol*, unstable

(cf. Ger. *wanken*, to totter), and ult. with ON. *vākr*, child, Norw. dial. *vækja*, little girl. For shortening cf. *much*, and for orig. common gender cf. *girl*. Like synon. F. *fille*, Ger. *dirne*, the word has degenerated, exc. in dial.

The wenche is nat dead, but slepith
(Wyc. *Matt.* ix. 24).

The xxij day of Maij was my wief delivered of a wenche (Hoby's *Autob.*).

wend. AS. *wendan*, to turn, causal of *wind*[2]. Com. Teut.; cf. Du. Ger. *wenden*, ON. *venda*, Goth. *wandjan*, all causals. Now only in to *wend one's way* and in past *went*.

Wend [*ethn.*]. Slav. race of NE. Germany. Orig. gen. Ger. name for Slavs, OHG. *Winid*, *Wined*, whence L. *Veneti* (Tacitus), *Vendi* (Pliny).

went. See *wend*.

wentletrap. Shellfish. Ger. *wendeltreppe*, lit. spiral stair, cogn. with *wind*[2], *trap*[1].

were. See *be*.

wergild [*hist.*]. Fine for manslaughter. AS. *wergild*, from *wer*, man, *gild*, payment (see *werwolf*, *yield*).

wert. See *be*.

Wertherism. From *Die Leiden des jungen Werther*, sentimental suicide novel by Goethe (1774). Cf. *Byronism*.

werwolf. AS. *werwulf*, man-wolf. First element is Aryan; cf. OHG. *wer*, ON. *verr*, Goth. *wair*, Welsh *gŵr*, L. *vir*, etc. For the compd. cf. G. λυκάνθρωπος, wolf-man. So also Norw. Dan. *varulv*, Du. *weerwolf*, MedL. *guerulfus*, whence OF. *garou*, replaced by pleon. *loup-garou*, "a mankind wolfe" (Cotg.). Explanation in quot. 2 is folk-etym.

Vidimus enim frequenter in Anglia per lunationes homines in lupos mutari, quod hominum genus *gerulfos* Galli nominant, Anglici vero *werewolf* dicunt: *were* enim Anglice "virum" sonat, *ulf* "lupum" (Gervase of Tilbury, 12 cent.).

Such wolves are called "warwolves," bicause a man had neede to beware of them
(Turbervile, 1576).

Wesleyan. Of *John Wesley* (†1791).

west. AS. *west*. Com. Teut.; cf. Du. *west*, Ger. *west(en)*, ON. *vestr*; cogn. with L. *vesper*, G. ἑσπέρα, evening. F. *ouest* is from Teut. *Western Empire* (*Church*) date from division of Roman Empire under Theodosius (395). Cf. *Latin* (*Greek*) *Church*. The *Western powers*, Britain, France, Italy, is a term from the Great War. With to *go west*, orig. US., a natural figure from the

setting sun, cf. G. proverb ὁ βίος ἑσπέραν ἄγει.

wet. AS. *wæt*; cf. ON. *vātr*, OFris. *wēt*; cogn. with *water*. In many fig. senses contrasted with *dry*.

The sub-committee of the [US. Democratic] Convention, which is making a preliminary draft platform, has rejected the proposal to introduce a "wet" plank (*Daily Chron.* July 1, 1920).

wether. AS. *wether*. Com. Teut.; cf. Du. *weder*, Ger. *widder*, ON. *vethr*, Goth. *withrus*, lamb; cogn. with L. *vitulus* (see *veal*), from an Aryan word for year that appears in L. *vetus*, old, G. ἔτος, year; thus orig. yearling.

wey. Unit of weight. AS. *wǣge*, weight.

wh-. Words in *wh-* are, apart from imit. formations, of Teut. origin. AS. *hw-*, OHG. *hw-*, ON. *hv-*, Goth. *hw-*, corresponding to L. *qu-*. In some words (*whelk*, *whisk*, *whole*, *whore*, etc.) the *-h-* or *-w-* is spurious.

whack. Imit. of resounding blow. Cf. *thwack*. For intens. use of *whacking* cf. *thumping*, *walloping*, etc.

whack: a share of a booty obtained by fraud. *A paddy whack*: a stout brawney Irishman (Grose).

whale[1]. Animal. AS. *hwæl*. Com. Teut.; cf. Du. *walvisch*, Ger. *walfisch* (OHG. also *wal*), ON. *hvalr*. *Whalebone*, earlier *whale's bone* (Layamon), was applied to the tooth of the *walrus* (q.v.) long before the days of whaling (see *harpoon*).

Ham. Do you see that cloud, that's almost in shape like a camel?
Pol. By the mass, and 'tis like a camel, indeed.
Ham. Methinks it is like a weasel.
Pol. It is backed like a weasel.
Ham. Or like a whale?
Pol. Very like a whale (*Haml.* iii. 2).

whale[2] [*US.*]. To thrash. See *wale*.

whang. Imit. of blow, with more of vibratory resonance than *bang*.

wharf. AS. *hwerf*; cf. Du. *werf*, Ger. *werft* (from LG.), Sw. *varf*. Orig. sense doubtful, but app. connected with AS. *hwearfian*, to turn, of which the Ger. cogn. *werben* implies any form of busy activity. Or it may have orig. meant simply shore, bank, as in poet. AS. *merehwearf*, sea-shore, with sense-development like that of *quay*. Shaks. uses it of river-bank (*Haml.* i. 5). Prob. originated in E. and spread like *dock*[3]. For *wharfinger* (earlier *wharfager*) cf. *scavenger*, *passenger*, etc.

what. AS. *hwæt*, neut. of *hwā*, who (q.v.). *What-not*, article of furniture, is intended to hold china, photographs...and *what not*.

To *give one what for* is to respond to his remonstrant *what for?* by further assault.

For wa I wist noght what was what
     (*Ywaine & Gawin*, 432).

whaup [*Sc.*]. Curlew. Imit. of cry.

wheal [*Corn.*]. Mine. Corn. *hwel*.

wheat. AS. *hwǣte*, cogn. with *white*. Com. Teut.; cf. Du. *weit*, Ger. *weizen*, ON. *hveiti*, Goth. *hwaiteis*.

wheatear. Bird. Imit. spelling of false sing. for *white-arse*. Cf. synon. F. *cul-blanc*, Du. *witstaart*, and such bird-names as *redstart* (q.v.); also G. πύγαργος, white-tailed eagle, from πυγή, rump, ἀργός, white.

wheedle. A 17 cent. word (Pepys, Jan. 10, 1668), described by early slang dicts. as a cant word, and mentioned by Locke, with *sham*, as a neol. It occurs several times in Littleton's *Lat. Dict.* (1677). The -h- is prob. spurious, and the date of introduction makes Ger. origin likely; hence it may be Ger. *wedeln*, to wag the tail, whence *anwedeln*, to fawn on, wheedle; cf. *fawn*[2] and see *adulation*. Cf. also G. σαίνειν, to wag the tail, fig. "to fawn upon, caress, wheedle" (Liddell & Scott).

wheel. AS. *hwēol*, earlier *hweogul*, ult. cogn. with *cycle*; cf. ON. *hvēl*, Du. *wiel*, Fris. *wēl*, spinning-wheel. One of the two Aryan words showing the antiquity of the device, the other being represented by L. *rota*, Du. Ger. *rad*, Sanskrit *ratha*, waggon, war-chariot. *The wheel comes full turn* is allusive to the *wheel of fortune*.

They four had one likeness, as if a wheel had been in the midst of a wheel (*Ezek.* x. 10).

The helm is usually composed of three parts, viz. the rudder, the tiller, and the wheel, except in small vessels, where the wheel is unnecessary
     (Falc.).

wheeze. AS. *hwēsan*, *hwǣsan*, past *hwēos*. Current sense of antiquated fabrication is quite mod., ? orig. of stale stage tricks.

whelk[1]. Shell-fish. Earlier *welk*, *wilk*, AS. *weoloc*, *weolc*, chiefly in ref. to purple dye, murex; cf. Du. *wulk*, *wilk*, *wullok*, etc. The -h- is spurious.

whelk[2]. Pimple. Only as echo of Shaks. (v.i.). AS. *hwylca*, tumour; cf. synon. Norw. *valk*. Cf. also obs. *wheal*, pimple.

His [Bardolph's] face is all bubukles, and whelks, and knobs, and flames of fire (*Hen. V*, iii. 6).

whelm [*poet.*]. ME. *whelmen*, *overwhelmen*, to turn, overturn, app. connected with AS. *āhwylfan*, to vault over, overwhelm, from *hwealf*, vault, concavity. Cf. Du. *welven*,

Ger. *wölben* (OHG. *welben*), ON. *velfa*, to vault[1], Goth. *hwilftri*, coffin. Cf. dial. *whelm*, to turn upside down, cover up. Thus orig. sense would be to cover up, smother. But the -m is obscure.

I whelme an holowe thyng over an other thyng: je mets dessus (Palsg.).

cooperio: to cover all over, to overwhelm (Litt.).

to whelve: cooperio (*ib.*).

whelp. AS. *hwelp*; cf. Du. *welp*, Ger. *welf* (OHG. *hwelf*, whence family name *Guelph*), ON. *hvelpr*. No connection with *wolf*.

when. AS. *hwænne*, cogn. with *who* (cf. relation of *then* and *the*); cf. Du. *wen*, Ger. *wann*, *wenn*, ON. *hvenar*, whene'er, Goth. *hwan*. *Whence* is ME. *whennes*, with adv. -s (cf. *thence*, *hence*). For *when* (time), *whence* (place), cf. *then*, *thence*.

where. AS. *hwār*, *hwǣr*, cogn. with *who* (v.s.); cf. Du. *waar*, Ger. *wo* (OHG. *wā*, earlier *war*, as in *worin*, *warum*), ON. *hvar*, Goth. *hwar*. Pronominal origin can be traced in compds. *whereas*, *wherefore*, *wherewithal*, etc. With the last cf. F. *de quoi*.

wherry. In 16 cent. also *whirry*, *werrie*, *wyrry*. Origin unknown.

whet. AS. *hwettan*, from *hwæt*, bold, sharp (cf. sense-development of *keen*). Com. Teut.; cf. Du. *wetten*, Ger. *wetzen* (from OHG. *was*, sharp), ON. *hvetja*; also Goth. *hwass*, sharp.

whether. Orig. pron. AS. *hwæther*, which of two, as still in Bibl. E. (*Matt.* xxvii. 21), from *who*, with same formation and development of function as *either*; cf. OHG. *hwedar*, ON. *hvārr* (for *hvatharr*), Goth. *hwathar*. The Aryan suffix appears in synon. G. πότερος. Cf. also *other*.

whew. Natural expression of ludicrous consternation or suggestive of a shiver.

whey. AS. *hwǣg*; cf. Du. LG. *wei*, Fris. *waey*, E. dial. (north.) *whig*.

which. AS. *hwilc* (cf. Sc. *whilk*), from -*līc*, like, and root of *who*; formed like *each*, *such*; cf. Du. *welk*, Ger. *welch*, ON. *hvīlīkr*, Goth. *hwēleiks*. In ME. used as relative pron. for mod. *who*, as still in Lord's Prayer.

whidah-bird. From *Whidah* in Dahomey (WAfr.).

whiff. Imit. of light puff. Hence used also of a light sculling-boat. *The whiff of grapeshot* is the title of Carlyle's chapter (*Revolution*, vii. 7) describing Bonaparte's method of countering mob-law.

Whig. "The name of a political faction" (Johns.). Orig. (c. 1667) a Covenanter,

Sc. rebel, for earlier *whiggamore*, said to have been applied to Sc. carters from the west who employed the word *whiggam* in sense of *gee-up!* In current sense, like *Tory*, from Revolution of 1689.

Those whom (by way of hatefull distinction) they call'd Whiggs and Trimmers (Evelyn, 1685).

while. Orig. noun. AS. *hwīl*, space of time, as still in *long while*, *worth while*, *between whiles*, etc. Com. Teut.; cf. Du. *wijl*, Ger. *weile*, ON. *hvīla*, rest, Goth. *hweila*. *Whilst* is for earlier *whiles* (cf. *against*, *amidst*), with adv. *-s*. With archaic *whilom*, AS. *hwīlum* (dat. pl.), cf. synon. Ger. *weiland*, with excrescent *-d* from OHG. *wīlōn*, *hwīlōm* (dat. pl.), and Du. *wijlen*. In to *while away the time* there may be association with *wile* (cf. F. *tromper l'heure*).

der weiland könig: the late king (Ludw.).

whim. Earlier (16 cent.) usu. *whim-wham*. The *-s* of *whimsy* (Milt.), *whimsical*, points to connection with Dan. *vimse*, to run about aimlessly, Dan. dial. *hvims*, giddy; cf. ON. *hvima*, to wander with the eyes.

whimbrel. Curlew. App. from cry; cf. *whimper*.

whimper. Frequent. of obs. *whimp*, ? ult. cogn. with *whine*; cf. Ger. *wimmern*, "to whimper or whine as a little child" (Ludw.).

whin[1]. Grass. ME. also *quin*. Cf. Norw. Dan. *hvene*, Sw. *hven*, Norw. dial. *kvein*; cogn. with Sw. dial. *hven*, boggy field (ON. *hvein* in place-names). Cf., for sense-development, Norw. Dan. *kjös*, sedge, from *kjos*, creek.

whin[2]. Sandstone. ME. *quin* (cf. *whin*[1]), but connection between the two seems unlikely.

whinchat. Bird. ? To *whin*[1] or *whin*[2]. Analogy of *stonechat* points to latter.

whine. AS. *hwīnan*; cf. ON. *hvīna*, to whiz, prob. of imit. origin. Not connected with Ger. *weinen*, to weep, which corresponds to AS. *wānian*, Du. *weenen*, ON. *veina*, prob. from the Teut. interj. represented by E. *woe*.

whinger. See *whinyard*.

whinny. For earlier *whinn*, "hinnio" (Litt.), of imit. origin; cf. *whine*, also F. *hennir* (see *hinny*[2]), Ger. *wiehern*, the latter cogn. with E. dial. *wicker*.

whinyard, whinger [*hist.*]. Short sword. A 16 cent. word, which I take to be corrupted, under influence of synon. *poniard* and *hanger*, from Ger. *weidner*, "a huntsman's hanger" (Ludw.), used also in sense of short stabbing sword. It is spelt *whynarde* by Skelton (*Bowge of Court*, 363), but the -*h*- is prob. intrusive. Boyer (1729) has *winyard*. The form *whinger* is Sc. (16 cent.). E. is very fond of -*yard*; cf. *halyard*, *lanyard*; Skelton even has *haynyarde*, OF. *haineur*, hater.

braquemar: a wood-knife, hangar, whineyard (Cotg.).

parazonium, pugio de zona pendens: Ger. stossstegen, weidner; Du. byhangende, dagghe, oft poniaert, een hesse, een hanger, een stootdegen (A. Junius).

whip. The -*h*- is prob. unoriginal, and ground-sense is quick and sudden movement (cf. to *whip off, out*); cf. Du. *wippen*, "to shake, or to wag" (Hexh.), Ger. *wippen*, to flog (from LG.), cogn. with *weifen*, to wind, whip (e.g. frills), with which cf. *guipure*; ult. cogn. with L. *vibrare*. Ger. *wipfel*, tree-top, is also connected, and LG. *wip*, bundle of twigs, suggests a possible origin of the current sense. Orig. sense appears in Du. *wipstaart*, wagtail, also in *whipple-tree* of cart, with which cf. *swingle-tree*, from *swing*. Though not recorded in AS., it is a true Teut. word, with Scand. cognates. Parl. use of *whip*, likening the elect of the people to fox-hounds, is characteristic of a sporting race. Cf. to *have the whip-hand of* (Dryden). *Whipper-snapper* (T. Brown, c. 1700), *whipster* (*Oth.* v. 2) app. suggest much noise (snapping of **whip**s) and little effect. The *whippoorwill* (US.) is named from its cry (cf. *bobolink*, *katydid*, *more-pork*).

He was first a whipper-in to the Premier, and then became Premier himself (*Ann. Reg.* 1771).

whippet. Prob. from *whip*, with idea of rapid movement. Applied in the Great War to light "tank."

To seize and take away all such greyhounds, beagles, or whippets as may any wise be offensive to his majestys game and disport
(*Royal Warrant*, 1636).

whir. Imit.; cf. *whiz*.

whirl. ON. *hvirfill*, ring, circuit, crown of head (cf. *vertex*); cogn. with Du. *wervel*, Ger. *wirbel*, vortex, whirlwind. Norw. Dan. has also verb *hvirre*, ON. *hverfa*, to turn, whence archaic Dan. *hvirrelwind*. Com. Teut.; cf. AS. *hweorfan*, to turn, Du. *werven*, Ger. *werben*, to be actively employed. For *whirligig* (*Prompt. Parv.*) see *gig*[1].

They have sown the wind, and they shall reap the whirlwind (*Hosea*, viii. 7).

whisk. ME. *wisk*, swift stroke. The noun is not found in AS., but cf. AS. *weoxian*, to clean (with a whisk or brush). Orig. sense appears in Ger. *wisch*, "a whisk or brush" (Ludw.), whence *wischen*, "to whisk, or wipe something" (*ib.*), *entwischen*, to slip away. For sense of blow cf. vulg. *wipe in the chops*, for that of rapid movement, e.g. to *whisk away*, cf. similar use of *brush*. Cognates are ON. *visk*, wisp, Du. *wisch*, in *stroowisch*, wisp of straw. Prob. cogn. with *wisp*. *Whisker* was orig. playful, "brusher." Here belongs also *whisky*, a light cart.

He kept a phaeton, a stylish Tim Whiskey
(Hickey's *Memoirs*, ii. 32).

whisker. See *whisk*. In 17–18 cents. *pair of whiskers* usu. = moustache.

whisker, or *mustache*: mystax (Litt.).

whisky[1]. Spirit. Short for *usquebaugh* (q.v.), the *i* being nearest E. sound to Celt. *u* (whence peculiar sound of F. *u*). It is curious that *brandy*, *gin*, *rum*, *whisky* are all clipped forms. *Whisky* thus means simply water (cf. *vodka*).

whisky[2]. Cart. See *whisk*.

whisper. AS. *hwisprian*, of imit. origin; cf. Ger. *wispeln*, ON. *hviskra*.

whist[1]. Interj. invoking silence. Natural exclamation better represented by *st* (cf. *sh* and *hush*). In Wyc. (*Judges*, xviii. 19).

whist[2]. Game. Earlier (17 cent.) *whisk*, from taking up the tricks. Altered (18 cent.) to *whist* on assumption that it was a silent game (v.s.).

whistle. AS. *wistle*, *hwistle*, noun, *wistlian*, *hwistlian*, verb; of imit. origin and cogn. with *whisper*; cf. ON. *hvīsla*, to whisper. Used also in ME. of the hissing of serpents (cf. F. *siffler*, to whistle, hiss). To *whistle for* (with small prospect of getting) is prob. from naut. *whistling for a wind*. In to *wet one's whistle* the word may orig. have meant pipe (cf. surname *Whistler* = *Piper*, and the use of AS. *hwistlere* for minstrel, *Matt.* ix. 23). To *pay too much for one's whistle* is from Franklin (cf. *axe to grind*).

So was hir joly whistle wel y-wet
(Chauc. A. 4155).

whit. AS. *wiht*, thing, wight[1] (q.v.), the former app. the older sense. Cf. *aught*, *naught*, *not*. Now always with neg., or in *every whit*, as in *AV*. (1 *Sam.* iii. 18).

Whit, Whitsun. The second form is due to wrong separation of *Whit-Sunday*, i.e. *White Sunday*, into *Whitsun-day* (cf. *Whit-Monday*). ? So called from white garments worn at baptisms usu. celebrated at this time. Late AS. *Hwīta-sunnan-dæg* (earlier is *Pentecosten*). Cf. ON. *Hvīta-dagar*, Pentecost, lit. white days, *Hvīta-daga-vika*, Whit week, *Hvīta-sunnu-dagr*, Whit-Sunday, etc.

white. AS. *hwīt*. Com. Teut.; cf. Du. *wit*, Ger. *weiss*, ON. *hvītr*, Goth. *hweits*; cogn. with *wheat*. In *whitebait*, the fry of the sprat, herring, and other fish, *bait* (q.v.) has the older sense of food. *Whiteboy* (hist.), Ir. secret society, so called from the white smocks used in raids, is 18 cent. The *White House* is the popular name of the "Executive Mansion" of the US. President at Washington. With current use of *white man* (US.), favourably contrasted with "coloured," cf. E. use of *sahib* in the Services. Pol. sense, opposed to *red* (Republican), dates from F. Revolution. With formation of *whitening* cf. *lightning*. With *whiting* cf. synon. Ger. *weissling*, Norw. *hvitting*. *White magic* (*witch*) is contrasted with the *black art* (q.v.). With fig. sense of *whitewash*, to conceal person's faults, give bankrupt fresh start, cf. earlier *blanch* (v.i.). The *white man's burden* is a poem by Kipling (*Times*, Feb. 4, 1899). *White hope* came into sporting use (c. 1912) in ref. to the quest for a white man capable of beating the negro champion pugilist, Jack Johnson.

To blanch and varnish her deformities (Milt.).

Before very long will begin White Bolshevism, the White Terror, the rule of the reactionaries
(*Daily Herald*, June 25, 1919).

Denikin and his Cossacks were the "white hopes" of the Anti-Bolshevists (*Obs*. Dec. 7, 1919).

Whitechapel. In various depreciatory senses (cf. *Billingsgate*), from what was once a pleasant London suburb where Pepys used to drive to take the air.

whither. AS. *hwider*, from root of *who*, with suffix as in *hither*, *thither*.

whitlow. Dial. forms, e.g. *quick-flaw*, *whick-flaw*, *white-flow*, *whitflaw*, etc., are due to folk-etym. My own conjecture is that it is a perversion of *outlaw*, which had in ME. a northern var. *wtelaw*. Cf. synon. *felon* (q.v.). A prefixed *w-* is not uncommon; cf. *one* and dial. *wuts*, oats.

Whitsun. See *Whit*.

whittle. From archaic *whittle*, knife, ME. *thwitel*, from AS. *thwītan*, to cut. Now esp. in to *whittle down*, reduce.

A Sheffeld thwitel baar he in his hose
                    (Chauc. A. 3933).

whiz. Imit.; cf. *whir*, *hiss*, etc.

who. AS. *hwā*, orig. inter. The dat. *whom*, AS. *hwām*, is now used as acc., for AS. *hwone*. The genitive *whose* is AS. *hwæs*. Aryan; cf. Du. *wie*, Ger. *wer*, ON. *hverr*, Goth. *hwas*, L. *quis*, Sanskrit *ka*, etc.

whoa. Interj. enjoining a halt. Opposite of *gee*. ? Not orig. of horses.

Then the Kyng [Ed. IV], perceyvyng the cruell assaile, cast his staff, and with high voice cried, "Whoo" (*Excerpta Hist.* 1467).

whole. AS. *hāl*, uninjured. Com. Teut.; cf. Du. *heel*, Ger. *heil*, ON. *heill*, Goth. *hails*. Orig. sense in *wholesome* (cf. Ger. *heilsam*) and in Bibl. E. (e.g. *Matt.* ix. 12). Spelling with *w-* (cf. *whore*) begins to appear from c. 1500, but is not found till much later in north. documents; cf. Sc. var. *haill* (from ON.). Cf. *hale*[1], *heal*, *holy*.

vendre en gros: to sell by great; to vent, or utter his commodities by whole-sale (Cotg.).

whom. See *who*.

whoop, whooping-cough. See *hoop*[2].

whop. Also *whap*. ? Imit. variation on *whip*. With intens. *whopping* cf. *thumping*, *spanking*, etc.

whore. ON. *hōra*; cf. Du. *hoer*, Ger. *hure*; also AS. *hōr*, adultery; cogn. with L. *carus*, dear. The *w-* is 16 cent. (cf. *whole*). So also, in 17 cent., Pepys writes always *Mr Whore* for *Mr Hoare*. Rahab the harlot is called in the two Wyc. versions *strompet* and *hoor*.

whorl. Also earlier *wharl*, ME. *wharwyl* of a spyndyl, "vertebrum" (*Prompt. Parv.*), from AS. *hweorfan*, to turn, whence also *hweorfa*, whorl of a spindle. Cf. *whirl*.

whortleberry. For earlier *hurtleberry* (q.v.), ? from AS. *hortan* (pl.), whortleberries, bilberries. Hence US. *huckleberry*.

whose. See *who*.

why. AS. *hwī*, instrument. of *who*, *what*; cf. OSax. *hwī*, Ger. *wie*, ON. *hvī*, Goth. *hvē*. As introductory word of surprise or expostulation from 16 cent.

wick[1]. Of candle. AS. *weoce*. WGer.; cf. Du. *wiek*, Ger. *wieche*; ? cogn. with LG. *wocken*, spinning-wheel, thus, thing spun.

wick[2] [*topogr.*]. AS. *wīc*, L. *vicus*, village, cogn. with G. οἶκος, house; cf. Du. *wijk*, OHG. *wīh*, Goth. *weihs*, all from L.

wicked. Extended from ME. *wikke*, wicked, feeble; cogn. with *weak*, *witch-elm*. Orig. applied to things as well as persons, e.g. *wicked ways* in *Piers Plowm.* for bad roads.

Som wikke aspect or disposicioun
Of Saturne (Chauc. A. 1087).

The wickedest wood that ever I was in in all my life (Purch. xvi. 42).

wicker. ME. *wikir*, osier; cf. Sw. dial. *vikker*, *vekker*; cogn. with Sw. *vika*, to bend and with *weak*.

vimen: a rodde, a wicker, an osier or twig (Coop.).

wicket. AF. *wiket*, F. *guichet*, "a wicket, or hatch of a doore" (Cotg.), also OF. *guiquet*. Earlier OF. *guischet*, Prov. *guisquet*, pointing to an orig. *-s-*, have suggested derivation from Ger. *wischen* (see *whisk*), with orig. sense of loop-hole (q.v.), convenience for escape. But the absence of the *-s-* in E. suggests that there may have been two synon. words in OF. The cricket *wicket* was orig. of the form of a little gate.

widdershins [*dial.*]. Contrary to course of sun or clock. For first element see *withers*, the second is ON. *sinni*, way (cogn. with *send*), with adv. *-s*.

wide. AS. *wīd*. Com. Teut.; cf. Du. *wijd*, Ger. *weit*, ON. *vīthr*. Sense has been limited in E. (see *far*). *Width* is of later formation (cf. *length*, *breadth*). *Wide of the mark*, whence the cricket *wide*, is from archery.

wide-awake: a broad-brimmed felt, or stuff hat, so called because it never had a *nap*, and never wants one (Hotten).

widgeon. Cf. F. *vigeon*, L. *vipio-n-*, small crane. For phonology cf. *pigeon*.

widow. AS. *wydewa*, *wuduwa*. Com. Teut.; cf Du. *weduwe*, Ger. *witwe*, *wittib*, Goth *widuwō*; cogn. with OIr. *fedb*, L. *viduus* bereft (cf. F. *veuve*, It. *vedova*, Sp. *viuda*), G. ἠΐθεος, unmarried, Sanskrit *vidhavā*, Welsh *gweddw*, all ult. from an Aryan root which appears in Sanskrit *vidh*, to be without, and perh. in Ger. *waise*, orphan. With later *widower* cf. Ger. *witwer*. Slang *the widow*, champagne, is from F. *Veuve Cliquot*, well-known firm of wine-merchants. *Widow's peak* is allusive to belief that hair growing to point on forehead is omen of early widowhood, app. because it suggests the "peak" of a widow's hood.

biquoquet: peake of a ladyes mourning heed [= hood] (Palsg.).

The abundant black hair, growing in a widow's peak (Kipling, *Brushwood Boy*).

width. See *wide*.

wield. AS. *gewieldan*, to control, dominate, causal of *wealdan*, to govern, wield. The latter is Com. Teut.; cf. OSax. *waldan*, Ger. *walten*, ON. *valda*, Goth. *waldan*; ? cogn. with L. *valēre*, to be strong.

Blessid be mylde men, for thei shuln welde the eerthe (Wyc. *Matt.* v. 5).

wife. AS. *wīf*, woman, wife. Com. Teut.; cf. Du. *wijf*, Ger. *weib*, ON. *vīf*, all neut. and with orig. sense of woman, as in *fishwife*, *old wives' tales*, etc. Cf. sense-development of F. *femme*, L. *femina*, woman. Perh. ult. the veiled being, in allusion to marriage custom; cf. ON. *vīfathr*, shrouded. The older Aryan word appears in *quean*.

Refuse profane and old wives' fables [*Vulg.* fabulae aniles] (1 *Tim.* iv. 7).

wig. Aphet. for *periwig* (q.v.). *Wigs on the green* describes a free fight in the village (v.i.). With *wigging* cf. F. *laver la tête*, *donner un savon*, Ger. *den kopf waschen*, also Sp. *peluca*, a severe reproof, lit. a periwig.

There were high words and some blows and pulling off of perriwiggs (Pepys, May 15, 1663).

einen mit scharffer lauge den kopf waschen: to chide, check or rebuke one soundly (Ludw.).

wigan. Fabric. From *Wigan*, Lancashire.

wiggle-waggle. Redupl. on *waggle*.

wight[1] [*archaic*]. Being. AS. *wiht*, creature, thing, whit (q.v.). Com. Teut.; cf. Du. *wicht*, small child, Ger. *wicht*, child, wight (esp. in *bösewicht*, rascal), ON. *vītr*, thing, goblin, Goth. *waihts*, thing. For double sense cf. *thing*, e.g. *a poor little thing*.

wight[2] [*archaic*]. Active, doughty. App. from neut. *vīgt* of ON. *vīgr*, doughty (cf. *want*, *thwart*[1]), cogn. with L. *vincere*, *vic-*, to conquer.

wyht, or delyver, or swyfte: agilis (*Prompt. Parv.*).

Oh for an hour of Wallace wight
Or well-skill'd Bruce to rule the fight
(*Marm.* vi. 20).

wigwam. NAmer. Ind. (Algonkin). From 17 cent. Orig. short for *wekuwomut*, in their house, where "*-om* is the sign of the possessive case, *-ut* of the locative" (James Platt, in *Notes & Queries*, Dec. 6, 1902).

wild. AS. *wilde*. Com. Teut.; cf. Du. Ger. *wild*, ON. *villr*, wandering, astray, Goth. *wiltheis*. Analogy of *savage* (q.v.) has suggested connection with Ger. *wald*, wood, weald, but this is uncertain, though noun *wild* has been confused with *weald* (q.v.).

Orig. sense was prob. ungoverned, etc., of persons, as in ME. *wildhedid*. *Wildfire* was orig. used of Greek fire. *Wild horses shall not...* alludes to old punishment of tearing victim asunder by means of horses. *Wild-cat scheme* dates from US. period of "frenzied finance" (1836). *Wild-goose chase* (*Rom. & Jul.* ii. 4) seems to have been a kind of follow-my-leader steeple-chase (Burton, *Anat.* ii. 2. 4).

Bryan Ochonour and Patric Omore, wyld Irishmen, were pardoned for theyr rebellyon
(*Privy Council Acts*, 1548).

wildebeest. Gnu (SAfr.). Du., wild beast.

wilder [*poet.*]. For *bewilder* (q.v.).

wilderness. Extended from earlier *wilderne*, wild place, from AS. *wilder*, wild animal, orig. *wild deer*. Cf. synon. Ger. *wildnis*, from *wild*.

wile. Late AS. *wīl*, ? representing ONF. **wile*, OF. *guile* (see *guile*), OHG. *wigila*. Hence *wily*.

Wilhelmstrasse [*hist.*]. Ger. Foreign Office. From address. Cf. *Quai d'Orsay*.

will. AS. *willan*. Com. Teut.; cf. Du. *willen*, Ger. *wollen*, ON. *vilja*, Goth. *wiljan*; cogn. with L. *velle*, to wish, Sanskrit *vṛ*, to choose. Pres. *will* was orig. past (cf. *may*, *can*, etc.). Noun is AS. *willa*, will, pleasure. Hence a fresh verb to *will* (pres. he *wills*, not he *will*), whence *willing*, orig. pres. part., as in *God willing*. For *willy-nilly* see *nill*. Current use of *will to* (*victory*, etc.) is after Ger. *Wilful* has degenerated like so many other adjs., e.g. Wyc. has *wilfully* for *AV.* gladly (*Acts*, xxi. 17). *Free will* is in Bacon. *Good will* (of a business) seems to have meant in 16 cent. power of nominating successor in tenancy.

The hye God on whom that we bileeve
In wilful poverte chees to lyve his lyf
(Chauc. D. 1178).

willet. NAmer. snipe. From cry, assimilated to surname.

william pear. For *Williams pear*, from name of grower (cf. *greengage*). Orig. *Williams' bon chrétien*, the F. pear being named in honour of Saint François de Sales.

william, sweet. Plant. Cf. *ragged robin* and hundreds of dial. plant-names.

armoires: the flowers called Sweet-Johns, or Sweet-Williams, Tolmeyners, and London-tufts (Cotg.).

will o' the wisp. See *wisp* and cf. *jack o' lantern*. The phenomenon is also called in dial. *Hob, Jenny, Joan, Peggy, Kitty*. See also *harlequin*.

willow. AS. *welig*, whence *wilig*, basket (mod. dial. *willy*); cf. Du. *wilg*, LG. *wilge*. For more usual Teut. name see *withy*. The *willow pattern*, imit. of, but not copied from, Chin. style, dates from 1780 (J. Turner).

willy-nilly. See *nill*.

wilt. App. dial. var. of **wilk, welk* (q.v.). The same confusion is seen in 16 cent. *Wilkshire*, for *Wiltshire*.

wily. See *wile*.

wimble [*archaic*]. Gimlet (q.v.). Cf. Dan. *vimmel*, from LG. *wimmel, wemel*, from a root indicative of quick movement whence also obs. E. *wimble*, active. F. *vilebrequin*, "a wimble" (Cotg.), is from ODu. dim. *wimbelkin*.

wimple [*archaic*]. Garment such as nuns wear (*Is.* iii. 22). AS. *wimpel, winpel*, garment for neck, perh. for **wind-pæll*, winding cloak, of which second element is L. *pallium*, mantle. Cf. Du. *wimpel*, OHG. *wimpal*, ON. *vimpill*. Synon. F. *guimpe*, OF. *guimple*, is from OHG.

win. AS. *gewinnan*, to acquire, gain, from *winnan*, to toil, suffer, orig. sense of latter appearing in intrans. to *win to* (*away, clear*, etc.). Com. Teut.; cf. Du. *winnen*, Ger. *gewinnen*, ON. *vinna*, Goth. *winnan*.

wince. Earlier *winch, wench*, AF. **wencher*, OF. *guenchir*, "to start, shrinke, or wrench aside, thereby to avoid a comming blow" (Cotg.), OLG. *wenkjan*; cf. Ger. *wanken*, to totter, cogn. with *winken*, to motion, wink. In ME. esp. of a jibbing, or kicking, horse.

wincey. Fabric. ? For **linsey-winsey*, riming variation on *linsey-woolsey*.

winch. AS. *wince*, pulley, cogn. with *wince*, with ground-sense of something turning, bending. Cf. *crank*[1].

wind[1]. Noun. AS. *wind*. Aryan; cf. Du. Ger. *wind*, ON. *vindr*, Goth. *winds*, L. *ventus*, Welsh *gwynt*, Sanskrit *vāta*; orig. pres. part. of Aryan verb which appears in Ger. *wehen*, to blow; ult. cogn. with *weather*. Numerous fig. uses, e.g. *near the wind*, *three sheets in the wind*, to *raise the wind*, to *take the wind out of one's sails*, to *get to windward of* (cf. *weather-gage*), *between wind and water* (Purch.), etc., are of naut. origin. To *get wind of, wind the game, something in the wind*, are from hunting. To *get the wind up* (neol.) is app. from aviation. Here belongs to *wind a horn*, of which past is prop. *winded* (Shaks.). For fig. sense of *windmill* see *tilt*[3]. *Windfall*, stroke of luck, is from

earlier sense of wood or fruit thrown down by the wind and free to all.

The said galliasse in schort tyme came on vynduart of the tothir schip (*Complaynt of Scotlande*, 1549).

bois chablis: wind-falls; the trees, or branches of trees, which the wind hath overthrowne (Cotg.).

wind[2]. Verb. AS. *windan*. Com. Teut.; cf. Du. Ger. *winden*, ON. *vinda*, Goth. *-windan* (in compds.); cf. *wend, wander*. From Teut. comes F. *guinder*, "to hoyse, or lift up on high" (Cotg.). To *wind up*, conclude (trans. & intrans.), is app. an early metaphor from wool-winding. For to *wind a horn* see *wind*[1].

windlass. ME. *windelas*, more usu. *windas*, ON. *vindāss*, from *vinda*, to wind, *āss*, pole; hence also archaic F. *guindas*.

Ther may no man out of the place it dryve
For noon engyn of wyndas ne polyve
　　　　　　　　　　　　(Chauc. F. 183).

windlestraw. AS. *windelstrēaw*, from *windel*, basket, from *winden*, to wind, plait.

window. ME. *wind-oge*, ON. *vind-auga*, lit. wind-eye, replacing AS. *ēagduru*, eye-door, *ēagthyrel*, eye-hole. Orig. unglazed hole in roof, the Teut. langs. usu. adopting, with introduction of glass, the L. name (*fenestra*), e.g. Du. *venster*, Ger. *fenster* (cf. F. *fenêtre*). *Window-dressing*, in fig. sense, is late 19 cent.

windsor chair. Made in Bucks and also called *wycombe chair*.

wine. AS. *wīn*, L. *vinum*, wine, vine, cogn. with G. οἶνος. Adopted early, with the art of vine-culture, by the Teut. langs.; cf. Du. *wijn*, Ger. Goth. *wein*; also OSlav. *vino*.

wing. ME. also *weng*, ON. *vængr*, replacing AS. *fethra* (pl.), with which cf. Ger. *fittich*, pinion. With to *wing*, wound, disable, cf. F. *en avoir dans l'aile*, to be hard hit. *Winged words* is after G. ἔπεα πτερόεντα (Homer).

wink. AS. *wincian*; cf. Ger. *winken*, to nod, beckon; cogn. with ON. *vanka*. Ground-sense of rapid movement (cf. *like winking*) points to connection with *wince* (q.v.). With to *wink at* cf. to *connive*. Langland has *wink*, nap, with which cf. *forty winks*.

And the times of this ignorance God winked at
　　　　　　　　　　　　(*Acts*, xvii. 30).

einem mit den augen wincken: to give one the wink, to tip him a wink, or the wink (Ludw.).

winkle. AS. *wincle*, in *winewincle* or *pinewincle*, periwinkle, cogn. with *winch, wince*, from convoluted shell; cf. AS. *wincel*, corner.

winnow. AS. *windwian*, from *wind*[1]; cf. L. *ventilare*, "to fanne, to winow corne" (Coop.), from *ventus*, wind.

And Y shal bringe in up on Elam foure wyndus fro the foure coestus of hevene, and Y shal wynewe [*var.* wyndewe] them in to alle these windus
(Wyc. *Jer.* xlix. 36).

winsome. AS. *wynsum*, from *wynn*, joy; ult. cogn. with *Venus*. Cf. Ger. *wonne*, joy, *wonnig*, winsome.

winter. AS. *winter*. Com. Teut.; cf. Du. Ger. *winter*, ON. *vetr*, Goth. *wintrus*. In primitive Teut. also in sense of year, as in AS. *ǣnetre* (*ān-wintre*), one-year-old, and still in dial. *twinter*, two-year old, for *two winter*; see *night, summer*.

Now is the winter of our discontent
Made glorious summer by this sun of York
(*Rich. III*, i. 1).

Winton. Signature of bishop of Winchester, AS. *Wintanceaster*.

wipe. AS. *wīpian*, cogn. with LG. *wīp*, wisp (of straw for rubbing down). For relation of *wipe* to *wisp* (twist of straw), cf. F. *torcher*, to wipe, from *torche*, torch, also "wreathed clowt, wispe, or wad of straw" (Cotg.). To *wipe out* (fig.) is US. For *wipe*, blow, cf. slang use of F. *torcher*, *frotter*, *brosser*.

To statesmen would you give a wipe,
You print it in Italic type (Swift).

wire. AS. *wīr*; cf. ON. *vīrr*, OHG. *wiara*, twisted ornament; ult. cogn. with L. *viriae*, armlets (of twisted wire), said by Pliny to be of Celt. origin. In sense of telegraph from c. 1880. *Wireless* dates from c. 1895. To *wire-draw* is to draw out metal into wire, hence to over-elaborate in length. *Wire-drawer* occurs as trade-description and surname in 13 cent. *Wire-pulling*, allusive to puppets, is US., for earlier *wire-working*. To *wire in* (colloq.), set to work vigorously, is mod. slang (? orig. pugil.).

A subject common, bare-worne, and wyer-drawne in a thousand bookes (Florio's *Montaigne*, i. 28).

wis [*pseudo-archaic*]. False pres. of *wist* (q.v.), through adv. *iwis*, certainly, orig. adj., AS. *gewiss* (cf. Ger. *gewiss*), being taken as *I wis*. See *wit*.

Y-wis, but if ich have my wille,
For deerne love of thee, lemman, I spille
(Chauc. A. 3277).

Where my morning haunts are he wisses not
(Milton, *Smectymnuus*).

wisdom. See *wise*[2]. With *wisdom tooth*, cut at age of wisdom, cf. F. *dent de sagesse* (Cotg.), Ger. *weisheitszahn*, G. σωφρονιστῆρες.

wise[1]. Noun. AS. *wīse*. Com. Teut.; cf. Du. *wijze*, Ger. *weise*, ON. *-vīs*, in *öthruvīs*; cogn. with *wise*[2], ground-sense of which is knowing the way. Cf. F. *guise*, from Teut. Hence also suffix *-wise*, as in *likewise*, *otherwise*, often used indifferently with *-ways*.

wise[2]. Adj. AS. *wīs*. Com. Teut.; cf. Du. *wijs*, Ger. *weise*, ON. *vīss*, Goth. *un-weis*; cogn. with *wit*. Hence *wisdom*.

-wise. See *wise*[1].

wiseacre. "One that knows or tells truth, but we commonly use it *in malam partem*, for a fool" (Blount). Via Du. from Ger. *weissager*, a prophet, altered, by analogy with Ger. *wahrsager*, a soothsayer (from *wahr*, true), from OHG. *wīzago*, cogn. with AS. *wītega*, wise man, prophet, from *witig*, witty, wise.

weissager: 1. *ein prophet*: a prophet; 2. *ein wahrsager*: a prognosticator, a witty fore-teller (Ludw.).

wish. AS. *wȳscan*, from *wūsc* (in *wūscbearn*), wish, whence ME. *wusch*, mod. noun being re-coined from verb. Com. Teut.; cf. Du. *wensch*, Ger. *wunsch*, ON. *ōsk*; cogn. with Sanskrit *vāṅkh*. The E. word has lost an *-n-* before the spirant (cf. *other, five*).

Thy wish was father, Harry, to that thought
(2 *Hen. IV*, iv. 5).

wishy-washy. Redupl. on *wash*. But cf. Ger. *wisch-wasch*, *wischi-waschi*, which may be equally well from *wisch*, wisp, fig. trash.

wisp. ME. also *wips* (cf. *wasp*), app. cogn. with *wipe* (q.v.). Ground-sense is something twisted, as in Goth. *waips*, crown. In *will o' the wisp*, the allusion is to a torch.

wist [*archaic*]. Past of *wit* (q.v.); cf. Ger. *wusste*, past of *wissen*, to know.

wistaria. Plant. Named from *C. Wistar*, US. anatomist (†1818).

wistful. ? Evolved from earlier adv. *wistly*, silently, earnestly (*Rich. II*, v. 4), ? from *whist*[1]. Later sense influenced by *wishful*.

wit. AS. *witt*, understanding, sense, from *witan*, to know, orig. sense surviving in *out of one's wits*, *five wits*, *wit's end*, etc. Replaced in early 16 cent., in higher senses, by *wisdom*. The verb survives in archaic *wot* (pres.), *wist* (past), *to wit* (cf. F. *à savoir*); cf. also *wittingly*, i.e. knowingly. The verb, an old pret., as is seen by absence of -s in *God wot*, is Aryan; cf. Du. *weten*, Ger. *wissen*, ON. *vita*, Goth. *witan*, L. *vidēre*, to see, G. ἰδεῖν, to see, Sanskrit *vid*, to perceive. For development of current sense of noun cf. Ger. *witz*, F. *esprit*. For *wit*, witty person, orig. sage, cf. *witenagemot*. *Witticism* (17 cent.) is due to *Anglicism*, *Gallicism*.

I am at my whyttys end (*Cely Papers*, 1482).

I find out knowledge of witty inventions [*Vulg.* eruditae cogitationes] (*Prov.* viii. 12).

It was about the time of Cowley that *Wit*, which had been till then used for *Intellection*, in contradistinction to *Will*, took the meaning, whatever it be, which it now bears (Johns.).

witch. AS. *wicca* (m.), *wicce* (f.), thought to be cogn. with Goth. *weihs*, holy, Ger. *weihen*, to consecrate, and L. *victima* (see *victim*). This, though not capable of proof, is very likely, as the priests of a suppressed religion naturally become magicians to its successors or opponents (? cf. *voodoo*). In ME. *witch* still meant also *wizard*, with which it is not etym. connected. *Witching* is usu. after *Haml.* iii. 2. Witches were liable to be burned till 1736.

There was a man in that citee whos name was Symount a witche (Wyc. *Acts*, viii. 9).

witch-elm, wych-elm. Pleon. for AS. *wice*, from *wícan*, to bend, give way; cf. *wicker*. So also *witch-alder*, *witch-hazel*.

witenagemot [*hist.*]. AS. *witena* (genitive pl.) -*gemōt*, lit. meeting of sages. See *wit*, *moot*.

with. AS. *with*, against, opposite, also *wither-*, as prefix. Has taken over sense of AS. *mid* (see *midwife*), which it has superseded. Orig. sense survives in verbs *withdraw*, *withhold*, *withsay*, *withstand*, corresponding also to AS. compds. of *wither-* and Ger. compds. of *wider-*, against. Cf. ON. *vith*, and see *withers*, *widdershins*. *With* is often treated as a conjunction (= *and*) by ungrammatical writers.

He with fiftie others were slaine (Purch.).

Lord Rhondda, who, with Lady Mackworth his daughter, were on board
(*Daily Chron.* May 7, 1918).

Damaris, with her old guardian and nurse, accept him without further wonderment
(*Times Lit. Supp.* May 29, 1919).

with-. See *with*.

withal. ME. *with alle*, for AS. *mid ealle*, wholly. Cf. OF. *atout* (*à tout*) in very similar sense. See *with*.

withe. See *withy*.

wither. ME. *wideren*, *wederen*, from *weder*, weather. Thus orig. sense is to change by exposure to weather, and a *withered leaf* and *weathered rock* are parallel.

withers. From ME. *wither*, AS. *withre*, resistance, cogn. with AS. *wither*, against (see *with*); cf. Du. *weder*, Ger. *wider*, against, *wieder*, again, ON. *vithr*, Goth. *withra*; cogn. with Sanskrit *vi*, apart, with suffix as in L. *inter*, *intra*. The *withers* are so called because they feel the pull of the vehicle. Cf. synon. Ger. *widerrist*, of which second element is cogn. with *wrist*.

Let the galled jade wince, our withers are unwrung
(*Haml.* iii. 2).

within, without. AS. *withinnan*, *withūtan*, lit. against the inside, outside (see *with*). With sense-development of *without* cf. that of F. *hors*, lit. outside.

withy, withe. AS. *wíthig*, willow, bond (*Judges*, xvi.). Com. Teut.; cf. Du. *weede*, hop-bine, Ger. *weide*, willow, ON. *vith*, *vithja*; prob. from an Aryan root meaning flexible which appears in L. *vitis*, vinetendril, *vimen*, osier, *vinum*, vine, G. ἰτέα, willow.

witness. AS. *witnes*, evidence (given of one's own knowledge or *wit*). For transition from abstract to personal cf. F. *témoin*, a witness, representing L. *testimonium*, evidence. With to *call to witness* cf. F. *prendre à témoin*, orig. sense of both phrases being abstract. Verb to *witness* is in *Piers Plowm*.

witticism, wittingly. See *wit*.

wittol [*archaic*]. Husband conniving at wife's infidelity. App. from bird-name *witewal*, *woodwale*, the green woodpecker, from a belief that it hatched the cuckoo's eggs and reared the cuckoo's young as its own. No doubt the application of the nickname was partly determined by a punning allusion to *wit*, knowledge, AS. *witol*, knowing (the old etymologists explained *wittol* as *wit-all*, i.e. know all). For a similar use of a bird-name cf. *cuckold* and also L. *curruca*, "the bird which hatcheth the cuckowes egges; also a cuckold, Juv. *Sat.* vi." (Holyoak). The bird-name is app. from *wood*, but the second element is obscure. It has been supposed to be cogn. with *Welsh* (q.v.) and to mean foreigner.

witwal, a bird: picus. *Witwal*, or *wittal*, a witting cuckold: Cornelius Tacitus (Litt.).

wivern [*her.*]. Dragon. AF. *wivre*, ONF. form of F. *guivre*, snake, L. *vipera*, viper. The -*n* is excrescent, as in *bittern*. The initial *gu-*, *w-* suggests that the word passed into F. via OHG.

wizard. ME. *wisard*, from *wise*[2], with pejorative suffix (cf. *dastard, sluggard*, etc.). Unconnected with *witch*.

wizened. From *wizen*, AS. *wisnian*, to wither, cogn. with *weornian*, to fade; cf. ON. *visinn*, wizened, whence *visna*, to wither, also OHG. *wesanēn*. ? Cogn. with Teut. *wesan*, to be, with sense of "has been" (cf. Ger. *verwesen*, decayed), ? or from Aryan root containing idea of destruction which appears in L. *virus*, poison. Also spelt *weazen-ed*.

woad. AS. *wād*; cf. Du. *weede*, Ger. *waid*; also F. *guède*, It. *guado*, from Teut. Prob. an ancient Aryan word represented in L. by *vitrum*.

wobble. For earlier *wabble*, frequent. of dial. *wap*, cogn. with ME. *quappen*, to tremble, and perh. ult. with *squab*.

woe. AS. *wā*, orig. interj. of dismay. Com. Teut.; cf. Du. *wee*, Ger. *weh*, ON. *vei*, Goth. *weh*; also L. *vae*. In *woe is me*, etc. the complement is dat. (cf. L. *vae victis*). Cf. *wail, welladay*. *Woebegone* preserves the p.p. of AS. *begān, begangan*, to surround, beset, take possession of, the *woe-* being instrument.

> Wo was this wrecched womman tho begon
>
> (Chauc. B. 918).

> "Go wei," quod the kok, "wo the bi-go!"
>
> (*Vox and Wolf*).

woiwode. See *voivode*.

wold. ME. *wald*, AS. *weald*. See *weald*. Orig. sense, like that of *forest*, was uncultivated or unenclosed ground. The northern *wolds* are usu. treeless, like the southern *downs*. Cf. *Cotswold*.

wolf. AS. *wulf*. Aryan; cf. Du. Ger. *wolf*, ON. *úlfr*, Goth. *wulfs*, L. *lupus*, G. λύκος, Sanskrit *vṛka*; cogn. with G. ἑλκεῖν, to tear (cf. *vulture*). The lost guttural of the Teut. forms survives in ON. *ylgr*, she-wolf. As the commonest of the predatory animals the wolf figures largely in metaphor and is an important element in Teut. names (*Ethelwulf, Wolfram*, etc.). As emblem of famine in *keep the wolf from the door*. See also *Tartar*.

> Veniunt ad vos in vestimentis ovium, intrinsecus autem sunt lupi rapaces (*Vulg. Matt.* vii. 15).

wolfram [*chem.*]. Ger., orig. personal name, "wolf raven." For application to mineral cf. *cobalt, nickel*.

wolverine. NAmer. glutton[2]. Irreg. from *wolf*.

woman. AS. *wīfmann*, wife man, i.e. female being, with pl. *wīfmen*. For loss of *-f-* cf. *leman*. Change of vowel is due to the init. *w-* (cf. *won't*), survival of orig. sound in pl. being app. due to unconscious tendency to differentiate, perh. also to assim. to second syllable (*wīmīn*).

> And she answered (all the woman in her flashing from her eyes),
> "You mustn't ask no questions, and you won't be told no lies!" (Gilbert, *Annie Protheroe*).

womb. AS. *wamb*, belly. Com. Teut.; cf. Du. *wam*, Ger. *wamme, wampe*, ON. *vömb*, Goth. *wamba*, all rather in gen. than in spec. E. mod. sense.

> And he covetide to fille his wombe of the coddis that the hoggis eeten (Wyc. *Luke*, xv. 16).

wombat. From native Austral. *womback*.

wonder. AS. *wundor*. Com. Teut.; cf. Du. *wonder*, Ger. *wunder*, ON. *undr*. *Wondrous* is altered from ME. *wonders*, adv. genitive of adj. *wonder*, which is a back-formation from adv. *wonderly*, AS. *wundorlic*. Cf. *righteous* for a similar adoption of *-ous*. *Wonderland* was popularized by Lewis Carroll (1865).

> The great world behold, lo, divided wonderly Into two regions (*Four Elements*, c. 1510).

wont. First as adj. With excrescent *-t* from ME. *wone, wune*, accustomed, AS. *gewun*, usual, cogn. with *wunian*, to dwell, continue, become habituated. Perh. also partly from the p.p. *woned* of the ME. verb. Cf. Ger. *gewohnt*, wont, OHG. *giwon*, of which earlier form survives in *gewohnheit*, habit, *gewöhnlich*, usually. Also ON. *vanr*, accustomed, *venja*, to accustom (see *wean*). The whole group perh. belongs to the Aryan root meaning pleasure which appears in *winsome, Venus*, etc.

> She never was to swiche gestes woned
>
> (Chauc. E. 339).

won't. For *will not*. For change of vowel after *w-* cf. *woman*. Perh. also influenced by *don't*.

woo. ME. *wowen*, AS. *wōgian*, also *wōgere*, wooer, with no known cognates.

wood. AS. *widu, wudu*, forest, timber (cf. double sense of Ger. *holz*); cogn. with ON. *vithr*, tree, OHG. *witu* (still in *wiedehopf*, hoopoe, wood-hen, lit. wood-hopper); also with OIr. *fid*, tree, Gael. *fiodh*, wood, Welsh *gwydd*, trees. For *woodbine* see *bine*. Second element of *woodruff*, AS. *wudurofe*, is obscure. The fact that it is a common surname (cf. *Woodward*) would point to some connection with *reeve*[1]; cf. Ger. *waldmeister*, "woodroof, woodrow, spurry" (Ludw.), lit. wood-master. The *wood-reeve* was an important official, and the bird-name *ruff*[4] (m.), *reeve*[3] (f.), suggests a possible ablaut relation between the vowels. *Not to see the wood for trees* has parallels in most langs.; cf. Ovid's *frondem in silvis non cernere*.

woodburytype [*phot.*]. Invented by *W. B. Woodbury* (†1885).

woodchuck. NAmer. marmot. NAmer. Ind. (Cree) *wuchak*, assimilated to *wood*. Longfellow's *ojeeg* (*Hiawatha*, xvi.) is the Odjibway form.

woof. Altered, under influence of *weave*, from ME. *oof*, "thred for webbynge; *trama*" (*Prompt. Parv.*), AS. *ōwef*, which is likewise altered under same influence from *ōwebb*, *āwebb*, whence dial. *abb* in same sense. The prefix of the last word is *on-*. See *web*.

wool. AS. *wull*. Com. Teut.; cf. Du. *wol*, Ger. *wolle*, ON. *ull*, Goth. *wulla*; cogn. with L. *villus*, *vellus*, Russ. *volna*, Welsh *gwlán* (whence *flannel*), Sanskrit *ūrṇā*. The *woolsack* is supposed by Evelyn to be emblematic of chief source of national wealth. Both he and Pepys use *wool-pack* of judges' bench in House of Lords. To *go woolgathering* (of wits), used by Flor., is perh. connected with the salving of wool from hedges and brambles, a task entrusted to the weak and inefficient.

And so his hyghness shall have thereoff but as hadd the man that sherid is hogge, muche crye and litill woll (*NED.* c. 1460).

The sons of Knipperdoling
Let all their senses run a-woolling
(Ward, *Hudibras Rediv.* 1715).

woold [*naut.*]. With excrescent -*d*, for earlier *wool*, Du. *woelen*, to wrap, orig. to wind; cogn. with *wallow*.

Hemp roopes for wulling of ordinance vj coyles (*Privy Council Acts*, 1547).

word. AS. *word*. Com. Teut.; cf. Du. *woord*, Ger. *wort*, ON. *orth*, Goth. *waurd*; cogn. with L. *verbum* (cf. *beard*, *red*). Also used for *word of honour*, e.g. *upon my word*, and for *watch-word*, e.g. *sharp's* (*mum's*) *the word*. Also collect. in *the word* (*of God*), *household word* (i.e. familiar expression). *Wordbook* is a foolish mod. imit. of Ger. *wörterbuch*, which is itself a 17 cent. "speech-purifying" substitute for *lexicon*.

work. Verb is AS. *wyrcan*, past *worhte* (whence *wrought*), from noun *weorc*. Com.

Teut.; cf. Du. Ger. *werk*, ON. *verk*; cogn. with *organ* and G. ἔργον, work. See also *wright*. Sense of fortification is found in AS. *Workday*, *workman*, *workhouse* are AS., the last in sense of *workshop*. *Workaday* is prob. for *working-day*. With mod. use of *works* as sing. cf. *United States* (v.i.), *shambles*, *golf-links*, etc.

O, how full of briers is this working-day world
(*As You Like It*, i. 3).

The United States has brought into existence a new steel-works (*Daily Chron.* May 1, 1919).

world. AS. *weorold*, *woruld*. Com. Teut.; cf. Du. *wereld*, Ger. *welt* (OHG. *weralt*), ON. *veröld*, all compds. of which first element means man (cf. *werwolf*), and second, cogn. with *old*, means age (cf. Goth. *alds*, world). Thus Ger. *weltalter*, epoch, is etym. pleon. Orig. sense was age, period, later development being imit. of L. *saeculum*, century, used, in early Church L., for (this) world in contrast with eternity (cf. *secular*, *temporal*). Orig. sense still in *world without end* = L. *in saecula saeculorum*. For extended senses cf. those of F. *monde*. Mod. pol. compds., e.g. *world-power*, (*-politics*), are adapted from Ger. (see *welt*[2]). With *all the world and his wife* (Swift) cf. F. *tout le monde et son père*.

worm. AS. *wyrm*, serpent, dragon, worm. Com. Teut.; cf. Du. *worm*, Ger. *wurm* (still meaning serpent in poet. *lindwurm*), ON. *ormr* (as in the *Great Orme*, i.e. dragon), Goth. *waurms*; cogn. with L. *vermis*, G. ῥόμος.

wormwood. Corrupt. of AS. *wermōd*, *weremōd*; cf. Du. *wermoet*, Ger. *wermut*. The two elements app. represent man (see *werwolf*, *world*) and courage (*mood*[1]), and I suggest that the name is due to the early use of the herb as an aphrodisiac. See quot. below, and cf. *skirret*.

Prosunt [absinthia] hominibus, spleni, virgaeque virili (Neckham, 12 cent.).

worry. AS. *wyrgan*, to strangle. WGer.; cf. Du. *worgen*, Ger. *würgen*. Orig. sense in to *worry sheep* (*prey*). Later sense appears to have been affected by obs. *warray*, *werrey* (see *war*); cf. sense-development of *harry*.

worse, worst. AS. *wiersa*, *wierrest*, used as compar. and superl. of *yfel*. Com. Teut.; cf. OSax. *wirs*, *wirsista*, OHG. *wirser*, *wirsist*, ON. *verri*, *verst*, Goth. *wairsiza* (compar.); survives only in E. & Scand. Sc. *waur* is from ON. With to *worst* cf. synon. to *best*. With vulgar *worser* cf. literary *better, lesser. If the worst comes to the worst* is 16 cent., but the first *worst* was perh. orig. *worse*.

I cannot hate thee worser than I do
(*Ant. & Cleop.* ii. 5).

worship. First as noun. AS. *weorthscipe*, "worth-ship," glory, dignity, orig. sense surviving in *your worship* (cf. *your lordship, honour, majesty,* etc., *the worshipful the Mayor*). Verb is ME. See quot. s.v. *worsted*.

worsted. Recorded from 13 cent. From *Worstead*, Norfolk, place of origin. See Chauc. A. 262. F. *ostade*, "the stuffe worsted, or woosted" (Cotg.), is from E.

I wold make my doblet all worsted for worship of Norffolk (*Paston Let.* ii. 235).

wort¹. Herb. Now chiefly in compds. (*cole-wort, mugwort,* etc.), otherwise replaced by *plant.* AS. *wyrt*, plant, root. Com. Teut.; cf. OSax. *wurt*, Ger. *wurz*, ON. *urt*, Goth. *waurts*; cogn. with *root¹*, and ult. also with L. *radix*, G. *ρίζα*. See also *wurzel*.

wort². Unfermented beer. AS. *wyrt*, in *max-wyrt*, mash-wort, app. ident. with *wort¹*; cf. OSax. *wurtia*, Ger. *würze*, spice, ON. *virtr*, beer-wort, cogn. but not ident. forms.

worth¹. Value. AS. *weorth* (noun & adj.). Com. Teut.; cf. Du. *waard*, Ger. *wert*, ON. *verth*, Goth. *wairths*; ? cogn. with *ware¹*. With later *worthy* cf. *swarthy, vasty, wary*. The suffix *-worth*, in *stalworth*, is cogn.

worth² [*archaic*]. In *woe worth the day*. Pres. subj. of AS. *weorthan*, to become, be. Com. Teut.; cf. Du. *worden*, Ger. *werden*, ON. *vertha*, Goth. *wairthan*; cogn. with L. *vertere*, to turn, ground-sense of taking direction appearing in cogn. *-ward(s)*. See also *weird*.

Thus saith the Lord God; Howl ye, Woe worth the day [*Vulg.* vae diei] (*Ezek.* xxx. 2).

worthy. See *worth¹*, and cf. Ger. *würdig*, ON. *verthugr*. Application to person, e.g. *a Tudor worthy*, appears in ME.

wot. See *wit*.

would. Past of *will* (q.v.).

wound. AS. *wund*. Com. Teut.; cf. Du. *wond*, Ger. *wunde*, ON. *und*, Goth. *wunds* (adj.). The adj. (AS. *wund*, Ger. *wund*) is perh. the older, and represents the pres. part. (cf. *friend, fiend*) of a Teut. verb, possibly represented by E. *win* (q.v.). Formerly rimed with *ground* (v.i.).

I'll sing thy [Charles I's] obsequies with trumpet sounds
And write thy epitaph with bloods and wounds
(Montrose).

wourali. See *curare*.

wr-. All words in *wr-* are of Teut. origin, the *w-* disappearing in Ger. & ON., though persisting as *v-* in mod. Scand. langs. The combination corresponds to G. *ρ-* for earlier *Fρ-*. A large proportion of *wr-* words belong to an Aryan root with sense of twisting.

wrack. ME. *wrac*, var. *wreck* (q.v.), from which it is now differentiated in sense; cf. Du. *wrak*; also F. *varech*, sea-weed, orig. "a sea-wrack or wrecke" (Cotg.), from E. See also *rack⁴*. *Wreck* is always *wrack* in early editions of Shaks.

The constable of the castel doun is fare
To seen this wrak, and al the ship he soghte
(Chauc. B. 512).

Wraf. Member of *Women's Royal Air Force* (1917). See *Waac* and cf. *Anzac*.

wraith. Orig. Sc. Earlier *wrath, wreth*, altered from *warth*, in orig. sense of guardian angel, ON. *vörthr*, guardian. See *ward*.

wrangle. ME. *wranglen*, cogn. with *wring*. Hence *wrangler* (univ.), disputant in schools, applied to first class in mathematical tripos.

wrap. App. for earlier *wlap*, for which see quot. s.v. *cratch*. This occurs passim in Wyc. where Tynd. has *wrap*. See also *develop*. It is possible that *wrapper* and *envelope* are ult. related. With fig. *wrapped up in* cf. *bound up with*. *Wrop* was once literary (v.i.).

The world was like a large and sumptuous shop,
Where God his goodly treasures did unwrap
(Sylv. *Furies*).

wrath. AS. *wrǣthu*, from *wrāth*, angry, whence *wroth*; cogn. with Du. *wreed*, angry, OHG. *rīdan*, to twist, ON. *reithr*, angry, and ult. with *writhe*.

wreak. AS. *wrecan*, to avenge (q.v.), orig. to drive, urge. Com. Teut.; cf. Du. *wreken*, Ger. *rächen*, ON. *reka*, to drive, pursue, Goth. *wrikan*, to persecute; cogn. with L. *urgēre*, G. *εἴργειν*, to shut in. To *wreak vengeance* is, compared with ME., pleon. Sometimes erron. used by mod. writers as though it were pres. of *wrought* (see *work*). See also *wreck, wretch*.

He wolde doon so ferforthly his myght
Upon the tiraunt Creon hem to wreke
(Chauc. A. 960).

The damage they have wreaked must be repaired to the uttermost farthing
(*Sunday Times*, Oct. 6, 1918).

wreath. AS. *wrǣth*, fillet, bandage, cogn. with *writhe*. Orig. sense of twisting in *wreath of* *smoke, face wreathed in smiles, wreathed horn* (Spenser, Wordsworth).

wreck. AS. *wræc*, exile, misery, from *wrecan*, to drive, wreak (q.v.). It later assumed sense of cogn. *wrack*, applied to anything driven ashore by the waves. Cf. *wretch*.

wren. AS. *wrenna*; cf. ON. *rindill*. ? From *Rindr, Vrindr*, one of the wives of Odin. Its names in other langs. are usu. royal, e.g. L. *regulus*, F. *roitelet*, Ger. *zaunkönig*, app. in allusion to golden crest.

Wren. Member of *Women's Royal Naval* (Div.).

wrench. AS. *wrenc*, artifice, trick, whence *wrencan*, to twist, wrench; cogn. with *wring* (q.v.). It is curious that the fig. sense (still in colloq. *wrinkle*) appears first in E. Logical order of senses appears in Ger. *ränke*, intrigue, pl. of *rank*, twist, cogn. with *renken*, to wrench, dislocate.

His wily wrenches thou ne mayst nat flee
               (Chauc. G. 1081).

wrest. AS. *wrǣstan*, to twist, cogn. with *wreath, writhe, wrist.* Twisting idea is still prominent in fig. sense.

The House is bent on wresting anything to his prejudice they can pick up (Pepys, Oct. 28, 1667).

wrestle. AS. *wrǣstlian*, from *wrest* (v.s.).

wretch. AS. *wrǣcca*, outcast, exile, from *wrecan*, to expel, "wreak"; for sense-development cf. Ger. *elend*, wretched, orig. exile, OHG. *eli-lenti*, of alien land. OHG. *recko, wreckeo*, bandit, outlaw, took in MHG. sense of warrior, whence poet. Ger. *recke*, revived by Wieland in 18 cent. With Pepys' regular "my wife, poor wretch" cf. quot. below. The word is still used somewhat endearingly in dial.

Excellent wretch! Perdition seize my soul,
But I do love thee (*Oth.* iii. 3).

wrick, rick. To twist. ME. *wrikken*, cogn. with *wriggle*. Cf. Du. *wrikken*, Norw. Dan. *vrikke*, Sw. *vricka*.

wriggle. Frequent. of obs. *wrig*, cogn. with *wrick* (v.s.) and with *wry, writhe*; cf. AS. *wrīgian*, to struggle forward.

wright. Now dial., exc. in compds. (*wheelwright, shipwright*, etc.), but very common as surname. AS. *wyrhta*, worker, from *wyrcan*, to work. Cf. OHG. *wurhta*, worker, also surviving in surnames, e.g. *Schuchardt*, shoe-wright.

Se wyrhta ys wyrthe hys metys
               (AS. *Gosp. Matt.* x. 10).

wring. AS. *wringan*, to twist. Com. Teut.; cf. Du. *wringen*, Ger. *ringen*, Norw. Dan.

vrang, contorted, Goth. *wruggō*, noose. Cogn. with *wrench, writhe*, etc.

wrinkle. AS. *wrincle*, cogn. with *wring, wrench*; cf. obs. Du. *wrinkel*, Ger. *runzel*, dim. of OHG. *runza* (for **wrunkza*); cogn. with L. *ruga*, furrow, wrinkle, and prob. also with *ruck*[2]. In sense of device, etc. (in *Euphues*), as in to *give one a wrinkle*, app. a direct dim. from *wrench* (q.v.).

wrist. AS. *wrist*, also *handwrist*, cogn. with *writhe*. For sense cf. Ger. *handgelenk*, wrist, from *lenken*, to turn. The Teut. sense is joint, articulation; cf. LG. *wrist*, Ger. *rist*, wrist and ankle in MHG., ON. *rist*, ankle.

writ. AS. *writ, gewrit*, a writing, legal document, scripture, from *write*. With *Holy writ* cf. *scripture*, F. *écritures saintes*, etc.

Ge dweliath, and ne cunnon hālige gewritu
             (AS. *Gosp. Matt.* xxii. 29).

The King's writ runs in Ireland
            (Lord Wimborne, Nov. 15, 1917).

write. AS. *wrītan*, to grave, draw, write. Com. Teut., though spec. sense, orig. to scratch runes on bark (see *book*), is not found in Du. & Ger.; cf. Du. *rijten*, Ger *reissen*, to tear, ON. *rīta*, to write, Goth. **wreitan* (inferred from *writs*, stroke of pen). Orig. sense of L. *scribere* was also to scratch (see *shrive*). Cf. also *character*.

writhe. AS. *wrīthan*, to twist. Com. Teut.; cf. archaic Du. *wrijten*, OHG. *rīdan* (whence F. *rider*, to wrinkle), ON. *rītha*. Orig. strong, as still in poet. p.p. *writhen*.

wrong. Late AS. *wrang*, injustice, from *wring*; cogn. with ON. *rangr* (for **wrangr*). As adj. still means lit. bent, crooked, in ME.

Ether of litil, ether of greet, and wrong [*Vulg.* tortus] nose (Wyc. *Lev.* xxi. 19).

Wrong is in French aptly called *Tort*, because wrong is wrested or crooked, being contrary to what is right and straight
            (Leigh, *Philologicall Commentary*).

wroth. See *wrath*.

wrought. See *work*.

wry. ME., bent, twisted, from *wrien*, to twist, etc., AS. *wrīgian*. Orig. sense survives in *awry*. See *wriggle*.

This Phebus gan aweyward for to wryen
            (Chauc. H. 262).

wurzel. Ger., root[1] (q.v.). Not a dim., but an orig. compd., OHG. *wurzala*, for **wurzwalu*, root-staff (see *wort*[1], *wale*); cf. AS. *wyrtwala*, root, stock, *wyrtwalian*, to plant. See also *mangel-wurzel*.

wyandotte. Breed of fowls from NAmer. Name of Red Ind. tribe.

wych-elm. See *witch-elm*.

Wykehamist. Member of Winchester College, founded (1378) by *William of Wykeham*, bishop of Winchester. Recorded from 16 cent.

wyvern. See *wivern*.

x-. All words in *x-*, exc. *xebec*, are of G. origin and learned formation. In the abbrevs. *Xmas*, *Xtian*, *X-* represents G. X (= *ch*); so also XP for G. Χριστός, Christ.

x. As symbol for 10 from L. In math. distortion of earlier crossed *r*, for L. *radix* (see *root*[1]) or *res*, as used by medieval mathematicians for the unknown quantity. Hence *x-rays*, from their unknown character (see *Röntgen rays*). On beer-barrels *XX*, *XXX* are said to be for *extra*.

Xanthippe. Shrew. Wife of Socrates.

xantho-. From G. ξανθός, yellow.

xebec. Vessel. Cf. F. *chabec*, *chebec*, It. *sciabecco*, *zambecco*, Sp. *jabeque*, Turk. *sumbakī*, all from Arab. *shabbak*.

xeno-. From G. ξένος, guest, stranger, foreigner.

xero-. From G. ξηρός, dry.

xipho-. From G. ξίφος, sword.

xylo-. From G. ξύλον, wood, timber.

xyster [*med.*]. Instrument for scraping bones. G. ξυστήρ, from ξύειν, to scrape.

xystus [*antiq.*]. Covered colonnade for use of athletes in winter. G. ξυστός, prop. adj., scraped (v.s.), from polished floor.

Y. Of various Y-shaped devices. Also *y-moth*, gamma-moth.

y-. In archaisms for AS. *ge-*. See *yclept*.

yacht. Du. *jacht*, earlier *jagt*, for *jagtschip*, from *jagen*, to hunt; cf. LG. *jageschip*. Used by Purch. (*jact*) in transl. from Du. Pepys (from 1659) has many allusions to the king's yacht, built as an improvement on his Du. pleasure-boat. *Yachting*, like skating (see *skate*[2]), came from Holland with Charles II. Also in F. (Colbert, 1666).

[We] anchored thwart of Sluis, where came on board us with his yachts [*MS.* yoathes] the Prince of Orange (Phineas Pett, 1613).

He is building the King's yacht, which will be a pretty thing, and much beyond the Dutchman
(Pepys, Jan. 13, 1661).

I sailed this morning with his Majesty in one of his yachts (or pleasure boats), vessels not known among us till the Dutch East India Company presented that curious piece to the king
(Evelyn, Oct. 1, 1661).

yager [*hist.*]. Du. *jager*, as *jäger* (q.v.). See also *yacht*.

yah. Natural expression of derision.

yahoo. Brute in human form. Coined by Swift (*Gulliver*), prob. from *yah*.

Yahveh, Yahvist. See *Jehovah*.

yak. Tibetan *gyak*.

yale lock. From name of US. inventor (19 cent.).

yam. Native WAfr. Spelt *inami*, *inani* by Hakl., *iniamo* by Purch.; cf. F. *iame* (*Paul et Virginie*), Port. *inhame*. Senegal *nyami*, to eat, "understood by foreigners as referring to the African 'staff of life'" (James Platt, *Notes & Queries*, March 24, 1900).

Saying in the true Creolian language and style, "No! me no can yam more"
(Hickey's *Memoirs*, ii. 64).

Yama. Hindu judge of the dead. Sanskrit.

yamen. See *Tsung-li-yamen*.

yank [*US.*]. To jerk abruptly. Origin unknown.

Yankee. Orig. (18 cent.) of limited application, and perh. first used of Du. inhabitants of New Amsterdam (New York). Prob. a dim. of Du. *Jan*, John (cf. *Jenkin*). It has also been suggested that it is a back-formation, like *Chinee*, *Portugee*, from Du. *Jan Kes*, lit. John Cornelius, both of which names are used as nicknames in Du. *Yankee doodle* was a pop. song during the War of Independence (1775–83).

And some be Scot, but the worst, God wot, and the boldest thieves, be Yank!
(Kipling, *Three Sealers*).

yap. Imit.; cf. F. *japper*, to yelp.

yard[1]. Measure. AS. *gierd*, rod, wand, measure of land; cf. Du. *gard*, rod, Ger. *gerte*, "a rod, switch, or wand" (Ludw.), Goth. *gazds*, stake; ? ult. cogn. with L. *hasta*, spear. For sense of measure cf. *rod*, *rood*, *pole*[1], *perch*[2]. Orig. sense still in naut. *yard*, *yard-arm*. Hanging at the *yard-arm* is recorded in Purch.

yard[2]. Enclosure. AS. *geard*. WAryan; cf. Du. *gaard*, OHG. *garto* (cf. *Stuttgart*), ON. *garthr* (see *garth*), Goth. *gards*, house, L. *hortus*, garden (q.v.), G. χόρτος, feeding-place, all with ground-sense of hedged enclosure; also OIr. *gort*, field, Russ. *gorod*, town (as in *Novgorod*), OSlav. *gradu* (*Belgrade*, *Petrograd*). For sense-development in other langs. cf. *town*.

yarn. AS. *gearn*. Com. Teut.; cf. Du. *garen*, Ger. ON. *garn*. Thought to come from an Aryan root containing idea of winding which appears in ON. *görn* (pl. *garner*), entrails, and L. *haru-spex*, "a divinour or soothsayer by looking in beastes bowels" (Coop.). Fig. sense from sailors' practice of telling tales while engaged in sedentary work such as yarn-twisting, with secondary allusion to length.

yarrow. AS. *gearwe*. WGer.; cf. Du. *gerw*, Ger. *garbe* (OHG. *garawa*).

yashmak. Moslem woman's veil. Arab.

yataghan. Earlier also *ataghan* (Byron). Turk. *yātāghān*, from *yātāq*, bed, ? thus a bedside weapon; cf. F. *épée de chevet*, lit. pillow-sword.

yaw [*naut.*]. ON. *jaga*, to sway (like a door on its hinges), supposed to be from Ger. *jagen*, to hunt (see *yacht*). In Shaks. (*Haml.* v. 2).

If any lose companie, and come in sight againe, to make three yawes, and strike the myson three times (Hawkins, 1564).

yawl[1]. Boat. Du. *jol*, "a Jutland boat" (Sewel); cf. LG. *jolle*, whence also Norw. Dan. *jolle*, Sw. *julle*, Ger. *jolle*, *jölle* (also *golle*, *gelle*), F. *yole*; ? ult. from ON. *kjöll*, barge, ship, keel[2]. Purch. has *joll*, in transl. from Du. *Jolly-boat* (q.v.) is unconnected.

yawl[2]. To yell, etc. Imit., cf. Ger. *jaulen*, ON. *gaula*.

yawn. AS. *gānian*, also *gīnan*, *geonian*. Com. Teut.; cf. Ger. *gähnen* (OHG. *ginēn*, *geinōn*), ON. *gīna* (cf. ON. *gin*, maw); also, without the *-n-* (orig. inflexional), Du. *geeuwen*, OHG. *giwēn*; cogn. with L. *hiare*, to gape, G. χειά, hole.

yaws. Tropical Afr. disease, framboesia. Orig. from Guiana, and prob. a Guarani (Brazil) word.

yclept. Now only facet., perh. owing to its use by Armado and Holofernes in *Love's Lab. Lost*. ME. (*y-* for AS. *ge-*) for AS. *gecliped*, p.p. of *clipian*, to call (out); cf. OFris. *klippa*, to ring, LG. *klippen*, to resound.

He conquered al the regne of Femenye,
That whilom was y-cleped Scithia (Chauc. A. 866).

ye. AS. *gē*, *gīe*, nom. pl., and as such distinguished from *you* in ME., though often confused with it in early mod. E., e.g. in *thankee* (*thank ye*). Aryan; cf. Du. *gij*, OHG. *ir* (*ihr*), ON. *ēr*, Goth. *jūs*, G. ὑμεῖς, Sanskrit *yūyam*. See *you*, *your*.

Blessed are ye, when men shall revile you, and persecute you (*Matt.* v. 11).

y[e]. Archaic printing for *the*, *y* being substituted for obs. symbol þ (= *th*). Cf. the substitution in Sc. of *z* for obs. ʒ (= *gh* or *y*) in *Mackenzie*, etc.

yea. AS. *gēa*. Com. Teut.; cf. Du. Ger. ON. Goth. *ja*; cogn. with G. ῆ, truly. See *yes*.

yean, ean [*archaic & dial.*]. To bring forth (a lamb), whence *yeanling*, young lamb. AS. *geēanian* and *ēanian*; cf. Du. *oonen*; ? ult. cogn. with L. *agnus*, lamb; cf. Welsh *oen*, OIr. *úan*, lamb.

year. AS. *gēar*, *gēr*. Com. Teut.; cf. Du. *jaar*, Ger. *jahr*, ON. *ār*, Goth. *jēr*. Also OPers. *yār-*. Orig. sense was prob. spring, turn of the year; cf. cogn. G. ὥρα, season, spring, Slav. *jaru*, spring. The true Aryan word for year appears in G. ἔτος, cogn. with L. *vetus*, old. For uninflected neut. pl., as still in *two-year-old*, etc., cf. *swine*.

yearn. AS. *giernan*, from *georn*, eager, desirous. Com. Teut.; cf. Du. *gaarne*, Ger. *gern* (adv., willingly), ON. *gjarn*, Goth. *gairns* (in *faihu-gairns*, avaricious); also Ger. *begehren*, to desire (from MHG. *geren*).

yeast. AS. *gist*. Com. Teut.; cf. Du. *gest*, Ger. *gischt*, earlier *gäscht* (cf. *gähren*, to ferment, causal from OHG. *jesen*), ON. *jastr*; cogn. with G. ζεῖν, to boil.

yelk. See *yolk*.

yell. AS. *gellan*. Com. Teut.; cf. Du. *gillen*, Ger. *gellen*, ON. *gjalla*; cogn. with AS. *galan*, to sing, and hence with *nightingale*. Of imit. origin.

yellow. AS. *geolu*, *geolw-*. WGer.; cf. Du. *geel*, Ger. *gelb* (OHG. *gelo*, *gelw-*); cogn. with ON. *gulr*, L. *helvus*, pale yellow, G. χλωρός, green, OPers. *zari-*, yellow. *Yellowhammer* is for *-ammer*, AS. *amore*, *emer*, with which cf. Ger. *goldammer*, *emmerling* (corruptly *hämmerling*), applied to various birds; perh. cogn. with OHG. *amar*, kind of corn (cf. hist. of *linnet*). The corrupt. may be partly due to the metallic note of the bird. The *yellow peril* was first formulated in Germany (*die gelbe gefahr*). Hence perh. also US. *yellow press* (1898), sensationally chauvinistic.

The yellow-hammers on the roof-tiles beat
Sweet little dulcimers to broken time
                (Francis Ledwidge).

yelp. AS. *gielpan*, to boast; cogn. with *yell*; cf. MHG. *gelfen*, ON. *gjālpa*. Of imit. origin.

yen. Jap. coinage unit. Chin. *yuen*, round, dollar.

yeoman. From 13 cent. App. for unrecorded AS. **gēa-mann* (cf. OFris. *gāman*, villager), with first element cogn. with archaic Ger. *gau*, region, country (as in *Rheingau, Breisgau, Aargau*, etc.), OHG. *gouwi*; cf. Goth. *gawi* and AS. *-gēa* (in place-names). ME. sense (Chauc. etc.) is that of trusted attendant and fighting-man of lower rank than squire, the order being "knight, squire, yeoman, knave." This survives in *yeoman service* (*Haml.* v. 2). We may compare Ger. *landsknecht*, foot-soldier, lit. land man. For later sense of small landholder cf. that of *squire*. *Yeomanry* is formed on *infantry, cavalry*, mil. organization dating from 1761. Mod. spelling attempts to reconcile the ME. forms *yemen, yoman*.

The flower of England's chivalry, her knights and yeomen, had perished
(Corbett-Smith, *Marne and after*).

yes. AS. *gēse*, ? for *gēa swā*, yea so, ? or *gēa sī*, yea be it. A much stronger affirmation than the simple *yea*. Cf. AS. *nese*, no. *Yes* does not occur in *AV.*, and in Shaks. is used esp., like F. *si*, in reply to a neg. question.

yesterday. AS. *giestrandæg*, with which cf. *giestranæfen*, whence poet. *yestre'en*. Com. Teut.; cf. Du. *gisteren*, Ger. *gestern*, also ON. *ī gær*, yesterday, to-morrow, Goth. *gistradagis*, to-morrow, ground-sense being the day other than to-day; cogn. with L. *heri, hesternus*, G. χθές, Sanskrit *hyas*.

Where are the snows of yester-year [*antan*]?
(Rossetti, *transl. of* Villon's *ballade*).

yet. AS. *gīet*. Ger. *jetzt*, now, MHG. *ietze, iezuo*, app. from *ie*, ay, ever, *zuo*, to, suggests that AS. *gīet* is a similar compd.

yew. AS. *īw, ēow*. Com. Teut.; cf. Du. *ijf*, Ger. *eibe* (OHG. *īwa*, whence F. *if*), ON. *ȳr*; cogn. with Welsh *yw*, OIr. *eo*. Association with bow is very early, ON. *ȳr* being used for bow, as *askr*, ash, is for spear.

Yggdrasil [*Norse myth.*]. Ash-tree binding together earth, heaven and hell. From *Yggr*, a name of Odin.

Yiddish [*ling.*]. Ger. *jüdisch*, Jewish.

yield. AS. *gieldan*, to pay, render, orig. strong (v.i.) and trans.; current sense of surrendering from reflex. use. Com. Teut.; cf. Du. *gelden*, Ger. *gelten*, to be worth (whence *geld*, money), ON. *gjalda*, Goth. *-gildan*, in compds.; cogn. with OIr. *gell*,

pledge. Earliest E. sense survives in noun *yield* (from investments, land, etc.).

And by the force of twenty is he take
Unyolden, and y-drawe unto the stake
(Chauc. A. 2641).

Clepe the workmen, and yelde to hem her hijre
(Wyc. *Matt.* xx. 8).

-yl [*chem.*]. G. ὕλη, material, orig. wood, timber, cogn. with L. *silva*, wood.

yodel. Ger. *jodeln*, used of the Swiss mountaineers. Of imit. origin.

yogi. Hindu devotee of *yoga*, ascetic meditation. Hind., Sanskrit, union. Fryer (17 cent.) has *Jogue, Jogi*.

yo-ho, yo-heave-ho [*naut.*]. Similar meaningless cries are recorded from c. 1300.

Your maryners shall synge arowe
Hey how and rumby lowe (*Squire of Low Degree*).

Al the marynalis ansuert of that samyn sound,
"hou, hou" (*Complaynt of Scotlande*, 1549).

yoicks. Earlier (18 cent.) also *hyke, hoix, heux*. Cf. *tally-ho*.

yoke. AS. *geoc*, yoke, yoke of oxen, measure of land. Aryan; cf. Du. *juk*, Ger. *joch*, ON. *ok*, Goth. *juk*, L. *jugum*, G. ζυγόν, Sanskrit *yuga*. See also *join*. A word from the earliest agricultural age of mankind. Sense of pair and fig. uses (*under the yoke*, etc.) are also common to Aryan langs.

Thou robed man of justice, take thy place;—
And thou, his yoke-fellow of equity,
Bench by his side (*Lear*, iii. 6).

yokel. Origin unknown. It is ident. in form with one of the dial. names of the *hickwall*, a kind of woodpecker (? cf. *silly cuckoo*). ? Or from *yoke* (of plough); cf. Ger. *flegel*, yokel, lit. flail.

yolk, yelk. AS. *geoloca*, from *geolu*, yellow.

yon, yonder. AS. *geon*, that, *geond*, thither, with suffix as in *hither, thither*; cf. *geondan*, beyond. Com. Teut.; cf. Ger. *jener*, ON. *enn, inn*, Goth. *jains*; cogn. with G. ἐκεῖνος. Now, exc. in dial. and poet. style, replaced ungrammatically by *that*.

yore. AS. *gēara*, genitive pl. of *gēar*, year. Orig. used without *of*.

Hoom to Surrye been they went ful fayn,
And doon hir nedes as they han doon yoore
(Chauc. B. 173).

yorker [*cricket*]. ? From *York*, as being a favourite ball with Yorkshire bowlers, ? or from dial. *yark*, to jerk.

you. Orig. dat. and acc. of *ye* (q.v.). AS. *ēow*. Its incorr. use for nom. and complete expulsion, exc. in dial. and poet. style, of the sing. *thou*, is peculiar to E.

young. AS. *geong.* Com. Teut.; cf. Du. *jong,*
Ger. *jung,* ON. *ungr,* Goth. *juggs;* cogn.
with L. *juvencus,* bullock, Welsh *ieuanc,*
OIr. *óac,* young, the earlier Aryan stem
appearing in L. *juvenis,* Sanskrit *yuvan.*
The limitation of sex of the *young person*
dates from c. 1750 and the myth of her
super-sensitiveness from Mr Podsnap. Pol.
sense, e.g. *Young England (Ireland, Turks,*
etc.), started c. 1840–50. *Youngster,* replacing ME. *youngling* (cf. Ger. *jüngling,*
youth), was perh. suggested by *younker,*
Du. *jonker, jong-heer* (see *Junker*). This is
used by Spenser of a knight, but current
sense app. started in naut. E.

Then came the men and women, yonge persones
[*Vulg.* juvenes] and children
(Coverd. *Judith,* vii. 12).

Her Majestie may in this enterprize [conquest of
Guiana] employ all the souldiers and gentlemen
that are younger brethren (Raleigh).

We spared him two of our men, namely Mortimer
Prittle, yonker, and Thomas Valens (Purch. 1614).

your, yours. AS. *ēower,* genitive of *ye* (q.v.);
cf. OSax. *iuwar,* Ger. *euer,* ON. *ythr,* Goth.
izwar. For function cf. *my, thy, our,* etc.
Often used, esp. in 16–17 cents., with
something of the force of the ethic dat.,
e.g. *No one is so quarrelsome as your convinced pacifist.* Cf. *our friend,* the person in
question, *my lady,* the minx under discussion.

youth. AS. *geogoth* (see *young*), the nasal
disappearing as in Du. *jeugd* (from *jong*),
Ger. *jugend* (from *jung*). The same Aryan
suffix appears in L. *juventus.* Sense of individual is peculiar to E., but F. *jeunesse*
is similarly used in familiar speech.

yprite [*hist.*]. Explosive used in war. Ger.
yprit, from *Ypres* (1915).

ytterbium, yttrium [*chem.*]. From *Ytterby,*
Sweden.

yucca. Flower. Sp., from native lang. of
Hayti. " *Yucca* is among the very earliest
native American words on record. It is
quoted by Amerigo Vespucci in his famous
'First Letter,' date 1497" (James Platt,
Notes & Queries, Apr. 12, 1902).

Yugo-Slav [*ethn.*]. Includes Serbs, Croats,
Slovenes. From *jug,* south, common to
Slav. langs., exc. Pol.

Yule. AS. *gēol* (*geohhol, geohel*), cogn. with
ON. *jól;* cf. AS. names for December,
January (q.v.), also Goth. *fruma juileis,*
November, ON. *ȳlir,* December. Orig.

name of heathen festival at winter solstice
adapted to Christian use by the missionaries (cf. *Easter*). See also *jolly.*

ywis [*archaic*]. See *wis.*

zabernism [*hist.*]. Military jackbootery. From
an incident at *Saverne* (Ger. *Zabern*) in
Alsace (1912), when an excited Ger.
subaltern cut down a lame cobbler who
smiled at him. Cf. *junkerism.*

zaffer [*chem.*]. F. *zafre,* from Arab.

zamindar. See *zemindar.*

zanana. See *zenana.*

zany. "A buffon, Meery-Andrew, or Jack-
Pudding" (*Gloss. Angl. Nova,* 1707). It.
zanni, dial. pet form of *Giovanni,* John;
earlier *zane,* "the name of John. Also a
sillie John, a gull, a noddie. Used also for
a simple vice, clowne, foole, or simple
fellowe in a plaie or comedie" (Flor.).
Orig. a charlatan's attendant buffoon in
the character of a peasant from Bergamo
(see *bergamask*). In Shaks. (*Love's Lab.
Lost,* v. 2). With obs. to *zany* cf. to *ape.*

He's like the zani to a tumbler,
That tries tricks after him to make men laugh
(Ben Jonson, *Every Man out of his
Humour,* iv. 1).

zaptieh. Turk. policeman. Turk.

Zarathustran. See *Zoroastrian.*

zariba, zareeba. Fenced camp, etc. (Sudan).
Arab. *zarība,* pen, fold.

Zarp [*hist.*]. SAfr. slang for member of Transvaal police. From letters *Z.A.R.P.* on cap,
Zuyd-Afrikaansch-Republik-Polizei.

zeal. F. *zèle,* L., G. ζῆλος, ? ult. cogn. with
yeast. Orig. rel. sense in *zealot* (see *Canaanite*).

zebra. Port., from native WAfr. name.

The zevera or zebra which is like an horse
(Andrew Battell, in Purch.).

zebu. Humped ox. F. *zébu,* ult. of Tibetan
origin.

On le montrait à la foire à Paris en 1752 sous le nom
de zebu; nous avons adopté ce nom (Buffon).

zedoary. Pungent root. OF. *zedoaire,* MedL.
zedoaria, Pers. *zadwār.* Hence also ME.
zedewal (*cetewale* in Chauc. A. 3207).

zeitgeist. Ger., spirit of the age. See *tide,
ghost.* ? Coined by Herder (18 cent.).

Zelanian [*geog.*]. From ModL. *Nova Zelania,*
New Zealand.

zemindar. Landholder. Hind., from Pers.
zamīndār, from *zamīn,* earth, *-dār,* possessing (cf. *sirdar, ressaldar,* etc.).

zemstvo. Russ. local council. For *zemskoe sobranje* (q.v.), land council, from *zemlja*, earth, land (as in *Nova Zemlja*).

The Revolution commands the Zemstvos and Town Councils (*Daily Chron.* Mar. 17, 1917).

zenana. Hind., from Pers. *zanāna*, from *zan*, woman, cogn. with G. γυνή, woman (see *quean, queen*).

Zend. Ancient Pers. lang. preserved in the *Zend-Avesta*, containing teaching of Zoroaster. *Avistāk va Zand* is used in Pahlavi for the Zoroastrian law and commentary, the origin of both words being obscure. Hence *Zend* (ling.) for OPers.

zenith. F. *zénith*, OSp. *zenith*, Arab. *samt*, way, road, L. *semita*, pathway; for *samt-ur-ras*, path over-head. Cf. *azimuth*.

zephyr. F. *zéphyr*, L., G. ζέφυρος, west wind.

zeppelin. Invented (early 20 cent.) by *Count Zeppelin* (†1917). In E. as gen. name for airship. Colloq. *zepp*.

zero. F. *zéro*, It. *zero*, Sp. *cero*, contr. from MedL. *zephyrum*, Arab. *çifr*, cipher (q.v.).

zest. Orig. piece of lemon-peel, etc. to give piquancy (cf. to *add a zest to*). F. *zeste, zest*, used esp. of membrane dividing sections of nut. Origin obscure. I do not know whether there is anything in conjecture below.

zest: segmentum corticis aurantiae [orange] in vinum per flammam lucernae expressum, q.d. ζεστόν [hot] (Litt.).

zeugma [*gram.*]. Ellipsis in which word has double function; cf. *syllepsis*. G. ζεῦγμα, bond, linking, cogn. with *yoke* (q.v.).

zibet. Asiatic civet. It. *zibetto*, civet (q.v.).

zigzag. F., Ger. *zick-zack*, redupl. on *zacken*, point, tooth. See *attach*.

zinc. Ger. *zink*, of unknown origin. Perh. coined by Paracelsus.

Zingaro. Gipsy. It., also *Zingano* (Flor.), MedL. *Zingari* (pl.), whence also Ger. *Zigeuner*, F. *tzigane* (q.v.). Origin unknown. Late G. ἀθίγγανοί, a sect of early Christian heretics, lit. non-touchers, has been suggested.

zinnia. Flower. From *J. G. Zinn*, Ger. botanist. Cf. *dahlia, fuchsia*, etc.

Zionism. Movement (late 19 cent.) for colonizing Palestine with Jews. From *Zion*, Jerusalem, Heb. *Tsīyōn*, lit. hill.

zircon [*min.*]. Arab. *zarqūn*, cinnabar, from Pers. *zar*, gold. See *jargoon*.

zither. Ger., cither (q.v.).

Zoar. Place of refuge (*Gen.* xix. 22).

zodiac. F. *zodiaque*, L., G. ζωδιακός (sc. κύκλος, circle), from ζῴδιον, small figure, dim. of ζῷον, animal, cogn. with ζωή, life, ζῆν, to live.

zoetrope. Rudimentary form of cinematograph, wheel of life. Irreg. from G. ζωή, life, τροπή, turn.

zoic [*geol.*]. G. ζωικός, of animals (v.s.).

Zoilus. Captious critic (3 cent. B.C.). Cf. *Aristarchus*.

Zolaism. Gross form of realism as in novels of *Émile Zola* (†1900).

zollverein. Ger., customs union, from *zoll*, toll[1] (q.v.), *vereinen*, to unite, from *ein*, one.

zone. F., L., G. ζώνη, belt.

Zoo. For *Zoological Gardens*. Cf. *Cri(terion)*, *Pav(ilion)*.

zoo-. From G. ζωός, living, from ζωή, life.

zoom [*aeron.*]. "Zooming means just merely lifting the machine to surmount an obstacle and immediately putting her nose down again" (*Daily Chron.* Feb. 2, 1917). Cf. *blimp*.

zorilla. Kind of skunk. Sp., dim. of *zorra*, fox, ? from Basque *zurra*, crafty.

Zoroastrian. Of *Zoroaster*, OPers. *Zarathustra*, rel. teacher of the Persians (7–6 cent. B.C.), founder of religion of the magi and of the Parsees.

zouave. F., orig. name, *Zaouavua*, of Kabyle tribe (Algeria) from which recruited. The *zouaves* are now F. soldiers, the native Algerian soldiers being called *Turcos*.

zounds [*archaic*]. For *God's-wounds*.

zucchetta [*eccl.*]. Skull cap. It., dim. of *zucca*, gourd.

zwieback. Ger., lit. two-bake. Cf. *biscuit*.

Zwinglian. Follower of Swiss Reformer *Zwingli* (†1531).

zygo-. From G. ζυγόν, yoke.

zymotic [*med.*]. G. ζυμωτικός, from ζύμη, leaven, fermentation, cogn. with ζεῖν, to boil.

A CATALOG OF SELECTED
DOVER BOOKS
IN ALL FIELDS OF INTEREST

DRAWINGS OF REMBRANDT, edited by Seymour Slive. Updated Lippmann, Hofstede de Groot edition, with definitive scholarly apparatus. All portraits, biblical sketches, landscapes, nudes. Oriental figures, classical studies, together with selection of work by followers. 550 illustrations. Total of 630pp. 9⅛ × 12¼.
21485-0, 21486-9 Pa., Two-vol. set $29.90

GHOST AND HORROR STORIES OF AMBROSE BIERCE, Ambrose Bierce. 24 tales vividly imagined, strangely prophetic, and decades ahead of their time in technical skill: "The Damned Thing," "An Inhabitant of Carcosa," "The Eyes of the Panther," "Moxon's Master," and 20 more. 199pp. 5⅜ × 8½.   20767-6 Pa. $4.95

ETHICAL WRITINGS OF MAIMONIDES, Maimonides. Most significant ethical works of great medieval sage, newly translated for utmost precision, readability. Laws Concerning Character Traits, Eight Chapters, more. 192pp. 5⅜ × 8½.
24522-5 Pa. $5.95

THE EXPLORATION OF THE COLORADO RIVER AND ITS CANYONS, J. W. Powell. Full text of Powell's 1,000-mile expedition down the fabled Colorado in 1869. Superb account of terrain, geology, vegetation, Indians, famine, mutiny, treacherous rapids, mighty canyons, during exploration of last unknown part of continental U.S. 400pp. 5⅜ × 8½.   20094-9 Pa. $8.95

HISTORY OF PHILOSOPHY, Julián Marías. Clearest one-volume history on the market. Every major philosopher and dozens of others, to Existentialism and later. 505pp. 5⅜ × 8½.   21739-6 Pa. $9.95

ALL ABOUT LIGHTNING, Martin A. Uman. Highly readable nontechnical survey of nature and causes of lightning, thunderstorms, ball lightning, St. Elmo's Fire, much more. Illustrated. 192pp. 5⅜ × 8½.   25237-X Pa. $5.95

SAILING ALONE AROUND THE WORLD, Captain Joshua Slocum. First man to sail around the world, alone, in small boat. One of great feats of seamanship told in delightful manner. 67 illustrations. 294pp. 5⅜ × 8½.   20326-3 Pa. $4.95

LETTERS AND NOTES ON THE MANNERS, CUSTOMS AND CONDITIONS OF THE NORTH AMERICAN INDIANS, George Catlin. Classic account of life among Plains Indians: ceremonies, hunt, warfare, etc. 312 plates. 572pp. of text. 6⅛ × 9¼.   22118-0, 22119-9, Pa., Two-vol. set $17.90

THE SECRET LIFE OF SALVADOR DALÍ, Salvador Dalí. Outrageous but fascinating autobiography through Dalí's thirties with scores of drawings and sketches and 80 photographs. A must for lovers of 20th-century art. 432pp. 6½ × 9¼. (Available in U.S. only)   27454-3 Pa. $9.95

THE BOOK OF BEASTS: Being a Translation from a Latin Bestiary of the Twelfth Century, T. H. White. Wonderful catalog of real and fanciful beasts: manticore, griffin, phoenix, amphivius, jaculus, many more. White's witty erudite commentary on scientific, historical aspects enhances fascinating glimpse of medieval mind. Illustrated. 296pp. 5⅜ × 8¼. (Available in U.S. only) 24609-4 Pa. $7.95

FRANK LLOYD WRIGHT: Architecture and Nature with 160 Illustrations, Donald Hoffmann. Profusely illustrated study of influence of nature—especially prairie—on Wright's designs for Fallingwater, Robie House, Guggenheim Museum, other masterpieces. 96pp. 9¼ × 10¾. 25098-9 Pa. $8.95

LIMBERT ARTS AND CRAFTS FURNITURE: The Complete 1903 Catalog, Charles P. Limbert and Company. Rare catalog depicting 188 pieces of Mission-style furniture: fold-down tables and desks, bookcases, library and octagonal tables, chairs, more. Descriptive captions. 80pp. 9⅜ × 12¼. 27120-X Pa. $6.95

YEARS WITH FRANK LLOYD WRIGHT: Apprentice to Genius, Edgar Tafel. Insightful memoir by a former apprentice presents a revealing portrait of Wright the man, the inspired teacher, the greatest American architect. 372 black-and-white illustrations. Preface. Index. vi + 228pp. 8¼ × 11. 24801-1 Pa. $10.95

THE STORY OF KING ARTHUR AND HIS KNIGHTS, Howard Pyle. Enchanting version of King Arthur fable has delighted generations with imaginative narratives of exciting adventures and unforgettable illustrations by the author. 41 illustrations. xviii + 313pp. 6⅛ × 9¼. 21445-1 Pa. $6.95

THE GODS OF THE EGYPTIANS, E. A. Wallis Budge. Thorough coverage of numerous gods of ancient Egypt by foremost Egyptologist. Information on evolution of cults, rites and gods; the cult of Osiris; the Book of the Dead and its rites; the sacred animals and birds; Heaven and Hell; and more. 956pp. 6⅛ × 9¼. 22055-9, 22056-7 Pa., Two-vol. set $22.90

A THEOLOGICO-POLITICAL TREATISE, Benedict Spinoza. Also contains unfinished *Political Treatise*. Great classic on religious liberty, theory of government on common consent. R. Elwes translation. Total of 421pp. 5⅜ × 8½. 20249-6 Pa. $7.95

INCIDENTS OF TRAVEL IN CENTRAL AMERICA, CHIAPAS, AND YUCATAN, John L. Stephens. Almost single-handed discovery of Maya culture; exploration of ruined cities, monuments, temples; customs of Indians. 115 drawings. 892pp. 5⅜ × 8½. 22404-X, 22405-8 Pa., Two-vol. set $17.90

LOS CAPRICHOS, Francisco Goya. 80 plates of wild, grotesque monsters and caricatures. Prado manuscript included. 183pp. 6⅝ × 9⅜. 22384-1 Pa. $6.95

AUTOBIOGRAPHY: The Story of My Experiments with Truth, Mohandas K. Gandhi. Not hagiography, but Gandhi in his own words. Boyhood, legal studies, purification, the growth of the Satyagraha (nonviolent protest) movement. Critical, inspiring work of the man who freed India. 480pp. 5⅜ × 8½. (Available in U.S. only) 24593-4 Pa. $6.95

ILLUSTRATED DICTIONARY OF HISTORIC ARCHITECTURE, edited by Cyril M. Harris. Extraordinary compendium of clear, concise definitions for over 5,000 important architectural terms complemented by over 2,000 line drawings. Covers full spectrum of architecture from ancient ruins to 20th-century Modernism. Preface. 592pp. 7½ × 9⅝. 24444-X Pa. $15.95

THE NIGHT BEFORE CHRISTMAS, Clement C. Moore. Full text, and woodcuts from original 1848 book. Also critical, historical material. 19 illustrations. 40pp. 4⅝ × 6. 22797-9 Pa. $2.50

THE LESSON OF JAPANESE ARCHITECTURE: 165 Photographs, Jiro Harada. Memorable gallery of 165 photographs taken in the 1930s of exquisite Japanese homes of the well-to-do and historic buildings. 13 line diagrams. 192pp. 8⅜ × 11¼. 24778-3 Pa. $10.95

THE AUTOBIOGRAPHY OF CHARLES DARWIN AND SELECTED LETTERS, edited by Francis Darwin. The fascinating life of eccentric genius composed of an intimate memoir by Darwin (intended for his children); commentary by his son, Francis; hundreds of fragments from notebooks, journals, papers; and letters to and from Lyell, Hooker, Huxley, Wallace and Henslow. xi + 365pp. 5⅜ × 8. 20479-0 Pa. $6.95

WONDERS OF THE SKY: Observing Rainbows, Comets, Eclipses, the Stars and Other Phenomena, Fred Schaaf. Charming, easy-to-read poetic guide to all manner of celestial events visible to the naked eye. Mock suns, glories, Belt of Venus, more. Illustrated. 299pp. 5¼ × 8¼. 24402-4 Pa. $8.95

BURNHAM'S CELESTIAL HANDBOOK, Robert Burnham, Jr. Thorough guide to the stars beyond our solar system. Exhaustive treatment. Alphabetical by constellation: Andromeda to Cetus in Vol. 1; Chamaeleon to Orion in Vol. 2; and Pavo to Vulpecula in Vol. 3. Hundreds of illustrations. Index in Vol. 3. 2,000pp. 6⅛ × 9¼. 23567-X, 23568-8, 23673-0 Pa., Three-vol. set $41.85

STAR NAMES: Their Lore and Meaning, Richard Hinckley Allen. Fascinating history of names various cultures have given to constellations and literary and folkloristic uses that have been made of stars. Indexes to subjects. Arabic and Greek names. Biblical references. Bibliography. 563pp. 5⅜ × 8½. 21079-0 Pa. $9.95

THIRTY YEARS THAT SHOOK PHYSICS: The Story of Quantum Theory, George Gamow. Lucid, accessible introduction to influential theory of energy and matter. Careful explanations of Dirac's anti-particles, Bohr's model of the atom, much more. 12 plates. Numerous drawings. 240pp. 5⅜ × 8½. 24895-X Pa. $6.95

CHINESE DOMESTIC FURNITURE IN PHOTOGRAPHS AND MEASURED DRAWINGS, Gustav Ecke. A rare volume, now affordably priced for antique collectors, furniture buffs and art historians. Detailed review of styles ranging from early Shang to late Ming. Unabridged republication. 161 black-and-white drawings, photos. Total of 224pp. 8⅜ × 11¼. (Available in U.S. only) 25171-3 Pa. $14.95

VINCENT VAN GOGH: A Biography, Julius Meier-Graefe. Dynamic, penetrating study of artist's life, relationship with brother, Theo, painting techniques, travels, more. Readable, engrossing. 160pp. 5⅜ × 8½. (Available in U.S. only) 25253-1 Pa. $4.95

HOW TO WRITE, Gertrude Stein. Gertrude Stein claimed anyone could understand her unconventional writing—here are clues to help. Fascinating improvisations, language experiments, explanations illuminate Stein's craft and the art of writing. Total of 414pp. 4⅝ × 6⅜. 23144-5 Pa. $6.95

ADVENTURES AT SEA IN THE GREAT AGE OF SAIL: Five Firsthand Narratives, edited by Elliot Snow. Rare true accounts of exploration, whaling, shipwreck, fierce natives, trade, shipboard life, more. 33 illustrations. Introduction. 353pp. 5⅜ × 8½. 25177-2 Pa. $9.95

THE HERBAL OR GENERAL HISTORY OF PLANTS, John Gerard. Classic descriptions of about 2,850 plants—with over 2,700 illustrations—includes Latin and English names, physical descriptions, varieties, time and place of growth, more. 2,706 illustrations. xlv + 1,678pp. 8½ × 12¼. 23147-X Cloth. $89.95

DOROTHY AND THE WIZARD IN OZ, L. Frank Baum. Dorothy and the Wizard visit the center of the Earth, where people are vegetables, glass houses grow and Oz characters reappear. Classic sequel to *Wizard of Oz*. 256pp. 5⅜ × 8. 24714-7 Pa. $5.95

SONGS OF EXPERIENCE: Facsimile Reproduction with 26 Plates in Full Color, William Blake. This facsimile of Blake's original "Illuminated Book" reproduces 26 full-color plates from a rare 1826 edition. Includes "The Tyger," "London," "Holy Thursday," and other immortal poems. 26 color plates. Printed text of poems. 48pp. 5¼ × 7. 24636-1 Pa. $3.95

SONGS OF INNOCENCE, William Blake. The first and most popular of Blake's famous "Illuminated Books," in a facsimile edition reproducing all 31 brightly colored plates. Additional printed text of each poem. 64pp. 5¼ × 7. 22764-2 Pa. $3.95

PRECIOUS STONES, Max Bauer. Classic, thorough study of diamonds, rubies, emeralds, garnets, etc.: physical character, occurrence, properties, use, similar topics. 20 plates, 8 in color. 94 figures. 659pp. 6⅛ × 9¼. 21910-0, 21911-9 Pa., Two-vol. set $21.90

ENCYCLOPEDIA OF VICTORIAN NEEDLEWORK, S. F. A. Caulfeild and Blanche Saward. Full, precise descriptions of stitches, techniques for dozens of needlecrafts—most exhaustive reference of its kind. Over 800 figures. Total of 679pp. 8⅛ × 11. 22800-2, 22801-0 Pa., Two-vol. set $26.90

THE MARVELOUS LAND OF OZ, L. Frank Baum. Second Oz book, the Scarecrow and Tin Woodman are back with hero named Tip, Oz magic. 136 illustrations. 287pp. 5⅜ × 8½. 20692-0 Pa. $5.95

WILD FOWL DECOYS, Joel Barber. Basic book on the subject, by foremost authority and collector. Reveals history of decoy making and rigging, place in American culture, different kinds of decoys, how to make them, and how to use them. 140 plates. 156pp. 7⅞ × 10¾. 20011-6 Pa. $14.95

HISTORY OF LACE, Mrs. Bury Palliser. Definitive, profusely illustrated chronicle of lace from earliest times to late 19th century. Laces of Italy, Greece, England, France, Belgium, etc. Landmark of needlework scholarship. 266 illustrations. 672pp. 6⅛ × 9¼. 24742-2 Pa. $16.95

ILLUSTRATED GUIDE TO SHAKER FURNITURE, Robert Meader. All furniture and appurtenances, with much on unknown local styles. 235 photos. 146pp. 9 × 12. 22819-3 Pa. $9.95

WHALE SHIPS AND WHALING: A Pictorial Survey, George Francis Dow. Over 200 vintage engravings, drawings, photographs of barks, brigs, cutters, other vessels. Also harpoons, lances, whaling guns, many other artifacts. Comprehensive text by foremost authority. 207 black-and-white illustrations. 288pp. 6 × 9. 24808-9 Pa. $9.95

THE BERTRAMS, Anthony Trollope. Powerful portrayal of blind self-will and thwarted ambition includes one of Trollope's most heartrending love stories. 497pp. 5⅜ × 8½. 25119-5 Pa. $9.95

ADVENTURES WITH A HAND LENS, Richard Headstrom. Clearly written guide to observing and studying flowers and grasses, fish scales, moth and insect wings, egg cases, buds, feathers, seeds, leaf scars, moss, molds, ferns, common crystals, etc.—all with an ordinary, inexpensive magnifying glass. 209 exact line drawings aid in your discoveries. 220pp. 5⅜ × 8½. 23330-8 Pa. $5.95

RODIN ON ART AND ARTISTS, Auguste Rodin. Great sculptor's candid, wide-ranging comments on meaning of art; great artists; relation of sculpture to poetry, painting, music; philosophy of life, more. 76 superb black-and-white illustrations of Rodin's sculpture, drawings and prints. 119pp. 8⅜ × 11¼. 24487-3 Pa. $7.95

FIFTY CLASSIC FRENCH FILMS, 1912–1982: A Pictorial Record, Anthony Slide. Memorable stills from Grand Illusion, Beauty and the Beast, Hiroshima, Mon Amour, many more. Credits, plot synopses, reviews, etc. 160pp. 8¼ × 11. 25256-6 Pa. $11.95

THE PRINCIPLES OF PSYCHOLOGY, William James. Famous long course complete, unabridged. Stream of thought, time perception, memory, experimental methods; great work decades ahead of its time. 94 figures. 1,391pp. 5⅜ × 8½. 20381-6, 20382-4 Pa., Two-vol. set $25.90

BODIES IN A BOOKSHOP, R. T. Campbell. Challenging mystery of blackmail and murder with ingenious plot and superbly drawn characters. In the best tradition of British suspense fiction. 192pp. 5⅜ × 8½. 24720-1 Pa. $5.95

CALLAS: Portrait of a Prima Donna, George Jellinek. Renowned commentator on the musical scene chronicles incredible career and life of the most controversial, fascinating, influential operatic personality of our time. 64 black-and-white photographs. 416pp. 5⅜ × 8¼. 25047-4 Pa. $8.95

GEOMETRY, RELATIVITY AND THE FOURTH DIMENSION, Rudolph Rucker. Exposition of fourth dimension, concepts of relativity as Flatland characters continue adventures. Popular, easily followed yet accurate, profound. 141 illustrations. 133pp. 5⅜ × 8½. 23400-2 Pa. $4.95

HOUSEHOLD STORIES BY THE BROTHERS GRIMM, with pictures by Walter Crane. 53 classic stories—Rumpelstiltskin, Rapunzel, Hansel and Gretel, the Fisherman and his Wife, Snow White, Tom Thumb, Sleeping Beauty, Cinderella, and so much more—lavishly illustrated with original 19th-century drawings. 114 illustrations. x + 269pp. 5⅜ × 8½. 21080-4 Pa. $4.95

SUNDIALS, Albert Waugh. Far and away the best, most thorough coverage of ideas, mathematics concerned, types, construction, adjusting anywhere. Over 100 illustrations. 230pp. 5⅜ × 8½.   22947-5 Pa. $5.95

PICTURE HISTORY OF THE NORMANDIE: With 190 Illustrations, Frank O. Braynard. Full story of legendary French ocean liner: Art Deco interiors, design innovations, furnishings, celebrities, maiden voyage, tragic fire, much more. Extensive text. 144pp. 8⅞ × 11¾.   25257-4 Pa. $11.95

THE FIRST AMERICAN COOKBOOK: A Facsimile of "American Cookery," 1796, Amelia Simmons. Facsimile of the first American-written cookbook published in the United States contains authentic recipes for colonial favorites—pumpkin pudding, winter squash pudding, spruce beer, Indian slapjacks, and more. Introductory Essay and Glossary of colonial cooking terms. 80pp. 5⅜ × 8½.
24710-4 Pa. $3.50

101 PUZZLES IN THOUGHT AND LOGIC, C. R. Wylie, Jr. Solve murders and robberies, find out which fishermen are liars, how a blind man could possibly identify a color—purely by your own reasoning! 107pp. 5⅜ × 8½. 20367-0 Pa. $2.95

ANCIENT EGYPTIAN MYTHS AND LEGENDS, Lewis Spence. Examines animism, totemism, fetishism, creation myths, deities, alchemy, art and magic, other topics. Over 50 illustrations. 432pp. 5⅜ × 8½.   26525-0 Pa. $8.95

ANTHROPOLOGY AND MODERN LIFE, Franz Boas. Great anthropologist's classic treatise on race and culture. Introduction by Ruth Bunzel. Only inexpensive paperback edition. 255pp. 5⅜ × 8½.   25245-0 Pa. $7.95

THE TALE OF PETER RABBIT, Beatrix Potter. The inimitable Peter's terrifying adventure in Mr. McGregor's garden, with all 27 wonderful, full-color Potter illustrations. 55pp. 4¼ × 5½.   22827-4 Pa. $1.75

THREE PROPHETIC SCIENCE FICTION NOVELS, H. G. Wells. *When the Sleeper Wakes, A Story of the Days to Come* and *The Time Machine* (full version). 335pp. 5⅜ × 8½. (Available in U.S. only)   20605-X Pa. $8.95

APICIUS COOKERY AND DINING IN IMPERIAL ROME, edited and translated by Joseph Dommers Vehling. Oldest known cookbook in existence offers readers a clear picture of what foods Romans ate, how they prepared them, etc. 49 illustrations. 301pp. 6⅛ × 9¼.   23563-7 Pa. $8.95

SHAKESPEARE LEXICON AND QUOTATION DICTIONARY, Alexander Schmidt. Full definitions, locations, shades of meaning of every word in plays and poems. More than 50,000 exact quotations. 1,485pp. 6½ × 9¼.
22726-X, 22727-8 Pa., Two-vol. set $31.90

THE WORLD'S GREAT SPEECHES, edited by Lewis Copeland and Lawrence W. Lamm. Vast collection of 278 speeches from Greeks to 1970. Powerful and effective models; unique look at history. 842pp. 5⅜ × 8½.   20468-5 Pa. $12.95

THE BLUE FAIRY BOOK, Andrew Lang. The first, most famous collection, with many familiar tales: Little Red Riding Hood, Aladdin and the Wonderful Lamp, Puss in Boots, Sleeping Beauty, Hansel and Gretel, Rumpelstiltskin; 37 in all. 138 illustrations. 390pp. 5⅜ × 8½. 21437-0 Pa. $6.95

THE STORY OF THE CHAMPIONS OF THE ROUND TABLE, Howard Pyle. Sir Launcelot, Sir Tristram and Sir Percival in spirited adventures of love and triumph retold in Pyle's inimitable style. 50 drawings, 31 full-page. xviii + 329pp. 6½ × 9¼. 21883-X Pa. $7.95

THE MYTHS OF THE NORTH AMERICAN INDIANS, Lewis Spence. Myths and legends of the Algonquins, Iroquois, Pawnees and Sioux with comprehensive historical and ethnological commentary. 36 illustrations. 5⅜ × 8½. 25967-6 Pa. $8.95

GREAT DINOSAUR HUNTERS AND THEIR DISCOVERIES, Edwin H. Colbert. Fascinating, lavishly illustrated chronicle of dinosaur research, 1820s to 1960. Achievements of Cope, Marsh, Brown, Buckland, Mantell, Huxley, many others. 384pp. 5¼ × 8¼. 24701-5 Pa. $8.95

THE TASTEMAKERS, Russell Lynes. Informal, illustrated social history of American taste 1850s–1950s. First popularized categories Highbrow, Lowbrow, Middlebrow. 129 illustrations. New (1979) afterword. 384pp. 6 × 9. 23993-4 Pa. $8.95

NORTH AMERICAN INDIAN LIFE: Customs and Traditions of 23 Tribes, Elsie Clews Parsons (ed.). 27 fictionalized essays by noted anthropologists examine religion, customs, government, additional facets of life among the Winnebago, Crow, Zuni, Eskimo, other tribes. 480pp. 6⅛ × 9¼. 27377-6 Pa. $10.95

AUTHENTIC VICTORIAN DECORATION AND ORNAMENTATION IN FULL COLOR: 46 Plates from "Studies in Design," Christopher Dresser. Superb full-color lithographs reproduced from rare original portfolio of a major Victorian designer. 48pp. 9¼ × 12¼. 25083-0 Pa. $7.95

PRIMITIVE ART, Franz Boas. Remains the best text ever prepared on subject, thoroughly discussing Indian, African, Asian, Australian, and, especially, Northern American primitive art. Over 950 illustrations show ceramics, masks, totem poles, weapons, textiles, paintings, much more. 376pp. 5⅜ × 8. 20025-6 Pa. $8.95

SIDELIGHTS ON RELATIVITY, Albert Einstein. Unabridged republication of two lectures delivered by the great physicist in 1920–21. *Ether and Relativity* and *Geometry and Experience*. Elegant ideas in nonmathematical form, accessible to intelligent layman. vi + 56pp. 5⅜ × 8½. 24511-X Pa. $3.95

THE WIT AND HUMOR OF OSCAR WILDE, edited by Alvin Redman. More than 1,000 ripostes, paradoxes, wisecracks: Work is the curse of the drinking classes, I can resist everything except temptation, etc. 258pp. 5⅜ × 8½. 20602-5 Pa. $4.95

ADVENTURES WITH A MICROSCOPE, Richard Headstrom. 59 adventures with clothing fibers, protozoa, ferns and lichens, roots and leaves, much more. 142 illustrations. 232pp. 5⅜ × 8½. 23471-1 Pa. $4.95

PLANTS OF THE BIBLE, Harold N. Moldenke and Alma L. Moldenke. Standard reference to all 230 plants mentioned in Scriptures. Latin name, biblical reference, uses, modern identity, much more. Unsurpassed encyclopedic resource for scholars, botanists, nature lovers, students of Bible. Bibliography. Indexes. 123 black-and-white illustrations. 384pp. 6 × 9. 25069-5 Pa. $9.95

FAMOUS AMERICAN WOMEN: A Biographical Dictionary from Colonial Times to the Present, Robert McHenry, ed. From Pocahontas to Rosa Parks, 1,035 distinguished American women documented in separate biographical entries. Accurate, up-to-date data, numerous categories, spans 400 years. Indices. 493pp. 6½ × 9¼. 24523-3 Pa. $11.95

THE FABULOUS INTERIORS OF THE GREAT OCEAN LINERS IN HISTORIC PHOTOGRAPHS, William H. Miller, Jr. Some 200 superb photographs capture exquisite interiors of world's great "floating palaces"—1890s to 1980s: *Titanic, Ile de France, Queen Elizabeth, United States, Europa,* more. Approx. 200 black-and-white photographs. Captions. Text. Introduction. 160pp. 8⅜ × 11¾. 24756-2 Pa. $10.95

THE GREAT LUXURY LINERS, 1927–1954: A Photographic Record, William H. Miller, Jr. Nostalgic tribute to heyday of ocean liners. 186 photos of *Ile de France, Normandie, Leviathan, Queen Elizabeth, United States,* many others. Interior and exterior views. Introduction. Captions. 160pp. 9 × 12. 24056-8 Pa. $12.95

A NATURAL HISTORY OF THE DUCKS, John Charles Phillips. Great landmark of ornithology offers complete detailed coverage of nearly 200 species and subspecies of ducks: gadwall, sheldrake, merganser, pintail, many more. 74 full-color plates, 102 black-and-white. Bibliography. Total of 1,920pp. 8⅜ × 11¼. 25141-1, 25142-X Cloth., Two-vol. set $100.00

THE COMPLETE "MASTERS OF THE POSTER": All 256 Color Plates from "Les Maîtres de l'Affiche", Stanley Appelbaum (ed.). The most famous compilation ever made of the art of the great age of the poster, featuring works by Chéret, Steinlen, Toulouse-Lautrec, nearly 100 other artists. One poster per page. 272pp. 9¼ × 12¼. 26309-6 Pa. $29.95

THE TEN BOOKS OF ARCHITECTURE: The 1755 Leoni Edition, Leon Battista Alberti. Rare classic helped introduce the glories of ancient architecture to the Renaissance. 68 black-and-white plates. 336pp. 8⅜ × 11¼. 25239-6 Pa. $14.95

MISS MACKENZIE, Anthony Trollope. Minor masterpieces by Victorian master unmasks many truths about life in 19th-century England. First inexpensive edition in years. 392pp. 5⅜ × 8½. 25201-9 Pa. $8.95

THE RIME OF THE ANCIENT MARINER, Gustave Doré, Samuel Taylor Coleridge. Dramatic engravings considered by many to be his greatest work. The terrifying space of the open sea, the storms and whirlpools of an unknown ocean, the ice of Antarctica, more—all rendered in a powerful, chilling manner. Full text. 38 plates. 77pp. 9¼ × 12. 22305-1 Pa. $4.95

THE EXPEDITIONS OF ZEBULON MONTGOMERY PIKE, Zebulon Montgomery Pike. Fascinating firsthand accounts (1805–6) of exploration of Mississippi River, Indian wars, capture by Spanish dragoons, much more. 1,088pp. 5⅜ × 8½. 25254-X, 25255-8 Pa., Two-vol. set $25.90

A CONCISE HISTORY OF PHOTOGRAPHY: Third Revised Edition, Helmut Gernsheim. Best one-volume history—camera obscura, photochemistry, daguerreotypes, evolution of cameras, film, more. Also artistic aspects—landscape, portraits, fine art, etc. 281 black-and-white photographs. 26 in color. 176pp. 8⅜ × 11¼.
25128-4 Pa. $14.95

THE DORÉ BIBLE ILLUSTRATIONS, Gustave Doré. 241 detailed plates from the Bible: the Creation scenes, Adam and Eve, Flood, Babylon, battle sequences, life of Jesus, etc. Each plate is accompanied by the verses from the King James version of the Bible. 241pp. 9 × 12.
23004-X Pa. $9.95

WANDERINGS IN WEST AFRICA, Richard F. Burton. Great Victorian scholar/ adventurer's invaluable descriptions of African tribal rituals, fetishism, culture, art, much more. Fascinating 19th-century account. 624pp. 5⅜ × 8½. 26890-X Pa. $12.95

HISTORIC HOMES OF THE AMERICAN PRESIDENTS, Second Revised Edition, Irvin Haas. Guide to homes occupied by every president from Washington to Bush. Visiting hours, travel routes, more. 175 photos. 160pp. 8¼ × 11.
26751-2 Pa. $9.95

THE HISTORY OF THE LEWIS AND CLARK EXPEDITION, Meriwether Lewis and William Clark, edited by Elliott Coues. Classic edition of Lewis and Clark's day-by-day journals that later became the basis for U.S. claims to Oregon and the West. Accurate and invaluable geographical, botanical, biological, meteorological and anthropological material. Total of 1,508pp. 5⅜ × 8½.
21268-8, 21269-6, 21270-X Pa., Three-vol. set $29.85

LANGUAGE, TRUTH AND LOGIC, Alfred J. Ayer. Famous, clear introduction to Vienna, Cambridge schools of Logical Positivism. Role of philosophy, elimination of metaphysics, nature of analysis, etc. 160pp. 5⅜ × 8½. (Available in U.S. and Canada only)
20010-8 Pa. $3.95

MATHEMATICS FOR THE NONMATHEMATICIAN, Morris Kline. Detailed, college-level treatment of mathematics in cultural and historical context, with numerous exercises. For liberal arts students. Preface. Recommended Reading Lists. Tables. Index. Numerous black-and-white figures. xvi + 641pp. 5⅜ × 8½.
24823-2 Pa. $11.95

HANDBOOK OF PICTORIAL SYMBOLS, Rudolph Modley. 3,250 signs and symbols, many systems in full; official or heavy commercial use. Arranged by subject. Most in Pictorial Archive series. 143pp. 8¼ × 11. 23357-X Pa. $8.95

INCIDENTS OF TRAVEL IN YUCATAN, John L. Stephens. Classic (1843) exploration of jungles of Yucatan, looking for evidences of Maya civilization. Travel adventures, Mexican and Indian culture, etc. Total of 669pp. 5⅜ × 8½.
20926-1, 20927-X Pa., Two-vol. set $13.90

DEGAS: An Intimate Portrait, Ambroise Vollard. Charming, anecdotal memoir by famous art dealer of one of the greatest 19th-century French painters. 14 black-and-white illustrations. Introduction by Harold L. Van Doren. 96pp. 5⅜ × 8½.
25131-4 Pa. $4.95

PERSONAL NARRATIVE OF A PILGRIMAGE TO AL-MADINAH AND MECCAH, Richard F. Burton. Great travel classic by remarkably colorful personality. Burton, disguised as a Moroccan, visited sacred shrines of Islam, narrowly escaping death. 47 illustrations. 959pp. 5⅜ × 8½.
21217-3, 21218-1 Pa., Two-vol. set $19.90

PHRASE AND WORD ORIGINS, A. H. Holt. Entertaining, reliable, modern study of more than 1,200 colorful words, phrases, origins and histories. Much unexpected information. 254pp. 5⅜ × 8½.
20758-7 Pa. $5.95

THE RED THUMB MARK, R. Austin Freeman. In this first Dr. Thorndyke case, the great scientific detective draws fascinating conclusions from the nature of a single fingerprint. Exciting story, authentic science. 320pp. 5⅜ × 8½. (Available in U.S. only)
25210-8 Pa. $6.95

AN EGYPTIAN HIEROGLYPHIC DICTIONARY, E. A. Wallis Budge. Monumental work containing about 25,000 words or terms that occur in texts ranging from 3000 B.C. to 600 A.D. Each entry consists of a transliteration of the word, the word in hieroglyphs, and the meaning in English. 1,314pp. 6⅜ × 10.
23615-3, 23616-1 Pa., Two-vol. set $35.90

THE COMPLEAT STRATEGYST: Being a Primer on the Theory of Games of Strategy, J. D. Williams. Highly entertaining classic describes, with many illustrated examples, how to select best strategies in conflict situations. Prefaces. Appendices. xvi + 268pp. 5⅜ × 8½.
25101-2 Pa. $7.95

THE ROAD TO OZ, L. Frank Baum. Dorothy meets the Shaggy Man, little Button-Bright and the Rainbow's beautiful daughter in this delightful trip to the magical Land of Oz. 272pp. 5⅜ × 8.
25208-6 Pa. $5.95

POINT AND LINE TO PLANE, Wassily Kandinsky. Seminal exposition of role of point, line, other elements in nonobjective painting. Essential to understanding 20th-century art. 127 illustrations. 192pp. 6½ × 9¼.
23808-3 Pa. $5.95

LADY ANNA, Anthony Trollope. Moving chronicle of Countess Lovel's bitter struggle to win for herself and daughter Anna their rightful rank and fortune—perhaps at cost of sanity itself. 384pp. 5⅜ × 8½.
24669-8 Pa. $8.95

EGYPTIAN MAGIC, E. A. Wallis Budge. Sums up all that is known about magic in Ancient Egypt: the role of magic in controlling the gods, powerful amulets that warded off evil spirits, scarabs of immortality, use of wax images, formulas and spells, the secret name, much more. 253pp. 5⅜ × 8½.
22681-6 Pa. $4.95

THE DANCE OF SIVA, Ananda Coomaraswamy. Preeminent authority unfolds the vast metaphysic of India: the revelation of her art, conception of the universe, social organization, etc. 27 reproductions of art masterpieces. 192pp. 5⅜ × 8½.
24817-8 Pa. $6.95

CHRISTMAS CUSTOMS AND TRADITIONS, Clement A. Miles. Origin, evolution, significance of religious, secular practices. Caroling, gifts, yule logs, much more. Full, scholarly yet fascinating; non-sectarian. 400pp. 5⅜ × 8½.
23354-5 Pa. $7.95

THE HUMAN FIGURE IN MOTION, Eadweard Muybridge. More than 4,500 stopped-action photos, in action series, showing undraped men, women, children jumping, lying down, throwing, sitting, wrestling, carrying, etc. 390pp. 7⅞ × 10⅝.
20204-6 Cloth. $24.95

THE MAN WHO WAS THURSDAY, Gilbert Keith Chesterton. Witty, fast-paced novel about a club of anarchists in turn-of-the-century London. Brilliant social, religious, philosophical speculations. 128pp. 5⅜ × 8½.
25121-7 Pa. $3.95

A CÉZANNE SKETCHBOOK: Figures, Portraits, Landscapes and Still Lifes, Paul Cézanne. Great artist experiments with tonal effects, light, mass, other qualities in over 100 drawings. A revealing view of developing master painter, precursor of Cubism. 102 black-and-white illustrations. 144pp. 8¾ × 6⅝.
24790-2 Pa. $6.95

AN ENCYCLOPEDIA OF BATTLES: Accounts of Over 1,560 Battles from 1479 B.C. to the Present, David Eggenberger. Presents essential details of every major battle in recorded history, from the first battle of Megiddo in 1479 B.C. to Grenada in 1984. List of Battle Maps. New Appendix covering the years 1967–1984. Index. 99 illustrations. 544pp. 6½ × 9¼.
24913-1 Pa. $14.95

AN ETYMOLOGICAL DICTIONARY OF MODERN ENGLISH, Ernest Weekley. Richest, fullest work, by foremost British lexicographer. Detailed word histories. Inexhaustible. Total of 856pp. 6½ × 9¼.
21873-2, 21874-0 Pa., Two-vol. set $19.90

WEBSTER'S AMERICAN MILITARY BIOGRAPHIES, edited by Robert McHenry. Over 1,000 figures who shaped 3 centuries of American military history. Detailed biographies of Nathan Hale, Douglas MacArthur, Mary Hallaren, others. Chronologies of engagements, more. Introduction. Addenda. 1,033 entries in alphabetical order. xi + 548pp. 6½ × 9¼. (Available in U.S. only)
24758-9 Pa. $13.95

LIFE IN ANCIENT EGYPT, Adolf Erman. Detailed older account, with much not in more recent books: domestic life, religion, magic, medicine, commerce, and whatever else needed for complete picture. Many illustrations. 597pp. 5⅜ × 8½.
22632-8 Pa. $9.95

HISTORIC COSTUME IN PICTURES, Braun & Schneider. Over 1,450 costumed figures shown, covering a wide variety of peoples: kings, emperors, nobles, priests, servants, soldiers, scholars, townsfolk, peasants, merchants, courtiers, cavaliers, and more. 256pp. 8⅜ × 11¼.
23150-X Pa. $9.95

THE NOTEBOOKS OF LEONARDO DA VINCI, edited by J. P. Richter. Extracts from manuscripts reveal great genius; on painting, sculpture, anatomy, sciences, geography, etc. Both Italian and English. 186 ms. pages reproduced, plus 500 additional drawings, including studies for *Last Supper, Sforza* monument, etc. 860pp. 7⅞ × 10¾.
22572-0, 22573-9 Pa., Two-vol. set $35.90

THE ART NOUVEAU STYLE BOOK OF ALPHONSE MUCHA: All 72 Plates from "Documents Decoratifs" in Original Color, Alphonse Mucha. Rare copyright-free design portfolio by high priest of Art Nouveau. Jewelry, wallpaper, stained glass, furniture, figure studies, plant and animal motifs, etc. Only complete one-volume edition. 80pp. 9⅜ × 12¼.   24044-4 Pa. $10.95

ANIMALS: 1,419 Copyright-Free Illustrations of Mammals, Birds, Fish, Insects, Etc., edited by Jim Harter. Clear wood engravings present, in extremely lifelike poses, over 1,000 species of animals. One of the most extensive pictorial sourcebooks of its kind. Captions. Index. 284pp. 9 × 12.   23766-4 Pa. $10.95

OBELISTS FLY HIGH, C. Daly King. Masterpiece of American detective fiction, long out of print, involves murder on a 1935 transcontinental flight—"a very thrilling story"—*NY Times*. Unabridged and unaltered republication of the edition published by William Collins Sons & Co. Ltd., London, 1935. 288pp. 5⅜ × 8½. (Available in U.S. only)   25036-9 Pa. $5.95

VICTORIAN AND EDWARDIAN FASHION: A Photographic Survey, Alison Gernsheim. First fashion history completely illustrated by contemporary photographs. Full text plus 235 photos, 1840–1914, in which many celebrities appear. 240pp. 6½ × 9¼.   24205-6 Pa. $8.95

THE ART OF THE FRENCH ILLUSTRATED BOOK, 1700–1914, Gordon N. Ray. Over 630 superb book illustrations by Fragonard, Delacroix, Daumier, Doré, Grandville, Manet, Mucha, Steinlen, Toulouse-Lautrec and many others. Preface. Introduction. 633 halftones. Indices of artists, authors & titles, binders and provenances. Appendices. Bibliography. 608pp. 8⅜ × 11¼.   25086-5 Pa. $24.95

THE WONDERFUL WIZARD OF OZ, L. Frank Baum. Facsimile in full color of America's finest children's classic. 143 illustrations by W. W. Denslow. 267pp. 5⅜ × 8½.   20691-2 Pa. $7.95

FOLLOWING THE EQUATOR: A Journey Around the World, Mark Twain. Great writer's 1897 account of circumnavigating the globe by steamship. Ironic humor, keen observations, vivid and fascinating descriptions of exotic places. 197 illustrations. 720pp. 5⅜ × 8½.   26113-1 Pa. $15.95

THE FRIENDLY STARS, Martha Evans Martin & Donald Howard Menzel. Classic text marshalls the stars together in an engaging, nontechnical survey, presenting them as sources of beauty in night sky. 23 illustrations. Foreword. 2 star charts. Index. 147pp. 5⅜ × 8½.   21099-5 Pa. $3.95

FADS AND FALLACIES IN THE NAME OF SCIENCE, Martin Gardner. Fair, witty appraisal of cranks, quacks, and quackeries of science and pseudoscience: hollow earth, Velikovsky, orgone energy, Dianetics, flying saucers, Bridey Murphy, food and medical fads, etc. Revised, expanded In the Name of Science. "A very able and even-tempered presentation."—*The New Yorker*. 363pp. 5⅜ × 8.

20394-8 Pa. $6.95

ANCIENT EGYPT: Its Culture and History, J. E. Manchip White. From predynastics through Ptolemies: society, history, political structure, religion, daily life, literature, cultural heritage. 48 plates. 217pp. 5⅜ × 8½.   22548-8 Pa. $5.95

SIR HARRY HOTSPUR OF HUMBLETHWAITE, Anthony Trollope. Incisive, unconventional psychological study of a conflict between a wealthy baronet, his idealistic daughter, and their scapegrace cousin. The 1870 novel in its first inexpensive edition in years. 250pp. 5⅜ × 8½.   24953-0 Pa. $6.95

LASERS AND HOLOGRAPHY, Winston E. Kock. Sound introduction to burgeoning field, expanded (1981) for second edition. Wave patterns, coherence, lasers, diffraction, zone plates, properties of holograms, recent advances. 84 illustrations. 160pp. 5⅜ × 8¼. (Except in United Kingdom)   24041-X Pa. $4.95

INTRODUCTION TO ARTIFICIAL INTELLIGENCE: Second, Enlarged Edition, Philip C. Jackson, Jr. Comprehensive survey of artificial intelligence—the study of how machines (computers) can be made to act intelligently. Includes introductory and advanced material. Extensive notes updating the main text. 132 black-and-white illustrations. 512pp. 5⅜ × 8½.   24864-X Pa. $10.95

HISTORY OF INDIAN AND INDONESIAN ART, Ananda K. Coomaraswamy. Over 400 illustrations illuminate classic study of Indian art from earliest Harappa finds to early 20th century. Provides philosophical, religious and social insights. 304pp. 6⅜ × 9⅜.   25005-9 Pa. $11.95

THE GOLEM, Gustav Meyrink. Most famous supernatural novel in modern European literature, set in Ghetto of Old Prague around 1890. Compelling story of mystical experiences, strange transformations, profound terror. 13 black-and-white illustrations. 224pp. 5⅜ × 8½.   25025-3 Pa. $7.95

PICTORIAL ENCYCLOPEDIA OF HISTORIC ARCHITECTURAL PLANS, DETAILS AND ELEMENTS: With 1,880 Line Drawings of Arches, Domes, Doorways, Facades, Gables, Windows, etc., John Theodore Haneman. Sourcebook of inspiration for architects, designers, others. Bibliography. Captions. 141pp. 9 × 12.
24605-1 Pa. $8.95

BENCHLEY LOST AND FOUND, Robert Benchley. Finest humor from early 30s, about pet peeves, child psychologists, post office and others. Mostly unavailable elsewhere. 73 illustrations by Peter Arno and others. 183pp. 5⅜ × 8½.
22410-4 Pa. $4.95

ERTÉ GRAPHICS, Erté. Collection of striking color graphics: *Seasons, Alphabet, Numerals, Aces* and *Precious Stones*. 50 plates, including 4 on covers. 48pp. 9⅜ × 12¼.
23580-7 Pa. $7.95

THE JOURNAL OF HENRY D. THOREAU, edited by Bradford Torrey, F. H. Allen. Complete reprinting of 14 volumes, 1837-61, over two million words; the sourcebooks for *Walden,* etc. Definitive. All original sketches, plus 75 photographs. 1,804pp. 8½ × 12¼.   20312-3, 20313-1 Cloth., Two-vol. set $130.00

CASTLES: Their Construction and History, Sidney Toy. Traces castle development from ancient roots. Nearly 200 photographs and drawings illustrate moats, keeps, baileys, many other features. Caernarvon, Dover Castles, Hadrian's Wall, Tower of London, dozens more. 256pp. 5⅜ × 8¼.   24898-4 Pa. $7.95

AMERICAN CLIPPER SHIPS: 1833–1858, Octavius T. Howe & Frederick C. Matthews. Fully-illustrated, encyclopedic review of 352 clipper ships from the period of America's greatest maritime supremacy. Introduction. 109 halftones. 5 black-and-white line illustrations. Index. Total of 928pp. 5⅜ × 8½.
25115-2, 25116-0 Pa., Two-vol. set $21.90

TOWARDS A NEW ARCHITECTURE, Le Corbusier. Pioneering manifesto by great architect, near legendary founder of "International School." Technical and aesthetic theories, views on industry, economics, relation of form to function, "mass-production spirit," much more. Profusely illustrated. Unabridged translation of 13th French edition. Introduction by Frederick Etchells. 320pp. 6⅛ × 9¼. (Available in U.S. only)
25023-7 Pa. $8.95

THE BOOK OF KELLS, edited by Blanche Cirker. Inexpensive collection of 32 full-color, full-page plates from the greatest illuminated manuscript of the Middle Ages, painstakingly reproduced from rare facsimile edition. Publisher's Note. Captions. 32pp. 9⅜ × 12¼. (Available in U.S. only)
24345-1 Pa. $5.95

BEST SCIENCE FICTION STORIES OF H. G. WELLS, H. G. Wells. Full novel *The Invisible Man*, plus 17 short stories: "The Crystal Egg," "Aepyornis Island," "The Strange Orchid," etc. 303pp. 5⅜ × 8½. (Available in U.S. only)
21531-8 Pa. $6.95

AMERICAN SAILING SHIPS: Their Plans and History, Charles G. Davis. Photos, construction details of schooners, frigates, clippers, other sailcraft of 18th to early 20th centuries—plus entertaining discourse on design, rigging, nautical lore, much more. 137 black-and-white illustrations. 240pp. 6⅛ × 9¼.
24658-2 Pa. $6.95

ENTERTAINING MATHEMATICAL PUZZLES, Martin Gardner. Selection of author's favorite conundrums involving arithmetic, money, speed, etc., with lively commentary. Complete solutions. 112pp. 5⅜ × 8½.
25211-6 Pa. $3.95

THE WILL TO BELIEVE, HUMAN IMMORTALITY, William James. Two books bound together. Effect of irrational on logical, and arguments for human immortality. 402pp. 5⅜ × 8½.
20291-7 Pa. $8.95

THE HAUNTED MONASTERY and THE CHINESE MAZE MURDERS, Robert Van Gulik. 2 full novels by Van Gulik continue adventures of Judge Dee and his companions. An evil Taoist monastery, seemingly supernatural events; overgrown topiary maze that hides strange crimes. Set in 7th-century China. 27 illustrations. 328pp. 5⅜ × 8½.
23502-5 Pa. $6.95

CELEBRATED CASES OF JUDGE DEE (DEE GOONG AN), translated by Robert Van Gulik. Authentic 18th-century Chinese detective novel; Dee and associates solve three interlocked cases. Led to Van Gulik's own stories with same characters. Extensive introduction. 9 illustrations. 237pp. 5⅜ × 8½.
23337-5 Pa. $5.95

Prices subject to change without notice.

Available at your book dealer or write for free catalog to Dept. GI, Dover Publications, Inc., 31 East 2nd St., Mineola, N.Y. 11501. Dover publishes more than 400 books each year on science, elementary and advanced mathematics, biology, music, art, literary history, social sciences and other areas.